West Academic Publishing's Emeritus Advisory Board

CYBERSECURITY LAW: AN EVOLVING FIELD

Second Edition

■ ■ ■

Michael S. Mireles

Professor of Law
University of the Pacific, McGeorge School of Law

Jack L. Hobaugh Jr.

Patent Attorney
Certified Information Systems Security Professional (CISSP)
Certified Information Privacy Professional—U.S. Private Sector (CIPP/US)
Certified Information Privacy Professional—Europe (CIPP/E)
Certified Information Privacy Technologist (CIPT)

AMERICAN CASEBOOK SERIES®

American Casebook Series is a trademark registered in the U.S. Patent and Trademark Office.

© 2021 LEG, Inc. d/b/a West Academic
© 2022 LEG, Inc. d/b/a West Academic
      444 Cedar Street, Suite 700
      St. Paul, MN 55101
      1-877-888-1330

West, West Academic Publishing, and West Academic are trademarks of West Publishing Corporation, used under license.

Printed in the United States of America

ISBN: 978-1-68561-064-7

Jack Hobaugh wishes to thank his wife Diana for her support, his parents, Violet and Jack, who sent their son on the path to education, and everyone who has mentored him over the years – too many to mention - but you know who you are.

Michael Mireles wishes to thank SS, EM, DM and GM; and his parents and in-laws. He is also grateful for his colleagues at University of the Pacific, McGeorge School of Law, in particular Associate Dean for Academic Affairs Mary-Beth Moylan, Dean Michael Hunter Schwartz, Associate Dean for Diversity Lawrence Levine and Associate Dean Franklin Gevurtz for support.

The authors wish to thank Madeline Orlando, Lauren Hirota, Tatum Kennedy, Anastasia Leach, Anya Leonard, Mark Cayaba, Oleksiy Gromov, Tracy Dudick, Kelsie Menefee and Charles Raub for their research and editing assistance. The authors are thankful for their Fall 2020 and 2021 Cybersecurity Law and Policy classes at the University of the Pacific. The authors also thank the Georgetown Journal of International Law, the Texas International Law Journal, the Lewis and Clark Law Review and the Brookings Institution for permission to reprint work originally published by them.

Table of Contents

Table of Cases

CYBERSECURITY LAW: AN EVOLVING FIELD

Second Edition

CHAPTER ONE. INTRODUCTION

1.1 Overview of This Casebook

The goal of this book is to provide law students, practicing attorneys, and in-house counsel with the necessary background to counsel others in the area of cybersecurity and cybersecurity law. The expansive and everchanging area of cybersecurity law requires an understanding of the intersection and interaction of cybersecurity, cybersecurity law, and privacy law. These three areas often overlap but never fully converge. To fully understand cybersecurity law, one must understand the relationships between cybersecurity, cybersecurity law, and privacy law. Throughout this book, the authors will identify and discuss those relationships. Moreover, we will delve into the various substantive areas of cybersecurity, cybersecurity law, and privacy law where those areas are coextensive, but sometimes where they are not.

The relevant substantive law covered by this book includes a patchwork of state, common law and federal laws. This book will analyze the regulations applied by cybersecurity regulators, such as the Federal Trade Commission and the Securities Exchange Commission. The substantive law reviewed also includes various statutory and common law causes of action brought by private parties for data breaches and other related cybersecurity issues. Notably, the book also covers the National Institute of Standards and Technology (NIST) Cybersecurity Frameworks, cybersecurity issues related to the Internet of Things, and data breach and other cybersecurity state laws. Finally, anti-hacking laws and international issues will be discussed. But first, a little computing history.

1.1[A] BRIEF HISTORY OF COMPUTING IN THE CYBERSECURITY CONTEXT

The first computers were standalone, non-connected machines. Hacking would have required physical access to the machine or the medium upon which the code was written before it was submitted to the machine. In those early days, programming code was written by punching holes in tape or punch card (keycards). Then the tape and cards were submitted to the computer operator for submission to the computer. Then came the connectivity between mainframe computers in an effort to connect military computers. Next, was the coming of age of standalone personal computers with hard drives and floppy disk drives. The internet was born, and dial-up modems were used to access the internet through internet service providers. Companies maintained mainframe computers connected to dumb terminals. Eventually, the dumb terminals were replaced with Personal Computers (PCs) in a client-server distributed configuration, where some of the processing could be moved off of the mainframe computer and onto the PC client.

With the success of the internet, companies needed to provide internet access to the public to remain competitive. Thus, companies had to figure out how to have a public facing computer presence while at the same time protecting their internal computing systems that contain sensitive non-public information. A protection zone between the public facing systems and the internal system (intranet) was created using gateways,[1] proxy servers,[2] and firewalls.[3] That zone is referred to as a DMZ. The security team spent a lot of time and effort making sure that the DMZ was not breached. This architecture today is referred to as a legacy system because companies are and have been moving away from that architecture by moving into the cloud.

The cloud provides a cost-effective way for a company to grow its computing resources. In the legacy system, if a company wanted to expand its computing power, it meant buying new systems, a costly endeavor. It was also hard for the information technology ("IT") team to size the systems for projected growth, and if the business had a slow period, it meant systems being underutilized. In contrast, cloud providers can provide extra computing resources on an ad hoc basis and cheaper than purchasing new equipment. With these cost-saving changes come additional challenges for companies to protect ever-increasingly valuable data. The term cloud conjures up a vision of a black box where computing power lives, but how it functions is not immediately visible to the user or company. Legacy systems gave the company control over their systems. Now in the cloud, companies have to rely on the cloud vendor to take over some of the responsibilities that the company had with the legacy systems. So, the company has traded efficiency for control by moving to the cloud.

Cloud vendors provide many different services to include:

- Software-as-a-Service ("SaaS");
- Platform-as-a-Service ("PaaS");
- Infrastructure-as-a-Service ("IaaS");
- Database-as-a-Service ("DBaaS");
- Container-as-a-Service ("CaaS");
- Function-as-a-Service ("FaaS");
- Ransomware-as-a-Service ("RaaS") and
- just about anything that can be offered as an outsourced software, hardware, and/or networking service.

If you own or use a personal computer, you likely are also using SaaS. SaaS is a service, normally offered as a subscription, and that service is located in the cloud. One example is Microsoft Office 365. Instead of purchasing the software and keeping the software on your personal computer, one can just purchase a subscription to the software through the SaaS model. One advantage of having the software in the cloud is that the subscription can cover many devices, such as PC, smart pad, smart phone, etc. Another advantage is that as a company adds employees, those employees can be easily added to the service through a subscription process. Cloud vendors take on the task of managing multiple customers in the same SaaS product.

---

[1] A "gateway" is a node such as router that data passes through in a network.

[2] "A proxy server acts as a gateway between you and the internet. It's an intermediary server separating end users from the websites they browse. Proxy servers provide varying levels of functionality, security, and privacy depending on your use case, needs, or company policy." Jeff Peters, *What is a Proxy Server and How Does it Work?*, VARONIS, https:///www.varonis.com/blog/what-is-a-proxy-server/ (last updated June 10, 2020).

[3] There are several different types of firewalls. Firewalls essentially operate to keep unwanted data or persons from accessing a computer. *See* ZACH CODINGS, COMPUTER PROGRAMMING AND CYBER SECURITY FOR BEGINNERS 268–269 (2019) (discussing packet filters firewall, application firewall, packet firewall and hybrid firewall).

There is nothing really mysterious about cloud computing architecture. Cloud vendors can offer services cheaper than the cost of legacy systems because of virtual machines. When a customer is accessing a virtual machine in the cloud, the customer does not see a difference between a dedicated machine and a virtual machine. But the machine is not dedicated to just one customer. The virtual machine is supporting many customers/clients through the use of a hypervisor. The hypervisor can be either hardware or software that divides the resources of the underlying machine among multiple customers. The vendor can bring down costs with a virtual machine model because the machine can be fully utilized.

PaaS is similar to SaaS, but instead of offering a service such as Microsoft Office 365, PaaS offers a platform for creating applications and other software. So, PaaS is a cloud offering that will likely be used by companies, and not individuals.

IaaS is an offering of infrastructure. DBaaS is an offering of a database service. Basically, a cloud provider has the technology to offer any type of service that is marketable.

CaaS is a cloud-based way of providing containers as a service. Operating System (OS) "virtualization techniques are primarily focused on providing a portable, reusable, and automatable way to package and run applications (apps). The terms application container or simply container are frequently used to refer to these technologies."[4]

FaaS "is a category of cloud computing services that provides a platform allowing customers to develop, run, and manage application functionalities without the complexity of building and maintaining the infrastructure typically associated with developing and launching an app."[5]

Most companies understand that they must invest in protecting digital assets whether they be legacy or cloud through targeted cybersecurity efforts. Thus, it is not surprising that the estimate for global cybersecurity spending will reach $10 billion by 2027.[6] Other interesting statistics include:

1) Small businesses are the target of half of cyber attacks;
2) Damages from cybersecurity attacks could reach $6 trillion by 2021;
3) 90% of cyber crimes go unreported every year in the US;
4) By 2024, the cybersecurity market is expected to be a $300 billion industry;
5) Ransomeware attacks likely occur every 14 seconds;
6) An Internet of Things (IoT) device may be attacked within 5 minutes of connecting to the Internet.[7]

---

[4] https://csrc.nist.gov/csrc/media/publications/sp/800-190/draft/documents/sp800-190-draft2.pdf.
[5] https://en.wikipedia.org/wiki/Function_as_a_service.
[6] Matt Powell, *11 Eye Opening Cyber Security Statistics for 2019*, CPO MAGAZINE (June 25, 2019), https://www.cpomagazine.com/cyber-security/11-eye-opening-cyber-security-statistics-for-2019/.
[7] *Id.*

1.1[B] INTRODUCTION TO THE RELATIONSHIP BETWEEN CYBERSECURITY, CYBERSECURITY LAW AND PRIVACY LAW AND "REASONABLE SECURITY MEASURES"

This is a text on cybersecurity law; it is not a book on privacy. Actually, the origin of privacy law had nothing to do with cyberspace. A well-known lawyer and socialite Samuel D. Warren living in the Boston area in the late 1800s became alarmed when another invention the Kodak camera became available to the public. That meant Mr. Warren could not socialize in public without the threat of his activities being photographed by anyone who had purchased a Kodak camera. Future Supreme Court Justice Louis Brandeis joined the fight for privacy, and in doing so created a privacy movement. Thus, in the beginning, computers and the internet were not even on the privacy law radar. Even today, one can violate privacy laws with just paper records. Yes, there can be a data breach with just paper records. Because privacy law predates cybersecurity law, it has been well covered in many texts.

With that said, it would be impossible to ignore privacy law because of its intersection and interaction with cybersecurity law. For example, the Health Insurance Portability and Accountability Act (HIPAA), Children's Online Privacy Protection Act (COPPA), and Gramm-Leach-Bliley Act (GLBA) are federal privacy laws that require the implementation of cybersecurity in some form or fashion. Most privacy books do not delve into the cybersecurity ramifications of these laws. This text does.

Often, cybersecurity and cybersecurity law deficiencies do not become apparent until a privacy law enforcement action has been triggered. For example, a data breach that negatively affects persons can trigger tort negligence actions, federal agency cybersecurity enforcement, state data breach notification (privacy) laws, and state AG cybersecurity investigation and enforcement actions. These events often disclose underlying cybersecurity deficiencies and cybersecurity law infractions that would have gone unnoticed without the breach, such as lack of encryption or "reasonable security measures" to safeguard data. It is often only after the discovery of the privacy infraction, that the underlying and arguably, more important cybersecurity law infractions surface.

This text will look at cybersecurity law through four different perspectives: the courts, the law, the enforcing party, and the defense. The defense will likely win or lose based on whether the cybersecurity measures were determined to be reasonable security measures. Some may argue that a security breach is evidence of negligence just as a plane crash has been argued to be negligence via *res ipsa loquitor*, because planes do not crash without some form of negligence. But, in our opinion, security (data) breaches are not automatically negligence because if a company has on-line systems, it is only a matter of time before those systems are breached, even without an act of negligence. A company can be diligent and implement reasonable security measures but still have a breach. Why? Because testing of software and hardware does not always find every bug.[8] How often do you update your smartphone operating system to fix newly

---

[8] Professors Jay P. Kesan and Carol M. Hayes note that, "Battles against security flaws are plagued by externality problems." *See* JAY P. KESAN & CAROL M. HAYES, CYBERSECURITY AND PRIVACY LAW IN A NUTSHELL 35 (West Academic 2019). Essentially, the overall harm from a security flaw is greater than any one user bears and each individual user may rely on others to address the harm. *Id.* "So, the social harm of cybersecurity is an externality not borne by the individual users, who have a more limited experience of harm." *Id.* Thus, creators of software are more focused on software functionality instead of security because that is what consumers demand. *Id.* at 35-36. Moreover, the authors note that one study

discovered bugs and security flaws? Testing software is hard because it is hard to foresee every use (and an attempted hack) of a software product. Yet, not imagining a test case does not equate to negligence.

There will be companies that have implemented reasonable security measures and companies that have not implemented reasonable security measures. Both will have breaches over time. The difference is that the company that implements reasonable security measures will have a valid argument for not breaching the reasonable security measures standard.

So, who will have the final say as to whether a company implemented reasonable security measures? Ultimately, it will be the courts. Because technology is ever-changing, what are reasonable security measures today, may not be tomorrow. As the technology progresses and threats from bad actors adapt, what are reasonable cybersecurity measures will also necessarily evolve over time. Each case will likely bring a new set of facts and nuances that will need to be processed by the court. It is unlikely that the judge or his/her clerks on the case will be versed in cybersecurity technology, similar to patent law cases that often address complex technology questions. Accordingly, cybersecurity cases will likely become a battle of the experts because the courts will not be equipped to determine whether cybersecurity measures were or were not reasonable on their own. Experts may opine on the content of the actions of a reasonable cybersecurity professional and this introduction provides some guidance as to the job duties of a cybersecurity professional. Reasonable measures to safeguard data will not be a static concept. Moreover, the question of what may be a reasonable measure may be informed by statutes, regulations, agency guidance and matters, court decisions and industry standards.

Many laws will not be pure cybersecurity laws but instead laws that contain cybersecurity law aspects. We will dissect the relevant laws and discuss the cybersecurity portions and how they are being applied. Enforcing parties may be individuals given rights of action, agencies through the law and regulations, and states' attorney generals through state law. We will discuss cases to determine what has not been successful, what was successful, and what actions are likely to be successful in the future.

1.2 What is Cybersecurity Law?

To better understand how to define cybersecurity law and how cybersecurity law fits into the legal landscape, we must first take a look at two closely related subjects: cybersecurity and privacy law. Cybersecurity is the protection of machines, digital data, and networks. The foundation of providing cybersecurity protection is based on maintaining the security triad of confidentiality, integrity, and availability, commonly referred to as CIA. Confidentiality is the protection of data, objects, and resources. Some

---

states that, "the average software developed in the United States has 6,000 software flaws per million lines of code, and between one and five percent of software flaws are security vulnerabilities." *Id.* at 16 (citing Carol Woody & Nancy Mead, *Using Quality Metrics and Security Methods to Predict Software Assurance*, SEI BLOG (June 20, 2016), https://insights.sei.cmu.edu/sei_blog/2016/06/using-quality-metrics-and-security-methods-to-predict-software-assurance.html).

authors focus mainly on data because privacy law focuses on sensitive data known as personally identifiable information (PII). Integrity is the protection of reliability and correctness of data. Availability is providing uninterrupted and timely access for those appropriately authenticated and authorized for data, objects, and resources. The European Union General Data Protection Regulation (GDPR) added a fourth category of Resilience to CIA that applies to the resilience "of processing systems and services." Thus, we may start to see CIAR instead of the normal CIA.

In contrast to cybersecurity, privacy law is about protecting the privacy of humans. The International Association of Privacy Professionals (IAPP) identifies four main areas of privacy: information privacy, bodily privacy, territorial privacy, and communications privacy. Information privacy is the "claim of individuals, groups or institutions to determine for themselves when, how and to what extent information about them is communicated to others."[9] Bodily privacy "focuses on a person's physical being and any invasion thereof. Such an invasion can take the form of genetic testing, drug testing or body cavity searches."[10] Territorial privacy is "concerned with placing limitations on the ability of one to intrude into another individual's environment. Environment is not limited to the home; it may be defined as the workplace or public space and environmental considerations can be extended to an international level. Invasion into an individual's territorial privacy typically comes in the form of video surveillance, ID checks and use of similar technology and procedures."[11] There is an obvious friction here between the implementation of cybersecurity in the form of video surveillance, ID checks, etc., and territorial privacy. Communications privacy "encompasses protection of the means of correspondence, including postal mail, telephone conversations, electronic e-mail and other forms of communicative behavior and apparatus."[12]

So, what is cybersecurity law and how does it relate to cybersecurity and privacy law? Although the term has been quickly adopted as an oft-used legal buzz word and big law is quickly adding cybersecurity law as a practice area, a well-adopted definition does not yet exist. As Professor Jeff Kosseff noted in his 2018 law review article, "Defining Cybersecurity Law", "the U.S. legal system lacks a consistent definition of the term 'cybersecurity law'."[13]

We expect the definition of cybersecurity law to morph over time as regulatory bodies continue to struggle with the term as they attempt to promulgate cybersecurity laws to protect their citizens. For the purposes of this book we define **cybersecurity law** as *any law that is promulgated towards the protection of machines, digital data, and networks*. In essence, cybersecurity law is any law that applies to cybersecurity. There is no protection of humans in our definition of cybersecurity law because that is the role of privacy law. But there is a relationship between privacy law and cybersecurity law. Moreover, this book will also cover some aspects of the protection of humans, but is not an exhaustive coverage of those issues.[14]

---

[9] IAPP Glossary of Privacy Terms, https://iapp.org/resources/glossary/#identifiability.

[10] IAPP Glossary of Privacy Terms, https://iapp.org/resources/glossary/#background-screening-checks.

[11] IAPP Glossary of Privacy Terms, https://iapp.org/resources/glossary/#t-closeness.

[12] IAPP Glossary of Privacy Terms, https://iapp.org/resources/glossary/#caching.

[13] Jeff Kosseff, *Defining Cybersecurity Law*, 103 IOWA L. REV. 985, 985 (2018).

[14] A computer virus called Stuxnet was used to disable the Iranian nuclear program by infecting computer systems controlling centrifuges. This is an example of a cyberattack impacting the operation of physical devices. For more information on Stuxnet, please see Kim Zetter, *An Unprecedented Look at Stuxnet, the*

And that relationship is easily seen in most of the laws that can be categorized as covering both privacy laws and cybersecurity laws. Upon closer examination, most of these laws are neither pure privacy laws nor pure cybersecurity laws, but instead, a combination of both. We will cover laws in the following chapters that contain separate sections for cybersecurity and privacy. All fifty states now have data breach notification laws. Data breach notification laws can be categorized as privacy laws because they set out requirements to notify people affected by the data breach, also known as customers, so that the people can take appropriate steps to protect their identity. States have also started promulgating data protection laws that go beyond just notification of a breach and towards the protection of the companies' digital assets. These laws can be categorized as cybersecurity laws because they address and enforce reasonable security measures for protecting digital assets. Some states keep these two laws separate, but there is at least one state, Alabama, a late comer to mandating notification, that has combined privacy and cybersecurity into one overarching law. The same is true for at least some of the federal laws, such as HIPAA, which obviously attempts to protect people's privacy but also requires technical safeguards that would fall into the cybersecurity category. We will look at these relationships in detail as we step through the federal and state laws.

QUESTIONS

A startup technology company (Techno) with an internet presence is concerned whether it could withstand the fallout from a hack. Techno, like many companies, collects data about its customers that could be considered personally identifiable information (PII). Techno, like many startup companies, has a lean budget and its engineers are focused on getting Techno products to market. Techno also has a Chief Information Officer (CIO) that is in charge of all systems and a General Counsel (GC), who is in charge of the legal department.

Should Techno hire a cybersecurity expert, perhaps a Chief Information Security Officer (CISO)? If yes, why?

Techno's GC is concerned with the recent uptick in FTC and state cases that use a "reasonable security measures" standard to determine if a company has cybersecurity liability. Would Techno benefit from cybersecurity counsel? Could cybersecurity counsel be a liaison between the CISO or CIO and GC? If so, how?

Techno's GC is also concerned about the collection of PII and the potential damages resulting from any breach of PII. Techno's GC understands that the PII has privacy implications. Should the GC enlist the help of cybersecurity counsel to plan for a potential breach?

1.3 Responsibilities of a Cybersecurity Professional

The core responsibility of the cybersecurity professional is the protection of machines, digital data, and networks through the application of the cybersecurity triad—CIA. Confidentiality, Integrity, and Availability (CIA) is the mantra of the cybersecurity professional. The cybersecurity professional strives to protect the

---

World's First Digital Weapon, WIRED, (November 3, 2014), https://www.wired.com/2014/11/countdown-to-zero-day-stuxnet/ (last updated October 9, 2020).

confidentiality, integrity, and availability of machines, data, and networks. Although protecting the machines, digital data, and networks is important, that protection should never be at the risk of the loss of human life.

The cybersecurity professional applies CIA across many layers of an organization starting with security governance through the implementation of principles, polices, and procedures. If a security incident or event occurs, the cybersecurity professional is a key member of the incident response team (IRT). The first step in achieving and maintaining CIA begins with identifying cybersecurity risks across all business processes and assets by using a risk management framework. The risk management framework is discussed in more detail in Chapter Ten. Next, each identified risk is either mitigated, avoided or accepted. Risks are specifically addressed through continuity of operations plans, business continuity plans, incident response plans and disaster recovery plans.

Quantifying and qualifying cybersecurity risk is a team effort that requires C-suite buy-in and multiple departments input. Risk is measured by threat * vulnerability. Input from the cybersecurity professional will be essential for determining what threats are out there that could affect the company's computing resources. Likewise, the cybersecurity professional's input will be essential for determining the company's computing resources vulnerabilities. The business departments and legal team will also be invaluable in determining how the risk could affect the company's business and how much resources should be applied to mitigating the risk.

1.3[A] VULNERABILITY ANALYSIS

The threats that a company faces are dynamic because the sources of the threats are dynamic and the cyber landscape of the company is dynamic. The cybersecurity professional must stay informed of the threats. Also, the cybersecurity professional must routinely perform vulnerability analysis of the machines, data and networks. A vulnerability is any type flaw that can be exploited.[15] Vulnerability analysis can be performed through scanning for flaws. Such scanning includes:

- Network Discovery Scanning that identifies open communication ports on a particular network. Open communication ports present the potential for bad actors to access a system through the open port.
- Web Vulnerability Scanning that looks for known vulnerabilities on Web-site applications.

If vulnerabilities are found, a next step can be penetration testing to see if the vulnerability can be exploited. The cybersecurity professional will be careful when using penetration testing because penetration testing can be disruptive to systems. Because of the potential for penetration testing to be disruptive, penetration testing should never be carried out without approval from company management.

Managing vulnerabilities is a complicated task for the cybersecurity professional, because the vulnerabilities can be found in many of the company's computing and networking assets. To name a few, vulnerabilities can be found in:

---

[15] A "zero day vulnerability" is a vulnerability that is unknown to the creator of the software and not addressed. A "zero day exploit" is a the use of the zero day vulnerability before it is addressed. Cybersecurity experts Yuri Diogenes and Erdal Ozkaya discuss past zero day exploits, including vulnerabilities in WhatsApp, Chrome, and Windows. *See* YURI DIOGENES & ERDAL OZKAYA, CYBERSECURITY – ATTACK AND DEFENSE STRATEGIES 180–182 (Packt 2018).

- Hardware such as microchips
- Firmware[16]
- Operating Systems
- Database Systems
- Every software application that the company has.
- Network nodes such as routers
- Firewalls
- Proxy Servers
- Gateways
- Human end users
- WiFi

Vulnerabilities are also found in personal computing devices such as laptops and smart phones. These devices can present a challenge for the cybersecurity professional in a bring-your-own-device (BYOD) architecture because these devices may not be managed by the company and the company may not be able to control the applications that are downloaded onto the device. Thus, the company may not have a good view of the vulnerabilities that are on the device and connected to the company's network. Counsel can be very helpful in advising companies before they decide to go to a BYOD architecture by making sure the employee agreement in such cases addresses giving the company rights to the necessary insight into the device to address vulnerabilities. Counsel should also limit the use of the device on the network, especially when an employee is accessing company data in the cloud. Users have been known to bypass secured applications in favor of using unapproved applications because the user prefers an unapproved application over the approved application.

Following is a discussion of cybersecurity risk by the U.S. Department of Homeland Security (DHS) Cybersecurity and Infrastructure Security Agency (CISA):

> Cyberspace and its underlying infrastructure are vulnerable to a wide range of risks stemming from both physical and cyber threats and hazards. Sophisticated cyber actors and nation-states exploit vulnerabilities to steal information and money and are developing capabilities to disrupt, destroy, or threaten the delivery of essential services. Cyberspace is particularly difficult to secure due to a number of factors: the ability of malicious actors to operate from anywhere in the world, the linkages between cyberspace and physical systems, and the difficulty of reducing vulnerabilities and consequences in complex cyber networks. Of growing concern is the cyber threat to critical infrastructure, which is increasingly subject to sophisticated cyber intrusions that pose new risks. As information technology becomes increasingly integrated with physical infrastructure operations, there is increased risk for wide scale or high-consequence events that could cause harm or disrupt services upon which our economy and the daily lives of millions of Americans depend. In light of the risk and potential consequences of cyber events, strengthening the security and resilience of cyberspace has become an important homeland security mission.[17]

---

[16] "Firmware" is "permanent" software programmed on hardware.

[17] *Cybersecurity*, CYBERSECURITY & INFRASTRUCTURE SECURITY AGENCY, https://www.cisa.gov/cybersecurity (last visited Aug. 28, 2020).

On March 31, 2021, "[DHS] Secretary Mayorkas outlined a bold vision for the Department's cybersecurity efforts to confront the growing threat of cyber-attacks, including a series of 60-day sprints to operationalize his vision, to drive action in the coming year, and to raise public awareness about key cybersecurity priorities."[18] Those sprints included:

- Ransomware
- Cybersecurity Workforce
- Industrial Control Systems (ICS)
- Elections Security
- International Cybersecurity

In addition to the series of 60-day springs, the Secretary will focus on four ongoing priorities: (1) cementing the resilience of democratic institutions, including the integrity of elections and institutions outside the executive branch, (2) building back better to strengthen the protection of civilian government networks, (3) advancing a risk-based approach to supply-chain security and exploiting new technologies to increase resilience, and (4) preparing for strategic, on-the-horizon challenges and emerging technology such as the transition to post-quantum encryption algorithms.[19]

The sharing of knowledge greatly helps the cybersecurity professional stay abreast of the ever-increasing list of vulnerabilities. The DHS maintains an online form and email address for disclosing vulnerabilities.[20] A list of common vulnerabilities is maintained by the MITRE Corporation and sponsored by CISA:

Common Vulnerabilities and Exposures (CVE®) is a list of common identifiers for publicly known cybersecurity vulnerabilities.

Use of CVE Entries, which are assigned by CVE Numbering Authorities (CNAs) from around the world, ensures confidence among parties when used to discuss or share information about a unique software or firmware vulnerability, provides a baseline for tool evaluation, and enables automated data exchange.

CVE is:

- One identifier for one vulnerability or exposure
- One standardized description for each vulnerability or exposure
- A dictionary rather than a database
- How disparate databases and tools can "speak" the same language
- The way to interoperability and better security coverage
- A basis for evaluation among services, tools, and databases

---

[18] https://www.dhs.gov/topic/cybersecurity (last visited Aug. 7, 2021).

[19] *Id.*

[20] https://www.dhs.gov/vulnerability-disclosure-form (last visited Aug. 7, 2021).

- Free for public download and use
- Industry-endorsed via the CVE Numbering Authorities, CVE Board, and numerous products and services that include CVE[21]

Various DHS departments provide information on cybersecurity.[22] Of special interest is the National Cybersecurity and Communications Integration Center (NCCIC):

NCCIC offers no-cost, subscription-based information products to stakeholders through the www.us-cert.gov and www.ics-cert.gov websites. CISA Central designed these products—part of the National Cyber Awareness System (NCAS)—to improve situational awareness among technical and non-technical audiences by providing timely information about cybersecurity threats and issues and general security topics. Products include technical alerts, control systems advisories and reports, weekly vulnerability bulletins, and tips on cyber hygiene best practices. Subscribers can select to be notified when products of their choosing are published.

Service benefits include:

- Current Activity provides up-to-date information about high-impact security activity affecting the community at-large.
- Alerts provide timely information about current security issues, vulnerabilities, and exploits.
- Advisories provide timely information about current ICS security issues, vulnerabilities, and exploits.
- Bulletins provide weekly summaries of new vulnerabilities. Patch information is provided when available.
- Tips provide guidance on common security issues.

For more information on available information products, visit www.us-cert.gov/ncas and www.ics-cert.us-cert.gov/. To subscribe to select products, visit public.govdelivery.com/accounts/USDHSUSCERT/subscriber/new.[23]

In October of 2009, DHS opened the National Cybersecurity and Communications Integration Center (NCCIC), "a 24 hour, DHS-led coordinated watch and warning center that will improve national efforts to address threats and incidents affecting the nation's critical information technology and cyber infrastructure."[24] NCCIC is now known as "CISA Central." The DHS has placed an emphasis on sharing

---

[21] *About CVE*, COMMON VULNERABILITIES AND EXPOSURES, https://cve.mitre.org/about/index.html (last updated Nov. 6, 2019).

[22] https://uscert.cisa.gov/nccic?__hstc=245485531.267f74747c9821ec26a48120809aad7e.1486339200049 .1486339200051.1486339200052.2&__hssc=245485531.1.1486339200052&__hsfp=528229161

[23] *Information Sharing and Awareness*, CYBERSECURITY & INFRASTRUCTURE SECURITY AGENCY, https://www.cisa.gov/information-sharing-and-awareness (last revised June 3, 2020).

[24] https://www.dhs.gov/news/2009/10/30/new-national-cybersecurity-center-opened (last visited Aug. 7, 2021).

cybersecurity information by creating the Cyber Information Sharing and Collaboration Program (CISCP):

> Cyber Information Sharing and Collaboration Program (CISCP) enables information exchange and the establishment of a community of trust between the Federal Government and critical infrastructure owners and operators. CISCP and its members can share cyber threat, incident, and vulnerability information in near real-time to collaborate and better understand cyber threats. By leveraging CISA Central, formerly known as the National Cybersecurity and Communications Integration Center (NCCIC), members can receive guidance on cyber-related threats to prevent, mitigate or recover from cyber incidents.

> CISCP membership provides access to the full suite of CISA Central products and services to support information exchange. Upon receiving indicators of observed cyber threat activity from its members, CISCP analysts redact proprietary information and collaborate with both government and industry partners to produce accurate, timely, actionable data and analytical products.[25]

CISA also maintains a webpage for tracking current activity.[26] Included on this webpage:
- Access to the National Cyber Awareness System
  - Current Activity
  - Alerts
  - Bulletins
  - Analysis Reports
- Recent Vulnerabilities
- Link to the National Vulnerability Database
- View of Vulnerability Notes
- Announcements
- Sections on:
  - reporting:
    - incidents
    - phishing
    - malware
    - vulnerabilities
- email signup to subscribe to alerts from US-CERT.

Below is an example of an email communication from US-CERT regarding a security update released by Adobe with instructions on how to update to protect against discovered vulnerabilities:

---

[25] https://www.cisa.gov/information-sharing-and-awareness (last Updated Date: June 29, 2021).
[26] https://us-cert.cisa.gov (last visited August 7, 2021).

++++++++++++++ start of email ++++++++++++++

US-CERT <US-CERT@ncas.us-cert.gov>
Thu 7/23/2020 3:49 PM
. . .
Adobe Releases Security Updates
07/22/2020 11:05 AM EDT

Original release date: July 22, 2020

Adobe has released security updates to address vulnerabilities in multiple Adobe products. An attacker could exploit some of these vulnerabilities to take control of an affected system.

The Cybersecurity and Infrastructure Security Agency (CISA) encourages users and administrators to review the following Adobe Security Bulletins and apply the necessary updates.

- Bridge APSB20-44
- Photoshop APSB20-45
- Prelude APSB20-46
- Reader Mobile APSB20-50

++++++++++++++ end of email ++++++++++++++
So, just how frequent are these communications? The communications are very frequent. Below is a one-week summary for just the "High Vulnerabilities":

High Vulnerabilities

Primary Vendor – Product	Description	Published	CVSS Score	Source & Patch Info
atlassian -- jira_server_and_data_center	Affected versions of Atlassian Jira Server and Data Center allow remote attackers to achieve template injection via the Web Resources Manager. The affected versions	2020-07-03	7.5	CVE-2020-14172 MISC

Primary Vendor – Product	Description	Published	CVSS Score	Source & Patch Info
	are before version 8.8.1.			
gog -- galaxy_client	An issue was discovered in GOG Galaxy Client 2.0.17. Local escalation of privileges is possible when a user installs a game or performs a verify/repair operation. The issue exists because of weak file permissions and can be exploited by using opportunistic locks.	2020-07-05	9.3	CVE-2020-15529 MISC
gog -- galaxy_client	An issue was discovered in GOG Galaxy Client 2.0.17. Local escalation of privileges is possible when a user starts or uninstalls a game because of weak file permissions and missing file integrity checks.	2020-07-05	9.3	CVE-2020-15528 MISC
google -- android	An issue was discovered on Samsung mobile devices with Q(10.0) software. Attackers	2020-07-07	7.1	CVE-2020-15584 CONFIRM

Primary Vendor – Product	Description	Published	CVSS Score	Source & Patch Info
	can trigger an out-of-bounds access and device reset via a 4K wallpaper image because ImageProcessHelper mishandles boundary checks. The Samsung ID is SVE-2020-18056 (July 2020).			
mobileiron -- core_and_connector	An Authentication Bypass vulnerability in MobileIron Core and Connector versions 10.6 and earlier that allows remote attackers to bypass authentication mechanisms via unspecified vectors.	2020-07-07	7.5	CVE-2020-15506 MISC
mobileiron -- core_and_connector	A remote code execution vulnerability in MobileIron Core and Connector versions 10.6 and earlier, and Sentry versions 9.8 and earlier that allows remote attackers to execute arbitrary code via unspecified vectors.	2020-07-07	7.5	CVE-2020-15505 MISC

Primary Vendor -- Product	Description	Published	CVSS Score	Source & Patch Info
mozilla -- firefox	In non-standard configurations, a JPEG image created by JavaScript could have caused an internal variable to overflow, resulting in an out of bounds write, memory corruption, and a potentially exploitable crash. This vulnerability affects Firefox < 78.	2020-07-09	7.6	CVE-2020-12422 MISC MISC
mozilla -- firefox	Mozilla developers reported memory safety bugs present in Firefox 76. Some of these bugs showed evidence of memory corruption and we presume that with enough effort some of these could have been exploited to run arbitrary code. This vulnerability affects Firefox < 77.	2020-07-09	9.3	CVE-2020-12411 MISC MISC
mozilla -- firefox	A VideoStreamEncoder may have been freed in a race condition with VideoBroadcaster::AddOrUpdateSink, resulting in a use-	2020-07-09	9.3	CVE-2020-12416 MISC MISC

Primary Vendor – Product	Description	Published	CVSS Score	Source & Patch Info
	after-free, memory corruption, and a potentially exploitable crash. This vulnerability affects Firefox < 78.			
mozilla -- firefox_and_firefox_esr_ and_thunderbird	Mozilla Developer Iain Ireland discovered a missing type check during unboxed objects removal, resulting in a crash. We presume that with enough effort that it could be exploited to run arbitrary code. This vulnerability affects Thunderbird < 68.9.0, Firefox < 77, and Firefox ESR < 68.9.	2020-07-09	9.3	CVE-2020-12406 MISC MISC MISC MISC
mozilla -- firefox_and_firefox_esr_ and_thunderbird	Mozilla developers reported memory safety bugs present in Firefox 76 and Firefox ESR 68.8. Some of these bugs showed evidence of memory corruption and we presume that with enough effort some of these could have been exploited to run arbitrary code. This vulnerability affects	2020-07-09	9.3	CVE-2020-12410 MISC MISC MISC MISC

Primary Vendor -- Product	Description	Published	CVSS Score	Source & Patch Info
	Thunderbird < 68.9.0, Firefox < 77, and Firefox ESR < 68.9.			
mozilla -- firefox_and_firefox_esr_and_thunderbird	When trying to connect to a STUN server, a race condition could have caused a use-after-free of a pointer, leading to memory corruption and a potentially exploitable crash. This vulnerability affects Firefox ESR < 68.10, Firefox < 78, and Thunderbird < 68.10.0.	2020-07-09	9.3	CVE-2020-12420 MISC MISC MISC MISC
mozilla -- firefox_and_firefox_esr_and_thunderbird	When processing callbacks that occurred during window flushing in the parent process, the associated window may die; causing a use-after-free condition. This could have led to memory corruption and a potentially exploitable crash. This vulnerability affects Firefox ESR < 68.10, Firefox < 78, and	2020-07-09	9.3	CVE-2020-12419 MISC MISC MISC MISC

Primary Vendor – Product	Description	Published	CVSS Score	Source & Patch Info
	Thunderbird < 68.10.0.			
mozilla -- firefox_and_firefox_esr_and_thunderbird	Due to confusion about ValueTags on JavaScript Objects, an object may pass through the type barrier, resulting in memory corruption and a potentially exploitable crash. *Note: this issue only affects Firefox on ARM64 platforms.* This vulnerability affects Firefox ESR < 68.10, Firefox < 78, and Thunderbird < 68.10.0.	2020-07-09	9.3	CVE-2020-12417 MISC MISC MISC MISC
phpzag -- phpzag	SQL injection with the search parameter in Records.php for phpzag live add edit delete data tables records with ajax php mysql	2020-07-07	7.5	CVE-2020-8519 MLIST MISC MISC
phpzag -- phpzag	SQL injection in order and column parameters in Records.php for phpzag live add edit delete data tables	2020-07-07	7.5	CVE-2020-8520 MLIST MISC MISC

Primary Vendor – Product	Description	Published	CVSS Score	Source & Patch Info
	records with ajax php mysql			
phpzag -- phpzag	SQL injection with start and length parameters in Records.php for phpzag live add edit delete data tables records with ajax php mysql	2020-07-07	7.5	CVE-2020-8521 MLIST MISC MISC
solarwinds -- serv-u_ftp_server	SolarWinds Serv-U FTP server before 15.2.1 allows remote command execution.	2020-07-05	7.5	CVE-2020-15541 MISC
we-com -- opendata_cms	We-com OpenData CMS 2.0 allows SQL Injection via the username field on the administrator login page.	2020-07-05	7.5	CVE-2020-15540 MISC MISC
webchess -- webchess	WebChess 1.0 allows SQL injection via the messageFrom, gameID, opponent, messageID, or to parameter.	2020-07-07	7.5	CVE-2019-20896 CONFIRM[27]

[27] *Bulletin (SB20-195)*, CYBERSECURITY & INFRASTRUCTURE SECURITY AGENCY (July 13, 2020), https://us-cert.cisa.gov/ncas/bulletins/sb20-195.

In another proactive cybersecurity step, CISA on July 30, 2021, announced the Vulnerability Disclosure Policy (VDP) Platform:

> CISA has announced the establishment of its Vulnerability Disclosure Policy (VDP) Platform for the federal civilian enterprise, which will allow the Federal Civilian Executive Branch to coordinate with the civilian security research community in a streamlined fashion. The VDP Platform provides a single, centrally managed website that agencies can leverage as the primary point of entry for intaking, triaging, and routing vulnerabilities disclosed by researchers. It enables researchers and members of the general public to find vulnerabilities in agency websites and submit reports for analysis.
>
> This new platform allows agencies to gain greater insights into potential vulnerabilities, which will improve their cybersecurity posture. This approach also means agencies no longer need to develop separate systems to enable vulnerability reporting and triage of identified vulnerabilities, providing government-wide cost savings that CISA estimates at over $10 million.
>
> For more details, see the blog post by CISA's Executive Assistant Director for Cybersecurity, Eric Goldstein.[28]

When a vulnerability is discovered, the proper patch or other solution, such as an adjustment to the configuration will be applied after proper testing of the patch or configuration. A patch is just a portion of new code that can be implemented into an existing operational system to fix a bug or vulnerability. Configuration is also known as settings on some devices. Most devices come with a default configuration recommended by the manufacturer. For example, users can then set the settings on their smart phone manually to meet their personal preferences. Hackers understand configuration settings and if a vulnerability is known for a particular setting, that setting can become a target for the hackers. For a major system, such as a server, there will be configuration files that can be tweaked by the IT department.

Testing is crucial because a company does not want to apply a patch or configuration that would break the company's system(s). The vendor should have thoroughly tested the patch or recommended configuration, but it is impossible to test for every environment that the patch may be placed into. There may be times when the risk and vulnerability are so grave that in-house testing may be passed over for expediency of a fix. Otherwise, the company will likely set up a testing sandbox to test the new patch or configuration. A sandbox is a secure area where code, patches, and configurations can be tested without the risk of contaminating any company systems already in operation. After successful sandbox testing, review, and management approval, the patch or configuration can be implemented into operational systems.

---

[28] https://us-cert.cisa.gov/ncas/current-activity/2021/07/30/cisa-announces-vulnerability-disclosure-policy-vdp-platform (last visited Aug. 7, 2021).

After adding the patch or adjusting the configuration, a new system baseline should be captured and backed up for future use. In the event of a system crash, the baseline can be used to restore the system to the proper setup. The baseline can also be used to set up a new system to ensure that all systems are equally configured and patched.

So, what if the software code was developed in-house? The first step is to investigate the source of the vulnerability. It could come from in-house, an ethical hacker (a good hacker, also sometimes known as a "white hat" (someone who works for the company) or "gray hat" (an independent or affiliated with another company) as opposed to a "black hat" (someone with nefarious purposes)), a blog entry, a complaint, or even a breach. Then it is up to the company's IT department to build a patch or a new configuration. The operational testing requirement remains the same.

Vulnerability tracking and responding with the implementation of new patches and configuration is a never-ending task and probably keeps the security professional awake at night because the security professional can never know for sure if all vulnerabilities have been discovered. It is a best effort task.

But vulnerability analysis is only part of the risk = vulnerability * threat analysis. Vulnerabilities are not an issue if there is no threat of attacking the vulnerability. The threat can come from many places. The threat can be external and originate from a hacker sitting in Russia or China or the United States.[29] The threat can be internal and originate from a disgruntled employee. Internal or external, the cybersecurity professional must understand and be aware of the threats, and where possible, take action to protect the company's resources from attack. The cybersecurity professional may not know the actual threat but instead understand the type of threat that may attack in the future. Or the cybersecurity professional may be informed of a known threat. For example, the cybersecurity professional may receive an alert, that identifies the vulnerability along with the threat, such as:

Alert (AA20-206A)
Threat Actor Exploitation of F5 BIG-IP CVE-2020-5902

Summary

The Cybersecurity and Infrastructure Security Agency (CISA) is issuing this alert in response to recently disclosed exploits that target F5 BIG-IP devices that are vulnerable to CVE-2020-5902. F5 Networks, Inc. (F5) released a patch for CVE-2020-5902 on June 30, 2020.[1]

Unpatched F5 BIG-IP devices are an attractive target for malicious actors. Affected organizations that have not applied the patch to fix this critical remote code execution (RCE) vulnerability risk an attacker exploiting CVE-2020-5902 to take control of their system. **Note:** F5's security advisory for CVE-2020-5902

---

[29] An "advanced persistent threat" is usually a prolonged attack that accesses a system repeatedly. It may be instigated by a nation-state.

states that there is a high probability that any remaining unpatched devices are likely already compromised.

CISA expects to see continued attacks exploiting unpatched F5 BIG-IP devices and strongly urges users and administrators to upgrade their software to the fixed versions. CISA also advises that administrators deploy the signature included in this Alert to help them determine whether their systems have been compromised.

This Alert also provides additional detection measures and mitigations for victim organizations to help recover from attacks resulting from CVE-2020-5902. CISA encourages administrators to remain aware of the ramifications of exploitation and to use the recommendations in this alert to help secure their organization's systems against attack.

Background

CISA has conducted incident response engagements at U.S. Government and commercial entities where malicious cyber threat actors have exploited CVE-2020-5902—an RCE vulnerability in the BIG-IP Traffic Management User Interface (TMUI)—to take control of victim systems. On June 30, F5 disclosed CVE-2020-5902, stating that it allows attackers to, "execute arbitrary system commands, create or delete files, disable services, and/or execute arbitrary Java code."

On July 4, open-source reporting indicated a proof-of-concept code was available and threat actors were exploiting the vulnerability by attempting to steal credentials. On July 5, security researchers posted exploits that would allow threat actors to exfiltrate data or execute commands on vulnerable devices. The risk posed by the vulnerability is critical.

Technical Details

CISA has observed scanning and reconnaissance, as well as confirmed compromises, within a few days of F5's patch release for this vulnerability. As early as July 6, 2020, CISA has seen broad scanning activity for the presence of this vulnerability across federal departments and agencies—this activity is currently occurring as of the publication of this Alert.

CISA has been working with several entities across multiple sectors to investigate potential compromises relating to this vulnerability. CISA has confirmed two compromises and is continuing to investigate. CISA will update this Alert with any additional actionable information.

Detection Methods

CISA recommends administrators see the F5 Security Advisory K52145254 for indicators of compromise and F5's CVE-2020-5902 IoC Detection Tool.[2]

CISA also recommends organizations complete the following actions in conducting their hunt for this exploit:

- Quarantine or take offline potentially affected systems
- Collect and review artifacts such as running processes/services, unusual authentications, and recent network connections
- Deploy the following CISA-created Snort signature to detect malicious activity:

alert tcp any any -> any $HTTP_PORTS (msg:"BIG-IP:HTTP URI GET contains '/tmui/login.jsp/..|3b|/tmui/':CVE-2020-5902"; sid:1; rev:1; flow:established,to_server; content:"/tmui/login.jsp/..|3b|/tmui/"; http_uri; fast_pattern:only; content:"GET"; nocase; http_method; priority:2; reference:url,github.com/yassineaboukir/CVE-2020-5902; reference:cve,2020-5902; metadata:service http;)

Mitigations

CISA strongly urges organizations that have not yet done so to upgrade their BIG-IP software to the corresponding patches for CVE-2020-5902. If organizations detect evidence of CVE-2020-5902 exploitation after patching and applying the detection measures in this alert, CISA recommends taking immediate action to reconstitute affected systems.

Should an organization's IT security personnel discover system compromise, CISA recommends they:

- Reimage compromised hosts
- Provision new account credentials
- Limit access to the management interface to the fullest extent possible
- Implement network segmentation
  - **Note:** network segmentation is a very effective security mechanism to help prevent an intruder from propagating exploits or laterally moving within an internal network. Segregation separates network segments based on role and functionality. A securely segregated network can limit the spread of malicious occurrences, reducing the impact from intruders that gain a foothold somewhere inside the network.[30]

---

[30] *Alert (AA20-206A)*, Cybersecurity & Infrastructure Security Agency (July 24, 2020), https://us-cert.cisa.gov/ncas/alerts/aa20-206a.

1.3[B] CYBERSECURITY TOOLS

These threat alerts and known vulnerability databases are extremely helpful to the cybersecurity professional. But the cybersecurity professional must also be proactive by using technology tools to protect the company's computing and network assets from harm because not every vulnerability will be discovered and placed in the database or every threat result in an email or SMS alert. For example, maybe the threat is internal, such as an employee sending confidential data over the company's network to an outside party. Or maybe the data meant for investor A is sent to Investor B without any nefarious intent, it was just a mistake. Or maybe an employee clicks on a link that the employee incorrectly thinks is valid and from the IT department, and that causes a cybersecurity breach. There are many communication channels, hosts, and endpoints that need to be monitored.

Some of the tools that are available to cybersecurity professional include:
- Intrusion Protection Systems (IPS)
- Intrusion Detection Systems (IDS)
- Data Loss Prevention (DLP)
- Security Information and Event Management systems (SIEM).

An IPS "is software that has all the capabilities of an intrusion detection system and can also attempt to stop possible incidents."[31]

An IDS "is software that automates the intrusion detection process."[32]

IPS technologies are differentiated from IDS technologies by one characteristic: IPS technologies can respond to a detected threat by attempting to prevent it from succeeding. They use several response techniques, which can be divided into the following groups:

- The IPS stops the attack itself. Examples of how this could be done are as follows:

  − Terminate the network connection or user session that is being used for the attack

  − Block access to the target (or possibly other likely targets) from the offending user account, IP address, or other attacker attribute

  − Block all access to the targeted host, service, application, or other resource.

- The IPS changes the security environment. The IPS could change the configuration of other security controls to disrupt an attack. Common

---

[31] Peter Mell & Karen Scarfone, *Guide to Intrusion Detection and Prevention Systems (IDPS) (Draft)*, NATIONAL INSTITUTE OF STANDARDS AND TECHNOLOGY 3 (July 2012), *available at* https://csrc.nist.gov/CSRC/media/Publications/sp/800-94/rev-1/draft/documents/draft_sp800-94-rev1.pdf.
[32] *Id.*

examples are reconfiguring a network device (e.g., firewall, router, switch) to block access from the attacker or to the target, and altering a host-based firewall on a target to block incoming attacks. Some IPSs can even cause patches to be applied to a host if the IPS detects that the host has vulnerabilities.

- The IPS changes the attack's content. Some IPS technologies can remove or replace malicious portions of an attack to make it benign. A simple example is an IPS removing an infected file attachment from an email and then permitting the cleaned email to reach its recipient. A more complex example is an IPS that acts as a proxy and normalizes incoming requests, which means that the proxy repackages the payloads of the requests, discarding header information. This might cause certain attacks to be discarded as part of the normalization process.[33]

For brevity, NIST uses the combined term of "intrusion detection and prevention systems (IDPS):[34]

There are many types of IDPS technologies. For the purposes of this document, they are divided into the following four groups based on the type of events that they monitor and the ways in which they are deployed:

- Network-Based, which monitors network traffic for particular network segments or devices and analyzes the network and application protocol activity to identify suspicious activity. It can identify many different types of events of interest. It is most commonly deployed at a boundary between networks, such as in proximity to border firewalls or routers, virtual private network (VPN) servers, remote access servers, and wireless networks. Section 4 contains extensive information on network- based IDPS technologies.
- Wireless, which monitors wireless network traffic and analyzes its wireless networking protocols to identify suspicious activity involving the protocols themselves. It cannot identify suspicious activity in the application or higher-layer network protocols (e.g., TCP, UDP) that the wireless network traffic is transferring. It is most commonly deployed within range of an organization's wireless network to monitor it, but can also be deployed to locations where unauthorized wireless networking could be occurring. More information on wireless IDPSs is presented in Section 5.
- Network Behavior Analysis (NBA), which examines network traffic to identify threats that generate unusual traffic flows, such as distributed denial of service (DDoS) attacks, certain forms of malware (e.g., worms, backdoors), and policy violations (e.g., a client system providing network services to other systems). NBA systems are most often deployed to monitor flows on an organization's internal networks, and are also sometimes deployed where they can monitor flows between an

---

[33] *Id.* at 5.
[34] *Id.* at 3.

organization's networks and external networks (e.g., the Internet, business partners' networks). NBA products are discussed in more detail in Section 6.

- Host-Based, which monitors the characteristics of a single host and the events occurring within that host for suspicious activity. Examples of the types of characteristics a host-based IDPS might monitor are network traffic (only for that host), system logs, running processes, application activity, file access and modification, and system and application configuration changes. Host-based IDPSs are most commonly deployed on critical hosts such as publicly accessible servers and servers containing sensitive information. Section 7 contains additional information on host-based IDPSs.[35]

Most IDPSs use multiple detection methodologies, either separately or integrated, to provide more broad and accurate detection. The primary classes of detection methodologies are as follows:

- Signature-based, which compares known threat signatures to observed events to identify incidents. This is very effective at detecting known threats but largely ineffective at detecting unknown threats and many variants on known threats. Signature-based detection cannot track and understand the state of complex communications, so it cannot detect most attacks that comprise multiple events.
- Anomaly-based detection, which compares definitions of what activity is considered normal against observed events to identify significant deviations. This method uses profiles that are developed by monitoring the characteristics of typical activity over a period of time. The IDPS then compares the characteristics of current activity to thresholds related to the profile. Anomaly-based detection methods can be very effective at detecting previously unknown threats. Common problems with anomaly-based detection are inadvertently including malicious activity within a profile, establishing profiles that are not sufficiently complex to reflect real-world computing activity, and generating many false positives.
- Stateful protocol analysis, which compares predetermined profiles of generally accepted definitions of benign protocol activity for each protocol state against observed events to identify deviations. Unlike anomaly-based detection, which uses host or network-specific profiles, stateful protocol analysis relies on vendor-developed universal profiles that specify how particular protocols should and should not be used. It is capable of understanding and tracking the state of protocols that have a notion of state, which allows it to detect many attacks that other methods cannot. Problems with stateful protocol analysis include that it is often very difficult or impossible to develop completely accurate models of protocols, it is very resource-intensive, and it cannot detect attacks that

---

[35] *Id.* at 9.

do not violate the characteristics of generally acceptable protocol behavior.[36]

A data loss prevention (DLP) system looks to recognize and block attempts at data exfiltration. A DLP can look at data classification or do pattern matching on data being removed from the system. Pattern matching can concentrate of such sensitive data as social security numbers or credit card numbers. DLP systems are normally focused on networks and endpoint-based computing assets. Key detection areas are emails and USB drives. Some operating systems can capture the attachment of a USB drive and record forensic information for further analysis. Upon detection, the DLP can take action to block. Encryption will defeat DLP systems.

A security information and event system (SIEM) is a system that collects data from many systems across the enterprise. The data is normally captured in a log file at an end point such as a personal work computer or from hosts such as servers or other points of interest with logging capability within the enterprise network. The SIEM can be configured to collect and review the data from all of these log files to look for trends or events of interest to determine if an incident has occurred.

All of these tools require constant fine-tuning for threats through proper configuration and follow-up analysis of captured events and incidents. The cybersecurity professional is to the daily operation of machines, data and networks as a doctor is to the ongoing diagnosis of a patient.

Some companies will also set up what is known as a honeypot, which is a decoy system that looks like it contains sensitive and important data but does not. The honeypot is a trap where information about the hacker can be collected while the hacker is probing the honeypot. And as long as the perpetrator is spending time in the honeypot, the perpetrator is ignoring the other valid and valuable systems.

Companies should remove all systems, applications, and services from the network when they are no longer needed. Leaving active but retired assets on the company's network allows unnecessary access ports and opportunity of entry.[37]

1.3[C] INHOUSE DEVELOPMENT OF PRODUCTS AND SERVICES

Many companies develop their own software in-house when it is cheaper than buying software or when software is not available commercially off the shelf with the feature set the company desires. Having an in-house development team is costly but it gives the company the flexibility to pursue the features they want in the software on their priority timetable. The application of reasonable security measures should start with the design and development of the software.

Privacy by Design is a phrase often used by privacy professionals. Privacy by Design is the concept whereby the designing stage for software incorporates privacy

---

[36] *Id.* at 10.

[37] A black hat hacker may access a computer or multiple computers to use them to attack another system. The utilized computers are sometimes called "bad bots" or "zombies." Cyber Blog Team, *Bots and Cybersecurity*, LIFARS (2020), www.lifars.com/2020/06/bots-and-cybersecurity/amp/. The group of bad bots or zombies may be called a "bot net." *Id.* A "bot net" can be used for a Distributed Denial of Service (DDoS) attack, which can overload a system. *Id.* A "bot net" attack can be used to steal personal information. *Id.*

considerations. As already noted, privacy considerations apply to the protection of data that could adversely affect a person if the data is compromised. Thus, Privacy by Design is data-centric and could be referred to as security by design. Just as important if not more so, would be the application of cybersecurity testing during the design and development phases of software.

Software has a Software Development Life Cycle (SDLC) that includes many phases from conception through the retirement of the software. Secure SDLC adds a focus on maintaining security through the SDLC. Security of the application should be addressed and monitored throughout the SDLC starting with the conception and design phase. Design teams along with development teams are often under a lot of pressure to produce code that works and is done on-time and on-budget to meet a particular market cycle. For example, a smartphone that goes to market after Christmas will miss market share. Sometimes, in that process, testing for security in addition to functionality can be overlooked. To remedy that situation, the cybersecurity team should establish a good relationship with the design and development teams. Cybersecurity counsel can also be helpful in being part of that relationship. The design and development teams may not fully understand the consequences of not incorporating security measures early on. Education of the development and design teams on the challenges faced by both counsel and the cybersecurity team can go a long way in providing a working partnership across all teams on addressing cybersecurity for the good of all.

The disconnect often stems from each team not understanding why something has to be done or how it affects the company as a whole. Because each team uses different terminology for communicating about their performance goals, communication can be difficult. Engineers will not understand the legal world and vice versa. Engineers may not understand the daily challenges of the cybersecurity team and vice versa. For example, one of the authors was brought into a case before the FTC. It became apparent early on that the engineers and the attorneys were very dedicated to solving issues that affected the company's bottom line but that neither side understood the challenges of the other's task. The engineers were designing communication devices that had a short shelf live and a new product pipeline had to be maintained to keep adding new product features and have new products delivered on time for seasonal markets. The legal department was focused on protecting the company against the enforcement powers of the FTC. The author was able to explain the issue to each side in their terms. The engineers were more than happy to cooperate after the issue was put into their language and after they understood the risk of cybersecurity was equivalent, if not greater than missing a product deadline.

A good relationship and partnership with operations is also crucial in maintaining good cybersecurity practices. This goal has led to the development and implementation of a DevOps solution.

The DevOps approach is a team effort between operations, development, and cybersecurity. Some may use the term Quality Assurance (QA) instead of cybersecurity. QA is fine as long as that team also has a focus on cybersecurity.

1.3[D] Incident Response Responsibilities

The cybersecurity professional responsibilities that we have discussed so far in this chapter are proactive protection and detection responsibilities. The cybersecurity professional also has incident response responsibilities. An incident response plan is crucial for a proper response to an incident. Events and incidents are distinguishable:

> An event is any observable occurrence in a system or network. Events include a user connecting to a file share, a server receiving a request for a web page, a user sending email, and a firewall blocking a connection attempt. Adverse events are events with a negative consequence, such as system crashes, packet floods, unauthorized use of system privileges, unauthorized access to sensitive data, and execution of malware that destroys data. This guide addresses only adverse events that are computer security- related, not those caused by natural disasters, power failures, etc.

> A computer security incident is a violation or imminent threat of violation of computer security policies, acceptable use policies, or standard security practices. Examples of incidents are:

> - An attacker commands a botnet to send high volumes of connection requests to a web server, causing it to crash.
> - Users are tricked into opening a "quarterly report" sent via email that is actually malware; running the tool has infected their computers and established connections with an external host.
> - An attacker obtains sensitive data and threatens that the details will be released publicly if the organization does not pay a designated sum of money.
> - A user provides or exposes sensitive information to others through peer-to-peer file sharing services.[38]

A good incident response plan will include personnel and associated responsibilities, communication information, steps to be taken in the event of an incident, and chain of command. The cybersecurity professional will likely be a member of the computer incident response team (CIRT), also known as computer security incident response team (CSIRT). NIST has developed an incident response life cycle that includes preparation, detection and analysis, containment eradication and recovery, and post-incident activity:[39]

NIST provides a checklist for the action to take for a suspected incident:[40]

---

[38] Paul Cichonski, et. al., *Computer Security Incident Handling Guide*, NATIONAL INSTITUTE STANDARDS AND TECHNOLOGY 6 (Aug. 2012), *available at* https://nvlpubs.nist.gov/nistpubs/SpecialPublications/NIST.SP.800-61r2.pdf.
[39] *Id.* at 21.
[40] *Id.* at 42.

	Action	Completed
Detection and Analysis		
1.	Determine whether an incident has occurred	
1.1	Analyze the precursors and indicators	
1.2	Look for correlating information	
1.3	Perform research (e.g., search engines, knowledge base)	
1.4	As soon as the handler believes an incident has occurred, begin documenting the investigation and gathering evidence	
2.	Prioritize handling the incident based on the relevant factors (functional impact, information impact, recoverability effort, etc.)	
3.	Report the incident to the appropriate internal personnel and external organizations	
Containment, Eradication, and Recovery		
4.	Acquire, preserve, secure, and document evidence	
5.	Contain the incident	
6.	Eradicate the incident	
6.1	Identify and mitigate all vulnerabilities that were exploited	
6.2	Remove malware, inappropriate materials, and other components	
6.3	If more affected hosts are discovered (e.g., new malware infections), repeat the Detection and Analysis steps (1.1, 1.2) to identify all other affected hosts, then contain (5) and eradicate (6) the incident for them	
7.	Recover from the incident	
7.1	Return affected systems to an operationally ready state	
7.2	Confirm that the affected systems are functioning normally	
7.3	If necessary, implement additional monitoring to look for future related activity	
Post-Incident Activity		
8.	Create a follow-up report	
9.	Hold a lessons learned meeting (mandatory for major incidents, optional otherwise)	

Even with a thorough IRP and checklist, do not expect the response to an incident to go smoothly. Expect the incident to happen on a Friday evening after everyone has left and are pursuing their weekend plans. Expect that responding to a verifiable incident will be stressful. Companies should conduct table-top exercises to give participants practice and to identify gaps in the plan or checklist. Companies should also provide training to potential participants. And it is a good idea to get the legal department involved at the beginning of the incident.

NOTES

Note 1

The Business News Daily in an article titled, Best InfoSec and Cybersecurity Certifications of 2020, set forth the five top certifications for cybersecurity-related professionals. The top five certifications include: 1) Certified Ethical Hacker (CEH); 2) Certified Information Security Manger (CISM); 3) CompTIA Security+; 4) Certified Information Systems Security Professional (CISSP); and 5) Certified Information

Security Auditor (CISA).[41]   The CEH is offered by the International Council of E-Commerce Consultants.   The Information Systems Audit and Control Association provides the CISM. CompTIA issues the Security + certification. The CISSP is provided by the International Information Systems Security Certification Consortium. Finally, the Information Systems Audit and Control Association also offers the CISA. According to the article, there are over 300,000 open cybersecurity professional positions in the United States in 2020.

Note 2

Do you think artificial intelligence and machine learning will be the panacea for cybersecurity woes?   While artificial intelligence may lead to efficient detection of vulnerabilities, malware and the assessment of risk, what are some fundamental problems with artificial intelligence tools in the cybersecurity space? *See* Danny Palmer, *AI is changing everything about cybersecurity, for better and for worse. Here's what you need to know*, ZDNet (March 2, 2020), https://www.zdnet.com/article/ai-is-changing-everything-about-cybersecurity-for-better-and-for-worse-heres-what-you-need-to-know/ (noting that AI could be used by hackers); Josephine Wolff, *How to Improve Cybersecurity for Artificial Intelligence*, Brookings Institution (June 9, 2020), https://www.brookings.edu/research/how-to-improve-cybersecurity-for-artificial-intelligence/ (noting that defensive AI systems can be hacked). In a technological arms race, artificial intelligence is also being used by hackers. Kat Jercich, *AI and machine learning: A gift, and a curse, for cybersecurity*, Healthcare IT News (October 20, 2020), https://www.healthcareitnews.com/news/ai-and-machine-learning-gift-and-curse-cybersecurity (noting sophistication of attackers using machine learning and AI).

Note 3

Quantum computing and blockchain are two technologies that may impact cybersecurity practices. One issue concerning quantum computing is how it may impact current encryption standards. *See Migration to Post-Quantum Cryptography*, National Institute of Standards. NIST provides a statement of the problem:

> The advent of quantum computing technology will compromise many of the current cryptographic algorithms, especially public-key cryptography, which is widely used to protect digital information. Most algorithms on which we depend are used worldwide in components of many different communications, processing, and storage systems. Once access to practical quantum computers becomes available, all public-key algorithms and associated protocols will be vulnerable to criminals, competitors, and other adversaries. It is critical to begin planning for the replacement of hardware, software, and services that use public-key algorithms now so that information is protected from future attacks. *Id.*

---

[41] Ed Tittel, Kim Lindros, & Mary Kyle, *Best InfoSec and Cybersecurity Certifications of 2020*, BUSINESS NEWS DAILY, https://www.businessnewsdaily.com/10708-information-security-certifications.html (last updated Feb. 3, 2020).

Private or public blockchain technology may enable better protection for the integrity of information. Additionally, blockchain technology can be used for access control. NIST states: "Blockchain technology offers high confidence and tamper resistance implemented in a distributed fashion without a central authority, which means that it can be a trustable alternative for enforcing access control policies." *Blockchain for Access Control Systems: Draft NISTIR 8403 Available for Comment*, NIST (December 20, 2021), available at https://www.nist.gov/news-events/news/2021/12/blockchain-access-control-systems-draft-nistir-8403-available-comment. NIST has produced a document concerning using blockchain for access control: "This document presents analyses of blockchain access control systems from the perspectives of properties, components, architectures, and model supports, as well as discussions on considerations for implementation." *Id.*

Note 4

In order to conceptualize the importance of cybersecurity, it may be helpful to think of personal data flows in the context of a hypothetical physical store. As you examine whether to enter the store, data is collected about you. When you walk in the store, data is collected about you. As you move through the store and examine items, data is collected about you. As you leave the store and perhaps purchase goods or services, data is collected about you. Entities are confronted with the issue of how to manage all of that data. As you will learn from this book, collecting only the information needed for your purpose is a cybersecurity and informational privacy best practice. What happens if the entity that collected data is purchased by another entity? Who may access data? What happens if the entity no longer wishes to keep data? How should the entity dispose of data?

Personal data, which may be protected by intellectual property law in some contexts, may not be the only valuable information subject to exfiltration or modification. Other types of product or service-related data protected by intellectual property laws may be at risk as well.

Note 5

One of the most significant threats to cybersecurity is social engineering. Social engineering generally involves the use of means to access a system by using deception against a human being such as phishing. One answer to protect against the problem of social engineering is excellent training. Should trained employees who fall for social engineering schemes be liable for the harm caused by such schemes? What if the employee makes multiple mistakes? Is that good cause for termination?

QUESTIONS

The C-suite management of a startup technology company (Techno) with an internet presence is concerned about the cost of hiring a full-time cybersecurity professional. How can the cost of a full-time cybersecurity professional be justified in the eyes of C-suite management?

1.4 Responsibilities of a Cybersecurity Counselor

We chose the term Cybersecurity Counselor over Cybersecurity Attorney because a counselor is a broader term that designates providing advice beyond just cybersecurity legalities. A cybersecurity counselor will have the opportunity to advise clients across a broad swath of cybersecurity-related issues. The cybersecurity counselor may be involved in all aspects of a company's cybersecurity lifecycle, including but not limited to the creation of initial cybersecurity policies, controls, guidance and procedure, risk analysis under a risk analysis framework, business continuity planning, disaster recovery planning, training, and incident response. A competent cybersecurity counselor can become a liaison or bridge between the C-suite or General Counsel's office and the cybersecurity professional.

As a cybersecurity counsel just joining the legal department of a company, you will need to understand the business models of your company. After understanding the business models, you will need to determine which regulators and agencies regulate your industry and/or business models. Once the regulators and agencies are identified, research must be done to establish which cybersecurity and privacy laws apply to your company along with the legal risk for each. Next, counsel should acquire an inventory of the company's data and cyber assets. With this information in hand, counsel must make a determination as to whether the company is in compliance and whether "reasonable security measures" are in place for the data and cyber assets. The chapter on the NIST Cybersecurity Framework provides a methodology for assessing what may be reasonable security measures under the specific circumstances involved. If the company is not in compliance with reasonable security measures, counsel must drive efforts to get into compliance and maintain reasonable security measures by ensuring the proper cybersecurity policies and procedures are developed and then maintained. Counsel must also determine whether the policies and procedures are being followed by all employees and provide proper training as needed on the policies and procedures. Indeed, one common source of cybersecurity issues involve employees who are not properly trained in recognizing attempts to breach a particular system. Efforts to breach systems by relying on humans is generally known as social engineering and may include phishing or even just searching through trash for passwords.

The cybersecurity in-house counsel will ideally be a liaison between General Counsel and the company person responsible for maintaining cybersecurity and responding to incidents. Cybersecurity counsel will maintain communication channels with cyber-related departments and business departments, whose business requirements are driving cyber-related efforts. By doing so, cybersecurity counsel should not be surprised when a new product is placed in the network. Also, when needed, cybersecurity counsel will manage outside cybersecurity legal-related efforts.

Counsel should also establish and maintain contacts and relationships with the FBI and Secret Service departments that pursue data breach incidents. Counsel should be prepared to advise on when to contact law enforcement, the FBI, or the Secret Service.

The cybersecurity landscape is dynamic. Counsel will also need to stay on top of changing and new laws at the federal and state levels. Companies are also dynamic.

Counsel will need to be aware of any upcoming mergers and then participate in the merger to make sure the company maintains it cybersecurity posture across the merger. In a smaller company, counsel may also be asked to take on privacy duties. Notably, cybersecurity counsel may be litigators and transactional attorneys. As we explore future chapters, cybersecurity litigation as well as transactions are important areas of cybersecurity legal work. Moreover, cybersecurity legal issues cross the public and private spheres as well as cut across all industries in the private arena.

 Most companies are transactional in nature. There are contracts for outsourcing, providing services to customers, and receiving services from vendors. In today's connected world, a majority of these contracts will have the need for a watchful cybersecurity eye and a cybersecurity legal eye. As mentioned *supra*, the move of company services to the cloud have presented good economic opportunities to save money, but there are also opportunities for security gaps. For example, who is responsible for every aspect of security, the cloud provider, the customer, or both? Counsel will need to understand whether the company is a controller or processor of data. Counsel will also need to verify that the vendor will handle sensitive data properly. Does the vendor meet compliance standards? Is the vendor ISO 27001 certified?[42] Has the vendor gone through SOC audits?[43] Were those SOC audits made available for review, and did they pass?

 As we have noted, the United States has a patchwork of regulations that cover privacy and cybersecurity law enforced by a number of agencies. In the following chapters, we will provide detail for those regulations and who is covered. The first step is determining the character and make-up of the client or company. Are they a pure investment firm covered by the SEC or do they dabble in many areas, covered by cybersecurity laws and regulations written for various agencies and enforced by many agencies?

NOTES

Note 1

---

[42] The Independent Standards Organization [ISO]:
> ISO is an independent, non-governmental international organization with a membership of 167 national standards bodies.
> Through its members, it brings together experts to share knowledge and develop voluntary, consensus-based, market relevant International Standards that support innovation and provide solutions to global challenges. ISO - About us

ISO 27001:
> ISO/IEC 27001 is widely known, providing requirements for an information security management system (ISMS), though there are more than a dozen standards in the ISO/IEC 27000 family. Using them enables organizations of any kind to manage the security of assets such as financial information, intellectual property, employee details or information entrusted by third parties. ISO - ISO/IEC 27001 — Information security management

[43] "SOC is an acronym that now stands for System and Organization Controls (previously Service Organization Controls) and is an audit of a companies controls that are in place to help ensure the Security, Availability, Processing Integrity, Confidentiality and Privacy of their customers data. The SOC control standards were created and overseen by the American Institute of Certified Public Accountants (AICPA)." Adsero Security, *Security 101, SOC Audit, What is a SOC Audit*, available at What is a SOC Audit? - Adsero Security (last visited May 23, 2022).

Some of you may have been exposed to the legal profession by working in a firm or taking legal courses such as Civil Procedure, Professional Responsibility, and Evidence. You can imagine how much confidential information is collected by law firms through their representation of clients. Indeed, law firms have been the victims of cybersecurity hacks and breaches. And, of course, those attorneys are subject to the cybersecurity rules that we will discuss. However, attorneys also have ethical obligations to ensure that data is properly protected by cybersecurity measures. For example, attorneys have duties to guard confidential information and to competently represent their clients. In ABA Ethics Formal Opinion 477R (May 22, 2017), the ABA noted:

Securing Communication of Protected Client Information

> A lawyer generally may transmit information relating to the representation of a client over the internet without violating the Model Rules of Professional Conduct where the lawyer has undertaken reasonable efforts to prevent inadvertent or unauthorized access. However, a lawyer may be required to take special security precautions to protect against the inadvertent or unauthorized disclosure of client information when required by an agreement with the client or by law, or when the nature of the information requires a higher degree of security.

In discussing the relevance of encrypting client communications, the ABA stated:

> However, cyber-threats and the proliferation of electronic communications devices have changed the landscape and it is not always reasonable to rely on the use of unencrypted email. For example, electronic communication through certain mobile applications or on message boards or via unsecured networks may lack the basic expectation of privacy afforded to email communications. Therefore, lawyers must, on a case-by-case basis, constantly analyze how they communicate electronically about client matters . . . to determine what effort is reasonable.

Notably, the ABA emphasized that attorneys must train employees on sensitivity to cybersecurity issues as well as ensure vendors utilize appropriate cybersecurity measures. Should lawyers use unencrypted emails when communicating with clients? If a lawyer is not going to encrypt all communications with a client, which type of communication should they not encrypt? Why?

Note 2

Why may cybersecurity counsel want to be involved in testing the company's cybersecurity systems? What may be learned about a company's cybersecurity system through testing? What about attorney client privilege or work product doctrine? What are the benefits of claiming confidentiality under those doctrines?

QUESTIONS

A startup technology company (Techno) with an internet presence is concerned with the new approach of state AGs and the FTC in using a reasonable security measures cause of action against companies that have published cybersecurity issues. Techno has been lucky so far, it has not had any cybersecurity incidents that it is aware of, but it assumes that ethical hackers have been visiting its websites looking for vulnerabilities. Techno believes it is doing the "right thing" when it comes to the cybersecurity protection of its systems, but it is concerned that it doesn't have enough of its cybersecurity programs captured in policy, controls, and procedure documents. It is also lacking a written business continuity plan and disaster recovery plan even though it believes it would be okay in a disaster because its staff is small and technically nimble. Management took an initial step toward solving the lack of documentation issue by purchasing cybersecurity control and policy document templates based on NIST and ISO frameworks from a vendor. Should Techno hire a cybersecurity counsel to edit and customize the templates for Techno's systems or is it ok to just rely on the IT department to edit and customize? Please advise.

Techno plans to offer goods online. Techno would like to utilize a vendor to design and operate its website. Techno would also like to use a vendor's software "in the cloud" to run its internal processes, such as human resources. What risks may exist for Techno? Please advise.

Techno was notified by a grey hat hacker that there is a vulnerability in its vendor's internal processing software. What should Techno do? Please advise.

1.5 Example of A Cybersecurity Problem

The following case excerpt is an example of a cybersecurity problem. The excerpt includes the facts from a securities case involving the Experian data breach. In the facts, you can see how badly Experian failed to adopt and maintain reasonable and appropriate security measures. We will examine the Experian case in detail in the Securities and Exchange Commission chapter.

In re Equifax Securities Litigation, 357 F.Supp.3d 1189 (2019).

OPINION AND ORDER
THOMAS W. THRASH, JR., United States District Judge
I. Background
. . .
As part of its business, Equifax collects, maintains, and sells a huge quantity of personal data about consumers and employees all over the world. This personally identifiable information is highly sensitive. It includes Social Security numbers, addresses, birthdays, employment history, driver's license information, detailed payment history, loans, credit card information, and more. Credit bureaus such as Equifax acquire this information from banks, mortgage lenders, credit card issuers, and other financing companies. This personally identifiable information is a highly valuable target for cybercriminals; it includes some of the most private information about consumers. This information can be used to enter into a mortgage, set up a bank account, change a phone number, and even more.

The Defendants recognized the importance of safeguarding this highly sensitive personal information. In its SEC filings, Equifax acknowledged that it collected and stored sensitive data, including the personally identifiable information of consumers, and stated that safeguarding this data was "critical" to its "business operations and strategy." It noted that its success was dependent upon its "reputation as a trusted steward of information." Equifax also acknowledged that it was a valuable target for cybercriminals due to the vast trove of information it collected. In its SEC filings, Equifax recognized that it was regularly the target of criminal hackers, and that a cybersecurity incident could subject it to a variety of serious consequences.

Acknowledging the importance of protecting the data in its custody, the Defendants made a number of statements during the class period regarding Equifax's networks and the security of the personal data in its custody. According to the Plaintiff, the Defendants issued statements concerning the strength of Equifax's cybersecurity systems, its compliance with data protection laws, and the integrity of its internal controls. For example, with regard to the strength of its data security, Equifax's website provided that the company employed "strong data security and confidentiality standards" and maintained "a highly sophisticated data information network that includes advanced security, protections and redundancies." With regard to Equifax's compliance with data protection laws, regulations, and standards, the Defendants stated in SEC filings that they continuously monitored federal and state legislative and regulatory activities "in order to remain in compliance" with those laws. The Defendants also certified in SEC filings during the class period that Equifax had effective internal controls that would provide "reasonable assurance regarding prevention or timely detection of unauthorized acquisition, use or disposition of our assets."

However, despite these assurances, Equifax's cybersecurity was dangerously deficient. The Data Breach, according to the Plaintiff, was the inevitable result of widespread shortcomings in Equifax's data security systems. According to the Plaintiff's allegations, Equifax's data protection measures were "grossly inadequate," "failed to meet the most basic industry standards," and "ran afoul of the well-established mandates of applicable data protection laws." These shortcomings spanned a number of facets of cybersecurity practices, including a failure to implement proper patching protocols, failure to encrypt sensitive information, the storage of sensitive data on public-facing servers, the use of inadequate network monitoring practices, the use of obsolete software, and more. Overall, according to cybersecurity experts, a "catastrophic breach of Equifax's systems was inevitable because of systemic organizational disregard for cybersecurity and cyber-hygiene best practices."

According to the Plaintiff, Equifax failed to implement an adequate patch management process, while also failing to remediate known deficiencies in its cybersecurity infrastructure. The company relied upon a single individual to manually implement its patching process across its entire network. This individual had no way to know where vulnerable software in need of patching was being run on Equifax's systems. This protocol was far less secure than the automatic patching processes that many other companies, including Equifax's peers, employ in their systems. According to cybersecurity experts, this patching process fell far short of industry standards.

Equifax also failed to encrypt sensitive data in its custody. According to the Amended Complaint, Equifax admitted that sensitive personal information relating to hundreds of millions of Americans was not encrypted, but instead was stored in plaintext, making it easy for unauthorized users to read and misuse. Not only was this information unencrypted, but it also was accessible through a public-facing, widely used website. This enabled any attacker that compromised the website's server to immediately have access to this sensitive personal data in plaintext. Smith also admitted during congressional testimony that, with respect to its core credit databases, Equifax failed to encrypt any of its data. It also failed to encrypt its highly vulnerable mobile applications, meaning that in addition to keeping sensitive data unencrypted in its own systems, it also failed to encrypt data being transmitted over the internet. This, according to experts, was a major security failure. And, when Equifax did encrypt data, it left the keys to unlocking the encryption on the same public-facing servers, making it easy to remove the encryption from the data. These inadequacies in Equifax's encryption protocol fell far short of industry standards and data security laws, and showed that Equifax did not "know what they were doing" with respect to data security.

Moreover, Equifax also failed to implement adequate authentication measures. Authentication measures are mechanisms, such as passwords, that verify that a party attempting to access a system or network is authorized to do so. According to the Amended Complaint, Equifax's authentication measures were insufficient to protect the sensitive personal data in its custody from unauthorized access. These mechanisms included weak passwords and security questions. For example, Equifax relied upon four digit pins derived from Social Security numbers and birthdays to guard personal information, despite the fact that these weak passwords had already been compromised in previous breaches. Furthermore, Equifax employed the username "admin" and the password "admin" to protect a portal used to manage credit disputes, a password that "is a surefire way to get hacked." This portal contained a vast trove of personal information. According to cybersecurity experts, these shortcomings demonstrated "poor security policy and a lack of due diligence." Equifax's authentication practices fell short of the data security standards, which recommend the use of multi-factor authentication. Equifax also failed to adequately monitor its networks and systems, which greatly exacerbated the fallout of the Data Breach. According to the Plaintiff, Equifax failed to establish mechanisms for monitoring its networks and systems to alert when a threat existed. Such mechanisms include maintaining activity logs, setting up processes for tracking malicious scripts, and implementing file integrity monitoring. According to cybersecurity experts, logging is a "simple but crucial cybersecurity technique" in which a company monitors its systems by continuously logging network access so as to identify unauthorized users. This failure by Equifax greatly compounded the magnitude of the Data Breach's impact. According to experts, a breach as large scale as this one would not have occurred if Equifax had implemented better monitoring systems. If adequate monitoring systems had been in place, Equifax could have identified the breach much earlier and prevented the exfiltration of consumer data from its network. Improved logging techniques also could have enabled Equifax to expel the hackers from its systems and minimize the impact of the breach. Instead, due in part to Equifax's failure to implement effective logging techniques, hackers were able to continuously access this sensitive personal data for over 75 days. Equifax's failure to utilize proper network monitoring, one of the most basic cybersecurity practices, demonstrates the fundamental deficiencies in its networks.

Equifax's handling of the sensitive data in its custody also reflected a poor cybersecurity regime. There were two main shortcomings as to this category. First, Equifax stored sensitive personal information, in unencrypted plaintext form, on public-facing servers and web portals. Second, it failed to partition this sensitive information to limit the exposure if a breach occurred. In contrast, standard security best practices recommend that companies ensure that sensitive data is stored on non-public servers and is inaccessible through public-facing networks. Equifax's failure to properly segment its networks also contravened standard cybersecurity practices. Experts note that network segmentation, which consists of dividing a network into smaller partitions, isolates critical assets from one another and controls the access to sensitive data. Equifax's failure to properly handle this sensitive data is another example of the deficiencies in its cybersecurity regime.

Many other aspects of Equifax's cybersecurity practices were also deficient. According to the Plaintiff, Equifax relied upon outdated security systems and software, allowed its "attack surface" to grow too big by leaving thousands of servers exposed on the internet; allowed unused data to accumulate and failed to dispose of unneeded data; failed to restrict access to sensitive data to only those employees whose job responsibilities required such access; failed to adequately train its security personnel; failed to perform adequate reviews of its systems, networks, and security; and failed to develop a data breach management plan. However, despite the woeful state of Equifax's cybersecurity, the Defendants made a number of statements touting the strength of Equifax's data systems and the cybersecurity practices that it employed.

According to the Plaintiff, the Defendants also ignored a number of warnings that Equifax's data security measures were inadequate. In 2014, KPMG performed a security audit of Equifax which found that, among other deficiencies, Equifax left encryption keys on the same public servers where encrypted data was stored. Then, in 2016, Equifax hired Deloitte to perform another security audit. Deloitte discovered several problems in its audit, including inadequate patching systems. However, according to former cybersecurity employees at Equifax, the company's management did not take the security audit seriously. Equifax employees and cybersecurity researchers continued to warn Equifax of deficiencies in its cybersecurity protocol. They warned Equifax about its inadequate patching systems, its failure to encrypt sensitive personal data, its storage of personal data on public-facing servers, and more. Furthermore, in March 2017, Equifax hired Mandiant, a cybersecurity firm, to investigate weaknesses in its data protection systems. This investigation, which was described as a "top-secret project," was personally overseen by Smith. Mandiant concluded that Equifax's data protection systems were grossly inadequate. Mandiant specifically identified Equifax's unpatched systems and "misconfigured security policies" as indicative of major problems. However, instead of heeding Mandiant's advice, Equifax squelched a broader review of Equifax's security systems.

Equifax also experienced other, smaller data breaches prior to the Data Breach here. According to the Plaintiff, these previous breaches should have warned the Defendants that Equifax's cybersecurity, including its authentication and network monitoring measures, was severely deficient. In April 2016, hackers breached Equifax's W2Express website, a service that offers downloadable W-2 forms for companies. The hackers were able to access the W-2 data of hundreds of thousands of employees of numerous companies that contracted with Equifax to use this service. The hackers were able to access this information by entering an employee's default PIN code, which was the last four digits of the employee's Social Security number and their four-digit birth year. According to cybersecurity experts, these authentication measures fell short of data security best practices. The hackers were also able to remain undetected in Equifax's networks for approximately one year before they were discovered, which the Plaintiff alleges reflected a failure to employ adequate network monitoring practices. Then, in February 2017, Equifax learned that another breach occurred in its Workforce Solutions segment. From April 2016 to March 2017, hackers were able to obtain wage and W-2 data maintained by Equifax's TALX division, now called Equifax Workforce Solutions. The hackers were again able to exploit Equifax's use of personal identifiers and weak four-digit PIN codes to protect this sensitive data. The hackers also were able to remain in Equifax's network for over a year. Cybersecurity experts opined that Equifax's authentication protections, which were exploited in this breach, were inadequate and failed to meet basic industry standards. After this incident Equifax promised to make improvements in its cybersecurity defenses, but failed to do so.

On or about March 7, 2017, security firms began issuing warnings that attackers were exploiting a vulnerability in Apache Struts, an open-source software application used to build interactive websites. This software is commonly used for websites where customers submit online forms. Apache Struts is widely used by large businesses, including a substantial percentage of the Fortune 100 companies. Equifax used Apache Struts at this time. Security firms began reporting that Apache Struts was vulnerable to a "remote code execution attack." This attack is a dangerous type of exploit that allows attackers to force the vulnerable systems into running computer programs written by the attackers, which can make it easy to either steal data or establish a foothold in the vulnerable system. This weakness in Apache Struts was not just highly dangerous – it was also especially easy to exploit. Due to both the dangerous nature of this vulnerability and the widespread use of Apache Struts in the business community, the vulnerability and the corresponding update to the software aimed at addressing the vulnerability were widely publicized. Both Apache itself and security firms publicized the vulnerability. By March 8, 2017, Apache released updated versions of Apache Struts to mitigate this vulnerability in the software.

In March 2017, hackers breached Equifax's network using the Apache Struts vulnerability. On or about May 13, 2017, the hackers accessed files containing Equifax usernames and passwords, which they then used to access documents and sensitive information in Equifax's "legacy environment," an area where it stored old data that it no longer used. The attackers accessed numerous databases and compromised multiple systems. The collection of information that the hackers obtained was so large that they had to break it up into smaller pieces to avoid setting off alarms. The hackers ultimately stole the names, Social Security numbers, birthdays, addresses, drivers license information, tax identification numbers, and other personal data of 148 million Americans, as well as personal information of nearly one million foreign consumers and employees. They also obtained the credit card information for 209,000 consumers.

On July 29 and 30 of 2017, Equifax discovered that criminal hackers had gained unauthorized access to its network. Susan Mauldin, Equifax's Chief Security Officer, notified John Kelly, Equifax's Chief Legal Officer, about the Data Breach on July 31. Mauldin informed Kelly that personally identifiable information may have been compromised in the Data Breach. Under Equifax's data security protocol, the chief of security is alerted about any issues, who then determines the severity of the breach. If the chief of security determines the breach to be severe, he or she then informs the executive leadership of the issue. On July 31, Smith was notified about the Data Breach. Kelly told Smith that Chief Information Officer David Webb would meet with him in person to discuss a data security issue. In this meeting, Webb notified Smith of the Data Breach, informing him that it had occurred in an online consumer dispute portal.

On August 2, 2017, Equifax notified the FBI of the Data Breach. It also retained legal counsel to guide its investigation into the breach. The same day, Equifax's legal counsel retained Mandiant to assist in the investigation into the incident. Experts would later note that these steps suggested that Equifax knew that the Data Breach was serious. . . .

On September 7, 2017, Equifax disclosed the Data Breach to the public for the first time. In a press release after the close of trading that day, Equifax revealed that it had suffered a data breach affecting the personal information of approximately 143 million American consumers. Equifax continued to make subsequent disclosures over the following days, ending on September 15, 2017, providing additional details concerning the Data Breach. The company stated that it had engaged Mandiant, a cybersecurity firm, to conduct a review, and that it had reported the breach to law enforcement. Experts, analysts, and the media immediately began to weigh in, with one analyst describing the breach as "one of the biggest cyber-attacks in US history." Cybersecurity experts opined that massive cybersecurity failures on Equifax's part resulted in the Data Breach, and that its public response and outreach were "haphazard and ill-conceived." Financial experts also began to weigh in. Some financial analysts predicted from the outset of this public revelation that, due to the unprecedented size of this incident, Equifax's stock price would decline. Other analysts predicted that Equifax would incur substantial costs relating to the Data Breach for years to come. . . .

On September 8, 2017, this action was commenced. In the Amended Complaint, the Plaintiff asserts one claim for violation of section 10(b) of the Exchange Act and Rule 10b–5 promulgated thereunder against all of the Defendants (Count I), and one claim for violation of section 20(a) of the Exchange Act against the Individual Defendants (Count II). The Plaintiff alleges that the Defendants made false or misleading statements on Equifax's website, in Equifax's SEC filings, and at Equifax Investor Conferences and Presentations. According to the Plaintiff, these false or misleading statements concerned the state of Equifax's cybersecurity, Equifax's compliance with data protection laws, regulations, and industry best practices, and Equifax's internal controls. On June 18, 2018, this Court modified the PSLRA's automatic stay of discovery to allow for limited case management and discovery planning activities. The Defendants now move to dismiss.

QUESTION

What specifically did Equifax fail to do that you think would constitute a failure to exercise and maintain "reasonable and appropriate security measures?"

NOTES

Note 1

Relatively small city governments have been the subject of ransomware attacks by hackers. In 2020, the city of Lafayette in Colorado had to deal with a ransomware attack. The City released the following statement, in part:

The ransomware that invaded the City's system was used by criminals to block access to the City's computer data until a sum of money is paid. The City was coerced into paying a $45,000 ransom to retrieve a "key" to unlock encrypted data. Ransom payment was not the direction the City wanted to go, and pursued all avenues to find alternative solutions. In a cost/benefit scenario of rebuilding the City's data versus paying the ransom, the ransom option far outweighed attempting to rebuild. The inconvenience of a lengthy service outage for residents was also taken into consideration.

While there is no way to eliminate the risk of these types of attacks, the City is taking steps to install crypto-safe backups, deploy additional cybersecurity systems, and implement regular vulnerability assessments to prevent future data threats.[44]

Why do you think small city governments are viable targets for ransomware attacks? On October 1, 2020, the U.S. Department of Treasury released a document titled, "Advisory on Potential Sanctions Risks for Facilitating Ransomware Payments," which warns that ransomware payments to certain individuals or entities may run afoul of laws and regulations concerning, for example, transactions with certain blocked entities and individuals, or countries with sanctions against them.[45] Should the government prohibit all ransomware payments? Why or why not?

Note 2

The Federal Trade Commission [FTC] released some demographic data concerning the victims of identity theft in 2005. The FTC reported, in relevant part:

- AGE: "The likelihood of a person who is 75 or over being a victim is 55 or 60 percent lower than that for someone who is between 35 and 44."
- INCOME: "Incomes in the $75,000 to $100,000 range are associated with at least a 50 percent increase in the risk of ID theft relative to the risk faced with an income of less than $25,000. Incomes over $100,000 are associated with an estimated increase of roughly 70 to 74 percent."
- GENDER: "The risk of experiencing some form of ID theft is just over 20 percent higher for women than for men . . . ."

---

[44] City of Lafayette, *Cyberattack Causes City Computer Outage* (August 4, 2020), https://cityoflafayette.com/civicalerts.aspx?AID=5729 (last updated October 9, 2020). For additional information concerning the Lafayette ransomware attack, please read: Tamara Cheung, *After a Small Colorado City Paid Cyber Attackers a Ransom, There's Concern About the Rest of the State*, Colorado Sun (Aug. 10, 2020), https://coloradosun.com/2020/08/10/cyber-attack-ransomware-small-towns-data-breach-malware-lafayette/ (last updated October 9, 2020).

[45] U.S. Department of Treasury, Advisory on Potential Sanctions Risks for Facilitating Ransomware Payments (Oct. 1, 2020), https://home.treasury.gov/system/files/126/ofac_ransomware_advisory_10012020_1.pdf.

- RACE/ETHNICITY: Non-Hispanic Whites are at 76.9%. Black and African Americans are at 8.6%. Asians at 2.1%. Hispanic at 6.7%.
- GEOGRAPHY: "The risk generally appears to be highest in Pacific states – California, Nevada, Washington, and those parts of Oregon and Idaho that are on Pacific time."[46]

Why do you think non-Hispanic Whites are significantly more likely to experience identity theft? Could this reflect the likelihood that other racial and ethnic groups may be poorer targets because they do not have the same access to credit for a variety of reasons? Why may some racial and ethnic groups have less access to credit than other racial and ethnic groups?

Note 3

The United States government is working to develop a cybersecurity workforce. In a September 2021 Aspen Institute report, titled, "Diversity, Equity and Inclusion in Cybersecurity," the authors pointed to the lack of racial and gender diversity in the cybersecurity field.[47] Importantly, the government is focusing on Historically Black Colleges and Universities (HBCUs). What may be the benefits of having HBCUs focused on producing a workforce for relatively high-paying cybersecurity positions? Some particularly important global competition issues concern maximizing the potential of available human capital and ensuring the availability of well-paying jobs to create a tax base to fund social programs and preserve confidence in democracy.

Note 4

Cybersecurity problems drive to the heart of our democracy. For example, as discussed *infra*, a target of cybersecurity breaches in some countries includes not only critical infrastructure, candidates for and holders of political office, the election ballot box, but also journalists. A major concern is the spread of misinformation and disinformation. Why is cybersecurity so important for journalists for democracy?

QUESTION

What do you think are some of the potential cybersecurity problems that exist given the number of employees and students who are now working from home given the global COVID-19 pandemic and its aftermath?

---

[46] Keith B. Anderson, Identify Theft: Does the Risk Vary with Demographics, WORKING PAPER NO. 279 (August 2005), https://www.ftc.gov/sites/default/files/documents/reports/identity-theft-does-risk-vary-demographics/wp279_0.pdf (last updated October 9, 2020).

[47] *Diversity, Equity and Inclusion in Cybersecurity*, ASPEN INSTITUTE (September 2021), available at Diversity-Equity-and-Inclusion-in-Cybersecurity_9.921.pdf (aspeninstitute.org).

CHAPTER TWO. FEDERAL TRADE COMMISSION ENFORCEMENT AND CYBERSECURITY LAW

2.1 Introduction

This Chapter reviews the Federal Trade Commission (FTC) enforcement actions concerning cybersecurity. The FTC is a federal agency tasked with protecting consumers and promoting competition.[48] In recent years the FTC has taken enforcement action against many companies, small and large, under "unfair or deceptive acts or practices in or affecting commerce" that have been clear-cut privacy enforcement actions. The "unfair or deceptive acts or practices in or affecting commerce" enforcement powers of the FTC come from Section 5 of the 1914 FTC Act. The FTC has been particularly successful in enforcing consumer privacy through the deceptive acts prong by pursuing companies that collect personal data beyond that which is disclosed in the companies' privacy notices. Of course, in 1914 cybersecurity was not envisioned as something that would be covered by the Act. But with the proliferation of computers and the connection of computers with the internet, cybersecurity has become a hot topic, and the FTC has been quick to find a way to add cybersecurity to its enforcement regiment.

Since 2002, the FTC has assumed a leading role in policing corporate cybersecurity practices. In that time, it has brought more than 60 cases against companies for unfair or deceptive practices that endanger the personal data of consumers.[49]

In 2002, the FTC started asserting claims based on "unfair" cybersecurity practices. For the next 10 years, all actions brought by the FTC resulted in negotiated consent agreements, with no company testing the FTC's statutory authority to regulate cybersecurity. While some companies questioned the FTC's authority, they all settled rather than engage in an embarrassing legal battle. That changed when the FTC sued Wyndham Worldwide Corp. in 2012.[50]

The HTC America Inc. ("HTC") case is a good example of the FTC consent agreements negotiated during that 10-year period.

HTC America Inc.

---

[48] *What We Do*, FEDERAL TRADE COMMISSION, https://www.ftc.gov/about-ftc/what-we-do (last visited Sept. 13, 2020).

[49] William R. Denny, *Cybersecurity as an Unfair Practice: FTC Enforcement under Section 5 of the FTC Act*, AMERICAN BAR ASSOCIATION (Sept. 19, 2018), https://www.americanbar.org/groups/business_law/publications/blt/2016/06/cyber_center_denny/.

[50] *Id.*

In the Matter of HTC America Inc., the FTC brought a complaint with one count of unfair security practices and two counts of deception. The FTC claimed that HTC failed to "employ reasonable security in the customization of its mobile devices." In paragraph 7 of the complaint the FTC asserted:

Until at least November 2011, respondent engaged in a number of practices that, taken together, failed to employ reasonable and appropriate security in the design and customization of the software on its mobile devices. Among other things, respondent:

(a) failed to implement an adequate program to assess the security of products it shipped to consumers; (b) failed to implement adequate privacy and security guidance or training for its engineering staff; (c) failed to conduct assessments, audits, reviews, or tests to identify potential security vulnerabilities in its mobile devices; (d) failed to follow well- known and commonly-accepted secure programming practices, including secure practices that were expressly described in the operating system's guides for manufacturers and developers, which would have ensured that applications only had access to users' information with their consent; and (e) failed to implement a process for receiving and addressing security vulnerability reports from third-party researchers, academics or other members of the public, thereby delaying its opportunity to correct discovered vulnerabilities or respond to reported incidents.[51]

Two points are noteworthy about this case and many other cases brought by the FTC. First, the FTC does not enumerate what comprises "reasonable and appropriate security." Such a road map could potentially box the FTC into a corner and allow an entity to escape the grasp of the FTC because the entity followed the enumerated factors but still failed to have adequate security based on other factors that the FTC may have not considered at the time it would have enumerated the factors. By not enumerating "reasonable and appropriate security" factors, the FTC can remain flexible in its complaints. Also, "reasonable and appropriate security" factors today may not be the same in the future after hackers evolve to circumvent today's reasonable and appropriate security" measures. The FTC methodology is somewhat similar to the Supreme Court's statement that the Court knows obscenity when it sees it.[52] Same for the FTC, it knows bad security practices when it sees it and may rely on industry standards to help define it. However, those standards evolve over time to react to some of the afore-mentioned changes.

---

[51] Complaint at 2, HTC America Inc., F.T.C. No. C-4406 (July 2, 2013).
[52] *See* Jacobellis v. State of Ohio, 84 S. Ct. 1676, 1683 (1964) (Stewart, J., concurring) ("I shall not today attempt to further define the kinds of material I understand to be embraced within that shorthand description; and perhaps I could never succeed in intelligibly doing so. But I know it when I see it, and the motion picture involved in this case is not that.").

Second, the FTC must rely on other sources to provide the evidence or at least point the FTC to the evidence of unreasonable or inappropriate security practices that lead to a potential finding of unfair security practices. In the HTC matter, it was security researchers who first notified HTC of the vulnerabilities and then went public after HTC failed to respond to the researchers input.[53] After the evidence is revealed to the FTC, it can be an aggressive bulldog in seeking enforcement, but the FTC does not have the resources to monitor inappropriate security practices. An entity that expects an FTC enforcement action because of negative publicity should immediately remedy the publicized cybersecurity shortcomings and any others that might surface during an FTC matter, and prepare to receive interrogatories from the FTC. In or about the time of the HTC matter, the FTC's string of cybersecurity consent agreements without a court challenge came to an end when the FTC went after Wyndham Worldwide Corp.

NOTES

Note 1

The FTC may start an administrative action or file a complaint in district court. The FTC describes its enforcement process in the following material:

[Administrative Enforcement and Adjudication]

In the administrative process, the Commission determines in an adjudicative proceeding whether a practice violates the law. Under Section 5(b) of the FTC Act, the Commission may challenge "unfair or deceptive act[s] or practice[s]," "unfair methods of competition," or violations of other laws enforced through the FTC Act, by instituting an administrative adjudication. When the Commission has "**reason to believe**" that a law violation has occurred, the Commission may issue a complaint setting forth its charges. If the respondent elects to settle the charges, it may sign a consent agreement (without admitting liability), consent to entry of a final order, and waive all right to judicial review. If the Commission accepts the proposed consent agreement, it places the order on the record for thirty days of public comment (or for such other period as the Commission may specify) before determining whether to make the order final.

If the respondent elects to contest the charges, the complaint is adjudicated before an administrative law judge ("ALJ") in a trial-type proceeding conducted under the Commission's Rules of Practice. The prosecution of a matter is conducted by FTC "complaint counsel," who are staff from the relevant bureau or a regional office. Upon conclusion of the hearing, the ALJ issues an "initial decision" setting forth his or her findings of fact and conclusions of law, and recommending either entry of an order to cease and desist or dismissal of the complaint. Either complaint counsel or respondent, or both, may appeal the initial decision

---

[53] John P. Mello Jr., *'Massive Security Vulnerability' in HTC Android Phones Claimed*, PCWORLD (Oct. 2, 2011), https://www.pcworld.com/article/240958/massive_security_vulnerability_in_htc_android_phones_claimed.html.

to the full Commission. In limited cases, including certain merger cases, the Commission's rules provide that the appeal is automatic.

Upon appeal of an initial decision, the Commission receives briefs, holds oral argument, and thereafter issues its own final decision and order. The Commission's final decision is appealable by any respondent against which an order is issued. The respondent may file a petition for review with any United States court of appeals within whose jurisdiction the respondent resides or carries on business or where the challenged practice was used. FTC Act Section 5(c), 15 U.S.C. Sec. 45(c). If the court of appeals affirms the Commission's order, the court enters its own order of enforcement. The party losing in the court of appeals may seek review by the Supreme Court. Commission decisions and orders are available on this site. . . .

Where the Commission has determined in a litigated administrative adjudicatory proceeding that a practice is unfair or deceptive and has issued a final cease and desist order, the Commission may obtain civil penalties from non-respondents who thereafter violate the standards articulated by the Commission. To accomplish this, the Commission must show that the violator had "actual knowledge that such act or practice is unfair or deceptive and is unlawful" under Section 5(a)(1) of the FTC Act. FTC Act Section 5(m)(1)(B), 15 U.S.C. Sec. 45(m)(1)(B). To prove "actual knowledge," the Commission typically shows that it provided the violator with a copy of the Commission determination about the act or practice in question, or a "synopsis" of that determination

Judicial Enforcement

Even where the Commission determines through adjudication that a practice violates consumer protection or competition law, the Commission must still seek the aid of a court to obtain civil penalties or consumer redress for violations of its orders to cease and desist or trade regulation rules (discussed below). In this section, we discuss the Commission's ability to challenge a practice directly in court, without first making a final agency determination that the challenged conduct is unlawful.

Section 13(b) of the FTC Act, 15 U.S.C. Sec. 53(b), authorizes the Commission to seek preliminary and permanent injunctions to remedy "any provision of law enforced by the Federal Trade Commission." Whenever the Commission has "reason to believe" that any party "is violating, or is about to violate" a provision of law enforced by the Commission, the Commission may ask the district court to enjoin the allegedly unlawful conduct, pending completion of an FTC administrative proceeding to determine whether the conduct is unlawful. Further, "in proper cases," the Commission may seek, and the court may grant, a permanent injunction.

The Commission makes widespread use of the permanent injunction proviso of Section 13(b) in its consumer protection program. In doing so, the Commission may seek not only permanent injunctions that bar unfair or deceptive practices, but also imposition of various kinds of monetary equitable relief (i.e., restitution and rescission of contracts) to remedy past violations. In some cases, the Commission may also seek to preserve the possibility of ultimate monetary equitable relief, by obtaining temporary restraining orders and preliminary injunctions that freeze assets and impose temporary receivers. See, e.g., *FTC v. U.S. Oil & Gas Corp.*, 748 F.2d 1431, 1432-35 (11th Cir. 1984) (per curiam); *FTC v. H.N. Singer, Inc.*, 668 F.2d 1107, 1110-13 (9th Cir. 1982).[54]

Federal Trade Commission Act [Enforcement Authority]

Cease and Desist	administrative cease and desist authority [§5(b) FTCA]
Injunctive (and Other Equitable) Relief	judicially ordered injunctive relief [§13(b) FTCA; also §5(l) FTCA (for violations of cease and orders)]
Redress	judicially ordered redress [§13(b) FTCA]
Rulemaking	[§6(g) FTCA]
Civil Penalties	judicially ordered civil penalties for violating cease and desist orders [§5(l) FTCA; Commission Rule 1.98(c)]
Criminal Penalties	referral to U.S. Department of Justice [§16(b) FTCA]

QUESTIONS

A mobile phone company (MobiPhone) produces mobile phones and preloads the phones with an operating system (OS) and some of its own apps from which it collects data about the user. MobiPhone's privacy policy is missing one or two of the data types collected by the homegrown apps because, well, the programmers made some changes and just forgot to inform the legal team. If you were a member of the legal team, how would you prevent this scenario from happening?

A mobile phone company (MobiPhone) produces mobile phones and preloads the phones with an operating system (OS) and some of its own apps from which it collects

---

[54] *A Brief Overview of the Federal Trade Commission's Investigative, law Enforcement, and Rulemaking Authority*, FEDERAL TRADE COMMISSION, https://www.ftc.gov/about-ftc/what-we-do/enforcement-authority (last revised Oct. 2019). The U.S. Court Appeals for the Seventh Circuit has challenged the FTC's ability to obtain restitution under section 13(b) injunctive relief. *See FTC v. Credit Bureau Center, LLC*, 937 F.3d 764 (7th Cir. 2019).

data about the user. The legal team is concerned that it cannot keep up with all of the changes that are being implemented in the new generation of MobiPhone's cell phones. The engineering team is working long hours of overtime to get the new phones to market so that the company can stay competitive. The legal team knows that the engineers are swamped and not focused on security. The legal team is monitoring blogs where ethical hackers exchange findings. Nothing has shown up on the blogs indicating that MobiPhone has any security issues and MobiPhone has not received any complaints. Are the legal team's actions "reasonable and appropriate security?" If not, what next steps should the legal team take?

2.2 Wyndham and Subsequent Enforcement Actions

The Wyndham case was the first court test of the FTC's unfair practices application of the "reasonable and appropriate security" standard. The court provides a significant amount of background information concerning the FTC's regulatory power.

Federal Trade Commission v. Wyndham, 799 F.3d 236 (3rd Cir. 2015).

The Federal Trade Commission Act prohibits "unfair or deceptive acts or practices in or affecting commerce." 15 U.S.C. § 45(a). In 2005 the Federal Trade Commission began bringing administrative actions under this provision against companies with allegedly deficient cybersecurity that failed to protect consumer data against hackers. The vast majority of these cases have ended in settlement.

On three occasions in 2008 and 2009 hackers successfully accessed Wyndham Worldwide Corporation's computer systems. In total, they stole personal and financial information for hundreds of thousands of consumers leading to over $10.6 million dollars in fraudulent charges. The FTC filed suit in federal District Court, alleging that Wyndham's conduct was an unfair practice and that its privacy policy was deceptive. The District Court denied Wyndham's motion to dismiss, and we granted interlocutory appeal on two issues: whether the FTC has authority to regulate cybersecurity under the unfairness prong of § 45(a); and, if so, whether Wyndham had fair notice its specific cybersecurity practices could fall short of that provision. We affirm the District Court.
. . .

The FTC alleges that, at least since April 2008, Wyndham engaged in unfair cybersecurity practices that, "taken together, unreasonably and unnecessarily exposed consumers' personal data to unauthorized access and theft."
. . .

III. FTC's Regulatory Authority Under § 45(a)
A. Legal Background

The Federal Trade Commission Act of 1914 prohibited "unfair methods of competition in commerce." Pub. L. No. 63-203, § 5, 38 Stat. 717, 719 (codified as amended at 15 U.S.C. § 45(a)). Congress "explicitly considered, and rejected, the notion that it reduce the ambiguity of the phrase 'unfair methods of competition' . . . by enumerating the particular practices to which it was intended to apply." FTC v. Sperry & Hutchinson

Co., 405 U.S. 233, 239–40 (1972) (citing S. Rep. No. 63-597, at 13 (1914)); see also S. Rep. No. 63-597, at 13 ("The committee gave careful consideration to the question as to whether it would attempt to define the many and variable unfair practices which prevail in commerce . . . . It concluded that . . . there were too many unfair practices to define, and after writing 20 of them into the law it would be quite possible to invent others." (emphasis added)). The takeaway is that Congress designed the term as a "flexible concept with evolving content," FTC v. Bunte Bros., 312 U.S. 349, 353 (1941), and "intentionally left [its] development . . . to the Commission," Atl. Ref. Co. v. FTC, 381 U.S. 357, 367 (1965).

After several early cases limited "unfair methods of competition" to practices harming competitors and not consumers, see, e.g., FTC v. Raladam Co., 283 U.S. 643 (1931), Congress inserted an additional prohibition in § 45(a) against "unfair or deceptive acts or practices in or affecting commerce," Wheeler-Lea Act, Pub. L. No. 75-447, § 5, 52 Stat. 111, 111 (1938).

For the next few decades, the FTC interpreted the unfair-practices prong primarily through agency adjudication. But in 1964 it issued a "Statement of Basis and Purpose" for unfair or deceptive advertising and labeling of cigarettes, 29 Fed. Reg. 8324, 8355 (July 2, 1964), which explained that the following three factors governed unfairness determinations:

> (1) whether the practice, without necessarily having been previously considered unlawful, offends public policy as it has been established by statutes, the common law, or otherwise— whether, in other words, it is within at least the penumbra of some common-law, statutory or other established concept of unfairness; (2) whether it is immoral, unethical, oppressive, or unscrupulous; [and] (3) whether it causes substantial injury to consumers (or competitors or other businessmen). *Id.*

Almost a decade later, the Supreme Court implicitly approved these factors, apparently acknowledging their applicability to contexts other than cigarette advertising and labeling. Sperry, 405 U.S. at 244 n.5. The Court also held that, under the policy statement, the FTC could deem a practice unfair based on the third prong— substantial consumer injury—without finding that at least one of the other two prongs was also satisfied. *Id.*

During the 1970s, the FTC embarked on a controversial campaign to regulate children's advertising through the unfair-practices prong of § 45(a). At the request of Congress, the FTC issued a second policy statement in 1980 that clarified the three factors. FTC Unfairness Policy Statement, Letter from the FTC to Hon. Wendell Ford and Hon. John Danforth, Senate Comm. on Commerce, Sci., and Transp. (Dec. 17, 1980), appended to Int'l Harvester Co., 104 F.T.C. 949, 1070 (1984) [hereinafter 1980 Policy Statement]. It explained that public policy considerations are relevant in determining whether a particular practice causes substantial consumer injury. *Id.* at 1074–76. Next, it "abandoned" the "theory of immoral or unscrupulous conduct . . . altogether" as an "independent" basis for an unfairness claim. Int'l Harvester Co., 104 F.T.C. at 1061 n.43;

1980 Policy Statement, supra at 1076 ("The Commission has . . . never relied on [this factor] as an independent basis for a finding of unfairness, and it will act in the future only on the basis of the [other] two."). And finally, the Commission explained that "[u]njustified consumer injury is the primary focus of the FTC Act" and that such an injury "[b]y itself . . . can be sufficient to warrant a finding of unfairness." 1980 Policy Statement, supra at 1073. This "does not mean that every consumer injury is legally 'unfair.'" *Id.* Indeed, [t]o justify a finding of unfairness the injury must satisfy three tests. [1] It must be substantial; [2] it must not be outweighed by any countervailing benefits to consumers or competition that the practice produces; and [3] it must be an injury that consumers themselves could not reasonably have avoided. *Id.*

In 1994, Congress codified the 1980 Policy Statement at 15 U.S.C. § 45(n):

The Commission shall have no authority under this section . . . to declare unlawful an act or practice on the grounds that such act or practice is unfair unless the act or practice causes or is likely to cause substantial injury to consumers which is not reasonably avoidable by consumers themselves and not outweighed by countervailing benefits to consumers or to competition. In determining whether an act or practice is unfair, the Commission may consider established public policies as evidence to be considered with all other evidence. Such public policy considerations may not serve as a primary basis for such determination.

FTC Act Amendments of 1994, Pub. L. No. 103-312, § 9, 108 Stat. 1691, 1695. Like the 1980 Policy Statement, § 45(n) requires substantial injury that is not reasonably avoidable by consumers and that is not outweighed by the benefits to consumers or competition. It also acknowledges the potential significance of public policy and does not expressly require that an unfair practice be immoral, unethical, unscrupulous, or oppressive. . . .

The court concluded that "[t]he three requirements in § 45(n) may be necessary rather than sufficient conditions of an unfair practice . . ."

B. Did Wyndham Have Fair Notice of the Meaning of § 45(a)?

Having decided that Wyndham is entitled to notice of the meaning of the statute, we next consider whether the case should be dismissed based on fair notice principles. We do not read Wyndham's briefs as arguing the company lacked fair notice that cybersecurity practices can, as a general matter, form the basis of an unfair practice under § 45(a). Wyndham argues instead it lacked notice of what *specific* cybersecurity practices are necessary to avoid liability. We have little trouble rejecting this claim.

To begin with, Wyndham's briefing focuses on the FTC's failure to give notice of its interpretation of the statute and does not meaningfully argue that the statute itself fails fair notice principles. We think it imprudent to hold a 100–year–old statute unconstitutional as applied to the facts of this case when we have not expressly been asked to do so.

Moreover, Wyndham is entitled to a relatively low level of statutory notice for several reasons. Subsection 45(a) does not implicate any constitutional rights here. *Vill. of Hoffman Estates v. Flipside, Hoffman Estates, Inc.,* 455 U.S. 489, 499, 102 S.Ct. 1186, 71 L.Ed.2d 362 (1982). It is a civil rather than criminal statute. And statutes regulating economic activity receive a "less strict" test because their "subject matter is often more narrow, and because businesses, which face economic demands to plan behavior carefully, can be expected to consult relevant legislation in advance of action." *Id.*

In this context, the relevant legal rule is not "so vague as to be 'no rule or standard at all.'" *CMR D.N. Corp.,* 703 F.3d at 632. Subsection 45(n) asks whether "the act or practice causes or is likely to cause substantial injury to consumers which is not reasonably avoidable by consumers themselves and not outweighed by countervailing benefits to consumers or to competition." While far from precise, this standard informs parties that the relevant inquiry here is a cost-benefit analysis, *Pa. Funeral Dirs. Ass'n v. FTC,* 41 F.3d 81, 89–92 (3d Cir.1994), that considers a number of relevant factors, including the probability and expected size of reasonably unavoidable harms to consumers given a certain level of cybersecurity and the costs to consumers that would arise from investment in stronger cybersecurity. We acknowledge there will be borderline cases where it is unclear if a particular company's conduct falls below the requisite legal threshold. But under a due process analysis a company is not entitled to such precision as would eliminate all close calls. *Cf. Nash v. United States,* 229 U.S. 373, 377, 33 S.Ct. 780, 57 L.Ed. 1232 (1913) ("[T]he law is full of instances where a man's fate depends on his estimating rightly, that is, as the jury subsequently estimates it, some matter of degree."). Fair notice is satisfied here as long as the company can reasonably foresee that a court could construe its conduct as falling within the meaning of the statute.

What appears to us is that Wyndham's fair notice claim must be reviewed as an as-applied challenge. Yet Wyndham does not argue that its cybersecurity practices survive a reasonable interpretation of the cost-benefit analysis required by § 45(n). One sentence in Wyndham's reply brief says that its "view of what data-security practices are unreasonable ... is not necessarily the same as the FTC's." Wyndham Reply Br. at 23. Too little and too late.

Wyndham's as-applied challenge falls well short given the allegations in the FTC's complaint. As the FTC points out in its brief, the complaint does not allege that Wyndham used *weak* firewalls, IP address restrictions, encryption software, and passwords. Rather, it alleges that Wyndham failed to use *any* firewall at critical network points, Compl. at ¶ 24(a), did not restrict specific IP addresses *at all, id.* at ¶ 24(j), did not use *any* encryption for certain customer files, *id.* at ¶ 24(b), and did not require some users to change their default or factory-setting passwords *at all, id.* at ¶ 24(f). Wyndham did not respond to this argument in its reply brief.

Wyndham's as-applied challenge is even weaker given it was hacked not one or two, but three, times. At least after the second attack, it should have been painfully clear to Wyndham that a court could find its conduct failed the cost-benefit analysis. That said, we leave for another day whether Wyndham's alleged cybersecurity practices do in fact fail, an issue the parties did not brief. We merely note that certainly after the second time Wyndham was hacked, it was on notice of the possibility that a court *could* find that its practices fail the cost-benefit analysis.

Several other considerations reinforce our conclusion that Wyndham's fair notice challenge fails. In 2007 the FTC issued a guidebook, *Protecting Personal Information: A Guide for Business,* FTC Response Br. Attachment 1 [hereinafter *FTC Guidebook*], which describes a "checklist[ ]" of practices that form a "sound data security plan." *Id.* at 3. The guidebook does not state that any particular practice is required by § 45(a),21 but it does counsel against many of the specific practices alleged here. For instance, it recommends that companies "consider encrypting sensitive information that is stored on [a] computer network ... [, c]heck ... software vendors' websites regularly for alerts about new vulnerabilities, and implement policies for installing vendor-approved patches." *Id.* at 10. It recommends using "a firewall to protect [a] computer from hacker attacks while it is connected to the Internet," deciding "whether [to] install a 'border' firewall where [a] network connects to the Internet," and setting access controls that "determine who gets through the firewall and what they will be allowed to see ... to allow only trusted employees with a legitimate business need to access the network." *Id.* at 14. It recommends "requiring that employees use 'strong' passwords" and cautions that "[h]ackers will first try words like ... the software's default password[ ] and other easy-to-guess choices." *Id.* at 12. And it recommends implementing a "breach response plan," *id.* at 16, which includes "[i]nvestigat[ing] security incidents immediately and tak[ing] steps to close off existing vulnerabilities or threats to personal information," *id.* at 23.

As the agency responsible for administering the statute, the FTC's expert views about the characteristics of a "sound data security plan" could certainly have helped Wyndham determine in advance that its conduct might not survive the cost-benefit analysis.

Before the attacks, the FTC also filed complaints and entered into consent decrees in administrative cases raising unfairness claims based on inadequate corporate cybersecurity. FTC Br. at 47 n.16. The agency published these materials on its website and provided notice of proposed consent orders in the Federal Register. Wyndham responds that the complaints cannot satisfy fair notice principles because they are not "adjudications on the merits." Wyndham Br. at 41. But even where the "ascertainable certainty" standard applies to fair notice claims, courts regularly consider materials that are neither regulations nor "adjudications on the merits." *See, e.g., United States v. Lachman,* 387 F.3d 42, 57 (1st Cir.2004) (noting that fair notice principles can be satisfied even where a regulation is vague if the agency "provide[d] a sufficient, publicly accessible statement" of the agency's interpretation of the regulation). That the FTC commissioners—who must vote on whether to issue a complaint, 16 C.F.R. § 3.11(a); ABA Section of Antitrust Law, *FTC Practice and Procedure Manual* 160–61 (2007)— believe that alleged cybersecurity practices fail the cost-benefit analysis of § 45(n) certainly helps companies with similar practices apprehend the possibility that their cybersecurity could fail as well.

Wyndham next contends that the individual allegations in the complaints are too vague to be relevant to the fair notice analysis. It does not, however, identify any specific examples. And as the Table below reveals, the individual allegations were specific and similar to those here in at least one of the four or five cybersecurity-related unfair-practice complaints that issued prior to the first attack.

CSS	Wyndham
1 Created unnecessary risks to personal information by storing it in a vulnerable format for up to 30 days, CSS at ¶ 6(1).	Allowed software at hotels to store payment card information in clear readable text, Comp. at ¶ 24(b).
2 Did not adequately assess the vulnerability of its web application and computer network to commonly known or reasonably foreseeable attacks, did not implement simple, low-cost and readily available defenses to such attacks, CSS at ¶ 6(2)-(3).	Failed to monitor network for the malware use in a previous intrusion, Compl. at ¶ 24(i), which was then resused by hackers later to access the system again, id. at 34.
3 Failed to use strong passwords to prevent a hacker from gaining control over computers on its computer network and access to personal information stored on the network, CSS at ¶ 6(4).	Did not employ common methods to require user IDs and passwords that are difficult for hackers to guess. E.g., allowed remote access to a hotel's property management system that used default/factory setting passwords, Comp. ¶ 24(f).
4 Did not use readily available security measures to limit access between computers on its network and between those computers and the Internet, CSS at ¶ 6(5).	Did not use readily available security measures, such as firewalls, to limit access between and among hotels' property management systems, the Wyndham network, and the Internet, Compl. at ¶ 24(a).
5 Failed to employ sufficient measures to detect unauthorized access to personal information or to conduct security investigations, CSS at ¶ 6(6).	Failed to employ reasonable measures to detect and prevent unauthorized access to computer network or to conduct security investigations, Compl. at ¶ 24(h).

Table: Comparing CSS and Wyndham Complaints

Wyndham also argues that, even if the individual allegations are not vague, the complaints "fail to spell out what specific cybersecurity practices ... actually triggered the alleged violation, ... provid[ing] only a ... description of certain alleged problems that, *'taken together,'* " fail the cost-benefit analysis. Wyndham Br. at 42 (emphasis in original). We part with it on two fronts. First, even if the complaints do not specify which allegations, in the Commission's view, form the necessary and sufficient conditions of the alleged violation, they can still help companies apprehend the possibility of liability under the statute. Second, as the Table below shows, Wyndham cannot argue that the complaints fail to give notice of the necessary and sufficient conditions of an alleged § 45(a) violation when all of the allegations in at least one of the relevant four or five complaints have close corollaries here. *See* Complaint, *CardSystems Solutions, Inc.,* No. C–4168, 2006 WL 2709787 (F.T.C.2006) [hereinafter CCS]. In sum, we have little trouble rejecting Wyndham's fair notice claim.

And with the Wyndham decision, the FTC no longer needed to add deception to its compliant to have an iron-clad case. Unfair security practices could now stand on their own as an action in the complaint.

NOTES

Note 1

The standard set forth by the FTC and *Wyndham* court for unfair cybersecurity practices is relatively undefined. Do you think that the standard fails to provide enough notice to companies concerning what level of cybersecurity they should adopt? What policy reasons favor a relatively undefined standard? For a discussion concerning the duty owed by companies concerning data security, please see William McGeveran, *The Duty of Data Security*, 103 Minn. L. Rev. 1135 (2019) and Justin (Gus) Hurwitz, *Response to McGeveran's The Duty of Data Security: Not the Objective Duty He Wants, Maybe the Subjective Duty We Need*, 103 Minn. L. Rev. Headnotes 139 (2019).

Note 2

In *Due Process and the FTC's Fair and Reasonable Approach to Data Protection: Response to Woodrow Hartzog and Daniel J. Solove*, 84 Geo. Wash. L. Rev. Arguendo 51, 55–56 (2016), Valdimir J. Semendyai discusses the usage of FTC consent agreements as notice of what may satisfy "reasonable security measures" in addressing Professors Hartzog and Solove's arguments in favor of those agreements. Mr. Semendvia disagrees that the FTC is providing constitutional fair notice. He states: "[T]he reasonableness of a given data protection strategy can be determined in advance by looking to the accepted practices of the industry itself and can be proven afterward in any legal action through data security expert testimony."

Professor Justin (Gus) Hurwitz also argues that the FTC agreements fail to provide a similar "body of law" to the common law. See Justin (Gus) Hurwitz, *Data Security and the FTC's Uncommon Law*, 101 Iowa L. Rev. 955 (2016) ("Perhaps most important, common-law courts shape legal norms because, and only where, they are required to do so. The FTC, on the other hand, has the option to develop legal norms using either quasi-judicial enforcement actions or quasi-legislative rulemaking processes.").

Note 3

In *The FTC, The Unfairness Doctrine, and Data Security Breach Litigation: Has the Commission Gone Too Far?*, Professor Michael D. Scott reviews the unfairness doctrine as applied to data security breach litigation matters involving the FTC. Notably, the author argues that, "[i]f Congress enacted legislation providing for specific FTC oversight of corporate data security under carefully constrained rules and regulations, the legislation could alleviate much of the uncertainty and negative effects of the FTC's seemingly ad hoc enforcement actions under the unfairness doctrine. . . ."[55]

Note 4

In an FTC publication titled, *The FTC's Use of Unfairness Authority: Its Rise, Fall, and Resurrection*, J. Howard Beals, discusses the modern unfairness doctrine and its application:

III. Modern Unfairness Summarized

As codified in 1994, in order for a practice to be unfair, the injury it causes must be (1) substantial, (2) without offsetting benefits, and (3) one that consumers cannot reasonably avoid. Each step involves a detailed, fact-specific analysis that must be carefully considered by the Commission. The primary purpose of the Commission's modern unfairness authority continues to be to protect consumer sovereignty by attacking practices that impede consumers' ability to make informed choices.

The first step in the unfairness analysis is to determine whether there has been substantial consumer injury. It can be economic harm, or a threat to health or safety. Substantial injury is an objective test. As the Commission noted in the policy statement, emotional distress is ordinarily insufficient. Substantial injury can consist of small harm to a large number of consumers, or significant harm to each affected individual. Even in the aggregate, total injury may not be large, as in cases when the company is small or the practice is one that creates unnecessary transaction costs. But relative to the benefits, the injury may still be substantial. To qualify as substantial, an injury must be real, and it must be large compared to any offsetting benefits.

---

[55] Michael D. Scott, *The FTC, The Unfairness Doctrine, and Data Security Breach Litigation: Has the Commission Gone Too Far?*, 60 ADMIN. L. REV. 127, 171 (2008).

Once it is determined that there is substantial consumer injury, the next step is to determine whether the harm is outweighed by countervailing benefits to consumers or competition. High prices, for example, are not unfair in part because they provide important signals to other market participants to reallocate resources in ways that ultimately benefit consumers, such as entering the market or increasing production if they are already in the market. Generally, it is important to consider both the costs of imposing a remedy (such as the cost of requiring a particular disclosure in advertising) and any benefits that consumers enjoy as a result of the practice, such as the avoided costs of more stringent authorization procedures and the value of consumer convenience.

Finally, a practice is only unfair if the injury is not one that a consumer can reasonably avoid. The Unfairness Policy Statement recognizes that the reasonable avoidance prong limits unfairness actions to those where the Commission seeks "to halt some form of seller behavior that unreasonably creates or takes advantage of an obstacle to the free exercise of consumer decision-making." If consumers could have made a different choice, but did not, the Commission should respect that choice. For example, starting from certain premises, one might argue that fast food or fast cars create significant harms that are not outweighed by countervailing benefits and should be banned. But the concept of reasonable avoidance keeps the Commission from substituting its paternalistic choices for those of informed consumers. If any institution is to make such decisions, it should be Congress, not the Commission. Unwise consumer choices are a strong argument for consumer education, but not for law enforcement.

Thus, the modern unfairness test reflects several common sense principles about the appropriate role for the Commission in the marketplace. First, the Commission's role is to promote consumer choices, not second-guess those choices. That's the point of the reasonable avoidance test. Second, the Commission should not be in the business of trying to second guess market outcomes when the benefits and costs of a policy are very closely balanced or when the existence of consumer injury is itself disputed. That's the point of the substantial injury test. And the Commission should not be in the business of making essentially political choices about which public policies it wants to pursue. That is the point of codifying the limited role of public policy.

An understanding of the relative roles of deception and unfairness is also important to make full and appropriate use of the Commission's unfairness authority. Although, in the past, they have sometimes been viewed as mutually exclusive legal theories, Commission precedent incorporated in the statutory codification makes clear that deception is properly viewed as a subset of unfairness. Both focus on preventing injury to consumers.

The criteria for deception are best understood as they seek to identify a set of cases that would pass a benefit/cost test. Material misleading claims prohibited by the Commission's deception authority almost invariably cause consumer injury because consumer choices are frustrated and their preferences are not satisfied. That injury is substantial as long as enough consumers are affected. Moreover, consumers cannot reasonably avoid the injury precisely because the seller misled them about the consequences of the choice.

Thus, the primary difference between full-blown unfairness analysis and deception analysis is that deception does not ask about offsetting benefits. Instead, it presumes that false or misleading statements either have no benefits, or that the injury they cause consumers can be avoided by the company at very low cost. In other words, deception analysis essentially creates a shortcut, assuming that, when a material falsehood exists, the practice would not pass the full benefit/cost analysis of unfairness, because there are rarely, if ever, countervailing benefits to deception.[56]

QUESTIONS

Did Wyndham do the FTC a big favor by bringing this case or did Wyndham have a good case? How much did the Wyndham case increase the power of the FTC in the area of cybersecurity?

Before Wyndham, would offering to permit the FTC to win on a sole unfair practices FTC charge (count) without adding a deception charge have been a good negotiating tactic? If the FTC had taken such an offer, would that consent decree carried the same weight as Wyndham?

Post *Wyndham* FTC Actions

After Wyndham the FTC began positioning some of its enforcement actions as data security actions. Numerous actions have been so designated by the FTC since 2016. The FTC maintains a list of the enforcement actions on its website. Here is a list of some of those actions:

- Residual Pumpkin Entity, LLC, formerly d/b/a CafePress, In the Matter of (February 1, 2021)

- SkyMed International, Inc., In the Matter of (December 16, 2020)

- Ascension Data & Analytics, LLC, In the Matter of (December 15, 2020)

- Zoom Video Communications, Inc., In the Matter of (November 9, 2020)

- NTT Global Data Centers Americas, Inc., In the Matter of (July 9, 2020)

---

[56] J. Howard Beales, *The FTC's Use of Unfairness Authority: Its Rise, Fall, and Resurrection*, FEDERAL TRADE COMMISSION (May 30, 2003), https://www.ftc.gov/public-statements/2003/05/ftcs-use-unfairness-authority-its-rise-fall-and-resurrection.

- Tapplock, Inc., In the Matter of (May 20, 2020)

- InfoTrax Systems, L.C. (November 12, 2019)

- LightYear Dealer Technologies, LLC, In the Matter of (September 6, 2019)

- LabMD, Inc. v. Federal Trade Commission (August 30, 2019)

- Equifax, Inc. (July 31, 2019)

- James V. Grago, Jr. doing business as ClixSense.com, In the Matter of (July 2, 2019)

- D-Link (July 2, 2019)

- Office Depot, Inc. (March 29, 2019)

- mResource LLC (Loop Works LLC), In the Matter of (November 19, 2018)

- VenPath, Inc., In the Matter of (November 19, 2018)

- SmartStart Employment Screening, Inc., In the Matter of (November 19, 2018)

- Uber Technologies, Inc., In the Matter of (October 29, 2018)

- IDmission LLC, In the Matter of (October 11, 2018)

- BLU Products and Samuel Ohev-Zion, In the Matter of (September 11, 2018)

- PayPal, Inc., In the Matter of (May 24, 2018)

- VTech Electronics Limited (January 8, 2018)

- TaxSlayer, In the Matter of (November 8, 2017)

- Ashley Madison (September 27, 2017)[57]

The following chart shows the counts (complaint basis) for each of the FTC enforcement actions listed above.

Matter	Date	Complaint Basis
In the Matter of Residual Pumpkin Entity, LLC, formerly d/b/a CafePress	February 1, 2021	Count I Data Security Misrepresentations; Count II Response to Data Security Incident Misrepresentations; Count III Unfair Data Security

---

[57] *Data Security*, FEDERAL TRADE COMMISSION, https://www.ftc.gov/datasecurity (last visited Aug. 5, 2020).

		Practices; Count IV Data Collection and Use Misrepresentation; Count V Misrepresentation Relating to Privacy Shield Frameworks; Count VI Misrepresentation Relating to Deletion of Consumer Data; Count VII Unfair Withholding of Payable Commissions After Security Breach
SkyMed International, Inc., In the Matter of	December 16, 2020	Count 1 Deception: HIPPA Seal Misrepresentation; Count 2 Deception: Security Incident Response Misrepresentation; Count 3 Unfairness: Unfair Information Security Practices
Ascension Data & Analytics, LLC, In the Matter of	December 15, 2020	Count 1: Violation of GLB Safeguards Rule
Zoom Video Communications, Inc., In the Matter of	November 9, 2020	Count 1: Deceptive Representation Regarding End-to-End Encryption; Count 2: Deceptive Representation Regarding Level of Encryption; Count 3: Deceptive Representation Regarding Secured Cloud Storage for Recorded Meetings; Count 4: Unfair Circumvention of Third-Party Privacy and Security Safeguard; Count 5 Deceptive Failure to Disclose; and Violations of the FTC Act
NTT Global Data Centers Americas, Inc., In the Matter of	July 9, 2020	Count 1: Privacy Shield Participation Misrepresentation; Count 2: Misrepresentation Regarding Verification; Count 3: Misrepresentation Regarding Dispute Resolution; Count 4: Misrepresentation

		Regarding Continuing Obligations; and Violations of FTC Act Section 5.
Tapplock, Inc., In the Matter of	May 20, 2020	Count 1: Deceptive Representation Regarding Security; Count 2: Deceptive Representation Regarding Protection of Personal Information
InfoTrax Systems, L.C.	November 12, 2019	Count 1: Unfairness: Failure to Employ Reasonable Data Security Practices: "Respondents' failure to employ reasonable data security practices to protect personal information—including names, addresses, SSNs, government identifiers, and financial account information—caused or is likely to cause substantial injury to consumers that is not outweighed by countervailing benefits to consumers or competition and is not reasonably avoidable by consumers themselves. This practice was, and is, an unfair act or practice."
LightYear Dealer Technologies, LLC	June 17, 2019	Count 1: Unfair Data Security Practices Count 2: Violation of the Safeguards Rule
James V. Grago, Jr. doing business as ClixSense.com	May 1, 2019	Count 1: Deception: Misrepresentation about Encryption Count 2: Deception: Misrepresentation about Latest Security Techniques Count 3: Unfairness: Failure to Employ Reasonable Security Practices
Unixiz, Inc. doing business as i-Dressup.com	April 24, 2019	Count 1: COPPA

Office Depot, Inc.	March 19, 2019	Count 1: Deceptive Representations Count 2: Means and Instrumentalities: false or misleading representations equating to deceptive acts or practices.
mResource LLC (Loop Works LLC)	November 19, 2018	Count 1: Privacy Misrepresentation
VenPath, Inc.	November 19, 2018	Count 1: Privacy Misrepresentation Count 2: Misrepresentation Regarding Continuing Obligations
SmartStart Employment Screening, Inc.	November 19, 2018	Count 1: Privacy Misrepresentation Count 2: Misrepresentation Regarding Continuing Obligations
LabMD, Inc.	November 19, 2018	FTC alleged LabMD engaged in an unfair act or practice "by failing to prevent unauthorized access to its patient information." Eleventh Circuit No. 14-12144 filed 1/20/2015.
Uber Technologies, Inc.	October 29, 2018	Count 1: Misrepresentation Count 2: False or misleading representation
IDmission, LLC	October 11, 2018	Count 1: Privacy Misrepresentation
BLU Products and Samuel Ohev-Zion	September 11, 2018	Count 1: Deceptive Representation Regarding Disclosure of Personal Information Count 2: Deceptive Representation Regarding Data Security Practices
PayPal, Inc.	May 24, 2018	Violations of the FTC Act: Count 1: deceptive act or practice Count 2: deceptive act or practice Count 3: deceptive act or practice Count 4: false or misleading representation on use of

		"bank grade security systems" Violation of the Privacy Rule and Reg. P Count 5: violation of Privacy Rule Count 6: violation of Safeguards Rule
Vtech Electronics Limited	January 8, 2018	Count 1: COPPA Count 2 : FTC Act: deception regarding encryption
TaxSlayer NOTE: This is FTC enforcement under the GLBA and demonstrates how there is overlap of privacy and security.	November 8, 2017	Count 1: Violations of the Privacy Rule and Reg. P Count 2: Violations of the Safeguards Rule
Lenovo, Inc.	September 13, 2017	Count 1: Deceptive Failure to Disclose Count 2: Unfair Preinstallation of Man-in-the-Middle Software Count 3: Unfair Security Practices: "Respondent's failure to take reasonable measures to assess and address security risks created by third-party software preinstalled on its laptops, caused or is likely to cause substantial injury to consumers, that is not offset by countervailing benefits to consumers or competition, and is not reasonably avoidable by consumers." [paragraph 37].
D-Link	May 22, 2017	Count 1: Unfairness by failing to take "reasonable steps to secure the software for their routers and IP cameras." Count 2: Security Event Response Policy Misrepresentation.

		Count 3: Router Promotional Misrepresentations. Count 4: IP Camera Promotional Misrepresentations. Count 5: Router GUI Misrepresentations.
LabMD, Inc. NOTE: fight over subject matter jurisdiction – healthcare.	September 13, 2017	Violation of the FTC Act by "respondent's failure to employ reasonable and appropriate measures to prevent unauthorized access to personal information. . ."
ASUSTeK Computer Inc.	July 28, 2016	Count 1: Router Security Misrepresentations Count 2: AiCloud Security Misrepresentations Count 3: AiDisk Security Misrepresentations Count 4: Firmware Upgrade Tool Misrepresentations Count 5: Unfair Security Practices: "respondent has failed to take reasonable steps to secure the software for its routers . . ." [paragraph 45]
Henry Schein Practice Solutions, Inc.	May 23, 2016	Count 1: Deceptive Claims of Encryption – Industry-Standard Count 2: Deceptive Claims of Encryption – Regulatory Obligations

The complaint counts fall into these basic areas:
1) Deception including deception regarding cybersecurity practices;
2) Misrepresentations including misrepresentations regarding cybersecurity practices;
3) Unfair security practices;
4) Violations of the Privacy Rule and Reg. P (FTC enforcement under the GLBA);
5) Violations of the Safeguards Rule (FTC enforcement under the GLBA); and
6) COPPA enforcement.

To understand how the FTC approaches claims of unfair security practices, we provide an overview of three cases that include claims of unfair security practices and the 2020 Zoom Communications complaint with deception and unfairness claims.

1) ASUSTeK Computer LLC;
2) James V. Grago, Jr. doing business as ClixSense.com; and
3) LightYear Dealer Technologies, LLC.

In the **ASUSTek Computer LLC** ("ASUSTek") complaint, Count 5 set forth the cause of action for unfair security practices:

UNFAIR SECURITY PRACTICES (Count 5)

45. As set forth in Paragraphs 4-36, respondent has failed to take reasonable steps to secure the software for its routers, which respondent offered to consumers for the purpose of protecting their local networks and accessing sensitive personal information. Respondent's actions caused or are likely to cause substantial injury to consumers in the United States that is not outweighed by countervailing benefits to consumers or competition and is not reasonably avoidable by consumers themselves. This practice is an unfair act or practice.

46. The acts and practices of respondent as alleged in this complaint constitute unfair or deceptive acts or practices in or affecting commerce in violation of Section 5(a) of the Federal Trade Commission Act, 15 U.S.C. § 45(a).

The FTC described ASUSTek as "a hardware manufacturer that, among other things, sells routers, and related software and services, intended for consumer use."[58]

The cybersecurity problems identified by the FTC in the ASUSTek products included:

RESPONDENT'S FAILURE TO REASONABLY SECURE ITS ROUTERS AND RELATED "CLOUD" FEATURES

30. Respondent has engaged in a number of practices that, taken together, failed to provide reasonable security in the design and maintenance of the software developed for its routers and related "cloud" features. Among other things, respondent failed to:

a. perform security architecture and design reviews to ensure that the software is designed securely, including failing to:

i. use readily-available secure protocols when designing features intended to provide consumers with access to their sensitive personal information. For example, respondent designed the AiDisk feature to use FTP rather than a protocol that supports transit encryption;

ii. implement secure default settings or, at the least, provide sufficient information that would ensure that consumers did not unintentionally expose sensitive personal information;

---

[58] Complaint at 1, ASUSTeK Computer Inc., F.T.C. No. C-4587 (July 18, 2016).

iii. prevent consumers from using weak default login credentials to protect critical security functions or sensitive personal information. For example, respondent allowed consumers to retain the weak default login credentials username "admin" and password "admin" for the admin console, and username "Family" and password "Family" for the AiDisk FTP server;

b. perform reasonable and appropriate code review and testing of the software to verify that access to data is restricted consistent with a user's privacy and security settings;

c. perform vulnerability and penetration testing of the software, including for wellknown and reasonably foreseeable vulnerabilities that could be exploited to gain unauthorized access to consumers' sensitive personal information and local networks, such as authentication bypass,[59] clear-text password disclosure,[60] cross-site scripting,[61] cross-site request forgery,[62] and buffer overflow vulnerabilities;[63]

---

[59] Editors: Authentication Bypass: authentication is the step of proving that the user who is attempting to access a system is who he/she/they says they are. A bypass would be going around this step.

[60] Editors: Clear-text Password Disclosure: Normally passwords are kept in an encrypted or hashed format. Clear-text is keeping the password as it was typed in from the keyboard. So if the password was typed in as "123", it would be stored as "123" and easily readable by anyone who has access to that storage.

[61] Editors: Cross-site Scripting (XSS): Basically, it is when the calling of a script is permitted on a web page through a normal text entry box. This permits the script to be run. The fix is input validation.

[62] Editors: "In short, CSRF abuses the trust relationship between browser and server. This means that anything that a server uses in order to establish trust with a browser (e.g., cookies, but also HTTP/Windows Authentication) is exactly what allows CSRF to take place - but this only the first piece for a successful CSRF attack.
The second piece is a web form or request which contains parameters predictable enough that an attacker could craft their own malicious form/request which, in turn, would be successfully accepted by the target service. Then, usually through social engineering or XSS, the victim would trigger that malicious form/request submission while authenticated to the legitimate service. This is where the browser/server trust is exploited." *Anti CSRF Tokens ASP.NET*, OWASP, https://owasp.org/www-community/Anti_CRSF_Tokens_ASP-NET (last visited Sept. 13, 2020).

[63] Editors: Buffer Overflow Vulnerabilities: Basically, a buffer is an area designated in volatile computer memory that can be sized for receiving input. If input is not properly validated, input that is too large can overflow its allocated portion of the buffer and overflow into another variable causing data corruption.

d. implement readily-available, low-cost protections against well-known and reasonably foreseeable vulnerabilities, as described in (c), such as input validation,[64] anti-CSRF tokens,[65] and session time-outs;[66]

e. maintain an adequate process for receiving and addressing security vulnerability reports from third parties such as security researchers and academics;

f. perform sufficient analysis of reported vulnerabilities in order to correct or mitigate all reasonably detectable instances of a reported vulnerability, such as those elsewhere in the software or in future releases; and

g. provide adequate notice to consumers regarding (i) known vulnerabilities or security risks, (ii) steps that consumers could take to mitigate such vulnerabilities or risks, and (iii) the availability of software updates that would correct or mitigate the vulnerabilities or risks.[67]

It is likely that the FTC did not gather all of the above information on day one. The FTC likely became interested either through consumer complaints as detailed in the complaint or through following scientific or watchdog blogs, or bulletins. The FTC would have also followed up the leads with specific interrogatories to the company. At the end of this process, the FTC has a long list of cybersecurity mistakes, mis-steps, and failures that it can list and compare against known industry cybersecurity practices to point out gaps in "reasonable security." Basically, here is what a reasonable company does regarding cybersecurity practices and here is what you did. In the end, the company is left with no choice but to agree to a consent agreement with the FTC.

QUESTIONS

Is there anything that ASUSTek could have done to mitigate its exposure to the FTC? If yes, when and what steps should ASUSTek have taken?

---

[64] Editors: Input Validation: Testing a user's input before accepting it as valid. A basic example is asking a user to input how many hours they worked this week and that answer will be put into an integer variable in the program. So, an answer of '40' would be valid but an answer of 'forty' would be rejected by the input validation code because 'forty' is a string and not an integer. In relationship to XSS, it would be testing for scripting by looking for "<SCRIPT>". If "<SCRIPT>" is found, the input is rejected.

[65] Editors: Anti-CSRF Tokens: "In order to prevent CSRF in ASP.NET, anti-forgery tokens (also known as request verification tokens) must be utilized. These tokens are simply randomly-generated values included in any form/request that warrants protection. Note that this value should be unique for every individual session. This guarantees that every form/request is tied to the authenticated user and, therefore, protected from CSRF.

Important: non-idempotent GET requests represent an anti-pattern where CSRF protection is concerned. Always use POST requests with anti-CSRF tokens for proper protection."

Anti CSRF Tokens ASP.NET, OWASP, https://owasp.org/www-community/Anti_CRSF_Tokens_ASP-NET (last visited Sept. 13, 2020).

[66] Editors: Session Time-outs: the amount of time that a session remains valid without activity after a successful log-in. If there is no activity within this period, the user is automatically logged out of the session.

[67] Complaint at 7–8, ASUSTeK Computer Inc., F.T.C. No. C-4587 (July 18, 2016).

In **James V. Grago, Jr.** ("ClixSense"), count 3 set forth the cause of action for unfair security practices:

"Count III – Unfairness: Failure to Employ Reasonable Security Practices

25. As described in Paragraphs 11 to 20, Respondent's failure to employ reasonable security practices caused or is likely to cause substantial injury to consumers that is not outweighed by countervailing benefits to consumers or competition and is not reasonably avoidable by consumers themselves. This practice is an unfair act or practice.

26. The acts and practices of Respondent as alleged in this complaint constitute unfair or deceptive acts or practices in or affecting commerce in violation of Section 5(a) of the FTC Act, 15 U.S.C § 45(a)."[68]

The cybersecurity problems identified by the FTC for ClickSense included:

11. Since 2010, Respondent has engaged in a number of unreasonable security practices that led to the breach described in Paragraphs 13 to 20, which caused or are likely to cause substantial consumer injury. Among other things, Respondent:

a. failed to implement readily available security measures to limit access between computers on ClixSense's network, and between such computers and the Internet;

b. permitted employees to store plain text user credentials in personal email accounts, and on ClixSense's laptops;

c. failed to change default login and password credentials for third-party company network resources; and

d. maintained consumers' personal information, including consumers' names, addresses, email addresses, dates of birth, gender, answers to security questions, login and password credentials, and Social Security numbers, in clear text on ClixSense's network and devices.

12. Respondent could have addressed each of the failures described in Paragraph 11 by implementing readily available and relatively low-cost security measures.

13. In November 2015, a ClixSense user informed Respondent about a publicly available web browser extension[69] that purportedly allowed users to automatically click on and view advertisements. The automated tool would potentially facilitate click fraud on Respondent, requiring Respondent to pay users for advertisements they did not view.

14. Without exercising precautions such as using a virtual machine[70] to segregate the software from network credentials or users' personal information, Respondent downloaded the unknown and potentially harmful browser extension onto the ClixSense network in February 2016. Security experts have long opined that companies should have appropriate segregation between systems to avoid exposure of such information.

---

[68] Complaint at 6, James V. Grago, Jr., doing business as ClixSense.com, F.T.C. No. C-4678 (July 2, 2019).

[69] Editors: web browser extension: code added to the web browser for customizing the browser. For example, an ad blocker that blocks commercial advertisements.

[70] Editors: virtual machine: Normally in the cloud, a server that contains a hypervisor through either a hardware or software implementation that divides the server's processing power among more than one entity and that virtual server appears to each entity as its own dedicated server.

15. Following the downloading of the browser extension, and continuing for many months, one or more hackers used the browser extension as an entry point to obtain information to attack ClixSense's computer network. The hacker(s) then engaged in activities on ClixSense's network that put Respondent on notice that ClixSense's network had been compromised, including deleting content from the ClixSense website; accessing documents, email accounts, and credentials stored on employee laptops; changing employees' logins and passwords; redirecting email notifications for multiple network accounts, including ClixSense's cloud and Domain Name System (DNS) host services; and redirecting visitors to the ClixSense website to an unaffiliated adult-themed website.

16. On or about September 6, 2016, the hacker(s) used a set of credentials obtained from an email message on a compromised employee's company laptop to access an old server that Respondent no longer used and that Respondent should have disconnected from the ClixSense network. These server credentials were the default credentials issued to ClixSense but never changed.

17. Because the old server was still connected to the ClixSense network, the hacker(s) was able to use it to connect to the active ClixSense server where consumer personal information was stored. The hacker(s) connected to ClixSense's active server and downloaded a copy of the ClixSense user table, which contained clear text information regarding 6.6 million consumers— including some 500,000 U.S. consumers.

18. Following this attack, the hacker(s) accessed and then published and offered for sale on a website known for posting of security exploits,[71] personal information pertaining to approximately 2.7 million consumers, including full names and physical addresses, dates of birth, gender, answers to security questions, email addresses and passwords, as well as hundreds of Social Security numbers. The public availability of this data increases the likelihood of identity theft or fraud for consumers whose information was posted.

19. Misuse of the types of personal information ClixSense collects—including Social Security numbers, dates of birth, full names, physical addresses, gender, email addresses, usernames, passwords, and answers to security questions—is likely to facilitate identity theft, privacy harms, and other consumer injuries.

20. On September 11, 2016, Respondent published a data breach announcement on ClixSense's website. Two months later, on November 14, 2016, Respondent sent individual breach notification emails to U.S. consumers. Prior to these notifications, consumers had no way of independently knowing about Respondent's security failures and could not reasonably have avoided possible harms from such failures.[72]

In **LightYear Dealer Technologies, LLC** ("LightYear"), count 1 set forth the cause of action for unfair security practices:
"Count 1 Unfair Data Security Practices
26. As described in Paragraphs 11 to 22, Respondent's failure to employ reasonable measures to protect personal information caused or is likely to cause substantial injury

---

[71] Editors: security exploits: Attempts at exploiting security vulnerabilities.
[72] Complaint at 3–5, James V. Grago, Jr., doing business as ClixSense.com, F.T.C. No. C-4678 (July 2, 2019).

to consumers that is not outweighed by countervailing benefits to consumers or competition and is not reasonably avoidable by consumers themselves. This practice is an unfair act or practice."[73]

The cybersecurity problems identified by the FTC for LightYear included:

Respondent's Data Security Practices
11. Until at least June 2017, Respondent engaged in a number of practices that, taken together, failed to provide reasonable security for the personal information stored on its network. Among other things, Respondent:
a. Failed to develop, implement, or maintain a written organizational information security policy;
b. Failed to implement reasonable guidance or training for employees or third-party contractors, regarding data security and safeguarding consumers' personal information;
c. Failed to assess the risks to the personal information stored on its network, such as by conducting periodic risk assessments or performing vulnerability and penetration testing of the network;
d. Failed to use readily available security measures to monitor its systems and assets at discrete intervals to identify data security events (e.g., unauthorized attempts to exfiltrate consumers' personal information across the company's network) and verify the effectiveness of protective measures;
e. Failed to impose reasonable data access controls, such as restricting inbound connections to known IP addresses, and requiring authentication to access backup databases;
f. Stored consumers' personal information on Respondent's computer network in clear text; and
g. Failed to have a reasonable process to select, install, secure, and inventory devices with access to personal information.[74]

In the Matter of Zoom Communications (FTC Complaint, November 9, 2020).

Founded in 2011, Zoom is a videoconferencing platform provider that provides customers with videoconferencing services and various add-on services, such as cloud storage. Zoom's 2019 annual revenue was $622.7 million; its Q1 2020 revenue was $328.2 million. Zoom has over 2,000 employees.

Zoom's core product is the Zoom "Meeting," which is a platform for one-on-one and group videoconferences. Zoom Meetings also have the capability, among other things, for accompanying chat messages, screen sharing, and the recording of videoconferences. Zoom offers certain customers the option to host Zoom's videoconferencing services on the customer's internal network through its "Connecter" product. . . .

---

[73] Complaint at 6, LightYear Dealer Technologies, LLC., F.T.C. No. C-4687 (Sept. 6, 2019).
[74] Complaint at 3, LightYear Dealer Technologies, LLC., F.T.C. No. C-4687 (Sept. 6, 2019).

Zoom routinely collects certain information about users, including: first and last name; email address; user name and password; approximate location; date of birth; technical information about users' devices, network, and internet connection; and in the case of a paid subscription, billing address and payment card information of the account holder. Zoom also collects and stores event details for all Zoom Meetings, including the date, time, and length of Meetings; the Meeting participants' usernames; and each participant's answers to any polling questions asked during a Meeting. Finally, Zoom also collects and stores information shared while using the service, such as recorded Meetings that users store on Zoom's cloud storage, voice mails, chat and instant messages, files, and whiteboards.

As of July 2019, Zoom had approximately 600,000 paid customers of its videoconferencing services. Approximately 88% of those customers were small businesses with ten or fewer employees. In December 2019, approximately 10 million people worldwide participated in a Zoom Meeting each day. By April 2020, that number had skyrocketed to 300 million daily meeting participants worldwide, in large part due to an increased demand for videoconferencing services as a result of social distancing recommendations and local government stay-at-home orders related to the novel coronavirus pandemic. In addition to Zoom's traditional business customers, individuals, doctors, mental health professionals, schools, and others began to use Zoom's videoconferencing services in greater numbers.

Users share sensitive information during Zoom meetings. This can include financial information, health information, proprietary business information, and trade secrets. For example, Zoom has been used for therapy sessions, Alcoholics Anonymous meetings, and telehealth appointments.

As reflected in Zoom's Security Guide, the security of users' Zoom communications relies not only on its Meeting encryption or similar features, but also on its internal network security. Malicious actors who infiltrate Zoom's internal network could gain access to Zoom's administrative controls and compromise Zoom users' personal information. Despite this, Zoom, among other things, has: a. Failed to implement a training program on secure software development principles; b. Failed to test, audit, assess, or review its applications for security vulnerabilities at certain key points, such as prior to releasing software updates, including failing to ensure that its software is free from commonly known or reasonably foreseeable attacks, such as "Structured Query Language" (SQL) injection attacks and "Cross-Site Scripting" (XSS) attacks; c. Failed to monitor service providers or other contractors who have access to Zoom's network; d. Failed to secure remote access to its networks and systems through multi-factor authentication or similar technology; e. Failed to use readily available measures to safeguard against anomalous activity and/or cybersecurity events across all of Zoom's systems, networks, and assets within those networks, including monitoring all of Zoom's networks and systems at discrete intervals, properly configuring firewalls, and segmenting its networks; f. Failed to implement a systematic process for incident response; g. Failed to implement a systematic process for inventorying, classifying, and deleting user data stored on Zoom's network; and h. Been a year or more behind in patching software in its commercial environment.

Respondent's Deceptive and Unfair Privacy and Security Practices

Zoom has made numerous, prominent representations touting the strength of the privacy and security measures it employs to protect users' personal information. For example, Zoom has claimed on its website, in Security Guides, and in its privacy policy, that it takes "security seriously," that it "places privacy and security as the highest priority," and that it "is committed to protecting your privacy."

The privacy and security of video communications, including the level of encryption used to secure those communications, is important to users and their decisions about which videoconferencing platform to use, the price to pay for such services, and/or how they use those services. In numerous blog posts, Zoom has pointed to its security as a reason for potential customers to use Zoom's videoconferencing services. In a January 2017 blog post, "Zoom: The Fastest Growing App on Okta," Zoom specifically cited, based on customer feedback, its security feature of "end-to-end AES 256 bit encryption" as important to businesses and one of the reasons for Zoom's growth.

Zoom's Deceptive End-to-End Encryption Claims

End-to-end encryption is a method of securing communications where an encrypted communication can only be deciphered by the communicating parties. No other persons can decrypt the communications because they do not possess the necessary cryptographic keys to do so. End-to-end encryption is intended to prevent communications from being read or modified by anyone other than the true sender and recipient(s).

Since at least June 2016, Zoom has represented in its App, on its website, in its Security Guides, in its HIPAA Compliance Guide, in blog posts, and in direct communications with customers, that it offered end-to-end encryption to secure videoconference communications between hosts and attendees during Zoom Meetings.

For example, Zoom has represented that it provided end-to-end encryption in the Zoom App. When a user hovered over a green padlock in the top left corner of a Meeting, the user would see a popup stating, "Zoom is using an end to end encrypted connection." Zoom also has represented that it employed end-to-end encryption for Zoom Meetings on the "meetings" and "security" pages of its public website, available at zoom.us/meetings and zoom.us/security. For example, on its "meetings" webpage, Zoom claimed that it offered end-to-end encryption for "all meetings"[.] . . . Zoom has made similar representations in its Security Guides, which are available through its public website at www.zoom.us/security. In its June 2019 Security Guide, Zoom explained that Meeting hosts could "Enable an end-to-end (E2E) encrypted meeting." Zoom likewise claimed in its June 2016 Security Guide that Meeting hosts could "Secure a meeting with end-to-end encryption (E2E)."

Zoom also claimed that it used "industry-standard end-to-end" encryption with AES 256-bit encryption as a way for its healthcare customers to comply with the Health Insurance Portability and Accountability Act (HIPAA)'s Security Rule. The HIPAA Security Rule applies to certain healthcare entities and contains federally mandated standards for protecting individuals' electronic personal health information. For example, on the "healthcare" webpage of Zoom's website, available at zoom.us/healthcare, Zoom claimed that its customers could "Achieve HIPAA (signed BAA) and PIPEDA/PHIPA compliance with complete end-to-end 256-bit AES encryption." Zoom similarly explained in its June 2016 and July 2017 HIPAA Compliance Guides, available through its public website at zoom.us/healthcare, that its end-to-end encryption, among other security features, supported its healthcare customers' compliance with the HIPAA Security Rule[.] . . . In a January 2019 white paper entitled "End to End Encryption," Zoom represented that it offered end-to-end encryption for Zoom Meetings as an "added layer of application security for Zoom meetings, webinars, and chat (instant messaging) sessions." Zoom explained that end-to-end encryption meant that Zoom Meetings, webinars, and chat sessions could only be decrypted by "authenticated participant(s) who have the key required for decryption." The white paper also explained that video, audio, and screen sharing were all "protected with the Advanced Encryption Standard (AES) 256-bit algorithm."

Zoom specifically touted its level of encryption as a reason for customers and potential customers to use Zoom's videoconferencing services in numerous blog posts on its website. For example, in an April 24, 2017 blog post, "Zoom Reporting Live from American Telemedicine Association 2017," Zoom promoted its "End-to-end AES 256-bit encryption of all meeting data and instant messages" as a reason for healthcare providers to use Zoom as their telehealth videoconferencing solution. Additionally, in response to inquiries from customers or potential customers who contacted Zoom directly to ask about Zoom's security practices and the level of encryption it employed for Zoom Meetings, Zoom informed them that it offers AES 256- bit, end-to-end encryption and directed them to its Security Guide that, as described above, made similar representations.

In fact, Zoom did not provide end-to-end encryption for any Zoom Meeting that was conducted outside of Zoom's "Connecter" product (which are hosted on a customer's own servers), because Zoom's servers—including some located in China—maintain the cryptographic keys that would allow Zoom to access the content of its customers' Zoom Meetings. Zoom has acknowledged that its Meetings were generally incapable of end-to end encryption in an April 2020 blog post by its Chief Product Officer[.] . . .

Zoom's Deceptive Claims Regarding Level of Encryption

Encrypting communications with the Advanced Encryption Standard (AES) and a 256-bit encryption key can be an effective way to secure communications and prevent eavesdropping. The 256-bit encryption key refers to the length of the key needed to decrypt the communications. Generally speaking, a longer encryption key provides more confidentiality protection than shorter keys because there are more possible key combinations, thereby making it harder to find the correct key and crack the encryption. Since at least June 2015, Zoom has made numerous and prominent claims that it encrypted Zoom Meetings, in part, by using AES, with a 256-bit encryption key ("AES 256-bit Encryption" or "256-bit Encryption"). For example, in a June 2015 blog post entitled "Why Zoom's Security Features Matter for your Business," available at https://blog.zoom.us/wordpress/2015/06/17/why-zoomssecurity-matter-for-business/,

Zoom explained that encryption was important for video communications because people "discuss sensitive things in unplanned moments," and touted "Zoom's use of AES 256 encryption" as making it "it impossible for a hacker to grab anything outside of a hopelessly garbled transmission..." (emphasis in original). On the "security" page of Zoom's website, available at zoom.us/security, Zoom also has claimed that it used 256-bit Encryption to protect user data[.] . . .

Zoom likewise claimed that it uses 256-bit Encryption in its Security Guide and in its online Help Center. For example, Zoom's June 2019 Security Guide stated, "Webinar contents and screen sharing are secured using AES 256 and communicate over secured network using 256-bit encryption standard." In Zoom's online Help Center, available at https://support.zoom.us/hc/en-us/articles/201362723-Encryption-for-Meetings, Zoom answered a "Frequently Asked Question[]" about its Meeting encryption by explaining, in part, that its Meetings were encrypted "by default" with AES 256-bit Encryption[.] . . .

In fact, Zoom used a lower level of encryption for securing Zoom Meetings, AES 128-bit encryption in Electronic Code Book ("ECB") mode. AES 128-bit encryption uses a shorter encryption key than AES 256-bit Encryption, and therefore provides less confidentiality protection because there are fewer possible values for the 128-bit key than for a 256-bit key. Reflecting the comparative strength of AES 256-bit Encryption and AES 128-bit Encryption, the National Security Agency has reported that AES 256-bit Encryption may be used for securing "TOP SECRET" materials, whereas AES 128-bit encryption may only be used for securing "SECRET" communications.

Zoom's Deceptive Claims Regarding Secure Storage for Zoom Meeting Recordings

Zoom offers customers the ability to record their Zoom Meetings and store such recordings on either the host's local device or, for paying customers, in Zoom's secure cloud storage ("Cloud Recordings"). In Zoom's June 2019 Security Guide, Zoom claims that Cloud Recordings are processed and stored in Zoom's cloud "after the meeting has ended," where they "are stored encrypted as well." Zoom's June 2016 Security Guide similarly claimed that Cloud Recordings "are processed and securely stored in Zoom's cloud once the meeting has ended." In fact, recorded Meetings are kept on Zoom's servers for up to 60 days, unencrypted, before Zoom transfers the recordings to its secure cloud storage, where they are then stored encrypted. . . .

VIOLATIONS OF THE FTC ACT

Count I Deceptive Representation Regarding End-to-End Encryption

. . . Zoom has represented, directly or indirectly, expressly or by implication, that it employed end-to-end encryption to secure the content of communications between participants using Zoom's video conferencing service. In fact, as described in Paragraph 24, Zoom did not employ end-to-end encryption to secure the content of communications between participants using Zoom's video conferencing service. Therefore, the representation set forth in Paragraph 54 is false or misleading.

Count II Deceptive Representation Regarding Level of Encryption

. . . Zoom has represented, directly or indirectly, expressly or by implication, that it employed 256-bit Encryption to secure the content of communications between participants using Zoom's video conferencing service.76 In fact . . . Zoom did not employ 256-bit Encryption to secure the content of communications between participants using Zoom's video conferencing service. Therefore, the representation set forth in Paragraph 56 is false or misleading.

Count III Deceptive Representation Regarding Secured Cloud Storage for Recorded Meetings

. . . Zoom has represented, directly or indirectly, expressly or by implication, that recorded Meetings are stored encrypted in Zoom's cloud storage immediately after a Meeting has ended. In fact, . . . recorded Meetings are not stored encrypted in Zoom's cloud storage immediately after a Meeting has ended. Therefore, the representation set forth in Paragraph 58 is false or misleading. . . .

Violations of the FTC Act

The acts and practices of Zoom as alleged in this complaint constitute unfair or deceptive acts or practices in or affecting commerce in violation of Section 5(a) of the Federal Trade Commission Act, 15 U.S.C. § 45(a).

The FTC's complaint for each of the above four cases was tailored to cover specific cybersecurity failures for each company. The FTC listed failures but did not give the public guidance on an all-inclusive specific list of what would be reasonable security measures in the complaints themselves. Even without a specific list, a couple of best security practices are evident such as:

1) Use readily available measures especially if they are low cost;
2) Do some vulnerability and penetration testing to identify weak areas;
3) Use encryption instead of clear text.

Each of the above would easily fit into a list of cybersecurity best practices. And the FTC has taken its guidance one step further by providing the business community with a "Start with Security – A Guide for Business – Lessons Learned from FTC Cases."[75]

The guidance covered in this short document include:
1) Start with security;
2) Control access to data sensibly;

---

[75] *Start with Security—A Guide for Business—Lessons Learned from FTC Cases*, FEDERAL TRADE COMMISSION, *available at* https://www.ftc.gov/system/files/documents/plain-language/pdf0205-startwithsecurity.pdf.

3) Require secure passwords and authentication;
4) Store sensitive personal information securely and protect it during transmission;
5) Segment your network and monitor who's trying to get in and out;
6) Secure remote access to your network;
7) Apply sound security practices when developing new products;
8) Make sure you service providers implement reasonable security measures;
9) Put procedures in place to keep your security current and address vulnerabilities that may arise;
10) Secure paper, physical media, and devices.[76]

As with the FTC cases, the above guidance is part of the normal best practices landscape practiced by cybersecurity professionals. It is also a clear signal that the FTC is and will be taking an active and proactive role in cybersecurity.

In *How Much Is Data Security Worth?*, Almudena Arcelus, Brian Ellman and Randal S. Milch discuss how businesses should evaluate whether to increase their cybersecurity. The authors point to several questions that should guide the cost benefit analysis of adopting better cybersecurity:

• What data do we currently collect and maintain, and how are the data stored and accessed? Which technology assets are most vulnerable?
• How necessary are the data for our business and for creating new sources of value for our customers? . . .
• Does our industry, firm size, and business model leave us any more or less vulnerable to a breach and/or associated costs?
• Do our data practices make us a more or less attractive target for illegal activity?
• Which measures should be implemented to lower the probability of a high-cost breach and to reduce the effects of a breach on our business and customers?[77]

NOTES

Note 1

In *Zoom Video Communications, Inc.*, the complaint also notes that Zoom had secretly deployed a web server in one of their updates that bypassed a third-party's security safeguards.[78] Apple's Safari browser had a prompt that asked it is users whether they would like to connect through third-party apps when clicking on certain websites

---

[76] *See id* (listing and describing the various steps businesses should take to ensure security).
[77] *See* Almudena Arcelus, Brian Ellman, and Randal S. Milch, *How Much is Data Security Worth?*, 15 ABASCITECH LAWYER 10, 11–14 (2019).
[78] *Id.* at 8.

or URLs that attempted to launch these apps.[79] In one of its updates in June 2018, Zoom secretly implemented "ZoomOpener," which bypassed the Safari browser safeguard and automatically launched the Zoom meeting.[80] It would also automatically activate the user's webcam upon joining the meeting.[81]

The FTC complaint criticized the implementation of ZoomOpener from many different cybersecurity angles.[82] The lack of compensating security measures from Zoom exposed users to phishing attacks that could lure users onto websites with Zoom Meetings to forcefully activate the webcam.[83] ZoomOpener also exposed users to potential Remote Control Execution attacks because it downloaded software updates without properly validating the software's source, as well as Denial of Service attacks from hackers targeting a Zoom user with invalid meeting join requests.[84]

Note 2

In the Matter of Residual Pumpkin Entity, the FTC alleged that CafePress, now doing business as Residual Pumpkin, failed to implement reasonable security measures, "including [not using] many low-cost protections, against well-known and reasonably foreseeable vulnerabilities" and "using the SHA-1 hashing algorithm, deprecated by the National Institute of Standards and Technology in 2011, instead of more secure algorithms, and failing to use a "salt"—random data that makes attacks (e.g., brute force, rainbow tables) against cryptographically protected passwords harder." Some of the well-known vulnerabilities included, ""Structured Query Language" ("SQL") injection, Cascading Style Sheets ("CSS") and HTML injection, cross-site scripting ("XSS"), and cross-site request forgery ("CSRF") attacks, that could be exploited to gain unauthorized access to Personal Information on its network".[85] The FTC also pointed to CafePress maintaining social security numbers in clear text.[86]

Note 3

In a paper published by the Brookings Institute titled, *The FTC Can Rise to the Privacy Challenge, but not Without Help from Congress*, Chris Jay Hoofnagle, Woodrow Hartzog and Daniel J. Solove, provide an explanation of the powers of the FTC and how it has successfully resisted capture by industry and ideological bias.[87] The authors

---

[79] *Id.*

[80] *Id.*

[81] *Id.*

[82] *Id.*

[83] *Id.* at 8-9.

[84] *Id.*

[85] Complaint, In the Matter of Residual Pumpkin Entity, LLC, FTC No. 1923209 (Mar. 15, 2022), www.ftc.gov/legal-library/browse/cases-proceedings/1923209-cafepress-matter.

[86] *Id.*

[87] Chris Jay Hoofnagle, Woodrow Hartzog, and Daniel J. Solove, *The FTC Can Rise to the Privacy Challenge, but not Without Help from Congress*, BROOKINGS INSTITUTE (Aug. 8, 2019),

believe that the FTC is the right agency to continue enforcing privacy actions particularly under its Section 5 power, and a similar assertion could be made with respect to cyber security actions. However, the authors argue that the FTC needs more resources and a clearer mandate from Congress to effectively pursue violations of Section 5. Notably, the authors state that:

> [The FTC] carries out this mission with a budget of just over $300 million and a total staff of about 1,100, of whom no more than 50 are tasked with privacy. In comparison, the U.K.'s Information Commissioner's Office (ICO) has over 700 employees and a £38 million budget for a mission focused entirely on privacy and data protection.[88]

The authors note that smaller companies may ignore the FTC because they essentially realize they are unlikely to be sued because of the relatively low resources of the FTC.[89] Do you think the FTC has sufficient resources to enforce cybersecurity infractions and effectively provide a coherent body of law for companies to follow?

Note 4

FTC Chair Lina M. Khan addressed the link between privacy and data security in an April 11, 2022, speech to the International Association of Privacy Professionals.[90] She alluded to an important concept in privacy and cybersecurity law concerning data minimization. Essentially, companies should be collecting only data that they need for a specific purpose and not any other data. Moreover, data should not be retained once the purpose has been fulfilled. Chair Khan noted that the FTC would be more involved in ensuring that entities are not involved in over-collecting or harvesting personal data. Additionally, Chair Khan noted that the FTC is considering additional rulemaking concerning privacy and cybersecurity. In looking forward, Chair Khan stated:

> [T]he realities of how firms surveil, categorize, and monetize user data in the modern economy invite us to consider how we might need to update our approach further yet. First, the Commission is considering initiating a rulemaking to address commercial surveillance and lax data security practices. Giving that our economy will only continue tofurther digitize, market-wide rules could help provide clear notice and render enforcement more impactful and efficient.
>
> Second, we need to reassess the frameworks we presently use to assess unlawful conduct. Specifically, I am concerned that present market realities may render the "notice and consent" paradigm outdated and insufficient. Many have noted the ways that this framework seems to fall

---

https://www.brookings.edu/blog/techtank/2019/08/08/the-ftc-can-rise-to-the-privacy-challenge-but-not-without-help-from-congress/.

[88] *Id.*

[89] *Id.*

[90] *See* Lina M. Khan, *Remarks of Chair Lina M. Khan, As Prepared for Delivery IAPP Global Privacy Summit 2022 Washington, D.C.* (April 11, 2022), https://www.ftc.gov/system/files/ftc_gov/pdf/Remarks%20of%20Chair%20Lina%20M.%20Khan%20at%20IAPP%20Global%20Privacy%20Summit%202022.pdf.

short, given both the overwhelming nature of privacy policies—and the fact that they may very well be beside the point. When faced with technologies that are increasingly critical for navigating modern life, users often lack a real set of alternatives and cannot reasonably forego using these tools.

Going forward, I believe we should approach data privacy and security protections by considering substantive limits rather than just procedural protections, which tend to create process requirements while sidestepping more fundamental questions about whether certain types of data collection and processing should be permitted in the first place. The central role that digital tools will only continue to play invites us to consider whether we want to live in a society where firms can condition access to critical technologies and opportunities on users surrendering to commercial surveillance. Privacy legislation from Congress could also help usher in this type of new paradigm.[91]

The United States Congress has been considering various proposed laws concerning privacy. A comprehensive federal privacy law may also address cybersecurity issues.

2.3 The Sufficiency of FTC Complaints: D-Link Systems

In *D-Link Systems*, the FTC challenged the security practices of a router and IP camera products made by D-Link Systems. The following materials include a copy of the FTC's complaint against D-Link Systems in the Northern District of California and a district court decision reviewing the sufficiency of the FTC's complaint.

FTC v. D-Link Systems Complaint for Permanent Injunctive and Other Equitable Relief in Federal District Court (March 20, 2017).

1. Plaintiff, the Federal Trade Commission ("FTC"), for its Complaint, brings this action under Section 13(b) of the Federal Trade Commission Act ("FTC Act"), 15 U.S.C. § 53(b), to obtain permanent injunctive relief and other equitable relief against Defendants for engaging in unfair or deceptive acts or practices in violation of Section 5(a) of the FTC Act, 15 U.S.C. § 45(a), in connection with Defendants' failure to take reasonable steps to secure the routers and Internet-protocol cameras they designed for, marketed, and sold to United States consumers.

JURISDICTION AND VENUE
2. This Court has subject matter jurisdiction pursuant to 28 U.S.C. §§ 1331, 1337(a), and 1345, and 15 U.S.C. §§ 45(a) and 53(b).
3. Venue in the Northern District of California is proper under 28 U.S.C. § 1391(b) and (c) and 15 U.S.C. § 53(b).

---

[91] *Id.* at 5-6.

PLAINTIFF

4. The FTC is an independent agency of the United States Government created by statute. 15 U.S.C. §§ 41-58. The FTC enforces Section 5(a) of the FTC Act, 15 U.S.C. § 45(a), which prohibits unfair or deceptive acts or practices in or affecting commerce.

5. The FTC is authorized to initiate federal district court proceedings, by its own attorneys, to enjoin violations of the FTC Act and to secure such other equitable relief as may be appropriate in each case. 15 U.S.C. §§ 53(b), 56(a)(2)(A).

DEFENDANTS

6. Defendant D-Link Corporation ("D-Link") is a Taiwanese corporation with its principal office or place of business at No. 289, Xinhu 3rd Rd., Neihu District, Taipei City, Taiwan 114. D-Link transacts or has transacted business in this district and throughout the United States. At all times material to this Complaint, acting alone or in concert with others, D-Link purposefully directed its activities to the United States by designing, developing, marketing, and manufacturing routers, Internet-protocol ("IP") cameras, and related software and services, intended for use by consumers throughout the United States.

7. Defendant D-Link Systems, Inc., ("DLS") is a California corporation with its principal office or place of business at 17595 Mt. Herrmann St., Fountain Valley, California 92708. DLS transacts or has transacted business in this district and throughout the United States. At all times material to this Complaint, acting alone or in concert with others, DLS has advertised, marketed, distributed, or sold routers, IP cameras, and related software and services, intended for use by consumers throughout the United States. The Chairman of DLS's Board of Directors has served as D-Link's Chief Executive Officer and the two entities have coordinated closely regarding the security of Defendants' routers and IP cameras.

8. The FTC's claims against D-Link and DLS arise from or relate to Defendants' acts or practices aimed at or taking place in the United States.

COMMERCE

9. At all times material to this Complaint, Defendants have maintained a substantial course of trade in or affecting commerce, as "commerce" is defined in Section 4 of the FTC Act, 15 U.S.C. § 44.

DEFENDANTS' BUSINESS PRACTICES

10. D-Link is a hardware device manufacturer that designs, develops, markets, and manufactures networking devices, including devices with core functions that relate to security, such as consumer routers and IP cameras. D-Link designs, develops, and manufactures these products, their marketing materials, and related software and services for distribution or sale to United States consumers through its subsidiary, DLS. D-Link is responsible for providing ongoing support to DLS for its products, including by remediating any design, usability, and security issues in Defendants' routers and IP cameras. D-Link also conducts security testing of the software for Defendants' routers and IP cameras. When releasing new software for such routers and IP cameras, D-Link uses a digital signature issued in its name, known as a "private key," to sign the software, in order to assure entities, such as browsers and operating systems, that the software comes from an authentic or "trusted" source and is not malware.

11. DLS is a subsidiary of D-Link and is nearly 98% owned by D-Link and its holding company, D-Link Holding Company, Ltd. DLS provides marketing and after-sale services integral to D-Link's operations, including by marketing and acting as the sole distributor of Defendants' routers and IP cameras throughout the United States. DLS also recommends to D-Link features that D-Link should include in products designed for the United States market. Among other services, DLS acts as the primary point-of-contact for problems that United States consumers have with Defendants' routers, IP cameras, or related software and services; conducts initial inquiries into the validity of security vulnerability reports for products sold in the United States; and transmits to D-Link any such reports that it believes may warrant software security updates from D-Link. DLS also assists in notifying United States consumers about the availability of security updates through means such as DLS's websites.

12. Defendants have provided software applications that enable users to access their routers and IP cameras from a mobile device ("mobile apps"), including a free "mydlink Lite" mobile app. Defendants designed the mydlink Lite app to require the user to enter a user name and password ("login credentials") the first occasion that a user employs the app on a particular mobile device. After that first occasion, the app stores the user's login credentials on that mobile device, keeping the user logged into the mobile app on that device.

DEFENDANTS' ROUTERS

13. Defendants' routers, like other routers, operate to forward data packets along a network. In addition to routing network traffic, they typically play a key role in securing consumers' home networks, functioning as a hardware firewall for the local network, and acting as the first line of defense in protecting consumer devices on the local network, such as computers, smartphones, IP cameras, and other connected appliances, against malicious incoming traffic from the Internet.

DEFENDANTS' IP CAMERAS

14. Defendants' IP cameras, akin to many such IP cameras, play a key security role for consumers, by enabling consumers to monitor private areas of their homes or businesses, to detect any events that may place the property or its occupants at risk. In many instances, Defendants offer them as a means to monitor the security of a home while consumers are away, or to monitor activities within the household, including the activities of young children, while a consumer is at home. Consumers seeking to monitor the security of their homes or the safety of young children may access live video and audio feeds ("live feeds") from their cameras over the Internet, using a mobile device or other computer.

DEFENDANTS' SECURITY FAILURES

15. Defendants have failed to take reasonable steps to protect their routers and IP cameras from widely known and reasonably foreseeable risks of unauthorized access, including by failing to protect against flaws which the Open Web Application Security Project has ranked among the most critical and widespread web application vulnerabilities since at least 2007.

Among other things:

a.   Defendants repeatedly have failed to take reasonable software testing and remediation measures to protect their routers and IP cameras against well known and easily preventable software security flaws, such as "hard-coded" user credentials[92] and other backdoors,[93] and command injection flaws,[94] which would allow remote attackers to gain control of consumers' devices;

b.   Defendant D-Link has failed to take reasonable steps to maintain the confidentiality of the private key that Defendant D-Link used to sign Defendants' software, including by failing to adequately restrict, monitor, and oversee handling of the key, resulting in the exposure of the private key on a public website for approximately six months; and

c.   Defendants have failed to use free software, available since at least 2008, to secure users' mobile app login credentials, and instead have stored those credentials in clear, readable text on a user's mobile device.

THOUSANDS OF CONSUMERS AT RISK

16. As a result of Defendants' failures, thousands of Defendants' routers and cameras have been vulnerable to attacks that subject consumers' sensitive personal information and local networks to a significant risk of unauthorized access. In fact, the press has reported that Defendants' routers and cameras have been vulnerable to a range of such attacks and have been compromised by attackers, including by being made part of large scale networks of computers infected by malicious software, known as "botnets."

17. The risk that attackers would exploit these vulnerabilities to harm consumers was significant. In many instances, remote attackers could take simple steps, using widely available tools, to locate and exploit Defendants' devices, which were widely known to be vulnerable. For example, remote attackers could search for vulnerable devices over the Internet and obtain their IP addresses using readily available tools, such as a popular search engine that can locate devices running particular software versions or operating in particular locations. Alternatively, attackers could use readily accessible scanning tools to identify vulnerable devices operating in particular areas or on particular networks. In many instances, an attacker could then take simple steps to exploit vulnerabilities in Defendants' routers and IP cameras, impacting not only consumers who purchased these devices, but also other consumers, who access the Internet in public or private locations served by the routers or who visit locations under the IP cameras' surveillance.

18. By creating these vulnerabilities, Defendants put consumers at significant risk of harm in a variety of ways. An attacker could compromise a consumer's router, thereby obtaining unauthorized access to consumers' sensitive personal information. For example, using a compromised router, an attacker could re-direct consumers seeking a

---

[92] Editors: hard-coded user credentials: Example would be a username and password that is already hard-coded into those fields so that the user does not have to log in. Dangerous and should be avoided. Effectively permits a user to use an application without logging in.

[93] Editors: "backdoors": A backdoor is code written by a programmer that permits that programmer access to the program without going through the authentication and authorization steps. This can be a method of giving the programmer access for debugging or for nefarious purposes so that the programmer would have access after leaving the company. Backdoors should not be tolerated. With today's debugging tools they are not necessary.

[94] Editors: command injection flaws: One example is SQL injection, where a user enters a semi-colon after a text answer plus a command following the semi-colon that could do harm to the data. This works because a semi-colon is used to separate multiple SQL commands in one text string. The cure is input validation that looks for semi-colons.

legitimate financial site to a spoofed website, where they would unwittingly provide the attacker with sensitive financial account information.   Alternatively, using a compromised router, an attacker could obtain consumers' tax returns or other files stored on the router's attached storage device or could use the router to attack other devices on the local network, such as computers, smartphones, IP cameras, or connected appliances. Similarly, by exploiting the vulnerabilities described in Paragraph 15, an attacker could compromise a consumer's IP camera, thereby monitoring consumers' whereabouts to target them for theft or other criminal activity or to observe and record over the Internet their personal activities and conversations or those of their young children. In many instances, attackers could carry out such exploits covertly, such that consumers would have no reason to know that an attack was ongoing. Finally, during the time Defendant D-Link's private key was available on a public website, consumers seeking to download legitimate software from Defendants were at significant risk of downloading malware, signed by malicious actors using D-Link's private key.

DEFENDANTS' SECURITY STATEMENTS
19. Defendants have disseminated or caused to be disseminated to consumers statements regarding the security of their products, including their routers and IP cameras.

SECURITY EVENT RESPONSE POLICY
20. From approximately December 2013 until early September 2015, after highly publicized security flaws were found to affect many of its products, Defendant DLS posted a Security Event Response Policy on its product support webpage, http://support.dlink.com/securityadvisories.aspx, in the general form of Exhibit 1. Within its Security Event Response Policy, under a bolded heading "D-Link's commitment to Product Security," Defendant DLS stated: D-Link prohibits at all times, including during product development by D-Link or its affiliates, any intentional product features or behaviors which allow unauthorized access to the device or network, including but not limited to undocumented account credentials, covert communication channels, 'backdoors' or undocumented traffic diversion. All such features and behaviors are considered serious and will be given the highest priority.

PROMOTIONAL CLAIMS
21. Defendants highlight their routers' security features in a wide range of materials available on Defendant DLS's website, including user manuals and promotional brochures, which describe these features alongside language that specifically references the device's "security". Such materials include, but are not limited to, brochures in the general form of Exhibits 2-5, which state:
a. Under a bolded, italicized, all-capitalized heading, "EASY TO SECURE," that the router: supports the latest wireless security features to help prevent unauthorized access, be it from over a wireless network or from the Internet. Support for WPATM and WPA2TM standards ensure that you will be able to use the best possible encryption, regardless of your client devices. In addition [the router] utilizes dual active firewalls (SPI and NAT) to prevent potential attacks from across the Internet.
Delivering great wireless performance, network security and coverage [the router] is ideal for upgrading your existing wireless network. (See PX 2).

b. Under a bolded, italicized, all-capitalized heading, "ADVANCED NETWORK SECURITY," that the router: ensures a secure Wi-Fi network through the use of WPA/WPA2 wireless encryption. Simply press the WPS button to quickly establish a secure connection to new devices. The [router] also utilizes dual-active firewalls (SPI and NAT) to prevent potential attacks and intrusions from across the Internet. (See PX 3).

c.   Under a bolded heading, "Advanced Network Security," that the router: supports the latest wireless security features to help prevent unauthorized access, be it from over a wireless network or from the Internet. Support for WPATM and WPA2TM standards ensure that you will be able to use the best possible encryption method. In addition, this [router] utilizes Stateful Packet Inspection Firewalls (SPI) to help prevent potential attacks from across the Internet. (See PX 4).

d.   Under a heading "128-bit Security Encryption," that the router: protects your network with 128-bit AES data security encryption – the same technology used in E-commerce or online banking. Create your own network name and password or put it at the tip of your fingers with 'Push Button Security' standard on every Amplifi device. With hassle-free plug and play installation, and advanced Wi-Fi protected setup, the [router] is not only one of the fastest routers available, its [sic] also one of the safest. (See PX 5).

22. Defendants highlight the security of their IP cameras in a wide range of materials available on Defendant DLS's website, including user manuals and promotional brochures, which describe these features alongside language that specifically references the device's "security". Such materials include, but are not limited to, brochures in the general form of Exhibit 6, which display the word "SECURITY" in large, capital letters, in a vividly colored footer across the bottom of each page. (See PX 6). In addition, Defendants have designed their IP camera packaging, including in the general form of Exhibit 7, to display security-related terms. Such terms include the words "secure connection," next to a lock icon, among the product features listed on the side of the box (see PX 7).

INTERACTIVE SECURITY FEATURES

23. Defendants' routers offer numerous security features that Defendants present alongside instructions that specifically reference the device's "security". In particular, in many instances, to begin using the router, users must access a graphical user interface (hereinafter, "Defendants' router GUI"), in the general form of Exhibits 8 and 9, which includes instructions, such as:

a.   "To secure your new networking device, please set and verify a password below" (see PX 8); and

b.   "It is highly recommended that you create a password to keep your router secure." (See PX 9).

24. Defendants' IP cameras offer numerous security features that Defendants present alongside language that specifically references the device's "security". In particular, to begin using the camera, in many instances, users must access a GUI (hereinafter "Defendants' IP camera GUI"), in the general form of Exhibits 10 and 11, which include language, such as:

a.   instructions to "Set up an Admin ID and Password" or "enter a password" in order "to secure your camera" (see PX 10); and

b.   security-related banners, including, but not limited to, the words "SECURICAM Network," alongside a lock icon, across the top of the GUI (see PX 11). . . .

VIOLATIONS OF THE FTC ACT

26. Section 5(a) of the FTC Act, 15 U.S.C. § 45(a), prohibits "unfair or deceptive acts or practices in or affecting commerce."

27. Acts or practices are unfair under Section 5 of the FTC Act if they cause or are likely to cause substantial injury to consumers that consumers cannot reasonably avoid themselves and that is not outweighed by countervailing benefits to consumers or competition. 15 U.S.C. § 45(n).

COUNT I
Unfairness

28. In numerous instances, Defendants have failed to take reasonable steps to secure the software for their routers and IP cameras, which Defendants offered to consumers, respectively, for the purpose of protecting their local networks and accessing sensitive personal information.

29. Defendants' practices caused, or are likely to cause, substantial injury to consumers in the United States that is not outweighed by countervailing benefits to consumers or competition and is not reasonably avoidable by consumers.

30. Therefore, Defendants' acts and practices as described in Paragraphs 15-18 of this Complaint constitute unfair acts or practices in or affecting commerce, in violation of Section 5 of the FTC Act, 15 U.S.C. §§ 45(a) and 45(n).

COUNT II
Security Event Response Policy Misrepresentation

31. Through the means described in Paragraph 20, Defendant DLS has represented, directly or indirectly, expressly or by implication, that Defendants took reasonable steps to secure their products from unauthorized access.

32. In truth and in fact, as described in Paragraphs 15-18, Defendants did not take reasonable steps to secure their products from unauthorized access.

33. Therefore, the making of the representation set forth in Paragraph 31 of this Complaint constitutes a deceptive act or practice, in or affecting commerce in violation of Section 5(a) of the FTC Act, 15 U.S.C. § 45(a).

COUNT III
Router Promotional Misrepresentations

34. Through the means described in Paragraph 21, Defendants have represented, directly or indirectly, expressly or by implication, that the routers described by these claims were secure from unauthorized access.

35. In truth and in fact, as described in Paragraphs 15-18, Defendants' routers were not secure from unauthorized access and control.

36. Therefore, the making of the representation set forth in Paragraph 34 of this Complaint constitutes a deceptive act or practice, in or affecting commerce in violation of Section 5(a) of the FTC Act, 15 U.S.C. § 45(a).

COUNT IV
IP Camera Promotional Misrepresentations

37. Through the means described in Paragraph 22, Defendants have represented, directly or indirectly, expressly or by implication, that the IP cameras described by these claims were secure from unauthorized access and control.

38. In truth and in fact, as described in Paragraphs 15-18, Defendants' IP cameras were not secure from unauthorized access and control.

39. Therefore, the making of the representation set forth in Paragraph 37 of this Complaint constitutes a deceptive act or practice, in or affecting commerce in violation of Section 5(a) of the FTC Act, 15 U.S.C. § 45(a).

COUNT V
Router GUI Misrepresentations

40. Through the means described in Paragraph 23, Defendants have represented, directly or indirectly, expressly or by implication, that the routers described by these claims were secure from unauthorized access.

41. In truth and in fact, as described in Paragraphs 15-18, Defendants' routers were not secure from unauthorized access and control.

42. Therefore, the making of the representation set forth in Paragraph 40 of this Complaint constitutes a deceptive act or practice, in or affecting commerce in violation of Section 5(a) of the FTC Act, 15 U.S.C. § 45(a).

COUNT VI
IP Camera GUI Misrepresentations

43. Through the means described in Paragraph 24, Defendants have represented, directly or indirectly, expressly or by implication, that the IP cameras described by these claims were secure from unauthorized access and control.

44. In truth and in fact, as described in Paragraphs 15-18, Defendants' IP cameras were not secure from unauthorized access and control.

45. Therefore, the making of the representation set forth in Paragraph 43 of this Complaint constitutes a deceptive act or practice, in or affecting commerce in violation of Section 5(a) of the FTC Act, 15 U.S.C. § 45(a).

CONSUMER INJURY

46. Consumers are likely to suffer substantial injury as a result of Defendants' violations of the FTC Act. Absent injunctive relief by this Court, Defendants are likely to injure consumers and harm the public interest.

THIS COURT'S POWER TO GRANT RELIEF

47. Section 13(b) of the FTC Act, 15 U.S.C. § 53(b), empowers this Court to grant injunctive and such other relief as the Court may deem appropriate to halt and redress violations of any provision of law enforced by the FTC.

PRAYER FOR RELIEF

Wherefore, Plaintiff FTC, pursuant to Section 13(b) of the FTC Act, 15 U.S.C. § 53(b), and the Court's own equitable powers, requests that the Court:

A. Enter a permanent injunction to prevent future violations of the FTC Act by Defendants; and

B. Award Plaintiff the costs of bringing this action, as well as such other and additional relief as the Court may determine to be just and proper.

In the following case, the D-Link Systems challenges the sufficiency of the pleading of the FTC's complaint.

Federal Trade Commission v. D-Link Systems, 2017 WL 4150873 (N.D. Cal. 2017).

JAMES DONATO, United States District Judge

In this enforcement action under Section 5(a) and Section 13(b) of the Federal Trade Commission Act ("FTC Act"), 15 U.S.C. §§ 45(a) and 53(b), the Federal Trade Commission ("FTC") alleges that defendant D-Link Systems ("DLS") engaged in unfair and deceptive practices in the marketing and sales of routers and Internet-protocol ("IP") cameras. . . . DLS moves to dismiss the complaint on a variety of grounds. The motion is granted in part and denied in part.

BACKGROUND

As alleged in the complaint, DLS sells router and IP camera products to consumers in the United States. DLS marketed these products as providing good data security because they featured "the latest wireless security features to help prevent unauthorized access" and "the best possible encryption" protections, among other safeguards. The FTC alleges that, in fact, DLS failed to protect its products from "widely known and reasonably foreseeable risks of unauthorized access" by not providing "easily preventable" measures against "'hard-coded' user credentials and other backdoors," not maintaining the confidentiality of the private key DLS used with consumers to validate software updates, and not deploying "free software, available since at least 2008, to secure users' mobile app login credentials." As a consequence, "consumers' sensitive personal information and local networks" are at significant risk of being accessed by unauthorized agents. DLS's practices constitute, in the FTC's view, unfair and deceptive conduct under the FTC Act.

DISCUSSION

I. PLEADING STANDARDS

DLS challenges the sufficiency of the complaint under Federal Rules of Civil Procedure 12(b)(6), 8(a), and 9(b).[95] The standards governing the application of Rule 12(b)(6) are straightforward. To meet the pleading requirements of Rule 8(a) and to survive a Rule 12(b)(6) motion to dismiss, a claim must provide "a short and plain statement ... showing that the pleader is entitled to relief," Fed. R. Civ. P. 8(a)(2), including "enough facts to state a claim ... that is plausible on its face." *Bell Atl. Corp. v. Twombly*, 550 U.S. 544, 570 (2007). A claim is plausible on its face if, accepting all factual allegations as true and construing them in the light most favorable to the plaintiff, the Court can reasonably infer that the defendant is liable for the misconduct alleged.

---

[95] Editors: Federal Rule of Civil Procedure 9(b) states: "**(b) Fraud or Mistake; Conditions of Mind.** In alleging fraud or mistake, a party must state with particularity the circumstances constituting fraud or mistake. Malice, intent, knowledge, and other conditions of a person's mind may be alleged generally." Fed. R. Civ. P. 9(b) (emphasis is original).

Ashcroft v. Iqbal, 556 U.S. 662, 678 (2009). The plausibility analysis is "context-specific" and not only invites but "requires the reviewing court to draw on its judicial experience and common sense." *Id.*

Whether the FTC's complaint should also meet the specificity requirements of Rule 9(b) is a more nuanced question. There is no doubt that the gravamen of the deception claims is that DLS misled consumers about the data safety and security features of its products. That core allegation sounds in fraud and would appear to fit squarely within the rule in our circuit that such claims must meet the heightened pleading standards of Rule 9(b). *See Vess v. Ciba-Geigy Corp. USA*, 317 F.3d 1097, 1103-04 (9th Cir. 2003). The wrinkle is that the circuit has not yet had occasion to determine whether *Vess* and similar decisions apply to FTC deception claims , and the FTC says that Rule 9(b) should not apply because "[u]nlike the elements of common law fraud, the FTC need not prove scienter, reliance, or injury to establish a § 5 violation."

This argument is not persuasive. In essence, the FTC contends Rule 9(b) is inapplicable because fraud is not an essential element of its deception claims. But that is precisely the truncated view of Rule 9(b) that our circuit has rejected. *Vess* requires a claim to satisfy Rule 9(b)'s specificity demands when the defendant is alleged to have engaged in fraudulent conduct, even though fraud is not a necessary element of the claim. Tellingly, *Vess* articulated this standard in the context of California's Unfair Competition Law ("UCL"), which like Section 5 outlaws deceptive practices without requiring fraud as an essential element. Our circuit has consistently held that UCL and similar consumer claims rooted in allegations of false or misleading statements about a product sound in fraud and must meet Rule 9(b)'s requirements. The FTC's deception claims are premised on exactly these types of misleading statements to consumers, and so Rule 9(b) must apply to them. Other district courts have reached the same conclusion.

Whether the FTC must also plead its unfairness claim under Rule 9(b) is more debatable. The parties have assumed that only Rule 8 applies. That was not necessarily unreasonable. Under Section 5(n), an act may be unfair if it: (1) causes or is likely to cause substantial injury to consumers; (2) is not reasonably avoidable by consumers; and (3) is not outweighed by countervailing benefits to consumers or competition. 15 U.S.C. § 45(n). There is little flavor of fraud in these elements, and the FTC has expressly stated that the unfairness claim against DLS is not tied to an alleged misrepresentation. *See* Section III, below. At the same time, however, the FTC has said that for all of its claims "the core facts overlap, absolutely," . . . and there is no doubt that the overall theme of the complaint is that DLS misled consumers about the data security its products provide. The FTC also acknowledges that DLS's misrepresentations are relevant to the unfairness claim because consumers could not have reasonably avoided injury in light of them.

Consequently, there is a distinct possibility that Rule 9(b) might apply to the unfairness claim. But the question presently is not ripe for resolution. As discussed below, the unfairness claim is dismissed under Rule 8. Whether it will need to satisfy Rule 9(b) will depend on how the unfairness claim is stated, if the FTC chooses to amend.

II. THE DECEPTION CLAIMS

Counts II through VI are grounded on allegedly deceptive practices by DLS. All are reviewed for sufficiency under Rule 9(b), with different outcomes depending on the specific allegations.

Count II states a plausible claim. This claim alleges that DLS has misrepresented the data security and protections its devices provide. Among other examples, the FTC alleges that DLS has made misleading statements to consumers about its data security policies and practices. The allegations in support of the claim identify specific statements DLS made at specific times between December 2013 and September 2015. *Id.*, PX 1. The allegations also specify why the statements are deceptive. Paragraphs 15-18 allege that DLS's routers and IP cameras do not protect against "critical and widespread web application vulnerabilities" identified since 2007, including " 'hard-coded' user credentials," "command injection flaws" and "other backdoors." These allegations, along with others in the complaint, amply provide "the who, what, when, where and how of the misconduct charged."

DLS says that Rule 9(b) requires an exacting identification of the IP camera models or router models with the alleged security flaws described in Paragraph 15. This goes too far. While mere labels, conclusions and "[b]road allegations that include no particularized supporting detail do not suffice" for Rule 9(b) purposes, "this standard does not require absolute particularity or a recital of the evidence.... [A] complaint need not allege 'a precise time frame,' 'describe in detail a single specific transaction' or identify the 'precise method' used to carry out the fraud." Count II identifies the time period during which DLS made the statements and provides specific reasons why the statements were false—for example, that the routers and IP cameras could be hacked through hard-coded user credentials or command injection flaws. That is all Rule 9(b) demands.

DLS's suggestion that the complaint should allege specific consumer reliance on the statements, . . . is also not well-taken. In this vein, DLS highlights that the security policy ends with a disclaimer: "It is up to the reader to determine the suitability of any directions or information in this document." It is certainly true that the ultimate determination of whether a statement was deceptive depends on whether it was likely to have misled consumers acting reasonably under the circumstances. But at this stage, the FTC simply needs to allege particularized facts leading to a plausible inference of liability, which it has done. Disclaimers, moreover, do not as a matter of law immunize statements that are otherwise deceptive. That point is particularly apt here, where the DLS disclaimer attempts a sweeping abandonment of responsibility that purports to dump on the consumer all of the risk that DLS may be wrong, reckless or outright lying about its data security features.

Counts III and VI also state plausible claims. The exhibits attached to the complaint identify the contents of the allegedly deceptive statements as well as the years those statements were made. Paragraphs 15-18 offer specific facts to explain why and how the types of statements contained in these materials are false or misleading.

Counts IV and V fare less well under Rule 9(b). These counts center on alleged misrepresentations in promotional materials for IP cameras and graphic user interfaces (GUI's) for routers. Exhibit 6, a promotional brochure for an IP camera, is the only dated exhibit supporting these counts, and even there the FTC has not alleged facts showing that such brochures are likely to mislead consumers. The brochure simply advertises a "surveillance camera" for the "home or small office" and contains no representations at all about digital security. It is not plausible that a reasonable consumer would believe the camera is secure from digital attacks just because the word "SECURITY" is printed on the bottom corner of the brochure. After all, the device is being marketed as a home security camera. The remaining exhibits contain more plausibly deceptive statements but fail to identify when those statements were made. These claims lack enough specificity to give DLS fair notice of its allegedly deceptive conduct, and are dismissed with leave to amend.

III. THE UNFAIRNESS CLAIM

The parties hotly contest the viability of Count I, which alleges unfair practices under the FTC Act. DLS raises several broad objections, starting with the contention that the unfairness claim as a whole is an ultra vires reach by the FTC to assert authority over general data security practices. "Section 5 says nothing about data security.... If Congress wanted the FTC to regulate data security for the entire economy, it would have clearly said so." This contention echoes similar arguments in other cases attacking the FTC's authority to regulate data security practices, particularly in the absence of rulemaking. *See, e.g., FTC v. Wyndham Worldwide Corp.*, 10 F. Supp. 3d 602 (D.N.J. 2014), *aff'd*, 799 F.3d 236 (3d Cir. 2015).

This type of challenge to the FTC's authority has been consistently rejected by other courts, with good reason. Congress intentionally made Section 5 open-ended, and "explicitly considered, and rejected, the notion that it reduce the ambiguity of the phrase 'unfair methods of competition' by tying the concept of unfairness to a common-law or statutory standard or by enumerating the particular practices to which it was intended to apply." *FTC v. Sperry & Hutchinson Co.*, 405 U.S. 233, 239-40 (citing and discussing Senate Report No. 597, 63d Cong., 2d Sess., 13 (1914)). The FTC is "charged with giving meaning to 'the elusive, but congressionally mandated standard of fairness,' *Sperry & Hutchinson Co.*, 405 U.S. at 244, which by its very nature, is 'a flexible concept with evolving content.' *FTC v. Bunte Bros., Inc.*, 312 U.S. 349, 353 (1941)." *FTC v. IFC Credit Corp.*, 543 F. Supp. 2d 925, 940 (N.D. Ill. 2008); *see also* 15 U.S.C. § 45(a)(2) ("The Commission is hereby empowered and directed" to prevent unfair practices). Consequently, the fact that data security is not expressly enumerated as within the FTC's enforcement powers is of no moment to the exercise of its statutory authority. *See also FTC v. Wyndham Worldwide Corp*, 799 F.3d 236, 259 (3d Cir. 2015) (finding that legislative acts affecting cybersecurity have not "reshaped the provision's [15 U.S.C. § 45(a)] meaning to exclude cybersecurity").

DLS's next broad objection goes to fair notice. DLS says that the FTC has not "promulgate[d] clear, unambiguous standards" for fair practices in data security, . . . and that fair notice requires that the FTC adopt standards before pursuing enforcement actions in federal court or at the Commission.

This misconstrues federal administrative law. Agencies are not required to anticipate problems and promulgate general rules before performing their statutory duties. While "quasi-legislative" rulemaking may be an optimal way for agencies to proceed, requiring it as a precedent to all enforcement actions would "stultify the administrative process" and render it "inflexible and incapable" of meeting its statutory commands. Consequently, the choice "between proceeding by general rule or by individual, ad hoc litigation is one that lies primarily in the informed discretion of the administrative agency." There can be no serious question that data security is a new and rapidly developing facet of our daily lives, and to require the FTC in all cases to adopt rules or standards before responding to data security issues faced by consumers is impractical and inconsistent with governing law. . . .

While DLS's general objections to the unfairness claim are unavailing, a specific issue of adequacy under Rule 8 has merit. As noted, Section 5(n) makes unfair an act or practice that "causes or is likely to cause substantial injury to consumers which is not reasonably avoidable by consumers themselves and not outweighed by countervailing benefits to consumers or to competition." 15 U.S.C. § 45(n). This statutory definition has been used by the courts and the Commission as setting out the three elements of an unfairness claim under Section 45(n).

The pleading problem the FTC faces concerns the first element of injury. The FTC does not allege any actual consumer injury in the form of a monetary loss or an actual incident where sensitive personal data was accessed or exposed. Instead, the FTC relies solely on the likelihood that DLS put consumers at "risk" because "remote attackers could take simple steps, using widely available tools, to locate and exploit Defendants' devices, which were widely known to be vulnerable." Dkt. No. 1 ¶ 17; *see also id.* ¶ 18 (attacker "could compromise" a router and thereby "could obtain" tax returns or other sensitive files).

That is effectively the sum total of the harm allegations, and they make out a mere possibility of injury at best. The FTC does not identify a single incident where a consumer's financial, medical or other sensitive personal information has been accessed, exposed or misused in any way, or whose IP camera has been compromised by unauthorized parties, or who has suffered any harm or even simple annoyance and inconvenience from the alleged security flaws in the DLS devices. The absence of any concrete facts makes it just as possible that DLS's devices are not likely to substantially harm consumers, and the FTC cannot rely on wholly conclusory allegations about potential injury to tilt the balance in its favor. The lack of facts indicating a likelihood of harm is all the more striking in that the FTC says that it undertook a thorough investigation before filing the complaint, . . . and that the DLS devices have had the challenged security flaws since 2011. This complaint stands in sharp contrast to complaints that have survived motions to dismiss in other cases involving data security issues. *See, e.g., FTC v. Wyndham Worldwide*, 799 F.3d 236, 242 (3d. Cir. 2015) (sustaining complaint that alleged data theft of personal information of hundreds of thousands of consumers with over $10.6 million in fraudulent charges).

The FTC nevertheless contends that dismissal is unwarranted because "[t]he degree of likely substantial injury is a question of fact inappropriate for this stage of the case," Dkt. No. 28 at 6, and cites this Court's holding in *Brickman v. Fitbit, Inc.*, No. 15-CV-02077-JD, 2016 WL 3844327, at *3 (N.D. Cal. July 15, 2016), to that end. This misunderstands *Brickman*. That decision, in a case which did not involve Section 5(n) or the FTC, held only that consumer reliance on the defendant's allegedly deceptive marketing statements entailed disputes of fact not suited for resolution on a Rule 12(b)(6) motion. That is not the question here, particularly since the FTC has expressly divorced the unfairness claim from any of DLS's representations to consumers. *Brickman* is not at all germane.

If the FTC had tied the unfairness claim to the representations underlying the deception claims, it might have had a more colorable injury element. A consumer's purchase of a device that fails to be reasonably secure—let alone as secure as advertised—would likely be in the ballpark of a "substantial injury," particularly when aggregated across a large group of consumers. *See Neovi*, 604 F.3d at 1157 ("An act or practice can cause substantial injury by doing a small harm to a large number of people") (citation and quotes omitted). But the FTC pursued a different and ultimately untenable track.

CONCLUSION

Counts I, IV, and V of the complaint are dismissed with leave to amend. The motion to dismiss is denied in all other respects. If the FTC would like to amend, it should file a revised complaint that is consistent with this order by **October 20, 2017**.

NOTES

Note 1

The *D-Link Systems* Court notes that the FTC could have tied its unfairness claim to deception representations which may have aided its argument concerning injury. Why would those alleged deceptive representations linked to the unfairness claim make it more likely there was injury for purposes of unfairness?

2.4 The LabMD Matter and D-Link Systems Order

The following two LabMD cases concern inadequate data security programs by a medical company. The first case is an opinion and order from the Federal Trade Commission. The second opinion is from a federal appellate court overturning the Federal Trade Commission's opinion and order. The last document is the stipulated order in the D-Link Systems matter.

In the Matter of LabMD, 2016 WL 4128215 (FTC 2016).

OPINION OF THE COMMISSION

By Chairwoman Edith Ramirez, for the Commission:

This case concerns the alleged failure by Respondent LabMD, Inc. to protect the sensitive personal information, including medical information, of consumers whose physicians had entrusted that information to the company. Specifically, Complaint Counsel alleges that LabMD failed to implement reasonable security measures to protect the sensitive consumer information on its computer network and therefore that its data security practices were unfair under Section 5 of the Federal Trade Commission Act. The Administrative Law Judge dismissed the Complaint following an administrative trial, holding that Complaint Counsel had not shown that LabMD's data security practices either caused or were likely to cause substantial injury.

As we explain below, we conclude that the ALJ applied the wrong legal standard for unfairness. We also find that LabMD's security practices were unreasonable, lacking even basic precautions to protect the sensitive consumer information maintained on its computer system. Among other things, it failed to use an intrusion detection system or file integrity monitoring; neglected to monitor traffic coming across its firewalls; provided essentially no data security training to its employees; and never deleted any of the consumer data it had collected. These failures resulted in the installation of file-sharing software that exposed the medical and other sensitive personal information of 9,300 consumers on a peer-to-peer network accessible by millions of users. LabMD then left it there, freely available, for 11 months, leading to the unauthorized disclosure of the information.

We therefore reverse the ALJ's decision and conclude that LabMD's data security practices constitute an unfair act or practice within the meaning of Section 5 of the FTC Act. We enter an order requiring that LabMD notify affected consumers, establish a comprehensive information security program reasonably designed to protect the security and confidentiality of the personal consumer information in its possession, and obtain independent assessments regarding its implementation of the program.

FACTUAL BACKGROUND

From 2001 until early 2014, LabMD operated as a clinical laboratory conducting tests on patient specimen samples and reporting the test results to its physician customers. Once patients' personal information had been downloaded to LabMD's network, physician-clients could order tests and access test results using LabMD's online portal. Over the course of its operations, LabMD collected sensitive personal information, including medical information, for over 750,000 patients. This information included names, addresses, dates of birth, Social Security numbers, insurance information, diagnosis codes, and physician orders for tests and services. In many instances, LabMD retrieved the personal information of all of the patients in its physician-clients' databases, regardless of whether LabMD performed tests for those patients.

As discussed in more detail below, from at least 2005 until 2010, LabMD did not have basic data security practices in place for its network. For instance, it had no file integrity monitoring or intrusion detection system in place and did not adequately monitor traffic coming across its firewalls. It failed to provide data security training to its information technology personnel or other employees, in violation of its own internal compliance program. LabMD also lacked a policy requiring strong passwords. For example, at least six employees used "labmd" as their login password. It also failed to take steps to update its software and protect against known vulnerabilities that could be exploited to gain unauthorized access to consumers' personal information.

Additionally, until at least the fall of 2009, management employees were given administrative rights over their workstations and sales employees had administrative rights over their laptop computers. This gave them the ability to change security settings and to download software applications and files of all types from the Internet, many of which - like peer-to-peer ("P2P") file-sharing applications and music files - were unrelated to LabMD's business.

In or about 2005, the P2P file-sharing program LimeWire was downloaded and installed on a computer used by LabMD's billing manager. It was widely known in the billing department that the billing manager and others in the department regularly used LimeWire while at work, primarily for downloading and listening to music.

Often used to share music, videos, and photographs, P2P file-sharing applications allow one computer user to search for and download all files that have been made available for sharing on a "host" computer that is also using the same file-sharing application. LimeWire was one of a number of common P2P applications that used the "Gnutella" P2P protocol. A user shares files on the Gnutella network by designating a directory on his or her computer as a shared directory, making all of the files within the directory freely available for downloading and viewing by other users of the network. Once a file is downloaded by a user from the Gnutella network, the file can be shared further without downloading it again from the original computer. Because of the ease of sharing, it can be extremely difficult or impossible to remove a file from the network once it has been downloaded. Between 2005 and 2010, the Gnutella network had between two and five million users online at any given time.

In February 2008, Richard Wallace, a forensic analyst employed by Tiversa Holding Company, a data security company, discovered and downloaded a copy of one of LabMD's insurance aging reports. Mr. Wallace testified that he used a P2P network and standard P2P application like LimeWire to download the file from a LabMD IP address in Atlanta, Georgia. IDF 121-22. This file, dated June 7, 2007 and referred to as the "1718 file," contained 1,718 pages of sensitive personal information for approximately 9,300 consumers, including their names, dates of birth, social security numbers, "CPT" codes designating specific medical tests and procedures for lab tests conducted by LabMD, and, in some instances, health insurance company names, addresses, and policy numbers. Using the "browse host" function on LimeWire, which enabled him to view all of the shared, downloadable files on LabMD's computer, Mr. Wallace downloaded other documents from the same IP address. Three of these documents also contained sensitive personal information from three consumers, including health insurance data, date of birth, and social security number.

In May 2008, Tiversa, with the aim of obtaining LabMD's business, informed LabMD that the 1718 file had been exposed through LimeWire. Tiversa repeatedly solicited LabMD, offering to sell its breach detection services, and later falsely claimed it had evidence that the 1718 file had spread further across P2P networks.

After being contacted by Tiversa, LabMD conducted an internal investigation to determine how the 1718 file had been exposed. It turned out that, during the time that LimeWire had been on the billing manager's computer, the entire contents of her "My Documents" folder had been designated for sharing. Although most of the 950 files in the shared folder were music or videos, the 1718 file and other documents were shared as well. Despite clear onscreen warnings from LimeWire that the documents were being shared, neither the billing manager nor anyone else who knew about the P2P file-sharing program did anything to protect the patient information that was being exposed until Tiversa notified LabMD of the disclosure. Once informed of the disclosure, LabMD never notified any of the consumers listed in the 1718 file that their personal information had been disclosed.

Later, in 2010, LabMD hired an independent security firm, ProviDyn, to perform penetration tests on its system and catalogue the vulnerabilities it found. ProviDyn identified a number of urgent and critical vulnerabilities on four of the seven servers it tested and rated the overall security of each server as poor. Among the four servers was the "Mapper" server that LabMD used to receive sensitive information of hundreds of thousands of consumers from physician clients.

Then, in 2012, the Sacramento California Police Department found 40 LabMD "day sheets" containing the names and social security numbers of 600 people, copied checks revealing the names, addresses, and bank numbers of nine individuals, and one money order payable to LabMD (collectively, the "Sacramento documents") while searching the home of individuals suspected of utility billing theft. The Sacramento Police Department collected the documents as evidence and arrested the two individuals who had possession of the documents; the arrested individuals later pled nolo contendere to identity theft.

In January 2014, LabMD stopped conducting lab tests and began winding down its business. It continues to preserve tissue samples and provide past test results to healthcare providers. LabMD has not destroyed or deleted any of the patient data it collected. As a result, it continues to maintain the personal data of hundreds of thousands of people on its computer system.

. . .

E. The ALJ's Initial Decision

Judge Chappell issued his Initial Decision on November 13, 2015. He focused on only the first of the unfairness standard's three elements, holding that Complaint Counsel had failed to prove that LabMD's computer data security practices "caused" or were "likely to cause" "substantial consumer injury," as required by Section 5(n) of the FTC Act. On that basis, he dismissed the Complaint.

In so holding, the ALJ defined the phrase "likely to cause" to mean "having a high probability of occurring or being true." Applying this standard, the ALJ rejected Complaint Counsel's argument that identity and medical identity theft-related harms were "likely" for consumers whose personal information was maintained on LabMD's computer network. He concluded that, ""[a]t best, Complaint Counsel has proven the 'possibility' of harm, but not any 'probability' or likelihood of harm."

According to the ALJ, neither the exposure of the 1718 file nor the Sacramento documents incident demonstrated that LabMD's security practices either caused or were likely to cause consumer injury. As to the 1718 file, he rejected Complaint Counsel's argument that the very disclosure of sensitive personal medical information, including lab tests for conditions such as HIV, prostate cancer, and herpes, itself represented substantial consumer injury. He concluded that "[e]ven if there were proof of such harm, this would constitute only subjective or emotional harm that, under the facts of this case, where there is no proof of other tangible injury, is not a 'substantial injury' within the meaning of Section 5(n)."

The ALJ also found there was little likelihood of future harm. He explained that Complaint Counsel had not shown that the 1718 file was downloaded by anyone other than Tiversa, and that Tiversa had shared the information only with an academic researcher and the FTC. He concluded that this, combined with the fact that there had been no consumer complaints or injuries linked to the disclosure of the 1718 file, indicated that there was little likelihood that the information in the file would be disclosed to additional individuals or would cause future harm.

With respect to the Sacramento incident, the ALJ concluded that Complaint Counsel had failed to establish a causal connection between the incident and any failure of LabMD to reasonably protect data on its computer network as alleged in the Complaint. The ALJ noted that the documents were found in hard copy form and that no evidence had been presented establishing that the documents were maintained on, or taken from, LabMD's computer network. Additionally, although the documents were discovered in the possession of identity thieves, the ALJ held that Complaint Counsel had not shown that the exposure of the Sacramento documents caused or was likely to cause substantial consumer harm. In particular, he highlighted the lack of evidence of consumer complaints or injuries resulting from the incident and reasoned that, because the documents had been booked into evidence by the Sacramento Police Department, there was also no likelihood of future injury.

The ALJ declined to address or make any findings of fact with respect to the other issues in the case, including the reasonableness of LabMD's data security practices and the two other unfairness elements - whether the alleged harm was reasonably avoidable by consumers and whether it was outweighed by countervailing benefits to consumers or competition. He also concluded that, in light of his holding, it was unnecessary to address LabMD's affirmative defenses.

Complaint Counsel appeal the ALJ's ruling, arguing that the ALJ misconstrued Section 5(n) by applying an unduly stringent substantial injury standard and failing to recognize that economic and physical harm are not the only forms of cognizable injury. They contend further that he erred by placing undue emphasis on the lack of evidence of particular consumers who suffered actual injury. Complaint Counsel also argue that the ALJ erred by requiring that the probability that consumers will suffer injury be precisely quantified.

LabMD, in turn, urges us to adopt the standard set forth in the ALJ's Initial Decision and affirm his dismissal of the Complaint. As alternative bases for dismissal of the Complaint, LabMD argues that the Commission's unfairness standard is unconstitutionally void for vagueness and fails to provide due process and fair notice. LabMD also claims that dismissal is warranted because the information Complaint Counsel obtained regarding the 1718 file and "all derivative evidence" are based on "unreliable, if not false evidence" provided by Tiversa.

STANDARD OF REVIEW

The Commission reviews the ALJ's findings of fact and conclusions of law de novo, considering "such parts of the record as are cited or as may be necessary to resolve the issues presented." Our de novo review applies to "both findings of fact and inferences drawn from those facts." We have nonetheless carefully considered the ALJ's factual findings and analysis in the course of conducting our own review.

ANALYSIS
I. The Unfairness Standard

Section 5 of the FTC Act authorizes the Commission to challenge "unfair or deceptive acts or practices in or affecting commerce." 15 U.S.C. §45(a). In 1994, Congress added Section 5(n) to the Act, providing that an act or practice may be deemed unfair if (1) it "causes or is likely to cause substantial injury to consumers"; (2) the injury "is not reasonably avoidable by consumers themselves"; and (3) the injury is "not outweighed by countervailing benefits to consumers or competition." 15 U.S.C. § 45(n).

This three-part test, derived from the Commission's 1980 Policy Statement on Unfairness, codifies the analytical framework for the Commission's application of its unfairness authority. Our resolution of this case turns in significant part on the meaning of the first prong of Section 5(n) and the relationships that tie the various elements of the unfairness standard together. In construing and applying Section 5(n), we draw considerable guidance from the Unfairness Statement and the many Commission actions and federal court rulings applying the unfairness standard. Within the framework set out by Congress, it is up to the Commission to determine, on a case-by-case basis, which practices should be condemned as """unfair." See FTC v. Wyndham Worldwide, Inc., 799 F.3d 236, 243 (3d Cir. 2015) ("Congress designed the term as a 'flexible concept with evolving content,' and 'intentionally left [its] development ... to the Commission."DD"). .
..

The central focus of any inquiry regarding unfairness is consumer injury. As reflected in the first prong of Section 5(n), a finding of unfairness requires that the injury in question be "substantial." It is well established that substantial injury may be demonstrated by a showing of a small amount of harm to a large number of people, as well as a large amount of harm to a small number of people. Additionally, in the Unfairness Statement, the Commission noted that most cases of unfairness involve economic harm or health and safety risks, and that "[e]motional impact and other more subjective types of harm ... will not ordinarily make a practice unfair." Unfairness Statement, 104 F.T.C. at 1073. The Commission, however, also recognized that, in extreme cases, subjective types of harm might well be considered as the basis for a finding of unfairness, citing as an example ""harassing late-night telephone calls" from debt collectors. Id. at 1073 n.16; see also SENATE REPORT at 13 (legislative history of Section 5(n) referring to ""abusive debt collection practices" and "high pressure sales tactics" as examples of contexts in which the unfairness standard may apply). Indeed, neither the Unfairness Statement nor Section 5(n) forecloses the possibility that an intangible but very real harm like a privacy harm resulting from the disclosure of sensitive health or medical information may constitute a substantial injury.

The first prong of Section 5(n) also includes a causation requirement that is satisfied where a practice "causes ... substantial injury." 15 U.S.C. § 45(n). The practice need not be the only or most proximate cause of an injury to meet this test. As the Third Circuit recently explained in Wyndham, "that a company's conduct was not the most proximate cause of an injury generally does not immunize liability from foreseeable harms." 799 F.3d at 246.

A practice may also meet the first prong of Section 5(n) if it is "likely to cause substantial injury." Congress therefore expressly authorized the Commission to address injuries that have not yet manifested. Id. ("[T]he FTC Act expressly contemplates the possibility that conduct can be unfair before actual injury occurs."). In determining whether a practice is "likely to cause a substantial injury," we look to the likelihood or probability of the injury occurring and the magnitude or seriousness of the injury if it does occur. Thus, a practice may be unfair if the magnitude of the potential injury is large, even if the likelihood of the injury occurring is low. For example, in Philip Morris, Inc., 82 F.T.C. 16 (1973), the Commission found unfair the unsolicited distribution of free sample razor blades in a manner that could lead the razors to fall into the hands of small children - even though no child had yet been injured. See also Int'l Harvester Co., 104 F.T.C. at 1064 (failure to include a warning label on a tractor gas cap was unfair where the likelihood of harm was low but the injuries were severe). As is the case for analysis of unfairness generally, this evaluation does not require precise quantification. What is important is obtaining an overall understanding of the level of risk and harm to which consumers are exposed. . . .

Under the second and third prongs of Section 5(n), we ask whether consumers could have reasonably avoided the asserted injury and whether it is outweighed by countervailing benefits. See Unfairness Statement, 104 F.T.C. at 1073-74; Orkin Exterminating Co., Inc. v. FTC, 849 F.2d 1354, 1363-64 (11th Cir. 1988) (Commission's "definition of 'unfairness' focuses upon unjustified consumer injury") (emphasis added).

Among the types of acts or practices the Commission has long challenged under its unfairness authority are unreasonable and inappropriate data security practices. The Third Circuit succinctly summarized how the three prongs of the unfairness test apply in the data security context in Wyndham, describing it as "a cost-benefit analysis" that "considers a number of relevant factors, including the probability and expected size of reasonably unavoidable harms to consumers given a certain level of cybersecurity and the costs to consumers that would arise from investment in stronger cybersecurity."

This framework dovetails with the analysis the Commission has consistently employed in its data security actions, which is encapsulated in the concept of "reasonable" data security. As the Commission has explained:

> The touchstone of the Commission's approach to data security is reasonableness: a company's data security measures must be reasonable and appropriate in light of the sensitivity and volume of consumer information it holds, the size and complexity of its business, and the cost of available tools to improve security and reduce vulnerabilities .... [T]he Commission has made clear that it does not require perfect security; reasonable and appropriate security is a continuous process of assessing and addressing risks; there is no one-size-fits-all data security program; and the mere fact that a breach occurred does not mean that a company has violated the law.

Commission Statement Marking the FTC's 50th Data Security Settlement, at 1 (Jan. 31, 2014) ("50th Settlement Statement").

Thus, we evaluate whether LabMD's data security practices, taken together, failed to provide reasonable and appropriate security for the sensitive personal information on its computer network, and whether that failure caused or was likely to cause substantial injury that consumers could not have reasonably avoided and that was not outweighed by benefits to consumers or competition.

We now present an overview of LabMD's data security practices and then apply each of the three prongs of Section 5(n) to the facts here.

II. LabMD's Data Security Practices

LabMD was entrusted with patients' sensitive medical and financial information, and was obligated to put reasonable security systems in place to guard against the risk of an unauthorized release of such information. As discussed below, LabMD did not employ basic risk management techniques or safeguards such as automated intrusion detection systems, file integrity monitoring software, or penetration testing. It also failed to monitor traffic coming across its firewalls. In addition, LabMD failed to provide its employees with data security training. And it failed to adequately limit or monitor employees' access to patients' sensitive information or restrict employee downloads to safeguard the network.

A. LabMD Failed to Protect its Computer Network or Employ Adequate Risk Assessment Tools

Widely known and accepted standards governing minimum reasonable data security practices have long established that risk assessment is an essential starting point. For example, as of 2003, regulations issued pursuant to the Health Insurance Portability and Accountability Act of 1996 ("HIPAA"), Pub. L. No. 104-191, 110 Stat, 1936 (1996), have required covered entities like LabMD that transmit health information to "[c]onduct an accurate and thorough assessment of the potential risks and vulnerabilities to the confidentiality, integrity, and availability of electronic protected health information held by the covered entity." While the requirements imposed by HIPAA do not govern whether LabMD met its obligations under Section 5 of the FTC Act, they do provide a useful benchmark for reasonable behavior. Similarly, since at least 2002, National Institute of Science and Technology ("NIST") guidelines provided a framework for risk management for information technology systems that included testing for the presence of vulnerabilities. Additionally, since at least 2005, IT practitioners commonly used intrusion detection systems and file integrity monitoring products to assess whether there were risks on networks. They also used "penetration tests," which are a series of audits that check for conditions such as whether a server's ports are unused and open or whether industry-known software bugs are unpatched, to spot vulnerabilities that criminals could exploit to obtain unauthorized access to sensitive information on the network.

Although LabMD had at least two IT employees on staff, it did none of this. It had no intrusion detection system or file integrity monitoring at all, and it employed penetration testing only after Tiversa had notified it that the 1718 file was available through LimeWire. The tools that LabMD used to help mitigate risk were antivirus programs, firewall logs, and manual computer inspections, which could identify only a limited scope of vulnerabilities and were often used in a manner that further reduced their effectiveness. For example, LabMD did not consistently update virus definitions or run and review scans. Also, LabMD's manual inspections were not used to detect security risks but merely responded to complaints about computer performance.

LabMD also failed to monitor its network for unauthorized intrusions or exfiltration, which is another common practice long employed by IT professionals. LabMD's firewalls were ineffective for the purpose of risk assessment for two reasons. First, they were not configured properly. Second, no one at LabMD reviewed firewall logs or network activity logs except in connection with troubleshooting a problem, such as with Internet speed or connectivity. For example, there was no attempt to monitor outgoing traffic for items like social security numbers.

One significant consequence of these failures by LabMD was that LimeWire ran undetected on the billing manager's computer between 2005 and 2008.35 File integrity monitoring or a more complete walk-around inspection could have detected the program, but these safeguards were not in place. Indeed, even after learning of the 1718 file breach in 2008, following which LabMD initiated daily "walk-around inspections," IT employees did not follow any written checklist and instead only asked employees if they were experiencing computer problems.

B. LabMD Failed to Provide Data Security Training to its Employees

Even where basic hardware and software data security mechanisms are in place, there is an increased likelihood of exposing consumers' personal information if employees are not adequately trained. HIPAA's Security Rule, for example, requires that covered entities "[i]mplement a security awareness and training program for all members of [the] workforce (including management)."

LabMD recognized the need for training, as acknowledged in its Compliance Manual which mandated that its compliance officer establish in-house training sessions regarding privacy and security, but it failed to provide such training to any of its employees including its IT personnel. As a result, employees, including sales representatives and billing staff, did not receive training regarding data security,

security mechanisms, or the consequences of reconfiguring security settings in applications. For example, the LabMD billing manager from May 2005 to May 2006 testified that she and other billing department employees did not receive any training from LabMD about protecting sensitive health data, stating that LabMD relied on the training that these employees received in their previous employment. Due in part to this lack of data security training, LabMD employees appear not to have understood the risk involved in using P2P file sharing software on LabMD's computers.

C. LabMD Failed to Adequately Restrict and Monitor the Computer Practices of Individuals Using Its Network

LabMD also did not adequately limit or monitor employees' access to the sensitive personal information of patients or restrict employee downloads to safeguard the network.

As the National Research Council has been emphasizing since 1997, "[p]rocedures should be in place that restrict users' access to only that information for which they have a legitimate need." Similarly, HIPAA requires that covered entities implement policies and procedures for authorizing "access to electronic protected information" and "to prevent those workforce members who do not have access ... from obtaining access to electronic protected health information." 45 C.F.R. § 164.308(a)(3)(i). LabMD's own 2004 employee handbook acknowledged that sharing health information unnecessarily was illegal and that the company was required to take "specific measures to ensure our compliance with this law."

Yet, LabMD failed to employ adequate measures to prevent employees from accessing personal information not needed to perform their jobs. In fact, LabMD turned off the feature of its laboratory information software, LabSoft, that allowed for distinct access settings for different users. Even college students hired on a part-time basis could access patients' medical and other sensitive information. In addition, LabMD's sales representatives were able to use physician-clients' login credentials to log in to LabSoft, which gave them access to patient information. Because LabMD had no data deletion policy and never destroyed any patient or billing information it received since it began operating, the amount of information on its network was extensive and included copies of personal checks and credit and debit card account numbers in addition to medical information.

Nor did LabMD adequately restrict or monitor what employees downloaded onto their work computers. Throughout the period at issue, it was widely recognized that downloading unauthorized applications to a computer was dangerous, and P2P programs in particular "presented a well-known and significant risk that files would be inadvertently shared." As the NRC also advised, "'Organizations should exercise and enforce discipline over user software. At a minimum, they should ... limit the ability of users to download or install their own software."

Until at least the fall of 2009, LabMD's management employees were given administrative rights over their workstations and its sales employees had administrative rights over their laptop computers, which allowed them to change security settings and download software applications and music files from the Internet. LabMD's Policy Manual included a Software Monitoring Policy that stated that users' "'add/remove' programs file will be reviewed for the appropriate applications for the specific user." If followed, this policy would have led to detection of the LimeWire program. CX0740 (Hill Report) ¶ 61(b).

In sum, if LabMD had followed proper data security protocols, LimeWire never would have been installed on the computer used by LabMD's billing manager in the first instance, or it would have been discovered and removed soon after downloading. Instead, LimeWire sat on the billing manager's computer for approximately three years and resulted in the exposure of the 1718 file.

III. LabMD's Data Security Practices Were Unfair in Violation of Section 5(n)

We now turn to whether LabMD's data security practices were unfair within the meaning of Section 5(n). As discussed above, we find that LabMD's lax security practices resulted in the unauthorized sharing of the 1718 file on LimeWire, exposing sensitive medical information of 9,300 consumers to millions of Gnutella users. For the reasons discussed below, we further find that, due to the exposure of the 1718 file, LabMD's data security practices caused and were likely to cause substantial injury that was not avoidable by consumers or outweighed by countervailing benefits and thus that LabMD's data security practices were unfair.

We note that Complaint Counsel argues that LabMD's security practices risked exposing the sensitive information of all 750,000 consumers whose information is stored on its computer network and therefore that they create liability even apart from the LimeWire incident. We find that the exposure of sensitive medical and personal information via a peer-to-peer file-sharing application was likely to cause substantial injury and that the disclosure of sensitive medical information did cause substantial injury. Therefore, we need not address Complaint Counsel's broader argument.

A. LabMD's Data Security Practices Caused and Were Likely to Cause Substantial Injury

1. LabMD's Unauthorized Disclosure of the 1718 File Itself Caused Substantial Injury

We address first whether the unauthorized disclosure of the 1718 file caused actual "substantial injury" to consumers. The ALJ held that "privacy harms, allegedly arising from an unauthorized exposure of sensitive medical information ... unaccompanied by any tangible injury such as monetary harm or health and safety risks, [do] not constitute 'substantial injury' within the meaning of Section 5(n)." We disagree.

It is undisputed that the 1718 file contained names, dates of birth, social security numbers, insurance company names, policy numbers, and codes for laboratory tests performed, including tests for HIV, herpes, prostate cancer, and testosterone levels. We also know that the file was downloaded by at least one unauthorized third-party - Tiversa - and then shared with an academic researcher.

Complaint Counsel introduced evidence of a range of harms that can and often do result from the unauthorized disclosure of sensitive personal information of the types contained in the 1718 file. One category encompasses economic harms resulting from identity theft and medical identity theft. This includes monetary losses due to financial fraud and time and resources expended by consumers in resolving fraud-related disputes. Medical identity theft associated with data breaches can also result in misdiagnosis or mistreatment of illness, and can thereby harm consumers' physical health and safety. There is no dispute that these economic and health and safety harms fall squarely within the types of injury encompassed by Section 5(n).

Because LabMD never notified any of the consumers identified in the 1718 file that their information had been disclosed, we do not know whether the breach of the 1718 file resulted in actual identity theft, medical identity theft, or physical harm for any of the consumers whose information was disclosed. We therefore evaluate whether the disclosure of sensitive medical information alone, in the absence of proven economic or physical harm, satisfies the "substantial injury" requirement.

We conclude that the disclosure of sensitive health or medical information causes additional harms that are neither economic nor physical in nature but are nonetheless real and substantial and thus cognizable under Section 5(n). For instance, Complaint Counsel's expert, Rick Kam, testified that disclosure of the mere fact that medical tests were performed irreparably breached consumers' privacy, which can involve "embarrassment or other negative outcomes, including reputational harm." Mr. Daugherty himself recognized the sensitivity of personal medical data and the gravity of its unauthorized disclosure. In fact, the protection of personal health information was seen as part of the service LabMD delivered to its customers, and the company trained its sales representatives to assure physician clients that their data would be maintained on secure servers (despite not following through with such protections). As LabMD's Vice President for Operations noted, it is vital for a lab to protect sensitive patient information.

Indeed, the Commission has long recognized that the unauthorized release of sensitive medical information harms consumers. The Commission brought its very first data security case against Eli Lilly to address lax security practices that resulted in the inadvertent disclosure of the email addresses of Prozac users. FTC v. Eli Lilly & Co., 133 F.T.C. 763, 767-68 (2002) (complaint and consent order). A more recent example involving sensitive medical information is GMR Transcription Services. There we alleged that the failure of GMR's service provider to implement reasonable security measures harmed consumers due to the disclosure of files containing notes from medical examinations on the Internet, which included information about psychiatric disorders, alcohol and drug abuse, and pregnancy loss. GMR Transcription Services, Inc., 2014 WL 4252393, *4 (Aug. 14, 2014) (complaint and consent order). And just last month we announced a settlement with Practice Fusion, a cloud-based electronic health record company, for soliciting consumer healthcare reviews in a manner that we alleged failed to adequately disclose that the reviews would be posted on the Internet. We alleged that these practices resulted in the unauthorized disclosure of some patients' sensitive personal and medical information, including health conditions, medications taken, medical procedures performed, and treatments received. Complaint, In re Practice Fusion, Inc., FTC File No. 142-3039 (June 8, 2015).

There is also broad recognition in federal and state law of the inherent harm in the disclosure of sensitive health and medical information. Section 5(n) expressly authorizes us to look to "established public policies" as additional evidence in support of a determination about whether a practice is unfair, including whether it causes substantial injury, and we do so here. Federal statutes such as HIPAA and the Health Information Technology for Economic and Clinical Health ("HITECH") Act, as well as state laws, establish the importance of maintaining the privacy of medical information in particular. See, e.g., HIPAA, 42 U.S.C. §§ 1320 et seq. (directing HHS to promulgate privacy and security rules for health information); 45 C.F.R. Parts 160 & 164 (privacy, data security, and related rules); HITECH Act, Pub. L. No. 111-5, 123 Stat. 226 (2009), codified at 42 U.S.C. §§ 300jj et seq.; §§ 17901 et seq., and revisions to 42 U.S.C. §§ 1320d--1320d(8); Freedom of Information Act, 5 U.S.C. § 552(b)(6) (restricting agencies from disclosing "personnel and medical files and similar files the disclosure of which would constitute a clearly unwarranted invasion of personal privacy"); Fair Credit Reporting Act, 15 U.S.C. §§ 1681a(i) & 1681b(g)(1) (generally prohibiting reporting agencies from releasing "a consumer report that contains medical information ... about a consumer" for employment, credit, or insurance purposes)); id. § 1681a(i) (defining "medical information"); Ga. Code Ann. § 31-33-2(d) (forbidding release of medical records without patient's signed written authorization); id. § 31-22-4(c) (restricting clinical labs' disclosure of test results); id. §§ 31-22-9.1(a)(2)(D), 24-12-21(b)(1) (limiting the release of "AIDS confidential information," including the fact that a person has submitted to an HIV test); id. § 24-12-21(o), (u) (imposing criminal liability for intentional or knowing disclosure of AIDS confidential information and permitting civil liability for "gross negligence").

Federal courts have similarly acknowledged the importance of protecting the confidentiality of sensitive medical information. See, e.g., Maracich v. Spears, 133 S. Ct. 2191, 2202 (2013) (recognizing that an individual's "medical and disability history" is among "the most sensitive kind of information" and characterizing its use in attorney solicitations as a "substantial ... intrusion on privacy"); Harris v. Thigpen, 941 F.2d 1495, 1513-14 (11th Cir. 1991) (expressing view that prison inmates' interest in preventing non-consensual disclosure of their HIV-positive diagnoses, although not absolute, is "significant" and "constitutionally-protected"). State courts, including those in Georgia, also have long recognized a right to privacy in sensitive medical information. See, e.g., Multimedia WMAZ, Inc. v. Kubach, 443 S.E. 2d 491 (Ga. App. 1994) (en banc) (affirming verdict awarding damages for public disclosure of AIDS diagnosis).

Tort law also recognizes privacy harms that are neither economic nor physical. As explained by the Restatement of Torts, when "intimate details of [one's] life are spread before the public gaze in a manner highly offensive to the ordinary reasonable man, there is an actionable invasion of his privacy, unless the matter is one of legitimate public interest." RESTATEMENT (SECOND) OF TORTS § 652D, Comment b (1977). Thus, one can be held liable for invasion of privacy if "the matter publicized is of a kind that[:] (a) would be highly offensive to a reasonable person, and (b) is not of legitimate concern to the public." Id. § 652D (summarizing tort of "publicity given to private life").

We therefore conclude that the privacy harm resulting from the unauthorized disclosure of sensitive health or medical information is in and of itself a substantial injury under Section 5(n), and thus that LabMD's disclosure of the 1718 file itself caused substantial injury.

2. LabMD's Unauthorized Exposure of the 1718 File Was Likely to Cause Substantial Injury

We now address whether, independent of our holding that the disclosure of sensitive medical information caused substantial injury under Section 5(n), the unauthorized exposure of the 1718 file for more than 11 months on LimeWire was also "likely to cause substantial injury." The ALJ interpreted "likely to cause" as requiring a showing that substantial consumer injury was "probable." He relied principally on the

Merriam Webster dictionary's statement that "the word 'likely' is 'used to indicate the chance that something will happen,' and is primarily defined as 'having a high probability of occurring or being true." On that basis, he concluded that Section 5(n) requires a showing that it is "probable that something will occur," not merely "possible," and that "at best, Complaint Counsel has proven the 'possibility' of harm." The ALJ's analysis does not withstand scrutiny.

As an initial matter, we are unpersuaded by the ALJ's reliance on a single dictionary definition to determine the meaning of the phrase "likely to cause" in Section 5(n). Different dictionaries define the phrase differently. See, e.g., Dictionary.com (defining "likely" as "reasonably to be believed or expected"). Some dictionaries define "likely" more broadly when used, as in Section 5(n), with an infinitive ("likely to cause"). Thus, Black's Law Dictionary defines "likely" in the phrase "likely to show" as "[s]howing a strong tendency; reasonably expected." Black's Law Dictionary (10th ed. 2014). Similarly, Collins English Dictionary defines "likely" when used as an adjective as "probable," but when used with an infinitive as "tending to or inclined." None of these dictionary definitions is dispositive. Where there is disagreement about the meaning of an important statutory term, dictionary definitions may not be particularly helpful. Bullock v. BankChampaign, N.A., 133 S. Ct. 1754, 1758 (2014). "It is a fundamental principle of statutory construction (and, indeed, of language itself) that the meaning of a word cannot be determined in isolation, but must be drawn" from the "specific context in which that language is used, and the broader context of the statute as a whole." Yates v. United States, 135 S. Ct. 1074, 1082.

Unlike the ALJ, we agree with Complaint Counsel that showing a "significant risk" of injury satisfies the "likely to cause" standard. In arriving at his interpretation of Section 5(n), the ALJ found that Congress had implicitly ""considered, but rejected," text in the Unfairness Statement stating that an injury "may be sufficiently substantial" if it "raises a significant risk of concrete harm." Yet the legislative history of Section 5(n) contains no evidence that Congress intended to disavow or reject this statement in the Unfairness Statement. Rather, it makes clear that in enacting Section 5(n) Congress specifically approved of the substantial injury discussion in the Unfairness Statement and existing case law applying the Commission's unfairness authority. See SENATE REPORT at 12-13; H.R. REP. NO. 103-617, at 12 (1994) (Conf. Rep.).

We conclude that the more reasonable interpretation of Section 5(n) is that Congress intended to incorporate the concept of risk when it authorized the Commission to pursue practices "likely to cause substantial injury." This reading is supported by prior Commission cases applying the unfairness standard, which also teach that the likelihood that harm will occur must be evaluated together with the severity or magnitude of the harm involved. In other words, contrary to the ALJ's holding that "likely to cause" necessarily means that the injury was "probable," a practice may be unfair if the magnitude of the potential injury is large, even if the likelihood of the injury occurring is low. For example, in International Harvester - the quintessential unfairness case - the Commission found the failure to include a warning label on a tractor gas cap to be unfair where harmful fuel geysering accidents had occurred at a "rate of less than .001 percent," but the injuries involved included death and severe disfigurement. Int'l Harvester Co., 104 F.T.C. at 1063; see also Philip Morris, 82 F.T.C. at 16 (finding unfairness based on severe health hazards without alleging any injuries had yet occurred).

The Third Circuit interpreted Section 5(n) in a similar way in Wyndham. It explained that defendants may be liable for practices that are likely to cause substantial injury if the harm was "foreseeable," Wyndham, 799 F.3d at 246, focusing on both the "probability and expected size" of consumer harm. This approach is consistent with the standard applied in negligence cases. As described in the Restatement of Torts, a "negligent act or omission may be one which involves an unreasonable risk of harm to another through ... the foreseeable action of ... a third person." RESTATEMENT (SECOND) OF TORTS § 302 (1965).

In this case, there was a significant risk of substantial injury. First, there was a high likelihood of harm because the sensitive personal information contained in the 1718 file was exposed to millions of online P2P users, many of whom could have easily found the file. The ALJ's contrary determination that the 1718 file could only have been found by a search of the file's exact name, IDF 77, was in error. Complaint Counsel's expert on the Gnutella network, Dr. Clay Shields, convincingly explained how the 1718 file could have been found through a variety of commonly-used search techniques that would not have required searching for its exact file name or components thereof.

For instance, Dr. Shields pointed out that malicious users can and do search for P2P users whose computers are misconfigured. As he explained, a computer may be misconfigured to share files that the user does not intend to share, such as all the files in the "My Documents" directory. Users do not need to have any information about the names of the files they hope to find; rather, they can look for common files that are placed in particular directories when installed (e.g., in "My Documents"). Finding such files suggests a high probability that the computer is misconfigured and is exposing files that the user does not intend to share. The searcher who locates such a computer can then use LimeWire's "browse host" function - which permits the searcher to see all the files the host computer is sharing, id. at ¶¶ 56-57 - to identify and download potentially sensitive files being inadvertently shared. "The LabMD computer, which was running LimeWire, would have been vulnerable to being found in this manner." CX0738 (Shields Rebuttal Report) at ¶ 67.

Dr. Shields explained further that these methods, including use of the browse host functionality, were not speculative - that P2P networks are often used by malicious persons who use these types of simple techniques to seek out information that has been inadvertently shared. A user could have received a search hit for some other file that was present on the billing manager's computer and then used the browse host function to examine and download other files. Dr. Shields explained that because LabMD's billing manager was using LimeWire to download and share popular music that could result in many search hits, her behavior "could easily have led to the 1,718 File being downloaded through browse host." He continued:

> In addition, the shared folders on [the billing manager's] computer contained other files that might have drawn the interest of potential thieves and could have been found through the basic search. For example, there was a file named "W-9 Form" being shared. A person who was interested in identity theft might have been searching [for] that term to find addresses and Social Security numbers. The browse host function could then be used to view and download the 1,718 File that was contained in the same shared folders.

Dr. Shields' conclusions are borne out by what actually occurred. Mr. Wallace did not discover the 1718 file by searching for its exact name. Rather, he located the 1718 file while conducting a general search for sensitive information on P2P networks, using standard P2P software. There is nothing in Mr. Wallace's testimony to suggest that he was searching for LabMD files specifically or that he knew - or even could have known - the 1718 file's exact name.

Dr. Shields also opined that "[w]hile it may be unlikely that any random user would choose to download the 1,718 File, this low probability must be balanced against the enormous number of users on the Gnutella system." In particular, he quotes the estimate of LabMD's expert, Adam Fisk, that "[a]t any one time on the LimeWire network there would be approximately 2 to 5 million users online," and opines that "[o]ver an extended period of time, such as weeks or months, even a 1 in 1,000,000 chance of someone downloading the 1,718 file would therefore result in it being downloaded many times." Dr. Shields' opinion, in combination with Mr. Wallace's actual experience, is persuasive evidence that LabMD's exposure of the 1718 file and other documents for sharing on the Gnutella network created a significant likelihood that sensitive medical and other information would be disclosed. Indeed, the sensitivity of the data in LabMD's possession made a breach particularly likely to occur. As Complaint Counsel's expert Mr. Van Dyke noted, the types of sensitive personal information found on the 1718 file are very attractive to identity thieves.

The ALJ nonetheless discounted Complaint Counsel's evidence that LabMD's practices were "likely to cause" harm in light of what he characterized as the """"inherently speculative nature of predicting 'likely' harm." He placed great weight on the fact that Complaint Counsel had "not ... identified even one consumer that suffered any harm as a result of Respondent's alleged unreasonable data security" and concluded that this "undermines the persuasiveness of Complaint Counsel's claim that such harm is nevertheless "'likely' to occur."

The ALJ's reasoning comes perilously close to reading the term "likely" out of the statute. When evaluating a practice, we judge the likelihood that the practice will cause harm at the time the practice occurred, not on the basis of actual future outcomes. This is particularly true in the data security context. Consumers typically have no way of finding out that their personal information has been part of a data breach. Furthermore, even if they do learn that their information has been exposed, it is very difficult for identity theft victims to find out which company was the source of the information that was used to harm them absent notification from the company. Here, given the absence of notification by LabMD, a lack of evidence regarding particular consumer injury tells us little about whether LabMD's security practices caused or were likely to cause substantial consumer injury. Moreover, Section 5 very clearly has a "prophylactic purpose" and authorizes the Commission to take "preemptive action." FTC v. Freecom Commc'ns, 401 F.3d 1192, 1203 (10th Cir. 2005). We need not wait for consumers to suffer known harm at the hands of identity thieves.

In addition to demonstrating a significant risk of harm in this case, Complaint Counsel also proved that the severity and magnitude of potential harm was high. As noted above, Complaint Counsel's expert witnesses identified a range of harms that can and do result from the unauthorized disclosure of consumers' sensitive personal information of the type maintained by LabMD on its computer network.

Mr. Kam focused on the consumer harms caused by medical identity theft, i.e., the unauthorized use of a consumer's personal health information such as health insurance policy information, test codes, and diagnosis codes, to fraudulently obtain medical services, prescription drugs, or other products or services, or to fraudulently bill health insurance providers. In particular, Mr. Kam reported the results of a Survey on Medical Identity Theft by the Ponemon Institute in 2013, showing the substantial out-of-pocket expenses that medical identity theft victims typically incur, including "reimbursement to healthcare providers for services received by the identity thief"; costs of "identity protection, credit counseling and legal counsel"; and "payment for medical services and prescriptions because of a lapse in healthcare coverage." He observed that victims typically have to spend significant time to resolve problems caused by medical identity theft, and often give up because the process is so difficult and time-consuming. He also noted that because "[t]here is no central 'medical identity bureau' where a consumer can set up a fraud alert, like they can with the credit bureaus," and as a result, ""identity thieves can continue to use a consumer's medical identity to commit identity crimes" for long periods of time.

Mr. Van Dyke emphasized that information like names, addresses, and Social Security numbers cannot be readily changed so that, once compromised, these types of personal information can often be used by malicious actors for an extended period and "could result in affected consumers suffering fraud in perpetuity." Mr. Van Dyke also cited data from a survey conducted by his firm, Javelin, showing the average amount of money that identity thieves steal, the average number of hours that victims spend to resolve specific categories of fraud, and the out-of-pocket costs that victims incur in the course of resolving them.

In addition, medical identity theft associated with data breaches can result in misdiagnosis or mistreatment of illness, and can thereby harm consumers' physical health and safety. Mr. Kam explained that a ""victim of medical identity theft may have the integrity of [his or her] electronic health record compromised if the health information of the identity thief has merged with that of the victim," and that "[t]he resulting inaccuracies may cause serious health and safety risks to the victim, such as the wrong blood type or life-threatening drug allergies." Medical identity theft victims have also reported other types of health and safety harms caused by the theft, such as delay in receiving medical treatment and incorrect pharmaceutical prescriptions. All of these types of harms are cognizable under Section 5(n).

Finally, given that we have found that the very disclosure of sensitive health or medical information to unauthorized individuals is itself a privacy harm, LabMD's sharing of the 1718 file on LimeWire for 11 months was also highly likely to cause substantial privacy harm to thousands of consumers, in addition to the harm actually caused by the known disclosure.

Having found that the unauthorized exposure of the 1718 file created a high likelihood of a large harm to consumers, we conclude that the unauthorized exposure of the 1718 file was "likely to cause substantial injury to consumers."

3. The Sacramento Incident

We do not find, however, that the security incident involving the Sacramento documents provides additional evidence that LabMD's computer security practices caused or were likely to cause substantial injury. LabMD does not dispute that the Sacramento Police Department discovered the documents in the possession of identity thieves. However, unlike with the 1718 file incident, the evidence does not establish any causal link between the exposed documents, which were found in hard copy form, and LabMD's computer security practices.

The fact that the documents were found in the hands of identity thieves strongly suggests that they viewed the information contained therein (including names and social security numbers) as valuable for their purposes. It also raises concerns that LabMD's lax security practices may not have been confined to its computers. Nonetheless, like the ALJ, we conclude that Complaint Counsel have not established that the Sacramento security incident was caused by deficiencies in LabMD's computer security practices, which were the sole practices challenged in the Complaint.

B. Consumers Could Not Reasonably Avoid the Injuries Resulting from LabMD's Data Security Practices

Turning to the second prong of Section 5(n), we find that consumers had no ability to avoid the harms caused by LabMD's practices. LabMD's clients were physicians or other health care providers. Most patients who provided blood or tissue samples for testing were not notified that their specimens would be given to LabMD for testing, or that LabMD would receive and retain other sensitive personal information as well. While some consumers eventually learned of LabMD's existence during the billing or collections process, even these consumers lacked any information about LabMD's data security practices, and thus had no opportunity to avoid injuries caused by these practices. In sum, victims of a LabMD data breach would have "no chance whatsoever to avoid the injury before it occurred." FTC v. Neovi, Inc., 598 F. Supp. 2d 1104, 1115 (S.D. Cal. 2008), aff'd, 604 F.3d 1150 (9th Cir. 2010).

LabMD nonetheless argues that consumers were reasonably capable of mitigating any injury "after the fact." We disagree. Our inquiry centers on whether consumers can avoid harm before it occurs. Second, even assuming arguendo that the ability to mitigate harm does factor into its avoidability, there is nothing LabMD has pointed to that demonstrates mitigation after the fact would have been possible here. Without notice of a breach, consumers can do little to mitigate its harms. LabMD would be the entity to provide such notice if a breach occurred on its network, yet it did not notify the relevant 9,300 consumers that their medical and other sensitive personal information had been exposed in the 1718 file. Moreover, even if consumers do receive notice that their information was involved in a breach, it may be difficult or impossible to mitigate or avoid further harm, since they have "little, if ... any, control over who may access that information" in the future, and tools such as credit monitoring and fraud alerts cannot foreclose the possibility of future identity theft over a long period of time. Furthermore, consumers cannot avoid or fully reverse certain categories of non-economic injury that may accompany the exposure of sensitive medical information. In short, there was no way for consumers to avoid the injury that was caused or likely to be caused by LabMD's inadequate data security practices.

C. The Injuries Were Not Outweighed by Countervailing Benefits to Consumers or to Competition

Finally, we must consider whether the consumer injury resulting from LabMD's data security practices is "outweighed by countervailing benefits to consumers or to competition." 15 U.S.C. § 45(n). A "benefit" can be in the form of lower costs and then potentially lower prices for consumers, and the Commission "will not find that a practice unfairly injures consumers unless it is injurious in its net effects." Unfairness Statement, 104 F.T.C. at 1073. This cost-benefit inquiry is particularly important in cases where the allegedly unfair practice consists of a party's failure to take actions that would prevent consumer injury or reduce the risk of such injury. Int'l Harvester Co., 104 F.T.C. at 1064. When a case concerns the failure to provide adequate data security in particular, "countervailing benefits" are the foregone costs of "investment in stronger cybersecurity" by comparison with the cost of the firm's existing "level of cybersecurity." Wyndham, 799 F.3d at 255.

Here, we conclude that whatever savings LabMD reaped by forgoing the expenses needed to remedy its conduct do not outweigh the "substantial injury to consumers" caused or likely to be caused by its poor security practices. For the data security failures we described above, the record contains detailed evidence of low-cost solutions that LabMD could have adopted to cure the deficiencies and render its practices reasonable and appropriate. LabMD has not disputed Complaint Counsel's showing as to the availability and cost of these alternatives.

For example, there were many free or low cost software tools and hardware devices available for detecting vulnerabilities, including antivirus programs, firewalls, vulnerability scanning tools, intrusion detection devices, penetration testing programs, and file integrity monitoring tools. LabMD could have maintained and updated operating systems of computers and other devices on its network at relatively low cost. Remediation processes and updates for vulnerabilities were widely available. These processes included free notifications from vendors, as well as the Computer Emergency Response Team ("CERT"), the Open Source Vulnerability Data Base, NIST, and others.

In addition, LabMD could have adequately trained employees to safeguard personal information at relatively low cost. Several nationally recognized organizations provided low-cost or free IT security training courses. For example, the SysAdmin Audit Network Security (SANS) Institute, formed in 1989, provides free security training webcasts. Additional free resources could be found online, and CERT at Carnegie Mellon University offered e- learning courses for IT professionals for as little as $850.

LabMD also could have limited employees' access to only the types of personal information that they needed to perform their jobs at relatively low cost. Because operating systems and applications already have access controls embedded in them, rectifying this issue would have required only the time of trained IT staff. In addition, LabMD could have purged the personal information of consumers for whom it never performed testing at relatively low cost. This could have been accomplished using LabMD's database applications, and would have required only the time of trained IT staff. We recognize that the time of trained IT staff can amount to a real cost, but LabMD already had multiple IT personnel on staff. Any such additional costs would be far outweighed by the likely adverse consequences to consumers of LabMD's lax security practices.

Finally, LabMD readily could have prevented the installation of LimeWire by simply providing the billing manager and other employees non-administrative accounts on their workstations. The Windows operating system that LabMD used included this functionality; LabMD could have made use of it with no monetary expense.

Consequently, the benefits resulting from LabMD's flawed practices are negligible because the costs to provide the appropriate data security would have been relatively low. The cost-benefit test "is easily satisfied 'when a practice produces clear adverse consequences for consumers that are not accompanied by an increase in services or benefits to consumers or by benefits to competition."D' Neovi, 598 F. Supp. 2d at 1116 (quoting FTC v. J.K. Publications, Inc., 99 F. Supp. 2d 1176, 1201 (C.D. Cal. 2000)). That is the case here.

. . . LabMD challenges this enforcement proceeding next on the ground that the Commission had "not prescribed regulations or legislative rules under Section 5 establishing medical data security standards" before issuing the complaint against LabMD. In our January 16, 2014 order, we noted that "longstanding case law confirm[s] that administrative agencies may - indeed, must - enforce statutes that Congress has directed them to implement, regardless whether they have issued regulations addressing the specific conduct at issue." Indeed, "complex questions relating to data security practices in an online environment are particularly well-suited to case-by-case development in administrative adjudications or enforcement proceedings." By the same token, "it is well-established that the common law of negligence does not violate due process simply because the standards of care are uncodified," and thus "courts and juries [routinely] subject companies to tort liability for violating uncodified standards of care."

Fundamentally, Section 5(n) provides reasonably clear and intelligible guidelines for companies to follow in designing their own data security programs. See Wyndham, 799 F.3d at 255. As discussed above, the FTC Act simply requires a company that maintains personal information about consumers to assess the risks that its actions could cause harm to those consumers and to implement reasonable measures to prevent or minimize such foreseeable harm.

We provided ample notice to the public of our expectations regarding reasonable and appropriate data security practices by issuing numerous administrative decisions finding specific companies liable for unreasonable data security practices. Our complaints, as well as our decisions and orders accepting consent decrees, which are published on our website and in the Federal Register, make clear that the failure to take reasonable data security measures may constitute an unfair practice. Those complaints, decisions, and orders also flesh out the specific types of security lapses that may be deemed unreasonable. These widely available materials "constitute a body of experience and informed judgment to which ... [parties] may properly resort for guidance." Gen. Elec. Co. v. Gilbert, 429 U.S. 125, 141-42 (1976). And even though they "are neither regulations nor 'adjudications on the merits," they are sufficient to afford fair notice of what was needed to satisfy Section 5(n). See Wyndham, 799 F.3d at 257. LabMD cannot seriously contend that it lacked notice that its security failures, which led to at least one documented breach of thousands of consumers' sensitive personal information - practices similar to those committed by other companies against which the FTC has taken action - could trigger Section 5 liability.

. . .

V. The Remedy is Appropriate and Required to Prevent Further Consumer Injury

Having found that LabMD violated the FTC Act, we enter an order that will ensure LabMD reasonably protects the security and confidentiality of the personal consumer information in its possession. 15 U.S.C. § 45(b). "The Commission is not limited to prohibiting the illegal practice in the precise form in which it is found to have existed in the past." FTC v. Colgate-Palmolive Co., 380 U.S. 374, 395 (1965). Rather, "[t]he Commission has wide latitude in fashioning orders to prevent ... respondents from pursuing a course of conduct similar to that found to have been unfair." Thompson Med. Co., 104 F.T.C. 648, 832-33 (1984), aff'd, 791 F.2d 189 (D.C. Cir. 1986). This discretion is subject to two constraints, however. First, the order must be sufficiently clear and precise to be understood by the violator. Second, the order must bear a reasonable relationship to the unlawful practice found to exist.

We enter an order similar to the Notice Order that was attached to the Complaint. The Order contains three provisions to prevent future violations by LabMD and remediate the risk of harm to consumers.

Part I of the Order requires LabMD to establish, implement, and maintain a comprehensive information security program that is reasonably designed to protect the security and confidentiality of consumers' personal information. The program must be in writing, and should contain administrative, technical, and physical safeguards appropriate to LabMD's size and complexity, the nature and scope of its activities, and the sensitive personal information maintained on LabMD's network. In light of the discussion in our opinion and the availability of guidance about comprehensive information security programs from HIPAA and organizations such as NIST and the SANS Institute, this provision is sufficiently clear and precise that its requirements can be readily understood and met.

Part II of the Order requires LabMD to obtain initial and then biennial assessments and reports regarding its implementation of the information security program. Each assessment must set forth the safeguards that LabMD implemented and maintained during the reporting period and certify that LabMD's security program is operating with sufficient effectiveness to provide reasonable assurance that the security, confidentiality, and integrity of personal information is protected. The assessments and reports must be provided by a qualified, objective, independent third-party professional. This provision will ensure that LabMD implements information security practices that are appropriate for LabMD's size, complexity, and the nature and scope of its activities and the sensitive personal information maintained on its network, and thereby complies with the Order. Courts have upheld the use of extensive assessment and monitoring requirements by an independent third party in final injunction orders.

These two provisions are reasonably related to the unlawful practices that form the basis for LabMD's liability - the failure by LabMD to implement reasonable and appropriate data security practices to protect consumers' sensitive medical and other information - and seek to ensure that this failure is remedied. The FTC has required these types of provisions in numerous final orders to settle actions involving data security practices that it charged were violations of Section 5(n). . . .

Part III of the Order requires LabMD to notify individuals whose personal information LabMD has reason to believe was or could have been exposed about the unauthorized disclosure of their personal information. LabMD must also notify the health insurance companies for these individuals of the information disclosure. Without notification, consumers would not know about the unauthorized disclosure of their sensitive information and would not know to take actions to reduce their risk of harm from identity or medical identity theft. LabMD acknowledges that this type of notice is required under HIPAA for disclosures of personal medical information that have occurred since 2010. Similarly, notice to affected consumers' insurance companies enables these insurers to protect consumers' identities from misuse. These notification requirements are consistent with relief obtained in other cases.

The remaining parts of the Order are standard recordkeeping and sunset provisions that are included in most Commission orders. Part IV is a record-keeping requirement. Part V establishes that copies of the Order be distributed to, among others, principals, managers, and employees of LabMD. . . . Part VII establishes compliance reporting requirements. . . .

LabMD contends that the relief in the Order is unnecessary and punitive. We disagree. Although LabMD stopped accepting specimen samples and conducting tests in January 2014, LabMD continues to exist as a corporation and has not ruled out a resumption of operations. Moreover, LabMD continues to maintain the personal information of approximately 750,000 consumers on its computer system. Because LabMD continues to hold consumers' personal information and may resume operations at some future time, the Order is appropriate and necessary. . . .

In addition, the Order takes account of LabMD's current limited operations. The Order requires that LabMD establish and implement a comprehensive information security program that provides administrative, technical and physical safeguards that are appropriate for the nature and scope of LabMD's activities. A reasonable and appropriate information security program for LabMD's current operations with a computer that is shut down and not connected to the Internet will undoubtedly differ from an appropriate comprehensive information security program if LabMD resumes more active operations.

Finally, we reject LabMD's claim that the Order is punitive. The Order merely requires measures reasonably necessary to ensure the protection of the personal information on its computer system and notice related to its unfair practices. An order that is purely remedial and preventative is not a penalty or forfeiture.

CONCLUSION

For the foregoing reasons, the Commission concludes that LabMD's data security practices were unreasonable and constitute an unfair act or practice in violation of Section 5 of the FTC Act. Consequently, we vacate the ALJ's Initial Decision and issue a Final Order requiring that LabMD notify affected individuals, establish a comprehensive information security program, and obtain assessments regarding its implementation of the program.

FINAL ORDER . . .
DEFINITIONS

For purposes of this order, the following definitions shall apply:
1. "Commerce" shall mean as defined in Section 4 of the Federal Trade Commission Act, 15 U.S.C. § 44.
2. Unless otherwise specified, "respondent" shall mean LabMD, Inc., and its successors and assigns.
3. "Affected Individual" shall mean any consumer whose personal information LabMD has reason to believe was, or could have been, accessible to unauthorized persons before July 28, 2016, including, but not limited to, consumers listed in the Insurance File and other documents available to a peer-to-peer file sharing network, but excluding consumers whom LabMD has notified, before July 28, 2016, of a data security breach.
4. "Insurance File" shall mean the file containing personal information about approximately 9,300 consumers, including names, dates of birth, Social Security numbers, health insurance company names and policy numbers, and medical test codes,

that was available to a peer-to-peer file sharing network through a peer-to-peer file sharing application installed on a computer on respondent's computer network.

5. "Personal information" shall mean individually identifiable information from or about an individual consumer including, but not limited to: (a) first and last name; (b) telephone number; (c) a home or other physical address, including street name and name of city or town; (d) date of birth; (e) Social Security number; (f) medical record number; (g) bank routing, account, and check numbers; (h) credit or debit card information, such as account number; (i) laboratory test result, medical test code, or diagnosis, or clinical history; (j) health insurance company name and policy number; or (k) a persistent identifier, such as a customer number held in a "cookie" or processor serial number.

I.

IT IS ORDERED that the respondent shall, no later than the date this order becomes final and effective, establish and implement, and thereafter maintain, a comprehensive information security program that is reasonably designed to protect the security, confidentiality, and integrity of personal information collected from or about consumers by respondent or by any corporation, subsidiary, division, website, or other device or affiliate owned or controlled by respondent. Such program, the content and implementation of which must be fully documented in writing, shall contain administrative, technical, and physical safeguards appropriate to respondent's size and complexity, the nature and scope of respondent's activities, and the sensitivity of the personal information collected from or about consumers, including:

A. the designation of an employee or employees to coordinate and be accountable for the information security program;

B. the identification of material internal and external risks to the security, confidentiality, and integrity of personal information that could result in the unauthorized disclosure, misuse, loss, alteration, destruction, or other compromise of such information, and assessment of the sufficiency of any safeguards in place to control these risks. At a minimum, this risk assessment should include consideration of risks in each area of relevant operation, including, but not limited to: (1) employee training and management; (2) information systems, including network and software design, information processing, storage, transmission, and disposal; and (3) prevention, detection, and response to attacks, intrusions, or other systems failures;

C. the design and implementation of reasonable safeguards to control the risks identified through risk assessment, and regular testing or monitoring of the effectiveness of the safeguards' key controls, systems, and procedures;

D. the development and use of reasonable steps to select and retain service providers capable of appropriately safeguarding personal information they receive from respondent, and requiring service providers by contract to implement and maintain appropriate safeguards; and

E. the evaluation and adjustment of respondent's information security program in light of the results of the testing and monitoring required by Subpart C, any material changes to respondent's operations or business arrangements, or any other circumstances that respondent knows or has reason to know may have a material impact on the effectiveness of its information security program.

II.

IT IS FURTHER ORDERED that, in connection with its compliance with Part I of this order, respondent shall obtain initial and biennial assessments and reports

("Assessments") from a qualified, objective, independent third-party professional, who uses procedures and standards generally accepted in the profession. Professionals qualified to prepare such assessments shall be: a person qualified as a Certified Information System Security Professional (CISSP) or as a Certified Information Systems Auditor (CISA); a person holding Global Information Assurance Certification (GIAC) from the SysAdmin, Audit, Network, Security (SANS) Institute; or a similarly qualified person or organization approved by the Associate Director for Enforcement, Bureau of Consumer Protection, Federal Trade Commission . . . Each Assessment shall:

A. set forth the specific administrative, technical, and physical safeguards that respondent has implemented and maintained during the reporting period;

B. explain how such safeguards are appropriate to respondent's size and complexity, the nature and scope of respondent's activities, and the sensitivity of the personal information collected from or about consumers;

C. explain how the safeguards that have been implemented meet or exceed the protections required by Part I of this order; and

D. certify that respondent's security program is operating with sufficient effectiveness to provide reasonable assurance that the security, confidentiality, and integrity of personal information is protected, and has so operated throughout the reporting period. Each Assessment shall be prepared and completed within sixty (60) days after the end of the reporting period to which the Assessment applies. Respondent shall provide the initial Assessment to the Associate Director for Enforcement, Bureau of Consumer Protection, Federal Trade Commission, Washington, D.C. 20580, within ten (10) days after the Assessment has been prepared. All subsequent biennial Assessments shall be retained by respondent until the order is terminated and provided to the Associate Director for Enforcement within ten (10) days of request. . . .

By the Commission. . . .
Issued: July 28, 2016

NOTES

Note 1

The Order reproduced in the FTC's LabMD matter *supra* also contains provisions concerning follow up reporting required by LabMD. The Order also requires notice to individuals impacted by the LabMD data breach.

Note 2

What is required for demonstrating "cause or likely to cause substantial injury?" Which approach do you prefer? Why?

Note 3

After reading the LabMD FTC opinion, what do you think of about Tiversa and grey hat hackers? By notifying LabMD of a security vulnerability, Tiversa is essentially asking LabMD to hire it to deal with the problem. This is classic grey hat behavior: A grey hat hacker has found a flaw and approaches the company with the flaw to offer to fix it. What happened when LabMD failed to hire Tiversa? Do the positives of allowing and indeed, encouraging, grey hat activity outweigh any potential negatives? Did Tiversa essentially try to blackmail LabMD? Or, is Tiversa a "good guy" who is helping to ensure that consumers are protected? What behavior should we be incentivizing?

Note 4

Notably, computer hacking tools are widely available online, including "how to" instructions for hacking. Ostensibly, this is for the benefit of white and grey hats or so-called ethical hackers, but it also benefits black hat hackers. Should we criminalize the possession and distribution of hacking tools and instructions? What policy and practical concerns exist? What do we want to encourage and "expose to the light?"

LabMD v. Federal Trade Commission, 894 F.3d 1221 (11th Cir. 2018).
Opinion

TJOFLAT, Circuit Judge:
This is an enforcement action brought by the Federal Trade Commission ("FTC" or "Commission") against LabMD, Inc., alleging that LabMD's data-security program was inadequate and thus constituted an "unfair act or practice" under Section 5(a) of the Federal Trade Commission Act (the "FTC Act" or "Act"), 15 U.S.C. § 45(a). Following a trial before an administrative law judge ("ALJ"), the Commission issued a cease and desist order directing LabMD to create and implement a variety of protective measures. LabMD petitions this Court to vacate the order, arguing that the order is unenforceable because it does not direct LabMD to cease committing an unfair act or practice within the meaning of Section 5(a). We agree and accordingly vacate the order.

I.
A.

LabMD is a now-defunct medical laboratory that previously conducted diagnostic testing for cancer. It used medical specimen samples, along with relevant patient information, to provide physicians with diagnoses. Given the nature of its work, LabMD was subject to data-security regulations issued under the Health Insurance Portability and Accountability Act of 1996, known colloquially as HIPAA. LabMD employed a data-security program in an effort to comply with those regulations.

Sometime in 2005, contrary to LabMD policy, a peer-to-peer file-sharing application called LimeWire was installed on a computer used by LabMD's billing manager. LimeWire is an application commonly used for sharing and downloading music and videos over the Internet. It connects to the "Gnutella" network, which during the relevant period had two to five million people logged in at any given time. Those using LimeWire and connected to the Gnutella network can browse directories and download files that other users on the network designate for sharing. The billing manager designated the contents of the "My Documents" folder on her computer for sharing, exposing the contents to the other users. Between July 2007 and May 2008, this folder contained a 1,718-page file (the "1718 File") with the personal information of 9,300 consumers, including names, dates of birth, social security numbers, laboratory test codes, and, for some, health insurance company names, addresses, and policy numbers. In February 2008, Tiversa Holding Corporation, an entity specializing in data security, used LimeWire to download the 1718 File. Tiversa began contacting LabMD months later, offering to sell its remediation services to LabMD. LabMD refused Tiversa's services and removed LimeWire from the billing manager's computer. Tiversa's solicitations stopped in July 2008, after LabMD instructed Tiversa to direct any further communications to LabMD's lawyer. In 2009, Tiversa arranged for the delivery of the 1718 File to the FTC.

B.

In August 2013, the Commission, following an extensive investigation, issued an administrative complaint against LabMD and assigned an ALJ to the case. The complaint alleged that LabMD had committed an "unfair act or practice" prohibited by Section 5(a) by "engag[ing] in a number of practices that, taken together, failed to provide reasonable and appropriate security for personal information on its computer networks." Rather than allege specific acts or practices that LabMD engaged in, however, the FTC's complaint set forth a number of data-security measures that LabMD failed to perform. LabMD answered the complaint, denying it had engaged in the conduct alleged and asserting several affirmative defenses, among them that the Commission lacked authority under Section 5 of the Act to regulate its handling of the personal information in its computer networks.

After answering the FTC's complaint, LabMD filed a motion to dismiss it for failure to state a case cognizable under Section 5. The motion essentially replicated the assertions in LabMD's answer. Under the FTC's Rules of Practice, the Commission, rather than the ALJ, ruled on the motion to dismiss. The Commission denied the motion, concluding that it had authority under Section 5(a) to prosecute the charge of unfairness asserted in its complaint. LabMD, Inc., 2014-1 Trade Cases P 78784 (F.T.C.), 2014 WL 253518 (Jan. 16, 2014).

Following discovery, LabMD filed a motion for summary judgment, presenting arguments similar to those made in support of its motion to dismiss. As before, the motion was submitted to the Commission to decide. It denied the motion on the ground that there were genuine factual disputes relating to LabMD's liability "for engaging in unfair acts or practices in violation of Section 5(a)," necessitating an evidentiary hearing. . . .

After considering the parties' submissions, the ALJ dismissed the FTC's complaint, concluding that the FTC failed to prove that LabMD had committed unfair acts or practices in neglecting to provide adequate security for the personal information lodged in its computer networks. Namely, the FTC failed to prove that LabMD's "alleged failure to employ reasonable data security ... caused or is likely to cause substantial injury to consumers," as required by Section 5(n) of the Act, 15 U.S.C. § 45(n). Because there was no substantial injury or likelihood thereof, there could be no unfair act or practice.

The FTC appealed the ALJ's decision, which under 16 C.F.R. § 3.52 brought the decision before the full Commission for review. In July 2016, reviewing the ALJ's findings of fact and conclusions of law de novo, see id. § 3.54, the FTC reversed the ALJ's decision.

The FTC first found that LabMD "failed to implement reasonable security measures to protect the sensitive consumer information on its computer network." Therefore, LabMD's "data security practices were unfair under Section 5." In particular, LabMD failed to adequately secure its computer network, employ suitable risk-assessment tools, provide data-security training to its employees, and adequately restrict and monitor the computer practices of those using its network. Because of these deficiencies, the Commission continued, LimeWire was able to be installed on the LabMD billing manager's computer, and Tiversa was ultimately able to download the 1718 File. The Commission then held that, contrary to the ALJ's decision, the evidence showed that Section 5(n)'s "substantial injury" prong was met in two ways: the unauthorized disclosure of the 1718 File itself caused intangible privacy harm, and the mere exposure of the 1718 File on LimeWire was likely to cause substantial injury. The FTC went on to conclude that Section 5(n)'s other requirements were also met.

Next, the Commission addressed and rejected LabMD's arguments that Section 5(a)'s "unfairness" standard—which, according to the Commission, is a reasonableness standard—is void for vagueness and that the Commission failed to provide fair notice of what data-security practices were adequate under Section 5(a). The FTC then entered an order vacating the ALJ's decision and enjoining LabMD to install a data-security program that comported with the FTC's standard of reasonableness. The order is to terminate on either July 28, 2036, or twenty years "from the most recent date that the [FTC] files a complaint ... in federal court alleging any violation of the order, whichever comes later." . . .

II.

Now, LabMD argues that the Commission's cease and desist order is unenforceable because the order does not direct it to cease committing an unfair "act or practice" within the meaning of Section 5(a).12 We review the FTC's legal conclusions de novo but give "some deference to [its] informed judgment that a particular commercial practice is to be condemned as 'unfair.'" We review the FTC's findings of facts under the "substantial evidence" standard, . . ., which requires "more than a mere scintilla" of evidence "but less than a preponderance. . .."

A.

Section 5(a) of the FTC Act authorizes the FTC to protect consumers by "prevent[ing] persons, partnerships, or corporations ... from using unfair ... acts or practices in or affecting commerce." The Act does not define the term "unfair." The provision's history, however, elucidates the term's meaning.

The FTC Act, passed in 1914, created the FTC and gave it power to prohibit "unfair methods of competition." Rather than list "the particular practices to which [unfairness] was intended to apply," Congress "intentionally left development of the term 'unfair' to the Commission" through case-by-case litigation—though, at the time of the FTC Act's inception, the FTC's primary mission was understood to be the enforcement of antitrust law. In 1938, the Act was amended to provide that the FTC had authority to prohibit "unfair ... acts or practices." This amendment sought to clarify that the FTC's authority applied not only to competitors but, importantly, also to consumers. Hence, the FTC possesses "unfairness authority" to prohibit and prosecute unfair acts or practices harmful to consumers.

In 1964, the FTC set forth three factors to consider in deciding whether to wield its unfairness authority. The FTC was to consider whether an act or practice (1) caused consumers, competitors, or other businesses substantial injury; (2) offended public policy as established by statute, the common law, or otherwise; and (3) was immoral, unethical, or unscrupulous. The Supreme Court cited these factors with apparent approval in dicta in the 1972 case FTC v. Sperry & Hutchinson, 405 U.S. 233, 244 n.5, 92 S.Ct. 898, 905 n.5, 31 L.Ed.2d 170 (1972).

"Emboldened" by Sperry & Hutchinson's dicta, "the Commission set forth to test the limits of the unfairness doctrine." This effort peaked in a 1978 attempt to "use unfairness to ban all advertising directed to children on the grounds that it was 'immoral, unscrupulous, and unethical' and based on generalized public policies to protect children." Congress and much of the public disapproved. Congressional backlash included refusing to fund the FTC, thus shutting it down for several days, and passing legislation that prevented the FTC from using its unfairness authority to promulgate rules that restrict children's advertising.

Following this episode, the Commission wrote a unanimous letter to two senators in 1980 placing gloss on the three 1964 unfairness factors that were recognized in Sperry & Hutchinson. As to the first factor, consumer injury, the FTC laid out a separate three-part test defining a qualifying injury. These consumer-injury factors would later be codified in Section 5(n). The FTC stated that to warrant a finding of unfairness, an injury "[1] must be substantial; [2] it must not be outweighed by any countervailing benefits to consumers or competition that the practice produces; and [3] it must be an injury that consumers themselves could not reasonably have avoided."

As to the second 1964 unfairness factor, public policy, the FTC specified that the policies relied upon "should be clear and well-established"—that is, "declared or embodied in formal sources such as statutes, judicial decisions, or the Constitution as interpreted by the courts, rather than being ascertained from the general sense of the national values." Put another way, an act or practice's "unfairness" must be grounded in statute, judicial decisions—i.e., the common law—or the Constitution. An act or practice that causes substantial injury but lacks such grounding is not unfair within Section 5(a)'s meaning. Finally, the FTC stated that it was nixing the third 1964 unfairness factor—whether a practice is immoral, unethical, or unscrupulous—because it was "largely duplicative" of the first two. Thus, an "unfair" act or practice is one which meets the consumer-injury factors listed above and is grounded in well-established legal policy.

B.

Here, the FTC's complaint alleges that LimeWire was installed on the computer used by LabMD's billing manager. This installation was contrary to company policy. The complaint then alleges that LimeWire's installation caused the 1718 File, which consisted of consumers' personal information, to be exposed. The 1718 File's exposure caused consumers injury by infringing upon their right of privacy. Thus, the complaint alleges that LimeWire was installed in defiance of LabMD policy and caused the alleged consumer injury. Had the complaint stopped there, a narrowly drawn and easily enforceable order might have followed, commanding LabMD to eliminate the possibility that employees could install unauthorized programs on their computers.

But the complaint continues past this single allegation of wrongdoing, adding that LimeWire's installation was not the only conduct that caused the 1718 File to be exposed. It also alleges broadly that LabMD "engaged in a number of practices that, taken together, failed to provide reasonable and appropriate security for personal information on its computer networks." The complaint then provides a litany of security measures that LabMD failed to employ, each setting out in general terms a deficiency in LabMD's data-security protocol. Because LabMD failed to employ these measures, the Commission's theory goes, LimeWire was able to be installed on the billing manager's computer. LabMD's policy forbidding employees from installing programs like LimeWire was insufficient.

The FTC's complaint, therefore, uses LimeWire's installation, and the 1718 File's exposure, as an entry point to broadly allege that LabMD's data-security operations are deficient as a whole. Aside from the installation of LimeWire on a company computer, the complaint alleges no specific unfair acts or practices engaged in by LabMD. Rather, it was LabMD's multiple, unspecified failures to act in creating and operating its data-security program that amounted to an unfair act or practice. Given the breadth of these failures, the Commission attached to its complaint a proposed order which would regulate all aspects of LabMD's data-security program—sweeping prophylactic measures to collectively reduce the possibility of employees installing unauthorized programs on their computers and thus exposing consumer information. The proposed cease and desist order, which is identical in all relevant respects to the order the FTC ultimately issued, identifies no specific unfair acts or practices from which LabMD must abstain and instead requires LabMD to implement and maintain a data-security program "reasonably designed" to the Commission's satisfaction. See generally Appendix.

The decision on which the FTC based its final cease and desist order exhibits more of the same. The FTC found that LabMD "failed to implement reasonable security measures to protect the sensitive consumer information on its computer network" and that the failure caused substantial consumer injury. In effect, the decision held that LabMD's failure to act in various ways to protect consumer data rendered its entire data-security operation an unfair act or practice. The broad cease and desist order now at issue, according to the Commission, was therefore justified.

* * *

The first question LabMD's petition for review presents is whether LabMD's failure to implement and maintain a reasonably designed data-security program constituted an unfair act or practice within the ambit of Section 5(a). The FTC declared that it did because such failure caused substantial injury to consumers' right of privacy, and it issued a cease and desist order to avoid further injury.

The Commission must find the standards of unfairness it enforces in "clear and well-established" policies that are expressed in the Constitution, statutes, or the common law. The Commission's decision in this case does not explicitly cite the source of the standard of unfairness it used in holding that LabMD's failure to implement and maintain a reasonably designed data-security program constituted an unfair act or practice. It is apparent to us, though, that the source is the common law of negligence. According to the Restatement (Second) of Torts § 281 (Am. Law Inst. 1965), Statement of the Elements of a Cause of Action for Negligence,

> [an] actor is liable for an invasion of an interest of another, if:
> (a) the interest invaded is protected against unintentional invasion, and
> (b) the conduct of the actor is negligent with respect to the other, or a class of persons within which [the other] is included, and
> (c) the actor's conduct is a legal cause of the invasion, and
> (d) the other has not so conducted himself as to disable himself from bringing an action for such invasion.

The gist of the Commission's complaint and its decision is this: The consumers' right of privacy is protected against unintentional invasion. LabMD unintentionally invaded their right, and its deficient data-security program was a legal cause. Section

5(a) empowers the Commission to "prevent persons, partnerships, or corporations ... from using unfair ... acts or practices." The law of negligence, the Commission's action implies, is a source that provides standards for determining whether an act or practice is unfair, so a person, partnership, or corporation that negligently infringes a consumer interest protected against unintentional invasion may be held accountable under Section 5(a). We will assume arguendo that the Commission is correct and that LabMD's negligent failure to design and maintain a reasonable data-security program invaded consumers' right of privacy and thus constituted an unfair act or practice.

The second question LabMD's petition for review presents is whether the Commission's cease and desist order, founded upon LabMD's general negligent failure to act, is enforceable. We answer this question in the negative. We illustrate why by first laying out the FTC Act's enforcement and remedial schemes and then by demonstrating the problems that enforcing the order would pose.

III.

The FTC carries out its Section 5(a) mission to prevent unfair acts or practices in two ways: formal rulemaking and case-by-case litigation.

The Commission is authorized under 15 U.S.C. § 57a to prescribe rules "which define with specificity" unfair acts or practices within the meaning of Section 5(a). Once a rule takes effect, it becomes in essence an addendum to Section 5(a)'s phrase "unfair ... acts or practices"; the rule puts the public on notice that a particular act or practice is unfair. The FTC enforces its rules in the federal district courts. Under 15 U.S.C. § 45(m)(1)(A), the Commission may bring an action to recover a civil penalty against any person, partnership or corporation that knowingly violates a rule.30 This case does not involve the enforcement of an FTC-promulgated rule.

What is involved here is the FTC's establishment of an unfair act or practice through litigation. Because Congress thought impossible the task of legislating a comprehensive list of unfair acts or practices, it authorized the Commission to establish unfair acts or practices through case-by-case litigation. In the litigation context, once an act or practice is adjudged to be unfair, the act or practice becomes in effect—like an FTC-promulgated rule—an addendum to Section 5(a).

The FTC Act provides two forums for such litigation. The Commission may choose to prosecute its claim that an act or practice is unfair before an ALJ, with appellate review before the full Commission and then in a federal court of appeals. See 15 U.S.C. § 45(b), (c); 16 C.F.R. § 3.1 et seq. Or, under Section 13(b) of the Act, 15 U.S.C. § 53(b), it may prosecute its claim before a federal district judge, with appellate review also in a federal court of appeals.

Assume a factual scenario in which the Commission believes a certain act or practice is unfair. It should not matter which of the two forums the Commission chooses to prosecute its claim. The result should be the same. As we explain below, the ALJ and the district judge use materially identical procedural rules in processing the case to judgment and both apply the same substantive law to the facts. Further, putting any venue differences aside, the same court of appeals reviews their decisions.

A.

We consider the Commission's first option, litigation before an ALJ. The Commission issues an administrative complaint against a party it has reason to believe is engaging in an unfair act or practice and seeks a cease and desist order. 16 C.F.R. §

3.13. The Commission prosecutes the complaint before an ALJ whom it designates, in accordance with its Rules of Practice. Id. § 3.1 et seq. Under these Rules, the complaint must provide, among other things, "[a] clear and concise factual statement sufficient to inform each respondent with reasonable definiteness of the type of acts or practices alleged to be in violation of the law." Id. § 3.11. If the respondent files a motion to dismiss the complaint, the motion is referred to the Commission for a ruling. If the motion is denied, the respondent files an answer. From that point on, the proceedings before the ALJ resemble the proceedings in an action for injunctive relief in federal district court. If the ALJ finds that the respondent has been engaging in the unfair act or practice alleged and will likely continue doing so, the ALJ enters a cease and desist order enjoining the respondent from engaging in the unfair conduct.33 If not, the ALJ dismisses the Commission's complaint. Either way, the ALJ's decision is appealable to the FTC, id. § 3.52, and the FTC's decision is in turn reviewable in a federal court of appeals, 15 U.S.C. § 45(c).

Suppose the Commission chooses the second option, litigation before a federal district judge under Section 13(b). If the Commission has reason to believe a party is engaging in an unfair act or practice, it seeks an injunction by filing in district court a complaint that sets forth "well-pleaded facts ... permit[ting] the court to infer more than the mere possibility of misconduct." Ashcroft v. Iqbal, 556 U.S. 662, 679, 129 S.Ct. 1937, 1950, 173 L.Ed.2d 868 (2009) (citing Fed. R. Civ. P. 8(a)(2)). Although the case is tried pursuant to the Federal Rules of Civil Procedure, not the FTC Rules of Practice, it is handled essentially as it would be before the ALJ. If the district judge finds that the defendant has been engaging in the unfair act or practice alleged and will likely continue doing so, the judge enjoins the defendant from engaging in such conduct. Whatever the court's decision, it is reviewable in the court of appeals.

Assume the result is the same in both litigation forums. The ALJ enters a cease and desist order; the district court issues an injunction. Appellate review would reach the same result regardless of the trial forum (assuming that venue is laid in the same court of appeals). Assume further that both coercive orders are affirmed by the court of appeals. The cease and desist order and the injunction address the same behavior and contain the same command: discontinue engaging in a specific unfair act or practice.

With the cease and desist order or the injunction in hand, the Commission may proceed in two ways against a party who violates its terms. The Commission may seek the imposition of either a civil penalty or civil-contempt sanction. We explain below the procedures the Commission invokes in pursuing these respective remedies.

B.
1.

Under Section 5(l), 15 U.S.C. § 45(l), the Commission may bring a civil-penalty action in district court should the respondent violate a final cease and desist order. The Commission's complaint would allege that the defendant is subject to an existing cease and desist order and has violated its terms. For each separate violation of the order—or, in the case of a continuing violation, for each day in violation—the district court may impose a penalty of up to $41,484.39 Id. Section 5(l) also empowers the district court to grant an injunction if the Commission proves that the violation is likely to continue and an injunction is necessary to enforce the order.

If the Commission has obtained an injunction in district court requiring the defendant to discontinue an unfair act or practice, it may invoke the district court's civil-contempt power should the defendant disobey. Rather than filing a complaint, as in a Section 5(l) action, the Commission simply moves the district court for an order requiring the defendant to show cause why it should not be held in contempt for engaging in conduct the injunction specifically enjoined. If the court is satisfied that the conduct is forbidden, it issues a show cause order. Then, if at the show cause hearing the Commission establishes by clear and convincing proof that the defendant engaged in the forbidden conduct and that the defendant "had the ability to comply" with the injunctive provision at issue, McGregor v. Chierico, 206 F.3d 1378, 1383 (11th Cir. 2000), the court may adjudicate the defendant in civil contempt and impose appropriate sanctions.

2.

The concept of specificity is crucial to both modes of enforcement. We start with civil penalties for violations of cease and desist orders. Nothing in the FTC Act addresses what content must go into a cease and desist order. The FTC Rule of Practice governing Commission complaints, however, states that a complaint must contain "[a] clear and concise factual statement sufficient to inform each respondent with reasonable definiteness of the type of acts or practices alleged to be in violation of the law." 16 C.F.R § 3.11. It follows that the remedy the complaint seeks must comport with this requirement of reasonable definiteness. Moreover, given the severity of the civil penalties a district court may impose for the violation of a cease and desist order, the order's prohibitions must be stated with clarity and precision. The United States Supreme Court emphasized this point in FTC v. Colgate-Palmolive Co., stating,

> [T]his Court has ... warned that an order's prohibitions should be clear and precise in order that they may be understood by those against whom they are directed, and that [t]he severity of possible penalties prescribed ... for violations of orders which have become final underlines the necessity for fashioning orders which are, at the outset, sufficiently clear and precise to avoid raising serious questions as to their meaning and application.

380 U.S. 374, 392, 85 S.Ct. 1035, 1046, 13 L.Ed.2d 904 (1965) (quotations and citations omitted). The imposition of penalties upon a party for violating an imprecise cease and desist order—up to $41,484 per violation or day in violation—may constitute a denial of due process.

Specificity is equally important in the fashioning and enforcement of an injunction consequent to an action brought in district court under Section 13(b). Federal Rule of Civil Procedure 65(d)(1) requires that an injunctive order state the reasons for its coercive provisions, state the provisions "specifically," and describe the acts restrained or required "in reasonable detail." The Supreme Court has stated that Rule 65(d)(1)'s "specificity provisions ... are no mere technical requirements. The Rule was designed to prevent uncertainty and confusion on the part of those faced with injunctive orders, and to avoid the possible founding of a contempt citation on a decree too vague to be understood." Indeed, "[t]he most fundamental postulates of our legal order forbid the imposition of a penalty for disobeying a command that defies comprehension." Int'l Longshoremen's Ass'n, Local 1291 v. Phila. Marine Trade Ass'n, 389 U.S. 64, 76, 88 S.Ct. 201, 208, 19 L.Ed.2d 236 (1967). Being held in contempt and sanctioned pursuant to an insufficiently specific injunction is therefore a denial of due process. See id. (reversing a civil-contempt judgment founded upon an order too vague to be understood).

In sum, the prohibitions contained in cease and desist orders and injunctions must be specific. Otherwise, they may be unenforceable. Both coercive orders are also governed by the same standard of specificity, as the stakes involved for a violation are the same—severe penalties or sanctions.

C.

In the case at hand, the cease and desist order contains no prohibitions. It does not instruct LabMD to stop committing a specific act or practice. Rather, it commands LabMD to overhaul and replace its data-security program to meet an indeterminable standard of reasonableness. This command is unenforceable. Its unenforceability is made clear if we imagine what would take place if the Commission sought the order's enforcement. As we have explained, the standards a district court would apply are essentially the same whether it is entertaining the Commission's action for the imposition of a penalty or the Commission's motion for an order requiring the enjoined defendant to show cause why it should not be adjudicated in contempt. For ease of discussion, we posit a scenario in which the Commission obtained the coercive order it entered in this case from a district court, and now seeks to enforce the order.

The Commission moves the district court for an order requiring LabMD to show cause why it should not be held in contempt for violating the following injunctive provision:

> [T]he respondent shall ... establish and implement, and thereafter maintain, a comprehensive information security program that is reasonably designed to protect the security, confidentiality, and integrity of personal information collected from or about consumers.... Such program ... shall contain administrative, technical, and physical safeguards appropriate to respondent's size and complexity, the nature and scope of respondent's activities, and the sensitivity of the personal information collected from or about consumers....

See Appendix at 2. The Commission's motion alleges that LabMD's program failed to implement "x" and is therefore not "reasonably designed." The court concludes that the Commission's alleged failure is within the provision's language and orders LabMD to show cause why it should not be held in contempt.

At the show cause hearing, LabMD calls an expert who testifies that the data-security program LabMD implemented complies with the injunctive provision at issue. The expert testifies that "x" is not a necessary component of a reasonably designed data-security program. The Commission, in response, calls an expert who disagrees. At this point, the district court undertakes to determine which of the two equally qualified experts correctly read the injunctive provision. Nothing in the provision, however, indicates which expert is correct. The provision contains no mention of "x" and is devoid of any meaningful standard informing the court of what constitutes a "reasonably designed" data-security program. The court therefore has no choice but to conclude that the Commission has not proven—and indeed cannot prove—LabMD's alleged violation by clear and convincing evidence. See McGregor, 206 F.3d at 1383.

If the court held otherwise and ordered LabMD to implement "x," the court would have effectively modified the injunction at a show cause hearing. This would open the door to future modifications, all improperly made at show cause hearings. Pretend that LabMD implemented "x" pursuant to the court's order, but the FTC, which is continually monitoring LabMD's compliance with the court's injunction, finds that "x" failed to bring the system up to the FTC's conception of reasonableness. So, the FTC again moves the district court for an order to show cause. This time, its motion alleges that LabMD failed to implement "y," another item the Commission thinks necessary to any reasonable data-security program. Does the court side with the Commission, modify the injunction, and order the implementation of "y"? Suppose "y" fails. Does another show cause hearing result in a third modification requiring the implementation of "z"?

The practical effect of repeatedly modifying the injunction at show cause hearings is that the district court is put in the position of managing LabMD's business in accordance with the Commission's wishes. It would be as if the Commission was LabMD's chief executive officer and the court was its operating officer. It is self-evident that this micromanaging is beyond the scope of court oversight contemplated by injunction law.

This all serves to show that an injunction identical to the FTC cease and desist order at issue would be unenforceable under a district court's contempt power. Because the standards governing the coercive enforcement of injunctions and cease and desist orders are the same, it follows that the Commission's cease and desist order is itself unenforceable.

IV.

In sum, assuming arguendo that LabMD's negligent failure to implement and maintain a reasonable data-security program constituted an unfair act or practice under Section 5(a), the Commission's cease and desist order is nonetheless unenforceable. It does not enjoin a specific act or practice. Instead, it mandates a complete overhaul of LabMD's data-security program and says precious little about how this is to be accomplished. Moreover, it effectually charges the district court with managing the overhaul. This is a scheme Congress could not have envisioned. We therefore grant LabMD's petition for review and vacate the Commission's order.
SO ORDERED.

NOTES

Note 1

The Eleventh Circuit's mention of Tiversa's role in bringing this matter to the FTC's attention is interesting. Do you think that influenced the decision of the Eleventh Circuit? Why or why not? What signals do you think the Eleventh Circuit may be sending to the FTC?

Note 2

In response to the decision in *LabMD v. Federal Trade Commission*, 894 F.3d 1221 (11th Cir. 2018), the FTC published a blog post outlining its efforts to improve orders concerning data security breaches:

When Chairman Simons and I arrived at the FTC, one of our first priorities was to strengthen the FTC's orders in data security cases. We've already made three major changes that improve data security practices and provide greater deterrence, within the bounds of our existing authority.

Since the early 2000s, our data security orders had contained fairly standard language. For example, these orders typically required a company to implement a comprehensive information security program subject to a biennial outside assessment. As part of the FTC's Hearings on Competition and Consumer Protection in the 21st Century, we held a hearing in December 2018 that specifically considered how we might improve our data security orders. We were also mindful of the 11th Circuit's 2018 LabMD decision, which struck down an FTC data security order as unenforceably vague.

Based on this learning, in 2019 the FTC made significant improvements to its data security orders. These improvements are reflected in seven orders announced this year against an array of diverse companies: ClixSense (pay-to-click survey company), i-Dressup (online games for kids), DealerBuilt (car dealer software provider), D-Link (Internet-connected routers and cameras), Equifax (credit bureau), Retina-X (monitoring app), and Infotrax (service provider for multilevel marketers).

The improvements fall into three categories.

First, the orders are more specific. They continue to require that the company implement a comprehensive, process-based data security program, and they require the company to implement specific safeguards to address the problems alleged in the complaint. Examples have included yearly employee training, access controls, monitoring systems for data security incidents, patch management systems, and encryption. These requirements not only make the FTC's expectations clearer to companies, but also improve order enforceability.

Second, the orders increase third-party assessor accountability. We still rely on outside assessors to review the comprehensive data security program required by the orders, and now we require even more rigor in these assessments. For example, the orders clearly and specifically require assessors to identify evidence to support their conclusions, including independent sampling, employee interviews, and document review. The assessors must retain documents related to the assessment, and cannot refuse to provide those documents to the FTC on the basis of certain privileges. When FTC staff can access working papers and other materials, they are better able to investigate compliance and enforce orders. Perhaps most importantly, our new orders give us the authority to approve and re-approve assessors every two years. If an assessor falls down on the job, we will withhold approval and force the company to hire a different assessor.

Third, the orders elevate data security considerations to the C-Suite and Board level. For example, every year companies must now present their Board or similar governing body with their written information security program — and, notably, senior officers must now provide annual certifications of compliance to the FTC. This will force senior managers to gather detailed information about the company's information security program, so they can personally corroborate compliance with an order's key provisions each year. Requiring these kinds of certifications under oath has been an effective compliance mechanism under other legal regimes (e.g., securities law), and we expect it will likewise ensure better year-round governance and controls regarding FTC data security orders.

Regarding that third point, research suggests the FTC's efforts to improve corporate governance on data security issues are timely and well founded. Boards are becoming increasingly involved in cybersecurity governance, as demonstrated by surveys of practitioners and the growth of literature aimed at educating board members on cybersecurity. Some studies suggest that Board attention to data security decisions can dramatically improve data safeguarding. For example, one study found a 35% decrease in the probability of information security breaches when companies include the Chief Information Security Officer (or equivalent) in the top management team and the CISO has access to the board. Our new orders are consistent with this research: they create additional incentives for high-level oversight of, and appropriate attention to, data security.[96]

Federal Trade Commission v. D-Link Systems, (Proposed) Stipulated Order for Injunction and Judgement (filed July 2, 2019).

Plaintiff, the Federal Trade Commission ("Commission"), filed its Complaint for Permanent Injunction and Other Equitable Relief pursuant to Section 13(b) of the Federal Trade Commission Act ("FTC Act"), 15 U.S.C. § 53(b). The Commission and Defendant stipulate, for the purpose of settlement, to the entry of this Stipulated Order for Injunction ("Order") to resolve all matters in dispute in this action between them. THEREFORE, IT IS ORDERED as follows:

FINDINGS
. . . 2. The Complaint charges that Defendant participated in deceptive acts or practices in violation of Section 5 of the FTC Act, 15 U.S.C. § 45, related to the security of the software in its IP cameras and Routers. . . .

DEFINITIONS
For the purpose of this Order, the following definitions apply:
1. "Approved Standard" shall mean the "Security for industrial automation and control systems – Part 4-1: Secure product development lifecycle requirements", attached hereto as Exhibit A, or, in the event that such standard no longer exists, any successor standard established or approved by the International Electrotechnical Commission, or any

---

[96] Andrew Smith, *New and improved FTC data security orders: Better guidance for companies, better protection for consumers*, FEDERAL TRADE COMMISSION (Jan. 6, 2020, 9:46 AM), https://www.ftc.gov/news-events/blogs/business-blog/2020/01/new-improved-ftc-data-security-orders-better-guidance.

successor entity thereto. In the event no such successor standard or successor entity exists, or at the election of Defendant, Approved Standard shall mean a standard of comparable scope and thoroughness approved, at his or her sole discretion, by the Associate Director for Enforcement, Bureau of Consumer Protection, Federal Trade Commission. Any decision not to approve a standard must be accompanied by a writing setting forth in detail the reasons for denying such approval.

2. "Defendant" means D-Link Systems, Inc. and its successors and assigns.

3. "Covered Device" shall mean any IP Camera or Router that Defendant sells on or after January 5, 2017, directly or through authorized re-sellers to consumers in the United States; provided that "Covered Device" does not include IP Cameras or Routers that Defendant can establish that Defendant offers primarily for enterprises and other commercial entities, including products identified in Exhibit B.

4. "IP Camera" shall mean any Internet Protocol ("IP") camera, cloud camera, or other Internet-accessible camera that transmits, or allows for the transmission of, video, audio, or audiovisual data over the Internet.

5. "Router" shall mean any network device that forwards IP data packets from one network to another or from a network to the Internet.

ORDER I. COMPREHENSIVE SOFTWARE SECURITY PROGRAM

IT IS ORDERED that Defendant shall, for a period of twenty (20) years after entry of this Order, continue with or establish and implement, and maintain, a comprehensive software security program ("Software Security Program") that is designed to provide protection for the security of its Covered Devices, unless Defendant ceases to market, distribute, or sell any Covered Devices. Subject to Section II.I of this Order, to satisfy this requirement, Defendant must, at a minimum:

A. Document in writing the content, implementation, and maintenance of the Software Security Program;

B. Provide the written program and any evaluations thereof or updates thereto to Defendant's board of directors or governing body or, if no such board or equivalent governing body exists, to a senior officer of Defendant responsible for Defendant's Software Security Program at least once every twelve (12) months;

C. Designate a qualified employee or employees to coordinate and be responsible for the Software Security Program;

D. Assess and document, at least once every twelve (12) months, internal and external risks to the security of Covered Devices that could result in the unauthorized disclosure, misuse, loss, theft, alteration, destruction, or other compromise of such information input into, stored on or captured with, accessed, or transmitted by a Covered Device;

E. Design, implement, maintain, and document safeguards, as a part of a secure software development process, that control for the internal and external risks Defendant identifies to the security of Covered Devices.

Such safeguards shall also include:

1. Engaging in security planning by enumerating in writing how functionality and features will affect the security of Covered Devices;

2. Performing threat modeling to identify internal and external risks to the security of data transmitted using Covered Devices;

3. Engaging in pre-release code review of every release of software for Covered Devices through the use of automated static analysis tools;

4. Conducting pre-release vulnerability testing of every release of software for Covered Devices;

5. Performing ongoing code maintenance by maintaining a database of shared code to be used to help find other instances of a vulnerability when a vulnerability is reported or otherwise discovered;

6. Remediation processes designed to address security flaws, or analogous instances of security flaws, identified at any stage of software development process;

7. Ongoing monitoring of security research for potential vulnerabilities that could affect Covered Devices;

8. A process for accepting vulnerability reports from security researchers, which shall include providing a designated point of contact for security researchers, appointing supervisory personnel to validate concerns;

9. Automatic firmware updates directly to the Covered Devices that are configured to receive automatic firmware updates;

10. At least 60 days prior to ceasing security updates for a Covered Device, a clear and conspicuous notice to consumers who registered their Covered Device, through the communication channel(s) the consumer chose at the time of registration, and a clear and conspicuous notice on the product information page of the Covered Device on Defendant's website that the Covered Device will no longer receive firmware updates; and

11. Biennial security training for personnel and vendors responsible for developing, implementing, or reviewing Covered Device software, including firmware updates.

F. Assess, at least once every twelve (12) months the sufficiency of any safeguards in place to address the risks to the security of Covered Devices, and modify the Software Security Program based on the results.

G. Test and monitor the effectiveness of the safeguards at least once every twelve (12) months, and modify the Software Security Program based on the results.

H. Select and retain service providers capable of maintaining security practices consistent with this Order, and contractually require service providers to implement and maintain safeguards consistent with this Order; and

I. Evaluate and adjust the Software Security Program in light of any changes to Defendant's operations or business arrangements, or any other circumstances that Defendant knows or has reason to know may have an impact on the effectiveness of the Software Security Program.

At a minimum, Defendant must evaluate the Software Security Program at least once every twelve (12) months and modify the Software Security Program based on the results. Except for Sections I.B and I.C, Defendant may select, appoint, and work with third parties that are contractually required to comply with the requirements of this Section I, provided that Defendant discloses all material facts and does not misrepresent any material facts to said third party. Defendant shall obtain from said third party all materials and documentation necessary to evaluate the effectiveness of the compliance with any provisions that the third party is contracted to comply with. However, Defendant shall be solely responsible for compliance with this Order.

II. SOFTWARE SECURITY ASSESSMENTS BY A THIRD PARTY

IT IS FURTHER ORDERED that, in connection with compliance with Defendant's Software Security Program, Defendant must obtain initial and biennial assessments ("Assessments"):

A. The Assessments must be obtained from a qualified, objective, independent third party professional ("Assessor"), who: (1) is qualified as a Certified Secure Software Lifecycle Professional (CSSLP) with professional experience with secure Internet-accessible devices; (2) uses procedures and standards generally accepted in the profession; (3) conducts an independent review of the Software Security Program, or, at the election of Defendant, an assessment of the Approved Standard; and (4) retains all documents considered for each Assessment for five (5) years after completion of such Assessment and will provide such documents to the Commission within fourteen (14) days of receipt of a written request from a representative of the Commission. No documents considered for an Assessment may be withheld on the basis of a claim of confidentiality, proprietary or trade secrets, work product or attorney client privilege.

B. For each Assessment, Respondent shall provide the Associate Director for Enforcement for the Bureau of Consumer Protection at the Federal Trade Commission with the name and affiliation of the person selected to conduct the Assessment, which the Associate Director shall have the authority to approve in his sole discretion. Any decision not to approve an individual selected to conduct such Assessment must be accompanied by a writing setting forth in detail the reasons for denying such approval.

C. The reporting period for the Assessments to FTC must cover: (1) from the entry of this Order to January 31, 2020, for the initial Assessment; and (2) each 2-year period thereafter for ten (10) years after entry of this Order for the biennial Assessments.

D. If Defendant elects to assess Defendant's compliance with the Software Security Program, the Assessment must: (1) determine whether Defendant has implemented and maintained the Software Security Program; (2) assess the effectiveness of Defendant's implementation and maintenance of sub-Sections I.A-I; (3) identify any gaps or weaknesses in the Software Security Program; (4) identify specific evidence (such as documents reviewed, sampling and testing performed, and interviews conducted) examined to make such determinations, assessments, and identifications, and explain why the evidence that the Assessor examined is sufficient to justify the Assessor's findings; or,

E. If Defendant elects to assess Defendant's compliance with the Approved Standard, the Assessment must certify compliance with the Approved Standard, including, but not limited to, the following provisions: (1) Part 6.4 ("SR-3: Product Security Requirements"); (2) Part 6.5 ("SR-4: Product security requirements content"); (3) Part 6.3 ("SR-2: Threat model"); (4) Part 8.3.1(c) ("Static Code Analysis"); (5) Part 9.4 ("SVV-3: Vulnerability Testing"); (6) Part 9.5 ("Penetration Testing"); (7) Part 10.4 ("DM-3: Assessing security-related issues"); (8) Part 10.5 ("DM-4: Addressing security-related issues"); (9) Part 10.2 ("DM-1: Receiving notifications of security-related issues"); (10) Part 11.6 ("SUM-5: Timely delivery of security patches"); (11) Part 10.6 ("DM-5: Disclosing security-related issues"); (12) Part 5.6 ("SM-4: Security expertise").

F. No finding of any Assessment shall rely solely on assertions or attestations by Defendant's management. The Assessment shall be signed by the Assessor and shall state that the Assessor conducted an independent review of the Software Security Program or the Approved Standard, and did not rely solely on assertions or attestations by Defendant's management.

G. To the extent that Defendant has selected, appointed, or worked with a third party to implement any of the criteria of the Software Security Program or any criteria of the Approved Standard, Defendant shall provide to the Assessor, or cause to be provided to the Assessor, in connection with the Assessment, all materials and documentation necessary for the Assessor to conduct the Assessment of the effectiveness of the Comprehensive Software Security Program or Approved Standard. All such materials and documentation shall be maintained and produced upon request pursuant to the provisions of this Order.

H. Each Assessment must be completed within sixty (60) days after the end of the reporting period to which the Assessment applies. Unless otherwise directed by a Commission representative in writing, Defendant must submit the initial Assessment to the Commission within twenty (20) days after the Assessment has been completed via email. . . . All subsequent biennial Assessments shall be retained by Defendant until the order is terminated and provided to the Associate Director for Enforcement within twenty (20) days of request.

I. If Defendant obtains an Assessment (i) certifying that the Software Security Program for the Covered Devices is in compliance with the Approved Standard and (ii) certifying that Defendant is in compliance with Section I.E.10, Defendant shall be deemed in compliance with Section I of this Order for two (2) years from the date of that Assessment or until the next January 31 Assessment deadline, whichever is earlier. Provided, however: 1. Defendant shall not be deemed in compliance with Section I of this Order based on a Section II Assessment if Defendant made a representation, express or implied, that either misrepresented or omitted a material fact and such misrepresentation or omission would likely affect a reasonable Assessor's decision about whether Defendant complied with the Approved Standard.

Further, in the event that such a misrepresentation or omission was made for the purpose of deceiving the Assessor, Defendant shall not be deemed in compliance with any portion of Section I or Section II of this Order based on that Assessment. 2. Defendant shall not be deemed in compliance with Section I of this Order based upon a Section II Assessment if Defendant materially changed its practices after the Assessment in question, unless, at the time of the material change, an Assessor qualified under this Section certifies that the material change does not cause Defendant to fall out of compliance with the Approved Standard on which the Assessment in question was based.

III. COOPERATION WITH THIRD-PARTY SOFTWARE SECURITY ASSESSOR

IT IS FURTHER ORDERED that Defendant, whether acting directly or indirectly, in connection with any Assessment required by Section II of this Order titled Software Security Assessments by a Third Party, must:

A. Disclose all material facts to the Assessor, and must not misrepresent in any manner, expressly or by implication, any fact material to the Assessor's Assessment; and

B. Provide or otherwise make available to the Assessor all information and material in its possession, custody, or control that is necessary to the Assessment for which there is no reasonable claim of privilege.

IV. ANNUAL CERTIFICATION

IT IS FURTHER ORDERED that, in connection with compliance with Defendant's Software Security Program, Defendant shall: A. One year after the entry of this Order, and each year thereafter, provide the Commission with a certification from a senior corporate manager, or, if no such senior corporate manager exists, a senior officer of Defendant responsible for Defendant's Software Security Program that: (1) the requirements of this Order have been established, implemented, and maintained; and (2) Defendant is not aware of any material noncompliance that has not been (a) corrected or (b) disclosed to the Commission. The certification must be based on the personal knowledge of the senior corporate manager, senior officer, or subject matter experts upon whom the senior corporate manager or senior officer reasonably relies in making the certification. Unless otherwise directed by a Commission representative in writing, submit all annual certifications to the Commission pursuant to this Order via email. . . .

V. SPECIFIC CONDUCT PROVISIONS

IT IS FURTHER ORDERED that
A. Defendant shall no longer sell, distribute, or host on its website the IP Camera setup wizard software containing the representations shown in Exhibit C attached hereto for any Covered Devices.
B. Within 60 days of the effective date of this Order, provide clear and conspicuous notice to all consumers who registered their Covered Devices, through the communication channel(s) the consumer chose at the time of registration, containing instructions for updating said device with the latest firmware update.

VI. ORDER ACKNOWLEDGMENTS

IT IS FURTHER ORDERED that Defendant obtains acknowledgments of receipt of this Order:
A. Defendant, within 7 days of entry of this Order, must submit to the Commission an acknowledgment of receipt of this Order sworn under penalty of perjury.
B. For three years after entry of this Order, Defendant must deliver a copy of this Order to: (1) all principals, officers, directors, and LLC managers and members; (2) all employees having managerial responsibilities for the security of Covered Devices and all agents and representatives who participate in the security of Covered Devices; and (3) any business entity resulting from any change in structure as set forth in the Section titled Compliance Reporting. Delivery must occur within 7 days of entry of this Order for current personnel. For all others, delivery must occur before they assume their responsibilities.
C. From each individual or entity to which a Defendant delivered a copy of this Order, that Defendant must obtain, within 30 days, a signed and dated acknowledgment of receipt of this Order.

VII. COMPLIANCE REPORTING

IT IS FURTHER ORDERED that Defendant makes timely submissions to the Commission:

A. On January 31, 2020, Defendant must submit a compliance report, sworn under penalty of perjury, which must: (1) identify the primary physical, postal, and email address and telephone number, as designated points of contact, which representatives of the Commission may use to communicate with Defendant; (2) identifies all of that Defendant's businesses by all of their names, telephone numbers, and physical, postal, email, and Internet addresses; (3) describes the activities of each business, including the security and marketing practices; (4) describes in detail whether and how Defendant is in compliance with each Section of this Order (either directly or, at Defendant's election, Defendant may, for the purpose of satisfying this requirement as to Sections I and II, incorporate a Section II initial Assessment); and (5) provides a copy of each Order Acknowledgment obtained pursuant to this Order, unless previously submitted to the Commission.

B. For ten (10) years after entry of this Order, Defendant must submit a compliance notice, sworn under penalty of perjury, within 14 days of any change in the following: (a) any designated point of contact; or (b) the structure of Defendant or any entity that Defendant has any ownership interest in or controls directly or indirectly that may affect compliance obligations arising under this Order, including: creation, merger, sale, or dissolution of the Defendant or any subsidiary, parent, or affiliate that Defendant has any ownership interest in or controls directly or indirectly that engages in any acts or practices subject to this Order.

C. Defendant must submit to the Commission notice of the filing of any bankruptcy petition, insolvency proceeding, or similar proceeding by or against such Defendant within 14 days of its filing.

D. Any submission to the Commission required by this Order to be sworn under penalty of perjury must be true and accurate and comply with 28 U.S.C. § 1746, such as by concluding: "I declare under penalty of perjury under the laws of the United States of America that the foregoing is true and correct. Executed on: _____" and supplying the date, signatory's full name, title (if applicable), and signature.

E. Unless otherwise directed by a Commission representative in writing, all submissions to the Commission pursuant to this Order must be emailed. . . .

VIII. RECORDKEEPING

IT IS FURTHER ORDERED that Defendant must create certain records for ten (10) years after entry of the Order, and retain each such record for 5 years. Specifically, Defendant must create and retain the following records:

A. accounting records showing the revenues from all goods or services sold;

B. Defendant's personnel records showing, for each person providing services, whether as an employee or otherwise, that person's: name; addresses; telephone numbers; job title or position; dates of service; and (if applicable) the reason for termination;

C. records of all consumer complaints and refund requests, whether received directly or indirectly, such as through a third party, concerning the subject matter of the Order;

D. all records necessary to demonstrate full compliance with each provision of this Order, including all submissions to the Commission; and

E. a copy of each unique advertisement or other marketing material by Defendant making a representation subject to this Order.

IX. COMPLIANCE MONITORING

IT IS FURTHER ORDERED that, for the purpose of monitoring Defendant's compliance with this Order:

A. Within 14 days of receipt of a written request from a representative of the Commission, Defendant must: submit additional compliance reports or other requested information, which must be sworn under penalty of perjury; appear for depositions; and produce documents for inspection and copying. The Commission is also authorized to obtain discovery, without further leave of court, using any of the procedures prescribed by Federal Rules of Civil Procedure 29, 30 (including telephonic depositions), 31, 33, 34, 36, 45, and 69. . . .

NOTES

Note 1

Please compare the Order attached to the FTC decision in LabMD with the 2019 D-Link Systems Order. What do you think the FTC will need to add and change in the Order attached to the FTC decision in LabMD?

Note 2

The Order in D-Link Systems is specific regarding security measures and references the International Electrotechnical Commission standards document titled, "Security for Industrial Automation and Control Systems Part 4-1 - Secure Product Development Lifecycle Requirements (2018)." Moreover, the order references some parts of the document specifically, including Part 6.4 ("SR-3: Product Security Requirements) and Part 10.6 ("DM-5: Disclosing security-related issues"). The International Electrotechnical Commission "is the world's leading organization for the preparation and publication of International Standards for all electrical, electronic and related technologies." Please note that the FTC can also apply a similar standard for compliance by D-Link Systems if the listed standard in the Order does not exist. Does this comply with the appellate court's decision in LabMD?

Note 3

At least one Federal Appellate Court in *In re SuperValu*, 925 F.3d 955 (8th Cir. 2019), has held that Illinois courts likely will not recognize a duty on behalf of retailers to safeguard customer data in a negligence claim concerning a data security breach. Moreover, that Court determined that the Federal Trade Commission Act does not create a duty on behalf of retailers. The Court stated, in relevant part:

> To state a claim for negligence under Illinois law, a complaint must allege "facts that establish the existence of a duty of care owed by the defendant to the plaintiff, a breach of that duty, and an injury proximately caused by that breach." Marshall v. Burger King Corp., 222 Ill.2d 422, 305 Ill.Dec. 897, 856 N.E.2d 1048, 1053 (2006). Holmes's claim is primarily premised on the view that SuperValu, as a retailer, had a duty to safeguard his credit-card information from cyberattacks. Whether

a defendant owes a legal duty to the plaintiff is a question of state law. See Iseberg v. Gross, 227 Ill.2d 78, 316 Ill.Dec. 211, 879 N.E.2d 278, 284 (2007). In Illinois, generally there is no affirmative duty to protect another from a criminal attack unless one of four historically recognized "special relationships" exists between the parties. See id., 316 Ill.Dec. 211, 879 N.E.2d at 284–85.

The parties agree that the Illinois Supreme Court has not yet addressed whether a retailer has a qualifying special relationship with its customers such that it is obligated to protect their financial information from hackers. In these circumstances, our role is to predict how that court would rule if faced with the issue. Blankenship v. USA Truck, Inc., 601 F.3d 852, 856 (8th Cir. 2010). The Seventh Circuit recently addressed the same question and predicted that Illinois would not impose such a duty on retailers like SuperValu. See Cmty. Bank of Trenton v. Schnuck Mkts., Inc., 887 F.3d 803, 816 (7th Cir. 2018). The Seventh Circuit based its ruling on Cooney v. Chicago Public Schools, an Illinois Appellate Court decision that appears to hold that the state does not recognize a duty in tort to safeguard sensitive personal information. See 407 Ill.App.3d 358, 347 Ill.Dec. 733, 943 N.E.2d 23, 28–29 (2010). Holmes has not drawn our attention to any Illinois authority contrary to Cooney. We agree with the Seventh Circuit's reading of Cooney and accordingly adopt its conclusion. The failure of Illinois law to impose this type of common-law duty on merchants mandates dismissal of Holmes's negligence claim.

In the alternative, Holmes argues that his negligence claim is premised on a duty imposed by federal statute, specifically the Federal Trade Commission Act (FTCA). The FTCA gives the Federal Trade Commission the authority to, among other things, enforce against "unfair or deceptive acts or practices in or affecting commerce." 15 U.S.C. § 45(a). The Commission has used this authority to bring a number of enforcement actions against companies that have purportedly failed to protect consumer financial data against hackers. See FTC v. Wyndham Worldwide Corp., 799 F.3d 236, 240 (3d Cir. 2015). The FTCA creates no private right of action. FTC v. Johnson, 800 F.3d 448, 452 (8th Cir. 2015).

Illinois courts have held that statutes "designed to protect human life or property" can establish the "standard of conduct required of a reasonable person" and therefore "fix the measure of legal duty" in a negligence action. Noyola v. Bd. of Educ., 179 Ill.2d 121, 227 Ill.Dec. 744, 688 N.E.2d 81, 84–85 (Ill. 1997). If a defendant violates such a statute, a right of action may be implied in tort if four conditions are met: (1) the plaintiff is a member of the class for whose benefit the statute was enacted, (2) the right of action is consistent with the underlying purpose of the statute, (3) the plaintiff's injury is one the statute was designed to prevent, and (4) the right of action is necessary to provide an adequate remedy for violations of the statute. Id., 227 Ill.Dec. 744, 688 N.E.2d at 85.

Several of these conditions are absent here. Congress empowered the Commission—and the Commission alone—to enforce the FTCA.

Implying a cause of action would be inconsistent with Congress's anticipated enforcement scheme. Holmes points to nothing suggesting that the Commission's enforcement efforts have been inadequate to redress violations of the statute in this area. At least one court has expressly rejected the proposition that § 45(a) creates a duty enforceable through an Illinois negligence action. See Cmty. Bank of Trenton v. Schnuck Mkts., Inc., 210 F. Supp. 3d 1022, 1041 (S.D. Ill. 2016). Holmes cites no authority to the contrary. We conclude that Illinois is unlikely to recognize a legal duty enforceable through a negligence action arising from the FTCA. The district court's dismissal of this claim was proper." *Id. See also In re Sonic Customer Data Security Breach Litigation*, 2020 WL 3577341 (N.D. Ohio 2020) ("The Court finds that because the FTC Act Section 5 does not lay out objective standards, it does not support a claim for negligence per se under Oklahoma law. By its terms, the statute only prohibits unfair competition or unfair or deceptive acts. While the FTC and other courts have interpreted Section 5's terms to apply to data security requirements, the statute's actual terms do not lay out positive, objective standards that, if violated, could give the standard for a negligence per se claim under Oklahoma law.").

Another court has found that the FTC Act can serve as the basis of a negligence per se claim in the data security breach context under Georgia law. See *In re Marriott International Customer Data Security Breach Litigation*, 2020 WL 869241 (D. Md. 2020). Moreover, the FTC Act can be used as evidence of foreseeable risk to demonstrate that a duty exists. See *In re Brinker Data Incident Litigation*, 2020 WL 691848, 9 (M.D. Fla. 2020).

Note 4

In "Prepared Remarks of Chairman Joseph J. Simons, Hearing on 'Oversight of the Federal Trade Commission: Strengthening Protections for American's Privacy and Data Security' Committee on Energy and Commerce Subcommittee on Consumer Protection and Commerce" on May 8, 2019, Chairman Simons highlighted gaps in FTC enforcement power concerning data security breaches and privacy matters and requests new legislation from Congress:

Our primary legal authority in this space is Section 5 of the FTC Act, which prohibits deceptive or unfair commercial practices. But Section 5 is an imperfect tool. For example, Section 5 does not allow the Commission to seek civil penalties for first-time privacy violations. It does not allow us to reach non-profits and common carriers, even when their practices have serious implications for consumer privacy and data security. These limitations have a critical effect on our ability to protect consumers, which is why we urge Congress to enact privacy and data security legislation, enforceable by the FTC, which grants the agency civil penalty authority, targeted APA rulemaking authority, and jurisdiction over non-profits and common carriers.[97]

Note 5

In a report titled, "Privacy and Data Security Update: 2019," the Federal Trade Commission discussed its actions concerning data security breaches:

> Since 2002, the FTC has brought more than 70 cases against companies that have engaged in unfair or deceptive practices involving inadequate protection of consumers' personal data. In 2019, the FTC strengthened its standard orders in data security cases. Each of the cases discussed below resulted in settlements that, among other things, required the companies to implement a comprehensive security program, obtain robust biennial assessments of the program, and submit annual certifications by a senior officer about the company's compliance with the order.
>
> The FTC's complaint against Equifax alleged that the company failed to secure the massive amount of personal information stored on its network. Among other things, the company allegedly failed to patch well-known software vulnerabilities, failed to segment its database servers, and stored Social Security numbers in unencrypted, plain text. According to the complaint, these failures led to a breach that affected more than 147 million people, and exposed millions of names and dates of birth, Social Security numbers, physical addresses, and other personal information that could lead to identity theft and fraud. The settlement, which totals between $575 million and $700 million, was part of a global resolution where Equifax settled matters with a consumer class action, the Consumer Financial Protection Bureau, and 50 states and territories.
>
> In July, the FTC announced a complaint and settlement against the operator of ClixSense.com, an online rewards website that pays its users to view advertisements, perform online tasks, and complete online surveys. The complaint alleged that the website's operator, James V. Grago, Jr., deceived consumers by falsely claiming that ClixSense "utilizes the latest security and encryption techniques to ensure the security of your account information." In fact, ClixSense failed to implement minimal data security measures and stored personal information—including Social Security numbers—in clear text with no encryption, according to the complaint. The FTC alleged that ClixSense's

---

[97] *Oversight of the Federal Trade Commission: Strengthening Protections for American's Privacy and Data Security: Hearing before the Subcomm. on Consumer Protection and Commerce of the H. Comm. on Energy and Commerce*, 116th Cong. 2–3 (May 8, 2019) (prepared remarks of Joseph J. Simons, Chairman of the Fed. Trade Comm'n). The FTC notes: "The Federal Trade Commission enforces a variety of antitrust and consumer protection laws affecting virtually every area of commerce, with some exceptions concerning banks, insurance companies, non-profits, transportation and communications common carriers, air carriers, and some other entities." *See What the FTC Does*, FEDERAL TRADE COMMISSION, https://www.ftc.gov/news-events/media-resources/what-ftc-does (last updated Nov. 21, 2020).

failures allowed hackers to gain access to the company's network, resulting in a breach of 6.6 million consumers' information.

The FTC settled charges against Unixiz, d/b/a i-Dressup.com, a dress-up games website, alleging that the company and its owners stored and transmitted users' personal information in plain text and failed to perform vulnerability testing of its network, implement an intrusion detection and prevention system, and monitor for potential security incidents. These failures led to a security breach in which a hacker accessed the information of approximately 2.1 million users—including approximately 245,000 users who indicated they were under 13.

[T]he FTC alleged that Retina-X, a company that sold socalled "stalking apps," and its owner claimed that "Your private information is safe with us." Despite this claim, the company and its owner failed to adopt and implement reasonable information security policies and procedures.

In its complaint against a provider of software to help auto dealers with management of their inventory, personnel, and customers, the FTC alleged that LightYear Dealer Technologies, LLC, d/b/a DealerBuilt failed to implement readily available and low-cost measures to protect the personal information it collected. These failures led to a data breach in which a hacker gained access to the unencrypted personal information— such as Social Security numbers and other sensitive data—of about 12.5 million consumers.

The FTC settled charges against InfoTrax Systems, a technology company that provides back-end operation services to multi-level marketers. The FTC alleged that a hacker infiltrated InfoTrax's server, along with websites maintained by the company on behalf of clients, more than 20 times and accessed the personal information of more than a million consumers. According to the complaint, InfoTrax and its former CEO, Mark Rawlins, failed to use reasonable, low-cost, and readily available security protections to safeguard the personal information they maintained on behalf of their clients.

Smart home products manufacturer D-Link Systems, Inc. agreed to implement a comprehensive software security program in order to settle FTC allegations over misrepresentations that the company took reasonable steps to secure its wireless routers and Internet-connected cameras. The settlement ended FTC litigation against D-Link stemming from a 2017 complaint in which the agency alleged that, despite claims touting device security, vulnerabilities in the company's routers and Internet-connected cameras left sensitive consumer information, including live video and audio feeds, exposed to third parties and vulnerable to hackers.[98]

Note 6

---

[98] *Privacy and Security Update: 2019*, FEDERAL TRADE COMMISSION 7 (2019), *available at* https://www.ftc.gov/system/files/documents/reports/privacy-data-security-update-2019/2019-privacy-data-security-report-508.pdf.

The FTC published a blog post titled, "$575 Million Equifax Settlement Illustrates Security Basics for Your Business." The blog post reviews the Equifax matter and provides advice concerning avoiding the mistakes made by Equifax:

Patch your software. Segment your network. Monitor for intruders. According to tech experts, those are security basics for businesses of any size. But when you're industry giant Equifax – a company in possession of staggering amounts of highly confidential information about more than 200 million Americans – it's almost unthinkable not to implement those fundamental protections. An FTC, CFPB, and State AG settlement of at least $575 million illustrates the injury to consumers when companies ignore reasonably foreseeable (and preventable) threats to sensitive data. Read on for security tips for your business and what consumers can do to get compensation for their losses and sign up for free credit monitoring.

The Equifax data breach has been in the headlines, but what happened behind the scenes? According to the complaint, in March 2017, US-CERT – Homeland Security's cyber experts – alerted Equifax and other companies about a critical security vulnerability in open-source software used to build Java web applications. The alert warned anyone using a vulnerable version of the software to update it immediately to a free patched version. It didn't take long before the press reported that hackers had already started to exploit the vulnerability.

Equifax's security team got the US-CERT alert on March 9, 2017, and sent it to more than 400 employees with instructions that the staffers responsible for the affected software should patch it within 48 hours, as required by the company's Patch Management Policy. Within a week, Equifax performed a scan intended to search for vulnerable forms of the software remaining on its network. But the scan Equifax conducted wasn't up to the task, which ultimately proved devastating to consumers. According to the complaint, the company used an improperly configured automatic scanner that failed to detect that the vulnerable software was alive and well on a part of the company's Automated Consumer Interview System (ACIS). The lawsuit alleges that Equifax didn't detect the "open sesame" vulnerability in its system for months.

How sensitive was the data stored on the ACIS portal? If it's been a while since you've made that hands-on-face shriek from "Home Alone," now may be the time because it was the portal where Equifax collected information about consumer disputes, including documentation uploaded by consumers. In addition, Equifax used that platform for consumer credit freezes, fraud alerts, and even requests for a free annual credit report. Thus, millions of consumers interacted with the ACIS portal every year. The complaint outlines the specifics, but suffice it to say that for infocrooks looking for Social Security numbers, dates of birth, credit card numbers, expiration dates, and the like, the data on ACIS was Grade A primo stuff.

Compounding the injury to consumers was the fact that ACIS was originally built in the 1980s and even in-house Equifax documents referred to it as "archaic" and "antiquated technology." What's more, the complaint alleges that when Equifax sent that email to more than 400 of its employees warning them about the need for the patch, the company didn't alert the staff member responsible for the part of ACIS with the vulnerability.

Equifax failed to discover the unpatched vulnerability for more than four months. In late July 2017, the company's security team spotted suspicious traffic on the ACIS portal. They blocked it, but identified additional questionable traffic the next day. That's when Equifax took the platform offline and hired a forensic consultant who determined that hackers had already exploited the vulnerability. But it gets worse. The consultant figured out that once inside the ACIS system, attackers were able to gain access to other parts of the network and rummage through dozens of unrelated databases also containing highly confidential information. In addition, they accessed a storage space connected to the ACIS databases that included administrative credentials stored in plain text, which they used to grab even more sensitive data. According to Equifax's forensic analysis, attackers were able to steal (among other things) approximately 147 million names and dates of birth, 145 million Social Security numbers, and 209,000 credit and debit card numbers and expiration dates.

The complaint alleges that a number of Equifax's actions – and failures to act – led to violations of the FTC Act and the Gramm-Leach-Bliley Safeguards Rule, which requires financial institutions to implement and maintain a comprehensive information security program. For example:

- Equifax didn't check to make sure employees followed through on the patching process;

- Equifax failed to detect that a patch was needed because the company used an automated scan that wasn't properly configured to check all the places that could be using the vulnerable software;

- Equifax failed to segment its network to limit how much sensitive data an attacker could steal;

- Equifax stored admin credentials and passwords in unprotected plain-text files;

- Equifax failed to update security certificates that had expired 10 months earlier; and

- Equifax didn't detect intrusions on "legacy" systems like ACIS.

The complaint cites those as factors that contributed to a breach of consumers' personal information of massive proportions.

The settlement requires Equifax to pay at least $300 million to a fund that will provide affected consumers with credit monitoring services, compensate people who bought credit or identity monitoring services from Equifax, and reimburse consumers for out-of-pocket expenses incurred as a result of the 2017 data breach. Equifax will add up to $125 million more to the fund if the initial payment isn't enough to compensate consumers for their losses. Equifax also will pay $175 million to 48 states, the District of Columbia and Puerto Rico, and a $100 million civil penalty to the CFPB. (The FTC doesn't have legal authority to get civil penalties in a case like this.)

Financial remedies are only part of the settlement. Under the order, Equifax must implement a comprehensive information security program requiring – among other things – that:

- Equifax must conduct annual assessments of internal and external security risks, implement safeguards to address them, and test the effectiveness of those safeguards;

- Equifax must assure that service providers with access to personal information stored by Equifax also implement appropriate security programs; and

- Equifax must get annual certifications from Equifax's Board of Directors saying, in effect, "Yes, I attest that the company is complying with the order's requirement of an appropriate information security program."

The Equifax settlement is a study in how basic security missteps can have staggering consequences. Here are some tips other companies can take from the case – and we didn't have to look far for advice. The quotes are all from the FTC's brochure, Start with Security.

"Update and patch third-party software." Companies should treat a security warning from US-CERT with the utmost seriousness. Equifax's 48-hour Patch Management Policy may have looked good on paper, but paper can't patch a critical software vulnerability. Of course, you should tell your IT team to implement appropriate patches and fixes. But you also need a belt-and-suspenders system to make sure your company follows through effectively.

"Ensure proper configuration." There's nothing inherently wrong with using an automated vulnerability scan, but if it's not set up to know where to look, it's just another collection of zeros and ones. The complaint alleges that Equifax compounded the problem by not maintaining an accurate inventory of what systems ran what software – a fundamental practice that would have made it easier to find the vulnerability in the ACIS platform.

"Monitor activity on your network." Who's coming in and what's going out? That's what an effective intrusion detection tool asks when it senses unauthorized activity. An effective system of intrusion detection could have helped Equifax detect the vulnerability sooner, thereby reducing the number of affected consumers.

"Segment your network." The idea behind ships' watertight compartments is that even if one portion of the structure sustains damage, the entire vessel won't go under. Segmenting your network – storing sensitive data in separate secure places on your system – can have a similar mitigating effect. Even if an attacker sneaks into one part of your system, an appropriately segmented network can help prevent a data oops from turning into a full-fledged OMG."[99]

Note 7

The FTC published a blog post concerning ways to protect data in the cloud:

For businesses, cloud services are kind of like clouds. At their best, they can be soothing and expansive. But for companies that fail to appreciate the security implications, their ethereal presence may hide dangerous storms within. As cloud computing has become business as usual for many businesses, frequent news reports about data breaches and other missteps should make companies think carefully about how they secure their data. The FTC has six tips for your business about making your use of cloud services safer – both for you and for the consumers who rely on you to safeguard their information.

1. Take advantage of the security features offered by cloud service companies. Cloud providers offer detailed guidance about their security controls and how to set up their services in a more secure fashion. But it's up to you to understand the options and configure those settings in the way best suited to your business. Keep in mind that it's not a matter of a simple on-and-off switch. Configuring your cloud security requires you to make thoughtful decisions that align with the sensitivity of the data you store and how you use it. In addition, think carefully about who at your company needs what data. Unless employees have a legitimate business reason, they shouldn't have access to your cloud resources. Require multi-factor authentication and strong passwords to protect against the risk of unauthorized access. Furthermore, never hard code passwords in cloud-based applications or source code. You may think you're saving steps, but it's the business equivalent of a "Hack me!" sign.

2. Take regular inventories of what you keep in the cloud. Some companies' cloud storage resembles a forgotten attic overdue for a spring cleaning. Whether you store data in the cloud, on your network, or in a file cabinet, you can't keep data safe if you don't know where it is. That's why up-to-date inventories are essential to data management. Many cloud services provide tools – for example, dashboards or management consoles – for just that purpose. But don't just set it and forget it. In addition to staying on top of what data is where, make sure your security configurations and access rights remain consistent with the sensitivity of

---

[99] Leslie Fair, *$575 Million Equifax Settlement Illustrates Security Basics for Your Business*, FEDERAL TRADE COMMISSION (July 22, 2019, 6:48 AM), https://www.ftc.gov/news-events/blogs/business-blog/2019/07/575-million-equifax-settlement-illustrates-security-basics.

what you've stored. As you add data that may require more protection, re-evaluate your security settings and amp them up accordingly. Also, don't take anything on faith. Actively test for misconfigurations or other security failings that could compromise your data and maintain robust log files so you can continuously monitor your cloud repositories. We've all read reports about sensitive data stored in a cloud repository open to the internet and you don't want your company name in the next headline.

3. Don't store personal information when it's not necessary. One upside of cloud storage is that it's often less expensive than other methods. But as people with big basements will tell you, the list of stuff deemed "essential" tends to expand in direct proportion to how much storage space is available. As you conduct that inventory of what you keep in the cloud, resist the temptation to hold on to data "just because." Instead, be ruthless in posing the question, "Do we have a legitimate need to store this information?" If the answer is no, dispose of it securely. No one can breach what you don't have.

4. Consider encrypting rarely used data. "There's some information I don't have to access regularly – back-ups, for example – but I do need to retain it." We hear you and we have a suggestion. As part of your defense-in-depth approach to security, consider whether to encrypt that data at rest. Indeed, if your data contains sensitive information, encrypting that data is a basic principle of security regardless of where it's stored.

5. Pay attention to credible warnings. Some cloud providers offer automated tools to remind you about cloud repositories that are open to the internet. Others may contact customers with warnings like that. In other instances, security researchers may contact companies when they find exposed data online. If you receive one of these warnings, pay attention. Investigate your cloud repositories and recheck your security settings.

6. Security is your responsibility. Using cloud services doesn't mean you can outsource security. Throughout the lifecycle of data in your company's possession, security remains your responsibility. Even if you rely on your cloud provider's security tools, you should still have a written data security program that lays out your company's process for securing consumers' personal information, and people on your staff knowledgeable about maintaining, monitoring, testing, and updating that program. Yes, you need to review your cloud contracts carefully to spell out your expectations and clearly establish who is primarily in charge of what. But keep in mind that if it's *your* data, it's ultimately *your* responsibility.[100]

Note 8

---

[100] Elisa Jillson and Andy Hasty, *Six steps toward more secure cloud computing*, FEDERAL TRADE COMMISSION (June 15, 2020, 9:30 AM), https://www.ftc.gov/news-events/blogs/business-blog/2020/06/six-steps-toward-more-secure-cloud-computing.

The FTC published a blog post exploring issues concerning a third party vendor's data security issues:

> Entrepreneurs wear a lot of hats. In addition to marketing their products, they're responsible for operational functions like inventory, ordering, and the protection of customer data. Rather than managing all that millinery, some businesses turn to third-party service providers to run things behind the scenes. But what steps are those companies taking to secure the confidential consumer information in their possession? That's one issue raised by the FTC's proposed settlement with Utah-based InfoTrax Systems.
>
> InfoTrax provides operations systems and online distributor tools for the direct sales industry. Multi-level marketers contract with InfoTrax to run their web portals. Through those portals, people register with MLMs as distributors, sign up new distributors, and place orders for themselves and for the consumers who buy from them.
>
> Those transactions involve large amounts of sensitive data – full names, credit and debit cards with expiration dates and three-digit CVV numbers, bank account data, Social Security numbers, user IDs and passwords, etc. Let's be clear: We're not talking about a name here or an account number there. By September 2016, InfoTrax stored personal information from approximately 11.8 million consumers. But according to the complaint, InfoTrax engaged in a series of data fails that created vulnerabilities on its network, weaknesses that allowed unauthorized access to confidential consumer information. Among other things, the FTC alleges that:
>
> - InfoTrax failed to perform adequate code review and penetration testing to assess cyber risks;
>
> - InfoTrax failed to take precautions to detect malicious file uploads;
>
> - InfoTrax failed to adequately limit where on its network third parties could upload unknown files;
>
> - InfoTrax failed to adequately segment its network to ensure that one client's distributors couldn't access another client's data;
>
> - InfoTrax failed to implement safeguards to detect suspicious activity – for example, the company didn't have an effective intrusion detection system to spot questionable queries; didn't use file integrity monitoring tools to determine when files had been altered, and didn't regularly monitor for unauthorized attempts to transfer sensitive data from its network;
>
> - InfoTrax stored confidential information, including Social Security numbers, credit and debit card numbers, user IDs, and passwords in clear, readable text; and

- InfoTrax didn't have a systematic process for deleting consumers' personal information it no longer had a business need to keep on its network.

What happened as a result of those failures shouldn't come as a surprise. According to the complaint, sometime in 2014 an intruder exploited security vulnerabilities on InfoTrax's server and a client's website to upload malicious code that gave the intruder remote access to data on InfoTrax's network – something that was done a total of 17 times in a two-year period, all without InfoTrax spotting the problem. You'll want to read the complaint for details, but the FTC alleges the intruder used multiple means to make off with highly sensitive financial information about InfoTrax's clients and end consumers.

Finally, on March 7, 2016, almost two years after the data thefts began, InfoTrax got an inkling of the multiple breaches. The tip-off came in the form of an alert that one of its servers had reached its maximum capacity, a warning the company received only because an intruder had created a data archive so massive that the disk ran out of space. The FTC says that only then did the company take steps to remove the intruder from its network. But even so, the intruder continued to grab data from InfoTrax's server for a few more weeks.

The complaint alleges that InfoTrax's failure to employ reasonable data security to protect personal information was an unfair practice, in violation of the FTC Act. The proposed order requires InfoTrax and then-CEO Mark Rawlins to implement a comprehensive information security program, get every-other-year assessments, and certify compliance annually. In addition, the settlement puts specific safeguards in place to address the security deficiencies alleged in the complaint. The FTC is accepting public comments about the proposed settlement.

What insights can other companies glean from the case?

Readily available security tools can reduce risks. The FTC alleges InfoTrax could have reduced the risk to sensitive data by implementing readily available, cost-effective protective measures. For example, security-conscious companies use tools to monitor unauthorized entries and exits on their network. Then there's input validation, which can determine if data from potentially untrusted sites is properly configured – a precaution that can reduce the risk of malicious code sneaking into, say, a data base on your network. In addition, file integrity tools may be able to spot if an intruder has altered information.

Inventory the data in your possession and securely dispose of it when there's no longer a need to maintain it. According to the FTC, one of the databases the intruder breached was a legacy file InfoTrax wasn't aware was still on its server. The complaint allegation demonstrates the importance of knowing what you have and where you have it. It also illustrates the wisdom of securely disposing of unnecessary information. You don't have to protect what you no longer have.

Consider the impact security failures have on clients and customers. Identity theft is always a risk when personal information is breached, but the complaint in this case adds a human perspective on the consequences of lax data security. For example, when one InfoTrax client hired a call center to assist with data breach response, consumers and distributors reported more than 280 instances of alleged fraud, including 238 complaints of unauthorized credit card charges, 34 complaints of new credit lines opened, 15 complaints of tax fraud, and 1 complaint of misuse of information for employment purposes. For third-party service providers with sensitive consumer data, security that's second to none should be a first-level priority."[101]

Note 9

Child Online Privacy and Protection Act
The Child Online Privacy Protection Act of 1998 is primarily a privacy law; however, it does include a cybersecurity provision:

§312.8 **Confidentiality, security, and integrity of personal information collected from children.**
The operator must establish and maintain reasonable procedures to protect the confidentiality, security, and integrity of personal information collected from children. The operator must also take reasonable steps to release children's personal information only to service providers and third parties who are capable of maintaining the confidentiality, security and integrity of such information, and who provide assurances that they will maintain the information in such a manner.
Moreover, the FTC expressly has enforcement authority:

§312.9 **Enforcement.**
Subject to sections 6503 and 6505 of the Children's Online Privacy Protection Act of 1998, a violation of a regulation prescribed under section 6502 (a) of this Act shall be treated as a violation of a rule defining an unfair or deceptive act or practice prescribed under section 18(a)(1)(B) of the Federal Trade Commission Act (15 U.S.C. 57a(a)(1)(B)).

While COPPA does not include a private right of action, some plaintiffs have attempted to use it as a basis for another cause of action. Recently, COPPA was used this way in a case involving ByteDance, the owner of TikTok, involving the collection of information concerning children. The case was settled for $1.1 million.[102] The article states: "In their complaint, the parents cited the Federal Trade Commission (FTC) action against the defendants based on similar allegations of COPPA violations, which resulted in the largest civil penalty ever obtained by the agency—$5.7 million—in a children's

---

[101] Lesley Fair, *When third-party service providers are party to sensitive data*, FEDERAL TRADE COMMISSION (Nov. 12, 2019, 12:02 PM), https://www.ftc.gov/news-events/blogs/business-blog/2019/11/when-third-party-service-providers-are-party-sensitive-data.

[102] *See* Jesse M. Brody, *Parents Sue TikTok for COPPA Violations, Settle for $1.1 M*, LEXOLOGY (Dec. 17, 2019), https://www.lexology.com/library/detail.aspx?g=dc66c9ac-e3b7-4e78-8402-847ba12c1562.

privacy case." [103] Ultimately, around 6 million parents "whose children used or signed up for Musical.ly or TikTok" will split $1.1 million.[104]

QUESTIONS

Did Wyndham open a pandora's box by permitting a federal agency to apply such a broad reasonable measures standard or is this just more of the same broad enforcement approach that was already normally available under the deception standard?

Based on the outcome of the recent FTC cybersecurity cases, what would be the likely outcomes for each of the following scenarios:

Scenario One: Startup technology company (Startup One) does not have a cybersecurity program in place. Startup One was founded in a garage by two engineers. They now have 8 total employees and are frantically working on getting the second version of their product to market to take advantage of the Christmas buying season. The engineers apply patches to existing systems without testing the patches when they are aware of the patch availability. They have a default firewall in place, but no-one is monitoring the firewall activity or the log files. Startup One has been lucky, it has been in business for two years and has not had a data breach. Assuming a breach will not occur over the next year, is Startup One at risk of being targeted by state attorney generals (AG) or federal agencies like the FTC?

Scenario Two: Startup technology company (Startup Two) is in the process of making the transition from a startup company to an operating company with a web presence. Startup Two understands the risk of not employing adequate cybersecurity and has hired cybersecurity personnel and cybersecurity counsel to put a robust cybersecurity solution in place. Startup Two decided to speed up the process by buying cybersecurity policy document templates that are based on industry standards. The templates address company cybersecurity controls and policy. After conforming the templates to its particular business, Startup Two added cybersecurity related procedures based on the controls and policies. Startup Two also followed through with providing training to its employees and keeping the documents and procedures up to date. A watchdog organization has discovered a flaw in Startup Two's cybersecurity firewall setup that potentially puts PII at risk. The watchdog notified Startup Two of the problem via its customer service center. The customer service center did not understand the significance of the problem and did not report the issue to management. What is the potential risk for Startup Two?

Scenario Three: a mature technology company (TechnoPlus) is in the process of transitioning its legacy computing to the cloud to save money. TechnoPlus is cloud service is a Platform as a Service (PaaS) solution which means that the cloud service provider will provide servers and operating systems, along with storage and networking but not the applications that sit on top of the operating system (OS). Cybersecurity occurs at the networking, OS and application levels. By using PaaS, TechnoPlus has given up the cybersecurity control it had over the OS and networking. Based on the

---

[103] *Id.*

[104] *Id.*

above FTC cases, what due diligence must be performed by TechnoPlus to ensure the cloud provider will meet best cybersecurity practices.

Do cybersecurity expert witnesses have a future role in FTC cases in that the expert can help a respondent argue what are reasonable measures, especially if the FTC views the measure as low cost but industry views it as a higher cost and even perhaps, not a necessary measure? At what point should a company enlist the services of such an expert?

CHAPTER THREE. THE GRAMM-LEACH-BLILEY ACT AND FTC SAFEGUARDS RULE

3.1 Introduction

The United States relies on a patch work of federal and state privacy and cybersecurity laws. The Gramm-Leach-Bliley Act (GLBA) is one of those laws. One might think of the GLBA as primarily a financial privacy law. However, there is also an important cybersecurity requirement called the Safeguards Rule that is enforced by the FTC regarding customer information handled by financial institutions. This chapter reviews the older FTC Safeguards Rule and the new FTC Safeguards Rule. In late October 2021, the FTC announced adoption of the new FTC Safeguards Rule which will not be completely effective until one year after publication in the Federal Register. There are other regulatory agencies that address financial institutions, such as banks and credit unions, that may not be subject to the FTC's GLBA enforcement authority.

This chapter reviews the regulations implementing the GLBA as well as FTC enforcement on behalf of customers. This chapter also examines case law concerning the GLBA and the Safeguards Rule in private litigation as well as standards regarding credit cards. Additionally, the chapter examines the New York Department of Financial Services cybersecurity rules and a case involving those rules. Finally, security regulations and enforcement by banking regulators related to the GLBA are reviewed.

3.2 FTC's Jurisdiction under GLBA

The regulations at Title 16, Chapter I, Subchapter C Part 314 identify the FTC's jurisdiction:

§314.1 Purpose and scope.

(a) *Purpose.* This part, which implements sections 501 and 505(b)(2) of the Gramm-Leach-Bliley Act, sets forth standards for developing, implementing, and maintaining reasonable administrative, technical, and physical safeguards to protect the security, confidentiality, and integrity of customer information.

(b) *Scope.* This part applies to the handling of customer information by all financial institutions over which the Federal Trade Commission ("FTC" or "Commission") has jurisdiction. This part refers to such entities as "you." This part applies to all customer information in your possession, regardless of whether such information pertains to individuals with whom you have a customer relationship, or pertains to the customers of other financial institutions that have provided such information to you.[105]

---

[105] 16 C.F.R. §314.1(a)-(b) (2002).

The first question is which entities are included in the phrase: "financial institutions over which the [FTC] has jurisdiction." The FTC provides advice concerning who may be covered by the GBLA:

> The definition of "financial institution" includes many businesses that may not normally describe themselves that way. In fact, the Rule applies to all businesses, regardless of size, that are "significantly engaged" in providing financial products or services. This includes, for example, check-cashing businesses, payday lenders, mortgage brokers, nonbank lenders, personal property or real estate appraisers, professional tax preparers, and courier services. The Safeguards Rule also applies to companies like credit reporting agencies and ATM operators that receive information about the customers of other financial institutions. In addition to developing their own safeguards, companies covered by the Rule are responsible for taking steps to ensure that their affiliates and service providers safeguard customer information in their care.[106]

As discussed *infra*, there are different regulators and agencies that have jurisdiction over other financial institutions that do not fall within the FTC's authority to regulate certain financial institutions.

Importantly, the FTC issued new implementing regulations on October 27, 2021. The two following sections will review the older regulations and the newer regulations. Notably, the new regulations are much more detailed in what is required for an information security program. All of the enforcement actions discussed *infra* concern enforcement under the older regulations. There are not any published decisions under the newer regulation as of the submission of this manuscript to the publisher.

3.3 The Older FTC Safeguards Rule

The regulations implementing the GLBA provides specific cybersecurity standards for safeguarding customer information by requiring a "comprehensive information security program." The Definitions section provides:

§314.2   Definitions.

(a) *In general.* Except as modified by this part or unless the context otherwise requires, the terms used in this part have the same meaning as set forth in the Commission's rule governing the Privacy of Consumer Financial Information, 16 CFR part 313.

(b) *Customer information* means any record containing nonpublic personal information as defined in 16 CFR 313.3(n), about a customer of a financial institution,

---

[106] *See Financial Institutions and Customer Information: Complying with the Safeguards Rule*, FEDERAL TRADE COMMISSION (Apr. 2006), https://www.ftc.gov/tips-advice/business-center/guidance/financial-institutions-customer-information-complying.

whether in paper, electronic, or other form, that is handled or maintained by or on behalf of you or your affiliates.

(c) *Information security program* means the administrative, technical, or physical safeguards you use to access, collect, distribute, process, protect, store, use, transmit, dispose of, or otherwise handle customer information.

(d) *Service provider* means any person or entity that receives, maintains, processes, or otherwise is permitted access to customer information through its provision of services directly to a financial institution that is subject to this part.[107]

§314.3   Standards for safeguarding customer information.

(a) *Information security program.* You shall develop, implement, and maintain a comprehensive information security program that is written in one or more readily accessible parts and contains administrative, technical, and physical safeguards that are appropriate to your size and complexity, the nature and scope of your activities, and the sensitivity of any customer information at issue. Such safeguards shall include the elements set forth in §314.4 and shall be reasonably designed to achieve the objectives of this part, as set forth in paragraph (b) of this section.

(b) *Objectives.* The objectives of section 501(b) of the Act, and of this part, are to:

(1) Insure the security and confidentiality of customer information;

(2) Protect against any anticipated threats or hazards to the security or integrity of such information; and

(3) Protect against unauthorized access to or use of such information that could result in substantial harm or inconvenience to any customer.[108]

§314.4   Elements.

In order to develop, implement, and maintain your information security program, you shall:

(a) Designate an employee or employees to coordinate your information security program.

(b) Identify reasonably foreseeable internal and external risks to the security, confidentiality, and integrity of customer information that could result in the unauthorized disclosure, misuse, alteration, destruction or other compromise of such information, and assess the sufficiency of any safeguards in place to control these risks. At a minimum, such a risk assessment should include consideration of risks in each relevant area of your operations, including:

(1) Employee training and management;

---

[107] 16 C.F.R. §314.2 (2002).
[108] 16 C.F.R. §314.3 (2002).

(2) Information systems, including network and software design, as well as information processing, storage, transmission and disposal; and

(3) Detecting, preventing and responding to attacks, intrusions, or other systems failures.

(c) Design and implement information safeguards to control the risks you identify through risk assessment, and regularly test or otherwise monitor the effectiveness of the safeguards' key controls, systems, and procedures.

(d) Oversee service providers, by:

(1) Taking reasonable steps to select and retain service providers that are capable of maintaining appropriate safeguards for the customer information at issue; and

(2) Requiring your service providers by contract to implement and maintain such safeguards.

(e) Evaluate and adjust your information security program in light of the results of the testing and monitoring required by paragraph (c) of this section; any material changes to your operations or business arrangements; or any other circumstances that you know or have reason to know may have a material impact on your information security program.[109]

In various documents, the FTC provides advice on complying with GLBA cybersecurity requirements:

> Many companies collect personal information from their customers, including names, addresses, and phone numbers; bank and credit card account numbers; income and credit histories; and Social Security numbers. The Gramm-Leach-Bliley (GLB) Act requires companies defined under the law as "financial institutions" to ensure the security and confidentiality of this type of information. As part of its implementation of the GLB Act, the Federal Trade Commission (FTC) issued the Safeguards Rule, which requires financial institutions under FTC jurisdiction to have measures in place to keep customer information secure.[110]
>
> The Safeguards Rule requires companies to assess and address the risks to customer information in all areas of their operation, including three areas that are particularly important to information security: Employee Management and Training; Information Systems; and Detecting and Managing System Failures. One of the early steps companies should take is to determine what information they are collecting and storing, and whether they have a business need to do so. You can reduce the risks to

---

[109] 16 C.F.R. §314.4 (2002).

[110] *See Financial Institutions and Customer Information: Complying with the Safeguards Rule*, FEDERAL TRADE COMMISSION (Apr. 2006), https://www.ftc.gov/tips-advice/business-center/guidance/financial-institutions-customer-information-complying.

customer information if you know what you have and keep only what you need.[111]

The Safeguards Rule requires companies to develop a written information security plan that describes their program to protect customer information. The plan must be appropriate to the company's size and complexity, the nature and scope of its activities, and the sensitivity of the customer information it handles. . . .

The requirements are designed to be flexible. Companies should implement safeguards appropriate to their own circumstances. For example, some companies may choose to put their safeguards program in a single document, while others may put their plans in several different documents — say, one to cover an information technology division and another to describe the training program for employees. Similarly, a company may decide to designate a single employee to coordinate safeguards or may assign this responsibility to several employees who will work together. In addition, companies must consider and address any unique risks raised by their business operations — such as the risks raised when employees access customer data from their homes or other off-site locations, or when customer data is transmitted electronically outside the company network.[112]

3.4 The New FTC Safeguards Rule (Adopted October 2021)

The new FTC Safeguards Rule is not completely effective until December 9, 2022.[113] The new FTC Safeguards Rule as well as commentary was published by the FTC in late October 2021.[114] The new FTC Safeguards Rule has several major changes to the prior rule. However, the main thrust of the Rule remains the same, which is to ensure the development, implementation and maintenance of a security information program that contains administrative, physical, and technical safeguards that are contextually applied depending on a number of factors. The main changes involve an extensive definitional section which, for example, includes a detailed definition of multi-factor authentication; and more specific requirements for the information security program. In the Notice of Proposed Rulemaking, the Federal Trade Commission explains each proposed change to what would specifically comply with creating an

---

[111] *See Financial Institutions and Customer Information: Complying with the Safeguards Rule*, FEDERAL TRADE COMMISSION (Apr. 2006), https://www.ftc.gov/tips-advice/business-center/guidance/financial-institutions-customer-information-complying.

[112] *Id.*

[113] 16 C.F.R. §314.5 (2021). That section provides: "Section 314.4(a), (b)(1), (c)(1) through (8), (d)(2), (e), (f)(3), (h), and (i) are effective as of December 9, 2022." *Id.*

[114] FEDERAL TRADE COMMISSION, 16 CFR Part 314, RIN 3084-AB35, *Standards for Safeguarding Customer Information* (October 27, 2021), available at Standards for Safeguarding Customer Information (ftc.gov).

information security program.[115] Some of the explanations have been provided in a footnote to the corresponding new change. Again, the general thrust of the Rules is the same.

PART 314—STANDARDS FOR SAFEGUARDING CUSTOMER INFORMATION

§ 314.1 Purpose and scope

(a) Purpose. This part, which implements sections 501 and 505(b)(2) of the Gramm–Leach–Bliley Act, sets forth standards for developing, implementing, and maintaining reasonable administrative, technical, and physical safeguards to protect the security, confidentiality, and integrity of customer information.

(b) Scope. This part applies to the handling of customer information by all financial institutions over which the Federal Trade Commission ("FTC" or "Commission") has jurisdiction. Namely, this part applies to those "financial institutions" over which the Commission has rulemaking authority pursuant to section 501(b) of the Gramm–Leach–Bliley Act. An entity is a "financial institution" if its business is engaging in an activity that is financial in nature or incidental to such financial activities as described in section 4(k) of the Bank Holding Company Act of 1956, 12 U.S.C. 1843(k), which incorporates activities enumerated by the Federal Reserve Board in 12 CFR 225.28 and 225.86. The "financial institutions" subject to the Commission's enforcement authority are those that are not otherwise subject to the enforcement authority of another regulator under section 505 of the Gramm–Leach–Bliley Act, 15 U.S.C. 6805. More specifically, those entities include, but are not limited to, mortgage lenders, "pay day" lenders, finance companies, mortgage brokers, account servicers, check cashers, wire transferors, travel agencies operated in connection with financial services, collection agencies, credit counselors and other financial advisors, tax preparation firms, non-federally insured credit unions, investment advisors that are not required to register with the Securities and Exchange Commission, and entities acting as finders. They are referred to in this part as "You." This part applies to all customer information in your possession, regardless of whether such information pertains to individuals with whom you have a customer relationship, or pertains to the customers of other financial institutions that have provided such information to you.[116]

§ 314.2 Definitions

(a) Authorized user means any employee, contractor, agent, customer, or other person that is authorized to access any of your information systems or data.

(b)(1) Consumer means an individual who obtains or has obtained a financial product or service from you that is to be used primarily for personal, family, or household purposes, or that individual's legal representative.

(2) For example:

---

[115] *Standards for Protecting Customer Information,* Federal Trade Commission (Apr. 4, 2019), *available at* https://www.federalregister.gov/documents/2019/04/04/2019-04981/standards-for-safeguarding-customer-information.

[116] Subsection b is a new addition to the regulation.

(i) An individual who applies to you for credit for personal, family, or household purposes is a consumer of a financial service, regardless of whether the credit is extended.

(ii) An individual who provides nonpublic personal information to you in order to obtain a determination about whether he or she may qualify for a loan to be used primarily for personal, family, or household purposes is a consumer of a financial service, regardless of whether the loan is extended.

(iii) An individual who provides nonpublic personal information to you in connection with obtaining or seeking to obtain financial, investment, or economic advisory services is a consumer, regardless of whether you establish a continuing advisory relationship.

(iv) If you hold ownership or servicing rights to an individual's loan that is used primarily for personal, family, or household purposes, the individual is your consumer, even if you hold those rights in conjunction with one or more other institutions. (The individual is also a consumer with respect to the other financial institutions involved.) An individual who has a loan in which you have ownership or servicing rights is your consumer, even if you, or another institution with those rights, hire an agent to collect on the loan.

(v) An individual who is a consumer of another financial institution is not your consumer solely because you act as agent for, or provide processing or other services to, that financial institution.

(vi) An individual is not your consumer solely because he or she has designated you as trustee for a trust.

(vii) An individual is not your consumer solely because he or she is a beneficiary of a trust for which you are a trustee.

(viii) An individual is not your consumer solely because he or she is a participant or a beneficiary of an employee benefit plan that you sponsor or for which you act as a trustee or fiduciary.

(c) Customer means a consumer who has a customer relationship with you.

(d) Customer information means any record containing nonpublic personal information about a customer of a financial institution, whether in paper, electronic, or other form, that is handled or maintained by or on behalf of you or your affiliates.

(e)(1) Customer relationship means a continuing relationship between a consumer and you under which you provide one or more financial products or services to the consumer that are to be used primarily for personal, family, or household purposes.

(2) For example:

(i) Continuing relationship. A consumer has a continuing relationship with you if the consumer:

(A) Has a credit or investment account with you;

(B) Obtains a loan from you;

(C) Purchases an insurance product from you;

(D) Holds an investment product through you, such as when you act as a custodian for securities or for assets in an Individual Retirement Arrangement;

(E) Enters into an agreement or understanding with you whereby you undertake to arrange or broker a home mortgage loan, or credit to purchase a vehicle, for the consumer;

(F) Enters into a lease of personal property on a non-operating basis with you;

(G) Obtains financial, investment, or economic advisory services from you for a fee;

(H) Becomes your client for the purpose of obtaining tax preparation or credit counseling services from you;

(I) Obtains career counseling while seeking employment with a financial institution or the finance, accounting, or audit department of any company (or while employed by such a financial institution or department of any company);

(J) Is obligated on an account that you purchase from another financial institution, regardless of whether the account is in default when purchased, unless you do not locate the consumer or attempt to collect any amount from the consumer on the account;

(K) Obtains real estate settlement services from you; or

(L) Has a loan for which you own the servicing rights.

(ii) No continuing relationship. A consumer does not, however, have a continuing relationship with you if:

(A) The consumer obtains a financial product or service from you only in isolated transactions, such as using your ATM to withdraw cash from an account at another financial institution; purchasing a money order from you; cashing a check with you; or making a wire transfer through you;

(B) You sell the consumer's loan and do not retain the rights to service that loan;

(C) You sell the consumer airline tickets, travel insurance, or traveler's checks in isolated transactions;

(D) The consumer obtains one-time personal or real property appraisal services from you; or

(E) The consumer purchases checks for a personal checking account from you.

(f) Encryption means the transformation of data into a form that results in a low probability of assigning meaning without the use of a protective process or key, consistent with current cryptographic standards and accompanied by appropriate safeguards for cryptographic key material.[117]

---

[117] The Notice of Proposed Rulemaking states: "Proposed paragraph (e) would define "encryption" as "the transformation of data into a form that results in a low probability of assigning meaning without the use of a protective process or key." This term is used in proposed section 314.4(c)(4), which generally requires financial institutions to encrypt customer information, with certain exceptions. This definition is

(g)(1) Financial product or service means any product or service that a financial holding company could offer by engaging in a financial activity under section 4(k) of the Bank Holding Company Act of 1956 (12 U.S.C. 1843(k)).

(2) Financial service includes your evaluation or brokerage of information that you collect in connection with a request or an application from a consumer for a financial product or service.

(h)(1) Financial institution means any institution the business of which is engaging in an activity that is financial in nature or incidental to such financial activities as described in section 4(k) of the Bank Holding Company Act of 1956, 12 U.S.C. 1843(k). An institution that is significantly engaged in financial activities, or significantly engaged in activities incidental to such financial activities, is a financial institution.

(2) Examples of financial institutions are as follows:

(i) A retailer that extends credit by issuing its own credit card directly to consumers is a financial institution because extending credit is a financial activity listed in 12 CFR 225.28(b)(1) and referenced in section 4(k)(4)(F) of the Bank Holding Company Act of 1956 (12 U.S.C. 1843(k)(4)(F)), and issuing that extension of credit through a proprietary credit card demonstrates that a retailer is significantly engaged in extending credit.

(ii) An automobile dealership that, as a usual part of its business, leases automobiles on a nonoperating basis for longer than 90 days is a financial institution with respect to its leasing business because leasing personal property on a nonoperating basis where the initial term of the lease is at least 90 days is a financial activity listed in 12 CFR 225.28(b)(3) and referenced in section 4(k)(4)(F) of the Bank Holding Company Act, 12 U.S.C. 1843(k)(4)(F).

(iii) A personal property or real estate appraiser is a financial institution because real and personal property appraisal is a financial activity listed in 12 CFR 225.28(b)(2)(i) and referenced in section 4(k)(4)(F) of the Bank Holding Company Act, 12 U.S.C. 1843(k)(4)(F).

(iv) A career counselor that specializes in providing career counseling services to individuals currently employed by or recently displaced from a financial organization, individuals who are seeking employment with a financial organization, or individuals who are currently employed by or seeking placement with the finance, accounting or audit departments of any company is a financial institution because such career counseling activities are financial activities listed in 12 CFR 225.28(b)(9)(iii) and referenced in section 4(k)(4)(F) of the Bank Holding Company Act, 12 U.S.C. 1843(k)(4)(F).

---

adopted from the Model Law and is intended to define the process of encryption while not requiring any particular technology or technique for achieving the protection provided by encryption. The Commission seeks comment on this definition." *Standards for Protecting Customer Information*, Federal Trade Commission (Apr. 4, 2019), *available at* https://www.federalregister.gov/documents/2019/04/04/2019-04981/standards-for-safeguarding-customer-information.

(v) A business that prints and sells checks for consumers, either as its sole business or as one of its product lines, is a financial institution because printing and selling checks is a financial activity that is listed in 12 CFR 225.28(b)(10)(ii) and referenced in section 4(k)(4)(F) of the Bank Holding Company Act, 12 U.S.C. 1843(k)(4)(F).

(vi) A business that regularly wires money to and from consumers is a financial institution because transferring money is a financial activity referenced in section 4(k)(4)(A) of the Bank Holding Company Act, 12 U.S.C. 1843(k)(4)(A), and regularly providing that service demonstrates that the business is significantly engaged in that activity.

(vii) A check cashing business is a financial institution because cashing a check is exchanging money, which is a financial activity listed in section 4(k)(4)(A) of the Bank Holding Company Act, 12 U.S.C. 1843(k)(4)(A).

(viii) An accountant or other tax preparation service that is in the business of completing income tax returns is a financial institution because tax preparation services is a financial activity listed in 12 CFR 225.28(b)(6)(vi) and referenced in section 4(k)(4)(G) of the Bank Holding Company Act, 12 U.S.C. 1843(k)(4)(G).

(ix) A business that operates a travel agency in connection with financial services is a financial institution because operating a travel agency in connection with financial services is a financial activity listed in 12 CFR 225.86(b)(2) and referenced in section 4(k)(4)(G) of the Bank Holding Company Act, 12 U.S.C. 1843(k)(4)(G).

(x) An entity that provides real estate settlement services is a financial institution because providing real estate settlement services is a financial activity listed in 12 CFR 225.28(b)(2)(viii) and referenced in section 4(k)(4)(F) of the Bank Holding Company Act, 12 U.S.C. 1843(k)(4)(F).

(xi) A mortgage broker is a financial institution because brokering loans is a financial activity listed in 12 CFR 225.28(b)(1) and referenced in section 4(k)(4)(F) of the Bank Holding Company Act, 12 U.S.C. 1843(k)(4)(F).

(xii) An investment advisory company and a credit counseling service are each financial institutions because providing financial and investment advisory services are financial activities referenced in section 4(k)(4)(C) of the Bank Holding Company Act, 12 U.S.C. 1843(k)(4)(C).

(xiii) A company acting as a finder in bringing together one or more buyers and sellers of any product or service for transactions that the parties themselves negotiate and consummate is a financial institution because acting as a finder is an activity that is financial in nature or incidental to a financial activity listed in 12 CFR 225.86(d)(1).

(3) Financial institution does not include:

(i) Any person or entity with respect to any financial activity that is subject to the jurisdiction of the Commodity Futures Trading Commission under the Commodity Exchange Act (7 U.S.C. 1 et seq.);

(ii) The Federal Agricultural Mortgage Corporation or any entity chartered and operating under the Farm Credit Act of 1971 (12 U.S.C. 2001 et seq.);

(iii) Institutions chartered by Congress specifically to engage in securitizations, secondary market sales (including sales of servicing rights) or similar transactions related to a transaction of a consumer, as long as such institutions do not sell or transfer nonpublic personal information to a nonaffiliated third party other than as permitted by §§ 313.14 and 313.15; or

(iv) Entities that engage in financial activities but that are not significantly engaged in those financial activities, and entities that engage in activities incidental to financial activities but that are not significantly engaged in activities incidental to financial activities.

(4) Examples of entities that are not significantly engaged in financial activities are as follows:

(i) A retailer is not a financial institution if its only means of extending credit are occasional "lay away" and deferred payment plans or accepting payment by means of credit cards issued by others.

(ii) A retailer is not a financial institution merely because it accepts payment in the form of cash, checks, or credit cards that it did not issue.

(iii) A merchant is not a financial institution merely because it allows an individual to "run a tab."

(iv) A grocery store is not a financial institution merely because it allows individuals to whom it sells groceries to cash a check, or write a check for a higher amount than the grocery purchase and obtain cash in return.

(i) Information security program means the administrative, technical, or physical safeguards you use to access, collect, distribute, process, protect, store, use, transmit, dispose of, or otherwise handle customer information.

(j) Information system means a discrete set of electronic information resources organized for the collection, processing, maintenance, use, sharing, dissemination or disposition of electronic information containing customer information or connected to a system containing customer information, as well as any specialized system such as industrial/process controls systems, telephone switching and private branch exchange systems, and environmental controls systems that contains customer information or that is connected to a system that contains customer information.[118]

---

[118] The Notice of Proposed Rule Making states: "Proposed paragraph (h) would define "information system" as "a discrete set of electronic information resources organized for the collection, processing, maintenance, use, sharing, dissemination or disposition of electronic information, as well as any specialized system such as industrial/process controls systems, telephone switching and private branch exchange systems, and environmental control systems." The term "information system" is used throughout the proposed amendments to designate the systems that must be covered by the information security program. This definition is designed to cover the systems, including hardware, software, and networks that financial institutions use to maintain, process, access and store customer information. It is meant to be a broad definition that covers any system that, if compromised, could result in unauthorized access to customer information." *Id.*

(k) Multi-factor authentication means authentication through verification of at least two of the following types of authentication factors:

(1) Knowledge factors, such as a password;

(2) Possession factors, such as a token; or

(3) Inherence factors, such as biometric characteristics.[119]

(l)(1) Nonpublic personal information means:

(i) Personally identifiable financial information; and

(ii) Any list, description, or other grouping of consumers (and publicly available information pertaining to them) that is derived using any personally identifiable financial information that is not publicly available.

(2) Nonpublic personal information does not include:

(i) Publicly available information, except as included on a list described in paragraph (l)(1)(ii) of this section; or

(ii) Any list, description, or other grouping of consumers (and publicly available information pertaining to them) that is derived without using any personally identifiable financial information that is not publicly available.

(3) For example:

(i) Nonpublic personal information includes any list of individuals' names and street addresses that is derived in whole or in part using personally identifiable financial information (that is not publicly available), such as account numbers.

(ii) Nonpublic personal information does not include any list of individuals' names and addresses that contains only publicly available information, is not derived, in whole or in part, using personally identifiable financial information that is not publicly available,

---

[119] The Notice of Proposed Rule Making states: "Proposed paragraph (i) would define "multi-factor authentication" as "authentication through verification of at least two of the following types of authentication factors: 1. Knowledge factors, such as a password; 2. possession factors, such as a token; or 3. inherence factors, such as biometric characteristics." This term is used in proposed section 314.4(c)(6), which requires financial institutions to implement multi-factor authentication for individuals accessing internal networks that contain customer information. This definition comes from the Cybersecurity Regulations and is designed to conform to current understanding of what constitutes multi-factor authentication while still allowing financial institutions considerable flexibility in designing systems to protect their networks. Under this definition, a system of multi-factor authentication would need to verify at least two of the three types of factors, but has considerable flexibility in how to implement each factor. For example, under the knowledge factor, financial institutions are not limited to requiring passwords for access to systems, but might also use biographical information, or other knowledge that should be limited to the authorized user. The possession factor, could include verifying that a recognized device is accessing the system, or the transmission of a one-time code to a device on file with the financial institution. For the inherence factors, fingerprints, retina scans, or voice prints can be used. The Commission seeks comment on whether this definition is sufficiently flexible, while still requiring the elements of meaningful multi-factor authentication." *Id.*

and is not disclosed in a manner that indicates that any of the individuals on the list is a consumer of a financial institution.

(m) Penetration testing means a test methodology in which assessors attempt to circumvent or defeat the security features of an information system by attempting penetration of databases or controls from outside or inside your information systems.[120]

(n)(1) Personally identifiable financial information means any information:

(i) A consumer provides to you to obtain a financial product or service from you;

(ii) About a consumer resulting from any transaction involving a financial product or service between you and a consumer; or

(iii) You otherwise obtain about a consumer in connection with providing a financial product or service to that consumer.

(2) For example:

(i) Information included. Personally identifiable financial information includes:

(A) Information a consumer provides to you on an application to obtain a loan, credit card, or other financial product or service;

(B) Account balance information, payment history, overdraft history, and credit or debit card purchase information;

(C) The fact that an individual is or has been one of your customers or has obtained a financial product or service from you;

(D) Any information about your consumer if it is disclosed in a manner that indicates that the individual is or has been your consumer;

(E) Any information that a consumer provides to you or that you or your agent otherwise obtain in connection with collecting on, or servicing, a credit account;

(F) Any information you collect through an internet "cookie" (an information collecting device from a web server); and

---

[120] The Notice of Proposed Rule Making states: "Proposed paragraph (j) would define "penetration testing" as a "test methodology in which assessors attempt to circumvent or defeat the security features of an information system by attempting penetration of databases or controls from outside or inside your information systems." This term is used in proposed section 314.4(d)(2), which requires financial institutions to continually monitor the effectiveness of their safeguards or to engage in annual penetration testing. The primary example of penetration testing is where a security expert uses common techniques in an attempt to breach the security of a financial institution's information system. As set forth in the proposed definition, this includes attempts where the penetration tester is acting as an outsider who must penetrate the system without any initial access to the system, and attempts where the tester acts as someone with limited access to the system—such as a contractor or employee—and tries to access information that such an insider is not authorized to access. The Commission believes that there is currently a commonly understood definition of these services and that this definition provides sufficient guidance to understand the requirements of the proposed amendments." *Id.*

(G) Information from a consumer report.

(ii) Information not included. Personally identifiable financial information does not include:

(A) A list of names and addresses of customers of an entity that is not a financial institution; and

(B) Information that does not identify a consumer, such as aggregate information or blind data that does not contain personal identifiers such as account numbers, names, or addresses.

(o)(1) Publicly available information means any information that you have a reasonable basis to believe is lawfully made available to the general public from:

(i) Federal, State, or local government records;

(ii) Widely distributed media; or

(iii) Disclosures to the general public that are required to be made by Federal, State, or local law.

(2) You have a reasonable basis to believe that information is lawfully made available to the general public if you have taken steps to determine:

(i) That the information is of the type that is available to the general public; and

(ii) Whether an individual can direct that the information not be made available to the general public and, if so, that your consumer has not done so.

(3) For example:

(i) Government records. Publicly available information in government records includes information in government real estate records and security interest filings.

(ii) Widely distributed media. Publicly available information from widely distributed media includes information from a telephone book, a television or radio program, a newspaper, or a website that is available to the general public on an unrestricted basis. A website is not restricted merely because an internet service provider or a site operator requires a fee or a password, so long as access is available to the general public.

(iii) Reasonable basis.

(A) You have a reasonable basis to believe that mortgage information is lawfully made available to the general public if you have determined that the information is of the type included on the public record in the jurisdiction where the mortgage would be recorded.

(B) You have a reasonable basis to believe that an individual's telephone number is lawfully made available to the general public if you have located the telephone number in the telephone book or the consumer has informed you that the telephone number is not unlisted.

(p) Security event means an event resulting in unauthorized access to, or disruption or misuse of, an information system, information stored on such information system, or customer information held in physical form.

(q) Service provider means any person or entity that receives, maintains, processes, or otherwise is permitted access to customer information through its provision of services directly to a financial institution that is subject to this part.

(r) You includes each "financial institution" (but excludes any "other person") over which the Commission has enforcement jurisdiction pursuant to section 505(a)(7) of the Gramm–Leach–Bliley Act.

§ 314.3 Standards for safeguarding customer information.

(a) Information security program. You shall develop, implement, and maintain a comprehensive information security program that is written in one or more readily accessible parts and contains administrative, technical, and physical safeguards that are appropriate to your size and complexity, the nature and scope of your activities, and the sensitivity of any customer information at issue. The information security program shall include the elements set forth in § 314.4 and shall be reasonably designed to achieve the objectives of this part, as set forth in paragraph (b) of this section.

(b) Objectives. The objectives of section 501(b) of the Act, and of this part, are to:

(1) Insure the security and confidentiality of customer information;

(2) Protect against any anticipated threats or hazards to the security or integrity of such information; and

(3) Protect against unauthorized access to or use of such information that could result in substantial harm or inconvenience to any customer.[121]

§ 314.4 Elements.[122]

In order to develop, implement, and maintain your information security program, you shall:

---

[121] The Notice of Proposed Rule Making states: "Proposed Amendment to Section 314.3: Standards for Safeguarding Customer Information. Current section 314.3 requires financial institutions to develop an information security program (subsection (a)) and sets forth the objectives of the Rule (subsection (b)). Proposed section 314.3 retains the current requirements of section 314.3 under subsection (a) and the existing statement of objectives under subsection (b). It would, however, change the requirement that "safeguards" be based on the elements set forth in section 314.4, by replacing "safeguards" with "information security program." This change is proposed to clarify that the elements set forth in section 314.4 are parts of the information security plan." *Id.*

[122] The Notice of Proposed Rule Making states: "Proposed Amendments to Section 314.4: Elements The proposed amendments to section 314.4 would alter existing required elements of an information security program and adds several new elements. Although the Commission believes the proposed approach is sufficiently flexible, it seeks comment on whether it creates unintended consequences for businesses, may be more stringent than necessary to achieve the objective, and/or unnecessarily modifies the current rule without creating a material benefit to security." *Id.*

(a) Designate a qualified individual responsible for overseeing and implementing your information security program and enforcing your information security program (for purposes of this part, "Qualified Individual"). The Qualified Individual may be employed by you, an affiliate, or a service provider. To the extent the requirement in this paragraph (a) is met using a service provider or an affiliate, you shall:

(1) Retain responsibility for compliance with this part;

(2) Designate a senior member of your personnel responsible for direction and oversight of the Qualified Individual; and

(3) Require the service provider or affiliate to maintain an information security program that protects you in accordance with the requirements of this part.[123]

(b) Base your information security program on a risk assessment that identifies reasonably foreseeable internal and external risks to the security, confidentiality, and integrity of customer information that could result in the unauthorized disclosure, misuse, alteration, destruction, or other compromise of such information, and assesses the sufficiency of any safeguards in place to control these risks.

(1) The risk assessment shall be written and shall include:

(i) Criteria for the evaluation and categorization of identified security risks or threats you face;

---

[123] The Notice of Proposed Rule Making states: "Proposed Paragraph (a)
Amended paragraph (a) would expand the current requirement of designating an "employee or employees to coordinate your information security program" by requiring the designation of a single qualified individual responsible for overseeing and implementing the financial institution's security program and enforcing its information security program. This individual is referenced in the Rule as a Chief Information Security Officer or "CISO." This title is for clarity in the proposed Rule; financial institutions would not be required to actually grant that title to the designated individual. The proposed amendment would no longer allow financial institutions to designate more than one employee to coordinate the information security program. The Commission is interested in hearing about the potential costs and benefits of this proposal. In particular, the Commission is interested in any data, research or case studies that the Commission could use to analyze whether this is the best approach. This proposed change is intended to ensure that a single individual is accountable for overseeing the entire information security program and to lessen the possibility that there will be gaps in responsibility between individuals. The Commission believes that requiring a single responsible individual will increase accountability for the security of financial institutions' information systems. *Id.*

Under the proposed amendment, the CISO need not be an employee of the financial institution, but can be an employee of an affiliate or a service provider. This proposed change is meant to accommodate financial institutions that may prefer to retain an outside expert, lack the resources to employ their own information security staff qualified to oversee a program, or decide to pool resources with affiliates to share staff to manage information security. To the extent a financial institution meets this requirement by using a service provider or affiliate, however, the proposed amendment would require that the financial institution still: 1. Retain responsibility for compliance with the Rule; 2. designate a senior member of its personnel to be responsible for direction and oversight of the CISO; and 3. require the service provider or affiliate to maintain an information security program that protects the financial institution in accordance with the Rule. These proposed amendments are designed to ensure that, even when the financial institution outsources the CISO function, the financial institution retains responsibility for its own information security." *Id.*

(ii) Criteria for the assessment of the confidentiality, integrity, and availability of your information systems and customer information, including the adequacy of the existing controls in the context of the identified risks or threats you face; and

(iii) Requirements describing how identified risks will be mitigated or accepted based on the risk assessment and how the information security program will address the risks.

(2) You shall periodically perform additional risk assessments that reexamine the reasonably foreseeable internal and external risks to the security, confidentiality, and integrity of customer information that could result in the unauthorized disclosure, misuse, alteration, destruction, or other compromise of such information, and reassess the sufficiency of any safeguards in place to control these risks.[124]

(c) Design and implement safeguards to control the risks you identity through risk assessment, including by: [125]

---

[124] The Notice for Proposed Rule Making states: "Proposed Paragraph (b)
The proposed amendments to paragraph (b) clarify that a financial institution must base its information security program on the findings of its risk assessment by changing the first sentence of existing paragraph (b) to read that financial institutions' "information security program shall be based on a risk assessment. . . ." This is intended to emphasize this requirement, which is already required under the existing Rule. In addition, the proposed amendment removes existing section 314.4(b)'s requirement that the risk assessment must include consideration of specific risks because these specific risks are set forth elsewhere in the proposed amendments.
    Proposed section 314.4(b)(1) would require that the risk assessments be written and based on criteria for evaluating the risks the institutions face based on their particular information systems and the customer information they hold.[82] In addition, revised paragraph (b)(1) would require that the risk assessment describe how the financial institution will mitigate or Start Printed Page 13166accept any identified risks and how the financial institution's information security program will address those risks. The Commission is proposing these requirements in order to encourage financial institutions to perform thorough and complete risk assessments. The proposed amendment would allow financial institutions to develop their own criteria suited to their needs, but generally the criteria should address the sensitivity and value of customer information collected, maintained or transmitted by the financial institution and possible vectors through which the security, confidentiality, and integrity of that information could be threatened.
    The proposed amendment to section 314.4(b) would also add a requirement that financial institutions "periodically perform additional risk assessments that reexamine the reasonably foreseeable internal and external risks to the security, confidentiality, and integrity of customer information that could result in the unauthorized disclosure, misuse, alteration, destruction or other compromise of such information, and reassess the sufficiency of any safeguards in place to control these risks. The Commission believes that in order to be effective, a risk assessment must be subject to periodic reevaluation to adapt to changes in both financial institutions' information systems and changes in threats to the security of those systems. The proposed amendment would not set forth a prescriptive schedule for the periodic risk assessment, but would require financial institutions to set their own schedule based on the needs and resources of their institution." *Id.*
[125] The Notice of Proposed Rule Making states: "Proposed paragraph (c) retains the existing Rule's requirement for financial institutions to design and implement safeguards to control the risks identified in the risk assessment. It also adds more detailed requirements for what these safeguards must include. The Commission believes that most financial institutions already implement such measures as part of their comprehensive information security programs under the existing Rule. The proposed amendment simply

(1) Implementing and periodically reviewing access controls, including technical and, as appropriate, physical controls to:

(i) Authenticate and permit access only to authorized users to protect against the unauthorized acquisition of customer information; and

(ii) Limit authorized users' access only to customer information that they need to perform their duties and functions, or, in the case of customers, to access their own information; [126]

(2) Identify and manage the data, personnel, devices, systems, and facilities that enable you to achieve business purposes in accordance with their relative importance to business objectives and your risk strategy; [127]

(3) Protect by encryption all customer information held or transmitted by you both in transit over external networks and at rest. To the extent you determine that encryption of customer information, either in transit over external networks or at rest, is infeasible, you may instead secure such customer information using effective alternative compensating controls reviewed and approved by your Qualified Individual; [128]

(4) Adopt secure development practices for in-house developed applications utilized by you for transmitting, accessing, or storing customer information and

---

makes these requirements explicit in order to clarify the Rule and ensure that financial institutions understand their obligations under the Rule." *Id.*

[126] The Notice of Proposed Rule Making states: "Amended paragraph (c)(1) would require financial institutions to place access controls on information systems, designed to authenticate users and permit access only to authorized individuals in order to protect customer information from unauthorized acquisition. The Commission views this as a fundamental requirement of all information security programs, which certainly would have been a part of any program that met the requirements of the existing Rule." *Id.*

[127] The Notice of Proposed Rule Making states: "Proposed paragraph (c)(2) would require financial institutions to "[i]dentify and manage the data, personnel, devices, systems, and facilities that enable [the financial institution] to achieve business purposes in accordance with their relative importance to business objectives and [the financial institution's] risk strategy." This requirement is designed to ensure that the financial institution inventories the data in its possession, inventories the systems on which that data is collected, stored or transmitted, and has a full understanding of the relevant portions of its information systems and their relative importance. For example, it would require a company to understand which devices and networks contain customer information, who has access to them, and how those systems are connected to each other and to external networks." *Id.*

[128] The Notice of Proposed Rule Making states: "Proposed paragraph (c)(4) would generally require financial institutions to encrypt all customer information, both in transit and at rest. The Commission believes that in most circumstances encryption is an appropriate and important way to protect customer information from unauthorized use and access. Recognizing that companies may need flexibility in certain unforeseen circumstances, the proposed amendment does, however, permit financial institutions to use alternative means to protect customer information, subject to review and approval by the CISO. This is similar to the approach taken by the Health Insurance Portability and Accountability Act Security Rule, which permits a covered entity to use an alternative to encryption if it determines that encryption is not reasonable and documents an equivalent alternative measure. The Commission seeks comment on this approach." *Id.*

procedures for evaluating, assessing, or testing the security of externally developed applications you utilize to transmit, access, or store customer information;[129]

(5) Implement multi-factor authentication for any individual accessing any information system, unless your Qualified Individual has approved in writing the use of reasonably equivalent or more secure access controls;[130]

(6)(i) Develop, implement, and maintain procedures for the secure disposal of customer information in any format no later than two years after the last date the information is used in connection with the provision of a product or service to the customer to which it relates, unless such information is necessary for business operations or for other legitimate business purposes, is otherwise required to be retained by law or regulation, or where targeted disposal is not reasonably feasible due to the manner in which the information is maintained; and

(ii) Periodically review your data retention policy to minimize the unnecessary retention of data;[131]

---

[129] The Notice of Proposed Rule Making states: "Proposed paragraph (c)(5) would establish a requirement that financial institutions "[a]dopt secure development practices for in-house developed applications utilized" for "transmitting, accessing, or storing customer information." This proposed amendment is designed to ensure that financial institutions address the security of software they develop to handle customer information, as distinct from the security of their networks that contain customer information. Financial institutions would be required to adopt practices designed to develop applications that do not subject customer information to unacceptable risk of unauthorized access. In addition, this amendment would require financial institutions to develop "procedures for evaluating, assessing, or testing the security of externally developed applications [they] utilize to transmit, access, or store customer information." This proposed provision is designed to ensure that financial institutions take steps to verify that applications they use to handle customer information are secure. Under this amendment, financial institutions would be required to take reasonable steps to assure themselves that applications they use to handle customer information are secure and will not expose customer information." *Id*.

[130] The Notice of Proposed Rule Making states: "Amended paragraph (c)(6) would require financial institutions to "implement multi-factor authentication for any individual accessing customer information" or "internal networks that contain customer information." The Commission views multi-factor authentication as a minimum standard to allowing access to customer information for most financial institutions. As discussed above, the Commission believes that the definition of multi-factor authentication is sufficiently flexible to allow most financial institutions to develop a system that is suited to their needs. Currently used forms of multifactor authentication, such as requiring both a password and the receipt of a one-time passcode on a registered device, would meet this proposed requirement. To the extent that a financial institution finds that a method other than multi-factor authentication offers reasonably equivalent or more secure access controls, the institution may adopt that method with the written permission of its CISO. The Commission seeks comment on this approach." *Id*.

[131] The Notice of Proposed Rule Making states: "Amended paragraph (c)(8) would require financial institutions to develop procedures for the secure disposal of customer information in any format that is no longer necessary for their business operations or other legitimate business purposes. The proposed amendment allows the retention of information when retaining the information is required by law or where targeted disposal is not feasible due to the manner in which the information is maintained, such as when the information is on paper records that cannot be destroyed without also destroying other information which is still necessary for business operations. The disposal of records, both physical and digital, can result in exposure of customer information if not performed properly. Similarly, if records are retained when they are no longer necessary, there is a risk that those records will be subject to

(7) Adopt procedures for change management;[132] and

(8) Implement policies, procedures, and controls designed to monitor and log the activity of authorized users and detect unauthorized access or use of, or tampering with, customer information by such users.[133]

(d)(1) Regularly test or otherwise monitor the effectiveness of the safeguards' key controls, systems, and procedures, including those to detect actual and attempted attacks on, or intrusions into, information systems.[134]

---

unauthorized access. This amendment would require financial institutions to reduce both of those risks by designing procedures to dispose of records that are no longer necessary and to do so securely and in a timely manner. The proposed amendment does not define "legitimate business purposes," as the Commission feels that the wide array of business models of financial institutions under its jurisdiction defies any such attempt.

The Commission seeks comment on whether the Rule should define legitimate business purposes to exclude certain uses of customer information, require the destruction of certain types of data after a fixed period, or require financial institutions to affirmatively demonstrate a current need for customer information that is retained. The Commission also seeks comment on whether the proposed amendment should include a requirement to develop procedures to limit the collection of customer information that is not necessary for business operation or other legitimate business purposes."

[132] The Notice of Proposed Rule Making states: "Proposed paragraph (c)(9) would require financial institutions to adopt procedures for change management. Change management procedures govern the addition, removal, or modification of elements of an information system. Under the proposed amendment, financial institutions would need to develop procedures to assess the security of devices, networks, and other items to be added to their information system or the effect of removing such items or otherwise modifying the information system. For example, a financial institution that acquired a new subsidiary and wished to combine the new subsidiary's network with its own would be required to assess the security of the new network and the effect of adding it to the existing network. Although the Commission believes the proposed approach is sufficiently balanced, it seeks comment on whether the proposal may be more stringent than necessary to achieve the objective, or unnecessarily modifies the current rule without creating a material benefit to security." *Id.*

[133] The Notice of Proposed Rule Making states: "Proposed paragraph (c)(10) would require financial institutions to implement policies and procedures designed "to monitor the activity of authorized users and detect unauthorized access or use of, or tampering with, customer information by such users." In addition to threats posed by outside actors, authorized users such as employees and contractors can pose a substantial risk to the security of customer information. This amendment would require financial institutions to take steps to monitor those users and their activities related to customer information in a manner adapted to the financial institution's particular operations and needs. The monitoring should allow financial institutions to identify inappropriate use of customer information by authorized users, such as transferring large amounts of data or accessing information for which the user has no legitimate use. This requirement is separate from the requirement to maintain "audit trails," which would require logging of unusual events." *Id.*

[134] The Notice of Proposed Rule Making states: "Proposed paragraph (d)(1) would retain the current Rule's requirement that financial institutions "[r]egularly test or otherwise monitor the effectiveness of the safeguards' key controls, systems, and procedures, including those to detect actual and attempted attacks on, or intrusions into, information systems." The Commission views testing and monitoring as an integral part of any information security program. Proposed paragraph (d)(2) provides further guidance noting that the monitoring should take the form of either "continuous monitoring" or "periodic penetration testing and vulnerability assessments." Continuous monitoring is any system that allows real-time, ongoing monitoring of an information system's security, including monitoring for security threats, misconfigured systems, and other vulnerabilities. The Commission seeks comment on whether these required

(2) For information systems, the monitoring and testing shall include continuous monitoring or periodic penetration testing and vulnerability assessments. Absent effective continuous monitoring or other systems to detect, on an ongoing basis, changes in information systems that may create vulnerabilities, you shall conduct:

(i) Annual penetration testing of your information systems determined each given year based on relevant identified risks in accordance with the risk assessment; and

(ii) Vulnerability assessments, including any systemic scans or reviews of information systems reasonably designed to identify publicly known security vulnerabilities in your information systems based on the risk assessment, at least every six months; and whenever there are material changes to your operations or business arrangements; and whenever there are circumstances you know or have reason to know may have a material impact on your information security program.

(e) Implement policies and procedures to ensure that personnel are able to enact your information security program by:

(1) Providing your personnel with security awareness training that is updated as necessary to reflect risks identified by the risk assessment;

(2) Utilizing qualified information security personnel employed by you or an affiliate or service provider sufficient to manage your information security risks and to perform or oversee the information security program;

(3) Providing information security personnel with security updates and training sufficient to address relevant security risks; and

(4) Verifying that key information security personnel take steps to maintain current knowledge of changing information security threats and countermeasures.[135]

---

enhancements are appropriate, as well as information about the potential costs or unintended consequences of this proposal.

   If a financial institution does not adopt effective continuous monitoring, under the proposed amendments it would be required to engage in periodic penetration testing and vulnerability assessment consisting of no less than annual penetration testing based on the financial institution's risk assessment and biannual vulnerability assessments designed to detect publicly known vulnerabilities. These tests may be performed directly by the financial institution or by third-party assessors, as long as they are designed to assess the systems that contain or can be used to access customer information and are performed effectively. The schedule of this required testing aligns with the requirements of the Cybersecurity Regulations. The Commission seeks comment on whether this schedule of penetration testing and vulnerability assessment is appropriate or whether the Rule should require these tasks to be performed more or less frequently. In particular, the Commission is interested in any data, research or case studies that the Commission could use to analyze what commenters advocate." *Id.*

[135] Proposed paragraph (e) would require financial institutions to implement policies and procedures "to ensure that personnel are able to enact [the financial institution's] information security program" through various forms of training and education. Training of employees is a critical part of information security, as employees will be the ones enforcing and implementing any information security program.

   First, financial institutions would be required to provide their personnel with "security awareness training that is updated to reflect risks identified by the risk assessment." This requirement would apply to all personnel that have the ability to handle, access, or dispose of customer information. The training

(f) Oversee service providers, by:

(1) Taking reasonable steps to select and retain service providers that are capable of maintaining appropriate safeguards for the customer information at issue;

(2) Requiring your service providers by contract to implement and maintain such safeguards; and

(3) Periodically assessing your service providers based on the risk they present and the continued adequacy of their safeguards.[136]

---

would be designed to inform personnel of the risks to customer information and the financial institution's policies and procedures to minimize those risks.

Second, financial institutions would be required to "[u]tiliz[e] qualified information security personnel," employed either by them or by affiliates or service providers, "to manage [their] information security risks and to perform or oversee the information security program." This amendment is designed to ensure that information security personnel used by financial institutions are qualified for their positions and that sufficient personnel are used.

Third, financial institutions would be required to "[p]rovid[e] information security personnel with security updates and training sufficient to address relevant security risks." Maintaining awareness of emerging threats and vulnerabilities is a critical aspect of information security that the Commission believes was already a part of any information security program that complies with the existing Safeguards Rule. This amendment formalizes the requirement that financial institutions provide information security personnel with ongoing training to stay abreast of such developments. It is separate from the requirement to train all personnel generally, reflected in paragraph (e)(1).

Fourth, financial institutions would be required to "[v]erify[ ] that key information security personnel take steps to maintain current knowledge of changing cybersecurity threats and countermeasures." For example, a financial institution could offer incentives or funds for key personnel to undertake continuing education that addresses recent developments, include a requirement to stay abreast of security research as part of their performance metrics, or conduct an annual assessment of key personnel's knowledge of threats related to their information system. This requirement would be in addition to the proposed requirement that data security personnel be provided ongoing training. The proposed amendment does not define "key personnel" as the Commission believes that which personnel are "key" will vary considerably from entity to entity and that each financial institution will need to determine which employees must maintain this knowledge based on their structure and risk assessments. In most cases, though, the Commission believes that at a minimum the CISO and senior cybersecurity personnel would be covered by this amendment. Although the Commission believes the proposed approach is sufficiently flexible, it seeks comment on whether these proposals create unintended consequences for businesses, may be more stringent than necessary to achieve the objective, and/or unnecessarily modifies the current rule without creating a material benefit to security. In particular, the Commission is interested in any data, research or case studies that the Commission could use to analyze what commenters advocate. *Id.*

[136] The Notice of Proposed Rule Making states: "Proposed paragraph (f) would retain the current Rule's requirement in existing paragraph (d) regarding the oversight of service providers, and add a requirement that financial institutions periodically assess service providers "based on the risk they present and the continued adequacy of their safeguards." The current Rule requires an assessment of service providers' safeguards only at the onboarding stage; the proposed addition is designed to require financial institutions to monitor their service providers on an ongoing basis to ensure that they are maintaining adequate safeguards to protect customer information that they possess or access. This ongoing oversight could include investigating red flags raised by service providers' practices or conducting periodic assessments of service provider practices, depending on the circumstances." *Id.*

(g) Evaluate and adjust your information security program in light of the results of the testing and monitoring required by paragraph (d) of this section; any material changes to your operations or business arrangements; the results of risk assessments performed under paragraph (b)(2) of this section; or any other circumstances that you know or have reason to know may have a material impact on your information security program.[137]

(h) Establish a written incident response plan designed to promptly respond to, and recover from, any security event materially affecting the confidentiality, integrity, or availability of customer information in your control. Such incident response plan shall address the following areas:

(1) The goals of the incident response plan;

(2) The internal processes for responding to a security event;

(3) The definition of clear roles, responsibilities, and levels of decision-making authority;

(4) External and internal communications and information sharing;

(5) Identification of requirements for the remediation of any identified weaknesses in information systems and associated controls;

(6) Documentation and reporting regarding security events and related incident response activities; and

(7) The evaluation and revision as necessary of the incident response plan following a security event.[138]

---

[137] The Notice of Proposed Rule Making states: "Proposed paragraph (g) would retain the language of existing paragraph (e) in the current Rule, which would continue to require financial institutions to evaluate and adjust their information security programs in light of the result of testing required by this section, material changes to their operations or business arrangements, or any other circumstances that they know or have reason to know may have a material impact on their information security program. While proposed paragraph (d) would amplify the testing required under the current Rule, the requirement to evaluate and adjust the program in light of such testing remains the same." *Id.*

[138] The Notice of Proposed Rule Making states: "Proposed paragraph (h) would require financial institutions to establish incident response plans. The written response plans would be required to be "designed to promptly respond to, and recover from, any security event materially affecting the confidentiality, integrity, or availability of customer information" in the financial institution's possession. The amendment would require the incident response plans to address the following areas: 1. The goals of the incident response plan; 2. the internal processes for responding to a security event; 3. the definition of clear roles, responsibilities and levels of decision-making authority; 4. external and internal communications and information sharing; 5. identification of requirements for the remediation of any identified weaknesses in information systems and associated controls; 6. documentation and reporting regarding security events and related incident response activities; and 7. the evaluation and revision as necessary of the incident response plan following a security event. The proposed incident response plan requirement focuses on preparing financial institutions to respond promptly and appropriately to security events and to mitigate any weaknesses in their information systems accordingly. It is not intended to create any independent reporting or notification requirements, nor to conflict with any such requirements to which financial institutions are already subject. The proposed requirement regarding "documentation

(i) Require your Qualified Individual to report in writing, regularly and at least annually, to your board of directors or equivalent governing body. If no such board of directors or equivalent governing body exists, such report shall be timely presented to a senior officer responsible for your information security program. The report shall include the following information:

(1) The overall status of the information security program and your compliance with this part; and

(2) Material matters related to the information security program, addressing issues such as risk assessment, risk management and control decisions, service provider arrangements, results of testing, security events or violations and management's responses thereto, and recommendations for changes in the information security program.[139]

---

and reporting regarding security events and related incident response activities" would require incident response plans to document any notification or reporting requirements imposed by other federal or state laws, but does not in itself impose any such requirement.

The Commission seeks comment on whether the proposed amendment should require that financial institutions report security events to the Commission. The Cybersecurity Regulations require covered entities to report security events to the superintendent of the Department of Financial Services, but the proposed rule does not have a similar provision. The Commission seeks comment on whether such a provision should be added and, if so, what the elements of such a provision should be. Specifically, the Commission seeks comment on 1. the appropriate deadline for reporting security events after discovery; 2. whether all security events should require notification or whether notification should be required only under certain circumstances, such as a determination of a likelihood of harm to customers or that the event affects a certain number of customers; 3. whether such reports should be made public; 4. whether the events involving encrypted information should be included in the requirement; and 5. whether the requirement should allow law enforcement agencies to prevent or delay notification if notification would affect law-enforcement investigations.

In addition to seeking comment on the content of the plan, the Commission seeks comment on whether the proposed amendment would conflict with breach notification or reporting laws already in existence. Some states have enacted breach notification laws that exempt companies that maintain breach response procedures that are compliant with certain federal regulations from having to meet the requirements of the state's breach notification law. For example, Delaware's breach notification law states:

A person that is regulated by state or federal law, including . . . the Gramm Leach Bliley Act . . . and that maintains procedures for a breach of security pursuant to the laws, rules, regulations, guidance, or guidelines established by its primary or functional state or federal regulator is deemed to be in compliance with this chapter if the person notifies affected Delaware residents in accordance with the maintained procedures when a breach of security occurs.

The Commission seeks comment on whether the introduction of the proposed requirement for an incident response plan would cause financial institutions to be exempt from this, or similar, state breach notification laws, and if so, how this should affect the Commission's decision about whether to require an incident response plan in the Rule. *Id.*

[139] The Notice of Proposed Rule Making states: "Proposed paragraph (i) would require a financial institution's CISO to "report in writing, at least annually, to [the financial institution's] board of directors or equivalent governing body" regarding the following information: 1. The overall status of the information security program and financial institution's compliance with the Safeguards Rule; and 2. material matters related to the information security program, addressing issues such as risk assessment, risk management and control decisions, service provider arrangements, results of testing, security events

§ 314.6 Exceptions.

Section 314.4(b)(1), (d)(2), (h), and (i) do not apply to financial institutions that maintain customer information concerning fewer than five thousand consumers.

NOTES

Note 1

In the Notice of Proposed Rulemaking, the FTC notes the arguments for and against adopting more definitive direction for following the Safeguards Rule to produce an information security program:

> Several commenters urged the Commission not to add more specific and prescriptive requirements for information security programs. These commenters stated that financial institutions are familiar with the Rule in its current form and have established practices and policies in reliance on it; that preserving the Rule's flexible guidelines for information security plans enables financial institutions to adapt quickly to the rapidly changing cybersecurity landscape; and that additional prescriptive requirements for information security plans would negatively impact innovation.

> Some commenters asserted that a more prescriptive regulatory approach for information security programs in the Rule would not necessarily make institutions more secure and cautioned that regulation that adopts a checklist approach to information security plans risks creating complacency among companies. A few commenters proposed that rather than amending the Rule to add more specific and prescriptive requirements for information security plans, the Commission should promote self-regulation as an appropriate tool to effectively promote information security.

---

or violations and management's responses thereto, and recommendations for changes in the information security program. For financial institutions that do not have a board of directors or equivalent, the CISO must make the report to a senior officer responsible for the financial institution's information security program. This amendment is designed to ensure that the governing body of the financial institution is engaged with and informed about the state of the financial institution's information security program. Likewise, an annual written report may create accountability for the CISO by requiring the CISO to set forth the status of information security program for the governing body. The Commission requests comment on whether the burden of a required annual report would outweigh the benefits, whether the report should have other required components, or whether particular components are unnecessary.

In addition, the Commission requests comments on whether the proposed rule should also require the Board or equivalent governing body to certify compliance with the Rule. The Commission seeks comment on whether such a requirement would appropriately increase the engagement of the governing body of the financial institution in the information security program or whether it would create too much burden on financial institutions to independently assess the program.

The Commission also requests comment on how such a requirement would impact corporate governance; what precedents exist for federally-mandated board reporting on specific management issues, and analyses of their efficacy; and what effect requiring reporting to the board or certification by it would have." *Id.*

On the other hand, some commenters recommended that the FTC strengthen the Rule by including more detailed security requirements. The Clearing House Association LLC ("The Clearing House"), a banking association and payments company that is owned by the largest commercial banks, argued that the Rule's requirements, at least with respect to large financial technology ("Fintech") companies, should be more akin to the rules applicable to banks under the Federal Financial Institutions Examination Council ("FFIEC") Interagency Guidelines. Among other things, these guidelines specify elements that financial institutions should include in a risk assessment; areas a financial institution must consider—such as access controls, encryption, and incident response—in developing security controls; and provisions that financial institutions must include in contracts with service providers. The Electronic Privacy Information Center ("EPIC") recommended that certain practices set forth in the FTC's Safeguards Rule Guidance, such as employee background checks, authentication requirements, and encryption, should be mandatory.

Having considered these comments, the Commission proposes to amend the Rule to include more specific security requirements. While the Commission agrees with those commenters that argued that the flexibility of the current Safeguards Rule is a strength that allows the Rule to adapt to changing technology and threats, the Commission believes that more specific requirements will benefit financial institutions by providing them more guidance and certainty in developing their information security programs, while largely preserving that flexibility. The Commission agrees that a checklist approach is not appropriate, which is why the proposed amendments retain the existing Rule's process-based approach, allowing companies to tailor their programs to their size and to the sensitivity and amount of customer information they collect. As to the commenters that stated that the current Rule works well and that companies have already developed compliance programs under it, the Commission does not believe the proposed new requirements would require an overhaul of existing compliance programs. Because the new requirements build on existing requirements, they will help companies benchmark and improve their current compliance programs, rather than having to start from scratch. Finally, the Commission recognizes that some of the financial institutions to which the Safeguards Rule applies— such as tax preparers or mortgage brokers—may be very small businesses with few customers. Accordingly, the proposed amendment would exempt smaller financial institutions from certain requirements of the amended Rule.

The Commission also agrees that very specific requirements for information security programs could become outdated and require frequent amendments. Accordingly, the proposed amendments provide more detailed requirements as to the issues and threats that must be addressed by the information security program, but do not require specific solutions to those problems. Instead, the proposed amendments retain the process-based approach of the Rule, while providing a more detailed map of what information security plans must address. As discussed in detail below, information security programs under the proposed amendments would still be based on risk assessments performed by the covered financial institutions and would be developed to address the specific risks and needs of the financial institution. The Commission continues to believe that a flexible, non-prescriptive Rule enables covered organizations to use it to respond to the changing landscape of security threats, to allow for innovation in security practices, and to accommodate technological changes and advances. The proposed amendments are designed to preserve that flexibility while doing more to ensure that financial institutions develop information security plans that are appropriate, reasonable, and designed to protect customer information. Although the Commission believes the proposed approach is sufficiently flexible, it seeks comment on whether the approach creates unintended consequences for businesses, may be more stringent than necessary to achieve the objective, and/or unnecessarily modifies language without creating a material benefit to security.[140]

QUESTIONS

1) What is different between the prior regulations and the new regulations? What are the benefits of the new regulations? What are the potential downsides of the new regulations?

2) What impact would these changes have on small businesses (like a car dealership) that rely on consulting services to implement their and monitor their security?

NOTES

Note 1

Two of the elements of the proposed regulations concerning the information security program were not adopted by the FTC. First, proposed §314.4 (c)(3) stated: "(3) Restrict access at physical locations containing customer information only to authorized individuals[.]" The Notice of Proposed Rule Making states: "Proposed paragraph (c)(3) would require that financial institutions restrict access to physical locations containing customer information only to authorized individuals. This element would require financial institutions to protect physical locations, as opposed to networks, that contain customer information and is designed to address the threat to physical copies of records. This would require financial institutions to protect paper files and control access to areas in which such files are stored. This may include restricting access to work areas where personnel are using hard copies of customer information or requiring physical locks on filing cabinets containing customer information and similar protections. It would also

---

[140] *Standards for Protecting Customer Information*, FEDERAL TRADE COMMISSION (Apr. 4, 2019), *available at* https://www.federalregister.gov/documents/2019/04/04/2019-04981/standards-for-safeguarding-customer-information.

include policies for securing physical devices that contain personal information, such as laptops, tablets, phones, and thumb drives."[141]

Second, proposed §314.4 (c)(7) stated: "(7) Include audit trails within the information security program designed to detect and respond to security events[.]" The Notice of Proposed Rule Making states: "Amended paragraph (c)(7) would require information systems under the Rule to include audit trails designed to detect and respond to security events. Audit trails are chronological logs that show who has accessed an information system and what activities the user engaged in during a given period. The proposed Rule does not require any specific type of audit trail, nor does it require that every transaction be recorded in its entirety. However, the audit trail must be designed to allow the financial institution to detect when the system has been compromised or when an attempt to compromise has been made. It must also provide sufficient information for the financial institution to reasonably respond to the event. The proposed amendment does not require that the audit trails be retained for any particular period, but the Commission believes that in order to allow the financial institution to detect and respond to security events, the audit trails will usually have to be maintained for some reasonable length of time. Financial institutions would need to determine the appropriate retention period for their operations. The Commission seeks comment on whether this requirement needs to be modified or eliminated for smaller firms, or narrowed to avoid undue burden."[142]

Note 2

In adopting additional detail concerning creating an information security program, the Federal Trade Commission explains that it is relying on two rules created by two other organizations:

> As discussed above, the Commission proposes to amend the Safeguards Rule to include more detailed requirements for the development and establishment of the information security program required under the Rule. These amendments are based primarily on the cybersecurity regulations issued by the New York Department of Financial Services, 23 NYCRR 500 ("Cybersecurity Regulations"), and the insurance data security model law issued by the National Association of Insurance Commissioners ("Model Law"). The Cybersecurity Regulations were issued in February 2017 after two rounds of public comment. The Model Law was issued in October 2017. The Commission believes that both the Cybersecurity Regulations and the Model Law maintain the balance between providing detailed guidance and avoiding overly prescriptive requirements for information security programs. The proposed amendments do not adopt either law wholesale, instead taking

---

[141] *Id.*
[142] *Id.*

portions from each and adapting others for the purposes of the Safeguards Rule.[143]

The New York Department of Financial Services Cybersecurity Regulations are discussed in a following note.

Note 3

The Federal Trade Commission also noted that it was rejecting reliance on other model standards and laws:

> The Commission sought comment on whether the Rule should reference or incorporate any other information security standards or frameworks, such as the National Institute of Standards and Technology's ("NIST") Cybersecurity Framework (the "Framework") or the Payment Card Industry Data Security Standard ("PCIDSS").

> The majority of commenters advocated against referring to or incorporating any other information security standard or framework, such as the NIST Framework or PCIDSS, into the Rule. Some commenters argued that the FTC should not adopt the NIST Framework as a binding set of obligations because it would lead to a "check the box" security mandate, and would add a layer of complexity to an already complex regulatory environment where institutions have to comply with numerous preexisting federal and state requirements. The Electronic Transactions Association ("ETA") argued that the Framework is "not designed to replace an organization's cybersecurity risk management" and that it is not intended to be a standard or checklist.

> A few commenters wrote in support of incorporating a reference to the NIST Framework in the Rule, while not requiring compliance with the Framework. For example, the Financial Services Roundtable/BITS ("FSR/BITS") argued that incorporating the NIST Framework in the Rule as an informative reference would help to address "the growing thicket of cybersecurity compliance obligations that are spreading across the financial services sector." FSR/BITS recommended further that the Commission modify the Rule so that financial institutions that use the NIST Framework would be found in *de facto* compliance with the Rule.

> With respect to the PCIDSS, numerous commenters opposed the Rule's reference or incorporation of PCIDSS. Commenters argued such an amendment has the possibility of undermining the Rule's flexibility by imposing a "one-size-fits-all" approach. MasterCard Worldwide, a co-founder and developer of PCIDSS, opposed this amendment to the Rule, highlighting that the PCIDSS was created by major card networks for participants in the card industry. Whereas the PCIDSS may be

---

[143] *Standards for Protecting Customer Information*, FEDERAL TRADE COMMISSION (Apr. 4, 2019), *available at* https://www.federalregister.gov/documents/2019/04/04/2019-04981/standards-for-safeguarding-customer-information.

appropriate for payment card issuers and acquirers, MasterCard argued, it would not necessarily apply well to other financial institutions. Other comments agreed that incorporating PCIDSS would be inappropriate. No commenters wrote in support of referencing or incorporating the PCIDSS into the Rule. Having considered these comments, the Commission declines to propose changing the Rule to incorporate or reference a particular security standard or framework. As noted above, for a variety of reasons, including questions about the applicability of the particular standards at issue to all financial institutions, the majority of commenters opposed referencing or incorporating any specific information security standard or framework into the Rule. Mandating that companies follow a particular security standard or framework would reduce the flexibility built into the current Rule. This proposal does not amend the Rule to allow compliance with such standards to serve as a safe harbor against Commission enforcement, as some commenters sought. The Commission seeks additional comment on how such a program could remain up to date and respond rapidly to changes in the security environment, and the workability of monitoring changing standards and adapting a safe harbor rule as needed.[144]

The NIST Framework is discussed in Chapter 9. The Payment Card Industry Data Security Standard is discussed in a following note.

Note 4

Payment Card Industry Data Security Standard is an industry standard created by the PCI Security Standards Organization. A recent version is the 2018 PCI Data Security Standard Document (version 3.2.1).[145] The Standard Document is over 130 pages long. The PCI Security Standards Organization website states the following goals and requirements:

PCI Security Standards

If you accept or process payment cards, the PCI Data Security Standards apply to you.

These standards cover technical and operational system components included in or connected to cardholder data.

Goals

PCI DSS Requirements

Build and Maintain a Secure Network

---

[144] *Id.*

[145] *See Document Library*, SECURITY STANDARDS COUNCIL, *available at* https://www.pcisecuritystandards.org/documents/PCI_DSS_v3-2-1.pdf?agreement=true&time=1595295980801 (last visited Sept. 21, 2020) (listing the various searchable documents).

1. Install and maintain a firewall configuration to protect cardholder data
2. Do not use vendor-supplied defaults for system passwords and other security parameters

Protect Cardholder Data

3. Protect stored cardholder data
4. Encrypt transmission of cardholder data across open, public networks

Maintain a Vulnerability Management Program

5. Use and regularly update anti-virus software or programs
6. Develop and maintain secure systems and applications

Implement Strong Access Control Measures

7. Restrict access to cardholder data by business need-to-know
8. Assign a unique ID to each person with computer access
9. Restrict physical access to cardholder data

Regularly Monitor and Test Networks

10. Track and monitor all access to network resources and cardholder data
11. Regularly test security systems and processes

Maintain an Information Security Policy

12. Maintain a policy that addresses information security for employees and contractors

For each goal and requirement, there is detailed guidance in the Standard Document. For example, with respect to firewalls, the Standard Document sets forth over fifteen requirements with corresponding testing procedures and guidance. The following sets forth the Requirements, Testing Procedures and Guidance for 1.3.1-2:

[Requirements:] Implement a DMZ to limit inbound traffic to only system components that provide authorized publicly accessible services, protocols, and ports. Limit inbound Internet traffic to IP addresses within the DMZ.

[Testing Procedures:] Examine firewall and router configurations to verify that a DMZ is implemented to limit inbound traffic to only system components that provide authorized publicly accessible services, protocols, and ports. Examine firewall and router configurations to verify that inbound Internet traffic is limited to IP addresses within the DMZ.

[Guidance:] Examine firewall and router configurations to verify that a DMZ is implemented to limit inbound traffic to only system components that provide authorized publicly accessible services, protocols, and ports.

The DMZ is that part of the network that manages connections between the Internet (or other untrusted networks), and services that an organization needs to have available to the public (like a web server). This functionality is intended to prevent malicious individuals from accessing the organization's internal network from the Internet, or from using services, protocols, or ports in an unauthorized manner. *Id.*

The website further provides "Quick Steps to Security:"

- Buy and use only approved PIN entry devices at your points-of-sale.

- Buy and use only validated payment software at your POS or website shopping cart.

- Do not store *any* sensitive cardholder data in computers or on paper.

- Use a firewall on your network and PCs.

- Make sure your wireless router is password-protected and uses encryption.

- Use strong passwords. Be sure to change default passwords on hardware and software – most are unsafe.

- Regularly check PIN entry devices and PCs to make sure no one has installed rogue software or "skimming" devices.

- Teach your employees about security and protecting cardholder data.

- Follow the PCI Data Security Standard.

Note 5

In *Biometrics and Banking: Assessing the Adequacy of the Gramm-Leach-Bliley Act*, 24 N.C. BANKING INST. 309 (2020), Meredith E. Bock argues that the GLBA likely does not adequately provide protections for biometric information, particularly for behavioral biometric technologies. "Behavioral biometrics analyze behaviors such as keystrokes, handwriting, and navigation of a webpage to verify a user's identity [and] create[s] a unique profile that is virtually impossible to replicate." Bock notes that this information is currently used by some financial institutions for fraud detection and to "evaluate the security risks within the company. . . ."

Note 6

On February 28, 2020, the Federal Student Aid Office of the The Department of Education of the United States issued a notice to educational institutions titled, "Enforcement of Cybersecurity Requirements under the Graham-Leach-Bliley Act."[146]

---

[146] *Enforcement of Cybersecurity Requirements under the Gramm-Leach-Bliley Act*, FEDERAL STUDENT AID, (Feb. 28, 2020), *available at* https://ifap.ed.gov/electronic-announcements/022820EnforcCyberReqGrammLeachBlileyAct.

The notice states in relevant part:

> . . . We expect all of our partners to maintain strong security policies and effective internal controls to prevent unauthorized access or disclosure of sensitive information. . . .The Federal Trade Commission (FTC) has enforcement authority for the requirements and has determined that institutions of higher education (institutions) are financial institutions under GLBA.
>
> Each institution has agreed to comply with GLBA in its Program Participation Agreement with the Department. In addition, as a condition of accessing the Department's systems, each institution and servicer must sign the Student Aid Internet Gateway (SAIG) Enrollment Agreement, which states that the institution must ensure that all federal student aid applicant information is protected from access by or disclosure to unauthorized personnel.
>
> Institutions and third-party servicers are also required to demonstrate administrative capability in accordance with 34 C.F.R. § 668.16, including the maintenance of adequate checks and balances in their systems of internal control. An institution or servicer that does not maintain adequate internal controls over the security of student information may not be considered administratively capable.
>
> In Dear Colleague Letter GEN-15-18 and GEN-16-12, we reminded institutions about the longstanding requirements of GLBA and notified them of our intention to begin enforcing legal requirements of GLBA through annual compliance audits. In Dear CPA Letter CPA-19-01, we explained the procedures for auditors to determine whether institutions were in compliance with GLBA. This announcement explains the Department's procedures for enforcing those requirements and the potential consequences for institutions or servicers that fail to comply.

Audit Findings

Auditors are expected to evaluate three information safeguard requirements of GLBA in audits of postsecondary institutions or third-party servicers under the regulations in 16 C.F.R. Part 314:

1. The institution must designate an individual to coordinate its information security program.

2. The institution must perform a risk assessment that addresses three required areas described in 16 C.F.R. 314.4(b):

    a)   Employee training and management;

    b)   Information systems, including network and software design, as well as information processing, storage, transmission and disposal; and

c)   Detecting, preventing and responding to
                                attacks, intrusions, or other systems
                                failures.

3. The institution must document a safeguard for each risk identified in
    Step 2 above.

    When an auditor determines that an institution or servicer has failed to
    comply with any of these GLBA requirements, the finding will be included
    in the institution's audit report.

Federal Trade Commission

When an audit report that includes a GLBA audit finding is received by
the Department, we will refer the audit to the FTC. Once the finding is
referred to the FTC, that finding will be considered closed for the
Department's audit tracking purposes. The FTC will determine what
action may be needed as a result of the GLBA audit finding.

Cybersecurity Team

Federal Student Aid's Postsecondary Institution Cybersecurity Team
(Cybersecurity Team) will also be informed of findings related to GLBA,
and may request additional documentation from the institution in order
to assess the level of risk to student data presented by the institution or
servicer's information security system.

If the Cybersecurity Team determines that the institution or servicer
poses substantial risk to the security of student information, the
Cybersecurity Team may temporarily or permanently disable the
institution or servicer's access to the Department's information systems.
Additionally, if the Cybersecurity Team determines that as a result of
very serious internal control weaknesses of the general controls over
technology that the institution's or servicer's administrative capability is
impaired or it has a history of non-compliance, it may refer the institution
to the Department's Administrative Actions and Appeals Service Group
for consideration of a fine or other appropriate administrative action by
the Department.

3.5 FTC GBLA/FTC Safeguards Rule Cases

Per the FTC's enforcement data base, the following cases are at least partially
categorized as GLBA cases since 2011.[147] Of course, that does not mean that every case

---

[147] *See Cases and Proceedings: Advanced Search*, FEDERAL TRADE COMMISSION,
https://www.ftc.gov/enforcement/cases-proceedings/advanced-
search?combine=&date_filter%5Bmax%5D%5Bdate%5D=&date_filter%5Bmin%5D%5Bdate%5D=&fi
eld_case_action_type_value=All&field_competition_topics_tid=All&field_consumer_protection_topics_
tid=250&field_enforcement_type_tid=All&field_federal_court_tid=All&field_industry_tid=All&field_m
atter_number_value=&field_mission_tid_1=All&field_release_date_value%5Bmax%5D%5Bdate%5D=

covers the Safeguard Rule because there are other causes of action under the GBLA such as the Privacy Rule and our focus is on the Safeguard Rule.

Updated	Title	FTC Matter/File No.
December 15, 2020	Ascension Data & Analytics, LLC, In the Matter of (Administrative)	192 3126
January 7, 2020	Mortgage Solutions FCS, Inc. (Federal)	182 3199
September 6, 2019	LightYear Dealer Technologies, LLC, In the Matter of (Administrative)	172 3051
July 31, 2019	Equifax, Inc. (Federal)	172 3203
May 24, 2018	PayPal, Inc., In the Matter of (Administrative)	162 3102
November 8, 2017	TaxSlayer, In the Matter of (Administrative)	1023172
November 7, 2012	PLS Financial Services, Inc., et al. (Federal)	1023172
August 19, 2011	ACRAnet, Inc., In the Matter of (Administrative)	092 3088
August 19, 2011	SettlementOne Credit Corporation (Administrative)	082 3208
August 19, 2011	Fajilan and Associates, Inc., also d/b/a Statewide Credit Services, In the Matter of (Administrative)	092 3089

One of the latest cases, Mortgage Solutions FCS, Inc. (January 7, 2020) relies on multiple causes of action in addition to the GBLA.

United States v. Mortgage Solutions FCS, Inc. (January 7, 2020) Complaint.

Plaintiff brings this action under Section 13(b) of the Federal Trade Commission Act ("FTC Act") . . . to obtain civil penalties, permanent injunctive relief, and other equitable relief for Defendants' acts or practices in violation of Section 5(a) of the FTC Act, 15 U.S.C. § 45(a); in violation of the FCRA, 15 U.S.C. §§ 1681–1681x; in violation of the rule regarding the Privacy of Consumer Financial Information ("Regulation P"), 12 C.F.R. Part 1016, issued pursuant to Title V, Subtitle A, of the Gramm-Leach-Bliley Act ("GLB Act") . . . ; and in violation of the rule regarding the Standards for Safeguarding

---

&field_release_date_value%5Bmin%5D%5Bdate%5D=&items_per_page=20 (last visited Sept. 21, 2020) (listing the different case names from most recent to least recent with an advanced search option).

Customer Information ("Safeguards Rule"), 16 C.F.R. Part 314, issued pursuant to Title V, Subtitle A, of the Gramm-Leach-Bliley Act ("GLB Act").[148]

The following material includes additional pertinent information concerning the Mortgage Solutions FCS, Inc (January 7, 2020) complaint:

Mortgage Solutions is a mortgage broker, serving as an intermediary between residential mortgage lenders and prospective borrowers. Consumers seeking to obtain mortgage financing submit loan applications through Mortgage Solutions, which then shops the applications around to various lenders. Lenders who choose to extend credit to a Mortgage Solutions customer compensate Mortgage Solutions at rates ranging from 1% to 1.5% of the amount of the offered loan.

Mortgage Solutions collects and maintains sensitive personal financial information from its customers and prospective customers, including names, Social Security numbers, dates of birth, income information, and credit history. Mortgage Solutions obtains personal financial information directly from its customers and also by obtaining and reviewing customers' consumer credit reports.

Between approximately June 2015 and August 2016, Defendant Walker, on behalf of Defendant Mortgage Solutions, published or caused to be published responses (the "Yelp responses") to negative consumer reviews about his services that appeared on the consumer review website Yelp.com.

In numerous instances, the Yelp responses, which are publicly viewable on the Yelp.com page for Mount Diablo Lending, contain personal information about the customers to whose reviews Walker responded, including but not limited to information about the consumers' sources of income, debt-to-income ratios, credit history, taxes, family relationships, and health. For example, the Yelp responses contain the following statements:

> "The truth of the matter is you didn't have one late 2 years ago. Your credit report shows 4 late payments from the Capital One account, 1 late from Comenity Bank which is Pier 1, another late from Credit First Bank, 3 late payments from an account named San Mateo. Not to mention the mortgage lates. All of these late payments are having an enormous negative impact on your credit score. Ty could not have known all of these negative items were on your credit report from the initial conversation."

> "The high debt to income ratio was caused by this borrower cosigning on multiple mortgages for his children. The borrower was also self employed and took high deductions from his business."

> "His mother-in-law was on title but not on the new loan. The new loan was only going to be in his and his wife's name. This was a cash out loan, he was supposedly using the funds to pay off his kids Med School bills. The notary that sat down to sign was concerned the mother-in-law who was signing her rights off of the property had dementia. This was never

---

[148] Complaint at 1–2, United States v. Mortgage Solutions FCS, Inc., No. 4:20-cv-110 (2020).

mentioned to us throughout the whole process....The funny thing is he admitted to me in one of our final conversations that his mother-in-law actually did have a 'slight' case of dementia.   OK SO WHAT THE NOTARY SAID IS TRUE!!!! The title company did try to work with him by saying if he could get a letter from a doctor stating his mother in-law was aware of what she was signing we could proceed. He didn't want to go that route, evidently she doesn't have the capacity to understand she is signing away her rights to the property.... I know you feel entitled to the funds from your mothers house as you clearly stated to me but unfortunately that is not the way the law works and there is nothing my company can do about it."

In numerous instances, in the Yelp responses, Defendants disclosed the reviewing consumers' first and last names. Even where Defendants did not disclose reviewing consumers' first and last names, however, the consumers are readily identifiable by users of the site, including reviewers' friends, family, and acquaintances. Several reviewing consumers' Yelp profiles include photographs and links to the consumers' other Yelp reviews.

As described below, Defendants' posting of negative financial information about consumers on Yelp, and their failures to provide adequate privacy notices or data security, violated their responsibilities under Regulation P, 12 C.F.R. § 1016.4(a), the Safeguards Rule, 16 C.F.R. Part 314, the Fair Credit Reporting Act, 15 U.S.C. § 1681b(f), and Section 5 of the FTC Act, 15 U.S.C. § 45.

. . .

27. Pursuant to section 621(a)(1) of the FCRA, 15 U.S.C. § 1681s(a)(1), a violation of the FCRA constitutes an unfair or deceptive act or practice in or affecting commerce, in violation of Section 5(a) of the FTC Act, 15 U.S.C. § 45(a).

28. Several of the Yelp responses contained information that was derived from a consumer report within the meaning of section 603(d) of the FCRA. 15 U.S.C. § 1681a(d). For instance, Defendant Walker made the following statements in response to a customer's review: "A lot of these charge offs were still on the clients credit profile which were discovered during the underwriting process. If I would have known this from the outset we wouldn't had proceeded with her loan."

29. None of the Yelp responses containing credit report information was communicated in connection with any pending credit decision related to the reviewing consumer, or for any other permissible purpose under the statute. Instead, Defendants revealed customers' sensitive, personal information on a publicly-viewable website.

INFORMATION-SECURITY PRACTICES

30. The Safeguards Rule, which implements Section 501(b) of the GLB Act, 15 U.S.C. § 6801(b), was promulgated by the FTC on May 23, 2002, and became effective on May 23, 2003. The Rule requires financial institutions to protect the security, confidentiality, and integrity of customer information by developing and implementing a comprehensive written "information security program" containing reasonable administrative, technical, and physical safeguards, including safeguards used to access, collect, distribute, process,

protect, store, use transmit, dispose of, or otherwise handle customer information. 16 C.F.R. § 314.3.

31. Among other things, the Safeguards Rule requires that financial institutions, in developing, implementing, and maintaining their information security programs, "regularly test or otherwise monitor the effectiveness of the safeguards' key controls, systems, and procedures." 16 C.F.R. § 314.4(c).

32. Mortgage Solutions is a "financial institution," as defined in Section 509(3)(A) of the GLB Act, 15 U.S.C. § 6809(3)(A), and is subject to FTC enforcement of the Safeguards Rule pursuant to Section 505 of the GLB Act, 15 U.S.C. § 6805(a)(7), 16 C.F.R. § 314.1, 16 C.F.R. § 314.2, and 12 C.F.R. § 1016.3(l)(3).

33. Defendant Mortgage Solutions did not implement an information security program until approximately September 2017.

34. Beginning in approximately September 2017, Defendant Mortgage Solutions implemented an "Information Security Plan." However, the Information Security Plan makes no provision for regularly testing or assessing its own effectiveness, and in fact Defendants have failed to engage in any regular testing or assessment of the effectiveness of the Information Security Plan's key controls, systems, and procedures.

VIOLATIONS OF REGULATION P

COUNT I

Failure to Provide Clear, Conspicuous, and Accurate Privacy Notices

41. As described in Paragraphs 18 and 19, from approximately October 2012 until approximately April 2018, Defendants failed to ensure that customers of Mortgage Solutions were provided with clear, conspicuous, and accurate privacy notices.

42. Defendants' acts and practices set forth in Paragraph 40 constitute a violation of Regulation P, 12 C.F.R. §§ 1016.4-1016.6.

COUNT II

Impermissible Disclosure of Nonpublic Personal Information

43. As described in Paragraphs 10-12, between approximately June 2015 and August 2016, Defendants publicly disclosed nonpublic personal information about several Mortgage Solutions customers by publishing this information in the Yelp responses.

44. As described in Paragraphs 18-21, during the time period when the Yelp responses were published, Defendants provided Mortgage Solutions customers with neither notice that their nonpublic personal information could be publicly disclosed nor an opportunity to opt out of such disclosures.

45. Defendants' acts and practices set forth in Paragraphs 42 and 43 constitute violations of Regulation P, 12 C.F.R. § 1016.10(a)(1).

VIOLATIONS OF THE FAIR CREDIT REPORTING ACT

COUNT III

Impermissible Use of Consumer Reports

46. In numerous instances, as described in Paragraphs 27 and 28, Defendants have used consumer reports for an impermissible purpose.

47. Defendants' acts or practices, as set forth in Paragraph 45, violate section 604(f) of the FCRA, 15 U.S.C. § 1681b(f).

48. Pursuant to section 621(a)(l) of the FCRA, 15 U.S.C. § 1681s(a)(1), the acts and practices alleged in Paragraph 46 also constitute unfair or deceptive acts or practices in violation of section 5(a) of the FTC Act, 15 U.S.C. § 45(a).

VIOLATIONS OF THE SAFEGUARDS RULE

COUNT IV

Failure to Develop and Implement an Information Security Program

49. As described in Paragraph 32, until approximately September 2017, Mortgage Solutions failed to implement an information security program.

50. Defendants' acts and practices set forth in Paragraph 48 constitute a violation of the Safeguards Rule, 16 C.F.R. § 314.3(a).

COUNT V

Inadequacy of Information Security Program

51. As described in Paragraph 33, in developing, implementing, and maintaining the Mortgage Solutions "Information Security Plan," Defendants have failed to regularly test or otherwise monitor the effectiveness of the Information Security Plan's key controls, systems, and procedures.

52. Defendants' acts and practices set forth in Paragraph 50 constitute a violation of the Safeguards Rule, 16 C.F.R. § 314.4(c).[149]

QUESTIONS

Count IV (failure to develop and implement an information security program) and Count V (Inadequacy of information security program) apply to the Safeguards Rule. The court also mentions administrative, technical, and physical controls for implementing the Safeguards Rule. Which of these controls should have been applied to keep Walker from disclosing sensitive information on Yelp?

The Defendants settled the case with the FTC and a stipulated order was entered. The following is the order.

United States v. Mortgage Solutions FCS, Inc. Stipulated Order for Permanent Injunction, Civil Penalties and Other Relief

---

[149] Complaint at 4–6, 8–12, United States v. Mortgage Solutions FCS, Inc., No. 4:20-cv-110 (2020).

. . . Plaintiff and Defendants stipulate to the entry of this Stipulation and Order ("Order") to resolve all matters in dispute in this action between them.

THEREFORE, IT IS ORDERED as follows:

FINDINGS

. . . 2. The Complaint charges that Defendants participated in deceptive and unfair acts or practices in violation of Section 5 of the FTC Act, 15 U.S.C. § 45; violated the Fair Credit Reporting Act, 15 U.S.C. §§ 1681-1681x (the "FCRA"); violated the rule regarding the Privacy of Consumer Financial Information ("Regulation P"), 12 C.F.R. Part 1016, issued pursuant to Title V, Subtitle A, of the Gramm-Leach-Bliley Act ("GLB Act"), 15 U.S.C. §§ 6801-6804; and violated of the rule regarding the Standards for Safeguarding Customer Information ("Safeguards Rule"), 16 C.F.R. Part 314, issued pursuant to Title V, Subtitle A, of the Gramm-Leach-Bliley Act ("GLB Act"), 15 U.S.C. §§ 6801(b), 6805(b)(2). Specifically, the Complaint charges that Defendants failed to accurately disclose their privacy practices, failed to develop and implement an adequate information security program, and improperly disclosed customers' sensitive personal financial information. . . .

DEFINITIONS

For the purpose of this Order, the following definitions apply: . . .

F. "Covered Incident" means any instance in which any United States federal, state, or local law or regulation requires a Covered Business or Individual Defendant, to notify any U.S. federal, state, or local government entity that Nonpublic Personal Information collected or received, directly or indirectly, by a Covered Business from or about an individual consumer was, or is reasonably believed to have been, accessed, acquired, or shared without authorization. . . .

M. "Information Security Program" means a comprehensive policy that is written in one or more readily accessible parts and contains administrative, technical, and physical safeguards that are appropriate to Defendants' size and complexity, the nature and scope of Defendants' activities, and the sensitivity of any customer information at issue.

N. "Nonpublic Personal Information" means

1. Personally Identifiable Financial Information;

2.   Any list, description, or other grouping of consumers (and publicly available information pertaining to them) that is derived using any Personally Identifiable Financial Information that is not publicly available.

O. "Opt Out Notice" means a Clear and Conspicuous notice that accurately explains consumers' right to opt out of disclosures of Nonpublic Personal Information to nonaffiliated Third parties. Such notice must state:

1.   That Defendants disclose or reserve the right to disclose Nonpublic Personal Information about the consumer to a nonaffiliated third party;

2. That the consumer has the right to Opt Out of that disclosure; and

3. A reasonable means by which the consumer may exercise the Opt Out right.

P. "Opt Out" means to direct that Defendants not disclose Nonpublic Personal Information about that consumer to a nonaffiliated third party, except for Excepted Disclosures.

Q. "Personally Identifiable Financial Information" means any information:

1.   That a consumer provides to Defendants to obtain a Financial Service from Defendants;

2.   About a consumer resulting from any transaction involving a Financial Service between Defendants and the consumer; or

3.   That Defendants otherwise obtain about a consumer in connection with providing a Financial Service to that consumer.

R. "Privacy Notice" means a Clear and Conspicuous notice that accurately reflects the defendant's privacy policies and practices and that Defendants provide to a consumer not later than upon entering into a Customer Relationship with the consumer or, in any event, before disclosing any Nonpublic Personal Information about the consumer to any nonaffiliated third party unless the disclosure is an Excepted Disclosure. Such notice shall include, at a minimum,

1. The categories of Nonpublic Personal Information that Defendants collect;

2. The categories of Nonpublic Personal Information that Defendants disclose;

3.   The categories of affiliates and nonaffiliated third parties to whom Defendants disclose Nonpublic Personal Information, other than parties to whom Defendants make Excepted Disclosures;

4.   The categories of Nonpublic Personal Information about Defendants' former customers that Defendants disclose and the categories of affiliates and nonaffiliated third parties to whom Defendants disclose Nonpublic Personal Information about former customers, other than those parties to whom Defendants make only Excepted Disclosures;

5. A separate statement of the categories of information Defendants disclose to Service Providers and the categories of Service Providers with whom Defendants have contracted;

6. An explanation of the consumer's right to opt out of the disclosure of Nonpublic Personal Information to nonaffiliated third parties, including the method(s) by which the consumer may exercise that right at that time and any disclosures to which the right does not apply; and

7. Defendants' policies and practices with respect to protecting the confidentiality and security of Nonpublic Personal Information.

S. "Service Provider" means a nonaffiliated third party to which Defendants disclose Nonpublic Personal Information so that the third party can perform services for Defendants or functions on Defendants' behalf, and with whom Defendants have entered into a contractual agreement that prohibits the third party from disclosing or using the information other than to carry out the purposes for which Defendants disclosed the information, including for a use that would qualify the disclosure as an Excepted Disclosure in the ordinary course of business.

ORDER

I. PROHIBITION AGAINST MISREPRESENTING PRIVACY PRACTICES

IT IS ORDERED that Defendants, Defendants' officers, agents, employees, and attorneys, and all other persons in active concert or participation with any of them, who receive actual notice of this Order, whether acting directly or indirectly, in connection with promoting or offering for sale any good or service, are permanently restrained and enjoined from misrepresenting, expressly or by implication, Defendants' privacy and data security practices, including whether, how, and for what purposes Defendants collect, use, transfer, and/or disclose personal information about consumers.

II. INJUNCTION CONCERNING USING OR OBTAINING CONSUMER REPORTS

IT IS FURTHER ORDERED that Defendants and Defendants' officers, agents, employees, and attorneys, and all other persons in active concert or participation with any of them, who receive actual notice of this Order, whether acting directly or indirectly, in connection with the sale of any good or service, are hereby permanently restrained and enjoined from using or obtaining a Consumer Report for any purpose other than For a Permissible Purpose.

III. INJUNCTION CONCERNING THE PROVISION OF PRIVACY NOTICES

IT IS FURTHER ORDERED that Defendants and Defendants' officers, agents, employees, and attorneys, and all other persons in active concert or participation with any of them, who receive actual notice of this Order, whether acting directly or indirectly, in connection with Defendants' provision of any Financial Service are hereby permanently restrained and enjoined from failing to provide a Privacy Notice to each consumer with whom Defendants form a Customer Relationship or about whom Defendants make a disclosure of Nonpublic Personal Information, other than an Excepted Disclosure, to a nonaffiliated third party.

IV. PROHIBITION AGAINST IMPROPER DISCLOSURE OF NONPUBLIC PERSONAL INFORMATION

IT IS FURTHER ORDERED that Defendants, Defendants' officers, agents, employees, and attorneys, and all other persons in active concert or participation with any of them, who receive actual notice of this Order, whether acting directly or indirectly, in connection with Defendants' provision of any Financial Service, are permanently restrained and enjoined from disclosing to any nonaffiliated third party any Nonpublic Personal Information about a consumer unless

A. The disclosure is to a Service Provider or is an Excepted Disclosure; or

B. Defendants have:

1. Clearly and Conspicuously disclosed to the consumer, separate and apart from any "privacy policy," "data use policy," "statement of rights and responsibilities" page, or other similar document, including any notice provided pursuant to Provision III of this order: (1) the categories of nonpublic personal information that will be disclosed to such third parties and (2) the identity or specific categories of such third parties; and 2. Obtained the relevant consumer's affirmative express consent.

V. MANDATED INFORMATION SECURITY PROGRAM

IT IS FURTHER ORDERED that each Covered Business shall not transfer, sell, share, collect, maintain, or store Nonpublic Personal Information unless the Covered Business establishes and implements, and thereafter maintains, a comprehensive Information Security Program that protects the security, confidentiality, and integrity of such Nonpublic Personal Information. To satisfy this requirement, each Covered Business must, at a minimum:

A. Document in writing the content, implementation, and maintenance of the Information Security Program;

B. Provide the written program and any evaluations thereof or updates thereto to a senior officer responsible for its Information Security Program at least once every twelve (12) months and promptly after a Covered Incident;

C. Designate a qualified employee or employees to coordinate and be responsible for the Information Security Program;

D. Assess and document, at least once every twelve (12) months and promptly following a Covered Incident, internal and external risks to the security, confidentiality, or integrity of Personal Information that could result in the unauthorized disclosure, misuse, loss, theft, alteration, destruction, or other compromise of such information;

E. Design, implement, maintain, and document safeguards that control the internal and external risks to the security, confidentiality, or integrity of Nonpublic Personal Information identified in response to sub-Provision VI.D. Each safeguard shall be based on the volume and sensitivity of the Personal Information that is at risk, and the likelihood that the risk could be realized and result in the unauthorized access, collection, use, alteration, destruction, or disclosure of the Personal Information.

F. Assess, at least once every twelve (12) months and promptly following a Covered Incident, the sufficiency of any safeguards in place to address the risks to the security, confidentiality, or integrity of Nonpublic Personal Information, and modify the Information Security Program based on the results;

G. Test and monitor the effectiveness of the safeguards at least once every twelve (12) months and promptly following a Covered Incident, and modify the Information Security Program based on the results;

H. Select and retain service providers capable of safeguarding Nonpublic Personal Information they access through or receive from each Covered Business, and contractually require service providers to implement and maintain safeguards for Personal Information; and

I. Evaluate and adjust the Information Security Program in light of any changes to its operations or business arrangements, a Covered Incident, or any other circumstances that Defendants know or have reason to know may have an impact on the effectiveness of the Information Security Program. At a minimum, each Covered Business must evaluate the Information Security Program at least once every twelve (12) months and modify the Information Security Program based on the results.

VI. INFORMATION SECURITY ASSESSMENTS BY A THIRD PARTY

IT IS FURTHER ORDERED that, in connection with compliance with Provision VI of this Order titled Mandated Information Security Program, Defendants must obtain, for each Covered Business, initial and biennial assessments ("Assessments"):

A. The Assessments must be obtained from a qualified, objective, independent third-party professional ("Assessor"), who: (1) uses procedures and standards generally accepted in the profession; (2) conducts an independent review of the Information Security Program; and (3) retains all documents relevant to each Assessment for five (5) years after completion of such Assessment and will provide such documents to the Commission within ten (10) days of receipt of a written request from a representative of the Commission. No documents may be withheld on the basis of a claim of confidentiality, proprietary or trade secrets, work product protection, attorney client privilege, statutory exemption, or any similar claim.

B. For each Assessment, Defendants shall provide the Associate Director for Enforcement for the Bureau of Consumer Protection at the Federal Trade Commission with the name and affiliation of the person selected to conduct the Assessment, which the Associate Director shall have the authority to approve in his sole discretion.

C. The reporting period for the Assessments must cover: (1) the first 180 days after the issuance date of the Order for the initial Assessment; and (2) each 2-year period thereafter for ten (10) years after issuance of the Order for the biennial Assessments.

D. Each Assessment must: (1) determine whether each Covered Business has implemented and maintained the Information Security Program required by Provision VI of this Order, titled Mandated Information Security Program; (2) assess the effectiveness of each Covered Business's implementation and maintenance of sub-Provisions VI.A-I; (3) identify any gaps or weaknesses in the Information Security Program; and (4) identify specific evidence (including, but not limited to documents reviewed, sampling and testing performed, and interviews conducted) examined to make such determinations, assessments, and identifications, and explain why the evidence that the Assessor examined is sufficient to justify the Assessor's findings. No finding of any Assessment shall rely solely on assertions or attestations by a Covered Business's management. The Assessment shall be signed by the Assessor and shall state that the Assessor conducted an independent review of the Information Security Program, and did not rely solely on assertions or attestations by a Covered Business's management.

E. Each Assessment must be completed within sixty (60) days after the end of the reporting period to which the Assessment applies. Unless otherwise directed by a Commission representative in writing, Defendants must submit each Assessment to the Commission within ten (10) days after the Assessment has been completed via email. . .

VII. COOPERATION WITH THIRD PARTY INFORMATION SECURITY ASSESSOR

IT IS FURTHER ORDERED that Defendants, whether acting directly or indirectly, in connection with any Assessment required by Provision VII of this Order titled Information Security Assessments by a Third Party, must:

A. Disclose all material facts to the Assessor, and must not misrepresent in any manner, expressly or by implication, any fact material to the Assessor's: (1) determination of whether Defendants have implemented and maintained the Information Security Program required by Provision VI of this Order, titled Mandated Information Security Program; (2) assessment of the effectiveness of the implementation and maintenance of sub-Provisions VI.A-I; or (3) identification of any gaps or weaknesses in the Information Security Program; and

B. Provide or otherwise make available to the Assessor all information and material in their possession, custody, or control that is relevant to the Assessment for which there is no reasonable claim of privilege.

VIII. ANNUAL CERTIFICATION

IT IS FURTHER ORDERED that, in connection with compliance with Provision VI of this Order titled Mandated Information Security Program, Defendants shall:

A. One year after the issuance date of this Order, and each year thereafter, provide the Commission with a certification from a senior corporate manager, or, if no such senior corporate manager exists, a senior officer of each Covered Business responsible for each Covered Business's Information Security Program that: (1) each Covered Business has established, implemented, and maintained the requirements of this Order; (2) each Covered Business is not aware of any material noncompliance that has not been (a) corrected or (b) disclosed to the Commission; and (3) includes a brief description of any Covered Incident. The certification must be based on the personal knowledge of the senior corporate manager, senior officer, or subject matter experts upon whom the senior corporate manager or senior officer reasonably relies in making the certification. . . .

IX. COVERED INCIDENT REPORTS

IT IS FURTHER ORDERED that Defendants, for any Covered Business, within a reasonable time after the date of discovery of a Covered Incident, but in any event no later than ten (10) days after the date the Covered Business first notifies any U.S. federal, state, or local government entity of the Covered Incident, must submit a report to the Commission. The report must include, to the extent possible:

A. The date, estimated date, or estimated date range when the Covered Incident occurred;

B. A description of the facts relating to the Covered Incident, including the causes of the

Covered Incident, if known;

C. A description of each type of information that triggered the notification obligation to the U.S. federal, state, or local government entity;

D. The number of consumers whose information triggered the notification obligation to the U.S. federal, state, or local government entity;

E. The acts that the Covered Business has taken to date to remediate the Covered Incident and protect Personal Information from further exposure or access, and protect affected individuals from identity theft or other harm that may result from the Covered Incident; . . .

X. MONETARY JUDGMENT FOR CIVIL PENALTY

IT IS FURTHER ORDERED that:

A. Judgment in the amount of one hundred and twenty thousand dollars ($120,000) is entered in favor of Plaintiff against Individual Defendant and Corporate Defendant, jointly and severally, as a civil penalty.

B. Defendants are ordered to pay to Plaintiff, by making payment to the Treasurer of the United States, one hundred and twenty thousand dollars ($120,000), which, as Defendants stipulate, their undersigned counsel holds in escrow for no purpose other than payment to Plaintiff. Such payment must be made within 7 days of entry of this Order by electronic fund transfer in accordance with instructions previously provided by a representative of Plaintiff. . . .

XIII. COMPLIANCE REPORTING

IT IS FURTHER ORDERED that Defendants make timely submissions to the Commission: One year after entry of this Order, each Defendant must submit a compliance report, worn under penalty of perjury:

1. Each Defendant must: (a) identify the primary physical, postal, and email address and telephone number, as designated points of contact, which representatives of the Commission and Plaintiff may use to communicate with Defendant; (b) identify all of that Defendant's businesses by all of their names, telephone numbers, and physical, postal, email, and Internet addresses; (c) describe the activities of each business, including the goods and services offered, and the involvement of any other Defendant (which Individual Defendants must describe if they know or should know due to their own involvement); (d) describe in detail whether and how that Defendant is in compliance with each Section of this Order; and (e)provide a copy of each Order Acknowledgment obtained pursuant to this Order, unless previously submitted to the Commission. . . .[150]

QUESTIONS

1) The order states that the safeguards should be based on the volume and sensitivity of data. Should volume matter?

2) The civil penalty assessed is $120,000. What is more costly to the company, the civil penalty or the years of ongoing compliance audits and mandatory reporting?

---

[150] Stipulated Order for Permanent Injunction, Civil Penalties, and Other Relief at 1–3, 5–7, 10–20, 22, 23, United States v. Mortgage Solutions FCS, Inc., No. 4:20-cv-00110 (2020).

3) Do you think this order complies with the requirements set forth in the Eleventh Circuit's LabMD opinion?

NOTES

Note 1

> In the Privacy and Data Security Update 2019, the FTC noted:
>
> The Gramm-Leach-Bliley (GLB) Act requires financial institutions to send customers initial and annual privacy notices and allow them to opt out of sharing their information with unaffiliated third parties. It also requires financial institutions to implement reasonable security policies and procedures. Since 2005, the FTC has brought about 35 cases alleging violations of the GLB Act and its implementing regulations. In 2019, the FTC brought the following cases:
>
> In the Equifax case, . . . the FTC alleged that the credit reporting agency violated the GLB Safeguards Rule. Specifically, the complaint alleged that Equifax failed to design and implement safeguards to address foreseeable internal and external risks to the security, confidentiality, and integrity of customer information; regularly test or monitor the effectiveness of the safeguards; and evaluate and adjust its information security program in light of the results of testing and monitoring, and other relevant circumstances. . . .[151]

Note 2

> The Federal Trade Commission discussed the lessons learned from the TaxSlayer matter:
>
> Under the Gramm-Leach-Bliley Act, "financial institutions" – more on what that means in a moment – must comply with the Privacy Rule and the Safeguards Rule. The Privacy Rule requires covered companies to provide notices to consumers that explain their privacy policies and practices. (The Privacy Rule has been around since 2001. In the wake of the Dodd-Frank Act, the Consumer Financial Protection Bureau became responsible for implementing the Rule. In 2014 the CFPB puts its version in place, called Reg P.)
>
> The Safeguards Rule mandates that financial institutions protect the security, confidentiality, and integrity of customer information by implementing and maintaining a comprehensive written information security program. A cut-and-paste job won't do. The program has to include administrative, technical, and physical safeguards appropriate to

---

[151] *Privacy and Data Security Update 2019*, FEDERAL TRADE COMMISSION (2019), *available at* https://www.ftc.gov/system/files/documents/reports/privacy-data-security-update-2019/2019-privacy-data-security-report-508.pdf.

the business' size, the nature and scope of its activities, and the sensitivity of the customer information at issue. For example, companies have to conduct an assessment of how customers' information could be at risk and then implement safeguards to address those risks.

Now back to what the FTC says TaxSlayer did – and didn't do – that violated the Rules. TaxSlayer offers consumers tax preparation and filing services that are both web-based and available through the company's app. Of course, to file a tax return, consumers have to input . . . [their] Social Security number, phone number, address, income, marital status, spouse, kids, debts, health insurance, bank names, account numbers, etc.

For a two-month period in 2015, TaxSlayer was subject to a list validation attack, which allowed remote attackers to access the accounts for about 8,800 TaxSlayer users. (A list validation attack, also known as credential stuffing, is where hackers steal login credentials from one site and then – banking on the fact that some consumers use the same password on multiple sites – use them to access accounts on other popular sites.) In an unknown number of cases, criminals used the data to commit tax identity theft. They filed fake returns with altered routing numbers and pocketed refunds they weren't owed. And what a mess that left for victimized consumers. Long delays in getting their rightful refunds, freezes or holds on their credit, and endless hours trying to unscramble the ID theft egg.

In the proposed complaint, the FTC alleges that TaxSlayer violated the Privacy Rule and Reg P by failing to give customers the privacy notices they were due. What's more, TaxSlayer violated the Safeguards Rule by failing to have a written information security program, failing to conduct the necessary risk assessment, and failing to put safeguards in place to control those risks – specifically, the risk that remote attackers would use stolen credentials to take over consumers' TaxSlayer accounts and commit tax identity theft.

Tracking the settlements in several other GLB cases, TaxSlayer must comply with the rules and will be subject to every-other-year independent assessments for the next decade. You can file a comment about the proposed settlement by September 29, 2017.

What does the TaxSlayer case mean for other companies?

1. **You or your clients may be covered by GLB and not even know it**. GLB's definition of "financial institution" is broader than a lot of businesses think. Sure, it covers companies with vaults, tellers, and chained ballpoint pens that rarely work. But if you have clients in the tax planning or tax prep business, chances are they're covered by the Gramm-Leach-Bliley Act, too. What steps have you taken to help them comply?

2. **Deliver your privacy notices**. Reg P requires that you deliver your privacy notice in a way that consumers are reasonably expected to actually receive it. A link to your privacy policy on your home page is

insufficient. There's a model notice that identifies the information you're required to provide.

3. **Use appropriate authentication procedures.** The Safeguards Rule includes concrete guidance about crafting your information security program and the FTC's complaint outlines instances where TaxSlayer's authentication practices allegedly fell short. According to the FTC, the credential stuffing attack on TaxSlayer ended when the company implemented multi-factor authentication – requiring users to type in their usernames and passwords and then to authenticate their device by entering a code the company sent to their email or phone. Have your clients considered the security advantages of multi-factor authentication?

4. **The Safeguards Rule doesn't build in any laurel-resting time.** Once covered companies have a written information security program in place, the Safeguards Rule includes ongoing obligations. For example, companies must evaluate and adjust their programs in light of changes to their business operations, the results of monitoring or testing, and other relevant factors. Your company or your clients may have put safeguards in place back in 2003 when GLB was the new kid on the block. But what have they done recently to keep their program current?"[152]

3.6 Private Cause of Action Using GLBA and Safeguards Rule

In the following case, a district court held that the GLBA and Safeguards Rule did not provide a private cause of action.

Thymes v. Gillman Companies, 2018 WL 1281852 (S.D. Tex. 2018).

SIM LAKE, UNITED STATES DISTRICT JUDGE

Pending before the court is Defendant's Motion to Dismiss Under Rules of Civil Procedure 12(b)(6) and 9(b). . . .

Plaintiff brings five causes of action: (1) violations of the Federal Trade Commission ("FTC") Safeguard Rule and the Gramm–Leach–Bliley Act ("GLBA"); . . . (3) disclosure of private consumer financial information in violation of the GLBA. . . . Defendant moves to dismiss all causes of action.

A. Causes of Action (1) and (3)

Having considered the arguments and authorities cited by the parties the court concludes that the Plaintiff has no cause of action under the GLBA, 15 U.S.C. § 68 01 et

---

[152] Lesley Fair, *4 Gramm-Leach-Bliley tips to take from FTC's TaxSlayer case*, FEDERAL TRADE COMMISSION BLOG (Aug. 29, 2017, 12:21 PM), https://www.ftc.gov/news-events/blogs/business-blog/2017/08/4-gramm-leach-bliley-tips-take-ftcs-taxslayer-case.

seq or under the FTC Safeguard Rule, 16 C.F.R. § 314.1 et seq. Neither the GLBA nor the FTC Safeguards Rule authorizes a private cause of action. Section 6805(a) of the GLBA provides an express enforcement mechanism that states:

> this subchapter and the regulations prescribed thereunder shall be enforced by the Bureau of Consumer Financial Protection, the Federal functional regulators, the State insurance authorities, and the Federal Trade Commission with respect to financial institutions and other persons subject to their jurisdiction under applicable law ...

15 U.S.C. § 6805(a). Section 314.1 of the FTC Safeguard Rule states that it "implements Sections [6801] and [6805(b)(2)] of the Gramm–Leach–Bliley Act." 16 C.F.R. § 314.1(a). Courts in the Northern District of Texas have held that the "GLBA does not create a private right of action." Hall v. Phenix Investigations, Inc., Civil Action No. 3:14–0665–D, 2014 WL 5697856, at *9 (N.D. Tex. Nov. 5, 2014). The court in Hall explained that "[c]onsidering that Congress expressly provided for administrative and criminal enforcement of GLBA, 'it is highly improbable that Congress absentmindedly forgot to mention an intended private action.' " Hall, 2014 WL 5697856 at *9. Based on the plain readings of the statute and the regulation, the court agrees with the holding[] of Hall . . . that the GLBA does not provide a private right of action.

Because the FTC Safeguards Rule implements the enforcement provision of the GLBA, and because the GLBA does not provide a private cause of action, the court concludes that the FTC Safeguards Rule does not provide a private cause of action. Therefore Plaintiff's claims under the GLBA and the FTC Safeguard Rule, causes of action number (1) and number (3), will be dismissed.

QUESTIONS

1) Should there be a private cause of action under the Safeguards Rule?

2) Would a private cause of action be manageable in the courts?

In the following case, the district court held that while the GLBA could not serve as the basis of a negligence per se claim, the Safeguards Rule could serve as the basis of such a claim in the data breach context.

In re Equifax Customer Data Security Breach Litigation, 371 F.Supp.3d 1150 (N.D. Ga. 2019).

THOMAS W. THRASH, JR. United States District Judge

This is a data breach case. It is before the Court on the Defendants' Motion to Dismiss the Financial Institutions' Consolidated Amended Complaint. For the reasons set forth below, the Defendants' Motion to Dismiss the Financial Institutions' Consolidated Amended Complaint [Doc. 435] is GRANTED in part and DENIED in part.

I. Background

On September 7, 2017, the Defendant Equifax Inc. announced that it was the subject of one of the largest data breaches in history. From mid-May through the end of July 2017, hackers stole the personal information of nearly 150 million Americans (the

"Data Breach"). This personally identifiable information included names, Social Security numbers, birth dates, addresses, driver's license numbers, images of taxpayer ID cards and passports, photographs associated with government-issued identification, payment card information, and more. This Data Breach, according to the Plaintiffs, was the direct result of Equifax's disregard for cybersecurity.

. . . Equifax Information Services collects and reports consumer information to financial institutions, including the Plaintiffs. The Plaintiffs are financial institutions that provide a range of financial services. The Plaintiffs depend greatly on the services provided by Equifax and other credit reporting agencies, since the information they provide is necessary to determine the credit-worthiness of their customers.

According to the Plaintiffs, the Data Breach was the direct result of Equifax's refusal to take the necessary steps to protect the personally identifiable information in its custody. Equifax was warned on numerous occasions that its cybersecurity was dangerously deficient, and that it was vulnerable to data theft and security breaches. In fact, Equifax had suffered multiple security breaches in the past, showing that the Data Breach was not an isolated incident. However, despite these warnings, Equifax did not take the necessary steps to improve its data security or prepare for the known cybersecurity risks.

On March 7, 2017, a vulnerability in the Apache Struts software, a popular open source software program, was discovered. Equifax used Apache Struts to run a dispute portal website. The same day that this vulnerability was announced, the Apache Foundation made available various patches to protect against this vulnerability. The Apache Foundation, along with the U.S. Department of Homeland Security, issued public warnings regarding the vulnerability and the need to implement these patches. Equifax received these warnings and disseminated them internally, but failed to implement the patch. Then, between May 13 and July 30, 2017, hackers exploited this vulnerability to enter Equifax's systems. These hackers were able to access multiple databases and exfiltrate sensitive personal information in Equifax's custody. In addition to obtaining this personal information, the hackers accessed 209,000 consumer credit card numbers. On July 29, 2017, Equifax discovered the Data Breach. Equifax's CEO, Richard Smith, was informed of the breach on July 31, 2017. On September 7, 2017, Equifax publicly announced that the Data Breach had occurred.

The Plaintiffs allege that the Data Breach undermined the credit reporting and verification system by exposing this personally identifiable information. According to the Plaintiffs, they were harmed because the Data Breach had a significant impact on financial institutions, including the measures they use to authenticate their customers. The Plaintiffs were forced to expend resources to assess the impact of the Data Breach and their ability to authenticate customers and detect fraud. They have also expended resources establishing new monitoring methods for preventing fraud and will continue to incur costs to develop new modes of preventing such activity. Twenty-three of the Plaintiffs also allege that they issued payment cards that were compromised in the Data Breach. The Plaintiffs assert claims for negligence, negligence per se, negligent misrepresentation, and claims under various state business practices statutes. The Defendants now move to dismiss.

. . .

D. Negligence Per Se

Next, the Defendants move to dismiss the Plaintiffs' negligence per se claim. In Count 2 of the Complaint, the Plaintiffs allege that Equifax violated the Gramm-Leach-Bliley Act, Section 5 of the FTC Act, and similar state statutes, by maintaining security programs and safeguards that "were not appropriate to Equifax's size and complexity" and by "mishandling consumer data and not using reasonable measures to protect PII and by not complying with applicable industry standards." "Georgia law allows the adoption of a statute or regulation as a standard of conduct so that its violation becomes negligence per se." In order to make a negligence per se claim, however, the plaintiff must show that it is within the class of persons intended to be protected by the statute and that the statute was meant to protect against the harm suffered.

1. GLBA

The Defendants first argue that the Gramm-Leach-Bliley Act (the "GLBA") and its implementing regulations cannot provide a basis for a negligence per se claim. The GLBA provides, in part, that "[i]t is the policy of the Congress that each financial institution has an affirmative and continuing obligation to respect the privacy of its customers and to protect the security and confidentiality of those customers' nonpublic personal information." In *Wells Fargo Bank, N.A. v. Jenkins*, the Georgia Supreme Court concluded that the GLBA could not form the basis of a negligence claim. The court noted that the GLBA "certainly ... expresses the goal that financial institutions respect the privacy, security, and confidentiality of customers." However, it explained that "[w]hile this is a clear Congressional policy statement, it is just that. It does not provide for certain duties or the performance of or refraining from any specific acts on the part of financial institutions, nor does it articulate or imply a standard of conduct or care, ordinary or otherwise." "Congress did not see fit to impose such a duty under 15 U.S.C. § 6801(a) ...."

This Court agrees. The GLBA does not provide a specific standard of conduct that is sufficient to give rise to a legal duty under Georgia law. The cases that the Plaintiffs rely upon do not support an argument to the contrary. In most of those cases, the issue of whether the GLBA imposes a legal duty of care was not at issue, or they contain no discussion of the standard of conduct that the GLBA actually imposes. Thus, the Court concludes that the Plaintiffs' negligence per se claims must be dismissed to the extent that they are predicated upon the GLBA.

However, the Plaintiffs also allege that the Defendants breached a statutory duty owed under the regulations implementing the GLBA. The Plaintiffs argue that the failure to maintain reasonable data security measures to protect consumer information violates the Safeguards Rule, which constitutes a violation of the GLBA. The Safeguards Rule, 16 C.F.R. § 314, implements the GLBA by setting forth "standards for developing, implementing, and maintaining reasonable administrative, technical, and physical safeguards to protect the security, confidentiality, and integrity of customer information." The Defendants contend that the Safeguards Rule, like the GLBA itself, cannot serve as the basis for a statutory duty because it merely provides general requirements for data security, and does not provide an ascertainable standard of conduct. In *Jenkins*, the Georgia Supreme Court, in rejecting a statutory duty under the GLBA, noted that "[t]here is no finding by the Court of Appeals of a violation of any regulation, directive, or standard authorized by 15 U.S.C. § 6801(b), to support Jenkins's claim of the Bank's negligence." It noted that "Jenkins points to certain provisions of the Code of Federal Regulations in support of the finding of a duty under 15 U.S.C. § 6801(a), specifically 16 C.F.R. § 314.1; however, the regulation was not part of the Court of Appeals analysis or its finding of duty under the GLBA. Furthermore, 16 C.F.R. § 314.1(a) expressly implements only sections 501 and 505(b)(2) of the GLBA and applies to those financial institutions over which the Federal Trade Commission has jurisdiction."

However, unlike the GLBA itself, the Court concludes that the Safeguards Rule provides an ascertainable standard of conduct permitting it to serve as the basis for a negligence per se claim. In *Jenkins*, the Georgia Supreme Court rejected such a claim under the GLBA because it did "not provide for certain duties or the performance of or refraining from any specific acts on the part of financial institutions, nor does it articulate or imply a standard of conduct or care, ordinary or otherwise." In contrast to the GLBA, the Safeguards Rule provides for certain duties that financial institutions must perform, and provides an ascertainable standard of conduct. For example, it provides that financial institutions should "[d]esignate an employee or employees to coordinate your information security program." It further requires these institutions to "[i]dentify reasonably foreseeable internal and external risks to the security, confidentiality, and integrity of customer information that could result in the unauthorized disclosure, misuse, alteration, destruction or other compromise of such information, and assess the sufficiency of any safeguards in place to control these risks." It explains that such a risk assessment should include consideration of "[e]mployee training and management," "[i]nformation systems, including network and software design, as well as information processing, storage, transmission and disposal," and "[d]etecting, preventing and responding to attacks, intrusions, or other systems failures." The Court finds that these provisions go beyond a mere policy statement and provide a specific standard of conduct.

The Defendants then contend that the Plaintiffs do not provide any allegations that the Defendants breached this standard of conduct. However, the Court concludes that the Plaintiffs' allegations are sufficient. The Plaintiffs allege that the Defendants breached their duty under the Safeguards Rule because their data security systems "were not adequate to: identify reasonably foreseeable internal and external risks, assess the sufficiency of safeguards in place to control for these risks, or to detect, prevent, or respond to a data breach." They further allege that "Equifax's security program and safeguards were inadequate to evaluate and adjust to events that would have a material impact on Equifax's information security program, such as the numerous prior data breaches that other retailers and Equifax itself had experienced and the notification to Equifax that an identified vulnerability in a software program it utilized would make Equifax particularly susceptible to a data breach." These allegations are sufficient to avoid dismissal.

NOTES

Note 1

In *USAA Federal Savings Bank v. PLS Financial Services*, 340 F.Supp.3d 721 (N.D. Ill. 2018), at least one district court has held that the Safeguards regulations under the Gramm Leach Bliley Act cannot serve as the basis of a negligence action. The district court stated:

> This does not mean, as USAA argues, that PLS had no duty to safeguard personal information and is "invulnerable to these laws." *See* Doc. 103 at 1, 9. It only means that USAA cannot enforce violations of these rules, with enforcement left instead to state and federal regulators. . . . Because the GLBA, the Privacy Rule, and the Safeguards Rule do not allow for a private right of action, following *Martin*, USAA's negligence claim based on these rules fails. *Id.*

Which court decision do you think is better supported by policy? Are the important policies encapsulated in GLB and the Safeguards Rule best protected by federal enforcement, private action or both?

3.7 The New York Department of Financial Services

As noted above, The New York Department of Financial Services has issued Cybersecurity Regulations. The Cybersecurity Regulations state, in part:

Section 500.02 Cybersecurity Program.

(a) Cybersecurity Program. Each Covered Entity shall maintain a cybersecurity program designed to protect the confidentiality, integrity and availability of the Covered Entity's Information Systems.

(b) The cybersecurity program shall be based on the Covered Entity's Risk Assessment and designed to perform the following core cybersecurity functions:

(1) identify and assess internal and external cybersecurity risks that may threaten the security or integrity of Nonpublic Information stored on the Covered Entity's Information Systems;

(2) use defensive infrastructure and the implementation of policies and procedures to protect the Covered Entity's Information Systems, and the Nonpublic Information stored on those Information Systems, from unauthorized access, use or other malicious acts;

(3) detect Cybersecurity Events;

(4) respond to identified or detected Cybersecurity Events to mitigate any negative effects;

(5) recover from Cybersecurity Events and restore normal operations and services; and

(6) fulfill applicable regulatory reporting obligations.

(c) A Covered Entity may meet the requirement(s) of this Part by adopting the relevant and applicable provisions of a cybersecurity program maintained by an Affiliate, provided that such provisions satisfy the requirements of this Part, as applicable to the Covered Entity.

(d) All documentation and information relevant to the Covered Entity's cybersecurity program shall be made available to the superintendent upon request.

Section 500.03 Cybersecurity Policy.

Cybersecurity Policy. Each Covered Entity shall implement and maintain a written policy or policies, approved by a Senior Officer or the Covered Entity's board of directors (or an appropriate committee thereof) or equivalent governing body, setting forth the Covered Entity's policies and procedures for the protection of its Information Systems and Nonpublic Information stored on those Information Systems. The cybersecurity policy shall be based on the Covered Entity's Risk Assessment and address the following areas to the extent applicable to the Covered Entity's operations:

(a) information security;

(b) data governance and classification;

(c) asset inventory and device management;

(d) access controls and identity management;

(e) business continuity and disaster recovery planning and resources;

(f) systems operations and availability concerns;

(g) systems and network security;

(h) systems and network monitoring;

(i) systems and application development and quality assurance;

(j) physical security and environmental controls;

(k) customer data privacy;

(l) vendor and Third Party Service Provider management;

(m) risk assessment; and

(n) incident response.

Section 500.05 Penetration Testing and Vulnerability Assessments.

The cybersecurity program for each Covered Entity shall include monitoring and testing, developed in accordance with the Covered Entity's Risk Assessment, designed to assess the effectiveness of the

Covered Entity's cybersecurity program. The monitoring and testing shall include continuous monitoring or periodic Penetration Testing and vulnerability assessments. Absent effective continuous monitoring, or other systems to detect, on an ongoing basis, changes in Information Systems that may create or indicate vulnerabilities, Covered Entities shall conduct:

(a) annual Penetration Testing of the Covered Entity's Information Systems determined each given year based on relevant identified risks in accordance with the Risk Assessment; and

(b) bi-annual vulnerability assessments, including any systematic scans or reviews of Information Systems reasonably designed to identify publicly known cybersecurity vulnerabilities in the Covered Entity's Information Systems based on the Risk Assessment.

Section 500.06 Audit Trail.

(a) Each Covered Entity shall securely maintain systems that, to the extent applicable and based on its Risk Assessment:

(1) are designed to reconstruct material financial transactions sufficient to support normal operations and obligations of the Covered Entity; and

(2) include audit trails designed to detect and respond to Cybersecurity Events that have a reasonable likelihood of materially harming any material part of the normal operations of the Covered Entity.

(b) Each Covered Entity shall maintain records required by section 500.06(a)(1) of this Part for not fewer than five years and shall maintain records required by section 500.06(a)(2) of this Part for not fewer than three years.

Section 500.07 Access Privileges.

As part of its cybersecurity program, based on the Covered Entity's Risk Assessment each Covered Entity shall limit user access privileges to Information Systems that provide access to Nonpublic Information and shall periodically review such access privileges.

Section 500.08 Application Security.

(a) Each Covered Entity's cybersecurity program shall include written procedures, guidelines and standards designed to ensure the use of secure development practices for in-house developed applications utilized by the Covered Entity, and procedures for evaluating, assessing or testing the security of externally developed applications utilized by the Covered Entity within the context of the Covered Entity's technology environment.

(b) All such procedures, guidelines and standards shall be periodically reviewed, assessed and updated as necessary by the CISO (or a qualified designee) of the Covered Entity.

Section 500.09 Risk Assessment.

(a) Each Covered Entity shall conduct a periodic Risk Assessment of the Covered Entity's Information Systems sufficient to inform the design of the cybersecurity program as required by this Part. Such Risk Assessment shall be updated as reasonably necessary to address changes to the Covered Entity's Information Systems, Nonpublic Information or business operations. The Covered Entity's Risk Assessment shall allow for revision of controls to respond to technological developments and evolving threats and shall consider the particular risks of the Covered Entity's business operations related to cybersecurity, Nonpublic Information collected or stored, Information Systems utilized and the availability and effectiveness of controls to protect Nonpublic Information and Information Systems.

(b) The Risk Assessment shall be carried out in accordance with written policies and procedures and shall be documented. Such policies and procedures shall include:

(1) criteria for the evaluation and categorization of identified cybersecurity risks or threats facing the Covered Entity;

(2) criteria for the assessment of the confidentiality, integrity, security and availability of the Covered Entity's Information Systems and Nonpublic Information, including the adequacy of existing controls in the context of identified risks; and

(3) requirements describing how identified risks will be mitigated or accepted based on the Risk Assessment and how the cybersecurity program will address the risks.

Section 500.10 Cybersecurity Personnel and Intelligence.

(a) Cybersecurity Personnel and Intelligence. In addition to the requirements set forth in section 500.04(a) of this Part, each Covered Entity shall:

(1) utilize qualified cybersecurity personnel of the Covered Entity, an Affiliate or a Third Party Service Provider sufficient to manage the Covered Entity's cybersecurity risks and to perform or oversee the performance of the core cybersecurity functions specified in section 500.02(b)(1)-(6) of this Part;

(2) provide cybersecurity personnel with cybersecurity updates and training sufficient to address relevant cybersecurity risks; and

(3) verify that key cybersecurity personnel take steps to maintain current knowledge of changing cybersecurity threats and countermeasures.

(b) A Covered Entity may choose to utilize an Affiliate or qualified Third Party Service Provider to assist in complying with the requirements set forth in this Part, subject to the requirements set forth in section 500.11 of this Part.

Section 500.11 Third Party Service Provider Security Policy.

(a) Third Party Service Provider Policy. Each Covered Entity shall implement written policies and procedures designed to ensure the security of Information Systems and Nonpublic Information that are accessible to, or held by, Third Party Service Providers. Such policies and procedures shall be based on the Risk Assessment of the Covered Entity and shall address to the extent applicable:

(1) the identification and risk assessment of Third Party Service Providers;

(2) minimum cybersecurity practices required to be met by such Third Party Service Providers in order for them to do business with the Covered Entity;

(3) due diligence processes used to evaluate the adequacy of cybersecurity practices of such Third Party Service Providers; and

(4) periodic assessment of such Third Party Service Providers based on the risk they present and the continued adequacy of their cybersecurity practices.

(b) Such policies and procedures shall include relevant guidelines for due diligence and/or contractual protections relating to Third Party Service Providers including to the extent applicable guidelines addressing:

(1) the Third Party Service Provider's policies and procedures for access controls, including its use of Multi-Factor Authentication as required by section 500.12 of this Part, to limit access to relevant Information Systems and Nonpublic Information;

(2) the Third Party Service Provider's policies and procedures for use of encryption as required by section 500.15 of this Part to protect Nonpublic Information in transit and at rest;

(3) notice to be provided to the Covered Entity in the event of a Cybersecurity Event directly impacting the Covered Entity's Information Systems or the Covered Entity's Nonpublic Information being held by the Third Party Service Provider; and

(4) representations and warranties addressing the Third Party Service Provider's cybersecurity policies and procedures that relate to the security of the Covered Entity's Information Systems or Nonpublic Information.

(c) Limited Exception. An agent, employee, representative or designee of a Covered Entity who is itself a Covered Entity need not develop its own Third Party Information Security Policy pursuant to this section if the agent, employee, representative or designee follows the policy of the Covered Entity that is required to comply with this Part.

Section 500.12 Multi-Factor Authentication.

(a) Multi-Factor Authentication. Based on its Risk Assessment, each Covered Entity shall use effective controls, which may include Multi-Factor Authentication or Risk-Based Authentication, to protect against unauthorized access to Nonpublic Information or Information Systems.

(b) Multi-Factor Authentication shall be utilized for any individual accessing the Covered Entity's internal networks from an external network, unless the Covered Entity's CISO has approved in writing the use of reasonably equivalent or more secure access controls.

Section 500.13 Limitations on Data Retention.

As part of its cybersecurity program, each Covered Entity shall include policies and procedures for the secure disposal on a periodic basis of any Nonpublic Information identified in section 500.01(g)(2)-(3) of this Part that is no longer necessary for business operations or for other legitimate business purposes of the Covered Entity, except where such information is otherwise required to be retained by law or regulation, or where targeted disposal is not reasonably feasible due to the manner in which the information is maintained.

Section 500.14 Training and Monitoring.

As part of its cybersecurity program, each Covered Entity shall:

(a) implement risk-based policies, procedures and controls designed to monitor the activity of Authorized Users and detect unauthorized access or use of, or tampering with, Nonpublic Information by such Authorized Users; and

(b) provide regular cybersecurity awareness training for all personnel that is updated to reflect risks identified by the Covered Entity in its Risk Assessment.

Section 500.15 Encryption of Nonpublic Information.

(a) As part of its cybersecurity program, based on its Risk Assessment, each Covered Entity shall implement controls, including encryption, to protect Nonpublic Information held or transmitted by the Covered Entity both in transit over external networks and at rest.

(1) To the extent a Covered Entity determines that encryption of Nonpublic Information in transit over external networks is infeasible, the Covered Entity may instead secure such Nonpublic Information using effective alternative compensating controls reviewed and approved by the Covered Entity's CISO.

(2) To the extent a Covered Entity determines that encryption of Nonpublic Information at rest is infeasible, the Covered Entity may instead secure such Nonpublic Information using effective alternative compensating controls reviewed and approved by the Covered Entity's CISO.

(b) To the extent that a Covered Entity is utilizing compensating controls under (a) above, the feasibility of encryption and effectiveness of the compensating controls shall be reviewed by the CISO at least annually.

Section 500.16 Incident Response Plan.

(a) As part of its cybersecurity program, each Covered Entity shall establish a written incident response plan designed to promptly respond to, and recover from, any Cybersecurity Event materially affecting the confidentiality, integrity or availability of the Covered Entity's Information Systems or the continuing functionality of any aspect of the Covered Entity's business or operations.

(b) Such incident response plan shall address the following areas:

(1) the internal processes for responding to a Cybersecurity Event;

(2) the goals of the incident response plan;

(3) the definition of clear roles, responsibilities and levels of decision-making authority;

(4) external and internal communications and information sharing;

(5) identification of requirements for the remediation of any identified weaknesses in Information Systems and associated controls;

(6) documentation and reporting regarding Cybersecurity Events and related incident response activities;

and

(7) the evaluation and revision as necessary of the incident response plan following a Cybersecurity Event.

The New York Department of Financial Services brought its first enforcement action in July of 2020 against **First American Title Insurance**. The Statement of Charges and Notice of Hearing states, in relevant part:

OVERVIEW

1. For more than four years, First American Title Insurance Company ("First American" or "Respondent") exposed tens of millions of documents that contained consumers' sensitive personal information including bank account numbers and statements, mortgage and tax records, Social Security numbers, wire transaction receipts, and drivers' license images. . . .

THE ROLE AND JURISDICTION OF THE DEPARTMENT OF FINANCIAL SERVICES

6. The Department of Financial Services is the insurance regulator in the State of New York. The Superintendent of Financial Services is responsible for ensuring the safety and soundness of New York's insurance industry and promoting the reduction and elimination of fraud, abuse, and unethical conduct with respect to insurance participants.

7. The Superintendent has the authority to conduct investigations, bring enforcement proceedings, levy monetary penalties and order injunctive relief against parties who have violated the relevant laws and regulations.

8. Among her many obligations to the public is the Superintendent's consumer protection function, which includes the protection of individuals' private and personally sensitive data from careless, negligent, or willful exposure by licensees of the Department.

9. To support this critical obligation to consumers, the Superintendent's Cybersecurity Regulation places on all DFS-regulated entities ("Covered Entities"), including First American, an obligation to establish and maintain a cybersecurity program designed to protect the confidentiality, integrity, and availability of its Information Systems and its customers' Nonpublic Information, as defined in 23 NYCRR 500.01(e) and 500.01(g), respectively.

10. To that end, the DFS Cybersecurity Regulation require Covered Entities to implement and maintain cybersecurity policies and procedures to address, to the extent applicable, consumer data privacy and other consumer protection issues with effective controls, secure access privileges, thorough and routine cybersecurity risk assessments, comprehensive training and monitoring for all employees and other users, and well-grounded governance processes to ensure senior attention to these important protections.

11. Every Covered Entity is required to base its cybersecurity policies and procedures on risk assessments to ensure ongoing evaluation of the risks that continuously threaten the security of Nonpublic Information, including sensitive personal information, and to further safeguard the Information Systems that are accessed or held by Third Party Service Providers. Encryption and multifactor authentication are further controls required under the Cybersecurity Regulation to ensure that Covered Entities thoroughly protect their customers' private data.

12. Respondent, a Nebraska-based stock insurance company, is a licensee of the Superintendent authorized to write title insurance in New York. As such, Respondent is a "Covered Entity" under 23 NYCRR Section 500.01(c) and is therefore subject to the requirements of the Cybersecurity Regulation.

13. Nonpublic Information ("NPI") means all electronic information that is not publicly available and is: (1) Business-related information of a Covered Entity the tampering with which, or unauthorized disclosure, access or use of which, would cause a material adverse impact to the business, operations or security of the Covered Entity; (2) Any information concerning an individual which because of name, number, personal mark, or other identifier can be used to identify such individual, in combination with any one

or more of the following data elements: (i) social security number, (ii) drivers' license number or non-driver identification card number, (iii) account number, credit or debit card number, (iv) any security code, access code or password that would permit access to an individual's financial account, or (v) biometric records; and (3) Any information or data, except age or gender, in any form or medium created by or derived from a health care provider or an individual and that relates to (i) the past, present or future physical, mental or behavioral health or condition of any individual or a member of the individual's family, (ii) the provision of health care to any individual, or (iii) payment for the provision of health care to any individual.

14. Pursuant to Section 404 of the Financial Services Law, the Consumer Protection and Financial Enforcement Division of the Department investigated whether First American was complying with the Superintendent's Cybersecurity Regulation, 23 NYCRR Part 500, which requires that all Department-regulated entities, including First American, have a cybersecurity program that, among other things, protects customer NPI. After such investigation, the Department hereby commences an administrative proceeding alleging that First American has committed the violations described below.

FACTUAL ALLEGATIONS

Respondent's Business Activities

15. Title insurance policies insure the interests of owners or lenders against defects in the title to real property. These defects include adverse ownership claims, liens, encumbrances, or other matters affecting title. Respondent is the second largest title insurance provider in the United States. In 2019, its Title Insurance and Services segment accounted for 91.5% of Respondent's $6.2 billion in consolidated revenue.

16. When a customer seeks to purchase title insurance, Respondent collects personal information from multiple sources in connection with the insurance application. The customer submits NPI in the form of applications and settlement or financial statements. Others involved in the transaction on behalf of the title customer, such as the real estate agent, lender, escrow, or settlement agent and attorney, also submit documents containing sensitive customer information.

In performing the ensuing title search, Respondent obtains, from its own or others' proprietary databases, documents that may also contain personal information such as appraisals, credit reports, escrow account balances, and account numbers. Respondent might also collect documents from public records such as tax assessments and liens to include as part of a title insurance package (the "package" or "title package").

17. Therefore, in the regular course of its business, Respondent collects, stores, and transmits the personal information of millions of buyers and sellers of real estate in the U.S. each year. Respondent stores this information in its main document repository, the FAST image repository, also known as "FAST." Documents can be loaded into FAST by Respondent's employees assigned to any of Respondent's business units. Respondent uses documents stored in FAST to transact title insurance and settlement orders.

18. FAST includes tens of millions of documents with sensitive personal information, such as social security numbers, bank account and wiring information, and mortgage and tax records. In April 2018, for example, FAST contained 753 million documents, 65

million of which had been tagged by Respondent's employees as containing NPI. A random sampling of 1,000 documents that were not tagged showed that 30% of those documents also contained NPI. As of May 2019, FAST contained over 850 million documents.

19. Respondent also created and maintains an application on its network known as EaglePro. EaglePro is a web-based title document delivery system that allows title agents and other Respondent employees to share any document in FAST with outside parties. EaglePro is intended to be used by title agents and others to share the title package with the parties to a real estate transaction. After a party to or a participant in a transaction selects documents from FAST to be shared with another participant of a real estate transaction, EaglePro emails the recipient a link to a website that allows him or her to access those documents. Anyone who had the link or the URL for the website could access the package without login or authentication.

Respondent's Data Exposure

20. In October 2014, Respondent updated the EaglePro system in a manner that gave rise to the Vulnerability. The URL for each website shared via EaglePro included an ImageDocumentID number, and each document in FAST was assigned a sequentially numbered ImageDocumentID. By changing the ImageDocumentID number in the URL by one or more digits, anyone could view the document corresponding to the revised ImageDocumentID. As a result, by simply typing in any ImageDocumentID, any document in FAST could be accessed regardless of whether the viewer had authorized access to those documents. Until May 2019, the URLs shared via EaglePro had no expiration date.

21. In other words, more than 850 million documents were accessible to anyone with a URL address providing access to a single document in the EaglePro-generated website. The Vulnerability thus led to exposure of a staggering volume of personal and financially sensitive documents, any number of which could be used by fraudsters to engage in identity theft and even outright theft of assets. Moreover, such theft could occur without individuals knowing their information had been stolen from Respondent.

22. In December 2018, First American's Cyber Defense Team discovered the EaglePro Vulnerability during a penetration test of the EaglePro application. The Cyber Defense Team's role was to conduct penetration tests on Respondent's applications — tests that simulated a cyberattack — in order to identify vulnerabilities that could be exploited.

23. In an email on December 17, 2018, a member of the Cyber Defense Team alerted the EaglePro Application Development team to the existence of the EaglePro Vulnerability, reporting "recently discovered important findings during the reconnaissance phase of our current penetration test of the EaglePro application that should be addressed." The email went on to describe the Vulnerability. Recognizing the urgency of the situation, the manager of the Application Development team responsible for EaglePro replied that the Vulnerability should be "address[ed] as soon as possible."

24. On January 11, 2019, the Cyber Defense Team distributed the final report of the EaglePro penetration test. The report described the Vulnerability in detail, including pages of screenshots demonstrating how the EaglePro website URL could be manipulated to display sensitive documents not intended for widespread viewing. The

penetration test report also showed that more than 5,000 documents exposed by EaglePro had been subjected to Google search engine indexing, i.e., collection and storage of data by Google to facilitate later information retrieval in the course of open-source Google searches by the public. Among the key findings in the Cyber Defense Team's report was the following warning: "using standard Internet search methods we were able to bypass authentication to retrieve documents that were found using Google searches" (emphasis in the original). The Cyber Defense Team reviewed 10 documents exposed by the Vulnerability, and, although none contained NPI, the Cyber Defense Team strongly recommended that the application team investigate further and determine whether sensitive documents were exposed. Despite this clear warning, this recommendation was ignored, and Respondent failed to conduct follow-up investigation.

25. Even more alarming, in the six months following discovery of the Vulnerability, Respondent failed to correct the Vulnerability even though hundreds of millions of documents were exposed. This lapse was caused by a cascade of errors that occurred substantially due to flaws in Respondent's vulnerability remediation program. Some of these flaws are illustrated below:

a. Respondent grossly underestimated the level of risk associated with the Vulnerability. During interviews with the Department, several Respondent employees revealed that the Vulnerability was not addressed, in part, because the problem was erroneously classified as "medium severity." The "medium severity" classification, in turn, rested on the mistaken belief that EaglePro could not transmit NPI. Respondent's Chief Information Security Officer, the senior most employee responsible for the security of Respondent's Information Systems, testified that she believed that data accessible in EaglePro was publicly available, and therefore did not constitute NPI. However, anyone with the barest familiarity with EaglePro understood that the application could be used to distribute any documents contained in FAST, including documents of a highly sensitive nature that clearly constituted NPI. Nonetheless, this error was never corrected.

b. Respondent failed to follow its own cybersecurity policies. Respondent's policies required a security overview report for each application and a risk assessment for data stored or transmitted by any application. No security overview or risk assessment was performed for EaglePro.

c. Respondent conducted an unacceptably minimal review of exposed documents, and thereby failed to recognize the seriousness of the security lapse. The Cyber Defense Team reviewed only 10 documents out of the hundreds of millions of documents exposed. While conducting such a preposterously minimal review, the Cyber Defense Team found no NPI in the 10 documents reviewed and thus failed to recognize the seriousness of the situation. As a result, the team erroneously classified the Vulnerability as merely "medium severity."

d. Respondent failed to heed advice proffered by its own in-house cybersecurity experts. The Cyber Defense Team recommended that the EaglePro application team conduct further review to determine if sensitive documents were exposed by the Vulnerability. No such review was conducted. Moreover, the application team knew that EaglePro could distribute the highly sensitive documents warehoused in FAST but nonetheless conducted no further investigation of the Vulnerability.

e. An apparent administrative error compounded the delay in the timeframe for remediating the Vulnerability. The director of the Cyber Defense Team inadvertently caused additional delay in the remediation by accidently re-classifying the vulnerability from "medium" to "low" severity when it was entered into Respondent's vulnerability tracking system in January 2019. Classified as "low severity," Respondent's policy inaccurately allowed 90 days for the remediation of the Vulnerability.

f. Respondent failed to adhere to its internal policies, and delayed addressing the Vulnerability for six months. Even if Respondent had correctly classified the Vulnerability, which Respondent failed to do by deeming it "low severity," Respondent failed to remediate within 90 days as the policy required even for "low severity " vulnerabilities. Instead, Respondent failed to address the Vulnerability for more than five months after its discovery, and even then, only after the Vulnerability was revealed by a media outlet. This failure occurred despite discovery of the Vulnerability, widespread internal circulation of a detailed report on the Vulnerability, and assignment of a 90-day deadline for remediation. Sworn testimony by Respondent's employees responsible for data security revealed internal confusion and an alarming lack of accountability with regard to responsibility for remediation of vulnerabilities.

g. Remediation was ineffectively assigned to an unqualified employee. Shortly after the EaglePro penetration test report was circulated on January 11, 2019, responsibility for remediating the Vulnerability was assigned to a new employee with little experience in data security (the "Accountable Remediation Owner"). The newly assigned Accountable Remediation Owner was never given a copy of the EaglePro penetration test detailing the Vulnerability. Moreover, the gravity of the Vulnerability was not highlighted to the employee, who was merely provided with a laundry list of EaglePro application vulnerabilities, mostly minor in nature. In addition, the new Accountable Remediation Owner was not provided with the applicable policies and standards for Respondent's data security and remediation, and was offered little support in performing these new responsibilities.

26. In addition to the failure to promptly detect and then remediate the Vulnerability, EaglePro and FAST generally lacked adequate controls to protect NPI.

27. Respondent knew that its procedure to identify and classify sensitive documents in FAST was significantly flawed. To identify and classify sensitive documents containing NPI, Respondent relied solely on a process in which title agents, in the course of uploading documents, manually added the prefix "SEC" to the name for each file containing NPI. EaglePro users were then instructed not to distribute any documents containing NPI. Moreover, Respondent was fully aware that this methodology — by a wide margin — failed to identify and protect documents containing NPI. For instance:

i. In April 2018, a presentation by senior members of Respondent's IT and information security management teams to the Board of Directors demonstrated that within a random sample of 1,000 documents stored in FAST, 30% of those documents contained NPI but were not tagged as such. At this error rate, potentially hundreds of millions of documents containing NPI were not designated properly.

ii. A June 1, 2019 email from Respondent's Vice President of Information Security discussing problems with the NPI controls in EaglePro likewise acknowledged that the manual process for designated NPI was "highly prone to error."

28. Despite these widely acknowledged control deficiencies, Respondent's staff responsible for EaglePro's application security — the Director of Vulnerability Remediation Management Team, the Director of Application Security, and the EaglePro Accountable Remediation Owner — testified that they were not aware that NPI was transmitted using EaglePro or that a 2018 sample of documents in FAST had revealed a significant error rate in the tagging of documents with NPI.

29. In June 2019, after a journalist publicized Respondent's data security vulnerabilities, Respondent's information security personnel recommended modifying EaglePro, limiting access to authenticated users.   Senior management rejected that recommendation. Respondent's information security personnel then recommended adding two technical controls to protect NPI.   First, they recommended disallowing transmission of tagged NPI documents in EaglePro via unsecured links.   Second, in recognition of the faulty nature of manually tagging documents, they recommended a scan of FAST for documents containing NPI but not tagged as sensitive.   Neither recommendation was implemented.

30. To this day, the sole control preventing EaglePro from being used to transmit NPI is merely an instruction to users not to send NPI. Respondent relies on training to ensure employees follow procedures, delegating responsibility for such training to individual business units.   At the same time, individual business units are left at their own discretion to design and conduct the training. This lack of centralized and coordinated training exists despite Respondent's professed awareness of inadequate controls.

31. When the Department asked Respondent's CISO why additional controls were not adopted to protect NPI, Respondent's CISO disavowed ownership of the issue, stating, among other reasons, that such controls were not the responsibility of Respondent's information security department.

32. Respondent also failed to timely encrypt documents containing NPI as required by the Department's Cybersecurity Regulation. 23 NYCRR Section 500.15 requires, among other things, documents containing NPI be encrypted. While encryption would not have prevented the data exposure of NPI due to the Vulnerability, the encryption requirement of 23 NYCRR Section 500.15 went into effect on September 1, 2018 – 18 months after the Part 500 regulation went into effect.   Nonetheless, Respondent did not encrypt the tens of millions of documents tagged as containing NPI until approximately December 2018, months after the relevant provisions of the Cybersecurity Regulation went into effect.   Moreover, the remainder of the documents in FAST — which Respondent knew included many documents containing NPI — were not fully encrypted until mid-2019.

Respondent's Data Exposure is Revealed

33. On May 24, 2019, Brian Krebs, a journalist who reports on cybersecurity issues, published an article revealing that Respondent had exposed 885 million documents — dating as far back as 2003 and many containing NPI — by rendering the documents openly accessible to the public. Mr. Krebs himself was easily able to view highly-

sensitive consumer data, including documents that contained NPI such as social security numbers, drivers' licenses, and tax and banking information.

34. In the days leading up to publication of his findings, Mr. Krebs and another individual who had stumbled upon the Vulnerability repeatedly reached out to First American to alert the firm of the Vulnerability.

35. After publication of Mr. Krebs's findings, Respondent reported the incident to the Department, as required under 23 NYCRR 500.17. Respondent also publicly disclosed that it "shut down external access to a production environment with a reported design defect that created the potential for unauthorized access to customer data." In an Incident Update addressed to Respondent's customers on May 31, 2019, Respondent conceded that documents containing NPI were potentially exposed.

36. After the disclosure by Mr. Krebs, Respondent conducted a forensic investigation into data exposure attributable to the Vulnerability but was unable to determine whether records were accessed prior to June 2018. Respondent's forensic investigation relied on a review of web logs retained from June 2018 onward. Respondent's own analysis demonstrated that during this 11-month period, more than 350,000 documents were accessed without authorization by automated "bots" or "scraper" programs designed to collect information on the Internet.

SPECIFICATIONS OF CHARGES

CHARGE I RESPONDENT VIOLATED 23 NYCRR 500.02

37. The allegations set forth in paragraphs 1 to 36 above are repeated and realleged as if fully set forth herein.

38. Section 500.02 of the Cybersecurity Regulation requires that each Covered Entity maintain a cybersecurity program designed to protect the confidentiality, integrity and availability of the Covered Entity's Information Systems. The cybersecurity program must be based on the Covered Entity's Risk Assessment and designed to perform core cybersecurity functions, including identifying and assessing internal and external cybersecurity risks that may threaten the security or integrity of NPI stored on the Covered Entity's Information Systems.

39. Respondent failed to perform risk assessments for data stored or transmitted within its Information Systems, specifically the FAST and EaglePro applications, despite those applications' transmission and storage of NPI. Respondent's acts or practices, for the period beginning on the effective date of this Section, March 1, 2017, through May 24, 2019, constitute a violation of 23 NYCRR 500.02.

CHARGE II RESPONDENT VIOLATED 23 NYCRR 500.03

40. The allegations set forth in paragraphs 1 to 39 above are repeated and realleged as if fully set forth herein.

41. Section 500.03 of the Cybersecurity Regulation, 23 NYCRR 500.03, requires that a Covered Entity maintain a written policy or policies, approved by a Senior Officer or the board of directors (or an appropriate committee thereof) or equivalent governing body, setting forth the Covered Entity's policies and procedures for the protection of its

Information Systems and the NPI stored on those Information Systems. Section 500.03 further requires that the cybersecurity policy shall be based on the Covered Entity's Risk Assessment and address the following areas, among others: data governance and classification, access controls and identity management, and risk assessment. § 500.03(b), (d), and (m).

42. Respondent failed to maintain and implement data governance and classification policies for NPI suitable to its business model and associated risks. Respondent's classification of EaglePro as an application that did not contain or transmit NPI was incorrect given that EaglePro could and did allow access to documents containing NPI.

43. Respondent did not maintain an appropriate, risk-based policy governing access controls for EaglePro. These inadequate access controls failed to prevent the exposure of NPI in millions of documents. Respondent's acts or practices for the period beginning on the effective date of the Section, March 1, 2017, through May 24, 2019, constitute violations of 23 NYCRR 500.03.

CHARGE III RESPONDENT VIOLATED 23 NYCRR 500.07

44. The allegations set forth in paragraphs 1 to 43 above are repeated and realleged as if fully set forth herein.

45. Section 500.07 of the Cybersecurity Regulation, 23 NYCRR 500.07, requires that a Covered Entity shall limit user access privileges to Information Systems that provide access to NPI and shall periodically review such access privileges.

46. The Vulnerability allowed unauthorized remote users to gain access to NPI in Respondent's FAST system. The Vulnerability existed due to a lack of reasonable access controls. Any person could access sensitive documents stored in FAST simply by altering an EaglePro URL. Respondent's acts or practices, for the period beginning on the effective date of the Section, March 1, 2017, through May 24, 2019, constitute a violation of 23 NYCRR 500.07.

CHARGE IV RESPONDENT VIOLATED 23 NYCRR 500.09

47. The allegations set forth in paragraphs 1 to 46 above are repeated and realleged as if fully set forth herein.

48. Section 500.09(a) of the Cybersecurity Regulation, 23 NYCRR 500.09(a), requires each Covered Entity to conduct a periodic Risk Assessment of the Covered Entity's Information Systems to inform the design of the cybersecurity program as required by 23 NYCRR Part 500. Such Risk Assessment shall be updated as reasonably necessary to address changes to the Covered Entity's Information Systems, NPI, or business operations. The Covered Entity's Risk Assessment shall allow for revision of controls to respond to technological developments and evolving threats and shall consider the particular risks of the Covered Entity's business operations related to cybersecurity, NPI collected or stored, Information Systems utilized and the availability and effectiveness of controls to protect NPI and Information Systems.

49. Section 500.09(b) requires that the Risk Assessment be carried out in accordance with written policies and procedures and shall be documented. Among other things, such policies and procedures shall include: criteria for the assessment of the confidentiality,

integrity, security, and availability of the Covered Entity's Information Systems and Nonpublic Information, including the adequacy of existing controls in the context of identified risks; and requirements describing how identified risks will be mitigated or accepted based on the Risk Assessment and how the cybersecurity program will address the risks.

50. The Risk Assessment was not sufficient to inform the design of the cybersecurity program as required by 23 NYCRR Part 500, as indicated not only by Respondent's failure to identify where NPI was stored and transmitted through its Information Systems, but also its failure to identify the availability and effectiveness of controls to protect NPI and Information Systems. Respondent's acts or practices, for the period beginning on the effective date of this Section, March 1, 2018, through May 24, 2019, constitute a violation of 23 NYCRR 500.09.

CHARGE V RESPONDENT VIOLATED 23 NYCRR 500.14(b)

51. The allegations set forth in paragraphs 1 to 50 above are repeated and realleged as if fully set forth herein.

52. Section 500.14(b) of the Cybersecurity Regulation, 23 NYCRR 500.14(b), requires that as part of its cybersecurity program, each Covered Entity is required to provide regular cybersecurity awareness training for all personnel, and such training must be updated to reflect risks identified by the Covered Entity in its Risk Assessment.

53. Respondent did not provide adequate data security training for Respondent's employees and affiliated title agents responsible for identifying and uploading sensitive documents into the FAST system and in using the EaglePro system. This failure was especially significant since both the process of identifying sensitive documents and the only control preventing NPI from being distributed through EaglePro depended solely on employees and users correctly identifying sensitive documents and treating them appropriately. As a result, Respondent did not adopt cybersecurity awareness training that reflected the risks inherent in its operations and led to the Vulnerability reported on May 24, 2019. Respondent's acts or practices, for the period beginning on the effective date of the Section, March 1, 2018, through May 24, 2019, constitute a violation of 23 NYCRR 500.14.

CHARGE VI RESPONDENT VIOLATED 23 NYCRR 500.15

54. The allegations set forth in paragraphs 1 to 53 above are repeated and realleged as if fully set forth herein.

55. Section 500.15 of the Cybersecurity Regulation requires that Covered Entities implement controls, including encryption, to protect NPI held or transmitted by the Covered Entity both in transit over external networks and at rest. This section allows for the use of effective alternative compensating controls to secure NPI in transit over external networks and at rest if encryption of such is infeasible. Such compensating controls must be reviewed and approved by the Covered Entity's CISO. To the extent that a Covered Entity is utilizing compensating controls, the feasibility of encryption and effectiveness of the compensating controls shall be reviewed by the CISO at least annually.

56. Until the end of 2018, Respondent failed to encrypt documents marked as sensitive within the FAST repository. Other documents that contained sensitive data but were erroneously not marked as sensitive– were not encrypted until mid-2019. Respondent did not implement controls suitable to protect the NPI stored or transmitted by it, both in transit over external networks and at rest, nor did Respondent implement suitable compensating controls approved by the CISO. Respondent's acts or practices, for the period beginning on the effective date of the Section, September 1, 2018, through May 24, 2019, constitute a violation of 23 NYCRR 500.15.[153]

QUESTIONS

1) The Chief Information Security Officer (CISO) attempts to dodge responsibility and place it on another department. Should the CISO been aware of what was happening and taken immediate action?

2) The lack of security on the documents existed from 2014 through 2018. A fundamental risk assessment and vulnerability analysis should have identified the issue back in 2014. Should the length of time that a vulnerability exists because of inaction be factored into the penalty?

3) How much responsibility for security should EaglePro be tasked with? Should EaglePro be added to this case as a respondent?

3.8 Other Legal Regulation Concerning Financial Institutions[154]

As one might expect, the focus of the FTC's GLBA enforcement is on protecting consumers, which is the normal jurisdiction of the FTC. But there are other federal agencies that have jurisdiction and oversight responsibilities over financial institutions and thus, are also empowered under the GLBA to promulgate and enforce cyber security guidelines within the direction of the GLBA. These federal agencies are known as federal banking agencies. Title 12 U.S. Code Section 1462 defines Federal Banking Agencies as:

Office of the Comptroller of the Currency (OCC)
Board of Governors of the Federal Reserve System and
Federal Deposit Insurance Corporation (FDIC)

These federal banking agencies[155] enforce cybersecurity standards for financial institutions within their jurisdiction through the Interagency Guidelines Establishing

---

[153] Statement of Charges and Notice of Hearing at 2–19. In the Matter of First American Title Insurance Company, No. 2020-0030-C (July 21, 2020).

[154] This section is not intended to be comprehensive.

[155] On March 29, 2022, the FDIC released the following letter concerning a new breach notification requirement for regulated banks:

On November 23, 2021, the Federal Deposit Insurance Corporation (FDIC), the Board of Governors of the Federal Reserve System, and the Office of the Comptroller of the

Information Security Standards, known as the "Security Guidelines."   The Security Guidelines apply to the following types of financial institutions:

> National banks, Federal branches and Federal agencies of foreign banks and any subsidiaries of these entities (except brokers, dealers, persons providing insurance, investment companies, and investment advisers) (OCC); member banks (other than national banks), branches and agencies of foreign banks (other than Federal branches, Federal agencies, and insured State branches of foreign banks), commercial lending companies owned or controlled by foreign banks, Edge and Agreement Act Corporations, bank holding companies and their nonbank subsidiaries or affiliates (except brokers, dealers, persons providing insurance, investment companies, and investment advisers) (Board); state non-member banks, insured state branches of foreign banks, and any subsidiaries of such entities (except brokers, dealers, persons providing insurance, investment companies, and investment advisers) (FDIC); and insured savings associations and any subsidiaries of such savings associations (except brokers, dealers, persons providing insurance, investment companies, and investment advisers) (OTS).[156]

Another Federal agency involved in financial institution cybersecurity standards is the Federal Financial Institutions Examination Council (FFIEC).   The FFIEC provides a nice summary[157] of the Federal agency enforcement actions by agency and type of financial institution:

Currency (collectively, the agencies) issued a joint final rule to establish computer-security incident notification requirements (Final Rule) for banking organizations and their bank service providers. Banks and their service providers must comply with the Final Rule starting May 1, 2022.

FDIC-supervised banks can comply with the rule by reporting an incident to their case manager, who serves as the primary FDIC contact for all supervisory-related matters, or to any member of an FDIC examination team if the event occurs during an examination. If a bank is unable to access its supervisory team contacts, the bank may notify the FDIC by email at: incident@fdic.gov.

Bank service providers must notify any affected FDIC-supervised banking organization customer as soon as possible when the bank service provider determines that it has experienced a computer-security incident that has materially disrupted or degraded, or is reasonably likely to materially disrupt or degrade, services provided to such banking organization for four or more hours. FEDERAL DEPOSIT INSURANCE CORPORATION, *Financial Institution Letter: Computer-Security Incident Notification Implementation* (March 29, 2022), available at https://www.fdic.gov/news/financial-institution-letters/2022/fil22012.html.

[156] *Interagency Guidelines Establishing Information Security Standards*, BOARD OF GOVERNORS OF THE FED. RES. SYS., https://www.federalreserve.gov/supervisionreg/interagencyguidelines.htm (last visited Nov. 2, 2020) (referring to FN 2).

[157] *Enforcement Actions and Orders*, FED. FIN. INST. EXAMINATION COUNCIL, https://www.ffiec.gov/enforcement.htm (last modified Apr. 15, 2020, 11:10 AM).

Enforcement actions and orders against institutions or their affiliated parties can be found at the website of the institution's regulator:

Board of Governors of the Federal Reserve System (FRB)	▶ State member banks ▶ Bank holding companies ▶ Nonbank subsidiaries of bank holding companies ▶ Savings and loan holding companies ▶ Edge and agreement corporations ▶ Branches and agencies of foreign banking organizations operating in the United States and their parent banks ▶ Officers, directors, employees, and certain other categories of individuals associated with the above banks, companies, and organizations (referred to as "institution-affiliated parties")
Federal Deposit Insurance Corporation (FDIC)	▶ Insured State chartered banks that are not members of the Federal Reserve System (State nonmember banks) ▶ Insured branches of foreign banks ▶ Officers, directors, employees, controlling shareholders, agents, and certain other categories of individuals (institution-affiliated parties) associated with such institutions
National Credit Union Administration (NCUA)	▶ Credit unions
Office of the Comptroller of the Currency (OCC)	▶ National banks and their subsidiaries ▶ Federally chartered savings associations and their subsidiaries ▶ Federal Branches and agencies of foreign banks ▶ Institution-affiliated parties (IAPs), including (a) Officers, directors, and employees, and (b) A bank's controlling stockholders, agents, and certain other individuals

The Financial Services Information Sharing and Analysis Center (FS-ISAC) is also worth noting. "FS-ISAC, or the Financial Services Information Sharing and Analysis Center, is the global financial industry's go to resource for cyber and physical threat intelligence analysis and sharing."[158] Additional information on FS-ISAC can be found at www.fsisac.com.

---

[158] *Applications for Deposit Insurance Additional Resources*, FED. DEPOSIT INS. CORP., https://www.fdic.gov/regulations/applications/depositinsurance/contact.html (last visited Nov. 2, 2020).

This section with first discuss security guidelines and then will address enforcement actions.

3.8[A] SECURITY GUIDELINES

The following material concerns the Security Guidelines.

"Background and Overview of Security Guidelines

The Security Guidelines implement section 501(b) of the Gramm-Leach-Bliley Act (GLB Act) and section 216 of the Fair and Accurate Credit Transactions Act of 2003 (FACT Act). The Security Guidelines establish standards relating to administrative, technical, and physical safeguards to ensure the security, confidentiality, integrity and the proper disposal of customer information.

Each of the requirements in the Security Guidelines regarding the proper disposal of customer information also apply to personal information a financial institution obtains about individuals regardless of whether they are the institution's customers ("consumer information"). Consumer information includes, for example, a credit report about: (1) an individual who applies for but does not obtain a loan; (2) an individual who guarantees a loan; (3) an employee; or (4) a prospective employee. A financial institution must require, by contract, its service providers that have access to consumer information to develop appropriate measures for the proper disposal of the information.

Under the Security Guidelines, each financial institution must:

Develop and maintain an effective information security program tailored to the complexity of its operations, and

Require, by contract, service providers that have access to its customer information to take appropriate steps to protect the security and confidentiality of this information.

The standards set forth in the Security Guidelines are consistent with the principles the Agencies follow when examining the security programs of financial institutions.[6] Each financial institution must identify and evaluate risks to its customer information, develop a plan to mitigate the risks, implement the plan, test the plan, and update the plan when necessary. If an Agency finds that a financial institution's performance is deficient under the Security Guidelines, the Agency may take action, such as requiring that the institution file a compliance plan."[159]

Each of the federal banking agencies has adopted amendments to their rules and regulations to address the Security Guidelines: 12 CFR part 30 for the Office of the Comptroller of the Currency; 12 CFR part 263 for the Board of Governors of the Federal

---

[159] *Interagency Guidelines Establishing Information Security Standards*, BOARD OF GOVERNORS OF THE FED. RES. SYS., https://www.federalreserve.gov/supervisionreg/interagencyguidelines.htm (last visited Nov. 2, 2020).

Reserve System; and, 12 CFR part 308, subpart R and 12 CFR part 391, subpart B for the Federal Deposit Insurance Corporation. Next is a review of 12 CFR part 30 as a representative example of the three agencies.

12 CFR Part 30 in relevant part states:

§30.1 Scope.

(a) The rules set forth in this part and the standards set forth in appendices A, B, C, D, and E to this part apply to national banks, Federal savings associations, and Federal branches of foreign banks that are subject to the provisions of section 39 of the Federal Deposit Insurance Act (section 39)(12 U.S.C. 1831p-1).

(b) The standards set forth in appendix B to this part also apply to uninsured national banks, Federal branches and Federal agencies of foreign banks, and the subsidiaries of any national bank, Federal savings association, and Federal branch and Federal agency of a foreign bank (except brokers, dealers, persons providing insurance, investment companies, and investment advisers). Violation of these standards may be an unsafe and unsound practice within the meaning of 12 U.S.C. 1818.

[66 FR 8633, Feb. 1, 2001, as amended at 70 FR 6332, Feb. 7, 2005; 79 FR 54543, Sept. 11, 2014; 81 FR 66800, Sept. 29, 2016]

§30.2 Purpose.

Section 39 of the FDI Act, 12 U.S.C. 1831p-1, requires the Office of the Comptroller of the Currency (OCC) to establish safety and soundness standards. Pursuant to section 39, a national bank or Federal savings association may be required to submit a compliance plan if it is not in compliance with a safety and soundness standard prescribed by guideline under section 39(a) or (b). An enforceable order under section 8 of the FDI Act, 12 U.S.C. 1818(b), may be issued if, after being notified that it is in violation of a safety and soundness standard prescribed under section 39, the national bank or Federal savings association fails to submit an acceptable compliance plan or fails in any material respect to implement an accepted plan. This part establishes procedures for requiring submission of a compliance plan and issuing an enforceable order pursuant to section 39. The Interagency Guidelines Establishing Standards for Safety and Soundness are set forth in appendix A to this part, and the Interagency Guidelines Establishing Information Security Standards are set forth in appendix B to this part. The OCC Guidelines Establishing Standards for Residential Mortgage Lending Practices are set forth in appendix C to this part. The OCC Guidelines Establishing Heightened Standards for Certain Large Insured National Banks, Insured Federal Savings Associations, and Insured Federal Branches are set forth in appendix D to this part. The OCC Guidelines Establishing Standards for Recovery Planning by Certain Large Insured National Banks, Insured Federal Savings Associations, and Insured Federal Branches are set forth in appendix E to this part.

[60 FR 35680, July 10, 1995, as amended at 63 FR 55488, Oct. 15, 1998; 64 FR 52641, Sept. 30, 1999; 66 FR 8633, Feb. 1, 2001; 70 FR 6332, Feb. 7, 2005; 79 FR 54543, Sept. 11, 2014; 81 FR 66800, Sept. 29, 2016]

§30.3 Determination and notification of failure to meet safety and soundness standards and request for compliance plan.

(a) *Determination.* The OCC may, based upon an examination, inspection, or any other information that becomes available to the OCC, determine that a national bank or Federal savings association has failed to satisfy the safety and soundness standards contained in the Interagency Guidelines Establishing Standards for Safety and Soundness set forth in appendix A to this part, the Interagency Guidelines Establishing Standards for Safeguarding Customer Information set forth in appendix B to this part, the OCC Guidelines Establishing Standards for Residential Mortgage Lending Practices set forth in appendix C to this part, the OCC Guidelines Establishing Heightened Standards for Certain Large Insured National Banks, Insured Federal Savings Associations, and Insured Federal Branches set forth in appendix D to this part, or the OCC Guidelines Establishing Standards for Recovery Planning by Certain Large Insured National Banks, Insured Federal Savings Associations, and Insured Federal Branches set forth in appendix E to this part.

(b) *Request for compliance plan.* If the OCC determines that a national bank or Federal savings association has failed to satisfy a safety and soundness standard pursuant to paragraph (a) of this section, the OCC may request, by letter or through a report of examination, the submission of a compliance plan and the bank or savings association shall be deemed to have notice of the deficiency three days after mailing of the letter by the OCC or delivery of the report of examination.

[60 FR 35680, July 10, 1995, as amended at 63 FR 55488, Oct. 15, 1998; 64 FR 52641, Sept. 30, 1999; 66 FR 8633, Feb. 1, 2001; 70 FR 6332, Feb. 7, 2005; 79 FR 54543, Sept. 11, 2014; 81 FR 66800, Sept. 29, 2016]

§30.4 Filing of safety and soundness compliance plan.

(a) *Schedule for filing compliance plan*—(1) *In general.* A national bank or Federal savings association shall file a written safety and soundness compliance plan with the OCC within 30 days of receiving a request for a compliance plan pursuant to §30.3(b) unless the OCC notifies the bank or savings association in writing that the plan is to be filed within a different period.

(2) *Other plans.* If a national bank or Federal savings association is obligated to file, or is currently operating under, a capital restoration plan submitted pursuant to section 38 of the FDI Act (12 U.S.C. 1831o), a cease-and-desist order entered into pursuant to section 8 of the FDI Act (12 U.S.C. 1818(b)), a formal or informal agreement, or a response to a report of examination or report of inspection, it may, with the permission of the OCC, submit a compliance plan under this section as part of that plan, order, agreement, or response, subject to the deadline provided in paragraph (a) of this section.

(b) *Contents of plan.* The compliance plan shall include a description of the steps the national bank or Federal savings association will take to correct the deficiency and the time within which those steps will be taken.

(c) *Review of safety and soundness compliance plans.* Within 30 days after receiving a safety and soundness compliance plan under this part, the OCC shall provide written notice to the national bank or Federal savings association of whether the plan has been approved or seek additional information from the bank or savings association regarding the plan. The OCC may extend the time within which notice regarding approval of a plan will be provided.

(d) *Failure to submit or implement a compliance plan*—(1) *Supervisory actions.* If a national bank or Federal savings association fails to submit an acceptable plan within the time specified by the OCC or fails in any material respect to implement a compliance plan, then the OCC shall, by order, require the bank or savings association to correct the deficiency and may take further actions provided in section 39(e)(2)(B). Pursuant to section 39(e)(3), the OCC may be required to take certain actions if the national bank or Federal savings association commenced operations or experienced a change in control within the previous 24-month period, or the bank or savings association experienced extraordinary growth during the previous 18-month period.

(2) *Extraordinary growth.* For purposes of paragraph (d)(1) of this section, extraordinary growth means an increase in assets of more than 7.5 percent during any quarter within the 18-month period preceding the issuance of a request for submission of a compliance plan, by a national bank or Federal savings association that is not well capitalized for purposes of section 38 of the FDI Act. For purposes of calculating an increase in assets, assets acquired through merger or acquisition approved pursuant to the Bank Merger Act (12 U.S.C. 1828(c)) will be excluded.

(e) *Amendment of compliance plan.* A national bank or Federal savings association that has filed an approved compliance plan may, after prior written notice to and approval by the OCC, amend the plan to reflect a change in circumstance. Until such time as a proposed amendment has been approved, the bank or savings association shall implement the compliance plan as previously approved.

[60 FR 35680, July 10, 1995, as amended at 79 FR 54543, Sept. 11, 2014]

§30.5 Issuance of orders to correct deficiencies and to take or refrain from taking other actions.

(a) *Notice of intent to issue order*—(1) *In general.* The OCC shall provide a national bank or Federal savings association prior written notice of the OCC's intention to issue an order requiring the bank or savings association to correct a safety and soundness deficiency or to take or refrain from taking other actions pursuant to section 39 of the FDI Act. The national bank or Federal savings association shall have such time to respond to a proposed order as provided by the OCC under paragraph (c) of this section.

(2) *Immediate issuance of final order.* If the OCC finds it necessary in order to carry out the purposes of section 39 of the FDI Act, the OCC may, without providing the notice prescribed in paragraph (a)(1) of this section, issue an order requiring a national bank

or Federal savings association immediately to take actions to correct a safety and soundness deficiency or take or refrain from taking other actions pursuant to section 39. A national bank or Federal savings association that is subject to such an immediately effective order may submit a written appeal of the order to the OCC. Such an appeal must be received by the OCC within 14 calendar days of the issuance of the order, unless the OCC permits a longer period. The OCC shall consider any such appeal, if filed in a timely manner, within 60 days of receiving the appeal. During such period of review, the order shall remain in effect unless the OCC, in its sole discretion, stays the effectiveness of the order.

(b) *Content of notice.* A notice of intent to issue an order shall include:

(1) A statement of the safety and soundness deficiency or deficiencies that have been identified at the national bank or Federal savings association;

(2) A description of any restrictions, prohibitions, or affirmative actions that the OCC proposes to impose or require;

(3) The proposed date when such restrictions or prohibitions would be effective or the proposed date for completion of any required action; and

(4) The date by which the national bank or Federal savings association subject to the order may file with the OCC a written response to the notice.

(c) *Response to notice—(1) Time for response.* A national bank or Federal savings association may file a written response to a notice of intent to issue an order within the time period set by the OCC. Such a response must be received by the OCC within 14 calendar days from the date of the notice unless the OCC determines that a different period is appropriate in light of the safety and soundness of the national bank or Federal savings association or other relevant circumstances.

(2) *Content of response.* The response should include:

(i) An explanation why the action proposed by the OCC is not an appropriate exercise of discretion under section 39;

(ii) Any recommended modification of the proposed order; and

(iii) Any other relevant information, mitigating circumstances, documentation, or other evidence in support of the position of the national bank or Federal savings association regarding the proposed order.

(d) *Agency consideration of response.* After considering the response, the OCC may:

(1) Issue the order as proposed or in modified form;

(2) Determine not to issue the order and so notify the national bank or Federal savings association; or

(3) Seek additional information or clarification of the response from the national bank or Federal savings association, or any other relevant source.

(e) *Failure to file response.* Failure by a national bank or Federal savings association to file with the OCC, within the specified time period, a written response to a proposed order shall constitute a waiver of the opportunity to respond and shall constitute consent to the issuance of the order.

(f) *Request for modification or rescission of order.* Any national bank or Federal savings association that is subject to an order under this part may, upon a change in circumstances, request in writing that the OCC reconsider the terms of the order, and

may propose that the order be rescinded or modified. Unless otherwise ordered by the OCC, the order shall continue in place while such request is pending before the OCC.
[60 FR 35680, July 10, 1995, as amended at 79 FR 54544, Sept. 11, 2014]

§30.6   Enforcement of orders.

(a) *Judicial remedies.* Whenever a national bank or Federal savings association fails to comply with an order issued under section 39, the OCC may seek enforcement of the order in the appropriate United States district court pursuant to section 8(i)(1) of the FDI Act, 12 U.S.C. 1818(i)(1).

(b) *Failure to comply with order.* Pursuant to section 8(i)(2)(A) of the FDI Act, 12 U.S.C. 1818(i)(2)(A), the OCC may assess a civil money penalty against any national bank or Federal savings association that violates or otherwise fails to comply with any final order issued under section 39 and against any institution-affiliated party who participates in such violation or noncompliance.

(c) *Other enforcement action.* In addition to the actions described in paragraphs (a) and (b) of this section, the OCC may seek enforcement of the provisions of section 39 or this part through any other judicial or administrative proceeding authorized by law.
[60 FR 35680, July 10, 1995, as amended at 79 FR 54544, Sept. 11, 2014]

. . .

Appendix B to Part 30—Interagency Guidelines Establishing Information Security Standards

Table of Contents

I. Introduction

The Interagency Guidelines Establishing Information Security Standards (Guidelines) set forth standards pursuant to section 39 of the Federal Deposit Insurance

Act (section 39, codified at 12 U.S.C. 1831p-1), and sections 501 and 505(b), codified at 15 U.S.C. 6801 and 6805(b) of the Gramm-Leach Bliley Act. These Guidelines address standards for developing and implementing administrative, technical, and physical safeguards to protect the security, confidentiality, and integrity of customer information. These Guidelines also address standards with respect to the proper disposal of consumer information, pursuant to sections 621 and 628 of the Fair Credit Reporting Act (15 U.S.C. 1681s and 1681w).

A. *Scope.* The Guidelines apply to customer information maintained by or on behalf of entities over which the OCC has authority. Such entities, referred to as "the national bank or Federal savings association," are national banks, Federal savings associations, Federal branches and Federal agencies of foreign banks, and any subsidiaries of such entities (except brokers, dealers, persons providing insurance, investment companies, and investment advisers). The Guidelines also apply to the proper disposal of consumer information by or on behalf of such entities.

B. *Preservation of Existing Authority.* Neither section 39 nor these Guidelines in any way limit the authority of the OCC to address unsafe or unsound practices, violations of law, unsafe or unsound conditions, or other practices. The OCC may take action under section 39 and these Guidelines independently of, in conjunction with, or in addition to, any other enforcement action available to the OCC.

C. *Definitions.*

1. Except as modified in the Guidelines, or unless the context otherwise requires, the terms used in these Guidelines have the same meanings as set forth in sections 3 and 39 of the Federal Deposit Insurance Act (12 U.S.C. 1813 and 1831p-1).

2. For purposes of the Guidelines, the following definitions apply:

a. *Board of directors,* in the case of a branch or agency of a foreign bank, means the managing official in charge of the branch or agency.

b. *Consumer information* means any record about an individual, whether in paper, electronic, or other form, that is a consumer report or is derived from a consumer report and that is maintained or otherwise possessed by or on behalf of the national bank or Federal savings association for a business purpose. Consumer information also means a compilation of such records. The term does not include any record that does not identify an individual.

i. *Examples.*

(1) *Consumer information* includes:

(A) A consumer report that a national bank or Federal savings association obtains;

(B) Information from a consumer report that the national bank or Federal savings association obtains from its affiliate after the consumer has been given a notice and has elected not to opt out of that sharing;

(C) Information from a consumer report that the national bank or Federal savings association obtains about an individual who applies for but does not receive a loan, including any loan sought by an individual for a business purpose;

(D) Information from a consumer report that the national bank or Federal savings association obtains about an individual who guarantees a loan (including a loan to a business entity); or

(E) Information from a consumer report that the national bank or Federal savings association obtains about an employee or prospective employee.

(2) *Consumer information* does not include:

(A) Aggregate information, such as the mean credit score, derived from a group of consumer reports; or

(B) Blind data, such as payment history on accounts that are not personally identifiable, that may be used for developing credit scoring models or for other purposes.

c. *Consumer report* has the same meaning as set forth in the Fair Credit Reporting Act, 15 U.S.C. 1681a(d).

d. *Customer* means any customer of the national bank or Federal savings association as defined in 12 CFR 1016.3(i).

e. *Customer information* means any record containing nonpublic personal information, as defined in 12 CFR 1016.3(p), about a customer, whether in paper, electronic, or other form, that is maintained by or on behalf of the national bank or Federal savings association.

f. *Customer information systems* means any methods used to access, collect, store, use, transmit, protect, or dispose of customer information.

g. *Service provider* means any person or entity that maintains, processes, or otherwise is permitted access to customer information or consumer information through its provision of services directly to the national bank or Federal savings association.

II. Standards for Information Security

A. *Information Security Program.* Each national bank or Federal savings association shall implement a comprehensive written information security program that includes administrative, technical, and physical safeguards appropriate to the size and complexity of the national bank or Federal savings association and the nature and scope of its activities. While all parts of the national bank or Federal savings association are not required to implement a uniform set of policies, all elements of the information security program must be coordinated.

B. *Objectives.* A national bank's or Federal savings association's information security program shall be designed to:

1. Ensure the security and confidentiality of customer information;

2. Protect against any anticipated threats or hazards to the security or integrity of such information;

3. Protect against unauthorized access to or use of such information that could result in substantial harm or inconvenience to any customer; and

4. Ensure the proper disposal of customer information and consumer information.

III. Development and Implementation of Information Security Program

A. *Involve the Board of Directors.* The board of directors or an appropriate committee of the board of each national bank or Federal savings association shall:

1. Approve the national bank's or Federal savings association's written information security program; and

2. Oversee the development, implementation, and maintenance of the national bank's or Federal savings association's information security program, including assigning specific responsibility for its implementation and reviewing reports from management.

B. *Assess Risk.* Each national bank or Federal savings association shall:

1. Identify reasonably foreseeable internal and external threats that could result in unauthorized disclosure, misuse, alteration, or destruction of customer information or customer information systems.

2. Assess the likelihood and potential damage of these threats, taking into consideration the sensitivity of customer information.

3. Assess the sufficiency of policies, procedures, customer information systems, and other arrangements in place to control risks.

C. *Manage and Control Risk.* Each national bank or Federal savings association shall:

1. Design its information security program to control the identified risks, commensurate with the sensitivity of the information as well as the complexity and scope of the national bank's or Federal savings association's activities. Each national bank or Federal savings association must consider whether the following security measures are appropriate for the national bank or Federal savings association and, if so, adopt those measures the national bank or Federal savings association concludes are appropriate:

a. Access controls on customer information systems, including controls to authenticate and permit access only to authorized individuals and controls to prevent employees from providing customer information to unauthorized individuals who may seek to obtain this information through fraudulent means.

b. Access restrictions at physical locations containing customer information, such as buildings, computer facilities, and records storage facilities to permit access only to authorized individuals;

c. Encryption of electronic customer information, including while in transit or in storage on networks or systems to which unauthorized individuals may have access;

d. Procedures designed to ensure that customer information system modifications are consistent with the national bank's or Federal savings association's information security program;

e. Dual control procedures, segregation of duties, and employee background checks for employees with responsibilities for or access to customer information;

f. Monitoring systems and procedures to detect actual and attempted attacks on or intrusions into customer information systems;

g. Response programs that specify actions to be taken when the national bank or Federal savings association suspects or detects that unauthorized individuals have gained access to customer information systems, including appropriate reports to regulatory and law enforcement agencies; and

h. Measures to protect against destruction, loss, or damage of customer information due to potential environmental hazards, such as fire and water damage or technological failures.

2. Train staff to implement the national bank's or Federal savings association's information security program.

3. Regularly test the key controls, systems and procedures of the information security program. The frequency and nature of such tests should be determined by the national bank's or Federal savings association's risk assessment. Tests should be conducted or reviewed by independent third parties or staff independent of those that develop or maintain the security programs.

4. Develop, implement, and maintain, as part of its information security program, appropriate measures to properly dispose of customer information and consumer information in accordance with each of the requirements of this paragraph III.

D. *Oversee Service Provider Arrangements.* Each national bank or Federal savings association shall:

1. Exercise appropriate due diligence in selecting its service providers;

2. Require its service providers by contract to implement appropriate measures designed to meet the objectives of these Guidelines; and

3. Where indicated by the national bank's or Federal savings association's risk assessment, monitor its service providers to confirm that they have satisfied their obligations as required by section D.2. As part of this monitoring, a national bank or Federal savings association should review audits, summaries of test results, or other equivalent evaluations of its service providers.

E. *Adjust the Program.* Each national bank or Federal savings association shall monitor, evaluate, and adjust, as appropriate, the information security program in light of any relevant changes in technology, the sensitivity of its customer information, internal or external threats to information, and the national bank's or Federal savings association's own changing business arrangements, such as mergers and acquisitions, alliances and joint ventures, outsourcing arrangements, and changes to customer information systems.

F. *Report to the Board.* Each national bank or Federal savings association shall report to its board or an appropriate committee of the board at least annually. This report should describe the overall status of the information security program and the national bank's or Federal savings association's compliance with these Guidelines. The reports should discuss material matters related to its program, addressing issues such as: risk assessment; risk management and control decisions; service provider arrangements; results of testing; security breaches or violations and management's responses; and recommendations for changes in the information security program.

G. *Implement the Standards.*

1. *Effective date.* Each national bank or Federal savings association must implement an information security program pursuant to these Guidelines by July 1, 2001.

2. *Two-year grandfathering of agreements with service providers.* Until July 1, 2003, a contract that a national bank or Federal savings association has entered into with a service provider to perform services for it or functions on its behalf satisfies the provisions of section III.D., even if the contract does not include a requirement that the servicer maintain the security and confidentiality of customer information, as long as the national bank or Federal savings association entered into the contract on or before March 5, 2001.

3. *Effective date for measures relating to the disposal of consumer information.* Each national bank or Federal savings association must satisfy these Guidelines with respect to the proper disposal of consumer information by July 1, 2005.

4. *Exception for existing agreements with service providers relating to the disposal of consumer information.* Notwithstanding the requirement in paragraph III.G.3., a national bank's or Federal savings association's contracts with its service providers that have access to consumer information and that may dispose of consumer information, entered into before July 1, 2005, must comply with the provisions of the Guidelines relating to the proper disposal of consumer information by July 1, 2006.

Supplement A to Appendix B to Part 30—Interagency Guidance on Response Programs for Unauthorized Access to Customer Information and Customer Notice

I. Background

This Guidance[160] interprets section 501(b) of the Gramm-Leach-Bliley Act ("GLBA") and the Interagency Guidelines Establishing Information Security Standards (the "Security Guidelines")[161] and describes response programs, including customer notification procedures, that a financial institution should develop and implement to address unauthorized access to or use of customer information that could result in substantial harm or inconvenience to a customer. The scope of, and definitions of terms used in, this Guidance are identical to those of the Security Guidelines. For example, the term "customer information" is the same term used in the Security Guidelines, and means any record containing nonpublic personal information about a customer, whether in paper, electronic, or other form, maintained by or on behalf of the institution.

A. Interagency Security Guidelines

---

[160] Editors: Footnote 1 of the document states: "This Guidance was jointly issued by the Board of Governors of the Federal Reserve System (Board), the Federal Deposit Insurance Corporation (FDIC), the Office of the Comptroller of the Currency (OCC), and the Office of Thrift Supervision (OTS). Pursuant to 12 U.S.C. 5412, the OTS is no longer a party to this Guidance." *Id.*

[161] Editors: Footnote 2 of the document states: "²12 CFR part 30, app. B (OCC); 12 CFR part 208, app. D-2 and part 225, app. F (Board); and 12 CFR part 364, app. B and 12 CFR 391.5 (FDIC). The "Interagency Guidelines Establishing Information Security Standards" were formerly known as "The Interagency Guidelines Establishing Standards for Safeguarding Customer Information." *Id.*

Section 501(b) of the GLBA required the Agencies to establish appropriate standards for financial institutions subject to their jurisdiction that include administrative, technical, and physical safeguards, to protect the security and confidentiality of customer information. Accordingly, the Agencies issued Security Guidelines requiring every financial institution to have an information security program designed to:

1. Ensure the security and confidentiality of customer information;

2. Protect against any anticipated threats or hazards to the security or integrity of such information; and

3. Protect against unauthorized access to or use of such information that could result in substantial harm or inconvenience to any customer.

B. Risk Assessment and Controls

1. The Security Guidelines direct every financial institution to assess the following risks, among others, when developing its information security program:

a. Reasonably foreseeable internal and external threats that could result in unauthorized disclosure, misuse, alteration, or destruction of customer information or customer information systems;

b. The likelihood and potential damage of threats, taking into consideration the sensitivity of customer information; and

c. The sufficiency of policies, procedures, customer information systems, and other arrangements in place to control risks.[162]

2. Following the assessment of these risks, the Security Guidelines require a financial institution to design a program to address the identified risks. The particular security measures an institution should adopt will depend upon the risks presented by the complexity and scope of its business. At a minimum, the financial institution is required to consider the specific security measures enumerated in the Security Guidelines,[163] and adopt those that are appropriate for the institution, including:

a. Access controls on customer information systems, including controls to authenticate and permit access only to authorized individuals and controls to prevent employees from providing customer information to unauthorized individuals who may seek to obtain this information through fraudulent means;

b. Background checks for employees with responsibilities for access to customer information; and

c. Response programs that specify actions to be taken when the financial institution suspects or detects that unauthorized individuals have gained access to customer information systems, including appropriate reports to regulatory and law enforcement agencies.[164]

C. Service Providers

The Security Guidelines direct every financial institution to require its service providers by contract to implement appropriate measures designed to protect against

---

[162] Editors: Footnote 3 of the document states: "*See* Security Guidelines, III.B." *Id.*

[163] Editors: Footnote 4 of the document states: "*See* Security Guidelines, III.C." *Id.*

[164] Editors: Footnote 5 of the document states: "*See* Security Guidelines, III.C." *Id.*

unauthorized access to or use of customer information that could result in substantial harm or inconvenience to any customer.[165]

II. Response Program

Millions of Americans, throughout the country, have been victims of identity theft. Identity thieves misuse personal information they obtain from a number of sources, including financial institutions, to perpetrate identity theft. Therefore, financial institutions should take preventative measures to safeguard customer information against attempts to gain unauthorized access to the information. For example, financial institutions should place access controls on customer information systems and conduct background checks for employees who are authorized to access customer information. However, every financial institution should also develop and implement a risk-based response program to address incidents of unauthorized access to customer information in customer information systems[166] that occur nonetheless. A response program should be a key part of an institution's information security program.[167] The program should be appropriate to the size and complexity of the institution and the nature and scope of its activities.

In addition, each institution should be able to address incidents of unauthorized access to customer information in customer information systems maintained by its domestic and foreign service providers. Therefore, consistent with the obligations in the Guidelines that relate to these arrangements, and with existing guidance on this topic issued by the Agencies,[168] an institution's contract with its service provider should require the service provider to take appropriate actions to address incidents of unauthorized access to the financial institution's customer information, including notification to the institution as soon as possible of any such incident, to enable the institution to expeditiously implement its response program.

A. Components of a Response Program

---

[165] Editors: Footnote 6 of the document states: "*See* Security Guidelines, II.B. and III.D. Further, the Agencies note that, in addition to contractual obligations to a financial institution, a service provider may be required to implement its own comprehensive information security program in accordance with the Safeguards Rule promulgated by the Federal Trade Commission ("FTC"), 16 CFR part 314." *Id.*

[166] Editors: Footnote 9 in the document states: "Under the Guidelines, an institution's *customer information systems* consist of all of the methods used to access, collect, store, use, transmit, protect, or dispose of customer information, including the systems maintained by its service providers. *See* Security Guidelines, I.C.2.d." *Id.*

[167] Editors: Footnote 10 in the document states: "*See* FFIEC Information Technology Examination Handbook, Information Security Booklet, Dec. 2002 available at *http://www.ffiec.gov/ffiecinfobase/html_pages/infosec_book_frame.htm.* Federal Reserve SR 97-32, Sound Practice Guidance for Information Security for Networks, Dec. 4, 1997; OCC Bulletin 2000-14, "Infrastructure Threats—Intrusion Risks" (May 15, 2000), for additional guidance on preventing, detecting, and responding to intrusions into financial institution computer systems." *Id.*

[168] Editors: Footnote 11 in the document states: "*See* Federal Reserve SR Ltr. 13-19, Guidance on Managing Outsourcing Risk, Dec. 5, 2013; OCC Bulletin 2013-29, "Third-Party Relationships—Risk Management Guidance," Oct. 30, 2013; and FDIC FIL 68-99, Risk Assessment Tools and Practices for Information System Security, July 7, 1999." *Id.*

1. At a minimum, an institution's response program should contain procedures for the following:

a. Assessing the nature and scope of an incident, and identifying what customer information systems and types of customer information have been accessed or misused;

b. Notifying its primary Federal regulator as soon as possible when the institution becomes aware of an incident involving unauthorized access to or use of *sensitive* customer information, as defined below;

c. Consistent with the Agencies' Suspicious Activity Report ("SAR") regulations, notifying appropriate law enforcement authorities, in addition to filing a timely SAR in situations involving Federal criminal violations requiring immediate attention, such as when a reportable violation is ongoing;

d. Taking appropriate steps to contain and control the incident to prevent further unauthorized access to or use of customer information, for example, by monitoring, freezing, or closing affected accounts, while preserving records and other evidence; and

e. Notifying customers when warranted.

2. Where an incident of unauthorized access to customer information involves customer information systems maintained by an institution's service providers, it is the responsibility of the financial institution to notify the institution's customers and regulator. However, an institution may authorize or contract with its service provider to notify the institution's customers or regulator on its behalf.

III. Customer Notice

Financial institutions have an affirmative duty to protect their customers' information against unauthorized access or use. Notifying customers of a security incident involving the unauthorized access or use of the customer's information in accordance with the standard set forth below is a key part of that duty. Timely notification of customers is important to manage an institution's reputation risk. Effective notice also may reduce an institution's legal risk, assist in maintaining good customer relations, and enable the institution's customers to take steps to protect themselves against the consequences of identity theft. When customer notification is warranted, an institution may not forgo notifying its customers of an incident because the institution believes that it may be potentially embarrassed or inconvenienced by doing so.

A. Standard for Providing Notice

When a financial institution becomes aware of an incident of unauthorized access to sensitive customer information, the institution should conduct a reasonable investigation to promptly determine the likelihood that the information has been or will be misused. If the institution determines that misuse of its information about a customer has occurred or is reasonably possible, it should notify the affected customer as soon as possible. Customer notice may be delayed if an appropriate law enforcement agency determines that notification will interfere with a criminal investigation and provides the institution with a written request for the delay. However, the institution should notify its customers as soon as notification will no longer interfere with the investigation.

1. Sensitive Customer Information

Under the Guidelines, an institution must protect against unauthorized access to or use of customer information that could result in substantial harm or inconvenience to any customer. Substantial harm or inconvenience is most likely to result from improper access to *sensitive customer information* because this type of information is most likely to be misused, as in the commission of identity theft. For purposes of this Guidance, *sensitive customer information* means a customer's name, address, or telephone number, in conjunction with the customer's social security number, driver's license number, account number, credit or debit card number, or a personal identification number or password that would permit access to the customer's account. *Sensitive customer information* also includes any combination of components of customer information that would allow someone to log onto or access the customer's account, such as user name and password or password and account number.

2. Affected Customers

If a financial institution, based upon its investigation, can determine from its logs or other data precisely which customers' information has been improperly accessed, it may limit notification to those customers with regard to whom the institution determines that misuse of their information has occurred or is reasonably possible. However, there may be situations where the institution determines that a group of files has been accessed improperly, but is unable to identify which specific customers' information has been accessed. If the circumstances of the unauthorized access lead the institution to determine that misuse of the information is reasonably possible, it should notify all customers in the group.

B. Content of Customer Notice

1. Customer notice should be given in a clear and conspicuous manner. The notice should describe the incident in general terms and the type of customer information that was the subject of unauthorized access or use. It also should generally describe what the institution has done to protect the customers' information from further unauthorized access. In addition, it should include a telephone number that customers can call for further information and assistance.[169] The notice also should remind customers of the need to remain vigilant over the next twelve to twenty-four months, and to promptly report incidents of suspected identity theft to the institution. The notice should include the following additional items, when appropriate:

a. A recommendation that the customer review account statements and immediately report any suspicious activity to the institution;

b. A description of fraud alerts and an explanation of how the customer may place a fraud alert in the customer's consumer reports to put the customer's creditors on notice that the customer may be a victim of fraud;

c. A recommendation that the customer periodically obtain credit reports from each nationwide credit reporting agency and have information relating to fraudulent transactions deleted;

---

[169] Editors: Footnote 14 of the document states: "The institution should, therefore, ensure that it has reasonable policies and procedures in place, including trained personnel, to respond appropriately to customer inquiries and requests for assistance." *Id.*

d. An explanation of how the customer may obtain a credit report free of charge; and

e. Information about the availability of the FTC's online guidance regarding steps a consumer can take to protect against identity theft. The notice should encourage the customer to report any incidents of identity theft to the FTC, and should provide the FTC's Web site address and toll-free telephone number that customers may use to obtain the identity theft guidance and report suspected incidents of identity theft.

2. The Agencies encourage financial institutions to notify the nationwide consumer reporting agencies prior to sending notices to a large number of customers that include contact information for the reporting agencies.

C. Delivery of Customer Notice

Customer notice should be delivered in any manner designed to ensure that a customer can reasonably be expected to receive it. For example, the institution may choose to contact all customers affected by telephone or by mail, or by electronic mail for those customers for whom it has a valid e-mail address and who have agreed to receive communications electronically.

[66 FR 8633, Feb. 1, 2001, as amended at 69 FR 77616, Dec. 28, 2004; 70 FR 15751, 15753, Mar. 29, 2005; 71 FR 5780, Feb. 3, 2006; 79 FR 54544, Sept. 11, 2014][170]

3.8[B] ENFORCEMENT

The Federal bank agencies and the NCUA can instigate enforcement actions in this field. Next, a review of OCC enforcement and an OCC consent order as an example.

3.8[B][I] OCC ENFORCEMENT

The OCC supervises the following entities and has the statutory authority to take enforcement actions against them:

National banks and their subsidiaries
Federally chartered savings associations and their subsidiaries
Federal branches and agencies of foreign banks
Institution-affiliated parties (IAPs), including:
    Officers, directors, and employees
    A bank's controlling stockholders, agents, and certain other individuals.[171]

The OCC maintains an enforcement group that:

---

[170] 12 C.F.R. § 30, app. B (1995).

[171] *Enforcement Actions Search Tool*, OFF. OF THE COMPTROLLER OF THE CURRENCY, https://apps.occ.gov/EASearch/?Search=capital+one&Category=&ItemsPerPage=10&Sort=&AutoCompl eteSelection= (last visited Nov. 2, 2020).

Serves as the OCC's counsel on matters related to investigations, enforcement actions, and administrative litigation:

Conducts formal and informal investigations;

Advises on whether OCC-supervised institutions and institution affiliated parties (IAPs) have engaged in unsafe or unsound banking practices, violations of laws and regulations, or breaches of fiduciary duty;

Handles matters involving Bank Secrecy Act/Anti-Money Laundering law violations, consumer law violations, and fraud related actions, among other areas;

Advises the OCC's supervisory, compliance, and licensing units on the legal requirements for enforcement actions and on enforcement-related policies and procedures;

Litigates all OCC enforcement actions before the Office of Financial Institution Adjudication (OFIA), including civil money penalties, prohibitions and removals, and cease-and-desist orders;

Refers criminal acts involving OCC-supervised institutions or IAPs to the U.S. Department of Justice; and

Coordinates with the federal banking agencies; and other regulatory agencies, including the Financial Crimes Enforcement Network, the U.S. Securities and Exchange Commission, and the Consumer Financial Protection Bureau on matters involving OCC-supervised institutions.[172]

The following is a recent example of an OCC consent order:

#2020-037

UNITED STATES OF AMERICA DEPARTMENT OF THE TREASURY OFFICE OF THE COMPTROLLER OF THE CURRENCY

In the Matter of:
Capital One, N.A. Mclean, Virginia
Capital One Bank (USA), N.A. Glen Allen, Virginia AA-EC-20-49

CONSENT ORDER

WHEREAS, the Office of the Comptroller of the Currency ("OCC") has supervisory authority over Capital One, N.A., McLean, Virginia and Capital One Bank (USA), N.A., Glen Allen, Virginia (collectively, the "Bank");

WHEREAS, the OCC intends to initiate cease and desist proceedings against the Bank pursuant to 12 U.S.C. § 1818(b), through the issuance of a Notice of Charges, for

---

[172] *Chief Counsel's Office*, OFF. OF THE COMPTROLLER OF THE CURRENCY, https://www.occ.gov/about/who-we-are/organizations/chief-counsels-office/index-chief-counsels-office.html (last visited Nov. 2, 2020).

engaging in unsafe or unsound practices, including those relating to information security, and noncompliance with 12 C.F.R. Part 30;

WHEREAS, in the interest of cooperation and to avoid additional costs associated with administrative and judicial proceedings with respect to the above matter, the Bank, by and through its duly elected and acting Board of Directors ("Board"), consents to the issuance of this Consent Order ("Order"), by the OCC through the duly authorized representative of the Comptroller of the Currency ("Comptroller"); and

NOW, THEREFORE, pursuant to the authority vested in the OCC by Section 8(b) of the Federal Deposit Insurance Act, as amended, 12 U.S.C. § 1818(b), the OCC hereby orders that:

ARTICLE I JURISDICTION

(1) The Bank is an "insured depository institution" as that term is defined in 12 U.S.C. § 1813(c)(2).

(2) The Bank is a national banking association within the meaning of 12 U.S.C. § 1813(q)(1)(A), and is chartered and examined by the OCC. *See* 12 U.S.C. § 1 *et seq.*

(3) The OCC is the "appropriate Federal banking agency" as that term is defined in 12 U.S.C. § 1813(q) and is therefore authorized to initiate and maintain this cease and desist action against the Bank pursuant to 12 U.S.C. § 1818(b).

ARTICLE II COMPTROLLER'S FINDINGS

The Comptroller finds, and the Bank neither admits nor denies, the following:

(1) In or around 2015, the Bank failed to establish effective risk assessment processes prior to migrating its information technology operations to the cloud operating environment. The Bank also failed to establish appropriate risk management for the cloud operating environment, including appropriate design and implementation of certain network security controls, adequate data loss prevention controls, and effective dispositioning of alerts.

(2) The Bank's internal audit failed to identify numerous control weaknesses and gaps in the cloud operating environment. Internal audit also did not effectively report on and highlight identified weaknesses and gaps to the Audit Committee.

(3) For certain concerns raised by internal audit, the Board failed to take effective actions to hold management accountable, particularly in addressing concerns regarding certain internal control gaps and weaknesses.

(4) By reason of the foregoing conduct, the Bank was in noncompliance with 12 C.F.R. Part 30, Appendix B, "Interagency Guidelines Establishing Information Security Standards," and engaged in unsafe or unsound practices that were part of a pattern of misconduct.

(5) The Bank has begun addressing the identified corrective action and has committed to providing resources to remedy the deficiencies.

ARTICLE III COMPLIANCE COMMITTEE

(1) By August 31, 2020, the Board shall appoint a Compliance Committee of at least three (3) members of which a majority shall be directors who are not employees or officers of the Bank or any of its subsidiaries or affiliates. The Board shall submit in writing to the Examiner- in-Charge the names of the members of the Compliance Committee

within ten (10) days of their appointment. In the event of a change of the membership, the Board shall submit in writing to the Examiner-in-Charge within ten (10) days the name of any new or resigning committee member. The Compliance Committee shall monitor and oversee the Bank's compliance with the provisions of this Order. The Compliance Committee shall meet at least quarterly and maintain minutes of its meetings.

(2) By October 30, 2020, and thereafter within forty-five (45) days after the end of each quarter, the Compliance Committee shall submit to the Board a written progress report setting forth in detail:

(a) A description of the corrective actions needed to achieve compliance with each Article of this Order;

(b) The specific corrective actions undertaken to comply with each Article of this Order; and

(c) The results and status of the corrective actions.

(3) Upon receiving each written progress report, the Board shall forward a copy of the report, with any additional comments by the Board, to the Examiner-in-Charge within ten (10) days of the first Board meeting following the Board's receipt of such report.

ARTICLE IV
COMPREHENSIVE ACTION PLAN

(1) Within sixty (60) days of the effective date of this Order, the Bank shall develop a written action plan detailing the remedial actions necessary to achieve compliance with Articles V through X of this Order ("Action Plan"), and submit the Action Plan to the Examiner-in- Charge for review and prior written determination of no supervisory objection by the Deputy Comptroller. To the extent the remedial actions and action plans identified in Articles V through X are already addressed in the Bank's four previously adopted actions plans ("Existing Bank Action Plans"), the Existing Bank Action Plans may be used to satisfy the Action Plan and action plans required in Articles V through X. The Action Plan, at a minimum, shall specify:

(a) A description of the corrective actions needed to achieve compliance with each Article of this Order;

(b) Reasonable and well-supported timelines for completion of the corrective actions required by this Order; and

(c) The person(s) responsible for completion of the corrective actions required by this Order.

(2) The timelines contained in the Action Plan shall be consistent with any deadlines set forth in this Order, including any modifications to the Order made pursuant to Article XIV, Paragraph (4).

(3) In the event the Deputy Comptroller requires changes to the Action Plan, the Bank shall incorporate the required changes into the Action Plan and submit the revised Action Plan to the Examiner-in-Charge for review and prior written determination of no supervisory objection by the Deputy Comptroller.

(4) Upon receipt of a written determination of no supervisory objection from the Deputy Comptroller, the Board shall ensure the Bank has timely adopted and implemented all

corrective actions required by this Order, and shall verify the Bank adheres to the Action Plan, including the timelines set forth within the Action Plan.

(5) The Bank shall not take any action that will cause a significant deviation from, or material change to, the Action Plan. Where the Bank considers modifications to the Action Plan appropriate, the Bank shall submit a revised Action Plan containing the proposed modifications to the Examiner-in-Charge for prior written determination of no supervisory objection from the Deputy Comptroller. Upon receipt of a written determination of no supervisory objection from the Deputy Comptroller, the Board shall ensure the Bank has timely adopted and implemented all corrective actions required by this Order, and shall verify the Bank adheres to the revised Action Plan.

(6) By October 30, 2020, and thereafter within forty-five (45) days after the end of each quarter, the Bank shall prepare, and shall submit to the Board, a written Action Plan progress report setting forth in detail:

> (a) The specific corrective actions undertaken to comply with each Article of this Order;
>
> (b) The results and status of the corrective actions; and
>
> (c) A description of the outstanding corrective actions needed to achieve compliance with each Article of this Order and the party or parties responsible for the completion of outstanding corrective actions.

The Board shall direct the Bank to forward a copy of the report, with any additional comments by the Board, to the appropriate OCC official within ten (10) days of the first Board meeting following the Board's receipt of such report.

ARTICLE V
BOARD AND MANAGEMENT OVERSIGHT

(1) Within ninety (90) days of the effective date of this Order, the Bank shall submit to the OCC, for review and prior written determination of no supervisory objection by the Examiner-in-Charge, a plan to improve oversight of the Bank's cloud operating environment information security program ("Board and Management Oversight Plan"). At a minimum, the Board and Management Oversight Plan shall require the Bank to:

> (a) Develop appropriate and effective risk assessment processes across all three lines of defense to identify and manage technology risks within the cloud operating environment, including risk assessment processes specific to technology changes;
>
> (b) Reassess the quality and content of Board reporting and improve transparency into the materiality and status of known technology and cyber risk issues;
>
> (c) Increase scrutiny, monitoring, and oversight of management's actions to address significant technology and cyber risk issues, including audit findings; and
>
> (d) Hold management accountable for the timely remediation of material risk issues identified by internal and external sources, including requiring management to explain why key issues and risks related to the cloud operating environment have not been addressed in a timely and effective manner.

ARTICLE VI
RISK ASSESSMENT

(1) Within ninety (90) days of the effective date of this Order, the Bank shall develop and submit to the OCC, for review and prior written determination of no supervisory objection by the Examiner-in-Charge, a plan to improve risk assessment for the Bank's cloud and legacy technology operating environments ("Risk Assessment Plan"). At a minimum, the Risk Assessment Plan shall require the Bank to:

> (a) Document expected and potential threats of material changes to the cloud and legacy technology environments and mitigating controls or remediation plans to address such threats;

> (b) Develop appropriate risk mitigation testing from the beginning and throughout new project life cycle;

> (c) Create a current threat inventory for use in risk assessment processes;

> (d) Maintain the current threat inventory through continuous updating and analyzing of information regarding new threats and vulnerabilities, actual attacks, and the effectiveness of existing security controls; and

> (e) Reassess critical business processes related to cyber and technology change activity to ensure they are appropriately captured and included in existing risk assessment processes.

(2) The Risk Assessment Plan shall expand existing risk assessment processes and supporting policies and procedures to include coverage and guidance on the criteria against which to perform targeted risk assessments of material cyber and technology change initiatives.

(3) The Risk Assessment Plan shall redesign the enterprise risk assessment framework to capture and aggregate results of all relevant risk identification and control effectiveness inputs to drive enterprise risk reporting of cyber and technology change risk.

(4) The Bank shall not implement a material technology or cyber change initiative before development and submission of a comprehensive risk assessment for the change initiative to the Examiner-in-Charge. This requirement is effective upon submission of the Bank's Risk Assessment Plan as detailed in this Article.

ARTICLE VII
CLOUD OPERATIONS RISK MANAGEMENT

(1) Within ninety (90) days of the effective date of this Order, the Bank shall submit to the OCC, for review and prior written determination of no supervisory objection by the Examiner-in-Charge, a plan to improve the Bank's Cloud Operations Risk Management ("Cloud Operations Risk Management Plan"). At a minimum, the Cloud Operations Risk Management Plan shall require the Bank to implement effective corrective actions required as a result of a 2019 OCC examination. The Cloud Operations Risk Management plan shall broadly require the Bank to:

> (a) Develop comprehensive security controls protecting the Bank's network perimeter;

(b) Develop effective controls to identify and protect sensitive customer information contained within the Bank's technology systems and applications;

(c) Develop comprehensive processes to prevent and detect unauthorized disclosure of sensitive information sent outside the Bank's technology environment; and

(d) Develop effective vulnerability and configuration management controls related to the containerization of objects within the Bank's cloud environment.

ARTICLE VIII INDEPENDENT RISK MANAGEMENT

(1) Within ninety (90) days of the effective date of this Order, the Bank shall submit to the OCC, for review and prior written determination of no supervisory objection by the Examiner-in-Charge, a plan to improve independent risk management of the cloud operating environment ("Independent Risk Management Plan"). At a minimum, the Independent Risk Management Plan shall require the Bank to:

(a) Assess inherent technology and cyber risks enterprise-wide and deploy appropriate and effective controls to mitigate these risks;

(b) Challenge inherent and residual cyber risks as identified by technology and cyber first line functions;

(c) Formally define and document a comprehensive cyber risk and control universe that captures all relevant risks; and

(d) Utilize control universe data to create and implement an appropriate risk- based control testing and validation plan.

ARTICLE IX INTERNAL CONTROLS TESTING

(1) Within ninety (90) days of the effective date of this Order, the Bank shall submit to the OCC, for review and prior written determination of no supervisory objection by the Examiner-in-Charge, a plan designed to enhance the Bank's internal controls testing in the cloud environment ("Internal Controls Plan"). At a minimum, the Internal Controls Plan shall require the Bank to:

(a) Develop a control inventory by identifying and documenting relevant controls within the Bank's cloud operating environment;

(b) Develop and implement a comprehensive risk-based testing and monitoring plan that is reconciled back to the inventory; and

(c) Track and remediate control gaps, or appropriately approve control gaps as a risk acceptance.

ARTICLE X INTERNAL AUDIT

(1) Within ninety (90) days of the effective date of this Order, the Bank shall submit to the Examiner-in-Charge for review and prior written determination of no supervisory objection a plan to enhance the Bank's internal audit program ("Internal Audit Plan"). At a minimum, the Internal Audit Plan shall require the Bank to:

(a) Reassess the cyber and technology risk assessment methodology and scoring system that ranks and evaluates business and control risks for significant business units, products, services, and security functions;

(b) Assess and validate the completeness and accuracy of management's documented inventory of technology assets and configurable devices and software;

(c) Map the existing audit universe to the concerns noted in the recent examination to identify coverage gaps and audit quality issues;

(d) Incorporate lessons-learned related to the cybersecurity breach root cause analysis;

(e) Revise the risk-based technology audit plan to address the gaps and weaknesses described in Article II and within audit's lessons-learned assessment to ensure appropriate coverage of cloud operations and related security controls; and

(f) Assess audit staff expertise and training needs.

(2) The Internal Audit Plan shall also include improved reporting to the Audit Committee to appropriately capture detailed technology risk issues and control themes and ineffective or untimely remediation efforts to provide the Board with sufficient information to make informed decisions regarding risks within the IT operating and control environment.

ARTICLE XI
GENERAL BOARD RESPONSIBILITIES

(1) The Board shall ensure that the Bank has timely adopted and implemented all corrective actions required by this Order, and shall verify that the Bank adheres to the corrective actions and they are effective in addressing the Bank's deficiencies that resulted in this Order.

(2) In each instance in which this Order imposes responsibilities upon the Board, it is intended to mean that the Board shall:

(a) Authorize, direct, and adopt corrective actions on behalf of the Bank as may be necessary to perform the obligations and undertakings imposed on the Board by this Order;

(b) Ensure the Bank has sufficient processes, management, personnel, control systems, and corporate and risk governance to implement and adhere to all provisions of this Order;

(c) Require that Bank management and personnel have sufficient training and authority to execute their duties and responsibilities pertaining to or resulting from this Order;

(d) Hold Bank management and personnel accountable for executing their duties and responsibilities pertaining to or resulting from this Order;

(e) Require appropriate, adequate, and timely reporting to the Board by Bank management of corrective actions directed by the Board to be taken under the terms of this Order; and

(f) Address any noncompliance with corrective actions in a timely and appropriate manner. . . .[173]

---

[173] Consent Order, Capital One, N.A. & Capital One Bank (USA), N.A., No. AA-EC-20-49 (2020).

3.8[B][I] FDIC ENFORCEMENT

The FDIC can also enforce the Security Guidelines:

SAFETY AND SOUNDNESS ORDERS

Section 39 of the FDI Act requires the federal banking authorities to establish various safety and soundness standards. The Act allows the FDIC to request corrective plans from financial institutions that do not meet the standards, which are set forth in Part 364 and the interagency guidelines in Appendix A and Appendix B to Part 364.

If the FDIC requests an informal compliance plan to correct identified deficiencies and the institution fails to submit an acceptable plan, or fails to adhere to a submitted plan, the FDIC will pursue an enforceable order under Section 8 of the FDI Act. In addition, the FDIC may require by order, other corrective measures, such as restricted asset growth, higher capital levels, limits on deposit interest rates, or any other measure deemed necessary to effect corrective action.[174]

Also, as one of the federal bank agencies, the Federal Reserve System can also enforce the Security Guidelines as part of unsafe or unsound practices.

The Federal Reserve supervises the following entities and has the statutory authority to take formal enforcement actions against them: State member banks[;] Bank holding companies[;] Savings and loan holding companies[;] Nonbank subsidiaries of bank holding companies and of savings and loan holding companies[;] Edge Act and agreement corporations[;] Branches and agencies of foreign banking organizations operating in the United States and their parent banks[;] Systemically important nonbank financial companies designated by the Financial Stability Oversight Council (FSOC) for supervision by the Federal Reserve[;] Officers, directors, employees, and certain other categories of individuals or entities associated with the above banks, companies, and organizations (referred to as "institution-affiliated parties").

Generally, the Federal Reserve takes formal enforcement actions against the above entities and individuals for violations of laws, rules, or regulations, unsafe or unsound practices, breaches of fiduciary duty, and violations of final orders. Formal enforcement actions include cease and desist orders, written agreements, prompt corrective action directives, removal and prohibition orders, and orders assessing civil money penalties. Since August 1989, the Federal Reserve has made all final enforcement orders public in accordance with the Financial Institutions Reform, Recovery, and Enforcement Act of

---

[174] FED. DEP'T OF INS. CORP., FORMAL ADMINISTRATIVE ACTIONS 8 (2016), *available at* https://www.fdic.gov/regulations/safety/manual/section15-1.pdf.

1989; since November 1990, it has made written agreements public in accordance with the Crime Control Act of 1990. Since July 21, 2011, the Federal Reserve has made public all final enforcement actions taken by the Federal Reserve regarding savings and loan holding companies. Formal enforcement actions taken by the Federal Reserve before August 1989 are not public.

Since 2008, the Federal Reserve has posted "Section 19 Letters" on the Board of Governors' public website. Reserve Banks send Section 19 Letters (referring to section 19 of the Federal Deposit Insurance Act, 12 U.S.C. § 1829) to individuals, generally institution-affiliated parties of entities supervised by the Federal Reserve, who have been convicted of a crime involving dishonesty, a breach of trust, or money laundering, or who have entered into a pretrial diversion or similar program in connection with a prosecution for such a crime. Section 19 prohibits any individual with such a conviction, or who has entered into such a program, from participating in the affairs of insured depository institutions, their holding companies, or credit unions without prior regulatory or judicial approval.[175]

3.8[C] NATIONAL CREDIT UNION ADMINISTRATION

The National Credit Union Administration (NCUA) also participates under the GBLA.

On June 6, 2000, the NCUA Board approved a proposal to revise 12 CFR part 748 to include requirements for administrative, technical, and physical safeguards for member records and information, as required by the GLB Act. 65 FR 37302, Jun. 14, 2000.[176]

12 CFR part 748 in relevant part:

§748.0 Security program.
(a) Each federally insured credit union will develop a written security program within 90 days of the effective date of insurance.
(b) The security program will be designed to:
(1) Protect each credit union office from robberies, burglaries, larcenies, and embezzlement;
(2) Ensure the security and confidentiality of member records, protect against the anticipated threats or hazards to the security or integrity of such records, and protect against unauthorized access to or use of such records that could result in substantial harm or serious inconvenience to a member;

---

[175] *Enforcement Actions: About*, BOARD OF GOVERNORS OF THE FED. RES. SYS., https://www.federalreserve.gov/apps/enforcementactions/default.aspx (last visited Nov. 2, 2020).
[176] NAT'L CREDIT UNION ADMIN., 12 CFR PART 748: GUIDELINES FOR SAFEGUARDING MEMBER INFORMATION, *available at* https://www.ffiec.gov/exam/infobase/documents/02-ncu-12_cfr_748_app_a_safeguard_info-010100.pdf.

(3) Respond to incidents of unauthorized access to or use of member information that could result in substantial harm or serious inconvenience to a member;

(4) Assist in the identification of persons who commit or attempt such actions and crimes, and

(5) Prevent destruction of vital records, as defined in 12 CFR part 749.

(c) Each Federal credit union, as part of its information security program, must properly dispose of any consumer information the Federal credit union maintains or otherwise possesses, as required under §717.83 of this chapter.

[50 FR 53295, Dec. 31, 1985, as amended at 53 FR 4845, Feb. 18, 1988; 66 FR 8161, Jan. 30, 2001; 69 FR 69274, Nov. 29, 2004; 70 FR 22778, May 2, 2005][177]

Appendix A to Part 748 in relevant part:
Appendix A to Part 748—Guidelines for Safeguarding Member Information

Table of Contents

I. Introduction

The Guidelines for Safeguarding Member Information (Guidelines) set forth standards pursuant to sections 501 and 505(b), codified at 15 U.S.C. 6801 and 6805(b), of the Gramm-Leach-Bliley Act. These Guidelines provide guidance standards for developing and implementing administrative, technical, and physical safeguards to protect the security, confidentiality, and integrity of member information. These Guidelines also address standards with respect to the proper disposal of consumer information pursuant to sections 621(b) and 628 of the Fair Credit Reporting Act (15 U.S.C. 1681s(b) and 1681w).

---

[177] 12 C.F.R. § 748.0 (2019).

A. *Scope.* The Guidelines apply to member information maintained by or on behalf of federally insured credit unions. Such entities are referred to in this appendix as "the credit union." These Guidelines also apply to the proper disposal of consumer information by such entities.

B. *Definitions.*

1. *In general.* Except as modified in the Guidelines or unless the context otherwise requires, the terms used in these Guidelines have the same meanings as set forth in 12 CFR part 1016.

2. For purposes of the Guidelines, the following definitions apply:

a. *Consumer information* means any record about an individual, whether in paper, electronic, or other form, that is a consumer report or is derived from a consumer report and that is maintained or otherwise possessed by or on behalf of the credit union for a business purpose. Consumer information also means a compilation of such records. The term does not include any record that does not identify an individual.

b. *Consumer report* has the same meaning as set forth in the Fair Credit Reporting Act, 15 U.S.C. 1681a(d). The meaning of consumer report is broad and subject to various definitions, conditions and exceptions in the Fair Credit Reporting Act. It includes written or oral communications from a consumer reporting agency to a third party of information used or collected for use in establishing eligibility for credit or insurance used primarily for personal, family or household purposes, and eligibility for employment purposes. Examples include credit reports, bad check lists, and tenant screening reports.

c. *Member* means any member of the credit union as defined in 12 CFR 1016.3(n).

d. *Member information* means any records containing nonpublic personal information, as defined in 12 CFR 1016.3(p), about a member, whether in paper, electronic, or other form, that is maintained by or on behalf of the credit union.

e. *Member information system* means any method used to access, collect, store, use, transmit, protect, or dispose of member information.

f. *Service provider* means any person or entity that maintains, processes, or otherwise is permitted access to member information through its provision of services directly to the credit union.

II. Standards for Safeguarding Member Information

A. *Information Security Program.* A comprehensive written information security program includes administrative, technical, and physical safeguards appropriate to the size and complexity of the credit union and the nature and scope of its activities. While all parts of the credit union are not required to implement a uniform set of policies, all elements of the information security program must be coordinated.

B. *Objectives.* A credit union's information security program should be designed to: ensure the security and confidentiality of member information; protect against any anticipated threats or hazards to the security or integrity of such information; protect against unauthorized access to or use of such information that could result in substantial harm or inconvenience to any member; and ensure the proper disposal of member information and consumer information. Protecting confidentiality includes honoring members' requests to opt out of disclosures to nonaffiliated third parties, as described in 12 CFR 1016.1(a)(3).

III. Development and Implementation of Member Information Security Program

A. *Involve the Board of Directors.* The board of directors or an appropriate committee of the board of each credit union should:

1. Approve the credit union's written information security policy and program; and

2. Oversee the development, implementation, and maintenance of the credit union's information security program, including assigning specific responsibility for its implementation and reviewing reports from management.

B. *Assess Risk.* Each credit union should:

1. Identify reasonably foreseeable internal and external threats that could result in unauthorized disclosure, misuse, alteration, or destruction of member information or member information systems;

2. Assess the likelihood and potential damage of these threats, taking into consideration the sensitivity of member information; and

3. Assess the sufficiency of policies, procedures, member information systems, and other arrangements in place to control risks.

C. *Manage and Control Risk.* Each credit union should:

1. Design its information security program to control the identified risks, commensurate with the sensitivity of the information as well as the complexity and scope of the credit union's activities. Each credit union must consider whether the following security measures are appropriate for the credit union and, if so, adopt those measures the credit union concludes are appropriate:

a. Access controls on member information systems, including controls to authenticate and permit access only to authorized individuals and controls to prevent employees from providing member information to unauthorized individuals who may seek to obtain this information through fraudulent means;

b. Access restrictions at physical locations containing member information, such as buildings, computer facilities, and records storage facilities to permit access only to authorized individuals;

c. Encryption of electronic member information, including while in transit or in storage on networks or systems to which unauthorized individuals may have access;

d. Procedures designed to ensure that member information system modifications are consistent with the credit union's information security program;

e. Dual controls procedures, segregation of duties, and employee background checks for employees with responsibilities for or access to member information;

f. Monitoring systems and procedures to detect actual and attempted attacks on or intrusions into member information systems;

g. Response programs that specify actions to be taken when the credit union suspects or detects that unauthorized individuals have gained access to member information systems, including appropriate reports to regulatory and law enforcement agencies; and

h. Measures to protect against destruction, loss, or damage of member information due to potential environmental hazards, such as fire and water damage or technical failures.

2. Train staff to implement the credit union's information security program.

3. Regularly test the key controls, systems and procedures of the information security program. The frequency and nature of such tests should be determined by the credit union's risk assessment. Tests should be conducted or reviewed by independent third parties or staff independent of those that develop or maintain the security programs.

4. Develop, implement, and maintain, as part of its information security program, appropriate measures to properly dispose of member information and consumer information in accordance with the provisions in paragraph III.

D. *Oversee Service Provider Arrangements.* Each credit union should:

1. Exercise appropriate due diligence in selecting its service providers;

2. Require its service providers by contract to implement appropriate measures designed to meet the objectives of these guidelines; and

3. Where indicated by the credit union's risk assessment, monitor its service providers to confirm that they have satisfied their obligations as required by paragraph D.2. As part of this monitoring, a credit union should review audits, summaries of test results, or other equivalent evaluations of its service providers.

E. *Adjust the Program.* Each credit union should monitor, evaluate, and adjust, as appropriate, the information security program in light of any relevant changes in technology, the sensitivity of its member information, internal or external threats to information, and the credit union's own changing business arrangements, such as mergers and acquisitions, alliances and joint ventures, outsourcing arrangements, and changes to member information systems.

F. *Report to the Board.* Each credit union should report to its board or an appropriate committee of the board at least annually. This report should describe the overall status of the information security program and the credit union's compliance with these guidelines. The report should discuss material matters related to its program, addressing issues such as: risk assessment; risk management and control decisions; service provider arrangements; results of testing; security breaches or violations and management's responses; and recommendations for changes in the information security program.

[66 FR 8161, Jan. 30, 2001, as amended at 69 FR 69274, Nov. 29, 2004; 77 FR 71085, Nov. 29, 2012; 78 FR 32545, May 31, 2013; 84 FR 1609, Feb. 5, 2019][178]

The NCUA also enforces:

In working to protect the credit union system and the Share Insurance Fund from losses, NCUA employs several supervisory tools and enforcement actions depending on the

---

[178] 12 C.F.R. §748, app. A (2019).

severity of the situation. Some of these tools include letters of understanding and agreement, administrative orders and consent orders.

Administrative Orders

The NCUA issues Administrative Orders when it finds that a credit union or persons affiliated with a credit union have violated a law, a rule or regulation, or engaged in an unsafe or unsound practice.

Letters of Understanding and Agreement

A Letters of Understanding is essentially a contract between the NCUA and a credit union, its officials or both, in which the credit union or officials agree to take, or not take, certain specified actions. NCUA also requires Letters of Understanding for newly chartered credit unions, and to grant permanent special assistance.

Consent Orders

NCUA assesses civil monetary penalties against credit unions that fail to file a Call Report on time. Here are lists of credit unions that agreed to civil monetary penalties for not submitting their quarterly Call Report information by the filing deadline. https://www.ncua.gov/regulation-supervision/enforcement-actions

Administrative Orders are formal enforcement orders issued by the NCUA pursuant to Section 206 of the Federal Credit Union Act (FCUA) (12 U.S.C. § 1786). Generally, the NCUA issues Administrative Orders when it finds that a credit union or persons affiliated with a credit union have violated a law, rule or regulation, breached a fiduciary duty, or <u>engaged in an unsafe or unsound practice</u>.

The three most common orders issued by the NCUA include:
An **Order to Cease and Desist**, which requires a party to take action (or refrain from taking action), including making restitution;
An **Order or Notice of Prohibition**, which prohibits a party from ever working for a federally insured financial institution; and
An **Order Assessing Civil Money Penalties**.
Prior to the issuance of an Administrative Order, the Federal Credit Union Act provides due process rights, which include the ability to have an administrative hearing before the Office of Financial Institution Adjudication, and to appeal the agency's decision to issue an order to the U.S. Circuit Court of Appeals.[179]

---

[179] *Administrative Orders*, NAT'L CREDIT UNION ADMIN., https://www.ncua.gov/regulation-supervision/enforcement-actions/administrative-orders (last visited Nov. 2, 2020) (emphasis added).

3.8[D] U.S. COMMODITY FUTURES TRADING COMMISSION

The U.S. Commodity Futures Trading Commission (CFTC) is another federal agency participating in the regulation of cybersecurity practices.

CFTC Press release last update on February 26, 2014:

> The U.S. Commodity Futures Trading Commission's (Commission) Division of Swap Dealer and Intermediary Oversight (Division) today issued a Staff Advisory that outlines recommended best practices for covered financial institutions to comply with Title V and Part 160 of the Commission's regulations concerning security safeguards.

> Congress enacted Title V of the Gramm-Leach-Bliley Act (GLBA) in 1999 to ensure that financial institutions respect the privacy of their customers and protect the security and confidentiality of nonpublic personal information. In enacting the GLBA, Congress directed certain Federal financial regulators to adopt and implement rules to achieve Title V's goals. These recommendations are consistent with guidelines and regulations issued by other Federal financial regulators. See CFTC Staff Advisory 14-21 under Related Links.[180]

The CFTC Staff Advisory 14-21 in relevant part:

CFTC Staff Advisory No. 14-21
Division of Swap Dealer and Intermediary Oversight
February 26, 2014

To:	**All CFTC Regulated Intermediaries**
Attention:	**Chief Financial Officer**
Subject:	**Gramm-Leach-Bliley Act Security Safeguards**

Congress enacted Title V of the Gramm-Leach-Bliley Act (GLBA) in 1999 to ensure that financial institutions respect the privacy of their customers and protect the security and confidentiality of nonpublic personal information. In enacting the GLBA, Congress directed certain Federal financial regulators to adopt and implement rules to achieve Title V's goals. Through the Commodity Futures Modernization Act of 2000, Congress added the Commodity Futures Trading Commission (Commission) as a Federal financial regulator with responsibility for implementing Title V. The Commission promulgated Title V privacy rules in 2001, and has updated those regulations over time to include additional types of covered financial institutions to ensure that the goals of Title V continue to be met.

---

[180] Press Release, Commodity Futures Trading Comm'n, CFTC's Division of Swap Dealer and Intermediary. Oversight Issues a Staff Advisory on Best Practices for Complying with the Gramm-Leach-Bliley Act Security. Safeguards (Feb. 26, 2014).

At this time, the Division of Swap Dealer and Intermediary Oversight (Division) believes it important to outline recommended best practices for covered financial institutions to comply with Title V and Part 160 of the Commission's regulations concerning security safeguards. These recommendations are consistent with guidelines and regulations issued by other Federal financial regulators.

Background

Under Part 160 of the Commission's regulations, futures commission merchants, commodity trading advisors, commodity pool operators, introducing brokers, retail foreign exchange dealers, swap dealers and major swap participants (covered entities) "must adopt policies and procedures that address administrative, technical and physical safeguards for the protection of customer records and information." As outlined in Part 160.30, those policies and procedures must:

> (1) insure the security and confidentiality of customer records and information;
>
> (2) protect against any anticipated threats or hazards to the security or integrity of such records; and
>
> (3) protect against unauthorized access to or use of such records or information which could result in substantial harm or inconvenience to any customer.
>
> Below are recommended best practices for the required "administrative, technical and physical safeguards."

Recommended Best Practices

Each covered entity should develop, implement and maintain a written information security and privacy program that is appropriate to its size and complexity, the nature and scope of its activities, and which requires it to, at a minimum:

> 1. Designate a specific employee with privacy and security management oversight responsibilities, who develops strategic organizational plans for implementing the required controls, is part of or reports directly to senior management or the Board of Directors, and designates employee(s) to coordinate, implement and regularly assess the effectiveness of the program.
>
> 2. Identify, in writing, all reasonably foreseeable internal and external risks to security, confidentiality, and integrity of personal information and systems processing personal information that could result in the unauthorized disclosure, misuse, alteration, destruction, or other compromise of such information or systems, and establish processes and controls to assess and mitigate such risks; also, identify such risks, and establish processes and controls to assess and mitigate risks, before implementing new or material changes to internal systems.
>
> 3. Design and implement safeguards to control the identified risks, and maintain a written record of such designs.

4. Train staff to implement the program, and provide regular refresher training.

5. Regularly test or otherwise monitor the safeguards' controls, systems, policies and procedures, and maintain written records of the effectiveness of the controls, including the effectiveness of:

    a.   Access controls on personal information;

    b.   Appropriate encryption of electronic information in storage and transit;

    c.   Controls to detect, prevent and respond to incidents of unauthorized access to or use of personal information; and

    d.   Employee training and supervision relating to the program.

6. At least once every two years, arrange for an independent party to test and monitor the safeguards' controls, systems, policies and procedures, maintaining written records of the effectiveness of the controls, as explained above.

7. To the extent that third party service providers have access to customer records and information, oversee service providers and document in writing that in such oversight the entity is:

    a.   Taking reasonable steps to select and retain service providers capable of maintaining appropriate safeguards; and

    b.   Contractually requiring service providers to implement and maintain appropriate safeguards.

8. Regularly evaluate and adjust the program in light of:

    a.   The results of the risk assessment process;

    b.   Relevant changes in technology and business processes;

    c.   Any material changes to operations or business arrangements; and

    d.   Any other circumstances that the entity knows or reasonably believes may have a material impact on the program.

9. Design and implement policies and procedures for responding to an incident involving unauthorized access, disclosure or use of personal information, including policies and procedures to:

    a.   Assess the nature and scope of any such incident, and maintain a written record of the systems and information involved;

    b.   Take appropriate steps to contain and control the incident to prevent further unauthorized access, disclosure or use, and maintain a written record of steps taken;

    c.   Promptly conduct a reasonable investigation, determine the likelihood that personal information has or will be misused, and maintain a written record of such determination; and

    d.   If the covered entity determines that misuse of information has occurred or is reasonably possible, then as soon as possible notify individuals whose information was or may be misused and notify the Commission in writing explaining the situation and possible risks (unless law enforcement requests in writing that notification be delayed).

10.   Provide the Board of Directors an annual assessment of the program, including updates to the program, the effectiveness of the program, and instances during the year of unauthorized access or disclosure of personal information.

The Division issues these recommended best practices with the expectation that the Division will enhance its audit and review standards as it continues to focus more resources on GLBA Title V compliance.[181]

3.8[E] FEDERAL FINANCIAL INSTITUTIONS EXAMINATION COUNCIL

Another Federal agency that is involved in financial institution cybersecurity standards is the Federal Financial Institutions Examination Council (FFIEC).

The Federal Financial Institutions Examination Council (FFIEC) was established on March 10, 1979, pursuant to title X of the Financial Institutions Regulatory and Interest Rate Control Act of 1978 (FIRA), Public Law 95-630. In 1989, title XI of the Financial Institutions Reform, Recovery and Enforcement Act of 1989 (FIRREA) established The Appraisal Subcommittee (ASC) within the Examination Council.

The Council is a formal interagency body empowered to prescribe uniform principles, standards, and report forms for the federal examination of financial institutions by the Board of Governors of the Federal Reserve System (FRB), the Federal Deposit Insurance Corporation (FDIC), the National Credit Union Administration (NCUA), the Office of the Comptroller of the Currency (OCC), and the Consumer Financial Protection Bureau (CFPB) and to make recommendations to promote uniformity in the supervision of financial institutions. To encourage the application of uniform examination principles and standards by the state and federal supervisory authorities, the Council established, in accordance with the requirement of the statute, the State Liaison Committee composed of five representatives of state supervisory agencies. In accordance with the Financial Services Regulatory Relief Act of 2006, a representative state regulator was added as a voting member of the Council in October 2006.

The Council is responsible for developing uniform reporting systems for federally supervised financial institutions, their holding companies, and the nonfinancial institution subsidiaries of those institutions and holding companies. It conducts schools for examiners employed by the five federal member agencies represented on the Council

---

[181] Letter from Gary Barnett, Dir., Div. of Swap Dealer and Intermediary Oversight, to Chief Financial Officers of all CFTC Regulated Intermediaries (Feb. 26, 2014).

and makes those schools available to employees of state agencies that supervise financial institutions.

The Council was given additional statutory responsibilities by section 340 of the Housing and Community Development Act of 1980 to facilitate public access to data that depository institutions must disclose under the Home Mortgage Disclosure Act of 1975 (HMDA) and the aggregation of annual HMDA data, by census tract, for each metropolitan statistical area (MSA).[182]

The Federal Financial Institutions Examination Council (FFIEC) members are taking a number of initiatives to raise the awareness of financial institutions and their critical third-party service providers with respect to cybersecurity risks and the need to identify, assess, and mitigate these risks in light of the increasing volume and sophistication of cyber threats.

Financial institutions are increasingly dependent on information technology and telecommunications to deliver services to consumers and business every day. Disruption, degradation, or unauthorized alteration of information and systems that support these services can affect operations, institutions, and their core processes, and undermine confidence in the nation's financial services sector.

In June 2013, the FFIEC announced the creation of the Cybersecurity and Critical Infrastructure Working Group to enhance communication among the FFIEC member agencies and build on existing efforts to strengthen the activities of other interagency and private sector groups. In addition, the FFIEC began assessing and enhancing the state of the industry preparedness and identifying gaps in the regulators' examination procedures and training that can be closed to strengthen the oversight of cybersecurity readiness.

The National Institute of Standards and Technology defines cybersecurity as "the process of protecting information by preventing, detecting, and responding to attacks." As part of cybersecurity, institutions should consider management of internal and external threats and vulnerabilities to protect information assets and the supporting infrastructure from technology-based attacks.[183]

---

[182] *About the FFIEC*, FED. FIN. INST. EXAMINATION COUNCIL, https://www.ffiec.gov/about.htm (last modified Apr. 15, 2020, 11:10 AM).

[183] *Cybersecurity Awareness*, FED. FIN. INST. EXAMINATION COUNCIL, https://www.ffiec.gov/cybersecurity.htm (last modified Aug. 13, 2020, 10:27 AM).

CHAPTER FOUR. U.S. SECURITIES AND EXCHANGE COMMISSION CYBERSECURITY

4.1 Introduction

Congress created the SEC through the Securities Act of 1934. Congress also passed the Securities Act of 1933. These congressional actions were designed to restore confidence during the Great Depression. As one might expect, cybersecurity was not on the minds of Congress during these actions. But with the advent of computers and computerized trading, the SEC has had to address cybersecurity.

This chapter includes an examination of regulations enforced by the SEC as well as that enforcement. This chapter also reviews private litigation involving securities fraud and cybersecurity and disclosure issues related to cybersecurity.

4.2 Regulation S-P and Regulation SCI

The main regulations that the SEC relies on for cybersecurity are: 1) Privacy of Consumer Financial Information (Regulation S-P), 17 CFR PART 248; 2) Regulation SCI (Systems; Compliance; Integrity) plus Form SCI, 17 CFR PARTS 240, 242, and 249.

REGULATION S-P

Regulation S-P, which became effect on November 13, 2000, "requires registered broker-dealers, investment companies, and investment advisers to 'adopt written policies and procedures that address administrative, technical, and physical safeguards for the protection of customer records and information.'"[184]

The SEC promulgated Regulation S-P in response to "section 504 of the Gramm-Leach-Bliley Act."

Section 504 requires the Commission and other federal agencies to adopt rules implementing notice requirements and restrictions on a financial institution's ability to disclose nonpublic personal information about consumers. Under the Gramm-Leach-Bliley Act, a financial institution must provide its customers with a notice of its privacy policies and practices, and must not disclose nonpublic personal information about a consumer to nonaffiliated third parties unless the

---

[184] 17 C.F.R. § 248.30 (2000).

institution provides certain information to the consumer and the consumer has not elected to opt out of the disclosure. The Act also requires the Commission to establish for financial institutions appropriate standards to protect customer information. The final rules implement these requirements of the Gramm-Leach-Bliley Act with respect to investment advisers registered with the Commission, brokers, dealers, and investment companies, which are the financial institutions subject to the Commission's jurisdiction under that Act.[185]

Amendments to Regulation S-P covering the Disposal of Consumer Report Information became effective on January 11, 2005.

The amended rule implements the provision in section 216 of the Fair and Accurate Credit Transactions Act of 2003 requiring proper disposal of consumer report information and records. Section 216 directs the Commission and other federal agencies to adopt regulations requiring that any person who maintains or possesses consumer report information or any compilation of consumer report information derived from a consumer report for a business purpose must properly dispose of the information. The amendments also require the policies and procedures adopted under the safeguard rule to be in writing.[186]

The relevant text of Regulation S-P can be found in section 248.30, entitled "Procedures to safeguard customer records and information; disposal of consumer report information."

§248.30 Procedures to safeguard customer records and information; disposal of consumer report information.

(a) Every broker, dealer, and investment company, and every investment adviser registered with the Commission must adopt written policies and procedures that address administrative, technical, and physical safeguards for the protection of customer records and information. These written policies and procedures must be reasonably designed to:

(1) Insure the security and confidentiality of customer records and information;

(2) Protect against any anticipated threats or hazards to the security or integrity of customer records and information; and

(3) Protect against unauthorized access to or use of customer records or information that could result in substantial harm or inconvenience to any customer.

---

[185] FINAL RULE: PRIVACY OF CONSUMER FINANCIAL INFORMATION, S.E.C. (Nov. 18, 2003), *available at* https://www.sec.gov/rules/final/34-42974.htm.

[186] FINAL RULE: DISPOSAL OF CONSUMER REPORT INFORMATION, S.E.C. (Dec. 2, 2004), *available at* https://www.sec.gov/rules/final/34-50781.htm.

(b) *Disposal of consumer report information and records—*
(1) *Definitions* (i) *Consumer report* has the same meaning as in section 603(d) of the Fair Credit Reporting Act (15 U.S.C. 1681a(d)).

(ii) *Consumer report information* means any record about an individual, whether in paper, electronic or other form, that is a consumer report or is derived from a consumer report. Consumer report information also means a compilation of such records. Consumer report information does not include information that does not identify individuals, such as aggregate information or blind data.

(iii) *Disposal* means:

(A) The discarding or abandonment of consumer report information; or

(B) The sale, donation, or transfer of any medium, including computer equipment, on which consumer report information is stored.

(iv) *Notice-registered broker-dealers* means a broker or dealer registered by notice with the Commission under section 15(b)(11) of the Securities Exchange Act of 1934 (15 U.S.C. 78o(b)(11)).

(v) *Transfer agent* has the same meaning as in section 3(a)(25) of the Securities Exchange Act of 1934 (15 U.S.C. 78c(a)(25)).

(2) *Proper disposal requirements—*(i) *Standard.* Every broker and dealer other than notice-registered broker-dealers, every investment company, and every investment adviser and transfer agent registered with the Commission, that maintains or otherwise possesses consumer report information for a business purpose must properly dispose of the information by taking reasonable measures to protect against unauthorized access to or use of the information in connection with its disposal.

(ii) *Relation to other laws.* Nothing in this section shall be construed:

(A) To require any broker, dealer, or investment company, or any investment adviser or transfer agent registered with the Commission to maintain or destroy any record pertaining to an individual that is not imposed under other law; or

(B) To alter or affect any requirement imposed under any other provision of law to maintain or destroy any of those records.[187]

---

[187] 17 C.F.R § 248.20 (2000).

While confidentiality, integrity, and availability (CIA) are common goals of cybersecurity, administrative, technical, and physical safeguards are a common theme in achieving those goals. And they can be thought of as providing a layered defense in depth. In other words, if the physical protections are breached then the perpetrator still has to get through the technical and administrative safeguards, as depicted in the figure below:

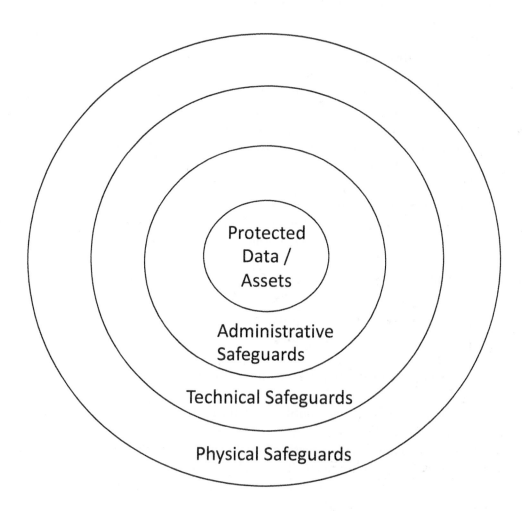

FIGURE 1: Defense in Depth

Because there are three layers of security applied, physical, technical (also known as logical), and administrative safeguards are also known as a defense in depth. Risk-adverse attorneys may relate this concept to the legal belt and suspenders preparation where the attorney does not rely on just one course of action.

Regulation SCI

In November 2014, the SEC adopted the Regulation Systems Compliance and Integrity and Form SCI. The goal was to "strengthen the technology infrastructure of the U.S. securities markets."

The rules were "designed to:
- Reduce the occurrence of systems issues;
- Improve resiliency when systems problems do occur;
- Enhance the Commission's oversight and enforcement of securities market technology infrastructure."

The regulation covers "SCI entities" that "includes self-regulatory organizations ('SROs'), including stock and options exchanges, registered clearing agencies, FINRA and the MSRB, alternative trading systems ('ATSs'), that trade NMS and non-NMS stocks exceeding specified volume thresholds, disseminators of consolidated market data ('plan processors'), and certain exempt clearing agencies."[188]

The regulation primarily covers "the systems of SCI entities that directly support any one of six key securities market functions – trading, clearance and settlement, order routing, market data, market regulation, and market surveillance . . ."[189]

Section 242.1001 Obligations related to policies and procedures of SCI entities

This section lays out the requirements for the capacity, integrity, resiliency, availability, and security for SCI systems:

(2) Policies and procedures required by paragraph (a)(1) of this section shall include, at a minimum:
(i) The establishment of reasonable current and future technological infrastructure capacity planning estimates;
(ii) Periodic capacity stress tests of such systems to determine their ability to process transactions in an accurate, timely, and efficient manner;
(iii) A program to review and keep current systems development and testing methodology for such systems;
(iv) Regular reviews and testing, as applicable, of such systems, including backup systems, to identify vulnerabilities pertaining to internal and external threats, physical hazards, and natural or manmade disasters;

---

[188] *Spotlight on Regulation SCI*, U.S. SECURITIES AND EXCHANGE COMMISSION, https://www.sec.gov/spotlight/regulation-sci.shtml (last modified Dec. 9, 2016).
[189] *Id.*

(v) Business continuity and disaster recovery plans that include maintaining backup and recovery capabilities sufficiently resilient and geographically diverse and that are reasonably designed to achieve next business day resumption of trading and two-hour resumption of critical SCI systems following a wide-scale disruption;

(vi) Standards that result in such systems being designed, developed, tested, maintained, operated, and surveilled in a manner that facilitates the successful collection, processing, and dissemination of market data; and

(vii) Monitoring of such systems to identify potential SCI events.

Notice that capacity, integrity, resiliency, availability, and security are very close to the CIA basic security tenants of confidentiality, integrity, and availability. These requirements are all about preventing system down-time because the financial markets would react negatively to systems not being available. Also notice that these requirements are similar to that of a private corporation, who's lifeblood may depend on its systems and where down systems can equate to lost revenue and lowered public opinion. So, basically, the SEC is giving notice that if a company wants to operate in this space, it must establish excellent business continuity planning. One interesting departure from CIA is capacity. Here the SEC is concerned about having enough capacity within the system, probably to handle high-volume situations that could cause market panic if the systems do not have enough capacity to handle all requests.

This section of 242.1001 lays out the requirements for the systems compliance:

(b) *Systems compliance.*

(1) Each SCI entity shall establish, maintain, and enforce written policies and procedures reasonably designed to ensure that its SCI systems operate in a manner that complies with the Act and the rules and regulations thereunder and the entity's rules and governing documents, as applicable.

(2) Policies and procedures required by paragraph (b)(1) of this section shall include, at a minimum:

(i) Testing of all SCI systems and any changes to SCI systems prior to implementation;

(ii) A system of internal controls over changes to SCI systems;

(iii) A plan for assessments of the functionality of SCI systems designed to detect systems compliance issues, including by responsible SCI personnel and by personnel familiar with applicable provisions of the Act and the rules and regulations thereunder and the SCI entity's rules and governing documents; and

(iv) A plan of coordination and communication between regulatory and other personnel of the SCI entity, including by responsible SCI personnel, regarding SCI systems design, changes, testing, and controls designed to detect and prevent systems compliance issues.

(3) Each SCI entity shall periodically review the effectiveness of the policies and procedures required by this paragraph (b), and take prompt action to remedy deficiencies in such policies and procedures.

(4) Safe harbor from liability for individuals. Personnel of an SCI entity shall be deemed not to have aided, abetted, counseled, commanded, caused, induced, or procured the violation by an SCI entity of this paragraph (b) if the person:

(i) Has reasonably discharged the duties and obligations incumbent upon such person by the SCI entity's policies and procedures; and

(ii) Was without reasonable cause to believe that the policies and procedures relating to an SCI system for which such person was responsible, or had supervisory responsibility, were not established, maintained, or enforced in accordance with this paragraph (b) in any material respect.

Section 242.1002 describes obligations related to SCI events. An SCI event per section 242.1000 "means and event at an SCI entity that constitutes:

(1) A systems disruption;

(2) A systems compliance issue; or

(3) A systems intrusion."

Section 242.1006 covers electronic filing and submission requirements including the use of Form SCI (found in section 249.1900).

It is worth noting at this point that Regulation S-P is focused on customer data, whereas Regulation SCI is focused on an entities' SCI systems. Accordingly, a company may be regulated under Regulation S-P because of its business plan and customer data, but not be regulated under Regulation SCI because its business model does not make it an SCI entity.

NOTES

Note 1

The SEC Office of Compliance Inspections and Examinations has released a document titled, "Cybersecurity and Resiliency Observations" on January 27, 2020. The document contains a collection of actions taken by regulated companies to comply with SEC regulations concerning cybersecurity. The document states, in relevant part:

"GOVERNANCE AND RISK MANAGEMENT
Effective cybersecurity programs start with the right tone at the top, with senior leaders who are committed to improving their organization's cyber posture through working with others to understand, prioritize, communicate, and mitigate cybersecurity risks. While the effectiveness of

any given cybersecurity program is fact-specific, we have observed that a key element of effective programs is the incorporation of a governance and risk management program that generally includes, among other things: (i) a risk assessment to identify, analyze, and prioritize cybersecurity risks to the organization; (ii) written cybersecurity policies and procedures to address those risks; and (iii) the effective implementation and enforcement of those policies and procedures.

OCIE has observed organizations utilizing the following risk management and governance measures:

• Senior Level Engagement. Devoting appropriate board and senior leadership attention to setting the strategy of and overseeing the organization's cybersecurity and resiliency programs.

• Risk Assessment. Developing and conducting a risk assessment process to identify, manage, and mitigate cyber risks relevant to the organization's business. This includes considering the organization's business model, as part of defining a risk assessment methodology, and working to identify and prioritize potential vulnerabilities, including remote or traveling employees, insider threats, international operations and geopolitical risks, among others.

• Policies and Procedures. Adopting and implementing comprehensive written policies and procedures addressing the areas discussed below and identified risks.

• Testing and Monitoring. Establishing comprehensive testing and monitoring to validate the effectiveness of cybersecurity policies and procedures on a regular and frequent basis. Testing and monitoring can be informed based on cyber threat intelligence.

• Continuously Evaluating and Adapting to Changes. Responding promptly to testing and monitoring results by updating policies and procedures to address any gaps or weaknesses and involving board and senior leadership appropriately.

• Communication. Establishing internal and external communication policies and procedures to provide timely information to decision makers, customers, employees, other market participants, and regulators as appropriate.

ACCESS RIGHTS AND CONTROLS

Access rights and controls are used to determine appropriate users for organization systems based on job responsibilities, and to deploy controls to limit access to authorized users. Access controls generally include: (i) understanding the location of data, including client information, throughout an organization; (ii) restricting access to systems and data to authorized users; and (iii) establishing appropriate controls to prevent and monitor for unauthorized access.

OCIE has observed strategies related to access rights and controls at organizations that perform the following:

• User Access. Developing a clear understanding of access needs to systems and data. This includes limiting access to sensitive systems and data, based upon the user's needs to perform legitimate and authorized activities on the organization's information systems, and requiring periodic account reviews.

• Access Management. Managing user access through systems and procedures that: (i) limit access as appropriate, including during onboarding, transfers, and terminations; (ii) implement separation of duties for user access approvals; (iii) re-certify users' access rights on a periodic basis (paying particular attention to accounts with elevated privileges including users, administrators, and service accounts); (iv) require the use of strong, and periodically changed, passwords; (v) utilize multi-factor authentication (MFA) leveraging an application or key fob to generate an additional verification code; and (vi) revoke system access immediately for individuals no longer employed by the organization, including former contractors.

• Access Monitoring. Monitoring user access and developing procedures that: (i) monitor for failed login attempts and account lockouts; (ii) ensure proper handling of customers' requests for user name and password changes as well as procedures for authenticating anomalous or unusual customer requests; (iii) consistently review for system hardware and software changes, to identify when a change is made; and (iv) ensure that any changes are approved, properly implemented, and that any anomalies are investigated.

DATA LOSS PREVENTION

Data loss prevention typically includes a set of tools and processes an organization uses to ensure that sensitive data, including client information, is not lost, misused, or accessed by unauthorized users.
OCIE has observed the following data loss prevention measures utilized by organizations:

• Vulnerability Scanning. Establishing a vulnerability management program that includes routine scans of software code, web applications, servers and databases, workstations, and endpoints both within the organization and applicable third party providers.

• Perimeter Security. Implementing capabilities that are able to control, monitor, and inspect all incoming and outgoing network traffic to prevent unauthorized or harmful traffic. These capabilities include firewalls, intrusion detection systems, email security capabilities, and web proxy systems with content filtering. Implementing an enterprise data loss prevention solution capable of monitoring and blocking access to personal email, cloud-based file sharing services, social media sites, and removable media such as USB and CDs.

• Detective Security. Implementing capabilities that are able to detect threats on endpoints. Considering products that can utilize both signature and behavioral based capabilities and can identify incoming fraudulent communications to prevent unauthorized software or malware from running. Establishing policies and procedures to capture and retain system logs from systems and applications for aggregation and analysis. For software that provides automated actions, such as macros and scripts, enabling optional security features or following the security guidance that may be offered by third party software providers.

• Patch Management. Establishing a patch management program covering all software (i.e., in-house developed, custom off-the-shelf, and other third party software) and hardware, including anti-virus and anti-malware installation.

• Inventory Hardware and Software. Maintaining an inventory of hardware and software assets, including identification of critical assets and information (i.e., know where they are located, and how they are protected).

• Encryption and Network Segmentation. Using tools and processes to secure data and systems, including: (i) encrypting data "in motion" both internally and externally; (ii) encrypting data "at rest" on all systems including laptops, desktops, mobile phones, tablets, and servers; and (iii) implementing network segmentation and access control lists to limit data availability to only authorized systems and networks.

• Insider Threat Monitoring. Creating an insider threat program to identify suspicious behaviors, including escalating issues to senior leadership as appropriate. Increasing the depth and frequency of testing of business systems and conducting penetration tests. Creating rules to identify and block the transmission of sensitive data (e.g., account numbers, social security numbers, trade information, and source code) from leaving the organization. Tracking corrective actions in response to findings from testing and monitoring, material changes to business operations or technology, and any other significant events.

• Securing Legacy Systems and Equipment. Verifying that the decommissioning and disposal of hardware and software does not create system vulnerabilities by using processes to: (i) remove sensitive information from and prompt disposal of decommissioned hardware and software; and (ii) reassess vulnerability and risk assessments as legacy systems are replaced with more modern systems.

MOBILE SECURITY

Mobile devices and applications may create additional and unique vulnerabilities. OCIE has observed the following mobile security measures at organizations utilizing mobile applications:

• Policies and Procedures. Establishing policies and procedures for the use of mobile devices.

• Managing the Use of Mobile Devices. Using a mobile device management (MDM) application or similar technology for an organization's business, including email communication, calendar, data storage, and other activities. If using a "bring your own device" policy, ensuring that the MDM solution works with all mobile phone/ device operating systems.

• Implementing Security Measures. Requiring the use of MFA for all internal and external users. Taking steps to prevent printing, copying, pasting, or saving information to personally owned computers, smartphones or tablets. Ensuring the ability to remotely clear data and content from a device that belongs to a former employee or from a lost device.

• Training Employees. Training employees on mobile device policies and effective practices to protect mobile devices.

INCIDENT RESPONSE AND RESILIENCY

Incident response includes: (i) the timely detection and appropriate disclosure of material information regarding incidents; and (ii) assessing the appropriateness of corrective actions taken in response to incidents. An important component of an incident response plan includes business continuity and resiliency (i.e., if an incident were to occur, how quickly can the organization recover and again safely serve clients?).

OCIE has observed that many organizations with incident response plans tend to include the following elements:

• Development of a Plan. Developing a risk-assessed incident response plan for various scenarios including denial of service attacks, malicious disinformation, ransomware, key employee succession, as well as extreme but plausible scenarios. Considering past cybersecurity incidents and current cyber-threat intelligence in developing business continuity plans and policies and procedures. Establishing and maintaining procedures that include: (i) timely notification and response if an event occurs; (ii) a process to escalate incidents to appropriate levels of management, including legal and compliance functions; and (iii) communication with key stakeholders.

• Addressing Applicable Reporting Requirements. Determining and complying with applicable federal and state reporting requirements for cyber incidents or events, such as requirements for financial institutions to file a suspicious activity report or for public companies to disclose material risks and incidents. For example, the organization should consider:

» Contacting local authorities or the FBI if an attack or compromise is discovered or suspected.

» Informing regulators and sharing information, including indicators of compromise (artifacts observed on a network or operating system indicating a potential intrusion), with the appropriate organizations.

» Notifying customers, clients, and employees promptly if their data is compromised.

• Assigning Staff to Execute Specific Areas of the Plan. Designating employees with specific roles and responsibilities in the event of a cyber incident. In doing so, identifying additional cybersecurity and recovery expertise in advance.

• Testing and Assessing the Plan. Testing the incident response plan and potential recovery times, using a variety of methods including tabletop exercises. If an incident does occur, implementing the plan and assessing the response after the incident to determine whether any changes to the procedures are necessary.

OCIE has observed the following strategies to address resiliency:

• Maintaining an Inventory of Core Business Operations and Systems. Identifying and prioritizing core business services. Understanding the impact on business services of an individual system or process failure. Mapping the systems and processes that support business services, including those over which the organization may not have direct control.

• Assessing Risks and Prioritizing Business Operations. Developing a strategy for operational resiliency with defined risk tolerances tailored to the organization. In developing a strategy, organizations consider: (i) determining which systems and processes are capable of being substituted during disruption so that business services can continue to be delivered; (ii) ensuring geographic separation of back-up data and avoid concentration risk; and (iii) the effects of business disruptions on both the institution's stakeholders and other organizations.

• Considering Additional Safeguards. Maintaining back-up data in a different network and offline. Evaluating whether cybersecurity insurance is appropriate for the organization's business.

VENDOR MANAGEMENT

Practices and controls related to vendor management generally include policies and procedures related to: (i) conducting due diligence for vendor selection; (ii) monitoring and overseeing vendors, and contract terms; (iii) assessing how vendor relationships are considered as part of the organization's ongoing risk assessment process as well as how the organization determines the appropriate level of due diligence to conduct on a vendor; and (iv) assessing how vendors protect any accessible client information.

OCIE has observed the following practices in the area of vendor management by organizations:
• Vendor Management Program. Establishing a vendor management program to ensure vendors meet security requirements and that appropriate safeguards are implemented. Leveraging questionnaires based on reviews of industry standards (e.g., SOC 2, SSAE 18) as well as independent audits. Establishing procedures for terminating or replacing vendors, including cloud-based service providers.
• Understanding Vendor Relationships. Understanding all contract terms including rights, responsibilities, expectations, and other specific terms to ensure that all parties have the same understanding of how risk and security is addressed. Understanding and managing the risks related to vendor outsourcing, including vendor use of cloud based services.
• Vendor Monitoring and Testing. Monitoring the vendor relationship to ensure that the vendor continues to meet security requirements and to be aware of changes to the vendor's services or personnel.

TRAINING AND AWARENESS

Training and awareness are key components of cybersecurity programs. Training provides employees with information concerning cyber risks and responsibilities and heightens awareness of cyber threats. OCIE has observed the following practices used by organizations in the area of cybersecurity training and awareness:
• Policies and Procedures as a Training Guide. Training staff to implement the organization's cybersecurity policies and procedures and engaging the workforce to build a culture of cybersecurity readiness and operational resiliency.
• Including Examples and Exercises in Trainings. Providing specific cybersecurity and resiliency training, including phishing exercises to help employees identify phishing emails. Including preventive measures in training, such as identifying and responding to indicators of breaches, and obtaining customer confirmation if behavior appears suspicious.

• Training Effectiveness. Monitoring to ensure employees attend training and assessing the effectiveness of training. Continuously re-evaluating and updating training programs based on cyber-threat intelligence.

Note 2

The OCIE released a risk alert titled, "Safeguarding Customer Records and Information in Network Storage – Use of Third Party Security Features," on May 23, 2019. The document states, in relevant part:

"During recent examinations, the Office of Compliance Inspections and Examinations ("OCIE")* identified security risks associated with the storage of electronic customer records and information by broker-dealers and investment advisers in various network storage solutions, including those leveraging cloud-based storage. Although the majority of these network storage solutions offered encryption, password protection, and other security features designed to prevent unauthorized access, examiners observed that firms did not always use the available security features. Weak or misconfigured security settings on a network storage device could result in unauthorized access to information stored on the device.

II. Summary of Examination Observations

OCIE staff has observed firms storing electronic customer records and information using various types of storage solutions, including cloud-based storage. During examinations, OCIE staff identified the following concerns that may raise compliance issues under Regulations S-P and S-ID:

• Misconfigured network storage solutions. In some cases, firms did not adequately configure the security settings on their network storage solution to protect against unauthorized access. In addition, some firms did not have policies and procedures addressing the security configuration of their network storage solution. Often, misconfigured settings resulted from a lack of effective oversight when the storage solution was initially implemented.

• Inadequate oversight of vendor-provided network storage solutions. In some cases, firms did not ensure, through policies, procedures, contractual provisions, or otherwise, that the security settings on vendor-provided network storage solutions were configured in accordance with the firm's standards.

• Insufficient data classification policies and procedures. In some cases, firms' policies and procedures did not identify the different types of data stored electronically by the firm and the appropriate controls for each type of data.

III. Examples of Effective Practices

The implementation of a configuration management program that includes policies and procedures governing data classification, vendor oversight, and security features will help to mitigate the risks incurred when implementing on-premise or cloud-based network storage solutions. During examinations, OCIE staff has observed several features of effective configuration management programs, data classification procedures, and vendor management programs, including:
• Policies and procedures designed to support the initial installation, on-going maintenance, and regular review of the network storage solution;
• Guidelines for security controls and baseline security configuration standards to ensure that each network solution is configured properly; and
• Vendor management policies and procedures that include, among other things, regular implementation of software patches and hardware updates followed by reviews to ensure that those patches and updates did not unintentionally change, weaken, or otherwise modify the security configuration.

4.3 SEC Enforcement

Now that we have covered the SEC security regulations, we will examine how the SEC enforces those regulations.

ENFORCEMENT ACTIONS –

The SEC uses its civil law authority to bring cyber-related enforcement actions that protect investors, hold bad actors accountable, and deter future wrongdoing. The Division of Enforcement's Cyber Unit was established in September 2017 and has substantial cyber-related expertise. The Cyber Unit focuses on violations involving digital assets, initial coin offerings and cryptocurrencies; cybersecurity controls at regulated entities; issuer disclosures of cybersecurity incidents and risks; trading on the basis of hacked nonpublic information; and cyber-related manipulations, such as brokerage account takeovers and market manipulations using electronic and social media platforms.[190]

---

[190] *See Spotlight on Cybersecurity, the SEC and You*, U.S. SECURITIES AND EXCHANGE COMMISSION, https://www.sec.gov/spotlight/cybersecurity (last modified Jan. 27, 2020).

However, SEC enforcement actions related to cyber security predate the creation of the Cyber Unit thus, it is apparent that the SEC was active in the cybersecurity law enforcement space long before the they created the Cyber Unit. Apparently, the creation of the Cyber Unit was a way to maintain focus on Cyber Security.

4.3[A] OVERVIEW OF SEC ENFORCEMENT ACTIONS

The SEC categorizes its cybersecurity enforcement actions as one of:

1) digital assets / initial coin offerings;
2) account intrusions;
3) hacker / insider trading;
4) market manipulation / false tweets / fake websites;
5) regulated entities – cybersecurity controls and safeguarding customer information;
6) public company disclosure and controls
7) trading suspensions

The following chart includes some of the actions brought by the SEC across the different potential categories of actions.[191] The review of this chart provides a general sense of the scope of cybersecurity actions brought by the SEC. The chart is also useful for research concerning past SEC enforcement actions.

Digital Assets/Initial Coin Offerings

Action Name	Description	Date Filed
SEC v. BitClave PTE Ltd.	The Commission filed settled cease-and-desist proceedings against BitClave PTE Ltd. for conducting an unregistered initial coin offering of digital asset securities, requiring company to return the proceeds from the $25.5 million offering and pay additional monetary relief to be distributed through a Fair Fund.	5/28/2020
SEC v. Dropil, Inc., et al.	The Commission filed a complaint against Dropil, Inc. and its three founders for allegedly conducting a fraudulent initial coin offering of unregistered digital asset securities raising money from thousands of investors.	4/23/2020

---

[191] *See Cyber Enforcement Actions*, U.S. SECURITIES AND EXCHANGE COMMISSION, https://www.sec.gov/spotlight/cybersecurity-enforcement-actions (last modified Sept. 15, 2020).

Action Name	Description	Date Filed
<u>SEC v. Meta 1 Coin Trust, et al.</u>	The Commission filed an emergency action against Meta 1 Coin Trust, a former state senator, and two others for allegedly conducting a fraudulent initial coin offering of unregistered digital asset securities.	3/20/2020
<u>Steven Seagal</u>	The Commission filed a settled cease-and-desist proceeding against an actor for failing to disclose payments he received for promoting an investment in an initial coin offering. ...	2/27/2020

Account Intrusions

Action Name	Description	Date Filed
<u>SEC v. Willner</u>	Day trader allegedly hacked into over 100 online customer brokerage accounts to manipulate the price of securities generating at least $700,000 in illicit profits	10/30/2017
<u>SEC v. Mustapha</u>	Overseas trader allegedly hacked into online customer brokerage accounts to manipulate stock prices through unauthorized trades	6/22/2016
<u>SEC v. Murmylyuk</u>	Trader allegedly hacked into online customer brokerage accounts to manipulate stock prices through unauthorized options trades	4/17/2012
<u>SEC v. Nagaicevs</u>	Overseas allegedly trader hacked into online customer brokerage accounts to manipulate stock prices through unauthorized trades	1/26/2012

Hacking/Insider Trading

Action Name	Description	Date Filed
<u>SEC v. Ieremenko, et al.</u>	The Commission filed a district court action alleging that Ieremenko, working with others, hacked into the SEC's EDGAR system and extracted test files containing nonpublic information about upcoming quarterly earnings announcement to use for illegal trading.	1/15/2019

Action Name	Description	Date Filed
SEC v. Hong, et al.	Overseas traders allegedly hacked into two U.S. law firms to obtain nonpublic information on which they traded	12/27/2016
SEC v. Ly	IT specialist allegedly hacked into the email accounts of senior executives of his employer to obtain nonpublic information on which he traded	12/5/2016
SEC v. Zavodchiko, et al.	Overseas trading ring allegedly hacked into the servers of newswire services to obtain nonpublic information on which they traded	2/18/2016
SEC v. Dubovoy, et al.	Overseas trading ring allegedly hacked into the servers of newswire services to obtain nonpublic information on which they traded	8/11/2015

Market Manipulation/False Tweets/Fake Websites

Action Name	Description	Date Filed
SEC v. Sotnikov, et al.	The Commission filed charges against a Russian national and entities he controlled for allegedly participating in a fraudulent scheme to lure U.S. investors into buying fictitious Certificates of Deposit (CDs) promoted through internet advertising and "spoofed" websites that mimic the actual sites of legitimate financial institutions.	3/13/2020
SEC v. Burns	U.S.-based trader allegedly filed false tender offer form on EDGAR to manipulate stock price	7/11/2018
SEC v. Murray	U.S.-based trader allegedly filed false tender offer form on EDGAR to manipulate stock price	5/19/2017
SEC v. Aly	Overseas trader allegedly manipulated stock price by filing false Schedule 13D form on EDGAR	5/24/2016
SEC v. Craig	Overseas trader allegedly disseminated false tweets to manipulate stock prices	11/6/2015

Action Name	Description	Date Filed
SEC v. PTG Capital Partners LTD, et al.	Overseas trader allegedly manipulated prices of stocks through false EDGAR filings	6/4/2015

Regulated Entities – Cybersecurity Controls and Safeguarding Customer Information

Action Name	Description	Date Filed
Virtu Americas LLC (f/k/a KCG Americas LLC)	The Commission filed a settled cease-and-desist proceeding against Virtu Americas LLC (f/k/a KCG Americas LLC) for failing to comply with certain provisions of Regulation SCI in connection with the dark pool formerly known as KCG MatchIt.	9/30/2019
The Options Clearing Corporation	The Commission filed a settled cease-and-desist and administrative proceeding against a registered clearing agency for violating Exchange Act Rules 17Ad-22(b)(2) and (e)(1), (3), (4), (6) and (7), Reg. SCI, and Section 19(b)(1) of the Exchange Act and Rule 19b-4(c) thereunder as a result of its failures to establish and enforce policies and procedures involving financial risk management, operational requirements and information-systems security and changing of policies on core risk management issues without obtaining the required SEC approval.	9/4/2019
Voya Financial Advisors	The Commission filed settled administrative proceedings against an Iowa-based broker-dealer and investment adviser related to its failures in cybersecurity policies and procedures surrounding a cyber intrusion that compromised personal information of thousands of its customers, in violation of Reg S-P and Reg S-ID.	9/26/2018
Morgan Stanley Smith Barney LLC	Failure to safeguard customer data from cyber-breaches in violation of Reg S-P stemming from a Morgan Stanley employee transferring confidential customer data to a personal server that was eventually hacked.	6/8/2016

Action Name	Description	Date Filed
RT Jones Capital Equities Management, Inc.	Failure to safeguard customer data from cyber-breaches in violation of Reg S-P as a result of an investment adviser's storage of sensitive customer information on a third-party hosted web server that was eventually hacked and its failure to adopt written policies and procedures reasonably designed to safeguard such customer information.	9/22/2015

Public Company Disclosure and Controls

Action Name	Description	Date Filed
Report of Investigation Pursuant to Section 21(a) of the Securities Exchange Act of 1934: Certain Cyber-Related Frauds Perpetrated Against Public Companies and Related Internal Accounting Controls Requirements	The Commission issued a Report of Investigation regarding certain cyber-related frauds and public company issuer internal accounting controls requirements. The Report discusses a type of cyber-fraud -- called "business email compromise" -- where perpetrators pretended in emails to be high-level company executives or vendors, and then convinced company personnel to transmit large wire transfers to accounts controlled by the perpetrators. The Report explains that public companies should consider cyber threats when implementing internal accounting controls.	10/16/2018
Altaba Inc., f/d/b/a Yahoo! Inc.	Failure to disclose December 2014 data breach in which Russian hackers stole personal data related to more than 500 million Yahoo! user accounts; the data breach was not disclosed until September 2016.	4/24/2018

Trading Suspensions

Action Name	Description	Date Filed
Bitcoin Generation, Inc.	The Commission suspended trading in the securities of BTGN, inter alia, because of concerns about the accuracy and adequacy of information contained in BTGN's public	4/29/2019

Action Name	Description	Date Filed
	statements and because of stock promotional activity relating to BTGN and the market impact of such promotional activity.	
American Retail Group, Inc. aka Simex, Inc.	The Commission suspended trading in the securities of ARGB amid questions surrounding statements claiming that the company had partnered with an SEC-qualified custodian for use with cryptocurrency transactions and that the company was conducting a token offering that was "officially registered in accordance [with] SEC requirements."	10/22/2018
Bitcoin Tracker One and Ether Tracker One	The Commission suspended trading in the securities of CXBTF and CETHF because of confusion among market participants regarding the true nature of these instruments.	9/9/2018
Evolution Blockchain Group Inc.	The Commission suspended trading in Evolution Blockchain Group Inc. because of questions about the accuracy of information contained in a press release and concerns about recent unusual and unexplained market activity in the company's common stock.	6/25/2018
IBITX Software Inc.	The Commission suspended trading in IBITX because of questions about the accuracy of assertions concerning the company's development of alternative forms of currency and its operation of a cryptocurrency platform.	4/20/2018
HD View 360 Inc.	The Commission suspended trading in this publicly-traded company because of concerns regarding the accuracy and adequacy of information about the company, including certain statements regarding enhancing a subsidiary with blockchain technology.	3/1/2018

. . .

4.3[B] SEC ENFORCEMENT ACTIONS IN DEPTH

In the Matter of Virtu America's LLC, the SEC relied on the Regulation Systems Compliance and Integrity (Regulation SCI) that went into effect on February 3, 2015 in bringing its enforcement action.[192]

In the Matter of Virtu America's LLC, Release No. 34-87155 (September 30, 2019).

ORDER INSTITUTING ADMINISTRATIVE AND CEASE-AND-DESIST PROCEEDINGS . . . AND IMPOSING REMEDIAL SANCTIONS AND A CEASE-AND-DESIST ORDER

I.

The Securities and Exchange Commission ("Commission") deems it appropriate and in the public interest that public administrative and cease-and-desist proceedings be, and hereby are, instituted pursuant to Sections 15(b) and 21C of the Securities Exchange Act of 1934 ("Exchange Act") against Virtu Americas LLC (f/k/a KCG Americas LLC) ("VAL" or "Respondent"). . . .

III.

On the basis of this Order and Respondent's Offer, the Commission finds that:

Summary

1. These proceedings arise out of the failure of VAL's predecessor entity, KCG Americas LLC ("KCGA"), to comply with Regulation Systems Compliance and Integrity ("Regulation SCI"). VAL owns and operates Virtu MatchIt, formerly known as KCG MatchIt, an alternative trading system ("ATS") commonly referred to as a "dark pool." Under Regulation SCI, an ATS that exceeds certain trading volume thresholds is defined as an SCI ATS and, thus, is required to comply with the substantive provisions of Regulation SCI. . . . Despite KCG MatchIt being subject to the requirements of Regulation SCI, KCGA did not comply with certain provisions of Regulation SCI.

Respondent

2. VAL is a Delaware entity with principal executive offices in New York, New York. It is a broker-dealer registered with the Commission. VAL is a subsidiary of Virtu Financial, Inc., which is incorporated in Delaware and headquartered in New York, New York. Virtu Financial, Inc. acquired KCG Holdings, Inc. on July 20, 2017. Prior to that acquisition, VAL was known as KCG Americas LLC (formerly known as Knight Capital Americas LLC). VAL owns and operates an ATS named Virtu MatchIt, formerly known as KCG MatchIt, which is a private execution venue that accepts, matches, and executes

---

[192] Order Instituting Administrative and Cease-and-Desist Proceedings, Virtu Americas LLC., No. 3-19563 (Sept. 30, 2019).

orders to buy and sell securities that it receives from ATS subscribers including VAL's clients and Virtu MatchIt direct subscribers.

Facts

3. Regulation SCI became effective on February 3, 2015 and applies to certain ATSs, self-regulatory organizations, plan processors, and exempt clearing agencies (collectively, "SCI entities").

4. The Commission enacted Regulation SCI to establish a formal regulatory structure to govern the automated systems of SCI entities and to mitigate certain concerns presented by technological developments in the securities markets. Specifically, Regulation SCI was intended to address the concern that "[g]iven the speed and interconnected nature of the U.S. securities markets, a seemingly minor systems problem at a single entity can quickly create losses and liability for market participants, and spread rapidly across the national market system, potentially creating widespread damage and harm to market participants, including investors." *See* Regulation Systems Compliance and Integrity, Final Rule, Exchange Act Release No. 73639, at p. 587 (Nov. 19, 2014).

5. Under Rule 1000 of Regulation SCI, an ATS can meet the definition of an SCI ATS in two ways. As relevant here, an SCI ATS is defined as "an alternative trading system ... which during at least four of the preceding six calendar months ... [had] with respect to NMS stocks ... [f]ive percent (5%) or more in any single NMS stock, and one-quarter percent (.25%) or more in all NMS stocks, of the average daily dollar volume reported by applicable transaction reporting plans."

6. If an ATS meets the definition of an SCI ATS in Rule 1000, it must comply with the requirements of Regulation SCI, including the obligations to:
> a. Establish, maintain, and enforce written policies and procedures reasonably designed to ensure that its applicable systems have levels of capacity, integrity, resiliency, availability, and security adequate to maintain their operational capability and promote the maintenance of fair and orderly markets, and that they operate in a manner that complies with the Exchange Act and the rules and regulations thereunder and the entity's rules and governing documents, as applicable.
> b. Mandate participation by designated members or participants in scheduled testing of the operation of their business continuity and disaster recovery plans, including backup systems, and to coordinate such testing on an industry- or sector-wide basis with other SCI entities.
> c. Take corrective action with respect to SCI events (defined to include systems disruptions, systems compliance issues, and systems intrusions), and notify the Commission of such events.

d. Disseminate information about certain SCI events to affected members or participants and, for certain major SCI events, to all members or participants of the SCI entity.

e. Conduct a review of their systems by objective, qualified personnel at least annually, submit quarterly reports regarding completed, ongoing, and planned material changes to their SCI systems to the Commission, and maintain certain books and records. . . .

11. Due to an error in the reporting logic that calculated execution volumes for KCG MatchIt, the Volume Monitoring System did not account for some trades on KCG MatchIt. As a result of that error, KCG MatchIt exceeded the Regulation SCI volume thresholds and was subject to Regulation SCI as of the effective date of February 3, 2015. Accordingly, KCG MatchIt met the definition of an SCI ATS as of the February 3, 2015 effective date and was required to comply with Regulation SCI by November 3, 2015.

12. KCG MatchIt continued to meet the definition of an SCI ATS after the February 3, 2015 effective date in additional securities during other periods between March 2015 and October 2016, when the SEC's Office of Compliance Inspections and Examinations ("OCIE") identified this issue during a routine exam. Each time KCG MatchIt crossed the Regulation SCI threshold, it met the definition of an SCI ATS and was required to comply with the substantive requirements of Regulation SCI.

13. Despite KCG MatchIt meeting the definition of an SCI ATS and thus being subject to the requirements of Regulation SCI, and as a result of the error described above, KCGA did not comply with certain provisions of Regulation SCI beginning on November 3, 2015. Specifically, KCGA did not: (a) establish the policies and procedures required by Regulation SCI; (b) file any quarterly or annual reports required by Regulation SCI; (c) conduct an annual Regulation SCI compliance review; (d) comply with various business continuity and disaster recovery plan requirements of Regulation SCI; or (e) maintain the books and records required by Regulation SCI.

14. Although the Final Rule contemplated that firms may use automated processes to stay below the volume thresholds, KCGA's systems did not operate as intended. As described above, KCGA attempted to stay below the volume thresholds that would define it as an SCI ATS to avoid the application of Regulation SCI. It had the obligation to monitor whether it was staying below the volume thresholds or whether it was in fact exceeding the volume thresholds and therefore subject to the requirements of Regulation SCI. *See* Regulation Systems Compliance and Integrity, Final Rule, Exchange Act Release No. 73639, at p. 63, fn. 167 (Nov. 19, 2014) . . . .

Violations

18. As a result of the conduct described above, VAL willfully violated:

a. Rule 1001(a)(1) of Regulation SCI, which requires each SCI entity to "establish, maintain, and enforce written policies and procedures reasonably designed to ensure that its SCI systems and, for purposes of security standards, indirect SCI systems, have levels of capacity, integrity, resiliency, availability, and security, adequate to maintain the SCI entity's operational capability and promote the maintenance of fair and orderly markets";

b. Rule 1001(b)(1) of Regulation SCI, which requires each SCI entity to "establish, maintain, and enforce written policies and procedures reasonably designed to ensure that its SCI systems operate in a manner that complies with the Act and the rules and regulations thereunder and the entity's rules and governing documents, as applicable";

c. Rule 1001(c) of Regulation SCI, which requires each SCI entity to "establish, maintain, and enforce reasonably designed written policies and procedures that include the criteria for identifying responsible SCI personnel, the designation and documentation of responsible SCI personnel, and escalation procedures to quickly inform responsible SCI personnel of potential SCI events";

d. Rule 1003(a)(1) of Regulation SCI, which requires each SCI entity to file a quarterly report with the Commission "describing completed, ongoing, and planned material changes to its SCI systems and the security of indirect systems, during the prior, current, and subsequent calendar quarters";

e. Rule 1003(b) of Regulation SCI, which requires each SCI entity to "[c]onduct an SCI review of the SCI entity's compliance with Regulation SCI not less than once each calendar year," "[s]ubmit a report of the SCI review...to senior management of the SCI entity for review no more than 30 calendar days after completion of such SCI review," and "[s]ubmit to the Commission, and to the board of directors of the SCI entity or the equivalent of such board, a report of the SCI review...together with any response by senior management, within 60 calendar days after its submission to senior management of the SCI entity";

f. Rule 1004(a) of Regulation SCI, which requires each SCI entity to "[e]stablish standards for the designation of those members or participants that the SCI entity reasonably determines are, taken as a whole, the minimum necessary for the maintenance of fair and orderly markets in the event of the activation of such [business continuity and disaster recovery] plans";

g. Rule 1004(b) of Regulation SCI, which requires each SCI entity to "[d]esignate members or participants...and require participation by such designated members or participants in scheduled functional and performance testing of the operation of such [business continuity and disaster recovery] plans, in the manner and frequency specified by the SCI entity, provided that such frequency shall not be less than once every 12 months";

h. Rule 1004(c) of Regulation SCI, which requires each SCI entity to "[c]oordinate the testing of such [business continuity and disaster recovery] plans on an industry- or sector-wide basis with other SCI entities"; and

i. Rule 1005 (b) of Regulation SCI, which requires each SCI entity that is not an SCI SRO to "[m]ake, keep, and preserve at least one copy of all documents...relating to its compliance with Regulation SCI, including, but not limited to, records relating to any changes to its SCI systems and indirect systems" and "[k]eep all such documents for a period of not less than five years, the first two years in a place that is readily accessible to the Commission or its representatives."

IV.

In view of the foregoing, the Commission deems it appropriate and in the public interest to impose the sanctions agreed to in Respondent's Offer.

Accordingly, pursuant to Sections 15(b) and 21C of the Exchange Act, it is hereby ORDERED that:

A. Respondent VAL cease and desist from committing or causing any violations and any future violations of Rules 1001, 1003, 1004, and 1005 of Regulation SCI, promulgated under the Exchange Act.

B. Respondent VAL is censured.

C. Respondent VAL shall, within 14 (fourteen) days of the entry of this Order, pay a civil money penalty in the amount of $1,500,000.00 to the Securities and Exchange Commission for transfer to the general fund of the United States Treasury, subject to Exchange Act Section 21F(g)(3). If timely payment is not made, additional interest shall accrue pursuant to 31 U.S.C. §3717. . . .

By the Commission.

Vanessa A. Countryman

Secretary

QUESTIONS

1) The term resiliency is used in conjunction with confidentiality, integrity, and availability (CIA). The term has also been adopted by the European General Data Protection Regulation (GDPR). Does availability necessarily contain the concept of resiliency? Is it possible to have availability without resiliency?

2) The SEC's Office of Compliance Inspections and Examinations ("OCIE") identified the volume issue during a routine exam. Should the FTC implement a similar OCIE for its jurisdiction?

3) What are the advantages and disadvantages of implementing SCI entity security from the inception of the product?

In the Matter of Voya Financial Advisors matter, the SEC identified cyber security deficiencies with policies and procedures found after a break-in that compromised customer data.

> The Securities and Exchange Commission today announced that a Des Moines-based broker-dealer and investment adviser has agreed to pay $1 million to settle charges related to its failures in cybersecurity policies and procedures surrounding a cyber intrusion that compromised personal information of thousands of customers.[193]

In the Matter of Voya Financial Advisors, Release No. 84288 (September 26, 2018).

ORDER INSTITUTING ADMINISTRATIVE AND CEASE-AND-DESIST PROCEEDINGS . . . AND IMPOSING REMEDIAL SANCTIONS AND A CEASE-AND-DESIST ORDER

I.

The Securities and Exchange Commission (the "Commission") deems it appropriate and in the public interest that public administrative and cease-and-desist proceedings be, and hereby are, instituted pursuant to Sections 15(b) and 21C of the Securities Exchange Act of 1934 (the "Exchange Act"), and Sections 203(e) and 203(k) of the Investment Advisers Act of 1940 (the ""Advisers Act"), against Voya Financial Advisors, Inc. ("VFA" or "Respondent"). . . .

III.

On the basis of this Order and Respondent's Offer, the Commission finds that:

Summary

1. These proceedings arise out of VFA's failure to adopt written policies and procedures reasonably designed to protect customer records and information, in violation of Rule 30(a) of Regulation S-P (17 C.F.R. § 248.30(a)) (the ""Safeguards Rule"), and VFA's failure to develop and implement a written Identity Theft Prevention Program as required by Rule 201 of Regulation S-ID (17 C.F.R. § 248.201) (the "Identity Theft Red Flags Rule").

---

[193] *SEC Charges Firm with Deficient Cybersecurity Procedures*, U.S. SECURITIES AND EXCHANGE COMMISSION (SEPT. 26, 2018), https://www.sec.gov/news/press-release/2018-213.

2. VFA is a dually registered broker-dealer and investment adviser. From at least 2013 through October 2017 (the "relevant period"), VFA gave its independent contractor representatives ("contractor representatives") access to its brokerage customer and advisory client (hereinafter, "customer") information through a proprietary web portal. . . .

6. The Safeguards Rule requires every broker-dealer and every investment adviser registered with the Commission to adopt written policies and procedures that address administrative, technical and physical safeguards for the protection of customer records and information. Those policies and procedures must be reasonably designed to: (1) insure the security and confidentiality of customer records and information; (2) protect against any anticipated threats or hazards to the security or integrity of customer records and information; and (3) protect against unauthorized access to or use of customer records or information that could result in substantial harm or inconvenience to any customer. . . .

8. The Identity Theft Red Flags Rule requires certain financial institutions and creditors, including broker-dealers and investment advisers registered or required to be registered with the Commission, to develop and implement a written Identity Theft Prevention Program that is designed to detect, prevent, and mitigate identity theft in connection with the opening of a covered account or any existing covered account. An Identity Theft Prevention Program must include reasonable policies and procedures to: identify relevant red flags for the covered accounts and incorporate them into the Identity Theft Prevention Program; detect the red flags that have been incorporated into the Identity Theft Prevention Program; respond appropriately to any red flags that are detected pursuant to the Identity Theft Prevention Program; and ensure that the Identity Theft Prevention Program is updated periodically to reflect changes in risks to customers from identity theft.

9. Although VFA adopted a written Identity Theft Prevention Program in 2009, VFA violated the Identity Theft Red Flags Rule because it did not review and update the Identity Theft Prevention Program in response to changes in risks to its customers or provide adequate training to its employees. In addition, the Identity Theft Prevention Program did not include reasonable policies and procedures to respond to identity theft red flags, such as those that were detected by VFA during the April 2016 intrusion.

Respondent

10. VFA is a Minnesota corporation headquartered in Des Moines, Iowa, and dually registered as a broker-dealer and investment adviser with the Commission. VFA has approximately 13 million customers and approximately $11 billion in regulatory assets under management. It is an indirect wholly-owned subsidiary of Voya.

Background

11. VFA offers a wide range of proprietary and non-proprietary investment products and services through a national network of independent contractor registered representatives. VFA has over 1,000 employees, including registered representatives, who work in its home and branch offices, as well as 3,800 other associated persons, including contractor representatives who work out of their own offices in approximately 1,200 locations throughout the United States. The contractor representatives make up the largest part of VFA's workforce and provide brokerage and investment advisory services to VFA's customers. In the course of providing these services, VFA contractor representatives regularly collect and access account information for VFA customers that contains PII.

12. During the relevant period, while VFA employees generally used information technology ("IT") equipment and IT systems provided by Voya, VFA contractor representatives generally used their own IT equipment and operated over their own networks.

13. During the relevant period, VFA contractor representatives typically accessed VFA customer information through a proprietary web portal called Voya for Professionals or VPro. By entering login credentials consisting of a username and password into VPro, the contractor representatives gained access to a number of web applications, including third-party applications such as SmartWorks, which is a customer and prospect relationship management system that contained PII and account information for VFA customers and prospects, and a customer account management system that enabled VFA employees and contractor representatives to, among other things, execute trades and initiate cash distributions.

VFA's Policies and Procedures Prior to the Intrusion Were Deficient
14. VFA had no cybersecurity staff of its own and outsourced most of its cybersecurity functions and some of its information technology functions to its parent company, Voya. Voya staff also serviced support call centers for VFA's customers and contractor representatives. Voya's Financial Application Support Team ("FAST") was responsible for responding to VFA contractor representatives' requests for assistance with respect to VPro and SmartWorks, among other systems.

15. Prior to the intrusion, over a dozen Voya policies and procedures relating to cybersecurity were supposed to govern the conduct of VFA. Among other things, these policies and procedures required: (a) manual account lock-outs for a user suspected of being involved in a security incident from web applications containing critical data, including customer PII; (b) a session timeout after 15 minutes of user inactivity in web applications containing customer PII; (c) a prohibition of concurrent web sessions by a single user in web applications containing customer PII; (d) multi-factor authentication ("MFA") for access to applications containing customer PII; (e) annual and ad-hoc review of cybersecurity policies; and (f) cybersecurity awareness training and updates for VFA employees and contractors.

16. VFA implemented these policies and procedures for the systems used by its associated persons that it classified as employees, including when those associated persons worked remotely.

17. Even though these policies and procedures were applicable to VFA's associated persons that it classified as independent contractors, including those working out of remote offices, these policies and procedures were not reasonably designed to apply to the systems they used. For example, VFA allowed its contractor representatives to maintain concurrent VPro sessions and did not apply 15-minute inactivity timeouts to VPro sessions. In addition, VFA did not have a procedure for terminating an individual VFA contractor representative's remote session. Further, VFA contractor representatives' web access to VPro was subject to MFA that required the user to answer previously-set security questions when a new device was connecting to the relevant VPro account. This form of MFA was rendered ineffective when users called the FAST team to request a reset of VPro passwords and FAST staff reset the security questions, which was what happened during the intrusion.

18. The password reset procedures for VPro allowed FAST staff to provide users who could not remember their passwords with a temporary password by phone, after the user provided at least two pieces of his or her PII. Temporary passwords were not required to be sent via secure email. Although these procedures did not authorize FAST staff to provide VPro usernames (in addition to passwords) to these users, the procedures did not explicitly prohibit it. These procedures remained in place at the time of the intrusion even though VFA was aware of prior fraudulent activity at Voya that involved attempts to impersonate its contractor representatives using their PII in calls to technical and customer support lines.

19. Voya kept a "monitoring list" of phone numbers suspected of having been used in connection with prior fraudulent activity at Voya. However, there was no written policy or procedure that required FAST and customer support call centers to use this list when responding to requests for password resets or other calls from the phone numbers on this list. Although Voya adopted an informal, unwritten procedure providing for the next-business-day review of phone calls from numbers on the "monitoring list" in January 2016, that procedure did not prevent someone from fraudulently obtaining access to confidential customer information at the time that the call was occurring, and the procedure was not consistently applied.

20. The contractor representatives' personal computers were supposed to be scanned for the existence of antivirus software, encryption, and certain software updates, but these scans were scheduled to occur only three times per year, and representatives often failed to take the actions that were necessary for the scans to occur. A third-party service provider scanned VFA contractor representatives' computers after a representative clicked a link sent by the service provider via email. However, some representatives

failed to click the link for extended periods of time, if at all. Among the computers that were scanned, the fail rate in each of 2015 and 2016 was approximately 30%, with half of those exhibiting critical failures, such as lack of encryption and antivirus software. VFA conducted no review or follow-up on failures of representatives to scan their computers or on the scans that identified security deficiencies.

21. The policies and procedures for protecting VFA customers' Voya.com profiles, which included the customers' personal and account information and provided users with the ability to change email and physical addresses of record as well as to document delivery preferences, were not reasonably designed. VFA did not provide notice to a customer when an initial profile was created for that customer and when contact information and document delivery preferences were changed for that customer. As a result, intruders could create and change customer profiles without customer detection, and they did so during the April 2016 attack.

22. VFA's policies and procedures to respond to a breach and mitigate identity theft in connection with an intrusion into VPro and SmartWorks were also not reasonably designed. They largely consisted of Voya's incident response procedures, which were not reasonably designed to deny or limit an unauthorized person's access to VFA customers' PII. For example, although incident response procedures required in general terms that potentially compromised user accounts be disabled or the relevant applications be shut down to prevent additional compromise, VFA's policies and procedures were not reasonably designed to accomplish these directives. Specifically, Voya IT security staff, who were responsible for responding to security incidents, were not provided with adequate training regarding the operation of VPro and erroneously believed that resetting a VPro password for a user would terminate that user's existing sessions. In fact, resetting VPro passwords did not terminate sessions, and existing sessions continued to proceed after password resets. VFA's incident response procedures also failed to ensure that the FAST and customer-facing call center staff were notified about an ongoing intrusion.

23. VFA's policies and procedures for designating compromised representatives' and customers' accounts for additional security measures during calls to support centers for VFA contractor representatives and customers they serviced were not reasonably designed. Although in January 2016, VFA informally adopted a procedure to place flags on such contractor representatives and customer accounts in the system, unbeknownst to the relevant security staff, such flags were erased from the system periodically in connection with unrelated automated system activities.

24. In 2009, before the Dodd-Frank Act of 2010 transferred to the Commission the rulemaking responsibility and enforcement authority under Section 615(e) of the Fair Credit Reporting Act with respect to the entities subject to its enforcement authority, VFA adopted an Identity Theft Prevention Program to comply with the then-applicable Red Flags Rule of the Federal Trade Commission (16 C.F.R. § 681.1). VFA's Identity

Theft Prevention Program required VFA to oversee the implementation and administration of the Identity Theft Prevention Program, to train its staff on the Identity Theft Prevention Program, and to have in place policies and procedures to periodically update the Identity Theft Prevention Program in response to changes in risks to VFA's customers.

25. Despite significant changes in external cybersecurity risks and in VFA's own risk profile, VFA did not substantively update the Identity Theft Prevention Program after 2009 and VFA's board of directors or a designated member of VFA's management did not administer and oversee the Identity Theft Prevention Program, as required by the Identity Theft Red Flags Rule. As a result, VFA's cyber incident response procedures were not reasonably designed to respond to identity theft red flags, such as those that were detected by Voya's staff prior to and during the April 2016 intrusion. For example, once VFA discovered that intruders had obtained access to the VPro system and customer PII, VFA did not have reasonable procedures to change security codes, employ other security devices, or modify existing procedures in order to deny unauthorized persons' access to VFA customer accounts. In addition, VFA failed to conduct training specific to the Identity Theft Prevention Program.[194]

The Intrusion and VFA's Response
26. On April 13, 14, and 18, 2016, one or more persons impersonating VFA contractor representatives subjected VFA to an intrusion that proceeded in several phases. In the course of this attack, the intruders exploited the weaknesses in VFA's cybersecurity policies and Identity Theft Prevention Program outlined above. Prior to the intrusion, between January and March 2016, VFA had been subject to other fraudulent activity in which unknown persons impersonated VFA representatives, including one of the representatives targeted in April 2016, sometimes using the same phone numbers and techniques as those used in the April 2016 intrusion.

27. Each of the three days began with a phone call to the FAST team, which was responsible for supporting VPro and SmartWorks. Two of the calls came from a phone number suspected of having been used in prior fraudulent activity at Voya. On each day, a caller impersonated a different VFA contractor representative, provided two forms of the representative's PII, and requested a reset of that contractor representative's VPro password. One of the representatives had been targeted during the prior fraudulent activity. On each occasion, FAST staff reset the password and provided a temporary password to the caller by phone. In two instances, FAST staff also provided the VFA contractor representative's VPro username to the caller. On each of the three days, the intruders used the contractor representative's VPro login credentials to access SmartWorks remotely. The intruders' sessions were not terminated when the authorized

---

[194] Editors: We did not remove the discussion of the Identity Theft Red Flags Rule to provide some exposure to that privacy rule.

users initiated new sessions, and their sessions were not timed out after several periods of inactivity of 15 minutes or longer.

28. Upon accessing SmartWorks, the intruders had access to PII of approximately 5,600 VFA customers, including address, date of birth, last four digits of the Social Security number, and email address. For at least 2,000 of these customers, the intruders viewed a full Social Security number and/or another government-issued identification number. The intruders also edited and ran reports containing customer information in SmartWorks. For all affected customers who held annuity contracts, the intruders had the ability to copy the unique contract numbers, which Voya customer service used as an identity authenticating factor during customer service calls. Through VPro, the intruders also had the ability to, but apparently did not, access a platform that VFA representatives and employees used to manage customer accounts, including to initiate distribution requests and execute trades.

29. Upon receipt of an email notification of password change, the first contractor representative notified FAST in the late morning of April 13, 2016 that he had not requested the change. The FAST member then reset that representative's VPro password and escalated the incident to a FAST manager, who reported it to Voya's security incident response team. The FAST manager emailed the entire FAST team the following morning, formally notifying the team of the incident and directing staffers not to provide usernames and temporary passwords by phone. However, in the intervening period, the intruders had obtained the second contractor representative's username, reset his password and gained access to SmartWorks. Moreover, the FAST manager's directive that no passwords be provided by phone and that the phone number monitoring list should be reviewed was not heeded on April 18, 2016, when a FAST team member provided a password to an intruder impersonating a third representative.

30. On the second day of the intrusion, Voya's security staff, which was charged with responding to the breach, identified certain IP addresses as likely involved in the intrusion. However, they failed to block these IP addresses or freeze the compromised representatives' SmartWorks sessions while the malicious sessions were in progress in part based on their mistaken belief that resetting the compromised VPro passwords would terminate these sessions. The intruders continued to have access to the PII of VFA customers for most of the day on the first two days of the intrusion and for more than two hours on the last day, until the intruders exited VFA's systems.

31. After the first contractor representative notified VFA of the fraudulent reset of his password, Voya's annuity customer service call center received five telephone calls from unknown callers impersonating one of that representative's customers and three calls from unknown callers impersonating the representative himself. These calls came in from four different phone numbers, which in six instances had area codes outside of the customer's and the representative's state of residence. Several of the calls came in from a number on the "monitoring list." The callers obtained account-level information from

technical support, changed the customer's email address of record to a "@yopmail.com" email address, and caused VFA to send certain of the customer's account documents to that address.

32. The intruders made other attempts to obtain customer-specific account information during the intrusion, and were successful in obtaining account documents for two additional VFA customers by establishing online Voya.com profiles, which provided them access to, among other things, account balances, account documents, tax documents, and other account information. Using these Voya.com profiles, the intruders changed the customers' email addresses of record to disposable email addresses (such as @yopmail.com and @@sharklasers.com), changed phone numbers of record, and changed the delivery method for statements and account confirmations to online and email, rather than by mail.

33. During the intrusion, Voya conducted testing of other contractor representatives' password resets in an effort to identify the scope of the intrusion and mitigate its impact in case other representatives were affected. This testing involved contacting the relevant representatives and inquiring whether they initiated the password resets. However, this testing was done only on the passwords reset between April 1 and 14, 2016, which included only the first half of the intrusion. There was no testing of passwords that were reset during the back half of the intrusion (April 15 through 18, 2016). In addition, 41% of the resets tested resulted in an "unable to reach" finding, and six of these resets occurred during the intrusion. There was no follow-up to these failures to reach the representatives whose passwords were reset during the intrusion.

34. After the intruders voluntarily left VFA's networks, VFA blocked two malicious IP addresses using its IPS/IDS systems. The intruders thereafter continued attempting to obtain distributions and information from the compromised accounts by contacting Voya's customer support call centers, as well other financial institutions, although no unauthorized transfers of funds or securities from VFA customer accounts are known to have occurred as a result of the attack.

Violations

35. As a result of the conduct described above, VFA willfully10 violated Rule 30(a) of Regulation S-P (17 C.F.R. § 248.30(a)), which requires every broker-dealer and every investment adviser registered with the Commission to adopt written policies and procedures that are reasonably designed to safeguard customer records and information.

36. As a result of the conduct described above, VFA willfully violated Rule 201 of Regulation S-ID (17 C.F.R. § 248.201), which requires registered broker-dealers and investment advisers that offer or maintain covered accounts to develop and implement a written Identity Theft Prevention Program that is designed to detect, prevent, and mitigate identity theft in connection with the opening of a covered account or any existing covered account.

VFA's Remedial Efforts

37. After the intrusion, VFA promptly undertook certain remedial acts, including: (a) blocking the malicious IP addresses; (b) revising its user authentication policy to prohibit provision of a temporary password by phone; (c) issuing breach notices to the affected customers, describing the intrusion and offering one year of free credit monitoring; and (d) implementing effective MFA for VPro.

38. Furthermore, on August 28, 2017, VFA named a new Chief Information Security Officer, who is responsible for creating and maintaining cybersecurity policies and procedures and an incident response plan tailored to VFA's business.

39. In determining to accept the Offer, the Commission considered the remedial acts undertaken by VFA.

Undertakings

40. Respondent has undertaken the following:

a. Retention of Compliance Consultant. Respondent shall retain, at its expense, an independent compliance consultant (the "Consultant") to conduct a comprehensive review of Respondent's policies and procedures for compliance with Regulation S-P and Regulation S-ID.

b. Respondent shall require the Consultant to enter into an agreement that provides that for the period of engagement and for a period of two years from completion of the engagement, the Consultant shall not enter into any employment, consultant, attorney-client, auditing or other professional relationship with Respondent, or any of its present or former affiliates, directors, officers, employees, or agents acting in their capacity. The agreement will also provide that the Consultant will require that any firm with which he/she is affiliated or of which he/she is a member, and any person engaged to assist the Consultant in performance of his/her duties under this Order shall not, without prior written consent of the Commission staff, enter into any employment, consultant, attorney-client, auditing or other professional relationship with Respondent, or any of its present or former affiliates, directors, officers, employees, or agents acting in their capacity as such for the period of the engagement and for a period of two years after the engagement.

c. Respondent shall cooperate fully with the Consultant.

d. Within three months after the date of the issuance of this Order, Respondent shall require the Consultant to submit a written Initial Report to Respondent and to the Commission staff. The Initial Report shall describe the review performed, the conclusions reached, and shall include any recommendations deemed necessary to make the policies and procedures and their implementation comply with applicable requirements.

e. Respondent shall adopt all recommendations contained in the Initial Report within 90 days of the date of its issuance, provided, however, that within 30 days of the issuance of the Initial Report, Respondent shall advise, in writing, the Consultant and the

Commission staff of any recommendations that Respondent considers to be unduly burdensome, impractical or inappropriate. With respect to any such recommendation, Respondent need not adopt that recommendation at that time but shall propose in writing an alternative policy, procedures or system designed to achieve the same objective or purpose. As to any recommendation on which Respondent and the Consultant do not agree, Respondent and the Consultant shall attempt in good faith to reach an agreement within 60 days after the issuance of the Initial Report. Within 15 days after the conclusion of the discussion and evaluation by Respondent and the Consultant, Respondent shall require that the Consultant inform Respondent and the Commission staff in writing of the Consultant's final determination concerning any recommendation that Respondent considers to be unduly burdensome, impractical, or inappropriate. Within 10 days of this written communication from Consultant, Respondent may seek approval from the Commission staff to not adopt recommendations that Respondent can demonstrate to be unduly burdensome, impractical, or inappropriate. Should the Commission staff agree that any proposed recommendations are unduly burdensome, impractical, or inappropriate, Respondent may adopt its proposed alternative policy, procedures or systems designed to achieve the same objective or purpose.

f. Within nine months after the date of issuance of this Order, Respondent shall require the Consultant to complete its review and issue a written Final Report to Respondent and the Commission staff. The Final Report shall describe the review performed, the conclusions reached, the recommendations made by the Consultant, any recommendations not adopted by Respondent pursuant to Paragraph 40(e), any proposals made by Respondent, any alternative policies, procedures or systems adopted by Respondent pursuant to Paragraph 40(e), and how Respondent is implementing the Consultant's final recommendations. . . .

IV.

In view of the foregoing, the Commission deems it appropriate and in the public interest to impose the sanctions agreed to in VFA's Offer. Accordingly, pursuant to Sections 15(b) and 21C of the Exchange Act and Sections 203(e) and 203(k) of the Advisers Act, it is hereby ORDERED that:

A. VFA cease and desist from committing or causing any violations and any future violations of Rule 30(a) of Regulation S-P (17 C.F.R. § 248.30(a)) and of Rule 201 of Regulation S-ID (17 C.F.R. § 248.201);

B. VFA is censured; and

C. VFA shall pay, within 10 (ten) business days of the entry of this Order, a civil money penalty in the amount of $1,000,000 to the Securities and Exchange Commission for transfer to the general fund of the United States Treasury, subject to Exchange Act Section 21F(g)(3). If timely payment is not made, additional interest shall accrue pursuant to 31 U.S.C. § 3717. . . .

By the Commission.
Brent J. Fields
Secretary

QUESTION

How should an entity control human mistakes that lead to security issues?

In an enforcement action concerning Regulation S-P, the SEC agreed to the following order with Morgan Stanley Smith Barney:

In the Matter of Morgan Stanley Smith Barney, Release No. 4415 (June 8, 2016).

ORDER INSTITUTING ADMINISTRATIVE AND CEASE- AND DESIST PROCEEDINGS . . . AND IMPOSING REMEDIAL SANCTIONS AND A CEASE-AND-DESIST ORDER

I.

The Securities and Exchange Commission (the "Commission") deems it appropriate and in the public interest that public administrative and cease-and-desist proceedings be, and hereby are, instituted pursuant to Sections 15(b) and 21C of the Securities Exchange Act of 1934 (the "Exchange Act"), and Sections 203(e) and 203(k) of the Investment Advisers Act of 1940 (the ""Advisers Act"), against Morgan Stanley Smith Barney LLC ("MSSB" or ""Respondent").

II.

In anticipation of the institution of these proceedings, Respondent has submitted an Offer of Settlement (the "Offer"), which the Commission has determined to accept. . . .

III.

On the basis of this Order and Respondent's Offer, the Commission finds that:

Summary

1. This proceeding arises out of MSSB's failure to adopt written policies and procedures reasonably designed to protect customer records and information, in violation of Rule 30(a) of Regulation S-P (17 C.F.R. § 248.30(a)) (the ""Safeguards Rule"). From at least August 2001 through December 2014, MSSB stored sensitive personally identifiable information ("PII") of individuals to whom MSSB provided brokerage and investment advisory services (referred to herein as "customers") on two of the firm's applications: the Business Information System ("BIS") Portal and the Fixed Income Division Select ("FID Select") Portal (collectively, "the Portals"). Galen Marsh ("Marsh"), then an MSSB employee, misappropriated data regarding approximately 730,000 customer accounts, associated with approximately 330,000 different households, by accessing the Portals

between 2011 and 2014. The misappropriated data included PII, such as customers' full names, phone numbers, street addresses, account numbers, account balances and securities holdings.

. . . 3. The Safeguards Rule, which the Commission adopted in 2000 and amended in 2005, requires, among others, every broker-dealer and investment adviser registered with the Commission to adopt written policies and procedures reasonably designed to: (1) insure the security and confidentiality of customer records and information; (2) protect against any anticipated threats or hazards to the security or integrity of customer records and information; and (3) protect against unauthorized access to or use of customer records or information that could result in substantial harm or inconvenience to any customer. . . .

Respondent

4. MSSB is a Delaware limited liability company and is registered with the Commission as a broker-dealer and an investment adviser. MSSB is an indirect wholly-owned subsidiary of Morgan Stanley and has its principal office and place of business in Purchase, New York.

Background

A. Confidential Customer Data at MSSB

5. In connection with its wealth management business, MSSB maintains hundreds of computer applications containing customers' PII. The two applications of relevance here are the BIS Portal and the FID Select Portal. The Portals were Web applications residing on MSSB's intranet that enabled certain MSSB employees to run reports that retrieved and organized customer data from underlying databases. At the relevant time, the BIS Portal could be used to run approximately 40 different reports, one of which was the Relationship Migration Book Analysis Report, which contained customers' full names, account numbers, phone numbers, states of residence and account balances.

6. The FID Select Portal was another Web application available on MSSB's intranet. This portal was used by MSSB Financial Advisors ("FAs"), who were usually the primary points of contact for customers, as well as the Client Service Associates ("CSAs") who supported the FAs, to obtain reports on the fixed income holdings in their customers' accounts. In particular, the Account Analysis Report available through the FID Select Portal provided customers' full names, account numbers, phone numbers, street addresses, account balances and information about specific fixed income holdings.

7. MSSB adopted certain policies and restrictions with respect to employees' access to and handling of confidential customer data available through the Portals. MSSB had written policies, including its Code of Conduct, that prohibited employees from accessing confidential information other than what employees had been authorized to access in

order to perform their responsibilities. In addition, MSSB designed and installed authorization modules that, if properly implemented, should have permitted each employee to run reports via the Portals only with respect to the data for customers whom that employee supported. These modules required FAs and CSAs to input numbers associated with the user's branch and FA or FA group number. MSSB's systems then should have permitted the user to access data only with respect to those customers whose data the user was properly entitled to view. Finally, MSSB installed and maintained technology controls that, among other things, restricted employees from copying data onto removable storage devices and from accessing certain categories of websites.

8. But MSSB failed to ensure the reasonable design and proper operation of its policies and procedures in safeguarding confidential customer data. In particular, the authorization modules were ineffective in limiting access with respect to one report available through the FID Select Portal and absent with respect to one of the reports available through the BIS Portal. Moreover, MSSB failed to conduct any auditing or testing of the authorization modules for the Portals at any point since their creation at least 10 years ago. Such auditing or testing would likely have revealed the deficiencies in these modules. Finally, MSSB did not monitor user activity in the Portals to identify any unusual or suspicious patterns.

B. Marsh's Identification and Exploitation of Flaws in the Portals

9. Marsh joined MSSB in April 2008 as a sales assistant. In 2010, Marsh entered MSSB's trainee program and eventually became a CSA based in the New York office. In this role, Marsh supported the work of the FAs in his group. In March 2014, Marsh was promoted to FA. In both his CSA and FA capacities, Marsh ran reports from several applications, including the Portals, that accessed and analyzed confidential customer data.

10. In or about June 2011, while he was employed as a CSA, Marsh discovered that the authorization module for the FID Select Portal did not work when he ran a particular report called the Account Analysis Report. Although the Portal should have restricted Marsh to accessing only customer data associated with the FAs whom he supported, Marsh noticed that he could run this report for all MSSB customers, including those outside his group. A programming flaw in the authorization module for the FID Select Portal caused the module to not interface properly with the employee data entitlements database applicable to that Portal. As a result, a CSA like Marsh was able to access customer data for any FA group throughout MSSB.

11. Marsh repeatedly exploited this programming flaw by first entering a branch ID number other than his own — numbers that were generally available throughout MSSB — and then entering various possible FA or FA group numbers until he discovered a combination that worked. At that point, Marsh was able to and did run reports containing PII of all customers of that FA or FA group. In addition, although Marsh's entitlements to access particular data were supposed to change when he was promoted

to FA in March 2014, MSSB failed to make such an entitlements change for the FID Select Portal, the entitlements for which were maintained in a database that was separate from the firm-wide entitlements database. Thus, Marsh continued his unauthorized accessing of confidential customer data until shortly before MSSB discovered his misconduct in late December 2014. From October 2013 through December 2014, Marsh conducted approximately 4,000 unauthorized searches of customer data using the FID Select Portal. By May 2014, Marsh began exploiting a separate and independent deficiency with respect to the BIS Portal — namely, that this portal lacked any authorization module whatsoever for its Relationship Migration Book Analysis Report. Thus, any CSA or FA was able to run this report and gather confidential customer data for other FAs' customers. In 2014, Marsh conducted approximately 1,900 unauthorized searches of customer data in the BIS Portal, using the same approach he used to access the FID Select Portal.

13. After downloading the data he accessed via the Portals, Marsh transferred the data to a personal server located at his home. MSSB had installed and maintained certain technology controls on its computer systems that, among other things, restricted employees from copying data onto removable storage devices and from accessing certain categories of websites. But Marsh transferred customer data to his personal server by accessing his personal website, galenmarsh.com, which had a feature that enabled Marsh to transfer data from his MSSB computer to his personal server. At the time, MSSB's Internet filtering software did not prevent employees from accessing such "uncategorized" websites from MSSB computers.

C. Data Breach and MSSB's Response

14. Between approximately December 15, 2014, and February 3, 2015, portions of the data downloaded by Marsh were posted to at least three Internet sites, purportedly for sale to a third party. MSSB discovered the data breach through one of its routine Internet sweeps on December 27, 2014. MSSB promptly took steps to remove this data from the Internet and notified law enforcement and other authorities.

15. After comparing certain data reports generated by Marsh to the information posted on the Internet, MSSB identified Marsh as the likely source of the data breach. On December 29 and 30, 2014, MSSB interviewed Marsh, who acknowledged that he had accessed and downloaded confidential customer data to his personal server. Marsh denied posting any of the data on the Internet. Subsequent forensic analysis of Marsh's personal server revealed that a third party likely hacked into the server and copied the confidential customer data that Marsh had downloaded. On January 5, 2015, MSSB began notifying those customers impacted by the data breach.

Violations

16. Adopted pursuant to the Exchange Act and the Advisers Act, among other statutes, the Safeguards Rule requires broker-dealers and investment advisers registered with the Commission to adopt written policies and procedures that address administrative, technical, and physical safeguards reasonably designed to: (1) insure the security and confidentiality of customer records and information; (2) protect against any anticipated threats or hazards to the security or integrity of customer records and information; and (3) protect against unauthorized access to or use of customer records or information that could result in substantial harm or inconvenience to any customer.

17. During the relevant period, MSSB maintained customer PII in numerous internal databases accessible by both the BIS Portal and the FID Select Portal. Although MSSB had adopted written policies and procedures relating to the protection of customer PII, those policies and procedures were not reasonably designed to safeguard its customers' PII as required by the Safeguards Rule. For example, MSSB's written policies and procedures failed to adequately address certain key administrative, technical and physical safeguards, such as: reasonably designed and operating authorization modules for the BIS Portal and the FID Select Portal to restrict employee access to only the confidential customer data as to which such employees had a legitimate business need; auditing and/or testing of the effectiveness of such authorization modules; and monitoring and analyzing of employee access to and use of the Portals.

18. As a result of the conduct described above, MSSB willfully violated Rule 30(a) of Regulation S-P (17 C.F.R. § 248.30(a)), which requires every broker-dealer and investment adviser registered with the Commission to adopt written policies and procedures that are reasonably designed to safeguard customer records and information.

Remedial Efforts

19. In determining to accept the Offer, the Commission has considered the remedial efforts promptly undertaken by Respondent and its cooperation afforded to the Commission Staff.

IV.

In view of the foregoing, the Commission deems it appropriate and in the public interest to impose the sanctions agreed to in Respondent's Offer.

Accordingly, pursuant to Sections 15(b) and 21C of the Exchange Act, and Sections 203(e) and 203(k) of the Advisers Act, it is hereby ORDERED that:

A. MSSB cease and desist from committing or causing any violations and any future violations of Rule 30(a) of Regulation S-P (17 C.F.R. § 248.30(a)).

B. MSSB is censured.

C. MSSB shall, within ten days of the entry of this Order, pay a civil money penalty in the amount of $1,000,000 to the Securities and Exchange Commission for transfer to the general fund of the United States Treasury, subject to Exchange Act Section 21F(g)(3). If timely payment is not made, additional interest shall accrue pursuant to 31 U.S.C. § 3717. . . .

By the Commission.

Brent J. Fields

Secretary

QUESTIONS

1) Both the FTC and SEC enforce parts of the Gramm-Leach-Bliley Act. Would it be more efficient to form a separate agency to enforce all of the GLBA? Or should it stay the way it is because the FTC and SEC each have skill sets with something different to offer?

2) Which of the following do you consider to be a stretch to be placed under cyber security:

> a) digital assets / initial coin offerings;

> b) account intrusions;

> c) hacker / insider trading;

> d) market manipulation / false tweets / fake websites;

> e) regulated entities – cybersecurity controls and safeguarding customer information;

> f) public company disclosure and controls

> g) trading suspensions

Why?

3) Initial coin offerings are definitely cyber-based. But why is it placed in the category of cyber security?

4) Market manipulation / false tweets / fake websites are definitely under the SEC, but just because it happens on the internet – does that make it within the realm of cyber security? Are false tweets and fake websites a cyber security issue or just criminal activities? Couldn't the perpetrators do the same thing with snail mail and brochures?

NOTES

Note 1

On October 16, 2018, the SEC released a document titled, "Report of Investigation Pursuant to Section 21(a) of the Securities Exchange Act of 1934 Regarding Certain Cyber-Related Frauds Perpetrated Against Public Companies and

Related Internal Accounting Controls Requirements." The Report stated, in pertinent part:

> The Division's investigation focused on the internal accounting controls of nine issuers that were victims of one of two variants of schemes involving spoofed or compromised electronic communications from persons purporting to be company executives or vendors. The issuers covered a range of sectors including technology, machinery, real estate, energy, financial, and consumer goods, reflecting the reality that every type of business is a potential target of 2 15 U.S.C. § 78m(b)(2)(B)(i) & (iii).

> At the time of the cyberscams, each issuer had substantial annual revenues and had securities listed on a national securities exchange. Each of the nine issuers lost at least $1 million; two lost more than $30 million. In total, the nine issuers lost nearly $100 million to the perpetrators, almost all of which was never recovered. Some of the investigated issuers were victims of protracted schemes that were only uncovered as a result of third-party actions, such as through detection by a foreign bank or law enforcement agency. Indeed, one company made 14 wire payments requested by the fake executive over the course of several weeks—resulting in over $45 million in losses—before the fraud was uncovered by an alert from a foreign bank. Another of the issuers paid eight invoices totaling $1.5 million over several months in response to a vendor's manipulated electronic documentation for a banking change; the fraud was only discovered when the real vendor complained about past due invoices.[195]

If the SEC issues a document such as the report above, what does that mean for public issuer companies?

Note 2

In a statement released by the SEC Chairman Jay Clayton on September 20, 2017, titled, "Statement on Cybersecurity," the Chairman noted that the SEC appears to have experienced cybersecurity breaches as well. The Statement provides, in relevant part:

> II.   Management of Internal Cybersecurity Risks

---

[195] S. E. C., No. 84429, REPORT OF INVESTIGATION PURSUANT TO SECTION 21(A) OF THE SECURITIES EXCHANGE ACT OF 1934 REGARDING CERTAIN CYBER-RELATED FRAUDS PERPETRATED AGAINST PUBLIC COMPANIES AND RELATED INTERNAL ACCOUNTING CONTROLS REQUIREMENTS (2018).

As described above, the Commission receives, stores and transmits substantial amounts of data, including sensitive and nonpublic data. Like many other governmental agencies, financial market participants and other private sector entities, we are the subject of frequent attempts by unauthorized actors to disrupt access to our public-facing systems, access our data, or otherwise cause damage to our technology infrastructure, including through the use of phishing, malware and other attack vectors. For example, with respect to our EDGAR system, we face the risks of cyber threat actors attempting to compromise the credentials of authorized users, gain unauthorized access to filings data, place fraudulent filings on the system, and prevent the public from accessing our system through denial of service attacks. We also face the risks of actors attempting to access nonpublic data relating to our oversight of, or enforcement actions against, market participants, which could then be used to obtain illicit trading profits. Similarly, with respect to CAT, we expect we will face the risk of unauthorized access to the CAT's central repository and other efforts to obtain sensitive CAT data. Through such access, intruders could potentially obtain, expose and profit from the trading activity and personally identifiable information of investors and other market participants.

Notwithstanding our efforts to protect our systems and manage cybersecurity risk, in certain cases cyber threat actors have managed to access or misuse our systems. In August 2017, the Commission learned that an incident previously detected in 2016 may have provided the basis for illicit gain through trading. Specifically, a software vulnerability in the test filing component of our EDGAR system, which was patched promptly after discovery, was exploited and resulted in access to nonpublic information. We believe the intrusion did not result in unauthorized access to personally identifiable information, jeopardize the operations of the Commission, or result in systemic risk. Our investigation of this matter is ongoing, however, and we are coordinating with appropriate authorities. As another example, our Division of Enforcement has investigated and filed cases against individuals who we allege placed fake SEC filings on our EDGAR system in an effort to profit from the resulting market movements.

In addition, like other organizations, we are subject to the risk of unauthorized actions or disclosures by Commission personnel. For example, a 2014 internal review by the SEC's Office of Inspector General ("OIG"), an independent office within the agency, found that certain SEC laptops that may have contained nonpublic information could not be located. The OIG also has found instances in which SEC personnel have transmitted nonpublic information through non-secure personal email accounts. We seek to mitigate this risk by requiring all personnel to complete privacy and security training and we have other relevant risk mitigation controls in place.

Similarly, we are subject to cybersecurity risk in connection with vendors we utilize. For example, a weakness in vendor systems or software products may provide a mechanism for a cyber threat actor to access SEC systems or information through trusted paths. Recent global supply chain security incidents such as compromises of reputable software update services are illustrative of this type of occurrence.

In light of the nature of the data at risk and the cyber-related threats faced by the SEC, the Commission employs an agency-wide cybersecurity detection, protection and prevention program for the protection of agency operations and assets. This program includes cybersecurity protocols and controls, network protections, system monitoring and detection processes, vendor risk management processes, and regular cybersecurity and privacy training for employees. That said, we recognize that cybersecurity is an evolving landscape, and we are constantly learning from our own experiences as well as the experiences of others. To aid in this effort, and notwithstanding limitations on our hiring generally, we expect to hire additional expertise in this area.[196]

4.4 Proposed SEC Rules Concerning Cybersecurity

Based on a rising concern with cybersecurity, the SEC has proposed new SEC rules concerning cybersecurity. In a March 9, 2022, document titled, "Cybersecurity Risk Management for Investment Advisers, Registered Investment Companies, and Business Development Companies," the SEC discusses the need for the new rules and sets forth the proposed rules.[197] The SEC states:

> An adviser or a fund may incur substantial remediation costs due to a cybersecurity incident. It may need to reimburse clients for cybersecurity-related losses as well as implement expensive organizational or technological changes to reinforce its ability to respond to and recover from a cybersecurity incident. It may also see an increase in its insurance premiums. In addition, an adviser or fund may face increased litigation, regulatory, or other legal and financial risks or suffer reputational damage, and any of these outcomes could cause its clients or investors to lose confidence in their adviser or fund, or the financial markets more generally. Cybersecurity risk management is therefore a

---

[196] Press Release, Jay Clayton, Chairman of S.E.C., Statement on Cybersecurity (Sept. 20, 2017).
[197] 87 FR 13524-01; 2022 WL 684547 (March 9, 2022).

critical area of focus for advisers and funds, and many advisers and funds have taken steps to address cybersecurity risks. . . .

While some funds and advisers have implemented cybersecurity programs under the existing regulatory framework [such as Regulation S-P], there are no Commission rules that specifically require firms to adopt and implement comprehensive cybersecurity programs. Based on our staff's examinations of advisers and funds, we are concerned that some funds and advisers that are registered with us have not implemented reasonably designed cybersecurity programs. As a result, these firms' clients and investors may be at greater risk of harm than those of funds and advisers that have in place appropriate plans to address cybersecurity risks.

To address these concerns, we are proposing rules 206(4)-9 under the Advisers Act and 38a-2 under the Investment Company Act, which would require advisers and funds that are registered or required to be registered with us to implement cybersecurity policies and procedures addressing a number of elements. Under the proposed rules, such an adviser's or fund's cybersecurity policies and procedures generally should be tailored based on its business operations, including its complexity, and attendant cybersecurity risks. Further, the proposed rules would require advisers and funds, at least annually, to review and evaluate the design and effectiveness of their cybersecurity policies and procedures, which would allow them to update them in the face of ever-changing cyber threats and technologies. We believe that advisers and funds should be required to adopt and implement policies and procedures that address a number of elements to increase the likelihood that they are prepared to face a cybersecurity incident (whether that threat comes from an outside actor or the firm's personnel), and that investors and other market participants are protected from a cybersecurity incident that could significantly affect a firm's operations and lead to significant harm to clients and investors.

To address cybersecurity more directly, we also are proposing amendments to adviser and fund disclosure requirements to provide current and prospective advisory clients and fund shareholders with improved information regarding cybersecurity risks and cybersecurity incidents. In particular, we propose amendments to Form ADV for advisers and Forms N-1A, N-2, N-3, N-4, N-6, N-8B-2, and S-6 for funds. We believe these proposed cybersecurity disclosure requirements would enhance investor protection by requiring that cybersecurity risk or incident-related information is available to increase understanding in these areas and help ensure that investors and clients can make informed investment decisions.

In addition, we are proposing to require advisers to report significant cybersecurity incidents affecting the adviser, or its fund or private fund clients, to the Commission on a confidential basis. These reports would bolster the efficiency and effectiveness of our efforts to protect investors in connection with cybersecurity incidents. This reporting would not only help the Commission monitor and evaluate the effects of a cybersecurity incident on an adviser and its clients or a fund and its investors, but also assess the potential systemic risks affecting financial markets more broadly.

Taken together, these reforms are designed to promote a more comprehensive framework to address cybersecurity risks for advisers and funds, thereby reducing the risk that advisers and funds would be not be able to maintain critical operational capability when confronted with a significant cybersecurity incident. These reforms also are designed to give clients and investors better information with which to make investment decisions, and to give the Commission better information with which to conduct comprehensive monitoring and oversight of ever-evolving cybersecurity risks and incidents affecting advisers and funds.

The proposed SEC rules address policies and procedures of some investment companies (also called "funds"), including the addition of language concerning cybersecurity incidents in the last two years, for example, in forms and prospectus documents.[198] There are also rules concerning reporting of cybersecurity incidents by

---

[198] One form includes the following language: **PART 274—FORMS PRESCRIBED UNDER THE INVESTMENT COMPANY ACT OF 1940**

. . . 12. Amend Form N-1A (referenced in §§ 239.15A and 274.11A) by revising General Instruction C.3.(g)(i) and (ii), and adding Item 10(a)(4). The revisions read as follows: . . .

Form N-1A

* * * * *

General Instructions

* * * * *

C. Preparation of the Registration Statement . . .

(g) Interactive Data File

(i) An Interactive Data File (rule 232.11 of Regulation S-T [17 CFR 232.11]) is required to be submitted to the Commission in the manner provided by rule 405 of Regulation S-T [17 CFR 232.405] for any registration statement or post-effective amendment thereto on Form N-1A that includes or amends information provided in response to Items 2, 3, 4, or 10(a)(4).

* * * * *

(ii) An Interactive Data File is required to be submitted to the Commission in the manner provided by rule 405 of Regulation S-T for any form of prospectus filed pursuant to paragraphs (c) or (e) of rule 497 under the Securities Act [17 CFR 230.497(c) or (e)] that includes information provided in response to Items 2, 3, 4, or 10(a)(4) that varies from the registration statement. All interactive data must be submitted with the filing made pursuant to rule 497.

* * * * *

Part A—INFORMATION REQUIRED IN A PROSPECTUS

* * * * *

Item 10. Management, Organization, and Capital Structure

* * * * *

and policy and procedure requirements for cybersecurity for investment advisers. Additionally, there are reporting forms for investment advisers.[199] In part, the proposed SEC rules state:

---

(4) Significant Fund Cybersecurity Incidents. Provide a description of any significant fund cybersecurity incident as defined by rule 38a-2 of the Investment Company Act (17 CFR 270.38a-2) that has or is currently affecting the Fund or its service providers.

Instructions

1. The disclosure must include all significant fund cybersecurity incidents that have occurred within the last 2 fiscal years, as well as any currently ongoing.

2. The description of each incident must include the following information to the extent known: The entity or entities affected; when the incident was discovered and whether it is ongoing; whether any data was stolen, altered, or accessed or used for any other unauthorized purpose; the effect of the incident on the Fund's operations; and whether the Fund or service provider has remediated or is currently remediating the incident.

[199] One form states: **FORM ADV-C INVESTMENT ADVISER CYBERSECURITY INCIDENT REPORT PURSUANT TO RULE 204-6 [17 CFR 275.206(4)-6]**

You must submit this Form ADV-C if you are registered with the Commission as an investment adviser within 48 hours after having a reasonable basis to conclude that a significant adviser cybersecurity incident or a significant fund cybersecurity incident (collectively, "significant cybersecurity incident") has occurred or is occurring in accordance with rule 204-6 under the Investment Advisers Act of 1940. Check the box that indicates what you would like to do (check all that apply):

○ Submit an initial report for a significant cybersecurity incident.

○ Submit an amended report for a significant cybersecurity incident.

○ Submit a final amended report for a significant cybersecurity incident.

(1) Investment Advisers Act SEC File Number: 801

(2) Your full legal name of investment adviser (if you are a sole proprietor, state last, first, middle name):

(3) Name under which your primarily conduct your advisory business, if different from above:

(4) Address of principal place of business (number, street, city, state, zip code):

(5) Contact information for an individual with respect to the significant cybersecurity incident being reported: (Name, title, address if different from above, phone, email address)

(6) Adviser reporting a:

Significant adviser cybersecurity incident

(a) If so, does the significant adviser cybersecurity incident involve any private funds?

(1) If yes, list the private fund ID number(s); \\

Significant fund cybersecurity incident

(b) If so, list each investment company registered under the Investment Company Act of 1940 or company that has elected to be a business development company pursuant to section 54 of that Act involved and their SEC file number(s) (811 or 814 number) and the series ID number of the specific fund if more than one series under the SEC file number.

(7) Approximate date(s) the significant cybersecurity incident occurred, if known:

(8) Approximate date the significant cybersecurity incident was discovered:

(9) Is the significant cybersecurity incident ongoing?

(a) If not, approximate date the significant cybersecurity incident was resolved or any internal investigation pertaining to such incident was closed.

(10) Has law enforcement or a government agency (other than the Commission) been notified about the significant cybersecurity incident?

(a) If yes, which law enforcement or government agencies have been notified?

(11) Describe the nature and scope of the significant cybersecurity incident, including any effect on the relevant entity's critical operations:

(12) Describe the actions taken or planned to respond to and recover from the significant cybersecurity incident:

PART 270—RULES AND REGULATIONS, INVESTMENT COMPANY ACT OF 1940

10. Section 270.38a-2 is added to read as follows:

17 CFR § 270.38a-2

§ 270.38a-2 Cybersecurity policies and procedures of certain investment companies.

(a) Cybersecurity policies and procedures. Each fund must adopt and implement written policies and procedures that are reasonably designed to address cybersecurity risks, including policies and procedures that:

(1) Risk assessment.

(i) Require periodic assessments of cybersecurity risks associated with fund information systems and fund information residing therein including requiring the fund to:

(A) Categorize and prioritize cybersecurity risks based on an inventory of the components of the fund information systems and fund information residing therein and the potential effect of a cybersecurity incident on the fund; and

(B) Identify the fund's service providers that receive, maintain, or process fund information, or are otherwise permitted to access fund information systems and any fund information

---

(13) Was any data was stolen, altered, or accessed or used for any other unauthorized purpose?
(a) If yes, describe the nature and scope of such information, including whether it was adviser information or fund information.
(14) Was any personal information lost, stolen, modified, deleted, destroyed, or accessed without authorization as a result of the significant cybersecurity incident?
(a) If yes, describe the nature and scope of such information.
(b) If yes, has notification been provided to persons whose personal information was lost, stolen, damaged, or accessed without authorization?
(i) If not, are such notifications planned?
(15) Has disclosure about the significant cybersecurity incident been made to the adviser's clients and/or to investors in any investment company registered under the Investment Company Act of 1940 or company that has elected to be a business development company pursuant to section 54 of that Act, or private funds advised by the adviser involved?
(a) If yes, when was such disclosure made?
(b) If not, explain why such disclosure has not be made?
(16) Is the significant cybersecurity incident covered under a cybersecurity insurance policy maintained by you or any investment company registered under the Investment Company Act of 1940 or company that has elected to be a business development company pursuant to section 54 of that Act, or any private fund?
(a) If yes, has the insurance company issuing the cybersecurity insurance policy been contacted about the significant cybersecurity incident?

residing therein, and assess the cybersecurity risks associated with the fund's use of these service providers.[200]

(ii) Require written documentation of any risk assessments.

(2) User security and access. Require controls designed to minimize user-related risks and prevent the unauthorized access to fund information systems and fund information residing therein including:

(i) Requiring standards of behavior for individuals authorized to access fund information systems and any fund information residing therein, such as an acceptable use policy;

(ii) Identifying and authenticating individual users, including implementing authentication measures that require users to present a combination of two or more credentials for access verification;

(iii) Establishing procedures for the timely distribution, replacement, and revocation of passwords or methods of authentication;

(iv) Restricting access to specific fund information systems or components thereof and fund information residing therein solely to individuals requiring access to such systems and information as is necessary for them to perform their responsibilities and functions on behalf of the fund; and

(v) Securing remote access technologies.

(3) Information protection.

---

[200] Risk assessment is fundamental to proper cybersecurity practices. The SEC reviews considerations concerning risk assessment:

An adviser or fund generally should assess, categorize, and prioritize the cybersecurity risks created by its information systems and information residing therein in light of the firm's particular operations. For example, advisers may be subject to different risks as a result of international operations, insider threats, or remote or traveling employees. Only after assessing, analyzing, categorizing, and prioritizing its risks can an adviser or fund develop and implement cybersecurity policies and procedures designed to mitigate those risks. The proposed cybersecurity risk management rules would also require advisers and funds to reassess and re-prioritize their cybersecurity risks periodically as changes that affect these risks occur. Due to the ongoing and emerging nature of cybersecurity threats, and the proposed requirement discussed below that advisers and funds review their cybersecurity policies and procedures no less frequently than annually, we are not proposing that such a reassessment occur at specified intervals. Instead, advisers and funds should reassess their cybersecurity risks as they arise to reflect internal changes, such as changes to its business, online presence, or client web access, or external changes, such as changes in the evolving technology and cybersecurity threat landscape, and inform senior officers of the adviser or fund of any material changes to the risk assessment. In assessing ongoing and emerging cybersecurity threats, advisers and funds generally should monitor and consider updates and guidance from private sector and governmental resources, such as the Financial Services Information Sharing and Analysis Center ("FS-ISAC") and the Department of Homeland Security's CISA. *Id.*

(i) Require measures designed to monitor fund information systems and protect fund information from unauthorized access or use, based on a periodic assessment of the fund information systems and fund information that resides on the systems that takes into account:

(A) The sensitivity level and importance of fund information to its business operations;

(B) Whether any fund information is personal information;

(C) Where and how fund information is accessed, stored and transmitted, including the monitoring of fund information in transmission;

(D) Fund information systems access controls and malware protection; and

(E) The potential effect a cybersecurity incident involving fund information could have on the fund and its shareholders, including the ability for the fund to continue to provide services.

(ii) Require oversight of service providers that receive, maintain, or process fund information, or are otherwise permitted to access fund information systems and any fund information residing therein and through that oversight document that such service providers, pursuant to a written contract between the fund and any such service provider, are required to implement and maintain appropriate measures, including the practices described in paragraphs (a)(1), (2), (3)(i), (4), and (5) of this section, that are designed to protect fund information and fund information systems.

(4) Cybersecurity threat and vulnerability management. Require measures to detect, mitigate, and remediate any cybersecurity threats and vulnerabilities with respect to fund information systems and the fund information residing therein.

(5) Cybersecurity incident response and recovery.

(i) Require measures to detect, respond to, and recover from a cybersecurity incident, including policies and procedures that are reasonably designed to ensure:

(A) Continued operations of the fund;

(B) The protection of fund information systems and fund information residing therein;

(C) External and internal cybersecurity incident information sharing and communications; and

(D) Reporting of a significant fund cybersecurity incident by the fund's adviser under § 275.204-6 (Rule 204-6 under the Investment Advisers Act of 1940).

(ii) Require written documentation of any cybersecurity incident, including the fund's response to and recovery from such an incident.

(b) Annual review. A fund must, at least annually, review and assess the design and effectiveness of the cybersecurity policies and procedures required by paragraph (a) of this section, including whether they reflect changes in cybersecurity risk over the time period covered by the review.

(c) Board oversight. A fund must:

(1) Obtain the initial approval of the fund's board of directors, including a majority of the directors who are not interested persons of the fund, of the fund's policies and procedures; and

(2) Provide, for review by the fund's board of directors, a written report prepared no less frequently than annually by the fund that, at a minimum, describes the review, the assessment, and any control tests performed, explains their results, documents any cybersecurity incident that occurred since the date of the last report, and discusses any material changes to the policies and procedures since the date of the last report.

(d) Unit investment trusts. If the fund is a unit investment trust, the fund's principal underwriter or depositor must:

(i) Approve the fund's policies and procedures; and

(ii) Receive all written reports required by paragraph (c) of this section.

(e) Recordkeeping. The fund must maintain:

(1) A copy of the policies and procedures that are in effect, or at any time within the past five years were in effect, in an easily accessible place;

(2) Copies of written reports provided to the board of directors pursuant to paragraph (c)(2) of this section (or, if the fund is a unit investment trust, to the fund's principal underwriter or depositor, pursuant to paragraph (d) of this section) for at least five years after the end of the fiscal year in which the documents were provided, the first two years in an easily accessible place;

(3) Any records documenting the review pursuant to paragraph (c)(2) of this section for at least five years after the end of the fiscal year in which the annual review was conducted, the first two years in an easily accessible place;

(4) Any report provided to the Commission pursuant to paragraph (a)(5) of this section for at least five years after the provision of the report, the first two years in an easily accessible place;

(5) Records documenting the occurrence of any cybersecurity incident, including records related to any response and recovery from such incident pursuant to paragraph (a)(5) of this section, for at least five years after the date of the incident, the first two years in an easily accessible place; and

(6) Records documenting the risk assessment pursuant to paragraph (a)(1) of this section for at least five years after the date of the assessment, the first two years in an easily accessible place.

(f) Definitions. For purposes of this section:

Cybersecurity incident means an unauthorized occurrence on or conducted through a fund's information systems that jeopardizes the confidentiality, integrity, or availability of a fund's information systems or any fund information residing therein.

Cybersecurity risk means financial, operational, legal, reputational, and other adverse consequences that could result from cybersecurity incidents, threats, and vulnerabilities.

Cybersecurity threat means any potential occurrence that may result in an unauthorized effort to adversely affect the confidentiality, integrity or availability of a fund's information systems or any fund information residing therein.

Cybersecurity vulnerability means a vulnerability in a fund's information systems, information system security procedures, or internal controls, including vulnerabilities in their design, configuration, maintenance, or implementation that, if exploited, could result in a cybersecurity incident.

Fund means a registered investment company or a business development company.

Fund information means any electronic information related to the fund's business, including personal information, received, maintained, created, or processed by the fund.

Fund information systems means the information resources owned or used by the fund, including physical or virtual infrastructure controlled by such information resources, or components thereof, organized for the collection, processing, maintenance, use, sharing, dissemination, or disposition of fund information to maintain or support the fund's operations.

Personal information means any information that can be used, alone or in conjunction with any other information, to identify an individual, such as name, date of birth, place of birth, telephone number, street address, mother's maiden name, Social Security number, driver's license number, electronic mail address, account number, account password, biometric records or other nonpublic authentication information.

Significant fund cybersecurity incident means a cybersecurity incident, or a group of related cybersecurity incidents, that significantly disrupts or degrades the fund's ability to maintain critical operations, or leads to the unauthorized access or use of fund information, where the unauthorized access or use of such information results in substantial harm to the fund or to an investor whose information was accessed.

PART 275—RULES AND REGULATIONS, INVESTMENT ADVISERS ACT OF 1940

21. Section 275.204-6 is added to read as follows:

17 CFR § 275.204-6

§ 275.204-6 Cybersecurity incident reporting.

(a) Every investment adviser registered or required to be registered under section 203 of the Act (15 U.S.C. 80b-3) shall:

(1) Report to the Commission any significant adviser cybersecurity incident or significant fund cybersecurity incident, promptly, but in no event

more than 48 hours, after having a reasonable basis to conclude that any such incident has occurred or is occurring by filing Form ADV-C electronically on the Investment Adviser Registration Depository (IARD).

(2) Amend any previously filed Form ADV-C promptly, but in no event more than 48 hours after:

(i) Any information previously reported to the Commission on Form ADV-C pertaining to a significant adviser cybersecurity incident or a significant fund cybersecurity becoming materially inaccurate;

(ii) Any new material information pertaining to a significant adviser cybersecurity incident or a significant fund cybersecurity incident previously reported to the Commission on Form ADV-C being discovered; or

(iii) Any significant adviser cybersecurity incident or significant fund cybersecurity incident being resolved or any internal investigation pertaining to such an incident being closed.

(b) For the purposes of this section:

Adviser information and cybersecurity incident have the same meanings as in § 275.206(4)-9 (Rule 206(4)-9 under the Investment Advisers Act of 1940).

Significant adviser cybersecurity incident means a cybersecurity incident, or a group of related cybersecurity incidents, that significantly disrupts or degrades the adviser's ability, or the ability of a private fund client of the adviser, to maintain critical operations, or leads to the unauthorized access or use of adviser information, where the unauthorized access or use of such information results in:

(i) Substantial harm to the adviser; or

(ii) Substantial harm to a client, or an investor in a private fund, whose information was accessed.

Significant fund cybersecurity incident has the same meaning as in § 270.38a-2 of this chapter (Rule 38a-2 under the Investment Company Act of 1940).

17 CFR § 275.206(4)-9

22. Section 275.206(4)-9 is added to read as follows:

17 CFR § 275.206(4)-9

§ 275.206(4)-9 Cybersecurity policies and procedures of investment advisers.

(a) Cybersecurity policies and procedures. As a means reasonably designed to prevent fraudulent, deceptive, or manipulative acts, practices, or courses of business within the meaning of section 206(4) of the Act (15 U.S.C. 80b6(4)), it is unlawful for any investment adviser registered or required to be registered under section 203 of the Investment Advisers Act of 1940 (15 U.S.C. 80b-3) to provide investment advice to clients unless the adviser adopts and implements written policies and procedures that are reasonably designed to address the adviser's cybersecurity risks, including policies and procedures that:

(1) Risk assessment.

(i) Require periodic assessments of cybersecurity risks associated with adviser information systems and adviser information residing therein, including requiring the adviser to:

(A) Categorize and prioritize cybersecurity risks based on an inventory of the components of the adviser information systems and adviser information residing therein and the potential effect of a cybersecurity incident on the adviser; and

(B) Identify the adviser's service providers that receive, maintain, or process adviser information, or are otherwise permitted to access adviser information systems and any adviser information residing therein, and assess the cybersecurity risks associated with the adviser's use of these service providers.

(ii) Require written documentation of any risk assessments.

(2) User security and access. Require controls designed to minimize user-related risks and prevent unauthorized access to adviser information systems and adviser information residing therein, including:

(i) Requiring standards of behavior for individuals authorized to access adviser information systems and any adviser information residing therein, such as an acceptable use policy;

(ii) Identifying and authenticating individual users, including implementing authentication measures that require users to present a combination of two or more credentials for access verification;

(iii) Establishing procedures for the timely distribution, replacement, and revocation of passwords or methods of authentication;

(iv) Restricting access to specific adviser information systems or components thereof and adviser information residing therein solely to individuals requiring access to such systems and information as is necessary for them to perform their responsibilities and functions on behalf of the adviser; and

(v) Securing remote access technologies.

(3) Information protection.

(i) Require measures designed to monitor adviser information systems and protect adviser information from unauthorized access or use, based on a periodic assessment of the adviser information systems and adviser information that resides on the systems that takes into account:

(A) The sensitivity level and importance of adviser information to its business operations;

(B) Whether any adviser information is personal information;

(C) Where and how adviser information is accessed, stored and transmitted, including the monitoring of adviser information in transmission;

(D) Adviser information systems access controls and malware protection; and

(E) The potential effect a cybersecurity incident involving adviser information could have on the adviser and its clients, including the ability for the adviser to continue to provide investment advice.

(ii) Require oversight of service providers that receive, maintain, or process adviser information, or are otherwise permitted to access adviser information systems and any adviser information residing therein and through that oversight document that such service providers, pursuant to a written contract between the adviser and any such service provider, are required to implement and maintain appropriate measures, including the practices described in paragraphs (a)(1), (2), (3)(i), (4), and (5) of this section, that are designed to protect adviser information and adviser information systems.

(4) Cybersecurity threat and vulnerability management. Require measures to detect, mitigate, and remediate any cybersecurity threats and vulnerabilities with respect to adviser information systems and the adviser information residing therein;

(5) Cybersecurity incident response and recovery.

(i) Require measures to detect, respond to, and recover from a cybersecurity incident, including policies and procedures that are reasonably designed to ensure:

(A) Continued operations of the adviser;

(B) The protection of adviser information systems and the adviser information residing therein;

(C) External and internal cybersecurity incident information sharing and communications; and

(D) Reporting of significant cybersecurity incidents under § 275.204-6 (Rule 204-6).

(ii) Require written documentation of any cybersecurity incident, including the adviser's response to and recovery from such an incident.

(b) Annual review. An adviser must, at least annually:

(1) Review and assess the design and effectiveness of the cybersecurity policies and procedures required by paragraph (a) of this section, including whether they reflect changes in cybersecurity risk over the time period covered by the review; and

(2) Prepare a written report that, at a minimum, describes the review, the assessment, and any control tests performed, explains their results, documents any cybersecurity incident that occurred since the date of the last report, and discusses any material changes to the policies and procedures since the date of the last report.

(c) Definitions. For purposes of this section:

Adviser information means any electronic information related to the adviser's business, including personal information, received, maintained, created, or processed by the adviser.

Adviser information systems means the information resources owned or used by the adviser, including physical or virtual infrastructure controlled by such information resources, or components thereof, organized for the collection, processing, maintenance, use, sharing, dissemination, or disposition of adviser information to maintain or support the adviser's operations.

Cybersecurity incident means an unauthorized occurrence on or conducted through an adviser's information systems that jeopardizes the confidentiality, integrity, or availability of an adviser's information systems or any adviser information residing therein.

Cybersecurity risk means financial, operational, legal, reputational, and other consequences that could result from cybersecurity incidents, threats, and vulnerabilities.

Cybersecurity threat means any potential occurrence that may result in an unauthorized effort to adversely affect the confidentiality, integrity, or availability of an adviser's information systems or any adviser information residing therein.

Cybersecurity vulnerability means a vulnerability in an adviser's information systems, information system security procedures, or internal controls, including vulnerabilities in their design, configuration, maintenance, or implementation that, if exploited, could result in a cybersecurity incident.

Personal information means:

(i) Any information that can be used, alone or in conjunction with any other information, to identify an individual, such as name, date of birth, place of birth, telephone number, street address, mother's maiden name, Social Security number, driver's license number, electronic mail address, account number, account password, biometric records or other nonpublic authentication information; or

(ii) Any other non-public information regarding a client's account.

NOTES

Note 1

The SEC solicits comments concerning the applicability of the rules to advisers and investment companies:

1. Should we exempt certain types of advisers or funds from these proposed cybersecurity risk management rules? If so, which ones, and why? For example, is there a subset of funds or advisers with operations so limited or staffs so small that the adoption of cybersecurity risk management programs is not beneficial?

2. Should we scale the proposed requirements based on the size of the adviser or fund? If so, which of the elements described below should not

be required for smaller advisers or funds? How would we define such smaller advisers or funds? For example, should we define such advisers and funds based on the thresholds that the Commission uses for purposes of the Regulatory Flexibility Act? Would using different thresholds based on assets under management, such as $150 million or $200 million, be appropriate? Would another threshold be more suitable, such as one based on an adviser's or fund's limited operations, staffing, revenues or management?

These questions raise fundamental issues with respect to cybersecurity requirements. There is a desire to maintain flexibility and to carefully consider the potentially burdensome nature of the requirements on smaller entities.

Note 2

The proposed SEC rules posit several questions soliciting comments concerning the cybersecurity risk management rules. The questions state:

3. Are the proposed elements of the cybersecurity policies and procedures appropriate? Should we modify or delete any of the proposed elements? Why or why not? For example, should advisers and funds be required, as proposed, to conduct a risk assessment as part of their cybersecurity policies and procedures? Should we require that a risk assessment include specific components (e.g., identification and documentation of vulnerabilities and threats, identification of the business effect of threats and likelihood of incidents occurring, identification and prioritization of responses), or require written documentation for risk assessments? Should the rules require policies and procedures related to user security and access, as well as information protection?

4. Should there be additional or more specific requirements for who would implement an adviser's or fund's cybersecurity program? For example, should we require an adviser or fund to specify an individual, such as a chief information security officer, or group of individuals as responsible for implementing the program or parts thereof? Why or why not? If so, should such an individual or group of individuals be required to have certain qualifications or experience related to cybersecurity, and if so, what type of qualifications or experience should be required?

5. The Investment Company Act compliance rule prohibits the fund's officers, directors, employees, adviser, principal underwriter, or any person acting under the direction of these persons, from directly or indirectly taking any action to coerce, manipulate, mislead or fraudulently influence the fund's chief compliance officer in the performance of her responsibilities under the rule in order to protect the chief compliance officer from undue influence by those seeking to conceal

non-compliance with the Federal securities laws. Should we adopt a similar prohibition for those administering a fund's or adviser's cybersecurity policies and procedures? Why or why not?

6. Would advisers and funds expect to use sub-advisers or other third parties to administer their cybersecurity programs? If so, to what extent and in what manner? Should there be additional or specific requirements for advisers and funds that delegate cybersecurity management responsibilities to a sub-adviser or third party? If so, what requirements and why?

7. Should we include any other cybersecurity program administration requirements? If so, what? For example, should we include a requirement for training staff responsible for day-to-day management of the program? If we require such training, should that involve setting minimum qualifications for staff responsible for carrying out the requirements of the program? Why or why not?

8. Are the proposed rules' definitions appropriate and clear? If not, how could these definitions be clarified within the context of the proposed rules? Should any be modified or eliminated? Are any of them proposed terms too broad or too narrow? Are there other terms that we should define?

9. What are best practices that commenters have developed or are aware of with respect to the types of measures that must be implemented as part of the proposed cybersecurity risk management rules or, alternatively, are there any measures that commenters have found to be ineffective or relatively less effective?

10. What user measures do advisers currently have for using mobile devices or other ways to access adviser or fund information systems remotely? Should we require advisers and funds to implement specific measures to secure remote access technologies?

11. Do advisers and funds currently conduct periodic assessments of their information systems to monitor and protect information from unauthorized use? If so, how often do advisers and funds conduct such assessments? Should the proposed rules specify a minimum assessment frequency, and if so, what should that frequency be?

12. Other than what is required to be reported under proposed rule 204-6, should we require any specific measures within an adviser's policies and procedures with respect to cybersecurity incident response and recovery?

13. Should we require that advisers and funds respond to cybersecurity incidents within a specific timeframe? If so, what would be an appropriate timeframe?

14. Should we require advisers and funds to assess the compliance of all service providers that receive, maintain, or process adviser or fund information, or are otherwise permitted to access adviser or fund

information systems and any adviser or fund information residing therein, with these proposed cybersecurity risk management rules? Should we expand or narrow this set of service providers? For example, with respect to funds, should this requirement only apply to "named service providers" as discussed above?

15. How do advisers and funds currently consider cybersecurity risks when choosing third-party service providers? What due diligence with respect to cybersecurity is involved in selecting a service provider?

16. How do advisers and funds reduce the risk of a cybersecurity incident transferring from the service provider (or a fourth party (i.e., a service provider used by one of an adviser's or fund's service providers)) to the adviser today?

17. Should we require advisers' and funds' cybersecurity policies and procedures to require oversight of certain service providers, including that such service providers implement and maintain appropriate measures designed to protect a fund's or an adviser's information and information systems pursuant to written contract? Do advisers and funds currently include specific cybersecurity and data protection provisions in their agreements with service providers? If so, what provisions are the most important? Do they address potential cybersecurity risks that could result from a cybersecurity incident occurring at a fourth party? Should any contractual provisions be specifically required as part of these rules? Should this requirement apply to a more limited subset of service providers? If so, which service providers? For example, should we require funds to include such provisions in their agreements with advisers that would be subject to proposed rule 206(4)-9? Are there other ways we should require protective actions by service providers?

18. Do advisers or funds currently consider their or their service providers' insurance policies, if any, when responding to cybersecurity incidents? Why or why not?

19. Are advisers and funds currently able to obtain information from or about their service providers' cybersecurity practices (e.g., policies, procedures, and controls) to effectively assess them? What, if any, challenges do advisers and funds currently have in obtaining such information? Are certain advisers or funds (e.g., smaller or larger firms) more easily able to obtain such information?

Note 3

The SEC also considers the broad economic impact of the proposed rules:

While advisers and funds have private incentives to maintain some level of cybersecurity hygiene, market failures can lead the privately optimal level to be inadequate from the perspective of overall economic efficiency:

Such market failures provide the economic rationale for regulatory intervention in advisers' and funds' cybersecurity practices. At the core of these market failures is asymmetric information about cybersecurity preparations and incidents as well as negative externalities to these incidents. Asymmetric information contributes to two main inefficiencies: First, because the production of cybersecurity defenses must constantly evolve, an adviser's or fund's inability to observe cyberattacks on its competitors inhibits the efficacy of its own cybersecurity preparations. Second, for a client or investor, the inability to observe an adviser's or fund's effort in cybersecurity preparation gives rise to a principal-agent problem that can contribute to an adviser or fund exerting too little effort (i.e., underinvesting or underspending) on cybersecurity preparations. Moreover, because there can be substantial negative externalities related to cybersecurity incidents, advisers' and funds' private incentives to exert effort on cybersecurity preparations are likely to be lower than optimal from a societal standpoint.

In the production of cybersecurity defenses, the main input is information. In particular, information about prior attacks and their degree of success is immensely valuable in mounting effective countermeasures. However, firms are naturally reluctant to share such information freely: Doing so can assist future attackers as well as lead to loss of customers, reputational harm, litigation, or regulatory scrutiny. Moreover, because disclosure of such information creates a positive information externality—the benefits of which accrue to society at large and which cannot be fully captured by the firm making the disclosure— an inefficient market equilibrium is likely to arise. In this market equilibrium, too little information about cybersecurity incidents is disclosed, leading to inefficiently low levels of cybersecurity defense production.

Asymmetric information also contributes to a principal-agent problem. The relationship between an adviser and its client or a fund and its investor is one where the principal (the client or fund investor) relies on an agent (the investment adviser or fund complex and its management) to perform services on the principal's behalf. Because principals and their agents do not have perfectly aligned preferences and goals, agents may take actions that increase their well-being at the expense of principals, thereby imposing "agency costs" on the principals. Although private contracts between principals and agents aim to minimize such costs, they are limited in their ability to do so; this limitation provides one rationale for regulatory intervention.

In the context of cybersecurity, the principal-agent problem is one of underspending in cybersecurity—agents exerting insufficient effort toward protecting the personal information, investments, or funds of the principals from being stolen or otherwise compromised. For example, in a recent survey of financial firms, 58% of the respondents self-reported "underspending" on cybersecurity. Several factors can contribute to this underspending. Agents (i.e., advisers and funds) may not be able to credibly signal to their principals (i.e., clients or investors) that they are better at addressing cybersecurity risks than their peers, reducing their incentives to bear such costs. At the same time, agents who do not bear the full cost of a cybersecurity failure (e.g., losses of their customers' information or assets) will prefer to avoid bearing costs—such as elaborate cybersecurity practices—the benefits of which accrue in large part to principals (i.e., clients and investors).

Agents' reputation motives—the fear of market-imposed loss of future profits—should generally work against the tendency for agents to underinvest in cybersecurity measures. However, for smaller agents—who do not enjoy economies of scale or scope, and generally have less valuable brands—the cost of implementing robust cybersecurity measures will be relatively high, while their reputation motives will be more limited. Thus, smaller agents can be expected to be especially prone to underinvestment.

Even in the absence of agency problems, advisers and funds may still underinvest in cybersecurity due to negative externalities or moral hazard. In the context of cybersecurity, negative externalities arise because a disruption to the operation or financial condition of one financial entity can have significant negative repercussions on the financial system broadly. For example, a cybersecurity incident at a large money market fund that affects its ability to process redemptions could disrupt the fund's shareholders' ability to access cash needed to satisfy other obligations, potentially leading those shareholders to default, which, in turn, could trigger further defaults by those shareholders' creditors. Alternatively, a cybersecurity incident may adversely affect market confidence and curtail economic activity through a confidence channel. As such costs would not be internalized by advisers and funds, advisers and funds would be expected to underinvest in measures aimed at avoiding such costs. In addition, advisers and funds may also underinvest in their cybersecurity measures due to moral hazard from expectations of government support. For example, a large fund may realize that it is an attractive target for sophisticated state actors aiming to disrupt the U.S. financial system. Protection against such "advanced persistent threats" from sophisticated actors is costly. A belief that such an attack would be met with government support could lead to moral hazard where the fund underinvests in defenses aimed at countering this threat.

The proposed amendments could mitigate these problems in several ways. First, establishing explicit requirements for cybersecurity policies and procedures could help ensure that investment advisers and funds devote a certain minimum amount of effort toward cybersecurity readiness. Second, the proposed disclosure and regulatory reporting requirements could help alleviate the information asymmetry problems by providing current and prospective investors and clients, third parties (e.g., fund rating services), and regulators with more information about funds' and advisers' cybersecurity exposure. The publicly disclosed information could in turn be used by investors, clients, and third parties to screen and monitor funds and investment advisers, while the confidential regulatory reports could be used by regulators to inform industry and law enforcement about ongoing threats. Finally, by reducing uncertainty about the effectiveness of funds' and investment advisers' cybersecurity measures, the proposed amendments could help level the competitive playing field for funds and advisers by simplifying prospective investors' and clients' decision making. By addressing important market imperfections, the proposed amendments could mitigate underinvestment in cybersecurity and improve the adviser and fund industry's ability to produce effective cybersecurity defenses through better information sharing, which could in turn lead to improved economic efficiency.

The effectiveness of the proposed amendments at mitigating the aforementioned problems would depend on several factors. It would depend on the extent to which the proposed amendments materially affect registrants' policies and procedures and disclosures. Insofar as the new requirements affect registrants' policies and procedures, the effectiveness of the proposed amendments would also depend on the extent to which the actions they induce alleviate cybersecurity underinvestment. The effectiveness of the proposed amendments would also depend on the extent to which the proposed disclosure requirements provide useful information to investors, clients, third parties, and regulators.

Note 4

The SEC also considered alternatives to the proposed rules reviewed *supra*. The SEC describes those alternatives as:

a. Require Only Disclosure of Cybersecurity Policies and Procedures Without Prescribing Elements

Rather than requiring registrants to adopt cybersecurity policies and procedures with specific enumerated elements, the Commission considered requiring advisers and funds to only provide explanations or summaries of their cybersecurity practices to their clients or investors.

We believe that such an approach would create weaker incentives to address potential underspending in cybersecurity measures as it would rely entirely on clients' and investors' (or third parties' providing analysis to clients and investors) ability to assess the effectiveness of registrants' cybersecurity practices from registrants' explanations. Given the cybersecurity risks of disclosing detailed explanations of cybersecurity practices, it is likely that such explanations would include only vague boilerplate language and provide little information that could be used by observers to infer the degree of cybersecurity preparedness. Such a "disclosure-only" regime is unlikely to be effective at resolving the underlying information asymmetry and would therefore be unlikely to affect meaningful change in registrants' cybersecurity practices. Moreover, not requiring specific enumerated elements in cybersecurity policies and procedures would likely result in less uniform cybersecurity preparedness across registrants, undermining clients' and investors' broader confidence in the fund and adviser industries. At the same time, the costs associated with this alternative would likely be minimal, as registrants would be unlikely to face pressure to adjust practices as a result of such disclosures.

b. Require Cybersecurity Policies and Procedures With More Limited Prescribed Elements

We also considered paring down some enumerated elements from the proposed cybersecurity policies and procedures requirement, more specifically the oversight of service providers component of the information protection element. In this regard, we considered narrowing the scope of the types of service providers to named service providers discussed further above and requiring a periodic review and assessment of a named service provider's cybersecurity policies and procedures in lieu of a written contract. We further considered requiring service providers that receive, maintain, or process adviser or fund information to provide security certifications in lieu of the written contract requirement.

Narrowing the scope of the types of service providers affected by the proposal could lower costs for registrants, especially smaller registrants who rely on generic service providers and would have difficulty effecting changes in contractual terms with such service providers. However, given that in the current technological context cybersecurity risk exposure of registrants is unlikely to be limited to (or even concentrated in) certain named service providers, narrowing the scope of service providers would likely lead to lower costs only insofar as it reduces effectiveness of the regulation. In other words, absent a written contractual arrangement with a service provider relating to the provider's cybersecurity practices, it is unlikely that registrants could satisfy their overarching obligations under the proposed rules.

Alternatively, maintaining the proposed scope but only requiring a standard, recognized, certification in lieu of a written contract could also lead to cost savings for registrants. However, we preliminarily believe that it would be difficult to prescribe a set of characteristics for such a "standard" certification that would sufficiently address the varied types of advisers and funds and their respective service providers.

c. Require Specific Prescriptive Requirements for Addressing Cybersecurity Risks

The Commission considered including more prescriptive elements in the cybersecurity policies and procedures requirement of the current proposal. For example, advisers and funds could have been required to implement particular controls (e.g., specific encryption protocols, network architecture, or authentication procedures) designed to address each general element of the required cybersecurity policies and procedures. Given the considerable diversity in the size, focus, and technical sophistication of affected registrants, any specific requirements would result in some registrants needing to substantially alter their cybersecurity policies and procedures.

The potential benefit of such an approach would be to provide assurance that advisers and funds have implemented certain specific cybersecurity hygiene practices. But this approach would also entail considerably higher costs as many registrants would need to adjust their existing practices. Considering the variety of advisers and funds registered with the Commission, it would be exceedingly difficult for the Commission to devise specific requirements that are appropriately suited for all registrants: A uniform set of requirements would certainly be both over- and under-inclusive, while providing varied requirements based on the circumstances of the registrant would be complex and impractical. For example, uniform prescriptive requirements that ensure reasonably designed cybersecurity policies and procedures for the largest, most sophisticated advisers and funds would likely be overly burdensome for smaller, less sophisticated advisers with more limited cybersecurity exposures. Conversely, if these uniform prescriptive requirements were tailored to advisers and funds with more limited operations or cybersecurity risk, such requirements likely would be inadequate to address larger registrants' cybersecurity risks appropriately. Alternatively, providing different requirements for different categories of registrants would involve considerable regulatory complexity in delineating the classes of advisers and defining the appropriate requirements for each class. More broadly, imposing detailed prescriptive requirements would effectively place the Commission in the role of dictating details of the IT practices of registrants without the benefit of the registrants' knowledge of their own particular circumstances. Moreover, given the complex and constantly evolving cybersecurity landscape, detailed regulatory requirements for cybersecurity practices would likely limit registrants' ability to adapt quickly to changes in the cybersecurity landscape.

d. Require Audits of Internal Controls Regarding Cybersecurity

Instead of requiring advisers and funds to adopt and implement cybersecurity policies and procedures, the Commission considered requiring advisers and funds to obtain audits of the effectiveness of their existing cybersecurity controls—for example, by obtaining service organization control audits with respect to their cybersecurity practices. This approach would not have required advisers and funds to adopt and implement cybersecurity policies and procedures as proposed, but instead would have required advisers and funds to engage an independent qualified third party to assess their cybersecurity controls and prepare a report describing its assessment and any potential deficiencies.

Under this alternative, an independent third party (e.g., an auditing firm) would certify to the effectiveness of the adviser's or fund's cybersecurity practices. If the firms providing such certifications have sufficient reputational motives to issue credible assessment, and if the scope of such certifications is not overly circumscribed, it is likely that registrants' cybersecurity practices would end up being more robust under this alternative than under the current proposal. By providing certification of a registrant's cybersecurity practices, a firm would—in effect—be "lending" its reputation to the registrant. Because "lenders" are naturally most sensitive to down-side risks (here, loss of reputation, lawsuits, damages, regulatory enforcement actions), one would expect them to avoid "lending" to registrants with cybersecurity practices whose effectiveness is questionable.

While certification by credible third parties could lead to more robust cybersecurity practices, the costs of such an approach would likely be considerably higher. Because of the aforementioned sensitivity to down-side risk, firms would likely be hesitant to provide cybersecurity certifications without a thorough understanding of a registrant's systems and practices; in many cases, developing such an understanding would involve considerable effort. In addition, it is possible that the inherent ambiguity of what represents "effective" practices in an evolving context like cybersecurity would lead to a reluctance among third parties to provide the necessary certification services.

e. Vary Requirements of the Proposed Rules on Cybersecurity and Procedures for Different Subsets of Advisers and Funds

The Commission considered requiring different elements in an adviser's or fund's cybersecurity policies and procedures based on characteristics of the adviser or fund. For example, advisers or funds with assets under management below a certain threshold or with only a limited number of clients or investors could have been required to implement more limited cybersecurity policies and procedures.

This approach could have scaled based on adviser or fund size, business or other criteria, with larger firms, for example, being required to address more elements in their cybersecurity policies and procedures or being required to implement more prescriptive cybersecurity measures. However, as discussed above, cybersecurity risks and vulnerabilities are likely to be unique to each adviser and fund depending on its particular operations, which could make it difficult to use any specific characteristics such as firm size, for example, as an effective proxy to determine the scope of their cybersecurity policies and procedures.

f. Administration and Oversight of Cybersecurity Policies and Procedures

The Commission considered various alternative requirements with respect to administration and oversight of an adviser's or fund's cybersecurity policies and procedures such as requiring advisers and funds to designate a CISO or requiring funds' boards to oversee directly a fund's cybersecurity policies and procedures. There is a broad spectrum of potential approaches to this alternative, ranging from the largely nominal (e.g., requiring registrants to designate someone to be a CISO) to the stringent (e.g., requiring a highly qualified CISO to attest to the effectiveness of the registrant's policies).

While employee designations and similar nominal requirements may improve accountability and enhance compliance in certain contexts, they are unlikely to lead to material improvements in highly technical aspects of business operations. Given the technical complexity of cybersecurity issues, imposing such nominal requirements is unlikely to do much to further the policy objectives or provide substantial economic benefit. At the same time, while such an approach would increase regulatory complexity, it would likely entail minimal costs for registrants.

On the other hand, stringent requirements such as requiring an attestation from a highly qualified CISO as to the effectiveness of a registrant's cybersecurity practices in specific enumerated areas could be quite effective. Expert practitioners in cybersecurity are in high demand and command high salaries. Thus, such an approach would impose substantial ongoing costs on registrants who do not already have appropriately qualified individuals on staff. This burden would be disproportionately borne by smaller registrants, for whom keeping a dedicated CISO on staff would be cost prohibitive. Allowing registrants to employ part-time CISOs would mitigate this cost burden, but such requirements would likely create a de facto "audit" regime. Such an audit regime would certainly be more effective if explicitly designed to function as such.

4.5 Private Litigation Concerning Securities Fraud for Data Breach

The following case concerns a major litigation brought by private parties concerning securities fraud for a significant data breach.

In re Equifax Securities Litigation, 357 F.Supp.3d 1189 (2019).

OPINION AND ORDER
THOMAS W. THRASH, JR., United States District Judge

This is a securities fraud class action. It is before the Court on the Defendants' Joint Motion to Dismiss. For the reasons set forth below, the Defendants' Joint Motion to Dismiss is GRANTED in part and DENIED in part.

I. Background

This case arises out of a massive data breach incident. On September 7, 2017, the Defendant Equifax Inc. announced that it was the subject of a data breach affecting more than 148 million Americans (the "Data Breach"). Criminal hackers breached Equifax's Computer network and obtained a vast amount of personally identifiable information in the company's custody. [The facts in this case are substantially similar to facts recited in Chapter One Introduction]

. . .

On September 7, 2017, Equifax disclosed the Data Breach to the public for the first time. In a press release after the close of trading that day, Equifax revealed that it had suffered a data breach affecting the personal information of approximately 143 million American consumers. Equifax continued to make subsequent disclosures over the following days, ending on September 15, 2017, providing additional details concerning the Data Breach. The company stated that it had engaged Mandiant, a cybersecurity firm, to conduct a review, and that it had reported the breach to law enforcement. Experts, analysts, and the media immediately began to weigh in, with one analyst describing the breach as "one of the biggest cyber-attacks in US history." Cybersecurity experts opined that massive cybersecurity failures on Equifax's part resulted in the Data Breach, and that its public response and outreach were "haphazard and ill-conceived." Financial experts also began to weigh in. Some financial analysts predicted from the outset of this public revelation that, due to the unprecedented size of this incident, Equifax's stock price would decline. Other analysts predicted that Equifax would incur substantial costs relating to the Data Breach for years to come.

On September 8, 2017, the price of Equifax's common stock dropped nearly fifteen percent, closing at $ 123.13 per share. There was also an extraordinarily high trading volume of 16.85 million shares of Equifax stock. On Monday, September 11, 2017, in response to more revelations made over the weekend, Equifax's stock price fell another nine percent to $ 113.32 per share. Over the course of the next few days, more information concerning Equifax's cybersecurity and the Data Breach was revealed to the public. By September 15, 2017, Equifax's stock price had fallen to $ 92.98, nearly a thirty-six percent decline since the initial public disclosure of the Data Breach.

On September 8, 2017, this action was commenced. In the Amended Complaint, the Plaintiff asserts one claim for violation of section 10(b) of the Exchange Act and Rule 10b–5 promulgated thereunder against all of the Defendants (Count I), and one claim for violation of section 20(a) of the Exchange Act against the Individual Defendants (Count II). The Plaintiff alleges that the Defendants made false or misleading statements on Equifax's website, in Equifax's SEC filings, and at Equifax Investor Conferences and Presentations. According to the Plaintiff, these false or misleading statements concerned the state of Equifax's cybersecurity, Equifax's compliance with data protection laws, regulations, and industry best practices, and Equifax's internal controls. On June 18, 2018, this Court modified the PSLRA's automatic stay of discovery to allow for limited case management and discovery planning activities. The Defendants now move to dismiss.

II. Legal Standard . . .

Complaints that allege fraud under federal securities law must satisfy the heightened pleading requirements of both Rule 9(b) and the Private Securities Litigation Reform Act of 1995. Rule 9(b) requires a complaint to "state with particularity the circumstances constituting fraud." "A complaint satisfies Rule 9(b) if it sets forth precisely what statements or omissions were made in what documents or oral representations, who made the statements, the time and place of the statements, the content of the statements and manner in which they misled the plaintiff, and what benefit the defendant gained as a consequence of the fraud."

The PSLRA also sets forth heightened pleading standards. This law was "enacted to cure perceived abuses in prosecuting class actions brought pursuant to federal securities laws." The PSLRA supplements Rule 9(b) in two ways. First, a plaintiff must specify "the reason or reasons why the statement is misleading, and, if an allegation regarding the statement or omission is made on information and belief, the complaint shall state with particularity all facts on which that belief is formed." Second, a plaintiff must set forth particular facts that give rise to a strong inference that the defendants acted with the required state of mind. Specifically, it requires that "the complaint shall, with respect to each act or omission alleged to violate this chapter, state with particularity facts giving rise to a strong inference that the defendant acted with the required state of mind." A complaint that fails to comply with any of these requirements must be dismissed.

III. Discussion

Section 10(b) of the Exchange Act of 1934 makes it unlawful "[t]o use or employ, in connection with the purchase or sale of any security ... any manipulative or deceptive device or contrivance in contravention of such rules and regulations as the Commission may prescribe." Rule 10b–5, promulgated thereunder by the Commission, states:

It shall be unlawful for any person, directly or indirectly, by use of any means or instrumentality of interstate commerce, or of the mails or of any facility of any national securities exchange, (a) To employ any device, scheme, or artifice to defraud, (b) To make any untrue statement of a material fact or to omit to state a material fact necessary in order to make the statements made, in the light of the circumstances under which they were made, not misleading, or (c) To engage in any act, practice, or course of business which operates or would operate as a fraud or deceit upon any person, in connection with the purchase or sale of any security.

To establish a securities fraud claim under these provisions, a plaintiff must allege: "(1) a material misrepresentation or omission; (2) made with scienter; (3) a connection with the purchase or sale of a security; (4) reliance on the misstatement or omission; (5) economic loss; and (6) a causal connection between the material misrepresentation or omission and the loss, commonly called 'loss causation.'"

The Defendants make four main arguments. First, they argue that the Plaintiff has failed to adequately plead that they made false or misleading statements. Second, they contend that the Plaintiff has failed to plead a strong inference of scienter, as required under the PSLRA. Third, they argue that the Plaintiff fails to adequately plead loss causation, an essential element of a section 10(b) claim. Finally, they argue that the Plaintiff's section 20(a) claim fails. The Court addresses each of these arguments in turn.

A. False or Misleading Statements

The Defendants first argue that the Plaintiff fails to sufficiently plead that the statements in question were false or misleading, as required by the PSLRA. Complaints alleging fraud must meet the heightened-pleading standards of Rule 9(b), which requires that in "alleging fraud or mistake, a party must state with particularity the circumstances constituting fraud or mistake." A fraud claim meets the requirements of Rule 9(b) if it sets forth precisely what statements or omissions were made in what documents or oral presentations, who made the statements, the time and place of the statements, the contents of the statements or manner in which they misled the plaintiff, and what the defendants gained as a consequence. Additionally, the PSLRA requires a securities-fraud plaintiff to "specify each statement alleged to have been misleading" and "the reason or reasons why the statement is misleading." "To show falsity, one typically juxtaposes an alleged misrepresentation to a contrary true fact." "A statement is misleading if in the light of the facts existing at the time of the statement a reasonable investor, in the exercise of due care, would have been misled by it." If an allegation regarding a statement or omission is made on information and belief, the complaint must state with particularity the facts on which the belief is formed.

This securities-fraud case is based primarily on the Defendants' alleged misrepresentations during the class period about the security of Equifax's networks and its efforts to ensure the protection of the data in its custody. The Defendants' purported misrepresentations can be grouped into three main categories: (1) statements concerning Equifax's cybersecurity and its efforts to protect consumer data; (2) statements concerning Equifax's compliance with data protection laws, regulations, and industry best practices; and (3) statements concerning Equifax's internal controls. The Defendants make four main arguments in favor of dismissal. First, they argue that many of the Plaintiff's claims allege mere corporate mismanagement. Second, they argue that the Plaintiff has not sufficiently pleaded the falsity of the alleged statements as required by the PSLRA. Third, they argue alleged statements of opinion or belief are not actionable. Fourth, they argue that they were under no duty to disclose the Data Breach prior to September 7, 2017. The Court addresses each of these.

1. Corporate Mismanagement

The Defendants first contend that many of the Plaintiff's allegations concern mere corporate mismanagement, which is not actionable under the federal securities laws. Specifically, the Defendants contend that "[a]llegations that Defendants should have implemented different or better security measures to protect data are, at most, allegations of 'mismanagement,' for which the securities laws do not provide a remedy." In Santa Fe Industries, Inc. v. Green, the Supreme Court held that allegations of corporate mismanagement are not actionable under section 10(b) because the federal securities laws do not regulate corporate fiduciary duties. There, the Supreme Court rejected a minority shareholder's claim that the company's majority shareholders violated section 10(b) by utilizing a short-form merger to eliminate the minority's interest. The Court concluded that the transaction at issue was not manipulative or deceptive within the meaning of section 10(b), and consequently not actionable. Thus, a plaintiff who alleges mere corporate mismanagement or breach of fiduciary duty does not state a claim under section 10(b). From this, the Defendants argue that many of the Plaintiff's claims fail because they merely make hindsight criticisms of the adequacy of Equifax's management of its data security efforts.

"However, 'false or misleading statements or omissions concerning material facts about management or internal operations may be actionable,' such as when a defendant 'makes certain statements while that defendant knows that existing mismanagement makes those statements false or misleading.'" Thus, while allegations that Equifax engaged in mismanagement would fail under section 10(b), allegations that the Defendants made false or misleading statements or omissions concerning such corporate mismanagement at Equifax can constitute basis for a section 10(b) claim. The Defendants misconstrue the Plaintiff's argument. The Plaintiff does not argue that the Defendants violated section 10(b) by failing to implement better cybersecurity practices. Instead, the Plaintiff contends that the Defendants violated section 10(b) by making false or misleading statements as to the strength and quality of Equifax's cybersecurity. Such a claim is not barred by Santa Fe.

2. The Adequacy of Equifax's Data Security

Next, the Defendants argue that the statements touting the strength of Equifax's data security systems and the adequacy of Equifax's efforts to promote cybersecurity do not constitute material misrepresentations. In the Amended Complaint, the Plaintiff alleges that the Defendants made a variety of material misrepresentations as to the state of Equifax's data security and Equifax's efforts to promote cybersecurity. For example, the Defendants allegedly stated that Equifax was a "trusted steward" of personal data and that it employed "strong data security and confidentiality standards on the data that we provide and on the access to that data." They allegedly stated that Equifax "maintain[ed] a highly sophisticated data information network that includes advanced security, protections and redundancies." According to the Plaintiff, the fundamental shortcomings in Equifax's cybersecurity, including a failure to take some of the most elementary precautions, render these statements false or misleading.

The Defendants make two main arguments for why these statements are not material misrepresentations. First, they argue that the alleged statements are not actually false or misleading because the facts pleaded do not show that Equifax's data security was actually inadequate. Second, they contend that these statements constitute inactionable puffery. According to the Defendants, these statements were vague, meaningless, statements of corporate optimism that no reasonable shareholder would rely upon in making investment decisions. The Court addresses each of these arguments in turn.

i. Falsity

The Defendants contend that the Plaintiff has failed to plead the falsity of each of the alleged statements concerning the strength of Equifax's systems. They argue that the Plaintiff has not shown that the statements boasting of the strength and complexity of Equifax's cybersecurity are actually false. Instead, according to the Defendants, the Plaintiff has only alleged that Equifax was the victim of a criminal attack that was out of its control. They contend that the fact that a company suffered a significant cyberattack does not necessarily mean that its cybersecurity was deficient, and thus does not render its prior statements about its commitment to data security false.

However, the Plaintiff alleges more than just the mere occurrence of the Data Breach. The Plaintiff has pleaded a multitude of specific, detailed factual allegations demonstrating that Equifax's cybersecurity systems were grossly deficient and outdated, despite the Defendants' various assurances to the contrary. In the Amended Complaint, the Plaintiff alleges that Equifax failed to implement even the most basic security measures, reflecting a "systemic organizational disregard for cybersecurity and cyber-hygiene best practices." Cybersecurity experts opined that Equifax's data security failures flowed from an inadequate "tone at the top" and that "the real problem was a very poor focus on information security at the highest levels of the company." For example, according to the Plaintiff, Equifax failed to implement an effective patch management process, relying upon a single employee to manually implement the company's patching process across its entire network. This process failed to meet the most basic industry standards – application of security patches is a critical cybersecurity practice. Because of this shortcoming, Equifax allegedly failed to remediate known deficiencies in its cybersecurity infrastructure, such as the Apache Struts vulnerability. Furthermore, according to the Plaintiff, Equifax failed to implement adequate encryption measures to protect sensitive information, in contrast to its representation that it encrypted confidential information. Equifax allegedly stored and transmitted the personal information of hundreds of millions of consumers in unencrypted, plaintext, making it easy for intruders to read and misuse.

Overall, the Plaintiff alleges that, among other things, Equifax: (1) failed to implement adequate patching processes; (2) failed to create adequate encryption measures to protect the information in its custody; (3) failed to implement adequate authentication measures to ensure that parties attempting to access its networks were authorized to do so; (4) failed to establish mechanisms for monitoring its networks for security breaches; (5) stored personal data in easily accessible public channels; (6) relied on outdated and obsolete software; and (7) failed to warehouse obsolete personal information. Together, according to the Plaintiff, each of these shortcomings created an inadequate cybersecurity system.

Given the dangerously deficient state of Equifax's cybersecurity, the Court concludes it was false, or at least misleading, for Equifax to tout its advanced cybersecurity protections. In contrast to the Defendants' representations that, among other things, Equifax employed a "highly sophisticated data information network" and "advanced security protections," Equifax's data security was dangerously lacking. While it is true that the mere occurrence of a data breach may not necessarily mean that a company's data security systems are inadequate, the Plaintiff here does not rely solely upon the occurrence of the Data Breach to establish that the Defendants' statements were false. Instead, the Plaintiff has pleaded a variety of facts showing that Equifax's cybersecurity systems were outdated, below industry standards, and vulnerable to cyberattack, and that Equifax did not prioritize data security efforts.

Furthermore, as the Plaintiff points out, a number of courts have come to a similar conclusion, holding that statements touting the strength or quality of an important business operation are false, and thus actionable, when those operations are, in reality, deficient. . . .

Similarly, the Defendants' representations that Equifax employed a highly sophisticated data information network are allegedly false given the actual state of its systems.

The case that the Defendants primarily rely upon, In re Heartland Payment Systems, Inc. Securities Litigation is distinguishable. In Heartland, the corporate defendant, a provider of bank card payment processing services to merchants, suffered a "Structured Query Language" attack by criminal hackers. This attack placed hidden, malicious software on the defendant's network, which infected its payment processing system. Because of this, hackers were able to steal 130 million credit card and debit card numbers. After this incident, the plaintiffs filed a securities action, alleging that the defendants misrepresented the state of Heartland's network security, that they concealed the occurrence of data breach from investors, and they made false statements concerning the adequacy of its security systems and the efforts they took for network security. Specifically, Heartland had stated that it "'place[d] significant emphasis on maintaining a high level of security' and maintained a network configuration that 'provides multiple layers of security to isolate our databases from unauthorized access.'" The plaintiffs argued that those statements were untruthful "because Heartland had suffered the SQL attack and had not fully resolved security issues arising out of that attack." The court concluded, however, that these statements were not false or misleading because there was "nothing inconsistent" between these statements and "the fact that Heartland had suffered an SQL attack." "The fact that a company has suffered a security breach does not demonstrate that the company did not 'place significant emphasis on maintaining a high level of security.'" The court further explained that it was "equally plausible" that Heartland did place a high emphasis upon security.

In contrast, the Plaintiff here has not alleged that the Defendants' statements concerning Equifax's cybersecurity practices are false merely because Equifax suffered a security breach. Instead, the Plaintiff has asserted specific factual allegations describing the poor state of Equifax's cybersecurity. These allegations depict a data security system that was dangerously deficient and fell far short of industry standards. Unlike in Heartland, where it was plausible that the company placed a high emphasis on security but nonetheless was a victim of a breach, Equifax's data security is alleged to have been in disrepair, in contrast to the Defendants' statements otherwise. Thus, Heartland is distinguishable.

The Defendants also argue that these allegations fail because the Plaintiff has failed to plead the falsity of the statements concerning the adequacy of cybersecurity with particularity. The PSLRA requires a plaintiff to specify "the reason or reasons why the statement is misleading." For example, the Defendants contend that the Plaintiff has not adequately alleged the falsity of the statement that the "Equifax network is reviewed on a continual basis by external security experts who conduct intrusion testing, vulnerability assessments, on-site inspections, and policy/incident management reviews." However, the Court concludes that the Plaintiff has satisfied its requirement to plead the falsity of these statements with particularity. The Plaintiff alleges in the Amended Complaint that this statement was false or misleading because Equifax "ignored advice issued by those external 'security experts' warning the Company about gross inadequacies in its cybersecurity," because Equifax "failed to heed the calls of its cybersecurity consultants to perform comprehensive system reviews," and because Equifax's vulnerability scanning was deficient since scans were performed "infrequently, examined only portions of Equifax's systems, relied on outdated technology, and lacked appropriate redundancies." The Defendants argue that these allegations merely second-guess the extent or efficacy of these efforts. However, the Court concludes that these allegations are sufficient because they explain why this statement was false, or at a minimum, misleading. These allegations explain that it was misleading to state that cybersecurity experts continually review Equifax's systems when Equifax ignored those experts' suggestions and used superficial vulnerability scanning.

The Defendants also challenge the statements that Equifax had a "rigorous enterprise risk management program" that targeted its cybersecurity risks, that Equifax used "a variety of technical, administrative and physical ways to keep personal credit data safe," that Equifax "regularly review[ed] and update[d] [its] security protocols," and that Equifax "develop[ed], maintain[ed], and enhance[d] secured proprietary information databases." According to the Defendants, the Plaintiff's allegations that Equifax's efforts were inadequate fail because they do not show that Equifax did not have a risk management program, or that it did not attempt to comply with data security regulations. However, the Plaintiff adequately alleges the falsity of each of these statements with particularity. With each of these statements, the Plaintiff explains how the context of Equifax's cybersecurity makes them false or misleading. The Plaintiff alleges that each of these areas of cybersecurity was so deficient that it was misleading for Equifax to assure investors that these efforts were promoting the security of its data systems. These statements do more than merely tell investors that a risk management program existed or that it used various cybersecurity techniques. Instead, Equifax used these statements to assure investors that they were taking cybersecurity seriously.

Furthermore, the Defendants also take many of these statements out of context in their brief. For example, the Defendants argue that the Plaintiff has not shown that it was false or misleading to state that Equifax had an enterprise risk management program. But, in the Amended Complaint, the Plaintiff alleges that Equifax stated that it has "a rigorous enterprise risk management program targeting ... data security." An assurance that Equifax employed a rigorous enterprise risk management program is more misleading to investors than simply affirming the existence of an enterprise risk management program. Similarly, the Defendants argue that the Plaintiff has not alleged that it was false to state that Equifax "regularly review[ed] and update[d] [its] security protocols," even if those efforts were not effective or to the necessary extent. However, in the Amended Complaint, the Plaintiff alleges that Equifax stated that "[w]e regularly review and update our security protocols to ensure that they continue to meet or exceed established best practices at all times." This statement does not merely state that Equifax reviewed and updated its security protocols, but instead that it did so to ensure that it met established best practices. Furthermore, the Defendants argue that the Plaintiff has not shown that the statement that Equifax "monitor[ed] federal and state legislative and regulatory activities that involve credit reporting, data privacy and security" is false, when in reality the Plaintiff alleges that Equifax stated that "[w]e continuously monitor federal and state legislative and regulatory activities that involve credit reporting, data privacy and security to identify issues in order to remain in compliance with all applicable laws and regulations." This context, omitted by the Defendants in their argument, is important in determining whether the statements were false or misleading.

ii. Puffery

Next, the Defendants argue that many of the challenged statements concerning Equifax's commitment to data security constitute inactionable puffery. Alleged misrepresentations must be based upon a material fact to give rise to a securities law violation. "Subjective characterizations of a company's current performance or predictions about future performance, absent a false misstatement of fact, are generally not actionable." Such statements of "corporate optimism" or "puffery" are not actionable because they both lack an underlying factual basis and also fail the materiality requirement of Rule 10b-5.216 Thus, "vague, optimistic statements are not actionable because reasonable investors do not rely on them in making investment decisions." Statements constitute "puffery" if they are "too general to cause a reasonable investor to rely upon them." According to the Defendants, many of the alleged statements reflected corporate optimism and aspiration that a reasonable investor would not rely upon, and thus constitute puffery. Such statements of puffery cannot serve as the basis for a section 10(b) claim because a reasonable investor would not rely upon them. For example, the Defendants contend that many of the statements "generally avow a commitment to data security or characterize security as a priority for Equifax." According to the Defendants, a reasonable investor would not rely upon statements such as these, which are "generalized, non-verifiable, and vague statements of commitment to and aspirations about data security."

However, the Court finds that these alleged statements are not inactionable puffery. An alleged misstatement or omission must be "so obviously unimportant to a reasonable investor that reasonable minds could not differ on the question of their importance" to be deemed inactionable puffery. For example, in the context of a drilling company's statements concerning its safety and training efforts, one court noted that it could not "say, as a matter of law, that Transocean's representation that such efforts were extensive was 'obviously unimportant' to GSF shareholders" since "[i]n an industry as dangerous as deepwater drilling, it is to be expected that investors will be greatly concerned about an operator's safety and training efforts." Likewise, the Court cannot say, as a matter of law, that Equifax's representations that its cybersecurity efforts were extensive or that it was "committed" to data security were so "obviously unimportant" to its shareholders that they should be considered immaterial. Furthermore, the fact that these statements relate to a core aspect of Equifax's business makes it even more likely that a reasonable investor would assign weight to them. Since data security plays an important part of a business such as Equifax, investors would be even more likely to find these types of representations important in making their investment decisions. For these reasons, the Court cannot, as a matter of law, conclude that these statements are obviously unimportant to Equifax's investors.

Moreover, the context of these alleged statements is important to this determination. Although the alleged statements, when viewed in isolation, might constitute puffery, the fact that they were made repeatedly to assure investors that Equifax's systems were secure could lead a reasonable investor to rely upon them as reflecting the state of Equifax's cybersecurity. Thus, the context of these supposedly "aspirational" statements matters: the Defendants repeatedly stated that cybersecurity, an important aspect of their business, was a top priority for senior management, despite the fact that Equifax failed to employ some of the most elementary cybersecurity practices. Even if, in a vacuum, each of these statements seems like a meaningless, corporate vaguery, when taken together a reasonable investor would rely upon them to conclude that Equifax made cybersecurity a serious priority. . . .

3. Failure to Disclose the Data Breach

Next, the Defendants move to dismiss the Plaintiff's allegations based upon their purported failure to disclose the Data Breach earlier. In the Amended Complaint, the Plaintiff alleges that some of the alleged statements were or became misleading by omission because the Defendants did not publicly disclose the Data Breach until September 7, 2017. According to the Plaintiff, the Defendants' statements after March 2017 lauding Equifax's data security were false or misleading because Equifax "knew or recklessly disregarded that hackers had already penetrated its databases."

However, the Court concludes that the Defendants were under no duty to disclose the Data Breach prior to becoming aware of the incident in July 2017. The Plaintiff has not alleged that the Defendants knew about the Data Breach before July 29, 2017, but instead argues that they were reckless as to its occurrence. It bases its argument upon warnings that the Defendants allegedly received as to the deficient state of Equifax's cybersecurity, its failure to employ adequate patching processes, and its failure to use proper network monitoring. These warnings might demonstrate that the Defendants knew of, or were reckless as to, Equifax's ability to prevent or detect a breach. However, these warnings do not establish that the Defendants knew, or were reckless to the existence of, the specific Data Breach at issue here. The allegations also do not demonstrate that the Defendants knew of, or were reckless as to the existence of, Equifax's failure to patch the Apache Struts vulnerability. Therefore, the Defendants were under no duty to disclose the existence of the Data Breach before they knew it had occurred.

Second, the Plaintiff argues that the Defendants were under a duty to correct their prior misstatements once they became aware of the Data Breach in July 2017. According to the Plaintiff, even if some of the Defendants' statements may not have been misleading at the time they were made, the Defendants had a duty to correct the statements once they learned that the Data Breach had occurred. A duty to disclose can be created by a defendant's previous decision to speak on the subject. "Where a defendant's failure to speak would render the defendant's own prior speech misleading or deceptive, a duty to disclose arises." According to the Plaintiff, the Defendants had a duty to disclose once they learned that their prior statements concerning the security of Equifax's systems became false due to the Data Breach.

However, the Court finds that the occurrence of the Data Breach did not itself make those prior statements false or misleading, and thus did not create a duty to disclose. As the Court noted above, the occurrence of a data breach does not necessarily imply that a company's data security is inadequate. In Heartland, the court concluded that the defendants were not under a duty to disclose the occurrence of a data breach because the plaintiffs had not alleged that the company's systems were actually deficient. The court noted that the occurrence of a data breach itself does not establish that a company's data security is inadequate. Similarly, here, the occurrence of the Data Breach itself did not necessarily render the Defendants' prior statements false, and thus did not impose a duty to correct those statements by disclosing the occurrence of the Data Breach. Therefore, the Court finds this argument unavailing.

4. Statements About Cybersecurity Risks

Next, the Defendants move to dismiss the Plaintiff's allegations regarding Equifax's warnings of its cybersecurity risks. In the Amended Complaint, the Plaintiff alleges that Equifax, Smith, and Gamble made false or misleading statements in SEC filings concerning the cybersecurity risks that Equifax faced. The Plaintiff alleges that Equifax stated in its 2015 and 2016 Forms 10-K that:

Despite our substantial investment in physical and technological security measures, employee training, contractual precautions and business continuity plans, our information technology networks and infrastructure or those of our third-party vendors and other service providers could be vulnerable to damage, disruptions, shutdowns, or breaches of confidential information due to criminal conduct, denial of service or other advanced persistent attacks by hackers[.]

However, according to the Plaintiff, it was false or misleading to state that Equifax "could be vulnerable" to a breach "when, in fact, Equifax was highly vulnerable to such an attack, as, in fact, Defendants had been warned on numerous occasions both before and during the Class Period."

The Defendants argue that these allegations fail to state a claim because, through these statements, the Defendants warned of the precise risk that caused the Plaintiff's losses. The Court finds that these statements are not actionable. The difference between disclosing that Equifax "could be vulnerable" and that it was "highly vulnerable" would not mislead a reasonable investor in making an investment decision. The case that the Plaintiff relies upon, In re Van der Moolen Holding N.V. Securities Litigation, is distinguishable. There, the court concluded that cautionary statements can give rise to a section 10(b) violation. The court noted that "to caution that it is only possible for the unfavorable events to happen when they have already occurred is deceit." However, that case is distinguishable. There, the defendant warned investors about regulatory risks, even though it knew or was recklessly ignorant that its employees were violating NYSE rules. Here, in contrast, the risk warned of is different. The Defendants warned that Equifax could be vulnerable to a data breach, but they did not fail to disclose the existence of a breach when they made that statement. Thus, unlike in Van der Moolen, the Defendants did not warn that Equifax could be at risk, when it in fact was suffering a data breach. Therefore, the Court finds these risk statements inactionable.

5. Equifax's Compliance With Data Protection Laws

Next, the Defendants move to dismiss the Plaintiff's claims concerning statements about Equifax's compliance with data protection laws, regulations, and best practices. In the Amended Complaint, the Plaintiff alleges that the Defendants made various statements assuring that Equifax complied with relevant data protection laws, regulations, standards, and best practices. For example, the Plaintiff alleges that Equifax stated on its website that it "takes great care to ensure that we use and process personal data in ways that comply with applicable regulations and respects individual privacy." Equifax also stated that "[w]e regularly review and update our security protocols to ensure that they continue to meet or exceed established best practices at all times" and that "[w]e continuously monitor federal and state legislative and regulatory activities that involve credit reporting, data privacy and security to identify issues in order to remain in compliance with all applicable laws and regulations." However, despite these affirmations, Equifax allegedly fell far short of complying with these regulatory requirements.

The Defendants first assert that these claims merely allege corporate mismanagement, which is not actionable under federal securities laws. However, as explained above, this argument fails. The Plaintiff does not allege that the Defendants violated section 10(b) by failing to comply with cybersecurity laws, regulations, and best practices. Instead, the Plaintiff argues that they violated section 10(b) by stating that Equifax was in compliance with these laws and regulations, when in fact it was not. As stated above, the Court finds that such a claim is actionable under federal securities laws. If the Plaintiff adequately alleged that Equifax made false statements concerning its compliance with these laws, regulations, and standards, then such claims would not be barred by Santa Fe.

The Defendants next argue that these alleged statements described Equifax's ongoing efforts to comply with data protection laws and standards, and that the statements did not guarantee compliance. According to the Defendants, the Plaintiff has not adequately alleged the falsity of these statements because the fact that they were not in compliance does not mean that they were not making efforts to comply. However, in the alleged statements, Equifax did more than just say that it made efforts to comply with these laws and standards. It stated that it monitored regulatory activities to "remain in compliance with all applicable laws and regulations," that it reviewed its security protocols to "ensure that they continue to meet or exceed established best practices," and that it took "great care" to ensure that it handled personal data in a way that complied with regulations. These statements go beyond merely stating that it made an effort to comply with laws, regulations, and industry standards, and instead assured that Equifax took steps to remain in compliance with laws and regulations and meet industry standards. According to the allegations in the Amended Complaint, Equifax in reality failed to live up to these assurances.

And even if these statements only conveyed that Equifax made an effort to comply with data security laws, regulations, and standards, they would still be false or misleading. A reasonable investor would understand these statements to assure that the company was making actual, good faith efforts to maintain a data security protocol that complied with these standards. In reality, according to the Amended Complaint, data security was not a priority at all for Equifax's management. The state of Equifax's cybersecurity reflected a "systemic organizational disregard for cybersecurity." Given this context, these statements were false or misleading. It is misleading to a reasonable investor to state that Equifax made an effort to comply with data laws, regulations, and standards when, in fact, Equifax demonstrated a systemic disregard for cybersecurity. For this reason, these statements concerning efforts to comply with data laws, regulations, and industry best practices are false or misleading.

The Defendants also argue that the fact Equifax experienced a cyberattack does not render their aspirational statements concerning their data security efforts and compliance false. However, as the Court explained with regard to the statements concerning the adequacy of Equifax's cybersecurity, the Plaintiff does not rely solely upon the occurrence of the Data Breach to show the falsity of the compliance statements. Instead, the Plaintiff alleges that these statements regarding Equifax's compliance with data security laws, regulations, and standards were false due to widespread deficiencies in Equifax's cybersecurity and data protocols. According to the Plaintiff, Equifax assured the public that it made efforts to remain in compliance with data laws, regulation, and standards, even though in reality its cybersecurity was in a state of disrepair. Therefore, under the facts alleged, these assurances that Equifax made efforts to comply with data protection laws and best practices were false or misleading.

Next, the Defendants also argue that these allegations fail because, unlike in the cases relied upon by the Plaintiff, the Plaintiff's allegations do not show that the Defendants had contemporaneous knowledge of the facts contradicting their statements concerning legal compliance. However, this argument addresses whether the Defendants acted with the requisite scienter, which is addressed below. Whether a statement is false or misleading, and whether a defendant made such a statement with the requisite state of mind, are two separate questions. As discussed above, the Plaintiff has adequately alleged that these statements were false or misleading.. . .

6. Statements Concerning Internal Controls

The Defendants next move to dismiss the Plaintiff's allegations concerning the Defendants' various statements about Equifax's internal controls. In the Amended Complaint, the Plaintiff alleges that Smith and Gamble certified in SEC filings, pursuant to the Sarbanes-Oxley Act, that Equifax maintained a system of internal controls that would provide "reasonable assurance regarding prevention or timely detection of unauthorized acquisition, use or disposition of our assets that could have a material effect on the financial statements." Nonetheless, according to the Plaintiff, these assurances in Equifax's 10-K and 10-Q filings concerning the quality of its internal controls were materially false or misleading because Equifax lacked adequate mechanisms for detecting and responding to data breaches. The Defendants move to dismiss the allegations concerning this category of statements. They argue that the Plaintiff has failed to plead the falsity of the challenged statements because they address Equifax's internal controls over financial reporting, as opposed to controls over data security. According to the Defendants, since these statements exclusively addressed financial reporting controls at Equifax, deficiencies in Equifax's cybersecurity mechanisms do not render these statements false. Thus, deficiencies in Equifax's data breach protocol do not establish that these statements were false.

The Court concludes that the Plaintiff has failed to show that these statements are false. "Congress enacted Sarbanes-Oxley to restore investor confidence in the wake of numerous, highly-publicized, cases of accounting fraud." The purpose of Sarbanes-Oxley certifications is to ensure that proper financial reporting processes are undertaken. In In re PetroChina Co. Ltd. Securities Litigation, the district court rejected a section 10(b) claim premised upon PetroChina's Sarbanes-Oxley certifications. The court noted that the plaintiffs' allegations, concerning bribery by PetroChina officials, did not "imply that the Company had flawed internal controls over financial reporting." The court explained that the plaintiffs did "not claim that PetroChina failed to evaluate its internal controls or disclose any weaknesses to its auditors," did not "assert that the certifying officers neglected to inform PetroChina's auditor of any relevant fraud," and did not "establish that PetroChina's internal controls in relation to financial reporting were insufficient; much less does the [complaint] make any allegation as to how or why PetroChina's internal controls were inadequate."

Likewise, the Plaintiff fails to allege that Equifax had flawed internal controls over its financial reporting. Even if Equifax's data breach protocol was vastly deficient, this does not establish that it had insufficient internal controls over financial reporting.

The Plaintiff has not raised any allegations concerning the accuracy of Equifax's accounting, books, or financial reporting. Therefore, the Plaintiff has not established that Equifax, Smith, or Gamble's statements concerning Equifax's internal controls over financial reporting were false. A reasonable investor would understand that certifications under Sarbanes-Oxley such as these are in the context of financial accounting scandals, and would recognize that it related to Equifax's financial reporting. A reasonable investor would not take assurances of internal controls to detect improprieties in accounting and bookkeeping to guarantee that there were systems in place to deal with cybersecurity breaches. Since the Plaintiff has not alleged that Equifax's financial reports were inaccurate in any way, its claims concerning Smith and Gamble's certification of proper internal controls pursuant to Sarbanes-Oxley fail. Therefore, the Plaintiff's claims are dismissed to the extent that they rely upon statements guaranteeing adequate internal controls pursuant to Sarbanes-Oxley.

7. Statements of Opinion and Belief

Next, the Defendants contend that many of the challenged statements are inactionable opinions or statements of belief. First, the Defendants contend that almost all of the alleged statements are inactionable, in part, because they are opinions. However, many of these statements that the Defendants contend are inactionable are not, in fact, opinions. For example, the Defendants contend that the following statement is an inactionable opinion: "As a trusted steward of consumer and business information, Equifax employs strong data security and confidentiality standards on the data we provide and on the access to that data. We maintain a highly sophisticated data information network that includes advanced security, protections and redundancies." While such statements use some indefinite language, they do not constitute a subjective opinion.

However, some of the allegedly false statements are closer calls. According to the Defendants, statements such as Smith's assurance that "I think we are in a very good position now" are not actionable because the Plaintiff has not shown that the Defendants did not in fact hold the stated opinions. The Plaintiff contends that this statement, even if an opinion, is actionable because it did not align with the information in his possession. "[C]ertain opinions may be actionable because 'if the real facts are otherwise, but not provided, the opinion statement will mislead its audience.'" An investor "expects not just that the issuer believes the opinion (however irrationally), but that it fairly aligns with the information in the issuer's possession at the time." Opinion statements can be "misleading in context," and thus "actionable," if they "conflict with what a reasonable investor would take from the statement itself."

As discussed in more detail below, the Plaintiff only alleges that Smith – not the other Individual Defendants – was given specific information as to the deficiencies in Equifax's cybersecurity. Around March 2017, Smith oversaw Mandiant's audit of Equifax's systems, where Mandiant warned that these systems were inadequate. The Plaintiff has not made specific allegations that Gamble, Ploder, or Dodge had information in their possession contradicting any opinion statements they issued. Without this knowledge, these opinion statements are not actionable. Furthermore, any opinion statements Smith made before receiving these warnings would also not be actionable.

B. Scienter

Next, the Defendants argue that the Plaintiff has failed to plead facts that give rise to a strong inference of scienter on the part of any of the Defendants. To state a section 10(b) claim, the PSLRA requires a plaintiff "to plead with particularity facts giving rise to a strong inference that the defendants either intended to defraud investors or were severely reckless when they made the allegedly materially false or incomplete statements." A "strong inference" is an inference that is "cogent and at least as compelling as any opposing inference one could draw from the facts alleged." This inquiry asks whether all of the facts alleged, taken as a whole, give rise to this strong inference of scienter. Thus, courts must consider the complaint in its entirety, and "not whether any individual allegation, scrutinized in isolation, meets that standard." This inquiry is "inherently comparative" because courts must take into account plausible opposing inferences. Where a lawsuit involves multiple defendants and multiple allegations, moreover, "scienter must be found with respect to each defendant and with respect to each alleged violation of the statute."

To move beyond the pleading state, a plaintiff "must allege facts sufficiently demonstrating each defendant's state of mind regarding his or her alleged violations." But, the PSLRA does permit the aggregation of facts to infer scienter. The factual allegations, taken as a whole, must give rise to this strong inference as to each Defendant and each alleged violation. Circumstantial evidence can be sufficient to establish a strong inference of scienter. Since scienter is highly fact-intensive inquiry, such questions are most appropriate for a fact finder. "In sum, the reviewing court must ask: When the allegations are accepted as true and taken collectively, would a reasonable person deem the inference of scienter at least as strong as any opposing inference?"

In the Eleventh Circuit, it is well established that section 10(b) and Rule 10b-5 require a showing of either an intent to deceive, manipulate, or defraud, or severe recklessness. The Eleventh Circuit has defined "severe recklessness" as:

> Severe recklessness is limited to those highly unreasonable omissions or misrepresentations that involve not merely simple or even inexcusable negligence, but an extreme departure from the standards of ordinary care, and that present a danger of misleading buyers or sellers which is either known to the defendant or is so obvious that the defendant must have been aware of it.

"Plaintiffs may prove such recklessness by providing evidence that defendants possessed knowledge of facts or access to information contradicting their public statements, so as to prove that defendants knew or should have known that they were misrepresenting material facts related to the corporation." "Facts indicating the scienter may include the particular times, dates, places, or other details of the alleged fraudulent activity." These particulars "are not required per se," but "their absence from the complaint may be indicative of the excessive generality of the allegations' supporting scienter." "With regard to Individual Defendants, the question is 'whether a reasonable person would infer that there was at least a fifty-fifty chance that the individual defendants knew about the alleged fraud (or were severely reckless in not knowing about it) based on its nature, duration, or amount.'"

Here, the Plaintiff attempts to plead scienter by alleging, among other things, that: (1) the Defendants received numerous warnings concerning the inadequacies of Equifax's cybersecurity; (2) the Defendants were aware of the breach by late July 2017, but failed to disclose the breach and continued to make false statements until September 7, 2017; (3) the false and misleading statements concerned one of the most significant issues and severe risks that Equifax faced; (4) the Defendants were in charge of cybersecurity and received routine updates about the state of Equifax's data security; (5) the egregiousness of the deficiencies in Equifax's data security practices supports an inference of scienter; (6) the sudden departure of high-ranking officers at Equifax after disclosure of the Data Breach supports a finding of scienter; and (7) suspicious stock sales by Gamble and Ploder support an inference of scienter. Since scienter is an essential element of a securities fraud claim, the Plaintiff must create a strong inference – one that is "cogent and compelling" – that the Defendants knew about the deficiencies in Equifax's cybersecurity, or were severely reckless in not knowing about it, when they made the allegedly false or misleading statements. The Court concludes that the allegations in the Amended Complaint establish a strong inference of scienter as to Equifax and Smith. However, these facts, even when taken together, do not give rise to a strong inference of scienter as to Gamble, Dodge, and Ploder.

1. Warnings About Data Security Deficiencies

First, the Defendants argues that alleged warnings of deficiencies in Equifax's cybersecurity fail to support a strong inference of scienter as to any of the Individual Defendants. In the Amended Complaint, the Plaintiff alleges that the "Defendants received numerous warnings ... that Equifax's cybersecurity was inadequate to protect the sensitive personal information in its custody" and that this contributes to a finding of scienter. Specifically, the Plaintiff alleges that: (1) Deloitte and KPMG issued audit reports detailing several problems with Equifax's cybersecurity, but Equifax's management did not take these reports seriously;(2) Smith oversaw a March 2017 investigation by security consulting firm Mandiant, in which Mandiant warned that Equifax's cybersecurity was inadequate and contained critical weaknesses;(3) security researchers warned Equifax that cybersecurity deficiencies existed, including an "immense cache of personal consumer information" that was accessible through public-facing websites;(4) Equifax received clear warnings about the Apache Struts vulnerability from both the government and its own employees;(5) Equifax employees warned "management" that the company's cybersecurity was inadequate, but data security was not a priority for management; and (6) Equifax prior breaches that revealed cybersecurity vulnerabilities to the Defendants. According to the Defendants, these allegations do not give rise to a strong inference of scienter because the Plaintiff has failed to plead facts showing that these supposed warnings were ever communicated to any of the Individual Defendants.

The Court finds that these allegations provide sufficient circumstantial evidence to conclude that Smith was aware of the warnings concerning the deficiencies in Equifax's cybersecurity. In the Amended Complaint, the Plaintiff alleges that Equifax hired Mandiant in early 2017 to conduct a cybersecurity audit after the W2Express breach in 2016. Specifically, the Plaintiff alleges that "Equifax hired cybersecurity firm Mandiant to investigate weaknesses in its data protection systems" and that "Smith was personally overseeing, and closely monitoring the progress of, this investigation." This allegation is based upon a Bloomberg report published in the wake of the Data Breach. The Plaintiff alleges that Mandiant "warned Equifax that its unpatched systems and misconfigured security policies could indicate major problems." However, instead of heeding Mandiant's advice, Equifax allegedly disputed the firm's findings and declined to engage in a broader review of Equifax's data security. Based upon this, the Court concludes that the Plaintiff adequately alleges that Smith knew, or was severely reckless as to the existence of, warnings of serious deficiencies in Equifax's cybersecurity after receiving Mandiant's warnings in early 2017.

The Defendants then argue that these allegations should not be given weight because they are based upon articles in Bloomberg and Motherboard that rely upon anonymous sources. In Mizzaro, the Eleventh Circuit addressed the question of how to weigh allegations based upon confidential witness reports. There, the court noted that "[a]lthough a whistleblower who demands confidentiality may be less credible than one who is willing to put his name behind his accusations," allegations based on such statements are not "heavily discounted" in all cases. It explained that "the weight to be afforded to allegations based on statements proffered by a confidential source depends on the particularity of the allegations made in each case, and confidentiality is one factor that courts may consider." "Confidentiality, however, should not eviscerate the weight given if the complaint otherwise fully describes the foundation or basis of the confidential witness's knowledge, including the position(s) held, the proximity to the offending conduct, and the relevant time frame."

In the Amended Complaint, the Plaintiff bases some of its allegations upon news articles citing anonymous sources. For example, the Plaintiff bases some of its allegations on a Bloomberg article reported on September 29, 2017.311 That article explained that the Mandiant investigation was "described internally as 'a top-secret project' and one that Smith was overseeing personally, according to one person with direct knowledge of the matter." The Plaintiff also premised some of its allegations upon an article published in Motherboard on October 26, 2017. Despite the fact that these news articles rely in part on anonymous sources, the Court declines to completely discount the allegations that rely upon them. This Court has previously noted that pleading requirements under the PSLRA can easily be satisfied with references to "internal memoranda" and "news articles." News articles, which frequently rely upon unnamed sources, constitute reliable bases for allegations. Therefore, the Court does not discount the allegations based upon these two articles merely because they cite anonymous sources. And, even if the Plaintiff did in fact rely solely upon information derived from an anonymous source, and not information from a news article, these allegations would still be entitled to weight. The Bloomberg article cites two independent sources, with direct knowledge, who corroborate each other's assertions. Furthermore, the Motherboard article provides statements from several former Equifax employees, providing both their positions and tenure in the company. The Court therefore finds that the allegations based upon these news articles are entitled to due consideration.

However, the Plaintiff's allegations of scienter fail as to the rest of the Individual Defendants. The Plaintiff has not provided sufficiently "particularized averments of fraud or scienter" as to Gamble, Ploder, and Dodge to give rise to a strong inference that they acted with knowledge or severe recklessness. "Claims of securities fraud cannot rest on speculation and conclusory allegations." The Plaintiff has not adequately pleaded that Gamble, Ploder or Dodge ever received any of these purported warnings as to the shortcomings in Equifax's data security. Instead, the Plaintiff relies upon general allegations that Equifax "management" was warned but did not heed experts' advice. Such generalities do not establish a strong inference of scienter. The Plaintiff has not alleged "which defendant knew what, how they knew it, or when" with regard to these warnings.

The Plaintiff relies upon In re ChoicePoint, Inc. Securities Litigation to support its argument that these allegations sufficiently plead scienter. However, that case is distinguishable. In ChoicePoint, the plaintiffs alleged that the defendants misrepresented the existence and severity of data security problems within the company prior to a data breach. The court concluded that the plaintiffs adequately alleged scienter. Specifically, the plaintiffs alleged that the individual defendants "had access to internal information demonstrating the falsity of the public statements and were confronted by employees," that employees specifically warned each of the individual defendants about the company's inadequate security procedures, and that some of the individual defendants learned of the company's data breach and subsequently sold millions of dollars of their company stock. In contrast, the Plaintiff has not alleged that Gamble, Dodge, and Ploder were specifically warned about the problems with Equifax's data security, and did not specifically allege that each of these defendants had access to information contradicting their public statements. Instead, the Plaintiff relies on general allegations that "management" was warned. Such an allegation requires the Court to assume that Gamble, Dodge, and Ploder were part of this group of "management" that received these warnings. This assumption does not give rise to a strong inference of scienter.

The Plaintiff also argues that this stringent requirement for scienter ignores recklessness as a way to establish scienter. According to the Plaintiff, it is not required to provide "smoking gun" evidence of scienter, but instead can establish recklessness through the Individual Defendants' "access to a plethora of information clearly and directly contradicting their public statements regarding cybersecurity." While it is true that the Plaintiff need not provide a "smoking gun" of scienter, it also cannot rely on generalities and chains of inferences. The Plaintiff must allege specific facts as to each defendant and each challenged statement that give rise to a strong inference of scienter. To establish a strong inference of recklessness, the Plaintiff must allege facts showing that the risk of misleading investors was so obvious that the Defendants must have been aware of it. The Plaintiff's allegations fail to meet this standard.

The Defendants also argue that, even if these warnings and concerns had been communicated to the Individual Defendants, the Plaintiff fails to plead facts establishing that they agreed with any of these concerns or were severely reckless in not believing them. Thus, with regard to Smith, even though he personally oversaw the Mandiant audit, the Plaintiff does not allege that he agreed with the firm's conclusion that Equifax's cybersecurity was deficient. However, the Plaintiff need not allege that Smith agreed subjectively with Mandiant's concerns to establish scienter. In Omnicare, the Supreme Court explained that an issuer's statement that its conduct is lawful, when made contrary to its lawyers' advice, can give rise to a section 10(b) claim.325 Similarly, Smith's statements touting Equifax's cybersecurity, despite his knowledge of experts' advice to the contrary, are actionable.

Next, the Defendants argue that the prior data breaches fail to establish a strong inference of scienter because they did not put them on notice of inadequacies in Equifax's systems. In the Amended Complaint, the Plaintiff alleges that the prior W2Express, LifeLock, and TALX breaches warned the Defendants that Equifax's cybersecurity was vulnerable. Thus, according to the Plaintiff, the Defendants knew or were severely reckless as to the deficient state of Equifax's cyberdefenses. According to the Defendants, the Plaintiff has not pleaded facts showing that these prior incidents were symptomatic of broader cybersecurity problems, and thus cannot be used to show that the Defendants were aware of the deficiencies in the data systems. The Defendants argue that these breaches did not put them on warning because none of them "remotely resemble[d]" the attack in the Data Breach. According to the Defendants, these prior breaches did not involve the same exact exploitation of unpatched software vulnerabilities.

The Court agrees with the Plaintiff that these prior breaches were symptomatic of a larger cybersecurity problem. The Amended Complaint details how these prior incidents were the result of many of the same problems that contributed to the Data Breach here. According to the Amended Complaint, these previous breaches resulted from, or were exacerbated by, poor authentication measures and inadequate network monitoring. In fact, after one of these incidents, Equifax acknowledged that it would need to implement additional monitoring and blocking measures to protect the data in its custody. Thus, Equifax understood that these deficiencies contributed to prior breaches. These prior breaches demonstrated the same, repeated network failures, and contrary to the Defendants' assertions, did depict fundamental problems in Equifax's cybersecurity.

Nonetheless, the Plaintiff has failed to allege that the Individual Defendants, except for Smith, knew, or were severely reckless to the fact that, these prior breaches were symptomatic of fundamental security problems. Although the Plaintiff adequately alleges that these prior breaches involved some of the same problems involved in the Data Breach, it has not alleged that Gamble, Dodge, or Ploder had specific knowledge, or access to specific facts, informing them that these prior breaches involved these specific issues. Absent such allegations, the Plaintiff has failed to allege that the Individual Defendants other than Smith knew that the prior breaches involved these authentication and monitoring issues, or that they were severely reckless as to this fact. Without knowing that these breaches were specifically caused by authentication and network monitoring issues, these Defendants would not have been put on notice that there were shortcomings in these areas of security. Without this knowledge, these previous breaches do not serve as warnings of the many cybersecurity deficiencies that the Plaintiff alleges in the Amended Complaint, and thus cannot establish scienter.

However, these prior breaches do help establish scienter as to Smith. As explained above, Equifax hired Mandiant in early 2017 in response to the TALX breach. Smith personally oversaw and closely monitored this investigation by Mandiant. Mandiant then confirmed in its review that Equifax's systems were grossly inadequate, and warned that Equifax's failure to patch vulnerabilities could present problems. Thus, Smith was personally aware of Mandiant's investigation and the results of this investigation, and knew that this investigation had been initiated due to the prior TALX breach. Thus, these allegations are sufficient to infer that Smith knew, or was severely recklessly as to the fact that, the TALX breach was the result of deficiencies in Equifax's cybersecurity. Therefore, the Court concludes that the TALX breach along with Mandiant's audit report contribute to a finding of scienter as to Smith. According to the Amended Complaint, the Mandiant investigation was a "top-secret project" that Smith was "overseeing personally." Smith, at least, had access to facts showing that the cybersecurity was seriously deficient, which would contribute to a conclusion that he was at least severely reckless in making statements touting Equifax's cybersecurity.

2. Knowledge of the Data Breach

Next, the Plaintiffs argue that Equifax Senior Management's knowledge of the Data Breach raises a strong inference of scienter. In the Amended Complaint, the Plaintiff alleges that Senior Management, including the Individual Defendants were "well aware" of the Data Breach by "late July 2017," but nonetheless failed to disclose the incident and continued to make false statements concerning Equifax's data security. Thus, according to the Plaintiff, the Defendants knowingly or recklessly made false statements because they knew of the Data Breach. The Defendants argue that these allegations concerning the Defendants' knowledge of the Data Breach fail to give rise to a strong inference of scienter.

First, the Defendants argue that each of the challenged statements attributed to Gamble, Ploder, and Dodge, and all but one of the statements attributed to Smith, are alleged to have been made on or before July 27, 2017. Thus, as to these statements, the Individual Defendants could not have known or been severely reckless as to the risk of misleading investors since they did not know of the existence of the Data Breach. The Court agrees. The Plaintiff has not shown that Gamble, Dodge, or Ploder made any of the challenged statements after they allegedly became aware of the Data Breach in late July 2017. Thus, these Individual Defendants' knowledge of the Data Breach does not establish scienter as to any of their specific alleged violations.

However, these allegations do support a finding of scienter as to Smith. On August 16, 2017, after discovery of the Data Breach, Smith made comments regarding Equifax's data security in a speech at the University of Georgia. The factual allegations in the Amended Complaint support a finding that Smith made these statements with the requisite scienter. By this point, Mandiant had already informed Smith that it was likely that a large amount of personally identifiable information had been compromised in the Data Breach. Furthermore, Smith had personally overseen the previous Mandiant investigation in March 2017, in which Mandiant concluded that Equifax's cybersecurity practices were grossly inadequate. Thus, Smith, despite knowing that the sensitive data had been compromised in the Data Breach, and despite personally overseeing this previous investigation by Mandiant, nonetheless stated that data security is "a huge priority for us" and that it was his "number one worry." These allegations are sufficient to raise a strong inference that Smith made this statement with the requisite scienter.

The Defendants argue that, even assuming Smith was aware of the Data Breach when he made this statement, "such knowledge would not reasonably have suggested that it would be misleading to state that data security was a 'huge priority' and 'his number one worry.' However, these arguments do not address whether Smith acted with the necessary scienter. Instead, they ask whether the statements were false or misleading – which is a separate inquiry. The Defendants conflate the two issues. As discussed above, these statements were false or misleading because a reasonable investor would understand this statement to convey that there was no significant security breach when it was made. The Defendants also argue that scienter as to this statement is not adequately alleged because the Plaintiff did not plead facts that Smith knew the statements were false or misleading. However, as explained above, Smith made these statements despite his knowledge of Mandiant's warnings concerning Equifax's deficiencies. Such knowledge, even if Smith disagreed with it, contributes to an inference of recklessness.

3. Core Business Operation

The Plaintiffs next argue that the fact that the alleged violations concerned one of the most critical risks facing Equifax contributes to a strong inference of scienter. However, the fact that an alleged fraud concerned a company's core business does not itself establish a strong inference of scienter. "[I]t is not automatically assumed that a corporate officer is familiar with certain facts just because these facts are important to the company's business; there must be other, individualized allegations that further suggest that the officer had knowledge of the fact in question." Instead, "a person's status as a corporate officer, when considered alongside other allegations, can help support an inference that that person is familiar with the company's most important operations."

However, this argument fails to establish scienter. It is insufficient for a plaintiff to make "conclusory allegations that the Defendants had access to the 'true facts' in order to demonstrate scienter, particularly where the complaint fails to allege 'which defendant knew what, how they knew it, or when.' " The Plaintiff's allegations that cybersecurity was critical to Equifax's business operations fail to establish scienter as to Dodge, Ploder, and Gamble. The Plaintiff must plead specific facts establishing that the Individual Defendants knew of, or were severely reckless as to, the existing deficiencies in Equifax's data systems. General allegations that cybersecurity is critical to Equifax's business may, in totality, contribute to a finding of scienter. However, absent allegations that Gamble, Ploder, or Dodge had access to specific facts showing these problems, this argument fails.

The Eleventh Circuit's decision in Garfield v. NDC Health Corporation is instructive. There, the plaintiff alleged that the defendants attended monthly operations meetings where every aspect of the business was discussed in detail, including "the aggressive channel stuffing and mounting problems with accounts recevable (sic)" that were at the center of the plaintiff's fraud allegations. The plaintiff also alleged that testimonial evidence by a former senior executive would show that the defendants knew of these problems. The court concluded that these allegations failed to establish scienter due to the absence of "particularized averments of fraud or scienter." The plaintiff's broad claims lacked the requisite detail because "it failed to allege what was said at the meeting, to whom it was said, or in what context." The court explained that "[a] general allegation that Individual Defendants promoted channel stuffing at a series of meetings does not establish scienter."

Here, the Plaintiff fails to establish a strong inference of scienter based upon Dodge, Ploder, and Gamble's roles in the company. The Amended Complaint fails to allege what warnings were given to each of these specific Individual Defendants, when those warnings were conveyed to these Individual Defendants, what was said in such warnings, and in what context those warnings were made. Generally, the Plaintiff alleges that these Individual Defendants, based upon their positions and their general duty to monitor the operations of Equifax's networks and systems, must have known about the deficient state of its cybersecurity. The Amended Complaint, however, fails to provide specific factual allegations as to a "time, place or manner" in which any of the Individual Defendants were specifically warned of these cybersecurity deficiencies. Therefore, these allegations are insufficient to support an inference of scienter.

The Plaintiff cites In re Ebix, Inc. Securities Litigation. There, the court concluded that the factual allegations gave rise to a strong inference that the defendants were at least severely reckless in their representations due to the defendants' "roles within the company (CEO and CFO), their active participation in press releases, earnings calls, and SEC filings dealing with the issues focused on in the [complaint], and the nature, duration and extent of the fraud alleged." However, Ebixis distinguishable from this case because there the plaintiff alleged "specific communications to and from the Individual Defendants regarding these issues." In contrast, the Plaintiff here has not alleged any specific communications to or from any of the Individual Defendants concerning the state of Equifax's cybersecurity. Without these types of specific allegations, the Plaintiff fails to establish a strong inference that the Individual Defendants were severely reckless in their representations concerning Equifax's data security.

Thus, these general allegations that cybersecurity was a core business operation do not support an inference that Dodge, Gamble, or Ploder knowingly or recklessly misrepresented the state of Equifax's networks when they stated that cybersecurity was one of Equifax's top priorities. These allegations do contribute to a finding of scienter as to Smith, when taken into account with the other, more specific allegations as to his knowledge of problems with Equifax's data security. However, on their own, these allegations do not establish a strong inference of scienter.

4. Defendants' Assurances

Next, the Plaintiff argues that the Defendants assured investors that they were focused on cybersecurity and compliance with data security laws, and that these assurances support an inference of scienter. The Plaintiff cites In re Theragenics Corp. Securities Litigation in support of this argument. However, the facts of that case are distinguishable. This Court in Theragenics did not hold that the defendants' assurances that they were monitoring their competitor's performance supported an inference of scienter. Instead, the plaintiffs there alleged that the defendants did in fact continually monitor the performance of their competitor, establishing that they knew their statements were false or misleading. In contrast, the Plaintiff here has not shown that the Individual Defendants, aside from Smith, were monitoring Equifax's cybersecurity or had access to specific information or warnings that would have established that they knew or were severely reckless as to the falsity of the statements they made.

In essence, the Plaintiff argues that the Defendants stated that they were closely monitoring Equifax's cybersecurity, and that from this, one can infer that they must have known about the problems with data security. However, the fact that the Defendants stated that they were closely monitoring Equifax's network security does not establish that they knew of, or were severely reckless to the existence of, these cybersecurity deficiencies. These allegations are too general. Instead, the more plausible inference is that the Individual Defendants, besides Smith, were negligent with regard to their management and monitoring of cybersecurity. In the cases relied upon by the Plaintiff, the plaintiffs alleged that the defendants were in fact monitoring the events underlying the false or misleading statements, and thus knew or were severely reckless to the fact that the statements made were false. Scienter was not established in those cases merely because the defendants assured investors that they were monitoring those underlying events, as the Plaintiff here alleges. This argument, which requires additional inferential steps, is insufficient to establish scienter as to Gamble, Ploder, and Dodge.

5. Egregiousness of Cybersecurity Deficiencies

The Defendants next contend that the Plaintiff's allegations as to the "egregiousness" of the shortcomings in Equifax's data security fail to support a strong inference of scienter. Instead, according to the Defendants, these allegations merely constitute hindsight criticism as to the manner in which Equifax managed cybersecurity. The Plaintiff argues that the magnitude, scope, and duration of the deficiencies in Equifax's cybersecurity systems were such that they could not have escaped the notice of the Defendants and other senior management, and that this supports an inference of scienter. And, according to the Plaintiff, this is compounded by the fact that the Defendants allegedly represented that they were "closely monitoring" Equifax's data security. The Court concludes, however, that the egregiousness of Equifax's cybersecurity problems, without more specific allegations, fails to establish scienter. Once again, as discussed above, the Plaintiff has failed to establish that Dodge, Gamble, or Ploder knew of or were severely reckless as to these egregious deficiencies. The severity of these problems, if taken into account with other specific factual allegations supporting scienter, could help establish an inference of scienter. However, here those other allegations are absent. Without those allegations, the Plaintiff has failed to establish an inference that is cogent and compelling, and just as likely as other, more innocent explanations. Even if these problems were severe and widespread, it is still more plausible to infer that these Individual Defendants were negligent, rather than something more insidious.

6. Stock Sales

Next, the Plaintiff argues that suspicious stock sales by Gamble and Ploder support an inference of scienter. "[T]he timing of stock trades by insiders also may be relevant to inferring scienter." "Stock sales or purchases timed to maximize returns on nonpublic information weigh in favor of inferring scienter; the lack of similar sales weighs against inferring scienter." "To demonstrate the relevance of stock trades to the issue of scienter, a plaintiff 'bear[s] the burden of showing that sales by insiders were in fact unusual or suspicious in amount and in timing.'"

Here, the Court concludes that the stock sales fail to establish scienter. First, the Plaintiff fails to allege that any of the other Individual Defendants, including Smith, the CEO, engaged in insider trading. This alone undermines any inference that these stock sales contribute to a finding of scienter. Second, the stock sales, which can constitute circumstantial evidence that Gamble and Ploder knew that Equifax's stock price was artificially inflated, cannot on their own establish scienter as to these Defendants. However, as discussed above, the Plaintiff has failed to provide more than general allegations that any of the Individual Defendants, besides Smith, made misstatements with knowledge or severe recklessness toward their falsity. This circumstantial evidence fails to meet the stringent pleading requirements under the PSLRA that the allegations give rise to a strong inference of scienter.

There is no doubt that these sales by Gamble and Ploder are suspicious, especially given their timing. They contribute to an inference of scienter, but they are not sufficient on their own to raise a strong inference of scienter with regard to Gamble and Ploder as to the alleged violations. The stock sales could have, when aggregated with other facts, contributed to a finding of a strong inference of scienter. However, they cannot establish this strong inference on their own. This is compounded by the fact that the other Individual Defendants, including Smith, did not engage in similarly suspicious stock sales. Thus, given the lack of other specific factual allegations establishing scienter as to these Defendants, the suspicious stock sales by Gamble and Ploder fail to give rise to a strong inference of scienter on their own.

7. Sudden Resignations of Equifax Officers

Next, the Plaintiff contends that the sudden departures of high-ranking Equifax executives support an inference of scienter. On September 15, 2017, about a week after public disclosure of the Data Breach, Chief Security Officer Susan Mauldin and Chief Information Officer David Webb resigned from Equifax. On September 26, 2017, Smith retired from Equifax, without severance, effective immediately. The Equifax Board of Directors announced that it had the power to retroactively classify Smith as having been fired for cause, which includes intentional or reckless misconduct. According to the Plaintiff, the circumstances surrounding these departures of senior executives establish a strong inference that "there were profound failures in [Equifax's] data protection practices that were the result of reckless or intentional misconduct."

Some courts have concluded that the resignation of corporate officers, in certain contexts, can support an inference of scienter. However, in those cases, the context of the executives' resignations was important. The fact that an executive resigned, on its own, does not support an inference of scienter. Instead, the circumstances of the resignation must suggest that intentional or reckless misconduct had occurred. For example, in In re Home Loan Servicing Solutions, Ltd. Securities Litigation, cited by the Plaintiff, the court concluded that scienter was established as to a defendant who, among other things, was "at the epicenter" of the business, who was "forced to resign," and who regulatory documents indicated was "engaged in improper transactions." Similarly, in In re OSG Securities Litigation, the court concluded that the resignations of two executives supported an inference of scienter when the "circumstances and timing of the resignations" suggest that both defendants were terminated in relation to the undisclosed tax issue underlying the fraud claims. The court noted that "[a]lthough the decision to terminate the defendants does not negate the possibility of mere negligence in mismanaging the Section 956 issue, it more likely suggests a higher level of wrongdoing approaching recklessness or even conscious malfeasance."

In contrast, the context of the resignations here does not suggest that Gamble, Ploder, or Dodge knew of, or were severely reckless as to, the false or misleading nature of their statements. The Plaintiff fails to explain how the resignations of Smith, Mauldin, and Webb show that Gamble, Ploder, or Dodge acted with the requisite state of mind. Nothing about the context of these resignations would lead one to infer that Gamble, Ploder, or Dodge must have known about the deficient state of Equifax's cybersecurity. Without such allegations, the resignations of Smith, Mauldin, and Webb fail to establish scienter as to these Individual Defendants.

However, Smith's resignation does contribute to a finding of scienter on his part. Taking all of these allegations into account, the following facts support a strong inference of scienter: Smith was warned by Mandiant, after a previous breach, that Equifax's cybersecurity was grossly inadequate; Smith, as CEO, would have likely followed many of the developments in Equifax's cybersecurity since it was an important aspect of its business; Smith learned of the Data Breach in late July 2017, but still continued to make statements touting the company's security; and after the public disclosure of the incident, Smith resigned his roles in the company, while the Board of Directors announced it may decide to retroactively terminate him "with cause." These allegations, taken together, give rise to a strong inference of scienter that Smith made these misstatements with knowledge or severe recklessness as to their falsity.

But, the Court concludes overall that the Plaintiff has failed to allege specific facts giving rise to a strong inference of scienter as to Gamble, Ploder, or Dodge. Instead, as to these Defendants, the Plaintiff relies upon inferences based upon their role in the company and the size of the fraud. These general allegations do not suffice. "[I]t is not enough to make conclusory allegations that the Defendants had access to the 'true facts' in order to demonstrate scienter, particularly where the complaint fails to allege 'which defendant knew what, how they knew it, or when.'" "Nor does a vague assertion that a defendant must have known about the fraud by virtue of his position of authority suffice to prove a strong inference of scienter." Without specific allegations that Gamble, Ploder, and Dodge had access to information that made them aware of the problems with Equifax's data security, the Amended Complaint fails to give rise to a strong inference of scienter as to these Individual Defendants. Thus, the Plaintiff fails to adequately plead scienter under the stringent requirements set forth in the PSLRA.

8. Equifax's State of Mind

Finally, the Defendants argue that the Plaintiff has failed to adequately plead scienter as to Equifax. However, failure to adequately plead scienter as to individual defendants does not automatically mean that scienter cannot be established against a corporation. "Corporations, of course, have no state of mind of their own. Instead, the scienter of their agents must be imputed to them." A plaintiff, in theory, can still create a strong inference that a corporate defendant such as Equifax acted with the requisite scienter, even if it has failed to prove scienter as to the individual defendants. Even if the Amended Complaint fails to raise a strong inference of scienter as to any of the named Individual Defendants, the Plaintiff can survive dismissal if it "raise[s] a strong inference that somebody responsible for the allegedly misleading statements must have known about the fraud." To do so, the Plaintiff must allege facts in the Amended Complaint creating a strong inference that unnamed Equifax officials "were both responsible for issuing the allegedly false public statements and were aware of the alleged fraud." It can do so through allegations relating the state of mind of corporate officials "who make or issue the statement (or order or approve it or its making or issuance, or who furnish information or language for inclusion therein, or the like)."

Here, the Plaintiff's claims as to Equifax survive to the extent that the claims against Smith survive dismissal. Furthermore, the Plaintiff has alleged that Equifax's employees warned "management" of the deficient state of the company's cybersecurity. While these allegations are insufficient to establish scienter as to the named Defendants other than Smith, they are sufficient to establish that some corporate officials at Equifax, who would have had a role in crafting many of the statements made by the company, knew of the data security problems in the company. This is especially true given the resignations of Webb and Mauldin, two corporate executives whose responsibilities included data security, and Smith, whose role as CEO would have encompassed data security. The Plaintiff alleges that Equifax employees warned "management" of the problems with the company's cybersecurity, and also alleges that Webb and Mauldin resigned after the Data Breach. This supports an inference that some corporate officials in Equifax knew, or were severely reckless, as to the fraudulent conduct. Thus, the Court concludes that the Amended Complaint still creates a strong inference that Equifax, the corporate defendant, acted with the requisite state of mind.

C. Loss Causation

Next, the Defendants argue that the Plaintiff has failed to adequately allege loss causation. The Plaintiff must allege facts demonstrating that the Defendants' misrepresentations caused the losses for which the Plaintiff seeks to recover. To prove loss causation in a section 10(b) claim, "a plaintiff must offer 'proof of a causal connection between the misrepresentation and the investment's subsequent decline in value.'" Essentially, the Plaintiff must show that the Defendants' fraud, and not some other factor, proximately caused its alleged losses. The loss causation element does not require a plaintiff to prove that a "fraudulent misrepresentation was the sole cause of a security's loss in value." But, "the plaintiff must still demonstrate that the fraudulent statement was a 'substantial' or 'significant' cause of the decline in price." "By ensuring that only losses actually attributable to a given misrepresentation are cognizable, the loss causation requirement ensures that the federal securities laws do not 'becom[e] a system of investor insurance that reimburses investors for any decline in the value of their investments.'" Section 10(b) is not a "prophylaxis" against the normal risks associated with investment in the stock market, but instead is designed solely to protect against fraud. The loss causation element is only subject to Rule 8's notice pleading standard, requiring a "short and plain" statement, and not the heightened pleading standards of the PSLRA.

In the Amended Complaint, the Plaintiff alleges that "the market for Equifax's securities was efficient" and that "the market for Equifax stock promptly digest current information regarding Equifax from all publicly available sources and reflected such information in Equifax's stock price." Thus, according to the Plaintiff, it is entitled to a presumption of reliance. The Plaintiff's claims therefore rely upon the fraud-on-the-market theory of causation, derived from the efficient market hypothesis. This hypothesis provides "that 'in an open and developed securities market, the price of a company's stock is determined by the available material information regarding the company and its business.'" "Because millions of shares change hands daily, and a critical mass of market makers study the available information and influence the stock price through trades and recommendations, an efficient capital market rapidly and efficiently digests all available information and translates that information into the processed form of a market price." "Just as an efficient market translates all available truthful information into the stock price, the market processes the publicly disseminated falsehood and prices it into the stock as well." "The market price of the stock will then include an artificial 'inflationary' value—the amount that the market mistakenly attributes to the stock based on the fraudulent misinformation."

This presumption is also relevant for loss causation. "While reliance focuses on the front-end causation question of whether the defendant's fraud induced or influenced the plaintiff's stock purchase, loss causation provides the 'bridge between reliance and actual damages.'" In a fraud-on-the-market case, the loss causation element requires the plaintiff to show "that the fraud-induced inflation that was baked into the plaintiff's purchase price was subsequently removed from the stock's price, thereby causing losses to the plaintiff." Plaintiffs often demonstrate loss causation in fraud-on-the-market cases circumstantially, by:

(1) identifying a "corrective disclosure" (a release of information that reveals to the market the pertinent truth that was previously concealed or obscured by the company's fraud); (2) showing that the stock price dropped soon after the corrective disclosure; and (3) eliminating other possible explanations for this price drop, so that the factfinder can infer that it is more probable than not that it was the corrective disclosure—as opposed to other possible depressive factors—that caused at least a "substantial" amount of the price drop.

Overall, "loss causation analysis in a fraud-on-the-market case focuses on the following question: even if the plaintiffs paid an inflated price for the stock as a result of the fraud (i.e., even if the plaintiffs relied), did the relevant truth eventually come out and thereby cause the plaintiffs to suffer losses?"

The Defendants argue that the announcements to the public of the Data Breach on and following September 7, 2017 did not "reveal" that the prior statements concerning Equifax's data security were false, and thus were not a corrective disclosure. Specifically, the Defendant contends that: (1) the initial announcement of the incident on September 7, 2017 did not reveal that prior statements referencing Equifax's commitment to data security, efforts to protect data, and compliance with laws and regulations were false; (2) the revelations on September 11, 2017 that Equifax lacked an effective data breach crisis management plan did not show that any of the challenged statements were false or misleading; (3) the revelations on September 12, 2017 that 11.5 million customers signed up for the identity protection plan offered by Equifax does not reveal the falsity of any prior statements; and (4) revelations on September 13 and 14, 2017 that the Apache Struts vulnerability caused the Data Breach did not reveal that any of the challenged statements were false or misleading.

However, as noted above, a disclosure need not precisely mirror an earlier misrepresentation, but instead must relate to the misrepresentation and not other negative information about the company. Furthermore, a corrective disclosure can come from any source, and can take any form from which the market would absorb the information and accordingly react. The Court concludes that the Plaintiff has adequately alleged loss causation. "Rule 8 is satisfied if plaintiff provides 'a short and plain statement adequate to give defendants some indication of the loss and the causal connection that the plaintiff has in mind.'" The Plaintiff alleges that the initial disclosure of the Data Breach, along with subsequent disclosures that Equifax's poor cybersecurity played a part in the incident, that Congress would be conducting a probe into Equifax's general cybersecurity practices, that millions of consumers were affected, and that a failure to implement a patch that had been available since March 2017 caused the Data breach, all combined to disclose the truth to investors. This, along with the wide variety of news reporting on the incident detailing Equifax's cybersecurity problems, slowly revealed the truth about the prior misstatements. This adequately puts the Defendants on notice as to the causal connection between the Defendants' misrepresentations and the class's losses.

The Plaintiff also argues that a corrective disclosure "may occur through the materialization of an event within the 'zone of risk' concealed by defendant's misstatements." Under this theory, "[i]f the significance of the truth is such as to cause a reasonable investor to consider seriously a zone of risk that would be perceived as remote or highly unlikely by one believing the fraud, and the loss ultimately suffered is within that zone, then a misrepresentation or omission as to that information may be deemed a foreseeable or proximate cause of the loss." The Eleventh Circuit "has never decided whether the materialization-of-concealed-risk theory may be used to prove loss causation in a fraud-on-the-market case." The Court declines to adopt this theory here. First, the Plaintiff failed to plead this theory of loss causation in the Amended Complaint. Second, the Plaintiff has failed to explain how the "materialization" of the Data Breach itself corrected prior misstatements touting the strength of Equifax's cybersecurity. Third, the Court need not adopt this theory since the Plaintiff has adequately alleged loss causation through corrective disclosures.

D. In Connection With

Next, the Defendants contend that the statements made by Smith in a speech at the University of Georgia were not made in connection with the purchase or sale of a security. To state a claim under section 10(b), the plaintiff must show that the false or misleading statement was made in connection with the purchase or sale of a security. In using this phrase, "Congress ... 'intended only that the device employed, whatever it might be, be of a sort that would cause reasonable investors to rely thereon, and, in connection therewith, so relying, cause them to purchase or sell a corporation's securities.'" "Moreover, when ... a claim is based on the fraud-on-the-market theory, a 'straightforward cause and effect' test is applied, under which it is sufficient that 'statements which manipulate the market are connected to resultant stock trading.'"

Here, the Plaintiff has adequately shown that Smith's statement was made in connection with the purchase or sale of a security. "As the Supreme Court has noted, 'market professionals generally consider most publicly announced material statements about companies, thereby affecting stock market prices.'" In In re Carter-Wallace, Inc. Securities Litigation, the court noted that "[t]echnical advertisements in sophisticated medical journals detailing the attributes of a new drug could be highly relevant to analysts evaluating the stock of the company marketing the drug," and thus it could not conclude that such statements, as a matter of law, were not made in connection with a securities transaction. Similarly, statements made by Equifax's CEO concerning a core business operation could be highly relevant to analysts evaluating Equifax's stock. The fact that Smith made this statement at a presentation at a college, and not in some other setting, does not change this conclusion. This is further bolstered by the Plaintiff's allegation that this presentation was uploaded to the popular website YouTube.com. The Court cannot say that this statement, which would be relevant to analysts studying Equifax's securities, was not made in connection with a securities transaction. This is especially true given the fact that the Plaintiff relies upon the fraud-on-the-market theory. Therefore, the Court finds the Defendants' argument unpersuasive.

E. Section 20(a) Claims

Finally, the Defendants argue that the Plaintiff's section 20(a) claims fail to state a claim for which relief can be granted. Section 20(a) of the Exchange Act extends liability for violations of Rule 10b–5 to controlling persons in the company. "To show control person liability under Section 20(a), a plaintiff must allege that: (1) the company violated § 10(b); (2) the defendant had the power to control the general affairs of the company; and (3) the defendant had the power to control the specific corporate policy that resulted in the primary violation."

The Defendants first argue that the Plaintiff's failure to plead any primary violation of section 10(b) by Equifax requires dismissal of the section 20(a) claims. However, as discussed above, the Plaintiff has adequately pleaded some of its section 10(b) claims as to Equifax. The Defendants next argue that the Plaintiff fails to adequately plead that the Individual Defendants control "specific corporate policy" that resulted in the alleged primary violations of section 10(b). Specifically, the Defendants argue that the Plaintiff has not alleged that any of the Individual Defendants had control over the content and dissemination of the unattributed statements made on Equifax's website during the class period, or any of the statements made by different Individual Defendants, or that they controlled the cybersecurity matters misrepresented. Furthermore, the Defendants argue that the Plaintiff has not alleged that Gamble, Ploder, or Dodge controlled Equifax's "general affairs."

The Court agrees that the Plaintiff has failed to allege that Gamble, Ploder, or Dodge exercised control over the specific cybersecurity policies that resulted in the alleged violations, or that they exercised control over any of the unattributed statements made or statements made by other Individual Defendants. Thus, the Plaintiff's section 20(a) claims should be dismissed as to these Individual Defendants. The Court concludes, however, that the Plaintiff has adequately alleged a section 20(a) claim as to Smith. Smith, as CEO, had the power to control the "general affairs" of Equifax. Smith also had the power to control the specific corporate policy that resulted in the section 10(b) violations. Smith had both the power to control Equifax's cybersecurity policy and the statements made by Equifax and the other Individual Defendants as to these cybersecurity policies. Thus, the Plaintiff has sufficiently stated a claim for control liability as to Smith.

IV. Conclusion

For the reasons stated above, the Defendants' Joint Motion to Dismiss [Doc. 62] is GRANTED in part and DENIED in part. It is GRANTED as to the Defendants Gamble, Ploder, and Dodge. It is DENIED as to the Defendants Equifax and Smith.

NOTES

Note 1

In an unpublished 2021 case in Delaware, plaintiffs brought a shareholder suit against Marriott's board of directors.[201] The shareholder derivative suit alleged that Marriott failed to adequately perform a due diligence of an acquired company's cybersecurity practices, which apparently were deficient and allegedly resulted in a large data breach.[202] The complaint made the following specific allegations against the board of directors:

> The claim is based on allegations that the individual defendants breached their fiduciary duties by (1) failing to "undertake cybersecurity and technology due diligence" during the Acquisition; (2) failing to implement adequate internal controls after the Acquisition; and (3) concealing the data security incident until November 30, 2018.[203]

In analyzing the plaintiff's claims, the court stated:

> "The decision whether to initiate or pursue a lawsuit on behalf of the corporation is generally within the power and responsibility of the board of directors." A stockholder plaintiff can pursue claims belonging to the corporation if (1) the corporation's directors wrongfully refused a demand to authorize the corporation to bring the suit or (2) a demand would have been futile because the directors were incapable of impartially considering the demand. Because the plaintiff did not make a demand on Marriott's Board, the Complaint must plead particularized factual allegations establishing that demand was excused.[204]

The court stated that there is a three-part test to determine whether the demand would be futile.[205] The court ultimately granted defendant's motion to dismiss, in part, because

---

[201] *Fireman's Retirement System of St. Louis v. Marriott*, 2021 WL 4593777 (Ct. of Chan. Del. October 5, 2021) (unpublished).

[202] *Id.* at *1-*6.

[203] *Id.* at *6.

[204] *Id.*

[205] *Id.* at *7. The Court stated:
Delaware courts should ask the following three questions on a director by-director basis when evaluating allegations of demand futility:
(i) whether the director received a material personal benefit from the alleged misconduct that is the subject of the litigation demand;
(ii) whether the director faces a substantial likelihood of liability on any of the claims that would be the subject of the litigation demand; and
(iii) whether the director lacks independence from someone who received a material personal benefit from the alleged misconduct that would be the subject of the litigation demand or who would face a substantial likelihood of liability on any of the claims that are the subject of the litigation demand.
Demand is excused as futile if "the answer to any of the questions is 'yes' for at least half of the members of the demand board." The "analysis is conducted on a claim by-claim basis." *Id.*

plaintiffs' pre-acquisition due diligence claims are time-barred.[206] On the post-acquisition claims concerning cybersecurity lapses, the court explained that:

> As often stated, oversight liability under *Caremark* is "possibly the most difficult theory in corporation law upon which a plaintiff might hope to win a judgment." To prevail, the plaintiff must plead particularized facts showing that either (1) "the directors utterly failed to implement any reporting or information system or controls" or (2) "having implemented such a system or controls, consciously failed to monitor or oversee its operations thus disabling themselves from being informed of risks or problems requiring their attention."

> Compliance risk oversight generally falls within the governance responsibilities of the board of directors. Key enterprise risks affecting a corporation's "mission critical" components has been a focus of Delaware courts in assessing potential oversight liability, particularly where a board has allegedly failed to implement reporting systems or controls to monitor those risks. Cybersecurity, however, is an area of consequential risk that spans modern business sectors. In the past several years alone, cyberattacks have affected thousands of companies and government agencies. High-profile data breaches have exposed customer data at businesses from Yahoo! to Target and Home Depot. Targeted attacks have shut down hospitals and taken offline major fuel pipelines. Regulators in the United States and abroad have become more active in issuing cybersecurity guidance and undertaking enforcement activities in response. The President of the United States has named cybersecurity a "top priority and essential to national and economic security."

> Delaware courts have not broadened a board's *Caremark* duties to include monitoring risk in the context of business decisions. Oversight violations are typically found where companies—particularly those operating within a highly regulated industry—violate the law or run afoul of regulatory mandates. But as the legal and regulatory frameworks governing cybersecurity advance and the risks become manifest, corporate governance must evolve to address them. The corporate harms presented by non-compliance with cybersecurity safeguards increasingly call upon directors to ensure that companies have appropriate oversight systems in place.

> The growing risks posed by cybersecurity threats do not, however, lower the high threshold that a plaintiff must meet to plead a *Caremark* claim. For either prong of *Caremark*, "a showing of bad faith conduct ... is essential to establish director oversight liability." Only a "sustained or systemic failure of the board to exercise oversight ... will establish the lack of good faith that is a necessary condition to liability." The Complaint in this case falls well short of demonstrating that the Post-

---

[206] *Id.* at *8-*11.

Acquisition Board members face a substantial likelihood of liability for a sustained, bad faith failure of oversight. Demand is therefore not futile on that basis.[207]

Notably, the court pointed to the oversight and controls concerning cybersecurity exercised by the board and noted that there was not an oversight or monitoring failure by the board.[208] This case is unpublished but provides some guidance as to how a court may apply demand futility in the context of a data breach.

4.6 SEC Order for Failure to Disclose Breach Under Securities Reporting Laws and SEC Proposed Cybersecurity Rules

First, this section discusses Yahoo!'s disclosure issues concerning cybersecurity. Second, this section discusses the SEC's proposed cybersecurity rules.

The following order concerns Yahoo!'s failure to disclose a cybersecurity breach under securities laws:

In the Matter of ALTABA INC., f/d/b/a YAHOO! INC., Release No. 3937 (SEC, April 24, 2018), available at https://www.sec.gov/litigation/admin/2018/33-10485.pdf.

I.

The Securities and Exchange Commission ("Commission") deems it appropriate that cease and-desist proceedings be, and hereby are, instituted pursuant to Section 8A of the Securities Act of 1933 (the "Securities Act") and Section 21C of the Securities Exchange Act of 1934 ("Exchange Act"), against Altaba Inc., f/d/b/a Yahoo! Inc. ("Yahoo" or "Respondent"). . . .

In anticipation of the institution of these proceedings, Respondent has submitted an Offer of Settlement (the "Offer") which the Commission has determined to accept. Solely for the purpose of these proceedings and any other proceedings brought by or on behalf of the Commission, or to which the Commission is a party, and without admitting or denying the findings herein, except as to the Commission's jurisdiction over it and the subject matter of these proceedings, which are admitted, Respondent consents to the entry of this Order Instituting Cease and-Desist Proceedings Pursuant to Section 8A of the Securities Act of 1933 and Section 21C of the Securities Exchange Act of 1934, Making Findings, and Imposing a Cease-and-Desist Order ("Order"), as set forth below.

III.

On the basis of this Order and Respondent's Offer, the Commission finds that:

---

[207] *Id.* at *11-*12.
[208] *Id.* at *13-*14.

SUMMARY

1. This matter concerns material misstatements and omissions by Yahoo, one of the world's largest Internet media companies, regarding a 2014 data breach affecting more than 500 million of its user accounts. . . .

FACTS
Yahoo's Disclosures Regarding Data Breaches

8. At all relevant times, Yahoo was one of the world's largest Internet media companies, providing over a billion users worldwide with an array of products and services, including Internet searching capabilities, communications services, including Internet-based email, and digital content products, such as Yahoo News and Yahoo Finance. Yahoo's products and services involved the storage and transmission of its users' personal information in its facilities and on its equipment, networks, and corporate systems.

9. As an Internet media company, Yahoo made certain risk factor disclosures pertaining to potential data breaches in its annual reports on Form 10-K for the fiscal years ended December 31, 2014 and December 31, 2015, and in its quarterly reports on Form 10-Q for the first three quarters of 2015 and the first two quarters of 2016.2 These disclosures included the following header concerning security breaches: "If our security measures are breached, our products and services may be perceived as not being secure, users and customers may curtail or stop using our products and services, and we may incur significant legal and financial exposure." The disclosures also stated that Yahoo's "products and services involve the storage and transmission of Yahoo's users' and customers' personal and proprietary information in our facilities and on our equipment, networks and corporate systems," and that "[s]ecurity breaches expose us to a risk of loss of this information, litigation, remediation costs, increased costs for security measures, loss of revenue, damage to our reputation, and potential liability." The company's risk factor disclosures were incorporated by reference into registration statements on Form S-8 filed with the Commission on September 9, 2009 and September 11, 2014 that registered Yahoo's sales of its common stock under its employee stock purchase and option plans, pursuant to which Yahoo received approximately $384 million in cash proceeds in 2014, 2015, and 2016.

10. In the summer of 2016, Yahoo engaged in negotiations to sell its operating business to Verizon. In response to queries regarding past data breaches by Verizon during due diligence, Yahoo created a spreadsheet that falsely represented to Verizon that it was only aware of four minor breaches in which its users' personally identifying information was exposed, but did not disclose the 2014 theft of hundreds of millions of users' personal data in its response. During a June 27, 2016 telephone call requested by Verizon to

discuss the four breaches disclosed by Yahoo in its due diligence responses, Yahoo further did not disclose the 2014 theft of its users' personal data.

11. Ultimately, on July 23, 2016, Yahoo agreed to transfer the operating business to Yahoo Holdings at close, and entered into a stock purchase agreement with Verizon, by which Yahoo sold all of the outstanding shares of Yahoo Holdings to Verizon for $4,825,800,000 in cash. In the stock purchase agreement, Yahoo again affirmatively represented and warranted the following, in relevant part:

> To the Knowledge of [Yahoo], there have not been any incidents of, or third party claims alleging, (i) Security Breaches, unauthorized access or unauthorized use of any of [Yahoo's] ... information technology systems or (ii) loss, theft, unauthorized access or acquisition, modification, disclosure, corruption, or other misuse of any Personal Data in [Yahoo]'s ... possession, or other confidential data owned by [Yahoo]..., in each case (i) and (ii) that could reasonably be expected to have a Business Material Adverse Effect. . . .

Yahoo's Contemporaneous Knowledge of the 2014 Breach

12. Despite the disclosures set forth above, in late 2014, Yahoo had learned of a massive breach of its user database that resulted in the theft, unauthorized access, or acquisition of hundreds of millions of its users' personal data. At this time, Yahoo's internal information security team became aware that the company's information technology networks and systems had suffered a severe and widespread intrusion by hackers associated with the Russian Federation.

13. By December 2014, Yahoo's information security team, including its Chief Information Security Officer, had determined that the hackers had stolen copies of Yahoo's user database files containing the personal data of at least 108 million users, and likely even Yahoo's entire user database of billions of users. The personal data in the stolen files included highly sensitive information that Yahoo's information security team referred to as Yahoo's "crown jewels": Yahoo usernames, email addresses, telephone numbers, dates of birth, hashed passwords, and security questions and answers. Yahoo's information security team, including its Chief Information Security Officer, also concluded that the hackers had successfully gained access to a separate source of data: the email accounts of 26 Yahoo users specifically targeted by the hackers because of their connections to Russia.

14. Within days after Yahoo's information security team reached these conclusions, members of Yahoo's senior management and legal teams received various internal reports from Yahoo's Chief Information Security Officer stating that the theft of hundreds of millions of Yahoo users' personal data had occurred. As Yahoo has stated, the company's "relevant legal team had sufficient information to warrant substantial further inquiry in 2014, and they did not sufficiently pursue it." Yahoo Form 10-K for FY2016 at 47 (filed with the Commission on March 1, 2017). . . . However, Yahoo senior

management and relevant legal staff did not properly assess the scope, business impact, or legal implications of the breach, including how and where the breach should have been disclosed in Yahoo's public filings or whether the fact of the breach rendered, or would render, any statements made by Yahoo in its public filings misleading.

15. Furthermore, Yahoo's senior management and legal teams did not share information regarding the breach with Yahoo's auditors or outside counsel in order to assess the company's disclosure obligations in its public filings. Yahoo did not maintain disclosure controls and procedures designed to ensure that reports from Yahoo's information security team raising actual incidents of the theft of user data, or the significant risk of theft of user data, were properly and timely assessed to determine how and where data breaches should be disclosed in Yahoo's public filings, including, but not limited to, in its risk factor disclosures or MD&A. To the extent that Yahoo shared information regarding the breach with affected users, they only notified the 26 users whose email accounts were accessed during the breach.

16. As a result of these failures, Yahoo did not disclose the theft of Yahoo users' personal data in its public filings. Instead, Yahoo's risk factor disclosures in its annual reports for the years ended December 31, 2014 and December 31, 2015, and in its quarterly reports for the first three quarters of 2015 and the first two quarters of 2016, misleadingly suggested that a significant data breach had not yet occurred, and that therefore the company only faced the risk of data breaches and any negative effects that might flow from future breaches. In addition, Yahoo's filings did not address the breach's potential impact on the company's business in its risk factors; nor did they address known trends or uncertainties with regard to liquidity or net revenue presented by any current or future expenses and losses related to the 2014 data breach in its MD&A.

17. After the 2014 breach, Yahoo's information security team determined that the same hackers were continuously targeting Yahoo's user database throughout 2015 and early 2016, and also received reports raising the possibility of a high volume of compromised Yahoo user credentials for sale on the dark web. Based on this information, by June 2016, Yahoo's new Information Security Officer (hired in October 2015) concluded that Yahoo's entire user database, including the personal data of its users, had likely been stolen by nation-state actors through several hacker intrusions (including the 2014 breach), and ultimately could be exposed on the dark web in the immediate future. The Chief Information Security Officer communicated these conclusions to at least one member of Yahoo's senior management as Yahoo was negotiating the sale of its operating business to Verizon. Despite this further evidence indicating the theft of Yahoo's user database, Yahoo affirmatively represented to Verizon that it was unaware of any security breaches with a "Business Material Adverse Effect" in its stock purchase agreement, which was subsequently filed as an exhibit to a Form 8-K on July 25, 2016.

18. Based on the foregoing, Yahoo acted negligently in filing materially misleading periodic reports with the Commission. In particular, Yahoo knew, or should have known,

that its risk factor disclosures and MD&A in its annual reports on Form 10-K for the fiscal years ended December 31, 2014 and December 31, 2015, and in its quarterly reports on Form 10-Q for the first three quarters of 2015 and the first two quarters of 2016, and its stock purchase agreement with Verizon (which was filed as an exhibit to a current report on Form 8-K), as incorporated into its Form S-8 registration statements, were materially misleading.

Yahoo's Disclosure of the 2014 Breach

19. On or about September 22, 2016, Yahoo disclosed the 2014 breach and the resulting theft of data involving 500 million of its user accounts in a press release attached to a Form 8-K, and also disclosed the existence of the theft to Verizon. The day after Yahoo publicly disclosed the breach—and despite its July announcement of the pending sale to Verizon—Yahoo's market capitalization fell nearly $1.3 billion by virtue of a 3% decrease in its stock price. After disclosure of the 2014 breach, and after renegotiation of the terms of the sale of Yahoo's operating business pursuant to the stock purchase and reorganization agreements, Verizon and Yahoo agreed to a reduction in the acquisition price for Yahoo's operating business of $350 million, representing a 7.25% discount.

20. Yahoo also amended its risk factor disclosures and MD&A to address the 2014 breach in its subsequent public filings. With respect to risk factors, Yahoo acknowledged in its Form 10-Q for the third quarter of 2016 (filed October 9, 2016) that the data breach "risk" had already materialized by virtue of the 2014 data breach (referred to as the "Security Incident"). Specifically, Yahoo stated "Our security measures may be breached, as they were in the Security Incident and user data accessed, which may cause users and customers to curtail or stop using our products and services, and may cause us to incur significant legal and financial exposure" (italics added). Yahoo also added a risk factor specific to the 2014 data breach indicating that "the full extent of its impact and the impact of related government investigations and civil litigation on our results of operation ... could be material." With respect to its MD&A, Yahoo disclosed in its Form 10-Q for the third quarter of 2016 that the company expected to incur expenses—including investigation, remediation, and legal costs—related to the 2014 breach.

21. Yahoo also corrected prior statements that its disclosure controls and procedures were effective. In each of its 2014 and 2015 Form 10-Ks and Form 10-Qs for the first three quarters of 2015 and the first two quarters of 2016, Yahoo stated that its principal executive officer and principal financial officer evaluated the effectiveness of its disclosure controls and procedures (as such term is defined in Rules 13a-15(e) under the Exchange Act) and, for each period covered by the foregoing reports, had concluded that Yahoo's disclosure controls and procedures were effective. In its 2016 Form 10-K, filed with the Commission on March 1, 2017, Yahoo disclosed that its principal executive officer and principal financial officer had concluded that, "due exclusively to deficiencies in the Company's existing security incident response protocols related to the 2014 Security Incident, the Company's disclosure controls and procedures for each of the

annual and quarterly periods ended December 31, 2014 through September 30, 2016 were not effective at the end of each such period."

. . .

IV.

In view of the foregoing, the Commission deems it appropriate to impose the sanctions agreed to in Respondent Yahoo's Offer.

Accordingly, it is hereby ORDERED that:

A. Pursuant to Section 8A of the Securities Act and Section 21C of the Exchange Act, Respondent cease and desist from committing or causing any violations and any future violations of Sections 17(a)(2) and 17(a)(3) of the Securities Act, Section 13(a) of the Exchange Act, and Rules 12b-20, 13a-1, 13a-11, 13a-13, and 13a-15 thereunder.

B. Respondent shall, within ten (10) days of the entry of this Order, pay a civil money penalty in the amount of $35,000,000.00 to the Securities and Exchange Commission for transfer to the general fund of the United States Treasury, subject to Exchange Act Section 21F(g)(3). If timely payment is not made, additional interest shall accrue pursuant to 31 U.S.C. §3717.

. . .

By the Commission. Brent J. Fields   Secretary

NOTES

Note 1

The SEC issued guidance titled, "Commission Statement and Guidance on Public Company Cybersecurity Disclosures," concerning disclosures related to cybersecurity in 2018. The guidance states, in relevant part:

I. Introduction

A. Cybersecurity

Cybersecurity risks pose grave threats to investors, our capital markets, and our country. Whether it is the companies in which investors invest, their accounts with financial services firms, the markets through which they trade, or the infrastructure they count on daily, the investing public and the U.S. economy depend on the security and reliability of information and communications technology, systems, and networks. Companies today rely on digital technology to conduct their business operations and engage with their customers, business partners, and other constituencies. In a digitally connected world, cybersecurity presents ongoing risks and threats to our capital markets and to companies operating in all industries, including public companies regulated by the Commission.

As companies' exposure to and reliance on networked systems and the internet have increased, the attendant risks and frequency of cybersecurity incidents also have increased. Today, the importance of data management and technology to business is analogous to the importance of electricity and other forms of power in the past century. Cybersecurity incidents can result from unintentional events or deliberate attacks by insiders or third parties, including cybercriminals, competitors, nation-states, and "hacktivists." Companies face an evolving landscape of cybersecurity threats in which hackers use a complex array of means to perpetrate cyber-attacks, including the use of stolen access credentials, malware, ransomware, phishing, structured query language injection attacks, and distributed denial-of-service attacks, among other means. The objectives of cyber-attacks vary widely and may include the theft or destruction of financial assets, intellectual property, or other sensitive information belonging to companies, their customers, or their business partners. Cyber-attacks may also be directed at disrupting the operations of public companies or their business partners. This includes targeting companies that operate in industries responsible for critical infrastructure.

Companies that fall victim to successful cyber-attacks or experience other cybersecurity incidents may incur substantial costs and suffer other negative consequences, which may include:
• Remediation costs, such as liability for stolen assets or information, repairs of system damage, and incentives to customers or business partners in an effort to maintain relationships after an attack; [FN6]
• increased cybersecurity protection costs, which may include the costs of making organizational changes, deploying additional personnel and protection technologies, training employees, and engaging third party experts and consultants;
• lost revenues resulting from the unauthorized use of proprietary information or the failure to retain or attract customers following an attack;
• litigation and legal risks, including regulatory actions by state and federal governmental authorities and non-U.S. authorities;
• increased insurance premiums;
• reputational damage that adversely affects customer or investor confidence; and
• damage to the company's competitiveness, stock price, and long-term shareholder value.

Given the frequency, magnitude and cost of cybersecurity incidents, the Commission believes that it is critical that public companies take all required actions to inform investors about material cybersecurity risks and incidents in a timely fashion, including those companies that are subject to material cybersecurity risks but may not yet have been the target of a cyber-attack. Crucial to a public company's ability to make any required disclosure of cybersecurity risks and incidents in the appropriate timeframe are disclosure controls and procedures that provide an appropriate method of discerning the impact that such matters may have on the company and its business, financial condition, and results of operations, as well as a protocol to determine the potential materiality of such risks and incidents.[FN8] In addition, the Commission believes that the development of effective disclosure controls and procedures is best achieved when a company's directors, officers, and other persons responsible for developing and overseeing such controls and procedures are informed about the cybersecurity risks and incidents that the company has faced or is likely to face.

Additionally, directors, officers, and other corporate insiders must not trade a public company's securities while in possession of material nonpublic information, which may include knowledge regarding a significant cybersecurity incident experienced by the company. Public companies should have policies and procedures in place to (1) guard against directors, officers, and other corporate insiders taking advantage of the period between the company's discovery of a cybersecurity incident and public disclosure of the incident to trade on material nonpublic information about the incident, and (2) help ensure that the company makes timely disclosure of any related material nonpublic information.[FN9] In addition, we believe that companies are well served by considering the ramifications of directors, officers, and other corporate insiders trading in advance of disclosures regarding cyber incidents that prove to be material. We recognize that many companies have adopted preventative measures to address the appearance of improper trading and we encourage companies to consider such preventative measures in the context of a cyber event.

... C. Purpose of Release

In light of the increasing significance of cybersecurity incidents, the Commission believes it is necessary to provide further Commission guidance. This interpretive release outlines the Commission's views with respect to cybersecurity disclosure requirements under the federal securities laws as they apply to public operating companies. While the Commission continues to consider other means of promoting appropriate disclosure of cyber incidents, we are reinforcing and expanding upon the staff's 2011 guidance. In addition, we address two topics not developed in the staff's 2011 guidance, namely the importance of cybersecurity policies and procedures and the application of insider trading prohibitions in the cybersecurity context.

First, this release stresses the importance of maintaining comprehensive policies and procedures related to cybersecurity risks and incidents. Companies are required to establish and maintain appropriate and effective disclosure controls and procedures that enable them to make accurate and timely disclosures of material events, including those related to cybersecurity. Such robust disclosure controls and procedures assist companies in satisfying their disclosure obligations under the federal securities laws.

Second, we also remind companies and their directors, officers, and other corporate insiders of the applicable insider trading prohibitions under the general antifraud provisions of the federal securities laws and also of their obligation to refrain from making selective disclosures of material nonpublic information about cybersecurity risks or incidents.

The Commission, and the staff through its filing review process, continues to monitor cybersecurity disclosures carefully.

II. Commission Guidance

A. Overview of Rules Requiring Disclosure of Cybersecurity Issues

1. Disclosure Obligations Generally; Materiality

Companies should consider the materiality of cybersecurity risks and incidents when preparing the disclosure that is required in registration statements under the Securities Act of 1933 ("Securities Act") and the Securities Exchange Act of 1934 ("Exchange Act"), and periodic and current reports under the Exchange Act.[FN15] When a company is required to file a disclosure document with the Commission, the requisite form generally refers to the disclosure requirements of Regulation S-K and Regulation S-X. Although these disclosure requirements do not specifically refer to cybersecurity risks and incidents, a number of the requirements impose an obligation to disclose such risks and incidents depending on a company's particular circumstances. For example:

• Periodic Reports: Companies are required to file periodic reports to disclose specified information on a regular and ongoing basis. . . . Companies must provide timely and ongoing information in these periodic reports regarding material cybersecurity risks and incidents that trigger disclosure obligations.

• Securities Act and Exchange Act Obligations: Securities Act and Exchange Act registration statements must disclose all material facts required to be stated therein or necessary to make the statements therein not misleading. Companies should consider the adequacy of their cybersecurity-related disclosure, among other things, in the context of Sections 11, 12, and 17 of the Securities Act, as well as Section 10(b) and Rule 10b-5 of the Exchange Act.

• Current Reports: In order to maintain the accuracy and completeness of effective shelf registration statements with respect to the costs and other consequences of material cybersecurity incidents, companies can provide current reports on Form 8-K or Form 6-K. Companies also frequently provide current reports on Form 8-K or Form 6-K to report the occurrence and consequences of cybersecurity incidents. The Commission encourages companies to continue to use Form 8-K or Form 6-K to disclose material information promptly, including disclosure pertaining to cybersecurity matters. This practice reduces the risk of selective disclosure, as well as the risk that trading in their securities on the basis of material non-public information may occur.

In addition to the information expressly required by Commission regulation, a company is required to disclose "such further material information, if any, as may be necessary to make the required statements, in light of the circumstances under which they are made, not misleading." The Commission considers omitted information to be material if there is a substantial likelihood that a reasonable investor would consider the information important in making an investment decision or that disclosure of the omitted information would have been viewed by the reasonable investor as having significantly altered the total mix of information available.

In determining their disclosure obligations regarding cybersecurity risks and incidents, companies generally weigh, among other things, the potential materiality of any identified risk and, in the case of incidents, the importance of any compromised information and of the impact of the incident on the company's operations. The materiality of cybersecurity risks or incidents depends upon their nature, extent, and potential magnitude, particularly as they relate to any compromised information or the business and scope of company operations. The materiality of cybersecurity risks and incidents also depends on the range of harm that such incidents could cause. This includes harm to a company's reputation, financial performance, and customer and vendor relationships, as well as the possibility of litigation or regulatory investigations or actions, including regulatory actions by state and federal governmental authorities and non-U.S. authorities.

This guidance is not intended to suggest that a company should make detailed disclosures that could compromise its cybersecurity efforts—for example, by providing a "roadmap" for those who seek to penetrate a company's security protections. We do not expect companies to publicly disclose specific, technical information about their cybersecurity systems, the related networks and devices, or potential system vulnerabilities in such detail as would make such systems, networks, and devices more susceptible to a cybersecurity incident. Nevertheless, we expect companies to disclose cybersecurity risks and incidents that are material to investors, including the concomitant financial, legal, or reputational consequences. Where a company has become aware of a cybersecurity incident or risk that would be material to its investors, we would expect it to make appropriate disclosure timely and sufficiently prior to the offer and sale of securities and to take steps to prevent directors and officers (and other corporate insiders who were aware of these matters) from trading its securities until investors have been appropriately informed about the incident or risk.

Understanding that some material facts may be not available at the time of the initial disclosure, we recognize that a company may require time to discern the implications of a cybersecurity incident. We also recognize that it may be necessary to cooperate with law enforcement and that ongoing investigation of a cybersecurity incident may affect the scope of disclosure regarding the incident. However, an ongoing internal or external investigation—which often can be lengthy—would not on its own provide a basis for avoiding disclosures of a material cybersecurity incident.

. . . Companies should consider whether they need to revisit or refresh previous disclosure, including during the process of investigating a cybersecurity incident.

We expect companies to provide disclosure that is tailored to their particular cybersecurity risks and incidents. As the Commission has previously stated, we "emphasize a company-by-company approach [to disclosure] that allows relevant and material information to be disseminated to investors without boilerplate language or static requirements while preserving completeness and comparability of information across companies." Companies should avoid generic cybersecurity-related disclosure and provide specific information that is useful to investors.

2. Risk Factors

Item 503(c) of Regulation S-K and Item 3.D of Form 20-F require companies to disclose the most significant factors that make investments in the company's securities speculative or risky. Companies should disclose the risks associated with cybersecurity and cybersecurity incidents if these risks are among such factors, including risks that arise in connection with acquisitions.

It would be helpful for companies to consider the following issues, among others, in evaluating cybersecurity risk factor disclosure:
• The occurrence of prior cybersecurity incidents, including their severity and frequency;
• the probability of the occurrence and potential magnitude of cybersecurity incidents;
• the adequacy of preventative actions taken to reduce cybersecurity risks and the associated costs, including, if appropriate, discussing the limits of the company's ability to prevent or mitigate certain cybersecurity risks;
• the aspects of the company's business and operations that give rise to material cybersecurity risks and the potential costs and consequences of such risks, including industry-specific risks and third party supplier and service provider risks;
• the costs associated with maintaining cybersecurity protections, including, if applicable, insurance coverage relating to cybersecurity incidents or payments to service providers;
• the potential for reputational harm;
• existing or pending laws and regulations that may affect the requirements to which companies are subject relating to cybersecurity and the associated costs to companies; and
• litigation, regulatory investigation, and remediation costs associated with cybersecurity incidents.

In meeting their disclosure obligations, companies may need to disclose previous or ongoing cybersecurity incidents or other past events in order to place discussions of these risks in the appropriate context. For example, if a company previously experienced a material cybersecurity incident involving denial-of-service, it likely would not be sufficient for the company to disclose that there is a risk that a denial-of-service incident may occur. Instead, the company may need to discuss the occurrence of that cybersecurity incident and its consequences as part of a broader discussion of the types of potential cybersecurity incidents that pose particular risks to the company's business and operations. Past incidents involving suppliers, customers, competitors, and others may be relevant when crafting risk factor disclosure. In certain circumstances, this type of contextual disclosure may be necessary to effectively communicate cybersecurity risks to investors.

3. MD&A of Financial Condition and Results of Operations

Item 303 of Regulation S-K and Item 5 of Form 20-F require a company to discuss its financial condition, changes in financial condition, and results of operations. These items require a discussion of events, trends, or uncertainties that are reasonably likely to have a material effect on its results of operations, liquidity, or financial condition, or that would cause reported financial information not to be necessarily indicative of future operating results or financial condition and such other information that the company believes to be necessary to an understanding of its financial condition, changes in financial condition, and results of operations. In this context, the cost of ongoing cybersecurity efforts (including enhancements to existing efforts), the costs and other consequences of cybersecurity incidents, and the risks of potential cybersecurity incidents, among other matters, could inform a company's analysis. In addition, companies may consider the array of costs associated with cybersecurity issues, including, but not limited to, loss of intellectual property, the immediate costs of the incident, as well as the costs associated with implementing preventative measures, maintaining insurance, responding to litigation and regulatory investigations, preparing for and complying with proposed or current legislation, engaging in remediation efforts, addressing harm to reputation, and the loss of competitive advantage that may result. Finally, the Commission expects companies to consider the impact of such incidents on each of their reportable segments.

4. Description of Business

Item 101 of Regulation S-K and Item 4.B of Form 20-F require companies to discuss their products, services, relationships with customers and suppliers, and competitive conditions. If cybersecurity incidents or risks materially affect a company's products, services, relationships with customers or suppliers, or competitive conditions, the company must provide appropriate disclosure.

5. Legal Proceedings

Item 103 of Regulation S-K requires companies to disclose information relating to material pending legal proceedings to which they or their subsidiaries are a party. Companies should note that this requirement includes any such proceedings that relate to cybersecurity issues. For example, if a company experiences a cybersecurity incident involving the theft of customer information and the incident results in material litigation by customers against the company, the company should describe the litigation, including the name of the court in which the proceedings are pending, the date the proceedings are instituted, the principal parties thereto, a description of the factual basis alleged to underlie the litigation, and the relief sought.

6. Financial Statement Disclosures

Cybersecurity incidents and the risks that result therefrom may affect a company's financial statements. For example, cybersecurity incidents may result in:

• Expenses related to investigation, breach notification, remediation and litigation, including the costs of legal and other professional services;

• loss of revenue, providing customers with incentives or a loss of customer relationship assets value;

• claims related to warranties, breach of contract, product recall/replacement, indemnification of counterparties, and insurance premium increases; and

• diminished future cash flows, impairment of intellectual, intangible or other assets; recognition of liabilities; or increased financing costs.

The Commission expects that a company's financial reporting and control systems would be designed to provide reasonable assurance that information about the range and magnitude of the financial impacts of a cybersecurity incident would be incorporated into its financial statements on a timely basis as the information becomes available.

7. Board Risk Oversight

Item 407(h) of Regulation S-K and Item 7 of Schedule 14A require a company to disclose the extent of its board of directors' role in the risk oversight of the company, such as how the board administers its oversight function and the effect this has on the board's leadership structure. The Commission has previously said that "disclosure about the board's involvement in the oversight of the risk management process should provide important information to investors about how a company perceives the role of its board and the relationship between the board and senior management in managing the material risks facing the company." A company must include a description of how the board administers its risk oversight function. To the extent cybersecurity risks are material to a company's business, we believe this discussion should include the nature of the board's role in overseeing the management of that risk.

In addition, we believe disclosures regarding a company's cybersecurity risk management program and how the board of directors engages with management on cybersecurity issues allow investors to assess how a board of directors is discharging its risk oversight responsibility in this increasingly important area.

B. Policies and Procedures

1. Disclosure Controls and Procedures

Cybersecurity risk management policies and procedures are key elements of enterprise-wide risk management, including as it relates to compliance with the federal securities laws. We encourage companies to adopt comprehensive policies and procedures related to cybersecurity and to assess their compliance regularly, including the sufficiency of their disclosure controls and procedures as they relate to cybersecurity disclosure. Companies should assess whether they have sufficient disclosure controls and procedures in place to ensure that relevant information about cybersecurity risks and incidents is processed and reported to the appropriate personnel, including up the corporate ladder, to enable senior management to make disclosure decisions and certifications and to facilitate policies and procedures designed to prohibit directors, officers, and other corporate insiders from trading on the basis of material nonpublic information about cybersecurity risks and incidents.

Pursuant to Exchange Act Rules 13a-15 and 15d-15, companies must maintain disclosure controls and procedures, and management must evaluate their effectiveness. These rules define "disclosure controls and procedures" as those controls and other procedures designed to ensure that information required to be disclosed by the company in the reports that it files or submits under the Exchange Act is (1) "recorded, processed, summarized and reported, within the time periods specified in the Commission's rules and forms," and (2) "accumulated and communicated to the company's management . . . as appropriate to allow timely decisions regarding required disclosure."

A company's disclosure controls and procedures should not be limited to disclosure specifically required, but should also ensure timely collection and evaluation of information potentially subject to required disclosure, or relevant to an assessment of the need to disclose developments and risks that pertain to the company's businesses. Information also must be evaluated in the context of the disclosure requirement of Exchange Act Rule 12b-20. When designing and evaluating disclosure controls and procedures, companies should consider whether such controls and procedures will appropriately record, process, summarize, and report the information related to cybersecurity risks and incidents that is required to be disclosed in filings. Controls and procedures should enable companies to identify cybersecurity risks and incidents, assess and analyze their impact on a company's business, evaluate the significance associated with such risks and incidents, provide for open communications between technical experts and disclosure advisors, and make timely disclosures regarding such risks and incidents.

Exchange Act Rules 13a-14 and 15d-14 require a company's principal executive officer and principal financial officer to make certifications regarding the design and effectiveness of disclosure controls and procedures, and Item 307 of Regulation S-K and Item 15(a) of Exchange Act Form 20-F require companies to disclose conclusions on the effectiveness of disclosure controls and procedures. These certifications and disclosures should take into account the adequacy of controls and procedures for identifying cybersecurity risks and incidents and for assessing and analyzing their impact. In addition, to the extent cybersecurity risks or incidents pose a risk to a company's ability to record, process, summarize, and report information that is required to be disclosed in filings, management should consider whether there are deficiencies in disclosure controls and procedures that would render them ineffective.

2. Insider Trading

Companies and their directors, officers, and other corporate insiders should be mindful of complying with the laws related to insider trading in connection with information about cybersecurity risks and incidents, including vulnerabilities and breaches. It is illegal to trade a security "on the basis of material nonpublic information about that security or issuer, in breach of a duty of trust or confidence that is owed directly, indirectly, or derivatively, to the issuer of that security or the shareholders of that issuer, or to any other person who is the source of the material nonpublic information." As noted above, information about a company's cybersecurity risks and incidents may be material nonpublic information, and directors, officers, and other corporate insiders would violate the antifraud provisions if they trade the company's securities in breach of their duty of trust or confidence while in possession of that material nonpublic information.

Beyond the antifraud provisions of the federal securities laws, companies and their directors, officers, and other corporate insiders must comply with all other applicable insider trading related rules. Many exchanges require listed companies to adopt codes of conduct and policies that promote compliance with applicable laws, rules, and regulations, including those prohibiting insider trading. We encourage companies to consider how their codes of ethics and insider trading policies take into account and prevent trading on the basis of material nonpublic information related to cybersecurity risks and incidents. The Commission believes that it is important to have well designed policies and procedures to prevent trading on the basis of all types of material non-public information, including information relating to cybersecurity risks and incidents.

In addition, while companies are investigating and assessing significant cybersecurity incidents, and determining the underlying facts, ramifications and materiality of these incidents, they should consider whether and when it may be appropriate to implement restrictions on insider trading in their securities. Company insider trading policies and procedures that include prophylactic measures can protect against directors, officers, and other corporate insiders trading on the basis of material nonpublic information before public disclosure of the cybersecurity incident. As noted above, we believe that companies would be well served by considering how to avoid the appearance of improper trading during the period following an incident and prior to the dissemination of disclosure.

3. Regulation FD and Selective Disclosure

Companies also may have disclosure obligations under Regulation FD in connection with cybersecurity matters. Under Regulation FD, "when an issuer, or person acting on its behalf, discloses material nonpublic information to certain enumerated persons it must make public disclosure of that information." The Commission adopted Regulation FD owing to concerns about companies making selective disclosure of material nonpublic information to certain persons before making full disclosure of that same information to the general public.

In cases of selective disclosure of material nonpublic information related to cybersecurity, companies should ensure compliance with Regulation FD. Companies and persons acting on their behalf should not selectively disclose material, nonpublic information regarding cybersecurity risks and incidents to Regulation FD enumerated persons before disclosing that same information to the public. We expect companies to have policies and procedures to ensure that any disclosures of material nonpublic information related to cybersecurity risks and incidents are not made selectively, and that any Regulation FD required public disclosure is made simultaneously (in the case of an intentional disclosure as defined in the rule) or promptly (in the case of a non-intentional disclosure) and is otherwise compliant with the requirements of that regulation.

By the Commission.
Dated: February 21, 2018.
Brent J. Fields, Secretary."

Securities Exchange Commission, Commission Statement and Guidance on Public Company Cybersecurity Disclosures, 83 FR 8166-01, 2018 WL 1035366 (February 26, 2018).

Around March 9, 2022, the SEC issued proposed regulations titled, "Cybersecurity Risk Management, Strategy, Governance, and Incident Disclosure."[209] The regulations are not only directed at ensuring that cybersecurity incidents are disclosed as noted supra, but also to provide updates regarding prior incidents. Importantly, the regulations require the provision of information to investors concerning cybersecurity governance and risk management policies and strategy. The document states: "We are also proposing to require periodic disclosures about a registrant's policies and procedures to identify and manage cybersecurity risks, management's role in implementing cybersecurity policies and procedures, and the board of directors' cybersecurity expertise, if any, and its oversight of cybersecurity risk." The following is a description of some of the proposed regulations.

> The SEC proposes modifying Form 8-K reporting requirements:[210]
> Specifically, we propose to amend Form 8-K by adding new Item 1.05 that would require a registrant to disclose the following information about a material cybersecurity incident, to the extent the information is known at the time of the Form 8-K filing: • When the incident was discovered and whether it is ongoing; • A brief description of the nature and scope of the incident; • Whether any data was stolen, altered, accessed, or used for any other unauthorized purpose; • The effect of the incident on the registrant's operations; and • Whether the registrant has remediated or is currently remediating the incident.

The SEC further discuses materiality and provides examples of incidents that may quality as material:

> • An unauthorized incident that has compromised the confidentiality, integrity, or availability of an information asset (data, system, or network); or violated the registrant's security policies or procedures. Incidents may stem from the accidental exposure of data or from a deliberate attack to steal or alter data; • An unauthorized incident that caused degradation, interruption, loss of control, damage to, or loss of operational technology systems; • An incident in which an unauthorized party accessed, or a party exceeded authorized access, and altered, or has stolen sensitive business information, personally identifiable

---

[209] https://www.sec.gov/rules/proposed/2022/33-11038.pdf.

[210] A similar proposal is made for Form 6-K for FPIs. The SEC states: "We are also proposing to amend Form 20-F to require FPIs to disclose on an annual basis information regarding any previously undisclosed material cybersecurity incidents that have occurred during the reporting period, including a series of previously undisclosed individually immaterial cybersecurity incidents that has become material in the aggregate."

information, intellectual property, or information that has resulted, or may result, in a loss or liability for the registrant; • An incident in which a malicious actor has offered to sell or has threatened to publicly disclose sensitive company data; or • An incident in which a malicious actor has demanded payment to restore company data that was stolen or altered.

The SEC additionally proposed to Regulation S-K that investors are updated regarding information concerning previously disclosed cybersecurity incidents: "Proposed Item 106(d)(1) provides a means for investors to receive regular updates regarding the previously reported incident when and for so long as there are material changes, additions, or updates during a given reporting period." There is also a list of non-exclusive examples of update information: "Any material impact of the incident on the registrant's operations and financial condition; • Any potential material future impacts on the registrant's operations and financial condition; • Whether the registrant has remediated or is currently remediating the incident; and • Any changes in the registrant's policies and procedures as a result of the cybersecurity incident, and how the incident may have informed such changes." That proposed item also notes that prior immaterial incidents may become material in the aggregate and then must be disclosed. The following includes the proposed cybersecurity regulations concerning disclosure:

Proposed §229.106 (Item 106) Cybersecurity.

(a) Definitions. For purposes of this section:

Cybersecurity incident means an unauthorized occurrence on or conducted through a registrant's information systems that jeopardizes the confidentiality, integrity, or availability of a registrant's information systems or any information residing therein. Cybersecurity threat means any potential occurrence that may result in, an unauthorized effort to adversely affect the confidentiality, integrity or availability of a registrant's information systems or any information residing therein.

Information systems means information resources, owned or used by the registrant, including physical or virtual infrastructure controlled by such information resources, or components thereof, organized for the collection, processing, maintenance, use, sharing, dissemination, or disposition of the registrant's information to maintain or support the registrant's operations.

(b) Risk management and strategy.

Disclose in such detail as necessary to adequately describe the registrant's policies and procedures, if it has any, for the identification and management of risks from cybersecurity threats, including, but not limited to: operational risk (i.e., disruption of business operations); intellectual property theft; fraud; extortion; harm to employees or customers; violation of privacy laws and other litigation and legal risk; and reputational risk. Disclosure under this section should include, as applicable, a discussion of whether: (1) The registrant has a cybersecurity risk assessment program, and if so, provide a description of such program; (2) The registrant engages assessors, consultants, auditors, or other third parties in connection with any cybersecurity risk assessment program; (3) The registrant has policies and procedures to oversee and identify the cybersecurity risks associated with its use of any third-party service provider, including, but not limited to, those providers that have access to the registrant's customer and employee data. If so, the registrant shall describe these policies and procedures, including whether and how cybersecurity considerations affect the selection and oversight of these providers and contractual and other mechanisms the company uses to mitigate cybersecurity risks related to these providers; (4) The registrant undertakes activities to prevent, detect, and minimize effects of cybersecurity incidents, and if so, provide a description of the types of activities undertaken; (5) The registrant has business continuity, contingency, and recovery plans in the event of a cybersecurity incident; (6) Previous cybersecurity incidents informed changes in the registrant's governance, policies and procedures, or technologies; (7) Cybersecurity-related risks and previous cybersecurity-related incidents have affected or are reasonably likely to affect the registrant's strategy, business model, results of operations, or financial condition and if so, how; and (8) Cybersecurity risks are considered as part of the registrant's business strategy, financial planning, and capital allocation, and if so, how.

(c) Governance.

(1) Describe the board's oversight of cybersecurity risk, including the following as applicable: (i) Whether the entire board, specific board members, or a board committee is responsible for the oversight of cybersecurity risks; (ii) The processes by which the board is informed about cybersecurity risks, and the frequency of its discussions on this topic; and (iii) Whether and how the board or board committee considers cybersecurity risks as part of its business strategy, risk management, and financial oversight.

(2) Describe management's role in assessing and managing cybersecurity-related risks, as well as its role in implementing the registrant's cybersecurity policies, procedures, and strategies. The description should include, but not be limited to, the following information: (i) Whether certain management positions or committees are responsible for measuring and managing cybersecurity risk, specifically the prevention, mitigation, detection, and remediation of cybersecurity incidents, and the relevant expertise of such persons or members in such detail as necessary to fully describe the nature of the expertise; (ii) Whether the registrant has a designated chief information security officer, or someone in a comparable position, and if so, to whom that individual reports within the registrant's organizational chart, and the relevant expertise of any such persons in such detail as necessary to fully describe the nature of the expertise; (iii) The processes by which such persons or committees are informed about and monitor the prevention, mitigation, detection, and remediation of cybersecurity incidents; and (iv) Whether and how frequently such persons or committees report to the board of directors or a committee of the board of directors on cybersecurity risk.

Instructions to Item 106(c): 1. In the case of a foreign private issuer with a two-tier board of directors, for purposes of paragraph (c) of this section, the term board of directors means the supervisory or non-management board. In the case of a foreign private issuer meeting the requirements of §240.10A-3(c)(3) of this chapter, for purposes of paragraph (c) of this Item, the term board of directors means the issuer's board of auditors (or similar body) or statutory auditors, as applicable.

2. Relevant experience of management in Item 106(c)(2)(i) and (ii) may include, for example: prior work experience in cybersecurity; any relevant degrees or certifications; any knowledge, skills, or other background in cybersecurity.

(d) Updated incident disclosure.

(1) If the registrant has previously provided disclosure regarding one or more cybersecurity incidents pursuant to Item 1.05 of Form 8-K, the registrant must disclose any material changes, additions, or updates regarding such incident in the registrant's quarterly report filed with the Commission on Form 10-Q (17 CFR 249.308a) or annual report filed with the Commission on Form 10-K (17 CFR 249.310) for the period (the registrant's fourth fiscal quarter in the case of an annual report) in which the change, addition, or update occurred. The description should also include, as applicable, but not be limited to, the following information: (i) Any material effect of the incident on the registrant's operations and financial condition; (ii) Any potential material future impacts on the registrant's operations and financial condition; (iii) Whether the registrant has remediated or is currently remediating the incident; and (iv) Any changes in the registrant's policies and procedures as a result of the cybersecurity incident, and how the incident may have informed such changes.

(2) The registrant should provide the following disclosure to the extent known to management when a series of previously undisclosed individually immaterial cybersecurity incidents has become material in the aggregate: (i) A general description of when the incidents were discovered and whether they are ongoing; (ii) A brief description of the nature and scope of the incidents; (iii) Whether any data was stolen or altered in connection with the incidents; (iv) The effect of the incidents on the registrant's operations; and (v) Whether the registrant has remediated or is currently remediating the incidents. (e) Structured Data Requirement. Provide the information required by this Item in an Interactive Data File in accordance with Rule 405 of Regulation S-T and the EDGAR Filer Manual.

Proposed §229.407 (Item 407) Corporate Governance.

* * * (j) Cybersecurity expertise.

(1) If any member of the registrant's board of directors has expertise in cybersecurity, disclose the name(s) of any such director(s), and provide such detail as necessary to fully describe the nature of the expertise. In determining whether a director has expertise in cybersecurity, the registrant should consider, among other things: (i) Whether the director has prior work experience in cybersecurity, including, for example, prior experience as an information security officer, security policy analyst, security auditor, security architect or engineer, security operations or incident response manager, or business continuity planner; (ii) Whether the director has obtained a certification or degree in cybersecurity; and (iii) Whether the director has knowledge, skills, or other background in cybersecurity, including, for example, in the areas of security policy and governance, risk management, security assessment, control evaluation, security architecture and engineering, security operations, incident handling, or business continuity planning.

(2) Safe harbor. (i) A person who is determined to have expertise in cybersecurity will not be deemed an expert for any purpose, including, without limitation, for purposes of Section 11 of the Securities Act (15 U.S.C. 77k), as a result of being designated or identified as a director with expertise in cybersecurity pursuant to this Item 407(j). (ii) The designation or identification of a person as having expertise in cybersecurity pursuant to this Item 407(j) does not impose on such person any duties, obligations or liability that are greater than the duties, obligations and liability imposed on such person as a member of the board of directors in the absence of such designation or identification. (iii) The designation or identification of a person as having expertise in cybersecurity pursuant to this Item 407(j) does not affect the duties, obligations, or liability of any other member of the board of directors.

(3) Structured Data Requirement. Provide the information required by this Item in an Interactive Data File in accordance with Rule 405 of Regulation S-T and the EDGAR Filer Manual.

CHAPTER FIVE. HEALTH INSURANCE PORTABILITY AND ACCOUNTABILITY ACT

5.1 Introduction

HIPAA is the Health Insurance Portability and Accountability Act of 1996. Most Americans are familiar with the term HIPAA and would probably classify it as a privacy law that protects their medical data. The U.S. Department of Health and Human Services (HHS) provides a Security Rule for the protection of electronic health information. This chapter reviews the Security Rule, its enforcement and private litigation concerning HIPAA in the cybersecurity context.

5.2 The HIPAA Security Rule and Breach Notification Rules

The U.S. Department of Health and Human Services (HHS) has recognized both a Privacy Rule and a Security Rule. The privacy side of HIPAA has been well documented and analyzed in various texts, memorandums, and forums. In this chapter we will focus on the Security Rule. The text of the Security Rule is contained in 45 CFR Part 160 and Part 164.

> The *Security Standards for the Protection of Electronic Protected Health Information* (the Security Rule) establish a national set of security standards for protecting certain health information that is held or transferred in electronic form. The Security Rule operationalizes the protections contained in the Privacy Rule by addressing the technical and non-technical safeguards that organizations called "covered entities" must put in place to secure individuals' "electronic protected health information" (e-PHI). Within HHS, the Office for Civil Rights (OCR) has responsibility for enforcing the Privacy and Security Rules with voluntary compliance activities and civil money penalties.[211]

The Security Rule, published on February 20, 2003, has become more important and necessary as the medical profession has recognized the efficiencies of computerization and have moved from paper-based records to computerized medical programs.

Today, providers are using clinical applications such as computerized physician order entry (CPOE) systems, electronic health records (EHR), and radiology,

---

[211] *See Summary of the HIPAA Security Rule*, U.S. DEPARTMENT OF HEALTH & HUMAN SERVICES, https://www.hhs.gov/hipaa/for-professionals/security/laws-regulations/index.html (last reviewed July 26, 2013).

pharmacy, and laboratory systems. Health plans are providing access to claims and care management, as well as member self-service applications. While this means that the medical workforce can be more mobile and efficient (i.e., physicians can check patient records and test results from wherever they are), the rise in the adoption rate of these technologies increases the potential security risks.[212]

These systems also give the patient immediate access to test results as they are posted by the medical provider and permit the doctor and patient to communicate via the medical application. While these improvements give the patient access to valuable information, the assets and data also need to be protected.

A major goal of the Security Rule is to protect the privacy of individuals' health information while allowing covered entities to adopt new technologies to improve the quality and efficiency of patient care. Given that the health care marketplace is diverse, the Security Rule is designed to be flexible and scalable so a covered entity can implement policies, procedures, and technologies that are appropriate for the entity's particular size, organizational structure, and risks to consumers' e-PHI.[213]

The Security Rule, which applies to only certain entities, relies on administrative, technical, and physical security procedures to maintain the confidentiality, integrity, and availability of electronic Personal Health Information (e-PHI). The entities to which the Security Rule applies are:

health plans, health care clearinghouses, and to any health care provider who transmits health information in electronic form in connection with a transaction for which the Secretary of HHS has adopted standards under HIPAA (the "covered entities") and to their business associates.[214]

Health plans would include:
- Health insurance companies
- HMOs, or health maintenance organizations
- Employer-sponsored health plans
- Government programs that pay for health care, like Medicare, Medicaid, and military and veterans' health programs[215]

---

[212] *Id.*

[213] *Id.*

[214] *Id.*

[215] *Are You a Covered Entity?*, CENTERS FOR MEDICARE & MEDICAID SERVICES, https://www.cms.gov/Regulations-and-Guidance/Administrative-Simplification/HIPAA-ACA/AreYouaCoveredEntity (last modified Aug. 2, 2020).

Health care clearinghouses include "organizations that process nonstandard health information to conform to standards for data content or format, or vice versa, on behalf of other organizations."[216] Providers include entities that submit HIPAA transactions electronically such as:

- Doctors
- Clinics
- Psychologists
- Dentists
- Chiropractors
- Nursing homes
- Pharmacies[217]

Business Associates include:

- Third-party administrator that assists a health plan with claims processing
- Consultant that performs utilization reviews for a hospital
- Health care clearinghouse that translates a claim from a nonstandard format into a standard transaction on behalf of a health care provider, and forwards the processed transaction to a payer
- Independent medical transcriptionist that provides transcription services to a physician[218]

Health Information Technology for Economic and Clinical Health (HITECH)

Privacy and security protections for e-PHI were further expanded when in 2009 the U.S. Department of Health and Human Services (HHS) Office for Civil Rights (OCR) enacted HITECH as part of the American Recovery and Reinvestment Act of 2009.[219] On January 25, 2013, a final rule was announced by HHS that "implemented a number of provisions of the HITECH Act to strengthen the privacy and security protections for health information established under HIPAA."[220]

SECURITY RULE STANDARDS

---

[216] *Id.*

[217] *Id.*

[218] *Id.*

[219] *Omnibus HIPAA Rulemaking*, U.S. DEPARTMENT OF HEALTH & HUMAN SERVICES, https://www.hhs.gov/hipaa/for-professionals/privacy/laws-regulations/combined-regulation-text/omnibus-hipaa-rulemaking/index.html (last reviewed Sept. 13, 2019).

[220] *See Combined Regulation Text of All Rules*, U.S. DEPARTMENT OF HEALTH & HUMAN SERVICES, https://www.hhs.gov/hipaa/for-professionals/privacy/laws-regulations/combined-regulation-text/index.html?language=es (last reviewed May 17, 2017).

The security standards of the Security Rule contain the familiar administrative (45 CFR 164.308), physical (45 CFR 164.310), and technical (45 CFR 164.312) safeguards categories to ensure confidentiality, integrity, and availability (CIA) of e-PHI.[221]

---

[221] 45 C.F.R. §164.304 contains definitions for terms included in the Security Rule Standards section: "As used in this subpart, the following terms have the following meanings:

Access means the ability or the means necessary to read, write, modify, or communicate data/information or otherwise use any system resource. (This definition applies to "access" as used in this subpart, not as used in subparts D or E of this part.)

Administrative safeguards are administrative actions, and policies and procedures, to manage the selection, development, implementation, and maintenance of security measures to protect electronic protected health information and to manage the conduct of the covered entity's or business associate's workforce in relation to the protection of that information.

Authentication means the corroboration that a person is the one claimed.

Availability means the property that data or information is accessible and useable upon demand by an authorized person.

Confidentiality means the property that data or information is not made available or disclosed to unauthorized persons or processes.

Encryption means the use of an algorithmic process to transform data into a form in which there is a low probability of assigning meaning without use of a confidential process or key.

Facility means the physical premises and the interior and exterior of a building(s).

Information system means an interconnected set of information resources under the same direct management control that shares common functionality. A system normally includes hardware, software, information, data, applications, communications, and people.

Integrity means the property that data or information have not been altered or destroyed in an unauthorized manner.

Malicious software means software, for example, a virus, designed to damage or disrupt a system.

Password means confidential authentication information composed of a string of characters.

Physical safeguards are physical measures, policies, and procedures to protect a covered entity's or business associate's electronic information systems and related buildings and equipment, from natural and environmental hazards, and unauthorized intrusion.

Security or Security measures encompass all of the administrative, physical, and technical safeguards in an information system.

Security incident means the attempted or successful unauthorized access, use, disclosure, modification, or destruction of information or interference with system operations in an information system.

45 C.F.R. § 164.306 Security standards: General rules.

(a) *General requirements.* Covered entities and business associates must do the following:

(1) Ensure the confidentiality, integrity, and availability of all electronic protected health information the covered entity or business associate creates, receives, maintains, or transmits.

(2) Protect against any reasonably anticipated threats or hazards to the security or integrity of such information.

(3) Protect against any reasonably anticipated uses or disclosures of such information that are not permitted or required under subpart E of this part.

(4) Ensure compliance with this subpart by its workforce.

45 C.F.R. § 164.308 Administrative safeguards.

(a) A covered entity or business associate must, in accordance with § 164.306:

(1)(i) Standard: Security management process. Implement policies and procedures to prevent, detect, contain, and correct security violations.

(ii) Implementation specifications:

(A) Risk analysis (Required). Conduct an accurate and thorough assessment of the potential risks and vulnerabilities to the confidentiality, integrity, and availability of electronic protected health information held by the covered entity or business associate.

(B) Risk management (Required). Implement security measures sufficient to reduce risks and vulnerabilities to a reasonable and appropriate level to comply with § 164.306(a).

(C) Sanction policy (Required). Apply appropriate sanctions against workforce members who fail to comply with the security policies and procedures of the covered entity or business associate.

(D) Information system activity review (Required). Implement procedures to regularly review records of information system activity, such as audit logs, access reports, and security incident tracking reports.

Technical safeguards means the technology and the policy and procedures for its use that protect electronic protected health information and control access to it.

User means a person or entity with authorized access.

Workstation means an electronic computing device, for example, a laptop or desktop computer, or any other device that performs similar functions, and electronic media stored in its immediate environment." *Id.*

(2) Standard: Assigned security responsibility. Identify the security official who is responsible for the development and implementation of the policies and procedures required by this subpart for the covered entity or business associate.

(3)(i) Standard: Workforce security. Implement policies and procedures to ensure that all members of its workforce have appropriate access to electronic protected health information, as provided under paragraph (a)(4) of this section, and to prevent those workforce members who do not have access under paragraph (a)(4) of this section from obtaining access to electronic protected health information.

(ii) Implementation specifications:

(A) Authorization and/or supervision (Addressable). Implement procedures for the authorization and/or supervision of workforce members who work with electronic protected health information or in locations where it might be accessed.

(B) Workforce clearance procedure (Addressable). Implement procedures to determine that the access of a workforce member to electronic protected health information is appropriate.

(C) Termination procedures (Addressable). Implement procedures for terminating access to electronic protected health information when the employment of, or other arrangement with, a workforce member ends or as required by determinations made as specified in paragraph (a)(3)(ii)(B) of this section.

(4)(i) Standard: Information access management. Implement policies and procedures for authorizing access to electronic protected health information that are consistent with the applicable requirements of subpart E of this part.

(ii) Implementation specifications:

(A) Isolating health care clearinghouse functions (Required). If a health care clearinghouse is part of a larger organization, the clearinghouse must implement policies and procedures that protect the electronic protected health information of the clearinghouse from unauthorized access by the larger organization.

(B) Access authorization (Addressable). Implement policies and procedures for granting access to electronic protected health information, for example, through access to a workstation, transaction, program, process, or other mechanism.

(C) Access establishment and modification (Addressable). Implement policies and procedures that, based upon the covered entity's or the business associate's access authorization policies, establish, document, review, and modify a user's right of access to a workstation, transaction, program, or process.

(5)(i) Standard: Security awareness and training. Implement a security awareness and training program for all members of its workforce (including management).

(ii) Implementation specifications. Implement:

(A) Security reminders (Addressable). Periodic security updates.

(B) Protection from malicious software (Addressable). Procedures for guarding against, detecting, and reporting malicious software.

(C) Log-in monitoring (Addressable). Procedures for monitoring log-in attempts and reporting discrepancies.

(D) Password management (Addressable). Procedures for creating, changing, and safeguarding passwords.

(6)(i) Standard: Security incident procedures. Implement policies and procedures to address security incidents.

(ii) Implementation specification: Response and reporting (Required). Identify and respond to suspected or known security incidents; mitigate, to the extent practicable, harmful effects of security incidents that are known to the covered entity or business associate; and document security incidents and their outcomes.

(7)(i) Standard: Contingency plan. Establish (and implement as needed) policies and procedures for responding to an emergency or other occurrence (for example, fire, vandalism, system failure, and natural disaster) that damages systems that contain electronic protected health information.

(ii) Implementation specifications:

(A) Data backup plan (Required). Establish and implement procedures to create and maintain retrievable exact copies of electronic protected health information.

(B) Disaster recovery plan (Required). Establish (and implement as needed) procedures to restore any loss of data.

(C) Emergency mode operation plan (Required). Establish (and implement as needed) procedures to enable continuation of critical business processes for protection of the security of electronic protected health information while operating in emergency mode.

(D) Testing and revision procedures (Addressable). Implement procedures for periodic testing and revision of contingency plans.

(E) Applications and data criticality analysis (Addressable). Assess the relative criticality of specific applications and data in support of other contingency plan components.

(8) Standard: Evaluation. Perform a periodic technical and nontechnical evaluation, based initially upon the standards implemented under this rule and, subsequently, in response to environmental or operational changes affecting the security of electronic protected health information, that establishes the extent to which a covered entity's or business associate's security policies and procedures meet the requirements of this subpart.

(b)(1) Business associate contracts and other arrangements. A covered entity may permit a business associate to create, receive, maintain, or transmit electronic protected health information on the covered entity's behalf only if the covered entity obtains satisfactory assurances, in accordance with § 164.314(a), that the business associate will appropriately safeguard the information. A covered entity is not required to obtain such satisfactory assurances from a business associate that is a subcontractor.

(2) A business associate may permit a business associate that is a subcontractor to create, receive, maintain, or transmit electronic protected health information on its behalf only if the business associate obtains satisfactory assurances, in accordance with § 164.314(a), that the subcontractor will appropriately safeguard the information.

(3) Implementation specifications: Written contract or other arrangement (Required). Document the satisfactory assurances required by paragraph (b)(1) or (b)(2) of this section through a written contract or other arrangement with the business associate that meets the applicable requirements of § 164.314(a).

45 C.F.R. § 164.310 Physical safeguards.

A covered entity or business associate must, in accordance with § 164.306:

(a)(1) Standard: Facility access controls. Implement policies and procedures to limit physical access to its electronic information systems and the facility or facilities in which they are housed, while ensuring that properly authorized access is allowed.

(2) Implementation specifications:

(i) Contingency operations (Addressable). Establish (and implement as needed) procedures that allow facility access in support of restoration of lost data under the disaster recovery plan and emergency mode operations plan in the event of an emergency.

(ii) Facility security plan (Addressable). Implement policies and procedures to safeguard the facility and the equipment therein from unauthorized physical access, tampering, and theft.

(iii) Access control and validation procedures (Addressable). Implement procedures to control and validate a person's access to facilities based on their role or function, including visitor control, and control of access to software programs for testing and revision.

(iv) Maintenance records (Addressable). Implement policies and procedures to document repairs and modifications to the physical components of a facility which are related to security (for example, hardware, walls, doors, and locks).

(b) Standard: Workstation use. Implement policies and procedures that specify the proper functions to be performed, the manner in which those functions are to be performed, and the physical attributes of the surroundings of a specific workstation or class of workstation that can access electronic protected health information.

(c) Standard: Workstation security. Implement physical safeguards for all workstations that access electronic protected health information, to restrict access to authorized users.

(d)(1) Standard: Device and media controls. Implement policies and procedures that govern the receipt and removal of hardware and electronic media that contain electronic protected health information into and out of a facility, and the movement of these items within the facility.

(2) Implementation specifications:

(i) Disposal (Required). Implement policies and procedures to address the final disposition of electronic protected health information, and/or the hardware or electronic media on which it is stored.

(ii) Media re-use (Required). Implement procedures for removal of electronic protected health information from electronic media before the media are made available for re-use.

(iii) Accountability (Addressable). Maintain a record of the movements of hardware and electronic media and any person responsible therefore.

(iv) Data backup and storage (Addressable). Create a retrievable, exact copy of electronic protected health information, when needed, before movement of equipment.

45 C.F.R. § 164.312 Technical safeguards.

A covered entity or business associate must, in accordance with § 164.306:

(a)(1) Standard: Access control. Implement technical policies and procedures for electronic information systems that maintain electronic protected health information to allow access only to those persons or software programs that have been granted access rights as specified in § 164.308(a)(4).

(2) Implementation specifications:

(i) Unique user identification (Required). Assign a unique name and/or number for identifying and tracking user identity.

(ii) Emergency access procedure (Required). Establish (and implement as needed) procedures for obtaining necessary electronic protected health information during an emergency.

(iii) Automatic logoff (Addressable). Implement electronic procedures that terminate an electronic session after a predetermined time of inactivity.

(iv) Encryption and decryption (Addressable). Implement a mechanism to encrypt and decrypt electronic protected health information.

(b) Standard: Audit controls. Implement hardware, software, and/or procedural mechanisms that record and examine activity in information systems that contain or use electronic protected health information.

(c)(1) Standard: Integrity. Implement policies and procedures to protect electronic protected health information from improper alteration or destruction.

(2) Implementation specification: Mechanism to authenticate electronic protected health information (Addressable). Implement electronic mechanisms to corroborate that electronic protected health information has not been altered or destroyed in an unauthorized manner.

(d) Standard: Person or entity authentication. Implement procedures to verify that a person or entity seeking access to electronic protected health information is the one claimed.

(e)(1) Standard: Transmission security. Implement technical security measures to guard against unauthorized access to electronic protected health information that is being transmitted over an electronic communications network.

(2) Implementation specifications:

(i) Integrity controls (Addressable). Implement security measures to ensure that electronically transmitted electronic protected health information is not improperly modified without detection until disposed of.

(ii) Encryption (Addressable). Implement a mechanism to encrypt electronic protected health information whenever deemed appropriate.

QUESTION

Is it helpful to have the requirements broken out as administrative, technical, and physical?

The term implementation specification as used in the appendix, equates to "specific requirements or instruction for implementing a standard.[222] **Appendix A to Subpart C of Part 164 - Security Standards: Matrix[223]**

NOTES

Note 1

Some implementation specifications are "required" and "addressable." The Health and Human Services Agency has provided some additional information concerning the meaning of the two terms:

> What is the difference between addressable and required implementation specifications in the Security Rule?
>
> Answer:
> If an implementation specification is described as "required," the specification must be implemented. The concept of "addressable implementation specifications" was developed to provide covered entities additional flexibility with respect to compliance with the security standards. In meeting standards that contain addressable implementation specifications, a covered entity will do one of the following for each addressable specification: (a) implement the addressable implementation specifications; (b) implement one or more alternative security measures to accomplish the same purpose; (c) not implement either an addressable implementation specification or an alternative. The covered entity's choice must be documented. The covered entity must decide whether a given addressable implementation specification is a reasonable and appropriate security measure to apply within its particular security framework. For example, a covered entity must implement an addressable implementation specification if it is reasonable and appropriate to do so, and must implement an equivalent alternative if the addressable implementation specification is unreasonable and inappropriate, and there is a reasonable and appropriate alternative. This decision will depend on a variety of factors, such as, among others, the entity's risk analysis, risk mitigation strategy, what security measures are already in place, and the cost of implementation. The decisions that a covered entity makes regarding addressable specifications must be documented in writing. The written

---

[222] *See* 45 C.F.R. § 160.103.
[223] 45 C.F.R. Appendix A to Subpart C of Part 164—Security Standards: Matrix, *available at* https://www.law.cornell.edu/cfr/text/45/appendix-A_to_subpart_C_of_part_164.

documentation should include the factors considered as well as the results of the risk assessment on which the decision was based.[224]

Should a covered entity choose not to adopt an "addressable" security measure? Why or why not?

45 C.F.R. § 164.316 Policies and procedures and documentation requirements.

A covered entity or business associate must, in accordance with § 164.306:

(a) Standard: Policies and procedures. Implement reasonable and appropriate policies and procedures to comply with the standards, implementation specifications, or other requirements of this subpart, taking into account those factors specified in § 164.306(b)(2)(i), (ii), (iii), and (iv). This standard is not to be construed to permit or excuse an action that violates any other standard, implementation specification, or other requirements of this subpart. A covered entity or business associate may change its policies and procedures at any time, provided that the changes are documented and are implemented in accordance with this subpart.

(b)(1) Standard: Documentation.

(i) Maintain the policies and procedures implemented to comply with this subpart in written (which may be electronic) form; and

(ii) If an action, activity or assessment is required by this subpart to be documented, maintain a written (which may be electronic) record of the action, activity, or assessment.

(2) Implementation specifications:

(i) Time limit (Required). Retain the documentation required by paragraph (b)(1) of this section for 6 years from the date of its creation or the date when it last was in effect, whichever is later.

(ii) Availability (Required). Make documentation available to those persons responsible for implementing the procedures to which the documentation pertains.

(iii) Updates (Required). Review documentation periodically, and update as needed, in response to environmental or operational changes affecting the security of the electronic protected health information.

QUESTIONS

1) What does a six year retention of policies and procedures provide?

2) Even without a requirement to keep past policies and procedures, is it a good idea to do so?

---

[224] *What is the difference between addressable and required implementation specifications in the Security Rule?*, U.S. DEPARTMENT OF HEALTH & HUMAN SERVICES, https://www.hhs.gov/hipaa/for-professionals/faq/2020/what-is-the-difference-between-addressable-and-required-implementation-specifications/index.html (last reviewed July 26, 2013).

The HHS has also provided regulations concerning what safeguards a business partner must adhere to if processing electronic patient information.

45 C.F.R. § 164.314 Organizational requirements.

(a)(1) Standard: Business associate contracts or other arrangements. The contract or other arrangement required by § 164.308(b)(3) must meet the requirements of paragraph (a)(2)(i), (a)(2)(ii), or (a)(2)(iii) of this section, as applicable.

(2) Implementation specifications (Required).

(i) Business associate contracts. The contract must provide that the business associate will—

(A) Comply with the applicable requirements of this subpart;

(B) In accordance with § 164.308(b)(2), ensure that any subcontractors that create, receive, maintain, or transmit electronic protected health information on behalf of the business associate agree to comply with the applicable requirements of this subpart by entering into a contract or other arrangement that complies with this section; and

(C) Report to the covered entity any security incident of which it becomes aware, including breaches of unsecured protected health information as required by § 164.410.

(ii) Other arrangements. The covered entity is in compliance with paragraph (a)(1) of this section if it has another arrangement in place that meets the requirements of § 164.504(e)(3).

(iii) Business associate contracts with subcontractors. The requirements of paragraphs (a)(2)(i) and (a)(2)(ii) of this section apply to the contract or other arrangement between a business associate and a subcontractor required by § 164.308(b)(4) in the same manner as such requirements apply to contracts or other arrangements between a covered entity and business associate.

(b)(1) Standard: Requirements for group health plans. Except when the only electronic protected health information disclosed to a plan sponsor is disclosed pursuant to § 164.504(f)(1)(ii) or (iii), or as authorized under § 164.508, a group health plan must ensure that its plan documents provide that the plan sponsor will reasonably and appropriately safeguard electronic protected health information created, received, maintained, or transmitted to or by the plan sponsor on behalf of the group health plan.

(2) Implementation specifications (Required). The plan documents of the group health plan must be amended to incorporate provisions to require the plan sponsor to—

(i) Implement administrative, physical, and technical safeguards that reasonably and appropriately protect the confidentiality, integrity, and availability of the electronic protected health information that it creates, receives, maintains, or transmits on behalf of the group health plan;

(ii) Ensure that the adequate separation required by § 164.504(f)(2)(iii) is supported by reasonable and appropriate security measures;

(iii) Ensure that any agent to whom it provides this information agrees to implement reasonable and appropriate security measures to protect the information; and

(iv) Report to the group health plan any security incident of which it becomes aware.

The HHS has provided a document titled, "Summary of HIPAA Security Rule," on the operation of the Security Rule on the HHS website.

Summary of HIPAA Security Rule
General Rules
- The Security Rule requires covered entities to maintain reasonable and appropriate administrative, technical, and physical safeguards for protecting e-PHI.

Specifically, covered entities must:
1. Ensure the confidentiality, integrity, and availability of all e-PHI they create, receive, maintain or transmit;
2. Identify and protect against reasonably anticipated threats to the security or integrity of the information;
3. Protect against reasonably anticipated, impermissible uses or disclosures; and
4. Ensure compliance by their workforce.

The Security Rule defines "confidentiality" to mean that e-PHI is not available or disclosed to unauthorized persons. The Security Rule's confidentiality requirements support the Privacy Rule's prohibitions against improper uses and disclosures of PHI. The Security rule also promotes the two additional goals of maintaining the integrity and availability of e-PHI. Under the Security Rule, "integrity" means that e-PHI is not altered or destroyed in an unauthorized manner. "Availability" means that e-PHI is accessible and usable on demand by an authorized person.

HHS recognizes that covered entities range from the smallest provider to the largest, multi-state health plan. Therefore the Security Rule is flexible and scalable to allow covered entities to analyze their own needs and implement solutions appropriate for their specific environments. What is appropriate for a particular covered entity will depend on the nature of the covered entity's business, as well as the covered entity's size and resources.

Therefore, when a covered entity is deciding which security measures to use, the Rule does not dictate those measures but requires the covered entity to consider:
5. Its size, complexity, and capabilities,
6. Its technical, hardware, and software infrastructure,
7. The costs of security measures, and
8. The likelihood and possible impact of potential risks to e-PHI.

Covered entities must review and modify their security measures to continue protecting e-PHI in a changing environment.

Risk Analysis and Management

- The Administrative Safeguards provisions in the Security Rule require covered entities to perform risk analysis as part of their security management processes. The risk analysis and management provisions of the Security Rule are addressed separately here because, by helping to determine which security measures are reasonable and appropriate for a particular covered entity, risk analysis affects the implementation of all of the safeguards contained in the Security Rule.
- A risk analysis process includes, but is not limited to, the following activities:
    - Evaluate the likelihood and impact of potential risks to e-PHI;
    - Implement appropriate security measures to address the risks identified in the risk analysis;
    - Document the chosen security measures and, where required, the rationale for adopting those measures; and
    - Maintain continuous, reasonable, and appropriate security protections.

Risk analysis should be an ongoing process, in which a covered entity regularly reviews its records to track access to e-PHI and detect security incidents, periodically evaluates the effectiveness of security measures put in place, and regularly reevaluates potential risks to e-PHI.

Administrative Safeguards

- **Security Management Process.** As explained in the previous section, a covered entity must identify and analyze potential risks to e-PHI, and it must implement security measures that reduce risks and vulnerabilities to a reasonable and appropriate level.
- **Security Personnel.** A covered entity must designate a security official who is responsible for developing and implementing its security policies and procedures.
- **Information Access Management.** Consistent with the Privacy Rule standard limiting uses and disclosures of PHI to the "minimum necessary," the Security Rule requires a covered entity to implement policies and procedures for authorizing access to e-PHI only when such access is appropriate based on the user or recipient's role (role-based access).
- **Workforce Training and Management.** A covered entity must provide for appropriate authorization and supervision of workforce members who work with e-PHI. A covered entity must train all workforce members regarding its security policies and procedures, and must have and apply appropriate sanctions against workforce members who violate its policies and procedures.
- **Evaluation.** A covered entity must perform a periodic assessment of how well its security policies and procedures meet the requirements of the Security Rule.

Physical Safeguards

- **Facility Access and Control.** A covered entity must limit physical access to its facilities while ensuring that authorized access is allowed.
- **Workstation and Device Security.** A covered entity must implement policies and procedures to specify proper use of and access to workstations and electronic media. A covered entity also must have in place policies and procedures regarding the transfer, removal, disposal, and re-use of electronic media, to ensure appropriate protection of electronic protected health information (e-PHI).

Technical Safeguards

- **Access Control.** A covered entity must implement technical policies and procedures that allow only authorized persons to access electronic protected health information (e-PHI).
- **Audit Controls.** A covered entity must implement hardware, software, and/or procedural mechanisms to record and examine access and other activity in information systems that contain or use e-PHI.
- **Integrity Controls.** A covered entity must implement policies and procedures to ensure that e-PHI is not improperly altered or destroyed. Electronic measures must be put in place to confirm that e-PHI has not been improperly altered or destroyed.
- **Transmission Security.** A covered entity must implement technical security measures that guard against unauthorized access to e-PHI that is being transmitted over an electronic network.

Required and Addressable Implementation Specifications

- Covered entities are required to comply with every Security Rule "Standard." However, the Security Rule categorizes certain implementation specifications within those standards as "addressable," while others are "required." The "required" implementation specifications must be implemented. The "addressable" designation does not mean that an implementation specification is optional. However, it permits covered entities to determine whether the addressable implementation specification is reasonable and appropriate for that covered entity. If it is not, the Security Rule allows the covered entity to adopt an alternative measure that achieves the purpose of the standard, if the alternative measure is reasonable and appropriate.

Organizational Requirements

- **Covered Entity Responsibilities.** If a covered entity knows of an activity or practice of the business associate that constitutes a material breach or violation of the business associate's obligation, the covered entity must take reasonable steps to cure the breach or end the violation. Violations include the failure to implement safeguards that reasonably and appropriately protect e-PHI.
- **Business Associate Contracts.** HHS developed regulations relating to business associate obligations and business associate contracts under the HITECH Act of 2009.

Policies and Procedures and Documentation Requirements
- A covered entity must adopt reasonable and appropriate policies and procedures to comply with the provisions of the Security Rule. A covered entity must maintain, until six years after the later of the date of their creation or last effective date, written security policies and procedures and written records of required actions, activities or assessments.
- **Updates.** A covered entity must periodically review and update its documentation in response to environmental or organizational changes that affect the security of electronic protected health information (e-PHI).

State Law
- **Preemption.** In general, State laws that are contrary to the HIPAA regulations are preempted by the federal requirements, which means that the federal requirements will apply. "Contrary" means that it would be impossible for a covered entity to comply with both the State and federal requirements, or that the provision of State law is an obstacle to accomplishing the full purposes and objectives of the Administrative Simplification provisions of HIPAA.

Enforcement and Penalties for Noncompliance
- **Compliance.** The Security Rule establishes a set of national standards for confidentiality, integrity and availability of e-PHI. The Department of Health and Human Services (HHS), Office for Civil Rights (OCR) is responsible for administering and enforcing these standards, in concert with its enforcement of the Privacy Rule, and may conduct complaint investigations and compliance reviews.[225]

. . . .

QUESTION

Could state law preemption potentially cause issues with some of the new state data protection laws that don't narrowly and specifically cover e-PHI, but instead cover broader consumer personally identifiable information (PII)?

Breach Notification Rules
    HIPAA also requires breach notification to patients, the media and HHS. The following regulations concern breach notification.[226]

---

[225] *See Summary of HIPAA Security Rule*, U.S. DEPARTMENT OF HEALTH & HUMAN SERVICES, https://www.hhs.gov/hipaa/for-professionals/security/laws-regulations/index.html (last reviewed July 26, 2013).
[226] 45 C.F.R. § 164.402 contains definitions concerning the breach notification part:

"As used in this subpart, the following terms have the following meanings:

45 C.F.R. § 164.404 Notification to individuals.

(a) Standard—

(1) General rule. A covered entity shall, following the discovery of a breach of unsecured protected health information, notify each individual whose unsecured protected health information has been, or is reasonably believed by the covered entity to have been, accessed, acquired, used, or disclosed as a result of such breach.

(2) Breaches treated as discovered. For purposes of paragraph (a)(1) of this section, §§ 164.406(a), and 164.408(a), a breach shall be treated as discovered by a covered entity as of the first day on which such breach is known to the covered entity, or, by exercising reasonable diligence would have been known to the covered entity. A covered entity shall be deemed to have knowledge of a breach if such breach is known, or by exercising reasonable diligence would have been known, to any person, other than the person

---

Breach means the acquisition, access, use, or disclosure of protected health information in a manner not permitted under subpart E of this part which compromises the security or privacy of the protected health information.

(1) Breach excludes:

(i) Any unintentional acquisition, access, or use of protected health information by a workforce member or person acting under the authority of a covered entity or a business associate, if such acquisition, access, or use was made in good faith and within the scope of authority and does not result in further use or disclosure in a manner not permitted under subpart E of this part.

(ii) Any inadvertent disclosure by a person who is authorized to access protected health information at a covered entity or business associate to another person authorized to access protected health information at the same covered entity or business associate, or organized health care arrangement in which the covered entity participates, and the information received as a result of such disclosure is not further used or disclosed in a manner not permitted under subpart E of this part.

(iii) A disclosure of protected health information where a covered entity or business associate has a good faith belief that an unauthorized person to whom the disclosure was made would not reasonably have been able to retain such information.

(2) Except as provided in paragraph (1) of this definition, an acquisition, access, use, or disclosure of protected health information in a manner not permitted under subpart E is presumed to be a breach unless the covered entity or business associate, as applicable, demonstrates that there is a low probability that the protected health information has been compromised based on a risk assessment of at least the following factors:

(i) The nature and extent of the protected health information involved, including the types of identifiers and the likelihood of re-identification;

(ii) The unauthorized person who used the protected health information or to whom the disclosure was made;

(iii) Whether the protected health information was actually acquired or viewed; and

(iv) The extent to which the risk to the protected health information has been mitigated.

Unsecured protected health information means protected health information that is not rendered unusable, unreadable, or indecipherable to unauthorized persons through the use of a technology or methodology specified by the Secretary in the guidance issued under section 13402(h)(2) of Public Law 111–5." *Id.*

committing the breach, who is a workforce member or agent of the covered entity (determined in accordance with the federal common law of agency).

(b) Implementation specification: Timeliness of notification. Except as provided in § 164.412, a covered entity shall provide the notification required by paragraph (a) of this section without unreasonable delay and in no case later than 60 calendar days after discovery of a breach.

(c) Implementation specifications: Content of notification—

(1) Elements. The notification required by paragraph (a) of this section shall include, to the extent possible:

(A) A brief description of what happened, including the date of the breach and the date of the discovery of the breach, if known;

(B) A description of the types of unsecured protected health information that were involved in the breach (such as whether full name, social security number, date of birth, home address, account number, diagnosis, disability code, or other types of information were involved);

(C) Any steps individuals should take to protect themselves from potential harm resulting from the breach;

(D) A brief description of what the covered entity involved is doing to investigate the breach, to mitigate harm to individuals, and to protect against any further breaches; and

(E) Contact procedures for individuals to ask questions or learn additional information, which shall include a toll-free telephone number, an e-mail address, Web site, or postal address.

(2) Plain language requirement. The notification required by paragraph (a) of this section shall be written in plain language.

(d) Implementation specifications: Methods of individual notification. The notification required by paragraph (a) of this section shall be provided in the following form:

(1) Written notice.

(i) Written notification by first-class mail to the individual at the last known address of the individual or, if the individual agrees to electronic notice and such agreement has not been withdrawn, by electronic mail. The notification may be provided in one or more mailings as information is available.

(ii) If the covered entity knows the individual is deceased and has the address of the next of kin or personal representative of the individual (as specified under § 164.502(g)(4) of subpart E), written notification by first-class mail to either the next of kin or personal representative of the individual. The notification may be provided in one or more mailings as information is available.

(2) Substitute notice. In the case in which there is insufficient or out-of-date contact information that precludes written notification to the individual under paragraph (d)(1)(i) of this section, a substitute form of notice reasonably calculated to reach the individual shall be provided. Substitute notice need not be provided in the case in which there is insufficient or out-of-date contact information that precludes written notification to the next of kin or personal representative of the individual under paragraph (d)(1)(ii).

(i) In the case in which there is insufficient or out-of-date contact information for fewer than 10 individuals, then such substitute notice may be provided by an alternative form of written notice, telephone, or other means.

(ii) In the case in which there is insufficient or out-of-date contact information for 10 or more individuals, then such substitute notice shall:

(A) Be in the form of either a conspicuous posting for a period of 90 days on the home page of the Web site of the covered entity involved, or conspicuous notice in major print or broadcast media in geographic areas where the individuals affected by the breach likely reside; and

(B) Include a toll-free phone number that remains active for at least 90 days where an individual can learn whether the individual's unsecured protected health information may be included in the breach.

(3) Additional notice in urgent situations. In any case deemed by the covered entity to require urgency because of possible imminent misuse of unsecured protected health information, the covered entity may provide information to individuals by telephone or other means, as appropriate, in addition to notice provided under paragraph (d)(1) of this section.

45 C.F.R. § 164.406 Notification to the media.

(a) Standard. For a breach of unsecured protected health information involving more than 500 residents of a State or jurisdiction, a covered entity shall, following the discovery of the breach as provided in § 164.404(a)(2), notify prominent media outlets serving the State or jurisdiction.

(b) Implementation specification: Timeliness of notification. Except as provided in § 164.412, a covered entity shall provide the notification required by paragraph (a) of this section without unreasonable delay and in no case later than 60 calendar days after discovery of a breach.

(c) Implementation specifications: Content of notification. The notification required by paragraph (a) of this section shall meet the requirements of § 164.404(c).

45 C.F.R. § 164.408 Notification to the Secretary.

(a) Standard. A covered entity shall, following the discovery of a breach of unsecured protected health information as provided in § 164.404(a)(2), notify the Secretary.

(b) Implementation specifications: Breaches involving 500 or more individuals. For breaches of unsecured protected health information involving 500 or more individuals, a covered entity shall, except as provided in § 164.412, provide the notification required by paragraph (a) of this section contemporaneously with the notice required by § 164.404(a) and in the manner specified on the HHS Web site.

(c) Implementation specifications: Breaches involving less than 500 individuals. For breaches of unsecured protected health information involving less than 500 individuals, a covered entity shall maintain a log or other documentation of such breaches and, not later than 60 days after the end of each calendar year, provide the notification required by paragraph (a) of this section for breaches discovered during the preceding calendar year, in the manner specified on the HHS web site.

5.3 Office of Civil Rights Enforcement Actions Concerning HIPAA

The OCR is tasked with enforcing the Privacy and Security Rules. The OCR uses the following methods:

- investigation of complaints filed with the OCR;
- determining if covered entities are in compliance by conducting compliance interviews;
- education and outreach programs to encourage compliance.[227]

Cases closed by the OCR falls into five categories:

1) Resolved after intake and review without investigation;
2) Technical Assistance without investigation;
3) After investigation, no violation is determined;
4) After investigation, corrective action is obtained;
5) Other because OCR may have decided not to investigate based on:

    a) referral to DOJ for prosecution;

    b) case was part of a natural disaster;

    c) case was resolved by prosecution by state authorities;

    d) steps were taken to comply and OCR decides not to use resources to pursue.

As we have seen with other federal agencies that enforce cybersecurity, the accused normally has the choice to come to terms with the OCR accusations and enter into a resolution agreement. With such an agreement, "the covered entity or business associate agrees to perform certain obligations and make reports to HHS, generally for a period of three years. During the period, HHS monitors the covered entity's compliance with its obligations. A resolution agreement may include the payment of a resolution amount."[228]

The following is a list of matters that the OCR has brought enforcement matters and settled, in some cases. The list demonstrates an approximate number and a type of matters handled by the OCR.

---

[227] *Enforcement Process*, U.S. DEPARTMENT OF HEALTH & HUMAN SERVICES, https://www.hhs.gov/hipaa/for-professionals/compliance-enforcement/enforcement-process/index.html (last reviewed June 7, 2017).

[228] *See Resolution Agreements*, U.S. DEPARTMENT OF HEALTH & HUMAN SERVICES, https://www.hhs.gov/hipaa/for-professionals/compliance-enforcement/agreements/index.html (last reviewed Oct. 7, 2020).

- Health Care Provider Pays $100,000 Settlement to OCR for Failing to Implement HIPAA Security Rule Requirements - March 3, 2020
- Ambulance Company Pays $65,000 to Settle Allegations of Longstanding HIPAA Noncompliance - December 30, 2019
- OCR Settles Second Case in HIPAA Right of Access Initiative - December 12, 2019
- OCR Secures $2.175 Million HIPAA Settlement After Hospitals Failed to Properly Notify HHS of a Breach of Unsecured Protected Health Information - November 26, 2019
- OCR Imposes a $1.6 Million Civil Money Penalty against Texas Health and Human Services Commission for HIPAA Violations - November 7, 2019
- Failure to Encrypt Mobile Devices Leads to $3 Million HIPAA Settlement - November 5, 2019
- OCR Imposes a $2.15 Million Civil Money Penalty against Jackson Health System for HIPAA Violations - October 23, 2019
- Dental Practice Pays $10,000 to Settle Social Media Disclosures of Patients' Protected Health Information - October 2, 2019
- OCR Settles First Case in HIPAA Right of Access Initiative - September 9, 2019
- Indiana Medical Records Service Pays $100,000 to Settle HIPAA Breach - May 23, 2019
- Tennessee Diagnostic Medical Imaging Services Company Pays $3,000,000 to Settle Breach Exposing Over 300,000 Patients' Protected Health Information - May 6, 2019
- OCR Concludes 2018 with All-Time Record Year for HIPAA Enforcement - February7, 2019
- Cottage Health Settles Potential Violations of HIPAA Rules for $3 Million - February 7, 2019
- Colorado hospital failed to terminate former employee's access to electronic protected health information - December 11, 2018
- Florida contractor physicians' group shares protected health information with unknown vendor without a business associate agreement - December 4, 2018
- Allergy Practice pays $125,000 to settle doctor's disclosure of patient information to a reporter - November 26, 2018
- Anthem pays OCR $16 Million in record HIPAA settlement following largest health data breach in history – October 15, 2018
- Unauthorized Disclosure of Patients' Protected Health Information During ABC Documentary Filming Results in Multiple HIPAA Settlements Totaling $999,000 – September 20, 2018
- Judge rules in favor of OCR and requires a Texas cancer center to pay $4.3 million in penalties for HIPAA violations - June 18, 2018
- Consequences for HIPAA violations don't stop when a business closes - February 13, 2018

- Five breaches add up to millions in settlement costs for entity that failed to heed HIPAA's risk analysis and risk management rules - February 1, 2018
- Failure to protect the health records of millions of people costs entity millions of dollars - December 28, 2017
- Careless handling of HIV information jeopardizes patient's privacy, costs entity $387k - May 23, 2017
- Texas health system settles potential HIPAA violations for disclosing patient information - May 10, 2017
- $2.5 million settlement shows that not understanding HIPAA requirements creates risk - April 24, 2017
- No Business Associate Agreement? $31K Mistake - April 20, 2017
- Overlooking risks leads to breach, $400,000 settlement - April 12, 2017
- $5.5 million HIPAA settlement shines light on the importance of audit controls - February 16, 2017
- Lack of timely action risks security and costs money - February 1, 2017
- HIPAA settlement demonstrates importance of implementing safeguards for ePHI - January 18, 2017
- First HIPAA enforcement action for lack of timely breach notification settles for $475,000 - January 9, 2017
- UMass settles potential HIPAA violations following malware infection - November 22, 2016
- $2.14 million HIPAA settlement underscores importance of managing security risk - October 17, 2016
- HIPAA settlement illustrates the importance of reviewing and updating, as necessary, business associate agreements - September 23, 2016
- Advocate Health Care Settles Potential HIPAA Penalties for $5.55 Million - August 4, 2016
- Multiple alleged HIPAA violations result in $2.75 million settlement with the University of Mississippi Medical Center (UMMC) - July 21, 2016
- Widespread HIPAA vulnerabilities result in $2.7 million settlement with Oregon Health & Science University - July 18, 2016
- Business Associate's Failure to Safeguard Nursing Home Residents' PHI Leads to $650,000 HIPAA Settlement - June 29, 2016
- Unauthorized Filming for "NY Med" Results in $2.2 Million Settlement with New York Presbyterian Hospital - April 21, 2016
- $750,000 settlement highlights the need for HIPAA business associate agreements
- Improper disclosure of research participants' protected health information results in $3.9 million HIPAA settlement - March 17, 2016
- $1.55 million settlement underscores the importance of executing HIPAA business associate agreements - March 16, 2016
- Physical therapy provider settles violations that it impermissibly disclosed patient information- February 16, 2016

- Administrative Law Judge rules in favor of OCR enforcement, requiring Lincare, Inc. to pay $239,800 - February 3, 2016
- $750,000 HIPAA Settlement Underscores the Need for Organization Wide Risk Analysis - December 14, 2015
- Triple-S Management Corporation Settles HHS Charges by Agreeing to $3.5 Million HIPAA Settlement - November 30, 2015
- HIPAA Settlement Reinforces Lessons for Users of Medical Devices - November 24, 2015
- 750,000 HIPAA Settlement Emphasizes the Importance of Risk Analysis and Device and Media Control Policies - August 31, 2015
- HIPAA Settlement Highlights Importance of Safeguards When Using Internet Applications - June 10, 2015
- HIPAA Settlement Highlights the Continuing Importance of Secure Disposal of Paper Medical Records - April 22, 2015
- HIPAA Settlement Underscores the Vulnerability of Unpatched and Unsupported Software - December 2, 2014
- $800,000 HIPAA Settlement in Medical Records Dumping Case - June 23, 2014
- Data Breach Results in $4.8 Million HIPAA Settlements - May 7, 2014
- Concentra Settles HIPAA Case for $1,725,220 - April 22, 2014
- QCA Settles HIPAA Case for $250,000 - April 22, 2014
- County Government Settles Potential HIPAA Violations - March 7, 2014
- Resolution Agreement with Adult & Pediatric Dermatology, P.C. of Massachusetts - December 20, 2013
- HHS Settles with Health Plan in Photocopier Breach Case - August 14, 2013
- WellPoint Settles HIPAA Security Case for $1,700,000 - July 11, 2013
- Shasta Regional Medical Center Settles HIPAA Privacy Case for $275,000 - June 13, 2013
- Idaho State University Settles HIPAA Security Case for $400,000 - May 21, 2013
- HHS announces first HIPAA breach settlement involving less than 500 patients - December 31, 2012
- Massachusetts Provider Settles HIPAA Case for $1.5 Million - September 17, 2012
- Alaska DHSS Settles HIPAA Security Case for $1,700,000 - June 26, 2012
- HHS Settles Case with Phoenix Cardiac Surgery for Lack of HIPAA Safeguards - April 13, 2012
- HHS settles HIPAA case with BCBST for $1.5 million - March 13, 2012
- Resolution Agreement with the University of California at Los Angeles Health System - July 6, 2011
- Resolution Agreement with General Hospital Corp. & Massachusetts General Physicians Organization, Inc. - February 14, 2011
- Civil Money Penalty issued to Cignet Health of Prince George's County, MD - February 4, 2011

- Resolution Agreement with Management Services Organization Washington, Inc. - December 13, 2010
- Resolution Agreement with Rite Aid Corporation - July 27, 2010
- Resolution Agreement with CVS Pharmacy, Inc. - January 16, 2009
- Resolution Agreement with Providence Health & Services - July 16, 2008[229]

The Health and Human Services Office of Civil Rights submitted a document to Congress which includes a discussion of the responsibilities and duties of the OCR in enforcement:

Health and Human Services Office of Civil Rights, Report to Congress on HIPAA Privacy, Security, and Breach Notification Rule Compliance For Calendar Years 2015, 2016

Enforcement Process

OCR enforces the HIPAA Rules by investigating written complaints filed with OCR, either on paper, by e-mail, or through its complaint portal. OCR also conducts compliance reviews of circumstances brought to its attention, to determine if covered entities or business associates are in compliance with the Rules. In addition, OCR's compliance activities include conducting audits and providing education and outreach to foster compliance with the Rules' requirements, which are discussed later in the report. When necessary, OCR has authority to issue subpoenas to compel cooperation with an investigation.

Complaints

Under the law, OCR may take action only on complaints that meet the following conditions:

• The alleged violation must have taken place after compliance with the Rules was required. OCR cannot investigate complaints regarding actions that took place before compliance with the HIPAA Rules was required.

• The complaint must be filed against an entity that is required by law to comply with the HIPAA Rules (i.e., either a covered entity or a business associate).

• The complaint must describe an activity that, if determined to have occurred, would violate the HIPAA Rules.

• The complaint must be filed within 180 days of when the individual submitting the complaint knew or should have known about the act or omission that is the subject of the complaint. OCR may waive this time limit if it determines that the individual submitting the complaint shows good cause for not submitting the complaint within the 180 day time frame (e.g., circumstances that made submitting the complaint within 180 days impossible).

---

[229] *Resolution Agreements*, U.S. DEPARTMENT OF HEALTH & HUMAN SERVICES, https://www.hhs.gov/hipaa/for-professionals/compliance-enforcement/agreements/index.html (last reviewed Oct. 7, 2020).

OCR must first determine whether a complaint presents an eligible case for enforcement of the HIPAA Rules, as described above. In many cases, OCR lacks jurisdiction under the HIPAA Rules because the complaint alleges a violation prior to the compliance date of the applicable Rule, alleges a violation by an entity not covered by the HIPAA Rules, was untimely or withdrawn, describes an activity that did not violate the HIPAA Rules, or alleges an activity that OCR could not independently substantiate. In addition, in many cases, OCR provides technical assistance to the covered entity or business associate to resolve the case quickly without further investigation.

Compliance Reviews

OCR may open compliance reviews of covered entities and business associates based on an event or incident brought to the attention of OCR, such as through a breach report or based on patterns identified through a series of complaints.

Investigations

Once OCR initiates an investigation, OCR collects evidence, through interviews, witness statements, requests for data from the entity involved, information from site visits, or other available, relevant documents. Covered entities and business associates are required by law to cooperate with complaint investigations and compliance reviews. If a complaint or other event implicates the criminal provision of HIPAA (42 U.S.C. 1320d-6), OCR may refer the complaint to the Department of Justice (DOJ) for investigation. If DOJ declines to open a case referred by OCR for criminal investigation, OCR reviews the case for potential civil violations of the HIPAA Rules and may investigate the case.

In some cases, OCR may determine, based on the evidence, that the covered entity or business associate did not violate the requirements of the HIPAA Rules. In such cases, OCR sends a closure letter to the parties involved explaining the results of the investigation.

In other cases, OCR may determine, based on the evidence, that the covered entity or business associate was not in compliance with the requirements of the HIPAA Rules. In such cases, OCR will generally first attempt to resolve the case with the covered entity or business associate by obtaining voluntary compliance through corrective action, which may include a resolution agreement.

Where corrective action is sought, OCR obtains satisfactory documentation and other evidence from the covered entity or business associate that the covered entity or business associate undertook the required corrective action to resolve the allegations. In the vast majority of cases, a covered entity or business associate will, through voluntary cooperation and corrective action, be able to demonstrate satisfactory compliance with the HIPAA Rules.

Resolution Agreements

Where OCR finds indications of noncompliance due to willful neglect, or where the nature and scope of the noncompliance warrants additional enforcement action, OCR pursues a resolution agreement with a payment of a settlement amount and an obligation to complete a corrective action plan. In these cases, OCR notifies the covered entity or business associate that, while OCR is prepared to assess a CMP with regard to the alleged violations of the HIPAA Rules, OCR is willing to negotiate the terms of a resolution agreement and corrective action plan to resolve the indications of noncompliance. These settlement agreements have involved the payment of a monetary amount that is some fraction of the potential CMPs for which the covered entity or business associate would be liable in the case. Additionally, in most cases, the resolution agreement includes a corrective action plan that requires the covered entity or business associate to fix remaining compliance issues; in many cases, the corrective action plan requires the covered entity or business associate to undergo monitoring of its compliance with the HIPAA Rules for a specified period of time. While this type of resolution still constitutes informal action on the part of OCR, resolution agreements and corrective action plans are powerful enforcement tools for OCR.

Civil Money Penalties

OCR has the discretion to proceed directly to a CMP in an appropriate case, such as one involving particularly egregious circumstances. Further, if OCR and a covered entity or business associate are unable to reach a satisfactory agreement to resolve the matter informally, or if a covered entity or business associate breaches the terms of a resolution agreement, OCR may pursue formal enforcement. In such cases, OCR notifies the covered entity or business associate of a proposed determination of a violation of the HIPAA Rules for which OCR is imposing CMPs. If CMPs are imposed, the covered entity or business associate may request a hearing in which a Departmental administrative law judge decides if the penalties are supported by the evidence in the case.

From the 2003 compliance date of the HIPAA Privacy Rule through the end of calendar year 2017, out of all the cases OCR attempted to resolve informally through a resolution agreement, three cases have resulted in the imposition of a CMP.

Audits

Section 13411 of the HITECH Act requires HHS to perform periodic audits of covered entity and business associate compliance with the HIPAA Rules. These audits are reviews of covered entities and business associates that are initiated not because of any particular event or incident indicating possible noncompliance on the part of the covered entity or business associate, but rather based on application of a set of objective selection criteria. The objective of the audits is to: 1) assess an entity's effort to comply with the Rules, 2) ensure covered entities and business associates are adequately safeguarding PHI, and 3) ensure individuals are provided the rights afforded to them by the Rules.

Through the use of funds available under the HITECH Act, OCR engaged the services of a professional public accounting firm to conduct the pilot audit program in 2011-2012. As part of this pilot, OCR established a comprehensive audit protocol containing the HIPAA regulatory requirements to be assessed in the audits.

Throughout 2013, OCR analyzed the findings of the pilot audits to uncover trends, potential best practices, and vulnerabilities. In addition, OCR engaged PriceWaterhouse Coopers (PWC) to conduct an evaluation of the pilot audit program. The evaluation included surveys of audited entities, review of the protocols, and examination of the audit program structure and documentation. OCR received the final report from PWC in November 2013. . . .

NOTES

Note 1

The HHS website has a helpful flowchart demonstrating the HIPAA Privacy and Security Rule Complaint Process.[230]

Note 2

The National Institutes of Standards and Technology, U.S. Department of Commerce, has produced a document, titled "An Introductory Resource Guide for Implementing the Health Insurance Portability and Accountability Act (HIPAA) Security Rule." The NIST document provides detailed guidance for complying with the HIPAA Security Rule. For example, the document states:

4. Considerations when Applying the HIPAA Security Rule

In this section, security measures from NIST publications that are relevant to each section of the Security Rule are presented. Each standard is presented in a consistent tabular format. The following tables, organized by HIPAA Security Rule standard, are designed to initiate the thought process for implementing the requirements of the Security Rule. These tables highlight information a covered entity may wish to consider when implementing the Security Rule; they are not meant to be prescriptive. The tables may also not be considered all-inclusive of the information available in NIST publications.[231]

Health and Human Services and Metropolitan Health Community Health Services Matter

Health and Human Services released the following on its website describing the HHS and Metropolitan Health Community Health Services Matter:

---

[230] *Enforcement Process*, U.S. DEPARTMENT OF HEALTH & HUMAN SERVICES, https://www.hhs.gov/hipaa/for-professionals/compliance-enforcement/enforcement-process/index.html (last reviewed June 7, 2017).

[231] *See* NAT'L INST. OF STANDARDS AND TECH., AN INTRODUCTORY RESOURCE GUIDE FOR IMPLEMENTING THE HEALTH INSURANCE PORTABILITY AND ACCOUNTABILITY ACT (HIPAA) SECURITY RULE (2008), *available at* https://www.hhs.gov/sites/default/files/ocr/privacy/hipaa/administrative/securityrule/nist80066.pdf?language=es. The document continues setting forth each HIPAA Security Standard with guidance.

"Small Health Care Provider Fails to Implement Multiple HIPAA Security Rule Requirements

Metropolitan Community Health Services (Metro), doing business as Agape Health Services, has agreed to pay $25,000 to the Office for Civil Rights (OCR) at the U.S. Department of Health and Human Services (HHS) and to adopt a corrective action plan to settle potential violations of the Health Insurance Portability and Accountability Act (HIPAA) Security Rule. Metro is a Federally Qualified Health Center that provides a variety of discounted medical services to the underserved population in rural North Carolina and these facts were taken into account in reaching this agreement.

On June 9, 2011, Metro filed a breach report regarding the impermissible disclosure of protected health information to an unknown email account. The breach affected 1,263 patients. OCR's investigation revealed longstanding, systemic noncompliance with the HIPAA Security Rule. Specifically, Metro failed to conduct any risk analyses, failed to implement any HIPAA Security Rule policies and procedures, and neglected to provide workforce members with security awareness training until 2016.

"Health care providers owe it to their patients to comply with the HIPAA Rules. When informed of potential HIPAA violations, providers owe it to their patients to quickly address problem areas to safeguard individuals' health information," said Roger Severino, OCR Director."[232]

Resolution Agreement and Corrective Action Plan between Health and Human Services and Metropolitan Health Community Health Services (2020).[233]

RESOLUTION AGREEMENT
I. Recitals

1. Parties. The Parties to this Resolution Agreement (Agreement) are

A.　　　The United Suites Department of Health and Human Services, Office for Civil Rights ("HHS" or "OCR"), which enforces the Federal standards that govern the privacy of individually identifiable health information (45 C.F.R. Part 160 and Subparts A and E of Part 164, the "Privacy Rule"), the Federal standards that govern the security of electronic individually identifiable health information (45 C.F.R. Part 160 and Subparts A and C of Part 164, the "Security Rule"), and the Federal standards for notification in the case of breach of unsecured protected health information (45 C.F.R. Part 160 and Subparts A and D of 45 C.F.R. Part 164, the "Breach Notification Rule"). HHS has the

---

[232] *Small Health Care Provider Fails to Implement Multiple HIPAA Security Rule Requirements*, U.S. DEPARTMENT OF HEALTH & HUMAN SERVICES (July 23, 2020), https://www.hhs.gov/about/news/2020/07/23/small-health-care-provider-fails-to-implement-multiple-hipaa-security-rule-requirements.html.

[233] RESOLUTION AGREEMENT AND CORRECTIVE ACTION PLAN BETWEEN HEALTH AND HUMAN SERVICES AND METROPOLITAN HEALTH COMMUNITY HEALTH SERVICES, U.S. DEPARTMENT OF HEALTH & HUMAN SERVICES (2020), *available at* https://www.hhs.gov/sites/default/files/metro-signed-agreement.pdf.

authority to conduct compliance reviews and investigations of complaints alleging violations of the Privacy, Security, and Breach Notification Rules (the "HIPAA Rules") by covered entities and business associates, and covered entities and business associates must cooperate with I II-I compliance reviews and investigations. Sec 45 C.F.R. §§ 160.306(c), 160.308. and 160.310(b).

B.   Metropolitan Community Health Services, Inc. ("MCHS"), d/b/a Agape Health Services, which is a covered entity, as defined at 45 C.F.R. § 160.103, and therefore is required to comply with the HIPAA Rules. MCHS is a 501 (c)(3) (nonprofit) Federally Qualified Health Center ("FQHC"). Since 1999, MCHS provides a wide range of healthcare services including on-site pharmacy, dental, behavioral health, gynecology, as well as primary and pediatric care to individuals in North Carolina. It employs approximately 43 people and serves approximately 3,100 patients annually. HHS and MCHS shall together be referred to herein as the "Parties."

2. Factual Background and Covered Conduct.

On June 9, 2011, OCR received a Breach Report from MCHS. During its investigation, OCR learned that MCHS has widespread compliance issues. OCR conducted a compliance review of MCHS to determine its compliance status and found that MCHS is not in compliance with the HIPAA rules. Specifically, OCR's investigation revealed MCHS's noncompliance with the Security Rule.

OCR's investigation indicated that the following conduct occurred ("Covered Conduct"):

A.   MCHS failed to implement HIPAA Security Rule policies and procedures. See 45 C.F.R. §164.316.

B.   Until June 30, 2016, MCHS failed to provide its workforce with HIPPA Security Awareness and Training. See 45 C.F.R. §164.308(a)(5).

C.   MCHS failed to conduct an accurate and thorough assessment of the potential risks and vulnerabilities to the confidentiality, integrity, and availability ePHI held by it. See 45 C.F.R. § 164.308(a)(l)(ii)(A). . . .

5. . . . This Agreement is intended to resolve HHS Transaction Number 11 -129212 and any violations of the HIPAA Rules related to the Covered Conduct specified in Section I, Paragraph 2 of this Agreement. . . .

II. Terms and Conditions

1.   Payment. MCHS agrees to pay to HHS the amount of $25,000 ("Resolution Amount"). MCHS agrees to pay the Resolution Amount on or before April 10, 2020, pursuant to written instructions to be provided by HHS.

2.   Corrective Action Plan. MCHS has entered into and agrees to comply with the Corrective Action Plan ("CAP"), attached as Appendix A, which is incorporated into this Agreement by reference. If MCHS breaches the CAP, and fails to cure the breach as set forth in the CAP, then MCHS will be in breach of this Agreement and HHS will not be subject to the Release set forth in Section II, Paragraph 3 of this Agreement.

3.   Release by HHS. In consideration and conditioned upon HHS's performance of its obligations under this Agreement. HHS releases MCHS from any actions it may have against MCHS under the HIPAA Rules for the Covered Conduct identified in Section I, Paragraph 2. HHS does not release MCHS from, nor waive any rights, obligations, or causes of action other than those specifically referred to or in that paragraph. This release does not extend to actions that may be brought under section 1177 of the Social Security Act, 42 C.S.C. § 1320d-6.

. . .

Appendix A
CORRECTIVE ACTION PLAN
BETWEEN THE UNITED STATES DEPARTMENT OF HEALTH AND HUMAN SERVICES AND METROPOLITAN COMMUNITIY HEALTH SERVICES, INC.

I. Preamble
Metropolitan Community Health Services . . . ("MCHS") . . ., hereby enters into this Corrective Action Plan ("CAP") with the United States Department of Health and Human Services, Office for Civil Rights ("HHS" or "OCR"). Contemporaneously with this CAP, MCHS is entering into a Resolution Agreement ("Agreement") with HHS, and this CAP is incorporated by reference into the Agreement as Appendix A. MCHS enters into this CAP as consideration for the release set forth in Section II, Paragraph 3 of the Agreement.

. . .

V. Corrective Action Obligations

MCHS agrees to the following:

A.   Risk Analysis and Risk Management

1.   MCHS shall conduct and complete an accurate, thorough, enterprise-wide analysis of security risks and vulnerabilities that incorporates all electronic equipment, data systems, programs and applications controlled, administered, owned, or shared by MCHS or its affiliates that are owned, controlled or managed by MCHS that contain, store, transmit or receive MCHS ePHI. As part of this process, MCHS shall develop a complete inventory of all electronic equipment, data systems, off-site data storage

facilities, and applications that contain or score ePHI which will then be incorporated in its Risk

2.   Within 30 days of the Effective Date, MCHS shall submit to HHS the scope and methodology by which it proposes to conduct the Risk Analysis. HHS shall notify MCHS whether the proposed scope and methodology is or is not consistent with C.F.R. § 164.308 (a)(ii)(A).

3.   MCHS shall provide the Risk Analysis, consistent with paragraph V.B.I , to HHS within 120 days of HHS' approval of the scope and methodology described in paragraph V.B.2 for HHS' review.

4.   Upon submission by MCHS, HHS shall review and recommend changes to the aforementioned risk analysis. If HHS requires revisions to the Risk Analysis, HHS shall provide MCHS with a detailed, written explanation of such required revisions and with comments and recommendations in order for MCHS to be able to prepare a revised Risk Analysis. Upon receiving HHS' recommended changes, MCHS shall have thirty (30) calendar days to submit a revised risk analysis. This process will continue until HHS provides final approval of the risk analysis.

5.   Within sixty (60) calendar days of HHS's approval of the Risk Analysis, MCHS shall develop an organization-wide risk management plan to address and mitigate any security risks and vulnerabilities identified in its risk analysis. The plan shall include a process and timeline for implementation, evaluation, and revision. The plan shall be forwarded to HHS for its review.

6.   HHS shall review and recommend changes to the aforementioned risk management plan. Upon receiving HHS' recommended changes, MCHS shall have thirty (30) calendar days to submit a revised plan. This process will continue until HHS provides final approval of the plan. Upon HHS approval, MCHS shall begin implementation of the plan and distribute to workforce members involved with the implementation of the plan.

7.   MCHS shall annually conduct an accurate and thorough assessment of the potential risks and vulnerabilities to the confidentiality, integrity, and availability of e-PII held by MCHS affiliates that are owned, controlled, or managed by MCHS, and its engaged business associates, and document the security measures MCHS implemented or is implementing to sufficiently reduce the identified risks and vulnerabilities to a reasonable and appropriate level. Subsequent risk analyses and corresponding management plans shall be submitted for review by HHS in the same manner as described in this section until the conclusion of the CAP. Revisions to policies and procedures to this section shall be made pursuant to Section V.0.5 below.

B.   Policies & Procedures

1.	MCHS shall review and revise its written policies and procedures to comply with the Privacy, Security, and Breach notification Rules, pursuant to 45 C.F.R. 160 and Subparts A, C and F, of Para 164. MCHS's policies and procedures shall include, but not be limited to, the minimum content set forth in Paragraph V.E below.

Privacy Rule Provision:

1.	Uses and Disclosures of PHI - 45 CFR § 164.502(a)
2.	Minimum necessary - 45 CFR § 164.502(b)
3.	Disclosures to Business Associates- -15 C.F.R. § 16-l.502(c)(l)
4.	Training - 45 C.F.R. § 164.530(b)(1)
5.	Safeguards - 45 C.F.R. § 164.530(c)(1)
6.	Changes to Policies and Procedures - 45 C.F.R. § 164.530(i)(2)

Safeguard Provisions:

7.	Administrative Safeguards, including all required and addressable implementation specifications - 45 C.F.R. § 164.308(a) and (b).
8.	Physical Safeguards, including all required and addressable implementation specifications - 45 C.F.R. § 164.310.
9.	Technical Safeguards, including all required and addressable implementation specifications - 45 C.F.R. § 164.312.

Breach Notification Provisions:

10.	Notification to Individuals, including all required and addressable implementation specifications - 45 C.F.R. § 164.404.
11.	Notification to the Media, including all required and addressable implementation specifications - 45 C.F.R. § 164.406.
12.	Notification to the Secretary of HHS, including all required and addressable implementation specifications - 45 C.F.R. § 164.408.

2.	As necessary and appropriate, MCHS shall create or revise policies and procedures in response to any findings in its risk analysis or implement actions required by the corresponding risk management plan completed pursuant to Paragraph B above.

3.	MCHS shall provide such policies and procedures to HHS within ninety (90) days of receipt of HHS' approval of the risk management plan required by Paragraph V.B above. Upon receiving any recommended changes to such policies and procedures from HHS, MCHS shall have 30 days to revise such policies and procedures accordingly and provide the revised policies and procedures to HHS for review and approval. This process shall continue until HHS approves the policies and procedures.

C.   Adoption. Distribution. and Updating of Policies and Procedures

1.   Within thirty (30) calendar days of obtaining HHS' approval of the policies and procedures required by Section V.C of this CAP, MCHS shall finalize and officially adopt the policies and procedures in accordance with the applicable administrative procedures.

2.   MCHS shall distribute the approved policies and procedures to all MCHS' workforce members, including all workforce members of covered entities that are owned, controlled or managed by MCHS, as appropriate.

3.   MCHS shall distribute the approved policies and procedures to all new workforce members -within fourteen (14) days of when they become workforce members MCHS. The approved policies and procedures shall be provided to business associates and vendors at or before the time service commences.

4.   At the time of distribution of policies and procedures, MCHS shall document that workforce members and business associates have read, understand, and shall abide by such policies and procedures. MCHS will not provide access to PHI unless and until this documentation is obtained. This documentation shall be retained in compliance with Section VII of this CAP.

5.   MCHS shall review the approved policies and procedures routinely and shall promptly update the policies and procedures to reflect changes in operations at MCHS, federal law, HHS guidance, and/or any material compliance issues discovered by MCHS that warrant a change in the policies and procedures. MCHS shall assess, update, and revise, as necessary, the policies and procedures at least annually. MCHS shall provide such revised policies and procedures to HHS for review and approval. Within thirty (30) days of any approved revisions, MCHS shall distribute such revised policies and procedures to all workforce members. MCHS shall document that workforce members have read, understand, and shall abide by such policies and procedures. MCHS will not provide access to PHI unless and until this documentation is obtained.

D.   Training

1.   Within sixty (60) days of HHS' approval of the revised policies and procedures reviewed by this CAP, MCHS shall submit its proposed training materials to HHS for its review and approval.

2.   HHS will inform MCHS in writing as to whether HHS approves or disapproves of the proposed training materials. If HHS disapproves of them, HHS shall provide

MCHS with corrections and required revisions. Upon receiving notice of any required revisions to the training materials from HHS, MCHS shall have thirty (30) calendar days in which to revise the training materials and then submit the revised training materials to HHS for review and approval. This process shall continue until HHS approves the training materials.

3.   Within thirty (30) days of HHS' approval of the training materials, MCHS shall provide training to all workforce members, in accordance with MCHS's approved procedures. Any new workforce members that are hired during or after the initial training period described in this paragraph shall be trained within fourteen (14) days of when they become workforce members of MCHS and in all cases before being provided access to PHI.

4.   MCHS shall continue to perform routine retraining using the training materials HHS approved under this CAP to all workforce members for the duration of the Compliance Term of this CAP and as required by MCHS approved training procedures.

5.   Each workforce member who is required to receive training shall certify, in electronic or written form, that he or she received the training. The training certification shall specify the date on which the training was received. All training materials and certifications shall be retained in compliance with Section VII of this CAP.

6.   MCHS shall be responsible for ensuring workforce members comply with training requirements and complete all required training.

7.   MCHS shall review the training materials annually, and. where appropriate, update the training to reflect changes in Federal law or HHS guidance, any issues discovered during audits or reviews, and any other relevant developments.

VI. Reportable Events and Annual Reports

A.   Reportable Events

1.   During the Compliance Term, upon receiving information that a workforce member may have failed to comply with any provision of the revised policies and procedures required by this CAP, MCHS shall promptly investigate the mailer. If MCHS determines that a workforce member has violated the revised policies and procedures required by this CAP, MCHS shall notify HHS in writing within thirty (30) days. Such violations shall be known as "Reportable Events." The report to HHS shall include the following:

a.   A complete description of the event, including relevant facts, the person(s) involved, and the implicated provision(s) of MCHS's Privacy, Security, and Breach Notification policies and procedures; and

b.   A description of actions taken and any further steps MCHS plans to take to address the matter, to mitigate the harm, and to prevent it from recurring, including the application of appropriate sanctions against workforce members who failed to comply with Privacy, Security, and Breach Notification policies and procedures.

2.   If no Reportable Events occur during any one Reporting Period, as defined in this CAP, MCHS shall so inform HHS in its Annual Report for that Reporting Period.

B.   Annual Reports

1.   The one year period after HHS' last approval of the policies and procedures required by Section V, Paragraph C of this CAP, and each subsequent one-year period during the Compliance Term, as defined in Section ITT of this CAP, shall each be known as a "Reporting Period." MCHS shall submit to HHS a response with respect to the status of and findings regarding its compliance with this CAP for each Reporting Period ("Annual Report"). MCHS shall submit each Annual Report to HHS no later than thirty (30) days after the end of each corresponding Reporting Period. Each Annual Report shall include:

a.   An attestation signed by an officer of MCHS attesting that the policies and procedures required by Section V of this CAP: (a) have been adopted; (b) are being implemented; and (c) have been distributed to all workforce members, business associates, and vendors;

b.   An updated accounting of business associates as required by Section V.A.;

c.   A copy of all training materials used for the workforce training required by Section V, Paragraph E of this CAP, a description of the training, including a summary of the topics covered, who conducted the training, who participated in the training, and a schedule of when the training session(s) were held;

d.   An attestation signed by an officer of MCHS attesting that it is maintaining written or electronic certifications from all workforce members that are required to receive training that they received the requisite training pursuant to the requirements set forth in this CAP and pursuant to MCHS's approved training procedures;

e.   Evidence demonstrating that MCHS has implemented security measures to reduce risks and vulnerabilities identified in its most recent risk analysis, which may include an updated risk management plan;

f.   An attestation signed by an officer of MCHS listing all of its locations, the name under which each location is doing business, the corresponding mailing address, phone number and fax number for each location, and attesting that each location has complied with the obligations of this CAP;

g.   A summary of Reportable Events identified during the Reporting Period and the status of any corrective or preventative action(s) taken by MCHS relating to each Reportable Event; and

h.   An attestation signed by an officer of MCHS stating that he or she has reviewed the Annual Report, has made a reasonable inquiry regarding its content, and believes that, upon such inquiry, the information is accurate and truthful.

VII. Document Retention

MCHS shall maintain for inspection and copying, and shall provide to HHS upon request, all documents and records relating to compliance with this CAP for six (6) years from the Effective Date. . . .

B.   Notice of Breach and Intent to Impose Civil Monetary Penalty (CMP).
The Parties agree that a breach of this CAP by MCHS constitutes a breach of the Resolution Agreement. Upon a determination by HHS that MCHS has breached this CAP, HHS may notify MCHS of (a) MCHS's breach; and (b) HHS's intent to impose a civil money penalty)' (CMP) pursuant Lo 45 C.F.R. Part 160 for the Covered Conduct set forth in Section I, Paragraph 2 of the Agreement and any other conduct that constitutes a violation of the HIPPA. Privacy, Security, or Breach Notification Rules (this notification is hereinafter referred to as the "Notice of Breach and Intent to Impose CMP").

C.   Response.
MCHS shall have thirty (30) days from the date of receipt of the Notice of Breach and Intent to Impose CMPs from HHS to demonstrate to the satisfaction of HHS that

1.   MCHS is in compliance with the obligations of this CAP that HHS cited as the basis for the breach;

2.   The alleged breach has been cured; or

3.   The alleged breach cannot be cured within the 30 day period. but that MCHS (a) has begun to take action to cure the breach; (b) is pursuing such action with due diligence; and (c) has provided to HHS a reasonable timetable for curing the breach.

D.   Imposition of CMP.

If at the conclusion of the 30 day period, MCHS fails to respond under the requirements of Section VIII, Paragraph C to the satisfaction of HHS, HHS may proceed with the imposition of a CMP against MCHS pursuant to 45 C.F.R. Part 160 for the Covered Conduct set forth 1n Section I, Paragraph 2 of the Agreement and any other conduct that constitutes a violation of the HIPAA Rules. HHS shall notify MCHS in writing of its determination to proceed with the imposition of a CMP.

QUESTIONS

1) How does the CMP of $25,000 compare to the other actions the respondent must take?

2) What is more important: cybersecurity for PHI or providing health care to a possibility indigent population? How do the HIPAA security rules attempt to find a balance? How well do the rules find a balance between the provision of healthcare and the protection of sensitive health information? What about the danger of release of information concerning indigent peoples? Is the risk of identify theft high? Why or why not?

NOTES

Note 1

The HHS released a chart noting the, "Top Five Issues in Investigated Cases Closed with Corrective Action, by Calendar Year."[234]

Year	Issue 1	Issue 2	Issue 3	Issue 4	Issue 5
2019	Impermissible Uses & Disclosures	Safeguards	Access	Administrative Safeguards	Minimum Necessary
2018	Impermissible Uses & Disclosures	Safeguards	Administrative Safeguards	Access	Technical Safeguards
2017	Impermissible Uses & Disclosures	Safeguards	Administrative Safeguards	Access	Technical Safeguards
2016	Access	Impermissible Uses & Disclosures	Safeguards	Administrative Safeguards	Technical Safeguards

---

[234] *Top Five Issues in Investigated Cases Closed with Corrective Action, by Calendar Year*, U.S. DEPARTMENT OF HEALTH & HUMAN SERVICES, https://www.hhs.gov/hipaa/for-professionals/compliance-enforcement/data/top-five-issues-investigated-cases-closed-corrective-action-calendar-year/index.html (last reviewed Mar. 30, 2020).

Note 2

One of the largest breaches violating HIPAA requirements concerns Anthem. The HHS published a press release on its website concerning the data breach incident:

Anthem Pays OCR $16 Million in Record HIPAA Settlement Following Largest U.S. Health Data Breach in History

Anthem, Inc. has agreed to pay $16 million to the U.S. Department of Health and Human Services, Office for Civil Rights (OCR) and take substantial corrective action to settle potential violations of the Health Insurance Portability and Accountability Act (HIPAA) Privacy and Security Rules after a series of cyberattacks led to the largest U.S. health data breach in history and exposed the electronic protected health information of almost 79 million people. The $16 million settlement eclipses the previous high of $5.55 million paid to OCR in 2016.

Anthem is an independent licensee of the Blue Cross and Blue Shield Association operating throughout the United States and is one of the nation's largest health benefits companies, providing medical care coverage to one in eight Americans through its affiliated health plans. This breach affected electronic protected health information (ePHI) that Anthem, Inc. maintained for its affiliated health plans and any other covered entity health plans.

On March 13, 2015, Anthem filed a breach report with the HHS Office for Civil Rights detailing that, on January 29, 2015, they discovered cyber-attackers had gained access to their IT system via an undetected continuous and targeted cyberattack for the apparent purpose of extracting data, otherwise known as an advanced persistent threat attack. After filing their breach report, Anthem discovered cyber-attackers had infiltrated their system through spear phishing emails sent to an Anthem subsidiary after at least one employee responded to the malicious email and opened the door to further attacks. OCR's investigation revealed that between December 2, 2014 and January 27, 2015, the cyber-attackers stole the ePHI of almost 79 million individuals, including names, social security numbers, medical identification numbers, addresses, dates of birth, email addresses, and employment information.

"The largest health data breach in U.S. history fully merits the largest HIPAA settlement in history," said OCR Director Roger Severino. "Unfortunately, Anthem failed to implement appropriate measures for detecting hackers who had gained access to their system to harvest passwords and steal people's private information." Director Severino continued, "We know that large health care entities are attractive targets for hackers, which is why they are expected to have strong password policies and to monitor and respond to security incidents in a timely fashion or risk enforcement by OCR."

In addition to the impermissible disclosure of ePHI, OCR's investigation revealed that Anthem failed to conduct an enterprise-wide risk analysis, had insufficient procedures to regularly review information system activity, failed to identify and respond to suspected or known security incidents, and failed to implement adequate minimum access controls to prevent the cyber-attackers from accessing sensitive ePHI, beginning as early as February 18, 2014.

In addition to the $16 million settlement, Anthem will undertake a robust corrective action plan to comply with the HIPAA Rules.[235] . . .

Note 3

The following resolution agreements concern important issues that may be raised concerning violations of the Security Rule. The following discussion of resolution agreements concerns covered business associates, due diligence, failing to encrypt laptops and the coverage of municipalities.

Covered business associates are also subject to the security rule. "CHSPSC LLC ("CHSPSC") is a business associate as defined at 45 C.F.R. §160.103" [and] "provides services to hospitals and clinics indirectly owned by Community Health Systems, Inc. ("CHS Affiliates"), including legal, compliance, accounting, operations, human resources, information technology (IT) and health information management services."[236] CHSPSC was subject to a cyberattack resulting in compromised electronic personal health information of millions of individuals served by CHS Affiliates:

On April 10, 2014, an Advanced Persistent Threat group, known as APT18, compromised administrative credentials and remotely accessed CHSPSC's information system through its virtual private network (VPN). CHSPSC was unaware of the intrusion until notified by the Federal Bureau of Investigation (FBI) on April 18, 2014. The last identified evidence of attacker activity occurred on August 18, 2014. It was determined that APT18's intrusion affected 237 covered entities served by CHSPSC and

---

[235] *See Anthem Pays OCR $16 Million in Record HIPAA Settlement Following Largest U.S. Health Data Breach in History*, U.S. DEPARTMENT OF HEALTH & HUMAN SERVICES (Oct. 15, 2018), https://www.hhs.gov/about/news/2018/10/15/anthem-pays-ocr-16-million-record-hipaa-settlement-following-largest-health-data-breach-history.html.

[236] Resolution Agreement and Corrective Action Plan between Health and Human Services and CHSPSC, U.S. Department of Health & Human Services (2021), *available at* https://www.hhs.gov/sites/default/files/chspsc-ra-cap.pdf. Twenty-eight state attorney generals also brought a multi-state action against CHSPSC resulting in a $5 million fine for the failure to adopt reasonable security measures. *See* HIPAA Journal, *HIPAA Enforcement by State Attorney Generals*, (Jan. 21, 2021), available at https://www.hipaajournal.com/hipaa-enforcement-by-state-attorneys-general/.

that APT18 exfiltrated the PHI of 6,121,158 individuals, including name, sex, date of birth, phone number, social security number, email, ethnicity, and emergency contact information.[237]

The potential violations included:

> A. The requirement to prevent unauthorized access to the ePHI of 6,121,158 individuals whose information was maintained in CHSPSC's network. . . . B. From April 18, 2014 to June 18, 2014, the requirement to respond to a known security incident; mitigate, to the extent practicable, harmful effects of the security incident; and document the security incident and its outcome. . . . C. The requirement to implement technical policies and procedures to allow access only to those persons or software programs that have been granted access rights to information systems maintained by CHSPSC. . . . D. The requirement to implement procedures to regularly review records of information system activity, such as audit logs, access reports, and security incident tracking reports. . . . E. The requirement to conduct accurate and thorough assessments of the potential risks and vulnerabilities to the confidentiality, integrity, and availability of ePHI held by CHSPSC.[238]

CHSPSC paid $2,300,000 and entered a Corrective Action Plan.[239]

Cybersecurity due diligence has become a very important issue with regard to acquisitions and mergers with other companies. HHS has uncovered failures to comply with the security rule with acquired companies. The HHS entered into a resolution agreement on April 21, 2021, involving Peachstate Health Management, Inc. d/b/a AEON Clinical Laboratories (Peachstate).[240] Peachstate is a covered entity and "provides, among other things, clinical and genetic testing services mainly through its publicly-traded parent company, AEON Global Health Corporation (AGHC)."[241] The HHS OCR began a compliance investigation and review into Peachstate's privacy and security practices after a data breach involving a parent company who acquired Peachstate.[242] Peachstate engaged in numerous potential violations related to the security rule:

---

[237] *Id.*

[238] *Id.*

[239] *Id.*

[240] Resolution Agreement and Corrective Action Plan between Health and Human Services and Peachstate Health Management, U.S. Department of Health & Human Services (2021), *available at* https://www.hhs.gov/sites/default/files/peachstate-ra-cap.pdf.

[241] *Id.*

[242] *Id.*

A. Peachstate failed to conduct an accurate and thorough assessment of the potential risks and vulnerabilities to the confidentiality, integrity, and availability of electronic PHI held by Peachstate. . . . B. Peachstate failed to implement security measures sufficient to reduce risks and vulnerabilities to a reasonable and appropriate level identified in its risk analysis or assessment. . . . C. Peachstate failed to implement hardware, software, and/or procedural mechanisms that record and examine activity in information systems that contain or use electronic PHI. . . . D. Peachstate failed to maintain policies and procedures to comply with Subpart C in written (which may be electronic) form and to maintain written (which may be electronic) record of any action, activity, or assessment required by Subpart C or these policies and procedures.[243]

Peachstate agreed to pay $25,000 and entered a Corrective Action Plan.[244]

Unsecured and unencrypted data on employee laptops can violate the security rule. In June of 2020, HHS also entered into a resolution agreement with Lifespan ACE ("Lifespan"), a non-profit health system that includes "three academic teaching hospitals: Rhode Island Hospital and its Hasbro Children's Hospital; The Miriam Hospital; and Bradley Hospital[,] . . . [and] Newport Hospital and Gateway Healthcare."[245] This matter involved the theft of a Lifespan employee's laptop.[246] The laptop contained cached emails on the hard drive, including "patient names, medical record numbers, demographic information, including partial address information, and the name of one or more medications that were prescribed or administered to patients."[247] The following potential violations related to the security rule:

A. Lifespan did not implement policies and procedures to encrypt all devices used for work purposes . . . ; B. Lifespan did not implement policies and procedures to track or inventory all devices that access the network or which contain ePHI . . . ; C. Lifespan did not have the proper business associate agreements in place between Lifespan Corporation and the Lifespan healthcare provider affiliates that are members of the Lifespan ACE . . .; and D. Lifespan impermissibly disclosed the PHI of 20,431 individuals . . ..[248]

---

[243] *Id.*

[244] *Id.*

[245] Resolution Agreement and Corrective Action Plan between Health and Human Services and Lifespan ACE, U.S. Department of Health & Human Services (2020), *available at* https://www.hhs.gov/sites/default/files/lifespan-ra-cap-signed.pdf.

[246] *Id.*

[247] *Id.*

[248] *Id.*

Lifespan paid $1,040,000 and agreed to a Corrective Action Plan.[249]

In another matter exemplifying the need to move quickly to effectively address a known continuously exploited vulnerability, Athens Orthopedics ("AOC") entered a resolution agreement with HHS.[250] The resolution agreement states:

> On June 26, 2016, a journalist from "www.databreaches.net" notified AOC that "a database of patient records" suspected to belong to AOC was posted online for sale. On June 28, 2016, a hacker group known as "The Dark Overlord" contacted AOC by email and demanded money in return for a complete copy of the database it stole without sale or further disclosure. It was determined, through computer forensic analysis, that the Dark Overlord had obtained a vendor's credentials to AOC's system and used them to gain access on June 14, 2016. While AOC terminated the compromised credentials on June 27, 2016, the Dark Overlord's continued intrusion was not effectively blocked until July 16, 2016. It was determined that 208,557 individuals were affected by this breach. Due to the breadth of system applications affected, a variety of protected health information (PHI) was exposed including patient demographic information (name, date of birth, social security number, etc.), clinical information (reason for visit, "social history," medications, test results, medical procedures, etc.), and financial/billing information (health insurance information, payment history).[251]

The OCR found numerous potential violations:

> A. The requirement to prevent unauthorized access to the ePHI of 208,557 individuals whose information was maintained in AOC's information systems. (See 45 C.F.R. §164.502(a)). B. Until August 2016, the requirement to maintain copies of AOC's HIPAA policies and procedures. See 45 C.F.R. § 164.530(i) and (j). C. From September 30, 2015 to December 15, 2016, the requirement to implement sufficient hardware, software, and/or procedural mechanisms that record and examine activity in information systems that contain or use ePHI. See 45 C.F.R. §§ 164.312(b). D. Until August 7, 2017, the requirement to enter into business associate agreements with three of its business associates, Quest Records LLC, Total Technology Solutions, and SRS Software LLC. See 45 C.F.R. § 164.308(b)(3). E. Until January 15, 2018, the requirement to provide its entire workforce with HIPAA training. See 45 C.F.R. §

---

[249] *Id.*

[250] Resolution Agreement and Corrective Action Plan between Health and Human Services and Athens Orthopedics, U.S. Department of Health & Human Services (2020), *available at* https://www.hhs.gov/sites/default/files/athens-orthopedic-ra-cap.pdf.

[251] *Id.*

164.530(b). F. The requirement to conduct an accurate and thorough assessment of the potential risks and vulnerabilities to the confidentiality, integrity, and availability of ePHI held by AOC. See 45 C.F.R. § 164.308(a)(1)(ii)(A). G. The requirement to implement security measures sufficient to reduce risks and vulnerabilities to a reasonable and appropriate level. See 45 C.F.R. § 164.308(a)(1)(ii)(B).[252]

AOC paid $100,000 and entered a Corrective Action Plan.[253]

Importantly, municipalities are covered by HIPAA's security rule under certain circumstances. The HHS entered into a resolution agreement with The City of New Haven, a covered entity.[254] The City of New Haven "provide[d] health care services in its public health clinic, including diagnoses and treatment for sexually transmitted diseases (STDs), tuberculosis testing, and adult and pediatric immunizations."[255] Additionally, patient "insurance is electronically billed" and The City of New Haven "therefore transmits health information in connection with covered transactions."[256] In response to a breach notification by the City of New Haven, the OCR began a compliance investigation.[257] OCR discovered that a terminated employee was able to access her office with a work key and was able to "log[] into her old computer, with her user name and password, and downloaded information off of her computer onto a USB drive."[258] Moreover, "[t]he former employee removed boxes containing personal items and paper documents.[259] The OCR identified the following potential violations related to the security rule:

A. The City impermissibly disclosed the PHI of 498 individuals . . .; B. During the period of December 1, 2014 to December 31, 2018, The City failed to implement Privacy Rule policies and procedures . . .; C. The City failed to conduct an accurate and thorough assessment of the potential risks and vulnerabilities to the confidentiality, integrity, and availability of electronic protected health information (ePHI) held by NHHD . . .; D. During the period of December 1, 2014 to December 31, 2018, The City failed to implement procedures for terminating access to ePHI when the employment of, or other arrangement with, a workforce member ends . . .; E. During the period of December 1, 2014 to December 31, 2018, The

---

[252] *Id.*
[253] *Id.*
[254] Resolution Agreement and Corrective Action Plan between Health and Human Services and City of New Haven, U.S. Department of Health & Human Services (2021), *available at* *https://www.hhs.gov/sites/default/files/new-haven-resolution-agreement-corrective-action-plan.pdf.*
[255] *Id.*
[256] *Id.*
[257] *Id.*
[258] *Id.*
[259] *Id.*

City failed to assign a unique name and/or number for identifying and tracking user identity. . ..[260]

The City of New Haven paid $202,400 and entered a Corrective Action Plan.[261]

Note 4

Advanced Persistent Threats and Zero Day Vulnerabilities

The Health and Human Services, Office of Civil Rights, released a Spring 2019 OCR Cybersecurity Newsletter addressing advanced persistent threats and zero day vulnerabilities.

Advanced Persistent Threats and Zero Day Vulnerabilities

An advanced persistent threat (APT) is a long-term cybersecurity attack that continuously attempts to find and exploit vulnerabilities in a target's information systems to steal information or disrupt the target's operations. Although individual APT attacks need not be technologically sophisticated, the persistent nature of the attack, as well as the attacker's ability to change tactics to avoid detection, make APTs a formidable threat.

APTs are a serious threat to any information technology (IT) system, but especially those that are part of the health care field. Healthcare services are part of a multibillion dollar industry that utilizes data to develop new drugs and treatments. Medical research information, experimental treatment testing results, and even genetic data are valuable targets for theft because of their value in driving innovation. Further, health information is used by healthcare providers and insurers to provide and pay for healthcare services for individuals.   If compromised, health information can be used for identify theft that could lead to financial fraud including theft of health insurance coverage benefits.   Also, because an individual's health information can contain details concerning the most private and personal aspects of one's life, the compromise of one's health information could also lead to an ability to blackmail an individual based on their sensitive health information. Any security incident impacting the confidentiality, integrity, or availability

---

[260] *Id.*
[261] *Id.*

of protected health information (PHI), can directly affect the health and safety of citizens. APTs have already been implicated in several cyberattacks on the healthcare sector in the U.S. and around the world.

Zero Day Exploits

One of the most dangerous tools in a hacker's arsenal is the "zero day" exploit or attack which takes advantage of a previously unknown hardware, firmware, or software vulnerability. Hackers may discover zero day exploits by their own research or probing or may take advantage of the lag between when an exploit is discovered and when a relevant patch or anti-virus update is made available to the public.

These exploits are especially dangerous because their novel nature makes them more difficult to detect and contain than standard hacking attacks. The possibility of such an attack emphasizes the importance of an organization's overall security management process which includes monitoring of anti-virus or cybersecurity software for detection of suspicious files or activity. Though hackers may exploit zero day vulnerabilities to gain unauthorized access to an organization's computer system, appropriate safeguards, including encryption and access controls, may mitigate or even prevent unauthorized access to, or loss of, protected information. Once zero day vulnerabilities are made public, this information becomes accessible to both good and bad actors alike which means entities should have measures in place to be aware of new patches and for assessing the need to apply them. In the event a timely patch is not available, or cannot be immediately implemented (such as when testing is needed to ensure that the patch works with components of an entity's information systems), an entity may consider adopting other protective measures such as additional access controls or network access limitations to mitigate the impact of the zero day vulnerability until a patch is available.

A Dangerous Combination

APTs and zero day threats are dangerous enough by themselves. An APT using a zero day exploit can threaten computers and data all over the world. One such example is the EternalBlue exploit. EternalBlue targeted vulnerabilities in several of Microsoft's Windows operating systems. Soon after the EternalBlue exploit became publicly known, the WannaCry ransomware was released and began spreading, eventually infecting hundreds of thousands of computers around the world. The damages due to WannaCry infections are estimated to be in the billions of dollars. Analysis of WannaCry found that it used EternalBlue to spread and infect other systems. One of the organizations most impacted was the United Kingdom's National Health Service (NHS) which had up to 70,000 devices infected, forcing healthcare providers to turn away patients and shut down certain services. Several HIPAA covered entities and business associates in the United States were also affected by this cyberattack.

What Can HIPAA Covered Entities and Business Associates Do?

There are many security measures that organizations can proactively implement to help mitigate or prevent the damage that an APT or zero day attack may cause. The HIPAA Security Rule requires security measures that can be helpful in preventing, detecting and responding to cyberattacks such as those perpetrated by APTs or hackers leveraging zero day exploits. The HIPAA Security Rule includes the following security measures that can reduce the impact of an APT or zero day attack: Conducting risk analyses to identify risks and vulnerabilities (See 45 CFR § 164.308(a)(1)(ii)(A)); Implementing a risk management process to mitigate identified risks and vulnerabilities (See 45 CFR § 164.308(a)(1)(ii)(B)); Regularly reviewing audit and system activity logs to identify abnormal or suspicious activity (See 45 CFR § 164.308(a)(1)(ii)(D)); Implementing procedures to identify and respond to security incidents (See 45 CFR § 164.308(a)(6)); Establishing and periodically testing contingency plans including data backup and disaster recovery plans to ensure data is backed up and recoverable (See 45 CFR § 164.308(a)(7)); Implementing access controls to limit access to ePHI (See 45 CFR § 164.312(a)); Encrypting ePHI, as appropriate, for data-at-rest and data-in-motion (See 45 CFR §§ 164.312(a)(2)(iv), (e)(2)(ii)); and Implementing a security awareness and training program, including periodic security reminders and education and awareness of implemented procedures concerning malicious software protection, for all workforce members (See 45 CFR § 164.308(a)(5)).[262]

Note 5

Cloud Computing Services and HIPAA

Health and Human Services Department released a document titled, "Guidance on HIPAA & Cloud Computing."[263]

Guidance on HIPAA & Cloud Computing

---

[262] *See* U.S. DEPARTMENT OF HEALTH & HUMAN SERVICES & OFFICE OF CIVIL RIGHTS, SPRING 2019 OCR CYBERSECURITY NEWSLETTER (2019), *available at* https://www.hhs.gov/sites/default/files/spring-2019-ocr-cybersecurity-newsletter.pdf.

[263] *Guidance on HIPAA & Cloud Computing*, U.S. DEPARTMENT OF HEALTH & HUMAN SERVICES, https://www.hhs.gov/hipaa/for-professionals/special-topics/cloud-computing/index.html (last reviewed Aug. 31, 2020).

Introduction

With the proliferation and widespread adoption of cloud computing solutions, HIPAA covered entities and business associates are questioning whether and how they can take advantage of cloud computing while complying with regulations protecting the privacy and security of electronic protected health information (ePHI). This guidance assists such entities, including cloud services providers (CSPs), in understanding their HIPAA obligations.

Cloud computing takes many forms. This guidance focuses on cloud resources offered by a CSP that is an entity legally separate from the covered entity or business associate considering the use of its services. CSPs generally offer online access to shared computing resources with varying levels of functionality depending on the users' requirements, ranging from mere data storage to complete software solutions (e.g., an electronic medical record system), platforms to simplify the ability of application developers to create new products, and entire computing infrastructure for software programmers to deploy and test programs. Common cloud services are on-demand internet access to computing (e.g., networks, servers, storage, applications) services. We encourage covered entities and business associates seeking information about types of cloud computing services and technical arrangement options to consult a resource offered by the National Institute of Standards and Technology; SP 800-145, The NIST Definition of Cloud Computing - PDF.

The HIPAA Privacy, Security, and Breach Notification Rules (the *HIPAA Rules*) establish important protections for individually identifiable health information (called *protected health information* or *PHI* when created, received, maintained, or transmitted by a HIPAA covered entity or business associate), including limitations on uses and disclosures of such information, safeguards against inappropriate uses and disclosures, and individuals' rights with respect to their health information. Covered entities and business associates must comply with the applicable provisions of the HIPAA Rules. A *covered entity* is a health plan, a health care clearinghouse, or a health care provider who conducts certain billing and payment related transactions electronically. A *business associate* is an entity or person, other than a member of the workforce of a covered entity, that performs functions or activities on behalf of, or provides certain services to, a covered entity that involve creating, receiving, maintaining, or transmitting PHI. A business associate also is any subcontractor that creates, receives, maintains, or transmits PHI on behalf of another business associate.

When a covered entity engages the services of a CSP to create, receive, maintain, or transmit ePHI (such as to process and/or store ePHI), on its behalf, *the CSP is a business associate* under HIPAA. Further, when a business associate subcontracts with a CSP to create, receive, maintain, or transmit ePHI on its behalf, the *CSP subcontractor itself is a business associate.* This is true even if the CSP processes or stores only encrypted ePHI and lacks an encryption key for the data. Lacking an encryption key does <u>not</u> exempt a CSP from business associate status and obligations under the HIPAA Rules. As a result, the covered entity (or business associate) and the CSP must enter into a HIPAA-compliant *business associate agreement (BAA),* and the CSP is both contractually liable for meeting the terms of the BAA and directly liable for compliance with the applicable requirements of the HIPAA Rules.

This guidance presents key questions and answers to assist HIPAA regulated CSPs and their customers in understanding their responsibilities under the HIPAA Rules when they create, receive, maintain or transmit ePHI using cloud products and services.

QUESTIONS

1. May a HIPAA covered entity or business associate use a cloud service to store or process ePHI?

Yes, provided the covered entity or business associate enters into a HIPAA-compliant business associate contract or agreement (BAA) with the CSP that will be creating, receiving, maintaining, or transmitting electronic protected health information (ePHI) on its behalf, and otherwise complies with the HIPAA Rules. Among other things, the BAA establishes the permitted and required uses and disclosures of ePHI by the business associate performing activities or services for the covered entity or business associate, based on the relationship between the parties and the activities or services being performed by the business associate. The BAA also contractually requires the business associate to appropriately safeguard the ePHI, including implementing the requirements of the Security Rule. OCR has created guidance on the elements of BAAs.

A covered entity (or business associate) that engages a CSP should understand the cloud computing environment or solution offered by a particular CSP so that the covered entity (or business associate) can appropriately conduct its own risk analysis and establish risk management policies, as well as enter into appropriate BAAs. See 45 CFR §§ 164.308(a)(1)(ii)(A); 164.308(a)(1)(ii)(B); and 164.502. Both covered entities and business associates must conduct risk analyses to identify and assess potential threats and vulnerabilities to the confidentiality, integrity, and availability of all ePHI they create, receive, maintain, or transmit. For example, while a covered entity or business associate may use cloud-based services of any configuration (public, hybrid, private, etc.), provided it enters into a BAA with the CSP, the type of cloud configuration to be used may affect the risk analysis and risk management plans of all parties and the resultant provisions of the BAA. In addition, a *Service Level Agreement (SLA)* is commonly used to address more specific business expectations between the CSP and its customer, which also may be relevant to HIPAA compliance. For example, SLAs can include provisions that address such HIPAA concerns as:

- System availability and reliability;
- Back-up and data recovery (e.g., as necessary to be able to respond to a ransomware attack or other emergency situation);
- Manner in which data will be returned to the customer after service use termination;
- Security responsibility; and
- Use, retention and disclosure limitations.

If a covered entity or business associate enters into a SLA with a CSP, it should ensure that the terms of the SLA are consistent with the BAA and the HIPAA Rules. For example, the covered entity or business associate should ensure that the terms of the SLA and BAA with the CSP do not prevent the entity from accessing its ePHI in violation of 45 CFR §§ 164.308(b)(3), 164.502(e)(2), and 164.504(e)(1).

In addition to its contractual obligations, the CSP, as a business associate, has regulatory obligations and is directly liable under the HIPAA Rules if it makes uses and disclosures of PHI that are not authorized by its contract, required by law, or permitted by the Privacy Rule. A CSP, as a business associate, also is directly liable if it fails to safeguard ePHI in accordance with the Security Rule, or fails to notify the covered entity or business associate of the discovery of a breach of unsecured PHI in compliance with the Breach Notification Rule.

For more information about the Security Rule, see OCR and ONC tools for small entities and OCR guidance on SR compliance.

QUESTION

Are Service Level Agreements (SLAs) only for specific business expectations?

2. If a CSP stores only encrypted ePHI and does not have a decryption key, is it a HIPAA business associate?

Yes, because the CSP receives and maintains (e.g., to process and/or store) electronic protected health information (ePHI) for a covered entity or another business associate. Lacking an encryption key for the encrypted data it receives and maintains does not exempt a CSP from business associate status and associated obligations under the HIPAA Rules. An entity that maintains ePHI on behalf of a covered entity (or another business associate) is a business associate, even if the entity cannot actually view the ePHI. Thus, a CSP that maintains encrypted ePHI on behalf a covered entity (or another business associate) is a business associate, even if it does not hold a decryption key and therefore cannot view the information. For convenience purposes this guidance uses the term *no-view services* to describe the situation in which the CSP maintains encrypted ePHI on behalf of a covered entity (or another business associate) without having access to the decryption key.

While encryption protects ePHI by significantly reducing the risk of the information being viewed by unauthorized persons, such protections alone cannot adequately safeguard the confidentiality, integrity, and availability of ePHI as required by the Security Rule. Encryption does not maintain the integrity and availability of the ePHI, such as ensuring that the information is not corrupted by malware, or ensuring through contingency planning that the data remains available to authorized persons even during emergency or disaster situations. Further, encryption does not address other safeguards that are also important to maintaining confidentiality, such as administrative safeguards to analyze risks to the ePHI or physical safeguards for systems and servers that may house the ePHI.

As a business associate, a CSP providing no-view services is not exempt from any otherwise applicable requirements of the HIPAA Rules. However, the requirements of the Rules are flexible and scalable to take into account the no-view nature of the services provided by the CSP.

Security Rule Considerations

All CSPs that are business associates must comply with the applicable standards and implementation specifications of the Security Rule with respect to ePHI. However, in cases where a CSP is providing only no-view services to a covered entity (or business associate) customer, certain Security Rule requirements that apply to the ePHI maintained by the CSP may be satisfied for both parties through the actions of one of the parties. In particular, where only the customer controls who is able to view the ePHI maintained by the CSP, certain access controls, such as authentication or unique user identification, may be the responsibility of the customer, while others, such as encryption, may be the responsibility of the CSP business associate. Which access controls are to be implemented by the customer and which are to be implemented by the CSP may depend on the respective security risk management plans of the parties as well as the terms of the BAA. For example, if a customer implements its own reasonable and appropriate user authentication controls and agrees that the CSP providing no-view services need not implement additional procedures to authenticate (verify the identity of) a person or entity seeking access to ePHI, these Security Rule access control responsibilities would be met for both parties by the action of the customer.

However, as a business associate, the CSP is still responsible under the Security Rule for implementing other reasonable and appropriate controls to limit access to information systems that maintain customer ePHI. For example, even when the parties have agreed that the customer is responsible for authenticating access to ePHI, the CSP may still be required to implement appropriate internal controls to assure only authorized access to the administrative tools that manage the resources (e.g., storage, memory, network interfaces, CPUs) critical to the operation of its information systems. For example, a CSP that is a business associate needs to consider and address, as part of its risk analysis and risk management process, the risks of a malicious actor having unauthorized access to its system's administrative tools, which could impact system operations and impact the confidentiality, integrity and availability of the customer's ePHI. CSPs should also consider the risks of using unpatched or obsolete administrative tools. The CSP and the customer should each confirm in writing, in either the BAA or other documents, how each party will address the Security Rule requirements. Note that where the contractual agreements between a CSP and customer provide that the customer will control and implement certain security features of the cloud service consistent with the Security Rule, and the customer fails to do so, OCR will consider this factor as important and relevant during any investigation into compliance of either the customer or the CSP. A CSP is not responsible for the compliance failures that are attributable solely to the actions or inactions of the customer, as determined by the facts and circumstances of the particular case.

Privacy Rule Considerations

A business associate may only use and disclose PHI as permitted by its BAA and the Privacy Rule, or as otherwise required by law. While a CSP that provides only no-view services to a covered entity or business associate customer may not control who views the ePHI, the CSP still must ensure that it itself only uses and discloses the encrypted information as permitted by its BAA and the Privacy Rule, or as otherwise required by law. This includes, for example, ensuring the CSP does not impermissibly use the ePHI by blocking or terminating access by the customer to the ePHI.

Further, a BAA must include provisions that require the business associate to, among other things, make available PHI as necessary for the covered entity to meet its obligations to provide individuals with their rights to access, amend, and receive an accounting of certain disclosures of PHI in compliance with 45 CFR § 164.504(e)(2)(ii)(E)-(G). The BAA between a no-view CSP and a covered entity or business associate customer should describe in what manner the no-view CSP will meet these obligations – for example, a CSP may agree in the BAA that it will make the ePHI available to the customer for the purpose of incorporating amendments to ePHI requested by the individual, but only the customer will make those amendments.

Breach Notification Rule Considerations

As a business associate, a CSP that offers only no-view services to a covered entity or business associate still must comply with the HIPAA breach notification requirements that apply to business associates. In particular, a business associate is responsible for notifying the covered entity (or the business associate with which it has contracted) of breaches of unsecured PHI. See 45 CFR § 164.410. *Unsecured PHI* is PHI that has not been destroyed or is not encrypted at the levels specified in HHS' *Guidance to Render Unsecured Protected Health Information Unusable, Unreadable, or Indecipherable to Unauthorized Individuals* [12] If the ePHI that has been breached is encrypted consistent with the HIPAA standards set forth in 45 CFR § 164.402(2) and HHS' *Guidance* the incident falls within the breach "safe harbor" and the CSP business associate is not required to report the incident to its customer. However, if the ePHI is encrypted, but not at a level that meets the HIPAA standards or the decryption key was also breached, then the incident must be reported to its customer as a breach, unless one of the exceptions to the definition of "breach" applies. See 45 CFR § 164.402. See also 45 CFR § 164.410 for more information about breach notification obligations for business associates.

3. Can a CSP be considered to be a "conduit" like the postal service, and, therefore, not a business associate that must comply with the HIPAA Rules?

Generally, no. CSPs that provide cloud services to a covered entity or business associate that involve creating, receiving, or maintaining (e.g., to process and/or store) electronic protected health information (ePHI) meet the definition of a business associate, even if the CSP cannot view the ePHI because it is encrypted and the CSP does not have the decryption key.

As explained in previous guidance, the conduit exception is limited to *transmission-only* services for PHI (whether in electronic or paper form), including any temporary storage of PHI incident to such transmission. Any access to PHI by a conduit is only *transient* in nature. In contrast, a CSP that maintains ePHI for the purpose of storing it will qualify as a business associate, and not a conduit, even if the CSP does not actually view the information, because the entity has more *persistent access* to the ePHI.

Further, where a CSP provides transmission services for a covered entity or business associate customer, in addition to maintaining ePHI for purposes of processing and/or storing the information, the CSP is still a business associate with respect to such transmission of ePHI. The conduit exception applies where the *only* services provided to a covered entity or business associate customer are for transmission of ePHI that do not involve any storage of the information other than on a temporary basis incident to the transmission service.

4. Which CSPs offer HIPAA-compliant cloud services?

OCR does not endorse, certify, or recommend specific technology or products.

5. What if a HIPAA covered entity (or business associate) uses a CSP to maintain ePHI without first executing a business associate agreement with that CSP?

If a covered entity (or business associate) uses a CSP to maintain (e.g., to process or store) electronic protected health information (ePHI) without entering into a BAA with the CSP, the covered entity (or business associate) is in violation of the HIPAA Rules. 45 C.F.R §§164.308(b)(1) and §164.502(e). OCR has entered into a resolution agreement and corrective action plan with a covered entity that OCR determined stored ePHI of over 3,000 individuals on a cloud-based server without entering into a BAA with the CSP.

Further, a CSP that meets the definition of a business associate – that is a CSP that creates, receives, maintains, or transmits PHI on behalf of a covered entity or another business associate – must comply with all applicable provisions of the HIPAA Rules, regardless of whether it has executed a BAA with the entity using its services. See 78 Fed. Reg. 5565, 5598 (January 25, 2013). OCR recognizes that there may, however, be circumstances where a CSP may not have actual or constructive knowledge that a covered entity or another business associate is using its services to create, receive, maintain, or transmit ePHI. The HIPAA Rules provide an affirmative defense in cases where a CSP takes action to correct any non-compliance within 30 days (or such additional period as OCR may determine appropriate based on the nature and extent of the non-compliance) of the time that it knew or should have known of the violation (e.g., at the point the CSP knows or should have known that a covered entity or business associate customer is maintaining ePHI in its cloud). 45 CFR 160.410. This affirmative defense does not, however, apply in cases where the CSP was not aware of the violation due to its own willful neglect.

If a CSP becomes aware that it is maintaining ePHI, it must come into compliance with the HIPAA Rules, or securely return the ePHI to the customer or, if agreed to by the customer, securely destroy the ePHI. Once the CSP securely returns or destroys the ePHI (subject to arrangement with the customer), it is no longer a business associate. We recommend CSPs document these actions.

While a CSP maintains ePHI, the HIPAA Rules prohibit the CSP from using or disclosing the data in a manner that is inconsistent with the Rules.

6. If a CSP experiences a security incident involving a HIPAA covered entity's or business associate's ePHI, must it report the incident to the covered entity or business associate?

Yes. The Security Rule at 45 CFR § 164.308(a)(6)(ii) requires business associates to identify and respond to suspected or known security incidents; mitigate, to the extent practicable, harmful effects of security incidents that are known to the business associate; and document security incidents and their outcomes. In addition, the Security Rule at 45 CFR § 164.314(a)(2)(i)(C) provides that a business associate agreement must require the business associate to report, to the covered entity or business associate whose electronic protected health information (ePHI) it maintains, any security incidents of which it becomes aware. A security incident under 45 CFR § 164.304 means the attempted or successful unauthorized access, use, disclosure, modification, or destruction of information or interference with system operations in an information system. Thus, a business associate CSP must implement policies and procedures to address and document security incidents, and must report security incidents to its covered entity or business associate customer.

The Security Rule, however, is flexible and does not prescribe the level of detail, frequency, or format of reports of security incidents, which may be worked out between the parties to the business associate agreement (BAA). For example, the BAA may prescribe differing levels of detail, frequency, and formatting of reports based on the nature of the security incidents – e.g., based on the level of threat or exploitation of vulnerabilities, and the risk to the ePHI they pose. The BAA could also specify appropriate responses to certain incidents and whether identifying patterns of attempted security incidents is reasonable and appropriate.

Note, though, that the Breach Notification Rule specifies the content, timing, and other requirements for a business associate to report incidents that rise to the level of a breach of unsecured PHI to the covered entity (or business associate) on whose behalf the business associate is maintaining the PHI. See 45 CFR § 164.410. The BAA may specify more stringent (e.g., more timely) requirements for reporting than those required by the Breach Notification Rule (so long as they still also meet the Rule's requirements) but may not otherwise override the Rule's requirements for notification of breaches of unsecured PHI.

For more information on this topic, see the FAQ about reporting security incidents (although directed to plan sponsors and group health plans, the guidance is also relevant to business associates); as well as OCR breach notification guidance.

7. Do the HIPAA Rules allow health care providers to use mobile devices to access ePHI in a cloud?

Yes. Health care providers, other covered entities, and business associates may use mobile devices to access electronic protected health information (ePHI) in a cloud as long as appropriate physical, administrative, and technical safeguards are in place to protect the confidentiality, integrity, and availability of the ePHI on the mobile device and in the cloud, and appropriate BAAs are in place with any third party service providers for the device and/or the cloud that will have access to the e-PHI. The HIPAA Rules do not endorse or require specific types of technology, but rather establish the standards for how covered entities and business associates may use or disclose ePHI through certain technology while protecting the security of the ePHI by requiring analysis of the risks to the ePHI posed by such technology and implementation of reasonable and appropriate administrative, technical, and physical safeguards to address such risks. OCR and ONC have issued guidance on the use of mobile devices and tips for securing ePHI on mobile devices.

8. Do the HIPAA Rules require a CSP to maintain ePHI for some period of time beyond when it has finished providing services to a covered entity or business associate?

No, the HIPAA Rules generally do not require a business associate to maintain electronic protected health information (ePHI) beyond the time it provides services to a covered entity or business associate. The Privacy Rule provides that a business associate agreement (BAA) must require a business associate to return or destroy all PHI at the termination of the BAA where feasible. 45 CFR § 164.504(e)(2)(J).

If such return or destruction is not feasible, the BAA must extend the privacy and security protections of the BAA to the ePHI and limit further uses and disclosures to those purposes that make the return or destruction of the information infeasible. For example, return or destruction would be considered "infeasible" if other law requires the business associate CSP to retain ePHI for a period of time beyond the termination of the business associate contract.

QUESTION

Does erasing data count as the same thing as destruction of data?

9. Do the HIPAA Rules allow a covered entity or business associate to use a CSP that stores ePHI on servers outside of the United States?

Yes, provided the covered entity (or business associate) enters into a business associate agreement (BAA) with the CSP and otherwise complies with the applicable requirements of the HIPAA Rules. However, while the HIPAA Rules do not include requirements specific to protection of electronic protected health information (ePHI) processed or stored by a CSP or any other business associate outside of the United States, OCR notes that the risks to such ePHI may vary greatly depending on its geographic location. In particular, outsourcing storage or other services for ePHI overseas may increase the risks and vulnerabilities to the information or present special considerations with respect to enforceability of privacy and security protections over the data. Covered entities (and business associates, including the CSP) should take these risks into account when conducting the risk analysis and risk management required by the Security Rule. See 45 CFR §§ 164.308(a)(1)(ii)(A) and (a)(1)(ii)(B). For example, if ePHI is maintained in a country where there are documented increased attempts at hacking or other malware attacks, such risks should be considered, and entities must implement reasonable and appropriate technical safeguards to address such threats.

10. Do the HIPAA Rules require CSPs that are business associates to provide documentation, or allow auditing, of their security practices by their customers who are covered entities or business associates?

No. The HIPAA Rules require covered entity and business associate customers to obtain satisfactory assurances in the form of a business associate agreement (BAA) with the CSP that the CSP will, among other things, appropriately safeguard the protected health information (PHI) that it creates, receives, maintains or transmits for the covered entity or business associate in accordance with the HIPAA Rules. The CSP is also directly liable for failing to safeguard electronic PHI in accordance with the Security Rule and for impermissible uses or disclosures of the PHI. The HIPAA Rules do not expressly require that a CSP provide documentation of its security practices to or otherwise allow a customer to audit its security practices. However, customers may require from a CSP (through the BAA, service level agreement, or other documentation) additional assurances of protections for the PHI, such as documentation of safeguards or audits, based on their own risk analysis and risk management or other compliance activities.

11. If a CSP receives and maintains only information that has been de-identified in accordance with the HIPAA Privacy Rule, is it is a business associate?

No. A CSP is not a business associate if it receives and maintains (e.g., to process and/or store) only information de-identified following the processes required by the Privacy Rule. The Privacy Rule does not restrict the use or disclosure of de-identified information, nor does the Security Rule require that safeguards be applied to de-identified information, as the information is not considered protected health information. See the OCR guidance on de-identification for more information.

Note 6

HIPAA and other relevant data security laws inadequate?

The College of Healthcare Information Management Executives (CHIME) sent a letter to Congressman Lamar Alexander with suggestions for preparing for the next pandemic after COVID-19. The letter addresses cybersecurity in the healthcare context. The letter states, in relevant part:

III. Strengthen Cybersecurity Infrastructure

Healthcare is deemed a critical infrastructure by the Department of Homeland Security (DHS) and as such, patient safety and patient data should be viewed as a public good; protecting those things should be a national priority. As we increase interoperability, additional threats to data integrity and patient safety will arise. Without proper safeguards, the safe and secure transmission of sensitive data will continue to be a challenge and will hinder efforts to improve outcomes.

The healthcare sector, despite making progress over the past several years, is ill-equipped to handle a concurrent pandemic and cyberattack. Unfortunately, that is what our nation's healthcare system could very well experience. Cyber criminals are fully aware of our vulnerabilities and experts are predicting they will capitalize on those vulnerabilities. Given the complexity of the ever-growing number of interconnected devices, it is important to guarantee the security of those devices and the networks they reside on. As 5G utilization grows, the industry must monitor its adoption for additional risks that may arise as the Internet of Medical Things (IoMT) continues to rapidly expand.

The added stress to our nation's healthcare providers as they treat those with or suspected to have COVID-19 brings heightened importance to fortifying their ability to maintain continuity of operations. One industry estimate found that since January there has been a "30,000% increase in phishing, malicious websites, and malware targeting remote users—all related to COVID-19" (Zscaler, April 2020).

Providers need additional support to fend off the growing and sophisticated attacks aimed at stealing intellectual property, extorting ransoms, threatening patients by targeting medical devices connected to patients and hindering their ability to deliver care overall.[264]

Note 7

The Health and Human Services Agency Office of Civil Rights in Action has released several resources to guide entities that develop healthcare-related Apps that may utilize ePHI, including a Mobile Apps Interactive Tool. The following materials include an HHS document titled, "Health App Use Scenarios and HIPAA," and "Health Information Technology: Frequently Asked Questions."

Health App Use Scenarios and HIPAA

These scenarios address two questions under the Health Insurance Portability and Accountability Act (HIPAA):

1. How does HIPAA apply to health information that a patient creates, manages or organizes through the use of a health app?

2. When might an app developer need to comply with the HIPAA Rules?

The answers to these questions are fact and circumstance specific. Each scenario below is based on a specific set of facts. Please keep this in mind as you review a scenario and apply it to your own circumstances. Change in a scenario may change the analysis and, as a result, change the determination of whether the app developer is required to comply with HIPAA. We hope this will help you identify the particular aspects to explore in your own analysis.

---

[264] Letter from Russell P. Branzwell, President and CEO of Chime, and John Kravitz, Chair of the CHIME Board of Trustees, to the Honorable Lamar Alexander, Chairman of the Sen. Comm. on Health, Educ., Labor & Pensions (June 20, 2020), *available at* https://chimecentral.org/wp-content/uploads/2020/06/CHIME-Comments-for-Preparing-for-the-Next-Pandemic-White-Paper.pdf

Background: Only health plans, health care clearinghouses and most health care providers are covered entities under HIPAA. If you work for one of these entities, and as part of your job you are creating an app that involves the use or disclosure of identifiable health information, the entity (and you, as a member of its workforce) must protect that information in compliance with the HIPAA Rules. For extensive information on the requirements of the HIPAA rules and how to comply with them, please see http://www.hhs.gov/hipaa/index.html.

However, even if you are not a covered entity, you may be a business associate if you are creating or offering the app on behalf of a covered entity (or one of the covered entity's contractors) – and in that case you are required to comply with certain provisions of the HIPAA Rules. In general, a business associate is a person [or entity] who creates, receives, maintains or transmits protected health information (PHI) on behalf of a covered entity or another business associate. PHI is defined in the HIPAA regulations, and, in general, is identifiable health information. So, most vendors or contractors (including subcontractors) that provide services to or perform functions for covered entities that involve access to PHI are business associates. For example, a company that is given access to PHI by a covered entity to provide and manage a personal health record or patient portal offered by the covered entity to its patients or enrollees is a business associate.

Note that the scenarios below address the application of HIPAA to the app developer. In all cases in which a covered entity is transmitting PHI, either itself or using a business associate, it must apply reasonable safeguards to protect the information and nothing in the analyses below relieves covered entities (e.g., providers) of their own, independent obligation to comply with HIPAA.
Scenario Based on the Facts . . .

Is App Developer a HIPAA Business Associate?
Consumer downloads a health app to her smartphone. She populates it with her own information. For example, the consumer inputs blood glucose levels and blood pressure readings she obtained herself using home health equipment.

No. Developer is not creating, receiving, maintaining or transmitting protected health information (PHI) on behalf of a covered entity or another business associate. The consumer is using the developer's app to help her manage and organize her information without any involvement of her health care providers.

Consumer downloads a health app to her smartphone that is designed to help her manage a chronic condition. She downloads data from her doctor's EHR through a patient portal, onto her computer and then uploads it into the app. She also adds her own information to the app.

No. Developer is not creating, receiving, maintaining or transmitting protected health information (PHI) on behalf of a covered entity or another business associate. Instead, the consumer obtains health information from her provider, combines it with health information she inputs, and uses the app to organize and manage that information for her own purposes. There is no indication the provider or a business associate of the provider hired the app developer to provide or facilitate this service. Doctor counsels patient that his BMI is too high, and recommends a particular app that tracks diet, exercise, and weight.

Consumer downloads app to his smartphone and uses it to send a summary report to his doctor before his next appointment.

No. Developer is not creating, receiving, maintaining or transmitting protected health information (PHI) on behalf of a covered entity or another business associate. The doctor's recommendation implies her trust in the app, but there is no indication that the doctor hired the app developer to provide services to patients involving the handling of PHI. The consumer's use of an app to transmit data to a covered entity does not by itself make the app developer a BA of the covered entity.

Consumer downloads a health app to her smartphone that is designed to help her manage a chronic condition. Health care provider and app developer have entered into an interoperability arrangement at the consumer's request that facilitates secure exchange of consumer information between the provider EHR and the app. The consumer populates information on the app and directs the app to transmit the information to the provider's EHR. The consumer is able to access test results from the provider through the app.

No. Developer is not creating, receiving, maintaining or transmitting protected health information (PHI) on behalf of a covered entity or another business associate. The interoperability arrangement alone does not create a BA relationship because the arrangement exists to facilitate access initiated by the consumer. The app developer is providing a service to the consumer, at the consumer's request and on her behalf. The app developer is transmitting data on behalf of the consumer to and from the provider; this activity does not create a BA relationship with the covered entity.

Scenario Based on the Facts

Is App Developer a HIPAA Business Associate?

At direction of her provider, patient downloads a health app to her smart phone. Provider has contracted with app developer for patient management services, including remote patient health counseling, monitoring of patients' food and exercise, patient messaging, EHR integration and application interfaces. Information the patient inputs is automatically incorporated into provider EHR.

Yes, the developer is a business associate of the provider, because it is creating, receiving, maintaining and transmitting protected health information (PHI) on behalf of a covered entity. In this case, the provider contracts with the app developer for patient management services that involve creating, receiving, maintaining and transmitting PHI, and the app is a means for providing those services.

Consumer downloads to her smart phone a mobile PHR app offered by her health plan that offers users in its network the ability to request, download and store health plan records and check the status of claims and coverage decisions. The app also contains the plan's wellness tools for members, so they can track their progress in improving their health. Health plan analyzes health information and data about app usage to understand effectiveness of its health and wellness offerings. App developer also offers a separate, direct-to-consumer version of the app that consumers can use to store, manage, and organize their health records, to improve their health habits and to send health information to providers.

Yes, with respect to the app offered by the health plan, and no, when offering the direct-to-consumer app. Developer is a business associate of the health plan, because it is creating, receiving, maintaining or transmitting protected health information (PHI) on behalf of a covered entity. Developer must comply with applicable HIPAA Rules requirements with respect to the PHI involved in its work on behalf of the health plan. But its "direct-to-consumer" product is not provided on behalf of a covered entity or other business associate, and developer activities with respect to that product are not subject to the HIPAA Rules. Therefore, as long as the developer keeps the health information attached to these two versions of the app separate, so that information from the direct-to-consumer version is not part of the product offering to the covered entity health plan, the developer does not need to apply HIPAA protections to the consumer information obtained through the "direct-to-consumer" app.

<u>Key Questions</u>

If you are an app vendor, and you are not already a covered entity, you should consider the following questions in determining whether or not you may be a business associate – i.e., an entity that creates, receives, maintains or transmits protected health information (PHI) on behalf of a covered entity or business associate:

x Does your health app create, receive, maintain, or transmit identifiable information?

x Who are your clients? How are you funded?

x Are your clients covered entities? e.g., o hospitals, doctor's offices, clinics, pharmacies, or other health care providers who conduct electronic transactions; o health insurance issuers; health or wellness program related to a health plan offered by an employer

x Were you hired by, or are you paid for your service or product by, a covered entity? Or another business contracted to a covered entity?

x Does a covered entity (or a business associate acting on its behalf) direct you to create, receive, maintain or disclose information related to a patient or health plan member?

If you are only offering services directly to and collecting information for or on behalf of consumers, and not on behalf a provider, health plan or health care clearinghouse, you are not likely to be subject to HIPAA as either a covered entity or business associate. x Is your app independently selected by a consumer?

x Does the consumer control all decisions about whether to transmit her data to a third party, such as to her health care provider or health plan?

 x Do you have no relationship with that third party entity (other than an interoperability relationship)?[265]

Health Information Technology: Frequently Asked Questions

. . .

<u>Safeguards – Health Information Technology</u>

---

[265] *Health App Use Scenarios & HIPPA*, U.S. Department of Health & Human Services (Feb. 2016), *available at* https://www.hhs.gov/sites/default/files/ocr-health-app-developer-scenarios-2-2016.pdf.

Does the HIPAA Privacy Rule permit a covered health care provider to e-mail or otherwise electronically exchange protected health information (PHI) with another provider for treatment purposes?

Yes. The Privacy Rule allows covered health care providers to share PHI electronically (or in any other form) for treatment purposes, as long as they apply reasonable safeguards when doing so. Thus, for example, a physician may consult with another physician by e-mail about a patient's condition, or health care providers may electronically exchange PHI to and through a health information organization (HIO) for patient care.

How may the HIPAA Privacy Rule's requirements for verification of identity and authority be met in an electronic health information exchange environment?

The Privacy Rule requires covered entities to verify the identity and authority of a person requesting protected health information (PHI), if not known to the covered entity. See 45 C.F.R. § 164.514(h). The Privacy Rule allows for verification in most instances in either oral or written form, although verification does require written documentation when such documentation is a condition of the disclosure. The Privacy Rule generally does not include specific or technical verification requirements and thus, can flexibly be applied to an electronic health information exchange environment in a manner that best supports the needs of the exchange participants and the health information organization (HIO). For example, in an electronic health information exchange environment:

- Participants can agree by contract or otherwise to keep current and provide to the HIO a list of authorized persons so the HIO can appropriately authenticate each user of the network.
- For persons claiming to be government officials, proof of government status may be provided by having a legitimate government e-mail extension (e.g., xxx.gov).
- Documentation required for certain uses and disclosures may be provided in electronic form, such as scanned images or pdf files.
- Documentation requiring signatures may be provided as a scanned image of the signed documentation or as an electronic document with an electronic signature, to the extent the electronic signature is valid under applicable law.

Does the HIPAA Privacy Rule permit health care providers to use e-mail to discuss health issues and treatment with their patients?

Yes. The Privacy Rule allows covered health care providers to communicate electronically, such as through e-mail, with their patients, provided they apply reasonable safeguards when doing so. See 45 C.F.R. § 164.530(c). For example, certain precautions may need to be taken when using e-mail to avoid unintentional disclosures, such as checking the e-mail address for accuracy before sending, or sending an e-mail alert to the patient for address confirmation prior to sending the message. Further, while the Privacy Rule does not prohibit the use of unencrypted e-mail for treatment-related communications between health care providers and patients, other safeguards should be applied to reasonably protect privacy, such as limiting the amount or type of information disclosed through the unencrypted e-mail. In addition, covered entities will want to ensure that any transmission of electronic protected health information is in compliance with the HIPAA Security Rule requirements at 45 C.F.R. Part 164, Subpart C.

Note that an individual has the right under the Privacy Rule to request and have a covered health care provider communicate with him or her by alternative means or at alternative locations, if reasonable. See 45 C.F.R. § 164.522(b). For example, a health care provider should accommodate an individual's request to receive appointment reminders via e-mail, rather than on a postcard, if e-mail is a reasonable, alternative means for that provider to communicate with the patient. By the same token, however, if the use of unencrypted e-mail is unacceptable to a patient who requests confidential communications, other means of communicating with the patient, such as by more secure electronic methods, or by mail or telephone, should be offered and accommodated.

Patients may initiate communications with a provider using e-mail. If this situation occurs, the health care provider can assume (unless the patient has explicitly stated otherwise) that e-mail communications are acceptable to the individual. If the provider feels the patient may not be aware of the possible risks of using unencrypted e-mail, or has concerns about potential liability, the provider can alert the patient of those risks, and let the patient decide whether to continue e-mail communications.

Does the HIPAA Privacy Rule allow covered entities participating in electronic health information exchange with a health information organization (HIO) to establish a common set of safeguards?

Yes. The Privacy Rule requires a covered entity to have in place appropriate administrative, technical, and physical safeguards to protect the privacy of protected health information (PHI), including reasonable safeguards to protect against any intentional or unintentional use or disclosure in violation of the Privacy Rule. See 45 C.F.R. § 164.530(c). Each covered entity can evaluate its own business functions and needs, the types and amounts of PHI it collects, uses, and discloses, size, and business risks to determine adequate safeguards for its particular circumstances.

With respect to electronic health information exchange, the Privacy Rule would allow covered entities participating in an exchange with a HIO to agree on a common set of privacy safeguards that are appropriate to the risks associated with exchanging PHI to and through the HIO. In addition, as a requirement of participation in the electronic health information exchange with the HIO, these commonly agreed to safeguards also could be extended to other participants, even if they are not covered entities. A common or consistent set of standards applied to the HIO and its participants may help not only to facilitate the efficient exchange of information, but also to foster trust among both participants and individuals.

Access Rights, Apps and APIs

Does a HIPAA covered entity that fulfills an individual's request to transmit electronic protected health information (ePHI) to an application or other software (collectively "app") bear liability under the HIPAA Privacy, Security, or Breach Notification Rules (HIPAA Rules) for the app's use or disclosure of the health information it received?

The answer depends on the relationship between the covered entity and the app. Once health information is received from a covered entity, at the individual's direction, by an app that is neither a covered entity nor a business associate under HIPAA, the information is no longer subject to the protections of the HIPAA Rules. If the individual's app – chosen by an individual to receive the individual's requested ePHI – was not provided by or on behalf of the covered entity (and, thus, does not create, receive, transmit, or maintain ePHI on its behalf), the covered entity would not be liable under the HIPAA Rules for any subsequent use or disclosure of the requested ePHI received by the app. For example, the covered entity would have no HIPAA responsibilities or liability if such an app that the individual designated to receive their ePHI later experiences a breach.

If, on the other hand, the app was developed for, or provided by or on behalf of the covered entity – and, thus, creates, receives, maintains, or transmits ePHI on behalf of the covered entity – the covered entity could be liable under the HIPAA Rules for a subsequent impermissible disclosure because of the business associate relationship between the covered entity and the app developer. For example, if the individual selects an app that the covered health care provider uses to provide services to individuals involving ePHI, the health care provider may be subject to liability under the HIPAA Rules if the app impermissibly discloses the ePHI received.

What liability does a covered entity face if it fulfills an individual's request to send their ePHI using an unsecure method to an app?

Under the individual right of access, an individual may request a covered entity to direct their ePHI to a third-party app in an unsecure manner or through an unsecure channel. See 45 CFR 164.524(a)(1), (c)(2)(ii), (c)(3)(ii). For instance, an individual may request that their unencrypted ePHI be transmitted to an app as a matter of convenience. In such a circumstance, the covered entity would not be responsible for unauthorized access to the individual's ePHI while in transmission to the app. With respect to such apps, the covered entity may want to consider informing the individual of the potential risks involved the first time that the individual makes the request.

Where an individual directs a covered entity to send ePHI to a designated app, does a covered entity's electronic health record (EHR) system developer bear HIPAA liability after completing the transmission of ePHI to the app on behalf of the covered entity?

The answer depends on the relationship, if any, between the covered entity, the EHR system developer, and the app chosen by the individual to receive the individual's ePHI. A business associate relationship exists if an entity creates, receives, maintains, or transmits ePHI on behalf of a covered entity (directly or through another business associate) to carry out the covered functions of the covered entity. A business associate relationship exists between an EHR system developer and a covered entity. If the EHR system developer does not own the app, or if it owns the app but does not provide the app to, through, or on behalf of, the covered entity – e.g., if it creates the app and makes it available in an app store as part of a different line of business (and not as part of its business associate relationship with any covered entity) – the EHR system developer would not be liable under the HIPAA Rules for any subsequent use or disclosure of the requested ePHI received by the app.

If the EHR system developer owns the app or has a business associate relationship with the app developer, and provides the app to, through, or on behalf of, the covered entity (directly or through another business associate), then the EHR system developer could potentially face HIPAA liability (as a business associate of a HIPAA covered entity) for any impermissible uses and disclosures of the health information received by the app. For example, if an EHR system developer contracts with the app developer to create the app on behalf of a covered entity and the individual later identifies that app to receive ePHI, then the EHR system developer could be subject to HIPAA liability if the app impermissibly uses or discloses the ePHI received.

Can a covered entity refuse to disclose ePHI to an app chosen by an individual because of concerns about how the app will use or disclose the ePHI it receives?

No. The HIPAA Privacy Rule generally prohibits a covered entity from refusing to disclose ePHI to a third-party app designated by the individual if the ePHI is readily producible in the form and format used by the app. See 45 CFR 164.524(a)(1), (c)(2)(ii), (c)(3)(ii). The HIPAA Rules do not impose any restrictions on how an individual or the individual's designee, such as an app, may use the health information that has been disclosed pursuant to the individual's right of access. For instance, a covered entity is not permitted to deny an individual's right of access to their ePHI where the individual directs the information to a third-party app because the app will share the individual's ePHI for research or because the app does not encrypt the individual's data when at rest. In addition, as discussed in a separate FAQ, the HIPAA Rules do not apply to entities that do not meet the definition of a HIPAA covered entity or business associate.

Does HIPAA require a covered entity or its EHR system developer to enter into a business associate agreement with an app designated by the individual in order to transmit ePHI to the app?

It depends on the relationship between the app developer, and the covered entity and/or its EHR system developer. A business associate is a person or entity who creates, receives, maintains or transmits PHI on behalf of (or for the benefit of) a covered entity (directly or through another business associate) to carry out covered functions of the covered entity. An app's facilitation of access to the individual's ePHI at the individual's request alone does not create a business associate relationship. Such facilitation may include API terms of use agreed to by the third-party app (i.e., interoperability arrangements).

HIPAA does not require a covered entity or its business associate (e.g., EHR system developer) to enter into a business associate agreement with an app developer that does not create, receive, maintain, or transmit ePHI on behalf of or for the benefit of the covered entity (whether directly or through another business associate).

However if the app was developed to create, receive, maintain, or transmit ePHI on behalf of the covered entity, or was provided by or on behalf of the covered entity (directly or through its EHR system developer, acting as the covered entity's business associate), then a business associate agreement would be required.

5.4 Private Litigation and HIPAA

In the following case, the district court found that representations by a health insurer concerning compliance with HIPPA privacy and security requirements could give rise to some tort, state statutory and contract claims in the data breach context.

In re: Premera Blue Cross Customer Data Security Breach Litigation, 2017 WL 539578 (D. Or. 2017).

Michael H. Simon, United States District Judge

Plaintiffs bring this putative class action against Defendant Premera Blue Cross ("Premera"), a healthcare benefits servicer and provider. On March 17, 2015, Premera publicly disclosed that its computer network had been breached. Plaintiffs allege that this breach compromised the confidential information of approximately 11 million current and former members, affiliated members, and employees of Premera. The compromised confidential information includes names, dates of birth, Social Security Numbers, member identification numbers, mailing addresses, telephone numbers, email addresses, medical claims information, financial information, and other protected health information (collectively, "Sensitive Information"). According to Plaintiffs, the breach began in May 2014 and went undetected for nearly a year. Plaintiffs allege that after discovering the breach, Premera unreasonably delayed in notifying all affected individuals. Based on these allegations, among others, Plaintiffs bring various state common law claims and state statutory claims.
. . . Specifically, Premera moves to dismiss Plaintiffs' amended fraud-based and contract claims. . . .

STANDARDS

A motion to dismiss for failure to state a claim may be granted only when there is no cognizable legal theory to support the claim or when the complaint lacks sufficient factual allegations to state a facially plausible claim for relief. . . .

DISCUSSION

A. Plaintiffs' Fraud–Based Claims

In its Motion, Premera challenges the allegations of fraud contained in Plaintiffs' first, seventh, and tenth claims. Premera argues that Plaintiffs' claims that "sound in fraud" continue to fail to comply with the heightened pleading requirements of Rule 9(b) of the Federal Rules of Civil Procedure and should be dismissed. Plaintiffs respond that their new allegations cure the deficiencies identified by the Court in Premera I. Plaintiffs further respond that their state Consumer Protection Act ("CPA") claims allege that Premera's conduct was both deceptive and unfair and that the allegation of "unfair" conduct does not "sound in fraud" and thus is not subject to Rule 9(b).

1. Affirmative Misrepresentation

"To satisfy Rule 9(b), a pleading must identify 'the who, what, when, where, and how of the misconduct charged,' as well as 'what is false or misleading about [the purportedly fraudulent] statement, and why it is false.'" Cafasso v. Gen. Dynamics C4 Sys., Inc., 637 F.3d 1047, 1055. In Premera I, the Court noted that Plaintiffs' allegations were unclear about whether Plaintiffs were alleging fraud by affirmative misrepresentation. To cure this deficiency, the Court directed that Plaintiffs must clearly and explicitly identify each specific affirmative misrepresentation alleged and provide all of the other information required under Rule 9(b).

Premera argues that Plaintiffs' allegations of fraud remain vague and lack the required specificity. Premera also argues that the statements are not false. Further, Premera states that Plaintiffs have not alleged that any of them even read, heard, saw or relied on any statement that could support a fraud claim. Plaintiffs respond that they have stated the alleged affirmative misrepresentations with sufficient specificity. Plaintiffs add that whether the alleged statements are true is an issue of fact not appropriate for resolution in a motion to dismiss. Plaintiffs do not directly respond to Premera's assertion that without a specific allegation that Plaintiffs actually read the alleged misrepresentations, Plaintiffs have not sufficiently alleged causation.

In their amended pleading, Plaintiffs allege that Premera's policy booklets, Notice of Privacy Practices ("Privacy Notice"), and Code of Conduct contain affirmative misrepresentations. Although Plaintiffs did not attach to their amended pleading copies of Premera's policy booklets, Privacy Notice, or Code of Conduct, Plaintiffs' amended pleading quotes from those documents and Plaintiffs provide identifying Bates numbers and web addresses showing precisely where these documents can be found. Premera has attached to its Motion a copy of its Notice of Privacy Practices dated November 20, 2015 (ECF 78–1), the two referenced policy booklets (ECF 78–3 and 78–4), and Premera's Code of Conduct dated May 2015 (ECF 78–5). The Court may consider these documents in ruling on Premera's Motion.

a. Causation and reliance

. . . Premera's argument essentially is that in an affirmative misrepresentation case, without any allegation that any plaintiff read and relied upon the allegedly false or misleading statements, a plaintiff cannot show the requisite causation. This argument, however, reads a reliance requirement into the causation element in a CPA claim that the Washington Supreme Court has not adopted.

. . .

Depending on the deceptive practice at issue and the relationship between the parties, the plaintiff may need to prove reliance to establish causation . . .. Most courts have concluded a private right of action under state consumer protection law does not necessarily require proof of reliance, consistently with legislative intent to ease the burden ordinarily applicable in cases of fraud. . . .

The Court holds that under the facts presented here, reliance is not required. The Washington CPA's purpose is "to protect the public and foster fair and honest competition." Wash. Rev. Code. § 19.86.020. It is intended to "ease the burden ordinarily applicable in cases of fraud." Panag, 166 Wash. 2d at 59 n.15. . . . Here, as discussed below, the Court is allowing the Policyholder Plaintiffs' affirmative misrepresentation claim to proceed for those plaintiffs who received the Preferred Select policy booklet, Privacy Notice, or Code of Conduct. Plaintiffs allege that the Privacy Notice was sent with the policy booklet. Thus, the relevant Policyholder Plaintiffs received the same alleged misrepresentations.

Under such circumstances, and because Washington does not require proof of reliance and holds that proximate causation is an issue of fact, the Court agrees with courts in other jurisdictions that have held that such claims should not be dismissed unless "it is clear that no reasonable person would be deceived by defendant's conduct." Smith v. Wells Fargo Bank, N.A., 158 F. Supp. 3d 91, 101 (D. Conn. 2016), aff'd, 2016 WL 7323985 (2d Cir. Dec. 16, 2016). . . .

Here, the Court declines to find that no reasonable person would be deceived by Premera's alleged conduct and representations. Thus, the court declines to dismiss Plaintiffs' affirmative misrepresentation claims for failing to allege causation, at least at the motion to dismiss stage of the proceedings.

b. Premera's policy booklets

Plaintiffs allege that Premera's policy booklets are sent to its members. Plaintiffs further allege that these booklets contain affirmative misrepresentations. Specifically, Plaintiffs assert that Premera's "Preferred Select" policy booklet states: "We protect your privacy by making sure your information stays confidential. We have a company confidentiality policy and we require all employees to sign it." The statement that Premera protects policyholders' privacy and makes sure information stays confidential is a sufficiently specific representation. Plaintiffs allege that this statement is false because Premera did not protect its policyholders' privacy and did not "make sure" that their information stays confidential. Plaintiffs also allege that Premera knew this statement was false at the time it made the statement because Premera knew of its inadequate data security measures. These allegations are sufficient under Rule 9(b) to allege a fraudulent misrepresentation for Policyholder Plaintiffs who were sent this booklet. Premera's argument that it did, in fact, reasonably protect the privacy of their policyholders' Sensitive Information presents a question that is inappropriate to resolve at this stage of the litigation.

Plaintiffs also allege that the "Preferred Bronze" policy contains a misrepresentation. This policy states: "To safeguard your privacy, we take care to ensure that your information remains confidential by having a company confidentiality policy and by requiring all employees to sign it." Plaintiffs argue that this statement is a promise to take care to ensure that the policyholders' information stays confidential and it is false because Premera did not take adequate care to protect data security. Plaintiffs' argument, however, overlooks the second half of the sentence. Premera promised that it would ensure confidentiality "by having a company confidentiality policy and by requiring employees to sign it." Thus, the Preferred Bronze policy contains a promise to have a company confidentiality policy and to have employees sign that policy. Plaintiffs do not allege that Premera did not have such a policy or did not require that its employees sign the policy. Thus, Plaintiffs' allegations are insufficient to allege fraud by misrepresentation based on the Preferred Bronze policy booklet.

c. Privacy Notice

Plaintiffs allege that Premera's Privacy Notice also was provided to its members. Plaintiffs allege in Paragraph 40 that the Privacy Notice contained misrepresentations, including:

- Premera is "committed to maintaining the confidentiality of your medical and financial information";
- Under federal law, Premera "must take measures to protect the privacy of your personal information" and "[i]n addition, other state and federal privacy laws may provide additional privacy protection";
- Premera "protect[s] your personal information in a variety of ways," including "authoriz[ing] access to your personal information ... only to the extent necessary to conduct our business of serving you";
- Premera "take[s] steps to secure our buildings and electronic systems from unauthorized access";
- Premera "train[s] our employees on our written confidentiality policy and procedures and employees are subject to discipline if they violate them";
- Premera "will protect the privacy of your information even if you no longer maintain coverage through us"; and
- Premera is required by law to protect the privacy of Sensitive Information, provide the Privacy Notice to members, and notify members following a breach of Sensitive Information.

Plaintiffs allege that these statements are false or misleading because Premera was not committed to protecting Plaintiffs' Sensitive Information, did not take the appropriate measures required under federal and state law, did not protect Plaintiffs' Sensitive Information, did not properly train its employees, and did not provide adequate notice of the breach. Some of these alleged representations are more appropriate for Plaintiffs' claim of fraud by omission or half-truth (e.g., that Premera represented that under federal law it was required to protect Plaintiffs' Sensitive Information while knowing that it was not adequately complying with those federal laws). Others, however, are representations that, if false, as Plaintiffs allege, are sufficient to allege a claim of affirmative misrepresentations (e.g., that Premera does not limit access to Sensitive Information, train and discipline its employees on data security, or protect privacy of Sensitive Information after a person no longer has coverage with Premera). Accordingly, for Plaintiffs who were provided Premera's Privacy Notice, Plaintiffs' adequately have alleged a claim of affirmative misrepresentation.

d. Code of Conduct

Plaintiffs allege that Premera's Code of Conduct is found on its website and available to Premera's members. Plaintiffs allege this Code of Conduct contains misrepresentations, including that: (1) Premera is "committed to complying with federal and state privacy laws"; (2) Premera uses "privacy principles to guide our actions," including that customers "should enjoy the full array of privacy protections"; (3) Premera uses, "where appropriate," technical and physical security safeguards; (4) Premera is "committed to ensuring the security of our facilities and electronic systems to prevent unauthorized access"; and (5) Premera is "expected to be aware of and follow established corporate policies, processes and procedures" to protect its buildings and computer systems in compliance with the Health Insurance Portability and Accountability Act of 1996 ("HIPAA").

To prevail on a CPA claim under Washington law, a plaintiff must establish each of the following elements: "(1) unfair or deceptive act or practice; (2) occurring in trade or commerce; (3) public interest impact; (4) injury to plaintiff in his or her business or property; [and] (5) causation." Hangman Ridge Training Stables, Inc. v. Safeco Title Ins. Co., 105 Wash. 2d 778, 785–93 (Wash. 1986). The first two elements "may be established by a showing that (1) an act or practice which has a capacity to deceive a substantial portion of the public (2) has occurred in the conduct of any trade or commerce." Id. at 785–86. "Whether an alleged act is unfair or deceptive presents a question of law." Walker v. Quality Loan Serv. Corp., 176 Wash. App. 294, 318 (2013), as modified (Aug. 26, 2013). " 'Implicit in the definition of 'deceptive' under the CPA is the understanding that the practice misleads or misrepresents something of material importance.' " Id.

Premera argues that its statements in the Code of Conduct are not deceptive both because they are mere "puffery" or expressions of corporate optimism and because they are not false. Premera cites to securities fraud cases in which courts have found statements in a code of conduct or code of ethics not to be material because they are merely expressions of corporate optimism. To show that an act or statement is "unfair or deceptive" under Washington's CPA, however, "[a] plaintiff need not show that the act in question was intended to deceive, but that the alleged act had the capacity to deceive a substantial portion of the public." Thus, the relevant inquiry is different than in traditional fraud cases—although materiality is an "implicit" element, the critical factor is whether the alleged statements contained in the Code of Conduct had the capacity to deceive a substantial portion of the public.

In looking at the statements contained in the Code of Conduct, the Court agrees with Premera that these are not guarantees and that they are closer being aspirational statements. Cf. Lorona v. Arizona Summit Law Sch., LLC, 151 F. Supp. 3d 978, 995 (D.

Ariz. 2015) (finding statement that a for-profit school "believes" lawyers should enter the workplace with sufficient preparation was aspirational); Nathanson v. Polycom, Inc., 87 F. Supp. 3d 966, 976 (N.D. Cal. 2015) (finding statements in a Code of Business Ethics that company funds must be used for company purposes, not personal gain, and that employees must ensure that the company receives good value for its expenditures were " 'inherently aspirational' and hence immaterial"); Cement & Concrete Workers Dist. Council Pension, 964 F. Supp. 2d 1128, 1138–39 (N.D. Cal. 2013) (finding statements in a code of ethics immaterial because they are merely vague statements of corporate optimism). . . .

For purposes of a Washington CPA claim, the Code of Conduct statements have the capacity to deceive if, as Plaintiffs' allege, Premera did not provide adequate data security. A reasonable person, reading these statements, would believe that Premera provides reasonable and adequate data security. Moreover, whether a company that will be receiving a person's most highly sensitive personal information will keep that information secure is an issue of material importance. Thus, Plaintiffs' adequately allege a claim under Washington's CPA for alleged deceptive statements in Premera's Code of Conduct. . . .

3. Fraud by Omission

In Premera I, the Court held that in Plaintiffs' claims of fraud by omission Plaintiffs adequately had alleged materiality, reliance, the duty to speak, and the duty to avoid making a material omission. The Court found, however, that Plaintiffs had not alleged a clear articulation of precisely what should have been disclosed to Plaintiffs in order to prevent the statements that Premera did make from being misleading, i.e. a half-truth. To cure this deficiency in their amended pleading, Plaintiffs add Paragraph 256, which alleges that Premera should have disclosed that it did not implement industry standard access controls, did not fix known vulnerabilities in its electronic security protocols, failed to protect against reasonably anticipated threats, and otherwise did not comport with its assurances regarding protecting information.

Premera argues that Plaintiffs' new allegations do not cure the deficiency identified by the Court and are unreasonably vague. The Court disagrees. Plaintiffs' allegations are sufficient to articulate what Plaintiffs allege should have been disclosed to prevent Premera's statements from being misleading. Premera also argues that its delay in notifying Plaintiffs was reasonable and necessary to prevent greater harm. Weighing the potential benefits and harm of earlier disclosure, however, raises an issue that is inappropriate to resolve in a motion to dismiss under Rule 12(b)(6). . . .

5. Conclusion

Plaintiffs sufficiently allege a claim for fraud by omission and claims based on alleged misrepresentations in statements made in Premera's Preferred Select policy booklet, Privacy Notice, and Code of Conduct. . . .

B. Plaintiffs' Contract–Based Claims

1. Breach of Express Terms in the Express Contract

In Premera I, the Court agreed with Premera that Plaintiffs had not identified any express provision in the parties' health benefit contracts that contains any promise relating to data security and that Plaintiffs' references to Premera's Privacy Notice and Code of Conduct give rise to the question of whether those documents are part of the parties' health benefits contract. In response, Plaintiffs added more specific allegations relating to the policy booklets, Privacy Notice, and Code of Conduct.

a. Policy booklets

The FAC identifies the specific provisions contained in the policy booklets that Plaintiffs contend were breached. For the reasons discussed in addressing Plaintiffs' claims of affirmative misrepresentation based on the policy booklets, the Court concludes that Plaintiffs adequately allege a breach of express contract for the Policyholder Plaintiffs who were sent the Preferred Select policy, but not those who were sent only the Preferred Bronze policy.

b. Privacy Notice

Plaintiffs also allege that Premera made promises in its Privacy Notice that were part of the health benefits contract and were materially breached. Plaintiffs allege that "Premera sends its Notice of Privacy Policy and its policy booklets to all members of the Nationwide Premera Policyholder and Plan Administration Subclass, forming an express contract." Premera argues that because Plaintiffs do not specifically allege that the Privacy Notice was attached to the policy booklet, Plaintiffs' allegations are insufficient to support a claim that the Privacy Notice was sent along with the policy booklet. The Court disagrees. It is a reasonable inference from Plaintiffs' allegations in Paragraph 181 that the two documents were sent together.

Premera also argues that even if the Privacy Notice was sent with the policy booklets, the policy booklets contain clauses that preclude interpreting any contract among the parties as including the Privacy Notice. The Preferred Select policy has an integration clause, titled "Entire Contract," which states that the contract includes the policy booklet, summary of costs, application, and "[a]ll attachments and endorsements included now or issued later." The Preferred Bronze policy does not have this specific clause. Instead, it states that Premera agrees to "the terms and conditions appearing on this and the following pages, including any endorsements, amendments, and addenda to this contract which are signed and issued by Premera Blue Cross."

The Court is persuaded by the reasoning stated by United States District Judge Ruben Castillo in the Northern District of Illinois in addressing similar arguments from the defendant insurance company moving to dismiss a breach of contract claim involving similar policy provisions and deciding whether a notice of privacy was included in the policy. Judge Castillo explained:

> The matter is complicated, however, because the policy also expressly incorporates by reference certain extraneous documents. Specifically, it defines "policy" as "this policy with any attached application(s), and any riders and endorsements." The policy's table of contents specifies that "[a] copy of the application and any riders and endorsements follow page 17."

As the documents have been submitted to the Court, there are several documents following page 17, including the Privacy Pledge.

Based on the manner in which the Privacy Pledge was given to her, Plaintiff argues that this document qualifies as an endorsement. Defendant responds that the Privacy Pledge could not possibly constitute an endorsement under the plain meaning of that term.

"[A]n endorsement has been defined as being merely an amendment to an insurance policy; a rider." A "rider," in turn, is defined as "[a]n attachment to some document, such as ... an insurance policy, that amends or supplements the document." BLACK'S LAW DICTIONARY (10th ed. 2014). The Court disagrees with Defendant that the Privacy Pledge could not possibly satisfy these definitions. Plaintiff alleges that the Privacy Pledge accompanied the policy that was mailed to her, and this document can be read to supplement the policy by providing additional benefits to insureds regarding the handling of their personal information. The policy does require that endorsements be approved by Defendant's president or one if its vice-presidents, but the Privacy Pledge states that it was authored by Defendant's "Chairman, President and Chief Executive Officer."

Defendant argues that "an endorsement must be properly attached to the policy so as to indicate that it and the policy are parts of the same contract and must be construed together." But again, Plaintiff alleges that the Privacy Pledge was sent to her along with the policy documents, and the Court must accept this allegation as true. The policy itself states that the documents following page 17 are considered part of the policy, which would appear to include the Privacy Pledge. Based on Plaintiff's allegations and the language of the policy, her claim that the policy incorporated the Privacy Pledge is not implausible.

Defendant could have avoided any ambiguity by clearly labeling the documents sent with the policy that were intended to be incorporated by reference, but it did not do so. Or Defendant could have drafted an integration clause that did not reference outside documents, in which case Plaintiff would have been precluded from relying on outside documents to assert a breach of contract claim. But that is not how the policy was drafted, and any ambiguities must be construed against Defendant. Therefore, the Court rejects Defendant's argument that the contract documents foreclose Plaintiff's claim as a matter of law.

The Court holds that Plaintiffs have sufficiently alleged that Premera's Privacy Notice was expressly attached to and incorporated in the health benefits contracts. Further, for the same reasons the Court found the representations in the Privacy Notice are sufficiently specific for a misrepresentation claim, they are also sufficient for a breach of contract claim.

c. Code of Conduct

Regarding the Code of Conduct, as Plaintiffs quote in their FAC, the policy booklets connect the assurances relating to the protection of policyholders' Sensitive Information to a "company confidentiality policy." Plaintiffs allege that the Code of

Conduct "appears to include the 'company confidentiality policy' referenced in the policy booklets." Premera argues that: (1) the mere reference to this policy is insufficient to incorporate clearly and unequivocally the terms of a company confidentiality policy for Premera employees into the contract between Premera and its policyholders; (2) the policy is not clearly identified and Plaintiffs are guessing that the Code of Conduct contains the policy; and (3) even if the Code of Conduct were incorporated, it does not contain any enforceable promises.

Under Washington law, "'[i]f the parties to a contract clearly and unequivocally incorporate by reference into their contract some other document, that document becomes part of their contract.'" Cedar River Water & Sewer Dist. v. King Cty., 178 Wash. 2d 763, 785, (2013). "It must also be clear that the parties to the agreement had knowledge of and assented to the incorporated terms." Swinerton Builders Nw., Inc. v. Kitsap Cty., 168 Wash. App. 1002 (2012) (quotation marks omitted).

Addressing Premera's first argument, the Preferred Select policy states: "We protect your privacy by making sure your information stays confidential. We have a company confidentiality policy and we require all employees to sign it." The Court concludes this is an enforceable promise to protect data security. It is not, however, an incorporation by reference to the company confidentiality policy. It contains a factual statement that a policy exists. It does not link any promise made to policyholders or obligation of Premera to the existence or terms of that confidentiality policy.

The Preferred Bronze policy, on the other hand, states: "To safeguard your privacy, we take care to ensure that your information remains confidential by having a company confidentiality policy and by requiring all employees to sign it." As discussed above, the Court holds that this is not an enforceable promise to protect data security in and of itself It does, however, incorporate by reference the confidentiality policy. The reason the Preferred Bronze policy, unlike the Preferred Select policy, incorporates the company confidentiality policy by reference is because Premera is promising to protect the privacy of policyholders' information by having a company confidentiality policy. Thus, the logical reading of this clause is that it is the terms of the confidentiality policy that will protect policyholders' private information and that the parties intended those terms to be incorporated by reference. . . .

The fact that policyholders are not parties to the confidentiality policy does not prohibit its incorporation by reference. In fact, "[i]ncorporation by reference allows the parties to 'incorporate contractual terms by reference to a separate ... agreement to which they are not parties, and including a separate document which is unsigned.'" W. Washington Corp. of Seventh–Day Adventists v. Ferrellgas, Inc., 102 Wash. App. 488, 494 (2000) (quoting 11 Williston on Contracts § 30:25, at 233–34 (4th ed. 1999)).

Regarding Premera's second argument, the Court agrees that Plaintiffs' allegation that the Code of Conduct "appears" to contain the confidentiality clause incorporated into the Preferred Bronze policy indicates some doubt by Plaintiffs. Dismissal for inarticulate pleading, however, is not appropriate. Plaintiffs' allegations sufficiently place Premera on notice of what document Plaintiffs are claiming is the confidentiality policy and how it has been breached. Premera's argument that the Code of Conduct might not actually contain the referenced confidentiality policy is more appropriate to consider at summary judgment or trial.

Premera's final argument, that the Code of Conduct does not contain any enforceable promises, is well taken. As discussed above, the representations in the Code of Conduct are not guarantees but are expressions of corporate optimism. Although these statements are sufficiently alleged to be "deceptive" under Washington's CPA, they are not enforceable promises sufficient to support Plaintiffs' express contract claim.

2. Breach of Implied Terms in the Express Contract

The FAC clarifies that, in the alternative to their claim for breach of express terms in the express contract, the Policyholder Plaintiffs allege that there was an implied term in their express contract. Specifically, the Policyholder Plaintiffs allege that the express contracts included "implied terms requiring Premera to implement data security adequate to safeguard and protect the confidentiality of their Sensitive Information, including in accordance with HIPAA regulations, federal, state and local laws, and industry standards."

Under Washington law, a court may imply an obligation into a contract when five requirements are met: (1) the implication must arise from the language used or it must be indispensable to effectuate the intention of the parties; (2) it must appear from the language used that it was so clearly within the contemplation of the parties that they deemed it unnecessary to express it; (3) implied covenants can only be justified on the grounds of legal necessity; (4) a promise can be implied only where it can be rightfully assumed that it would have been made if attention had been called to it; (5) there can be no implied covenant where the subject is completely covered by the contract. Brown v. Safeway Stores, 94 Wash. 2d 359, 370 (1980). . . .

The Court agrees with Plaintiffs that under the circumstances of this case, it is apparent that the parties intended that Plaintiffs or their health care providers would give Plaintiffs' Sensitive Information to Premera and that Premera would take reasonable and adequate steps to protect the confidentiality of that information. Thus, under Oregon law, this is an appropriate circumstance in which to follow Section 204 and imply Plaintiffs' proposed omitted essential term into the parties' contract. The Court also notes that although Premera argues that nowhere did it indicate that it would follow state law or industry standards, that argument is contradicted by the documents submitted by Premera. For example, the Privacy Notice and Code of Conduct both expressly reference state law protecting confidential information, and the Code of Conduct also notes that Premera is expected to be aware of and follow established corporate policies and procedures to protect confidential information.

Premera's final argument is that implying a data security term into the parties' contract would frustrate the purpose of Congress in not allowing a private right of action under HIPAA. The fact that there is no private right of action under HIPAA, however, does not preclude causes of action under state law, even if such a cause of action requires as an element that HIPAA was violated. . . .

Here, however, the policy booklets are not government contracts that merely confirm a statutory obligation or opt-in to a federal statutory scheme. Plaintiffs ask the

Court to imply a term that Premera has agreed to provide reasonable and adequate data security, including data security that complies with HIPAA as well as with state and local laws and industry standards. This goes beyond merely confirming Premera's obligations under HIPAA and thus the fact that HIPAA does not provide a private right of action does not preclude the Court from implying this proposed term. See In re: Cmty. Health Sys., Inc., 2016 WL 4732630, at *23 (N.D. Ala. Sept. 12, 2016) (evaluating breach of contract claims for breaching contractual promises reasonably to protect data and allowing such claims to proceed); Dolmage, 2016 WL 754731, at *9 (same); In re Anthem, Inc. Data Breach Litig., 162 F. Supp. 3d 953, 1010–11 (N.D. Cal. 2016) ("Anthem I") (rejecting the argument that under the relevant statute exclusive enforcement lies with the government and finding the plaintiffs could pursue breach of contract claims as third-party beneficiaries because the contract terms established that the defendant "could be held to privacy Standards above and beyond the standards required under federal law"); accord In re Anthem, Inc. Data Breach Litig., 2016 WL 3029783, at *20 (N.D. Cal. May 27, 2016) ("Anthem II") ("A breach of contract claim based solely upon a pre-existing legal obligation to comply with HIPAA cannot survive dismissal." (emphasis in original)); Wiebe v. NDEX West, LLC, 2010 WL 2035992, *3 (CD. Cal. May 17, 2010) (noting that "plaintiffs must ... do something more to allege a breach of contract claim than merely point to allegations of a statutory violation").

3. Breach of Implied-in–Fact Contract

Plaintiffs also allege in the alternative to their express contract claim that by "providing their Sensitive Information, and upon Defendant's acceptance of such information, [the parties] entered into implied-in-fact contracts for the provision of data security, separate and apart from any express contracts." Plaintiffs further allege that the implied contracts "obligated Defendant to take reasonable steps to secure and safeguard Class members' Sensitive Information," that "[t]he terms of these implied contracts are further described in the federal laws, state law, local laws, and industry standards," and that Premera assented to these terms through its Privacy Notice, Code of Conduct, and other public statements.

As the Court explained in Premera I, Washington law recognizes contracts that are implied in fact. Such contracts are an agreement between parties "arrived at from their acts and conduct viewed in the light of surrounding circumstances, ... it grows out of the intentions of the parties to the transaction, and there must be a meeting of the minds." Milone & Tucci, Inc. v. Bona Fide Builders, Inc., 49 Wash. 2d 363, 367–68 (1956). An implied-in-fact contract still requires an offer, acceptance within the terms of the offer and communicated to the offeror, mutual intention to contract, and a meeting of the minds.

Premera argues that Plaintiffs continue to fail adequately to allege that there was a meeting of the minds with respect to the alleged implied contract. Specifically, Premera asserts that because this claim is alleged on behalf of every plaintiff in the putative class, it includes persons whose Sensitive Information came into Premera's possession without any relationship between the parties, such as persons who obtained medical treatment in Washington state who had a health benefits provider other than

Premera and may not have known that Premera was given their Sensitive Information. At least for such persons, Premera argues, Plaintiffs fail to allege the formation of an implied-in-fact contract.

Plaintiffs respond that they have alleged that all Plaintiffs "gave" their sensitive information to Premera and thus Premera did not just "come into possession" of the information. Although Plaintiffs allege in a conclusory fashion that all of them provided their Sensitive Information to Premera, Plaintiffs do not allege facts that plausibly suggest that Plaintiffs other than the Policyholder Plaintiffs gave information to Premera, as opposed to merely obtaining medical treatment in the state of Washington, giving their Sensitive Information to the Washington provider, who then may have sent that information to Premera for processing. There are no allegations of (1) an offer by Premera to accept Sensitive Information from those Plaintiffs, (2) a mutual intention to agree with those Plaintiffs regarding data security, or (3) any meeting of the minds between Premera and those plaintiffs regarding data security. Thus, there are insufficient allegations for any Plaintiffs or putative class members who are not Policyholder Plaintiffs to demonstrate the formation of an implied-in-fact contract relating to data security. Plaintiffs' claim of such an implied-in-fact contract for Plaintiffs other than the Policyholder Plaintiffs is therefore dismissed.

To the extent Premera intends to assert this argument against Policyholder Plaintiffs, however, the Court rejects Premera's position. For those Plaintiffs, there are sufficient allegations to support an alternative claim of a contract implied-in-fact. The policy booklets, Code of Conduct, and Privacy Notice all demonstrate Premera's commitment and intent to take reasonable and adequate steps to safeguard the Sensitive Information of its policyholders. Because the contractual relationship between Premera and the Policyholder Plaintiffs necessarily requires those Plaintiffs (and their doctors) to provide their Sensitive Information to Premera, Plaintiffs' allegations that they did so with an understanding and the intent that Premera would adequately protect that data is a plausible inference. . . .

4. Conclusion

The Policyholder Plaintiffs have sufficiently alleged claims for breach of express contract for alleged breach of Premera's obligations contained in the Preferred Select policy and Privacy Notice. Plaintiffs have not sufficiently alleged claims for breach of express contract for promises or obligations contained in the Preferred Bronze policy or Code of Conduct. Under Oregon law, Plaintiffs adequately allege breach of an implied term in their express contract, but this claim is not adequately alleged under the common law of contract in Washington. In addition, the Policyholder Plaintiffs sufficiently allege an alternative claim for breach of an implied-in-fact contract, but the non–Policyholder Plaintiffs have not.

In the following case, the district court rejected the plaintiffs breach of contract claims, but found that the plaintiffs sufficiently alleged unfair business practices under California law in the data breach context based on violations of HIPAA.

In re Anthem, Inc. Data Breach Litigation, 162 F.Supp.3d 953 (N.D. Cal. 2016).

LUCY H. KOH, United States District Judge

Plaintiffs bring this putative class action against Anthem, Inc., 28 Anthem affiliates, Blue Cross Blue Shield Association, and 17 non-Anthem Blue Cross Blue Shield Companies. The Court shall refer to Anthem, Inc. and the Anthem affiliates as the "Anthem Defendants," and shall refer to Blue Cross Blue Shield Association and the non-Anthem Blue Cross Blue Shield Companies as the "Non-Anthem Defendants." The Court shall refer to the Anthem and Non-Anthem Defendants collectively as "Defendants."

Before the Court are separate motions to dismiss Plaintiffs' consolidated amended complaint ("CAC") filed by the Anthem and Non-Anthem Defendants. . . .

I. BACKGROUND

A. Factual Background

Defendant Anthem, Inc. ("Anthem") is one of the largest health benefits and health insurance companies in the United States. Anthem serves its members through various Blue Cross Blue Shield ("BCBS") licensee affiliates and other non-BCBS affiliates. Anthem also cooperates with the Blue Cross Blue Shield Association ("BCBSA") and several independent BCBS licensees via the BlueCard program. "Under the BlueCard program, members of one BCBS licensee may access another BCBS licensee's provider networks and discounts when the members are out of state."

In order to provide certain member services, the Anthem and Non-Anthem Defendants "collect, receive, and access their customers' and members' extensive individually identifiable health record information." "These records include personal information (such as names, dates of birth, Social Security numbers, health care ID numbers, home addresses, email addresses, and employment information, including income data) and individually-identifiable health information (pertaining to the individual claims process, medical history, diagnosis codes, payment and billing records, test records, dates of service, and all other health information that an insurance company has or needs to have to process claims)." The Court shall refer to members' personal and health information as Personal Identification Information, or "PII."

Anthem maintains a common computer database which contains the PII of current and former members of Anthem, Anthem's affiliates, BCBSA, and independent BCBS licensees. In total, Anthem's database contains the PII of approximately 80 million individuals. According to Plaintiffs, both the Anthem and Non-Anthem Defendants promised their members that their PII would be protected. Blue Cross of California, for instance, mailed the following privacy notice to its members:

> We keep your oral, written and electronic [PII] safe using physical, electronic, and procedural means. These safeguards follow federal and state laws. Some of the ways we keep your [PII] safe include securing

offices that hold [PII], password-protecting computers, and locking storage areas and filing cabinets. We require our employees to protect [PII] through written policies and procedures.... Also, where required by law, our affiliates and nonaffiliates must protect the privacy of data we share in the normal course of business. They are not allowed to give [PII] to others without your written OK, except as allowed by law and outlined in this notice.

In February 2015, Anthem announced to the public that "cyberattackers had breached the Anthem Database, and [had] accessed [the PII of] individuals in the Anthem Database." This was not the first time that Anthem had experienced problems with data security. In late 2009, approximately 600,000 customers of Wellpoint (Anthem's former trade name) "had their personal information and protected healthcare information compromised due to a data breach." In addition, in 2013, the U.S. Department of Health and Human Services fined Anthem $1.7 million for various HIPAA violations related to data security. Finally, in 2014, the federal government informed Anthem and other healthcare companies of the possibility of future cyberattacks, and advised these companies to take appropriate measures, such as data encryption and enhanced password protection.

Plaintiffs allege that Defendants did not sufficiently heed these warnings, which allowed cyberattackers to extract massive amounts of data from Anthem's database between December 2014 and January 2015. After Anthem discovered the extent of this data breach, it proceeded to implement various containment measures. The cyberattacks ceased by January 31, 2015. In addition, after learning of the cyberattacks, Anthem proceeded to retain Mandiant, a cybersecurity company, "to assist in assessing and responding to the Anthem Data Breach and to assist in developing security protocols for Anthem." Mandiant's work culminated in the production of an Intrusion Investigation Report ("Mandiant Report"), which Mandiant provided to Anthem in July 2015.

According to Plaintiffs, the Mandiant Report found that "Anthem and [its] Affiliates [had] failed to take reasonable measures to secure the [PII] in their possession." Likewise, Plaintiffs allege that "Anthem and Anthem Affiliates [ ] lacked reasonable encryption policies." Additionally, "BCBSA and non-Anthem BCBS allowed the [PII] that their current and former customers and members had entrusted with them to be placed into the Anthem Database even though there were multiple public indications and warnings that the Anthem and Anthem Affiliates' computer systems and data security practices were inadequate." Plaintiffs further aver that although Anthem publicly disclosed the data breach in February 2015, many affected customers were not personally informed until March 2015, if at all. Finally, Plaintiffs contend that Anthem still has not disclosed whether it has made any changes to its security practices to prevent a future cyberattack.

B. Procedural History

A number of lawsuits were filed against the Anthem and Non-Anthem Defendants in the wake of the Anthem data breach. In general, these lawsuits bring putative class action claims alleging (1) failure to adequately protect Anthem's data systems, (2) failure to disclose to customers that Anthem did not have adequate security practices, and (3) failure to timely notify customers of the data breach.

. . . On November 23, 2015, the Anthem Defendants and Non-Anthem Defendants filed their respective motions to dismiss. ECF No. 410 ("Anthem Mot."); ECF No. 413 ("Non-Anthem Mot."). . . .

II. LEGAL STANDARD

A. Motion to Dismiss

Pursuant to Federal Rule of Civil Procedure 12(b)(6), a defendant may move to dismiss an action for failure to allege "enough facts to state a claim to relief that is plausible on its face." *Bell Atl. Corp. v. Twombly*, 550 U.S. 544, 570, 127 S.Ct. 1955, 167 L.Ed.2d 929 (2007). . . .

III. DISCUSSION

C. California Breach of Contract (against Anthem Defendants)

The consolidated amended complaint asserts against the Anthem Defendants a breach of contract claim under California law. Specifically, Plaintiffs allege that "Anthem and Anthem Affiliates did not satisfy their promises and obligations to Plaintiffs and Statewide Class Members under the contracts in that they did not take reasonable measures to keep Plaintiffs' and Statewide Class Members' [PII] secure and confidential and did not comply with the applicable laws, regulations, and industry standards." In moving to dismiss Plaintiffs' claim, the Anthem Defendants contend that "(a) the CAC fails to identify the contractual provisions that allegedly were breached, (b) the CAC fails to allege facts showing any breach caused Plaintiffs to suffer damages that are cognizable under California law. . . .

As to whether the consolidated amended complaint identifies the contractual provisions that were breached, the Court observes that, "[u]nder California law, to state a claim for breach of contract a plaintiff must plead the contract, plaintiffs' performance (or excuse for nonperformance), defendant's breach, and damage to plaintiff therefrom." *Low v. LinkedIn Corp.*, 900 F.Supp.2d 1010, 1028 (N.D.Cal.2012) (internal quotation marks omitted). With respect to this first requirement—the need to plead the contract— a plaintiff must, in actions involving breach of a written contract, "allege the specific provisions in the contract creating the obligation the defendant is said to have breached." *Young v. Facebook, Inc.*, 790 F.Supp.2d 1110, 1117 (N.D.Cal.2011). . . .

The Court finds that the consolidated amended complaint fails to satisfy this requirement, based on a review of (1) the language in the consolidated amended complaint, (2) the language on Anthem's public websites and in various privacy notices, (3) the exhibits submitted in connection with the consolidated amended complaint. . . . The Court addresses these four areas in detail below.

1. Language in Consolidated Amended Complaint

First, with respect to the language in the consolidated amended complaint, Plaintiffs allege that class members "who purchased individual insurance plans from Anthem Affiliates or who received health insurance...under a contract between an employer...and Anthem or Anthem Affiliates had valid, binding, and enforceable express, third party beneficiary, or implied contracts with Anthem and Anthem Affiliates."

However, under the section of the consolidated amended complaint titled "Breach of Contract," Plaintiffs do not refer to any contractual language or any contractual provisions that the Anthem Defendants allegedly breached. Instead, Plaintiffs state—without reference to an underlying contract or other documents—that class members provided "Anthem and/or Anthem Affiliates with their [PII]." In exchange, the Anthem Defendants promised "to protect [class members' PII] in compliance with federal and state laws and regulations, including HIPAA, and industry standards." In the very next paragraph, Plaintiffs state that "[t]he terms of Plaintiffs' and Statewide Class Members' contracts with Anthem and Anthem Affiliates that concern the protection of Plaintiffs' [PII] [are] set forth above." However, this paragraph does not refer specifically to any other part of the consolidated amended complaint. The remaining paragraphs in this section do no better. One paragraph addresses Plaintiffs' implied contract theory, another paragraph alleges that Plaintiffs "fully performed their obligations under their contracts," and several paragraphs address the damages that Plaintiffs seek. Considered together, none of these paragraphs identify a specific contractual provision that the Anthem Defendants breached.

These stray allegations mirror the facts in *Young v. Facebook*, where plaintiff stated in the complaint that "Facebook did not perform in accordance with the terms of [the] agreement in their Statement of Rights and Responsibilities contract by arbitrarily and impulsively handling [plaintiff's] member account." *Young*, 790 F.Supp.2d at 1117. However, as the district court pointed out, plaintiff's "complaint [did] not allege any provision of the contract prohibiting Facebook from terminating an account in the manner alleged." *Id.* Because plaintiff had failed to identify a relevant contractual provision that was breached, the *Young* court granted Facebook's motion to dismiss plaintiff's California breach of contract claim. *Id.* (finding that plaintiff had failed to "allege the specific provisions in the contract creating the obligation the defendant is said to have breached."). As in *Young*, Plaintiffs' conclusory statements in the "Breach of Contract" section of the consolidated amended complaint are insufficient to survive a motion to dismiss.

2. Language on Public Websites and in Privacy Notices

Plaintiffs, however, contend that the paragraphs discussed above constitute "only...the summary language [of Plaintiffs'] breach of contract count." Instead, Plaintiffs note, "specific promises...regarding data security" are located in paragraphs 161 through 170. These paragraphs include language from the public websites of the Anthem Defendants and from statements made by the Anthem Defendants in various privacy notices. The website for every Anthem BCBS affiliate, for instance, states:

> **[PII] (including Social Security Number) Privacy Protection Policy [Name of Anthem BCBS Affiliate] maintains policies that protect the confidentiality of [PII], including Social Security numbers, obtained from its members and associates in the course of its regular business functions.** [Name of Anthem BCBS Affiliate] is committed to protecting information about its customers and associates, especially the confidential nature of their [PII].

CAC ¶ 166 (second and fourth alterations in original). Likewise, Blue Cross of California mailed the following privacy notice to customers:

> **We keep your oral, written and electronic [PII] safe using physical, electronic, and procedural means. These safeguards follow federal and state laws.** Some of the ways we keep your [PII] safe include securing offices that hold [PII], **password-protecting computers**, and locking storage areas and filing cabinets. We require our employees to protect [PII] through written policies and procedures. **These policies limit access to [PII] to only those employees who need the data to do their job.** Employees are also required to wear ID badges to help keep people who do not belong out of areas where sensitive data is kept. **Also, where required by law, our affiliates and nonaffiliates must protect the privacy of data we share in the normal course of business.** They are not allowed to give [PII] to others without your written OK, except as allowed by law and outlined in this notice.

Id. ¶ 163. Although this language is more specific than the conclusory paragraphs discussed above, this language still does not give rise to a viable California breach of contract claim.

First, the consolidated amended complaint provides no information on when the language at issue was posted onto the Anthem Defendants' websites and when the various privacy notices were sent to class members. Clearly, such notices would be of little assistance to Plaintiffs' claim if Plaintiffs received these notices *after* the data breach at issue.

More importantly, the consolidated amended complaint makes no attempt to connect the language in paragraphs 161 through 170 with the terms of Plaintiffs' alleged contracts. At no point in paragraphs 161 through 170 do Plaintiffs allege that the privacy notices or public website statements were part of or were incorporated by reference into Plaintiffs' contracts with the Anthem Defendants. In fact, the word "contract" does not appear at all in paragraphs 161 through 170. By this same token, under the section of the consolidated amended complaint titled "Breach of Contract," Plaintiffs do not at any point refer to the privacy notices or public websites discussed in paragraphs 161 through 170.

Plaintiffs cannot bring a breach of contract claim based on language from documents that might have been issued after the alleged breach and based on language from documents that might not even have been part of the alleged contract. In reaching this conclusion, the Court returns to the legal principle discussed above: that, "[i]n an action for breach of a written contract, a plaintiff must allege the specific provisions in the contract creating the obligation the defendant is said to have breached." *Young*, 790 F.Supp.2d at 1117. Plaintiffs have failed to identify any such contractual provision because Plaintiffs have made no effort to connect the language in paragraphs 161 through 170 with the terms in Plaintiffs' contracts with the Anthem Defendants. On this basis alone, the Court finds that dismissal of Plaintiffs' California breach of contract claim is warranted. Below, the Court addresses additional bases upon which Plaintiffs' California breach of contract claim is unavailing.

3. Exhibits Submitted in Connection With Consolidated Amended Complaint

Plaintiffs have failed to submit any relevant exhibits, such as a copy of the contract between an Anthem Defendant and a California Plaintiff, which might counsel against dismissal. Although Plaintiffs are not required to submit such exhibits, these exhibits would certainly provide clarity on the scope and nature of the Anthem Defendants' obligations. Thus, in *Young*, plaintiff included a copy of Facebook's Statement of Rights and Responsibility with the complaint. 790 F.Supp.2d at 1118. Likewise, in *Zepeda v. PayPal, Inc.*, 777 F.Supp.2d 1215, 1220 (N.D.Cal.2011), plaintiff included Paypal's user agreement as an exhibit to accompany the complaint. In *Woods v. Google Inc.*, 2011 WL 3501403, *3–4 (N.D.Cal. Aug. 10, 2011), plaintiff also filed a copy of Google's advertising contract with the complaint. In all of these cases—*Young*, *Zepeda*, and *Woods*—the district court, after reviewing the allegations made in the complaint and the terms of the pertinent agreement, determined that the plaintiff could not maintain a cause of action for breach of contract under California law. Here, on the other hand, there is nothing for the Court to review as Plaintiffs have submitted no contracts or other materials for the Court to examine.

In fact, the only possibly relevant exhibits filed were submitted by the Anthem Defendants, not Plaintiffs. The Anthem Defendants, for instance, filed a copy of the Summary Plan Description under which Plaintiffs Daniel and Kelly Tharp allegedly received coverage. *See* ECF No. 411 at 1–2. This Plan Description includes a five page "Privacy Notice." *See* ECF No. 411-4 at 58–62. This Privacy Notice provides a list of specific circumstances where Anthem or an Anthem affiliate might disclose a member's personal health information. *Id.* The Notice further provides that "[o]ther than as stated above, the Health Plan will not disclose your health information other than with your written authorization." *Id.* at 61. Moreover, "[t]he Health Plan is required by law to maintain the privacy of your health information and to provide you with this Notice of the Plan's legal duties and privacy practices with respect to your health information. If you participate in an insured plan option, you will receive a notice directly from the Insurer." *Id.* at 62. This final statement in the Summary Plan Description could plausibly be taken to incorporate by reference future privacy notices sent to class members.

However, the problem with relying on this Summary Plan Description is that Plaintiffs have, in the consolidated amended complaint, stated that such documents do not represent the contract between class members and the Anthem Defendants. *See* CAC ¶ 303(b) ("With respect to contracts between employers and Anthem and/or Anthem

Affiliates, the applicable contract is the services agreement between the employer and Anthem and/or Anthem Affiliates, not the employer benefits plan document."). Plaintiffs repeat this assertion in opposing the Anthem Defendants' motion to dismiss. *See* Anthem Opp'n at 25 (describing Summary Plan Description documents as "non-enforceable"). Given Plaintiffs' position, the Court can not rely upon the Summary Plan Description to save Plaintiffs' breach of contract of claim from dismissal.

4. Incorporation of Applicable State and Federal Law

As a final point, Plaintiffs state that, "[u]nder California law, Defendants' contracts necessarily incorporate applicable laws even absent specific promises." This contention alone, however, does not save Plaintiffs' breach of contract claim.

First, the consolidated amended complaint provides little guidance as to which "applicable laws" were incorporated into the contract. Instead, the consolidated amended complaint merely alleges that the Anthem Defendants were required to comply with "federal and state laws and regulations, including HIPAA, and industry standards." In other words, outside of a single passing reference to HIPAA, Plaintiffs have provided little detail on what other laws, regulations, or standards the Anthem Defendants might have violated. As other district courts have noted, "plaintiffs must...do something more to allege a breach of contract claim than merely point to allegations of a statutory violation." *Wiebe v. NDEX West, LLC*, 2010 WL 2035992, *3 (C.D.Cal. May 17, 2010). The consolidated amended complaint fails to meet this requirement.

Second, Plaintiffs' breach of contract claim reaches beyond mere violation of "applicable laws." Plaintiffs, for instance, also allege that the Anthem Defendants' actions ran afoul of certain "industry standards." Thus, simply stating that Defendants' contracts incorporate applicable laws does not accurately reflect the nature of Plaintiffs' breach of contract claim.

In sum, after examining the consolidated amended complaint, the exhibits (or lack thereof) filed in connection with the consolidated amended complaint, and relevant case law and statutory authority, the Court finds that Plaintiffs have failed to identify the specific contractual provisions that were breached, as Plaintiffs must do in order to bring a breach of written contract claim under California law.

. . .

F. California Unfair Competition Law (against Anthem and Non-Anthem Defendants)

California's Unfair Competition Law ("UCL") provides a cause of action for business practices that are (1) unlawful, (2) unfair, or (3) fraudulent. Cal. Bus & Prof. Code § 17200, et seq. "The UCL's coverage is sweeping, and its standard for wrongful business conduct intentionally broad." Moore v. Apple, Inc., 73 F.Supp.3d 1191, 1204 (N.D.Cal.2014). "Although the UCL targets a wide range of misconduct, its remedies are limited because UCL actions are equitable in nature." Pom Wonderful LLC v. Welch Foods, Inc., 2009 WL 5184422, *2 (C.D.Cal. Dec. 21, 2009). "Remedies for private individuals bringing suit under the UCL are limited to restitution and injunctive relief." *Id.*

Each prong of the UCL provides a separate and distinct theory of liability, and Plaintiffs assert that Defendants' conduct was unlawful, unfair, and fraudulent. Before addressing whether Plaintiffs have sufficiently pleaded liability under these three prongs, however, the Court must first determine whether Plaintiffs have standing to bring suit. In order to establish standing under the UCL, "a plaintiff must make a twofold showing: he or she must demonstrate injury in fact and a loss of money or property caused by unfair competition." Susilo v. Wells Fargo Bank, N.A., 796 F.Supp.2d 1177, 1195–96 (C.D.Cal.2011). The California Supreme Court has referred to these elements as the "economic injury" and "caus[ation]" requirement. Kwikset Corp. v. Superior Court, 51 Cal.4th 310, 120 Cal.Rptr.3d 741, 246 P.3d 877, 885 (2011).

1. Standing

a. Economic Injury

As to whether Plaintiffs have demonstrated "injury in fact" and "a loss of money or property caused by unfair competition," Susilo, 796 F.Supp.2d at 1195–96, the California Supreme Court has stated that "[t]here are innumerable ways in which economic injury from unfair competition may be shown," Kwikset, 246 P.3d at 885. A plaintiff may, for instance,

> (1) surrender in a transaction more, or acquire in a transaction less, than he or she otherwise would have; (2) have a present or future property interest diminished; (3) be deprived of money or property to which he or she has a cognizable claim; or (4) be required to enter into a transaction, costing money or property, that would otherwise have been unnecessary
> Id. at 885–86.

Here, Plaintiffs seek recovery under the UCL for three types of economic injury: "Loss of Benefit of the Bargain," "Out of Pocket Costs," and "Imminent Risk of Further Costs." Plaintiffs' request for "Loss of Benefit of the Bargain" mirrors the California Supreme Court's determination in Kwikset that a plaintiff who has "surrender[ed] in a transaction more, or acquire[d] in a transaction less, than he or she otherwise would have" may bring a UCL claim. 246 P.3d at 885; see also CAC ¶ 309 ("As a result of Anthem and Anthem Affiliates' failure to implement the security measures required by the contracts, Plaintiffs and Statewide Class Members did not receive the full benefit of their bargain, and instead received health insurance and/or related health care services that were less valuable than what they paid for.").

Moreover, more recent case law within the data breach context confirms that benefit of the bargain damages represent economic injury for purposes of the UCL. See In re Adobe Sys., Inc. Privacy Litig., 66 F.Supp.3d 1197, 1224 (N.D.Cal.2014) (finding standing under the UCL because "[f]our of the six [p]laintiffs allege they personally spent more on Adobe products than they would had they known Adobe was not providing the reasonable security Adobe represented it was providing."); In re LinkedIn User Privacy Litig., 2014 WL 1323713, *4 (N.D.Cal. Mar. 28, 2014) (finding that benefit of the bargain losses are "sufficient to confer...statutory standing under the UCL."). Taken together, Kwikset, In re Adobe, and In re LinkedIn demonstrate that benefit of the bargain losses, as alleged in the consolidated amended complaint, constitute economic injury cognizable under the UCL.

Incidentally, the fact that Plaintiffs have sufficiently pleaded benefit of the bargain losses also establishes that Plaintiffs may seek restitution under the UCL. "[I]n the context of the UCL, 'restitution' is limited to the return of property or funds in which the plaintiff has an ownership interest (or is claiming through someone with an ownership interest)." Madrid v. Perot Sys. Corp., 130 Cal.App.4th 440, 30 Cal.Rptr.3d 210, 219 (Ct.App.2005). "Under the UCL, an individual may recover profits unfairly obtained to the extent that these profits represent monies given to the defendant or benefits in which the plaintiff has an ownership interest." Pom Wonderful, 2009 WL 5184422, *2 (internal quotation marks omitted). In requesting benefit of the bargain damages, Plaintiffs allege (1) that Defendants promised to undertake reasonable data security measures in accordance with the law, (2) that some portion of Plaintiffs' plan premiums went towards data security, and (3) that Defendants failed to undertake the promised data security measures. Plaintiffs therefore "overpa[id]" for their health insurance. In other words, Defendants profited from their lax security measures. Because Plaintiffs seek to "recover profits unfairly obtained," Pom Wonderful, 2009 WL 5184422, *2, Plaintiffs have sufficiently established that they may seek restitution in the instant action.

Defendants' reliance on In re Sony Gaming Networks & Customer Data Sec. Breach Litig. ("Sony I"), 903 F.Supp.2d 942 (S.D.Cal.2012), to challenge this conclusion is misplaced. In Sony I, defendants provided users with access to the Playstation Network ("PSN") free of charge. Because the Sony I plaintiffs "received the PSN services free of cost," the district court concluded that "[p]laintiffs have not alleged 'lost money or profits,' " as required to seek restitution under the UCL. In contrast, in the instant action, Plaintiffs did pay Defendants for their health benefits. Moreover, Plaintiffs understood that some portion of this payment would be directed "to protect Plaintiffs' and Statewide Class Members' [PII] in compliance with federal and state laws and regulations." Based on these allegations, Plaintiffs have established that Defendants received money in exchange for protecting Plaintiffs' data and that Plaintiffs now seek recovery of this money. . . .

b. Causation

"Generally, to prove that a data breach caused identity theft, the pleadings must include allegations of a nexus between the two instances beyond allegations of time and sequence." Resnick v. AvMed, Inc., 693 F.3d 1317, 1326 (11th Cir.2012). "[P]urely temporal connections are often insufficient to establish causation." Stollenwerk v. Tri–West Health Care All., 254 Fed.Appx. 664, 668 (9th Cir.2007). Instead, the "pleadings must indicate a logical connection between the two incidents." Resnick, 693 F.3d at 1327.

Here, the consolidated amended complaint sufficiently establishes a logical connection between the Anthem data breach and the harm suffered by Plaintiffs. Every Plaintiff was at one point enrolled in a health plan administered by a Defendant. As a condition of this enrollment, each Plaintiff provided his or her PII to a Defendant, which was thereafter inputted into Anthem's database. Defendants do not contest that each

Plaintiff had his or her PII stolen as a result of the Anthem data breach. Finally, many Plaintiffs allege that third parties used Plaintiffs' PII in the wake of the data breach. . . . These allegations—that each Plaintiff was enrolled in a health plan administered by a Defendant, that each Plaintiff had his or her PII stolen, and that specific aspects of Plaintiff's PII were used for illicit financial gain after the breach—establish the requisite logical and temporal connection necessary to demonstrate causation.

Defendants' contentions to the contrary lack merit. Defendants argue that Plaintiffs "rel[y] ...on tenuous temporal relationships that fail to connect the cyberattack and the alleged injuries, rather than stating sufficient facts to show economic injury caused by the unfair business practice." As the Court has pointed out, however, Plaintiffs do more than simply allege a temporal relationship between their economic injury and the data breach at issue. Rather, Plaintiffs state that (1) they were enrolled in a particular health plan administered by a Defendant, (2) that they provided their PII to Anthem, (3) that their PII was compromised as a result of the data breach, and (4) that their PII was used for illicit financial gain. Taken together, these allegations "plausibly link Plaintiffs' purported injuries to the Anthem cyberattack."

On this particular point, the Court also observes that Defendants have argued that "[s]cores of other cyber intrusions and data thefts have compromised the personal information of tens of millions of individuals." In support of this argument, Defendants point to recent data breaches at eBay, Target, Home Depot, Neiman Marcus, and various other entities. This contention fails for multiple reasons. First, Defendants' argument relies upon facts taken from a Forbes magazine article—an article not cited or referred to in the consolidated amended complaint. Defendants' argument thus represents little more than an end around the rule that, on a motion to dismiss, the Court may generally "consider only the contents of the complaint." Cooper v. Pickett, 137 F.3d 616, 622 (9th Cir.1997).

Second, and more importantly, under Defendants' theory, a company affected by a data breach could simply contest causation by pointing to the fact that data breaches occur all the time, against various private and public entities. This would, in turn, create a perverse incentive for companies: so long as enough data breaches take place, individual companies will never be found liable. No part of the UCL, the relevant authority addressing causation, or the specific facts of this case support such a legal theory. . . .

To summarize, the Court finds that Plaintiffs have sufficiently demonstrated both a logical and temporal relationship necessary to establish causation. Defendants' attempts to direct the Court to the facts (1) that many other data breaches occurred during the relevant time period and (2) that a named Plaintiff did not receive notice from an Anthem or Non-Anthem Defendant do not negate this finding. Thus, by demonstrating both causation and economic loss, Plaintiffs have sufficiently established standing under the UCL.

2. Unlawful

"The unlawful prong of the UCL prohibits anything that can properly be called a business practice and that at the same time is forbidden by law." In re Adobe, 66

F.Supp.3d at 1225 (internal quotation marks omitted). "Generally, violation of almost any law may serve as a basis for a UCL claim." Antman v. Uber Technologies, Inc., 2015 WL 6123054, *6 (N.D.Cal. Oct. 19, 2015). However, a UCL claim "must identify the particular section of the statute that was violated, and must describe with reasonable particularity the facts supporting the violation." Baba v. Hewlett–Packard Co., 2010 WL 2486353, *6 (N.D.Cal. June 16, 2010).

Plaintiffs allege that, with respect to the UCL's unlawful prong, Defendants' actions violated the Federal Trade Commission Act, HIPAA, the Gramm-Leach-Bliley Act, California's Confidentiality of Medical Information Act, California's unfair insurance practices statutes, California's Insurance Information and Privacy Protection Act, and California's data breach statute. In support of this contention, the consolidated amended complaint identifies specific provisions of HIPAA, the Gramm-Leach-Bliley Act, the Federal Trade Commission Act, and California's data breach statute, that were allegedly violated. Such references directly rebut Defendants' claim that the consolidated amended complaint "references...statutes only generally, and does not specify how ...Defendants supposedly violated them." Instead, a review of the complaint demonstrates that Plaintiffs' allegations "identify the particular section of the statute that was violated," and other allegations in the consolidated amended complaint "describe with reasonable particularity the facts supporting the violation." Accordingly, the Court finds that Plaintiffs' claim survives under the UCL's unlawful prong.

3. Unfair

"The 'unfair' prong of the UCL creates a cause of action for a business practice that is unfair even if not proscribed by some other law." In re Adobe, 66 F.Supp.3d at 1225. "The UCL does not define the term 'unfair.'...[And] the proper definition of 'unfair' conduct against consumers 'is currently in flux' among California courts."

Some California appellate courts apply a balancing approach, which requires courts to "weigh the utility of the defendant's conduct against the gravity of the harm to the alleged victim." Davis v. HSBC Bank Nevada, N.A., 691 F.3d 1152, 1169 (9th Cir.2012). Other California appellate courts have held that "unfairness must be tethered to some legislatively declared policy or proof of some actual or threatened impact on competition." Lozano, 504 F.3d at 735. Finally, at least one California appellate court has adopted and applied the three-part test set forth in § 5 of the Federal Trade Commission Act: "(1) the consumer injury must be substantial; (2) the injury must not be outweighed by any countervailing benefits to consumers or competition; and (3) it must be an injury that consumers themselves could not reasonably have avoided." Camacho v. Auto. Club of Southern California, 142 Cal.App.4th 1394, 48 Cal.Rptr.3d 770, 777 (Ct.App.2006). The Court shall refer to these tests as the "balancing test," the "tethering test," and the "FTC test," respectively.

In challenging whether Plaintiffs have sufficiently pleaded a UCL claim under the unfair prong, Defendants argue that the consolidated amended complaint "does not allege facts that support the conclusion that Defendants' failure to prevent the cyberattack resulted from immoral, unethical, oppressive, or unscrupulous conduct on

Defendants' part." Defendants' singular focus on whether their actions were immoral, unethical, oppressive, or unscrupulous, however, is misplaced.

None of the three tests for unfairness require plaintiffs to plead that defendants acted in an immoral, unethical, oppressive, or unscrupulous manner. With respect to the balancing test, for instance, the California Courts of Appeal have stated that "an unfair business practice occurs when it offends an established public policy or when the practice is immoral, unethical, oppressive, unscrupulous or substantially injurious to consumers." Bardin v. Daimlerchrysler Corp., 136 Cal.App.4th 1255, 39 Cal.Rptr.3d 634, 638 (Ct.App.2006). In other words, parties may proceed with a UCL claim under the balancing test by either alleging immoral, unethical, oppressive, unscrupulous, or substantially injurious conduct by Defendants or by demonstrating that Defendants' conduct violated an established public policy. Similarly, with respect to the tethering test, parties need not show immoral, unethical, oppressive, unscrupulous, or substantially injurious conduct in order to move forward with a UCL claim. The tethering test only requires parties to show "that the public policy which is a predicate to a consumer unfair competition action under the 'unfair' prong of the UCL [is] tethered to specific constitutional, statutory, or regulatory provisions." In re Adobe, 66 F.Supp.3d at 1226. Finally, the FTC test also does not require parties to show immoral, unethical, oppressive, unscrupulous, or substantially injurious conduct by Defendants.

In any event, the Court finds dismissal of Plaintiffs' UCL claim under the unfair prong unwarranted. In In re Adobe, this Court observed that various California statutes—including several statutes upon which Plaintiffs rely here—reflect "California's public policy of protecting customer data." Based on the allegations in the consolidated amended complaint, Defendants' actions violated this public policy. Whether Defendants' public policy violation is outweighed by the utility of their conduct under the balancing test is a question to be resolved at a later stage in this litigation. Thus, based on the balancing test alone, the Court DENIES Defendants' motion to dismiss Plaintiffs' UCL claim under the unfair prong.

4. Fraudulent

"To state a claim under the 'fraud' prong of [the UCL], a plaintiff must allege facts showing that members of the public are likely to be deceived by the alleged fraudulent business practice." Antman, 2015 WL 6123054, *6. Claims stated under the fraud prong of the UCL are subject to the particularity requirements of Federal Rule of Civil Procedure 9(b). Under this Rule, "[i]n alleging fraud or mistake, a party must state with particularity the circumstances constituting fraud or mistake." Fed. R. Civ. P. 9(b). Plaintiffs must include "an account of the time, place, and specific content of the false representations" at issue.

The gravamen of Plaintiffs' fraud claim is that Defendants promised to carry out reasonable security measures, but ultimately failed to carry through with this promise. At first blush, these allegations appear sufficient to state a claim under the fraud prong of the UCL: Defendants represented to Plaintiffs that they would do one thing, but ended up doing another. In general, such allegations constitute a misrepresentation in the most classic sense.

However, Plaintiffs' fraud claim suffers from one notable flaw: as with Plaintiffs' breach of contract claims, Plaintiffs have not "include[d] an account of the time...of the false representations" at issue. Instead, Plaintiffs once again direct the Court to review statements made by Defendants in various privacy notices and on Defendants' public websites. As the Court has explained, the consolidated amended complaint does not specify when these privacy notices were received or when certain statements were made on Defendants' websites. In fact, for several of the statements at issue, the only date identified in the consolidated amended complaint is October 19, 2015, the last day that Plaintiffs visited Defendants' websites. That date postdates the Anthem data breach and does not establish that Plaintiffs relied upon or were deceived by promises that Defendants made to Plaintiffs prior to the data breach.

Consistent with the Court's reasoning with respect to Plaintiffs' breach of contract claims, it is possible that Plaintiffs may amend the complaint to state with particularity the time that the specific misrepresentations occurred. Accordingly, the Court finds that Plaintiffs have not stated a fraud claim under the UCL, but that Plaintiffs may be able to do so after amendment. Thus, Plaintiffs' fraud claim under the UCL is DISMISSED with leave to amend. Plaintiffs, however, have sufficiently established standing under the UCL and have sufficiently stated a UCL claim to survive dismissal under the unlawful and unfair prongs. Defendants' motion to dismiss Plaintiffs' UCL claim is therefore GRANTED in part and DENIED in part.

NOTES

Note 1

Please note the differences in the treatment of the contract claims by the courts under the *Premera* and *Anthem* cases. How can holders of confidential data protect themselves from contract claims by users? Would you recommend a tightly written merger clause? What about clauses limiting liability and disclaiming any warranties? How would you phrase language concerning data security? Is it too easy to use contract terms to insulate an entity from a data breach of contract claim? What is the advantage of the general approach of Judge Koh's ruling in *Anthem* concerning statutory unfairness and unlawfulness claims from a policy perspective focused on the protection of consumer data rather than reliance on contract claims? Moreover, can you think of other arguments why potential language in website terms and conditions may not be binding perhaps providing consternation to either party depending on the circumstances?

Note 2

In *Weinberg v. Advanced Data Processing*, the district court held that violations of HIPPA cannot serve as the basis of a negligence per se claim under Florida law because HIPPA does not provide a private right of action. See Weinberg v. Advanced Data Processing, 147 F.Supp.3d 1359, 1366 (S.D. Fla. 2015).

CHAPTER SIX. STUDENT DATA PROTECTION LAW

6.1 Introduction

The COVID pandemic accelerated a move to online student applications and resources. With COVID, schools closed and were forced to implement and adapt to remote learning and the associated remote learning online tools. Even prior to computers becoming ubiquitous, the United States Department of Education had a focus on protecting education records through the Family Education Rights and Privacy Act (FERPA). As more student data became available online, the states also promulgated statutes and regulations to protect their students' online data.

The Family Education Rights and Privacy Act (FERPA) has a "reasonable methods" standard for cybersecurity controls. Moreover, FERPA and its regulations do not provide specific security measures.[266] Indeed, FERPA and its regulations have significantly less specificity than the Graham-Leach Bliley Act, Securities and Exchange Commission and Health Insurance Portability Accountability Act areas. Some educational institutions are also governed by the Graham-Leach Bliley Act, which is mostly enforced by the Federal Trade Commission. Additionally, the Department of Education, Office of the Inspector General has overlapping responsibility concerning FERPA. This chapter also provides selected coverage of different agencies concerning various industry sectors.

State student data privacy laws are an extension of FERPA. By name, one might expect state laws to be primarily privacy laws. But these laws are a perfect example of how privacy cannot exist without the implementation of risk-based security measures. A closer look at FERPAA and state laws demonstrates that these are truly cybersecurity-centric laws.

Although protecting student data is important, exfiltration of student data does not always amount to a risk of identity theft. The following case grapples with whether the exposure of student data carries with it the risk of identity theft.

---

[266] *See Data Security: K-12 and Higher Education*, U.S. DEP'T OF EDUCATION, https://studentprivacy.ed.gov/Security (last visited April 23, 2022).

6.2 Student Data and Identity Theft Risk

Kylie S., et al. v. Pearson, et al., d/b/a Pearson Clinical Assessment, 475 F.Supp.3d 844 (N.D. Ill. 2020).

John Z. Lee, United States District Judge

Pearson PLC, NCS Pearson, Inc., and Pearson Education, Inc. (collectively "Pearson") operate AIMSweb, an educational testing platform that stores students' names, emails, and birthdays, among other information. In 2018, hackers slipped past Pearson's defenses and gained access to the data hosted on AIMSweb. No credit cards, social security numbers, health records, or other sensitive information was compromised, and none of the affected students have reported fraudulent charges or other fallout attributable to the data breach.

Believing that Pearson neglected to implement security measures that would have thwarted the hackers, a group of Illinois and Colorado parents initiated this putative class action. At this stage, Pearson has moved to dismiss the complaint. Because Plaintiffs have not established Article III standing, the motion is granted.

I. Background

A. The AIMSweb Platform

Pearson PLC publishes educational materials. Am. Compl. Pearson Education, Inc., one of Pearson PLC's subsidiaries, supplies testing services. NCS Pearson, Inc., another subsidiary, software.

Working together, AIMSweb, a "digital education technology assessment platform licensed to schools and school districts." As part of the curriculum, schools that license the platform instruct their students to complete tests on AIMSweb. To do so, students must share "their first and last names, dates of birth, email addresses, unique student identification numbers, home addresses and telephone numbers." In a privacy policy that covers AIMSweb, Pearson accepted "full responsibility for the information we hold" and promised to "protect [student] privacy at all times."

B. The Data Breach

Sometime in late 2018, hackers penetrated AIMSweb's defenses and gained access to the data stored on the platform. But it was not until early 2019, when the FBI detected the incident, that Pearson realized that AIMSweb had been compromised.

In a preliminary analysis, the FBI estimated that the intruders could have accessed information related to roughly 900,000 students at about 13,000 schools. The disclosed data included "first name, last name, and in some instances ... date of birth and/or email address," along with students' "unique student identification numbers."

About four months after the FBI discovered the problem, Pearson issued a public notice acknowledging that a data breach had occurred. Pearson assured customers that it "do[es] "not have any evidence that th[e] information has been misused." "[A]s a precaution," however, it "offer[ed] to compensate victims in the form of one year of complimentary credit monitoring services."

C. Plaintiffs' Claims

Based on Pearson's failure to prevent the data breach, Plaintiffs assert a dozen different common law and statutory claims. They accuse Pearson of common law negligence, negligence per se, breach of an express contract, breach of an implied contract, unjust enrichment, and intrusion upon seclusion. They also allege that Pearson violated the Illinois Personal Information and Protection Act, 815 Ill. Comp. Stat. § 530/1 *et seq.* ; Illinois Consumer Fraud and Deceptive Business Practices Act, 815 Ill. Comp. Stat. § 505/1, *et seq.* ; Illinois Uniform Deceptive Trade Practices Act, 815 Ill. Comp. Stat. § 510/1, *et seq.* ; Colorado Security Breach Notification Act, Colo. Rev. Stat. §§ 6-1-716, *et seq.* ; Colorado Consumer Protection Act, Colo. Rev. Stat. §§ 6-1-101, *et seq.* ; and Colorado Student Data Transparency and Security Act, Colo. Rev. Stat. §§ 22-16-101, *et seq.*

For its part, Pearson maintains that the complaint should be dismissed for lack of subject-matter jurisdiction, want of personal jurisdiction, and failure to state a claim. The Court's analysis begins—and, in this case, ends—with the question of subject-matter jurisdiction.

II. Legal Standard

Under Federal Rule of Civil Procedure 12(b)(1), a defendant may move to dismiss claims over which a federal court lacks subject-matter jurisdiction. *See Apex Digital, Inc. v. Sears, Roebuck & Co.,* 572 F.3d 440, 443 (7th Cir. 2009); *Perry v. Vill. of Arlington Heights,* 186 F.3d 826, 829 (7th Cir. 1999). In analyzing a Rule 12(b)(1) motion, courts accept as true all well-pleaded facts, draw all reasonable inferences in the plaintiff's favor, and look beyond the jurisdictional allegations to evidence submitted on the issue of subject-matter jurisdiction. *See St. John's United Church of Christ v. City of Chi.,* 502 F.3d 616, 625 (7th Cir. 2007).

III. Analysis

Pearson contends that Plaintiffs lack standing to bring this suit. It is well-established that "[s]tanding is an essential component of Article III's case-or-controversy requirement." *Apex Digital, Inv. v. Sears, Roebuck & Co.,* 572 F.3d 440, 443 (7th Cir. 2009).

To support standing, a claimant must allege: "(1) an injury in fact, (2) that is fairly traceable to the challenged conduct of the defendant, and (3) that is likely to be redressed by a favorable judicial decision." *Spokeo, Inc. v. Robins,* —— U.S. ——, 136 S. Ct. 1540, 1547, 194 L.Ed.2d 635 (2016). "[A] plaintiff, as the party invoking federal jurisdiction, bears the burden of establishing these elements." *Id.* (citation omitted). At issue here is whether Plaintiffs have adequately pleaded an injury-in-fact.

An injury-in-fact refers to a particularized and concrete, actual or imminent invasion of a legally- protected interest. *See Lujan v. Defenders of Wildlife,* 504 U.S. 555, 560, 112 S.Ct. 2130, 119 L.Ed.2d 351 (1992). "For an injury to be 'particularized,' it 'must affect the plaintiff in a personal and individual way.' " *Spokeo,* —— U.S. ——, 136 S Ct. at 1548 (citation omitted). For an injury to be "concrete," it must "actually exist." *Id.* "This does not mean, however, that [a] risk of real harm cannot satisfy the requirement of concreteness." *Id.* at 1549. So long as the plaintiff faces "a substantial risk" of injury, the concreteness component is present.

In arguing that they suffered an injury-in-fact, Plaintiffs articulate three distinct theories. First, they submit that the data breach exacerbated their vulnerability to identity theft. Second, they suggest that the breach reduced the market value of their data. Finally, they contend that certain statutes dictate that any disclosure of student records is a legally-cognizable injury, even if no economic harm results.

A. Increased Risk of Identity Theft

Plaintiffs' primary argument is that the data breach made them easier targets for identity thieves. In *Remijas v. Neiman Marcus Group, LLC,* the Seventh Circuit recognized that a substantial risk of identity theft qualifies as an injury-in-fact. 794 F.3d

688 (7th Cir. 2015). There, "hackers deliberately targeted Neiman Marcus in order to obtain [shoppers'] credit card information." *Id.* at 693. All told, the attackers absconded with about 300,000 credit and debit card numbers. *Id.* at 690. They promptly placed fraudulent charges on 9,000 of the stolen cards. *Id.* Under those conditions, the Court of Appeals held that all of the shoppers had pleaded an injury-in-fact sufficient to survive a Rule 12(b)(1) motion. *Id.* at 693.

Whether a data breach exposes consumers to a material threat of identity theft turns on two factors that derive from *Remijas*: (1) the sensitivity of the data in question, see, e.g., *In re Vtech Data Breach Litig.*, No. 15 C 10889, 2017 WL 2880102, at *4 (N.D. Ill. July 5, 2017), and (2) the incidence of "fraudulent charges" and other symptoms of identity theft, see *Lewert v. P.F. Chang's China Bistro, Inc.*, 819 F.3d 963, 967 (7th Cir. 2016).

Particularly relevant here, *Vtech* applied these factors to a breach that exposed children's data. In that case, a toy company disclosed millions of "children's names, genders, birthdates" along with their parents' "email and mailing addresses, IP addresses, download and purchase histories" and other account information. *Vtech*, 2017 WL 2880102, at *2. Distinguishing *Remijas*, the court reasoned that "the data stolen here did not include credit-card or debit-card information, or any other information that could easily be used in fraudulent transactions." *Id.* at *3–4. At the same time, the court also found it significant that the breach had not "resulted in fraudulent charges" or any other "fallout." *Id.* "With respect to this data breach," the court concluded, "plaintiffs have not plausibly alleged a substantial risk of harm sufficient to confer standing." *Id.* at *4.

Similar logic explains why Plaintiffs' identity-theft theory fails in this case. What matters most is that the data disclosed here is far less likely to facilitate identity theft than the credit and debit card numbers at issue in *Remijas*. As the Seventh Circuit has observed, "the information stolen from payment cards can be used to open new cards in the consumer's name." *Lewert*, 819 F.3d at 967 (citing *Remijas*, 794 F.3d at 692–93). Here, by contrast, the names, emails, and dates of birth of registered students cannot "easily be used in fraudulent transactions." *Vtech*, 2017 WL 2880102, at *4. If anything, the data at issue here is less sensitive than in *Vtech,* which featured "passwords" and "secret questions and answers" that might be used to access other online accounts. *Id.*

This is not to say that the data taken from Pearson's servers could never enable identity theft. In a tactic that cybersecurity experts call "social engineering," hackers sometimes collect relatively benign information about consumers and contact "IT help desk [personnel]" at various companies in an effort to obtain more sensitive information, such as credit card or social security numbers. Under the circumstances alleged in the complaint, however, any theory that the data would facilitate social engineering depends on a "highly attenuated chain of possibilities" that "does not satisfy [Article III]." *Clapper v. Amnesty Int'l USA,* 568 U.S. 398, 410, 133 S.Ct. 1138, 185 L.Ed.2d 264 (2013).

To see why this is so, it is helpful to put oneself in the shoes of the hackers responsible for the Pearson breach. They now have a list of students' names, birthdays, and email addresses. But they have no way of knowing which students hold bank or credit card accounts at which company. And, even if the hackers guess that a specific student patronizes a particular financial institution, they will need to persuade that institution's IT staff that they represent the student. Given that names, birthdays, and emails are not usually viewed as reliable indicators of identity in and of themselves, that will be a difficult task. Should the hackers succeed, IT staff may still refuse to disclose sensitive information over the phone, preferring to send it to the students' email or physical addresses, over which the hackers have no control.

As this example illustrates, Plaintiffs' social engineering theory involves a "long sequence of uncertain contingencies involving multiple independent actors." *Attias v. Carefirst, Inc.*, 865 F.3d 620, 629 (D.C. Cir. 2017). In other words, social engineering only poses a threat if exceptionally determined hackers encounter especially credulous IT personnel. While that combination is theoretically possible, nothing in the complaint establishes that it exposes Plaintiffs to a substantial risk. *See Whitmore v. Ark.*, 495 U.S. 149, 158, 110 S.Ct. 1717, 109 L.Ed.2d 135 (1990) ("Allegations of possible future injury do not satisfy the requirements of Art[icle] III.").

Plaintiffs' inability to identify any consequences of the data breach reinforces that conclusion. More than a year after the breach, Plaintiffs cannot point to a single instance of identity theft affecting any of the 900,000 members of the putative class. Am. Compl. ¶ 1. By comparison, the *Remijas* plaintiffs alleged that thousands of shoppers had reported fraudulent charges on their credit card statements. 794 F.3d at 690. And, although Plaintiffs cite an FBI warning that "collection of student data could have ... safety implications" for children, they do not spotlight any safety incident attributable to the Pearson breach. Am. Compl. ¶ 32. Nor do they "allege that the hacker is a predator, or that the hacker disseminated the information broadly, to predators or anyone else who would harm the children." *Vtech*, 2017 WL 2880102, at *4. Ultimately, Plaintiffs' failure to describe any "fallout" underscores the relatively minimal danger posed by the data breach. *Id.* at *3–4.

In resisting that conclusion, Plaintiffs make much of Pearson's offer to supply students with free credit monitoring services in the wake of the breach. In *Remijas*, the court interpreted a similar offer as an admission that the risk of identity theft was not "so ephemeral that it can safely be disregarded." 794 F.3d at 694. Seizing on that language, Plaintiffs read *Remijas* as holding that a firm's provision of identity protection services is enough to establish that a breach poses a material danger.

But neither Seventh Circuit case law nor common sense support that conclusion. When the *Remijas* court analyzed the risk of identity theft, it repeatedly highlighted the sensitive nature of the compromised data and the actual incidences of fraudulent charges, much more so than the fact that the defendant had offered credit monitoring services to its customers. *See, e.g., id.* at 690, 691, 692. And in subsequent opinions, the Court of Appeals has assessed the threat posed by data breaches without even mentioning the presence or absence of any offers to provide credit monitoring. *See Lewert*, 819 F.3d at 967 ; *Tierney v. Advocate Health & Hosps. Corp.*, 797 F.3d 449, 451 (7th Cir. 2015). At most, Seventh Circuit precedent suggests that the provision of credit monitoring plays a minor part in standing analysis, not the decisive role Plaintiffs' envision.

Two practical considerations confirm the wisdom of that approach. First, the availability of free credit monitoring is an unreliable indicator of risk. The premise underlying Plaintiffs' argument is that firms only offer post-breach services when identity theft poses a serious threat. But firms may have other incentives to offer such services even when a data breach presents little or no risk, such as the need to placate and retain customers. According to a report cited in the complaint, for example, engaging those services has emerged as the "standard" response to data breaches in some industries. Am. Compl. ¶ 29 n.8 (citing Government Accountability Office, *Data Breaches —Range of Consumer Risks Highlights Limitations of Identity Theft Services*, at *11, https://www.gao.gov/assets/700/697985.pdf.). It follows that the provision of free services reveals relatively little about the degree of risk created by a breach.

Second, recognizing an injury-in-fact whenever firms supply identity protection services would create perverse incentives. Most of the time, courts "exclude[ ] evidence of subsequent remedial measures as proof of an admission of fault." Fed. R. Evid. 407, advisory committee's notes. A contrary rule would "discourag[e] [defendants] from taking steps in furtherance of added safety." *Id.* As the Third and Fourth Circuits have recognized, similar logic militates against placing substantial weight on a firm's decision to offer post-breach services. *See In re Horizon Healthcare Servs. Inc. Data Breach Litig.* , 846 F.3d 625, 634 n.12 (3d Cir. 2017) ; *Beck v. McDonald* , 848 F.3d 262, 276 (4th Cir. 2017). To do otherwise risks "disincentiviz[ing] companies from offering [free] services in the wake of a breach." *Horizon*, 846 F.3d at 634 n.12.

In short, Plaintiffs' theory fails because the disclosed data is not sensitive enough to materially increase the risk of identity theft. That none of the affected students seems to have suffered adverse consequences from the breach confirms this diagnosis, and Pearson's provision of credit monitoring services is not a reliable enough indicator of risk to undermine it. The result is that Plaintiffs cannot demonstrate Article III standing on this basis.

B. Diminution in Value of Personal Data

In the alternative, Plaintiffs assert that the data breach reduced the market value of their personal information. "[A]n economic market existed for Plaintiffs' and Class Members' [data]," their theory goes, and "the value of that data decreased as a result of its availability on the black market." Pls.' Resp. at 12, ECF No. 33. What is missing from the complaint, however, are any allegations that the Pearson hackers have attempted to trade the compromised data for anything of value. *See, e.g., In re Yahoo! Inc. Customer Data. Sec. Breach Litig.*, No. 16-MD-02752-LHK, 2017 WL 3727318, at *14 (N.D. Cal. Aug. 30, 2017) (identifying an injury-in fact because the complaint "include[d] several examples of hackers selling [personal identification information] from Yahoo accounts on the dark web"). Nor do Plaintiffs plead that they have ever sold their data or that they would even consider doing so. *See* Am. Compl. ¶ 26; *Khan v. Children's Nat'l Health Sys.*, 188 F. Supp. 3d 524, 533 (D. Md. 2016). Those deficiencies make this theory "too speculative" to confer standing. *See Clapper*, 568 U.S. at 401, 133 S.Ct. 1138.

C. Standing Based on Statutory Violations

Finally, Plaintiffs insist that certain statutes establish that any disclosure of student data counts as an injury, regardless of whether it leads to economic loss. As a general rule, legislatures "have the power to enact statutes creating legal rights, the invasion of which creates standing, even though no injury would exist without the statute." *Gaylor v. Mnuchin*, 919 F.3d 420, 426 (7th Cir. 2019) (citing *Sterk v. Redbox Automated Retail, LLC*, 770 F.3d 618, 623 (7th Cir. 2014)). For a statute to confer standing, however, a claimant must clear two hurdles. First, he must "allege[ ] a violation of a legally protected interest" established by the statute. *Sterk*, 770 F.3d at 623. Second, he must show that the statute protects a "substantive" rather than a "procedural" interest. *Bryant v. Compass Grp., USA, Inc.*, No. 20-1443, 958 F.3d 617, 620 (7th Cir. 2020).

In analyzing the first step, the Seventh Circuit distinguishes between statutes that award "statutory damages" and those that "require[ ] an actual injury." *Diedrich v. Ocwen Loan Servicing, LLC*, 839 F.3d 583, 589 (7th Cir. 2016). If the relevant legislation grants statutory damages, courts generally proceed to the second step. *See CS Wang &*

Assoc. v. Wells Fargo Bank, N.A., 305 F. Supp. 3d 864, 880 (N.D. Ill. 2018) ("[It is] telling, though not dispositive, that [a statute] gives injured persons the right to sue for ... statutory damages"). But if the statute calls for "actual injury," then "the injury requirement for standing overlaps with the injury requirement under the statute," and there is "no need to perform a separate [analysis]" of statutory standing. *Diedrich*, 839 F.3d at 589.

Plaintiffs falter at the first step. In claiming that they retain a legally-protected interest in the compromised records, Plaintiffs invoke the Family Education Rights and Privacy Act ("FERPA"), 20 U.S.C. § 1232g, and the Illinois School Student Records Act ("ISSRA"), 105 Ill. Comp. Stat. § 10/1 *et seq.* At a minimum, however, statutory standing demands that the claimant plead a violation of the cited statute. *See Sterk*, 770 F.3d at 623. And, while the complaint elaborates a dozen different causes of action, it does not allege that Pearson ran afoul of FERPA or ISSRA.

A more fundamental problem is that neither statute treats the disclosure of student data as an injury unless the plaintiff suffers actual damages. To be sure, ISSRA empowers "[a]ny person injured by plaintiff for the plaintiff's damages, the costs of the action and reasonable attorneys' fees," and nothing more. *Id.* § 10/9(c). Because ISSRA limits recovery to "the plaintiff's damages," *id.*, and makes no provision for statutory or nominal damages, the Court concludes that an claim brought under ISSRA "requires an actual injury." *Diedrich*, 839 F.3d at 589.

FERPA is similarly unhelpful to Plaintiffs. Nearly two decades ago, the Supreme Court held that FERPA's "nondisclosure provisions fail to confer enforceable rights." *Gonzaga Univ. v. Doe*, 536 U.S. 273, 287, 122 S.Ct. 2268, 153 L.Ed.2d 309 (2002). That means that FERPA does not "creat[e] legal rights, the invasion of which creates standing." *Gaylor*, 919 F.3d at 426; *see Kyles v. J.K. Guardian Sec. Servs., Inc.*, 222 F.3d 289, 294 (7th Cir. 2000) (explaining that statutory standing "depends in great measure on the particular rights conferred").

Perhaps anticipating these problems, Plaintiffs have submitted a supplemental memorandum. *See* Supp. Not. at 1–2, ECF No. 55. Although that memorandum purports to alert this Court to the Seventh Circuit's recent decision in *Bryant*, 958 F.3d 617, 626, Plaintiffs also use it as an opportunity to raise arguments they left out of their response brief. Specifically, they claim that Illinois's Personal Information Protection Act ("PIPA"), *see* 815 Ill. Comp. Stat. § 530/1, *et seq.*, and Colorado's Security Breach Notification Act, *see* Colo. Rev. Stat. § 6-1-716, *et seq.*, confer standing.

Putting aside the procedural dodginess of the filing, neither statute saves Plaintiffs. For one thing, *Remijas* determined that PIPA fails to "provide the basis for finding an injury for Article III standing" because it "requires actual damages." 794 F.3d at 695–96 (citing *People ex rel. Madigan v. United Const. of Am., Inc.*, 367 Ill.Dec. 79, 981 N.E.2d 404, 411 (Ill. App. Ct. 2012)). And, like FERPA, the Colorado notification law does not create a private right of action. *See* Colo. Rev. Stat. § 6-1-716(g)(4).

Ultimately, then, the injury-in-fact element hinges on whether the breach caused economic loss by magnifying the danger of identity theft or diminishing the value of Plaintiffs' data. Because Plaintiffs have failed to sustain either of those theories, they cannot support Article III standing. As a result, the complaint is dismissed without prejudice for lack of subject-matter jurisdiction. *See Remijas*, 794 F.3d at 690 ("Where federal subject matter jurisdiction does not exist, federal courts do not have the power to dismiss with prejudice.") (citation omitted). Given that Plaintiffs have only amended their complaint once, and that they may be able to introduce facts that establish standing, the Court will allow them to revise their allegations a second and final time.

IV. Conclusion

For the reasons stated above, the motion to dismiss is granted. Pearson's motion to strike the class claims and Plaintiffs' motion to strike certain declarations submitted by Pearson are denied as moot. If Plaintiffs choose, they may submit a second amended complaint by August 21, 2020. If they do not do so, the Court will assume that Plaintiffs no longer wish to pursue this litigation and will terminate the case.

IT IS SO ORDERED.

6.3 FERPA

The Family Education Rights and Privacy Act (FERPA) is another act that appears on the surface to be all about privacy, but a closer look reveals a "reasonable methods" standard for cybersecurity controls. Some educational institutions are also governed by the Graham-Leach Bliley Act, which is mostly enforced by the Federal Trade Commission. Additionally, the Department of Education, Office of the Inspector General has overlapping responsibility concerning FERPA.

The Department of Education is committed to helping the education community better safeguard the security of student data in schools at all levels. While FERPA does not require institutions to adopt specific security controls, it does require the use of "reasonable methods" to safeguard student records (34 CFR § 99.31). Despite this requirement, hundreds of educational data breaches happen every year. Not only does the disclosure of this information potentially violate FERPA, but disclosures can expose students to a host of negative consequences such as identity theft, fraud, and extortion.[267]

The DOE provides an overview of FERPA:

"The Family Educational Rights and Privacy Act (FERPA) (20 U.S.C. § 1232g; 34 CFR Part 99) is a Federal law that protects the privacy of student education records. The law applies to all schools that receive funds under an applicable program of the U.S. Department of Education.

FERPA gives parents certain rights with respect to their children's education records. These rights transfer to the student when he or she reaches the age of 18 or attends a school beyond the high school level. Students to whom the rights have transferred are "eligible students."

Parents or eligible students have the right to inspect and review the student's education records maintained by the school. Schools are not required to provide copies of records unless, for reasons such as great distance, it is impossible for parents or eligible students to review the records. Schools may charge a fee for copies.

Parents or eligible students have the right to request that a school correct records which they believe to be inaccurate or misleading. If the school decides not to amend the record, the parent or eligible student then has the right to a formal hearing. After the hearing, if the school still decides not to amend the record, the parent or eligible student has the right to place a statement with the record setting forth his or her view about the contested information.

---

[267] *See Data Security: K-12 and Higher Education*, U.S. DEPARTMENT OF EDUCATION, https://studentprivacy.ed.gov/Security (last visited Oct. 12, 2020).

Generally, schools must have written permission from the parent or eligible student in order to release any information from a student's education record.

However, FERPA allows schools to disclose those records, without consent, to the following parties or under the following conditions (34 CFR § 99.31):

School officials with legitimate educational interest;

Other schools to which a student is transferring;

Specified officials for audit or evaluation purposes;

Appropriate parties in connection with financial aid to a student;

Organizations conducting certain studies for or on behalf of the school;

Accrediting organizations;

To comply with a judicial order or lawfully issued subpoena;

Appropriate officials in cases of health and safety emergencies; and

State and local authorities, within a juvenile justice system, pursuant to specific State law.

Schools may disclose, without consent, "directory" information such as a student's name, address, telephone number, date and place of birth, honors and awards, and dates of attendance. However, schools must tell parents and eligible students about directory information and allow parents and eligible students a reasonable amount of time to request that the school not disclose directory information about them. Schools must notify parents and eligible students annually of their rights under FERPA. The actual means of notification (special letter, inclusion in a PTA bulletin, student handbook, or newspaper article) is left to the discretion of each school.[268]

34 CFR Part 99.31(a)(1)(ii) requires a minimum of effective administrative policy for controlling access to education records:

(ii) An educational agency or institution must use reasonable methods to ensure that school officials obtain access to only those education records in which they have legitimate educational interests. An educational agency or institution that does not use physical or technological access controls must ensure that its administrative policy for controlling access to education records is effective and that it remains in compliance with the legitimate educational interest requirement in paragraph (a)(1)(i)(A) of this section.[269]

Paragraph (a)(1)(i)(A) states:

(A) The disclosure is to other school officials, including teachers, within the agency or institution whom the agency or institution has determined to have legitimate educational interests.

The authors find it interesting that an educational agency or institution is permitted to rely on administrative policy without physical or technological controls. Moreover, there is not a data breach notification requirement for students in FERPA. Additionally, FERPA does not include a private right of action.

---

[268] *Family Educational Rights and Privacy Act (FERPA)*, U.S. DEPARTMENT OF EDUCATION, https://www2.ed.gov/policy/gen/guid/fpco/ferpa/index.html (last modified Mar. 1, 2018).

[269] 34 C.F.R. § 99.31.

6.3[A] DOE GUIDANCE FROM THE PRIVACY TECHNICAL ASSISTANCE CENTER

The following documents are from the DOE Privacy Technical Assistance Center and provide guidance concerning data security.

The Privacy Technical Assistance Center of the DOE released a document[270] setting forth information for training personnel concerning data security:

Security Training Content

Encouraging awareness about data and IT security issues and developing a properly trained staff requires that many content areas be addressed through a comprehensive training program. When developing a security program it will be helpful to include the following essential categories:

• Risk assessment, including the identification of system threats and vulnerabilities. • Physical security (e.g., locked doors and windows), desktop security (e.g., password protected computers), mobile device security (e.g., no sensitive data on easily misplaced storage media), and network security (e.g., secure data exchange). • Access controls, including how to password protect files, encrypt transmissions and files, and authenticate users. • Good practices related to the use of email, software/applications, and the internet. • Phishing, hoaxes, malware, viruses, worms, and spyware. • Remote access to data and systems. • Data backup and disaster recovery. • Data security breach notification protocols. • Directions for viewing written data security procedures and principles, and providing a forum to answer questions about such guidance as needed to ensure compliance.

The Privacy Technical Assistance Center of the DOE released a document[271] setting forth best practices for identify authentication:

What are Some Reasonable Authentication Practices?

Educational agencies and institutions are required to use "reasonable" authentication methods for all disclosures of PII from education records under FERPA.

---

[270] PRIVACY TECHNICAL ASSISTANCE CENTER, DATA SECURITY AND MANAGEMENT TRAINING: BEST PRACTICE CONSIDERATIONS 3 (2015), *available at*
https://studentprivacy.ed.gov/sites/default/files/resource_document/file/Data%20Security%20and%20Management%20Training_1.pdf.
[271] PRIVACY TECHNICAL ASSISTANCE CENTER, IDENTITY AUTHENTICATION BEST PRACTICES: BEST PRACTICE CONSIDERATIONS 4–6 (2015), *available at*

This includes disclosures of PII made with the written consent of a parent or eligible student, as required under FERPA (34 CFR §99.30), as well as disclosures made without consent under one of the FERPA exceptions listed in 34 CFR §99.31(a). An educational agency or institution must also identify and authenticate the identity of a parent or student before allowing them to inspect and review the student's own records, as permitted under FERPA (34 CFR §99.10). No individual or entity should be allowed unauthenticated access to confidential education records or data at any time.

While the Department does not mandate any specific requirements regarding reasonable methods, some best practice suggestions include • conducting privacy risk assessments to determine potential threats to the data; • selecting authentication levels based on the risk to the data (the higher the risk, the more stringent the authentication); • developing a process to securely manage any secret authenticating information, or "authenticators" (e.g., passwords), throughout their creation, use, and disposal; • enforcing policies to reduce the possibility of authenticator misuse (e.g., encrypting stored passwords, locking out accounts with suspicious activity, etc.); and • managing user identities through creation, provisioning, use, and disposal (with periodic account recertification to confirm that a user account has been properly authorized and is still required by the user.)

The following section provides more specific recommendations for applying effective authentication procedures; see also NIST Special Publications 800-63, Digital Identity Guidelines and other resources at the end of this document for additional suggestions. As these are best practices, it is up to individual organizations to determine which actions are the most appropriate based on the specific circumstances, including the sensitivity level of the data and the risk of harm associated with unauthorized disclosure.

What Specific Methods for Effective Authentication Can PTAC Recommend?

Depending on the level of assurance required, an educational agency or institution might determine that an application, which allows parents to gain access to "less sensitive" education data, such as attendance records, by using single-factor authentication (for example, a username and a unique PIN generated upon registration with the system) provides the necessary level of identity authentication. The same organization may have other systems that allow access to "more sensitive" data, such as student financial aid information, health information, or SSNs. In addition to a username and a PIN, these systems might choose to employ additional authentication factors. For example, a school may require parents requesting online access to a student's transcript to answer security questions or confirm their identity by retrieving a one-time password sent to the mobile device they have previously registered with the institution.

It is important to remember that authentication factors like PINs, passwords, and security tokens are only effective if the user is the only party who knows this information or possesses the token. This sometimes makes it difficult to recover a user's ability to access the data from a system if the user has forgotten the password or misplaced his or her token. No agency officials should be able to recover passwords or security tokens for any reason. With that in mind, full, unencrypted passwords in plain

---

https://studentprivacy.ed.gov/sites/default/files/resource_document/file/Identity_Authentication_Best_Practices_0.pdf.

text should never be stored within electronic systems. We recommended that you work with your Information Technology (IT) Administrator or Security Officer to ensure that stored passwords are encrypted using a strong cryptographic algorithm. This approach reduces the risk of password data leakage and prevents administrators or school officials from being able to access actual passwords, increasing the assurance level of the system.

In most cases, establishing identity authentication for electronic transactions is more complex than for transactions conducted in person or by phone. Each educational agency or institution must assess its own policies and systems to determine appropriate identity authentication measures based on its own combination of technology, the sensitivity of the data, and applicable data security policies. The risks and privacy impacts may differ significantly by organization depending on the type of data an agency or an institution maintains and on the potential harm caused by the failure to properly secure the data. For example, a school that does not share student records electronically would have a vastly different disclosure risk than a school or an agency that routinely shares education data with partner organizations and offers students online access to their own records. Please keep in mind that an organization may have multiple information systems, which house data of differing sensitivities and privacy impact.

For electronic systems, well-designed account recovery mechanisms and cryptographic protection of the authentication process are of great importance and should be incorporated into the system development process. One unwavering fact of electronic data systems is that users will, at some point, lose or forget their account password, PIN, or other authenticating information. It is important that these systems include the ability to safely recover or reset the authenticating information without negatively impacting the integrity of the authentication system. The method might be as simple as an email-based recovery option that asks alternate security questions created during user registration. This type of recovery procedure relies on the knowledge of the security questions, which the user created upon registration, and requires the party being authenticated to have access to the email account utilized for the registration. These two factors together increase the security of the transaction and allow a user to recover information without delay. (Additional authentication is not necessary when utilizing a mail or delivery process that authenticates the recipient's identity, because it is structured to deliver the information only to the intended recipient.)

Identity authentication relies on the secrecy of authentication factors. Consequently, it is advisable that all exchanges of passwords or other authenticating information be sent through encrypted channels using a secure transfer protocol, such as Transport Layer Security. For online systems, organizations should implement basic authentication controls to reduce the ability of an attacker to guess at authentication credentials until the correct combination is achieved (known as "brute force password guessing") by introducing mechanisms to lockout or prevent repetitive failed authentication attempts. The most popular solution is to implement an account lockout mechanism, whereby an account or system is automatically locked after a predefined number of unsuccessful log-on attempts (the account can then be unlocked only by a system administrator or help desk). This approach can help to reduce the threat of brute-force attacks.

Care should be taken when developing and implementing authentication systems within web applications to ensure that the applications are built using secure coding and session management techniques along with thorough validation of user input to prevent attacks like SQL injection, Cross Site Scripting, and Cross Site Request Forgery among others (see Glossary for definitions of these terms). (For additional data security tips, see the PTAC brief Data Security: Top Threats to Data Protection).

The Privacy Technical Assistance Center of the DOE released a document[272] stating Data Security Checklist:

Data Security Checklist

Policy and governance. Develop a comprehensive data governance plan that outlines organizational policies and standards regarding data security and individual privacy protection. The plan should clearly identify staff responsibilities for maintaining data security and empower employees by providing tools they can use to minimize the risks of unauthorized access to PII. Refer to PTAC's Data Governance Checklist for more information.

Personnel security. Create an Acceptable Use Policy that outlines appropriate and inappropriate uses of Internet, Intranet, and Extranet systems. Incorporate security policies in job descriptions and specify employee responsibilities associated with maintaining compliance with these policies. Conduct regular checks and trainings to ensure employee understanding of the terms and conditions of their employment. Confirm the trustworthiness of employees through the use of personnel security screenings, policy training, and binding confidentiality agreements.

Physical security. Make computing resources physically unavailable to unauthorized users. This includes securing access to any areas where sensitive data (i.e., data that carry the risk for harm1 from an unauthorized or inadvertent disclosure) are stored and processed, such as buildings and server rooms. An unlocked server room is an invitation for malicious or accidental damage. Monitor access to these areas to prevent intrusion attempts (e.g., by administering identification badges and requiring staff and visitors to log in prior to entering the premises or accessing the resources).

Network mapping. Network mapping provides critical understanding of the enterprise (servers, routers, etc.) and its connections. Furthermore, network mapping can capture applications and associated data. A robust mapping capability will map the dependencies between applications, data, and network layers, and highlight potential vulnerabilities. There are a number of network mapping tools available.

Inventory of assets. The inventory should include both authorized and unauthorized devices used in your computing environment. These devices are often scanned and discovered by automated programs (continuously searching the internet for vulnerabilities) and if unsecured devices are discovered they can be compromised. Inventorying, when used in conjunction with network mapping, will give your organization a better understanding of the security requirements needed to protect your assets.

Authentication. The ways in which someone may be authenticated fall into three categories: something you know, something you have, or something you are. Two-factor authentication (TFA) combines two of these elements and is more costly, but provides more security. Consider TFA for remote users or privileged "super users."

---

[272] PRIVACY TECHNICAL ASSISTANCE CENTER, DATA SECURITY CHECKLIST 1–4 (2015), available at https://studentprivacy.ed.gov/sites/default/files/resource_document/file/Data%20Security%20Checklist_0.pdf

Authentication technologies provide assurance that the person is authorized to access network assets, services, and information.

Provide a layered defense. Employ a "Defense in Depth" architecture that uses a wide spectrum of tools arrayed in a complementary fashion. The most common layers to protect are hosts (individual computers), application, network, and perimeter. There are specific security controls that are suited for use at each of these layers. Relying on a firewall alone to protect your network is never adequate.

Secure configurations. It is a best practice not to put any hardware or software onto your network until it has been security tested and configured to optimize its security. Continuous scanning to ensure system components remain in a secure state is a critical capability that will enhance data security protection. Proactive management of security risks also involves establishing a comprehensive change management program to analyze and address security and privacy risks introduced by new technology or business processes.

Access control. Securing data access includes requiring strong passwords and multiple levels of user authentication, setting limits on the length of data access (e.g., locking access after the session timeout), limiting logical access to sensitive data and resources, and limiting administrative privileges. Role-based access is essential for protecting PII and sensitive data; defining specified roles and privileges for users is a required security procedure. Sensitive data that few personnel have access to should not be stored on the same server as other types of data used by more personnel without additional protections for the data (e.g., encryption).

Firewalls and Intrusion Detection/Prevention Systems (IDPS). A firewall is a device designed to permit or deny network transmissions based upon a set of rules. Firewalls are frequently used to protect networks from unauthorized access, while permitting legitimate communications to pass. An IDPS is a monitoring device that is designed to detect malicious activity on the network. Although some automatically take remediation action, most report suspicious activity to a central monitoring point for further analysis.

Automated vulnerability scanning. When new vulnerabilities (to hardware, operating systems, applications, and other network devices) are discovered, hackers immediately scan networks for these vulnerabilities. Scanning your network and systems on a regular basis will minimize the time of exposure to known vulnerabilities.

Patch management. Patch management is the process of using a strategy and plan for the testing and roll out of software updates and patches on a regular basis. The plan should address how patches will be applied to which systems at a specified time. A patch is a piece of code that protects computers and applications by updating the security state against new threats or vulnerabilities. Used in conjunction with vulnerability scanning, the enterprise can quickly shut down any vulnerability discovered.

Shut down unnecessary services. Each port, protocol, or service is a potential avenue for ingress into your enterprise. A best practice, which should be part of a secure configuration, should include shutting down all services and ports that are not required in your computing environment. A secure enterprise will continually monitor for the use of unapproved ports, protocols or services.

Mobile devices. When sensitive data are stored on servers or on mobile devices, such as laptops or smart phones, the data should be encrypted. There are far too many examples of mobile devices being lost or stolen and the subsequent exposure of the sensitive information stored on those devices in the public domain.

Emailing confidential data. Consider the sensitivity level of the data to be sent over the email. Emailing unprotected PII or sensitive data poses a high security risk. It is recommended that organizations use alternative practices to protect transmissions of these data. These practices include mailing paper copies via secure carrier, de-sensitizing data before transmission, and applying technical solutions for transferring files electronically (e.g., encrypting data files and/or encrypting email transmissions themselves).

Incident handling. When an incident does occur it is critical to have a process in place to both contain and fix the problem. Procedures for users, security personnel, and managers need to be established to define the appropriate roles and actions. Outside experts may be required to do a forensics investigation of the incident, but having the correct procedures in place initially will minimize the impact and damage.

Audit and compliance monitoring. Audits are used to provide an independent assessment of your data protection capabilities and procedures (see Data Stewardship: Managing Personally Identifiable Information in Electronic Student Education Records) and should be performed periodically. Auditors that are familiar with Family Educational Rights and Privacy Act statutory and regulatory requirements can further assist you in determining whether your systems are in compliance.

The Privacy Technical Assistance Center of the DOE released a document[273] titled Protecting Student Privacy While Using Online Educational Services: Model Terms of Service:

The document points to terms and conditions that educational institutes should pay special attention to when dealing with vendors who offer online education services. In particular, the document discusses security controls and states that best practices would include the following clause:

> Provider will store and process Data in accordance with industry best practices. This includes appropriate administrative, physical, and technical safeguards to secure Data from unauthorized access, disclosure, and use. Provider will conduct periodic risk assessments and remediate any identified security vulnerabilities in a timely manner. Provider will also have a written incident response plan, to include prompt notification of the [School/District] in the event of a security or privacy incident, as well as best practices for responding to a breach of PII. Provider agrees to share its incident response plan upon request.

The document further cautions that, "The lack of a security controls provision, or inclusion of a provision that sets a lower standard for Provider's security of Data, would be a bad practice and potentially violate FERPA [and f]ailure to provide security to students' PII is not a best practice and could lead to a FERPA violation."

The document also addresses data mining and makes clear that targeted advertising based on data mining by a vendor could lead to a FERPA violation.

---

[273] PRIVACY TECHNICAL ASSISTANCE CENTER, PROTECTING STUDENT PRIVACY WHILE USING ONLINE EDUCATIONAL SERVICES: MODEL TERMS OF SERVICE 8 (2016), *available at* https://studentprivacy.ed.gov/sites/default/files/resource_document/file/TOS_Guidance_Mar2016.pdf.

The Privacy Technical Assistance Center of the DOE released a document[274] titled Frequently Asked Questions: Cloud Computing:

Question: Are there recommended best practices to help agencies decide whether they should move to the cloud? Can the Department recommend which cloud solution to use?

Answer: The Department cannot recommend any specific cloud solution over another. Deciding which solution is the best for your organization should be made on a case-by-case basis, after conducting a careful risk management assessment. Some security questions to consider include, but are not limited to:

1. Does the cloud solution offer equal or greater data security capabilities than those provided by your organization's data center? To determine this, you should review and compare available solutions, including firewalls, patch management procedures, security monitoring and response methods, and other relevant data security measures.

2. Have you taken into account the vulnerabilities of the cloud solution? You should consider that cloud services are an increasingly attractive target for hackers. Some clouds have experienced direct malicious attacks, potentially exposing any information stored there. In other instances, the clouds have been the targets of denial of service attacks.

3. Have you considered that incident detection and response can be more complicated in a cloud-based environment? You should evaluate your existing incident response capabilities and determine if changes are needed before deciding whether to move to the cloud. Organizational policies and procedures may need to be updated to accommodate anticipated changes introduced by the addition of a cloud-based system. Any such changes should be made well in advance of the implementation and updated regularly.

4. Have you considered that metrics collection and system performance and security monitoring are more difficult in the cloud? You should define what metrics you need to collect and determine the desired level of security monitoring as part of the planning process of a potential move to the cloud.

In addition to security considerations, there are many other factors to keep in mind when deciding whether to move your data to the cloud. Potential concerns span a range of domains, including privacy, legal, and compliance issues. Several specific questions to consider include:

1. How will your agency exercise control over the data within the cloud to ensure that the data are available and that confidentiality and integrity of the data remain protected? Are there appropriate access and use controls in place to provide proper level of accountability? Are there any concerns regarding screening and monitoring of contractor staff and their activities?

2. Have you evaluated potential legal concerns associated with outsourcing data management to a cloud provider? Legal considerations may include ensuring proper protection of intellectual property and various contractual issues, such as end of service

---

[274] PRIVACY TECHNICAL ASSISTANCE CENTER, FREQUENTLY ASKED QUESTIONS: CLOUD COMPUTING 2–4 (2015), *available at*
https://studentprivacy.ed.gov/sites/default/files/resource_document/file/FAQ_Cloud_Computing_0.pdf.

matters. For example, your organization must have a way to get the data back in a secure and timely manner in case a cloud provider goes out of business.

3. Have you considered what measures you will need to implement to ensure that the cloud provider complies with all applicable federal, state, and local privacy laws, including FERPA? For example, have you made sure that storing data on the cloud does not interfere with your ability to provide parents and eligible students with access to their education records, should they choose to exercise their FERPA right to inspect and review them? Other considerations related to compliance with FERPA include ensuring that the cloud provider follows proper data use, re-disclosure, and destruction procedures, specified at 34 CFR §§99.33(a) and 99.35(b).

You should evaluate existing protection capabilities that your organization and its partners use to secure organizational systems and applications before deciding whether to migrate to a cloud-based solution. Such an evaluation will help to establish a baseline level of protection with which to evaluate potential benefits and risks associated with moving to a cloud-based alternative. While FERPA does not directly address the viability of specific cloud solutions, the Department recognizes that their use is a growing trend and has piloted its own cloud computing solutions.

Question: For educational agencies that have already selected a preferred cloud solution, are there recommended best practices when moving to the cloud?

Answer: The Department encourages educational agencies to focus on ensuring continuing protection of the privacy and security of students' records and minimizing the risk of unauthorized disclosure of the data by developing a cloud computing migration strategy that addresses the organization's specific privacy and security needs. This strategy involves carefully evaluating existing privacy, security, and compliance requirements and establishing expectations of prospective cloud service providers in terms of necessary levels of service and security before engaging with them. Agencies should carefully consider how moving to a cloud solution will affect their existing privacy and security controls. Transitioning to the cloud may present an opportunity for improving the effectiveness and efficiency of existing procedures as an agency is making the changes necessary to implement and manage a cloud-based solution. Moving data into the cloud can also significantly change the agency's legal requirements for the protection and handling of data. It is important to consult with your organization's legal counsel to fully understand the ramifications of implementing a cloud solution and the effect it may have on your organization's operations. Please see a list of resources at the end of this document for additional best practices information.

The Privacy Technical Assistance Center of the DOE released a document[275] titled Best Practices for Data Destruction:

. . . FERPA does not provide any specific requirements for educational agencies and institutions regarding disposition or destruction of the data they collect or maintain themselves, other than requiring them to safeguard FERPA-protected data from

---

[275] PRIVACY TECHNICAL ASSISTANCE CENTER, BEST PRACTICES FOR DATA DESTRUCTION 2–8 (2014), *available at*
https://studentprivacy.ed.gov/sites/default/files/resource_document/file/Best%20Practices%20for%20Dat a%20Destruction%20%282019-3-26%29.pdf.

unauthorized disclosure, and not to destroy any education records if there is an outstanding request to inspect or review them. When educational agencies and institutions disclose (or "share") PII from education records with third parties under an applicable exception to FERPA's written consent requirement, however, additional legal requirements regarding destruction of that PII may apply.

Under the "school official" exception, FERPA requires that the school or district maintain direct control over the authorized recipient's maintenance and use of the PII from education records, and that the recipient protect the PII from further or unauthorized disclosure. While these general requirements for protection of and direct control over the maintenance of the PII imply adequate destruction of that PII when no longer needed, FERPA's school official exception leaves it to the educational agency or institution to establish specific terms for the protection of and direct control over the maintenance of the PII from education records (including its eventual destruction).

Two commonly used exceptions to FERPA's written consent requirement provide more specificity regarding data destruction. FERPA's "studies" and "audit or evaluation" exceptions require the disclosing agency or institution to enter into a written agreement with the third party receiving the PII from education records. Under these exceptions, the agreement must (among other things) specify that the PII must be destroyed when no longer needed for the specific purpose for which it was disclosed and a time period for that destruction. While FERPA does not provide any technical standards for destruction, the audit or evaluation exception does require that the disclosing entity use "reasonable methods" to ensure that the PII from education records is properly protected by the recipient. (For more information on these two exceptions, the other requirements for written agreements, or additional guidance on what constitutes "reasonable methods," visit the PTAC website at https://studentprivacy.ed.gov).

While FERPA is silent on specific technical requirements governing data destruction, methods discussed in this document should be viewed as best practice recommendations for educational agencies and institutions to consider adopting when establishing record retention and data governance policies to follow internally, and also for inclusion in any written agreements and contracts they make with third parties to whom they are disclosing PII.

It should also be noted that while FERPA does not require that particular methods of data destruction be used, other applicable Federal, State, or local privacy laws and regulations may require specific secure data disposal methods. When creating data sharing agreements, check with your legal counsel to fully understand what requirements apply and how to proceed.

Depending on the type of data involved and the context in which the data are being used, there may be a number of specific requirements with which educational agencies and institutions must comply. For example, Part B of the Individuals with Disabilities Education Act (IDEA) requires public agencies to inform a student's parents when any PII collected, maintained, or used thereunder is no longer needed to provide educational services to the child. Subsequently, the information must be destroyed at the request of the parents (though a permanent record of a student's name, address, and phone number, his or her grades, attendance record, classes attended, grade level completed, and year completed may be maintained without time limitation. 34 CFR § 300.624(a) and (b)). Part B of the IDEA defines the term "destruction" as the "physical destruction or removal of personal identifiers from information so that the information is no longer personally identifiable." 34 CFR § 300.611(a)

Lastly, methods discussed in this guidance are intended as examples and should not be considered to be exhaustive. More detailed technical information can be found in the National Institute of Standards and Technology (NIST) Special Publication 800-88 Revision 1: Guidelines for Media Sanitization.

What is Data Destruction?

Data should be appropriately managed across the entire data lifecycle, from capture to destruction. Planning for data destruction is an integral part of a high quality data management program.

Data in any of their forms move through stages during their useful life and ultimately are either archived for later use, or destroyed when their utility has been exhausted. Establishing policies and procedures governing the management and use of data allows an organization to more efficiently and safely protect its data (see PTAC's resources on Data Governance at https://studentprivacy.ed.gov). When data are no longer needed, the destruction of the data becomes a critical, and often required, component of an effective data governance program. Data destruction is the process of removing information in a way that renders it unreadable (for paper records) or irretrievable (for digital records).

Because some methods of data destruction are more complicated, time-consuming, or resource intensive than others, it is common to select the method based on the underlying sensitivity of the data being destroyed, or the potential harm they could cause if they are recovered or inadvertently disclosed. For very low risk information, this may mean simply deleting electronic files or using a desk shredder for paper documents. However, these types of destruction methods can be undone, by a determined and motivated individual, making these methods inappropriate for more sensitive data. For more sensitive data, stronger methods of destruction at a more granular level may need to be employed to assure that the data are truly irretrievable.

How Long Should Data Be Retained Before They Are Destroyed?

FERPA does not require educational agencies and institutions to destroy education records maintained as a part of the regular school or agency operations, and in fact, many jurisdictions require lengthy retention periods for student attendance and graduation records. For other student records, in order to minimize information technology (IT) costs and reduce the likelihood of inadvertent disclosure of student information, schools and districts will often elect to establish their own record retention policies, including time frames for eventual destruction of the records. Minimizing the amount of data you retain, by destroying them when no longer needed, is a key element of the Fair Information Practice Principles (FIPPs), and is widely considered to be a best practice for protecting individuals' privacy and for lessening the potential impact of a data breach or inadvertent disclosure. For more information on FIPPs (including Data Minimization), see http://www.nist.gov/nstic/NSTIC-FIPPs.pdf.

Under the "studies" and "audit or evaluation" exceptions, FERPA requires that PII from education records be destroyed when no longer needed for the specific purpose for which it was disclosed, and that the written agreement specify the time period for destruction. When drafting these agreements, it may be difficult to accurately predict the appropriate destruction period in advance. In these cases, the parties may wish to consider establishing a time period for destruction of the PII, and then modifying the written agreement, if needed, to postpone the destruction date or move it sooner than initially specified. This can be especially important for longitudinal studies, which may span many decades. While FERPA requires that there be an end date upon which any

PII from education records disclosed under the studies or audit or evaluation exception must be destroyed, it does not specify a maximum time limit. In determining the appropriate time frame for the destruction of PII for a given study or audit or evaluation, some important issues should be considered. For example, for the purposes of verification and repeatability of findings, it may not be feasible to immediately destroy all of the PII involved in a study. In these cases, consider adding provisions within the agreement for the retention of PII needed for repeatability for an additional specified length of time. Additionally, an educational agency or institution might consider using a strategy in which the third party returns the research dataset to the educational agency or institution for archiving. In these cases, the third party would then destroy residual PII, leaving the educational agency or institution with the study dataset.

Under the school official exception, it is a best practice for schools and districts to require the third party receiving the PII to destroy it upon termination of the school official relationship (e.g., when the contract ends), or when no longer needed for the purpose for which it was disclosed (whichever comes first).

When PII from education records is disclosed under any of FERPA's other exceptions, unless legal requirements specify otherwise, it is a best practice for educational agencies and institutions to require the recipient to destroy the PII when no longer needed for the purpose for which it was disclosed.

Please note that other Federal, state, and local privacy laws and regulations may contain more stringent data retention and/or destruction requirements, so it is important to consider and comply with all applicable requirements when determining the appropriate time period for retention and destruction of data.

Best Practices for Data Destruction

The information below contains some common best practices for data destruction. This guidance should not be considered comprehensive. Many additional technologies and methodologies exist which may or may not apply to your specific needs. While this document provides high level recommendations, the National Institute of Standards and Technology (NIST) provides in-depth guidance and best practices for the implementation of effective methods of data destruction in their Guidelines for Media Sanitation.

Modern electronic data storage devices are extremely resilient, and data recovery techniques and technology are highly advanced. Data are routinely recovered from media which have been burned, crushed, submerged in water, or impacted from great heights. In effect, it really is quite difficult to permanently get rid of data, but the permanent and irreversible destruction of data is a cornerstone of protecting the privacy and security of students' education records. Data destruction encompasses a wide variety of media, including electronic and paper records. The choice of destruction methodology should be based on the risk posed by the sensitivity of the data being destroyed and the potential impact of unauthorized disclosure. For example, the negative impact from the disclosure of a file containing directory information, such as names of honor roll students, might not be as severe as the negative impact from the disclosure of a file containing students' Social Security Numbers, names, and dates of birth. Therefore, the approach to data destruction in these two scenarios might be different. While the negative impact from the disclosure of de-identified data may warrant only their deletion from a disk or other media, the negative impact and risk of unauthorized disclosure of sensitive PII typically would warrant stronger methods of data destruction. In the latter case, the organization might use a software or hardware technique that completely cleans the hard disk containing the PII to the point that the data cannot be retrieved, even forensically.

The table below identifies three major categories of data destruction. The table is arranged according to the degree of assurance each category provides, with "clear" providing the least amount of assurance and "destroy" providing the most assurance that the information is irretrievable. Organizations should make risk-based decisions on which method is most appropriate based on the data type, risk of disclosure, and the impact if that data were to be disclosed without authorization.

Data Destruction Categories

Clear

A method of sanitization that applies programmatic, software based techniques to sanitize data in all user-addressable storage locations for protection against simple non-invasive data recovery techniques; typically applied through the standard Read and Write commands to the storage device, such as by rewriting with a new value or using a menu option to reset the device to the factory state (where rewriting is not supported).

Purge

A method of sanitization that applies physical or logical techniques that render Target Data recovery infeasible using state of the art laboratory techniques.

Destroy

A method of sanitization that renders Target Data recovery infeasible using state of the art laboratory techniques and results in the subsequent inability to use the media for storage of data.

Adapted from NIST Draft Special Publication 800-88 Rev 1: Guidelines for Media Sanitization; Section 2.5 – Types of Sanitization

More information about the specific technical requirements for data destruction for various hardware and media types can be found in NIST's Guidelines for Media Sanitation, Appendix A: "Minimum Sanitization Recommendations."

No matter which method of destruction you choose, consider following these general best practices for data destruction:

When drafting written agreements with third parties, include provisions that specify that all PII that was provided to the third party must be destroyed when no longer needed for the specific purpose for which it was provided, including any copies of the PII that may reside in system backups, temporary files, or other storage media.

Ensure accountability for destruction of PII by using certification forms which are signed by the individual responsible for performing the destruction and contain detailed information about the destruction.

Remember that PII may also be present in non-electronic media. Organizations should manage non-electronic records in a similar fashion to their electronic data. When data are no longer required, destroy non-electronic media using secure means to render it safe for disposal or recycling. Commonly used methods include cross-cut shredders, pulverizers, and incinerators.

Depending on the sensitivity of the data being shared, be specific in the written agreement as to the type of destruction to be carried out.

When destroying electronic data, use appropriate data deletion methods to ensure the data cannot be recovered. Please note that simple deletion of the data is not effective. Often, when a data file is deleted, only the reference to that file is removed from the media. The actual file data remain on the disk and are available for recovery until overwritten. Talk to your IT professional to ensure proper deletion of records consistent with technology best practice standards.

Avoid using file deletion, disk formatting, and "one way" encryption to dispose of sensitive data—these methods are not effective because they leave the majority of the data intact and vulnerable to being retrieved by a determined person with the right tools.

Destroy CDs, DVDs, and any magneto-optical disks by pulverizing, cross-cut shredding, or burning.

Address in a timely manner sanitization of storage media which might have failed and need to be replaced under warranty or service contract. Many data breaches result from storage media containing sensitive information being returned to the manufacturer for service or replacement.

Create formal, documented processes for data destruction within your organization and require that partner organizations do the same.

Best Practices in Data Destruction – An Example

A school district wants to evaluate how its former elementary students are doing in its high school to improve its elementary school instruction. The district decides to contract with a research organization to perform a study to determine ways to improve instruction in its elementary school.

The district enters into a written agreement with the research organization under the FERPA studies exception. The agreement establishes clear guidelines and data management requirements to protect the privacy and confidentiality of the data, specifying that:

the study will take eight months to complete,

the data provided by the district are to be used only for the express purposes outlined in the study,

the research organization must put in place controls to limit access to the data and use secure file transfer process in accordance with the industry's standards for strong encryption mechanisms, and the data will be destroyed when no longer needed to conduct the study and by the end of the eight month contract.

In addition, the district stipulates in the written agreement that at the end of the contract the research dataset used for the study will be securely returned to the district, which will archive the file in case it is needed for future replication or evaluation of the findings, and that any remaining district data held by the research organization must be destroyed. The written agreement also stipulates the specific data destruction method that the research organization will use: in this case, a secure overwrite utility that overwrites the data files with random information, thus rendering the entirety of the data unrecoverable.

The written agreement explicitly identifies the person within the research organization who is responsible for the data while they are being used for the study, and the individual accountable for their destruction at the end of the project. The agreement also includes a destruction certification form on which the research organization must inventory the data destruction efforts, to be signed by the person responsible for destroying the data.

At the end of the contract, the research organization securely returns the study dataset back to the district and conducts the destruction of any remaining data using the agreed-upon tool to overwrite the data. The destruction is annotated on the form provided by the district and signed by the individual responsible for the destruction. The transport media that the district provided to the research organization for the purposes of conducting the study are securely returned to the district with the completed verification form.

NOTES

Note 1

A late 2020 ransomware cyberattack on a Nevada school district in Las Vegas resulted in the cybercriminal posting personal information, including grades, names, addresses, social security numbers and financial information, on a hacker website after the Clark County School District refused to pay the ransom. The Business Insider notes that there have been at least 60 ransomware attacks on school districts and universities.[276] Should FERPA include more stringent requirements for cybersecurity? What is the harm from the release of student information, including social security numbers, and grades? Are there inadequate incentives for school districts to increase their level of cybersecurity?

6.3[B] ADDITIONAL CYBERSECURITY REQUIREMENTS FOR TITLE IV SCHOOLS

There are additional cyber security requirements for Title IV schools. Title IV schools are essentially schools which process federal financial aid.

Title IV schools should be aware that:

"Under their Program Participation Agreement (PPA) and the Gramm-Leach-Bliley Act (15 U.S. Code § 6801), they must protect student financial aid information, with particular attention to information provided to institutions by the Department of Education or otherwise obtained in support of the administration of the Title IV Federal student financial aid programs authorized under Title IV of the Higher Education Act, as amended (the HEA). Summary information about the GLBA requirements is provided later in this letter; and

Under their Student Aid Internet Gateway (SAIG) Enrollment Agreement, they *"[m]ust ensure that all users are aware of and comply with all of the requirements to protect and secure data from Departmental sources using SAIG."*[277]

20 U.S. Code 1094 covers program participation agreements.[278]

The GLBA requires institutions to, among other things:

Develop, implement, and maintain a written information security program;

---

[276] Aaron Holmes, *A hacker published thousands of students' grades and private information after a Nevada school district refused to pay ransom*, BUSINESS INSIDER (Sept. 28, 2020, 8:09 AM), https://www.businessinsider.com/hacker-publishes-students-grades-private-info-after-demanding-ransom-2020-9.

[277] Letter from Ted Mitchell, Undersecretary, Fed. Student Aid, U.S. Dep't. of Educ., to colleagues (July 1, 2016), *available at* https://ifap.ed.gov/dear-colleague-letters/07-01-2016-gen-16-12-subject-protecting-student-information.

[278] *See* 20 U.S.C. § 1094.

Designate the employee(s) responsible for coordinating the information security program;

Identify and assess risks to customer information;

Design and implement an information safeguards program;

Select appropriate service providers that are capable of maintaining appropriate safeguards; and

Periodically evaluate and update their security program.

Under these GLBA requirements, Presidents and Chief Information Officers of institutions should have, at a minimum, evaluated and documented their current security posture against the requirements of GLBA and have taken immediate action to remediate any identified deficiencies.[279]

The Department of Education encourages Title IV schools to use NIST SP 800-171 for cyber security guidance:

The Department strongly encourages institutions to review and understand the standards defined in the NIST SP 800-171, the recognized information security publication for protecting "Controlled Unclassified Information (CUI)," a subset of Federal data that includes unclassified information that requires safeguarding or dissemination controls pursuant to and consistent with law, regulations, and Federal policies. NIST SP 800-171 identifies specific recommended requirements for non-Federal entities that handle CUI, including:

Limit information system access to authorized users (Access Control Requirements);

Ensure that system users are properly trained (Awareness and Training Requirements);

Create information system audit records (Audit and Accountability Requirements);

Establish baseline configurations and inventories of systems (Configuration Management Requirements);

Identify and authenticate users appropriately (Identification and Authentication Requirements);

Establish incident-handling capability (Incident Response Requirements);

Perform appropriate maintenance on information systems (Maintenance Requirements);

Protect media, both paper and digital, containing sensitive information (Media Protection Requirements);

Screen individuals prior to authorizing access (Personnel Security Requirements);

Limit physical access to systems (Physical Protection Requirements);

Conduct risk assessments (Risk Assessment Requirements);

Assess security controls periodically and implement action plans (Security Assessment Requirements);

---

[279] Letter from Ted Mitchell, Undersecretary, Fed. Student Aid, U.S. Dep't. of Educ., to colleagues (July 1, 2016), *available at* https://ifap.ed.gov/dear-colleague-letters/07-01-2016-gen-16-12-subject-protecting-student-information

Monitor, control, and protect organizational communications (System and Communications Protection Requirements); and

Identify, report, and correct information flaws in a timely manner (System and Information Integrity Requirement).[280]

We will cover National Institute of Standards and Technology (NIST) in detail in the next chapter.

NOTES

Note 1

The Federal Student Aid Office of the Department of Education has online resources concerning cybersecurity. Notably, the website includes a data breach reporting form and alerts of threats.[281]

Note 2

The Federal Student Aid Office of the Department of Education released a letter concerning cybersecurity issues:

Instances of data breaches at organizations entrusted with personally identifiable information (PII) continue to proliferate and reinforce the need for focused action by the U.S. Government to combat cybersecurity threats and to strengthen the Government's cybersecurity infrastructure. Ensuring the confidentiality, security and integrity of Title IV financial aid information depends on cooperation among FSA, institutions of higher education ("institutions") and other entities including state grant agencies, lenders, contractors and third-party servicers.

Our expectation is that all FSA partners will quickly assess and implement strong security policies and controls and undertake ongoing monitoring and management for the systems, databases and processes that support all aspects of the administration of Federal student financial aid programs authorized under Title IV of the Higher Education Act of 1965, as amended (the HEA). Such systems, databases and processes include all systems that collect, process, and distribute information – including PII – in support of applications for and receipt of Title IV student assistance.

The Student Aid Internet Gateway (SAIG) Enrollment Agreement entered into by each Title IV participating institution includes a provision that the institution *"[m]ust ensure that all Federal Student Aid applicant information is protected from access by or disclosure to unauthorized personnel."* Institutions are reminded that under various Federal and state laws and other authorities, including the HEA; the Family Educational Rights and Privacy Act (FERPA); the Privacy Act of 1974, as amended; the Gramm-Leach-Bliley Act; state data breach and privacy laws; and potentially other laws, they may be responsible for losses, fines and penalties (including criminal penalties) caused by data breaches.

---

[280] *Id.*

[281] *FSA Cybersecurity Compliance*, FEDERAL STUDENT AID, U.S. DEPARTMENT OF EDUCATION, https://ifap.ed.gov/fsa-cybersecurity-compliance (last visited Oct. 12, 2020).

To support the expectation and the SAIG requirements described above, FSA strongly encourages institutions to follow industry standards and best practices in managing information and information systems and in securing PII. Those standards and practices include:

Assessing the risk and magnitude of harm that could result from unauthorized access, use, disclosure, disruption, modification or destruction of information or information systems;

Determining the levels of information security appropriate to protect information and information systems;

Implementing policies and procedures to cost-effectively reduce risks to an acceptable level; and

Regularly testing and evaluation of information security controls and techniques to ensure effective implementation and improvement of such controls and techniques.

Such standards and practices also include collaborating with, and utilizing the resources of, US-CERT and other organizations dedicated to protection of information systems and the sensitive data they process.

The SAIG Agreement also includes a provision that in the event of an unauthorized disclosure or an actual or suspected breach of applicant information or other sensitive information (such as PII) the institution must immediately notify FSA at CPSSAIG@ed.gov. This provision is especially important as it helps FSA identify risks and breaches that impact multiple institutions and other entities.

In addition to other provisions within the SAIG Agreement, FSA requires institutions to comply with the Gramm-Leach-Bliley Act. Under Title V of the Gramm-Leach-Bliley Act, financial services organizations, including institutions of higher education, are required to ensure the security and confidentiality of customer records and information. This requirement was recently added to the Program Participation Agreement and is reflected in the Federal Student Aid Handbook.

The HEA also requires institutions to maintain appropriate institutional capability for the sound administration of the Title IV programs. Such capability would include satisfactory policies, safeguards, monitoring and management practices related to information security. Further, FERPA generally prohibits institutions from having policies or practices that permit the disclosure of education records or PII contained therein without the written consent of the student, unless an exception applies. Any data breach resulting from a failure of an institution to maintain appropriate and reasonable information security policies and safeguards could also constitute a FERPA violation.

Finally, we note that institutions frequently enter into contractual arrangements with other organizations to fulfill institutional obligations with respect to the Title IV federal student financial assistance programs. If your institution has entered into such an arrangement, we remind you of 34 CFR §668.25, which includes a provision that the institution remains liable for any action by its third-party servicers.[282]

Note 3

---

[282] Letter from James W. Runcie, Chief Operating Officer, Federal Student Aid, U.S. Dep't. of Educ., and Ted Mitchell, Undersecretary, Federal Student Aid, U.S. Dep't. of Educ., to colleague (July 29, 2015) *available at* https://ifap.ed.gov/dear-colleague-letters/07-29-2015-protecting-student-information.

In *Roberts v. Maricopa County Community College District*, the plaintiffs brought a class action lawsuit against Maricopa County Community College District based on at least two data breach incidents involving student PII. One data breach incident was discovered by the FBI and a second data breach incident involved the attempted sale of PII on the dark web. The plaintiffs raised numerous claims, including negligence, breach of fiduciary duty and breach of privacy. Notably, the plaintiffs' allegations included statements that the County College District represented that it complied with FERPA and GLB.[283]

Note 4

On February 28, 2020, the Federal Student Aid Office of the The Department of Education of the United States issued a notice to educational institutions titled, "Enforcement of Cybersecurity Requirements under the Graham-Leach-Bliley Act."[284]

The notice states in relevant part:

. . . We expect all of our partners to maintain strong security policies and effective internal controls to prevent unauthorized access or disclosure of sensitive information. . . .The Federal Trade Commission (FTC) has enforcement authority for the requirements and has determined that institutions of higher education (institutions) are financial institutions under GLBA.

Each institution has agreed to comply with GLBA in its Program Participation Agreement with the Department. In addition, as a condition of accessing the Department's systems, each institution and servicer must sign the Student Aid Internet Gateway (SAIG) Enrollment Agreement, which states that the institution must ensure that all federal student aid applicant information is protected from access by or disclosure to unauthorized personnel.

Institutions and third-party servicers are also required to demonstrate administrative capability in accordance with 34 C.F.R. § 668.16, including the maintenance of adequate checks and balances in their systems of internal control. An institution or servicer that does not maintain adequate internal controls over the security of student information may not be considered administratively capable.

In Dear Colleague Letter GEN-15-18 and GEN-16-12, we reminded institutions about the longstanding requirements of GLBA and notified them of our intention to begin enforcing legal requirements of GLBA through annual compliance audits. In Dear CPA Letter CPA-19-01, we explained the procedures for auditors to determine whether institutions were in compliance with GLBA. This announcement explains the Department's procedures for enforcing those requirements and the potential consequences for institutions or servicers that fail to comply.

Audit Findings

---

[283] *See generally* Class Action Complaint, Roberts v. Maricopa County Community College District, No. CV2014-007411 (Apr. 28, 2014).

[284] FEDERAL STUDENT AID, US DEP'T. OF EDUC., ENFORCEMENT OF CYBERSECURITY REQUIREMENTS UNDER THE GRAMM-LEACH-BLILEY ACT (Feb. 28, 2020), *available at* https://ifap.ed.gov/electronic-announcements/022820EnforcCyberReqGrammLeachBlileyAct.

Auditors are expected to evaluate three information safeguard requirements of GLBA in audits of postsecondary institutions or third-party servicers under the regulations in 16 C.F.R. Part 314:

The institution must designate an individual to coordinate its information security program.

The institution must perform a risk assessment that addresses three required areas described in 16 C.F.R. 314.4(b):

    a)   Employee training and management;

    b)   Information systems, including network and software design, as well as information processing, storage, transmission and disposal; and

    c)   Detecting, preventing and responding to attacks, intrusions, or other systems failures.

The institution must document a safeguard for each risk identified in Step 2 above.

When an auditor determines that an institution or servicer has failed to comply with any of these GLBA requirements, the finding will be included in the institution's audit report.

Federal Trade Commission

When an audit report that includes a GLBA audit finding is received by the Department, we will refer the audit to the FTC. Once the finding is referred to the FTC, that finding will be considered closed for the Department's audit tracking purposes. The FTC will determine what action may be needed as a result of the GLBA audit finding.

Cybersecurity Team

Federal Student Aid's Postsecondary Institution Cybersecurity Team (Cybersecurity Team) will also be informed of findings related to GLBA, and may request additional documentation from the institution in order to assess the level of risk to student data presented by the institution or servicer's information security system.

If the Cybersecurity Team determines that the institution or servicer poses substantial risk to the security of student information, the Cybersecurity Team may temporarily or permanently disable the institution or servicer's access to the Department's information systems. Additionally, if the Cybersecurity Team determines that as a result of very serious internal control weaknesses of the general controls over technology that the institution's or servicer's administrative capability is impaired or it has a history of non-compliance, it may refer the institution to the Department's Administrative Actions and Appeals Service Group for consideration of a fine or other appropriate administrative action by the Department.[285]

6.3[C] Office of Inspector General U.S. Department of Education Technology Crimes Division

The mission and jurisdiction of the Technology Crimes Division goes beyond just Title IV schools. The Office of Inspector General (OIG) is an "independent component of Federal agencies created by Congress" that "reports to [the] Head of the Agency and

---

[285] *Id.*

Congress."[286]   After the President appoints an Inspector General (IG), the IG is confirmed by the Senate. The Technology Crimes Division of the U.S. Department of Education investigates "crimes and criminal cyber threats against" the U.S. Department of Education's "IT infrastructure, or criminal activity in cyber space that threatens the Department's administration of Federal education assistance funds."[287] The Technology Crimes Division's "investigative jurisdiction encompasses any IT system used in the administration of Federal money originating from the Department of Education."[288]

The case examples include:

Grade hacking

Computer Intrusions

Criminal Forums online selling malware

ID/Credential theft to hijack Student Aid applications

Misuse of Department systems to obtain personal information

Falsifying student aid applications by U.S. government employees

Child Exploitation material trafficking[289]

The Department of Justice describes the responsibilities of the Technology Crimes Division as follows:

Technology Crimes Division

The Technology Crimes Division (TCD) is the OIG component responsible for investigating computer security incidents within ED, as well as, conducting forensic analysis of computer systems and other electronic media in support of criminal investigations. In addition, it is responsible for the coordination, tracking, and conduct of proactive data mining activities and projects; referring the results of those efforts to the field for investigation. TCD is comprised of fill-time Computer Crime Investigators (CCIs), technical professionals, and program analysts. All CCIs have full statutory law enforcement authority as granted by Congress.

In performing its responsibilities, the Division:

Perform cybercrime investigations in response to attacks against, as well as unauthorized access of, Department of Education information systems, networks, computer systems, or databases.

Investigates the criminal misuse of Departmental computers, which could include the accessing of child pornography.

Performs forensic analysis of computer media in support of criminal investigations by both TCD and OIG Investigation Services.

Develop policies and procedures on the application of advanced evidence collection, preservation, and analysis techniques.

Performs the intermediate step of validation of data query results to reduce or eliminate false positives, cross-checking data with other publicly and privately available databases, conducting sophisticated link analysis, and ultimately generating productive investigative referrals for Investigation Services field offices.

---

[286] *See* OFFICE OF THE INSPECTOR GENERAL, US DEP'T. OF EDUC., CYBER SECURITY FOR TITLE IV SCHOOLS, *available at* https://www.ren-isac.net/events/attachments/TB_Apr21_2017.pdf .

[287] *Id.*

[288] *Id.*

[289] *Id.*

Conducts proactive data mining initiatives and is responsible for the project management of those products, which includes coordination with field offices, tracking efforts, and reporting results.[290]

NOTES

Note 1

The following is a Press Release concerning a cybersecurity case in Philadelphia concerning the attempt to obtain President Donald Trump's tax returns:

PHILADELPHIA – United States Attorney William M. McSwain announced that Justin Hiemstra, 22, of St. Paul Park, Minnesota, and Andrew Harris, 23, of Philadelphia, Pennsylvania were both sentenced today to two years' probation and 200 hours of community service by United States District Judge Cynthia M. Rufe. In August 2019, Hiemstra pled guilty to using a school computer and someone else's username without that person's permission in an attempt to illegally obtain then-Presidential candidate Donald Trump's tax returns from the Internal Revenue Service. Harris pled guilty to the same charges in September 2019.

These charges arose out of a plot between the defendants, then students at Haverford College, to use computers at the school's computer lab and the Free Application for Student Aid (FAFSA) website to illegally access the tax returns. Hiemstra and Harris opened a false FAFSA application in the name of a member of the Trump family and found that someone else had already obtained a username and password for Donald Trump. In order to reset the password, the defendants were prompted to answer challenge questions, which the original person had created when setting up the account. The defendants were able to answer the questions and reset the password. They then used the President's personal identifying information, including his social security number and date of birth, to attempt to import the President's federal tax information into the bogus FAFSA application. Ultimately, this illegal attempt failed.

"Hiemstra and Harris thought they could manipulate and outsmart the FAFSA application process in order to obtain Donald Trump's tax returns for their own purposes. As it turns out, that was not such a smart move: they committed a serious violation of privacy rights and a federal crime in the process," said U.S. Attorney McSwain. "Now they have both been held accountable. And those who complete the FAFSA application, please take note: this Office takes these kinds of cybersecurity breaches seriously and we are doing everything we can to keep your personal information safe."[291]

Note 2

---

[290] *Archived Information: US Department of Education Principal office Functional Statements*, U.S. DEPARTMENT OF EDUCATION, https://www2.ed.gov/about/offices/list/om/fs_po/oig/it.html (last modified May 20, 2020).

[291] *Former Haverford College Students Sentenced for Attempting to Access President Trump's Tax Returns*, U.S. ATTORNEY'S OFFICE, EASTERN DISTRICT OF PENNSYLVANIA (Dec. 16 2019), https://www.justice.gov/usao-edpa/pr/former-haverford-college-students-sentenced-attempting-access-president-trump-s-tax.

The Office of Inspector General published a brochure[292] explaining in relative detail its duties:

The Federal government disburses billions of dollars each year to individuals and local, State, and national entities—so who makes sure that those recipients use Federal dollars as required by law? The answer: the offices of inspectors general—a cadre of Federal employees focused on protecting the integrity of our government and working to detect and prevent fraud, waste, abuse, and criminal activity involving Federal funds. We are the Office of Inspector General (OIG) for the U.S. Department of Education, and we help ensure that America's tax dollars are used effectively and efficiently. Ours is no small task: the U.S. Department of Education (ED) is one of the largest financial institutions in the country, managing a loan portfolio worth more than $1.2 trillion. Its program participants and funding recipients include all States and territories, school districts, schools, colleges and universities, other education services providers, and more than 13 million student aid and loan recipients each year. But each year, people steal or intentionally misuse ED funds—Federal student aid, special education money, or Title I funds to school districts with low-income families. They intentionally abuse ED programs, unlawfully access ED computer systems and databases, or use ED funding to support terrorism. It's our job to stop them. And that is what OIG Investigation Services is all about.

OIG Investigation Services

OIG Investigation Services is the law enforcement arm of ED. This team of professionals is responsible for criminal, civil, and administrative investigative activities relating to ED's programs and operations—from examining allegations of wrongdoing to aggressively pursuing those who seek to enrich themselves at the expense of our nation's students. Our criminal investigators exercise full law enforcement authority— carrying firearms, executing arrest and search warrants, and taking sworn statements. They also employ the full spectrum of traditional law enforcement techniques, such as conducting surveillance and undercover operations. ED OIG investigators work side-by-side with their colleagues in other law enforcement agencies, as well as with Federal, State, and local prosecutors. OIG Investigation Services has put a stop to thousands of schemes and scams involving ED programs, operations, and funds. We have unraveled multimillion dollar fraud schemes by high-ranking school officials, unscrupulous school owners, and other people placed in positions of trust to educate our children.

Investigation

What the OIG Investigates ED administers more than 120 programs and most Federal education assistance throughout the country. The OIG examines allegations of wrongdoing and conducts investigations in all of them, including the following. • Embezzlement, bribery, serious mismanagement, or other public corruption involving ED funds • Theft or misuse of Federal student aid • Identity theft • Fraudulent or other misinformation contained on a Free Application for Federal Student Aid (FAFSA) • Fraud, waste, or abuse involving a financial aid administrator, other school officials, student loan servicers, or collection agencies • Schools not complying with regulations or laws involving Federal student aid or other ED programs • Conflicts of interest • Contract and procurement irregularities • Theft or abuse of government property •

---

[292] U.S. DEP'T. OF EDUC., THE OFFICE OF INSPECTOR GENERAL, INVESTIGATION SERVICES, *available at* https://www2.ed.gov/about/offices/list/oig/invtreports/isgeneralbrochureonline.pdf.

Misconduct, abuse of authority, or ethics violations by ED employees or officials • Other violations of Federal laws, rules, and regulations pertaining to ED programs and funding In addition, the OIG Technology Crimes Division uses highly specialized techniques and methods such as digital evidence examination and proactive data analytics to investigate criminal activity that targets information technology systems, including the following. • Unauthorized access or fraudulent misuse of any information technology system used to administer, process, disburse, or manage Federal funds originating from ED • Theft or misuse of credentials to unlawfully access ED information technology systems, including the National Student Loan Data System and the FAFSA submission Web site • Identification and referral of cyber vulnerabilities in ED's systems and programs.

Note 3

The Department of Education Federal Student Aid office provides a list of resources for cybersecurity compliance. One of those resources is a link to the FedRAMP program concerning cybersecurity and cloud services offered by vendors for Federal Agencies:

The Federal Risk and Authorization Management Program (FedRAMP) is a government-wide program that provides a standardized approach to security assessment, authorization, and continuous monitoring for cloud products and services. This approach uses a "do once, use many times" framework that saves cost, time, and staff required to conduct redundant Agency security assessments. . . .

FedRAMP is mandatory for Federal Agency cloud deployments and service models at the low, moderate, and high risk impact levels. Private cloud deployments intended for single organizations and implemented fully within federal facilities are the only exception. Additionally, Agencies must submit a quarterly report in PortfolioStat listing all existing cloud services that do not meet FedRAMP requirements with the appropriate rationale and proposed resolutions for achieving compliance.

. . . The FedRAMP security controls are based on NIST SP 800-53 Revision 4 baselines and contain controls above the NIST baseline that address the unique elements of cloud computing.[293]

6.4 State Student Data Protection Laws

Before examining the individual state laws, a discussion of organized consortiums and their role in advancing student data protection laws. At no time in history are students more connected to their learning institutions via the internet than today. The COVID-19 pandemic forced school districts to rely on remote learning and cyber learning tools even more. Prior to COVID-19, K-12 districts and higher institutions of education were already relying on connected systems to aid in teaching and maintaining educational data, and to connect with student parents and guardians. Companies in this portion of the cyberspace are growing and providing more and more bundled educational services online. This is an area of tremendous growth and

---

[293] *Frequently Asked Questions*, FEDRAMP, https://www.fedramp.gov/faqs/ (last visited Oct. 13, 2020).

opportunity, both for companies and schools. And with this growth, the states have taken action to protect student online data.

When a school district signs a contract to implement a third-party system to store student data and provide features and functions to manipulate that data, the provider of the third-party system is not normally the collector of that data. That may seem counterintuitive because the students, parents, teachers, and school administrators are typing or uploading data directly into the third-party's system. If the third-party is not the collector, then who is the collector? The school district or higher education institution is the collector. The school district is the collector and controller of the student data because the school district contracts for the system and implements the system and provides the student accounts. Because the school district is the collector, the school district must manage the necessary relationships between the school district and the users. Where consent is required, the school district must receive that consent for the third-party to process that data. The third-party is a processor of the data and not a collector. This is also true for collecting data from students who fall under COPPA. The district must collect the necessary consents from the parents. To this end, most if not all third-party contracts require the school district to warrant that it will only permit data into the system with the proper consent, whether express or implied under FERPA.

Because the school district is the collector and the system owner is the processor, the school district is ordinarily responsible for meeting the requirements of the state student data laws. Although the processor is also viewed as a FERPA school official in its processing of the data and cannot escape the state student data laws, the school district still has certain responsibilities and duties in holding its processors accountable. This is accomplished through the contract language and proper vetting of the processor. Large companies have legal departments to handle such contractual issues, but school districts that are funded with taxpayer dollars cannot always afford to maintain a legal staff experienced in cybersecurity matters. To help in this area, organizations with school districts as members have formed to fill the void. It makes sense for an organization with like-minded members with identical tasks to combine their efforts and resources to produce a solution template for all. The Student Data Privacy Consortium is such an organization.

The Student Data Privacy Consortium (SDPC) provides tools and resources, acts as a clearinghouse for student data privacy operational issues, identifies projects that need attention, and leverages the combined power of its members.[294] One of the SDPC provided resources is a National Data Privacy Agreement. Data privacy agreements ("DPA") are agreements between the school district as a data collector (in GDPR terms, a controller) and the data processor. The DPA is sometimes also called a data processing agreement or data protection agreement. In reality, the DPA is more of a data security agreement than a data privacy agreement for the simple fact that student data privacy cannot be achieved without adequate security measures. The DPA is normally negotiated as an addendum or separate agreement to a main contract vehicle. Early on, the SDPC realized the need for a DPA template that all members could use. From this effort sprung 25 state alliances and a National DPA.[295] The current states that have

---

[294] *See About the Consortium, available at* https://privacy.a4l.org/privacy-community/ (last visited April 30, 2022).

[295] *See National Data Privacy Agreement, available at* https://privacy.a4l.org/national-dpa/ (last visited April 30, 2022).

alliance website pages are: AR, AZ, CA, FL, IA, IL, MA, ME, MN, MO, MT, NC, NE, NH, OH, OR, RI, TN, TX, UT, VA, VT, WA, WI, and WY.[296] The alliance webpage for these particular states presents that alliance's approved standard DPA. For example, the California page makes the CA-NDPA-V1 version of a DPA available to members. Each state alliance's DPA is customized to address the student data protection laws of that state. To be clear, not every district in a state belongs to the state alliance.

The main body of the NDPA covers the following areas:[297]

purpose and scope

data ownership and authorized access

duties of the school district (also called a Local Education Agency ("LEA"))

duties of processor (also called "provider")

data provisions to cover data storage, audits, data security, data breach.

The attached exhibits can cover:[298]

a description of the services provided by the processor

a schedule of data including the category of data and data elements definitions

directions for end of agreement deposition of data

contract vehicle for other district member to sign on to the same DPA after signing a main agreement

data security requirements – these can be met by maintaining a cybersecurity framework based on National Institute of Standard and Technology (NIST) Cybersecurity Framework Version 1.1, ISO 27000 series or others.

School districts that are not a member of the consortium or an alliance may use another version of a DPA or rely on the processor to provide a DPA. Regardless of the source, the DPA will normally be negotiated by the school district and the processor because templates do not always provide a perfect fit. Negotiators on both sides should recognize that the negotiation is not a winner-take-all effort but a win-win endeavor because the school district and processor must operate as partners in protecting student data. Negotiators for the processor should realize that the school district's hands may be tied on some points because some requirements may be mandated by state law, or its board and are not negotiable. Negotiators for the school district should realize that a successful processor could have thousands of customers and that the storage may be cloud-based making some areas of support standardized for the processor and thus non-negotiable. A thousand one-off customized security agreements could become quickly unmanageable for a processor. Also, keep in mind that the processor may use and negotiate DPAs with its subprocessors, such as cloud storage providers and any negotiation agreed to with the district must also work with the subprocessor. Cloud storage providers also have thousands of customers and cannot negotiate a separate security arrangement for each customer, such as the processor. What should be expected of processors and subprocessors is a commitment to providing industry standard security measures that focus on maintaining the confidentiality, integrity, and availability of the school district's data through industry standard physical, administrative, and

---

[296] https://sdpc.a4l.org/view_alliance.php?state=CA (last visited April 30, 2022).

[297] *See Standard Student Data Privacy Agreement (NDPA Standard Version 1.0), available at* https://cdn.ymaws.com/www.a4l.org/resource/resmgr/files/sdpc-publicdocs/final_sdpc_ndpa_v1-7.pdf.

[298] *Id.*

technological safeguards. Remember, the school district and the processor and subprocessors are on the same team. All want to safeguard the student data.

With an understanding of DPAs, we now look at individual state education and student data protection laws that are focused on protecting student data.

6.4[A] CALIFORNIA (SOPIPA)

For protecting student online data in California, there are two relevant acts: the California Online Personal Information Protection Act ("SOPIPA") and the California Education Code section 49073.1 ("Privacy of Pupil Records").

Section 49073.1(a) states:

A local education agency may, pursuant to a policy adopted by its governing board or, in the case of a charter school, its governing body, enter into a contract with a third party for either or both of the following purposes: (1) To provide services, including cloud-based services, for the digital storage, management, and retrieval of pupil records. (2) To provide digital educational software that authorizes a third-party provider of digital educational software to access, store, and use pupil records in accordance with the contractual provisions listed in subdivision (b).[299]

Subdivision (b) lists the contract requirements.

The SOPIPA expands on these requirements. Section (d) outlines the security requirements for the processor (operator):

(d) An operator shall:

(1) Implement and maintain reasonable security procedures and practices appropriate to the nature of the covered information, and protect that information from unauthorized access, destruction, use, modification, or disclosure.

(2) Delete a student's covered information if the school or district requests deletion of data under the control of the school or district.[300]

6.4[B] ILLINOIS (SOPPA)

In the summer of 2021, the state of Illinois updated its August 24, 2017 Student Online Personal Protection Act ("SOPPA").

For state data breach notification laws, the definition of personally identifiable information ("PII") is very narrow when compared to "covered information" for student data protection laws. The following very broad SOPPA definition of covered information is typical of state student data protection laws:

"Covered information" means personally identifiable information or material or information that is linked to personally identifiable information or material in any media or format that is not publicly available and is any of the following:

(1) Created by or provided to an operator by a student or the student's parent in the course of the student's or parent's use of the operator's site, service, or application for K through 12 school purposes.

---

[299]https://leginfo.legislature.ca.gov/faces/codes_displaySection.xhtml?sectionNum=49073.1.&lawCode=EDC.

[300] https://leginfo.legislature.ca.gov/faces/billNavClient.xhtml?bill_id=201320140SB1177.

(2) Created by or provided to an operator by an employee or agent of a school or school district for K through 12 school purposes.

(3) Gathered by an operator through the operation of its site, service, or application for K through 12 school purposes and personally identifies a student, including, but not limited to, information in the student's educational record or electronic mail, first and last name, home address, telephone number, electronic mail address, or other information that allows physical or online contact, discipline records, test results, special education data, juvenile dependency records, grades, evaluations, criminal records, medical records, health records, a social security number, biometric information, disabilities, socioeconomic information, food purchases, political affiliations, religious information, text messages, documents, student identifiers, search activity, photos, voice recordings, or geolocation information.[301]

The 2021 amendment added specific operator duties with a focus on security:

Sec. 15. Operator duties. An operator shall do the following:

(1) Implement and maintain reasonable security procedures and practices that otherwise meet or exceed industry standards designed to protect covered information from unauthorized access, destruction, use, modification, or disclosure.

(2) Delete, within a reasonable time period, a student's covered information if the school or school district requests deletion of covered information under the control of the school or school district, unless a student or his or her parent consents to the maintenance of the covered information.[302]

With the exception of nonpublic schools, the amendment requires a written agreement with the operator that must include the following:

(A) A listing of the categories or types of covered information to be provided to the operator.

(B) A statement of the product or service being provided to the school by the operator.

(C) A statement that, pursuant to the federal Family Educational Rights and Privacy Act of 1974, the operator is acting as a school official with a legitimate educational interest, is performing an institutional service or function for which the school would otherwise use employees, under the direct control of the school, with respect to the use and maintenance of covered information, and is using the covered information only for an authorized purpose and may not re-disclose it to third parties or affiliates, unless otherwise permitted under this Act, without permission from the school or pursuant to court order.

(D) A description of how, if a breach is attributed to the operator, any costs and expenses incurred by the school in investigating and remediating the breach will be allocated between the operator and the school. The costs and expenses may include, but are not limited to:

(i) providing notification to the parents of those students whose covered information was compromised and to regulatory agencies or other entities as required by law or contract;

---

[301] 105 ILCS 85/ Student Online Personal Protection Act.
[302] *Id.*

(ii) providing credit monitoring to those students whose covered information was exposed in a manner during the breach that a reasonable person would believe that it could impact his or her credit or financial security;

(iii) legal fees, audit costs, fines, and any other fees or damages imposed against the school as a result of the security breach; and

(iv) providing any other notifications or fulfilling any other requirements adopted by the State Board or of any other State or federal laws.

(E) A statement that the operator must delete or transfer to the school all covered information if the information is no longer needed for the purposes of the written agreement and to specify the time period in which the information must be deleted or transferred once the operator is made aware that the information is no longer needed for the purposes of the written agreement.

(F) If the school maintains a website, a statement that the school must publish the written agreement on the school's website. If the school does not maintain a website, a statement that the school must make the written agreement available for inspection by the general public at its administrative office. If mutually agreed upon by the school and the operator, provisions of the written agreement, other than those under subparagraphs (A), (B), and (C), may be redacted in the copy of the written agreement published on the school's website or made available at its administrative office.[303]

The above requirements would likely be addressed in a DPA. The DPA will also likely address the school district's duties under the law:

(e) Each school must implement and maintain reasonable security procedures and practices that otherwise meet or exceed industry standards designed to protect covered information from unauthorized access, destruction, use, modification, or disclosure. Any written agreement under which the disclosure of covered information between the school and a third party takes place must include a provision requiring the entity to whom the covered information is disclosed to implement and maintain reasonable security procedures and practices that otherwise meet or exceed industry standards designed to protect covered information from unauthorized access, destruction, use, modification, or disclosure. The State Board must make available on its website a guidance document for schools pertaining to reasonable security procedures and practices under this subsection.

---

[303] *Id.*

6.4[C] COLORADO

The governor of Colorado signed House Bill 16-1423 into law on June 10, 2016. Article 16 covers Student Data Transparency and Security.[304] Student PII is again broadly defined:

(13) "Student Personally Identifiable Information" means information that, alone or in combination, personally identifies an individual student or the student's parent or family, and that is collected, maintained, generated, or inferred by a public education entity, either directly or through a school service, or by a school service contract provider or school service on-demand provider."[305]

Under C.R.S. 22-16-104, the state board of education duties are enumerated including developing a detailed security plan that includes:

(I) GUIDANCE for authorizing access to the student data system and to individual student PERSONALLY IDENTIFIABLE INFORMATION, including GUIDANCE for authenticating authorized access;

(II)Privacy compliance standards;

(III) Privacy and security audits;

(IV) Security breach planning, notice, and procedures;

(V) STUDENT PERSONALLY IDENTIFIABLE INFORMATION retention and DESTRUCTION policies, which must include specific REQUIREMENTS for identifying when and how the STUDENT PERSONALLY IDENTIFIABLE INFORMATION will be destroyed;

(VI) Guidance for school districts and staff regarding STUDENT PERSONALLY IDENTIFIABLE INFORMATION use;

(VII) Consequences for security breaches; and

(VIII) Staff training regarding the policies;[306]

The law also enumerates Colorado Department of Education duties. Under C.R.S. 22-16-106:

The department shall develop data security guidance that may be used by local education PROVIDERS. The department's data security guidance must include:

(a) Guidance for authorizing access to the student data system and to STUDENT PERSONALLY IDENTIFIABLE INFORMATION, including guidance for authenticating authorized access;

(b)Privacy compliance standards;

(c) BEST PRACTICES FOR privacy and security audits;

(d) Security breach planning, notice, and procedures;

(e) Data retention and DESTRUCTION procedures;

(f) Data collection and sharing procedures;

(g) Recommendations that any contracts that affect databases, assessments, or instructional supports that include student or personally identifiable INFORMATION and are outsourced to vendors include express provisions that safeguard privacy and security and include penalties for noncompliance;

(h) Best security practices for privacy when using online education services, including websites and applications;

---

[304] https://www.cde.state.co.us/dataprivacyandsecurity/crs22-16-101.

[305] *Id.*

[306] *Id.*

(i) Guidance for contracts involving the outsourcing of educational services;

(j) Guidance for contracts involving online education services;

(k) Guidance for publishing a list of vendors that local education PROVIDERS contract with that hold student PERSONALLY IDENTIFIABLE INFORMATION;

(l) Consequences for security breaches; and

(m) EXAMPLES OF staff training regarding the procedures.[307]

Under C.R.S. 22-16-107. Local education providers – data collection – data security policy, local education providers are also given specific guidance regarding security. Under C.R.S. 22-16-110 School server contract provider – data security – data destruction:

(1) Each school service contract provider shall maintain a comprehensive information security program that is reasonably designed to protect the security, privacy, confidentiality, and integrity of student personally identifiable information. The information security program must make use of appropriate administrative, technological, and physical safeguards.[308]

The Colorado law is interesting in that it affects many levels of the education system, from the Colorado Department of Education down to the vendors that process student data. No entity is left untouched and rightly so because creating and maintaining cybersecurity takes a team effort at all levels.

6.4[D] TEXAS

Texas Education Code, Sec. 32.151 covers "Student Information." The "covered information" is similarly broad and resembles that of the Illinois SOPPA:

(1) "Covered information" means personally identifiable information or information that is linked to personally identifiable information, in any media or format, that is not publicly available and is:

(A) created by or provided to an operator by a student or the student's parent in the course of the student's or parent's use of the operator's website, online service, online application, or mobile application for a school purpose;

(B) created by or provided to an operator by an employee of a school district or school campus for a school purpose; or

(C) gathered by an operator through the operation of the operator's website, online service, online application, or mobile application for a school purpose and personally identifies a student, including the student's educational record, electronic mail, first and last name, home address, telephone number, electronic mail address, information that allows physical or online contact, discipline records, test results, special education data, juvenile delinquency records, grades, evaluations, criminal records, medical records, health records, social security number, biometric information, disabilities, socioeconomic information, food purchases, political affiliations, religious information, text messages, student identifiers, search activity, photograph, voice recordings, or geolocation information.[309]

---

[307] *Id.*

[308] *Id.*

[309] https://statutes.capitol.texas.gov/Docs/ED/pdf/ED.32.pdf.

The following section specifies the security protection measures for covered information that remains in effect until September 1, 2023:

Sec. 32.155. PROTECTION OF COVERED INFORMATION. An operator must implement and maintain reasonable security procedures and practices designed to protect any covered information from unauthorized access, deletion, use, modification, or disclosure.

The above guidance is greatly expanded in the amended version that becomes effective on September 01, 2023,

Sec. 32.155. PROTECTION OF COVERED INFORMATION.

(a) An operator must implement and maintain reasonable security procedures and practices designed to protect any covered information from unauthorized access, deletion, use, modification, or disclosure.

(b) Any operator that has been approved by the agency or had a product adopted by the agency and possesses any covered information must use the unique identifier established by the Texas Student Data System (TSDS) or a successor data management system maintained by the agency for any account creation, data upload, data transmission, analysis, or reporting to mask all personally identifiable student information. The operator shall adhere to a state-required student data sharing agreement that includes an established unique identifier standard for all operators as prescribed by the agency.

(c) In addition to including the unique identifier in releasing information as provided by Subsection (b), an operator may include any other data field identified by the agency or by a school district, open-enrollment charter school, regional education service center, or other local education agency as necessary for the information being released to be useful.

(d) A school district, open-enrollment charter school, regional education service center, or other local education agency may include additional data fields in an agreement with an operator or the amendment of an agreement with an operator under this section. An operator may agree to include the additional data fields requested by a school district, open-enrollment charter school, regional education service center, or other local education agency but may not require that additional data fields be included.

(e) A school district, open-enrollment charter school, regional education service center, or other local education agency may require an operator that contracts directly with the entity to adhere to a state-required student data sharing agreement that includes the use of an established unique identifier standard for all operators as prescribed by the agency.

(f) A national assessment provider who receives covered information from a student or from a school district or campus on behalf of a student is not required to comply with Subsection (b) or (e) if the provider receives the covered information solely to provide access to:

(1) employment, educational scholarships, financial aid, or postsecondary educational opportunities; or

(2) educational resources for middle school, junior high school, or high school students.

(g) The commissioner may adopt rules as necessary to administer this section.[310]

6.4[E] NEW YORK

New York is a state that has very specific cybersecurity requirements for protecting online student data that can be found in New York Education Law section 2-d and 8NYCRR Part 121.

Section 2-d, unauthorized release of personally identifiable information, provides definitions for "Personally identifiable information", "Student data", and "Teacher or principal data."

"Personally identifiable information," as applied to student data, means personally identifiable information as defined in section 99.3 of title thirty-four of the code of federal regulations implementing the family educational rights and privacy act, section twelve hundred thirty-two-g of title twenty of the United States code, and, as applied to teacher or principal data, means "personally identifying information" as such term is used in subdivision ten of section three thousand twelve-c of this chapter.

"Student data" means personally identifiable information from student records of an educational agency.

"Teacher or principal data" means personally identifiable information from the records of an educational agency relating to the annual professional performance reviews of classroom teachers or principals that is confidential and not subject to release under the provisions of section three thousand twelve-c of this chapter.

Section 2-d also requires a school to publish a parents bill of rights for data privacy and security:

Parents bill of rights for data privacy and security. a. A parents bill of rights for data privacy and security shall be published on the website of each educational agency and shall be included with every contract an educational agency enters into with a third party contractor where the third party contractor receives student data or teacher or principal data.

The parents bill of rights for data privacy and security must be stated in clear and plain English that explains:

(1) A student's personally identifiable information cannot be sold or released for any commercial purposes;

(2) Parents have the right to inspect and review the complete contents of their child's education record;

(3) State and federal laws protect the confidentiality of personally identifiable information, and safeguards associated with industry standards and best practices, including but not limited to, encryption, firewalls, and password protection, must be in place when data is stored or transferred;

(4) A complete list of all student data elements collected by the State is available for public review at (insert website address here) or by writing to (insert mailing address here); and

---

[310] *Id.*

(5) Parents have the right to have complaints about possible breaches of student data addressed. Complaints should be directed to (insert phone number, email and mailing address here).

The parents bill of rights for data privacy and security must also include supplemental information regarding contracts with third parties that process student, teacher, or principal data:

(1) the exclusive purposes for which the student data or teacher or principal data will be used;

(2) how the third party contractor will ensure that the subcontractors, persons or entities that the third party contractor will share the student data or teacher or principal data with, if any, will abide by data protection and security requirements;

(3) when the agreement expires and what happens to the student data or teacher or principal data upon expiration of the agreement;

(4) if and how a parent, student, eligible student, teacher or principal may challenge the accuracy of the student data or teacher or principal data that is collected; and

(5) where the student data or teacher or principal data will be stored (described in such a manner as to protect data security), and the security protections taken to ensure such data will be protected, including whether such data will be encrypted.

The commission with the chief privacy officer are responsible for promulgating regulations that establish standards for educational agency data security including the development of a model policy for educational agencies' use. The standards must include:

(1) data privacy protections, including criteria for determining whether a proposed use of personally identifiable information would benefit students and educational agencies, and processes to ensure that personally identifiable information is not included in public reports or other public documents;

(2) data security protections, including data systems monitoring, data encryption, incident response plans, limitations on access to personally identifiable information, safeguards to ensure personally identifiable information is not accessed by unauthorized persons when transmitted over communication networks, and destruction of personally identifiable information when no longer needed; and

(3) application of all such restrictions, requirements and safeguards to third-party contractors.

In establishing the above, the commissioner must use the input of experts from security, cybersecurity, and personal data protection.

In contracting with third-party processors, the contract must contain provisions for data sharing and maintaining confidentiality in accordance with applicable federal, state, and local law. To that end, the third-party processors must provide a data security and privacy plan that includes a requirement that any officers or employees who have access to data are trained or will receive training on the governing federal and state law. Additionally, the third-party processor must agree to:

(1) limit internal access to education records to those individuals that are determined to have legitimate educational interests;

(2) not use the education records for any other purposes than those explicitly authorized in its contract;

(3) except for authorized representatives of the third party contractor to the extent they are carrying out the contract, not disclose any personally identifiable information to any other party:

(i) without the prior written consent of the parent or eligible student; or

(ii) unless required by statute or court order and the party provides a notice of the disclosure to the department, district board of education, or institution that provided the information no later than the time the information is disclosed, unless providing notice of the disclosure is expressly prohibited by the statute or court order;

(4) maintain reasonable administrative, technical and physical safeguards to protect the security, confidentiality and integrity of personally identifiable student information in its custody;

(5) uses encryption technology to protect data while in motion or in its custody from unauthorized disclosure using a technology or methodology specified by the secretary of the United States departmentof health and human services in guidance issued under Section 13402(H)(2) of Public Law 111-5.

Part 121 – Strengthening Data Privacy and Security in NY State Educational Agencies to Protect Personally Identifiable Information – was an amendment to Education Law sections 2-d, 101, 207, and 305. Section 121.5 provides the Data Security and Privacy Standard that had to be adopted by New York education agencies by July 1, 2020. Significantly, in Part 121, the Education Department adopted the NIST Cybersecurity Framework (CSF) Version 1.1 "as the standard for data security and privacy for educational agencies." Other states have also been adopting the NIST CSF 1.1 as a valid framework for demonstrating reasonable cybersecurity standard. In addition to NIST CSF 1.1, many state DPAs have also adopted NIST Special Publication guidelines for demonstrating particular areas of cybersecurity strength and compliance. On January 16, 2020, NIST published version 1.0 of its NIST Privacy Framework that will likely become a companion document to the NIST CSF 1.1 and thus, also a source of standards for vendors to meet.

Section 121.6 – Data and Security and Privacy Plan – brought significant requirements for the capturing of processor security capabilities in vendor contract language:

(a) Each educational agency that enters into a contract with a third-party contractor shall ensure that the contract includes the third-party contractor's data security and privacy plan that is accepted by the educational agency. The data security and privacy plan shall, at a minimum:

(1) outline how the third-party contractor will implement all state, federal, and local data security and privacy contract requirements over the life of the contract, consistent with the educational agency's data security and privacy policy;

(2) specify the administrative, operational and technical safeguards and practices it has in place to protect personally identifiable information that it will receive under the contract;

(3) demonstrate that it complies with the requirements of Section 121.3(c) [bill of rights] of this Part;

(4) specify how officers or employees of the third-party contractor and its assignees who have access to student data, or teacher or principal data receive or will receive training on the federal and state laws governing confidentiality of such data prior to receiving access;

(5) specify if the third-party contractor will utilize sub-contractors and how it will manage those relationships and contracts to ensure personally identifiable information is protected;

(6) specify how the third-party contractor will manage data security and privacy incidents that implicate personally identifiable information including specifying any plans to identify breaches and unauthorized disclosures, and to promptly notify the educational agency;

(7) describe whether, how and when data will be returned to the educational agency, transitioned to a successor contractor, at the educational agency's option and direction, deleted or destroyed by the third-party contractor when the contract is terminated or expires.

Under Section 121.11 – Third Party Contractor Civil Penalties, a contractor may be subject to penalties:

(a) Each third party contractor that receives student data or teacher or principal data pursuant to a contract or other written agreement with an educational agency shall be required to notify such educational agency of any breach of security resulting in an unauthorized release of such data by the third party contractor or its assignees in violation of applicable state or federal law, the parents bill of rights for student data privacy and security, the data privacy and security policies of the educational agency and/or binding contractual obligations relating to data privacy and security, in the most expedient way possible and without unreasonable delay. Each violation of this paragraph by a third-party contractor shall be punishable by a civil penalty of the greater of $5,000 or up to $10 per student, teacher, and principal whose data was released, provided that the latter amount shall not exceed the maximum penalty imposed under General Business Law §899-aa (6) (a).

(b) Except as otherwise provided in subdivision (a) each violation of Education Law §2-d by a third-party contractor or its assignee shall be punishable by a civil penalty of up to $1,000.00; a second violation by the same third party contractor involving the same data shall be punishable by a civil penalty of up to $5,000; any subsequent violation by the same third party contractor involving the same data shall be punishable by a civil penalty of up to $10,000. Each violation shall be considered a separate violation for purposes of civil penalties and the total penalty shall not exceed the maximum penalty imposed under General Business Law §899-aa (6) (a).

6.4[F] VIRGINIA

Virginia code section 22.1-289.01. School service providers; school-affiliated entities; student personal information, provides rules for online school service providers. The lawmakers in Virginia felt the need to define a rather common technical term, "Machine-readable format" to mean "a structured format that can automatically be read and processed by a computer such as comma-separated values (CSV), Javascript Object

Notation (JSON), or Extensible Markup Language (XML). "Machine-readable format" does not include portable document format (PDF)."

This code section requires providers to "[M]aintain a comprehensive information security program that is reasonably designed to protect the security, privacy, confidentiality, and integrity of student personal information and makes use of appropriate administrative, technological, and physical safeguards."

As demonstrated by a look at a few of the state laws that apply to on-line education security measures, one can see that the requirements are not uniform across all states. Also, adding to the challenge is the rapidly changing landscape with regard to these laws. To be sure, states are watching closely the actions taken in other states and there is Even if a counselor had a perfect photographic memory, it is well advised for counsel to review the specific state law before giving advice.

CHAPTER SEVEN. ADDITIONAL FEDERAL REGULATION CONCERNING CYBERSECURITY

7.1 Introduction

The federal government has followed a sector specific approach to cybersecurity. Notably, various agencies which regulate different segments of the economy have provided guidance for entities operating in those industries. This chapter provides an overview of some regulations concerning selected areas of the economy that have not been previously covered. Moreover, the Biden Administration issued an Executive Order in 2021 aimed at improving cybersecurity across the federal agencies themselves as well as influencing companies that contract with the federal government through procurement regulation. This chapter provides an overview and some specific portions of the Executive Order. A brief review of some of the developments since the issuance of the Executive Order is also provided. Finally, this chapter covers the federal Cyber Incident Reporting for Critical Infrastructure Act of 2022.

7.2 Additional Federal Cybersecurity Regulation

As discussed *supra*, the United States follows a sectoral approach to privacy and cybersecurity regulation. Other sectors of the U.S. economy are regulated by various agencies.[311] This section provides a brief overview of some of the regulation of other agencies concerning specific sectors of the U.S. economy.[312] For example, the Department of Labor, Employee Benefits Security Administration; Department of

---

[311] The Executive Branch can drive improved cybersecurity practices through executive order. In a May 12, 2021 Executive Order, the Biden Administration essentially directed federal agencies to require improved cybersecurity practices from federal contractors. *See* THE WHITE HOUSE, *Executive Order on Improving the Nation's Cybersecurity* (May 12, 2021), available at https://www.whitehouse.gov/briefing-room/presidential-actions/2021/05/12/executive-order-on-improving-the-nations-cybersecurity/. Notably, the Executive Order also addresses software supply chain issues, in part, by requiring a Software Bill of Materials to purchasers. *Id.*

[312] For example, the Food and Drug Administration shares in responsibility for the regulation of cybersecurity for medical devices. *See* FOOD AND DRUG ADMINISTRATION, *FDA Fact Sheet: The FDA's Role in Medical Device Cybersecurity*, available at https://www.fda.gov/media/123052/download ("The FDA has published premarket and postmarket guidances that offer recommendations for comprehensive management of medical device cybersecurity risks, continuous improvement throughout the total product life-cycle, and incentivize changing marketed and distributed medical devices to reduce risk.").

Transportation, Federal Aviation Administration; Federal Communications Commission; and Food and Drug Administration may have cybersecurity requirements. The Department of Transportation, Federal Aviation Administration regulates aircrafts.[313] For example, the Federal Aviation Administration has an Aircraft Network Security Program requirement [ANSP].[314] The ANSP requirement was adopted to address the internet connectivity risks associated with aircraft.[315] Notably, the Flight Standards Information Management System states that preexisting regulations fail to specifically address electronic risks associated with connected aircraft.[316] The Flight Standards Information Management System sets forth the risks associated with connected aircraft:

> A. External Systems Access. The architecture of this airborne network may allow read and/or write access to and/or from external systems and networks, such as wireless airline operations and maintenance systems, satellite communications, email, the internet, etc. Onboard wired and wireless devices may also have access to portions of the aircraft's digital data buses (DDB) that provide flight critical functions. . . .
>
> B. Risk. Connected aircraft have the capability to reprogram flight critical avionics components wirelessly and via various data transfer mechanisms. This capability alone, or coupled with passenger connectivity on the aircraft network, may result in cybersecurity vulnerabilities from intentional or unintentional corruption of data and/or systems critical to the safety and continued airworthiness of the airplane. Credible examples of risks include the potential for:

---

[313] The Department of Transportation also regulates other areas such as trains and automobiles. For example, the Federal Railroad Administration regulates connected trains and released a document titled, "Cybersecurity Risk Management and Railroads." DEP'T OF TRANSPORTATION, FEDERAL RAILROAD ADMINISTRATION, *Cybersecurity Risk Management and Railroads* (June 22, 2020), available at https://railroads.dot.gov/elibrary/cyber-security-risk-management-connected-railroads. Moreover, the Department of Transportation issued a document titled, "Cybersecurity Best Practices for the Safety of Modern Vehicles" for public comment. *See* DEP'T OF TRANSPORTATION, *Cybersecurity Best Practices for the Safety of Modern Vehicles* (January 12, 2021), available at https://www.transportation.gov/regulations-fr/notices/2021-00390. The Department of Homeland Security, Transportation Security Administration (TSA) also provides cybersecurity requirements and guidance. For example, the TSA has issued cybersecurity directives involving critical pipeline networks. *See* DEP'T OF HOMELAND SECURITY, *DHS Announces New Cybersecurity Requirements for Critical Pipeline Owners and Operators* (July 20, 2021), available at https://www.dhs.gov/news/2021/07/20/dhs-announces-new-cybersecurity-requirements-critical-pipeline-owners-and-operators. The TSA has also issued cybersecurity directives concerning railroad and surface transportation. *See* DEP'T OF HOMELAND SECURITY, *Surface Transportation Cybersecurity Toolkit*, available at https://www.tsa.gov/for-industry/surface-transportation-cybersecurity-toolkit (last visited May 18, 2022). The Department of Homeland Security has also issued a roadmap for dealing with the threat of quantum computing in the cybersecurity space. *See* DEP'T OF HOMELAND SECURITY, *Post-Quantum Cryptography*, available at https://www.dhs.gov/quantum (last visited October 12, 2021).

[314] *See* Flight Standards Information Management System, Vol. 3 *General Technical Administration*, Chapter 61 *Aircraft Network Security Program* (June 5, 2019), available at https://fsims.faa.gov/PICDetail.aspx?docId=8900.1,Vol.3,Ch61,Sec1_SAS.

[315] *Id.*

[316] *Id.*

- Malware to infect an aircraft system,
- An attacker to use onboard wireless to access aircraft system interfaces,
- Denial of service of wireless interfaces,
- Denial of service of safety critical systems,
- Misuse of personal devices that access aircraft systems, and
- Misuse of off-board network connections to access aircraft system interfaces.[317]

The requirements for an ANSP state, in part:

OPERATOR ACTION.

A.   Develop an ANSP. Operators of connected aircraft must develop and maintain an ANSP that is sufficiently comprehensive in scope and detail to accomplish the following:

1)   Ensure that security protection is sufficient to prevent access by unauthorized sources external to the aircraft.

2)   Ensure that security threats specific to the certificate holder's operations are identified and assessed, and that risk mitigation strategies are implemented to ensure the continued airworthiness of the aircraft.

3)   Prevent inadvertent or malicious changes to the aircraft network, including those possibly caused by maintenance activity.

4)   Prevent unauthorized access from sources onboard the aircraft.

NOTE: The Security and Privacy Risk Management Staff will be the focal point for verifying the items in subparagraphs A1) through A4) above.

B.   Guidelines for Authorization. Operators of connected aircraft during initial certification (including the addition of new types of connected aircraft) should ensure that the initial compliance statement clearly describes the procedures that the operator will use for the ANSP. The operator must develop a section in its General Maintenance Manual (GMM) or other appropriate manual that provides detailed instruction on:

- Roles and responsibilities, including persons with authority and responsibility;
- Training/qualifications;
- Control of maintenance laptop/ground support equipment access and use;
- Control of access to airport wired and wireless service network;
- Controlling access to Loadable Software Airplane Part (LSAP) librarian resources;
- Creating secure parts signing process and controlling access to private keys;
- Control/monitor of physical access to aircraft;
- Control of aircraft conformity to type design, as amended;
- Provisions for parts pooling and parts borrowing;
- Procedures for part exchanges within its own fleet;
- Event recognition and response;

---

[317] *Id.*

- Event evaluation process with considerations for program improvements; and
- Security environment description.

B. Verify. The PAI should encourage the operator to submit the request for authorization for OpSpec D301, along with a complete ANSP document package at least 90 days prior to planned operation of the connected aircraft. Working with the Avionics Branch, the PAI will verify that the operator has established appropriate event recognition, response processes, and security awareness training within their respective program area.[318]

The Department of Labor, Employee Benefits Administration has released cybersecurity best practices for ERISA retirement plan fiduciaries.[319] Given the sensitive nature of the information held by ERISA retirement plan fiduciaries, the best practices require a relatively robust cybersecurity program.[320] The following is the Cybersecurity Program Best Practices document.

EMPLOYEE BENEFITS SECURITY ADMINISTRATION
UNITED STATES DEPARTMENT OF LABOR
CYBERSECURITY PROGRAM BEST PRACTICES[321]

ERISA-covered plans often hold millions of dollars or more in assets and maintain personal data on participants, which can make them tempting targets for cyber-criminals. Responsible plan fiduciaries have an obligation to ensure proper mitigation of cybersecurity risks. The Employee Benefits Security Administration has prepared the following best practices for use by recordkeepers and other service providers responsible for plan-related IT systems and data, and for plan fiduciaries making prudent decisions on the service providers they should hire. Plans' service providers should:

1. Have a formal, well documented cybersecurity program.
2. Conduct prudent annual risk assessments.
3. Have a reliable annual third party audit of security controls.
4. Clearly define and assign information security roles and responsibilities.
5. Have strong access control procedures.
6. Ensure that any assets or data stored in a cloud or managed by a third party service provider are subject to appropriate security reviews and independent security assessments.
7. Conduct periodic cybersecurity awareness training.
8. Implement and manage a secure system development life cycle (SDLC) program.

---

[318] *Id.*

[319] *See* DEP'T OF LABOR, EMPLOYEE BENEFITS SECURITY ADMINISTRATION, *Cybersecurity Program Best Practices*, https://www.dol.gov/sites/dolgov/files/ebsa/key-topics/retirement-benefits/cybersecurity/best-practices.pdf (last visited October 1, 2020).

[320] *Id.*

[321] *Id.*

9. Have an effective business resiliency program addressing business continuity, disaster recovery, and incident response.
10. Encrypt sensitive data, stored and in transit.
11. Implement strong technical controls in accordance with best security practices.
12. Appropriately respond to any past cybersecurity incidents.

1. A Formal, Well Documented Cybersecurity Program.

A sound cybersecurity program identifies and assesses internal and external cybersecurity risks that may threaten the confidentiality, integrity, or availability of stored nonpublic information. Under the program, the organization fully implements well-documented information security policies, procedures, guidelines, and standards to protect the security of the IT infrastructure and data stored on the system. A prudently designed program will: Protect the infrastructure, information systems and the information in the systems from unauthorized access, use, or other malicious acts by enabling the organization to: • Identify the risks to assets, information and systems. • Protect each of the necessary assets, data and systems. • Detect and respond to cybersecurity events. • Recover from the event. • Disclose the event as appropriate. • Restore normal operations and services.

Establish strong security policies, procedures, guidelines, and standards that meet the following criteria: • Approval by senior leadership. • Review at least annually with updates as needed. • Terms are effectively explained to users. • Review by an independent third party auditor who confirms compliance. • Documentation of the particular framework(s) used to assess the security of its systems and practices. • Formal and effective policies and procedures governing all the following: 1. Data governance and classification. 2. Access controls and identity management. 3. Business continuity and disaster recovery. 4. Configuration management. 5. Asset management. 6. Risk assessment. 7. Data disposal. 8. Incident response. 9. Systems operations. 10. Vulnerability and patch management. 11. System, application and network security and monitoring. 12. Systems and application development and performance. 13. Physical security and environmental controls. 14. Data privacy. 15. Vendor and third party service provider management. 16. Consistent use of multi-factor authentication. 17. Cybersecurity awareness training, which is given to all personnel annually. 18. Encryption to protect all sensitive information transmitted and at rest.

2. Prudent Annual Risk Assessments.

A Risk Assessment is an effort to identify, estimate, and prioritize information system risks. IT threats are constantly changing, so it is important to design a manageable, effective risk assessment schedule. Organizations should codify the risk assessment's scope, methodology, and frequency.

A risk assessment should: • Identify, assess, and document how identified cybersecurity risks or threats are evaluated and categorized. • Establish criteria to evaluate the confidentiality, integrity, and availability of the information systems and nonpublic information, and document how existing controls address the identified risks. • Describe how the cybersecurity program will mitigate or accept the risks identified. • Facilitate the revision of controls resulting from changes in technology and emerging threats. • Be kept current to account for changes to information systems, nonpublic information, or business operations.

3. A Reliable Annual Third Party Audit of Security Controls.

Having an independent auditor assess an organization's security controls provides a clear, unbiased report of existing risks, vulnerabilities, and weaknesses. As part of its review of an effective audit program, EBSA would expect to see: • Audit reports, audit files, penetration test reports and supporting documents, and any other analyses or review of the party's cybersecurity practices by a third party. • Audits and audit reports prepared and conducted in accordance with appropriate standards. • Documented corrections of any weaknesses identified in the independent third party analyses.

4. Clearly Defined and Assigned Information Security Roles and Responsibilities.

For a cybersecurity program to be effective, it must be managed at the senior executive level and executed by qualified personnel. As a senior executive, the Chief Information Security Officer (CISO) would generally establish and maintain the vision, strategy, and operation of the cybersecurity program which is performed by qualified personnel who should meet the following criteria: • Sufficient experience and necessary certifications. • Initial and periodic background checks. • Regular updates and training to address current cybersecurity risks. • Current knowledge of changing cybersecurity threats and countermeasures.

5. Strong Access Control Procedures.

Access control is a method of guaranteeing that users are who they say they are and that they have the appropriate access to IT systems and data. It mainly consists of two components: authentication and authorization.

The following are best security practices for access control: • Access to systems, assets and associated facilities is limited to authorized users, processes, devices, activities, and transactions. • Access privileges (e.g., general user, third party administrators, plan administrators, and IT administrators) are limited based on the role of the individual and adhere to the need-to-access principle. • Access privileges are reviewed at least every three months and accounts are disabled and/or deleted in accordance with policy. • All employees use unique, complex passwords. • Multi-factor authentication is used wherever possible, especially to access the internal networks from an external network, unless a documented exception exists based on the use of a similarly effective access control methodology. • Policies, procedures, and controls are implemented to monitor the activity of authorized users and detect unauthorized access, use of, or tampering with, nonpublic information. • Procedures are implemented to ensure that any sensitive information about a participant or beneficiary in the service provider's records matches the information that the plan maintains about the participant. • Confirm the identity of the authorized recipient of the funds.

6. **Assets or Data Stored in a Cloud or Managed by a Third Party Service Provider are Subject to Appropriate Security Reviews and Independent Security Assessments.**

Cloud computing presents many unique security issues and challenges. In the cloud, data is stored with a third-party provider and accessed over the internet. This means visibility and control over that data is limited. Organizations must understand the security posture of the cloud service provider in order to make sound decisions on using the service. Best practices include: • Requiring a risk assessment of third party service providers. • Defining minimum cybersecurity practices for third party service providers. • Periodically assessing third party service providers based on potential risks. • Ensuring that guidelines and contractual protections at minimum address the following: » The third party service provider's access control policies and procedures including the use of multi-factor authentication. » The third party service provider's encryption policies and procedures. » The third party service provider's notification protocol for a cybersecurity event which directly impacts a customer's information system(s) or nonpublic information.

7. **Cybersecurity Awareness Training Conducted at Least Annually for All Personnel and Updated to Reflect Risks Identified by the Most Recent Risk Assessment.**

Employees are often an organization's weakest link for cybersecurity. A comprehensive cybersecurity security awareness program sets clear cybersecurity expectations for all employees and educates everyone to recognize attack vectors, help prevent cyber-related incidents, and respond to a potential threat. Since identity theft is a leading cause of fraudulent distributions, it should be considered a key topic of training, which should focus on current trends to exploit unauthorized access to systems. Be on the lookout for individuals falsely posing as authorized plan officials, fiduciaries, participants or beneficiaries.

8. **Secure System Development Life Cycle Program (SDLC).**

A secure SDLC process ensures that security assurance activities such as penetration testing, code review, and architecture analysis are an integral part of the system development effort. Best practices include: • Procedures, guidelines, and standards which ensure any in-house applications are developed securely. This would include such protections as: » Configuring system alerts to trigger when an individual's account information has been changed. » Requiring additional validation if personal information has been changed prior to request for a distribution from the plan account. » Requiring additional validation for distributions (other than a rollover) of the entire balance of the participant's account. • Procedures for evaluating or testing the security of externally developed applications including periodic reviews and updates. • A vulnerability management plan, including regular vulnerability scans. • Annual penetration tests, particularly with respect to customer-facing applications.

9. A Business Resiliency Program which Effectively Addresses Business Continuity, Disaster Recover, and Incident Response.

Business resilience is the ability an organization has to quickly adapt to disruptions while maintaining continuous business operations and safeguarding people, assets, and data. The core components of a program include the Business Continuity Plan, Disaster Recovery Plan, and Incident Response Plan. • The Business Continuity Plan is the written set of procedures an organization follows to recover, resume, and maintain business functions and their underlying processes at acceptable predefined levels following a disruption. • The Disaster Recovery Plan is the documented process to recover and resume an organization's IT infrastructure, business applications, and data services in the event of a major disruption. • The Incident Response Plan is a set of instructions to help IT staff detect, respond to, and recover from security incidents.
An effective Business Resiliency Program should: •Reasonably define the internal processes for responding to a cybersecurity event or disaster. •Reasonably define plan goals. •Define the documentation and reporting requirements regarding cybersecurity events and responses. •Clearly define and describe the roles, responsibilities, and authority levels. • Describe external and internal communications and information sharing, including protocols to notify plan sponsor and affected user(s) if needed. •Identify remediation plans for any identified weaknesses in information systems. • Include after action reports that discuss how plans will be evaluated and updated following a cybersecurity event or disaster. •Be annually tested based on possible risk scenarios.

10. Encryption of Sensitive Data Stored and in Transit.

Data encryption can protect nonpublic information. A system should implement current, prudent standards for encryption keys, message authentication and hashing to protect the confidentiality and integrity of the data at rest or in transit.

11. Strong Technical Controls Implementing Best Security Practices.

Technical security solutions are primarily implemented and executed by the information system through mechanisms contained in the hardware, software, or firmware components of the system. Best security practices for technical security include: •Hardware, software and firmware models and versions that are kept up to date. •Vendor-supported firewalls, intrusion detection and prevention appliances/tools. •Current and regularly updated antivirus software. •Routine patch management (preferably automated). •Network segregation. •System hardening. •Routine data backup (preferably automated).

12. Responsiveness to Cybersecurity Incidents or Breaches.

When a cybersecurity breach or incident occurs, appropriate action should be taken to protect the plan and its participants, including: •Informing law enforcement. •Notifying the appropriate insurer. •Investigating the incident. •Giving affected plans and participants the information necessary to prevent/reduce injury. • Honoring any contractual or legal obligations with respect to the breach, including complying with agreed upon notification requirements. • Fixing the problems that caused the breach to prevent its recurrence.

The Federal Communications Commission has released a planning tool used to specifically help small business with developing effective cybersecurity plans called, "Cyberplanner." A user can enter various terms in the Cyberplanner such as Network Security, Website Security, and Privacy and Data Security.[322] In response to those terms, the Cyberplanner will provide specific inquiries and guidance concerning cybersecurity. The Federal Communications Commission has also released a best practices guide.[323] Moreover, the Federal Communications Commission has a Communications, Security, Reliability, and Interoperability Council (CSRIC). The CSRIC "make[s] recommendations to the Commission to promote the security, reliability, and resiliency of the Nation's communications systems." The Council consists of working groups who are tasked with specific inquires. In 2021, working groups were convened on numerous topics some of which included: Managing Security Risk in the Transition to 5G; Managing Security Risk in Emerging 5G Implementations; and Security Vulnerabilities during the IP Transition. The Managing Security Risk in the Transition to 5G description states:

> As Fifth Generation (5G) wireless technology is widely deployed by wireless service providers in the United States and around the world, its evolutionary design will incorporate a number of existing standards from previous generations. This approach risks the persistence in 5G of security issues that exist in currently deployed networks. For example, researchers have identified several vulnerabilities in the attach, detach, and paging procedures of earlier generation wireless technology that may negatively affect the confidentiality, integrity, and availability of wireless networks and continued challenges in avoiding fake base stations in 5G networks.
> The FCC directs CSRIC VII to review risks to 5G wireless technologies that may carry over from existing vulnerabilities in earlier wireless technologies that can lead to the loss of confidentiality, integrity, and availability of wireless network devices. CSRIC VII will recommend best practices to mitigate the risks for each vulnerability it identifies and address recently proposed solutions by security researchers. Additionally, the FCC directs CSRIC VII to recommend any updates, if appropriate, to the 3GPP SA3 (security working group) standards, including digital certificates and pre-provisioned Certificate Authorities, to mitigate these risks and then place the vulnerabilities on a scale that accounts for both risk level and remediation expense. Finally, the FCC directs CSRIC VII to identify optional features in 3GPP standards that

---

[322] *See* FEDERAL COMMUNICATIONS COMMISSION, Cyberplanner, available at https://www.fcc.gov/cyberplanner (last visited October 1, 2021).
[323] *See* FEDERAL COMMUNICATIONS COMMISSION, *Ten Cybersecurity Tips for Small Businesses*, available at DOC-306595A1.pdf (last visited October 1, 2021).

can diminish the effectiveness of 5G security, and recommendations to address these gaps.[324]

CSRIC also provides best practices documents[325] and reports.[326]

The FDA has issued numerous documents concerning cybersecurity and medical devices. Connected health devices raise very serious issues concerning cybersecurity and are also discussed *infra* in Chapter 12 concerning the Internet of Things. For example, imagine the connected pacemaker and the potential health risks to a user of a hacked device.

In April of 2022, the FDA issued proposed guidance concerning cybersecurity requirements for medical devices, which include "software or programmable logic," for comment. The guidance is not limited to network connected devices. The guidance is titled, "Cybersecurity in Medical Devices: Quality System Considerations and Content of Premarket Submissions Draft Guidance for Industry and Food and Drug Administration Staff"[327] and provides suggested nonbinding recommendations. The new guidance is intended to update prior FDA guidance concerning cybersecurity. The guidance addresses cybersecurity concerns for the Total Product Lifecycle, which is "achieved . . . through the implementation and adoption of a Secure Product Development Framework (SPDF)."[328] "An SPDF is a set of processes that reduce the number and severity of vulnerabilities in products throughout the device lifecycle."[329] In discussing the SPDF, the guidance provides overviews of Security Risk Management; Security Architecture[330] and Cybersecurity Testing.[331] The guidance finally discusses

---

[324] FEDERAL COMMUNICATIONS COMMISSION, *CSRIC VII Working Group Descriptions*, available at https://www.fcc.gov/files/csric7wgdescriptionsdocx (last visited October 4, 2021).

[325] FEDERAL COMMUNICATIONS COMMISSION, *CSRIC Best Practices*, available at https://opendata.fcc.gov/Public-Safety/CSRIC-Best-Practices/qb45-rw2t/data (last visited October 4, 2021).

[326] FEDERAL COMMUNICATIONS COMMISSION, *CSRIC Reports*, available at https://www.fcc.gov/CSRICReports (last visited October 4, 2021).

[327] DRAFT -Cybersecurity Guidance (April 8, 2022) (fda.gov), available at https://www.fda.gov/media/119933/download.

[328] *Id.*

[329] *Id.*

[330] "A security architecture, like a system architecture, defines the system and all end-to-end connections into and/or out of the system." *Id.* The Security Architecture section describes Implementation of Security Controls and Security Architecture Views. *Id.* Security Controls include: "Authentication; Authorization; Cryptography; Code, Data, and Execution Integrity; Confidentiality; Event Detection and Logging; Resiliency and Recovery; and Updatability and Patchability." *Id.* Appendix 1 contains specific recommendations concerning Security Controls. *Id.* Security Architecture Views include: "Global System View; Multi-Patient Harm View; Updateability/Patchability View; and Security Use Case View(s)." *Id.* "[S]ecurity architecture views should: Identify security-relevant system elements and their interfaces; Define security context, domains, boundaries, and external interfaces of the system; Align the architecture with (a) the system security objectives and requirements, (b) security design characteristics; and Establish traceability of architecture elements to user and system security requirements." *Id.*

[331] The guidance discusses cybersecurity testing:

transparency, including labeling. Notably, the Security Risk Management section reviews threat modeling, third party software components, and a software bill of materials.

As discussed *infra*, the concept of a software bill of materials is discussed in the 2021 Biden Administration Executive Order concerning cybersecurity. One of the important issues concerning connected devices is related to supply chain security with respect to software used in a device. The following is a portion of the FDA's proposed guidance addressing Security Risk Management.

Cybersecurity in Medical Devices: Quality System Considerations and Content of Premarket Submissions Draft Guidance for Industry and Food and Drug Administration Staff

A. Security Risk Management

Security testing documentation and any associated reports or assessments should be submitted in the premarket submission. FDA recommends that the following types of testing, among others, be provided in the submission:

a. Security requirements
   o Manufacturers should provide evidence that each design input requirement was implemented successfully.
   o Manufacturers should provide evidence of their boundary analysis and rationale for their boundary assumptions.

b. Threat mitigation
   o Manufacturers should provide details and evidence of testing that demonstrates effective risk control measures according to the threat models provided in the system, use case, and call-flow views.
   o Manufacturers should ensure the adequacy of each cybersecurity risk control (e.g., security effectiveness in enforcing the specified security policy, performance for maximum traffic conditions, stability and reliability, as appropriate).

c. Vulnerability Testing (such as section 9.4 of ANSI/ISA 62443-4-1)
   o Manufacturers should provide details and evidence of the following testing pertaining to known vulnerabilities:
   Abuse case, malformed, and unexpected inputs,
       • Robustness
       • Fuzz testing
   Attack surface analysis,
   Vulnerability chaining,
   Closed box testing of known vulnerability scanning,
   Software composition analysis of binary executable files, and
   Static and dynamic code analysis, including testing for credentials that are "hardcoded," default, easily-guessed, and easily compromised.

d. Penetration testing
   o The testing should identify and characterize security-related issues via tests that focus on discovering and exploiting security vulnerabilities in the product.
   Penetration test reports should be provided and include the following elements: Independence and technical expertise of testers, Scope of testing, Duration of testing, Testing methods employed, and Test results, findings, and observations.
   Id.

To fully account for cybersecurity risks in devices, the safety and security risks of each device should be assessed within the context of the larger system in which the device operates. In the context of cybersecurity, security risk management processes are critical because, given the evolving nature of cybersecurity threats and risks, no device is, or can be, completely secure. Security risk management should be part of a manufacturer's quality system. Specifically, the QSR requires, among other things, that manufacturers' processes address design (21 CFR 299 820.30), validation of the production processes (21 CFR 820.70), and corrective or preventive actions (21 CFR 820.100). These processes entail the technical, personnel, and management practices, among others, that manufacturers use to manage potential risks to their devices and ensure that their devices remain safe and effective, which includes security.

The process for performing security risk management is a distinct process from performing safety risk management as described in ISO 14971:2019. This is due to the scope of possible harm and the risk assessment factors in the context of security may be different than those in the context of safety. Also, while safety risk management focuses on physical injury or damage to property or the environment, security risk management may include not only risks that can result in patient harm but also those risks that are outside of FDA's assessment of safety and effectiveness such as those related to business or reputational risks.

Effective security risk management also addresses that cybersecurity-related failures do not occur in a probabilistic manner where an assessment for the likelihood of occurrence for a particular risk could be estimated based on historical data or modeling. This non-probabilistic approach is not the fundamental approach described in safety risk management under ISO 316 14971:2019. Instead, security risk assessment processes focus on exploitability, or the ability to exploit vulnerabilities present within a device and/or system. Additional discussion on exploitability assessments for the security risk assessment can be found in the FDA's Postmarket Cybersecurity Guidance. Exploitability for a cybersecurity risk during a premarket assessment may be different compared to a risk assessment performed for a postmarket vulnerability. For example, some of the exploitability factors discussed in the guidance (e.g., Exploit Code Maturity, Remediation Level, Report Confidence) may not be applicable to unreleased software. In these instances, a premarket exploitability assessment could either assume a worst-case assessment and implement appropriate controls, or provide a justification for a reasonable exploitability assessment of the risk throughout the total product lifecycle and how the risk is controlled.

FDA recommends that manufacturers establish a security risk management process that encompasses design controls (21 CFR 820.30), validation of production processes (21 CFR 820.70), and corrective and preventive actions (21 CFR 820.100) to ensure both safety and security risks are adequately addressed. For completeness in performing risk analyses under 21 CFR 820.30(g), FDA recommends that device manufacturers conduct both a safety risk assessment per ISO 14971:2019 and a separate, accompanying security risk assessment to ensure a more comprehensive identification and management of patient safety risks. The scope and objective of a security risk management process, in conjunction with other SPDF processes (e.g., security testing), is to expose how threats, through vulnerabilities, can manifest patient harm and other potential risks. These processes should also ensure that risk control measures or one type of risk assessment do not inadvertently introduce new risks in the other.

Known vulnerabilities should be mitigated in the design of the device. For marketed devices, if comprehensive design mitigations are not possible, compensating controls should be considered. All devices, when any known vulnerabilities are only partially mitigated or unmitigated by the device design, they should be assessed as reasonably foreseeable risks in the risk assessment and be assessed for additional control measures or risk transfer to the user/operator, or, if necessary, the patient. Risk transfer, if appropriate, should only occur when all relevant risk information is known, assessed, and appropriately communicated to users and includes risks inherited from the supply chain as well as how risk transfer will be handled when the device/system reaches end of support and end of life and whether or how the user is able to take on that role (e.g., if the user may be a patient).

Specific security risk management documentation where FDA has recommendations regarding their scope and/or content are discussed in the subsections below. The documentation FDA recommends manufacturers provide in their premarket submissions is summarized in the Security Risk Management Documentation below (Section V.A.4.).

1. Threat Modeling

Threat modeling includes a process for identifying security objectives, risks, and vulnerabilities across the system, and then defining countermeasures to prevent, or mitigate the effects of, threats to the system throughout its lifecycle. It is foundational for optimizing system, product, network, application, and connection security when applied appropriately and comprehensively.

With respect to security risk management, and in order to identify appropriate security risks and controls for the system, FDA recommends that threat modeling be performed to inform and support the risk analysis activities. As part of the risk assessment, FDA recommends threat modeling be performed throughout the design process and be inclusive of all system elements.

The threat model should: • identify system risks and mitigations as well as inform the pre- and post-mitigation risks considered as part of the security risk assessment; • state any assumptions about the system or environment of use (e.g. hospital networks are inherently hostile, therefore manufacturers are recommended to assume that an adversary controls the network with the ability to alter, drop, and replay packets); and • capture cybersecurity risks introduced through the supply chain, manufacturing, deployment, interoperation with other devices, maintenance/update activities, and decommission activities that might otherwise be overlooked in a traditional safety risk assessment processes.

FDA recommends that premarket submissions include threat modeling documentation to demonstrate how the risks assessed and controls implemented for the system address questions of safety and effectiveness. There are a number of methodologies and/or combinations of methods for threat modeling that manufacturers may choose to use. Rationale for the methodology(ies) selected should be provided with the threat modeling documentation. Additional recommendations on how threat modeling documentation should be submitted to FDA are discussed in Section V.B. below. Threat modeling activities can be performed and/or reviewed during design reviews. FDA recommends that threat modeling documentation include sufficient information on threat modeling activities performed by the manufacturer to assess and review the security features built into the device such that they holistically evaluate the device and the system in which the device operates, for the safety and effectiveness of the system.

2. Third-Party Software Components

As discussed in the FDA guidances "Off-The-Shelf (OTS) Software Use in Medical Devices"[332] and "Cybersecurity for Networked Medical Devices Containing Off-the-Shelf (OTS) Software,"[333] medical devices commonly include third-party software components including off the-shelf and open source software. When these components are incorporated, security risks of the software components become factors of the overall medical device system risk management processes and documentation.

As part of demonstrating compliance with quality system design controls under 21 CFR 404 820.30(g), and to support supply chain risk management processes, all software, including that developed by the device manufacturer ("proprietary software") and obtained from third parties should be assessed for cybersecurity risk and that risk should be addressed. Accordingly, device manufacturers are expected to document all software components of a device and to mitigate risks associated with these software components.

In addition, under 21 CFR 820.50, manufacturers must put in place processes and controls to ensure that their suppliers conform to the manufacturer's requirements. Such information is documented in the Design History File, required by 21 CFR 820.30(j), and Design Master Record, required by 21 CFR 820.181. This documentation demonstrates the device's overall compliance with the QSR, as well as that the third-party components meet specifications established for the device. Security risk assessments that include analyses and considerations of cybersecurity risks that may exist in or be introduced by third-party software and the software supply chain may help demonstrate that manufacturers have adequately ensured such compliance and documented such history.

As part of configuration management, device manufacturers should have custodial control of source code through source code escrow and source code backups.[334] While

---

[332] Editors: Footnote 25 in the guidance provides: "See FDA guidance Off-The-Shelf (OTS) Software Use in Medical Devices available at: https://www.fda.gov/regulatory-information/search-fda-guidance-documents/shelf-software-use-medical-devices." *Id.*

[333] Editors: Footnote 26 in the guidance provides: "See FDA guidance Cybersecurity for Networked Medical Devices Containing Off-the-Shelf (OTS) Software available at: https://www.fda.gov/regulatory-information/search-fda-guidance-documents/cybersecurity-networkedmedical-devices-containing-shelf-ots-software." *Id.*

[334] Editors: Footnote 28 in the guidance provides: "While some suppliers may not grant access to source code, manufacturers may consider adding to their purchasing controls acquisition of the source code

source code is not provided in premarket submissions, if this control is not available based on the terms in supplier agreements, the manufacturer should include in premarket submissions a plan of how the third party software component could be updated or replaced should support for the software end. The device manufacturer is also expected to provide to users whatever information is necessary to allow users to manage risks associated with the device.

One tool to help manage supply chain risk as well as clearly identify and track the software incorporated into a device is a Software Bill of Materials (SBOM), as described below.

(a) Software Bill of Materials

A Software Bill of Materials (SBOM) can aid in the management of cybersecurity risks that exist throughout the software stack. A robust SBOM includes both the device manufacturer developed components and third-party components (including purchased/licensed software and open-source software), and the upstream software dependencies that are required/depended upon by proprietary, purchased/licensed, and open-source software. An SBOM helps facilitate risk management processes by providing a mechanism to identify devices that might be affected by vulnerabilities in the software components, both during development (when software is being chosen as a component) and after it has been placed into the market throughout all other phases of a product's life.

Because vulnerability management is a critical part of a device's security risk management processes, an SBOM or an equivalent capability should be maintained as part of the device's configuration management, be regularly updated to reflect any changes to the software in marketed devices, and should support 21 CFR 820.30(j) (Design History File) and 820.181 447 (Design Master Record) documentation.
To assist FDA's assessment of the device risks and associated impacts on safety and 450 effectiveness related to cybersecurity, FDA recommends that premarket submissions include SBOM documentation as outlined below. SBOMs can also be an important tool for transparency with users of potential risks as part of labeling as addressed later in Section VI.

(b) Documentation Supporting Software Bill of Materials

FDA's guidance documents "Off-The-Shelf (OTS) Software Use in Medical Devices" and "Cybersecurity for Networked Medical Devices Containing Off-the-Shelf (OTS) Software" describe information that should be provided in premarket submissions for software components for which a manufacturer cannot claim complete control of the software lifecycle. In addition to the information recommended in those guidances, for each OTS component, the following should also be provided in a machine-readable format in premarket submissions.

---

should the purchased software reach end of support or end of life from the supplier earlier than the intended end of support or end of life of the medical device." *Id.*

A. The asset(s) where the software component resides;
B. The software component name;
C. The software component version;
D. The software component manufacturer;
E. The software level of support provided through monitoring and maintenance from the software component manufacturer;
F. The software component's end-of-support date; and
G. Any known vulnerabilities.[335]

Industry-accepted formats of SBOMs can be used to provide this information to FDA; however, if any of the above elements are not captured in such an SBOM, we recommend that those items also be provided, typically as an addendum, to FDA for the purposes of supporting premarket submission review. Additional examples of the type of information to include in a SBOM can be found in the Joint Security Plan - Appendix G ("Example Customer Security Documentation")[336] and Sections 2.3.17 and 2.3.18 of the Manufacturer Disclosure Statement for Medical Device Security (referred to as MDS2 or MDS2).[337]

As part of the premarket submission, manufacturers should also describe how the known vulnerabilities (item (G) above) were discovered to demonstrate whether the assessment methods were sufficiently robust. For third-party components with known vulnerabilities, device manufacturers should provide in premarket submissions: · A safety and security risk assessment of each known vulnerability; and · Details of applicable safety and security risk controls to address the vulnerability. If risk controls include compensating controls, those should be described in an appropriate level of detail.

For additional information and discussion regarding proprietary and third-party components, see 491 section V.B.2., Security Architecture Views, below.

3. Security Assessment of Unresolved Anomalies

FDA's Premarket Software Guidance, recommends that device manufacturers provide a list of software anomalies (e.g., bugs or defects) that exist in a product at the time of submission. For each of these anomalies, FDA recommends that device manufacturers conduct an assessment of the anomaly's impact on safety and effectiveness, and consult the Premarket Software Guidance to assess the associated documentation recommended for inclusion in such device's premarket submission.

---

[335] Editors: Footnote 32 in the guidance provides: "Known vulnerabilities are vulnerabilities that are published in the public National Vulnerability Database (NVD) or similar software vulnerability and/or weakness database. NVD is available at https://nvd.nist.gov/vuln/full-listing." *Id.*
[336] Editors: Footnote 33 in the guidance provides: "Medical Device and Health IT Joint Security Plan (JSP) is available at https://healthsectorcouncil.org/the-jointsecurity-plan/." *Id.*
[337] Editors: Footnote 34 in the guidance provides: "The Manufacturer Disclosure Statement for Medical Device Security is available at https://www.nema.org/standards/view/manufacturer-disclosure-statement-for-medical-device-security." *Id.*

Some anomalies discovered during development or testing may have security implications and may also be considered vulnerabilities. As a part of ensuring a complete security risk assessment under 21 CFR Part 820.30(g), the assessment for impacts to safety and effectiveness may include an assessment for the potential security impacts of anomalies. The assessment should also include consideration of any present Common Weakness Enumeration (CWE) categories. For example, a clinical user may inadvertently reveal the presence of a previously unknown software anomaly during normal use, where the impact of the anomaly might occur sporadically and be assessed to be acceptable from a software risk perspective. Conversely, a threat might seek out these types of anomalies, and identify means to exploit them in order to manifest the anomaly's impact continuously, which could significantly impact the acceptability of the risk when compared to an anomaly assessment that didn't include security considerations.

The criteria and rationales for addressing the resulting anomalies with security impacts should be provided as part of the security risk assessment documentation in the premarket submission.

4. Security Risk Management Documentation

To help demonstrate the safety and effectiveness of the device, manufacturers should provide the outputs of their security risk management processes in their premarket submissions, including their security risk management plan and security risk management report. A plan and report such as those described in AAMI TIR57, inclusive of the system threat modeling, SBOM and associated documentation, and unresolved anomaly assessment(s) described above, should be sufficient to support the security risk management process aspect of demonstrating a reasonable assurance of safety and effectiveness.

The security risk management report should: • summarize the risk evaluation methods and processes, detail the security risk assessment, and detail the risk mitigation activities undertaken as part of a manufacturer's risk management processes; and • provide traceability between the security risks, controls and the testing reports that ensure the device is reasonably secure.

5. [Total Product Life Cycle] TPLC Security Risk Management

Cybersecurity risks may continue to be identified throughout the device's TPLC. Manufacturers should ensure they have appropriate resources to identify, assess, and mitigate cybersecurity vulnerabilities as they are identified throughout the supported device lifecycle.

As part of using an SPDF, manufacturers should update their security risk management report as new information becomes available, such as when new threats, vulnerabilities, assets, or adverse impacts are discovered during development and after the device is released. When maintained throughout the device lifecycle, this documentation (e.g., threat modeling) can be used to quickly identify vulnerability impacts once a device is released and to support timely Corrective and Preventive Action (CAPA) activities described in 21 CFR 820.100.

Over the service life of a device, FDA recommends that the risk management documentation account for any differences in the risk management for fielded devices (e.g., marketed devices or devices no longer marketed but still in use). For example, if an update is not applied automatically for all fielded devices, then there will likely be different risk profiles for differing software configurations of the device. FDA recommends that vulnerabilities be assessed for any differing impacts for all fielded versions to ensure patient risks are being accurately assessed. Additional information as to whether a new premarket submission (e.g., PMA [Premarket Approval Applications], PMA supplement, 552 or 510(k)) or 21 CFR Part 806 reporting is needed based on postmarket vulnerabilities and general postmarket cybersecurity risk management are discussed in the Postmarket Cybersecurity Guidance.

To demonstrate the effectiveness of a manufacturer's processes, FDA recommends that a manufacturer track and record the measures and metrics below, and report them in premarket submissions and PMA annual reports (21 CFR 814.84), when available. Selecting appropriate measures and metrics for the processes that define an SPDF is important to ensure that device design appropriately addresses cybersecurity in compliance with QSR [Quality System Regulation in 21 CFR Part 820]. At a minimum, FDA recommends tracking the following measures and metrics: • Percentage of identified vulnerabilities that are updated or patched (defect density). • Time from vulnerability identification to when it is updated or patched. • Time from when an update or patch is available to complete implementation in devices deployed in the field. Averages of the above measures should be provided if multiple vulnerabilities are identified and addressed. These averages may be provided over multiple time frames based on volume or in response to process or procedure changes to increase efficiencies of these measures over time.

7.3 President Biden Executive Order on Improving the Nation's Cybersecurity

A significant issue confronting the federal government has been improving cybersecurity across federal government agencies. In August of 2021, Senators Portman and Peters released a bipartisan report that builds up prior reports which found that many federal agencies have deficient cybersecurity practices.[338] A press release concerning the report stated:

- According to agency inspectors general, the average grade of the large federal agencies' overall information security maturity was a C-.
- Six agencies operated systems without current authorizations to operate;
- Seven agencies used legacy systems or applications no longer supported by the vendor with security updates;

---

[338] Federal Cybersecurity - America's Data Still at Risk (FINAL).pdf (senate.gov), available at https://www.hsgac.senate.gov/imo/media/doc/Federal%20Cybersecurity%20-%20America's%20Data%20Still%20at%20Risk%20(FINAL).pdf.

- Six agencies failed to install security patches and other vulnerability remediation controls quickly;
- Seven agencies failed to maintain accurate and comprehensive information technology asset inventories; and
- Seven agencies failed to protect personally identifiable information adequately.
- Since the 2019 Portman-Carper report evaluating the same eight agencies, only the Department of Homeland Security (DHS) established an effective information security program. Three agencies – the Department of Transportation (DOT), Department of Education, and Social Security Administration (SSA) – showed very little improvement since the Subcommittee's report in 2019.
- There is no single point of accountability for federal cybersecurity. Instead, cybersecurity responsibilities are highly federated, making government-wide information security improvements difficult. Additionally, the federal government lacks a unified cybersecurity strategy to combat the current threat landscape.
- The DHS Inspector General failed to submit its annual evaluation to Congress prior to this report's release. Of the eight agencies examined by the Committee, the DHS OIG was the only agency which failed to do so.
- The federal government's continued overreliance on costly and difficult-to-secure legacy technology diverts critical funding away from other security efforts.
- DHS's flagship cybersecurity program for federal agencies—the National Cybersecurity Protection System (NCPS), operationally known as EINSTEIN—suffers from significant limitations in detecting and preventing intrusions.
- Agencies consistently failed to implement certain key cybersecurity requirements including encryption of sensitive data, limiting each user's access to the information and systems needed to perform their job, and multi-factor authentication, or to certify to Congress that the system is nonetheless secure.[339]

On May 12, 2021, the Biden Administration issued an Executive Order titled, "Executive Order on Improving the Nation's Cybersecurity." The Executive Order, among other goals, seeks to leverage the federal government contracting and acquisition process to improve cybersecurity across industries that work with the federal government. This approach holds promise to raise cybersecurity levels across many industries. The Executive Order contains timelines for agencies to report and comply with the directives of the Executive Order. Importantly, the Executive Order has several main components, including: 1) Policy; 2) Removing Barriers to Sharing Threat Information; 3) Modernizing Federal Cybersecurity; 4) Enhancing Software Supply

---

[339] Minority Media | Homeland Security & Governmental Affairs Committee | Homeland Security & Governmental Affairs Committee (senate.gov), available at
https://www.hsgac.senate.gov/media/minority-media/new-bipartisan-portman-peters-report-shows-federal-agencies-cybersecurity-failures-leaving-americans-personal-information-at-risk.

Chain Security; 5) Cyber Safety Review Board; 6) Standardizing the Federal Government's Playbook for Responding to Cybersecurity Vulnerabilities and Incidents; 7) Improving Detection of Cybersecurity Vulnerabilities and Incidents on Federal Government Networks; 8) Improving the Federal Government's Investigative and Remediation Capabilities; and 9) National Security Systems.

First, the Policy section provides the reasoning for the Executive Order. Specifically, the Policy Section notes that the federal government and private sector must cooperate in order to improve cybersecurity across the digital infrastructure. Moreover, President Biden believes that the Federal Government should lead the effort to raise cybersecurity standards through effective "prevention, detection, assessment and remediation of cyberattacks" across "systems that process data (information technology (IT)) and those that run the vital machinery that ensures our safety (operational technology (OT))." The Federal Government's cybersecurity standards should "meet or exceed" the directives in the Executive Order.

Second, the Executive Order seeks to improve the reporting of cyber incidents involving federal contractors with respect to their information and operational security. First, Section 2 seeks to remove barriers to sharing threat or incident information with CISA, FBI and "other elements of the Intelligence Community (IC)" that are imposed by contractual obligations. Section 2 requires a review of contractual requirements and recommendations to change those contracts.[340] The Executive Order contains specific direction concerning the design of the "recommended contract language and requirements":

> (i) service providers collect and preserve data, information, and reporting relevant to cybersecurity event prevention, detection, response, and investigation on all information systems over which they have control, including systems operated on behalf of agencies, consistent with agencies' requirements;
> (ii) service providers share such data, information, and reporting, as they relate to cyber incidents or potential incidents relevant to any agency with which they have contracted, directly with such agency and any other agency that the Director of OMB, in consultation with the Secretary of Defense, the Attorney General, the Secretary of Homeland Security, and the Director of National Intelligence, deems appropriate, consistent with applicable privacy laws, regulations, and policies;
> (iii) service providers collaborate with Federal cybersecurity or investigative agencies in their investigations of and responses to incidents or potential incidents on Federal Information Systems, including by implementing technical capabilities, such as monitoring

---

[340] Section 2(b) Within 60 days of the date of this order, the Director of the Office of Management and Budget (OMB), in consultation with the Secretary of Defense, the Attorney General, the Secretary of Homeland Security, and the Director of National Intelligence, shall review the Federal Acquisition Regulation (FAR) and the Defense Federal Acquisition Regulation Supplement contract requirements and language for contracting with IT and OT service providers and recommend updates to such requirements and language to the FAR Council and other appropriate agencies. The recommendations shall include descriptions of contractors to be covered by the proposed contract language.

networks for threats in collaboration with agencies they support, as needed; and

(iv) service providers share cyber threat and incident information with agencies, doing so, where possible, in industry-recognized formats for incident response and remediation.

Section 2 further provides timeline information for implementation of the recommended contract language.[341] The Secretary of Homeland Security and the Director of the OMB are required to ensure that "to the greatest extent possible that service providers share data with agencies, CISA, and the FBI as may be necessary for the Federal Government to respond to cyber threats, incidents, and risks." Section 2 sets forth the Federal Government's policy that ICT service providers "must promptly report" cyber incidents to the relevant contracting agency as well as CISA. Any reports concerning "National Security Systems . . . must be received and managed by the appropriate agency under g(i)(E) of this section." Additionally, specific recommended contract language to the FAR Council should be developed by the "Secretary of Homeland Security, in consultation [with] the Director of the [NSA], the Attorney General, and the Director of OMB." The contract language should identify:

(A) the nature of cyber incidents that require reporting;
(B) the types of information regarding cyber incidents that require reporting to facilitate effective cyber incident response and remediation;
(C) appropriate and effective protections for privacy and civil liberties;
(D) the time periods within which contractors must report cyber incidents based on a graduated scale of severity, with reporting on the most severe cyber incidents not to exceed 3 days after initial detection;
(E) National Security Systems reporting requirements; and
(F) the type of contractors and associated service providers to be covered by the proposed contract language.

A timeline is also provided for FAR Council review of the recommendations and publication for public comment. Additionally, a process for sharing those reports is to be developed by "the Director of the NSA, the Attorney General, the Secretary of Homeland Security, and the Director of National Intelligence."

Third, the Executive Order attempts to provide direction to federal agencies to modernize their cybersecurity practices. Importantly, section 3 notes that the Federal Government "must adopt security best practices; advance toward Zero Trust Architecture; accelerate movement to secure cloud services, including Software as a Service (SaaS), Infrastructure as a Service (IaaS), and Platform as a Service (PaaS); centralize and streamline access to cybersecurity data to drive analytics for identifying and managing cybersecurity risks; and invest in both technology and personnel to match these modernization goals."[342] At the same time, the Federal Government should strive

---

[341] Section 2(d) Within 90 days of receipt of the recommendations described in subsection (b) of this section, the FAR Council shall review the proposed contract language and conditions and, as appropriate, shall publish for public comment proposed updates to the FAR.
[342] The Executive Order defines Zero Trust Architecture:

to protect civil liberties. A timeline is provided for each agency to "prioritize resources for the adoption and use of cloud technology" and "develop a plan to implement Zero Trust Architecture, which shall incorporate, as appropriate, the migration steps that the National Institute of Standards and Technology (NIST) within the Department of Commerce has outlined in standards and guidance."[343] Section 3 further requires that agencies moving to the cloud must take into account the Federal Government's ability "to prevent, detect, assess, and remediate cyber incidents" by requiring CISA to work with "the Federal Risk and Authorization Management Program (FedRAMP) within the General Services Administration, shall develop security principles governing Cloud Service Providers (CSPs) for incorporation into agency modernization efforts." This includes, "for the FCEB, cloud-security technical reference architecture documentation that illustrates recommended approaches to cloud migration and data protection for agency data collection and reporting [and] a cloud-service governance framework." Section 3 also mandates adoption of "multi-factor authentication and encryption for data at rest and in transit, to the maximum extent consistent with Federal records laws and other applicable laws." A timeline is included for reporting and implementing multi-factor authentication and encryption.

> [T]he term "Zero Trust Architecture" means a security model, a set of system design principles, and a coordinated cybersecurity and system management strategy based on an acknowledgement that threats exist both inside and outside traditional network boundaries. The Zero Trust security model eliminates implicit trust in any one element, node, or service and instead requires continuous verification of the operational picture via real-time information from multiple sources to determine access and other system responses. In essence, a Zero Trust Architecture allows users full access but only to the bare minimum they need to perform their jobs. If a device is compromised, zero trust can ensure that the damage is contained. The Zero Trust Architecture security model assumes that a breach is inevitable or has likely already occurred, so it constantly limits access to only what is needed and looks for anomalous or malicious activity. Zero Trust Architecture embeds comprehensive security monitoring; granular risk-based access controls; and system security automation in a coordinated manner throughout all aspects of the infrastructure in order to focus on protecting data in real-time within a dynamic threat environment. This data-centric security model allows the concept of least-privileged access to be applied for every access decision, where the answers to the questions of who, what, when, where, and how are critical for appropriately allowing or denying access to resources based on the combination of sever. *Id.*

[343] On May 6, 2022, the NIST issued a White Paper titled, "Planning for a Zero Trust Architecture: A Planning Guide for Federal Administrators." *See* Scott Rose, *Planning for a Zero Trust Architecture: A Planning Guide for Federal Administrators*, National Institute of Standards (May 6, 2022), available at https://nvlpubs.nist.gov/nistpubs/CSWP/NIST.CSWP.20.pdf. The abstract of the White Paper provides:

> NIST Special Publication 800-207 defines zero trust as a set of cybersecurity principles used when planning and implementing an enterprise architecture. These principles apply to endpoints, services, and data flows. Input and cooperation from various stakeholders in an enterprise is needed for a zero trust architecture to succeed in improving the enterprise security posture. Some of these stakeholders may not be familiar with risk analysis and management. This document provides an overview of the NIST Risk Management Framework (NIST RMF) and how the NIST RMF can be applied when developing and implementing a zero trust architecture. *See* https://csrc.nist.gov/publications/detail/white-paper/2022/05/06/planning-for-a-zero-trust-architecture/final

Section 3 requires development of a "framework to collaborate on cybersecurity and incident response activities related to FCEB cloud technology, in order to ensure effective information sharing among agencies and between agencies and CSPs[,]" which notably includes participation by the Director of the FBI. FedRAMP is also to be modernized.

Fourth, the Executive Order contains direction to improve the cybersecurity of the software supply chain. Importantly, this section discusses the Software Bill of Materials.[344] The Executive Order section concerning the software supply chain provides:

Sec. 4. Enhancing Software Supply Chain Security.

(a) The security of software used by the Federal Government is vital to the Federal Government's ability to perform its critical functions. The development of commercial software often lacks transparency, sufficient focus on the ability of the software to resist attack, and adequate controls to prevent tampering by malicious actors. There is a pressing need to implement more rigorous and predictable mechanisms for ensuring that products function securely, and as intended. The security and integrity of "critical software" — software that performs functions critical to trust (such as affording or requiring elevated system privileges or direct access to networking and computing resources) — is a particular concern. Accordingly, the Federal Government must take action to rapidly improve the security and integrity of the software supply chain, with a priority on addressing critical software.

(b) Within 30 days of the date of this order, the Secretary of Commerce acting through the Director of NIST shall solicit input from the Federal Government, private sector, academia, and other appropriate actors to identify existing or develop new standards, tools, and best practices for complying with the standards, procedures, or criteria in subsection (e) of this section. The guidelines shall include criteria that can be used to evaluate software security, include criteria to evaluate the security practices of the developers and suppliers themselves, and identify innovative tools or methods to

---

[344] The Executive Order defines the Software Bill of Materials:

[T]he term "Software Bill of Materials" or "SBOM" means a formal record containing the details and supply chain relationships of various components used in building software. Software developers and vendors often create products by assembling existing open source and commercial software components. The SBOM enumerates these components in a product. It is analogous to a list of ingredients on food packaging. An SBOM is useful to those who develop or manufacture software, those who select or purchase software, and those who operate software. Developers often use available open source and third-party software components to create a product; an SBOM allows the builder to make sure those components are up to date and to respond quickly to new vulnerabilities. Buyers can use an SBOM to perform vulnerability or license analysis, both of which can be used to evaluate risk in a product. Those who operate software can use SBOMs to quickly and easily determine whether they are at potential risk of a newly discovered vulnerability. A widely used, machine-readable SBOM format allows for greater benefits through automation and tool integration. The SBOMs gain greater value when collectively stored in a repository that can be easily queried by other applications and systems. Understanding the supply chain of software, obtaining an SBOM, and using it to analyze known vulnerabilities are crucial in managing risk. *Id.*

demonstrate conformance with secure practices.

(c) Within 180 days of the date of this order, the Director of NIST shall publish preliminary guidelines, based on the consultations described in subsection (b) of this section and drawing on existing documents as practicable, for enhancing software supply chain security and meeting the requirements of this section.

(d) Within 360 days of the date of this order, the Director of NIST shall publish additional guidelines that include procedures for periodic review and updating of the guidelines described in subsection (c) of this section.

(e) Within 90 days of publication of the preliminary guidelines pursuant to subsection (c) of this section, the Secretary of Commerce acting through the Director of NIST, in consultation with the heads of such agencies as the Director of NIST deems appropriate, shall issue guidance identifying practices that enhance the security of the software supply chain. Such guidance may incorporate the guidelines published pursuant to subsections (c) and (i) of this section. Such guidance shall include standards, procedures, or criteria regarding:

(i) secure software development environments, including such actions as:

(A) using administratively separate build environments;

(B) auditing trust relationships;

(C) establishing multi-factor, risk-based authentication and conditional access across the enterprise;

(D) documenting and minimizing dependencies on enterprise products that are part of the environments used to develop, build, and edit software;

(E) employing encryption for data; and

(F) monitoring operations and alerts and responding to attempted and actual cyber incidents;

(ii) generating and, when requested by a purchaser, providing artifacts that demonstrate conformance to the processes set forth in subsection (e)(i) of this section;

(iii) employing automated tools, or comparable processes, to maintain trusted source code supply chains, thereby ensuring the integrity of the code;

(iv) employing automated tools, or comparable processes, that check for known and potential vulnerabilities and remediate them, which shall operate regularly, or at a minimum prior to product, version, or update release;

(v) providing, when requested by a purchaser, artifacts of the execution of the tools and processes described in subsection (e)(iii) and (iv) of this section, and making publicly available summary information on completion of these actions, to include a summary description of the risks assessed and mitigated;

(vi) maintaining accurate and up-to-date data, provenance (i.e., origin) of software code or components, and controls on internal and third-party software components, tools, and services present in software development processes, and performing audits and enforcement of these controls on a recurring basis;

(vii) providing a purchaser a Software Bill of Materials (SBOM) for each product directly or by publishing it on a public website;

(viii) participating in a vulnerability disclosure program that includes a reporting and disclosure process;

(ix) attesting to conformity with secure software development practices; and

(x) ensuring and attesting, to the extent practicable, to the integrity and provenance of open source software used within any portion of a product.

(f) Within 60 days of the date of this order, the Secretary of Commerce, in coordination with the Assistant Secretary for Communications and Information and the Administrator of the National Telecommunications and Information Administration, shall publish minimum elements for an SBOM.

(g) Within 45 days of the date of this order, the Secretary of Commerce, acting through the Director of NIST, in consultation with the Secretary of Defense acting through the Director of the NSA, the Secretary of Homeland Security acting through the Director of CISA, the Director of OMB, and the Director of National Intelligence, shall publish a definition of the term "critical software" for inclusion in the guidance issued pursuant to subsection (e) of this section. That definition shall reflect the level of privilege or access required to function, integration and dependencies with other software, direct access to networking and computing resources, performance of a function critical to trust, and potential for harm if compromised.[345]

(h) Within 30 days of the publication of the definition required by subsection (g) of this section, the Secretary of Homeland Security acting through the Director of CISA, in consultation with the Secretary of Commerce acting through the Director of NIST, shall identify and make available to agencies a list of categories of software and software products in use or in the acquisition process meeting the definition of critical software issued pursuant to subsection (g) of this section.

(i) Within 60 days of the date of this order, the Secretary of Commerce acting through the Director of NIST, in consultation with the Secretary of Homeland Security acting through the Director of CISA and with the Director of OMB, shall publish guidance outlining security measures for critical software as defined in subsection (g) of this section, including applying practices of least privilege, network segmentation, and proper configuration.

(j) Within 30 days of the issuance of the guidance described in subsection (i) of this section, the Director of OMB acting through the Administrator of the Office of Electronic Government within OMB shall take appropriate steps to require that agencies comply with such guidance.

(k) Within 30 days of issuance of the guidance described in subsection (e) of this section, the Director of OMB acting through the Administrator of the Office of

---

[345] Editors: NIST has issued a definition for critical software:

> EO-critical software is defined as any software that has, or has direct software dependencies upon, one or more components with at least one of these attributes: • is designed to run with elevated privilege or manage privileges; • has direct or privileged access to networking or computing resources; • is designed to control access to data or operational technology; • performs a function critical to trust; or, • operates outside of normal trust boundaries with privileged access.
>
> The definition applies to software of all forms (e.g., standalone software, software integral to specific devices or hardware components, cloud-based software) purchased for, or deployed in, production systems and used for operational purposes. Other use cases, such as software solely used for research or testing that is not deployed in production systems, are outside of the scope of this definition. See National Institutes of Standards, Definition of Critical Software Under Executive Order (EO) 14028 (October 13, 2021), available at https://www.nist.gov/system/files/documents/2021/10/13/EO%20Critical%20FINAL.pdf.

That NIST document includes a chart concerning types of software as well as frequently asked questions with answers. *Id.*

Electronic Government within OMB shall take appropriate steps to require that agencies comply with such guidelines with respect to software procured after the date of this order.

(l) Agencies may request an extension for complying with any requirements issued pursuant to subsection (k) of this section. Any such request shall be considered by the Director of OMB on a case-by-case basis, and only if accompanied by a plan for meeting the underlying requirements. The Director of OMB shall on a quarterly basis provide a report to the APNSA identifying and explaining all extensions granted.

(m) Agencies may request a waiver as to any requirements issued pursuant to subsection (k) of this section. Waivers shall be considered by the Director of OMB, in consultation with the APNSA, on a case-by-case basis, and shall be granted only in exceptional circumstances and for limited duration, and only if there is an accompanying plan for mitigating any potential risks.

(n) Within 1 year of the date of this order, the Secretary of Homeland Security, in consultation with the Secretary of Defense, the Attorney General, the Director of OMB, and the Administrator of the Office of Electronic Government within OMB, shall recommend to the FAR Council contract language requiring suppliers of software available for purchase by agencies to comply with, and attest to complying with, any requirements issued pursuant to subsections (g) through (k) of this section.

(o) After receiving the recommendations described in subsection (n) of this section, the FAR Council shall review the recommendations and, as appropriate and consistent with applicable law, amend the FAR.

(p) Following the issuance of any final rule amending the FAR as described in subsection (o) of this section, agencies shall, as appropriate and consistent with applicable law, remove software products that do not meet the requirements of the amended FAR from all indefinite delivery indefinite quantity contracts; Federal Supply Schedules; Federal Government-wide Acquisition Contracts; Blanket Purchase Agreements; and Multiple Award Contracts.

(q) The Director of OMB, acting through the Administrator of the Office of Electronic Government within OMB, shall require agencies employing software developed and procured prior to the date of this order (legacy software) either to comply with any requirements issued pursuant to subsection (k) of this section or to provide a plan outlining actions to remediate or meet those requirements, and shall further require agencies seeking renewals of software contracts, including legacy software, to comply with any requirements issued pursuant to subsection (k) of this section, unless an extension or waiver is granted in accordance with subsection (l) or (m) of this section.

(r) Within 60 days of the date of this order, the Secretary of Commerce acting through the Director of NIST, in consultation with the Secretary of Defense acting through the Director of the NSA, shall publish guidelines recommending minimum standards for vendors' testing of their software source code, including identifying recommended types of manual or automated testing (such as code review tools, static and dynamic analysis, software composition tools, and penetration testing).[346]

---

[346] On July 7, 2021, the NIST issued a White Paper, titled, "Recommended Minimum Standards for Vendor or Developer Verification (Testing) of Software Under Executive Order (EO) 14028." *See* Paul E. Black, Barbara Guttman & Vadim Okun, *Recommended Minimum Standards for Vendor or Developer*

(s) The Secretary of Commerce acting through the Director of NIST, in coordination with representatives of other agencies as the Director of NIST deems appropriate, shall initiate pilot programs informed by existing consumer product labeling programs to educate the public on the security capabilities of Internet-of-Things (IoT) devices and software development practices, and shall consider ways to incentivize manufacturers and developers to participate in these programs.

(t) Within 270 days of the date of this order, the Secretary of Commerce acting through the Director of NIST, in coordination with the Chair of the Federal Trade Commission (FTC) and representatives of other agencies as the Director of NIST deems appropriate, shall identify IoT cybersecurity criteria for a consumer labeling program, and shall consider whether such a consumer labeling program may be operated in conjunction with or modeled after any similar existing government programs consistent with applicable law. The criteria shall reflect increasingly comprehensive levels of testing and assessment that a product may have undergone, and shall use or be compatible with existing labeling schemes that manufacturers use to inform consumers about the security of their products. The Director of NIST shall examine all relevant information, labeling, and incentive programs and employ best practices. This review shall focus on ease of use for consumers and a determination of what measures can be taken to maximize manufacturer participation.[347]

(u) Within 270 days of the date of this order, the Secretary of Commerce acting through the Director of NIST, in coordination with the Chair of the FTC and

---

Verification (Testing) of Software Under Executive Order (EO) 14028 (July 7, 2021), available at https://nvlpubs.nist.gov/nistpubs/ir/2021/NIST.IR.8397.pdf. The abstract of the White Paper states:

> This document describes eleven recommendations for software verification techniques as well as providing supplemental information about the techniques and references for further information. It recommends the following techniques: • Threat modeling to look for design-level security issues • Automated testing for consistency and to minimize human effort • Static code scanning to look for top bugs • Heuristic tools to look for possible hardcoded secrets • Use of built-in checks and protections • "Black box" test cases • Code-based structural test cases • Historical test cases • Fuzzing • Web app scanners, if applicable • Address included code (libraries, packages, services) The document does not address the totality of software verification, but instead, recommends techniques that are broadly applicable and form the minimum standards. *Id.*

[347] On February 4, 2022, the NIST issued a White Paper, titled, "Recommended Criteria for Cybersecurity Labeling for Consumer Internet of Things (IoT) Products." *Id.* (February 4, 2022), available at https://nvlpubs.nist.gov/nistpubs/CSWP/NIST.CSWP.02042022-2.pdf. The abstract of the White Paper states:

> Executive Order (EO) 14028, "Improving the Nation's Cybersecurity," tasks the National Institute of Standards and Technology (NIST), in coordination with the Federal Trade Commission (FTC) and other agencies, to initiate pilot programs for cybersecurity labeling. NIST is, among other actions, directed "… to identify IoT cybersecurity criteria for a consumer labeling program…" This document seeks to fulfill this directive by recommending consumer IoT product label criteria, label design and consumer education considerations, and conformity assessment considerations for use by a scheme owner to inform a consumer Internet of Things (IoT) product labeling program. *See* https://csrc.nist.gov/publications/detail/white-paper/2022/02/04/criteria-for-cybersecurity-labeling-for-consumer-iot-products/final

representatives from other agencies as the Director of NIST deems appropriate, shall identify secure software development practices or criteria for a consumer software labeling program, and shall consider whether such a consumer software labeling program may be operated in conjunction with or modeled after any similar existing government programs, consistent with applicable law. The criteria shall reflect a baseline level of secure practices, and if practicable, shall reflect increasingly comprehensive levels of testing and assessment that a product may have undergone. The Director of NIST shall examine all relevant information, labeling, and incentive programs, employ best practices, and identify, modify, or develop a recommended label or, if practicable, a tiered software security rating system. This review shall focus on ease of use for consumers and a determination of what measures can be taken to maximize participation.

(v) These pilot programs shall be conducted in a manner consistent with OMB Circular A-119 and NIST Special Publication 2000-02 (Conformity Assessment Considerations for Federal Agencies).

(w) Within 1 year of the date of this order, the Director of NIST shall conduct a review of the pilot programs, consult with the private sector and relevant agencies to assess the effectiveness of the programs, determine what improvements can be made going forward, and submit a summary report to the APNSA.

(x) Within 1 year of the date of this order, the Secretary of Commerce, in consultation with the heads of other agencies as the Secretary of Commerce deems appropriate, shall provide to the President, through the APNSA, a report that reviews the progress made under this section and outlines additional steps needed to secure the software supply chain.

Fifth, the Executive Order establishes a Cyber Safety Review Board that reviews "significant' cybersecurity incidents concerning Federal Civilian Executive Branch Agencies, which includes almost all non-military agencies such as the Department of State, Federal Trade Commission, NASA and the U.S. Commission on Civil Rights. The Board also reviews significant cybersecurity incidents related to, "non-Federal systems, threat activity, vulnerabilities, mitigation activities, and agency responses." The Board is also responsible for making recommendations concerning cybersecurity incidents as of December 2020.

Sixth, the Executive Order attempts to standardize incident response across the various agencies. The Executive Order calls for a standardized playbook for "operational procedures . . . to be used in planning and conducting a cybersecurity vulnerability and incident response activity" which shall include:

(i) incorporate all appropriate NIST standards;
(ii) be used by FCEB Agencies; and
(iii) articulate progress and completion through all phases of an incident response, while allowing flexibility so it may be used in support of various response activities.

Additionally, "the playbook shall define key terms and use such terms consistently with any statutory definitions of those terms, to the extent practicable, thereby providing a shared lexicon among agencies using the playbook."

Seventh, the Executive Order directs the Federal Government to improve detection of cybersecurity vulnerabilities and incidents on Federal Government Networks. "FCEB Agencies shall deploy an Endpoint Detection and Response (EDR) initiative to support proactive detection of cybersecurity incidents within Federal Government infrastructure, active cyber hunting, containment and remediation, and incident response." The seventh section further provides for the sharing of information concerning vulnerabilities and incidents with CISA.

Eight, the executive order provides for the collection and maintenance of data necessary for investigating and remediating cybersecurity issues, including '[i]nformation from network and system logs on Federal Information Systems (for both on-premises systems and connections hosted by third parties, such as CSPs)." Notably, "[d]ata shall be retained in a manner consistent with all applicable privacy laws and regulations."

Finally, "the Secretary of Defense acting through the National Manager, in coordination with the Director of National Intelligence and the CNSS, and in consultation with the APNSA, shall adopt National Security Systems requirements that are equivalent to or exceed the cybersecurity requirements set forth in this order that are otherwise not applicable to National Security Systems."

NOTES

Note 1

On January 26, 2022, the Executive Office of the President issued a memorandum titled, "Moving the U.S. Government Toward Zero Trust Cybersecurity Principles." The memorandum states:

> This memorandum sets forth a Federal zero trust architecture (ZTA) strategy, requiring agencies to meet specific cybersecurity standards and objectives by the end of Fiscal Year (FY) 2024 in order to reinforce the Government's defenses against increasingly sophisticated and persistent threat campaigns. Those campaigns target Federal technology infrastructure, threatening public safety and privacy, damaging the American economy, and weakening trust in Government.[348]

Note 2

---

[348] EXECUTIVE OFFICE OF THE PRESIDENT, *Moving the U.S. Government Toward Zero Trust Cybersecurity Principles* (January 26, 2022), available at https://www.whitehouse.gov/wp-content/uploads/2022/01/M-22-09.pdf.

On October 6, 2021, the Department of Justice announced a new Civil Cyber Fraud Initiative.[349] The announcement stated, in part:

> The Civil Cyber-Fraud Initiative will utilize the False Claims Act to pursue cybersecurity related fraud by government contractors and grant recipients. The False Claims Act is the government's primary civil tool to redress false claims for federal funds and property involving government programs and operations. The act includes a unique whistleblower provision, which allows private parties to assist the government in identifying and pursing fraudulent conduct and to share in any recovery and protects whistleblowers who bring these violations and failures from retaliation.
>
> The initiative will hold accountable entities or individuals that put U.S. information or systems at risk by knowingly providing deficient cybersecurity products or services, knowingly misrepresenting their cybersecurity practices or protocols, or knowingly violating obligations to monitor and report cybersecurity incidents and breaches. The benefits of the initiative will include:
> - Building broad resiliency against cybersecurity intrusions across the government, the public sector and key industry partners.
> - Holding contractors and grantees to their commitments to protect government information and infrastructure.
> - Supporting government experts' efforts to timely identify, create and publicize patches for vulnerabilities in commonly-used information technology products and services.
> - Ensuring that companies that follow the rules and invest in meeting cybersecurity requirements are not at a competitive disadvantage.
> - Reimbursing the government and the taxpayers for the losses incurred when companies fail to satisfy their cybersecurity obligations.
> - Improving overall cybersecurity practices that will benefit the government, private users and the American public.
> The department will work closely on the Initiative with other federal agencies, subject matter experts and its law enforcement partners throughout the government.[350]

Note 3

The U.S. General Services Administration [GSA] supports agencies across the federal government with providing services and maintaining buildings, for example. The GSA has produced a Buyer's Guide for U.S. agencies to acquire products and services that utilize Zero Trust Architecture. The Buyer's Guide sets forth the seven tenets of Zero Trust Architecture:

---

[349] *See* U.S. DEP'T OF JUSTICE, *Deputy Attorney General Lisa O. Monaco Announces New Civil Cyber-Fraud Initiative*, (October 6, 2021), available at https://www.justice.gov/opa/pr/deputy-attorney-general-lisa-o-monaco-announces-new-civil-cyber-fraud-initiative.

[350] *Id.*

1. Rigorously enforce authentication and authorization – All resources require mandatory authentication, often paired with technologies such as multifactor authentication (MFA), before granting access. According to Zero Trust principles, no account has implicit access without explicit permission.

2. Maintain data integrity – Enterprises measure and monitor the security and integrity of all owned and associated assets, assess their vulnerabilities, patch levels, and other potential cybersecurity threats.

3. Gather data for improved security – Enterprises should collect current information from multiple sources, such as network infrastructure and communication, to regulate and improve security standards.

4. Consider every data source and computing device as a resource – Enterprises should consider any device with access to an enterprise-level network as a resource.

5. Keep all communication secured regardless of network location – Physical network locations alone should never imply trust. People connecting via enterprise and non-enterprise networks must undergo the same security requirements for resource access.

6. Grant resource access on a per-session basis – Enterprises should enforce a least-privilege policy: a user should only be granted the minimum privileges required to complete a task. Every access request requires evaluation and, when granted, does not immediately provide access to other resources. Users will need to submit a separate request for subsequent data access.

7. Moderate access with a dynamic policy – Enterprises need to protect resources with a transparent policy that continuously defines resources, accounts, and the type of privileges linked to each account. The process may involve attributes, such as device characteristics (i.e., software versions) and network locations.[351]

Note 4

The Department of Defense has issued a Zero Trust Architecture document:

Zero Trust focuses on protecting critical data and resources, not just the traditional network or perimeter security. Zero Trust implements continuous multi-factor authentication, micro-segmentation, encryption, endpoint security, analytics, and robust auditing to DAAS seven pillars to deliver cyber resiliency. As the Department evolves to become a more agile, more mobile, cloud-instantiated workforce, collaborating with multiple federal and non-governmental organizations (NGO) entities for a variety of missions, a hardened perimeter defense can no longer suffice as an effective means of enterprise security. In a world of increasingly

---

[351] GENERAL SERVICES ADMINISTRATION, *Zero Trust Architecture Buyer's Guide* (June 2021), available at https://www.gsa.gov/cdnstatic/Zero%20Trust%20Architecture%20Buyers%20Guide%20 v11%2020210610%20(2).pdf.

sophisticated threats, a Zero Trust framework reduces the attack surface, reduces risk, and ensures that if a device, network, or user/credential is compromised, the damage is quickly contained and remediated.

State-funded hackers are well trained, well-resourced, and persistent. The use of new tactics, techniques, and procedures combined with more invasive malware can enable motivated malicious personas to move with previously unseen speed and accuracy. Any new security capability must be resilient to evolving threats and effectively reduce threat vectors, internal and external.

Zero Trust end-user capabilities improve visibility, control, and risk analysis of infrastructure, application and data usage. This provides a secure environment for mission execution. Enabling Zero Trust capabilities address the following high-level goals:

• **Modernize Information Enterprise to Address Gaps and Seams.** Over time, DOD networks have been decentralized and arguably underfunded, as each Service component and organization faces competing financial priorities. Usability and security challenges stem from years of building infrastructure along organizational, operational and doctrinal boundaries, with multiple security and support tiers, enclaves and networks. Capabilities developed in silos have inevitably resulted in disconnects and gaps in the command structure and processes that preclude establishing a comprehensive, dynamic, and near-real time common operating picture (COP). Adversaries have exploited these logical, technological, and organizational gaps and seams.

• **Simplify Security Architecture.** A fragmented approach to information technology and cybersecurity has led to excessive technical complexity, which creates vulnerabilities in our cyber hygiene, inadequately addresses internal and lateral threats and results in high levels of latency. Complex security techniques render the user experience painfully unresponsive and unusable.

• **Produce Consistent Policy.** This is a critical lesson-learned from industry that automated cybersecurity policies must be consistently applied across environments (on/off premises) for maximum effectiveness. Technology leaders have relied on perimeter defense systems that fetter access and grant implicit trust based on network location. Waivers and exceptions to written policies, based on short term operational needs, have led to inconsistently managed, reconfigured, and/or disabled security systems, thereby making them porous and ineffective.

• **Optimize Data Management Operations.** The success of DOD missions, ranging from payroll to missile defense, are increasingly dependent on structured and tagged data. Advanced analytics also depend on this. While data standards and policy exist, they are disparate and inconsistently implemented. This results in: o Interoperability challenges between applications, organizations, and with external partners, o Inherent system inefficiencies and vulnerabilities, o Poor/frustrating user experience, and o Hampered abilities to fully leverage the benefits of cloud computing, data analytics, machine learning, and artificial intelligence

· **Provide Dynamic Credentialing and Authorization.** Persona based identities, credentials, and attributes are not dynamic or context aware and come from disparate sources. Two factor authentications, in the form of the Common Access Card (CAC), has not kept pace with multi-factor authentication advances in industry. Non-person identities are not widely addressed, nor are identities for bots and the Internet of Things (IoT). The ICAM Reference Design will provide further specifics on credentialing implementations consumed by Zero Trust Architectures.[352]

Note 5

On October 26, 2021, the U.S. Department of Justice announced that it would enforce cybersecurity requirements in federal contracts and grants through the False Claims Act:

Civil Cyber-Fraud Initiative Details

The Civil Cyber-Fraud Initiative will utilize the False Claims Act to pursue cybersecurity related fraud by government contractors and grant recipients. The False Claims Act is the government's primary civil tool to redress false claims for federal funds and property involving government programs and operations. The act includes a unique whistleblower provision, which allows private parties to assist the government in identifying and pursing fraudulent conduct and to share in any recovery and protects whistleblowers who bring these violations and failures from retaliation.

The initiative will hold accountable entities or individuals that put U.S. information or systems at risk by knowingly providing deficient cybersecurity products or services, knowingly misrepresenting their cybersecurity practices or protocols, or knowingly violating obligations to monitor and report cybersecurity incidents and breaches. The benefits of the initiative will include:

- Building broad resiliency against cybersecurity intrusions across the government, the public sector and key industry partners.
- Holding contractors and grantees to their commitments to protect government information and infrastructure.
- Supporting government experts' efforts to timely identify, create and publicize patches for vulnerabilities in commonly-used information technology products and services.
- Ensuring that companies that follow the rules and invest in meeting cybersecurity requirements are not at a competitive disadvantage.
- Reimbursing the government and the taxpayers for the losses incurred when companies fail to satisfy their cybersecurity obligations.

---

[352] DEPARTMENT OF DEFENSE, *Zero Trust Reference Architecture* (February 2021), available at https://dodcio.defense.gov/Portals/0/Documents/Library/(U)ZT_RA_v1.1(U)_Mar21.pdf.

- Improving overall cybersecurity practices that will benefit the government, private users and the American public.
The department will work closely on the Initiative with other federal agencies, subject matter experts and its law enforcement partners throughout the government.[353]

On March 8, 2022, the U.S. Department of Justice announced the first settlements under the initiative:

> Comprehensive Health Services LLC (CHS), located in Cape Canaveral, Florida, has agreed to pay $930,000 to resolve allegations that it violated the False Claims Act by falsely representing to the State Department and the Air Force that it complied with contract requirements relating to the provision of medical services at State Department and Air Force facilities in Iraq and Afghanistan. This is the Department of Justice's first resolution of a False Claims Act case involving cyber fraud since the launch of the department's Civil Cyber-Fraud Initiative, which aims to combine the department's expertise in civil fraud enforcement, government procurement and cybersecurity to combat new and emerging cyber threats to the security of sensitive information and critical systems.
>
> CHS is a provider of global medical services that contracted to provide medical support services at government-run facilities in Iraq and Afghanistan. Under one of the contracts, CHS submitted claims to the State Department for the cost of a secure electronic medical record (EMR) system to store all patients' medical records, including the confidential identifying information of United States service members, diplomats, officials and contractors working and receiving medical care in Iraq. The United States alleged that, between 2012 and 2019, CHS failed to disclose to the State Department that it had not consistently stored patients' medical records on a secure EMR system. When CHS staff scanned medical records for the EMR system, CHS staff saved and left scanned copies of some records on an internal network drive, which was accessible to non-clinical staff. Even after staff raised concerns about the privacy of protected medical information, CHS did not take adequate steps to store the information exclusively on the EMR system.
>
> . . .
>
> "This settlement demonstrates the department's commitment to use its civil enforcement tools to pursue government contractors that fail to follow required cybersecurity standards, particularly when they put confidential medical records at risk," said Principal Deputy Assistant Attorney General Brian M. Boynton, head of the Justice Department's Civil Division. "We will continue to ensure that those who do business

---

[353] DEPARTMENT OF JUSTICE, *Attorney General Lisa O. Monaco Announced New Civil Cyber-Fraud Initiative* (October 26, 2021), available at https://www.justice.gov/opa/pr/deputy-attorney-general-lisa-o-monaco-announces-new-civil-cyber-fraud-initiative.

with the government comply with their contractual obligations, including those requiring the protection of sensitive government information."

. . .

The civil settlement includes the resolution of two actions brought under the *qui tam* or whistleblower provisions of the False Claims Act against CHS. Under the *qui tam* provisions of the False Claims Act, a private party can file an action on behalf of the United States and receive a portion of the settlement if the government takes over the case and reaches a monetary agreement with the defendant. The *qui tam* cases are captioned *United States ex rel. Lawler v. Comprehensive Health Servs., Inc. et al.,* Case No. 20-cv-698 (E.D.N.Y.), and *United States ex rel. Watkins et al. v. CHS Middle East, LLC,* Case No. 17-cv-4319 (E.D.N.Y.).[354]

7.4 Cyber Incident Reporting for Critical Infrastructure Act of 2022

On March 15, 2022, President Biden signed the Cyber Incident Reporting for Critical Infrastructure Act of 2022 [Reporting Act of 2022].[355] The Reporting Act of 2022 requires cybersecurity incident reporting for critical infrastructure. The National Cybersecurity and Communications Integration Center [NCCIC] of the Department of Homeland Security is primarily responsible for receiving and analyzing incident reports, including those related to ransomware. NCCIC is also responsible for sharing information to relevant entities. The Reporting Act of 2022 has several main provisions, including: Section 2242. Required Reporting of Certain Cyber Incidents; Section 2243. Voluntary Reporting of Other Cyber Incidents; Section 2244. Noncompliance with Required Reporting; Section 2245. Information Shared with or Provided to the Federal Government; Section 2246. Cyber Incident Reporting Council; Section 104 Federal Sharing of Incident Reports; Section 105. Ransomware Vulnerability Warning Pilot Program; and Section 106. Ransomware Threat Mitigation Activities.

The key parts are Section 2242. Required Reporting of Certain Cyber Incidents which is codified at 6 U.S.C. 681(b). Section 2243. Voluntary Reporting of Other Cyber Incidents allows the submission of reports that are not required under Section 2242, and importantly, the protections provided for submission of required reports are also provided to voluntary reports. Section 2243. Noncompliance with Required Reporting includes the ability of the Attorney General to bring a civil action to enforce a subpoena to obtain information concerning an unreported incident or ransomware payment after

---

[354] DEPARTMENT OF JUSTICE, *Medical Services Contractor Pays $930,000 to Settle False Claims Act Allegations Relating to Medical Services Contracts at State Department and Air Force Facilities in Iraq and Afghanistan* (March 8, 2022), available at https://www.justice.gov/opa/pr/medical-services-contractor-pays-930000-settle-false-claims-act-allegations-relating-medical.

[355] Cyber Incident Reporting for Critical Infrastructure Act of 2022, codified as amended at 6 U.S.C. §§681-681g.

a failure of a covered entity to respond or inadequately respond to a request. Section 2245. Information Shared with or Provided to the Federal Government specifically delineates the purposes to which the information provided in incident reports can be used by the federal government.[356] Importantly, Section 2245 also provides an exemption from liability related to the submission of an incident report.[357] Section 104 authorizes the sharing of incident reports among federal agencies. Section 105. Ransomware Vulnerability Warning Pilot Program allows the creation of a warning program regarding ransomware designed "to leverage existing authorities and technology to specifically develop processes and procedures for, and to dedicate resources to, identifying information systems that contain security vulnerabilities associated with common ransomware attacks, and to notify the owners of those vulnerable systems of their security vulnerability." Section 106. Ransomware Threat Mitigation Activities authorizes the creation of a "Joint Ransomware Task Force to coordinate an ongoing nationwide campaign against ransomware attacks, and identify and pursue opportunities for international cooperation."

Section 2242. Required Reporting of Certain Cyber Incidents provides, in relevant part:

(a) In general

---

[356] That provision further provides protections for the information:

(b) PROTECTIONS FOR REPORTING ENTITIES AND INFORMATION.—Reports describing covered cyber incidents or ransom payments submitted to the Agency by entities in accordance with section 2242, as well as voluntarily-submitted cyber incident reports submitted to the Agency pursuant to section 2243, shall—
(1) be considered the commercial, financial, and proprietary information of the covered entity when so designated by the covered entity;
(2) be exempt from disclosure under section 552(b)(3) of title 5, United States Code (commonly known as the 'Freedom of Information Act'), as well as any provision of State, Tribal, or local freedom of information law, open government law, open meetings law, open records law, sunshine law, or similar law requiring disclosure of information or records;
(3) be considered not to constitute a waiver of any applicable privilege or protection provided by law, including trade secret protection; and
(4) not be subject to a rule of any Federal agency or department or any judicial doctrine regarding ex parte communications with a decision-making official. *Id.*

[357] That provision specifically states, in relevant part:

(c) LIABILITY PROTECTIONS.—
(1) IN GENERAL.—No cause of action shall lie or be maintained in any court by any person or entity and any such action shall be promptly dismissed for the submission of a report pursuant to section 2242(a) that is submitted in conformance with this subtitle and the rule promulgated under section 2242(b), except that this subsection shall not apply with regard to an action by the Federal Government pursuant to section 2244(c)(2).
(2) SCOPE.—The liability protections provided in this subsection shall only apply to or affect litigation that is solely based on the submission of a covered cyber incident report or ransom payment report to the Agency. *Id.*

(1) Covered cyber incident[358] reports

    (A) In general

A covered entity[359] that experiences a covered cyber incident shall report the covered cyber incident to the Agency not later than 72 hours after the covered entity reasonably believes that the covered cyber incident has occurred.

    (B) Limitation

The Director may not require reporting under subparagraph (A) any earlier than 72 hours after the covered entity reasonably believes that a covered cyber incident has occurred.

(2) Ransom payment reports

    (A) In general

A covered entity that makes a ransom payment as the result of a ransomware attack[360] against the covered entity shall report the payment to the Agency not later than 24 hours after the ransom payment has been made.

---

[358] Section 681 of Title 6 provides a definition for "cyber incident": ". . . **(A)** has the meaning given the term 'incident' in section 659 of this title; and **(B)** does not include an occurrence that imminently, but not actually, jeopardizes--**(i)** information on information systems; or **(ii)** information systems." Section 659 provides: "**(5)** the term "incident" means an occurrence that actually or imminently jeopardizes, without lawful authority, the integrity, confidentiality, or availability of information on an information system, or actually or imminently jeopardizes, without lawful authority, an information system." A "covered cyber incident" will be defined by subsequent rule making. *See* 6 U.S.C. § 681(4) ("The term "covered cyber incident" means a substantial cyber incident experienced by a covered entity that satisfies the definition and criteria established by the Director in the final rule issued pursuant to section 681b(b) of this title.").

[359] Section 681 of Title 6 provides a definition for "covered entity": ". . . means an entity in a critical infrastructure sector, as defined in Presidential Policy Directive 21, that satisfies the definition established by the Director in the final rule issued pursuant to section 681b(b) of this title." Presidential Policy Directive 21 provides a very broad definition of critical infrastructure which includes: "systems and assets, whether physical or virtual, so vital to the United States that the incapacity or destruction of such systems and assets would have a debilitating impact on security, national economic security, national public health or safety, or any combination of those matters." THE WHITE HOUSE, *Presidential Policy Directive -- Critical Infrastructure Security and Resilience* (February 12, 2013), available at https://obamawhitehouse.archives.gov/the-press-office/2013/02/12/presidential-policy-directive-critical-infrastructure-security-and-resil. The Policy Directive 21 also provides a list of critical infrastructure sectors: Chemical; Commercial Facilities; Communications; Critical Manufacturing; Dams; Defense Industrial Base; Emergency Services; Energy; Financial Services; Food and Agriculture; Government Facilities; Healthcare and Public Health; Information Technology; Nuclear Reactors, Materials, and Waste; Transportation Systems; Water and Wastewater Systems. *Id.*
The complete definition will be provided by subsequent rule making.

[360] Section 681 of Title 6 provides a definition for "ransomware attack":

> . . . **(A)** means an incident that includes the use or threat of use of unauthorized or malicious code on an information system, or the use or threat of use of another digital mechanism such as a denial of service attack, to interrupt or disrupt the operations of an information system or compromise the confidentiality, availability, or integrity of electronic data stored on, processed by, or transiting an information system to extort a demand for a ransom payment; and
> **(B)** does not include any such event where the demand for payment is--
> **(i)** not genuine; or
> **(ii)** made in good faith by an entity in response to a specific request by the owner or operator of the information system. *Id.*

(B) Application

The requirements under subparagraph (A) shall apply even if the ransomware attack is not a covered cyber incident subject to the reporting requirements under paragraph (1).

(3) Supplemental reports

A covered entity shall promptly submit to the Agency an update or supplement to a previously submitted covered cyber incident report if substantial new or different information becomes available or if the covered entity makes a ransom payment after submitting a covered cyber incident report required under paragraph (1), until such date that such covered entity notifies the Agency that the covered cyber incident at issue has concluded and has been fully mitigated and resolved.

(4) Preservation of information

Any covered entity subject to requirements of paragraph (1), (2), or (3) shall preserve data relevant to the covered cyber incident or ransom payment in accordance with procedures established in the final rule issued pursuant to subsection (b).

(5) Exceptions

(A) Reporting of covered cyber incident with ransom payment

If a covered entity is the victim of a covered cyber incident and makes a ransom payment prior to the 72 hour requirement under paragraph (1), such that the reporting requirements under paragraphs (1) and (2) both apply, the covered entity may submit a single report to satisfy the requirements of both paragraphs in accordance with procedures established in the final rule issued pursuant to subsection (b).

(B) Substantially similar reported information

(i) In general

Subject to the limitation described in clause (ii), where the Agency has an agreement in place that satisfies the requirements of section 681g(a) of this title, the requirements under paragraphs (1), (2), and (3) shall not apply to a covered entity required by law, regulation, or contract to report substantially similar information to another Federal agency within a substantially similar timeframe.

(ii) Limitation

The exemption in clause (i) shall take effect with respect to a covered entity once an agency agreement and sharing mechanism is in place between the Agency and the respective Federal agency, pursuant to section 681g(a) of this title.

(iii) Rules of construction

Nothing in this paragraph shall be construed to--

(I) exempt a covered entity from the reporting requirements under paragraph (3) unless the supplemental report also meets the requirements of clauses (i) and (ii) of this paragraph;

(II) prevent the Agency from contacting an entity submitting information to another Federal agency that is provided to the Agency pursuant to section 681g of this title; or

(III) prevent an entity from communicating with the Agency.

(C) Domain name system

The requirements under paragraphs (1), (2) and (3) shall not apply to a covered entity or the functions of a covered entity that the Director determines constitute critical infrastructure owned, operated, or governed by multi-stakeholder organizations that develop, implement, and enforce policies concerning the Domain Name System, such as the Internet Corporation for Assigned Names and Numbers or the Internet Assigned Numbers Authority.

(6) Manner, timing, and form of reports

Reports made under paragraphs (1), (2), and (3) shall be made in the manner and form, and within the time period in the case of reports made under paragraph (3), prescribed in the final rule issued pursuant to subsection (b).

(7) Effective date

Paragraphs (1) through (4) shall take effect on the dates prescribed in the final rule issued pursuant to subsection (b).

(b) Rulemaking

(1) Notice of proposed rulemaking

Not later than 24 months after March 15, 2022, the Director, in consultation with Sector Risk Management Agencies, the Department of Justice, and other Federal agencies, shall publish in the Federal Register a notice of proposed rulemaking to implement subsection (a).

(2) Final rule

Not later than 18 months after publication of the notice of proposed rulemaking under paragraph (1), the Director shall issue a final rule to implement subsection (a).

(3) Subsequent rulemakings

(A) In general

The Director is authorized to issue regulations to amend or revise the final rule issued pursuant to paragraph (2).

(B) Procedures

Any subsequent rules issued under subparagraph (A) shall comply with the requirements under chapter 5 of Title 5, including the issuance of a notice of proposed rulemaking under section 553 of such title.

(c) Elements

The final rule issued pursuant to subsection (b) shall be composed of the following elements:

(1) A clear description of the types of entities that constitute covered entities, based on--

(A) the consequences that disruption to or compromise of such an entity could cause to national security, economic security, or public health and safety;

(B) the likelihood that such an entity may be targeted by a malicious cyber actor, including a foreign country; and

(C) the extent to which damage, disruption, or unauthorized access to such an entity, including the accessing of sensitive cybersecurity vulnerability information or penetration testing tools or techniques, will likely enable the disruption of the reliable operation of critical infrastructure.

(2) A clear description of the types of substantial cyber incidents that constitute covered cyber incidents, which shall--

(A) at a minimum, require the occurrence of--

(i) a cyber incident that leads to substantial loss of confidentiality, integrity, or availability of such information system or network, or a serious impact on the safety and resiliency of operational systems and processes;

(ii) a disruption of business or industrial operations, including due to a denial of service attack, ransomware attack, or exploitation of a zero day vulnerability, against

(I) an information system or network; or

(II) an operational technology system or process; or

(iii) unauthorized access or disruption of business or industrial operations due to loss of service facilitated through, or caused by, a compromise of a cloud service provider, managed service provider, or other third-party data hosting provider or by a supply chain compromise;

(B) consider--

(i) the sophistication or novelty of the tactics used to perpetrate such a cyber incident, as well as the type, volume, and sensitivity of the data at issue;

(ii) the number of individuals directly or indirectly affected or potentially affected by such a cyber incident; and

(iii) potential impacts on industrial control systems, such as supervisory control and data acquisition systems, distributed control systems, and programmable logic controllers; and

(C) exclude--

(i) any event where the cyber incident is perpetrated in good faith by an entity in response to a specific request by the owner or operator of the information system; and

(ii) the threat of disruption as extortion, as described in section 681(14)(A) of this title.

(3) A requirement that, if a covered cyber incident or a ransom payment occurs following an exempted threat described in paragraph (2)(C)(ii), the covered entity shall comply with the requirements in this part in reporting the covered cyber incident or ransom payment.

(4) A clear description of the specific required contents of a report pursuant to subsection (a)(1), which shall include the following information, to the extent applicable and available, with respect to a covered cyber incident:

(A) A description of the covered cyber incident, including--

(i) identification and a description of the function of the affected information systems, networks, or devices that were, or are reasonably believed to have been, affected by such cyber incident;

(ii) a description of the unauthorized access with substantial loss of confidentiality, integrity, or availability of the affected information system or network or disruption of business or industrial operations;

(iii) the estimated date range of such incident; and

(iv) the impact to the operations of the covered entity.

(B) Where applicable, a description of the vulnerabilities exploited and the security defenses that were in place, as well as the tactics, techniques, and procedures used to perpetrate the covered cyber incident.

(C) Where applicable, any identifying or contact information related to each actor reasonably believed to be responsible for such cyber incident.

(D) Where applicable, identification of the category or categories of information that were, or are reasonably believed to have been, accessed or acquired by an unauthorized person.

(E) The name and other information that clearly identifies the covered entity impacted by the covered cyber incident, including, as applicable, the State of incorporation or formation of the covered entity, trade names, legal names, or other identifiers.

(F) Contact information, such as telephone number or electronic mail address, that the Agency may use to contact the covered entity or an authorized agent of such covered entity, or, where applicable, the service provider of such covered entity acting with the express permission of, and at the direction of, the covered entity to assist with compliance with the requirements of this part.

(5) A clear description of the specific required contents of a report pursuant to subsection (a)(2), which shall be the following information, to the extent applicable and available, with respect to a ransom payment:

(A) A description of the ransomware attack, including the estimated date range of the attack.

(B) Where applicable, a description of the vulnerabilities, tactics, techniques, and procedures used to perpetrate the ransomware attack.

(C) Where applicable, any identifying or contact information related to the actor or actors reasonably believed to be responsible for the ransomware attack.

(D) The name and other information that clearly identifies the covered entity that made the ransom payment or on whose behalf the payment was made.

(E) Contact information, such as telephone number or electronic mail address, that the Agency may use to contact the covered entity that made the ransom payment or an authorized agent of such covered entity, or, where applicable, the service provider of such covered entity acting with the express permission of, and at the direction of, that covered entity to assist with compliance with the requirements of this part.

(F) The date of the ransom payment.

(G) The ransom payment demand, including the type of virtual currency or other commodity requested, if applicable.

(H) The ransom payment instructions, including information regarding where to send the payment, such as the virtual currency address or physical address the funds were requested to be sent to, if applicable.

(I) The amount of the ransom payment.

(6) A clear description of the types of data required to be preserved pursuant to subsection (a)(4), the period of time for which the data is required to be preserved, and allowable uses, processes, and procedures.

(7) Deadlines and criteria for submitting supplemental reports to the Agency required under subsection (a)(3), which shall--

(A) be established by the Director in consultation with the Council;

(B) consider any existing regulatory reporting requirements similar in scope, purpose, and timing to the reporting requirements to which such a covered entity may also be subject, and make efforts to harmonize the timing and contents of any such reports to the maximum extent practicable;

(C) balance the need for situational awareness with the ability of the covered entity to conduct cyber incident response and investigations; and

(D) provide a clear description of what constitutes substantial new or different information.

(8) Procedures for--

(A) entities, including third parties pursuant to subsection (d)(1), to submit reports required by paragraphs (1), (2), and (3) of subsection (a), including the manner and form thereof, which shall include, at a minimum, a concise, user-friendly web-based form;

(B) the Agency to carry out--

(i) the enforcement provisions of section 681d of this title, including with respect to the issuance, service, withdrawal, referral process, and enforcement of subpoenas, appeals and due process procedures;

(ii) other available enforcement mechanisms including acquisition, suspension and debarment procedures; and

(iii) other aspects of noncompliance;

(C) implementing the exceptions provided in subsection (a)(5); and

(D) protecting privacy and civil liberties consistent with processes adopted pursuant to section 1504(b) of this title and anonymizing and safeguarding, or no longer retaining, information received and disclosed through covered cyber incident reports and ransom payment reports that is known to be personal information of a specific individual or information that identifies a specific individual that is not directly related to a cybersecurity threat.

(9) Other procedural measures directly necessary to implement subsection (a).

(d) Third party report submission and ransom payment

(1) Report submission

A covered entity that is required to submit a covered cyber incident report or a ransom payment report may use a third party, such as an incident response company, insurance provider, service provider, Information Sharing and Analysis Organization, or law firm, to submit the required report under subsection (a).

(2) Ransom payment

If a covered entity impacted by a ransomware attack uses a third party to make a ransom payment, the third party shall not be required to submit a ransom payment report for itself under subsection (a)(2).

(3) Duty to report

Third-party reporting under this subparagraph does not relieve a covered entity from the duty to comply with the requirements for covered cyber incident report or ransom payment report submission.

(4) Responsibility to advise

Any third party used by a covered entity that knowingly makes a ransom payment on behalf of a covered entity impacted by a ransomware attack shall advise the impacted covered entity of the responsibilities of the impacted covered entity regarding reporting ransom payments under this section.

NOTES

Note 1

Section (g) of The Reporting Act of 2022 specifically states:

(g) Rule of construction[.] Nothing in this section shall affect the authorities of the Federal Government to implement the requirements of Executive Order 14028 (86 Fed. Reg. 26633; relating to improving the nation's cybersecurity), including changes to the Federal Acquisition Regulations and remedies to include suspension and debarment.

Do you think that the Executive Order discussed *supra* is redundant of The Reporting Act of 2022?

Note 2

Do you think that The Reporting Act of 2022 should include a broader exemption from liability concerning reported incidents? What type of incentives may a very broad exemption create?

Note 3

Section (e) of The Reporting Act of 2022 directs the agency to engage in "an outreach and education campaign to inform likely covered entities, entities that offer or advertise as a service to customers to make or facilitate ransom payments on behalf of covered entities impacted by ransomware attacks and other appropriate entities of the requirements of paragraphs (1), (2), and (3) of subsection (a)."

Note 4

Should The Reporting Act of 2022 require direct reporting of incidents to the FBI?[361] Why not?

Note 5

U.S. CISA has also created a vulnerability disclosure policy platform for federal civilian agencies and the cybersecurity community:

CISA has announced the establishment of its Vulnerability Disclosure Policy (VDP) Platform for the federal civilian enterprise, which will allow the Federal Civilian Executive Branch to coordinate with the civilian security research community in a streamlined fashion. The VDP Platform provides a single, centrally managed website that agencies can leverage as the primary point of entry for intaking, triaging, and routing vulnerabilities disclosed by researchers. It enables researchers and members of the general public to find vulnerabilities in agency websites and submit reports for analysis.

This new platform allows agencies to gain greater insights into potential vulnerabilities, which will improve their cybersecurity posture. This

---

[361] *See* Ines Kagubare, *DOJ Officials Criticize Senate-passed Cyber Bill*, THE HILL (March 3, 2022), available at https://thehill.com/policy/cybersecurity/596736-doj-officials-criticize-cyber-bill/.

approach also means agencies no longer need to develop separate systems to enable vulnerability reporting and triage of identified vulnerabilities, providing government-wide cost savings that CISA estimates at over $10 million.[362]

---

[362] *CISA Announces Vulnerability Disclosure Policy Platform*, CISA (July 30, 2021), available at https://www.cisa.gov/uscert/ncas/current-activity/2021/07/30/cisa-announces-vulnerability-disclosure-policy-vdp-platform.

CHAPTER EIGHT. STATE CYBERSECURITY LAWS

8.1 Introduction

As discussed in the preceding chapters, the United States does not have one overarching cybersecurity law but instead relies on a collection of privacy and cybersecurity laws that each cover a specific area. For example, the Health Insurance Portability and Accountability Act (HIPAA) focuses on an individual's protected health information and the medical industry. In contrast, the Gramm–Leach–Bliley Act (GLBA), also known as the Financial Services Modernization Act of 1999, focuses on the financial industry. The states have been able to promulgate cybersecurity and privacy laws where the federal government has left a void. There are basically two types of laws enacted in this space: 1) data breach notification laws; and 2) cybersecurity laws concerning standards for the security of data, networks and computers. This Chapter will review some select data breach notification and more specific cybersecurity laws promulgated by the states.

8.2 State Breach Notification Laws

All 50 states, with California being the first, have adopted privacy data breach notification laws that mandate the timing and content of the data breach notification to those who may have been affected by the data breach. Many states have followed the California model for data breach notification. Normally, a data breach notification will be sent to customers in all 50 states plus the US territories. For the most part, the data breach notification contains an explanation of what happened, unless the state mandates that information not be revealed due to an ongoing investigation. The data breach notification will also likely contain an outsourced call-center number where the customer can receive more information, and identity theft programs that the company may be offering. The law also normally mandates whether and how soon the state Attorney General should be notified and how soon the data breach notification should be mailed after the discovery of the data breach. The law may also have a threshold number of customers to require notification. The majority of the states' data breach notification laws are similar, so it becomes a matter of knowing the states that are not similar to make sure notification violations do not occur. Also note that in some states, encryption of the breached data may negate the need for breach notification.

8.2[A] Selected State Data Breach Notification Laws

The following are excerpts of some state data breach notification laws. Specifically, the laws of Maryland and Massachusetts are below. In reviewing both sets of laws, please note the similarities and differences between the two pieces of legislation.

Maryland requires the following:

MD Code, State Government, §10–1305.

(a) (1) In this section, "breach of the security of a system" means the unauthorized acquisition of computerized data that compromises the security, confidentiality, or integrity of the personal information maintained by a unit.

(2) "Breach of the security of a system" does not include the good faith acquisition of personal information by an employee or agent of a unit for the purposes of the unit, provided that the personal information is not used or subject to further unauthorized disclosure.

(b) (1) If a unit that collects computerized data that includes personal information of an individual discovers or is notified of a breach of the security of a system, the unit shall conduct in good faith a reasonable and prompt investigation to determine whether the unauthorized acquisition of personal information of the individual has resulted in or is likely to result in the misuse of the information.

(2) (i) Except as provided in subparagraph (ii) of this paragraph, if after the investigation is concluded, the unit determines that the misuse of the individual's personal information has occurred or is likely to occur, the unit or the nonaffiliated third party, if authorized under a written contract or agreement with the unit, shall notify the individual of the breach.

(ii) Unless the unit or nonaffiliated third party knows that the encryption key has been broken, a unit or the nonaffiliated third party is not required to notify an individual under subparagraph (i) of this paragraph if:

1. the personal information of the individual was secured by encryption or redacted; and

2. the encryption key has not been compromised or disclosed.

(3) Except as provided in subsection (d) of this section, the notification required under paragraph (2) of this subsection shall be given as soon as reasonably practicable after the unit conducts the investigation required under paragraph (1) of this subsection.

(4) If, after the investigation required under paragraph (1) of this subsection is concluded, the unit determines that notification under paragraph (2) of this subsection is not required, the unit shall maintain records that reflect its determination for 3

years after the determination is made.

(c)   (1)   A nonaffiliated third party that maintains computerized data that includes personal information provided by a unit shall notify the unit of a breach of the security of a system if the unauthorized acquisition of the individual's personal information has occurred or is likely to occur.

(2)   Except as provided in subsection (d) of this section, the notification required under paragraph (1) of this subsection shall be given as soon as reasonably practicable after the nonaffiliated third party discovers or is notified of the breach of the security of a system.

(3)   A nonaffiliated third party that is required to notify a unit of a breach of the security of a system under paragraph (1) of this subsection shall share with the unit information relating to the breach.

(d)   (1)   The notification required under subsection (b) of this section may be delayed:

(i)   if a law enforcement agency determines that the notification will impede a criminal investigation or jeopardize homeland or national security; or

(ii)   to determine the scope of the breach of the security of a system, identify the individuals affected, or restore the integrity of the system.

(2)   If notification is delayed under paragraph (1)(i) of this subsection, notification shall be given as soon as reasonably practicable after the law enforcement agency determines that the notification will not impede a criminal investigation and will not jeopardize homeland or national security.

(e)   The notification required under subsection (b) of this section may be given:

(1)   by written notice sent to the most recent address of the individual in the records of the unit;

(2)   by electronic mail to the most recent electronic mail address of the individual in the records of the unit if:

(i)   the individual has expressly consented to receive electronic notice; or

(ii)   the unit conducts its duties primarily through Internet account transactions or the Internet;

(3)   by telephonic notice, to the most recent telephone number of the individual in the records of the unit; or

(4)   by substitute notice as provided in subsection (f) of this section if:

(i)   the unit demonstrates that the cost of providing notice would exceed $100,000 or that the affected class of individuals to be notified exceeds 175,000; or

(ii)   the unit does not have sufficient contact information to give notice in accordance with item (1), (2), or (3) of this subsection.

(f)   Substitute notice under subsection (e)(4) of this section shall consist of:

(1)   electronically mailing the notice to an individual entitled to notification under subsection (b) of this section if the unit has an electronic mail address for the individual to be notified;

(2)   conspicuous posting of the notice on the Web site of the unit if the unit maintains a Web site; and

(3)   notification to appropriate media.

(g)   The notification required under subsection (b) of this section shall include:

(1)   to the extent possible, a description of the categories of information that were, or are reasonably believed to have been, acquired by an unauthorized person, including which of the elements of personal information were, or are reasonably believed to have been, acquired;

(2)   contact information for the unit making the notification, including the unit's address, telephone number, and toll–free telephone number if one is maintained;

(3)   the toll–free telephone numbers and addresses for the major consumer reporting agencies; and

(4)   (i)   the toll–free telephone numbers, addresses, and Web site addresses for:

1.   the Federal Trade Commission; and

2.   the Office of the Attorney General; and

(ii)   a statement that an individual can obtain information from these sources about steps the individual can take to avoid identity theft.

(h)   (1)   Before giving the notification required under subsection (b) of this section, a unit shall provide notice of a breach of the security of a system to the Office of the Attorney General.

(2)   In addition to the notice required under paragraph (1) of this subsection, a unit, as defined in § 10–1301(f)(1) of this subtitle, shall provide notice of a breach of security to the Department of Information Technology.

(i)   A waiver of any provision of this section is contrary to public policy and is void and unenforceable.

(j)   Compliance with this section does not relieve a unit from a duty to comply with any other requirements of federal law relating to the protection and privacy of personal information.[363]

For comparison, Massachusetts notification requires the following:

Section 3: Duty to report known security breach or unauthorized use of personal information

Section 3. (a) A person or agency that maintains or stores, but does not own or license data that includes personal information about a resident of the commonwealth, shall provide notice, as soon as practicable and without unreasonable delay, when such person or agency (1) knows or has reason to know of a breach of security or (2) when the person or agency knows or has reason to know that the personal information of such resident was acquired or used by an unauthorized person or used for an unauthorized purpose, to the owner or licensor in accordance with this chapter. In addition to providing notice as provided herein, such person or agency shall cooperate with the owner or licensor of such information. Such cooperation shall include, but not be limited to, informing the owner or licensor of the breach of security or unauthorized acquisition or use, the date or approximate date of such incident and the nature thereof, and any steps the person or agency has taken or plans to take relating to the incident, except that such cooperation shall not be deemed to require the disclosure of confidential business information or trade secrets, or to provide notice to a resident that may have been affected by the breach of security or unauthorized acquisition or use.

(b) A person or agency that owns or licenses data that includes personal information about a resident of the commonwealth, shall provide notice, as soon as practicable and without unreasonable delay, when such person or agency (1) knows or has reason to know of a breach of security or (2) when the person or agency knows or has reason to know that the personal information of such resident was acquired or used by an unauthorized person or used for an unauthorized purpose, to the attorney general, the director of consumer affairs and business regulation and to such resident, in accordance with this chapter. The notice to be provided to the attorney general and said director, and consumer reporting agencies or state agencies if any, shall include, but not be limited to: (i) the nature of the breach of security or unauthorized acquisition or use; (ii) the number of residents of the commonwealth affected by such incident at the time of notification; (iii) the name and address of the person or agency that experienced the breach of security; (iv) name and title of the person or agency reporting the breach of security, and their relationship to the person or agency that experienced the breach of security; (v) the type of person or agency reporting the breach of security; (vi) the person responsible for the breach of security, if known; (vii) the type of personal information compromised, including, but not limited to, social security number, driver's license number, financial account number, credit or debit card number or other data; (viii) whether the person or agency maintains a written information security program; and

---

[363] MD. CODE ANN., STATE GOV'T §10-1305 (West 2014).

(ix) any steps the person or agency has taken or plans to take relating to the incident, including updating the written information security program. A person who experienced a breach of security shall file a report with the attorney general and the director of consumer affairs and business regulation certifying their credit monitoring services comply with section 3A.

Upon receipt of this notice, the director of consumer affairs and business regulation shall identify any relevant consumer reporting agency or state agency, as deemed appropriate by said director, and forward the names of the identified consumer reporting agencies and state agencies to the notifying person or agency. Such person or agency shall, as soon as practicable and without unreasonable delay, also provide notice, in accordance with this chapter, to the consumer reporting agencies and state agencies identified by the director of consumer affairs and business regulation.

The notice to be provided to the resident shall include, but shall not be limited to: (i) the resident's right to obtain a police report; (ii) how a resident may request a security freeze and the necessary information to be provided when requesting the security freeze; (iii) that there shall be no charge for a security freeze; and (iv) mitigation services to be provided pursuant to this chapter; provided, however, that said notice shall not include the nature of the breach of security or unauthorized acquisition or use, or the number of residents of the commonwealth affected by said breach of security or unauthorized access or use. The person or agency that experienced the breach of security shall provide a sample copy of the notice it sent to consumers to the attorney general and the office of consumer affairs and business regulation. A notice provided pursuant to this section shall not be delayed on grounds that the total number of residents affected is not yet ascertained. In such case, and where otherwise necessary to update or correct the information required, a person or agency shall provide additional notice as soon as practicable and without unreasonable delay upon learning such additional information.

(c) As practicable and as not to impede active investigation by the attorney general or other law enforcement agency, the office of consumer affairs and business regulation shall: (i) make available electronic copies of the sample notice sent to consumers on its website and post such notice within 1 business day upon receipt from the person that experienced a breach of security; (ii) update the breach of security notification report on its website as soon as practically possible after the information has been verified by said office but not more than 10 business days after receipt unless the information provided is not verifiable; provided, however, that the office shall post said notice as soon as verified; (iii) amend, on a recurring basis, the breach of security notification report to include new information discovered through the investigation process or new subsequent findings from a previously reported breach of security; and (iv) instruct consumers on how they may file a public records request to obtain a copy of the notice provided to the attorney general and said director from the person who experienced a breach of security.

(d) If the person or agency that experienced a breach of security is owned by another person or corporation, the notice to the consumer shall include the name of the parent or affiliated corporation.

(e) If an agency is within the executive department, it shall provide written notification of the nature and circumstances of the breach of security or unauthorized acquisition or use to the executive office of technology services and security and the division of public records in the office of the state secretary as soon as practicable and without unreasonable delay following the discovery of a breach of security or unauthorized acquisition or use, and shall comply with all policies and procedures adopted by the executive office of technology services and security pertaining to the reporting and investigation of such an incident.

(f) The department of consumer affairs and business regulation may promulgate regulations interpreting and applying this section.[364]

8.2[B] NATIONAL CONFERENCE OF STATE LEGISLATURES ON SECURITY BREACH NOTIFICATION LAWS

The National Conference of State Legislatures maintains a database of state privacy laws, which includes breach notification. As states are constantly modifying their privacy laws, the following table is a good starting point for an attorney to keep track of current breach notification laws. Notably, there are 50 states with security breach notification laws. Moreover, Puerto Rico, the Virgin Islands, District of Columbia and Guam have security breach notification laws. The database of state privacy laws includes the state name along with the citation and link to the relevant law. The following is an excerpt of the database with some states removed.

Security Breach Notification Laws[365]

7/17/2020 . . .

State	Citation
California	Cal. Civ. Code §§ 1798.29, 1798.82
Florida	Fla. Stat. §§ 501.171, 282.0041, 282.318(2)(i)
Illinois	815 ILCS §§ 530/1 to 530/25, 815 ILCS 530/55 (2020 S.B. 1624)

---

[364] MASS. GEN. LAWS ch. 93H, §3 (2019).
[365] *Security Breach Notification Laws*, NAT'L CONF. OF STATE LEG., https://www.ncsl.org/research/telecommunications-and-information-technology/security-breach-notification-laws.aspx (last updated July 17, 2020).

State	Citation
New York	N.Y. Gen. Bus. Law § 899-AA
Texas	Tex. Bus. & Com. Code §§ 521.002, 521.053
Washington	Wash. Rev. Code §§ 19.255.010, 42.56.590

8.2[C] An Analysis of Data Breach Laws Across the 50 States

Cybersecurity expert Carol M. Hayes provides an analysis of the data breach laws across the 50 states and a model law concerning data breach. The following material is an excerpt of her article.

Carol M. Hayes, Comparative Analysis of Data Breach Laws: Comprehension, Interpretation, and External Sources of Legislative Text, 23 Lewis & Clark L. Rev. 1221 (2020).[366]

B. Step 0: Why?

Analysis of statutory trends must consider the purpose of the law. Punitive laws can either have a victim-centered purpose or a perpetrator-centered purpose. In the case of data breach laws, legislatures overwhelmingly focus on the commerce or consumer protection implications. Data breach notification laws are thus generally imbued with a victim-centered purpose. Previous work on this topic has examined the nature of the injury caused by a data breach. Recent scholarship has argued that data insecurity causes anxiety on the part of victims whose sensitive information has been compromised. Laws governing data breaches should thus emphasize the implications for victims who for our purposes will generally be referred to as "data subjects."

Data breach laws are often couched in terms of preventing identity theft. But what is the social value that we protect with identity theft laws? Is the emphasis on protecting the individual or punishing the wrongdoer? Identity theft laws are often inconsistent on this point. The general wisdom is that identity theft laws are victim-centered, and many identity theft laws address specific remedies available to identity theft victims, like identity theft passports. On the other hand, a review of state identity theft laws finds that eighteen states include pretending to be a dead person as identity theft, in which case the motivation to protect the victim is weaker. More significantly, at least five states recognize the crime of identity theft when the "stolen" identity is fictitious, and eleven states recognize the crime of identity theft when the stolen identity

---

[366] This article was originally published in the Lewis and Clark Law Review.

is used to obtain employment. In those two situations, a victim-centered analysis falls apart because the injury is ambiguous at best. Including the use of a stolen identity to obtain employment is most likely a reference to undocumented laborers, and pretending to be a fake person only potentially harms the person being deceived.

Statutory organization is an element of statutory interpretation that is often ignored, but it can be informative in discerning the underlying purpose. Data breach laws are most often situated either in a consumer protection or trade regulation code section. This indicates that data breaches are seen as an economic issue in these states. On the other hand, four states placed their data breach notification laws within a statutory section on crime, and four states placed data breach provisions in code sections about network security or privacy. These placements suggest a focus on the data subject as something other than an economic actor. Of course, placement does not always signal content. Arizona examines data breaches under the same statutory chapter as other network security issues and has an entire title of its state code dedicated to information technology. Yet in spite of this contextual focus on information technology, Arizona's data breach law does not require covered entities to adopt reasonable security measures.

C. Step 1: Prevention

A federal or model data breach law needs to address preventative measures in addition to notification requirements. Encryption is a bare minimum practice that almost all states include in their data breach laws. Wyoming is the singular exception, as the language of the Wyoming statute only refers to redaction of personal information, not encryption.

Most often, encryption is addressed in the context of when a notification is *not* required, but it is discussed in this Section because encryption is a basic preventative measure. The data breach law in the District of Columbia does not require notification if the data was "rendered secure," which can fairly be read as including encryption. Twenty-seven states require notification when encrypted information is affected if the means of decrypting the data was also included in the breach.

State data breach laws that address prevention may also do so by requiring reasonable security practices, as 16 states do, or by addressing the disposal of records, as is the case in 23 states. Records disposal can be and often is addressed elsewhere in a state's code, but for this study, only records disposal provisions that were in the textual proximity of data breach laws were counted. Nevada is one of the states that requires some reasonable security practices, but Nevada also goes further by exempting entities from data breach liability if they comply with the security requirements and if the breach incident was not caused by gross negligence.

Of the 16 states that require the adoption of reasonable security practices, eight states also require covered entities to ensure that the third parties they send data to have reasonable security measures. Oregon does not address data transfers broadly, but requires "service providers" that work with the covered entity to be subject to contract terms requiring safeguards and practices to protect personal information.

Massachusetts and Oregon have the most detailed security requirements among state data breach laws. Of the two, Massachusetts is more detailed about technology, and Oregon is more detailed about administrative protocol. Massachusetts requires secure authentication protocols, secure access control measures, encryption, ongoing monitoring of systems that contain personal information, firewalls to protect systems that contain personal information, up-to-date antivirus software, and employee education on the security of personal information. Oregon requires three categories of protection: administrative safeguards, technical safeguards, and physical safeguards. Administrative safeguards include employee training, regular review of user access privileges, and risk management practices. Technical safeguards include security updates, regular tests of the effectiveness of security, and requirements to monitor, detect, prevent, and respond to cyberattacks and system failures. Physical safeguards include relevant risk assessment, monitoring, and safeguards for the disposal of records.

D. Step 2: The Breach

Data breach statutes are activated by security events. In analyzing statutory language, attention was paid to how the statutes defined a breach of security. A majority of statutes, 28 of 51, defined a breach as an incident that "compromises the security, confidentiality, or integrity" (SCI) of protected information. Seven states require that the incident "materially" compromise the SCI of protected information. Eight states omit data integrity as a factor. In two of those eight, the incident must materially compromise the security or confidentiality of protected information. Eight other states do not include SCI language in their definition of a breach of security.

A wide majority, 50 of 51, tie breaches to the unauthorized acquisition of protected data. Sixteen states tie breaches to the unauthorized access to protected data. Of those 16, New Jersey is the only one that does not also connect breaches to unauthorized acquisition. Maine and North Carolina include the unauthorized release of information in their breach definitions, and unauthorized use is part of the breach definition in both Maine and Massachusetts. Alabama, New York, and Vermont include some guidelines for determining whether protected information has been subjected to unauthorized acquisition.

Data breach laws are almost always focused on the breach of personal information that could facilitate identity theft. The standard formula is the last name and first initial plus a social security number, driver's license number, or financial account information and the means to access that account, such as a password or PIN. Biometric data is included in the definition of personal information in a minority of states, including Arizona, Colorado, and Illinois. In Connecticut, biometric data is listed as a protected type of "confidential information" in Section 4e-70, which pertains to state contractors who receive confidential information, but *not* as a type of "personal information" under Section 36a-701b, which is the state's primary data breach law. Delaware and Wisconsin include not just biometric indicators, but also an individual's DNA profile as an example of personal information.

Data breach laws often focus on "personal information," though some use the term "personal identifying information." Michigan's law defines the two terms separately and uses "personal identifying information" in the provisions about the commission of identity theft crimes. The more narrowly defined "personal information" appears in the data breach notification law and is defined by the standard formula presented above: name, social security number, driver's license number, and financial account information. Michigan's definition of "personally identifiable information" includes additional elements, including mother's maiden name, passport number, and biometric data. Thus in Michigan, biometric data is relevant for the crime of identity theft, but not for the data breach notification law.

Data breach laws also include exceptions. Two prominent exceptions that almost always appear are the good faith employee exception and the public records exception. The good faith employee exception typically appears in the statute's definition of a breach and says that it does not count as a breach if a good faith employee acquired the personal information and there was no subsequent misuse of the information. Forty-seven states and the District of Columbia include this exception. Oregon uses a less permissive form of this exception, only excluding the inadvertent acquisition by employees, not good faith acquisition.

The public records exception typically appears in the definition of personal information and says that information from public records does not count as personal information for the purpose of the data breach law. This exception is worded to apply to government records. Public records generally include information "lawfully made available to the general public from federal, state, or local government records." Twenty-two states also consider sources other than government records to be part of the public records exception. References to "widely distributed media" are common in the "government records plus" version of the public records exception.

E. Step 3: The Notification

Data breach laws often contain a variety of notification provisions. For simplicity, this Article categorizes some of the major notification requirements as who, what, when, and how.

Who	Who must be notified?	Does the breach law also apply to government agencies and third parties?
What	What information must the notice include?	What type of injury is sufficient to require notice?
When	When must the notification be made?	When may notification be delayed?
How	How may the entity provide notice?	How does the data breach law interact with other laws?

Table 1. Major notification provisions

1. Who?

Consider the first question: who must be notified? There are three main recipients of data breach notifications: the consumer, the state Attorney General, and credit reporting agencies. State data breach laws always address notification to the data subject, as this is part of the laws' fundamental purpose. Thirty-two states require that notification also be submitted to the AG's office or other government agency. While most states allow the AG notification to be made at the same time as the notice to consumers, Maryland and New Jersey both require the AG to be notified before the consumers are notified. Additionally, 36 states require credit reporting agencies to be notified, though the notice sent to the agencies may sometimes be required to omit specific information.

The second question asks: who is bound by the requirements? The party most likely to be subject to the requirements is the data owner. Most of the data breach laws in the United States require third parties who maintain data owned by someone else to notify the data owner in the event of a breach, and then it will be the responsibility of the data owner to follow the notification requirements. Data owners are thus generally responsible for notifications, even if the data owner entered into an agreement with a third party to process or store some of its data.

In a minority of states, the data breach law appears to not apply to breaches of government systems. New Mexico is the only state that explicitly states that the data breach provisions do not apply to government agencies. Most of the other laws in this category instead use language referencing business and exclude government agencies by implication. In Connecticut, there is a data breach law that applies to state contractors, and the primary data breach law applies only to persons doing business in the state, so breaches at the state agencies themselves seem to not be subject to either set of requirements. Some states that subject government agencies to the same notification requirements do so in a separate section specifically about government data breaches.

2. What?

The first major "what" question: what must the notice include? Twenty-five states address this question. Wisconsin does not list what must be included, but does say that a person who receives a notification of a data breach can submit a written request to learn what personal information was acquired. This makes it clear that Wisconsin law does not require the notification to include details about the personal information acquired. Still, Wisconsin residents are likely to receive that information as part of a notification from an out of state business, because most states with content requirements do require information about the type of personal information acquired. New Mexico, for example, specifically requires information about what personal information was affected. California's law also requires such information, and goes further than other data breach laws by providing a model notice in the statutory text.

The second major "what" question concerns the injury caused by the breach. Commonly, a data breach law's notification requirements will not trigger in the absence of a certain type of risk or injury. The data breach laws of nine states are written broadly enough that the notification requirement appears to be triggered by the mere inclusion of personal information in a breach, but most states require something more. In 13 states, the data holder must notify when the compromised information has or could result in identity theft or similar fraud affecting the data subject. Some states use broader language. Eighteen breach notification laws are triggered when the breach creates a risk of harm for the data subject. Most of the states that focus on harm look for a reasonable risk of harm. The requirement in Alabama, though, is triggered by a substantial risk of harm, and the requirement in South Carolina is triggered by a material risk of harm. Michigan requires a risk of substantial loss or injury and also provides guidance for determining if this threshold is met. Notification requirements in Arizona and Iowa are triggered based on the likelihood of financial harm specifically. In Wyoming, a breach is defined as including an unauthorized data acquisition that "causes or is reasonably believed to cause loss or injury" to a state resident. Fourteen states focus on the risk of misuse of the information rather than harm or identity theft. Maine requires an investigation to consider the likelihood of misuse, but does not explicitly tie the concept of misuse to the notice requirement.

These two questions illustrate the potential for conflict between state laws based on linguistic choices. Only 11 states require data owners to document instances where they determined that a notification was not required. Wyoming's requirements seem to not be tied to risk or likelihood but to a reasonable belief that a loss or injury was caused. Data owners that do business in multiple states have many considerations. If they are concerned about the public relations implications from announcing a data breach, they may look to minimize the number of notifications sent out. It may not be in society's best interest if data owners only report breaches to the minimum extent required by law, and only 11 states require data owners to document cases where there was a breach, an investigation, and a conclusion that a notification was not required.

A third "what" question concerns the format of the information. In most of the analyzed data breach laws, the definition of a breach is limited to electronic files. The language of the laws in 30 states refers only to electronic files. Some of the other laws explicitly apply data breach language to other formats, while others treat personal information differently depending on whether it is implicated by the data breach requirements or the sections governing records disposal. This is a substantive issue that must be addressed in any federal data breach legislation or model law.

3. When?

A failure to notify data subjects of a breach in a timely manner is generally considered to be a violation of a data breach law. Thirty-two of the data breach laws analyzed for this Article do not provide a specific timeframe, instead requiring the notice to be made without unreasonable delay. Texas requires notifications to be sent "as quickly as possible," while New Hampshire uses the language "as soon as possible." The unreasonable delay language is preferable to the latter two, because it allows for reasonableness considerations to be a factor in enforcement.

The focus on unreasonable delays implies that there could be a reasonable delay. Forty-two of the analyzed laws include language suggesting that a reasonable delay would include time to recover from the breach. This is commonly phrased to include time to determine the scope of the breach and time to restore system integrity. All of the analyzed data breach laws included explicit language allowing for delays due to a law enforcement investigation related to the breach.

The "notification clock" for data breaches often starts running at the discovery of the breach. As noted above, 34 data breach laws use flexible language for notification deadlines, most commonly "without unreasonable delay." The other 16 are divided across 30 days, 45 days, 60 days, and 90 days. As the Figure 2 shows, 45 days is the most common deadline. . . .

There are some states that require the data owner to investigate the data breach, and subsequent deadlines may be based on the date that investigation is completed. Maryland, for example, requires a "reasonable and prompt investigation." The notification clock in Maryland starts upon completion of this investigation. Maryland is one of the states that does not use "without unreasonable delay" language, instead requiring that notices be sent within 45 days. Some states reference investigations by the data owner without creating a formal requirement.

4. How?

Data breach laws typically spend considerable space describing appropriate processes for notification. The type of notice permitted varies somewhat across different statutes. Primary means of notice generally include written notice, telephonic notice, and electronic notice that complies with the standards for electronic signatures and electronic records in 15 U.S.C. § 7001.267

Substitute notice methods generally become available when the cost of notifying affected individuals exceeds a threshold amount, when the number of individuals to be notified exceeds a threshold number, or when the data owner lacks sufficient contact information to provide notice. The dollar amounts that make a notification eligible for substitute notice range from $5,000 to $500,000. The requirement for affected individuals ranges from 1,000 to 500,000, and some statutory language is ambiguous about whether that requirement is just for state residents or if the count of individuals to be notified includes all states. While the thresholds for substitute notice may not make a huge difference in the application of the laws, these broad ranges suggest that legislatures likely have different priorities when it comes to data breach notifications. Wyoming's law includes an explicit carve-out that lowers the substitute notice thresholds for Wyoming-based businesses. This can either be interpreted as a recognition that in-state businesses are generally smaller businesses and need to have less burdensome options available for legal notice, or it might be a little bit of protectionism to favor Wyoming-based businesses over others since substitute notice is likely to be cheaper.

Substitute notice must generally include notice via email if the email address is known, conspicuous posting on the data owner's website, and notification to major statewide media. Florida is one of a few states where sending the notification to an email address, without reference to Section 7001, is considered a form of direct notice.

Data owners would benefit from a consistent set of requirements. Thirty-nine of the data breach laws analyzed include language allowing data owners to use their own notification procedures if they are otherwise compliant. Consider a business that currently operates in a state that permits data owners to follow their own otherwise compliant procedures, like South Carolina. The neighboring state of North Carolina does not include this language in its data breach law. If a business wants to expand to North Carolina, it may have to evaluate and adjust its data breach practices. An important benefit of a federal data breach law is that it would standardize the process. . . .

Data breach laws also differ in how they address interactions with other laws. There are four major sources of law that data breach laws might address: consumer protection law, contract law, local law, and federal law. Twenty-four of the analyzed data breach statutes say that a violation of the data breach law is an unfair or deceptive act or an unlawful trade practice under state law. Texas also references its deceptive trade practice law, but only for a violation of the prohibition on unauthorized possession or use of personal information. Seventeen data breach laws emphasize that the requirements of the data breach law cannot be waived by contract, and seven data breach laws explicitly state that the data breach law preempts local ordinances.

Data breach laws vary on which federal laws or guidelines they address by name, but two common players are the Gramm-Leach-Bliley Act (GLBA) and the Health Insurance Portability and Accountability Act (HIPAA). The GLBA addresses data privacy issues affecting financial institutions and HIPAA concerns medical information.

Interaction with federal law and privacy standards gets a little linguistically sticky. Thirty-four data breach laws indicate that if the data owner is regulated by the specified laws, compliance with those laws counts as compliance with the data breach law. In six data breach laws, the language indicates that entities are exempt from application of the law if they are regulated by and comply with other specified laws.

Twelve data breach laws use broader language that seemingly allows for an exemption from the data breach law just for being regulated by specified laws or entities. Three of those, though, limit the exemption to the requirement to notify a credit report agency (CRA) about the breach. The data breach laws of New Hampshire, West Virginia, and the District of Columbia say that the CRA notification requirement does not apply to entities regulated by Title V of the GLBA, which also addresses CRA notifications. Similarly, California's exemption only applies to the provisions about data security. These exemptions apply to entities regulated by California's Confidentiality of Medical Information Act, California's Financial Information Privacy Act, and HIPAA. Outside of data security requirements, other references within California's law follow the more common "compliance there is compliance here" model.

Arkansas's law seems to provide a broad exemption, but it also includes conflicting language. In Section 4-110-106(a)(1), the law states:

The provisions of this chapter do not apply to a person or business that is regulated by a state or federal law that provides greater protection to personal information and at least as thorough disclosure requirements for breaches of the security of personal information than that provided by this chapter.

But then immediately following this broad "do not apply" language, the law immediately goes on in (a)(2): "Compliance with the state or federal law shall be deemed compliance with this chapter with regard to the subjects covered by this chapter." This distinction between exemption and compliance creates ambiguity.

There are some other regulatory interactions considered in a minority of states. In Nevada and Washington, compliance with the Payment Card Industry Data Security Standards (PCI DSS) can mitigate some of a data owner's liability. In both Maryland and Massachusetts, the data breach laws note that compliance is not transitive--that is, while compliance with another law might count as compliance with the data breach law, compliance with the data breach law does not count as compliance with the other law.

F. Step 4: Enforcement and Follow-Up

Enforcement of data breach laws varies widely. The previous Section noted that a lot of data breach laws reference state unfair trade practice laws in the context of enforcement. This simplifies matters for the state, because if a failure to notify is an unfair trade practice, no new legal process is needed because it fits into existing law. Again, though, this creates a variety of enforcement standards. Relying on unfair trade practice regulations to swallow data breach violations may also be inadvisable at a federal level because of resources. If a new breach law calls a notification violation an unfair trade practice, this indicates that much of the enforcement would be by the Federal Trade Commission (FTC), an agency that is increasingly being given responsibility for emerging data protection issues. Instead, perhaps a new office should be created to address data privacy and information technology regulatory issues.

In the analyzed data breach laws, the Attorneys General are often central players in enforcement, whether through authority over unfair trade practices or other sources of authority. Thirty-eight states and the District of Columbia assign the responsibilities of enforcement to the Attorney General. Oregon takes a slightly different approach by giving authority directly to the Director of the Department of Consumer and Business Services. Some of these provisions explicitly say that actions by the Attorney General are the exclusive method of enforcement. Some of the laws state that no private action is created, while others emphasize that no private action is lost.

Data breach laws also frequently address whether individuals affected by a data breach can recover from the data owner. Ten data breach laws establish a private cause of action, while other states make explicit that the data breach law does not create a private cause of action in at least some contexts. Nevada is one of the states whose data breach law does not create a private cause of action. However, Nevada does create a private cause of action for "data collectors" to recover notification costs from a party that obtained or benefited from the breached personal information. This means that a cause of action is created for the party whose systems are breached, but not the data subject, raising the question of who should be seen as the "victim" of a data breach. The language of Wisconsin's law denies the creation of a new civil action, but says that violation of the notification provisions can be used as "evidence of negligence or a breach of a legal duty."

Twenty-seven data breach laws address civil penalties. In Louisiana's administrative code, the civil penalty for a violation of the notification provisions is $5,000. Georgia mentions civil penalties, but the penalty appears to apply only to violations of the credit freeze provisions, so this may be superseded by recent changes to federal law. Similarly, Massachusetts includes civil penalties, but only for violations of the records disposal law. Washington State's data breach law does not address civil penalties, but it does highlight costs that the owner of the breached system may be required to pay. In Washington, data processors that did not "take reasonable care to guard against unauthorized access" can also be required to reimburse financial institutions for the cost of reissuing credit and debit cards to affected data subjects.

Advocates for a federal data breach law sometimes suggest including a requirement for a breached data owner to provide free credit monitoring. Such a policy is not yet widely adopted in the states. Connecticut is the only state that unambiguously requires free credit monitoring. Delaware requires free credit monitoring to be offered, but only if social security numbers were compromised. California's data breach law includes language requiring a minimum length of time when credit monitoring is offered, but there is an ambiguous "if any" in the middle of the provision: "If the person or business providing the notification was the source of the breach, an offer to provide appropriate identity theft prevention and mitigation services, if any, shall be provided at no cost to the affected person for not less than 12 months."

In Oregon, if a data owner offers credit monitoring services, the offer cannot be conditioned on the consumer providing a credit card number. Additionally, Oregon law requires that any related paid services must be addressed separately from the free credit monitoring. Montana's data breach law warns data owners that if they are going to tell data subjects about the breach and also inform the data subjects that they can contact CRAs, the data owners should let the CRAs know in advance.

A few state data breach laws address general data practices as well. Nevada's data breach law includes language requiring transparency in online data collection. Georgia, Maine, and Vermont also address the role of data brokers. Companies that aggregate data play a prominent role in electronic commerce, and the inclusion of data brokers in a data breach law indicates an awareness of these dynamics and the potential threats to personal information. Colorado and Illinois both have data breach laws that prohibit data owners from passing off the cost of notification to the data subjects of the breach.

G. Model Data Breach Laws

As noted elsewhere, the Uniform Law Commission is a major source for model legislation language. ULC formed a Data Breach Notification Committee (DBNC) in 2017, and at the July 2018 Annual Meeting of the Committee on Scope and Program, the DBNC recommended that a model data breach law be drafted. The Committee on Scope and Program did not approve the request, instead asking the DNBC to provide more information at the Committee's next midyear meeting in January 2019. In July 2019, the ULC authorized the creation of a drafting committee to focus on the collection and use of personally identifiable information. ULC has thus shown interest in a uniform data breach law, but has not finalized a proposal. The American Law Institute (ALI) similarly has a current project examining data privacy, which has a tentative draft available. The tentative draft was approved by ALI in 2019. It is unclear the extent to which data breach laws and model language will be addressed in the final version of this text.

SAMPLE PROVISION	ENACTED	SAMPLE PROVISION	ENACTED
Acquisition over time by the same entity counts as one breach	1	Approves of delays necessary to determine the scope of the breach and restore reasonable data integrity	43
This law preempts local ordinances on data breaches	7	Addresses interactions with other privacy laws that address breaches	45
Breach definition only covers threats to security and confidentiality, not integrity	8	Addresses electronic files only	46
Notification required when the stolen information has or could result in identity theft or fraud affecting information subject	13	Information in public records doesn't count as PII or accessing public records isn't a breach	48
Unauthorized access	16	Data breach law also applies to government agencies	48
Publicly available information, defined more broadly than public records	23	Good faith acquisitions by employees are not breaches	49

Violating statute's requirements is an unfair or deceptive act or unlawful trade practice	25	Unauthorized acquisition of data or PII	50
If the breach included the encryption key, you must disclose	27	Personal information is name PLUS something else	50
Civil penalties addressed in data breach law	29	Third party agents of covered entity experience a breach of data belonging to covered entity	50
Redaction and truncation	33	Financial account info PLUS means to access the account if needed (PIN, password, etc)	51
Entities regulated by other specified laws are deemed compliant with these requirements if they're compliant with their applicable laws	34	Encryption (e.g., PII definition excludes encrypted information, or notification is only required if the data was not encrypted)	51
Notification window starts at discovery of breach	37	Provision for delaying notice	51
You can use your own notification procedures if you're otherwise compliant	38	Law enforcement reasons to delay notification	51
AG can enforce data breach law	40	How to give notice	51

Instead, this Article analyzes the model language provided by another outside drafter, ALEC. The ALEC proposal was first posted in 2006 and was most recently updated in 2012. ALEC's model data breach law includes 28 of the traits that were coded for in the larger study of data breach laws. The following table lists these traits alongside how many enacted data breach statutes include similar or equivalent language.

Table 2. Commonality of provisions in enacted legislation

As the table shows, most of the statutory traits noted in the ALEC model appear in a majority of enacted statutes. Many of these traits are described at high levels of generality. Readers are cautioned to avoid making assumptions about the influence of the model law based on these numbers, as it creates a chicken and egg problem. The current research identified 121 individual traits in data breach legislation, and ALEC's proposal contained only 28 of the "hard-coded" traits. ALEC's model also sides with eight states that omit risks to data integrity from the definition of a data breach, and 34 states that require notifications to be made without unreasonable delay. The ALEC model also joins five states and the District of Columbia by making substitute notice available when the cost of notification would exceed $50,000 or there are over 100,000 affected individuals.

ALEC's accessibility increases its value as an example. Analyzing ALEC's model data breach language is instructive because it underscores many of the common threads across data breach laws. This Article's primary goal is to quantify some of these threads to enable the weaving of an efficient, unified data breach law. . . .

VI. CONCLUSION

Data breaches are a modern threat, and this Article has attempted to quantify some elements of policy responses to the threat. Language comprehension and statutory interpretation principles provide valuable context for the way that language shapes policy debates. Data breaches also lend themselves to analysis that considers extra-legislative origins of statutory text.

This Article empirically demonstrates that a unified data breach law is sorely needed. Such a law should focus on prevention, notification, and enforcement. A data breach law should require reasonable security practices and perhaps also adoption of the "best available security technology." The NIST Cybersecurity Framework can be applied to improve adoption of technology, though probably on a voluntary basis as an initial matter. A unified data breach law should focus on notification of the consumer and the regulator without unreasonable delay. Future research should examine the optimal role of credit report agencies in a data breach regime. Finally, a unified data breach law should have a mechanism for enforcement that ensures the protection of individual rights without imposing inefficiencies.

8.2[D] EXAMPLE PRIVATE CAUSE OF ACTIONS CASES BROUGHT UNDER STATE BREACH NOTIFICATION LAWS

The following materials include some private right of action cases that demonstrate confusion by the courts concerning how to deal with cybersecurity deficiencies and demonstrate the need for state cybersecurity laws that provide a right of action to adequately protect its citizens from data breaches. Indeed, citizens and their data are not protected by poorly conceived or drafted cybersecurity laws, or a failure to enact cybersecurity laws.

The selected cases include excerpts from decisions from Georgia, Oregon, Delaware and Pennsylvania. The Georgia, Oregon and Delaware cases reject a private negligence right of action for various reasons. The Pennsylvania case includes an appellate court decision rejecting a private negligence right of action; however, the Supreme Court of Pennsylvania overruled that decision.

McConnell et al. v. George Department of Labor, 814 S.E.2d 790 (Ga. 2018).

[McConnell was unsuccessful in using a tort cause of action based on existing Georgia privacy law. The court found that McConnel's cause of action failed because the Georgia legislature had not yet "proscribe[d] any conduct in storing data or protecting data security." In other words, the privacy law, which is a notification law, is missing the cybersecurity law piece that would be necessary to create the duty of care in a tort case.]

McConnell contends that a common law duty exists to safeguard and protect the personal information of another and argues that OCGA § § 10-1-393.8 and 10-1-910 help establish the duty of care to be exercised by those who collect or hold personal information. In OCGA § § 10-1-910, the General Assembly set out legislative findings underlying the Georgia Personal Identity Protection Act, OCGA § § 10-1-910 through 10-1-915 (the "GPIPA"), enacted in 2005. In the GPIPA, the General Assembly found, inter alia, that "[t]he privacy and financial security of individuals is increasingly at risk, due to the ever more widespread collection of personal information by both the private and public sectors[,]" that "[i]dentity theft is one of the fastest growing crimes committed in this state[,]" and that "[i]dentity theft is costly to the marketplace and to consumers[.]" OCGA § 10-1-910 (1), (6). Because "[v]ictims of identity theft must act quickly to minimize the damage[,] ... expeditious notification of unauthorized acquisition and possible misuse of a persons personal information is imperative." OCGA § 10-1-910 (7). In line with these findings, the GPIPA requires that affected persons be given certain notice of a data breach and the right and ability to place a security freeze on their credit report. McConnell contends that in codifying these findings the General Assembly demonstrated its intent to protect citizens from the adverse effects of disclosure of personal information and created a general duty to preserve and protect personal information. Notably, however, despite the General Assembly's aspirational recognition of the harm caused by identity theft, the GPIPA does not proscribe any conduct in storing data or protecting data security. Rather the GPIPA proscribes particular conduct, that is, notification and the placement of a security freeze, only after a (known or suspected) data security breach has occurred. Because the GPIPA does not impose any standard of conduct in implementing and maintaining data security practices, we conclude that it can not serve as the source of a general duty to safeguard personal information. Wells Fargo Bank, N.A. v. Jenkins, 293 Ga. 162, 165, 744 S.E.2d 686 (2013).

Similarly, we conclude that OCGA § 10-1-393.8, which is part of the Fair Business Practices Act of 1975 (the "FBPA") as amended, can not serve as the source of such a general duty to safeguard and protect the personal information of another. That Code section provides that, except as otherwise provided, "a person, firm, or corporation shall not: ... [p]ublicly post or publicly display in any manner an individuals social security number.... [P]ublicly post or publicly display means to intentionally communicate or otherwise make available to the general public[.]" OCGA § 10-1-393.8. As the trial court noted in the appealed order, the FBPA expressly prohibits intentionally communicating a persons' social security number, while McConnell alleges that the Department negligently disseminated his SSN by failing "to take the necessary precautions required to safeguard and protect the personal information from unauthorized disclosure." Although the FBPA imposes a standard of conduct to refrain from intentionally and publicly posting or displaying SSNs,[15] a legal [814 S.E.2d 799] duty to refrain from doing something intentionally is not equivalent to a duty to exercise a degree of care to avoid doing something unintentionally, which falls within the ambit of negligence. The trial court correctly concluded that McConnell's complaint is premised on a duty of care to safeguard personal information that has no source in Georgia statutory law or caselaw and that his complaint therefore failed to state a claim of negligence. Diamond v. Dept. of Transp., 326 Ga.App. 189, 195-196 (2), 756 S.E.2d 277 (2014).

Given the General Assembly's stated concern about the cost of identity theft to the marketplace and to consumers, as well as the fact that it created certain limited duties with regard to personal information (e. g., the duty to notify affected persons of data breaches and the duty not to intentionally communicate information such as SSNs to the general public), it may seem surprising that our legislature has so far not acted to establish a standard of conduct intended to protect the security of personal information, as some other jurisdictions have done in connection with data protection and data breach notification laws. It is beyond the scope of judicial authority, however, to move from aspirational statements of legislative policy to an affirmative legislative enactment sufficient to create a legal duty.

Laurie Paul v. Providence Health System-Oregon, 351 Or. 587 (Or. 2012).

The issue in this case is whether a healthcare provider can be liable in damages when the provider's negligence permitted the theft of its patients' personal information, but the information was never used or viewed by the thief or any other person. Plaintiffs claimed economic and noneconomic damages for financial injury and emotional distress that they allegedly suffered when, through defendant's alleged negligence, computer disks and tapes containing personal information from an estimated 365,000 patients (including plaintiffs) were stolen from the car of one of defendant's employees. The trial court and Court of Appeals held that plaintiffs had failed to state claims for negligence or for violation of the Unlawful Trade Practices Act (UTPA), ORS 646.605 to 646.652. We conclude that, in the absence of allegations that the stolen information was used in any way or even was viewed by a third party, plaintiffs have not suffered an injury that would provide a basis for a negligence claim or an action under the UTPA. We therefore affirm, although our analysis differs in some respects from that of the Court of Appeals. . . .

A. Damages for Economic Loss

Under the economic loss doctrine, " [O]ne ordinarily is not liable for negligently causing a stranger's purely economic loss without injuring his person or property." Hale v. Groce, 304 Or. 281, 284, 744 P.2d 1289 (1987). Damages for purely economic losses, however, are available when a defendant has a duty to guard against the economic loss that occurred. Onita, 315 Or. at 159, 843 P.2d 890. A duty to protect against economic loss can arise " from a defendant's particular status or relationships, or from legislation, beyond the generalized standards that the common law of negligence imposes on persons at large." Fazzolari v. Portland School Dist. No. 1J, 303 Or. 1, 10, 734 P.2d 1326 (1987). . . .

To the extent that plaintiffs seek damages for future harm to their credit or financial well- being, Lowe forecloses such a claim because " ' the threat of future harm, by itself, is insufficient as an allegation of damage in the context of a negligence claim,' " 344 Or. at 410, 183 P.3d 181 (quoting Zehr v. Haugen, 318 Or. 647, 656, 871 P.2d 1006 (1994)).

Affy Tapple LLC v. Shopvisible, LLC and Aptos Inc., 2019 WL 1324500 (Del. Super. Ct. Mar. 7, 2019).

COUNT IX- Gross Negligence

In Delaware, there is a statutory duty imposed on businesses to protect the security of personal information:

Any person who conducts business in this State and owns, licenses, or maintains personal information shall implement and maintain reasonable procedures and practices to prevent the unauthorized acquisition, use, modification, disclosure, or destruction of personal information collected or maintained in the regular course of business.

Many states have enacted similar statutes in order to protect confidential information. Delaware's statute imposes a statutory duty on businesses to safely manage personal information. However, the statute authorizes enforcement only by the Delaware Attorney General and does not create a private right of action:

Pursuant to the enforcement duties and powers of the Director of Consumer Protection of the Department of Justice under Chapter 25 of Title 29, the Attorney General may bring an action in law or equity to address the violations of this chapter and for other relief that may be appropriate to ensure proper compliance with this chapter or to recover direct economic damages resulting from a violation, or both. . . .

Affy Tapple's claim for gross negligence is a rehash of its claim for breach of the MSA. Because Affy Tapple has not brought a separate claim for gross negligence and because any breach of a statutory duty imposed on Aptos does not give rise to a private right of action, Affy Tapple's Count IX for gross negligence must be dismissed.

Dittman v. UPMC Commonwealth Court of Pennsylvania, 2015 WL 13779479 (May 28, 2015).

[In data protection negligence cases, the courts are also nervous about usurping the legislature in the area of data protection and will likely grapple with the reasonableness standard implemented by legislatures without guidance.]

COUNT I-NEGLIGENCE

In Count I-Negligence-plaintiffs allege that UPMC had a duty to exercise reasonable care to protect and secure its employees' personal and financial information within its possession or control from being compromised, stolen, lost, misused, and/or disclosed to unauthorized parties.

Paragraphs 52-62 of plaintiffs' negligence count read as follows: 52. Plaintiffs incorporate and re-allege each and every allegation contained above as if fully set forth herein. 53. UPMC had a duty to exercise reasonable care to protect and secure Plaintiffs' and the members of the proposed Classes' personal and financial information within its possession or control from being compromised, lost, stolen, misused, and/or disclosed to unauthorized parties. This highly confidential personal and financial information includes but is not limited to Social Security numbers, dates of birth, full legal names, addresses, bank account information, and other personal information. 54. UPMC's duty included, among other things, designing, maintaining, and testing its security systems to ensure that Plaintiffs' and the members of the proposed Classes personal and financial information in their possession was adequately secured and protected. 55. UPMC further had a duty to implement processes that would detect a breach of its security systems in a timely manner. 56. In light of the special relationship between Plaintiffs and members of the proposed Classes and UPMC, whereby UPMC required Plaintiffs and members of the proposed Classes to provide highly sensitive confidential personal and financial information as a condition of their employment, UPMC undertook a duty of care to ensure the security of such information, 57. Through its acts or omissions, UPMC breached its duty to use reasonable care to protect and secure Plaintiffs' and the members of the proposed Classes' personal and financial information within its possession or control. UPMC breached its duty by failing to adopt, implement, and maintain adequate security measures to safeguard Plaintiffs' and members of the proposed Classes' personal and financial information, failing to adequately monitor the security of its network, allowing unauthorized access to Plaintiffs' and the members of the proposed Classes' personal and financial information, and failing to recognize in a timely manner that Plaintiffs' and members of the proposed Classes' personal and financial information had been compromised. 58. UPMC's failure to comply with widespread industry standards relating to data security, as well as the delay between the date of the intrusion and the date Plaintiffs and members of the proposed Classes were informed of the Data Breach further evidence UPMC's negligence in failing to exercise reasonable care in safeguarding and protecting Plaintiffs' and the members of the proposed Classes' personal and financial information in its possession or control. 59. But for UPMC's wrongful and negligent breach of the duties owed to Plaintiffs and the members of the proposed Classes, the Data Breach would not have occurred and Plaintiffs' and the members of the proposed Classes' personal and financial information would not have been compromised. 60. The injury and harm suffered by Plaintiffs and the members of the proposed Classes was the reasonably foreseeable and probable result of UPMC's failure to exercise reasonable care in safeguarding and protecting Plaintiffs' and the members of the proposed Classes' personal and financial information in its possession or control. UPMC knew or should have known that its systems and technologies for processing and securing Plaintiffs' and members of the proposed Classes' personal and financial information had significant vulnerabilities. 61. As a result of UPMC's negligence, Plaintiffs and the members of the proposed Classes have incurred damages relating to fraudulently filed tax returns. 62. As a result of UPMC's negligence, Plaintiffs and the members of the proposed Classes are at an increased and imminent risk of becoming victims of identity theft crimes, fraud and abuse.

This negligence count is based on plaintiffs' contention that UPMC owed a duty of care to UPMC employees who were victims of third-party criminal activity. However, the only losses that the UPMC employees sustained are economic losses. Under the economic loss doctrine, no cause of action exists for negligence that results solely in economic losses unaccompanied by physical injury or property damage. Excavation Technologies, Inc. v. Columbia Gas Co. of Pa., 985 A.2d 840, 841 (Pa. 2009); Adams v. Copper Beach Townhome Communities, L.P., 816 A.2d 301 (Pa. Super. 2003). Bilt-Rite Contractors, Inc. v. The Architectural Studio, 866 A.2d 270 (Pa. 2005), does not apply because, as explained in the Supreme Court's Opinion in Excavation Technologies at 843, Bilt- Rite served to "clarify the elements of the tort as they apply to those in the business of supplying information to others for pecuniary gain." Id. at 843, quoting Bilt-Rite at 280. See Sovereign Bank v. B.J.'s Wholesale Club, Inc., 533 F.3d 162, 177-78 (3d Cir. 2008) ("The Pennsylvania Supreme Court [in Bilt-Rite] never suggested that it intended to severely weaken or undermine the economic loss doctrine in a case such as this. It simply carved out a narrow exception when losses result from the reliance on the advice of professionals.").

The present case does not involve defendants in the business of supplying information for economic gain.

Plaintiffs contend that a duty of care should be imposed on UPMC to protect the confidential information of its employees. Plaintiffs rely on Pennsylvania Supreme Court case law (most recently Seebold v. Prison Health Servs., Inc., 57 A.3d 1232 (Pa. 2012)), discussing the factors a court should consider in determining whether to impose a duty of care:

The common pleas court sustained PHS's preliminary objections based on the no-duty contention. Initially, the court recited that, in determining whether a defendant owes a duty of care to a plaintiff, several factors are considered, including: (1) the relationship between the parties; (2) the social utility of the actor's conduct; (3) the nature of the risk imposed and foreseeability of the harm incurred; (4) the consequences of imposing a duty upon the actor; and (5) the overall public interest in the proposed solution. See Seebold v. Prison Health Servs., Inc., No. 07-00024, slip op. at 2 (C.P. Lycoming, Dec. 4, 2008) (citing Althaus v. Cohen, 562 Pa. 547, 553, 756 A.2d 1166, 1169 (2000)).
Where only economic losses are involved, the Pennsylvania appellate courts have already balanced the competing interests through the adoption of the economic loss

doctrine. Thus, the Seebold/Althaus factors should not be considered where the plaintiff seeks to recover only economic losses.

Moreover, even when I consider the factors described in Seebold/Althaus, I do not find that the courts should impose a new affirmative duty of care that would allow data breach actions to recover damages recognized in common law negligence actions.

In the fact situation in which a person's confidential information was made available to third persons through a data breach, I find that the controlling factors are the consequences of imposing a duty upon the actor and the overall public interest in the proposed solution. Plaintiffs' proposed solution is the creation of a private negligence cause of action to recover actual damages, including damages for increased risks, upon a showing that the plaintiff's confidential information was made available to third persons through a data breach.

The public interest is not furthered by this proposed solution. Data breaches are widespread. They frequently occur because of sophisticated criminal activity of third persons. There is not a safe harbor for entities storing confidential information. The creation of a private cause of action could result within Pennsylvania alone of the filing each year of possibly hundreds of thousands of lawsuits by persons whose ' confidential information may be in the hands of third persons. Clearly, the judicial system is not equipped to handle this increased caseload of negligence actions. Courts will not adopt a proposed solution that will overwhelm Pennsylvania's judicial system.

Also, assuming that liability is not absolute, there are not any generally accepted reasonable care standards. Use of "expert" testimony and jury findings to develop standards as to what constitutes reasonable care is not a viable method for resolving the difficult issue of the minimum requirements of care that should be imposed in data breach litigation, assuming that any minimum' requirements should be imposed.

Under plaintiffs' proposed solution, in Pennsylvania alone, perhaps hundreds of profit and nonprofit entities would be required to expend substantial resources responding to the resulting lawsuits. These entities are victims of the same criminal activity as the plaintiffs. The courts should not, without guidance from the Legislature, create a body of law that does not allow entities that are victims of criminal activity to get on with their businesses.

In Seebold, the Pennsylvania Supreme Court stated that more is involved in a court's decision as to whether to create a new duty than considering the five Seebold/Althaus factors. The Seebold Opinion stated: "To the extent that the task of rendering duty versus no-duty decisions continues to reside with jurists, we acknowledge that it is one to which we are the least well suited." Id. at 1245. "[W]e have often recognized the superior tools and resources available to the Legislature in making social policy judgments, including comprehensive investigations and policy hearings." Id. Thus, the five factors should be considered in the context of court rulings adopting "the default position that, unless the justifications for and consequences of judicial policymaking are reasonably clear with the balance of factors favorably predominating, we will not impose new affirmative duties." Id. "Before a change in the law is made, a court, if it is to act responsibly must be able to see with reasonable clarity the results of its decision and to say with reasonable certainty that the change will serve the best interests of society." Id., quoting Hoven v. Kelble, 256 N.W.2d 379, 392 (Wis. 1977). See also Lance v. Wyeth, 85 A.3d 434, 454 (Pa. 2014).

I cannot say with reasonable certainty that the best interests of society would be served through the recognition of new affirmative duties of care imposing liability on health care providers and other entities electronically storing confidential information, the financial impact of which could even put these entities out of business. Entities storing confidential. information already have an incentive to protect confidential information because any breach will affect their operations. An "improved" system for storing confidential information will not necessarily prevent a breach of the system. These entities are also victims of criminal activity.

It is appropriate for courts to consider the creation of a new duty where what the court is considering is sufficiently narrow that it is not on the radar screen of the Legislature, In that situation, the courts are filling gaps that are not likely to be filled by the Legislature. However, where the Legislature is already considering what courts are being asked to consider, in the absence of constitutional issues, courts must defer to the Legislature.

The Legislature is aware of and has considered the issues that plaintiffs want this court to consider. As of this date, the only legislation which the General Assembly has chosen to enact requires entities that suffer a breach of their security systems to provide notification. Furthermore, the Legislature gives the Office of Attorney General exclusive authority to bring an action for violation of the notification requirement (i.e., no private actions are permitted).

See pages 14-15 set forth below of UPMC's Supplemental Brief in Support of Preliminary Objections, which describe the General Assembly's consideration of data breaches:
2. The General Assembly has considered the creation of civil liability for data breaches and decided against the imposition of such a duty.

The Pennsylvania General Assembly extensively considered data breaches and the issues related thereto prior to enacting the Breach of Personal Information Notification Act (the "Data Breach Act"]. 73 P.S. § 2301, et seq. (effective June 20, 2006). Ultimately, the General Assembly did not, by way of the Data Breach Act, enact legislation establishing a duty of protection or providing individuals with a private cause of action in the event of a data breach. Instead, the General Assembly mandated only that entities which suffer a "breach of the security of the system" must provide notification of the disclosure of personal information, £g§ 73 P.S. § 2303 ("Any entity that maintains, store or manages computerized data that includes personal information shall provide notice of any breach of the security of the system following discovery of the breach .... ").

In the Data Breach Act, the General Assembly also established an enforcement action - expressly reserved for the Attorney General of Pennsylvania - for violation of the notification requirement. 73 P.S. § 2308 ("The Office of Attorney General shall have exclusive authority to bring an action .., ."). Significantly, the General Assembly did not adopt or establish (1) a duty to protect or safeguard the security of computerized data against malicious and criminal attacks by third parties or (2) a cause of action for private litigants in the event of unauthorized access to the individuals' personal information.

Indeed, review of the legislative history of Pennsylvania's Data Breach Act reveals that the General Assembly considered incorporating an expansive civil liability provision, which would have permitted a person to recover "actual damages." S.B. 712, Printer's No. 859, § 8. The initial version of the bill was referred to the Communications and Technology Committee on June 3, 2005. History of S.B. 712 of 2005. Thereafter, on June 13, 2005, the bill was reported as amended by committee and the "Civil Relief provision was amended to reflect its current form. S.B. 712, Printer's No. 898, § 8.2 Under its current form, only a failure to notify is actionable and only the Attorney General may assert the claim. 73 P.S. § 2308. Numerous iterations of the law were proposed in the House of Representatives and the Senate, some of which provided an even more expansive array of damages to individuals victimized by data breaches. For example, H.B. 2006 of the 2005-2006 session of the Genera) Assembly provided for the award of actual damages and a One of up to $150, 000.00. H.B. 2006, Printer's No. 2925. The General Assembly chose by collective action, however, to enact a version without such provisions. (Emphasis in original.)

In summary, the General Assembly has considered and continues to consider the same issues that plaintiffs are requesting this court to consider under the Seebold/Althaus line of cases. The only duty that the General Assembly has chosen to impose as of today is notification of a data breach. It is not for the courts to alter the direction of the General Assembly because public policy is a matter for the Legislature.

I find to be persuasive the Opinion of an Illinois appellate court in Cooney v. Chicago Pub. Sch., 943 N.E.2d 23, 28-29 (Ill. App. Ct. 2010), which rejected the plaintiffs' request that the court create a new common law duty to protect and safeguard confidential information because the Legislature had already imposed a duty of notification:

While we do not minimize the importance of protecting this information, we do not believe that the creation of a new legal duty beyond legislative requirements already in place is part of our role on appellate review. As noted, the legislature has specifically addressed the issue and only required the [defendant] to provide notice of the disclosure. Cooney, 943 N.E.2d at 29.

For these reasons, I dismiss Count I of plaintiffs' Complaint.

Dittman et al. v. UPMC et al., 196 A.3d 1036 (Pa. 2018).

[This decision is the appeal of the prior case to the Supreme Court of Pennsylvania. The Supreme Court held that defendants did "owe a duty to Employees to use reasonable care to safeguard their sensitive personal data in collecting and storing it on an internet-accessible computer system."]

We granted discretionary review in this matter to determine whether an employer has a legal duty to use reasonable care to safeguard its employee's sensitive personal information that the employer stores on an internet-accessible computer system. We also examine the scope of Pennsylvania's economic loss doctrine, specifically whether it permits recovery in negligence for purely pecuniary damages. For the reasons discussed below, we hold that an employer has a legal duty to exercise reasonable care to safeguard its employee's sensitive personal information stored by the employer on an internet-accessible computer system. We further hold that, under Pennsylvania's economic loss doctrine, recovery for purely pecuniary damages is permissible under a negligence theory provided that the plaintiff can establish the defendants breach of a legal duty arising under common law that is independent of any duty assumed pursuant to contract. As the Superior Court came to the opposite conclusions, we now vacate its judgment. . . .

We granted allowance of appeal to address the following issues, as stated by Employees: a. Does an employer have a legal duty to use reasonable care to safeguard sensitive personal information of its employees when the employer chooses to store such information on an internet accessible computer system? b. Does the economic loss doctrine permit recovery for purely pecuniary damages which result from the breach of an independent legal duty arising under common law, as opposed to the breach of a contractual duty? Dittman v. UPMC, 642 Pa. 572, 170 A.3d 1042 (2017) (per curiam). . . .

Employees have sufficiently alleged that UPMCs affirmative conduct created the risk of a data breach. Thus, we agree with Employees that, in collecting and storing Employees data on its computer systems, UPMC owed Employees a duty to exercise reasonable care to protect them against an unreasonable risk of harm arising out of that act. . . .

Based on the foregoing, we conclude that the lower courts erred in finding that UPMC did not owe a duty to Employees to exercise reasonable care in collecting and storing their personal and financial information on its computer systems. This conclusion notwithstanding, Employees claim cannot proceed if we nonetheless hold that it is barred by the economic loss doctrine. Thus, we turn to our analysis of that doctrine. . . .

C. Conclusion

Based on the foregoing, we conclude that the courts below erred in determining that UPMC did not owe a duty to Employees to use reasonable care to safeguard their sensitive personal data in collecting and storing it on an internet-accessible computer system. We further hold that the lower courts erred in concluding that Pennsylvania's economic loss doctrine bars Employees negligence claim. Accordingly, we vacate the judgment of the Superior Court, reverse the order of the trial court, and remand the matter to the trial court for further proceedings consistent with this opinion.

8.3 Data Security Laws

As data breaches have become more common, state AGs have come to realize that they lacked power to address some of the root causes of some of the data breaches. The AGs did not have the authority to pursue companies that lacked proper cybersecurity and had to rely on teaming with the FTC to go after the bad actors. Many state legislatures have fixed that problem by promulgating data security laws that give the AG a channel to go after bad actors without the help of a federal agency.

8.3[A] NATIONAL CONFERENCE OF STATE LEGISLATURES TABLE ON DATA SECURITY LAWS

The NCLS has created a table on data security laws. [367] The table contains references to 25 state laws which are private sector data security laws. The table includes the state name, the statutory citation with a link, information about who it covers and the security measure that is required. The following is an excerpt of part of the table with some states and the section on who it applies to removed.

Data Security Laws | Private Sector

5/29/2019

State	Statutory Citation/Link	Security Measures Required
Florida	Fla. Stat. § 501.171(2)	Reasonable measures to protect and secure data in electronic form containing personal information.
Illinois	815 ILCS 530/45	Implement and maintain reasonable security measures to protect those records from unauthorized access, acquisition, destruction, use, modification, or disclosure. A contract for the disclosure of personal information must include a provision requiring the person to whom the information is disclosed to implement and maintain reasonable security measures.

---

[367] *Data Security Laws: Private Sector*, NAT'L. CONF. OF STATE LEG., https://www.ncsl.org/research/telecommunications-and-information-technology/data-security-laws.aspx (last updated May 29, 2019).

New York	New York Gen. Bus. Law § 899-BB	Develop, implement and maintain reasonable safeguards to protect the security, confidentiality and integrity of private information including, but not limited to, disposal of data.
Ohio	Ohio Rev. Stat. § 1354.01 to 1354.05 (2018 S.B. 220)	To qualify for an affirmative defense to a cause of action alleging a failure to implement reasonable information security controls resulting in a data breach, an entity must create, maintain, and comply with a written cybersecurity program that contains administrative, technical, and physical safeguards for the protection of personal information as specified (e.g., conforming to an industry-recognized cybersecurity framework as listed in the act).

8.3[B] SPECIFIC DATA SECURITY LAWS

As previously noted, some states have enacted data security laws or data breach notification laws with data security elements. The following materials include the text of data security related laws from Alabama, Massachusetts, Colorado and California.

Alabama Data Breach Notification Act of 2018

Alabama was one of the last two states to adopt a data breach notification law. Because they were late to the table in promulgating a notification law, they were able to add cybersecurity measures in addition to just breach notification requirements.

TITLE: Consumer protection, Alabama Data Breach Notification Act

March 28, 2018

SB318

An Act, Relating to consumer protection; to require certain entities to provide notice to certain persons upon a breach of security that results in the unauthorized acquisition of sensitive personally identifying information.

BE IT ENACTED BY THE LEGISLATURE OF ALABAMA:

Section 1. This act may be cited and shall be known as the Alabama Data Breach Notification Act of 2018.

Section 2. For the purposes of this act, the following terms have the following meanings:

(1) BREACH OF SECURITY or BREACH. The unauthorized acquisition of data in electronic form containing sensitive personally identifying information. Acquisition occurring over a period of time committed by the same entity constitutes one breach. The term does not include any of the following:

a. Good faith acquisition of sensitive personally identifying information by an employee or agent of a covered entity, unless the information is used for a purpose unrelated to the business or subject to further unauthorized use.

b. The release of a public record not otherwise subject to confidentiality or nondisclosure requirements.

c. Any lawful investigative, protective, or intelligence activity of a law enforcement or intelligence agency of the state, or a political subdivision of the state.

(2) COVERED ENTITY. A person, sole proprietorship, partnership, government entity, corporation, nonprofit, trust, estate, cooperative association, or other business entity that acquires or uses sensitive personally identifying information.

(3) DATA IN ELECTRONIC FORM. Any data stored electronically or digitally on any computer system or other database, including, but not limited to, recordable tapes and other mass storage devices.

(4) GOVERNMENT ENTITY. The State, a county, or a municipality or any instrumentality of the state, a county, or a municipality.

(5) INDIVIDUAL. Any Alabama resident whose sensitive personally identifying information was, or the covered entity reasonably believes to have been, accessed as a result of the breach.

(6) SENSITIVE PERSONALLY IDENTIFYING INFORMATION.

a. Except as provided in paragraph b., an Alabama resident's first name or first initial and last name in combination with one or more of the following with respect to the same Alabama resident:

1. A non-truncated Social Security number or tax identification number.

2. A non-truncated driver's license number, state-issued identification card number, passport number, military identification number, or other unique identification number issued on a government document used to verify the identity of a specific individual.

3. A financial account number, including a bank account number, credit card number, or debit card number, in combination with any security code, access code, password, expiration date, or PIN, that is necessary to access the financial account or to conduct a transaction that will credit or debit the financial account.

4. Any information regarding an individual's medical history, mental or physical condition, or medical treatment or diagnosis by a health care professional.

5. An individual's health insurance policy number or subscriber identification number and any unique identifier used by a health insurer to identify the individual.

6. A user name or email address, in combination with a password or security question and answer that would permit access to an online account affiliated with the covered entity that is reasonably likely to contain or is used to obtain sensitive personally identifying information.

b. The term does not include either of the following:

1. Information about an individual which has been lawfully made public by a federal, state, or local government record or a widely distributed media.

2. Information that is truncated, encrypted, secured, or modified by any other method or technology that removes elements that personally identify an individual or that otherwise renders the information unusable, including encryption of the data, document, or device containing the sensitive personally identifying information, unless the covered entity knows or has reason to know that the encryption key or security credential that could render the personally identifying information readable or useable has been breached together with the information.

(7) THIRD-PARTY AGENT. An entity that has been contracted to maintain, store, process, or is otherwise permitted to access sensitive personally identifying information in connection with providing services to a covered entity.

Section 3. (a) Each covered entity and third-party agent shall implement and maintain reasonable security measures to protect sensitive personally identifying information against a breach of security.

(b) Reasonable security measures means security measures practicable for the covered entity subject to subsection (c), to implement and maintain, including consideration of all of the following:

(1) Designation of an employee or employees to coordinate the covered entity's security measures to protect against a breach of security. An owner or manager may designate himself or herself.

(2) Identification of internal and external risks of a breach of security.

(3) Adoption of appropriate information safeguards to address identified risks of a breach of security and assess the effectiveness of such safeguards.

(4) Retention of service providers, if any, that are contractually required to maintain appropriate safeguards for sensitive personally identifying information.

(5) Evaluation and adjustment of security measures to account for changes in circumstances affecting the security of sensitive personally identifying information.

(6) Keeping the management of the covered entity, including its board of directors, if any, appropriately informed of the overall status of its security measures; provided, however, that the management of a government entity subject to this subdivision may be appropriately informed of the status of its security measures through a properly convened execution session under the Open Meetings Act pursuant to Section 36-25A-7, Code of Alabama 1975.

(c) An assessment of a covered entity's security shall be based upon the entity's reasonable security measures as a whole and shall place an emphasis on data security failures that are multiple or systemic, including consideration of all the following:

(1) The size of the covered entity.

(2) The amount of sensitive personally identifying information and the type of activities for which the sensitive personally identifying information is accessed, acquired, maintained, stored, utilized, or communicated by, or on behalf of, the covered entity.

(3) The covered entity's cost to implement and maintain the reasonable security measures to protect against a breach of security relative to its resources.

Section 4. (a) If a covered entity determines that a breach of security has or may have occurred in relation to sensitive personally identifying information that is accessed, acquired, maintained, stored, utilized, or communicated by, or on behalf of, the covered entity, the covered entity shall conduct a good faith and prompt investigation that includes all of the following:

(1) An assessment of the nature and scope of the breach.

(2) Identification of any sensitive personally identifying information that may have been involved in the breach and the identity of any individuals to whom that information relates.

(3) A determination of whether the sensitive personally identifying information has been acquired or is reasonably believed to have been acquired by an unauthorized person, and is reasonably likely to cause substantial harm to the individuals to whom the information relates.

(4) Identification and implementation of measures to restore the security and confidentiality of the systems compromised in the breach.

(b) In determining whether sensitive personally identifying information has been acquired or is reasonably believed to have been acquired by an unauthorized person without valid authorization, the following factors may be considered:

(1) Indications that the information is in the physical possession and control of a person without valid authorization, such as a lost or stolen computer or other device containing information.

(2) Indications that the information has been downloaded or copied.

(3) Indications that the information was used by an unauthorized person, such as fraudulent accounts opened or instances of identity theft reported.

(4) Whether the information has been made public.

Section 5. (a) A covered entity that is not a third-party agent that determines under Section 4 that, as a result of a breach of security, sensitive personally identifying information has been acquired or is reasonably believed to have been acquired by an unauthorized person, and is reasonably likely to cause substantial harm to the individuals to whom the information relates, shall give notice of the breach to each individual.

(b) Notice to individuals under subsection (a) shall be made as expeditiously as possible and without unreasonable delay, taking into account the time necessary to allow the covered entity to conduct an investigation in accordance with Section 4. Except as provided in subsection (c), the covered entity shall provide notice within 45 days of the covered entity's receipt of notice from a third party agent that a breach has occurred or upon the covered entity's determination that a breach has occurred and is reasonably likely to cause substantial harm to the individuals to whom the information relates.

(c) If a federal or state law enforcement agency determines that notice to individuals required under this section would interfere with a criminal investigation or national security, the notice shall be delayed upon the receipt of written request of the law enforcement agency for a period that the law enforcement agency determines is necessary. A law enforcement agency, by a subsequent written request, may revoke the delay as of a specified date or extend the period set forth in the original request made under this section if further delay is necessary.

(d) Except as provided by subsection (e), notice to an affected individual under this section shall be given in writing, sent to the mailing address of the individual in the records of the covered entity, or by email notice sent to the email address of the individual in the records of the covered entity. The notice shall include, at a minimum, all of the following:

(1) The date, estimated date, or estimated date range of the breach.

(2) A description of the sensitive personally identifying information that was acquired by an unauthorized person as part of the breach.

(3) A general description of the actions taken by a covered entity to restore the security and confidentiality of the personal information involved in the breach.

(4) A general description of steps an affected individual can take to protect himself or herself from identity theft.

(5) Information that the individual can use to contact the covered entity to inquire about the breach.

(e)(1) A covered entity required to provide notice to any individual under this section may provide substitute notice in lieu of direct notice, if direct notice is not feasible due to any of the following:

a. Excessive cost. The term includes either of the following:

1. Excessive cost to the covered entity relative to the resources of the covered entity.

2. The cost to the covered entity exceeds five hundred thousand dollars ($500,000).

b. Lack of sufficient contact information for the individual required to be notified.

c. The affected individuals exceed 100,000 persons.

(2) a. Substitute notice shall include both of the following:

1. A conspicuous notice on the Internet website of the covered entity, if the covered entity maintains a website, for a period of 30 days.

2. Notice in print and in broadcast media, including major media in urban and rural areas where the affected individuals reside.

b. An alternative form of substitute notice may be used with the approval of the Attorney General.

(f) If a covered entity determines that notice is not required under this section, the entity shall document the determination in writing and maintain records concerning the determination for no less than five years.

Section 6. (a) If the number of individuals a covered entity is required to notify under Section 5 exceeds 1,000, the entity shall provide written notice of the breach to the Attorney General as expeditiously as possible and without unreasonable delay. Except as provided in subsection (c) of Section 5, the covered entity shall provide the notice within 45 days of the covered entity's receipt of notice from a third party agent that a breach has occurred or upon the entity's determination that a breach has occurred and is reasonably likely to cause substantial harm to the individuals to whom the information relates.

(b) Written notice to the Attorney General shall include all of the following:

(1) A synopsis of the events surrounding the breach at the time that notice is provided.

(2) The approximate number of individuals in the state who were affected by the breach.

(3) Any services related to the breach being offered or scheduled to be offered, without charge, by the covered entity to individuals, and instructions on how to use the services.

(4) The name, address, telephone number, and email address of the employee or agent of the covered entity from whom additional information may be obtained about the breach.

(c) A covered entity may provide the Attorney General with supplemental or updated information regarding a breach at any time.

(d) Information marked as confidential that is obtained by the Attorney General under this section is not subject to any open records, freedom of information, or other public record disclosure law.

Section 7. If a covered entity discovers circumstances requiring notice under Section 5 of more than 1,000 individuals at a single time, the entity shall also notify, without unreasonable delay, all consumer reporting agencies that compile and maintain files on consumers on a nationwide basis, as defined in the Fair Credit Reporting Act, 15 U.S.C. 1681a, of the timing, distribution, and content of the notices.

Section 8. In the event a third-party agent has experienced a breach of security in the system maintained by the agent, the agent shall notify the covered entity of the breach of security as expeditiously as possible and without unreasonable delay, but no later than 10 days following the determination of the breach of security or reason to believe the breach occurred. After receiving notice from a third-party agent, a covered entity shall provide notices required under Sections 5 and 6. A third-party agent, in cooperation with a covered entity, shall provide information in the possession of the third-party agent so that the covered entity can comply with its notice requirements. A covered entity may enter into a contractual agreement with a third-party agent whereby the third-party agent agrees to handle notifications required under this act.

Section 9. (a) A violation of the notification provisions of this act is an unlawful trade practice under the Alabama Deceptive Trade Practices Act, Chapter 19, Title 8, Code of Alabama 1975, but does not constitute a criminal offense under Section 8-19-12, Code of Alabama 1975. The Attorney General shall have the exclusive authority to bring an action for civil penalties under this act.

(1) A violation of this act does not establish a private cause of action under Section 8-19-10, Code of Alabama 1975. Nothing in this act may otherwise be construed to affect any right a person may have at common law, by statute, or otherwise.

QUESTION

The Alabama statute states that the "Attorney General shall have the exclusive authority to bring an action for civil penalties under this act." The act also "does not establish a private cause of action. . ." What other rights may come into play?

Massachusetts Regulations Concerning Cybersecurity

Massachusetts was one of the earlier adopters of a cybersecurity law. Note that the following law is fairly narrow in that it provides specific security measures on how to comply with the law:

201 CMR 17: Standards for the protection of personal information of residents of the Commonwealth[368]

Section

17.01: Purpose and Scope

17.02: Definitions

17.03: Duty to Protect and Standards for Protecting Personal Information

17.04: Computer System Security Requirements

17.05: Compliance Deadline

17.01: Purpose and Scope

(1) Purpose. 201 CMR 17.00 implements the provisions of M.G.L. c. 93H relative to the standards to be met by persons who own or license personal information about a resident of the Commonwealth of Massachusetts. 201 CMR 17.00 establishes minimum standards to be met in connection with the safeguarding of personal information contained in both paper and electronic records. The objectives of 201 CMR 17.00 is to insure the security and confidentiality of customer information in a manner fully consistent with industry standards; protect against anticipated threats or hazards to the security or integrity of such information; and protect against unauthorized access to or use of such information that may result in substantial harm or inconvenience to any consumer.

(2) Scope. 201 CMR 17.00 applies to all persons that own or license personal information about a resident of the Commonwealth.

17.02: Definitions

The following words as used in 201 CMR 17.00 shall, unless the context requires otherwise, have the following meanings:

---

[368] 201 MASS. CODE REGS. 17 (2009).

Breach of Security, the unauthorized acquisition or unauthorized use of unencrypted data or, encrypted electronic data and the confidential process or key that is capable of compromising the security, confidentiality, or integrity of personal information, maintained by a person or agency that creates a substantial risk of identity theft or fraud against a resident of the commonwealth. A good faith but unauthorized acquisition of personal information by a person or agency, or employee or agent thereof, for the lawful purposes of such person or agency, is not a breach of security unless the personal information is used in an unauthorized manner or subject to further unauthorized disclosure.

Electronic, relating to technology having electrical, digital, magnetic, wireless, optical, electromagnetic or similar capabilities.

Encrypted, the transformation of data into a form in which meaning cannot be assigned without the use of a confidential process or key.

Owns or Licenses, receives, stores, maintains, processes, or otherwise has access to personal information in connection with the provision of goods or services or in connection with employment.

Person, a natural person, corporation, association, partnership or other legal entity, other than an agency, executive office, department, board, commission, bureau, division or authority of the Commonwealth, or any of its branches, or any political subdivision thereof.

Personal Information, a Massachusetts resident's first name and last name or first initial and last name in combination with any one or more of the following data elements that relate to such resident:

(a) Social Security number;

(b) driver's license number or state-issued identification card number; or

(c) financial account number, or credit or debit card number, with or without any required security code, access code, personal identification number or password, that would permit access to a resident's financial account; provided, however, that "Personal information" shall not include information that is lawfully obtained from publicly available information, or from federal, state or local government records lawfully made available to the general public.

Record or Records, any material upon which written, drawn, spoken, visual, or electromagnetic information or images are recorded or preserved, regardless of physical form or characteristics.

Service Provider, any person that receives, stores, maintains, processes, or otherwise is permitted access to personal information through its provision of services directly to a person that is subject to 201 CMR 17.00.

17.03: Duty to Protect and Standards for Protecting Personal Information

(1) Every person that owns or licenses personal information about a resident of the Common- wealth shall develop, implement, and maintain a comprehensive information security program that is written in one or more readily accessible parts and contains administrative, technical, and physical safeguards that are appropriate to:

(a) the size, scope and type of business of the person obligated to safeguard the personal information under such comprehensive information security program;

(b) the amount of resources available to such person;

(c) the amount of stored data; and

(d) the need for security and confidentiality of both consumer and employee information.

The safeguards contained in such program must be consistent with the safeguards for protection of personal information and information of a similar character set forth in any state or federal regulations by which the person who owns or licenses such information may be regulated.

(2) Without limiting the generality of the foregoing, every comprehensive information security program shall include, but shall not be limited to:

(a) Designating one or more employees to maintain the comprehensive information security program;

(b) Identifying and assessing reasonably foreseeable internal and external risks to the security, confidentiality, and/or integrity of any electronic, paper or other records containing personal information, and evaluating and improving, where necessary, the effectiveness of the current safeguards for limiting such risks, including but not limited to:

1. ongoing employee (including temporary and contract employee) training;

2. employee compliance with policies and procedures; and

3. means for detecting and preventing security system failures.

(c) Developing security policies for employees relating to the storage, access and transportation of records containing personal information outside of business premises.

(d)Imposing disciplinary measures for violations of the comprehensive information security program rules.

(e) Preventing terminated employees from accessing records containing personal information.

(f) Oversee service providers, by:

1. Taking reasonable steps to select and retain third-party service providers that are capable of maintaining appropriate security measures to protect such personal information consistent with 201 CMR 17.00 and any applicable federal regulations; and

2. Requiring such third-party service providers by contract to implement and maintain such appropriate security measures for personal information; provided, however, that until March 1, 2012, a contract a person has entered into with a third party service provider to perform services for said person or functions on said person's behalf satisfies the provisions of 201 CMR 17.03(2)(f)2. even if the contract does not include a requirement that the third party service provider maintain such appropriate safeguards, as long as said person entered into the contract no later than March 1, 2010.

(g)Reasonable restrictions upon physical access to records containing personal information, and storage of such records and data in locked facilities, storage areas or containers.

(h) Regular monitoring to ensure that the comprehensive information security program is operating in a manner reasonably calculated to prevent unauthorized access to or unauthorized use of personal information; and upgrading information safeguards as necessary to limit risks.

(i) Reviewing the scope of the security measures at least annually or whenever there is a material change in business practices that may reasonably implicate the security or integrity of records containing personal information.

(j) Documenting responsive actions taken in connection with any incident involving a breach of security, and mandatory post-incident review of events and actions taken, if any, to make changes in business practices relating to protection of personal information.

17.04: Computer System Security Requirements

Every person that owns or licenses personal information about a resident of the Commonwealth and electronically stores or transmits such information shall include in its written, comprehensive information security program the establishment and maintenance of a security system covering its computers, including any wireless system, that, at a minimum, and to the extent technically feasible, shall have the following elements:

(1) Secure user authentication protocols including:

(a) control of user IDs and other identifiers;

(b) a reasonably secure method of assigning and selecting passwords, or use of unique identifier technologies, such as biometrics or token devices;

(c) control of data security passwords to ensure that such passwords are kept in a location and/or format that does not compromise the security of the data they protect;

(d) restricting access to active users and active user accounts only; and

(e) blocking access to user identification after multiple unsuccessful attempts to gain access or the limitation placed on access for the particular system;

(2) Secure access control measures that:

(a) restrict access to records and files containing personal information to those who need such information to perform their job duties; and

(b) assign unique identifications plus passwords, which are not vendor supplied default passwords, to each person with computer access, that are reasonably designed to maintain the integrity of the security of the access controls;

(3) Encryption of all transmitted records and files containing personal information that will travel across public networks, and encryption of all data containing personal information to be transmitted wirelessly.

(4) Reasonable monitoring of systems, for unauthorized use of or access to personal information;

(5) Encryption of all personal information stored on laptops or other portable devices;

(6) For files containing personal information on a system that is connected to the Internet, there must be reasonably up-to-date firewall protection and operating system security patches, reasonably designed to maintain the integrity of the personal information.

(7) Reasonably up-to-date versions of system security agent software which must include malware protection and reasonably up-to-date patches and virus definitions, or a version of such software that can still be supported with up-to-date patches and virus definitions, and is set to receive the most current security updates on a regular basis.

(8) Education and training of employees on the proper use of the computer security system and the importance of personal information security.

17.05: Compliance Deadline

(1) Every person who owns or licenses personal information about a resident of the Commonwealth shall be in full compliance with 201 CMR 17.00 on or before March 1, 2010.

QUESTION

Is the Massachusetts law too specific?

Colorado Cybersecurity Law

Other states, such as Colorado, who promulgated its law years later, took a broader approach because it did not want to be boxed in by a narrow law. The following is the relevant text from that law.

Effective: September 1, 2018

C.R.S.A. § 6-1-713.5. Protection of personal identifying information— definition

(1) To protect personal identifying information, as defined in section 6-1-713(2), from unauthorized access, use, modification, disclosure, or destruction, a covered entity that maintains, owns, or licenses personal identifying information of an individual residing in the state shall implement and maintain reasonable security procedures and practices that are appropriate to the nature of the personal identifying information and the nature and size of the business and its operations.

(2) Unless a covered entity agrees to provide its own security protection for the information it discloses to a third-party service provider, the covered entity shall require that the third-party service provider implement and maintain reasonable security procedures and practices that are:

(a) Appropriate to the nature of the personal identifying information disclosed to the third-party service provider; and

(b) Reasonably designed to help protect the personal identifying information from unauthorized access, use, modification, disclosure, or destruction.

(3) For the purposes of subsection (2) of this section, a disclosure of personal identifying information does not include disclosure of information to a third party under circumstances where the covered entity retains primary responsibility for implementing and maintaining reasonable security procedures and practices appropriate to the nature of the personal identifying information and the covered entity implements and maintains technical controls that are reasonably designed to:

(a) Help protect the personal identifying information from unauthorized access, use, modification, disclosure, or destruction; or

(b) Effectively eliminate the third party's ability to access the personal identifying information, notwithstanding the third party's physical possession of the personal identifying information.

(4) A covered entity that is regulated by state or federal law and that maintains procedures for protection of personal identifying information pursuant to the laws, rules, regulations, guidances, or guidelines established by its state or federal regulator is in compliance with this section.

(5) For the purposes of this section, "third-party service provider" means an entity that has been contracted to maintain, store, or process personal identifying information on behalf of a covered entity.

NOTES

Note 1

The Colorado legislature purposely did not define "reasonable security procedures and practices that are appropriate to the nature of the personal identifying information and the nature and size of the business and its operations." This gives the Colorado AG FTC-like broad powers. This is what the AG wanted. Case law will continue to define what are reasonable cybersecurity practices. Unfortunately, entities can still roll the dice and not implement "reasonable" cybersecurity practices because they will only get caught if they have a reportable breach. Otherwise the AG does not have insight into what is happening at the entity unless perhaps if a whistle blower comes forward.

California Consumer Privacy Act as modified by the California Privacy Rights Act

California continues to lead the nation on protecting the consumer and has recently promulgated the California Consumer Privacy Act (CCPA). This law along with the European General Data Protection (GDPR) have changed the way companies do business. The CCPA is primarily a privacy law that gives individual customers rights to control how their data is collected, used, and disposed of. But the CCPA also gives a private right of action to hold companies accountable regarding reasonable cybersecurity measures. The California Privacy Rights Act, which was passed by the California voters on November 3, 2020, maintains the cybersecurity portion of the CCPA with some slight modifications and creates a new privacy agency. The following section of the California Privacy Rights Act has a focus on cybersecurity measures.

SEC. 16. Section 1798.150 of the Civil Code is amended to read:

1798.150, Personal Information Security Breaches

(a) (1) Any consumer whose nonencrypted **and** non redacted personal information, as defined in subparagraph (A) of paragraph (1) of subdivision (d) of Section 1798.81.5, **or whose email address in combination with a password or security question and answer that would permit access to the account**, is subject to an unauthorized access and exfiltration, theft, or disclosure as a result of the business's violation of the duty to implement and maintain reasonable security procedures and practices appropriate to the nature of the information to protect the personal information may institute a civil action for any of the following:

(A) To recover damages in an amount not less than one hundred dollars ($100) and not greater than seven hundred and fifty ($750) per consumer per incident or actual damages, whichever is greater.

(B) Injunctive or declaratory relief.

(C) Any other relief the court deems proper.

(2) In assessing the amount of statutory damages, the court shall consider any one or more of the relevant circumstances presented by any of the parties to the case, including, but not limited to, the nature and seriousness of the misconduct, the number of violations, the persistence of the misconduct, the length of time over which the misconduct occurred, the willfulness of the defendant's misconduct, and the defendant's assets, liabilities, and net worth.

(b) Actions pursuant to this section may be brought by a consumer if, prior to initiating any action against a business for statutory damages on an individual or class-wide basis, a consumer provides a business 30 days' written notice identifying the specific provisions of this title the consumer alleges have been or are being violated. In the event a cure is possible, if within the 30 days the business actually cures the noticed violation and provides the consumer an express written statement that the violations have been cured and that no further violations shall occur, no action for individual statutory damages or class-wide statutory damages may be initiated against the business. **The Implementation and maintenance of reasonable security procedures and practices pursuant to Section 1798.81.5[369] following a breach does not constitute a cure with respect to that breach**. No notice shall be required prior to an individual consumer initiating an action solely for actual pecuniary damages suffered as a result of the alleged violations of this title. If a business continues to violate this title in breach of the express written statement provided to the consumer under this section, the consumer may initiate an action against the business to enforce the written statement and may pursue statutory damages for each breach of the express written statement, as well as any other violation of the title that postdates the written statement.

(c) The cause of action established by this section shall apply only to violations as defined in subdivision (a) and shall not be based on violations of any other section of this title. Nothing in this title shall be interpreted to serve as the basis for a private right of action under any other law. This shall not be construed to relieve any party from any duties or obligations imposed under other law or the United States or California Constitution. [Emphasis added to additions made by the California Privacy Rights Act to the CCPA.]

---

[369] Editors: California Civil Code section 1798.81.5 provides in relevant part: "(b) "A business that owns, licenses, or maintains personal information about a California resident shall implement and maintain reasonable security procedures and practices appropriate to the nature of the information, to protect the personal information from unauthorized access, destruction, use, modification, or disclosure.""

NOTES

Note 1

The phrase "result of the business's violation of the duty to implement and maintain reasonable security procedures and practices appropriate to the nature of the information to protect the personal information may institute a civil action" raises some very interesting questions. How can an individual determine what are reasonable security procedures and practices? Will this lead to customers assuming that if a breach occurred then by default there were not reasonable security procedures and practices in place?

In *What Is a "Reasonable Security Procedure and Practice" Under the California Consumer Privacy Act's Safe Harbor* in 73 Consumer Financial Law Quarterly Report 173 (2019), Scott Hyman, Genevieve R. Walser-Jolly and Elizabeth Farrell argue that there is a lack of clarity with respect to the definition of "reasonable security standards" in the CCPA without regulatory guidance. *Id.* at 201. The authors note that a reliance on industry standards may be unhelpful because of the changing nature of those standards. *Id.* The authors state:

> Due care requires avoiding "any 'unreasonable risk,' which means 'unduly dangerous conduct.' The basic question is whether the risk of danger to others outweighs the utility of the act or the manner in which it is done; if so, the risk is unreasonable and the act is negligent." The burden of precautionary policies and practices should be measured alongside industry standards, but not dogmatically governed by them. A reasonableness analysis that considers the marginal utility of each level of cost of increased security--the financial and non-monetary burden to implement additional security procedures--provides the flexibility that tort law, and the concept of reasonableness, envisions." *Id.* at 201-02.

Note 2

There is also a 30-day cure provision for fixing security issues and notifying the customer "that no further violations shall occur." It seems rather dangerous for a company to state that "no further violations shall occur" after the fix. No matter how good the fix is, there is always the risk of a new hack on the same system. This statement is also very broad and vague. It will be interesting to see how this is litigated.

Note 3

In a Complaint for: (1) Violation of the California Consumer Privacy Act s 1798.150; (2) Violation of California's Unfair Competition Law, Cal. Bus. & Prof. Code s 17200, et seq.; (3) Negligence; (4) Breach of Contract; (5) Breach of Implied Contract in Atkinson et al. v. Minted, Inc., 2020 WL 3254373; No. 3:20-cv-03869 (N.D. Cal. June 11, 2020), plaintiffs seek relief under the CCPA as well as other laws. The allegations of the complaint, in relevant part, state:

Violation of the CCPA, Cal. Civ. Code § 1798.150

. . . 73. Defendant violated § 1798.150 of the CCPA by failing to prevent Plaintiffs' and Class members' nonencrypted PII from unauthorized access and exfiltration, theft, or disclosure as a result of Defendant's violations of its duty to implement and maintain reasonable security procedures and practices appropriate to the nature of the information.

74. Defendant collects consumers' personal information as defined in Cal. Civ. Code § 1798.140. Defendant has a duty to implement and maintain reasonable security procedures and practices to protect this personal information. As identified herein, Defendant failed to do so. As a direct and proximate result of Defendant's acts, Plaintiffs' and Class members' personal information, including unencrypted names, emails and passwords among other information, was subjected to unauthorized access and exfiltration, theft, or disclosure.

75. Plaintiffs and Class members seek injunctive or other equitable relief to ensure Defendant hereinafter adequately safeguards customers' PII by implementing reasonable security procedures and practices. Such relief is particularly important because Defendant continues to hold customers' PII, including Plaintiffs' and Class members' PII. These individuals have an interest in ensuring that their PII is reasonably protected.

76. On June 9, 2020, Plaintiffs' counsel sent a notice letter to Minted's registered service agent via UPS Next Day Air. Plaintiffs' counsel also emailed a copy of the notice to the *help@minted.com* email address on June 11. Assuming Minted cannot cure the Data Breach within 30 days, and Plaintiffs believe such cure is not possible under these facts and circumstances, then Plaintiffs intend to promptly amend this complaint to seek actual damages and statutory damages of $750 per customer record subject to the Data Breach on behalf of the California Class as permitted by the CCPA."

Note 4

In a 2016 California Data Breach Report that pre-dates the CCPA, former California Attorney General Kamala Harris discusses recommendations to address cybersecurity data breaches. The Report states that entities should comply with the Center for Internet Security Controls. The Report summarizes those Controls:

Count Connections

Know the hardware and software connected to your network. (CSC 1, CSC 2)

Configure Securely

Implement key security settings. (CSC 3, CSC 11)

Control Users

Limit user and administrator privileges. (CSC 5, CSC 14)

Update Continuously

Continuously assess vulnerabilities and patch holes to stay current. (CSC 4)

Protect Key Assets

Secure critical assets and attack vectors. (CSC 7, CSC 10, CSC 13)

Implement Defenses

Defend against malware and boundary intrusions. (CSC 8, CSC 12)

Block Access

Block vulnerable access points. (CSC 9, CSC 15, CSC 18)

Train Staff

Provide security training to employees and vendors with access. (CSC 17)

Monitor Activity

Monitor accounts and network audit logs. (CSC 6, CSC 16)

Test and Plan Response

Conduct tests of your defenses and be prepared to respond promptly and effectively to security incidents. (CSC 19, CSC 20)

The Report also recommends the use of multi-factor authentication and encryption for data in transit.[370]

Note 5

Several bills concerning a federal scheme for privacy have been brought before Congress, some of which include cybersecurity provisions. Notably, one of the most important issues concerns preemption of state privacy laws. The U.S. Senate Committee on Commerce, Science and Transportation held hearings on September 23, 2020, concerning privacy titled, "Revisiting the Need for Federal Privacy Data Privacy

---

[370] CALIFORNIA DATA BREACH REPORT, CAL. DEP'T OF JUST. (2016), *available at* https://oag.ca.gov/sites/all/files/agweb/pdfs/dbr/2016-data-breach-report.pdf.

Legislation."[371] Professor William Kovacic, Former Chairman and Commissioner of the Federal Trade Commission, offered his written testimony titled, "The Redesign of the U.S. Privacy Policy Institutional Framework."[372] In that testimony, Professor Kovacic provides an outline of the various institutions involved in privacy regulation in the United States and importantly notes that there is coordination between those institutions. He further notes the importance of California and its approach to policy as having an international impact and role. California Attorney General Xavier Becerra also offered written testimony making several points, including noting how the CCPA is a first step, a private right of action is needed, technology companies should create tools to make data control by the user easier and that the Congress should not preempt state law in this field.[373]

Note 6

The Uniform Law Commission issued the Uniform Personal Data Protection Act [UPDPA] in 2021.[374] The Act contains a provision requiring controllers and processors to conduct and maintain privacy and data security assessments. Importantly, Section 10 assessments require an analysis of the likelihood of issues with respect to the confidentiality and integrity of consumer information, including a recitation of the "efforts to mitigate the risks" and "the extent to which the data practices" are in compliance with the Act. The contents of the assessments are considered confidential and not available through state public record act requests or civil discovery. As of the time of publication of this book, the UPDPA has not been adopted by any state.

QUESTIONS

After reviewing the first chapters in this book concerning the different schemes for cybersecurity protection, as well as state statutes, do you think that the federal government should create an agency responsible for all cybersecurity matters? What are the costs and benefits of a single federal government agency taking over cybersecurity? Do you think a federal legislative one-size-fits-all cybersecurity scheme that would preempt state law would be beneficial to consumers? Why do you think a former chairman of the FTC would favor a strong state approach? There have been numerous proposed federal privacy laws, but none have been adopted. See Gopal Ratnam, *2018 CQ Roll Call Washington Data Privacy Briefing 0653* (""In the past 100 years no industry has improved security without being forced" because the marketplace

---

[371] Revisiting the Need for Federal Data Privacy Legislation: Hearing Before the Comm. on Com., Sci., and Transp., 116th Cong. (2020).

[372] Revisiting the Need for Federal Data Privacy Legislation: Hearing Before the Comm. on Com., Sci., and Transp., 116th Cong. (2020) (testimony of William E. Kovacic, Professor of L. and Pol'y, Geo. Wash. U. L. Sch.).

[373] Revisiting the Need for Federal Data Privacy Legislation: Hearing Before the Comm. on Com., Sci., and Transp., 116th Cong. (2020) (testimony of Xavier Becerra, Cal. Att'y Gen.).

[374] UNIFORM LAW COMMISSION, UNIFORM PERSONAL DATA PROTECTION ACT (2021), available at https://www.uniformlaws.org/viewdocument/final-act?CommunityKey=28443329-e343-4cbc-8c72-60b12fd18477&tab=librarydocuments.

doesn't reward safety and security while it favors risk takers who can make quick and cheap technologies, said Bruce Schneier, who also teaches at Harvard Law School and recently wrote a book, "Click Here to Kill Everybody: Security and Survival in a Hyper-connected World."").

CHAPTER NINE. ADDITIONAL PRIVATE CAUSES OF ACTION FOR CYBERSECURITY BREACHES

9.1 Introduction

This Chapter reviews private causes of action for security breaches of information also known as data breaches. Private causes of action may be brought after a data breach has occurred. For example, actions could be brought against companies who serve as a repository of customer data or companies responsible for securing the data of other companies. Causes of action for data breaches may include negligence, breach of contract, misrepresentation, unjust enrichment, general unfair trade practices, breach of warranty, breach of fiduciary duty and other statutory-based claims. Depending on the scope of the breach, plaintiffs may bring class action lawsuits for data breaches relying on the aforementioned causes of action. The purpose of this chapter is to provide a brief of overview of some of the common causes of action as well as reoccurring issues raised by these suits. One of the most important issues concerning causes of action for data breaches includes standing.

9.2 Standing

Reilly v. Ceridian Corp., 664 F.3d 38 (3d. Cir. 2011).

ALDISERT, Circuit Judge. . . .

I. A.

Ceridian is a payroll processing firm with its principal place of business in Bloomington, Minnesota. To process its commercial business customers' payrolls, Ceridian collects information about its customers' employees. This information may include employees' names, addresses, social security numbers, dates of birth, and bank account information.

Reilly and Pluemacher were employees of the Brach Eichler law firm, a Ceridian customer, until September 2003. Ceridian entered into contracts with Appellants' employer and the employers of the proposed class members to provide payroll processing services.

On or about December 22, 2009, Ceridian suffered a security breach. An unknown hacker infiltrated Ceridian's Powerpay system and potentially gained access to personal and financial information belonging to Appellants and approximately 27,000 employees at 1,900 companies. It is not known whether the hacker read, copied, or understood the data.

Working with law enforcement and professional investigators, Ceridian determined what information the hacker may have accessed. On about January 29, 2010, Ceridian sent letters to the potential identity theft victims, informing them of the breach:

"[S]ome of your personal information ... may have been illegally accessed by an unauthorized hacker.... [T]he information accessed included your first name, last name, social security number and, in several cases, birth date and/or the bank account that is used for direct deposit." App. 00039. Ceridian arranged to provide the potentially affected individuals with one year of free credit monitoring and identity theft protection. Individuals had until April 30, 2010, to enroll in the free program, and Ceridian included instructions on how to do so within its letter.

B.

On October 7, 2010, Appellants filed a complaint against Ceridian, on behalf of themselves and all others similarly situated, in the United States District Court for the District of New Jersey. Appellants alleged that they: (1) have an increased risk of identity theft, (2) incurred costs to monitor their credit activity, and (3) suffered from emotional distress.

On December 15, 2010, Ceridian filed a motion to dismiss pursuant to Rules 12(b)(1) and 12(b)(6), Federal Rules of Civil Procedure, for lack of standing and failure to state a claim. On February 22, 2011, the District Court granted Ceridian's motion, holding that Appellants lacked Article III standing. The Court further held that, assuming Appellants had standing, they nonetheless failed to adequately allege the damage, injury, and ascertainable loss elements of their claims. Appellants timely filed their Notice of Appeal on March 18, 2011.

II.

We have jurisdiction to review the District Court's final judgment pursuant to 28 U.S.C. § 1291. But "[a]bsent Article III standing, a federal court does not have subject matter jurisdiction to address a plaintiff's claims, and they must be dismissed." Taliaferro v. Darby Twp. Zoning Bd., 458 F.3d 181, 188 (3d Cir.2006). Hence, we exercise plenary review over the District Court's jurisdictional determinations, see Graden v. Conexant Sys. Inc., 496 F.3d 291, 294 n. 2 (3d Cir.2007), "review[ing] only whether the allegations on the face of the complaint, taken as true, allege facts sufficient to invoke the jurisdiction of the district court," Common Cause of Penn. v. Pennsylvania, 558 F.3d 249, 257 (3d Cir.2009). We also review de novo a district court's grant of a motion to dismiss for failure to state a claim under Rule 12(b)(6). See Vallies v. Sky Bank, 432 F.3d 493, 494 (3d Cir.2006).

Because the District Court dismissed Appellants' claims pursuant to Rules 12(b)(1) and 12(b)(6), we accept as true all well-pleaded allegations and construe the complaint in the light most favorable to the non-moving party. See Lewis v. Atlas Van Lines, Inc., 542 F.3d 403, 405 (3d Cir.2008).

III.

Appellants' allegations of hypothetical, future injury do not establish standing under Article III. For the following reasons we will therefore affirm the District Court's dismissal.

A.

Article III limits our jurisdiction to actual "cases or controversies." U.S. Const. art. III, § 2. One element of this "bedrock requirement" is that plaintiffs "must establish that they have standing to sue." Raines v. Byrd, 521 U.S. 811, 818, 117 S.Ct. 2312, 138 L.Ed.2d 849 (1997). It is the plaintiffs' burden, at the pleading stage, to establish standing. See Lujan v. Defenders of Wildlife, 504 U.S. 555, 561, 112 S.Ct. 2130, 119 L.Ed.2d 351 (1992). Although "general factual allegations of injury resulting from the defendant's conduct may suffice," Lujan, 504 U.S. at 561, 112 S.Ct. 2130, the complaint must still "clearly and specifically set forth facts sufficient to satisfy" Article III. Whitmore v. Arkansas, 495 U.S. 149, 155, 110 S.Ct. 1717, 109 L.Ed.2d 135 (1990).

"[T]he question of standing is whether the litigant is entitled to have the court decide the merits of the dispute or of particular issues." Elk Grove Unified Sch. Dist. v. Newdow, 542 U.S. 1, 11 (2004). Standing implicates both constitutional and prudential limitations on the jurisdiction of federal courts. See Storino, 322 F.3d at 296. Constitutional standing requires an "injury-in-fact, which is an invasion of a legally protected interest that is (a) concrete and particularized, and (b) actual or imminent, not conjectural or hypothetical." Danvers Motor Co. v. Ford Motor Co., 432 F.3d 286, 290–291 (3d Cir.2005). An injury-in-fact "must be concrete in both a qualitative and temporal sense. The complainant must allege an injury to himself that is 'distinct and palpable,' as distinguished from merely 'abstract,' and the alleged harm must be actual or imminent, not 'conjectural' or 'hypothetical.'" Whitmore, 495 U.S. at 155, 110 S.Ct. 1717.

Allegations of "possible future injury" are not sufficient to satisfy Article III. Whitmore, 495 U.S. at 158, 110 S.Ct. 1717; see also Lujan, 504 U.S. at 564 n. 2, 112 S.Ct. 2130 (stating that allegations of a future harm at some indefinite time cannot be an "actual or imminent injury"). Instead, "[a] threatened injury must be 'certainly impending,' " and "proceed with a high degree of immediacy, so as to reduce the possibility of deciding a case in which no injury would have occurred at all," Lujan, 504 U.S. at 564 n. 2, 112 S.Ct. 2130; Whitmore, 495 U.S. at 155, 110 S.Ct. 1717 (explaining that the imminence requirement "ensures that courts do not entertain suits based on speculative or hypothetical harms"). A plaintiff therefore lacks standing if his "injury" stems from an indefinite risk of future harms inflicted by unknown third parties.

B.

We conclude that Appellants' allegations of hypothetical, future injury are insufficient to establish standing. Appellants' contentions rely on speculation that the hacker: (1) read, copied, and understood their personal information; (2) intends to commit future criminal acts by misusing the information; and (3) is able to use such information to the detriment of Appellants by making unauthorized transactions in Appellants' names. Unless and until these conjectures come true, Appellants have not suffered any injury; there has been no misuse of the information, and thus, no harm.

The Supreme Court has consistently dismissed cases for lack of standing when the alleged future harm is neither imminent nor certainly impending. For example, the

Lujan Court addressed whether plaintiffs had standing when seeking to enjoin the funding of activities that threatened certain species' habitats. The Court held that plaintiffs' claim that they would visit the project sites "some day" did not meet the requirement that their injury be "imminent." 504 U.S. at 564 n. 2, 112 S.Ct. 2130 ("[W]e are at a loss to see how, as a factual matter, the standard can be met by respondents' mere profession of an intent, some day, to return."). Appellants' allegations here are even more speculative than those at issue in Lujan. There, the acts necessary to make the injury "imminent" were within plaintiffs' own control, because all plaintiffs needed to do was travel to the site to see the alleged destruction of wildlife take place. Yet, notwithstanding their stated intent to travel to the site at some point in the future—which the Court had no reason to doubt—their harm was not imminent enough to confer standing. See id. Here, Appellants' alleged increased risk of future injury is even more attenuated, because it is dependent on entirely speculative, future actions of an unknown third-party.

The requirement that an injury be "certainly impending" is best illustrated by City of Los Angeles v. Lyons, 461 U.S. 95, 103 S.Ct. 1660, 75 L.Ed.2d 675 (1983). There, the Court held that a plaintiff lacked standing to enjoin the Los Angeles Police Department from using a controversial chokehold technique on arrestees. Although the plaintiff had already once been subjected to this maneuver, the future harm he sought to enjoin depended on the police again arresting and choking him. See id. at 105, 103 S.Ct. 1660. Unlike the plaintiff in Lyons, Appellants in this case have yet to suffer any harm, and their alleged increased risk of future injury is nothing more than speculation. As such, the alleged injury is not "certainly impending." Lujan, 504 U.S. at 564 n. 2, 112 S.Ct. 2130.

Our Court, too, has refused to confer standing when plaintiffs fail to allege an imminent injury-in-fact. For example, although the plaintiffs in Storino contended that a municipal ordinance would eventually result in a commercially undesirable zoning change, we held that the allegation of future economic damage was too conjectural and insufficient to meet the "injury in fact" requirement. As we stated in that case, "one cannot describe how the [plaintiffs] will be injured without beginning the explanation with the word 'if.' The prospective damages, described by the [plaintiffs] as certain, are, in reality, conjectural." Similarly, we cannot now describe how Appellants will be injured in this case without beginning our explanation with the word "if": if the hacker read, copied, and understood the hacked information, and if the hacker attempts to use the information, and if he does so successfully, only then will Appellants have suffered an injury.

C.

In this increasingly digitized world, a number of courts have had occasion to decide whether the "risk of future harm" posed by data security breaches confers standing on persons whose information may have been accessed. Most courts have held that such plaintiffs lack standing because the harm is too speculative. See Amburgy v. Express Scripts, Inc., 671 F.Supp.2d 1046, 1051–1053 (E.D.Mo.2009); see also Key v.

DSW Inc., 454 F.Supp.2d 684, 690 (S.D.Ohio 2006). We agree with the holdings in those cases. Here, no evidence suggests that the data has been—or will ever be—misused. The present test is actuality, not hypothetical speculations concerning the possibility of future injury. Appellants' allegations of an increased risk of identity theft resulting from a security breach are therefore insufficient to secure standing.

Principally relying on Pisciotta v. Old National Bancorp, 499 F.3d 629 (7th Cir.2007), Appellants contend that an increased risk of identity theft is itself a harm sufficient to confer standing. In Pisciotta, plaintiffs brought a class action against a bank after its website had been hacked, alleging that the bank failed to adequately secure the personal information it solicited (such as names, addresses, birthdates, and social security numbers) when consumers applied for banking services on its website. The named plaintiffs did not allege "any completed direct financial loss to their accounts" nor that they "already had been the victim of identity theft as a result of the breach." The court, nonetheless, held that plaintiffs had standing, concluding, without explanation, that the "injury-in-fact requirement can be satisfied by a threat of future harm or by an act which harms the plaintiff only by increasing the risk of future harm that the plaintiff would have otherwise faced, absent the defendant's actions."

Appellants rely as well on Krottner v. Starbucks Corp., 628 F.3d 1139 (9th Cir.2010), in which the Court of Appeals for the Ninth Circuit conferred standing under circumstances much different from those present here. There, plaintiffs' "names, addresses, and social security numbers were stored on a laptop that was stolen from Starbucks." The court concluded that plaintiffs met the standing requirement through their allegations of "a credible threat of real and immediate harm stemming from the theft of a laptop containing their unencrypted personal data." Appellants here contend that we should follow Pisciotta and Krottner and hold that the "credible threat of real and immediate harm" stemming from the security breach of Ceridian's Powerpay system satisfies the standing requirement.

But these cases have little persuasive value here; in Pisciotta and Krottner, the threatened harms were significantly more "imminent" and "certainly impending" than the alleged harm here. In Pisciotta, there was evidence that "the [hacker's] intrusion was sophisticated, intentional and malicious." In Krottner, someone attempted to open a bank account with a plaintiff's information following the physical theft of the laptop. Here, there is no evidence that the intrusion was intentional or malicious. Appellants have alleged no misuse, and therefore, no injury. Indeed, no identifiable taking occurred; all that is known is that a firewall was penetrated. Appellants' string of hypothetical injuries do not meet the requirement of an "actual or imminent" injury.

D.

Neither Pisciotta nor Krottner, moreover, discussed the constitutional standing requirements and how they apply to generalized data theft situations. Indeed, the Pisciotta court did not mention—let alone discuss—the requirement that a threatened injury must be "imminent" and "certainly impending" to confer standing. Instead of making a determination as to whether the alleged injury was "certainly impending," both courts simply analogized data-security-breach situations to defective-medical-device, toxic-substance-exposure, or environmental-injury cases.

Still, Appellants urge us to adopt those courts' skimpy rationale for three reasons. First, Appellants here expended monies on credit monitoring and insurance to protect their safety, just as plaintiffs in defective-medical-device and toxic-substance-exposure cases expend monies on medical monitoring. See Sutton v. St. Jude Med. S.C., Inc., 419 F.3d 568, 570–575 (6th Cir.2005). Second, members of this putative class may very well have suffered emotional distress from the incident, which also represents a bodily injury, just as plaintiffs in the medical-device and toxic-tort cases have suffered physical injuries. See In re Paoli R.R. Yard PCB Litig., 916 F.2d 829, 850 (3d Cir.1990) (explaining that "courts have begun to recognize claims like medical monitoring, which can allow plaintiffs some relief even absent present manifestations of physical injury" and that "in the toxic tort context, courts have allowed plaintiffs to recover for emotional distress suffered because of the fear of contracting a toxic exposure disease"). Third, injury to one's identity is extraordinarily unique and money may not even compensate one for the injuries sustained, just as environmental injury is unique and monetary compensation may not adequately return plaintiffs to their original position. See Cent. Delta Water Agency v. United States, 306 F.3d 938, 950 (9th Cir.2002) (holding that "monetary compensation may well not adequately return plaintiffs to their original position" because harms to the environment "are frequently difficult or impossible to remedy"). Based on these analogies, Appellants contend they have established standing here. These analogies do not persuade us, because defective-medical-device and toxic-substance-exposure cases confer standing based on two important factors not present in data breach cases.

First, in those cases, an injury has undoubtedly occurred. In medical-device cases, a defective device has been implanted into the human body with a quantifiable risk of failure. See Sutton, 419 F.3d at 574. Similarly, exposure to a toxic substance causes injury; cells are damaged and a disease mechanism has been introduced. See In re Paoli R.R. Yard PCB Litig., 916 F.2d at 851, 851–852 (explaining that "persons exposed to toxic chemicals emanating from the landfill have an increased risk of invisible genetic damage and a present cause of action for their injury" because "in a toxic age, significant harm can be done to an individual by a tortfeasor, notwithstanding latent manifestation of that harm"). Hence, the damage has been done; we just cannot yet quantify how it will manifest itself.

In data breach cases where no misuse is alleged, however, there has been no injury—indeed, no change in the status quo. Here, Appellants' credit card statements are exactly the same today as they would have been had Ceridian's database never been hacked. Moreover, there is no quantifiable risk of damage in the future. See id. at 852 ("As a proximate result of exposure [to the toxic substance], plaintiff suffers a significantly increased risk of contracting a serious latent disease."). Any damages that may occur here are entirely speculative and dependent on the skill and intent of the hacker.

Second, standing in medical-device and toxic-tort cases hinges on human health concerns. See Sutton, 419 F.3d at 575. Courts resist strictly applying the "actual injury" test when the future harm involves human suffering or premature death. As the Sutton court explained, "there is something to be said for disease prevention, as opposed to disease treatment. Waiting for a plaintiff to suffer physical injury before allowing any redress whatsoever is both overly harsh and economically inefficient." Id. The deceased, after all, have little use for compensation. This case implicates none of these concerns. The hacker did not change or injure Appellants' bodies; any harm that may occur—if all of Appellants' stated fears are actually realized—may be redressed in due time through money damages after the harm occurs with no fear that litigants will be dead or disabled from the onset of the injury. See Key, 454 F.Supp.2d at 690 ("[T]hose [medical monitoring] cases not only act as a narrow exception to the general rule of courts rejecting standing based on increased risk of future harm, but are also factually distinguishable from the present case [of a data security breach].").

An analogy to environmental injury cases fails as well. As the Court of Appeals for the Ninth Circuit explained in Central Delta Water Agency, standing is unique in the environmental context because monetary compensation may not adequately return plaintiffs to their original position. See id. at 950 ("The extinction of a species, the destruction of a wilderness habitat, or the fouling of air and water are harms that are frequently difficult or impossible to remedy [by monetary compensation]."). In a data breach case, however, there is no reason to believe that monetary compensation will not return plaintiffs to their original position completely—if the hacked information is actually read, copied, understood, and misused to a plaintiff's detriment. To the contrary, unlike priceless "mountains majesty," the thing feared lost here is simple cash, which is easily and precisely compensable with a monetary award. We therefore decline to analogize this case to those cases in the medical device, toxic tort or environmental injury contexts.

E.

Finally, we conclude that Appellants' alleged time and money expenditures to monitor their financial information do not establish standing, because costs incurred to watch for a speculative chain of future events based on hypothetical future criminal acts are no more "actual" injuries than the alleged "increased risk of injury" which forms the basis for Appellants' claims. See Randolph v. ING Life Ins. & Annuity Co., 486 F.Supp.2d 1, 8 (D.D.C.2007) ("[T]he 'lost data' cases ... clearly reject the theory that a plaintiff is entitled to reimbursement for credit monitoring services or for time and money spent monitoring his or her credit."). That a plaintiff has willingly incurred costs to protect against an alleged increased risk of identity theft is not enough to demonstrate a "concrete and particularized" or "actual or imminent" injury. Id.; see also Amburgy, 671 F.Supp.2d at 1053 (holding plaintiff lacked standing even though he allegedly spent time and money to protect himself from risk of future injury); Hammond v. Bank of N.Y. Mellon Corp., No. 08–6060, 2010 WL 2643307, at *4, *7 (S.D.N.Y. June 25, 2010) (noting that plaintiffs' "out-of-pocket expenses incurred to proactively safeguard and/or repair their credit" and the "expense of comprehensive credit monitoring" did not confer standing); Allison v. Aetna, Inc., No. 09–2560, 2010 WL 3719243, at *5 n. 7 (E.D.Pa. Mar. 9, 2010) (rejecting claims for time and money spent on credit monitoring due to a perceived risk of harm as the basis for an injury in fact).

Although Appellants have incurred expenses to monitor their accounts and "to protect their personal and financial information from imminent misuse and/or identity theft," App. 00021, they have not done so as a result of any actual injury (e.g. because their private information was misused or their identities stolen). Rather, they prophylactically spent money to ease fears of future third-party criminality. Such misuse is only speculative—not imminent. The claim that they incurred expenses in anticipation of future harm, therefore, is not sufficient to confer standing.

IV.

The District Court correctly held that Appellants failed to plead specific facts demonstrating they have standing to bring this suit under Article III, because Appellants' allegations of an increased risk of identity theft as a result of the security breach are hypothetical, future injuries, and are therefore insufficient to establish standing. For the reasons set forth, we will AFFIRM the District Court's order granting Ceridian's motion to dismiss.

NOTES

Note 1

Please recall the *LabMD* case in Chapter 2 concerning FTC enforcement. Do you think that the *Reilly* appellate court would have arrived at a different result if medical information was involved such as in *LabMD*? In *LabMD*, the FTC opinion noted that social security numbers are difficult if not impossible to change. Do you think the *Reilly* appellate court adequately considered the sensitivity of the loss of financial information? What cybersecurity incentives does this decision set up? Does it create an incentive to notify customers and provide aid immediately as was done in the case by the defendants?

Transunion LLC v. Rameriz, 141 S.Ct. 2190 (2021).

Justice KAVANAUGH delivered the opinion of the Court.

To have Article III standing to sue in federal court, plaintiffs must demonstrate, among other things, that they suffered a concrete harm. No concrete harm, no standing. Central to assessing concreteness is whether the asserted harm has a "close relationship" to a harm traditionally recognized as providing a basis for a lawsuit in American courts— such as physical harm, monetary harm, or various intangible harms including (as relevant here) reputational harm. *Spokeo, Inc. v. Robins*, 578 U. S. 330, 340–341, 136 S.Ct. 1540, 194 L.Ed.2d 635 (2016).

In this case, a class of 8,185 individuals sued TransUnion, a credit reporting agency, in federal court under the Fair Credit Reporting Act. The plaintiffs claimed that TransUnion failed to use reasonable procedures to ensure the accuracy of their credit files, as maintained internally by TransUnion. For 1,853 of the class members,

TransUnion provided misleading credit reports to third-party businesses. We conclude that those 1,853 class members have demonstrated concrete reputational harm and thus have Article III standing to sue on the reasonable-procedures claim. The internal credit files of the other 6,332 class members were *not* provided to third-party businesses during the relevant time period. We conclude that those 6,332 class members have not demonstrated concrete harm and thus lack Article III standing to sue on the reasonable-procedures claim.

In two other claims, all 8,185 class members complained about formatting defects in certain mailings sent to them by TransUnion. But the class members other than the named plaintiff Sergio Ramirez have not demonstrated that the alleged formatting errors caused them any concrete harm. Therefore, except for Ramirez, the class members do not have standing as to those two claims.

Over Judge McKeown's dissent, the U. S. Court of Appeals for the Ninth Circuit ruled that all 8,185 class members have standing as to all three claims. The Court of Appeals approved a class damages award of about $40 million. In light of our conclusion that (i) only 1,853 class members have standing for the reasonable-procedures claim and (ii) only Ramirez himself has standing for the two formatting claims relating to the mailings, we reverse the judgment of the Ninth Circuit and remand the case for further proceedings consistent with this opinion.

I

In 1970, Congress passed and President Nixon signed the Fair Credit Reporting Act. 84 Stat. 1127, as amended, 15 U.S.C. § 1681 *et seq.* The Act seeks to promote "fair and accurate credit reporting" and to protect consumer privacy. § 1681(a). To achieve those goals, the Act regulates the consumer reporting agencies that compile and disseminate personal information about consumers.

The Act "imposes a host of requirements concerning the creation and use of consumer reports." *Spokeo, Inc.* v. *Robins*, 578 U. S. 330, 335, 136 S.Ct. 1540, 194 L.Ed.2d 635 (2016). Three of the Act's requirements are relevant to this case. *First*, the Act requires consumer reporting agencies to "follow reasonable procedures to assure maximum possible accuracy" in consumer reports. § 1681e(b). *Second*, the Act provides that consumer reporting agencies must, upon request, disclose to the consumer "[a]ll information in the consumer's file at the time of the request." § 1681g(a)(1). *Third*, the Act compels consumer reporting agencies to "provide to a consumer, with each written disclosure by the agency to the consumer," a "summary of rights" prepared by the Consumer Financial Protection Bureau. § 1681g(c)(2).

The Act creates a cause of action for consumers to sue and recover damages for certain violations. The Act provides: "Any person who willfully fails to comply with any requirement imposed under this subchapter with respect to any consumer is liable to that consumer" for actual damages or for statutory damages not less than $100 and not more than $1,000, as well as for punitive damages and attorney's fees. § 1681n(a).

TransUnion is one of the "Big Three" credit reporting agencies, along with Equifax and Experian. As a credit reporting agency, TransUnion compiles personal and financial information about individual consumers to create consumer reports. TransUnion then sells those consumer reports for use by entities such as banks, landlords, and car dealerships that request information about the creditworthiness of individual consumers.

Beginning in 2002, TransUnion introduced an add-on product called OFAC Name Screen Alert. OFAC is the U. S. Treasury Department's Office of Foreign Assets Control. OFAC maintains a list of "specially designated nationals" who threaten America's national security. Individuals on the OFAC list are terrorists, drug traffickers, or other serious criminals. It is generally unlawful to transact business with any person on the list. 31 C.F.R. pt. 501, App. A (2020). TransUnion created the OFAC Name Screen Alert to help businesses avoid transacting with individuals on OFAC's list.

When this litigation arose, Name Screen worked in the following way: When a business opted into the Name Screen service, TransUnion would conduct its ordinary credit check of the consumer, and it would also use third-party software to compare the consumer's name against the OFAC list. If the consumer's first and last name matched the first and last name of an individual on OFAC's list, then TransUnion would place an alert on the credit report indicating that the consumer's name was a "potential match" to a name on the OFAC list. TransUnion did not compare any data other than first and last names. Unsurprisingly, TransUnion's Name Screen product generated many false positives. Thousands of law-abiding Americans happen to share a first and last name with one of the terrorists, drug traffickers, or serious criminals on OFAC's list of specially designated nationals.

Sergio Ramirez learned the hard way that he is one such individual. On February 27, 2011, Ramirez visited a Nissan dealership in Dublin, California, seeking to buy a Nissan Maxima. Ramirez was accompanied by his wife and his father-in-law. After Ramirez and his wife selected a color and negotiated a price, the dealership ran a credit check on both Ramirez and his wife. Ramirez's credit report, produced by TransUnion, contained the following alert: "***OFAC ADVISOR ALERT - INPUT NAME MATCHES NAME ON THE OFAC DATABASE." App. 84. A Nissan salesman told Ramirez that Nissan would not sell the car to him because his name was on a "'terrorist list.'" *Id.*, at 333. Ramirez's wife had to purchase the car in her own name.

The next day, Ramirez called TransUnion and requested a copy of his credit file. TransUnion sent Ramirez a mailing that same day that included his credit file and the statutorily required summary of rights prepared by the CFPB. The mailing did not mention the OFAC alert in Ramirez's file. The following day, TransUnion sent Ramirez a second mailing—a letter alerting him that his name was considered a potential match to names on the OFAC list. The second mailing did not include an additional copy of the summary of rights. Concerned about the mailings, Ramirez consulted a lawyer and ultimately canceled a planned trip to Mexico. TransUnion eventually removed the OFAC alert from Ramirez's file.

In February 2012, Ramirez sued TransUnion and alleged three violations of the Fair Credit Reporting Act. *First*, he alleged that TransUnion, by using the Name Screen product, failed to follow reasonable procedures to ensure the accuracy of information in his credit file. See § 1681e(b). *Second*, he claimed that TransUnion failed to provide him with *all* the information in his credit file upon his request. In particular, TransUnion's first mailing did not include the fact that Ramirez's name was a potential match for a name on the OFAC list. See § 1681g(a)(1). *Third*, Ramirez asserted that TransUnion violated its obligation to provide him with a summary of his rights "with each written disclosure," because TransUnion's second mailing did not contain a summary of Ramirez's rights. § 1681g(c)(2). Ramirez requested statutory and punitive damages.

Ramirez also sought to certify a class of all people in the United States to whom TransUnion sent a mailing during the period from January 1, 2011, to July 26, 2011, that was similar in form to the second mailing that Ramirez received. TransUnion opposed certification. The U. S. District Court for the Northern District of California rejected TransUnion's argument and certified the class. 301 F.R.D. 408 (2014).

Before trial, the parties stipulated that the class contained 8,185 members, including Ramirez. The parties also stipulated that only 1,853 members of the class (including Ramirez) had their credit reports disseminated by TransUnion to potential creditors during the period from January 1, 2011, to July 26, 2011. The District Court ruled that all 8,185 class members had Article III standing. 2016 WL 6070490, *5 (Oct. 17, 2016).

At trial, Ramirez testified about his experience at the Nissan dealership. But Ramirez did not present evidence about the experiences of other members of the class.

After six days of trial, the jury returned a verdict for the plaintiffs. The jury awarded each class member $984.22 in statutory damages and $6,353.08 in punitive damages for a total award of more than $60 million. The District Court rejected all of TransUnion's post-trial motions.

The U. S. Court of Appeals for the Ninth Circuit affirmed in relevant part. 951 F.3d 1008 (2020). The court held that all members of the class had Article III standing to recover damages for all three claims. The court also concluded that Ramirez's claims were typical of the class's claims for purposes of Rule 23 of the Federal Rules of Civil Procedure. Finally, the court reduced the punitive damages award to $3,936.88 per class member, thus reducing the total award to about $40 million.

Judge McKeown dissented in relevant part. As to the reasonable-procedures claim, she concluded that only the 1,853 class members whose reports were actually disseminated by TransUnion to third parties had Article III standing to recover damages. In her view, the remaining 6,332 class members did not suffer a concrete injury sufficient for standing. As to the two claims related to the mailings, Judge McKeown would have held that none of the 8,185 class members other than the named plaintiff Ramirez had standing as to those claims.

We granted certiorari. 592 U. S. ——, 141 S.Ct. 972, 208 L.Ed.2d 504 (2020).

II

The question in this case is whether the 8,185 class members have Article III standing as to their three claims. In Part II, we summarize the requirements of Article III standing—in particular, the requirement that plaintiffs demonstrate a "concrete harm." In Part III, we then apply the concrete-harm requirement to the plaintiffs' lawsuit against TransUnion.

A

The "law of Art. III standing is built on a single basic idea—the idea of separation of powers." *Raines v. Byrd*, 521 U.S. 811, 820, 117 S.Ct. 2312, 138 L.Ed.2d 849 (1997) (internal quotation marks omitted). Separation of powers "was not simply an abstract generalization in the minds of the Framers: it was woven into the document that they drafted in Philadelphia in the summer of 1787." *INS v. Chadha*, 462 U.S. 919, 946, 103 S.Ct. 2764, 77 L.Ed.2d 317 (1983) (internal quotation marks omitted).

Therefore, we start with the text of the Constitution. Article III confines the federal judicial power to the resolution of "Cases" and "Controversies." For there to be a case or controversy under Article III, the plaintiff must have a "'personal stake'" in the case—in other words, standing. *Raines*, 521 U.S., at 819, 117 S.Ct. 2312. To demonstrate their personal stake, plaintiffs must be able to sufficiently answer the question: "'What's it to you?'" Scalia, The Doctrine of Standing as an Essential Element of the Separation of Powers, 17 Suffolk U. L. Rev. 881, 882 (1983).

To answer that question in a way sufficient to establish standing, a plaintiff must show (i) that he suffered an injury in fact that is concrete, particularized, and actual or imminent; (ii) that the injury was likely caused by the defendant; and (iii) that the injury would likely be redressed by judicial relief. *Lujan v. Defenders of Wildlife*, 504 U.S. 555, 560–561, 112 S.Ct. 2130, 119 L.Ed.2d 351 (1992). If "the plaintiff does not claim to have suffered an injury that the defendant caused and the court can remedy, there is no case or controversy for the federal court to resolve." *Casillas v. Madison Avenue Assocs., Inc.*, 926 F.3d 329, 333 (CA7 2019) (Barrett, J.).

Requiring a plaintiff to demonstrate a concrete and particularized injury caused by the defendant and redressable by the court ensures that federal courts decide only "the rights of individuals," *Marbury v. Madison*, 1 Cranch 137, 170, 5 U.S. 137, 2 L.Ed. 60 (1803), and that federal courts exercise "their proper function in a limited and separated government," Roberts, Article III Limits on Statutory Standing, 42 Duke L. J. 1219, 1224 (1993). Under Article III, federal courts do not adjudicate hypothetical or abstract disputes. Federal courts do not possess a roving commission to publicly opine on every legal question. Federal courts do not exercise general legal oversight of the Legislative and Executive Branches, or of private entities. And federal courts do not issue advisory opinions. As Madison explained in Philadelphia, federal courts instead decide only matters "of a Judiciary Nature." 2 Records of the Federal Convention of 1787, p. 430 (M. Farrand ed. 1966).

In sum, under Article III, a federal court may resolve only "a real controversy with real impact on real persons." *American Legion* v. *American Humanist Assn.*, 588 U. S. ——, ——, 139 S.Ct. 2067, 2103, 204 L.Ed.2d 452 (2019).

B

The question in this case focuses on the Article III requirement that the plaintiff 's injury in fact be "concrete"—that is, "real, and not abstract." *Spokeo, Inc.* v. *Robins*, 578 U. S. 330, 340, 136 S.Ct. 1540, 194 L.Ed.2d 635 (2016).

What makes a harm concrete for purposes of Article III? As a general matter, the Court has explained that "history and tradition offer a meaningful guide to the types of cases that Article III empowers federal courts to consider." *Sprint Communications Co.* v. *APCC Services, Inc.*, 554 U.S. 269, 274, 128 S.Ct. 2531, 171 L.Ed.2d 424 (2008). And with respect to the concrete-harm requirement in particular, this Court's opinion in *Spokeo* v. *Robins* indicated that courts should assess whether the alleged injury to the plaintiff has a "close relationship" to a harm "traditionally" recognized as providing a basis for a lawsuit in American courts. 578 U. S., at 341, 136 S.Ct. 1540. That inquiry asks whether plaintiffs have identified a close historical or common-law analogue for their asserted injury. *Spokeo* does not require an exact duplicate in American history and tradition. But *Spokeo* is not an open-ended invitation for federal courts to loosen Article III based on contemporary, evolving beliefs about what kinds of suits should be heard in federal courts.

As *Spokeo* explained, certain harms readily qualify as concrete injuries under Article III. The most obvious are traditional tangible harms, such as physical harms and monetary harms. If a defendant has caused physical or monetary injury to the plaintiff, the plaintiff has suffered a concrete injury in fact under Article III.

Various intangible harms can also be concrete. Chief among them are injuries with a close relationship to harms traditionally recognized as providing a basis for lawsuits in American courts. *Id.*, at 340–341, 136 S.Ct. 1540. Those include, for example, reputational harms, disclosure of private information, and intrusion upon seclusion. See, *e.g.*, *Meese v. Keene*, 481 U.S. 465, 473, 107 S.Ct. 1862, 95 L.Ed.2d 415 (1987) (reputational harms); *Davis v. Federal Election Comm'n*, 554 U.S. 724, 733, 128 S.Ct. 2759, 171 L.Ed.2d 737 (2008) (disclosure of private information); see also *Gadelhak v. AT&T Services, Inc.*, 950 F.3d 458, 462 (CA7 2020) (Barrett, J.) (intrusion upon seclusion). And those traditional harms may also include harms specified by the Constitution itself. See, *e.g.*, *Spokeo*, 578 U. S., at 340, 136 S.Ct. 1540 (citing *Pleasant Grove City v. Summum*, 555 U.S. 460, 129 S.Ct. 1125, 172 L.Ed.2d 853 (2009) (abridgment of free speech), and *Church of Lukumi Babalu Aye, Inc. v. Hialeah*, 508 U.S. 520, 113 S.Ct. 2217, 124 L.Ed.2d 472 (1993) (infringement of free exercise)).

In determining whether a harm is sufficiently concrete to qualify as an injury in fact, the Court in *Spokeo* said that Congress's views may be "instructive." 578 U. S., at 341, 136 S.Ct. 1540. Courts must afford due respect to Congress's decision to impose a statutory prohibition or obligation on a defendant, and to grant a plaintiff a cause of action to sue over the defendant's violation of that statutory prohibition or obligation. See *id.,* at 340–341, 136 S.Ct. 1540. In that way, Congress may "elevate to the status of legally cognizable injuries concrete, *de facto* injuries that were previously inadequate in law." *Id.,* at 341, 136 S.Ct. 1540 (alterations and internal quotation marks omitted); see *Lujan,* 504 U.S. at 562–563, 578, 112 S.Ct. 2130; cf., *e.g., Allen v. Wright,* 468 U.S. 737, 757, n. 22, 104 S.Ct. 3315, 82 L.Ed.2d 556 (1984) (discriminatory treatment). But even though "Congress may 'elevate' harms that 'exist' in the real world before Congress recognized them to actionable legal status, it may not simply enact an injury into existence, using its lawmaking power to transform something that is not remotely harmful into something that is." *Hagy v. Demers & Adams,* 882 F.3d 616, 622 (CA6 2018) (Sutton, J.) (citing *Spokeo,* 578 U. S., at 341, 136 S.Ct. 1540).

Importantly, this Court has rejected the proposition that "a plaintiff automatically satisfies the injury-in-fact requirement whenever a statute grants a person a statutory right and purports to authorize that person to sue to vindicate that right." *Spokeo,* 578 U. S., at 341, 136 S.Ct. 1540. As the Court emphasized in *Spokeo,* "Article III standing requires a concrete injury even in the context of a statutory violation." *Ibid.*

Congress's creation of a statutory prohibition or obligation and a cause of action does not relieve courts of their responsibility to independently decide whether a plaintiff has suffered a concrete harm under Article III any more than, for example, Congress's enactment of a law regulating speech relieves courts of their responsibility to independently decide whether the law violates the First Amendment. Cf. *United States v. Eichman,* 496 U.S. 310, 317–318, 110 S.Ct. 2404, 110 L.Ed.2d 287 (1990). As Judge Katsas has rightly stated, "we cannot treat an injury as 'concrete' for Article III purposes based only on Congress's say-so." *Trichell v. Midland Credit Mgmt., Inc.,* 964 F.3d 990, 999, n. 2 (CA11 2020) (sitting by designation).

For standing purposes, therefore, an important difference exists between (i) a plaintiff's statutory cause of action to sue a defendant over the defendant's violation of federal law, and (ii) a plaintiff's suffering concrete harm because of the defendant's violation of federal law. Congress may enact legal prohibitions and obligations. And Congress may create causes of action for plaintiffs to sue defendants who violate those legal prohibitions or obligations. But under Article III, an injury in law is not an injury in fact. Only those plaintiffs who have been *concretely harmed* by a defendant's statutory violation may sue that private defendant over that violation in federal court. As then-Judge Barrett succinctly summarized, "Article III grants federal courts the power to redress harms that defendants cause plaintiffs, not a freewheeling power to hold defendants accountable for legal infractions." *Casillas,* 926 F.3d at 332.

To appreciate how the Article III "concrete harm" principle operates in practice, consider two different hypothetical plaintiffs. Suppose first that a Maine citizen's land is polluted by a nearby factory. She sues the company, alleging that it violated a federal environmental law and damaged her property. Suppose also that a second plaintiff in Hawaii files a federal lawsuit alleging that the same company in Maine violated that same environmental law by polluting land in Maine. The violation did not personally harm the plaintiff in Hawaii.

Even if Congress affords both hypothetical plaintiffs a cause of action (with statutory damages available) to sue over the defendant's legal violation, Article III standing doctrine sharply distinguishes between those two scenarios. The first lawsuit may of course proceed in federal court because the plaintiff has suffered concrete harm to her property. But the second lawsuit may not proceed because that plaintiff has not suffered any physical, monetary, or cognizable intangible harm traditionally recognized as providing a basis for a lawsuit in American courts. An uninjured plaintiff who sues in those circumstances is, by definition, not seeking to remedy any harm to herself but instead is merely seeking to ensure a defendant's "compliance with regulatory law" (and, of course, to obtain some money via the statutory damages). *Spokeo,* 578 U. S., at 345, 136 S.Ct. 1540 (THOMAS, J., concurring) (internal quotation marks omitted); see *Steel Co.,* 523 U.S., at 106–107, 118 S.Ct. 1003. Those are not grounds for Article III standing.[1]

As those examples illustrate, if the law of Article III did not require plaintiffs to demonstrate a "concrete harm," Congress could authorize virtually any citizen to bring a statutory damages suit against virtually any defendant who violated virtually any federal law. Such an expansive understanding of Article III would flout constitutional text, history, and precedent. In our view, the public interest that private entities comply with the law cannot "be converted into an individual right by a statute that denominates it as such, and that permits all citizens (or, for that matter, a subclass of citizens who suffer no distinctive concrete harm) to sue." *Lujan,* 504 U.S., at 576–577, 112 S.Ct. 2130.[2]

A regime where Congress could freely authorize *unharmed* plaintiffs to sue defendants who violate federal law not only would violate Article III but also would infringe on the Executive Branch's Article II authority. We accept the "displacement of the democratically elected branches when necessary to decide an actual case." Roberts, 42 Duke L. J., at 1230. But otherwise, the choice of how to prioritize and how aggressively to pursue legal actions against defendants who violate the law falls within the discretion of the Executive Branch, not within the purview of private plaintiffs (and their attorneys). Private plaintiffs are not accountable to the people and are not charged with pursuing the public interest in enforcing a defendant's general compliance with regulatory law. See *Lujan,* 504 U.S., at 577, 112 S.Ct. 2130.

In sum, the concrete-harm requirement is essential to the Constitution's separation of powers. To be sure, the concrete-harm requirement can be difficult to apply in some cases. Some advocate that the concrete-harm requirement be ditched altogether, on the theory that it would be more efficient or convenient to simply say that a statutory violation and a cause of action suffice to afford a plaintiff standing. But as the Court has often stated, "the fact that a given law or procedure is efficient, convenient, and useful in facilitating functions of government, standing alone, will not save it if it is contrary to the Constitution." *Chadha*, 462 U.S., at 944, 103 S.Ct. 2764. So it is here.[3]

III

We now apply those fundamental standing principles to this lawsuit. We must determine whether the 8,185 class members have standing to sue TransUnion for its alleged violations of the Fair Credit Reporting Act. The plaintiffs argue that TransUnion failed to comply with statutory obligations (i) to follow reasonable procedures to ensure the accuracy of credit files so that the files would not include OFAC alerts labeling the plaintiffs as potential terrorists; and (ii) to provide a consumer, upon request, with his or her complete credit file, including a summary of rights.

Some preliminaries: As the party invoking federal jurisdiction, the plaintiffs bear the burden of demonstrating that they have standing. See *Lujan v. Defenders of Wildlife*, 504 U.S. 555, 561, 112 S.Ct. 2130, 119 L.Ed.2d 351 (1992). Every class member must have Article III standing in order to recover individual damages. "Article III does not give federal courts the power to order relief to any uninjured plaintiff, class action or not." *Tyson Foods, Inc. v. Bouaphakeo*, 577 U.S. 442, 466, 136 S.Ct. 1036, 194 L.Ed.2d 124 (2016) (ROBERTS, C. J., concurring).[4] Plaintiffs must maintain their personal interest in the dispute at all stages of litigation. *Davis v. Federal Election Comm'n*, 554 U.S. 724, 733, 128 S.Ct. 2759, 171 L.Ed.2d 737 (2008). A plaintiff must demonstrate standing "with the manner and degree of evidence required at the successive stages of the litigation." *Lujan*, 504 U.S., at 561, 112 S.Ct. 2130. Therefore, in a case like this that proceeds to trial, the specific facts set forth by the plaintiff to support standing "must be supported adequately by the evidence adduced at trial." *Ibid.* (internal quotation marks omitted). And standing is not dispensed in gross; rather, plaintiffs must demonstrate standing for each claim that they press and for each form of relief that they seek (for example, injunctive relief and damages). *Davis*, 554 U.S., at 734, 128 S.Ct. 2759.

A

We first address the plaintiffs' claim that TransUnion failed to "follow reasonable procedures to assure maximum possible accuracy" of the plaintiffs' credit files maintained by TransUnion. 15 U.S.C. § 1681e(b). In particular, the plaintiffs argue that TransUnion did not do enough to ensure that OFAC alerts labeling them as potential terrorists were not included in their credit files.

Assuming that the plaintiffs are correct that TransUnion violated its obligations under the Fair Credit Reporting Act to use reasonable procedures in internally maintaining the credit files, we must determine whether the 8,185 class members suffered concrete harm from TransUnion's failure to employ reasonable procedures.[5]

1

Start with the 1,853 class members (including the named plaintiff Ramirez) whose reports were disseminated to third-party businesses. The plaintiffs argue that the publication to a third party of a credit report bearing a misleading OFAC alert injures the subject of the report. The plaintiffs contend that this injury bears a "close relationship" to a harm traditionally recognized as providing a basis for a lawsuit in American courts—namely, the reputational harm associated with the tort of defamation. *Spokeo, Inc.* v. *Robins*, 578 U. S. 330, 341, 136 S.Ct. 1540, 194 L.Ed.2d 635 (2016).

We agree with the plaintiffs. Under longstanding American law, a person is injured when a defamatory statement "that would subject him to hatred, contempt, or ridicule" is published to a third party. *Milkovich v. Lorain Journal Co.*, 497 U.S. 1, 13, 110 S.Ct. 2695, 111 L.Ed.2d 1 (1990) (internal quotation marks omitted); *Gertz v. Robert Welch, Inc.*, 418 U.S. 323, 349, 94 S.Ct. 2997, 41 L.Ed.2d 789 (1974); see also Restatement of Torts § 559 (1938). TransUnion provided third parties with credit reports containing OFAC alerts that labeled the class members as potential terrorists, drug traffickers, or serious criminals. The 1,853 class members therefore suffered a harm with a "close relationship" to the harm associated with the tort of defamation. We have no trouble concluding that the 1,853 class members suffered a concrete harm that qualifies as an injury in fact.

TransUnion counters that those 1,853 class members did not suffer a harm with a "close relationship" to defamation because the OFAC alerts on the disseminated credit reports were only misleading and not literally false. See *id.*, § 558. TransUnion points out that the reports merely identified a consumer as a *potential* match" to an individual on the OFAC list—a fact that TransUnion says is not technically false.

In looking to whether a plaintiff's asserted harm has a "close relationship" to a harm traditionally recognized as providing a basis for a lawsuit in American courts, we do not require an exact duplicate. The harm from being labeled a "potential terrorist" bears a close relationship to the harm from being labeled a "terrorist." In other words, the harm from a misleading statement of this kind bears a sufficiently close relationship to the harm from a false and defamatory statement.

In short, the 1,853 class members whose reports were disseminated to third parties suffered a concrete injury in fact under Article III.

2

The remaining 6,332 class members are a different story. To be sure, their credit files, which were maintained by TransUnion, contained misleading OFAC alerts. But the parties stipulated that TransUnion did not provide those plaintiffs' credit information to any potential creditors during the class period from January 2011 to July 2011. Given the absence of dissemination, we must determine whether the 6,332 class members suffered some other concrete harm for purposes of Article III.

The initial question is whether the mere existence of a misleading OFAC alert in a consumer's internal credit file at TransUnion constitutes a concrete injury. As Judge Tatel phrased it in a similar context, "if inaccurate information falls into" a consumer's credit file, "does it make a sound?" *Owner-Operator Independent Drivers Assn., Inc. v. United States Dept. of Transp.*, 879 F.3d 339, 344 (CADC 2018).

Writing the opinion for the D. C. Circuit in *Owner-Operator*, Judge Tatel answered no. Publication is "essential to liability" in a suit for defamation. Restatement of Torts § 577, Comment *a*, at 192. And there is "no historical or common-law analog where the mere existence of inaccurate information, absent dissemination, amounts to concrete injury." *Owner-Operator*, 879 F.3d at 344–345. "Since the basis of the action for words was the loss of credit or fame, and not the insult, it was always necessary to show a publication of the words." J. Baker, An Introduction to English Legal History 474 (5th ed. 2019). Other Courts of Appeals have similarly recognized that, as Judge Colloton summarized, the "retention of information lawfully obtained, without further disclosure, traditionally has not provided the basis for a lawsuit in American courts," meaning that the mere existence of inaccurate information in a database is insufficient to confer Article III standing. *Braitberg v. Charter Communications, Inc.*, 836 F.3d 925, 930 (CA8 2016); see *Gubala v. Time Warner Cable, Inc.*, 846 F.3d 909, 912 (CA7 2017).

The standing inquiry in this case thus distinguishes between (i) credit files that consumer reporting agencies maintain internally and (ii) the consumer credit reports that consumer reporting agencies disseminate to third-party creditors. The mere presence of an inaccuracy in an internal credit file, if it is not disclosed to a third party, causes no concrete harm. In cases such as these where allegedly inaccurate or misleading information sits in a company database, the plaintiffs' harm is roughly the same, legally speaking, as if someone wrote a defamatory letter and then stored it in her desk drawer. A letter that is not sent does not harm anyone, no matter how insulting the letter is. So too here.[6]

Because the plaintiffs cannot demonstrate that the misleading information in the internal credit files itself constitutes a concrete harm, the plaintiffs advance a separate argument based on an asserted *risk of future harm*. They say that the 6,332 class members suffered a concrete injury for Article III purposes because the existence of misleading OFAC alerts in their internal credit files exposed them to a material risk that the information would be disseminated in the future to third parties and thereby cause them harm. The plaintiffs rely on language from *Spokeo* where the Court said that "the risk of real harm" (or as the Court otherwise stated, a "material risk of harm") can sometimes "satisfy the requirement of concreteness." 578 U. S., at 341–342, 136 S.Ct. 1540 (citing *Clapper v. Amnesty Int'l USA*, 568 U.S. 398, 133 S.Ct. 1138, 185 L.Ed.2d 264 (2013)).

To support its statement that a material risk of future harm can satisfy the concrete-harm requirement, *Spokeo* cited this Court's decision in *Clapper*. But importantly, *Clapper* involved a suit for *injunctive relief*. As this Court has recognized, a person exposed to a risk of future harm may pursue forward-looking, injunctive relief to prevent the harm from occurring, at least so long as the risk of harm is sufficiently imminent and substantial. See *Clapper*, 568 U.S., at 414, n. 5, 133 S.Ct. 1138; *Los*

Angeles v. Lyons, 461 U.S. 95, 102, 103 S.Ct. 1660, 75 L.Ed.2d 675 (1983); see also *Gubala*, 846 F.3d, at 912.

But a plaintiff must "demonstrate standing separately for each form of relief sought." *Friends of the Earth*, 528 U.S., at 185, 120 S.Ct. 693. Therefore, a plaintiff's standing to seek injunctive relief does not necessarily mean that the plaintiff has standing to seek retrospective damages.

TransUnion advances a persuasive argument that in a suit for damages, the mere risk of future harm, standing alone, cannot qualify as a concrete harm—at least unless the exposure to the risk of future harm itself causes a *separate* concrete harm. Brief for Petitioner 39, n. 4; Tr. of Oral Arg. 36.[7] TransUnion contends that if an individual is exposed to a risk of future harm, time will eventually reveal whether the risk materializes in the form of actual harm. If the risk of future harm materializes and the individual suffers a concrete harm, then the harm itself, and not the pre-existing risk, will constitute a basis for the person's injury and for damages. If the risk of future harm does *not* materialize, then the individual cannot establish a concrete harm sufficient for standing, according to TransUnion.

Consider an example. Suppose that a woman drives home from work a quarter mile ahead of a reckless driver who is dangerously swerving across lanes. The reckless driver has exposed the woman to a risk of future harm, but the risk does not materialize and the woman makes it home safely. As counsel for TransUnion stated, that would ordinarily be cause for celebration, not a lawsuit. *Id.*, at 8. But if the reckless driver crashes into the woman's car, the situation would be different, and (assuming a cause of action) the woman could sue the driver for damages.

The plaintiffs note that *Spokeo* cited libel and slander *per se* as examples of cases where, as the plaintiffs see it, a mere risk of harm suffices for a damages claim. But as Judge Tatel explained for the D.C. Circuit, libel and slander *per se* "require evidence of *publication*." *Owner-Operator*, 879 F.3d, at 345. And for those torts, publication is generally presumed to cause a harm, albeit not a readily quantifiable harm. As *Spokeo* noted, "the law has long permitted recovery by certain tort victims *even if their harms may be difficult to prove or measure*." 578 U. S., at 341, 136 S.Ct. 1540 (emphasis added). But there is a significant difference between (i) an actual harm that has occurred but is not readily quantifiable, as in cases of libel and slander *per se*, and (ii) a mere risk of future harm. By citing libel and slander *per se*, *Spokeo* did not hold that the mere risk of future harm, without more, suffices to demonstrate Article III standing in a suit for damages.

Here, the 6,332 plaintiffs did not demonstrate that the risk of future harm materialized—that is, that the inaccurate OFAC alerts in their internal TransUnion credit files were ever provided to third parties or caused a denial of credit. Nor did those plaintiffs present evidence that the class members were independently harmed by their exposure to the risk itself—that is, that they suffered some other injury (such as an emotional injury) from the mere risk that their credit reports would be provided to third-party businesses. Therefore, the 6,332 plaintiffs' argument for standing for their damages claims based on an asserted risk of future harm is unavailing.

Even apart from that fundamental problem with their argument based on the risk of future harm, the plaintiffs did not factually establish a sufficient risk of future harm to support Article III standing. As Judge McKeown explained in her dissent, the risk of future harm that the 6,332 plaintiffs identified—the risk of dissemination to third parties—was too speculative to support Article III standing. 951 F.3d 1008, 1040 (CA9 2020); see *Whitmore v. Arkansas*, 495 U.S. 149, 157, 110 S.Ct. 1717, 109 L.Ed.2d 135 (1990). The plaintiffs claimed that TransUnion could have divulged their misleading credit information to a third party at any moment. But the plaintiffs did not demonstrate a sufficient likelihood that their individual credit information would be requested by third-party businesses and provided by TransUnion during the relevant time period. Nor did the plaintiffs demonstrate that there was a sufficient likelihood that TransUnion would otherwise intentionally or accidentally release their information to third parties. "Because no evidence in the record establishes a serious likelihood of disclosure, we cannot simply presume a material risk of concrete harm." 951 F.3d, at 1040 (opinion of McKeown, J.).

Moreover, the plaintiffs did not present any evidence that the 6,332 class members even *knew* that there were OFAC alerts in their internal TransUnion credit files. If those plaintiffs prevailed in this case, many of them would first learn that they were "injured" when they received a check compensating them for their supposed "injury." It is difficult to see how a risk of future harm could supply the basis for a plaintiff's standing when the plaintiff did not even know that there was a risk of future harm.

Finally, the plaintiffs advance one last argument for why the 6,332 class members are similarly situated to the other 1,853 class members and thus should have standing. The 6,332 plaintiffs note that they sought damages for the entire 46-month period permitted by the statute of limitations, whereas the stipulation regarding dissemination covered only 7 of those months. They argue that the credit reports of many of those 6,332 class members were likely also sent to third parties outside of the period covered by the stipulation because all of the class members requested copies of their reports, and consumers usually do not request copies unless they are contemplating a transaction that would trigger a credit check.

That is a serious argument, but in the end, we conclude that it fails to support standing for the 6,332 class members. The plaintiffs had the burden to prove at trial that their reports were actually sent to third-party businesses. The inferences on which the argument rests are too weak to demonstrate that the reports of any particular number of the 6,332 class members were sent to third-party businesses. The plaintiffs' attorneys could have attempted to show that some or all of the 6,332 class members were injured in that way. They presumably could have sought the names and addresses of those individuals, and they could have contacted them. In the face of the stipulation, which pointedly failed to demonstrate dissemination for those class members, the inferences on which the plaintiffs rely are insufficient to support standing. Cf. *Interstate Circuit, Inc. v. United States*, 306 U.S. 208, 226, 59 S.Ct. 467, 83 L.Ed. 610 (1939) ("The production of weak evidence when strong is available can lead only to the conclusion that the strong would have been adverse").

In sum, the 6,332 class members whose internal TransUnion credit files were not disseminated to third-party businesses did not suffer a concrete harm. By contrast, the 1,853 class members (including Ramirez) whose credit reports were disseminated to third-party businesses during the class period suffered a concrete harm.

B

We next address the plaintiffs' standing to recover damages for two other claims in the complaint: the disclosure claim and the summary-of-rights claim. Those two claims are intertwined.

In the disclosure claim, the plaintiffs alleged that TransUnion breached its obligation to provide them with their complete credit files upon request. According to the plaintiffs, TransUnion sent the plaintiffs copies of their credit files that omitted the OFAC information, and then in a second mailing sent the OFAC information. See § 1681g(a)(1). In the summary-of-rights claim, the plaintiffs further asserted that TransUnion should have included another summary of rights in that second mailing— the mailing that included the OFAC information. See § 1681g(c)(2). As the plaintiffs note, the disclosure and summary-of-rights requirements are designed to protect consumers' interests in learning of any inaccuracies in their credit files so that they can promptly correct the files before they are disseminated to third parties.

In support of standing, the plaintiffs thus contend that the TransUnion mailings were formatted incorrectly and deprived them of their right to receive information in the format required by statute. But the plaintiffs have not demonstrated that the format of TransUnion's mailings caused them a harm with a close relationship to a harm traditionally recognized as providing a basis for a lawsuit in American courts. See *Spokeo*, 578 U. S., at 341, 136 S.Ct. 1540. In fact, they do not demonstrate that they suffered any harm *at all* from the formatting violations. The plaintiffs presented no evidence that, other than Ramirez, "a single other class member so much as *opened* the dual mailings," "nor that they were confused, distressed, or relied on the information in any way." 951 F.3d, at 1039, 1041 (opinion of McKeown, J.) (emphasis added). The plaintiffs put forth no evidence, moreover, that the plaintiffs would have tried to correct their credit files—and thereby prevented dissemination of a misleading report—had they been sent the information in the proper format. *Ibid.* Without any evidence of harm caused by the format of the mailings, these are "bare procedural violation[s], divorced from any concrete harm." *Spokeo*, 578 U. S., at 341, 136 S.Ct. 1540. That does not suffice for Article III standing.[8]

The plaintiffs separately argue that TransUnion's formatting violations created a risk of future harm. Specifically, the plaintiffs contend that consumers who received the information in this dual-mailing format were at risk of not learning about the OFAC alert in their credit files. They say that they were thus at risk of not being able to correct their credit files before TransUnion disseminated credit reports containing the misleading information to third-party businesses. As noted above, the risk of future harm on its own does not support Article III standing for the plaintiffs' damages claim. In any event, the plaintiffs made no effort here to explain how the formatting error prevented them from contacting TransUnion to correct any errors before misleading credit reports were disseminated to third-party businesses. To reiterate, there is no evidence that "a single other class member so much as opened the dual mailings," "nor that they were confused, distressed, or relied on the information in any way." 951 F.3d, at 1039, 1041 (opinion of McKeown, J.).

For its part, the United States as *amicus curiae*, but not the plaintiffs, separately asserts that the plaintiffs suffered a concrete "informational injury" under several of this Court's precedents. See *Federal Election Comm'n v. Akins*, 524 U.S. 11, 118 S.Ct. 1777, 141 L.Ed.2d 10 (1998); *Public Citizen v. Department of Justice*, 491 U.S. 440, 109 S.Ct. 2558, 105 L.Ed.2d 377 (1989). We disagree. The plaintiffs did not allege that they failed to receive any required information. They argued only that they received it *in the wrong format*. Therefore, *Akins* and *Public Citizen* do not control here. In addition, those cases involved denial of information subject to public-disclosure or sunshine laws that entitle all members of the public to certain information. This case does not involve such a public-disclosure law. See *Casillas v. Madison Avenue Assocs., Inc.*, 926 F.3d 329, 338 (CA7 2019); *Trichell v. Midland Credit Mgmt., Inc.*, 964 F.3d 990, 1004 (CA11 2020). Moreover, the plaintiffs have identified no "downstream consequences" from failing to receive the required information. *Trichell*, 964 F.3d at 1004. They did not demonstrate, for example, that the alleged information deficit hindered their ability to correct erroneous information before it was later sent to third parties. An "asserted informational injury that causes no adverse effects cannot satisfy Article III." *Ibid.*

* * *

No concrete harm, no standing. The 1,853 class members whose credit reports were provided to third-party businesses suffered a concrete harm and thus have standing as to the reasonable-procedures claim. The 6,332 class members whose credit reports were not provided to third-party businesses did not suffer a concrete harm and thus do not have standing as to the reasonable-procedures claim. As for the claims pertaining to the format of TransUnion's mailings, none of the 8,185 class members other than the named plaintiff Ramirez suffered a concrete harm.

We reverse the judgment of the U. S. Court of Appeals for the Ninth Circuit and remand the case for further proceedings consistent with this opinion. In light of our conclusion about Article III standing, we need not decide whether Ramirez's claims were typical of the claims of the class under Rule 23. On remand, the Ninth Circuit may consider in the first instance whether class certification is appropriate in light of our conclusion about standing.

It is so ordered.

NOTES

Note 1

In *Spokeo v. Robins*, 136 S.Ct. 1540 (2016), the U.S. Supreme Court emphasized that for allegations to confer standing the injury must be "concrete" and not just particularized in considering a claim under the Fair Credit Reporting Act. The Supreme Court stated:

> "Concrete" is not, however, necessarily synonymous with "tangible." Although tangible injuries are perhaps easier to recognize, we have confirmed in many of our previous cases that intangible injuries can nevertheless be concrete.

> In determining whether an intangible harm constitutes injury in fact, both history and the judgment of Congress play important roles. Because the doctrine of standing derives from the case-or-controversy requirement, and because that requirement in turn is grounded in historical practice, it is instructive to consider whether an alleged intangible harm has a close relationship to a harm that has traditionally been regarded as providing a basis for a lawsuit in English or American courts. In addition, because Congress is well positioned to identify intangible harms that meet minimum Article III requirements, its judgment is also instructive and important. Thus, we said in *Lujan* that Congress may "elevat[e] to the status of legally cognizable injuries concrete, *de facto* injuries that were previously inadequate in law." Similarly, Justice Kennedy's concurrence in that case explained that "Congress has the power to define injuries and articulate chains of causation that will give rise to a case or controversy where none existed before."

> Congress' role in identifying and elevating intangible harms does not mean that a plaintiff automatically satisfies the injury-in-fact requirement whenever a statute grants a person a statutory right and purports to authorize that person to sue to vindicate that right. Article III standing requires a concrete injury even in the context of a statutory violation. For that reason, Robins could not, for example, allege a bare procedural violation, divorced from any concrete harm, and satisfy the injury-in-fact requirement of Article III.

> This does not mean, however, that the risk of real harm cannot satisfy the requirement of concreteness. For example, the law has long permitted recovery by certain tort victims even if their harms may be difficult to prove or measure. Just as the common law permitted suit in such instances, the violation of a procedural right granted by statute can be sufficient in some circumstances to constitute injury in fact. In other

words, a plaintiff in such a case need not allege any *additional* harm beyond the one Congress has identified.

In the context of this particular case, these general principles tell us two things: On the one hand, Congress plainly sought to curb the dissemination of false information by adopting procedures designed to decrease that risk. On the other hand, Robins cannot satisfy the demands of Article III by alleging a bare procedural violation. A violation of one of the FCRA's procedural requirements may result in no harm. For example, even if a consumer reporting agency fails to provide the required notice to a user of the agency's consumer information, that information regardless may be entirely accurate. In addition, not all inaccuracies cause harm or present any material risk of harm. An example that comes readily to mind is an incorrect zip code. It is difficult to imagine how the dissemination of an incorrect zip code, without more, could work any concrete harm.

Because the Ninth Circuit failed to fully appreciate the distinction between concreteness and particularization, its standing analysis was incomplete. It did not address the question framed by our discussion, namely, whether the particular procedural violations alleged in this case entail a degree of risk sufficient to meet the concreteness requirement. We take no position as to whether the Ninth Circuit's ultimate conclusion—that Robins adequately alleged an injury in fact—was correct. *Id.* at 1549-1550.

Note 2

On March 9, 2022, the SEC issued proposed regulations titled, "Cybersecurity Risk Management, Strategy, Governance, and Incident Disclosure." The SEC noted some of the costs associated with a cybersecurity incident:

> Costs due to business interruption, decreases in production, and delays in product launches; • Payments to meet ransom and other extortion demands; • Remediation costs, such as liability for stolen assets or information, repairs of system damage, and incentives to customers or business partners in an effort to maintain relationships after an attack; • Increased cybersecurity protection costs, which may include increased insurance premiums and the costs of making organizational changes, deploying additional personnel and protection technologies, training employees, and engaging third-party experts and consultants; • Lost revenues resulting from intellectual property theft and the unauthorized use of proprietary information or the failure to retain or attract customers following an attack; • Litigation and legal risks, including regulatory actions by state and federal governmental authorities and non-U.S. authorities; • Harm to employees and customers, violation of privacy laws, and reputational damage that adversely affects customer or

investor confidence; and • Damage to the company's competitiveness, stock price, and long-term shareholder value.

Note 3

In a pre-*TransUnion* decision, the DC Circuit in *In re Office of Personnel Management Data Security Breach Litigation*, 928 F.3d 42 (DC Cir. 2019) held that plaintiff government workers had met standing requirements:

> We begin with N[ational Treasury Employees Union] Plaintiffs. For standing purposes, we assume that NTEU Plaintiffs have, as they claim, a "constitutional right to informational privacy" that was violated "the moment that [cyberattackers stole] their inherently personal information * * * from OPM's deficiently secured databases." Furthermore, given NTEU Plaintiffs' allegations regarding OPM's continued failure to adequately secure its databases, it is reasonable to infer that there remains a "substantial risk" that their personal information will be stolen from OPM again in the future. With respect to this claim, the loss of a constitutionally protected privacy interest itself would qualify as a concrete, particularized, and actual injury in fact. And the ongoing and substantial threat to that privacy interest would be a concrete, particularized, and imminent injury in fact. Both claimed injuries are plausibly traceable to OPM's challenged conduct, and the latter is redressable either by a declaration that the agency's failure to protect NTEU Plaintiffs' personal information is unconstitutional or by an order requiring OPM to immediately correct deficiencies in its cybersecurity programs. Cf. ACLU v. Clapper, 785 F.3d 787, 801 (2d Cir. 2015) (holding that, where plaintiffs allege a Fourth Amendment "injury [stemming] from the very collection of their telephone metadata," they "have suffered a concrete and particularized injury fairly traceable to the challenged program and redressable by a favorable ruling"). Accordingly, NTEU Plaintiffs have standing based on their claimed constitutional injury.

However, the DC Circuit held that the "NTEU Plaintiffs have failed to state a claim that flaws in OPM's information-storage measures violated the Constitution:"

> Finally, we turn to NTEU Plaintiffs' constitutional claim. In that claim, NTEU Plaintiffs do not allege that OPM intentionally disclosed the records at issue or performed the functional equivalent of such a disclosure. See, e.g., NTEU Plaintiffs' Compl. ¶ 97, J.A. 186 (alleging "reckless indifference"). Instead, NTEU Plaintiffs challenge OPM's internal record-management and storage practices and policies as unconstitutionally trenching on their asserted constitutional right to privacy. See, e.g., id. at 3, J.A. 155 ("Although on notice of serious flaws in its data system security, OPM failed to adequately secure personal information in its possession—a failure that was reckless under the

circumstances."). They appear to rely on two closely related threads of constitutional doctrine, one couched in terms of privacy and relying mainly on dicta from Whalen v. Roe, 429 U.S. 589, 97 S.Ct. 869, 51 L.Ed.2d 64 (1977), the other phrased more directly in terms of substantive due process and relying mainly on cases providing relief for persons harmed through government neglect of their personal safety. We address them in that order.

A

As NTEU Plaintiffs see it, the Constitution creates a "zone of privacy" that protects an individual's "interest in avoiding disclosure of personal matters." This putative right to "informational privacy," they contend, is violated not only where government agents intentionally disclose an individual's personal information, but where, as alleged here, the agents "reckless[ly]" fail to prevent a third party from stealing it.

Even assuming "without deciding[ ] that the Constitution protects" some "sort" of privacy "interest in avoiding disclosure of personal matters," NTEU Plaintiffs have failed to state a legally cognizable claim. There is no authority for their contention that the Constitution imposes on the government an affirmative duty—untethered to specific constitutional provisions such as the First Amendment, to "safeguard personal information" from the criminal acts of third parties.

The asserted duty to "adequately secure" government computer networks finds no support in the Constitution or our history. Not once do NTEU Plaintiffs quote the very document from which they purport to derive their claimed right: the Constitution of the United States. Nor, for that matter, do they invoke this "Nation's history and tradition,"—an integral part of the formula for identifying unenumerated rights.

NTEU Plaintiffs instead ground their claim in a single line of Supreme Court dictum from more than 40 years ago that describes "[t]he cases sometimes characterized as protecting 'privacy' " as involving, among other interests, a vague "individual interest in avoiding disclosure of personal matters." But neither we nor the Supreme Court has ever held that this interest is a constitutional right. Both courts have, so far, steadfastly rejected all informational privacy claims purporting to rest on the Constitution, while simply "assum[ing]"—but never "deciding"—that the Constitution protects a "right of the sort mentioned in Whalen." Indeed, neither this court nor the Supreme Court has ever elaborated on the rationale for—or even defined the "precise contours of"—the putative right to informational privacy. Rather, we have underlined its "ambiguity."

Other circuits, to be sure, have embraced a form of the putative right. See, e.g., In re Crawford, 194 F.3d 954, 958 (9th Cir. 1999); see also NASA, 562 U.S. at 146 n.9, 131 S.Ct. 746 (collecting cases). But see Doe v. Wigginton, 21 F.3d 733, 740 (6th Cir. 1994). But NTEU Plaintiffs have identified no case in which the government has been held to have violated the alleged right without having "affirmatively provid[ed] the protected information to those unauthorized to view it." Neither have we. Absent any plausible mooring in the Constitution's text or the Nation's history and tradition, we join the district court in declining to recognize the proposed constitutional right to informational privacy that would be violated not only when information is intentionally disclosed (or the functional equivalent), but also "when a third party steals it."

Troubled as we are by NTEU Plaintiffs' allegations regarding the severity and scope of OPM's data security shortcomings, we are nonetheless reluctant to constitutionalize an information security code for the government's "internal operations." OPM "collect[ed] and store[d]" the information at issue here not as sovereign, but as employer—in "its role as the federal civil service's personnel manager." In this capacity—" 'as proprietor' and manager of [the government's] 'internal operation,' "— OPM was "dealing 'with citizen employees,'" and thus had a "much freer hand" than it would have had if it had brought "its sovereign power to bear on citizens at large,". That "freer hand" exists for good reason. Whereas the "Constitution requires that a President chosen by the entire Nation oversee the execution of the laws," albeit by a "vast and varied federal bureaucracy," constitutionally micromanaging employment records management systems, reaching down to the details of "how [best] to protect" the "information systems" holding employee data, would shift a material part of that oversight function to the judiciary, which generally lacks established standards or guideposts for making such administrative judgments—at least in the absence of congressional direction.

Another reason counsels hesitation. Establishing judicial supervision over the security of the government's employee data would "short-circuit" the response that Congress has already launched. As the Supreme Court observed in NASA, Congress has in the Privacy Act adopted significant "protections against disclosure" of personal information that " 'evidence a proper concern' for individual privacy." Here, as there, the Act limits the government's ability to maintain records "about an individual," 5 U.S.C. § 552a(e)(1), and "imposes criminal liability for willful violations of its nondisclosure obligations,". NTEU Plaintiffs, of course, allege that OPM has "fail[ed] to satisfy" these obligations, and argue that their "inherently personal information remains at substantial risk of additional breaches because" of OPM's failures. But if NTEU Plaintiffs are right (as we must assume in the current posture of the case), then they may invoke the remedial provisions found by Congress to best balance privacy and competing interests. See 5 U.S.C. § 552a(g)(1)(D), (g)(4).

Establishing a freestanding constitutional right to informational privacy that creates a duty to safeguard personal information from unauthorized access by third parties would force us to develop a labyrinth of technical rules. For example, does the Constitution require data "encrypt[ion]"? If so, must all data be encrypted in transit, as well as at rest? What of the encryption key: Is 256 bits necessary—or would 128 bits scrape by, constitutionally speaking? See Orin S. Kerr & Bruce Schneier, Encryption Workarounds, 106 Geo. L.J. 989, 993 (2018) (illustrating the difference). How about "personal identity verification (PIV) credentials"—are they constitutionally mandated? And most significant: What "tools" should "federal courts * * * use to answer" these questions? NTEU Plaintiffs do not say; more important, neither does the Constitution.

We therefore hold that, assuming (without deciding) the existence of a constitutional right to informational privacy, it affords relief only for intentional disclosures or their functional equivalent—which NTEU Plaintiffs do not allege.

QUESTION

The DC Circuit states, "Finally, we agree with the district court that, assuming a constitutional right to informational privacy, NTEU Plaintiffs have not alleged any violation of such a right."

Is there a constitutional right to informational privacy?

9.3 Other Common Law and Statutory Causes of Action

The following cases set forth numerous causes of action that may be brought based on data security breaches. Notably, the cases involve the well-known Target and Equifax security breaches. Indeed, one of the largest data breaches involved the Target Corporation. Supposedly over 70 class action lawsuits were filed against Target based on the data breach. After surviving challenges to standing, the district court found that plaintiffs sufficiently pled certain causes of action against Target based on a massive data security breach. The district court further certified the class action and was affirmed on appeal.

In re Target Corporation Customer Data Security Breach Litigation, 64 F.Supp.3d 1304 (D. Minn. 2014).

PAUL A. MAGNUSON, District Judge.

This matter is before the Court on Defendant Target Corporation's Motion to Dismiss the Consolidated Amended Class Action Complaint (Docket No. 163) in the

Financial Institution Cases. For the reasons that follow, the Motion is granted in part and denied in part.

BACKGROUND

In December 2013, Defendant Target Corporation, a Minnesota-headquartered retailer that is one of the nation's largest retail chains, announced that over a period of more than three weeks during the busy Christmas holiday shopping season, computer hackers had stolen credit- and debit-card information for approximately 110 million of Target's customers. Lawsuits soon followed this announcement, and ultimately the Judicial Panel on Multidistrict Litigation consolidated all federal lawsuits into this litigation. The multidistrict litigation consists of two distinct types of claims: those brought by consumers and those brought by financial institutions. The Motion at issue here seeks to dismiss only the Consolidated Amended Class Action Complaint filed in the financial institution cases.

The court in another consumer data breach case has succinctly described the nation's credit- and debit-card system as follows:

> Every day, merchants swipe millions of customers' payment cards. In the seconds that pass between the swipe and approval (or disapproval), the transaction information goes from the point of sale, to an acquirer bank, across the credit-card network, to the issuer bank, and back. Acquirer banks contract with merchants to process their transactions, while issuer banks provide credit to consumers and issue payment cards. The acquirer bank receives the transaction information from the merchant and forwards it over the network to the issuer bank for approval. If the issuer bank approves the transaction, that bank sends money to cover the transaction to the acquirer bank. The acquirer bank then forwards payment to the merchant.

In re Heartland Payment Sys., Inc. Customer Data Sec. Breach Litig., 834 F.Supp.2d 566, 574 (S.D.Tex.2011) (footnote omitted), *rev'd in part sub nom. Lone Star Nat'l Bank, N.A. v. Heartland Payment Sys., Inc.*, 729 F.3d 421 (5th Cir.2013). Plaintiffs here are a putative class of issuer banks whose customers' data was stolen in the Target data breach.

Plaintiffs' Complaint consists of four claims against Target. Count One contends that Target was negligent in failing to provide sufficient security to prevent the hackers from accessing customer data. Count Two asserts that Target violated Minnesota's Plastic Security Card Act, and Count Three alleges that this violation constitutes negligence per se. Count Four claims that Target's failure to inform Plaintiffs of its insufficient security constitutes a negligent misrepresentation by omission.

Target now seeks dismissal of all claims, arguing that Plaintiffs have failed to plead sufficient facts to establish any of their claims.

DISCUSSION . . .

A. Negligence

The parties agree that, at least for the purposes of this Motion, Minnesota law governs Plaintiffs' negligence claim. A claim of negligence under Minnesota law requires a plaintiff to allege four elements: duty, breach, causation, and injury. Target contends that Plaintiffs have failed to sufficiently allege that Target owed them a duty or that Target breached any duty.

1. Duty

Minnesota law imposes a duty "to act with reasonable care for the protection of others" in two situations:

> First, ... general negligence law imposes a general duty of reasonable care when the defendant's own conduct creates a foreseeable risk of injury to a foreseeable plaintiff.

> Second, a defendant owes a duty to protect a plaintiff when action by someone other than the defendant creates a foreseeable risk of harm to the plaintiff and the defendant and plaintiff stand in a special relationship. In other words, although a defendant generally does not have a duty "to warn or protect others from harm caused by a third party's conduct," an exception to this rule exists when the parties are in a special relationship and the harm to the plaintiff is foreseeable. The existence of a duty is a question of law.

Target contends that Plaintiffs' claims must be analyzed as falling under the third-party-harm type of negligence, so that to be liable Target and Plaintiffs must stand in a "special relationship" with one another. Target asks the Court to find as a matter of law that Target had no duty to Plaintiffs because there is no special relationship between Plaintiffs and Target and, in any event, "'a person has no duty under Minnesota law to protect another from the harmful conduct, including criminal conduct, of a third person.'"

Plaintiffs argue that this case is not a third-party-harm case but rather is a straightforward negligence case: Target's own conduct, in failing to maintain appropriate data security measures and in turning off some of the features of its security measures, created a foreseeable risk of the harm that occurred, and Plaintiffs were the foreseeable victims of that harm.

Plaintiffs also argue that, even if this situation is a third-party-harm situation where a special relationship between Plaintiffs and Target is required, they have pled such a special relationship here. But as Target points out, Minnesota has recognized this "separate and distinct" special relationship doctrine, in a very few, limited situations that are not applicable here. Moreover, the Minnesota Supreme Court has cautioned against extending those situations further.

At this preliminary stage of the litigation, Plaintiffs have plausibly pled a general negligence case. Although the third-party hackers' activities caused harm, Target played a key role in allowing the harm to occur. Indeed, Plaintiffs' allegation that Target purposely disabled one of the security features that would have prevented the harm is itself sufficient to plead a direct negligence case: Plaintiffs allege that Target's "own conduct create[d] a foreseeable risk of injury to a foreseeable plaintiff." Thus, the Court must determine whether Plaintiffs have sufficiently pled that Target owed Plaintiffs a duty of care under general negligence principles.

Minnesota courts have considered the following factors when determining whether a defendant owed a duty of care in a general negligence case: (1) the foreseeability of harm to the plaintiff, (2) the connection between the defendant's conduct and the injury suffered, (3) the moral blame attached to the defendant's conduct, (4) the policy of preventing future harm, and (5) the burden to the defendant and community of imposing a duty to exercise care with resulting liability for breach. The duty to exercise reasonable care arises from the probability or foreseeability of injury to the plaintiff. "Although in most cases the question of foreseeability is an issue for the jury, the foreseeability of harm can be decided by the court as a matter of law when the issue is clear." The Court evaluates Plaintiffs' allegations regarding these factors in the light most favorable to Plaintiffs, keeping in mind that this Motion tests only the sufficiency of those allegations and not the ultimate success of Plaintiffs' legal theories.

Plaintiffs have plausibly alleged that Target's actions and inactions—disabling certain security features and failing to heed the warning signs as the hackers' attack began—caused foreseeable harm to Plaintiffs. Plaintiffs have also plausibly alleged that Target's conduct both caused and exacerbated the harm they suffered. And Plaintiffs' allegation that Target was solely able and solely responsible to safeguard its and Plaintiffs' customers' data is also plausible. Imposing a duty on Target in this case will aid Minnesota's policy of punishing companies that do not secure consumers' credit-and debit-card information. And despite Target's dire warnings about the burden of imposing such a duty, it is clear that the institutional parties to credit- and debit-card transactions have already voluntarily assumed similar duties toward one another. *See, e.g., In re Heartland,* 834 F.Supp.2d at 588 (noting that Visa and MasterCard Card Operating Regulations, which apply between merchants, issuer banks, and acquirer banks, specify procedures for issuer banks to make claims in the event of data breaches).

That Plaintiffs have plausibly alleged a duty on Target's part is bolstered by the existence of Minnesota's Plastic Card Security Act, discussed in more detail below. While courts are reluctant to recognize duties of care in the absence of legislative imprimatur, the duty to safeguard credit- and debit-card data in Minnesota has received that legislative endorsement. And the legislature specifically acknowledged the availability of other causes of action arising out of a Minnesota company's failure to safeguard customers' information, stating that the remedies under the PCSA "are cumulative and do not restrict any other right or remedy otherwise available" to the issuer banks. Minn.Stat. § 325E.64, subd. 3. Plaintiffs have adequately pled that Target owed them a duty of care, and their negligence claim will not be dismissed on this basis.

2. Breach

Having determined that Plaintiffs have plausibly alleged the existence of a duty, there can be no doubt that Plaintiffs have also plausibly alleged that Target breached that duty by failing to safeguard Plaintiffs' customers' information. Because Target does not challenge Plaintiffs' allegations with respect to the elements of causation and damages, Plaintiffs' negligence claim succeeds in stating a claim on which relief can be granted.

B. Negligent Omission

Plaintiffs' negligent-misrepresentation-by-omission claim alleges that Target "failed to disclose material weaknesses in its data security systems and procedures" that it had an obligation to disclose. According to Target, this claim fails for multiple reasons: Target had no duty to disclose anything to Plaintiffs; Plaintiffs have failed to plead this claim with the particularity Rule 9(b) requires; a negligent misrepresentation claim does not lie with respect to statements about Target's intent; and Plaintiffs have failed to allege reliance, which is an essential element of a negligent-misrepresentation-by-omission claim.

1. Duty

"As a general rule, one party to a transaction has no duty to disclose material facts to the other." This rule applies "unless (1) there existed a fiduciary or confidential relationship between the parties; (2) one party was in possession of special facts that could not have been discovered by the other; or (3) one party who chooses to speak omits information so as to make the information actually disclosed misleading."

Plaintiffs have not alleged that there is a fiduciary or confidential relationship between Target and Plaintiffs. Rather, Plaintiffs contend that Target knew facts about its ability to repel hackers that Plaintiffs could not have known, and that Target's public representations regarding its data security practices were misleading. Target takes issue with Plaintiffs' allegations in this regard, but on a Motion to Dismiss, the Court must determine only whether the allegations are plausible. The allegations meet that plausibility standard, and Plaintiffs have adequately pled a duty of care.

2. Rule 9(b)

Target also argues that Plaintiffs' negligent omission claim should be dismissed for failure to comply with the stricter pleading requirements of Rule 9(b). The Rule requires that, "[i]n alleging fraud or mistake, a party must state with particularity the circumstances constituting fraud or mistake." Fed.R.Civ.P. 9(b). These heightened pleading requirements apply to negligent-misrepresentation-by-omission claims. In the context of a claim of negligent omission, the Rule is satisfied "if the omitted information is identified and 'how or when' the concealment occurred."

Plaintiffs have identified the omitted information, namely Target's failure to disclose that its data security systems were deficient and in particular that Target had purposely disengaged one feature of those systems that would have detected and potentially stopped the hackers at the inception of the hacking scheme. Plaintiffs contend that these omissions were made in representations such as Target's online Privacy Policy and in Target's agreement to comply with Visa and MasterCard's Card Operating Regulations and other security requirements.

Although these allegations are not as detailed as Target would like, at this early stage of the litigation they are sufficient to allege the "how or when" the information regarding Target's data security practices was omitted from disclosure. Plaintiffs have complied with 9(b).

3. Omissions

Target argues that Plaintiffs' claim is not cognizable because it is founded on alleged omissions regarding what Target intended to do with respect to data security. Target contends that an omission regarding Target's "present intention to act in the future" is not actionable because it cannot be proved false. But Target misconstrues Plaintiffs' claim. Plaintiffs' negligent-omission claim is not premised on any statement about Target's future intentions or even on Target's statements about the data breach itself, but rather on the fact that Target held itself out as having secure data systems when Target knew that it did not have secure systems and had taken affirmative steps to make its systems more vulnerable to attack. At this stage of the case, this allegation is sufficient to state a claim for negligent omission.

4. Reliance

Finally, Target contends that Plaintiffs have failed to plead any reliance on the alleged omissions. Plaintiffs respond that reliance is not required, citing Judge Nelson's recent *Smith* decision. But *Smith* did not hold that reliance is not a required element for a negligent omission claim. Rather, *Smith* found that reliance was a "fact-intensive" inquiry inappropriate for resolution on a motion to dismiss. . . .

The Complaint contains no indication that Plaintiffs relied on any of the alleged omissions. Rather, the Complaint merely avers that Plaintiffs "suffered injury" "as a direct and proximate result of Target's negligent misrepresentations by omission." This is insufficient to plead reliance, and Plaintiffs' negligent-misrepresentation-by-omission claim must therefore be dismissed. Assuming that there are facts supporting Plaintiffs' reliance on the alleged omissions, Plaintiffs may file an amended complaint within 30 days that fully and plausibly alleges all of the required elements of a negligent-misrepresentation-by-omission claim.

C. Plastic Card Security Act

Minnesota's Plastic Card Security Act provides:

> No person or entity conducting business in Minnesota that accepts a [ ] [credit or debit card] in connection with a transaction shall retain the card security code data, the PIN verification code number, or the full contents

of any track of magnetic stripe data, subsequent to the authorization of the transaction or in the case of a PIN debit transaction, subsequent to 48 hours after authorization of the transaction.

* * * *

Whenever there is a breach of the security of the system of a person or entity that has violated this section ... that person or entity shall reimburse the financial institution that issued any [credit or debit cards] affected by the breach for the costs of reasonable actions undertaken by the financial institution as a result of the breach in order to protect the information of its cardholders or to continue to provide services to cardholders....

Count Two of the Complaint alleges a violation of this section, and Count Three contends that as a result of the alleged violation of the PCSA, Target is negligent per se.

Target raises two challenges to Plaintiffs' PCSA claims. First, Target contends that the PCSA applies only to transactions that occur in Minnesota, making the Act inapplicable to the majority of transactions about which Plaintiffs complain. Second, Target argues that the PCSA only prohibits the retention of customer data, and because the customer data at issue here was stolen when the consumer's card was used at a Target store and was not stolen from Target's database, Target's alleged retention of that data did not cause Plaintiffs' claimed harm.

Target's first argument is not well taken. The Act does not apply only to business transactions that take place in Minnesota. By its terms, it applies to the data retention practices of any person or entity "conducting business in Minnesota." Minn.Stat. § 325E.64, subd. 2. Target is a Minnesota company that conducts business in Minnesota, and thus its data retention practices are governed by the Act. And contrary to Target's assertions, the application of the PCSA to out-of-state transactions does not implicate the dormant Commerce Clause. The PCSA does not discriminate between in-state and out-of-state transactions or economic interests. Rather, it applies only to Minnesota companies' data security practices and does not purport to regulate the practices of any non-Minnesota company. And it applies equally to the Minnesota companies' data retention practices with respect to in-state and out-of-state transactions. The dormant Commerce Clause does not render the application of the PCSA in this situation unconstitutional.

Target's second argument is that, even if Target violated the retention provisions of the Act as Plaintiffs allege, Target's allegedly illegal activities did not cause the harm of which Plaintiffs complain. There is no dispute that the hackers who stole Target's customers' data did so by installing malware on Target's computer servers that read the data from customers' credit and debit cards at the moment those cards were swiped in Target's stores. Thus, according to Target, the fact that Target may also have stored that data longer than the PCSA allows is irrelevant, because the hackers did not steal the data from Target's data storage but rather stole it directly from the cards as they were used in Target's stores. Plaintiffs' response to this argument is two-fold. First, they allege that the hackers' malware did not immediately transmit the stolen data to the hackers' servers, but rather stored the stolen data on Target's own servers for up to six days before transmitting that data to the hackers. Thus, Plaintiffs contend that Target's servers did "retain" the data within the meaning of the PCSA, and that retention allowed the hackers to steal that data. Plaintiffs also contend that the hackers would have been unable to steal all of the magnetic stripe information, in particular the card's CVV code, without accessing the customer data Target regularly stored on its servers. In other words, Plaintiffs assert that the hackers gathered some data from the use of the card and other data from Target's servers, making the data breach even more serious.

Plaintiffs and Target disagree over which definition of "retain" the Court should use in interpreting the PCSA's requirements. Plaintiffs urge the Court to adopt the Oxford Dictionary's definition of retain, which is to "continue to have something." Target, on the other hand, contends that the correct definition of "retain" must be read in the context of technical data retention, and is "the storage of data for future usage."

Whether the Court interprets "retain" to mean "to continue to have" or "storage for future use" is immaterial to the outcome of the Motion to Dismiss. Plaintiffs allege that Target stored data for longer than the PCSA allows, and that the hackers were able to access some of this stored data, namely the CVV codes, without which the breach would not have been as serious. In other words, although the hackers received some data directly from consumers' cards, they also retrieved other data from Target's servers. Even if Target is correct that the hackers' storage of stolen data on Target's servers does not implicate the PCSA, Plaintiffs' claims undoubtedly state a PCSA violation. The Motion to Dismiss this Count must be denied.

Because Target's only argument regarding the negligence per se claim is that it fails because the PCSA claim fails, the negligence per se claim likewise survives this Motion.

CONCLUSION

Plaintiffs have plausibly pled a claim for negligence, a violation of the PCSA, and negligence per se. Plaintiffs failed to plead reliance, however, and therefore their negligent-misrepresentation claim must be dismissed without prejudice. . . .

QUESTION

These cases turn on the fact that data of the plaintiff was breached. In the case where data was not breached, and plaintiffs' data was not breached, but plaintiff found out about a security vulnerability within a company that was not fixed, would the plaintiff still have standing?

NOTES

Note 1

Negligence per se is found when a party violates a statute that provides a duty and the standard of care. See Restatement of Torts (Third) Ch. 3, §14 (2020) ("An actor is negligent if, without excuse, the actor violates a statute that is designed to protect against the type of accident the actor's conduct causes, and if the accident victim is within the class of persons the statute is designed to protect."). Negligence per se is raised in data breach private actions which may be based upon federal or state statutes. In addition to negligence per se, the breach of statutes may also provide evidence of the breach of the standard of care.

Note 2

A privacy law that may be implicated in a suit involving a data breach which may uncover a company's illegal practices is the Illinois Biometric Information Privacy Act. In *Rivera v. Google*, 238 F.Supp.3d 1088 (E.D. Ill. 2017), the district court summarized the applicability of the Act:

> The Illinois Biometric Information Privacy Act forbids the unauthorized collection and storing of some types of biometric data. 740 ILCS 14/1 *et seq.* A private entity cannot gather and use someone's "biometric identifier"—defined as retinal or iris scans, fingerprints, voiceprints, or hand or face geometry scans—unless that person has consented. *Id.* § 14/10. The Act also bans the non-consensual collection and storage of information (the Act labels it "biometric information") that is "based on" those biometric identifiers.

In July of 2020, Facebook paid $650 million to settle a class action lawsuit under the Illinois Biometric Information Privacy Act.[375]

In the Equifax matter, plaintiffs brought multiple causes of action based on cybersecurity data breaches.

In re Equifax Customer Data Security Breach Litigation, 362 F.Supp.3d 1295 (2019).

THOMAS W. THRASH, JR., United States District Judge

This is a data breach case. It is before the Court on the Defendants' Motion to Dismiss the Consolidated Consumer Class Action Complaint [Doc. 425]. For the reasons set forth below, the Defendants' Motion to Dismiss the Consolidated Consumer Class Action Complaint [Doc. 425] is GRANTED in part and DENIED in part.

I. Background

[The facts in this case are substantially similar to facts recited in Chapter One Introduction] The Plaintiffs here are a putative class of consumers whose personal

---

[375] Sara Morrison, *Facebook's sad summer continues with a $650 million settlement*, Vox (July 23, 2020, 5:30 PM), https://www.vox.com/recode/2020/7/23/21335806/facebook-settlement-illinois-facial-recognition-photo-tagging.

information was stolen during the Data Breach. The class alleges that it has been harmed by having to take measures to combat the risk of identity theft, by identity theft that has already occurred to some members of the class, by expending time and effort to monitor their credit and identity, and that they all face a serious and imminent risk of fraud and identity theft due to the Data Breach. The putative class brings a number of nationwide claims, along with a number of state claims. The class also seeks declaratory and injunctive relief. The Defendants now move to dismiss. . . .

III. Discussion . . .

B. Fair Credit Reporting Act

The Defendants first move to dismiss the Consumer Plaintiffs' claims under the Fair Credit Reporting Act ("FCRA"). Under the FCRA, a "consumer reporting agency may furnish a consumer report" only under limited circumstances provided for in the statute. In Count 1 of the Complaint, the Consumer Plaintiffs allege that the Defendants "furnished Class members' consumer reports" in violation of section 1681b of the FCRA and "failed to maintain reasonable procedures designed to limit the furnishing of Class members' consumer reports to permitted purposes, and/or failed to take adequate security measures that would prevent disclosure of Class members' consumer reports to unauthorized entities or computer hackers" in violation of section 1681e of the FRCA. The Defendants move to dismiss, arguing that Equifax did not "furnish" any consumer information within the meaning of the statute, and that the stolen personally identifying information is not a "consumer report" within the meaning of the statute. They also argue that since the Consumer Plaintiffs' section 1681b claim fails to state a claim, their section 1681e also necessarily fails. The Court agrees that the Consumer Plaintiffs fail to state a claim under the FCRA.

First, the Defendants argue that Equifax did not "furnish" the Plaintiffs' personal information within the meaning of the FCRA. The FCRA provides that a consumer reporting agency may only "furnish" a consumer report under limited circumstances. However, the statute does not further define "furnish." Generally, courts have held that information that is stolen from a credit reporting agency is not "furnished" within the meaning of the FCRA. For example, in In re Experian Data Breach Litigation, the court explained that "[a]lthough 'furnish' is not defined in the FCRA, courts generally use the term to describe the active transmission of information to a third-party rather than a failure to safeguard the data." In such a case, the data is stolen by a third party, and not furnished to the third party. Other courts have come to the same conclusion. The Plaintiffs acknowledge that the caselaw supports Equifax's argument, but contend nonetheless that Equifax's conduct was "so egregious" that it should be considered akin to furnishing. The Plaintiffs fail to offer a discernable criteria by which to determine when conduct becomes so egregious that it becomes akin to furnishing. Even assuming Equifax's conduct was egregious, the Court concludes that the Plaintiffs have not alleged facts showing that Equifax "furnished" the Plaintiffs' consumer reports to the hackers.

Next, the Defendants argue that the personally identifying information stolen during the Data Breach is not a "consumer report" within the meaning of the FCRA. The

Court agrees. Section 1681b of the FCRA prohibits the furnishing of "consumer reports," except under limited circumstances.60 The FCRA defines "consumer report," in general, to mean:

> [A]ny written, oral, or other communication of any information by a consumer reporting agency bearing on a consumer's credit worthiness, credit standing, credit capacity, character, general reputation, personal characteristics, or mode of living which is used or expected to be used or collected in whole or in part for the purpose of serving as a factor in establishing the consumer's eligibility for--(A) credit or insurance to be used primarily for personal, family, or household purposes; (B) employment purposes; or (C) any other purpose authorized under section 1681b of this title.

Equifax argues – and the Plaintiffs do not dispute this – that the hackers did not obtain access to the active credit files maintained by one of the Equifax subsidiaries. The hackers got only "legacy" data. Courts, facing similar factual circumstances, have concluded that information such as that taken in the Data Breach does not constitute a "consumer report," but instead is "header information." Such information is not a "consumer report" because it does not bear on an individual's credit worthiness. Information, such as a consumer's "name, phone number, social security number, date of birth, driver's license, current address, and time spent at that address" does not, itself, constitute such a credit report. The Plaintiffs' argument that the information stolen in the Data Breach could bear on their credit worthiness is not persuasive. Therefore, the Court concludes that the Plaintiffs fail to allege facts showing that the information stolen was a "credit report."

Finally, since the Consumer Plaintiffs' section 1681b claim fails, their section 1681e claim must also necessarily fail. Section 1681e requires consumer reporting agencies to "maintain reasonable procedures designed to avoid violations of section 1681c of this title and to limit the furnishing of consumer reports to the purposes listed under section 1681b of this title." However, a plaintiff bringing a claim that a reporting agency violated the "reasonable procedures" requirement of section 1681e must first show that the reporting agency released the report in violation of section 1681b.66 Therefore, since the Plaintiffs' claims under section 1681b fail, their claims under section 1681e also fail. . . .

C. Legally Cognizable Injury

The Defendants next argue that all of the Plaintiffs' tort claims, including their negligence, negligence per se, and state consumer protection act violations, fail because they have not sufficiently alleged injury and proximate causation. According to the Defendants, the Plaintiffs' injuries are not legally cognizable harms, and even if they were, the Plaintiffs have failed to adequately allege that the Defendants proximately caused their harms. Finally, the Defendants argue that the Plaintiffs' tort claims are all barred by the economic loss doctrine.

1. Non-Harms and Speculative Future Harms

First, the Defendants contend that the Plaintiffs have not pleaded legally cognizable harms because their purported injuries only include "non-harms" and "speculative future harms." "It is well-established Georgia law that before an action for a tort will lie, the plaintiff must show he sustained injury or damage as a result of the negligent act or omission to act in some duty owed to him." "Although nominal damages can be awarded where there has been an injury but the injury is small, ... where there is no evidence of injury accompanying the tort, an essential element of the tort is lacking, thereby entitling the defendant to judgment in his favor."

The Defendants first contend that the compromise of personally identifiable information itself is not an injury. Each of the Plaintiffs alleges that his or her personally identifiable information was compromised in the Data Breach. Such an injury is legally cognizable under Georgia law. The cases relied upon by the Defendants are distinguishable. The Defendants cite Rite Aid of Georgia, Inc. v. Peacock for the proposition that a plaintiff suffers no injury from the illegal sale of personally identifiable information. However, as the Plaintiffs point out, the plaintiff in that case did not allege that this information was misused, or likely to be misused. In Rite Aid, the plaintiff's pharmacy records were sold from Rite Aid to Walgreens when a Rite Aid store was closing. The plaintiff sought certification of a class of all individuals whose information had been sold to Walgreens. The court concluded that class certification was not proper, in part, because the plaintiff had not alleged an injury from the sale of his information from one pharmacy to the other, and instead only alleged a violation of law. In contrast, the Plaintiffs here have alleged that they have been harmed by having to take measures to combat the risk of identity theft, by identity theft that has already occurred to some members of the class, by expending time and effort to monitor their credit and identity, and that they all face a serious and imminent risk of fraud and identity theft due to the Data Breach. These allegations of actual injury are sufficient to support a claim for relief.

The Defendants also cite Finnerty v. State Bank & Trust Company for the proposition that fear of future damages from identity theft is too speculative to form a basis of recovery. However, as the Plaintiffs emphasize, that case involved an invasion of privacy claim by an individual whose Social Security number was included in a public court filing. The court concluded that this claim failed because, to state a claim for invasion of privacy, a plaintiff must show that there was a public disclosure in which information is distributed to the public at large. There, the claimant failed to allege that anyone actually saw his Social Security number, and thus did not prove that there was a public disclosure. Thus, the court there did not hold that the disclosure of personal information is, as a matter of law, not a legally cognizable injury. Instead, it concluded that one of the elements of an invasion of privacy claim was not met, making it distinguishable from this case. And, in contrast to the inadvertent disclosure of a Social Security number in a single public court filing, the compromise of a huge amount of personally identifying information by criminal hackers presents a much more significant risk of identity fraud.

The Defendants also cite Randolph v. ING Life Insurance and Annuity Company. There, the plaintiffs sued after a laptop computer containing their personal information was stolen from the home of one of the defendant's employees, alleging that there was a substantial risk of identity theft and other dangers due to the possible unauthorized use of their personal information. In that case, there was no evidence that the theft occurred for the specific purpose of obtaining the information on the laptop as opposed to the computer itself. Here, by contrast, the Plaintiffs allege that their information was specifically targeted and has already been misused. The Plaintiffs have adequately alleged facts showing actual cognizable injury.

The Defendants also cite Collins v. Athens Orthopedic Clinic in their reply brief. There, the defendant's patients sued after a cyberhacker stole their personal information from the defendant's systems. The court concluded that the plaintiffs did not allege a legally cognizable harm. It explained that:

> Plaintiffs allege that their information has been compromised and that they have spent time placing fraud or credit alerts on their accounts and "anticipate" spending more time on these activities. Plaintiffs claim damages, specifying only the cost of identity theft protection, credit monitoring, and credit freezes to be maintained "over the course of a lifetime." While credit monitoring and other precautionary measures are undoubtedly prudent, we find that they are not recoverable damages on the facts before us because Plaintiffs seek only to recover for an increased risk of harm.

Thus, according to the Defendants, the Plaintiffs' claims must fail, since costs associated with protecting the plaintiffs' personal information in Collins failed to establish a sufficient injury.

However, Collins is distinguishable. There, the plaintiffs alleged only an "increased risk of harm" associated with taking precautionary measures. The mere risk of harm, and not the type of injuries alleged, led the court to conclude that the plaintiffs' allegations as to injuries failed. In contrast, the Plaintiffs here have not pleaded merely an increased risk of harm. Instead, they have alleged that they have already incurred significant costs in response to the Data Breach. Many of the Plaintiffs have also already suffered forms of identity theft. Moreover, the Plaintiffs here have sufficiently alleged a substantial and imminent risk of impending identity fraud due to the vast amount of information that was obtained in the Data Breach. The Court concludes that these allegations are sufficient.

The Defendants also argue that the Plaintiffs that allege payment card fraud have failed to allege a sufficient injury. Plaintiffs Alvin Alfred Kleveno Jr., Maria Martucci, and Robert J. Etten allege that they experienced unauthorized charges on their payment cards as a result of the Data Breach. The Defendants contend that these allegations are insufficient because these Plaintiffs have not alleged the date on which these fraudulent charges were made, and because they failed to allege that they were not reimbursed for those charges. However, under Rule 8's requirement of a plain and simple statement, these Plaintiffs need not allege the specific date on which these fraudulent charges occurred. The Plaintiffs' allegations that such charges occurred are sufficient, and the Defendants cite no authority holding otherwise. Furthermore, contrary to the Defendants' assertions, these Plaintiffs also need not allege that they were not reimbursed for these fraudulent charges to adequately allege an injury. The Plaintiffs' allegations that they suffered unauthorized charges on their payment cards as a result of the Data Breach are actual, concrete injuries that are legally cognizable under Georgia law.

2. Proximate Causation

The Defendants next contend that the Plaintiffs have failed to adequately allege that Equifax proximately caused their injuries. "[B]efore any negligence, even if proven, can be actionable, that negligence must be the proximate cause of the injuries sued upon." "To establish proximate cause, a plaintiff must show a legally attributable causal connection between the defendant's conduct and the alleged injury." A plaintiff must establish "that it is more likely than not that the conduct of the defendant was a cause in fact of the result." "A mere possibility of such causation is not enough; and when the matter remains one of pure speculation or conjecture, or the probabilities are at best evenly balanced, it becomes the duty of the court to grant summary judgment for the defendant."

First, the Defendants argue that the Plaintiffs fail to allege that any injuries resulting from identity theft, payment-card fraud, or other similar theories resulted specifically from the Equifax Data Breach, and not some other data breach or fraudulent conduct. According to the Defendants, the Plaintiffs highlight dozens of other security breaches dating to 2013 in the Complaint, and the Defendants assert that over 1,500 data breaches occurred in 2017 alone. Thus, since the Plaintiffs have failed to allege that their injuries resulted directly from their personal information being obtained in this specific Data Breach, their theory of causation is "guesswork at best."

However, the Court finds this argument unpersuasive. Many of the Plaintiffs have alleged in the Complaint that they suffered some form of identity theft or other fraudulent activity as a result of the Data Breach. Such an allegation is sufficient at the pleading stage to establish that the Data Breach was the proximate cause of this harm. The Plaintiffs need not explicitly state that other breaches did not cause these alleged injuries, since their allegations that this Data Breach did cause their injuries implies such an allegation. Furthermore, allowing the Defendants "to rely on other data breaches to defeat a causal connection would 'create a perverse incentive for companies: so long as enough data breaches take place, individual companies will never be found liable.' The Court declines to create such a perverse incentive.

Many of the Plaintiffs also allege in the Complaint that they purchased credit monitoring and incurred other costs in direct response to the Data Breach. Thus, even assuming their identity theft injuries resulted from previous breaches, these separate injuries resulted only from the occurrence of the Data Breach. Finally, even assuming that such an argument could disprove proximate causation, it presents a factual dispute most appropriate for a jury to consider. The Plaintiffs have alleged that the Data Breach caused their identities to be stolen, while the Defendants contend prior breaches caused these injuries. This is purely a dispute of fact that is not appropriate for resolution at this stage of the litigation. Therefore, the Court concludes that the Plaintiffs have adequately alleged that the Data Breach proximately caused their injuries. The Plaintiffs plausibly allege that Equifax had custody of their personally identifiable information, that Equifax's systems were hacked, that these hackers obtained this personal information, and that as a result of this breach, they have become the victims of identity theft and other fraudulent activity. This is sufficient.

Next, the Defendants contend that the Plaintiffs' injuries were proximately caused by an "unidentified third party's criminal acts," and not Equifax itself. According to the Defendants, the unforeseeable criminal acts of third parties "insulate" defendants from liability. "Generally, there is no duty to prevent the unforeseeable 'intervening criminal act of a third person.'" Under Georgia law, "when a defendant claims that its negligence is not the proximate cause of the plaintiff's injuries, but that an act of a third party intervened to cause those injuries, the rule is 'that an intervening and independent wrongful act of a third person producing the injury, and without which it would not have occurred, should be treated as the proximate cause, insulating and excluding the negligence of the defendant.'"

However, "this rule does not insulate the defendant 'if the defendant had reasonable grounds for apprehending that such wrongful act would be committed.'" "[I]f the character of the intervening act claimed to break the connection between the original wrongful act and the subsequent injury was such that its probable or natural consequences could reasonably have been anticipated, apprehended, or foreseen by the original wrong-doer, the causal connection is not broken, and the original wrong-doer is responsible for all of the consequences resulting from the intervening act." Thus, if the Defendants had reasonable grounds to anticipate the criminal act, then they are not insulated from liability. "In determining whether a third party criminal act is foreseeable, Georgia courts have held that 'the incident causing the injury must be substantially similar in type to the previous criminal activities ... so that a reasonable person would take ordinary precautions to protect his or her customers or tenants against the risk posed by that type of activity.'" The question of reasonable foreseeability of a criminal attack is generally for a jury to determine. However, it may not be in this case because of the many public statements by Equifax that it knew how valuable its information was to cyber criminals and its susceptibility to hacking attempts.

In Home Depot, this Court allowed a negligence claim premised upon a data breach to continue, noting that the defendant "knew about a substantial data security risk dating back to 2008 but failed to implement reasonable security measures to combat it." Similarly, in Arby's, the court noted that the defendant knew about potential data breach threats but failed to implement reasonable security measures. Thus, according to the court, the criminal acts of the cyberhackers were reasonably foreseeable, and thus the plaintiffs' negligence claims could proceed. In Arby's, the court compared criminal data breaches to the "peculiarly similar context of premises liability," where the Georgia

Supreme Court has held that if a proprietor "has reason to anticipate a criminal act," then he or she has a duty to "exercise ordinary care to guard against injury from dangerous characters."

The Court concludes that, as in Arby's and Home Depot, the criminal acts of the hackers were reasonably foreseeable to the Defendants, and thus do not insulate them from liability. In the Complaint, the Plaintiffs allege that the Defendants observed major data breaches at other corporations, such as Target, Anthem, and Experian. Equifax itself even experienced prior data breaches. Furthermore, Equifax ignored warnings from cybersecurity experts that its data systems were dangerously deficient, and that there was a substantial risk of an imminent breach. These allegations are sufficient to establish that the acts of the third party cyberhackers were reasonably foreseeable. Thus, the causal chain is not broken.

The Defendants also assert that future identity theft and fraud is a second intervening cause that insulates them from liability. According to the Defendants, the Plaintiffs have not pleaded that this fraudulent conduct is the probable consequence of a data breach, and thus was not foreseeable. However, the Court concludes that the Plaintiffs have adequately alleged that such conduct was reasonably foreseeable. In the Complaint, the Plaintiffs allege that the Defendants knew the "likelihood and repercussions" of cybersecurity threats, and had stayed informed as to other well-publicized breaches. The Complaint details the Defendants' alleged awareness of the risks that data breaches pose, including the risks that the compromise of personal information entails. Equifax knew that fraudulent activity had resulted from other, well-publicized data breaches. Thus, the Plaintiffs have adequately alleged that this criminal conduct was reasonably foreseeable.

3. Economic Loss Doctrine

The Defendants next argue that the economic loss doctrine bars the Plaintiffs' tort claims. "The 'economic loss rule' generally provides that a contracting party who suffers purely economic losses must seek his remedy in contract and not in tort." In other words, "a plaintiff may not recover in tort for purely economic damages arising from a breach of contract." Where, however, "an independent duty exists under the law, the economic loss rule does not bar a tort claim because the claim is based on a recognized independent duty of care and thus does not fall within the scope of the rule." Here, the independent duty exception would bar application of the economic loss rule. "It is well-established that entities that collect sensitive, private data from consumers and store that data on their networks have a duty to protect that information[.]" As discussed below, the Defendants owed the Plaintiffs a duty of care to safeguard their personal information. Therefore, since an independent duty existed, the economic loss rule does not apply.

D. Negligence

Next, the Defendants move to dismiss the Plaintiffs' negligence claim. In Count 2 of the Complaint, the Plaintiffs allege that Equifax owed a duty to the Plaintiffs to "exercise reasonable care in obtaining, retaining, securing, safeguarding, deleting and protecting their Personal Information in its possession from being compromised, lost, stolen, accessed and misused by unauthorized persons." The Plaintiffs also allege that Equifax had a duty of care that arose from Section 5 of the Federal Trade Commission Act (the "FTC Act"), and the FCRA. The Defendants contend that they were under no duty of care toward the Plaintiffs.

In Georgia, "[a] cause of action for negligence requires (1) [a] legal duty to conform to a standard of conduct raised by the law for the protection of others against unreasonable risks of harm; (2) a breach of this standard; (3) a legally attributable causal connection between the conduct and the resulting injury; and, (4) some loss or damage flowing to the plaintiff's legally protected interest as a result of the alleged breach of the legal duty." "The threshold issue in any cause of action for negligence is whether, and to what extent, the defendant owes the plaintiff a duty of care." Whether such a duty exists is a question of law. Georgia recognizes a general duty "to all the world not to subject them to an unreasonable risk of harm."

The Defendants contend that Georgia law does not impose a duty of care to safeguard personal information. The Defendants rely primarily upon a recent Georgia Court of Appeals case, McConnell v. Georgia Department of Labor. In McConnell, the plaintiff filed a class action against the Georgia Department of Labor after one of its employees sent an email to 1,000 Georgians who had applied for unemployment benefits. This email included a spreadsheet with the name, Social Security number, phone number, email address, and age of 4,000 Georgians who had registered for services with the agency. The plaintiff, whose information was disclosed, filed a class action, asserting, among other claims, a claim for negligence.

A brief overview of McConnell's procedural history is helpful in understanding the court's decision in that case. In June 2016, the Georgia Court of Appeals initially rejected the plaintiff's claims. In McConnell I, the plaintiff, recognizing that such a duty had not been expressly recognized in Georgia caselaw, contended that such a duty arose from two statutory sources. The court concluded that neither of these statutory sources gave rise to a duty to safeguard personal information. The court explained that "McConnell's complaint is premised on a duty of care to safeguard personal information that has no source in Georgia statutory law or caselaw and that his complaint therefore failed to state a claim of negligence." However, in doing so, the court expressly distinguished this Court's prior holding in Home Depot, noting that this Court "found a duty to protect the personal information of the defendant's customers in the context of allegations that the defendant failed to implement reasonable security measures to combat a substantial data security risk of which it had received multiple warnings dating back several years and even took affirmative steps to stop its employees from fixing known security deficiencies" and explaining that "[t]here are no such allegations in this case."

Then, the Georgia Supreme Court vacated McConnell I, holding that the Court of Appeals could not decide whether the plaintiff failed to state a claim without first considering whether the doctrine of sovereign immunity barred his claims. On remand, the Georgia Court of Appeals, after deciding that sovereign immunity did not bar the plaintiff's claims, once again concluded that the plaintiff's negligence claim failed because "McConnell's complaint is premised on a duty of care to safeguard personal information that has no source in Georgia statutory law or caselaw and that his complaint therefore failed to state a claim of negligence." Examining both the Georgia Personal Identity Protection Act and the Georgia Fair Business Practices Act, the court concluded that neither gave rise to a duty to safeguard personal information. Although the legislature showed a "concern about the cost of identity theft to the marketplace" through these statutes, it did not act to "establish a standard of conduct intended to protect the security of personal information, as some other jurisdictions have done in connection with data protection and data breach notification laws."

The Defendants contend that McConnell III confirms that there is no duty under Georgia law, common law or statutory, to safeguard personally identifiable information. The Georgia Supreme Court has granted certiorari in the case. The Defendants, at oral argument, asked the Court to delay ruling upon the Motion to Dismiss until a ruling by the Georgia Supreme Court. However, it seems very unlikely to me that the Georgia Supreme Court will adopt a rule of law that tells hundreds of millions of consumers in the United States that a national credit reporting agency headquartered in Georgia has no obligation to protect their confidential personal identifying data. Unlike the Georgia Department of Labor, Equifax and the other national credit reporting agencies are heavily regulated by federal law. As noted previously, the Fair Credit Reporting Act strictly limits the circumstances under which a credit reporting agency may disclose consumer credit information. The failure to maintain reasonable and appropriate data security for consumers' sensitive personal information can constitute an unfair method of competition in commerce in violation of the Federal Trade Commission Act. The Gramm–Leach–Bliley Act * required the FTC to establish standards for financial institutions to protect consumers' personal information. The FTC has done that.

The Plaintiffs contend that, under Georgia law, allegations that a company knew of a foreseeable risk to its data security systems are sufficient to establish a duty of care. The Plaintiffs rely primarily upon Home Depot and Arby's for this proposition. In Home Depot, this Court denied the defendant's motion to dismiss a negligence claim arising out of a data breach. The Court concluded that Home Depot had a duty to safeguard customer information because it "knew about a substantial data security risk dating back to 2008 but failed to implement reasonable security measures to combat it." The Court, citing the Georgia Supreme Court's decision in Bradley Center, Inc. v. Wessner, came to this conclusion by expounding upon the general duty to "all the world not to subject them to an unreasonable risk of harm." The Court noted that "to hold that no such duty existed would allow retailers to use outdated security measures and turn a blind eye to the ever-increasing risk of cyber attacks, leaving consumers with no recourse to recover damages even though the retailer was in a superior position to safeguard the public from such a risk."

Then, in Arby's, the court declined to dismiss a plaintiff's negligence claim arising out of a data breach. The court explained that "[u]nder Georgia law and the standard articulated in Home Depot, allegations that a company knew of a foreseeable risk to its data security systems are sufficient to establish the existence of a plausible legal duty and survive a motion to dismiss." The court held that Arby's was under a duty to safeguard its customers' personal data due to allegations that it knew about potential problems and failed to implement reasonable security measures, knew about other highly-publicized data breaches, and was aware that its parent company had suffered a significant breach using the same computer system. The Arby's court also distinguished McConnell I, explaining that it was not "expressly inconsistent" with Home Depot because Home Depot found a duty to protect personal information in the context of the defendant's failure to implement reasonable security measures to combat a foreseeable risk, while there were no such allegations in McConnell I. The court also explained that the McConnell I court's characterization of Wessner as a narrow holding did not change its conclusion since McConnell I did not change the general duty that arises from foreseeable criminal acts.

The parties' interpretations of this caselaw diverge greatly. The Defendants contend that McConnell III, the latest decision of all of these cases, clarified this caselaw and affirmatively stated that there is no duty to safeguard personal information. Thus, according to the Defendants, Home Depot and Arby's are no longer good law. The Plaintiffs, in turn, argue that due to the factual differences between McConnell III, on the one hand, and Arby's and Home Depot, on the other hand, McConnell III does not conflict with these two cases. According to the Plaintiffs, there were no allegations in McConnell III that the state agency should have known that its employee would inadvertently disclose this personal information. In contrast, Home Depot and Arby's premised their holdings on the detailed allegations that the data breaches were foreseeable. Finally, the Plaintiffs argue that, despite the Defendants' characterizations, they are not asking this Court to recognize a new duty under Georgia law, but instead are asking it to apply traditional tort and negligence principles to the facts of this case.

The Court concludes that, under the facts alleged in the Complaint, Equifax owed the Plaintiffs a duty of care to safeguard the personal information in its custody. This duty of care arises from the allegations that the Defendants knew of a foreseeable risk to its data security systems but failed to implement reasonable security measures. McConnell III does not alter this conclusion. As the court in McConnell I noted, a critical distinction between these cases is that the duty in Home Depot arose from allegations that the defendant failed to implement reasonable security measures in the face of a known security risk. Such allegations did not exist in the McConnell line of cases. The McConnell III court came to the same conclusion as the McConnell I court, and did nothing to dispel this distinction made in McConnell III. Furthermore, given this mention of Home Depot in McConnell I, and the court's subsequent holding in Arby's, the McConnell III court's silence on this issue suggests a tacit approval of this distinction. And, as this Court noted in Home Depot, to hold otherwise would create perverse incentives for businesses who profit off of the use of consumers' personal data to turn a blind eye and ignore known security risks.

The Defendants go to great lengths to distinguish the Georgia Supreme Court's decision in Bradley Center, Inc. v. Wessner. Both Home Depot and Arby's relied, in part, upon Wessner to conclude that the defendants were under a duty to take reasonable measures to avoid a foreseeable risk of harm from a data breach incident. In Wessner, a man who voluntarily committed himself to a psychiatric hospital made statements to the hospital's staff that he desired to harm his wife. Despite these statements, the man was issued a weekend pass by the staff, and he subsequently obtained a gun, confronted his wife and another man, and killed them both. The Georgia Supreme Court concluded that the hospital owed a duty of care to the man's wife. The court explained that "[t]he legal duty in this case arises out of the general duty one owes to all the world not to subject them to an unreasonable risk of harm."

The Defendants argue that the holding in Wessner is much narrower than this. According to them, Wessner merely stands for the narrow proposition that a physician owes a legal duty when, in the course of treating a mental health patient, that physician exercises control over the patient and knows or should know that the patient is likely to cause harm to others. The Defendants further assert that the Wessner court's references to general negligence principles were done in an effort to explain why the case was a negligence case, and not a medical malpractice case. However, despite the Defendants' efforts to minimize the importance of Wessner, the Court finds that Wessner supports the conclusion that the Defendants owed a legal duty to take reasonable measures to prevent a reasonably foreseeable risk of harm due to a data breach incident. Nowhere in the Wessner decision does the Georgia Supreme Court limit its holding to the narrow proposition that the Defendants assert. In fact, in Wessner, the court explained that it was not creating a "new tort," but instead that it was applying "our traditional tort principles of negligence to the facts of this case." Other Georgia cases have similarly applied these same general principles. Likewise, this Court concludes that, under traditional negligence principles, the Defendants owed a legal duty to the Plaintiffs to take reasonable precautions due to the reasonably foreseeable risk of danger of a data breach incident.

The Defendants then argue that they did not "voluntarily" undertake a duty. In the Complaint, the Plaintiffs allege that Equifax's duty also arose from its "unique position as one of three nationwide credit-reporting companies that serve as linchpins of the financial system" and that Equifax "undertakes its collection of highly sensitive information generally without the knowledge or consent of consumers." The Defendants contend that this claim fails because under Georgia's "good Samaritan" provision, an undertaken duty extends only to preventing physical harm to another's person or property. The Plaintiffs do not respond to this argument. Therefore, to the extent that the Plaintiffs assert a duty premised upon the Defendants' voluntary undertaking such a responsibility, that claim should be dismissed.

E. Negligence Per Se

Next, the Defendants move to dismiss the Plaintiffs' negligence per se claim. In Count 3 of the Complaint, the Plaintiffs allege that Equifax violated Section 5 of the FTC Act, and similar state statutes, by "failing to use reasonable measures to protect Personal Information and not complying with industry standards," and that such violation constitutes negligence per se. "Georgia law allows the adoption of a statute or regulation as a standard of conduct so that its violation becomes negligence per se." In order to make a negligence per se claim, however, the plaintiff must show that it is within the class of persons intended to be protected by the statute and that the statute was meant to protect against the harm suffered.

The Defendants argue that the Plaintiffs fail to identify statutory text that imposes a duty with specificity upon the Defendants. Here, the Plaintiffs allege that Equifax violated Section 5 of the FTC Act. The Defendants argue that Section 5 cannot form the basis of a negligence per se claim. The failure to maintain reasonable and appropriate data security for consumers' sensitive personal information can constitute an unfair method of competition in commerce in violation of the Federal Trade Commission Act. The Consolidated Class Action Complaint here adequately pleads a violation of Section 5 of the FTC Act, that the Plaintiffs are within the class of persons intended to be protected by the statute, and that the harm suffered is the kind the statute meant to protect. Additionally, one Georgia case and one case applying Georgia law both suggest that the FTC Act can serve as the basis of a negligence per se claim. The Defendants' motion to dismiss the negligence per se claim should be denied.

Second, the Defendants argue that LabMD, Inc. v. Fed. Trade Comm'n, should lead this Court to a different conclusion. That was a direct enforcement action. There, the Eleventh Circuit noted that "standards of unfairness" must be found "in 'clear and well-established' policies that are expressed in the Constitution, statutes, or the common law." The court explained that the FTC in that case did "not explicitly cite the source of the standard of unfairness" it used in holding that LabMD's failure to implement a reasonable data security program was an unfair act or practice, but concluded that it was "apparent" that "the source is the common law of negligence." The court then vacated the FTC's order because the order was too vague to be enforced. It did not hold that inadequate data security cannot be regulated under Section 5.

Next, the Defendants argue that the Plaintiffs have not sufficiently alleged injury or proximate causation. Under Georgia law, negligence per se is "not liability per se." Even if negligence per se is shown, a plaintiff must still prove proximate causation and actual damage to recover. As discussed above, the Court concludes that the Plaintiffs have sufficiently alleged both a legally cognizable injury and proximate causation. Therefore, this argument is unavailing.

F. Georgia Fair Business Practices Act

Next, the Defendants move to dismiss the Plaintiffs' claims under the Georgia Fair Business Practices Act. The Georgia Fair Business Practices Act prohibits, generally, "unfair or deceptive acts or practices in the conduct of consumer transactions and consumer acts or practices in trade or commerce." In Count 4 of the Complaint, the

Plaintiffs allege that the Defendants violated multiple provisions of the Georgia Fair Business Practices Act, including O.C.G.A. §§ 10-1-393(a), 10-1-393(b)(5), 10-1-393(b)(7), 10-1-393(b)(9).201 The Defendants make multiple arguments in favor of dismissal.

The Defendants first argue that the Georgia Fair Business Practices Act does not require the safeguarding of personally identifiable information.202 According to the Defendants, McConnell III would have been decided differently if the Georgia Fair Business Practices Act contained such a requirement. In McConnell III, the court concluded that part of the Georgia Fair Business Practices Act, O.C.G.A. § 10-1-393.8, "can not serve as the source of such a general duty to safeguard and protect the personal information of another." That provision prohibited "intentionally communicating a person's social security number." The court rejected the plaintiff's claim, noting that he had alleged that the defendant negligently disseminated his social security number.

The Plaintiffs make multiple arguments in response. However, the Court finds these arguments unpersuasive. First, they argue that Arby's II, decided after McConnell III, held that data breach victims can pursue a claim under the Georgia Fair Business Practices Act. However, that decision only considered whether the plaintiffs had adequately alleged reliance. Thus, the court's reasoning does not bear on whether McConnell III precluded recovery under the Georgia Fair Business Practices Act. Second, the Plaintiffs contend that McConnell III only stands for the proposition that the Georgia Fair Business Practices Act is not the basis of a general tort duty. However, McConnell III's holding was broader than that. In McConnell III, the court, after examining parts of the Georgia Fair Business Practices Act, along with the Georgia Personal Identity Protection Act, concluded that there is no statutory basis for a duty to safeguard personal information in Georgia. It further explained that the Georgia legislature has not acted to establish a standard of conduct to protect the security of personal information, unlike other jurisdictions with data protection and data breach laws. Even though McConnell III examined the Georgia Fair Business Practices Act in the context of its provisions dealing with Social Security numbers specifically, it concluded that the entire Act, along with the rest of Georgia statutory law, did not require the safeguarding of personal information. Therefore, the Court concludes that the Georgia Fair Business Practices Act does not require businesses to safeguard personally identifiable information. This issue may be revisited depending upon the ruling of the Georgia Supreme Court in McConnell III.

G. Unjust Enrichment

The Defendants next move to dismiss the Plaintiffs' unjust enrichment claim. In Count 5 of the Complaint, the Plaintiffs allege that Equifax has been unjustly enriched by benefitting from and profiting off of the sale of the Plaintiffs' personally identifiable information, all at the Plaintiffs' expense. Unjust enrichment is an equitable doctrine that "applies when as a matter of fact there is no legal contract, but where the party sought to be charged has been conferred a benefit by the party contending an unjust enrichment which the benefitted party equitably ought to return or compensate for." Thus, in order to state a claim for unjust enrichment, the Plaintiffs must show that "(1) a benefit has been conferred, (2) compensation has not been given for receipt of the benefit, and (3) the failure to so compensate would be unjust."

The Defendants argue that, with regard to most of the Plaintiffs, personally identifiable information was conferred on Equifax by third parties, and not by the Plaintiffs themselves. Instead, only the Contract Plaintiffs gave their information to Equifax. Thus, according to the Defendants, the unjust enrichment claims of these non-Contract Plaintiffs fail because they do not allege that they conferred anything of value on Equifax.

The Plaintiffs first cite Arby's, contending that the court in that case "sustain[ed]" the plaintiffs' claim for unjust enrichment. However, the court in Arby's did not consider the merits of the plaintiffs' unjust enrichment claim. Instead, it merely decided that the plaintiffs could assert a claim for unjust enrichment in the alternative to their contract claims. Therefore, this case does not provide guidance as to whether the Plaintiffs have made allegations that satisfy each element of an unjust enrichment claim. The Plaintiffs also cite Sackin v. TransPerfect Global, Inc. However, the plaintiffs in that case asserted an unjust enrichment claim under New York law, which contains different elements than such a claim under Georgia law.

The Court concludes that the non-Contract Plaintiffs fail to establish the necessary elements of an unjust enrichment claim. The Georgia Court of Appeals has explained that "for unjust enrichment to apply, the party conferring the labor and things of value must act with the expectation that the other will be responsible for the cost. Otherwise, that party, like one who volunteers to pay the debt of another, has no right to an equitable recovery." For example, in Sitterli v. Csachi, the court concluded that for unjust enrichment to apply, the party conferring things of value must act with the expectation that the other will be responsible for the cost. The Plaintiffs have failed to show that they conferred a thing of value, namely their personally identifiable information, upon the Defendants with the expectation that Equifax would be responsible for the cost. The non-Contract Plaintiffs have failed to allege that they had any such expectation.

The Defendants also argue that the Contract Plaintiffs' unjust enrichment claims must be dismissed because those Plaintiffs have also pleaded breach of contract claims. Under Georgia law, "[a] party can only recover for a claim of unjust enrichment if there is not an express contract that governs the dispute." However, "[w]hile a party, indeed, cannot recover under both a breach of contract and unjust enrichment theory, a plaintiff may plead these claims in the alternative." Thus, the Contract Plaintiffs may assert inconsistent contract and unjust enrichment theories at this stage of the proceedings.

H. Breach of Contract

Next, the Defendants move to dismiss the Contract Plaintiffs' breach of contract claims. Nineteen Plaintiffs allege that they formed a contract with Equifax, either express or implied, when they obtained credit monitoring or identity theft protection services from the company. According to these Contract Plaintiffs, Equifax's Privacy

Policy constituted an agreement between Equifax and those individuals who provided personal information to it, including the Contract Plaintiffs. Equifax's Privacy Policy states that Equifax "restrict[s] access to personally identifiable information ... that is collected about you to only those who have a need to know that information in connection with the purpose for which it is collected and used." Equifax allegedly breached this contract by failing to take steps to protect the Contract Plaintiffs' personal information.

The Defendants argue that the Privacy Policy is not a contract, and even if it is, it did not impose the obligations that the Plaintiffs assert. They argue that the Contract Plaintiffs' purchases were governed by an express contract, with a merger clause, that does not incorporate the Privacy Policy. Under Georgia law, "a merger clause operates as a disclaimer of all representations not made on the face of the contract." The Equifax Product Agreement and Terms of Use, which the Defendants contend was the sole contract entered into between Equifax and the Contract Plaintiffs, provides that "[t]his Agreement constitutes the entire agreement between You and Us regarding the Products and information contained on or acquired through this Site or provided by Us." However, even if this is a valid merger clause, the Equifax Terms of Use go on to provide that these terms are "[s]ubject to the conditions described on the privacy page of this Web Site." Therefore, the Court concludes that the merger clause in the Terms of Use does not preclude the Contract Plaintiffs' claims.

The Contract Plaintiffs argue that they adequately pleaded that the Privacy Policy constituted a contract when they purchased services from Equifax, obtained their credit files, disputed their entries, or more. Courts have concluded that a business's privacy policy can constitute a stand-alone contract. However, the Contract Plaintiffs have not explicitly alleged that they read the Privacy Policy, or otherwise relied upon or were aware of the representations and assurances made in the Privacy Policy when choosing to use the Defendants' services. Without such a showing, the Plaintiffs have failed to establish the essential element of mutual assent. The Plaintiffs also assert that the Product Agreement and Terms of Use incorporated the Privacy Policy. However, even if the Plaintiffs establish that the Privacy Policy was part of this express contract, the terms of the agreement provide that Equifax will not "be liable to any party for any direct, indirect, special or other consequential damages for any use of or reliance upon the information found at this web site." Thus, even assuming the Privacy Policy was incorporated by reference, under the terms of this agreement the Plaintiffs cannot seek damages relating to the information in Equifax's custody.

The Plaintiffs alternatively assert an implied contract claim. However, this claim fails. As discussed above, the Equifax Terms of Use contained a valid merger clause. Such a clause precludes the assertion of an implied contract claim. Furthermore, the Plaintiffs have failed to allege facts establishing the necessary elements of an implied contract claim. The Georgia Court of Appeals has explained that, for both express and implied contract claims, "[t]he concept of a contract requires that the minds of the parties shall meet and accord at the same time, upon the same subject matter, and in the same sense." "In the absence of this meeting of the minds, there is no special contractual provisions between the alleged contracting parties." An implied contract only differs from an express contract in the type of proof used to prove its existence. The same element of mutual assent is required. The Contract Plaintiffs allege that an implied contract was formed because "Equifax agreed to safeguard and protect the Personal Information of Plaintiffs and Class members and to timely and accurately notify them if their Personal Information was breached or compromised." This conclusory allegation fails to establish the necessary element of mutual assent. This allegation, which contains a legal conclusion instead of a factual allegation, fails to show that the Defendants and the Contract Plaintiffs had a meeting of the minds, as required by Georgia law. Therefore, the Contract Plaintiffs' implied contract claim fails to state a claim.

I. State Statutes

1. State Business Fraud and Consumer Protection Statutes

The Defendants move to dismiss the Plaintiffs' claims under a variety of state business fraud and consumer protection statutes. The Defendants first argue that these statutes cannot apply to conduct that took place entirely in Georgia. Second, they contend that the Plaintiffs have not adequately alleged fraud, scienter, or injury. Third, they contend that the Plaintiffs have failed to establish that they had "consumer transactions," as many statutes require. Fourth, the Defendants assert that the Plaintiffs fail to allege that they were under a duty to disclose. Fifth, the Defendants argue that the Plaintiffs' claims for damages fail under statutes that provide only for equitable relief. Then, the Defendants contend that the Plaintiffs assert many claims under statutes that do not provide a private right of action. Finally, the Defendants contend that the Plaintiffs' claims under the Georgia Uniform Deceptive Trade Practices Act must fail. The Court addresses each of these arguments in turn.

. . .

iii. Scienter and Injury

Then, the Defendants argue that the Plaintiffs have failed to adequately plead scienter as to their state fraud and consumer protection statutes. According to the Defendants, the Plaintiffs repeatedly assert in the Complaint that Equifax "intended to mislead" the Plaintiffs, but provide no specific factual allegations in support of this conclusion. However, the Court finds the Defendants' argument unpersuasive. The Complaint provides a number of factual allegations demonstrating Equifax's knowledge and intent with regard to its cybersecurity. For instance, the Plaintiffs allege that Equifax was aware of the importance of data security and of the previous well-publicized data breaches. It also provides allegations that, despite this knowledge of cybersecurity risks, Equifax sought to capitalize on the increased number of breaches by providing identity theft protection, instead of taking steps to improve deficiencies in its cybersecurity. The Court finds that these allegations are sufficient.

The Defendants also contend that the Plaintiffs have failed to adequately allege injury. However, as explained above, the Plaintiffs have adequately alleged a legally cognizable injury. The Defendants cite one case for the proposition that "numerous" state statutes require that an injury be "ascertainable and monetary." However, the Court concludes that the Plaintiffs have largely asserted claims that are ascertainable and monetary. The vast majority of Plaintiffs assert that they spent money taking steps to guard their identity. Furthermore, the Plaintiffs who have alleged that they were victims of identity fraud also allege injuries that are ascertainable and monetary. And, to the extent that any Plaintiffs do not plead injuries that are clearly ascertainable and monetary, the Court concludes that those claims should not be dismissed. As the Plaintiffs emphasize, this requirement comes from one District Court case in California, which has been rejected by numerous other District Courts.

Next, the Defendants contend that the Plaintiffs' claims under state consumer protection statutes requiring "consumer transactions" fail because the non-Contract Plaintiffs do not allege that they engaged in a consumer transaction with Equifax. Although many of these state statutes provide that unfair or deceptive conduct must be done in connection with a consumer transaction, courts have interpreted these requirements liberally. Courts have concluded variously that some of these statutes do not require privity, that some of them do not require a plaintiff to be a direct purchaser of a consumer good, or that the "consumer transaction" language in some of the statutes do not actually impose a requirement for plaintiffs to meet. Therefore, the Court concludes that the state unfair and deceptive trade practices claims under statutes including "consumer transaction" language should not be dismissed.

iv. Duty to Disclose

Next, the Defendants contend that seventeen of the state consumer-fraud statutes do not impose liability for omissions unless there was a duty to disclose. The Court agrees. "In the absence of a confidential relationship, no duty to disclose exists when parties are engaged in arm's-length business negotiations; in fact, an arm's-length relationship by its nature excludes a confidential relationship." The Plaintiffs contend that Equifax was under a duty to disclose due to statements it voluntarily made touting its cybersecurity. However, the vast majority of the Plaintiffs do not even allege that they were in an arms-length transaction with Equifax. Instead, most of the Plaintiffs had no relationship with Equifax. Absent such a relationship, even with these statements touting its cybersecurity, Equifax was under no general duty to disclose to the entire world.

v. Equitable Relief

Next, the Defendants contend that the Plaintiffs seek money damages under four statutes that only provide for injunctive relief. According to the Defendants, the Plaintiffs cannot seek monetary damages under the Illinois, Maine, Minnesota, and Nebraska statutes. The Plaintiffs concede that they do not seek monetary damages under the Maine, Minnesota, and Nebraska Uniform Trade Secrets Acts. The Plaintiffs contend, however, that violation of the Illinois Personal Information Protection Act constitutes a violation of the Illinois Consumer Fraud and Deceptive Trade Practices Act, which expressly permits damages suits. The Court agrees. Since the Illinois Consumer Fraud and Deceptive Trade Practices Act allows for monetary damages, the

Plaintiffs' claims for violation of the Personal Information Protection Act can also seek recovery of monetary damages.

vi. Private Rights of Action

Finally, the Defendants contend that some of the Plaintiffs' claims arise under laws that do not provide a private right of action. Specifically, the Defendants contend that the Massachusetts Consumer Protection Act and the Nevada Deceptive Trade Practices Act do not provide for private rights of action. However, the Court finds these arguments unpersuasive. Both the Massachusetts statute and the Nevada statute are privately enforceable. Therefore, these claims should not be dismissed.

vii. Georgia Uniform Deceptive Trade Practices Act

The Defendants next argue that the Plaintiffs' claims under the Georgia Uniform Deceptive Trade Practices Act, in Count 27, must fail for the same reason that their claims under the Georgia Fair Business Practices Act also fail. The Court agrees. In McConnell III, the Georgia Court of Appeals concluded that there is no statutory basis under Georgia law for a duty to safeguard personal information.

2. State Data Breach Notification Statutes

Next, the Defendants move to dismiss the Plaintiffs' claims under state data breach notification statutes. The Defendants contend that twelve of the data breach statutes under which the Plaintiffs assert claims do not allow private rights of action. According to the Defendants, the data breach statutes of Colorado, Delaware, Florida, Iowa, Kansas, Maryland, Michigan, Montana, New Jersey, New York, Wisconsin, and Wyoming do not permit private actions, and the Georgia statute is silent as to whether a private right of action exists.

The Plaintiffs contend that, with regard to the statutes of Iowa, Michigan, and New York, this argument ignores the statutory language. According to the Plaintiffs, courts have interpreted these statutes to be ambiguous as to this question, or that they provide non-exclusive remedies. Iowa's data-breach statute provides that "[a] violation of this chapter is an unlawful practice pursuant to section 714.16 and, in addition to the remedies provided to the attorney general pursuant to section 714.16, subsection 7, the attorney general may seek and obtain an order that a party held to violate this section pay damages to the attorney general on behalf of a person injured by the violation."290 However, it further provides that "[t]he rights and remedies available under this section are cumulative to each other and to any other rights and remedies available under the law." In Target, the court concluded that "[t]his is at least ambiguous as to whether private enforcement is permissible," and thus the Iowa claims should not be dismissed. The Defendants contend that this Court should not follow Target where its reasoning is "plainly and persuasively contradicted by other courts or the statutes themselves." However, the Defendants have provided no cases contradicting this reasoning, and the Target holding is not inconsistent with the language of the statute. Therefore, this Court likewise concludes that the Plaintiffs' claims under the Iowa data-breach statute should not be dismissed for this reason.

Similarly, Michigan's data-breach statute provides that "a person that knowingly fails to provide any notice of a security breach required under this section may be ordered to pay a civil fine of not more than $ 250.00 for each failure to provide notice" and that "[t]he attorney general or a prosecuting attorney may bring an action to recover a civil fine under this section." However, this statute also provides that "Subsections (12) and (13) do not affect the availability of any civil remedy for a violation of state or federal law." In Target, the court concluded that this "implies that consumers may bring a civil action to enforce Michigan's data-breach notice statute through Michigan's consumer-protection statute or other laws," and thus this "claim will not be dismissed." Absent any compelling reasoning to the contrary provided by the Defendants, the Court agrees with the Target court. The Plaintiffs' claims under the Michigan data-breach statute should not be dismissed due to a lack of a private right of action.

Next, New York's statute provides that "whenever the attorney general shall believe from evidence satisfactory to him that there is a violation of this article he may bring an action in the name and on behalf of the people of the state of New York, in a court of justice having jurisdiction to issue an injunction, to enjoin and restrain the continuation of such violation." The statute also provides that "the remedies provided by this section shall be in addition to any other lawful remedy available." At first glance, these claims should survive for the same reasons the Iowa and Michigan claims survived in Target. However, this statute also provides that "[t]he provisions of this section shall be exclusive and shall preempt any provisions of local law, ordinance or code, and no locality shall impose requirements that are inconsistent with or more restrictive than those set forth in this section." A New York state court interpreted this provision to preclude a private action, reasoning that the "language ... militates against any implied private right of action" because it would be inconsistent with the legislative scheme. The Court agrees with this reasoning. Thus, since no private right of action exists under New York's data-breach statute, the Plaintiffs' claims under section 899-aa should be dismissed.

The Plaintiffs then contend that four of the data-breach statutes, those of Connecticut, Maryland, Montana, and New Jersey, are enforceable through those states' consumer-protection statutes, even though the data-breach statutes themselves do not contain a private right of action. The Plaintiffs contend that violation of Connecticut's data-breach statute constitutes an unfair trade practice enforceable through its unfair trade practices statute. However, section 36a-701b explicitly states that "[f]ailure to comply with the requirements of this section shall constitute an unfair trade practices for purposes of section 42-110b and shall be enforced by the Attorney General." The Plaintiffs, in their brief, conspicuously omit the last part of this provision, which explicitly limits enforcement to the Attorney General. Thus, the Plaintiffs' claims under section 36a-701b should be dismissed. Similarly, the Maryland and Montana data breach statutes are also privately enforceable through those states' unfair trade practices statutes.

The Court similarly concludes that New Jersey's statute provides a private right of action. New Jersey's data breach statute requires any business that conducts business in the state to "disclose any breach of security of ... computerized records following discovery or notification of the breach to any customer who is a resident of New Jersey whose personal information was, or is reasonably believed to have been, accessed by an unauthorized person." The language of the statute does not explicitly allow for a private right of action. The Defendants cite Holmes v. Countrywide Financial Corp., where the court concluded that "[i]nsofar as the Court can tell, § 56:8–163 does not provide a private right of action for citizens to enforce its provisions." The Plaintiffs respond that violation of this notification statute is considered an unfair trade practice and thus can be privately enforced through the state's consumer protection statute. The Court agrees. Section 56:8-166 provides that violation of such a statute constitutes an unfair trade practice. Thus, this statute provides for a private right of action.

Furthermore, the data breach statutes of Colorado, Delaware, Kansas, and Wyoming contain ambiguous language as to private enforceability or provide that the statute's remedies are "non-exclusive." In Target, the court noted that this permissive language is "at least ambiguous as to whether there is a private right of action" and concluded that, "absent any authority construing this ambiguity to exclude private rights of action," the claims should not be dismissed. The Court finds this reasoning persuasive. The Defendants have not identified any authority construing this language as precluding private rights of action. Absent such authority, the Court declines to dismiss the Plaintiffs' claims under the Colorado, Delaware, Kansas, and Wyoming data breach statutes.

Next, the parties disagree as to the Wisconsin data-breach statute. The Defendants contend that the statute does not permit suit by a private plaintiff, while the Plaintiffs contend that the statute is silent. The Court agrees that the statute is silent as to this question. The provision that the Defendants cite, section 134.98(4), provides that "[f]ailure to comply with this section is not negligence or a breach of any duty, but may be evidence of negligence or a breach of a legal duty." This language does not prohibit a private action. Thus, the Court must decide whether this silence precludes, or supports, a private right of action. Neither party cites authority answering this question. The Plaintiffs cite Target, where the court allowed a claim under this statute to survive because neither party cited a case regarding how to interpret silence as to enforcement under Wisconsin law. The court concluded that, absent any such authority, the plaintiffs' claim should survive. Likewise, the Court here concludes that, without any authority suggesting otherwise, this claim should survive.

. . .

Next, the Defendants argue that the Plaintiffs have failed to adequately allege a violation of any of the state data breach notification statutes. According to the Defendants, the Complaint alleges that 41 days elapsed between Equifax's discovery of the Data Breach and the disclosure of the incident to the public. The Defendants contend these state data-breach statutes permit an entity time to determine the scope of a breach before notification, and several of the statutes even establish specific time limits. Therefore, according to the Defendants, their notification met the requirements of these statutes.

However, the Court concludes that the Plaintiffs have adequately alleged a violation of many of these statutes. Theses statutes require notification, for example, in "the most expedient time possible and without unreasonable delay" and, for example, within a reasonable time. The Plaintiffs have alleged facts from which a jury could conclude that the Defendants did not provide notice within a reasonable time, as these notification statutes require. Therefore, the Court concludes that the Plaintiffs have adequately stated a claim.

The Defendants next argue that the Plaintiffs have failed to adequately allege a claim under the Maryland Social Security Number Privacy Act. This statute prohibits publicly posting or displaying an individual's Social Security number, requiring the individual to transmit his or her Social Security number over the internet unless the connection is secure, initiating the transmission of an individual's Social Security number over the internet unless the connection is secure, and more. In Count 47 of the Complaint, the Plaintiffs allege that the Defendants violated the Maryland Social Security Number Privacy Act by "transmitt[ing] Plaintiff's and Maryland Subclass members' Social Security numbers over the Internet on unsecure connections and/or without encrypting the Social Security Numbers." According to the Defendants, these allegations fail to state a claim because they do not establish that Equifax "initiated" the transmission of any of the Plaintiffs' Social Security numbers over the internet. The Court agrees. The Plaintiffs, analogizing their arguments under the FCRA, argue that Equifax's conduct was so egregious that it was essentially an active participant in initiating the transmission of the Plaintiffs' Social Security numbers. However, by suffering a criminal hack, the Defendants did not "initiate" the transmission of these Social Security numbers. While the Defendants may have been negligent, the Plaintiffs have not shown that they "initiated the transmission" of their Social Security numbers, or engaged in any other conduct prohibit by this statute. Therefore, this claim should be dismissed.

Finally, the Defendants contend that the Plaintiffs have failed to allege any injury resulting from a delay in notification. According to the Defendants, the Plaintiffs have not alleged when any injury occurred, and thus have not alleged any damage occurring between the time that Equifax should have notified them of the Data Breach, and the time that Equifax did publicly disclose the Data Breach. However, the Target court rejected this exact argument. There, the court reasoned that such an argument is premature at this stage and that plaintiffs need only plead "a 'short and plain statement' of their claims" under Rule 8.326 The Plaintiffs note that they could have frozen their credit earlier, or taken other precautions. At this stage of the litigation, such allegations are sufficient. . . .

IV. Conclusion

For the reasons stated above, the Defendants' Motion to Dismiss the Consolidated Consumer Class Action Complaint [Doc. 425] is GRANTED in part and DENIED in part.

QUESTION

State data breach notification statutes are designed to notify individuals in each state of a data breach that may have contained the individual's personal data. The timing of the notification can depend on many factors such as an ongoing investigation into the breach and how many people in a particular state are affected. Should a plaintiff be able to succeed on this claim?

NOTES

Note 1

The economic loss doctrine may bar a tort claimant. Restatement (Third) of Torts: Liability for Economic Harm, section 3 states: "Except as provided elsewhere in this Restatement, there is no liability in tort for economic loss caused by negligence in the performance or negotiation of a contract between the parties." Similarly to the Equifax cases discussed *supra*, the Supreme Court of Pennsylvania in Dittman v. UMPC, 649 Pa. 496 (2018), held that the economic loss doctrine did not preclude a negligence cause of action in the data security breach context. The court stated:

> Here, Employees have asserted that UPMC breached its common law duty to act with reasonable care in collecting and storing their personal and financial information on its computer systems. As this legal duty exists independently from any contractual obligations between the parties, the economic loss doctrine does not bar Employees' claim.

Note 2

On May 20, 2019, the Georgia Supreme Court decided the *Department of Labor v. McConnell*, 305 Ga. 812 (2019) case referenced in the *Equifax* opinion as on appeal at the time of the issuance of that opinion. In discussing the question of negligence under Georgia law, the Georgia Supreme Court stated:

> Negligence is premised on, among other things, a duty owed by the defendant to the plaintiff. The complaint alleged that the Department owed a duty to McConnell and the other proposed class members to safeguard and protect their personal information, which McConnell argues is based on a purported common law duty "to all the world not to subject [others] to an unreasonable risk of harm," *Bradley Center v. Wessner*, 250 Ga. 199, 201, 296 S.E.2d 693 (1982) (opinion of Gregory, J.), and two statutes, OCGA §§ 10-1-393.8 and 10-1-910.

In *Bradley Center*, the lead opinion, which only two Justices joined, said that everyone owes a general duty not to subject others to an "unreasonable risk of harm" and may be liable for any breach of that duty that causes harm to another. However, the language in *Bradley Center* on which McConnell relies was not a holding concurred in by a majority of this Court, was not supported by the only authority that the lead opinion cited, was not a correct statement of the law, did not control the result in that case (which was based on a "special relationship" between the plaintiff and the defendant), and has never been endorsed in a decision of this Court that qualifies as precedent. Accordingly, we hereby disapprove *Bradley Center* to the extent that it created a general legal duty "to all the world not to subject [others] to an unreasonable risk of harm." 250 Ga. at 201, 296 S.E.2d 693.4 We therefore reject McConnell's reliance upon *Bradley Center*.

McConnell also argues that two statutes, OCGA §§ 10-1-910 and 10-1-393.8, created a legal duty on the part of the Department to safeguard his and the other proposed class members' personal information. But OCGA § 10-1-910 does not explicitly establish any duty, nor does it prohibit or require any conduct at all. Rather, the statute recites a series of legislative findings about the vulnerability of personal information and the risk of identity theft. And while OCGA § 10-1-393.8 (a) (1) says that no "person, firm, or corporation" shall "[p]ublicly post or publicly display in any manner an individual's social security number," the statute then immediately adds, "As used in this Code section, 'publicly post' or 'publicly display' means to intentionally communicate or otherwise make available to the general public." The complaint alleged only a negligent disclosure, not an intentional one. Even assuming that OCGA § 10-1-393.8 (a) (1) creates a duty enforceable in tort to refrain from intentionally disclosing social security numbers, McConnell has not shown that the Department owed him or the other proposed class members a duty to protect their information against negligent disclosure. Accordingly, the Court of Appeals correctly held that the complaint failed to state a claim for negligence. *Id.* at 815-17.

In *Collins v. Athens Orthopedic Clinic*, P.A. 307 Ga. 555 (December 23, 2019), a case decided after the *McConnell* case referenced above, the Georgia Supreme Court determined that a plaintiff sufficiently pled injury in a data breach case against a private defendant where there were allegations concerning the criminal's hacking. However, the Georgia Supreme Court noted that, "showing injury as a result of the exposure of data is easier in a case like this, where the data exposure occurs as a result of an act by a criminal whose likely motivation is to sell the data to others. But that easier showing of injury may well be offset by a more difficult showing of breach of duty." *Id.* at 315-16. The court then cited its recent decision in the *McConnell* case and noted that "[t]his case is at the motion to dismiss stage, and the Court of Appeals's decision did not turn on this issue, so we leave it for another day." *Id.* at 316. In a District Court of Maryland decision after the Georgia Supreme Court's *McConnell* opinion, the District Court determined that a negligence per se action based on a data breach and FTC Section 5 survived a motion to dismiss in light of the Georgia Supreme Court's McConnell decision. *See In re Marriott Int'l Customer Data Security Breach Litigation*, 440 F.Supp.3d 447, 478-482 (D. Md. 2020).

Note 3

In *Privacy Remedies*, Professor Scholz argues that underenforcement of the privacy right has resulted from failure of courts and commentators to consider restitution as the quintessential remedy choice for privacy matters. *See* Lauren Henry Scholz, *Privacy Remedies*, 94 Ind. L.J. 653 (2019).

Note 4

Assume that Equifax contracted with a vendor to provide cloud services and cybersecurity for the data collected by Equifax. What clauses in the contract would you include to protect Equifax from liability for cybersecurity data breaches as best as possible under the law? Would you require the vendor to include a clause promising to adhere to industry standards and to comply with the relevant law? Would you require the vendor to acquire insurance as well as provide representations concerning indemnification? What about choice of law or forum clauses? Would you require a clause allowing Equifax to inspect the cybersecurity policies, practices and procedures of the vendor?

Note 5

As alluded to in the last note, cybersecurity insurance is available to provide coverage for liability for cybersecurity data breaches. The U.S. Cybersecurity & Infrastructure Security Agency discusses cybersecurity insurance in the following:

> Cybersecurity insurance is designed to mitigate losses from a variety of cyber incidents, including data breaches, business interruption, and network damage. A robust cybersecurity insurance market could help reduce the number of successful cyber attacks by: (1) promoting the adoption of preventative measures in return for more coverage; and (2) encouraging the implementation of best practices by basing premiums on an insured's level of self-protection. Many companies forego available policies, however, citing as rationales the perceived high cost of those policies, confusion about what they cover, and uncertainty that their organizations will suffer a cyber attack. In recent years, the Cybersecurity and Infrastructure Security Agency (CISA) has engaged key stakeholders to address this emerging cyber risk area.

Traditional commercial general liability and property insurance policies typically exclude cyber risks from their terms, leading to the emergence of cybersecurity insurance as a "stand alone" line of coverage. That coverage provides protection against a wide range of cyber incident losses that businesses may suffer directly or cause to others, including costs arising from data destruction and/or theft, extortion demands, hacking, denial of service attacks, crisis management activity related to data breaches, and legal claims for defamation, fraud, and privacy violations. Few cybersecurity insurance policies, however, provide businesses with coverage for an area of growing private and public concern: the physical damage and bodily harm that could result from a successful cyber attack against critical infrastructure.[376]

How can the government encourage the development of the cybersecurity insurance market and the spread of the risk of data breaches? What impact will a robust cybersecurity insurance market have on raising cybersecurity standards and deterring cybersecurity breaches? *See* Jay P. Kesan and Carol M. Hayes, *Strengthening Cybersecurity with Cyberinsurance Markets and Better Risk Assessment*, 102 Minn. L. Rev. 191 (2017) ("Done well, a cyberinsurance market could provide a fundamentally private market solution to some of the most pressing cybersecurity problems by urging the development and adoption of new security protections. A poorly designed cyberinsurance market, on the other hand, could aggravate existing failings, reward free riders, create moral hazards, and inadvertently limit the cyberinsurance market to market participants that are at greatest risk for cyberattacks. . . ."). For additional analysis concerning cybersecurity insurance policies, please see Asaf Lubin, *The Insurability of Cyber Risk* [Unpublished Manuscript] (2019), https://papers.ssrn.com/sol3/papers.cfm?abstract_id=3452833. CyberInsureOne is a company which provides help matching companies with cybersecurity insurance providers.[377]

Notably, in 2021, hackers targeted the cyber insurance industry. According to an article by Frank Bajak titled, *"In Crosshairs of Ransomware Crooks, Cyber Insurers Struggle,"*: "It's teetering on the edge of profitability, upended by a more than 400% rise last year in ransomware cases and skyrocketing extortion demands. As a percentage of premiums collected, cyber insurance payouts now top 70%, the break-even point." *See* Frank Bajak, *In the Crosshairs of Ransomware Crooks, Cyber Insurers Struggle*, Associated Press (July 5, 2021), available at https://apnews.com/article/kaseya-ransomware-attack-0705-4c2272cdd428ddfa1f3644d513566c06.

Note 6

Can you waive away cybersecurity protection for your data? For an interesting discussion of consent in the privacy context, please see Neil Richards & Woodrow

---

[377] https://cyberinsureone.com/about-us/.

Hartzog, *The Pathologies of Digital Consent*, 96 Wash. U. L. Rev. 1461 (2019) ("[T]he pathologies of consent show how consumers can be nudged and manipulated by powerful companies against their actual interests, and this phenomenon is easier when the legal regime that purports to protect consumers falls far from the gold standard [and] the solution is . . . to look to other mechanisms that are more sensitive to relationships and power differentials, such as those designed to inspire the social trust that makes consent less necessary.").

9.4 Class Certification

As previously noted and discussed in some of the cases supra, many data breach lawsuits are consolidated and class actions. Federal Rules of Civil Procedure, Rule 23, provides in relevant part:

(a) Prerequisites. One or more members of a class may sue or be sued as representative parties on behalf of all members only if:

(1) the class is so numerous that joinder of all members is impracticable;

(2) there are questions of law or fact common to the class;

(3) the claims or defenses of the representative parties are typical of the claims or defenses of the class; and

(4) the representative parties will fairly and adequately protect the interests of the class.

(b) Types of Class Actions. A class action may be maintained if Rule 23(a) is satisfied and if:

(1) prosecuting separate actions by or against individual class members would create a risk of:

(A) inconsistent or varying adjudications with respect to individual class members that would establish incompatible standards of conduct for the party opposing the class; or

(B) adjudications with respect to individual class members that, as a practical matter, would be dispositive of the interests of the other members not parties to the individual adjudications or would substantially impair or impede their ability to protect their interests;

(2) the party opposing the class has acted or refused to act on grounds that apply generally to the class, so that final injunctive relief or corresponding declaratory relief is appropriate respecting the class as a whole; or

(3) the court finds that the questions of law or fact common to class members predominate over any questions affecting only individual members, and that a class action is superior to other available methods for fairly and efficiently adjudicating the controversy. The matters pertinent to these findings include:

(A) the class members' interests in individually controlling the prosecution or defense of separate actions;

(B) the extent and nature of any litigation concerning the controversy already begun by or against class members;

(C) the desirability or undesirability of concentrating the litigation of the claims in the particular forum; and

(D) the likely difficulties in managing a class action.

The following three cases explore the requirements for maintaining a class action in the data security breach context.

In re Hannaford Brothers Data Security Breach Litigation, 293 F.R.D. 21 (2013).

DECISION AND ORDER ON PLAINTIFFS' REVISED AND SUPPLEMENTED MOTION FOR CLASS CERTIFICATION

D. BROCK HORNBY, District Judge.

Hannaford grocery stores suffered a massive technological intrusion at their retail points of sale during the period December 7, 2007 through March 10, 2008. Customers' debit and credit card data was stolen, and many lawsuits against Hannaford followed. After rulings by the Maine Supreme Judicial Court sitting as the Law Court and by the Court of Appeals for the First Circuit, the claims against Hannaford have been pared down to negligence and breach of implied contract, and the damages are limited to out-of-pocket expenditures customers made in reasonable attempts to mitigate against economic injury. Four named plaintiffs now have moved for certification of a Rule 23(b)(3) class to pursue claims for fees to obtain new cards; fees paid to expedite delivery of new cards; and fees paid for identity theft insurance and credit monitoring. The defendant Hannaford has objected. After oral argument on November 30, 2012, I find that the plaintiffs fail to meet the predominance requirement of Rule 23(b)(3) and Deny the motion for class certification.

Procedural History

The plaintiffs are grocery store customers of the defendant Hannaford.1 They claim that a third party criminally breached Hannaford's information technology systems at the retail point of sale and gained access to the customers' confidential financial and personal information during a 3–month period as a result of negligence and breach of implied contract on Hannaford's part. They filed class action lawsuits in this District and in other Districts. The Judicial Panel on Multidistrict Litigation transferred all the lawsuits here.

The plaintiffs then filed a consolidated complaint that alleged seven claims against Hannaford. Hannaford moved under Rule 12(b)(6) to dismiss all claims for failure to state a cause of action.

I dismissed four of the plaintiffs' seven claims for failure to state a claim. I allowed three to proceed, but only as to a plaintiff who, as a result of the intrusion, had incurred fraudulent charges and had not been reimbursed. Otherwise, I ruled that the plaintiffs had suffered no injury cognizable under Maine law. Thereafter, the plaintiffs stipulated that in fact that particular plaintiff had received reimbursement. I then dismissed the consolidated class action complaint in its entirety either for failure to state a claim or for lack of cognizable injury, but I delayed entry of judgment while I certified to the Maine Supreme Judicial Court sitting as the Law Court the question:

> (1) In the absence of physical harm or economic loss or identity theft, do time and effort alone, spent in a reasonable effort to avoid or remediate reasonably foreseeable harm, constitute a cognizable injury for which damages may be recovered under Maine law of negligence and/or implied contract?

In re Hannaford Bros. Co. Customer Data Sec. Breach Litig., 671 F.Supp.2d 198, 201 (D.Me.2009).

The Law Court answered no, agreeing with me that time and effort alone do not constitute a cognizable harm under Maine Law. In re Hannaford Bros. Co. Customer Data Sec. Breach Litig., 4 A.3d 492, 498 (Me.2010). I then entered judgment in favor of Hannaford, dismissing all claims.

On appeal, the First Circuit upheld my dismissal of five claims. But on negligence and breach of implied contract—where I ruled that the plaintiffs had stated a claim, but had not alleged cognizable injury for which to obtain relief—the Circuit ruled that the plaintiffs had sufficiently alleged categories of damages that were not time and effort alone and that were reasonably foreseeable mitigation costs that constitute cognizable harm under Maine law. Those were the fees for replacing cards and the cost of data theft protection products. As a result, the First Circuit ruled, the plaintiffs could proceed on their negligence and breach of implied contract claims, and it vacated and remanded accordingly. Anderson v. Hannaford Bros. Co., 659 F.3d 151 (1st Cir.2011).

Upon remand, the plaintiffs filed this new motion for class certification under Rule 23(b)(3), recasting their proposed class in light of the law of the case. The proposed class now is:

> All persons or entities anywhere in the United States who made purchases at stores owned or operated by Defendant or for which Defendant provided electronic payment processing services, during the period from December 7, 2007 through March 10, 2008, using debit or

credit cards, and who made reasonable out of pocket expenditures in mitigation of the consequences to them of an electronic breach of Defendant's data security during this period consisting of 1) payment of fees to obtain prompt replacement of cancelled cards and 2) purchase of security products such as credit monitoring and identity theft insurance.

In other words, the proposed class now is limited to Hannaford customers who incurred out-of-pocket costs in mitigation efforts that they undertook in response to learning of the data intrusion.

Analysis

I proceed to assess whether the plaintiffs satisfy the Rule 23(a) and (b)(3) criteria:

A. Rule 23(a)

1. Numerosity

The proposed class consists of those customers who spent money to obtain prompt replacement of their cards and/or purchased credit monitoring and identity theft insurance. Is their number sufficient to satisfy the numerosity requirement?

The numerosity requirement is satisfied when "the class is so numerous that joinder of all members is impracticable." Fed.R.Civ.P. 23(a)(1). There is no strict numerical test; "[t]he numerosity requirement requires examination of the specific facts of each case and imposes no absolute limitations." Gen. Tel. Co. v. EEOC, 446 U.S. 318 (1980). Although numbers alone are "not usually determinative," the sheer number of potential litigants in a class can be the only factor needed to satisfy numerosity. In re Relafen Antitrust Litig., 218 F.R.D. 337, 342 (D.Mass.2003) (("forty individuals [are] generally found to establish numerosity"); 1 Herbert Newberg & Alba Conte, Newberg on Class Actions § 3.05, at 3–25 (3d ed. 1992) (generally impracticable to join 40 plaintiffs and therefore a class of 40 should normally satisfy the numerosity requirement). While the named plaintiffs need not plead or prove the exact number of class members, speculation is insufficient, and they must positively show the impracticability of joinder.

Here, the named plaintiffs rely on data from three representative card issuers that dealt with Hannaford customers, Discover, KeyBank and Bank of America. This data shows fees associated with card replacement, expedited replacement, and identity theft protection products during the year following the Hannaford data breach. The data from Bank of America shows that approximately 12,000 card holders whose data was "reportedly subject to a security breach at Hannaford" purchased identity theft protection in the year following the Hannaford data breach. The number of Bank of America cardholders who purchased identity theft protection doubled from December 2007 to January 2008 and then the number continued increasing until April 2009. In May 2009, the number of Bank of America cardholders who purchased new identity theft protection policies began to decline, but did not drop to prebreach numbers until November 2009. The data from Discover shows that approximately five thousand card holders whose Discover cards may have been compromised purchased identity theft protection products in the year following the Hannaford data breach. The number of Discover cardholders who purchased new identity theft protection products increased after December 2007 and did not return to prebreach levels until July 2008. The data from KeyBank shows that approximately 14,000 cardholders were charged replacement fees in the year following the Hannaford data breach.

I conclude that this data satisfies the numerosity requirement, and that the numbers alone demonstrate impracticality of joinder. I recognize that correlation does not demonstrate causation, and that I cannot be confident that the Hannaford incident was the sole cause for all these expenses. But at this stage of class certification the challenge is to predict whether the class will be large. When assessing the size of the putative class, courts may "draw reasonable inferences from the facts presented to find the requisite numerosity." Given the patterns shown here for these card issuers and the absence of alternative persuasive explanations for those patterns, I conclude that the number of Hannaford customers who incurred these fees as a result of the breach is sufficient to satisfy Rule 23(a)(1).

In opposing the numerosity finding, Hannaford points to In re Heartland Payment Sys., Inc. Customer Sec. Breach Litig., 851 F.Supp.2d 1040, 1047 & n. 2, 1050 (S.D.Tex.2012). That was a case also involving a credit card data breach. There were 130 million potential class members in Heartland Payment. Yet after settlement, only 290 filed claims, and of those, only 11 claims were valid. Hannaford argues that there is no basis to assume that a larger number of class members will ultimately assert claims in this lawsuit than in Heartland Payment, and that in fact Hannaford already established a generous refund program following the data intrusion here. Hannaford points out that one former named plaintiff testified that she did not know whether KeyBank refunded the $5 fee it charged her for a replacement card, and that she had not checked on the refund because it was not worth her time to verify whether she received it. Hannaford seems to characterize this projected lack of interest as inability to demonstrate impracticability of joinder because, Hannaford claims, few customers will want to be part of the class.

I am certainly concerned that if this case proceeds as a class action, few class members will ultimately be interested in taking the time to file the paperwork necessary to obtain the very small amount of money that may be available if there is a recovery. I also note that the recovery of generous fees for plaintiffs' attorneys and large cy pres awards with little money going to actual class members call into question the integrity of the class action process for resolving lawsuits. Nevertheless, those are policy issues for Congress or for the Federal Rules drafters. There is no precedent for my deciding the numerosity issue based upon how many claimants care about recovery, or are likely to come forward to make a claim. This portion of the Rule is concerned only with whether the class as defined is composed of sufficient numbers to warrant class action treatment. My uneasiness based on the Heartland Payment outcome, and my concern here that this is a de minimis class action where virtually no one will bother to make a claim and that any recovery will serve solely the lawyers (and perhaps some modest measure of corporate deterrence) present questions for those who write the class action rules and for Congress, not for this individual judge applying the language of the Rule.

2. Commonality

To meet the commonality requirement under Rule 23(a)(2), the named plaintiffs must show that "there are questions of law or fact common to the class." Fed.R.Civ.P. 23(a)(2). The claims of the class "must depend upon a common contention ... that it is capable of classwide resolution-which means that determination of its truth or falsity will resolve an issue that is central to the validity of each one of the claims in one stroke." Wal–Mart Stores, Inc. v. Dukes, —— U.S. ——, 131 S.Ct. 2541, 2551, 180 L.Ed.2d 374 (2011). "What matters to class certification ... is not the raising of common questions—even in droves—but, rather the capacity of a classwide proceeding to generate common answers apt to drive the resolution of the litigation. Dissimilarities within the proposed class are what have the potential to impede the generation of common answers." Id.

Whether Hannaford's conduct was negligent or a contractual breach and whether it caused a data security breach that resulted in theft of customers' data and reasonably prompted customers to take mitigation measures are questions that are common among all the class members. Answering these questions will resolve issues that are "central to the validity of each one of the claims in one stroke." While the losses of each class member may not be identical in amount or type, Hannaford's action or inaction that allegedly produced the loss is the same, and the economic injuries are similar. Thus, there are questions of law and fact common to the class, and the commonality requirement is satisfied.

3. Typicality

Rule 23(a)(3) requires that "the claims or defenses of the representative parties [be] typical of the claims or defenses of the class." Fed.R.Civ.P. 23(a)(3). The typicality analysis is designed to ensure that class representatives, in pursuing their own interests, concurrently will advance those of the class. Class representatives' claims are "typical" when their claims "arise from the same event or practice or course of conduct that gives rise to the claims of other class members, and ... are based on the same legal theory." The purpose of the typicality inquiry is to "align the interests of the class and the class representatives so that the latter will work to benefit the entire class through the pursuit of their own goals."

As I said under commonality, the named plaintiffs here, like each member of the class, need to show that Hannaford was negligent or breached an implied contract, that Hannaford's conduct caused the data breach, that the data breach affected their debit or credit cards, and that they took reasonable mitigating efforts as a result. The named plaintiffs are entirely typical of the class in those respects. Two of the named plaintiffs incurred fees for card replacement; one incurred fees for prompt card replacement; and two incurred fees to purchase credit monitoring or identity theft insurance.

Where things differ is in the economic impact on various class members. Some Hannaford customers had fraudulent charges; others did not; some bought insurance or credit monitoring; others did not; some paid a fee for a new card; others did not; some paid for rush delivery; others did not. The class is limited to those who incurred one or another of these fees, but Hannaford asserts that the differences entail individual evidence of causation as to each class member's need to take mitigation efforts, that resolution of any named plaintiff's claim will leave unresolved the claims of any other putative class member, and that the named plaintiffs therefore cannot satisfy the typicality standard. For support Hannaford relies on In re TJX Cos. Retail Sec. Breach Litigation, 246 F.R.D. 389 (D.Mass.2007), where the court denied class certification of a negligent misrepresentation claim by credit card issuers against data security companies. TJX held that where reliance is an element of a claim, a presumption of reliance is never appropriate because "[p]roving the element of reliance will necessarily involve individual questions of fact." Hannaford argues that the same reasoning applies here to proof of expenditures made to mitigate damages, the premise of the class damages claim.

As an abstract proposition, there is some force to Hannaford's argument. But to accept it under the typicality analysis at this stage of the proceedings would be unfaithful to the First Circuit's decision that remanded the case to me. That court read the plaintiffs' complaint as establishing the following:

> This case involves a large-scale criminal operation conducted over three months and the deliberate taking of credit and debit card information by sophisticated thieves intending to use the information to their financial advantage. Unlike the cases cited by Hannaford, this case does not involve inadvertently misplaced or lost data which has not been accessed or misused by third parties. Here, there was actual misuse, and it was apparently global in reach. The thieves appeared to have expertise in accomplishing their theft, and to be sophisticated in how to take advantage of the stolen numbers. The data was used to run up thousands of improper charges across the globe to the customers' accounts. The card owners were not merely exposed to a hypothetical risk, but to a real risk of misuse.

Further, there is no suggestion there was any way to sort through to predict whose accounts would be used to ring up improper charges. By the time Hannaford acknowledged the breach, over 1,800 fraudulent charges had been identified and the plaintiffs could reasonably expect that many more fraudulent charges would follow. Hannaford did not notify its customers of exactly what data, or whose data, was stolen. It reasonably appeared that all Hannaford customers to have used credit or debit cards during the class period were at risk of unauthorized charges.

That many banks or issuers immediately issued new cards is evidence of the reasonableness of replacement of cards as mitigation. Those banks thought the cards would be subject to unauthorized use, and cancelled those cards to mitigate their own losses in what was a commercially reasonable judgment. That other financial institutions did not replace cards immediately does not make it unreasonable for cardholders to take steps to protect themselves.

[For the negligence claim] It was foreseeable, on these facts, that a customer, knowing that her credit or debit card data had been compromised and that thousands of fraudulent charges had resulted from the same security breach, would replace the card to mitigate against misuse of the card data. It is true that the only plaintiffs to allege having to pay a replacement card fee, Cyndi Fear and Thomas Fear, do not allege that they experienced any unauthorized charges to their account, but the test for mitigation is not hindsight. Similarly, it was foreseeable that a customer who had experienced unauthorized charges to her account, such as plaintiff Lori Valburn, would reasonably purchase insurance to protect against the consequences of data misuse.

....

[For the implied contract claim] Plaintiffs' claims for identity theft insurance and re-placement card fees involve actual financial losses from credit and debit card misuse. Under Maine contract law, these financial losses are recoverable as mitigation damages so long as they are reasonable. I read that language by the First Circuit as establishing that, on the facts that the plaintiffs asserted, a jury could find that every customer "knowing that her credit or debit card data had been compromised and that thousands of fraudulent charges had resulted from the same security breach" was entitled to mitigate by replacing the card, and that every customer "who had experienced unauthorized charges to her account" was entitled to mitigate by purchasing insurance. That entitlement to mitigate under the circumstances alleged makes the named plaintiffs' claims of injury typical of the class. To be sure, the plaintiffs may be unsuccessful in proving at trial or on summary judgment all of the facts that they alleged, but that is the premise of the lawsuit before me after remand, and this First Circuit holding suffices for this trial judge's determination of typicality.

4. Adequacy

Adequacy of representation requires that "the representative parties will fairly and adequately protect the interests of the class." Fed.R.Civ.P. 23(a)(4). There are two elements to the adequacy inquiry. First, there must be an absence of potential conflict between the named plaintiffs and the potential class members, and, second, the lawyers chosen by the class representative must be "qualified, experienced, and able to vigorously conduct the proposed litigation."

Specifically, of the four named plaintiffs one paid a fee for replacement of his Key Bank card and an additional fee to expedite delivery of his replacement card after his card was cancelled because of a fraudulent charge. Another was required to pay a fee to obtain a new card when she cancelled her Key Bank debit card in the wake of a fraudulent charge. The other two both purchased identity theft insurance products offered to them by Discover. One bought Discover's Identity Theft Protection ("ITP") product when he learned about the Hannaford data security breach. The other bought

Discover's Wallet Protection product when she experienced fraudulent activity with her Discover card number. These named plaintiffs appear to have no interests antagonistic to the other class members.

Nevertheless, Hannaford asserts in general that the named plaintiffs are not adequate because they have chosen to participate in class litigation rather than apply to Hannaford for refund gift cards. This path, Hannaford claims, "needlessly reduces the recovery for the putative class [and] contravenes the representatives' duty to protect the class." The Seventh Circuit seems to have accepted this argument. In re Aqua Dots Prods. Liability Litig., 654 F.3d 748, 752 (7th Cir.2011). Hannaford has not referred to any other Circuit that has done so. Although reasonable people can certainly maintain that as a matter of policy other solutions are preferable to litigation, I do not see how that argument has a place in the class certification decision under the current Rule. A named plaintiff can represent a class only by filing a lawsuit; that is what the Federal Rules of Civil Procedure (and Rule 23 in particular) are for. Named plaintiffs are hardly adequate representatives of a class by not filing a lawsuit, because then they are not class representatives at all! Moreover, members of a class under 23(b)(3) who determine that their interests are better served otherwise (as by an individual lawsuit or by applying for a refund from Hannaford) are free to opt out of the class. Fed.R.Civ.P. 23(c)(3)(B). This "opt out" provision is designed to ensure that even in a class action that meets all the prerequisites of Rule 23, "the individual interest is respected." Advisory Committee Notes to the 1966 Amendments. So, regardless of whether Hannaford customers are better advised to apply directly to Hannaford to reimburse the fees they paid, I find that the named plaintiffs are adequate under the language of the Rule.

. . . Since the named plaintiffs meet both parts of the adequacy of representation test, Rule 23(a)(4) is satisfied.

B. Rule 23(b)(3)

Rule 23(b)(3) provides for class certification where "questions of law or fact common to class members predominate over any questions affecting only individual members, and ... a class action is superior to other available methods for fairly and efficiently adjudicating the controversy." Rule 23(b)(3) (emphasis added). The objective behind both requirements is the promotion of economy and efficiency. See Rule 23(b)(3) Advisory Committee notes.

1. Predominance

Do "questions of law or fact common to class members predominate over any questions affecting only individual members" with respect to the class claims here?

The common questions of liability on the plaintiffs' negligence and implied contract claims concern whether Hannaford breached a duty to securely maintain its customers' credit and debit card information and whether that breach caused the intrusion, affected the plaintiffs' electronic data and reasonably led them to take protective measures that cost money.

As I said earlier, where things differ is in the actual impact on particular cardholders (for example, whether their particular accounts suffered fraudulent charges or not) and the actual mitigating steps they took and the costs they incurred.

Here, the appellate caselaw does not give clear guidance. On the one hand, the First Circuit has said that variations in damages do not prevent class certification and has reversed a court that said they did. See Smilow v. Southwestern Bell Mobile Sys., Inc., 323 F.3d 32, 40 (1st Cir.2003) ("The individuation of damages in consumer class actions is rarely determinative under Rule 23(b)(3). Where, as here, common questions predominate regarding liability, then courts generally find the predominance requirement to be satisfied even if individual damages issues remain."). Other circuits and authorities often say the same thing. On the other hand, if the issue is phrased as causation (of damages), the courts demand common proof.

Which label applies here, causation where common proof is required, or damages where individuation is allowed? Hannaford argues that causation is at issue, and that there can be a huge variation among customers in whether and how many fraudulent charges they suffered, the steps they took as a result, what alternative resources were available to them, etc. The plaintiffs, on the other hand, say that Hannaford caused the problem, and the only issue where there might be individualized proof is the amount of damage that each customer suffered. This labeling distinction is not a particularly useful method for deciding predominance. While the fact that damages may have to be ascertained on an individual basis is not, standing alone, sufficient to defeat class certification, it is nonetheless a factor that I consider in deciding whether, in the words of the Rule, the controversy can be fairly and efficiently adjudicated as a class action. McLaughlin v. American Tobacco Co., 522 F.3d 215, 231 (2d Cir.2008). As a trial judge, in my assessment of predominance I turn instead to how the trial will work (or not work) if this lawsuit proceeds as a class action.

Here, the plaintiffs tell me that the trial will be straightforward; the issues of standard of care, breach, and what happened as a result of the intrusion are all the same. And they say that they will prove by statistical proof the total damages caused to the class. In that respect, they say that they have card issuers' records that isolate the category of customers who shopped at Hannaford. As I described under numerosity, they say that these records show cards replaced and fees charged, instances of rush delivery charges, and instances of the purchase of insurance or credit monitoring services. These are chronological, they say, and show a pattern of escalation around the time of the Hannaford incident and soon thereafter. In addition, they say, they have evidence of "industry and institutional averages and trends." Pls.' Reply Mem. in Support of Class Certification at 10 (ECF No. 168). The plaintiffs go on to say that they can find experts who will be able to testify by statistical probability what proportion of the fees incurred are attributable to the Hannaford intrusion, as distinguished from other causes (like card loss or theft, other things in the news, marketing of services, etc.). They say that with this evidence they will ask the jury for a lump sum damage award that reflects the total fees that Hannaford caused. Later, they say, it will be a matter of typical class administration to distribute the proceeds to those who claim a share and qualify.

Hannaford, on the other hand, says that such a trial would violate the Rules Enabling Act, deprive it of its constitutional right to due process, and be fundamentally unfair. It insists on the right to be able to cross-examine each class member individually to ascertain whether he/she actually had fraudulent charges on his/her account, what really motivated his/her decision to incur certain fees, whether the decision was unreasonable under all the circumstances, and to determine for each class member what alternatives were available (AAA membership or credit union insurance that would provide coverage at no extra cost) to him/her. Hannaford asserts that cardholders regularly replace their cards for reasons unrelated to the Hannaford intrusion, that there is always "fraud in the electronic payment system from known and unknown causes," that individual plaintiffs may have had other motivations for buying insurance products or replacing a card, and that consumers purchase theft protection products even in the absence of a criminal data intrusion on their accounts. Thus, these issues that will affect entitlement to recovery, Hannaford asserts, can only be determined on an individual cardholder basis.

There are difficulties with both sides' arguments. Hannaford's position, construed broadly, would basically eliminate consumer class actions, if every consumer's damage must be assessed individually before the jury in a class action. But cases that support the plaintiffs' lump sum jury verdict procedure do not easily fit the record here. Generally in those cases, the plaintiffs already had an expert who had looked at the data and stated his/her ability to testify what the total damages would be. That is missing in this case. Although the plaintiffs have told me they will find such an expert, they have not presented that expert or that expert's opinion. Certainly I cannot take judicial notice that there will be such an expert. The plaintiffs bear the burden at class certification, General Telephone Co. of Southwest v. Falcon, 457 U.S. 147, 156, 102 S.Ct. 2364, 72 L.Ed.2d 740 (1982), and I conclude that their lack of an expert opinion on their ability to prove total damages to the jury is fatal. Without an expert, they cannot prove total damages, and the alternative (which even they do not advocate) is a trial involving individual issues for each class member as to what happened to his/her data and account, what he/she did about it, and why.

In the absence of expert opinion testimony, I conclude that the plaintiffs have not shown predominance. Nevertheless, in the event that the Circuit disagrees, I proceed to the final factor.

2. Superiority

The Rule lists four nonexhaustive factors relevant to superiority:

> (A) the class members' interest in individually controlling the prosecution or defense of separate actions;

> (B) the extent and nature of any litigation concerning the controversy already begun by or against class members;

(C) the desirability or undesirability of concentrating the litigation of the claims in the particular forum; and

(D) the likely difficulties in managing a class action.

All four lead to the conclusion that a class action is the superior method for adjudicating this controversy. Given the size of the claims, individual class members have virtually no interest in individually controlling the prosecution of separate actions (A); all the litigation has been transferred here (B and C); if I am wrong in my predominance ruling such that the plaintiffs should be allowed to find their expert later and do find one who can testify about lump sum damages, the difficulties of managing the class action (D) are then manageable.

Trial then would focus on the data theft, Hannaford's responsibility to have avoided it, and perhaps the reasonableness of customer concern after learning of it. Individual damages will vary, but a lump sum verdict against Hannaford would establish the fund against which class members could make claims and prove their eligibility.

As I have said previously, Hannaford asserts that it created a refund program for fees related to credit card replacement arising out of the data theft. It argues that its program provides a superior method of recovery. Hannaford representatives say that the refund program provides Hannaford gift cards to customers who paid fees associated with replacing their cards and with promptly obtaining a new card and does not require proof of causation or even loss. The gift cards, Hannaford contends, afford class members a comparable or even better remedy than they could hope to achieve in court. Hannaford relies on a handful of district court cases that conclude that where a defendant by "allow[ing] consumers to obtain refunds" is offering the very relief that plaintiffs seek, then "a class action is not superior." Webb v. Carter's Inc., 272 F.R.D. 489, 504–05 (C.D.Cal.2011) ("Where the defendant 'is already offering the very relief that Plaintiffs seek' by 'allow[ing] consumers to obtain refunds,' then 'a class action is not superior.' ").

Although I appreciate the policy preference of my colleagues in these cases and much as I too favor parties being able to resolve their controversies without expensive litigation, I observe that Rule 23(b)(3) does not address superiority as a matter of abstract economic choice analysis, but asks if a class action is "superior to other available methods for fairly and efficiently adjudicating the controversy"—i.e., other possible adjudication methods such as individual lawsuits or a consolidated lawsuit. Indeed, all four enumerated factors in this portion of the Rule deal with adjudication. See also the language of the Advisory Committee note in the 1966 amendment that added this provision. Recently, the Seventh Circuit recognized this language in holding that a refund program cannot be considered a method of "adjudicating the controversy" under 23(b)(3). I agree, and I conclude that Hannaford may or may not have a good program to satisfy aggrieved customers, but that the Hannaford program is not relevant to my superiority determination under the class certification decision.

Finally, Hannaford asserts that the class cannot be "ascertained by objective criteria prior to litigation." In Crosby, the First Circuit rejected a class defined as "all claimants who have not had a hearing or decision on their [Social Security] disability claim 'within a reasonable time.'" Crosby, 796 F.2d at 579–80. Because the Supreme Court had held that determination of whether a reasonable time violation occurred "can be made only on a case-by-case basis," the First Circuit concluded that members of such a class could not be identified prior to individualized fact-finding and litigation, and thus could not qualify as a class. That is not this case. Here, Hannaford customers during the data intrusion can be identified and those who made out-of-pocket expenditures as a result of the intrusion also can be identified. Whether their expenditures were reasonable is a typical damages issue that does not prevent class action treatment. This class can be ascertained before individualized fact-finding and litigation.

Using representative plaintiffs, a jury can determine what was a reasonable amount of money to spend to get a card replaced or for the purchase of some form of theft protection policy. Regardless of the circumstances of the individual customers, if the jury determines that it was reasonable to cancel and replace the exposed cards, then the jury can also determine what costs associated with the replacement of the card are reasonable mitigation expenses. Likewise, a jury can determine based on the representative plaintiffs whether the credit security products offered by the victim's card-issuing financial institution were a reasonable outlay in mitigation of threatened harm.

Conclusion

Accordingly, the plaintiffs satisfy the criteria for a Rule 23(b)(3) class in all respects but one, predominance. Because they fail to satisfy predominance, their motion for class certification is Denied.

So Ordered.

In re Target Corporation Customer Data Security Breach Litigation, 2017 WL 2178306 (May 17, 2017).

MEMORANDUM AND ORDER

Paul A. Magnuson, United States District Court Judge

This matter is before the Court on limited remand from the Eighth Circuit Court of Appeals. For following reasons, Consumer Plaintiffs' renewed Motion to Certify Class in Accordance with Limited Remand Order is granted.

BACKGROUND

On November 17, 2015, after nearly two years of litigation, this Court approved the settlement of the consumer cases in this multi-track Multi–District Litigation arising out of a massive data breach that involved tens of millions of Target customers' personal financial information. In doing so, the Court overruled the objections of Objector Leif

Olson that the settlement class was not appropriately certified under Rule 23. Olson appealed, and the Eighth Circuit Court of Appeals determined that this Court's evaluation of class certification was not the "rigorous analysis" that precedent required. In re Target Corp. Customer Data Sec. Breach Litig., 847 F.3d 608, 612 (8th Cir. 2017). The Eighth Circuit thus remanded the matter for a more detailed analysis of one of Olson's objections to certification, specifically whether class representatives and class counsel can adequately represent the class as a whole.

As the Eighth Circuit stated, this Court must "evaluate upon remand" the following issues:

> First, whether an intraclass conflict exists when class members who cannot claim money from a settlement fund are represented by class members who can. Second, if there is a conflict, whether it prevents the class representatives "from fairly and adequately protecting the interests of all of the class members." Third, if the class is conflicted, whether the conflict is "fundamental" and requires certification of one or more subclasses with independent representation.

Id. at 613.

Plaintiffs then brought a renewed Motion to Certify Class in accordance with the limited remand. Olson opposes the Motion. The Court held a hearing on the Motion on May 10, 2017, at which Plaintiffs, Olson, and Target weighed in on the issues.

DISCUSSION

A. The Class and Settlement

The class as preliminarily and finally certified consists of Target customers in the United States "whose credit or debit card information and/or whose personal information was compromised as a result of the [December 2013] data breach." The parties estimate that the personal information of nearly 100 million American consumers was compromised in the breach.

Target agreed to settle the consumers' claims by paying $10 million directly to class members, instituting substantial reforms to prevent the occurrence of another data breach, paying all expenses of class notice and settlement administration in addition to the $10 million settlement payment, and paying attorney's fees of slightly less than 30% of the total fund—also separate from the $10 million settlement payment.

The settlement provides for consumers to be reimbursed for all of their documented losses from the Target data breach, up to a maximum of $10,000. Customers who did not suffer any direct loss but who purchased identity theft protection or credit monitoring services after the data breach are eligible for reimbursement of those expenses. And, once all claims and class representative service awards are paid, the settlement funds will be distributed on a pro-rata basis to individuals who do not have any documented proof of loss. At the time of the final settlement approval hearing,

Consumer Plaintiffs estimated that such payments would amount to approximately $40 per claimant.

Since the November 2015 settlement approval, more than 225,000 individuals have submitted claims for reimbursement under the settlement. No claims have yet been paid, however, because of the pending appeals by Olson and one other objector.

B. Rule 23

A district court may not certify a class until it "is satisfied, after a rigorous analysis," that Rule 23(a)'s certification prerequisites are met. Wal–Mart Stores, Inc. v. Dukes, 564 U.S. 338, 351 (2011). Consistent with the Supreme Court's premise that "actual, not presumed, conformance with Rule 23(a) remains ... indispensable," after initial certification, the duty remains with the district court to assure that the class continues to be certifiable throughout the litigation. Where, as here, adequacy of class representation is at issue, "close scrutiny" in the district court is even more important given the need to protect the due process rights of absent class members.

As the Eighth Circuit repeatedly emphasized, this Court must conduct a "rigorous analysis" of the requirements for class certification. That analysis must examine whether the named representatives have common interests with the class, and whether those representatives will prosecute those interests vigorously through class counsel.

1. Intra–Class Conflict

There are two components to the class-conflict analysis. First is whether there are class representatives who have suffered the same or similar injury as the class members they seek to represent. Second is whether some class representatives and class counsel have interests that are so at odds with other class representatives and class members that a singular class is inappropriate.

The class representatives in this case include individuals who suffered no demonstrable or quantifiable injury. Indeed, there are numerous class representatives who, like Olson, allege only that their personal information was stolen in the data breach and do not allege any other element of damages. The class representatives thus meet the first factor in the conflict analysis.

Olson insists that there is a fundamental conflict between class members who suffered monetary loss in the Target data breach and those who did not. Under Olson's theory, any difference in the injuries class members suffered means that there is a conflict requiring separate subclasses and separate representation. But the question is not whether there is any potential or theoretical conflict among class members, it is whether class members' different interests are antagonistic to each other. See U.S. Fid. & Guar. Co. v. Lord, 585 F.2d 860, 873 (8th Cir. 1978) (noting that adequacy of representation requires that "the plaintiff must not have interests antagonistic to those of the class"); see also Ward v. Dixie Nat'l Life Ins. Co., 595 F.3d 164, 180 (4th Cir. 2010) ("For a conflict of interest to defeat the adequacy requirement, 'that conflict must be fundamental.' ... Moreover, a conflict will not defeat the adequacy requirement if it is 'merely speculative or hypothetical.' ").

As the Eighth Circuit has determined, "the antagonism which will defeat maintenance of a class action must relate to the subject matter in controversy, as when the representative's claim conflicts with the economic interests of the class ...." Sperry Rand Corp. v. Larson, 554 F.2d 868, 874 (8th Cir. 1977). Olson's oft-repeated mantra that some class members were "frozen out" of a recovery, does not substitute for evidence of an actual, fundamental conflict of interest that relates to the subject matter at issue. See Reynolds, 584 F.2d at 286 (noting that objectors presented "[n]o evidence ... of improper actions or actual conflict of interest on the part of the named plaintiffs or their counsel"). Moreover, "the mere fact that some members of a class may not receive a direct payment is not dispositive" of the fairness of the settlement to all class members. Olson presents no evidence regarding an actual, fundamental conflict because he has none, only rank speculation that a conflict exists.3 Olson has not established that the representatives' claims conflict with the economic interests of the class.

a. Amchem and Ortiz

Olson contends that the different interests among class members in this case is similar to those found to require subclasses with separate representation in two Supreme Court decisions, Amchem Products, Inc. v. Windsor, 521 U.S. 591 (1997), and Ortiz v. Fibreboard Corporation, 527 U.S. 815 (1999). Those cases, which both involved wide-ranging global settlements in the massive nationwide asbestos litigation, instead establish that any differences in class members' interests here are not fundamental and do not require subclasses, separate representation, or decertification of the class.

In Amchem, plaintiffs and defendants presented to the district court on the same day a class-action complaint, answer, proposed settlement agreement, and a joint motion for class certification. 521 U.S. at 601–02.4 The single "sprawling" class included individuals who had been diagnosed with an asbestos-related illness as well as individuals who had been exposed to asbestos either personally or through a parent or spouse but had not been diagnosed with any illness as a result. Id. at 602; see also id. at 624 ("No settlement class called to our attention is as sprawling as this one."). The settlement provided that class members who suffered certain diseases would receive monetary relief. It also waived all class members' claims for loss of consortium and medical monitoring. The damages awards were not adjustable for inflation, and did not include any provision for advancement in medical monitoring for asbestos injuries. Only class members who suffered from a compensable disease were entitled to an award under the settlement, and the settlement limited the number of individuals who could opt out of the settlement in a given year.

Large numbers of putative class members objected to the settlement. The objectors argued that there was a fundamental conflict between claimants whose injuries had become manifest and claimants without such injuries, so that the district court should have appointed independent counsel and should have divided the class into subclasses. The Supreme Court agreed, finding that the interests of currently injured plaintiffs and exposure-only plaintiffs were adverse to one another, because those with current injuries would seek only to maximize current payments, while those with future injuries would sacrifice immediate payment for a stable and ample future fund available to pay them in the event they developed a compensable disease.

The holding in Ortiz stems from the same concern, albeit in the very different context of a mandatory limited-fund class action under Rule 23(b)(1).5 The class in Ortiz also included those with present injuries and "exposure-only" plaintiffs, and attempted to bind all of these plaintiffs to a limited fund, with no opportunity to opt out of the settlement. In addition to the substantial due process problems such a settlement presented, the Court reiterated that Amchem required:

> that a class divided between holders of present and future claims (some of the latter involving no physical injury and attributable to claimants not yet born) requires division into homogeneous subclasses under Rule 23(c)(4)(B), with separate representation to eliminate conflicting interests of counsel.

Ortiz, 527 U.S. at 856 . Olson latches onto this statement to insist that, in every case involving both present and future injuries, subclasses are required. Olson overlooks, however, the substantial and dispositive differences between the two subclasses Amchem and Ortiz described and subclasses Olson urges on the Court in this case. See, e.g., Prof'l Firefighters Ass'n of Omaha, Local 385 v. Zalewski, 678 F.3d 640, 647 (8th Cir. 2012) ("The conflicts appellant describes are far from the 'extraordinarily various' injuries that sharply divided the interests of present and future claim holders in attempting to allocate the limited funds available in Amchem and Ortiz.").

First, as Ortiz noted, the future-injury subclass included individuals who were not yet born, and in both Amchem and Ortiz the future-injury class included individuals who might not be or could not be aware of their membership in the class. A court's overarching concern is with affording such individuals due process, and thus the prospect of foreclosing these individuals' claims without guarantees that they could be notified of the litigation gave the Court great pause. See Amchem, 521 U.S. at 628 ("[W]e recognize the gravity of the question whether class action notice sufficient under the Constitution and Rule 23 could ever be given to legions so unselfconscious and amorphous."). Here, in contrast, there are no unascertainable members of the class, and no attendant due process concerns, because all class members received adequate notice and had the opportunity to protect their own interests by opting out of the class.

In addition, although Olson tries to equate uninjured class members in this case with the future-injury subclasses in Ortiz and Amchem, as a practical matter there are no remaining future injuries in the class here. See Petrovic, 200 F.3d at 1146 (noting difference between "stark conflicts" in Amchem and Ortiz and the class at issue in Petrovic, which was "discrete and identified" and had "suffered a harm the extent of which has largely been ascertained"). Nearly four years after the data breach, all those whose personal financial information was stolen both know that their information was stolen and have suffered any injury they are reasonably likely to suffer. Plaintiffs who have suffered a monetary injury have had the opportunity to seek compensation for that injury. Plaintiffs who have not suffered any monetary injury likely have no claim to any future payment and thus the equitable relief from the settlement, in addition to the possible pro-rata share of the remaining settlement fund, constitutes all of the relief they could hope to reap from this litigation.

The Amchem and Ortiz global classes failed the adequacy test because the settlements in those cases disadvantaged one group of plaintiffs to the benefit of another. There is no evidence that the settlement here is similarly weighted in favor of one group to the detriment of another. Rather, the settlement accounts for all injuries suffered. Plaintiffs who can demonstrate damages, whether through unreimbursed charges on their payment cards, time spent resolving issues with their payment cards, or the purchase of credit-monitoring or identity-theft protection, are reimbursed for their actual losses, up to $10,000. Plaintiffs who have no demonstrable injury receive the benefit of Target's institutional reforms that will better protect consumers' information in the future, and will also receive a pro-rata share of any remaining settlement fund. It is a red herring to insist, as Olson does, that the no-injury Plaintiffs' interests are contrary to those of the demonstrable-injury Plaintiffs. All Plaintiffs are fully compensated for their injuries.

Thus, this case is not akin to In re Literary Works in Electronic Databases Copyright Litigation, 654 F.3d 242 (2d Cir. 2011). The In re Literary Works settlement divided the class into three claimant groups, called categories A, B, and C. The settlement capped the defendants' total liability and provided that, if the claims exceeded that cap, the compensation for category C claims would be reduced pro rata. Id. at 246. In other words, the settlement protected the category A and B claims at the expense of category C claims, providing that those claims could be reduced to zero depending on the amount of category A and B claims. The Second Circuit determined that the interests of category C claimants were fundamentally antagonistic to the interests of the other claimants and a single class could not adequately represent those antagonistic interests. See id. at 252 (describing the settlement as "[t]he selling out of one category of claim for another").

But the mere fact that one group of claimants recovers less than another group does not mean that a single class is inadequate to represent both groups. Id. at 253 ("We therefore disagree with objectors to the extent that they cite Category C's inferior recovery as determinative evidence of inadequate representation."); see also Dewey v. Volkswagen Aktiengesellschaft, 681 F.3d 170, 186–87 (3d Cir. 2012) ("To hold that [ ] differing valuations by themselves render the representative plaintiff inadequate would all but eviscerate the class action device."). The adequacy of representation is called into question when there is no way, absent independent representation, for a court (or plaintiffs) to assess the value of the different claims. In re Literary Works, 654 F.3d at 253. This danger is not present here, where claims either have demonstrable value or they do not—the value of all Plaintiffs' claims is easily ascertainable and independent representation is not required for Plaintiffs to understand the damages they suffered.

Consideration of the fairness of the settlement does not, as Olson insists, improperly conflate Rule 23(a)(4)'s adequacy of representation requirement and Rule 23(e)(2)'s fairness, adequacy, and reasonableness analysis. Whether the representation of named Plaintiffs and class counsel is adequate under Rule 23(a)(4) "cannot be determined solely by finding that the settlement meets the aggregate interests of the class or 'fairly' compensates the different types of claims at issue." In re Literary Works, 654 F.3d at 254. The adequacy of representation in this case is evidenced by much more than the settlement. It is evidenced by the relief sought in the Complaint, the fact that Plaintiffs insisted on receiving substantial equitable relief as part of their negotiations, and the fact that Plaintiffs sought to ensure that all class members were fully compensated for whatever type of demonstrable injury they suffered, whether in the form of impermissible charges on their payment cards, the time a class member had to spend to remedy fraudulent charges or other identity-theft-related issues, and payment for any credit monitoring or identity-theft protection a class member felt compelled to purchase because of the Target data breach. Olson has failed to establish either that the interests of the no-demonstrable-injury Plaintiffs fundamentally conflict with the interests of the demonstrable-injury Plaintiffs, or that the representation any Plaintiffs received was inadequate.

b. Injury

Olson's argument also ignores the fact that all class members in this case suffered the same injury. All class members were the victims of the theft of their personal information and suffered the attendant fear that this information might find its way into the wrong hands on the Internet's black market. The class therefore has an identity of interests not found in the cases on which Olson relies. Moreover, Olson ignores the Eighth Circuit's determination that "[t]he interests of the various plaintiffs do not have to be identical to the interests of every class member; it is enough that they share common objectives and legal or factual positions." Petrovic, 200 F.3d at 1148. As in Petrovic, class members here "seek essentially the same things:" compensation for whatever monetary damages they suffered and reassurance that their information will be safe in Target's hands in the future.

c. Statutory Damages

Although he did not raise this issue in his initial objections to the settlement, and thus did not preserve the issue for appellate review or for purposes of the limited remand, Olson now also contends that the presence of class members from California, Rhode Island, and the District of Columbia results in a fundamental intraclass conflict. These three jurisdictions offer their citizens statutory damages for violations of the jurisdiction's consumer-protection laws. According to Olson, the fact that class members from these jurisdictions have access to additional or different measures of damages mandates subclasses to ensure that these class members' interests are adequately represented.

In Rhode Island, consumers may recover actual damages or statutory damages of $200 for a violation of the state's unfair trade practices law. R.I. Gen. Laws § 6–13.1–

5.2(a). California's citizens may recoup statutory damages of $500, or $1,000 in a class action. Cal. Civ. Code §§ 1780(a)(1), 1798.84(c). And in the District of Columbia, a consumer injured by a violation of the consumer-protection laws can recover treble damages, or up to $1,500, whichever is greater. D.C. Code § 28–3905(k)(2)(A).

The availability of potential statutory damages for members of the class from California, Rhode Island, and the District of Columbia does not, by itself, mean that the interests of these class members are antagonistic to the interests of class members from other jurisdictions. Class actions nearly always involve class members with non-identical damages. See, e.g., Petrovic, 200 F.3d at 1148 (holding that named plaintiffs' interests "do not have to be identical" to those of every class member); Zalewski, 678 F.3d at 647 (affirming adequacy of representation where interests were "not entirely consistent").

Olson's argument in this regard ignores the substantial barriers to any individual class member actually recovering statutory damages. Class members from these three jurisdictions willingly gave up their uncertain potential recovery of statutory damages for the certain and complete recovery, whether monetary or equitable, the class settlement offered. Contrary to Olson's belief, this demonstrates the cohesiveness of the class and the excellent result named Plaintiffs and class counsel negotiated, not any intraclass conflict.

2. Adequacy of Representation

In addition to the possibility of an intra-class conflict, the Eighth Circuit directed this Court to address whether, if there was such a conflict, the class representatives fairly and adequately protected the class's interest. The Court has determined, after a rigorous analysis, that there is no intra-class conflict here. But even if there was such a conflict, the class representatives and their counsel more than adequately protected the class's interests.

This class suffered the same injury—theft of personal financial information—and the same risk of future injury. The only difference among class members is in the quantifiable damages suffered, not in the underlying injury. There is no danger of arbitrary line-drawing, as the objectors argued in Petrovic. And the settlement is structured to remedy all damages suffered, both actual and future. Thus, there is no danger of an "allocative conflict of interest" that caused the Third Circuit to determine that class certification was improper. Dewey, 681 F.3d at 188.

Dewey is instructive. In that case, the settlement divided the plaintiff class into two groups—those whose vehicles were more likely to have suffered leakage around their Volkswagen vehicle's sunroof, and those whose vehicles were less likely to have suffered leakage—and gave the first group of claimants priority in seeking reimbursement under the settlement, with the remaining claimants receiving payments only if there was sufficient money in the settlement fund (the so-called "residual" group). The objectors argued, as Olson does here, that the two groups were similar to the past-damage claimants and future-damage claimants found to require subclasses and separate representation in Amchem and Ortiz. Id. at 185. The Third Circuit disagreed, finding that "the alignment of interests is not so starkly problematic" as it was in Amchem and Ortiz, because a claimant in the reimbursement group "can continue to suffer injury into the future to the same extent as a future claimant." Id. Thus, the reimbursement-group claimants had "an interest in obtaining redress for future damage or avoiding future damage" and that interest aligned with those class members in the residual group.

The court found that the settlement itself and the structure of the negotiations evidenced the reimbursement claimants' adequate representation of residual claimaints' interest. Id. As the court stated, and as this Court has noted in this matter, the objectors' contentions regarding a conflict were "unduly speculative." Moreover, the court determined that, "even if the representative plaintiffs did value protections for future claimants less than other members of the class, ... their different valuations [do not] create a fundamental conflict sufficient to undermine their ability to adequately represent the class."

Olson relies heavily on the opinion in Dewey, because the Third Circuit ultimately determined that the class representatives were not adequate and remanded to the district court for possible certification of subclasses. See id. at 190 (noting that district court on remand could either decide to allow all claimants to seek reimbursement with no difference in priority or could certify subclasses). But Olson ignores the reasons behind the Third Circuit's decision. First, all class representatives came from the reimbursement group, and none from the residual group. Here, of course, there are some class representatives who suffered quantifiable injuries and some who did not.

In addition, the Dewey representative plaintiffs conducted a sampling of vehicle models, determined which models were more likely to have leakage problems, and then drew a line at an arbitrary midpoint, putting some vehicle models into the reimbursement group and others into the residual group. It was "this line-drawing exercise that exacerbated the adequacy problem," because "representative plaintiffs had an interest in excluding other plaintiffs from the reimbursement group, while plaintiffs in the residual group had an interest in being included in the reimbursement group."

The line-drawing in Dewey did not reflect the actual injuries any class member suffered, but instead reflected the judgment of class representatives and class counsel regarding which vehicles should receive priority in compensation. This was problematic because all class representatives' vehicles happened to fall into the reimbursement group with accompanying payment priority. In such a situation, Rule 23 requires representation for all plaintiffs' interests, to ensure that the line-drawing is not unduly prejudicial to one group of plaintiffs at the expense of another.

This is a far cry from the situation here, where the settlement draws no lines, much less arbitrary lines. If a class member suffered a monetary loss in the data breach, they are compensated for that loss. All class members' fears of future harm are remedied both by the compensation available for purchase of credit-monitoring/identity-theft protection and by the steps Target agreed to take to secure its customers' data in the future. Unlike in Dewey, there are no conflicts that prevent representative Plaintiffs, some of whom suffered quantifiable damages and others who did not, from adequately representing the class.

3. Subclasses and Separate Representation.

Finally, even if Olson is correct that a conflict exists, that conflict is not fundamental and does not require certification of separate subclasses with separate representation. "A fundamental conflict exists where some [class] members claim to have been harmed by the same conduct that benefitted other members of the class." Valley Drug Co. v. Geneva Pharms., Inc., 350 F.3d 1181, 1189 (11th Cir. 2003). Olson points to no harm that one group of Plaintiffs has suffered from the settlement's benefits to another group. The settlement is not a limited fund that is inadequate to pay the damages claims, it draws no lines between groups of claimants, and it does not reduce any group's compensation to the benefit of another group's.

As in Dewey, Plaintiffs in this case who have suffered demonstrable damages have the same potential for future injury as Olson and those Plaintiffs with no demonstrable damages. All Plaintiffs therefore had the same incentive to maximize the protections against future injuries. The equitable relief the settlement provides evidences the class's incentive to maximize those future protections. And as Target's counsel described, this relief was not "an easy get for the Plaintiffs and it was not an easy give for Target" but was the product of "days of mediation and negotiation." Indeed, as counsel stated, "No company likes to commit its resources to a five-year future relief" plan in a class action, but Target did so here. In agreeing to the substantial equitable relief in the settlement, Target agreed to make "significant investments" that "benefit[ ] all Target guests, including every member of the settlement class in this case." Olson has not established that there is a conflict here, or that any alleged conflict requires subclasses and separate representation.

CONCLUSION

The named class representatives in this case "have common interests with the members of the class" and have "vigorously prosecute[d] the interests of the class through qualified counsel." In re Target, 847 F.3d at 613. Olson has not established that there are any "conflicts of interest between the named parties and the class they seek to represent." "Again, it is not enough for objectors to point to differences in claims, allocation amounts, or state laws without identifying how such differences demonstrate a conflict of interest." Although Olson is highly critical of the settlement and the representation of named Plaintiffs and class counsel, he has utterly failed to demonstrate any conflict of interest.

In the end, it is insufficient to merely argue that a settlement is not good enough. To establish that the representation of class representatives and the settlement they negotiated is not fair or adequate, Olson must offer actual evidence of the conflict he claims. His failure to do so, or to offer any alternative potential—and reasonably achievable—recoveries shows that the representation was fair and adequate, and the settlement was as good a settlement as any class member could hope. Those who suffered monetary losses will, in the main, be compensated for all of the losses they suffered. Those who did not suffer any monetary loss will benefit from the heightened protections Target agreed to put in place to safeguard its customers' personal information. And any class member whose fear of identity theft compelled them to purchase protection for such theft can seek reimbursement for those costs from the settlement fund. It is difficult to imagine a settlement that more comprehensively addresses all of the harm suffered by a class as the settlement here. And the comprehensive nature of the settlement, in turn, reflects the adequacy, indeed the superiority, of the representation the class received from its named Plaintiffs and from class counsel.

Accordingly, IT IS HEREBY ORDERED that Consumer Plaintiffs' renewed Motion to Certify Class in Accordance with Limited Remand Order (Docket No. 775) is GRANTED.

In re Target Corporation Customer Data Security Breach Litigation, 892 F.3d 968 (8th Cir. 2018).

SHEPHERD, Circuit Judge.

This case is back to us after our reversal of the certification of a class composed of individuals whose payment card information was compromised as a result of the 2013 Target security breach. See In re Target Corp. Customer Data Sec. Breach Litig., 847 F.3d 608, 613 (8th Cir. 2017). On remand, the district court re-certified the class after conducting a rigorous analysis. Class member Leif Olson again objects to the certification on a number of grounds. In addition, class member Jim Sciaroni objects to the district court's approval of the settlement agreement. We see no error and affirm.

I. Background

In 2015, the district court certified a class of "[a]ll persons in the United States whose credit or debit card information and/or whose personal information was compromised as a result of the data breach that was first disclosed by Target on December 19, 2013." As has become common, the class was certified solely for the purpose of entering into a settlement agreement. The parties presented such an agreement to the court in short order.

Under the terms of this agreement, Target agreed to pay $10 million to settle the claims of all class members and waived its right to appeal an award of attorney's fees less than or equal to $6.75 million.[3] For those class members with documented proof of loss, the agreement called for full compensation of their actual losses up to $10,000 per claimant. For those class members with undocumented losses, the agreement directed a pro rata distribution of the amounts remaining after payments to documented-loss claimants and class representatives. Additionally, Target agreed to implement a number of data-security measures and to pay all class notice and administration expenses.

There were two primary objectors to the court's certification of the class and approval of the settlement agreement: Leif Olson and Jim Sciaroni. In the original appeal of this matter, Olson argued that the court failed to conduct the appropriate pre-certification analysis, and Sciaroni objected to the court's approval of the settlement. We agreed with Olson's argument and therefore remanded to the district court without considering Sciaroni's objections.

On remand, the court again certified the class. Olson appeals that decision, claiming the district court factually misunderstood the settlement agreement and failed to account for a number of alleged conflicts of interest between class counsel and class members and among competing subgroups of class members. In addition, Sciaroni's original objections to the settlement are before us. We first address Olson's claims before moving to Sciaroni's objections.

II. Olson

On appeal, Olson raises two principal challenges to the district court's certification order. First, he contends the district court fundamentally misunderstood the structure of the settlement agreement. Next, he argues that there is an intraclass conflict between class members who suffered verifiable losses from the data breach and those, like Olson, who have not, and that this conflict necessitates separate legal counsel. We address each argument in turn, applying the deferential abuse of discretion standard. See Petrovic v. Amoco Oil Co., 200 F.3d 1140, 1145 (8th Cir. 1999).

A.

Olson first launches a factual challenge to the district court's order. Under the terms of the settlement, the proceeds are first distributed to those individuals who submit proof of actual loss, up to a total amount of $10,000 per claimant. Next, the class representative awards are paid. Then any remaining proceeds are distributed in equal amounts to those claimants with undocumented losses. The district court accurately presented this structure on page 3 of its order, but it later made two comments which form the basis of Olson's attack:

> Plaintiffs who have not suffered any monetary injury likely have no claim to any future payment and thus the equitable relief from the settlement, in addition to the possible pro-rata share of the remaining settlement fund, constitutes all of the relief they could hope to reap from this litigation.

....

Plaintiffs who have no demonstrable injury receive the benefit of Target's institutional reforms that will better protect consumers' information in the future, and will also receive a pro-rata share of any remaining settlement fund.

Proceeding from these statements, Olson contends the district court fundamentally misunderstood the settlement structure because it apparently believed that those claimants in the zero-loss subclass would receive a share of remaining settlement proceeds. Under Olson's view, "that error alone warrants reversal." We disagree.

To be sure, as Olson points out, we have stated that "[t]he district court ... abuses its discretion if its conclusions rest on clearly erroneous factual determinations." Blades v. Monsanto Co., 400 F.3d 562, 566 (8th Cir. 2005). But here we have no indication that the district court rested its conclusions on the above statements. In fact, the court had already determined that no intraclass conflict existed four pages prior to making the above statements, so it stretches credulity to assert that its conclusion depended on a statement made thereafter. We need not define at what point an erroneous factual statement constitutes reversible error. In this case, it was obvious that the district court did not rely on an erroneous understanding of the settlement, and thus no abuse of discretion occurred.

B.

Olson next argues that there is an intraclass conflict between class members who suffered verifiable losses from the data breach and those, like Olson, who have not. Olson uses different names for this latter subclass, sometimes referring to it as a zero-recovery subgroup[6] and other times calling it a future-damages subclass. In substance, Olson's contention is that under the Supreme Court's asbestos decisions in Amchem and Ortiz, the district court's ruling was legally deficient because, even assuming there were named representatives from the zero-loss subclass, separate legal counsel was required to protect that subclass's interests. See, e.g., Ortiz v. Fibreboard Corp., 527 U.S. 815, 856, 119 S.Ct. 2295, 144 L.Ed.2d 715 (1999) ("[I]t is obvious after Amchem that a class divided between holders of present and future claims (some of the latter involving no physical injury and attributable to claimants not yet born) requires division into homogeneous subclasses under Rule 23(c)(4)(B), with separate representation to eliminate conflicting interests of counsel.").

We need look no further than the language of Amchem itself to refute this assertion. Describing the then-current state of asbestos litigation, the Court noted:

> [This] is a tale of danger known in the 1930s, exposure inflicted upon millions of Americans in the 1940s and 1950s, injuries that began to take their toll in the 1960s, and a flood of lawsuits beginning in the 1970s. On the basis of past and current filing data, and because of a latency period that may last as long as 40 years for some asbestos related diseases, a continuing stream of claims can be expected. The final toll of asbestos related injuries is unknown. Predictions have been made of 200,000 asbestos disease deaths before the year 2000 and as many as 265,000 by the year 2015.

Amchem Prods., Inc. v. Windsor, 521 U.S. 591, 598 (1997). Against this backdrop, the Court was confronted with a class certification and settlement offer that "proposed to settle, and to preclude nearly all class members from litigating against [certain asbestos] companies, all claims not filed before January 15, 1993, involving compensation for present and future asbestos-related personal injury or death."

After finding that Rule 23(b)(3)'s predominance requirement was not satisfied by the proposed class, the Court focused on Rule 23(a)(4)'s adequacy inquiry with the goal of uncovering whether there were "conflicts of interest between named parties and the class they seek to represent." Because "named parties with diverse medical conditions sought to act on behalf of a single giant class rather than on behalf of discrete subclasses," the Court found that such conflicts existed. More specifically, the Court reasoned that "for the currently injured, the critical goal is generous immediate payments[,] [and] [t]hat goal tugs against the interest of exposure-only plaintiffs in ensuring an ample, inflation-protected fund for the future." In the context of a nationwide phenomenon involving "millions of Americans" and "a latency period that may last as long as 40 years for some asbestos related diseases," this conclusion is sound because there was a real expectation that the exposure-only plaintiffs would fall ill after the date specified in the settlement. As a result of the fact that no exposure-only plaintiff could estimate with any certainty the extent of his or her future injury, the settlement offered no assurance that sufficient funds would remain to protect the interests of that group.

Olson struggles to analogize the present case to <u>Amchem</u> and <u>Ortiz</u>, asserting that class members with verified losses are attempting to maximize their recovery at the expense of those who "might only have future ... damages." His attempts are futile. As the Supreme Court noted, "[i]n contrast to mass torts involving a single accident, class members in this case were exposed to different asbestos-containing products, in different ways, over different periods, and for different amounts of time; some suffered no physical injury, others suffered disabling or deadly diseases." . We therefore believe the present case is more similar to our decision in Petrovic, 200 F.3d at 1146, where we distinguished <u>Amchem</u> and <u>Ortiz</u> by "not[ing] that the injuries involved in those cases were extraordinarily various, both in terms of the harm sustained and the duration endured."

Here, we have "a discrete and identified class that has suffered a harm the extent of which has largely been ascertained." <u>Id.</u> As Olson himself states, "all class members suffered the same injury, i.e., compromise of their personal and financial information from the data breach." Thus, similar to the mass tort cases the Supreme Court discussed in <u>Amchem</u>, we have one accident here—the data breach—that caused a series of events leading to the plaintiffs' injuries. But all class members had the ability to register for credit monitoring, and all of the compromised payment cards undoubtedly were cancelled and replaced by the issuing banks. Any risk of future harm is therefore entirely speculative, which is perhaps best illustrated by Olson's inability to direct the court—even generally—to a concrete type of future harm that the settlement fails to consider.

Of course, it is hypothetically possible that a member of the zero-loss subclass will suffer some future injury; for example, a line of credit could be opened using the personal information compromised in the breach. But this is just as likely to happen to a member of the subclass with documented losses. Accordingly, the interests of the two subclasses here are more congruent than disparate, and there is no fundamental conflict requiring separate representation. <u>See</u> DeBoer v. Mellon Mortg. Co., 64 F.3d 1171, 1175 (8th Cir. 1995) ("There is no indication that DeBoer's interest was antagonistic to the remainder of the class or that the claims were not vigorously pursued."); cf. Dewey, 681 F.3d at 185-86.

The district court did not abuse its discretion in certifying the class.

III. Sciaroni

Having found the district court properly certified the class, we now turn to Sciaroni's challenges to the district court's original order concerning the settlement in this case. Sciaroni first launches a two-fold challenge to the court's award of attorney's fees, arguing at the outset that the court erred by considering the costs of notice and administration expenses as a benefit to the class and then challenging the overall reasonableness of the award. Next, Sciaroni contends that the court erred in approving the settlement.

A.

Sciaroni first urges us to adopt the Seventh Circuit's approach to determine whether administrative fees and costs are a benefit to the class as a whole. See Redman v. RadioShack Corp., 768 F.3d 622, 630 (7th Cir. 2014) ("[T]he roughly $2.2 million in administrative costs should not have been included in calculating the division of the spoils between class counsel and class members. Those costs are part of the settlement but not part of the value received from the settlement by the members of the class."). During the pendency of this case, however, we issued two opinions that reached the opposite conclusion. See Huyer v. Buckley, 849 F.3d 395, 398 (8th Cir. 2017) ("[T]he district court did not abuse its discretion by basing its fee award on the total settlement fund, which included administrative costs."); In re Life Time Fitness, Inc., Tel. Consumer Prot. Act (TCPA) Litig., 847 F.3d 619, 623 (8th Cir. 2017) ("[T]he district court did not abuse its discretion by including approximately $750,000 in fund administration costs as part of the 'benefit' when calculating the percentage-of-the-benefit fee amount."). Accordingly, the same is true here: the district court acted within its discretion when it included notice and administrative expenses in its calculation of the total benefit to the class.

Sciaroni next challenges the reasonableness of the total fee award. "Decisions of the district court regarding attorney fees in a class action settlement will generally be set aside only upon a showing that the action amounted to an abuse of discretion." Petrovic, 200 F.3d at 1156. The court awarded counsel attorney's fees and expenses of $6.75 million, determining that amount was "not unreasonable under either the lodestar or percentage-of-the-fund methodology." Under our precedent, the district court has discretion to use either method, and the ultimate reasonableness of the award is evaluated by "consider[ing] relevant factors from the twelve factors listed in Johnson v. Ga. Highway Express, Inc., 488 F.2d 714, 719-20 (5th Cir. 1974)."

Perfunctory as its analysis may have been, we cannot say the district court failed to meet its burden "to provide a concise but clear explanation of its reasons for the fee award." Hensley, 461 U.S. at 437, 103 S.Ct. 1933. The court voiced its opinion that this "case has been hard-fought and heavily litigated since its inception" and that the award was "reasonable in light of the complexities and vagaries of this case." Though it did not mention Johnson, the court expressed its view—based on the above statements—that the award was justified by the time and labor required, the difficulty of the matter, the skills necessary to prevail (or to reach the current settlement agreement), and the length of the representation. Additionally, the court noted that "[t]he request amounts to a negative lodestar multiplier of .74, and ... is 29% of the total monetary payout Target is required to make as part of the settlement." Both of these figures are well within amounts we have deemed reasonable in the past. Cf. Huyer, 849 F.3d at 399-400 (collecting cases and noting "courts have frequently awarded attorneys' fees ranging up to 36% in class actions" and that a lodestar "multiplier [of 1.82] is well within the range of multipliers awarded in this and other circuits"). The court did not abuse its discretion.

B. Approval of the Settlement

Finally, Sciaroni takes issue with the district court's approval of the settlement, arguing that the court awarded "worthless objective relief," inadequately compensated class members, and ignored "subtle signs of collusion." Looking past the labels he uses, the thrust of Sciaroni's argument is that the settlement was unfair. As a prerequisite to approval, a district court must find that a settlement is "fair, reasonable, and adequate," and we will set aside this finding "[o]nly upon the clear showing that the district court abused its discretion." Prof'l Firefighters Ass'n of Omaha v. Zalewski, 678 F.3d 640, 645 (8th Cir. 2012) (internal quotation marks omitted). On review, "[w]e afford the district court's views '[g]reat weight' because the district court 'is exposed to the litigants, and their strategies, positions and proofs.' [It] is aware of the expense and possible legal bars to success." Id.

In determining whether a settlement agreement is fair, "a district court should consider (1) the merits of the plaintiff's case[ ] weighed against the terms of the settlement, (2) the defendant's financial condition, (3) the complexity and expense of further litigation, and (4) the amount of opposition to the settlement."[8] In re Uponor, Inc., F1807 Plumbing Fittings Prods. Liab. Litig., 716 F.3d 1057, 1063 (8th Cir. 2013). "The first factor, 'a balancing of the strength of the plaintiff's case against the terms of the settlement,' is '[t]he single most important factor.'" Keil, 862 F.3d at 695. "[M]indful of the limited scope of our review ... [w]e ask whether the District Court considered all relevant factors, whether it was significantly influenced by an irrelevant factor, and whether in weighing the factors it committed a clear error of judgment." Marshall v. Nat'l Football League, 787 F.3d 502, 508 (8th Cir. 2015).

The district court did not abuse its discretion. Indeed, despite the brevity of its reasoning on other questions, the court gave a carefully reasoned and complete analysis of all four Van Horn factors. On the first, it accurately noted the uphill battle facing the plaintiffs if this litigation were to proceed: standing issues being the most prevalent given the glaring fact that most of the plaintiffs suffered no concrete injury as a result of the breach. Weighed against this consideration, the monetary and non-monetary relief offered under the settlement likely offers the plaintiffs "the only conceivable remedies they could expect." <u>See</u> In re Uponor, Inc., 716 F.3d at 1063. It thus is unclear why Sciaroni strenuously argues that the non-monetary relief is inadequate, especially in light of his concession that "[w]hile some class members filed a claim, the vast majority of the millions of the class members are entitled only to injunctive relief." <u>Cf.</u> Marshall, 787 F.3d at 509 ("[W]e have never required that a settlement agreement specifically provide for a direct financial payment to each class member, and the mere fact that some members of a class may not receive a direct payment is not dispositive.").

Discussing the second factor, the court noted that Target has ample means to pay the settlement and therefore considered this neutral in the analysis. The court then discussed the third factor, commenting that "[f]urther litigation ... would undoubtedly be expensive and complex" in light of the impending "voluminous discovery" and the fact that the plaintiffs' consumer-protection claims arise under state law in nearly every jurisdiction in the country. <u>Cf.</u> Keil, 862 F.3d at 698 ("Class actions, in general, place an enormous burden of costs and expense upon parties. Here, the application of numerous states' laws made this a particularly complex case." (citation omitted) (internal quotation marks omitted)). Finally, the fourth factor weighed in favor of the settlement given that only 11 people out of the 80 million class members objected to the settlement. <u>Cf.</u> <u>id.</u> ("[O]ut of a class of approximately 3.5 million households, ... only fourteen class members submitted timely objections[,] [and] none of the named plaintiffs objected to the settlement. Thus, the amount of opposition is minuscule when compared with other settlements that we have approved.").

Sciaroni argues the worthless objective relief, combined with the presence of "clear-sailing" and "kicker" clauses in the agreement, subtly shows that the settling parties are guilty of collusion. A clear-sailing provision is one where "the defendants agree[ ] not to oppose the request for attorney fees," Johnston v. Comerica Mortg. Corp., 83 F.3d 241, 243 (8th Cir. 1996), and a kicker provision means that unused assets from the settlement are returned to the defendants instead of being distributed to the class, In re Bluetooth Headset Prods. Liab. Litig., 654 F.3d 935, 947 (9th Cir. 2011). Although Sciaroni's principal brief expressly states that both types of provisions are found in the current agreement, his reply brief substantially backs off of those assertions by conceding that the agreement "may not have a 'strict' clear sailing provision" and only "effectively" has a kicker clause. At any rate, Sciaroni's position simply voices generalized grievances with these provisions: nowhere does he explain *how* the clauses, even assuming they are present, operated to the detriment of the class. Sciaroni directs us to no authority that such provisions are per se unlawful, and he has likewise failed to provide any clear evidence of collusion. Accordingly, because he has not demonstrated that the settlement was unfair or inequitable, we affirm the court's approval of the settlement agreement.

IV. Conclusion

For the aforementioned reasons, we affirm the rulings of the district court.

NOTES

Note 1

In *Zappos.com Customer Data Security Breach Litigation*, 893 F.Supp.2d 1058 (2012), the district court found that a "browsewrap" arbitration clause did not apply because of a lack of consent and that it was illusory. Essentially, the class action could continue in court. The district court stated:

> Where, as here, there is no evidence that plaintiffs had actual knowledge of the agreement, "the validity of a browsewrap contract hinges on whether the website provides reasonable notice of the terms of the contract." *Van Tassell,* 795 F.Supp.2d at 791 (citing *Specht,* 306 F.3d at 32).

> Here, the Terms of Use hyperlink can be found on every Zappos webpage, between the middle and bottom of each page, visible if a user scrolls down. (Carton Decl. Ex. 1 (# 10–9).) For example, when the Zappos.com homepage is printed to hard copy, the link appears on page 3 of 4. (*Id.*) The link is the same size, font, and color as most other non-significant links. (*Id.*) The website does not direct a user to the Terms of Use when creating an account, logging in to an existing account, or making a purchase. (*Id.;* Carton Decl. Ex. 2 (# 10–10), Ex. 3 (# 10–11), Ex. 4 (# 10–12)., Ex. 5 (# 10–13); Ex. 6 (# 10–14), Ex. 7 (# 10–15).) Without direct evidence that Plaintiffs click on the Terms of Use, we cannot conclude that Plaintiffs ever viewed, let alone manifested assent to, the Terms of Use. The Terms of Use is inconspicuous, buried in the middle to bottom of every Zappos.com webpage among many other links, and the website never directs a user to the Terms of Use. No reasonable user would have reason to click on the Terms of Use, even those users who have alleged that they clicked and relied on statements found in adjacent links, such as the site's "Privacy Policy." . . . Where, as here, there is no acceptance by Plaintiffs, no meeting of the minds, and no manifestation of assent, there is no contract pursuant to Nevada law. . . .

> Plaintiffs argue that the Arbitration Clause is illusory because Zappos can avoid the promise to arbitrate simply by amending the provision, while Zappos.com users are simultaneously bound to arbitration.

> Most federal courts that have considered this issue have held that if a party retains the unilateral, unrestricted right to terminate the arbitration agreement, it is illusory and unenforceable, especially where there is no obligation to receive consent from, or even notify, the other parties to the contract. . . . Because the Terms of Use binds consumers to arbitration while leaving Zappos free to litigate or arbitrate wherever it sees fit, there exists no mutuality of obligation. We join those other

federal courts that find such arbitration agreements illusory and therefore unenforceable.

CHAPTER TEN. CYBERSECURITY RISK ASSESSMENT AND NATIONAL INSTITUTE OF STANDARDS AND TECHNOLOGY RISK MANAGEMENT FRAMEWORK

10.1 Introduction

This chapter covers risk assessment and the National Institute of Standards and Technology (NIST) Risk Management Framework. Cybersecurity frameworks provide the foundation for creating and maintaining industry standard practices for a robust cybersecurity program. The information security (infosec) department will normally own the cybersecurity framework. Although infosec will own the framework, it will take every department from development to legal to implement and maintain the framework. If you are a cybersecurity attorney, you will come to know the framework by heart. A huge part of the framework is risk assessment. If there was not risk in doing business, there would be no need for a framework or infosec. But with the coming of the internet age, came job security for those in the infosec field because with more connectivity and online presence came more cybersecurity risk. This chapter will also address various frameworks with a focus on the National Institute of Standards and Technology (NIST) Cybersecurity Framework (CSF) version 1.1 and the NIST Privacy Framework version 1.0. This chapter also discusses the FBI and Secret Services role in investigating cybersecurity issues.

10.2 Risk Assessment

As we have seen in previous chapters, many agencies use a reasonable security measures standard to determine the liability for a company after a data breach or other cybersecurity mishap that affects the public or after the uncovering of a potential cybersecurity issue that does not result in a breach but that draws the attention of an enforcement agency. The reasonable security measures standard will be a moving target over time as technology advances and bad actors become even more efficient, effective, and intrusive. We also expect the courts to further define over time and cases, the reasonable security measures standard.

Also, states are stepping in to fill the areas left unprotected by the federal agencies by promulgating privacy laws that follow the EU General Data Protection Regulation in protecting data subject rights. To protect those rights states have come to realize that stricter cybersecurity safeguards are needed and that it isn't that helpful to only notify those affected by a breach, more proactive measure are needed. State have also realized the power of relying on cybersecurity frameworks instead of having to dive into the details of technologies that can vary across industries. It is safer to designate a framework than to try to regulate the details of cybersecurity in a connected world that changes daily. Instead, designate a framework(s) that is designed to be flexible as to the technology and the industry. Let the company worry about keeping up with industry standard solutions by staying within the guidelines of the framework.

How can companies ensure that they are maintaining a reasonable security measures standard? Adopt a cybersecurity framework and follow it. Populating the adopted framework has many steps and areas, but there is no more important step than the risk assessment or risk analysis.

10.2[A] RISK ANALYSIS

This section concerns risk analysis impacting the lifeblood of many companies: data. The goal is to protect the data by maintaining confidentiality, integrity, and availability (CIA) of the data. If possible, the data must be protected at rest, in use and in transit. Protecting data at rest and in transit are easily achievable. Protecting data in use will require ubiquitous homomorphic encryption.[378] That is for the future. The Federal Information Security Management Act of 2022 (FISMA) describes CIA as:

> The FISMA defines three security objectives for information and information systems:
>
> CONFIDENTIALITY "Preserving authorized restrictions on information access and disclosure, including means for protecting personal privacy and proprietary information..." [44 U.S.C., Sec. 3542] A loss of confidentiality is the unauthorized disclosure of information.
>
> INTEGRITY "Guarding against improper information modification or destruction, and includes ensuring information non-repudiation and authenticity..." [44 U.S.C., Sec. 3542] A loss of integrity is the unauthorized modification or destruction of information.
>
> AVAILABILITY "Ensuring timely and reliable access to and use of information..." [44 U.S.C., SEC. 3542] A loss of availability is the disruption of access to or use of information or an information system.[379]

What is the risk in each of these categories in maintaining CIA? Risk can be measured by multiplying the threat times the vulnerability.

$$risk = threat * vulnerability$$

---

[378] "Homomorphic encryption algorithms are a type of encryption algorithm designed to allow mathematical operations to be performed on encrypted data." *See* Keyfactor, *What is homomorphic encryption, and why isn't it mainstream?* (July 26, 2021), available at What is homomorphic encryption, and why isn't it mainstream? – Keyfactor.

[379] STANDARDS FOR SECURITY CATEGORIZATION OF FEDERAL INFORMATION AND INFORMATION SYSTEMS, FED. INFO. PROCESSING STANDARDS PUBL'N 2 (2004), *available at* https://nvlpubs.nist.gov/nistpubs/FIPS/NIST.FIPS.199.pdf.

Reducing either the threat or the vulnerability will reduce the risk. Thus, to understand risk, we must be able to identify threats and vulnerabilities. Potential threats can include:

- Phishing
- Ransomware
- Cryptojacking
- Cyber-physical attacks
- State-sponsored attacks
- IoT attacks
- Smart medical devices and electronic medical records (EMRs)
- Third Parties (Vendor, Contractors Partners)
- Connected cars and semi-autonomous vehicles
- Social Engineering
- Severe shortage of cybersecurity professionals[380]

Assessing Risk will require input from many departments, including the legal department, and should be sponsored by upper management. The legal department must be involved to advise on risks associated with failing to meet laws, regulations, and contract obligations. Laws and regulations are self-explanatory, but contracts are not. A company may have thousands of customers for which a contact was entered into between the parties for data processing. The contracts will necessarily meet the letter of the law, but there are other risk considerations that may be negotiated in the contract, such as:

- How will the data be destroyed at the end of the contract or must it be returned?

- Are subprocessors permitted?

- Can the processing be assigned to a third-party?

- What are the cybersecurity safeguards required that may go beyond the law and regulations?

- Who is responsible for gathering user consent?

- Can the data be used after being aggregated or de-identified?

- Do data breaches amount to the level of a material breach?

- Who pays for user notifications in the event of a data breach?

- Are audits of the process permitted?

- Does the processor need to maintain a SOC II audit?[381]

---

[380] *See* Michelle Moore, *Top Cybersecurity Threats in 2020*, U. OF SAN DIEGO
https://onlinedegrees.sandiego.edu/top-cyber-security-threats/ (last visited Oct. 22, 2020).
[381] "A SOC 2 audit assesses a service organization's internal controls governing its services and data. These controls are called the Trust Services Principles and include security, availability, processing

- Does the processor maintain a training program?

- Does the processor require confidentiality commitments from its employees and contractors?

- Does the processor maintain an industry standard cybersecurity framework?

- Liability clauses

- Indemnity clauses

- Cybersecurity insurance requirement.

Simply stated, the contract becomes a vehicle for cybersecurity risk negotiation. Only counsel will fully understand these risks. But even seasoned cybersecurity counsel cannot make these risk-based decisions unassisted. Product must inform counsel of what the product can and cannot accomplish and InfoSec must inform of security capabilities. Determining risk is an important team effort that is hard to quantify for the bottom line, but left undone can undo the bottom line.

Sometimes risk can be measured (Quantitative Risk Analysis) but other times, it is left to a Qualitative Analysis.

Quantitative assessments typically employ a set of methods, principles, or rules for assessing risk based on the use of numbers—where the meanings and proportionality of values are maintained inside and outside the context of the assessment. This type of assessment most effectively supports cost-benefit analyses of alternative risk responses or courses of action.[382]

In contrast to quantitative assessments, *qualitative* assessments typically employ a set of methods, principles, or rules for assessing risk based on nonnumerical categories or levels (e.g., very low, low, moderate, high, very high).[383]

Conducting risk assessments includes the following specific tasks:

- Identify threat sources that are relevant to organizations;

- Identify threat events that could be produced by those sources;

---

integrity, confidentiality, and privacy as outlined by the American Institute of Certified Public Accountants (AICPA)." *See* strongDM, Everything You Need to Know About SOC 2 Audits (March 18, 2022), available at SOC 2 Audits: Everything You Need to Know | strongDM.
[382] INFORMATION SECURITY, NAT'L INST. OF STANDARDS AND TECH. 14 (2012), *available at* https://nvlpubs.nist.gov/nistpubs/Legacy/SP/nistspecialpublication800-30r1.pdf.
[383] *Id.*

- Identify vulnerabilities within organizations that could be exploited by threat sources through specific threat events and the predisposing conditions that could affect successful exploitation;

- Determine the likelihood that the identified threat sources would initiate specific threat events and the likelihood that the threat events would be successful;

- Determine the adverse impacts to organizational operations and assets, individuals, other organizations, and the Nation resulting from the exploitation of vulnerabilities by threat sources (through specific threat events); and

- Determine information security risks as a combination of likelihood of threat exploitation of vulnerabilities and the impact of such exploitation, including any uncertainties associated with the risk determinations.[384]

Counsel must keep in mind that in the event of litigation, the risk analysis may likely be discoverable. It is likely that most of the risk analysis team members will not be thinking of future litigation. But the risk analysis documentation could pose problems in court. For example, if the risk analysis identifies a significant risk and it is not addressed in the company's security measures, a company may have issues with making a case that it took reasonable security measures. Another issue could be identifying the "extent of loss if realized." For example, if a company identified the amount of loss in a data breach, it may be hard for the company to argue against that amount in court. For this reason, the authors recommend against putting any sort of precise damage figure on certain assets, particularly, personally identifiable information (PII) data records because this figure could be used against the company in court.

Now that the risks have been identified and analyzed, the company's next step is to determine what action should or should not be taken for each of the identified risks. The following are the possible responses:
- Mitigate
- Assign to an outside party such as an insurance company
- Accept as part of the risk of doing business

For the last response - Accept - no security measures are taken. The reasoning for this response must be well documented because it does not provide a security measure. If a security measure is not applied, it may be hard to argue and meet the threshold defense of providing reasonable security measure without convincing documentation as to why no action was taken. The cost/benefit analysis is extremely helpful in deciding a risk response, but could give a misleading answer if potential future legal action is not adequately priced in.

Data is often at the core of risk analysis with the objective being maintaining the confidentiality, integrity, and availability of the data. But there are many assets (physical, administrative, technology) that go into the protection of data such as:
- Maintaining the facility that houses the data

---

[384] *Id.* at 29.

- Assessing the physical, administrative, and technological safeguards of contracted for services, such as cloud storage providers or subprocessors
- Providing the proper environment for housing the machines that contain the data
- Managing access to the facility and machines
- Protecting the machines, operating system and software that provides access to the data
- Protecting the network that transports the data
- Maintaining backups of the data
- Maintaining business continuity and disaster recovery plans

A simple example of a risk analysis using the quantitative method could be as follows: What is the risk that a company's facility located in the Midwest could be affected by an earthquake? This would be a physical risk. To calculate using a quantitative approach, we must know the probability for an earthquake to occur in the Midwest region. Let's say the probability is .01 times in a year. And let's guess that the damage caused by an earthquake to the facility would be $50,000. Taking $50,000 time .01 gives us a $500 risk per year. Now, please assume the facility is in northern California on the fault line and the probability of an earthquake in a year is .5 or one earthquake every two years. We can also assume that the damage might be higher based on a more severe earthquake, so we may guess it might be $200,000 for one earthquake. Taking $200,000 times .5 for one year equals a $100,000 risk per year.

Of course, the facility is only one company asset. This exercise must be conducted for all significant company assets and all potential risks. For example, what would happen to all assets if a power outage occurred? That would answer the question as to whether a second source of power is needed such as a diesel generator. Or what happens when a hacker takes essential systems down for multiple days?

QUESTIONS

1) Outline the steps you would take to conduct a risk assessment of sensitive data being stored by a cloud service provider.

2) Assume that there is a high risk of data that is stored by a cloud service provider becoming unavailable for short but significant periods of time. Plan for continued business continuity.

3) You are an in-house cybersecurity attorney for a medium-sized investment firm. The firm is growing by merging with other investment firms, but your firms remains the main firm in the merger transactions. Your investment firm just merged with a smaller, but successful firm that has recently added an alternate trading platform. You have been assigned to a core team that has the responsibility for doing a risk assessment of the merger. The team consists of business area department leads, marketing, IT, engineering, cybersecurity, you are representing the legal team.

a) what is your role on the team?

b) what areas of risk should you be addressing?

c) What questions should you be asking?

d) What does your final risk assessment product look like?

The next section examines the NIST Risk Management Framework that can be used as a guide for forming a company's security policies and procedures.

10.3 Cybersecurity Frameworks

There are several cybersecurity frameworks available. Some, such as the ISO:27001:2013 require a third-party certification. Others, such as the NIST CSF v. 1.1 may be self-attested or can be attested to by a third-party audit. The NIST CSF v. 1.1 also has four tiers that enable a company to start with a tier one attestation and work towards the other, more difficult to achieve tiers. The following frameworks have been pre-approved as adequate by the California NDPA in its Exhibit F:[385]

- NIST CSF v 1.1

- NIST SP 800-53, Cybersecurity Framework for Improving Critical Infrastructure Cybersecurity, Special Publication 800-71

- ISO: 27001, 27002 by International Standards Organization

- Secure Controls Framework (SCF) by Secure Controls Framework Council, LLC

- CIS Critical Security Controls (CSC, CIS Top 20) by Center for Internet Security

- Cybersecurity Maturity Model Certification (CMMC) by Office of the Under Secretary of Defense for Acquisition and Sustainment (OUSD(A&S))

The ISO framework, which must be purchased, is adopted primarily by the European Union and European Economic Areas with more companies in the United States adopting the free NIST CSF v. 1.1.

10.4 National Institute of Standards and Technology (NIST) Risk Management Framework

The NIST CSF v 1.1, along with other NIST publications are widely recognized as a useful tool for analyzing and managing risk in the context of cybersecurity issues. The NIST CSF v 1.1 is mentioned in the New York Part 121 education statute and in many contracts. It has become shorthand for reasonable security measures. NIST has been working on cybersecurity guidelines for a long time. Next a look at that history.

---

[385] *See* California Student Privacy Alliance, at https://sdpc.a4l.org/view_alliance.php?state=CA (last visited Oct. 9, 2021).

10.4[A] INTRODUCTION AND OVERVIEW OF THE NIST RISK MANAGEMENT FRAMEWORK

Congress created NIST on March 3, 1901. After enacting the Computer Fraud and Abuse Act (CFAA) in 1986, Congress reviewed computer security in the federal government systems. That led to Congress promulgating the Computer Security Act (CSA) of 1987. The CSA mandated baseline security requirements for all federal agencies:

> Section 2 (b) SPECIFIC PURPOSES.-The purposes of this Act are--
> (1) by amending the Act of March 3, 1901, to assign to the National Bureau of Standards responsibility for developing standards and guidelines for Federal computer systems, including responsibility for developing standards and guidelines needed to assure the cost-effective security and privacy of sensitive information in Federal computer systems, drawing on the technical advice and assistance (including work products) of the National Security Agency, where appropriate;
>
> (2) to provide for promulgation of such standards and guidelines by amending section 111(d) of the Federal Property and Administrative Services Act of 1949;
>
> (3) to require establishment of security plans by all operators of Federal computer systems that contain sensitive information; and
>
> (4) to require mandatory periodic training for all persons involved in management, use, or operation of Federal computer systems that contain sensitive information.[386]

The Department of Defense (DoD) was also active in the 1980s in creating computer security standards. Most notable is the set of standards known as the rainbow series, because each book had a separate color.

> The **Rainbow Series** (sometimes known as the **Rainbow Books**) is a series of computer security standards and guidelines published by the United States government in the 1980s and 1990s. They were originally published by the U.S. Department of Defense Computer Security Center, and then by the National Computer Security Center.[387]

These brightly colored books were easy to recognize, and security professionals normally referred to a particular book by its color, for example, the orange book, instead

---

[386] Computer Security Act of 1987, 15 U.S.C. §§ 271, 278g-3, 278h.

[387] *Rainbow Series*, WIKIPEDIA, https://en.wikipedia.org/wiki/Rainbow_Series (last visited Oct. 22, 2020).

of its title. The rainbow series has been overtaken by more modern computer security efforts.

The Rainbow Series of Department of Defense standards is outdated, out of print, and provided here for historical purposes only. The following is a partial list--a more complete collection is available from the Federation of American Scientists:

DoD 5200.28-STD "Orange Book", DoD Trusted Computer System Evaluation Criteria (December 26, 1985)

CSC-STD-002-85 "Green Book", DoD Password Management Guideline (April 12, 1985)

CSC-STD-003-85 "Light Yellow Book", Computer Security Requirements: Guidance for Applying the Department of Defense Trusted Computer System Evaluation Criteria in Specific Environments (June 25, 1985)

CSC-STD-004-85 "Yellow Book II", Technical Rationale Behind CSC-STD-003-85: Computer Security Requirement (June 25, 1985)

NCSC-TG-001 "Tan Book", A Guide to Understanding Audit in Trusted Systems (July 28, 1987)

NCSC-TG-002, Version 1 "Bright Blue Book", Trusted Product Security Evaluation Program: a Guide for Vendors (March 1, 1988)

NCSC-TG-003 "Neon Orange Book", A Guide to Understanding Discretionary Access Control in Trusted Systems (September 30, 1987)

NCSC-TG-004, Version 1 "Aqua Book", Glossary of Computer Security Terms (October 21, 1988)

NCSC-TG-005, Version 1 "Red Book", Trusted Network Interpretation (July 31, 1987)

NCSC-TG-006, Version 1 "Orange Book", A Guide to Understanding Configuration Management in Trusted Systems (March 28, 1988)

NCSC-TG-008 "Lavender Book", A Guide to Understanding Trusted Distribution in Trusted Systems (December 15, 1988)

NCSC-TG-014 "Purple Book", Guidelines for Formal Verification Systems(April 1, 1989)

NCSC-TG-015 "Brown Book", Guide to Understanding Trusted Facility Management (June 1989)

NCSC-TG-019, Version 1 "Blue Book", Trusted Product Evaluation Questionnaire (October 16, 1989)[388]

The Federal Information Security Management Act (FISMA) of 2002 resulted in the FISMA Implementation Project.

> The FISMA Implementation Project was established in January 2003 to produce key security standards and guidelines required by Congressional legislation. These publications include FIPS 199, FIPS 200, and NIST Special Publications 800-53, 800-59, and 800-60. Additional security guidance documents supporting this project include NIST Special Publications 800-37, 800-39, 800-171, 800-53A and NIST Interagency Report 8011. It should be noted that the Computer Security Division continues to produce other security standards and guidelines in support of FISMA.[389]

FISMA was amended in 2014 by the Federal Information Security Modernization Act.

> The Federal Information Security Modernization Act of 2014 amends the Federal Information Security Management Act of 2002 (FISMA) provides several modifications that modernize Federal security practices to address evolving security concerns. These changes result in less overall reporting, strengthens the use of continuous monitoring in systems, increased focus on the agencies for compliance, and reporting that is more focused on the issues caused by security incidents.

> FISMA, along with the Paperwork Reduction Act of 1995 and the Information Technology Management Reform Act of 1996 (Clinger-Cohen Act), explicitly emphasizes a risk-based policy for cost-effective security. In support of and reinforcing this legislation, the Office of Management and Budget (OMB) through Circular A-130, "Managing Federal Information as a Strategic Resource,"[1] requires executive agencies within the federal government to:

- Plan for security

- Ensure that appropriate officials are assigned security responsibility

- Periodically review the security controls in their systems

---

[388] *See White Paper, DoD Rainbow* Series, Nat'l Inst. of Standards and Tech. (Dec. 26, 1985), https://csrc.nist.gov/publications/detail/white-paper/1985/12/26/dod-rainbow-series/final (listing various abstracts for the Rainbow Series of Department of Defense).

[389] *FISMA Implementation Project*, NAT'L INST. OF STANDARDS AND TECH., https://csrc.nist.gov/projects/risk-management (last updated Oct. 13, 2020).

- Authorize system processing prior to operations and, periodically, thereafter[390]

The need for cybersecurity standards and best practices that address interoperability, usability and privacy continues to be critical for the nation. NIST's cybersecurity programs seek to enable greater development and application of practical, innovative security technologies and methodologies that enhance the country's ability to address current and future computer and information security challenges.[391]

This chapter contains references to two NIST risk management frameworks, one for cybersecurity covering federal computer systems as mandated by FISMA (2002) that could also be applied by private companies and one for critical infrastructure cybersecurity as directed by 2013 Executive Order 13636. Both fundamentally rely on the same risk management principles outlined in the NIST Special Publications discussed later. The NIST Framework for Improving Critical Infrastructure Cybersecurity was encouraged by Executive Order 13636 in February 2013, was updated to version 1.1 in 2018. This is commonly referred to as NIST Cybersecurity Framework version 1.1 (NIST CSF v. 1.1) and as noted above has been adopted by many companies for their cybersecurity framework regardless of whether the company is considered to be part of the critical infrastructure. NIST CSF v. 1.1 is further described below.[392] Importantly, the NIST CSF v. 1.1 did not obsolete the NIST Special Publications as those continue to be updated. Also, the NIST Special Publications can be used in conjunction with the NIST CSF v. 1.1.

Executive Order 13636 defines "Critical Infrastructure" as:
"Sec. 2. Critical Infrastructure. As used in this order, the term critical infrastructure means systems and assets, whether physical or virtual, so vital to the United States that the incapacity or destruction of such systems and assets would have a debilitating impact on security, national economic security, national public health or safety, or any combination of those matters."

Ordinarily one might think of critical infrastructure as the electrical power grid, communications, and pipelines. But critical infrastructure is quite broad.

There are 16 critical infrastructure sectors whose assets, systems, and networks, whether physical or virtual, are considered so vital to the United States that their incapacitation or destruction would have a debilitating effect on security, national economic security, national public

---

[390] *FISMA Implementation Project, FISMA Background*, NAT'L INST. OF STANDARDS AND TECH. https://csrc.nist.gov/Projects/risk-management/detailed-overview (last updated Oct. 13, 2020).

[391] *Cybersecurity*, NAT'L INST. OF STANDARDS AND TECH., https://www.nist.gov/topics/cybersecurity (last visited Oct. 22, 2020).

[392] FRAMEWORK FOR IMPROVING CRITICAL INFRASTRUCTURE CYBERSECURITY, NAT'L. INST. OF STANDARDS AND TECH. (2018), *available at* https://nvlpubs.nist.gov/nistpubs/CSWP/NIST.CSWP.04162018.pdf.

health or safety, or any combination thereof. Presidential Policy Directive 21 (PPD-21): Critical Infrastructure Security and Resilience advances a national policy to strengthen and maintain secure, functioning, and resilient critical infrastructure.[393]

The Sectors include:

- Chemical

- Commercial Facilities

- Communications

- Critical Manufacturing

- Dams

- Defense Industrial Base

- Emergency Services

- Energy

- Financial Services

- Food and Agriculture

- Government Facilities

- Healthcare and Public Health

- Information Technology

- Nuclear Reactors, Materials, and Waste

- Transportation Systems

- Water and Wastewater Systems[394]

There are also subsectors within the sectors.

Also, in February 2013:

[T]he President issued Presidential Policy Directive 21 (PPD-21), *Critical Infrastructure Security and Resilience,* which explicitly calls for an update to the National Infrastructure Protection Plan (NIPP). This update is informed by significant evolution in the critical infrastructure risk, policy, and operating environments, as well as experience gained and lessons learned since the NIPP was last issued in 2009. The *National Plan* builds upon previous NIPPs by emphasizing the complementary goals of

---

[393] https://www.cisa.gov/critical-infrastructure-sectors (last updated Oct. 21, 2020).
[394] *Id.*

security and resilience for critical infrastructure. To achieve these goals, cyber and physical security and the resilience of critical infrastructure assets, systems, and networks are integrated into an enterprise approach to risk management.

The integration of physical and cyber security planning is consistent with Executive Order 13636, *Improving Critical Infrastructure Cybersecurity,* which directs the Federal Government to coordinate with critical infrastructure owners and operators to improve information sharing and collaboratively develop and implement risk-based approaches to cybersecurity. In describing activities to manage risks across the five national preparedness mission areas of prevention, protection, mitigation, response, and recovery, the *National Plan* also aligns with the National Preparedness System called for in Presidential Policy Directive 8 (PPD-8), *National Preparedness.*[395]

The COVID-19 pandemic has focused a spotlight on one of the subsectors of the Government Facilities Sector, the Education Facilities Subsector. During the pandemic students migrated from building to remote learning and supporting on-line services. The concerns of educating K through 12 students during the pandemic has been front and center. With the migration of students to remote learning, the threat of cyber attacks have also increased:

> The Cybersecurity and Infrastructure Security Agency (CISA) has seen an increase in malicious activity with ransomware attacks against K-12 educational institutions. Malicious cyber actors are targeting school computer systems, slowing access, and rendering the systems inaccessible to basic functions, including remote learning. In some instances, ransomware actors stole and threatened to leak confidential student data unless institutions paid a ransom.

> Since March, uninvited users have disrupted live-conferenced classroom settings by verbally harassing students, displaying pornography and violent images, and doxing meeting attendees.

> For detailed information on these threats and actions to take, visit the Joint Cybersecurity Advisory on this topic, jointly developed by CISA, FBI, and the Multi-State Information Sharing and Analysis Center.[396]

On October 8, 2021, the K-12 Cybersecurity Act of 2021 went into law:

> The *K-12 Cybersecurity Act* directs DHS's Cybersecurity and Infrastructure Security Agency (CISA) to work with teachers, school administrators, other federal departments, and private sector

---

[395] https://www.cisa.gov/sites/default/files/publications/national-infrastructure-protection-plan-2013-508.pdf.

[396] https://www.cisa.gov/publication/cyber-threats-k-12-remote-learning-education.

organizations to complete a study of cybersecurity risks specific to K-12 educational institutions, including risks related to securing sensitive student and employee records and challenges related to remote-learning. Following the completion of that study, the bill directs CISA to develop cybersecurity recommendations and an online toolkit to help schools improve their cybersecurity hygiene. These voluntary tools would be made available on the DHS website along with other DHS school safety information.[397]

The Executive Order also directed NIST to lead the development of a framework for critical infrastructure:

Sec. 7. Baseline Framework to Reduce Cyber Risk to Critical Infrastructure. (a) The Secretary of Commerce shall direct the Director of the National Start Printed Page 11741Institute of Standards and Technology (the "Director") to lead the development of a framework to reduce cyber risks to critical infrastructure (the "Cybersecurity Framework"). The Cybersecurity Framework shall include a set of standards, methodologies, procedures, and processes that align policy, business, and technological approaches to address cyber risks. The Cybersecurity Framework shall incorporate voluntary consensus standards and industry best practices to the fullest extent possible. The Cybersecurity Framework shall be consistent with voluntary international standards when such international standards will advance the objectives of this order, and shall meet the requirements of the National Institute of Standards and Technology Act, as amended (15 U.S.C. 271 et seq.), the National Technology Transfer and Advancement Act of 1995 (Public Law 104-113), and OMB Circular A-119, as revised.[398]

Following through on its guidance from the Executive Order, NIST created a Cybersecurity Framework concerning Critical Infrastructure for adoption by government and private organizations. The NIST states:

The Framework for Improving Critical Infrastructure Cybersecurity ("The Framework") provides a prioritized, flexible, repeatable, performance-based, and cost-effective approach to managing cybersecurity risk at all levels in an organization. It is applicable to organizations of all sizes and sectors. The Framework provides a common language for understanding, managing, and expressing cybersecurity risk both internally and externally. It can be used to help identify and prioritize actions for reducing cybersecurity risk, and it is a tool for

---

[397] https://www.rosen.senate.gov/rosen-backed-bipartisan-bill-strengthen-k-12-school-cybersecurity-passes-senate.

[398] Exec. Order No. 13636 (2013).

aligning policy, business, and technological approaches to managing that risk.[399]

Thus, the Framework can not only be used by government, but also for any organization in different industries. There is the ability to customize the Framework to account for variability in need and industry.[400] The Risk Based Framework provides objectives or outcomes.[401] The Framework is also considered a "living" document that can be modified over time because of changes to technology as well as regulation.[402] One way to think about the Framework is to consider it as a way to thoughtfully consider cybersecurity issues and importantly to demonstrate that one is "compliant" with their own cybersecurity policy.[403]

> The Framework focuses on using business drivers to guide cybersecurity activities and considering cybersecurity risks as part of the organization's risk management processes. The Framework consists of three parts: the Framework Core, the Implementation Tiers, and the Framework Profiles. The Framework Core is a set of cybersecurity activities, outcomes, and informative references that are common across sectors and critical infrastructure. Elements of the Core provide detailed guidance for developing individual organizational Profiles. Through use of Profiles, the Framework will help an organization to align and prioritize its cybersecurity activities with its business/mission requirements, risk tolerances, and resources. The Tiers provide a mechanism for organizations to view and understand the characteristics of their approach to managing cybersecurity risk, which will help in prioritizing and achieving cybersecurity objectives.[404]

The NIST CSF v. 1.1 was designed with flexibility in mind. The NIST CSF v. 1.1 is adaptable across different industries and areas:

> The Framework offers a flexible way to address cybersecurity, including cybersecurity's effect on physical, cyber, and people dimensions. It is applicable to organizations relying on technology, whether their cybersecurity focus is primarily on information technology (IT), industrial control systems (ICS), cyber-physical systems (CPS), or connected devices more generally, including the Internet of Things (IoT). The Framework can assist organizations in addressing cybersecurity as it affects the privacy of customers, employees, and other parties. Additionally, the Framework's outcomes serve as targets for workforce development and evolution activities.

---

[399] *Cybersecurity Framework Version 1.1. Overview*, NAT'L INST. OF STANDARDS AND TECH. (May 1, 2018), https://www.nist.gov/video/cybersecurity-framework-version-11-overview.
[400] *Id.*
[401] *Id.*
[402] *Id.*
[403] *Id.*
[404] https://nvlpubs.nist.gov/nistpubs/CSWP/NIST.CSWP.04162018.pdf at page v.

The Framework is not a one-size-fits-all approach to managing cybersecurity risk for critical infrastructure. Organizations will continue to have unique risks – different threats, different vulnerabilities, different risk tolerances. They also will vary in how they customize practices described in the Framework. Organizations can determine activities that are important to critical service delivery and can prioritize investments to maximize the impact of each dollar spent. Ultimately, the Framework is aimed at reducing and better managing cybersecurity risks.[405]

Adapting and using the NIST CSF v. 1.1, like any good cybersecurity framework is not a one and done effort. The framework is a living document that will require updating as threats, vulnerabilities, and the company evolves:

The Framework is a living document and will continue to be updated and improved as industry provides feedback on implementation. NIST will continue coordinating with the private sector and government agencies at all levels. As the Framework is put into greater practice, additional lessons learned will be integrated into future versions. This will ensure the Framework is meeting the needs of critical infrastructure owners and operators in a dynamic and challenging environment of new threats, risks, and solutions.[406]

The NIST CSF v. 1.1 can be a good starting point for startups and established companies that wish to adopt a framework to manage its cybersecurity risks. There is lots of support available on the NIST website and from others that have implemented the free standard. With its tiered approach and flexible criteria, the NIST CSF v. 1.1 allows a company that is starting from scratch to implement a risk standard that does not require perfection at the start. With four tiers, a company can start with tier one and then progress to a higher tier. Here is an overview of the components:

The *Framework Core* is a set of cybersecurity activities, desired outcomes, and applicable references that are common across critical infrastructure sectors. The Core presents industry standards, guidelines, and practices in a manner that allows for communication of cybersecurity activities and outcomes across the organization from the executive level to the implementation/operations level. The Framework Core consists of five concurrent and continuous Functions—Identify, Protect, Detect, Respond, Recover. When considered together, these Functions provide a high-level, strategic view of the lifecycle of an organization's management of cybersecurity risk. The Framework Core then identifies underlying key Categories and Subcategories – which are discrete outcomes – for each Function, and matches them with example Informative References such as existing standards, guidelines, and practices for each Subcategory.

---

[405] *Id.* at page vi.
[406] *Id.*

Framework Implementation Tiers ("Tiers") provide context on how an organization views cybersecurity risk and the processes in place to manage that risk. Tiers describe the degree to which an organization's cybersecurity risk management practices exhibit the characteristics defined in the Framework (e.g., risk and threat aware, repeatable, and adaptive). The Tiers characterize an organization's practices over a range, from Partial (Tier 1) to Adaptive (Tier 4). These Tiers reflect a progression from informal, reactive responses to approaches that are agile and risk-informed. During the Tier selection process, an organization should consider its current risk management practices, threat environment, legal and regulatory requirements, business/mission objectives, and organizational constraints.

A *Framework Profile* ("Profile") represents the outcomes based on business needs that an organization has selected from the Framework Categories and Subcategories. The Profile can be characterized as the alignment of standards, guidelines, and practices to the Framework Core in a particular implementation scenario. Profiles can be used to identify opportunities for improving cybersecurity posture by comparing a "Current" Profile (the "as is" state) with a "Target" Profile (the "to be" state). To develop a Profile, an organization can review all of the Categories and Subcategories and, based on business/mission drivers and a risk assessment, determine which are most important; it can add Categories and Subcategories as needed to address the organization's risks. The Current Profile can then be used to support prioritization and measurement of progress toward the Target Profile, while factoring in other business needs including cost- effectiveness and innovation. Profiles can be used to conduct self-assessments and communicate within an organization or between organizations.[407]

The framework can be downloaded from: https://www.nist.gov/cyberframework/framework.

As the authors acknowledged in the beginning of this book, cybersecurity, cybersecurity law, and privacy law overlap. Privacy cannot be achieved without cybersecurity. Some have confused information privacy law with the protecting the privacy of data. Data does not have privacy protection; people have privacy protection. Data has cybersecurity protection. But without protecting the data, humans cannot achieve privacy. On the heels of cybersecurity frameworks have developed privacy frameworks. Privacy frameworks acknowledge and incorporate and build upon the cybersecurity frameworks. The NIST Privacy Framework Version: A Tool for Improving Privacy Through Enterprise Risk Management, Version 1.0 was introduced on January 16, 2020.[408]

---

[407] *Id.* at pages 3-4.
[408] https://nvlpubs.nist.gov/nistpubs/CSWP/NIST.CSWP.01162020.pdf.

The Privacy Framework follows the structure of the Framework for Improving Critical Infrastructure Cybersecurity (Cybersecurity Framework) to facilitate the use of both frameworks together. Like the Cybersecurity Framework, the Privacy Framework is composed of three parts: Core, Profiles, and Implementation Tiers. Each component reinforces privacy risk management through the connection between business and mission drivers, organizational roles and responsibilities, and privacy protection activities.

- The Core enables a dialogue—from the executive level to the implementation/operations level—about important privacy protection activities and desired outcomes.

- Profiles enable the prioritization of the outcomes and activities that best meet organizational privacy values, mission or business needs, and risks.

- Implementation Tiers support decision-making and communication about the sufficiency of organizational processes and resources to manage privacy risk.

In summary, the Privacy Framework is intended to help organizations build better privacy foundations by bringing privacy risk into parity with their broader enterprise risk portfolio.[409]

For those using the ISO:27001:2013 cybersecurity framework, ISO has also developed a privacy framework to be using in conjunction, ISO:27701.

Both privacy frameworks mentioned contain a cybersecurity core and a risk-based approach. Reader is cautioned that privacy compliance requires more than a risk-based approach. Risk-based framework are a great starting place for privacy compliance but for full privacy compliance, subject matter rights must also be addressed.

In 2015, cybersecurity experts Scott J. Shackelford, Andrew A. Proia, Brenton Martell and Amanda N. Craig, in *Toward a Global Cybersecurity Standard of Care? Exploring the Implications of the 2014 NIST Cybersecurity Framework on Shaping Reasonable National and International Cybersecurity Practices*, 50 Tex. Int'l L. J. 305 (2015),[410] discussed the creation and major components of the NIST Cybersecurity Framework, including attempts to encourage its adoption by private industry:

"II. Introducing and Examining the NIST Cybersecurity Framework

Prior to President Obama's 2013 State of the Union Address and Executive Order 13636, efforts to update the regulatory provisions addressing critical infrastructure insecurity had largely stalled. In 2011, for instance, the Obama Administration released for consideration a comprehensive cybersecurity legislative proposal that intended to

---

[409] *Id.* at pages i-ii.

[410] This article was originally published in the Texas International Law Journal.

improve critical infrastructure protection. Portions of the Administration's 2011 proposal had been introduced in both the House and the Senate, but largely to no avail. The Cybersecurity Act of 2012 would have tasked a new National Cybersecurity Counsel to work with private sector critical infrastructure owners and operators to identify critical cyber infrastructure, conduct sector-by-sector cyber risk assessments, and establish a voluntary, outcome-based cybersecurity program for critical infrastructure. However, the bill faced opposition from the private sector and failed to pass the Senate. The recommendations issued by the House of Representatives House Republicans Cybersecurity Task Force have also failed to result in legislation as of March 2015. This legislative inertia prompted executive action by the Obama Administration.

A. Executive Order 13636 and the Objectives of the NIST Framework

Executive Order 13636, effective in February 2013, intended to balance effective critical infrastructure security measures with the maintenance of a cyber-environment that encourages efficiency, innovation, and economic prosperity. The major directives of the Order included enhancing the scope and efficiency of cybersecurity information sharing programs, assessing and coordinating privacy and civil liberties protections in cybersecurity activities, and implementing a baseline framework and voluntary program to reduce cyber risk to critical infrastructure. The Order itself provided a number of overarching objectives for the Cybersecurity Framework to fulfill. For example, it placed the Director of NIST in charge of developing a voluntary Framework that "include[s] a set of standards, methodologies, procedures, and processes that align policy, business, and technological approaches to address cyber risks." The Framework would use cybersecurity best practices, at both a national and international level, in order to provide a "prioritized, flexible, repeatable, performance-based, and cost-effective approach" that could help critical infrastructure manage cybersecurity risks. The Framework's creators were tasked with developing an approach that could adapt well to future, unknown technologies while also allowing the Framework to be used across industries. The Framework was also intended to mature over time, allowing areas of improvement to be recognized and accounted for in future Framework variations.

Privacy and civil liberties protections are also specifically emphasized within the Framework. The Order called for the Cybersecurity Framework and its associated information security measures to identify, assess, and mitigate the impact that security practices within the Framework may have on business confidentiality, individual privacy, and civil liberties. It also requested agencies to coordinate and ensure that privacy and civil liberties protections are incorporated into all activities mandated by the Order generally. Specifically, "[P]rotections shall be based upon the Fair Information Practice Principles and other privacy and civil liberties policies, principles, and frameworks as they apply to each agency's activities."

Executive Order 13636 provided NIST one year to develop the Cybersecurity Framework. To help with this process, NIST held five framework workshops throughout 2013, bringing together a large and diverse contingent of stakeholders, including academics, government officials, and private sector industry members. Meetings were held, webinars were presented, and informal sessions were scheduled to provide feedback throughout the course of the Framework's development.

These efforts resulted in the release of a preliminary draft of the Framework on October 22, 2013, just prior to the fifth workshop, which was held in November 2013. The preliminary Framework would undergo relatively few adjustments before it was released in its final version in early 2014. Among the more significant revisions was the removal of verbiage designed to signal whether an organization has successfully implemented the Framework, stressing the "voluntary" nature of the Framework. Certain terms, such as "adoption," were removed, and greater emphasis was placed on the Framework's focus on critical infrastructure. The most significant change came from the removal of the preliminary Framework's "Privacy Methodology," a detailed approach designed to address privacy and civil liberties considerations surrounding the deployment of cybersecurity activities. Reflecting a concern among stakeholders that "the methodology did not reflect consensus private sector practices and therefore might limit use of the Framework," NIST incorporated an alternative privacy methodology developed by Hogan Lovells's partner Harriet Pearson. The new privacy methodology, contained within the final version of the Framework, removes the organizational chart that would have corresponded to the Framework Core and instead provides a "general set of considerations and processes since privacy and civil liberties implications may differ by sector or over time and organizations may address these considerations and processes with a range of technical implementations." Overall, the preliminary Framework provided the foundation for what would become version 1.0 of the final Framework.

B. Breakdown of the NIST Cybersecurity Framework

The Cybersecurity Framework takes a risk-based approach for organizations to detect, mitigate, and respond to cyber threats. Rather than developing new cybersecurity standards and risk management processes, the Cybersecurity Framework "relies on a variety of existing standards, guidelines, and practices to enable critical infrastructure providers to achieve resilience," which allows the Framework to "scale across borders, acknowledge the global nature of cybersecurity risks, and evolve with technological advances and business requirements." The Cybersecurity Framework provides a "common language" for entities to evaluate their current cybersecurity posture, determine their targeted state for cybersecurity, prioritize opportunities for improvement, assess progress toward their targeted state, and establish sufficient methods of communication among internal and external stakeholders about cybersecurity risk. The substance of the Cybersecurity Framework is composed of three parts: (1) The Framework Core, (2) The Framework Implementation Tiers, and (3) The Framework Profile. We investigate each element in turn.

1. Framework Core

The Cybersecurity Framework begins by laying out the Framework Core, which "provides a set of activities to achieve specific cybersecurity outcomes, and references examples of guidance to achieve those outcomes." Neither an exhaustive list nor a checklist, the Framework Core is an organizational map of industry-recognized cybersecurity practices that are helpful in managing cybersecurity risk, and it provides unified terminology for organizations to understand successful cybersecurity practice outcomes. The Framework Core is broken down into four elements -- Functions,

Categories, Subcategories, and Informative References -- that assist in mapping applicable cybersecurity standards, guidelines, and best practices.

The Core begins by delineating essential cybersecurity activities "at their highest level," referred to as Functions. The Framework recognizes five Functions -- Identify, Protect, Detect, Respond, and Recover -- that are intended to assist an organization in expressing its management of cybersecurity risk by organizing practices into these key areas. Each Function contains more detailed subsets of overarching practices, referred to as Categories, which are "groups of cybersecurity outcomes, closely tied to programmatic needs and particular activities." Each Category assists an organization's approach to mapping the key Functions underlying the Cybersecurity Framework. Each Category provides a brief description to more efficiently place it within the context of its corresponding Function, as well as to guide further categorization within the remaining Core elements. For example, the "Identify" Function contains within it the "Asset Management" Category, which articulates practice outcomes to identify and manage the "data, personnel, devices, systems, and facilities that enable the organization to achieve business purposes . . . consistent with their relative importance to business objectives and the organization's risk strategy."

Function	Category	Subcategory	Informative References
IDENTIFY (ID)	Asset Management (ID. AM): The data, personnel, devices, systems, and facilities that enable the organization to achieve business purposes are identified and managed consistent with their relative importance to business objectives and the organization's risk strategy.	ID.AM-1: Physical devices and systems within the organization are inventoried	CCS CSC 1 COBIT 5 BAI09.01, BAI09.02 ISA 62443-2-1:2009 4.2.3.4 ISA 62443-3-3:2013 SR 7.8 ISO/IEC 27001:2013 A.8.1.1, A.8.1.2 NIST SP 800-53 Rev. 4 CM-8

Further subdividing the Framework Core are "specific outcomes of technical and/or management activities" referred to within the Framework as Subcategories. These subcategories provide further detail for organizations to address each overarching Category. Building off of our previous example, one Subcategory of the "Identify" Function's "Asset Management" Category is the practice of keeping inventory of all organization devices and systems, articulated in the above example as ID.AM-1. Each of these Subcategories receives a reference to the corresponding "standards, guidelines, and practices common among critical infrastructure sectors" that would provide methods for accomplishing the stated Subcategory practice, referred to as "Informative Reference[s]." An organization, for example, looking for an established standard or guideline for device inventory related to federal systems and organizations could look to the Framework's suggested NIST Special Publication 800-53. Specifically, the Framework directs an entity to the publication's "Configuration Management-8:

Information System Component Inventory" within the publication's security controls. It is within this document that an organization can review the specific control requirements, supplemental guidance to the control, and stated "control enhancements." The Framework's Informative References are not intended to be an exhaustive list, and companies are encouraged to continue to identify new or revised standards, guidelines, or practices as the cybersecurity landscape evolves.

2. The Framework Implementation Tiers

After mapping common cybersecurity activities and the various standards and practices employed to conduct these activities, the Framework provides a method for an organization to understand the degree to which its cybersecurity risk management practices match the characteristics described within the Framework, known as the Framework Implementation Tiers. The Tiers provide a measurement for how organizations view and manage cybersecurity risk, taking into consideration an organization's current practices, the cyber threat environment, legal and regulatory requirements, business objectives, and organizational constraints, among other considerations. Based upon an organization's evaluation of its practices, the organization can identify to which Tier it belongs. The Implementation Tiers consist of a range of four Tiers: Partial, Risk Informed, Repeatable, and Adaptive.

Each Tier definition is broken down into three general subsections: (1) Risk Management Process; (2) Integrated Risk Management Program; and (3) External Participation. These subsection definitions assist an organization in selecting its appropriate Tier. The Risk Management Process subsection addresses the extent to which an organization's cybersecurity risk management practices are formalized, the breadth of these formalized practices, and the extent to which the practices actively adjust to the changing cybersecurity landscape. The Integrated Risk Management Program subsection evaluates the level of awareness that managers and employees have of an organization's risk management practices, the level of involvement that managers and employees have in mitigating cybersecurity risks, and the level of cybersecurity information sharing that occurs within the organization. Finally, the External Participation subsection evaluates the extent to which organizations coordinate and collaborate with other external entities to share threat information.

3. The Framework Profile

While the Framework's Implementation Tiers gauge the degree and sophistication of an organization's overall cybersecurity risk management practices, the Framework Profiles are meant to align the particular Framework Core Functions, Categories, and Subcategories with an organization's own implementation scenarios. For example, an organization could create a "Current Profile" that would indicate "the cybersecurity outcomes that are currently being achieved" and a "Target Profile" that would specify "the outcomes needed to achieve the desired cybersecurity risk management goals." Comparing these Profiles would allow an organization to reveal "gaps" that should be addressed to meet the organization's cybersecurity risk management objectives and assist the organization in establishing a roadmap for achieving its Target Profile.

Overall, the drafters expressed that "successful implementation" of the Framework is based on an organization's ability to achieve its Targeted Profiles.

	Risk Management Process	Integrated Program	External Participation
Tier 1: Partial	Organizational cybersecurity risk management practices are not formalized, and risk is managed in an *ad hoc* and sometimes reactive manner. Prioritization of cybersecurity activities may not be directly informed by organizational risk objectives, the threat environment, or business/mission requirements.	There is limited awareness of cybersecurity risk at the organizational level and an organization-wide approach to managing cybersecurity risk has not been established. The organization implements cybersecurity risk management on an irregular, case-by-case basis due to varied experience or information gained from outside sources. The organization may not have processes that enable cybersecurity information to be shared within the organization.	An organization may not have the processes in place to participate in coordination or collaboration with other entities.
Tier 2: Risk-Informed	Risk management practices are approved by management but may not be established as organizational-wide policy. . . .	There is an awareness of cybersecurity risk at the organizational level but an organization-wide approach to managing cybersecurity risk has not been established. Risk-informed, management-approved processes and procedures are defined and implemented, and staff has adequate resources to perform their cybersecurity duties. Cybersecurity information is shared	The organization knows its role in the larger ecosystem, but has not formalized its capabilities to interact and share information externally.

within the organization on an informal basis.

Tier			
Tier 3: Risk-Informed and Repeatable	The organization's risk management practices are formally approved and expressed as policy. Organizational cybersecurity practices are regularly updated based on the application of risk management processes to . . . a changing threat and technology landscape.	There is an organization-wide approach to manage cybersecurity risk. Risk-informed policies, processes, and procedures are defined, implemented as intended, and reviewed. Consistent methods are in place to respond effectively to changes in risk. Personnel possess the knowledge and skills to perform their appointed roles and responsibilities.	The organization understands its dependencies and partners and receives information from these partners that enables collaboration and risk-based management decisions within the organization in response to events.
Tier 4: Adaptive	The organization adapts its cybersecurity practices based on lessons learned and predictive indicators derived from previous . . . cybersecurity activities. Through a process of continuous improvement . . . the organization actively adapts to a changing cybersecurity landscape and responds to evolving and sophisticated threats in a timely manner.	There is an organization-wide approach to managing cybersecurity risk that uses risk-informed policies, processes, and procedures to address potential cybersecurity events. Cybersecurity risk management is part of the organizational culture and evolves from an awareness of previous activities, information shared by other sources, and continuous awareness of activities on their systems and networks.	The organization manages risk and actively shares information with partners to ensure that accurate, current information is being distributed and consumed to improve cybersecurity before a cybersecurity event occurs.

Fig. 2: NIST Framework Implementation Tiers Definitions

C. Implementing the NIST Cybersecurity Framework

Articulating the basic components is only a portion of the Framework. Even more critical is how an organization implements the Framework. Understanding that organizations and industries vary significantly, and that cyber threats evolve rapidly, the Framework was developed in such a way as to allow implementation throughout myriad critical infrastructure settings. First, the Framework was developed to be organizationally comprehensive, emphasizing coordination of the Framework throughout every level of an organization. Second, the Framework was created to be flexible, allowing it to supplement an organization's already existing cybersecurity risk management program or to guide an organization in implementing such a risk management program for the first time. Third, the Framework was organized to be adaptable to changing circumstances and environments so that future versions of the Framework could be created as the cybersecurity landscape evolves.

The Framework stresses the coordination of risk management activities within every level of an organization. Early on in the Framework's development, stakeholders emphasized the importance of the Framework's implementation into all levels of an organization -- from senior leadership to employees, partners, and customers. Thus, the Framework explains how the executive level, the business and process level, and the implementation and operations level of an organization can contribute to the implementation of the Framework. Additionally, the Framework's flexibility is intended to allow its approach to address cybersecurity risks regardless of the organization, industry, or country. As the Framework stresses, it is "not a one-size-fits-all approach to managing cybersecurity risk for critical infrastructure." Instead, it assembles effective national and international cybersecurity practices, giving organizations the autonomy to adopt the Framework in a manner that fits the organization's business requirements and current risk management practices.

Further, because the NIST Framework "references globally recognized standards for cybersecurity, the Framework can also be used by organizations located outside the United States and can serve as a model for international cooperation on strengthening critical infrastructure cybersecurity." One region of significance is Europe. In 2013, a EU cybersecurity directive was proposed; it would require that companies harden their security policies to meet EU-developed standards -- a development that could cause any firm providing online services in Europe to "fundamentally have to change the way its business operates." Moreover, U.S.-EU policymakers are in regular discussions, meaning that the NIST Framework could be influential in shaping EU efforts in this space and could even help shape a global duty of cybersecurity care . . ..

The Framework provides a seven-step implementation process and may be used either as a reference guide to create a new risk management program or to supplement an already existing program. For instance, AT&T has stated that it will begin assessing how the Framework "best complements [its] existing cyber-risk management program." At the same time, IBM announced the creation of the IBM Industrial Controls Cybersecurity Consulting service that will assist companies in utilizing the Framework by "educat[ing] clients on details and mechanics of the NIST Cybersecurity Framework and perform[ing] a comprehensive assessment of a client's security maturity relative to the guidelines, best practices and international standards referenced in the Framework."

Finally, the Framework's adaptability to changing circumstances allows it to evolve as the cybersecurity landscape continues to mature. The Framework is a "living document" that will be amended, updated, and improved as companies begin implementing the Framework and feedback begins to surface. On the day the Framework was released, a "roadmap" was issued that discussed the Framework's "next steps" and identified "key areas of development, alignment, and collaboration." NIST plans to relinquish its role as "convener and coordinator" to private industry, but it plans to continue its current leadership into at least version 2.0.

D. Framework Incentives and C-Cubed Voluntary Program

A difficulty with any voluntary program is encouraging participation. While advocated as a "cost-effective" approach, implementing the Framework's practices will inevitably require time, money, and resources on the part of critical infrastructure organizations, especially those organizations that are currently without a cybersecurity risk management program. At the outset, increasing organizational participation in the Framework was approached in two ways: (1) reviewing current regulatory authorities to determine if establishing requirements based upon the Cybersecurity Framework would be permissible under current authority; and (2) researching a set of implementation incentives and developing a voluntary program to support the adoption of the Framework.

First, Executive Order 13636 called on agencies with "responsibility for regulating the security of critical infrastructure [to] engage in a consultative process with [the] DHS, [the Office of Management and Budget], and the National Security Staff to review the . . . Framework and determine if current cybersecurity regulatory requirements are sufficient given current and projected risks." These agencies are instructed to report to the President "whether or not the agency has clear authority to establish requirements based upon the Cybersecurity Framework to sufficiently address current and projected cyber risks to critical infrastructure, the existing authorities identified, and any additional authority required."

However, not every organization that may fall within the ambit of "critical infrastructure" has clear regulatory requirements related to cybersecurity. To maintain the voluntary nature of the Framework, Executive Order 13636 tasked the Secretary of Homeland Security, "in coordination with Sector-Specific Agencies," to develop a "voluntary program" to support adoption of the Framework by critical infrastructure organizations and other interested entities. Coinciding with the release of the Cybersecurity Framework, the DHS announced the Critical Infrastructure Cyber Community C³ Voluntary Program (C-Cubed Program). The C-Cubed Program aims to "assist stakeholders with understanding use of the Framework and other cyber risk management efforts, and support development of general and sector-specific guidance for Framework implementation."

In addition to creating a voluntary program, Executive Order 13636 tasked the Secretary of Homeland Security, the Secretary of the Treasury, and the Secretary of Commerce with establishing "a set of incentives designed to promote participation in the Program." The Departments' recommendations provided overlapping suggestions on how best to encourage the Framework's adoption as well as consensus on eight recommendations: cybersecurity insurance, grant funds, government service process preferences, liability limitations, streamlining and unifying regulations, public recognition of voluntary participation, rate recovery for price regulated industries, and increased cybersecurity research. Comments from the Obama Administration suggest it believes that market-based incentives and encouragement through the C-Cubed Voluntary Program will be the most successful drivers for organizations to adopt the Cybersecurity Framework. One senior Administration official stated:

'[W]e believe that the best drivers for adoption or use of the framework will ultimately be market based. Don't get me wrong, I think the government-based incentives are really important for us to pursue. But at the end of the day, it's the market that's got to drive the business case for the Cybersecurity Framework. The federal government is going to do its best to make the costs of using the framework lower, and the benefits of the framework higher, but it's the market that's going to ultimately make this work.'"

. . .

QUESTIONS

What are the advantages of adopting a flexible framework for assessing and responding to cybersecurity risks? What are the disadvantages? Do you think a flexible framework provides adequate certainty for companies to participate in the digital economy in light of cybersecurity risk? Why or why not? Does the framework provide adequate incentives for innovation concerning cybersecurity technology? What about necessary incentives for developing a trained cybersecurity workforce? Does the framework approach provide the necessary cybersecurity protection for critical infrastructure that is often controlled by private enterprise in the United States?

10.5 The NIST Risk Management Framework: Selected Information

This section provides materials from the NIST concerning the Risk Management Framework. The Risk Management Framework document is supplemented by many guidance documents provided by the NIST.

10.5[A] GLOSSARY OF THE RISK MANAGEMENT FRAMEWORK FOR CRITICAL INFRASTRUCTURE

Appendix B of the Risk Management Framework provides a helpful Glossary of terms.

"Appendix B: Glossary . . .

Category

The subdivision of a Function into groups of cybersecurity outcomes, closely tied to programmatic needs and particular activities. Examples of Categories include "Asset Management," "Access Control," and "Detection Processes."

Critical Infrastructure

Systems and assets, whether physical or virtual, so vital to the United States that the incapacity or destruction of such systems and assets would have a debilitating impact on cybersecurity, national economic security, national public health or safety, or any combination of those matters.

Cybersecurity

The process of protecting information by preventing, detecting, and responding to attacks.

Cybersecurity Event

A cybersecurity change that may have an impact on organizational operations (including mission, capabilities, or reputation).

Detect (function)

Develop and implement the appropriate activities to identify the occurrence of a cybersecurity event.

Framework

A risk-based approach to reducing cybersecurity risk composed of three parts: the Framework Core, the Framework Profile, and the Framework Implementation Tiers. Also known as the "Cybersecurity Framework."

Framework Core

A set of cybersecurity activities and references that are common across critical infrastructure sectors and are organized around particular outcomes. The Framework Core comprises four types of elements: Functions, Categories, Subcategories, and Informative References.

Framework Implementation Tier

A lens through which to view the characteristics of an organization's approach to risk—how an organization views cybersecurity risk and the processes in place to manage that risk.

Framework Profile

A representation of the outcomes that a particular system or organization has selected from the Framework Categories and Subcategories.

Function

One of the main components of the Framework. Functions provide the highest level of structure for organizing basic cybersecurity activities into Categories and Subcategories. The five functions are Identify, Protect, Detect, Respond, and Recover.

Identify (function)

Develop the organizational understanding to manage cybersecurity risk to systems, assets, data, and capabilities.

Informative Reference

A specific section of standards, guidelines, and practices common among critical infrastructure sectors that illustrates a method to achieve the outcomes associated with each Subcategory. An example of an Informative Reference is ISO/IEC 27001 Control A.10.8.3, which supports the "Data-in-transit is protected" Subcategory of the "Data Security" Category in the "Protect" function.

Mobile Code

A program (e.g., script, macro, or other portable instruction) that can be shipped unchanged to a heterogeneous collection of platforms and executed with identical semantics.

Protect (function)

Develop and implement the appropriate safeguards to ensure delivery of critical infrastructure services.

Privileged User

A user that is authorized (and, therefore, trusted) to perform security- relevant functions that ordinary users are not authorized to perform.

Recover (function)

Develop and implement the appropriate activities to maintain plans for resilience and to restore any capabilities or services that were impaired due to a cybersecurity event.

Respond (function)

Develop and implement the appropriate activities to take action regarding a detected cybersecurity event.

Risk

A measure of the extent to which an entity is threatened by a potential circumstance or event, and typically a function of: (i) the adverse impacts that would arise if the circumstance or event occurs; and (ii) the likelihood of occurrence.

Risk Management

The process of identifying, assessing, and responding to risk.

Subcategory

The subdivision of a Category into specific outcomes of technical and/or management activities. Examples of Subcategories include "External information systems are catalogued," "Data-at-rest is protected," and "Notifications from detection systems are investigated."[411]

10.5[B] NIST 800 SERIES OF SPECIAL PUBLICATIONS

The NIST publishes the 800 series of Special Publications for guidance in providing computer security for the federal government.[412] These Special Publications were a result of the Federal Information Security Management Act (FISMA) of 2002 that resulted in the FISMA Implementation Project.

Other risk management frameworks have been developed by notable organizations such as: Operationally Critical Threat, Asset and Vulnerability Evaluation (OCTAVE)[413]; Factor Analysis Information Risk (FAIR)[414]; and Intel's Threat Agent Risk Assessment (TARA).[415]

Attorneys and security engineers alike, both share an aversion to risk. Risk is always at the forefront of any business action or transaction. In the cybersecurity world, risk is defined as "A measure of the extent to which an entity is threatened by a potential

---

[411] FRAMEWORK FOR IMPROVING CRITICAL INFRASTRUCTURE CYBERSECURITY, NAT'L. INST. OF STANDARDS AND TECH. 37–38 (2014) (Diagrams and footnotes omitted).

[412] *See Computer Security Resource Center*, NAT'L INST. OF STANDARDS AND TECH. https://csrc.nist.gov/publications/sp800 (last visited Oct. 22, 2020) (listing the series of special publications for guidance in a searchable list).

[413] *See CTAVE FORTE: Establish a More Adaptable and Robust Risk Program*, CARNEGIE MELLON UNIVERSITY: SOFTWARE ENGINEERING INSTITUTE (June 2020), *available at* https://resources.sei.cmu.edu/library/asset-view.cfm?assetid=643959.

[414] *See What is the FAIR Institute*, FAIR INSTITUTE, https://www.fairinstitute.org (last visited Oct. 22, 2020).

[415] *See* JACKSON WYNN, ET AL., THREAT ASSESSMENT & REMEDIATION ANALYSIS (TARA), MITRE (Oct. 2011), *available at* https://www.mitre.org/sites/default/files/pdf/11_4982.pdf

circumstance or event, and typically a function of: (i) the adverse impacts that would arise if the circumstance or event occurs; and (ii) the likelihood of occurrence."[416]

The cybersecurity professional, through the use of controls and/or countermeasures, seeks to reduce or eliminate vulnerabilities, or where the vulnerabilities cannot be reduced or eliminated, then to reduce the effect of possible threats through the management of Organizational risk.

> The Risk Management Framework provides a process that integrates security, privacy, and cyber supply chain risk management activities into the system development life cycle. The risk-based approach to control selection and specification considers effectiveness, efficiency, and constraints due to applicable laws, directives, Executive Orders, policies, standards, or regulations. Managing organizational risk is paramount to effective information security and privacy programs; the RMF approach can be applied to new and legacy systems, any type of system or technology (e.g., IoT, control systems), and within any type of organization regardless of size or sector.[417]

As in-house counsel, you may have the chief information security officer (CISO) reporting to the legal department or even directly to the CEO, such is the importance of the CISO mission. Other parts of the organization that may be involved in risk management of information systems include engineering, application development, and operations. The application development team focus is on developing an application on time and ready for market distribution or in-house use. The development team is often under stress to deliver on time. Implementing security measures in the application can be viewed as a nuisance that is keeping the team from meeting its goals. The CISO is not part of the development team, but has a vested interest in making sure that security is properly implemented in the application. And the legal department has a huge interest in making sure that the implemented application security measures will meet legal requirements. Your job as counsel may depend on being able to communicate effectively with all of these departments. What makes counsel's task even tougher is that each department may speak its own language just as counsel has its own language of motions, injunctions, summary judgement, complaints, for example, that an engineer may not appreciate. The next few paragraphs are an attempt at giving counsel a foundation in understanding application/software development.

Software development can happen in house or be outsourced to an entity anywhere in the world. Or if a commercial application that exists that meets a company's requirements it can be purchased. This is called Commercial Off The Shelf (COTS) software. COTS can usually be configured or modified by the purchaser to provide an even closer requirements fit. It bears mentioning that adding security to an application may require a balancing act of not having the security take over the

---

[416] GUIDE FOR CONDUCTING RISK ASSESSMENTS, NAT'L INST. OF STANDARDS AND TECH. B-9 (2012), *available at* https://nvlpubs.nist.gov/nistpubs/Legacy/SP/nistspecialpublication800-30r1.pdf.

[417] *NIST Risk Management Framework (RMF)*, NAT'L INST. OF STANDARDS AND TECH., https://csrc.nist.gov/projects/risk-management/rmf-overview (last updated Sep. 28, 2021).

functionality or user-friendliness of the final product. As one might expect, the security/risk team should be involved as soon as possible in the process of either acquiring COTS or the System Development Life Cycle (SDLC).

There is no one-size-fits-all approach to the System Development Life Cycle and several methods exist. One method that is long in the tooth is the waterfall model. It can be envisioned as the results from the first step falling into the second step and then the results from the third step falling into the fourth step and so forth, with the steps being:
- Collection of system requirements
- Collection of software requirements
- Preliminary design
- Detailed design
- Coding and debugging of the code through unit testing of each module
- Testing of complete code
- Placing code into operations
- Maintaining the code through bug fixes and feature enhancements.

The waterfall approach can be a long process depending on the size of the system and can take years to completion. Each step may have a walkthrough of the results before passing it onto the next step. If issues are found, it stays in the same step, the issue is resolved, and another walkthrough takes place. A walkthrough is normally a team sitting around a conference table reviewing pages and pages of results. The advantage of waterfall development is that there is abundant documentation to follow and review. The disadvantage is that by the time the product is delivered, the requirements may have changed over time and the user is unhappy because the system no longer meets their current requirements.

Rapid Application Prototyping (RAD) was introduced to remedy some of the waterfall shortcomings. The goal of RAD was to produce a quick and dirty prototype based on the user's requirements that could be shown to the user for immediate feedback. This is an iterative process. It may start with just mocked up screenshots being shown to the user for feedback. Eventually after enough iterations, a final product is produced for the user group that is not a surprise to the users because the users have been intimately involved in the process from the start.

Another model that has become popular today is the Agile Software Development. The core tenants of Agile is:

> Individual and interactions over processes and tools; Working software over comprehensive documentation; Customer collaboration over contract negotiation; Responding to change over following a plan. That is, while there is value in the items on the right, we value the items on the left more.[418]

---

[418] Kent Beck, et al., *Manifesto for Agile Software Development*, AGILE, http://agilemanifesto.org (last visited Oct. 22, 2020).

Notice that in the above models, security is not a specific step or called out as a core tenant. This is probably because the code will function without security measures. There is likely a lot of legacy code in production today that was developed before the focus on cybersecurity. For example, the programming language COBOL is 60 years old and still prevalent in many systems today.[419] This is part of the challenge for the CISO and counsel. They must educate the development teams on the importance of reasonable security measures and the potential cost for not applying those measures. Often, when the importance of proper security measures is explained in engineering English and the risk of not applying the measure, and not legalese, the development team is more likely to take the measures to heart. Afterall, engineers are just as risk adverse as attorneys.

The 800 series of Special Publications for guidance in providing computer security is a risk-based approach that can be used with a system development life cycle.[420] Following is a high-level view of the Risk Management Framework Steps:

As an overarching step, the prepare step covers "[e]ssential activities to prepare the organization to manage security and privacy risks."[421]

The categorize step categorizes "the system and the information processed, stored, and transmitted based on an impact analysis."[422]

The select step is "Select the set of NIST SP 800-53 controls to protect the system based on risk assessment(s)."[423]

The implement step is "Implement the controls and document how controls are deployed."[424]

The assess step is "to determine if the controls are in place, operating as intended, and producing the desired results."[425]

In the authorize step a "Senior official makes a risk-based decision to authorize the system (to operate)."[426]

For the monitor step "Continuously monitor control implementation and risks to the system."[427]

---

[419] *See* Charles R. Martin, *Brush up your COBOL: Why is a 60 year old language suddenly in demand?*, THE OVERFLOW (Apr. 20, 2020), https://stackoverflow.blog/2020/04/20/brush-up-your-cobol-why-is-a-60-year-old-language-suddenly-in-demand/.

[420] *See* Risk-Based Approach, *available at* https://csrc.nist.gov/projects/risk-management/rmf-overview.

[421] *About the Risk Management Framework (RMF)*, NAT'L INST. OF STANDARDS AND TECH., https://csrc.nist.gov/projects/risk-management/rmf-overview (last updated Sep. 28, 2021).

[422] *Id.*

[423] *Id.*

[424] *Id.*

[425] *Id.*

[426] *Id.*

[427] *Id.*

FEDERAL INFORMATION PROCESSING STANDARDS, NIST SPECIAL PUBLICATIONS AND NIST INTERAGENCY REPORTS

This section contains a closer look at each of the Federal Information Processing Standards (FIPS) Publications, NIST Special Publications and NIST Interagency Reports. Although these documents were originally created for protecting federal assets, they have been adopted as guidelines by non-government businesses. This is a lot of material. The goal here is not to make Counsel an expert on each of these documents, but instead to give Counsel enough knowledge that Counsel will be able to participate in a knowledgeable conversation with the security team. Counsel may also have to dive into and understand a number of these documents if counsel is negotiating technical contracts or data privacy agreements because contracts often defer to NIST documents as the industry standard for measuring cybersecurity.

FIPS 199: Standards for Security Categorization of Federal Information and Information Systems

FIPS 199 is focused on the standards used "to categorize all information and information systems . . . based on the objectives of providing appropriate levels of information security according to a range of risk levels."[428]

FIPS 199 looks at the potential impact on organizations and individuals if the CIA [44 U.S.C., Sec. 3542] for information and information systems is breached.[429] The potential impact is divided into three categories, low, moderate, and high.[430]

Low potential impact is defined as "[t]he loss of confidentiality, integrity, or availability could be expected to have a **limited** adverse effect on organizational operations, organizational assets, or individuals."[431] Moderate potential impact is "[t]he loss of confidentiality, integrity, or availability could be expected to have a **serious** adverse effect on organizational operations, organizational assets, or individuals."[432] High potential impact is "[t]he loss of confidentiality, integrity, or availability could be expected to have a **severe or catastrophic** adverse effect on organizational operations, organizational assets, or individual."[433]

FIPS 199 provides examples to help in categorization. This categorization exercise could be very helpful to a company that is in risk analysis phase.

FIPS 199 provides in relevant part:

Potential Impact on Organizations and Individuals

---

[428] STANDARDS FOR SECURITY CATEGORIZATION OF FEDERAL INFORMATION AND INFORMATION SYSTEMS, NAT'L INST. OF STANDARDS AND TECH. 1 (2004), *available at* https://nvlpubs.nist.gov/nistpubs/FIPS/NIST.FIPS.199.pdf.
[429] *Id.* at 2.
[430] *Id.* at 2.
[431] *Id.* at 2.
[432] *Id.* at 2.
[433] *Id.* at 3.

FIPS Publication 199 defines three levels of potential impact on organizations or individuals should there be a breach of security (i.e., a loss of confidentiality, integrity, or availability). The application of these definitions must take place within the context of each organization and the overall national interest.

The potential impact is LOW if— – The loss of confidentiality, integrity, or availability could be expected to have a limited adverse effect on organizational operations, organizational assets, or individuals. AMPLIFICATION: A limited adverse effect means that, for example, the loss of confidentiality, integrity, or availability might: (i) cause a degradation in mission capability to an extent and duration that the organization is able to perform its primary functions, but the effectiveness of the functions is noticeably reduced; (ii) result in minor damage to organizational assets; (iii) result in minor financial loss; or (iv) result in minor harm to individuals.

The potential impact is MODERATE if— – The loss of confidentiality, integrity, or availability could be expected to have a serious adverse effect on organizational operations, organizational assets, or individuals. AMPLIFICATION: A serious adverse effect means that, for example, the loss of confidentiality, integrity, or availability might: (i) cause a significant degradation in mission capability to an extent and duration that the organization is able to perform its primary functions, but the effectiveness of the functions is significantly reduced; (ii) result in significant damage to organizational assets; (iii) result in significant financial loss; or (iv) result in significant harm to individuals that does not involve loss of life or serious life threatening injuries. Adverse effects on individuals may include, but are not limited to, loss of the privacy to which individuals are entitled under law.

The potential impact is HIGH if— – The loss of confidentiality, integrity, or availability could be expected to have a severe or catastrophic adverse effect on organizational operations, organizational assets, or individuals. AMPLIFICATION: A severe or catastrophic adverse effect means that, for example, the loss of confidentiality, integrity, or availability might: (i) cause a severe degradation in or loss of mission capability to an extent and duration that the organization is not able to perform one or more of its primary functions; (ii) result in major damage to organizational assets; (iii) result in major financial loss; or (iv) result in severe or catastrophic harm to individuals involving loss of life or serious life threatening injuries.

Security Categorization Applied to Information Types The security category of an information type can be associated with both user information and system information and can be applicable to information in either electronic or non-electronic form. It can also be used as input in considering the appropriate security category of an information system (see description of security categories for information systems below). Establishing an appropriate security category of an information type essentially requires determining the potential impact for each security objective associated with the particular information type.

The generalized format for expressing the security category, SC, of an information type is:

SC information type = {(confidentiality, impact), (integrity, impact), (availability, impact)}, where the acceptable values for potential impact are LOW, MODERATE, HIGH, or NOT APPLICABLE.4

EXAMPLE 1: An organization managing public information on its web server determines that there is no potential impact from a loss of confidentiality (i.e., confidentiality requirements are not applicable), a moderate potential impact from a loss of integrity, and a moderate potential impact from a loss of availability. The resulting security category, SC, of this information type is expressed as:

SC public information = {(confidentiality, NA), (integrity, MODERATE), (availability, MODERATE)}.

EXAMPLE 2: A law enforcement organization managing extremely sensitive investigative information determines that the potential impact from a loss of confidentiality is high, the potential impact from a loss of integrity is moderate, and the potential impact from a loss of availability is moderate. The resulting security category, SC, of this information type is expressed as:

SC investigative information = {(confidentiality, HIGH), (integrity, MODERATE), (availability, MODERATE)}.

EXAMPLE 3: A financial organization managing routine administrative information (not privacy-related information) determines that the potential impact from a loss of confidentiality is low, the potential impact from a loss of integrity is low, and the potential impact from a loss of availability is low. The resulting security category, SC, of this information type is expressed as:

SC administrative information = {(confidentiality, LOW), (integrity, LOW), (availability, LOW)}.

System information (e.g., network routing tables, password files, and cryptographic key management information) must be protected at a level commensurate with the most critical or sensitive user information being processed, stored, or transmitted by the information system to ensure confidentiality, integrity, and availability. The potential impact value of not applicable only applies to the security objective of confidentiality.

Security Categorization Applied to Information Systems Determining the security category of an information system requires slightly more analysis and must consider the security categories of all information types resident on the information system. For an information system, the potential impact values assigned to the respective security objectives (confidentiality, integrity, availability) shall be the highest values (i.e., high water mark) from among those security categories that have been determined for each type of information resident on the information system.

The generalized format for expressing the security category, SC, of an information system is:

SC information system = {(confidentiality, impact), (integrity, impact), (availability, impact)}, where the acceptable values for potential impact are LOW, MODERATE, or HIGH.

Note that the value of not applicable cannot be assigned to any security objective in the context of establishing a security category for an information system. This is in recognition that there is a low minimum potential impact (i.e., low water mark) on the loss of confidentiality, integrity, and availability for an information system due to the fundamental requirement to protect the system-level processing functions and information critical to the operation of the information system.

EXAMPLE 4: An information system used for large acquisitions in a contracting organization contains both sensitive, pre-solicitation phase contract information and routine administrative information. The management within the contracting organization determines that: (i) for the sensitive contract information, the potential impact from a loss of confidentiality is moderate, the potential impact from a loss of integrity is moderate, and the potential impact from a loss of availability is low; and (ii) for the routine administrative information (non-privacy-related information), the potential impact from a loss of confidentiality is low, the potential impact from a loss of integrity is low, and the potential impact from a loss of availability is low. The resulting security categories, SC, of these information types are expressed as:

SC contract information = {(confidentiality, MODERATE), (integrity, MODERATE), (availability, LOW)}, and SC administrative information = {(confidentiality, LOW), (integrity, LOW), (availability, LOW)}.

The resulting security category of the information system is expressed as:

SC acquisition system = {(confidentiality, MODERATE), (integrity, MODERATE), (availability, LOW)}, representing the high water mark or maximum potential impact values for each security objective from the information types resident on the acquisition system.

It is recognized that information systems are composed of both programs and information. Programs in execution within an information system (i.e., system processes) facilitate the processing, storage, and transmission of information and are necessary for the organization to conduct its essential mission-related functions and operations. These system processing functions also require protection and could be subject to security categorization as well. However, in the interest of simplification, it is assumed that the security categorization of all information types associated with the information system provide an appropriate worst case potential impact for the overall information system—thereby obviating the need to consider the system processes in the security categorization of the information system.

EXAMPLE 5: A power plant contains a SCADA (supervisory control and data acquisition) system controlling the distribution of electric power for a large military installation. The SCADA system contains both real-time sensor data and routine administrative information. The management at the power plant determines that: (i) for the sensor data being acquired by the SCADA system, there is no potential impact from a loss of confidentiality, a high potential impact from a loss of integrity, and a high potential impact from a loss of availability; and (ii) for the administrative information being processed by the system, there is a low potential impact from a loss of confidentiality, a low potential impact from a loss of integrity, and a low potential impact from a loss of availability. The resulting security categories, SC, of these information types are expressed as:

SC sensor data = {(confidentiality, NA), (integrity, HIGH), (availability, HIGH)},

and

SC administrative information = {(confidentiality, LOW), (integrity, LOW), (availability, LOW)}.

The resulting security category of the information system is initially expressed as:

SC SCADA system = {(confidentiality, LOW), (integrity, HIGH), (availability, HIGH)}, representing the high water mark or maximum potential impact values for each security objective from the information types resident on the SCADA system. The management at the power plant chooses to increase the potential impact from a loss of confidentiality from low to moderate reflecting a more realistic view of the potential impact on the information system should there be a security breach due to the unauthorized disclosure of system-level information or processing functions. The final security category of the information system is expressed as:

SC SCADA system = {(confidentiality, MODERATE), (integrity, HIGH), (availability, HIGH)}.[434]

FIPS 200: Minimum Security Requirements for Federal Information and Information Systems

FIPS 200 "specifies minimum security requirements for federal information and information systems in seventeen security-related areas," and "must meet the minimum security requirements . . . through the use of security controls in accordance with NIST Special Publication 800-53."[435]

FIPS 200 relies on the categorization for information and systems from the potential impact analysis of FIPS 199. pages 1-2. Because the impact analysis categorizes CIA, and CIA may not receive the same categorization across all three components of CIA, there is an opportunity for three different impact scores. For example, Confidentiality could be categorized as high, Integrity as moderate, and Availability as low. In determining the minimum security requirement for a particular item, the highest impact score (high water mark) across CIA prevails.[436]

The minimum security requirements cover seventeen security-related areas with regard to protecting the confidentiality, integrity, and availability of federal information systems and the information processed, stored, and transmitted by those systems.[437]

The 17 minimum security specifications include:
- Access Control (AC)
- Awareness and Training (AT)
- Audit and Accountability (AU)
- Certification, Accreditation, and Security Assessments (CA)
- Configuration Management (CM)
- Contingency Planning (CP)
- Identification and Authentication (IA)
- Incident Response (IR)
- Maintenance (MA)
- Media Protection (MP)
- Physical and Environmental Protection (PE)
- Planning (PL)

---

[434] STANDARDS FOR SECURITY CATEGORIZATION OF FEDERAL INFORMATION AND INFORMATION SYSTEMS, NAT'L INST. OF STANDARDS AND TECH. 2–5 (2004), *available at* https://nvlpubs.nist.gov/nistpubs/FIPS/NIST.FIPS.199.pdf.

[435] MINIMUM SECURITY REQUIREMENTS FOR FEDERAL INFORMATION AND INFORMATION SYSTEMS, NAT'L. INST. OF STANDARDS AND TECH. iv (2006), *available at* https://nvlpubs.nist.gov/nistpubs/FIPS/NIST.FIPS.200.pdf.

[436] *Id.* at 2.

[437] *Id.*

- Personnel Security (PS)
- Risk Assessment (RA)
- System and Services Acquisition (SA)
- System and Communications Protection (SC)
- System and Information Integrity (SI)[438]

The minimum security requirements are met "by selecting the appropriate security controls and assurance requirements as described in NIST Special Publication 800-53, *Recommended Security Controls for Federal Information Systems.*"[439]

FIPS 200 provides in relevant part:

1.PURPOSE

The E-Government Act of 2002 (Public Law 107-347), passed by the one hundred and seventh Congress and signed into law by the President in December 2002, recognized the importance of information security to the economic and national security interests of the United States. Title III of the E-Government Act, entitled the Federal Information Security Management Act (FISMA) of 2002, tasked NIST with the responsibility of developing security standards and guidelines for the federal government including the development of: • Standards for categorizing information and information systems1 collected or maintained by or on behalf of each federal agency based on the objectives of providing appropriate levels of information security according to a range of risk levels; • Guidelines recommending the types of information and information systems to be included in each category; and • Minimum information security requirements for information and information systems in each such category.

FIPS Publication 199, Standards for Security Categorization of Federal Information and Information Systems, approved by the Secretary of Commerce in February 2004, is the first of two mandatory security standards required by the FISMA legislation. FIPS Publication 200, the second of the mandatory security standards, specifies minimum security requirements for information and information systems supporting the executive agencies of the federal government and a risk-based process for selecting the security controls necessary to satisfy the minimum security requirements. This standard will promote the development, implementation, and operation of more secure information systems within the federal government by establishing minimum levels of due diligence for information security and facilitating a more consistent, comparable, and repeatable approach for selecting and specifying security controls for information systems that meet minimum security requirements.

---

[438] *Id.*
[439] *Id.*

2. INFORMATION SYSTEM IMPACT LEVELS

FIPS Publication 199 requires agencies to categorize their information systems as low-impact, moderate-impact, or high-impact for the security objectives of confidentiality, integrity, and availability. The potential impact values assigned to the respective security objectives are the highest values (i.e., high water mark) from among the security categories that have been determined for each type of information resident on those information systems. The generalized format for expressing the security category (SC) of an information system is:

SC information system = {(confidentiality, impact), (integrity, impact), (availability, impact)}, where the acceptable values for potential impact are low, moderate, or high.

Since the potential impact values for confidentiality, integrity, and availability may not always be the same for a particular information system, the high water mark concept must be used to determine the overall impact level of the information system. Thus, a low-impact system is an information system in which all three of the security objectives are low. A moderate-impact system is an information system in which at least one of the security objectives is moderate and no security objective is greater than moderate. And finally, a high-impact system is an information system in which at least one security objective is high. The determination of information system impact levels must be accomplished prior to the consideration of minimum security requirements and the selection of appropriate security controls for those information systems.

3. MINIMUM SECURITY REQUIREMENTS

The minimum security requirements cover seventeen security-related areas with regard to protecting the confidentiality, integrity, and availability of federal information systems and the information processed, stored, and transmitted by those systems. The security-related areas include: (i) access control; (ii) awareness and training; (iii) audit and accountability; (iv) certification, accreditation, and security assessments; (v) configuration management; (vi) contingency planning; (vii) identification and authentication; (viii) incident response; (ix) maintenance; (x) media protection; (xi) physical and environmental protection; (xii) planning; (xiii) personnel security; (xiv) risk assessment; (xv) systems and services acquisition; (xvi) system and communications protection; and (xvii) system and information integrity. The seventeen areas represent a broad-based, balanced information security program that addresses the management, operational, and technical aspects of protecting federal information and information systems.

Policies and procedures play an important role in the effective implementation of enterprise-wide information security programs within the federal government and the success of the resulting security measures employed to protect federal information and information systems. Thus, organizations must develop and promulgate formal, documented policies and procedures governing the minimum security requirements set forth in this standard and must ensure their effective implementation.

Specifications for Minimum Security Requirements

Access Control (AC): Organizations must limit information system access to authorized users, processes acting on behalf of authorized users, or devices (including other information systems) and to the types of transactions and functions that authorized users are permitted to exercise.

Awareness and Training (AT): Organizations must: (i) ensure that managers and users of organizational information systems are made aware of the security risks associated with their activities and of the applicable laws, Executive Orders, directives, policies, standards, instructions, regulations, or procedures related to the security of organizational information systems; and (ii) ensure that organizational personnel are adequately trained to carry out their assigned information security-related duties and responsibilities.

Audit and Accountability (AU): Organizations must: (i) create, protect, and retain information system audit records to the extent needed to enable the monitoring, analysis, investigation, and reporting of unlawful, unauthorized, or inappropriate information system activity; and (ii) ensure that the actions of individual information system users can be uniquely traced to those users so they can be held accountable for their actions.

Certification, Accreditation, and Security Assessments (CA): Organizations must: (i) periodically assess the security controls in organizational information systems to determine if the controls are effective in their application; (ii) develop and implement plans of action designed to correct deficiencies and reduce or eliminate vulnerabilities in organizational information systems; (iii) authorize the operation of organizational information systems and any associated information system connections; and (iv) monitor information system security controls on an ongoing basis to ensure the continued effectiveness of the controls.

Configuration Management (CM): Organizations must: (i) establish and maintain baseline configurations and inventories of organizational information systems (including hardware, software, firmware, and documentation) throughout the respective system development life cycles; and (ii) establish and enforce security configuration settings for information technology products employed in organizational information systems.

Contingency Planning (CP): Organizations must establish, maintain, and effectively implement plans for emergency response, backup operations, and post-disaster recovery for organizational information systems to ensure the availability of critical information resources and continuity of operations in emergency situations.

Identification and Authentication (IA): Organizations must identify information system users, processes acting on behalf of users, or devices and authenticate (or verify) the identities of those users, processes, or devices, as a prerequisite to allowing access to organizational information systems.

Incident Response (IR): Organizations must: (i) establish an operational incident handling capability for organizational information systems that includes adequate preparation, detection, analysis, containment, recovery, and user response activities; and (ii) track, document, and report incidents to appropriate organizational officials and/or authorities.

Maintenance (MA): Organizations must: (i) perform periodic and timely maintenance on organizational information systems; and (ii) provide effective controls on the tools, techniques, mechanisms, and personnel used to conduct information system maintenance.

Media Protection (MP): Organizations must: (i) protect information system media, both paper and digital; (ii) limit access to information on information system media to authorized users; and (iii) sanitize or destroy information system media before disposal or release for reuse.

Physical and Environmental Protection (PE): Organizations must: (i) limit physical access to information systems, equipment, and the respective operating environments to authorized individuals; (ii) protect the physical plant and support infrastructure for information systems; (iii) provide supporting utilities for information systems; (iv) protect information systems against environmental hazards; and (v) provide appropriate environmental controls in facilities containing information systems.

Planning (PL): Organizations must develop, document, periodically update, and implement security plans for organizational information systems that describe the security controls in place or planned for the information systems and the rules of behavior for individuals accessing the information systems.

Personnel Security (PS): Organizations must: (i) ensure that individuals occupying positions of responsibility within organizations (including third-party service providers) are trustworthy and meet established security criteria for those positions; (ii) ensure that organizational information and information systems are protected during and after personnel actions such as terminations and transfers; and (iii) employ formal sanctions for personnel failing to comply with organizational security policies and procedures.

Risk Assessment (RA): Organizations must periodically assess the risk to organizational operations (including mission, functions, image, or reputation), organizational assets, and individuals, resulting from the operation of organizational information systems and the associated processing, storage, or transmission of organizational information.

System and Services Acquisition (SA): Organizations must: (i) allocate sufficient resources to adequately protect organizational information systems; (ii) employ system development life cycle processes that incorporate information security considerations; (iii) employ software usage and installation restrictions; and (iv) ensure that third-party providers employ adequate security measures to protect information, applications, and/or services outsourced from the organization.

System and Communications Protection (SC): Organizations must: (i) monitor, control, and protect organizational communications (i.e., information transmitted or received by organizational information systems) at the external boundaries and key internal boundaries of the information systems; and (ii) employ architectural designs, software development techniques, and systems engineering principles that promote effective information security within organizational information systems.

System and Information Integrity (SI): Organizations must: (i) identify, report, and correct information and information system flaws in a timely manner; (ii) provide protection from malicious code at appropriate locations within organizational information systems; and (iii) monitor information system security alerts and advisories and take appropriate actions in response.

4. SECURITY CONTROL SELECTION

Organizations must meet the minimum security requirements in this standard by selecting the appropriate security controls and assurance requirements as described in NIST Special Publication 800-53, Recommended Security Controls for Federal Information System. The process of selecting the appropriate security controls and assurance requirements for organizational information systems to achieve adequate security is a multifaceted, risk-based activity involving management and operational personnel within the organization. Security categorization of federal information and information systems, as required by FIPS

Publication 199, is the first step in the risk management process. Subsequent to the security categorization process, organizations must select an appropriate set of security controls for their information systems that satisfy the minimum security requirements set forth in this standard. The selected set of security controls must include one of three, appropriately tailored security control baselines from NIST Special Publication 800-53 that are associated with the designated impact levels of the organizational information systems as determined during the security categorization process. - For low-impact information systems, organizations must, as a minimum, employ appropriately tailored security controls from the low baseline of security controls defined in NIST Special Publication 800-53 and must ensure that the minimum assurance requirements associated with the low baseline are satisfied. - For moderate-impact information systems, organizations must, as a minimum, employ appropriately tailored security controls from the moderate baseline of security controls defined in NIST Special Publication 800-53 and must ensure that the minimum assurance requirements associated with the moderate baseline are satisfied. - For high-impact information systems, organizations must, as a minimum, employ appropriately tailored security controls from the high baseline of security controls defined in NIST Special Publication 800-53 and must ensure that the minimum assurance requirements associated with the high baseline are satisfied.

Organizations must employ all security controls in the respective security control baselines unless specific exceptions are allowed based on the tailoring guidance provided in NIST Special Publication 800-53.

To ensure a cost-effective, risk-based approach to achieving adequate security across the organization, security control baseline tailoring activities must be coordinated with and approved by appropriate organizational officials (e.g., chief information officers, senior agency information security officers, authorizing officials, or authorizing officials designated representatives). The resulting set of security controls must be documented in the security plan for the information system.[440]

NIST Special Publication 800-53 addresses security controls base on whether the system is low-impact, moderate-impact, or high-impact. NIST Special Publication 800-53 is covered in its own section below.

The NIST 800 series of Special Publications is focused on Computer Security. Related series include Special Publications 1800 that covers Cybersecurity practice

---

[440] MINIMUM SECURITY REQUIREMENTS FOR FEDERAL INFORMATION AND INFORMATION SYSTEMS, NAT'L INST. OF STANDARDS AND TECH. (2006), *available at* https://nvlpubs.nist.gov/nistpubs/FIPS/NIST.FIPS.200.pdf.

guides, and Special Publication 500 that covers Information technology.[441] Next, we take a closer look at each relevant document of the 800 series.

SP 800-18 Revision 1: Guide for Developing Security Plans for Federal Information Systems

It is always good to have a plan and SP 800-18 provides guidance of developing such a security plan.

> The purpose of the system security plan is to provide an overview of the security requirements of the system and describe the controls in place or planned for meeting those requirements. The system security plan also delineates responsibilities and expected behavior of all individuals who access the system. The system security plan should be viewed as documentation of the structured process of planning adequate, cost-effective security protection for a system. It should reflect input from various managers with responsibilities concerning the system, including information owners, the system owner, and the senior agency information security officer (SAISO). Additional information may be included in the basic plan and the structure and format organized according to agency needs, so long as the major sections described in this document are adequately covered and readily identifiable.[442]

SP 800-30 Revision 1: Guide for Conducting Risk Assessments

> The purpose of Special Publication 800-30 is to provide guidance for conducting risk assessments of federal information systems and organizations, amplifying the guidance in Special Publication 800-39. Risk assessments, carried out at all three tiers in the risk management hierarchy, are part of an overall risk management process—providing senior leaders/executives with the information needed to determine appropriate courses of action in response to identified risks. In particular, this document provides guidance for carrying out each of the steps in the risk assessment process (i.e., preparing for the assessment, conducting the assessment, communicating the results of the assessment, and maintaining the assessment) and how risk assessments and other organizational risk management processes complement and inform each other. Special Publication 800-30 also provides guidance to organizations on identifying specific risk factors to monitor on an ongoing basis, so that organizations can determine whether risks have increased to

---

[441] *See Publications*, NAT'L INST. OF STANDARDS AND TECH., https://csrc.nist.gov/publications (last visited Oct. 22, 2020).

[442] GUIDE FOR DEVELOPING SECURITY PLANS FOR FEDERAL INFORMATION SYSTEMS, NAT'L INST. OF STANDARDS AND TECH. (2006), *available at* https://nvlpubs.nist.gov/nistpubs/Legacy/SP/nistspecialpublication800-18r1.pdf.

unacceptable levels (i.e., exceeding organizational risk tolerance) and different courses of action should be taken.[443]

SP 800-34 Revision 1: Contingency Planning Guide for Federal Information Systems

The importance of contingency planning cannot be understated, whether it be government systems and data or private business systems and data. Planning can make the difference between survival or ruin for a commercial enterprise.

This guide defines the following seven-step contingency planning process that an organization may apply to develop and maintain a viable contingency planning program for their information systems. These seven progressive steps are designed to be integrated into each stage of the system development life cycle.

1. **Develop the contingency planning policy statement.** A formal policy provides the authority and guidance necessary to develop an effective contingency plan.

2. **Conduct the business impact analysis (BIA).** The BIA helps identify and prioritize information systems and components critical to supporting the organization's mission/business processes. A template for developing the BIA is provided to assist the user.

3. **Identify preventive controls.** Measures taken to reduce the effects of system disruptions can increase system availability and reduce contingency life cycle costs.

4. **Create contingency strategies.** Thorough recovery strategies ensure that the system may be recovered quickly and effectively following a disruption.

5. **Develop an information system contingency plan.** The contingency plan should contain detailed guidance and procedures for restoring a damaged system unique to the system's security impact level and recovery requirements.

6. **Ensure plan testing, training, and exercises.** Testing validates recovery capabilities, whereas training prepares recovery personnel for plan activation and exercising the plan identifies planning gaps; combined, the activities improve plan effectiveness and overall organization preparedness.

---

[443] GUIDE FOR CONDUCTING RISK ASSESSMENTS, NAT'L INST. OF STANDARDS AND TECH. 2 (2012), *available at* https://nvlpubs.nist.gov/nistpubs/Legacy/SP/nistspecialpublication800-30r1.pdf.

7. **Ensure plan maintenance.** The plan should be a living document that is updated regularly to remain current with system enhancements and organizational changes.[444]

One of the most import steps is conducting the Business Impact Analysis.

Some key metrics in understanding business impact analysis are:

Working directly with mission/business process owners, departmental staff, managers, and other stakeholders, estimate the downtime factors for consideration as a result of a disruptive event.

- **Maximum Tolerable Downtime (MTD).** The MTD represents the total amount of time leaders/managers are willing to accept for a mission/business process outage or disruption and includes all impact considerations. Determining MTD is important because it could leave continuity planners with imprecise direction on (1) selection of an appropriate recovery method, and (2) the depth of detail which will be required when developing recovery procedures, including their scope and content.

- **Recovery Time Objective (RTO).** RTO defines the maximum amount of time that a system resource can remain unavailable before there is an unacceptable impact on other system resources, supported mission/business processes, and the MTD. Determining the information system resource RTO is important for selecting appropriate technologies that are best suited for meeting the MTD.

- **Recovery Point Objective (RPO).** The RPO represents the point in time, prior to a disruption or system outage, to which mission/business process data must be recovered (given the most recent backup copy of the data) after an outage.[445]

Because contingency planning covers many areas of the business, there are several plan types available, such as:
- Business Continuity Plan (BCP)
- Continuity of Operations Plan (COOP)
- Crisis Communication Plan
- Critical Infrastructure Protection (CIP) Plan
- Cyber Incident Response Plan
- Disaster Recovery Plan (DRP)
- Information System Contingency Plan (ISCP)
- Occupant Emergency Plan (OEP)[446]

---

[444] CONTINGENCY PLANNING GUIDE FOR FEDERAL INFORMATION SYSTEMS, NAT'L INST. OF STANDARDS AND TECH. ES-1 (2010), *available at*
https://nvlpubs.nist.gov/nistpubs/Legacy/SP/nistspecialpublication800-34r1.pdf.
[445] *Id.* at B-3
[446] *Id.* at 9-10.

The following table from NIST summarizes each of the above stated plans. MEF stands for Mission Essential Functions.

Plan	Purpose	Scope	Plan Relationship
Business Continuity Plan (BCP)	Provides procedures for sustaining mission/business operations while recovering from a significant disruption.	Addresses mission/business processes at a lower or expanded level from COOP MEFs.	Mission/business process focused plan that may be activated in coordination with a COOP plan to sustain non-MEFs.
Continuity of Operations (COOP) Plan	Provides procedures and guidance to sustain an organization's MEFs at an alternate site for up to 30 days; mandated by federal directives.	Addresses MEFs at a facility; information systems are addressed based only on their support of the mission essential functions.	MEF focused plan that may also activate several business unit-level BCPs, ISCPs, or DRPs, as appropriate.
Crisis Communications Plan	Provides procedures for disseminating internal and external communications; means to provide critical status information and control rumors.	Addresses communications with personnel and the public; not information system-focused.	Incident-based plan often activated with a COOP or BCP, but may be used alone during a public exposure event.
Critical Infrastructure Protection (CIP) Plan	Provides policies and procedures for protection of national critical infrastructure components, as defined in the National Infrastructure Protection Plan.	Addresses critical infrastructure components that are supported or operated by an agency or organization.	Risk management plan that supports COOP plans for organizations with critical infrastructure and key resource assets.
Cyber Incident Response Plan	Provides procedures for mitigating and correcting a cyber attack, such as a virus, worm, or Trojan horse.	Addresses mitigation and isolation of affected systems, cleanup, and minimizing loss of information.	Information system-focused plan that may activate an ISCP or DRP, depending on the extent of the attack.

Disaster Recovery Plan (DRP)	Provides procedures for relocating information systems operations to an alternate location.	Activated after major system disruptions with long-term effects.	Information system-focused plan that activates one or more ISCPs for recovery of individual systems.
Information System Contingency Plan (ISCP)	Provides procedures and capabilities for recovering an information system.	Addresses single information system recovery at the current or, if appropriate alternate location.	Information system-focused plan that may be activated independent from other plans or as part of a larger recovery effort coordinated with a DRP, COOP, and/or BCP .
Occupant Emergency Plan (OEP)	Provides coordinated procedures for minimizing loss of life or injury and protecting property damage in response to a physical threat.	Focuses on personnel and property particular to the specific facility; not mission/business process or information system-based.	Incident-based plan that is initiated immediately after an event, preceding a COOP or DRP activation.

Figure 4.[447]

Although we are focused on protecting cyber-related assets, we should never forget that protecting human life is the number one priority. Protecting systems come after protecting human life.

SP 800-37 Revision 2: Risk Management Framework for Information Systems and Organizations, A System Life Cycle Approach for Security and Privacy

SP 800-37 "describes the RMF and provides guidelines for managing security and privacy risks and applying the RMF to information systems and organizations."[448]

SP 800-39: Managing Information Security Risk, Organization, Mission, and Information System View

---

[447] *Id.* at 11.

[448] RISK MANAGEMENT FRAMEWORK FOR INFORMATION SYSTEMS AND ORGANIZATIONS: A SYSTEM LIFE CYCLE APPROACH FOR SECURITY AND PRIVACY, NAT'L INST. OF STANDARDS AND TECH. 3 (2018), *available at* https://nvlpubs.nist.gov/nistpubs/SpecialPublications/NIST.SP.800-37r2.pdf.

The risk management approach described in this publication is supported by a series of security standards and guidelines necessary for managing information security risk. In particular, the Special Publications developed by the Joint Task Force Transformation Initiative supporting the unified information security framework for the federal government include:

- Special Publication 800-37, *Guide for Applying the Risk Management Framework to Federal Information Systems: A Security Life Cycle Approach*;

- Special Publication 800-53, *Recommended Security Controls for Federal Information Systems and Organizations*;

- Special Publication 800-53A, *Guide for Assessing the Security Controls in Federal Information Systems and Organizations*; and

- Draft Special Publication 800-30, *Guide for Conducting Risk Assessments*.

In addition to the Joint Task Force publications listed above, the International Organization for Standardization (ISO) and the International Electrotechnical Commission (IEC) publish standards for risk management and information security including:

- ISO/IEC 31000, *Risk management – Principles and guidelines*;

- ISO/IEC 31010, *Risk management – Risk assessment techniques*;

- ISO/IEC 27001, *Information technology – Security techniques – Information security management systems – Requirements*; and

- ISO/IEC 27005, *Information technology – Security techniques – Information security risk management systems*.

NIST's mission includes harmonization of international and national standards where appropriate. The concepts and principles contained in this publication are intended to implement for federal information systems and organizations, an information security management system and a risk management process similar to those described in ISO/IEC standards. This reduces the burden on organizations that must conform to both ISO/IEC standards and NIST standards and guidance.[449]

SP-800-39 breaks risk management into three tiers, tier 1, tier 2, and tier 3. The following figure shows the relationship between the tiers:

---

[449] MANAGING INFORMATION SECURITY RISK: ORGANIZATION, MISSION, AND INFORMATION SYSTEM VIEW, NAT'L INST. OF STANDARDS AND TECH. 4 (2011), *available at* https://nvlpubs.nist.gov/nistpubs/Legacy/SP/nistspecialpublication800-39.pdf.

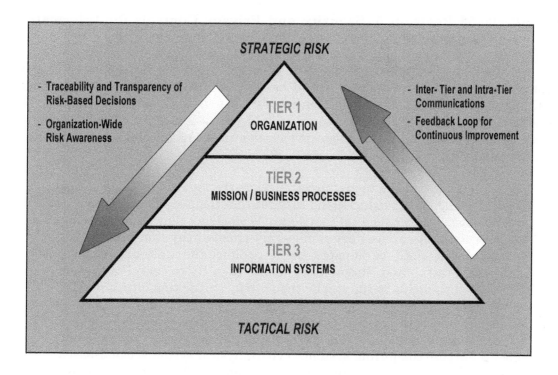

Figure 6.[450]

SP 800-47 Revision 1: Managing the Security of Information Exchanges

SP 800-47 Revision 1, first published in August 2002 replaced SP 800-47: Security Guide for Interconnecting Information Technology Systems in July 2021. The title change also suggests the changes that have occurred over the last 19 years regarding protecting data. The interconnection of systems was once a significant task. Today, interconnection is easily achieved and the security of exchanging information has become the more important task.

> This publication provides guidance for managing (i.e., planning, establishing, maintaining, and discontinuing) the security of information exchanges between systems that are owned and operated by different organizations or are within the same organization but with different authorization boundaries, including organizations within a single federal agency. Organizations manage the security of the information being exchanged by applying security controls and entering into agreements designed to manage risk and protect the information being exchanged at the same or similar level.[451]

---

[450] *Id.* at 9.

[451] MANAGING THE SECURITY OF INFORMATION EXCHANGES, NAT'L INST. OF STANDARDS AND TECH. (2021), *available at* https://nvlpubs.nist.gov/nistpubs/SpecialPublications/NIST.SP.800-47r1.pdf at 1.

SP 800-53 Revision 5: Security and Privacy Controls for Information Systems and Organizations

SP 800-53 is a significant document. This document is so large because it gives guidance on how to apply a tailored set of baseline security controls. As one might expect, applying the baseline security controls is not a small task. And this is a key document because one cannot have reasonable security measures without applying adequate security controls. Also, notice the large number of revisions, a testament to the ever-changing cybersecurity landscape.

> There is an urgent need to further strengthen the underlying information systems, component products, and services that the Nation depends on in every sector of the critical infrastructure— ensuring that those systems, components, and services are sufficiently trustworthy and provide the necessary resilience to support the economic and national security interests of the United States. This update to NIST Special Publication (SP) 800-53 responds to the call by the DSB by embarking on a proactive and systemic approach to develop and make available to a broad base of public and private sector organizations a comprehensive set of safeguarding measures for all types of computing platforms, including general purpose computing systems, cyber-physical systems, cloud-based systems, mobile devices, Internet of Things (IoT) devices, weapons systems, space systems, communications systems, environmental control systems, super computers, and industrial control systems. Those safeguarding measures include implementing security and privacy controls to protect the critical and essential operations and assets of organizations and the privacy of individuals. The objectives are to make the information systems we depend on more penetration-resistant, limit the damage from attacks when they occur, make the systems cyber-resilient and survivable, and protect individuals' privacy.[452]

SP 800-53A Revision 4: Assessing Security and Privacy Controls in Federal Information Systems and Organizations, Building Effective Assessment Plans

SP 800-53A, "a companion guideline to Special Publication 800-53," was "written to facilitate security control assessments and privacy control assessments conducted within and effective risk management framework."[453]

---

[452] SECURITY AND PRIVACY CONTROLS FOR INFORMATION SYSTEMS AND ORGANIZATIONS, NAT'L INST. OF STANDARDS AND TECH. (2020), *available at* https://nvlpubs.nist.gov/nistpubs/SpecialPublications/NIST.SP.800-53r5.pdf.

[453] ASSESSING SECURITY AND PRIVACY CONTROLS IN FEDERAL INFORMATION SYSTEMS AND ORGANIZATIONS: BUILDING EFFECTIVE ASSESSMENT PLANS, NAT'L INST. OF STANDARDS AND TECH. xi (2014), *available at* https://nvlpubs.nist.gov/nistpubs/SpecialPublications/NIST.SP.800-53Ar4.pdf.

Also, SP 800-53A "is designed to support Special Publication 800-37, *Guide for Applying the Risk Management Framework to Federal Information Systems: A Security Life Cycle Approach.*"[454]

As with SP 800-53, SP 80053A goes into great detail on how to assess. The figure below gives a condensed version.[455]

[454] *Id.* at 4.
[455] *Id.* at 28.

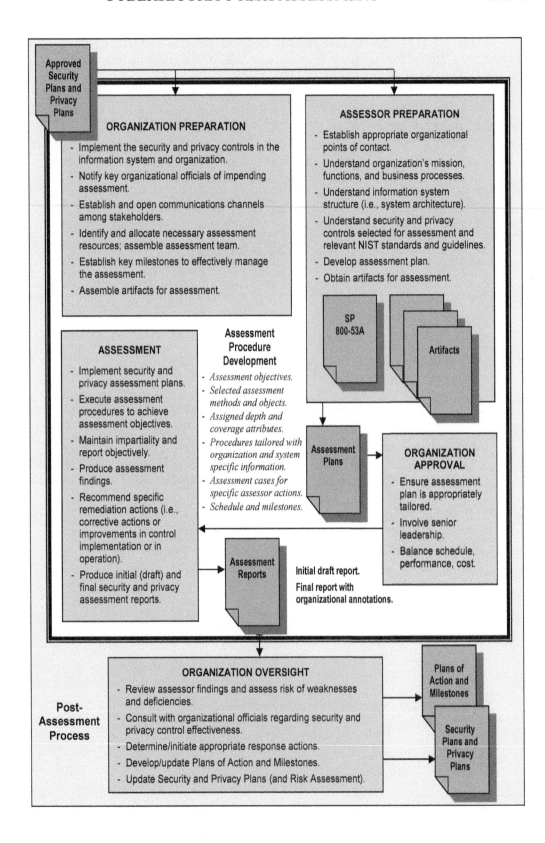

SP 800-59: Guideline for Identifying an Information System as a National Security System

This document provides guidelines developed in conjunction with the Department of Defense, including the National Security Agency, for identifying an information system as a national security system. The basis for these guidelines is the Federal Information Security Management Act of 2002 (FISMA, Title III, Public Law 107-347, December 17, 2002), which provides government-wide requirements for information security, superseding the Government Information Security Reform Act and the Computer Security Act.[456]

SP 800-60 Revision 1: Guide for Mapping Types of Information and Information Systems to Security Categories

The identification of information processed on an information system is essential to the proper selection of security controls and ensuring the confidentiality, integrity, and availability of the system and its information. The National Institute of Standards and Technology (NIST) Special Publication (SP) 800-60 has been developed to assist Federal government agencies to categorize information and information systems.[457]

SP 800-61 Revision 2: Computer Security Incident Handling Guide

The National Institute of Standards and Technology (NIST) has published the final version of its guide for managing computer security incidents. Based on best practices from government, academic and business organizations, this updated guide includes a new section expanding on the important practice of coordination and information sharing among agencies.

Government agencies face daily threats to their computer networks. The Federal Information Security Management Act requires government agencies to establish incident response competencies, and NIST researchers revised the guidance in *Computer Security Incident Handling Guide* to cover challenges related to today's evolving threats.

During the chaotic first minutes when a computer system is under attack, having a well-prepared incident response plan to follow ensures that

---

[456] GUIDELINE FOR IDENTIFYING AN INFORMATION SYSTEM AS A NATIONAL SECURITY SYSTEM, NAT'L INST. OF STANDARDS AND TECH. 1 (2003), *available at* https://nvlpubs.nist.gov/nistpubs/Legacy/SP/nistspecialpublication800-59.pdf.

[457] VOLUME I: GUIDE FOR MAPPING TYPES OF INFORMATION AND INFORMATION SYSTEMS TO SECURITY CATEGORIES, NAT'L INST. OF STANDARDS AND TECH. 1 (2008), *available at* https://nvlpubs.nist.gov/nistpubs/Legacy/SP/nistspecialpublication800-60v1r1.pdf.

steps such as alerting other agencies or law enforcement occur in the correct order.

The revised NIST guide provides step-by-step instructions for new, or well-established, incident response teams to create a proper policy and plan. NIST recommends that each plan should have a mission statement, strategies and goals, an organizational approach to incident response, metrics for measuring the response capability, and a built-in process for updating the plan as needed. The guide recommends reviewing each incident afterward to prepare for future attacks and to provide stronger protections of systems and data.

"This revised version encourages incident teams to think of the attack in three ways," explains co-author Tim Grance. "One is by method—what's happening and what needs to be fixed. Another is to consider an attack's impact by measuring how long the system was down, what type of information was stolen and what resources are required to recover from the incident. Finally, share information and coordination methods to help your team and others handle major incidents."

A draft version of the guide covered agencies sharing and coordinating information, but public comments called for more detailed information in this area, and the authors added a section on this topic to meet the requests. The guidance suggests that information about threats, attacks and vulnerabilities can be shared by trusted organizations before attacks so each organization can learn from others. By reaching out to the trusted group during an attack, one of the partners may recognize the unusual activity and make recommendations to quash the incident quickly. Also, some larger agencies with greater resources may be able to help a smaller agency respond to attacks.

The guide provides recommendations for agencies to consider before adding coordination and information sharing to the incident response plan, including how to determine what information is shared with other organizations and consulting with legal departments.[458]

Not all cybersecurity incidents are serious. Many cybersecurity incidents can easily be handled internally by the incident response team. But when a serious cybersecurity incident occurs, there are several outside sources that can be called for assistance. Those contacts and under what circumstances, and approvals to call should be contained in the incident response plan (IRP). Outside counsel could be one of those contacts. Local law enforcement, if they are equipped to handle cyber security incidents could be another. At a national and regional field-office level, the Secret Service and the

---

[458] COMPUTER SECURITY INCIDENT HANDLING GUIDE: RECOMMENDATIONS OF THE NATIONAL INSTITUTE OF STANDARDS AND TECHNOLOGY, NAT'L INST. OF STANDARDS AND TECH. (2012), *available at* http://nvlpubs.nist.gov/nistpubs/SpecialPublications/NIST.SP.800-61r2.pdf.

Federal Bureau of Investigation (FBI) can be valuable resources for cybersecurity incidents, and also for keeping informed on potential incident risks. As a cybersecurity in-house counsel, it would be advisable to build relationships with all of these resources and to understand under which circumstances each of these resources can be of assistance.

The Secret Service

The Secret Service can be a good resource to turn to for assistance after a cybersecurity incident:

> The U.S. Secret Service has a long and storied history of safeguarding America's financial and payment systems from criminal exploitation. The agency was created in 1865 to combat the rise of counterfeit currency following the Civil War. As the U.S. financial system has evolved - from paper currency to plastic credit cards to, now, digital information - so too have our investigative responsibilities.

> Today, Secret Service agents, professionals, and specialists work in field offices around the world to fight the 21st century's financial crimes, which are increasingly conducted through cyberspace. These investigations continue to address counterfeit, which still undermines confidence in the U.S. dollar, but it is credit card fraud, wire and bank fraud, computer network breaches, ransomware, and other cyber-enabled financial crimes, that have become the focus of much of the Secret Service investigative work.[459]

The FBI

As one might expect, the FBI has become heavily involved in a broad range of cybersecurity topics:

> Malicious cyber activity threatens the public's safety and our national and economic security. The FBI's goal is to change the behavior of criminals and nation-states who believe they can compromise U.S. networks, steal financial and intellectual property, and put critical infrastructure at risk without facing risk themselves. To do this, we use our unique mix of authorities, capabilities, and partnerships to impose consequences against our cyber adversaries.

> The FBI is the lead federal agency for investigating cyber attacks and intrusions. We collect and share intelligence and engage with victims

---

[459] *The Investigative Mission*, U. S. SECRET SERVICE, https://www.secretservice.gov/investigation/#menu-collapse-press (last visited Oct. 22, 2020).

while working to unmask those committing malicious cyber activities, wherever they are.[460]

The FBI is particularly focused on the following cybersecurity areas:

- **Business e-mail compromise (BEC)** scams exploit the fact that so many of us rely on e-mail to conduct business—both personal and professional—and it's one of the most financially damaging online crimes.

- **Identity theft** happens when someone steals your personal information, like your Social Security number, and uses it to commit theft or fraud.
- **Ransomware** is a type of malicious software, or malware, that prevents you from accessing your computer files, systems, or networks and demands you pay a ransom for their return.
- **Spoofing and phishing** are schemes aimed at tricking you into providing sensitive information to scammers.
- **Online predators** are a growing threat to young people.[461]

How the FBI is combating the cybersecurity threat:

Our adversaries look to exploit gaps in our intelligence and information security networks. The FBI is committed to working with our federal counterparts, our foreign partners, and the private sector to close those gaps.

These partnerships allow us to defend networks, attribute malicious activity, sanction bad behavior, and take the fight to our adversaries overseas. The FBI fosters this team approach through unique hubs where government, industry, and academia form long-term trusted relationships to combine efforts against cyber threats.

Within government, that hub is the National Cyber Investigative Joint Task Force (NCIJTF). The FBI leads this task force of more than 30 co-located agencies from the Intelligence Community and law enforcement. The NCIJTF is organized around mission centers based on key cyber threat areas and led by senior executives from partner agencies. Through these mission centers, operations and intelligence are integrated for maximum impact against U.S. adversaries.

---

[460] *The Cyber Threat*, FED. BUREAU OF INVESTIGATION, https://www.fbi.gov/investigate/cyber (last visited Oct. 22, 2020).
[461] *Id.*

Only together can we achieve safety, security, and confidence in a digitally connected world.[462]

The FBI's efforts in the cybersecurity area are extensive:

Whether through developing innovative investigative techniques, using cutting-edge analytic tools, or forging new partnerships in our communities, the FBI continues to adapt to meet the challenges posed by the evolving cyber threat.

- The FBI has specially trained cyber squads in each of our 56 field offices, working hand-in-hand with interagency task force partners.
- The rapid-response Cyber Action Team can deploy across the country within hours to respond to major incidents.
- With cyber assistant legal attachés in embassies across the globe, the FBI works closely with our international counterparts to seek justice for victims of malicious cyber activity.
- The Internet Crime Complaint Center (IC3) collects reports of Internet crime from the public. Using such complaints, the IC3's Recovery Asset Team has assisted in freezing hundreds of thousands of dollars for victims of cyber crime.
- CyWatch is the FBI's 24/7 operations center and watch floor, providing around-the-clock support to track incidents and communicate with field offices across the country.[463]

To gather complaints, the FBI maintains an Internet Crime Complaint Center (IC3):

The mission of the Internet Crime Complaint Center is to provide the public with a reliable and convenient reporting mechanism to submit information to the Federal Bureau of Investigation concerning suspected Internet-facilitated criminal activity and to develop effective alliances with law enforcement and industry partners. Information is analyzed and disseminated for investigative and intelligence purposes to law enforcement and for public awareness.

Since 2000, the IC3 has received complaints crossing the spectrum of cyber crime matters, to include online fraud in its many forms including Intellectual Property Rights (IPR) matters, Computer Intrusions (hacking), Economic Espionage (Theft of Trade Secrets), Online Extortion, International Money Laundering, Identity Theft, and a growing list of Internet facilitated crimes. It has become increasingly evident that, regardless of the label placed on a cyber crime matter, the

---

[462] *Id.*
[463] *Id.*

potential for it to overlap with another referred matter is substantial. Therefore, the IC3, formerly known as the Internet Fraud Complaint Center (Internet Fraud Complaint Center), was renamed in October 2003 to better reflect the broad character of such matters having an Internet, or cyber, nexus referred to the IC3, and to minimize the need for one to distinguish "Internet Fraud" from other potentially overlapping cyber crimes.[464]

The IC3 websites provides a web page for filing a complaint. But counsel should develop a relationship with the regional FBI cybersecurity agent so that counsel will have direct access during an incident. The agent can also be a good resource for keeping informed of potential cybersecurity risks. Indeed, the FBI encourages direct contact after a corporation has an incident.

SP 800-63-3: Digital Identity Guidelines

In today's connected society, most of us have at least one digital identity.

Digital identity is the online persona of a subject, and a single definition is widely debated internationally. The term persona is apropos as a subject can represent themselves online in many ways. An individual may have a digital identity for email, and another for personal finances. A personal laptop can be someone's streaming music server yet also be a worker-bot in a distributed network of computers performing complex genome calculations. Without context, it is difficult to land on a single definition that satisfies all.

Digital identity as a legal identity further complicates the definition and ability to use digital identities across a range of social and economic use cases. Digital identity is hard. Proving someone is who they say they are — especially remotely, via a digital service — is fraught with opportunities for an attacker to successfully impersonate someone. As correctly captured by Peter Steiner in The New Yorker, "On the internet, nobody knows you're a dog." These guidelines provide mitigations to the vulnerabilities inherent online, while recognizing and encouraging that when accessing some low-risk digital services, "being a dog" is just fine; while other, high-risk services need a level of confidence that the digital identity accessing the service is the legitimate proxy to the real-life subject.[465]

This recommendation and its companion volumes, Special Publication (SP) 800-63A, SP 800- 63B, and SP 800-63C, provide

---

[464] *Internet Crime Complaint Center (IC3)*, FED. BUREAU OF INVESTIGATION, https://www.ic3.gov/Home/About (last visited Oct. 25, 2020).
[465] https://nvlpubs.nist.gov/nistpubs/SpecialPublications/NIST.SP.800-63-3.pdf at iv.

technical guidelines to agencies for the implementation of digital authentication.[466]

SP 800-88 Revision 1: Guidelines for Media Sanitization

Transactional attorneys will likely be asked at some point in their work to review a contract that asks for compliance with this NIST document, especially if the entity collects or processes sensitive data.

This document will assist organizations in implementing a media sanitization program with proper and applicable techniques and controls for sanitization and disposal decisions, considering the security categorization of the associated system's confidentiality.

The objective of this special publication is to assist with decision making when media require disposal, reuse, or will be leaving the effective control of an organization. Organizations should develop and use local policies and procedures in conjunction with this guide to make effective, risk-based decisions on the ultimate sanitization and/or disposition of media and information.

The information in this guide is best applied in the context of current technology and applications. It also provides guidance for information disposition, sanitization, and control decisions to be made throughout the system life cycle. Forms of media exist that are not addressed by this guide, and media are yet to be developed and deployed that are not covered by this guide. In those cases, the intent of this guide outlined in the procedures section applies to all forms of media based on the evaluated security categorization of the system's confidentiality according to FIPS 199.[467]

SP 800-122: Guide to Protecting the Confidentiality of Personally Identifiable Information (PII)

Sometimes you might see contract language that has a requirement to protect the security and privacy of data. The attorney or contract manager who wrote that phrase does not understand the difference between cybersecurity and privacy. Data does not have privacy concerns. Data doesn't have to worry about identity theft. Data doesn't have a credit score or a bank account. People do. People must worry about privacy and identity theft. The concern for data is security. Because without data security, there will be no privacy.

The escalation of security breaches involving personally identifiable information (PII) has contributed to the loss of millions of records over the past few years. Breaches involving PII are hazardous to

---

[466] *Id.* at 1.

[467] https://nvlpubs.nist.gov/nistpubs/SpecialPublications/NIST.SP.800-88r1.pdf at 1.

both individuals and organizations. Individual harms may include identity theft, embarrassment, or blackmail. Organizational harms may include a loss of public trust, legal liability, or remediation costs. To appropriately protect the confidentiality of PII, organizations should use a risk-based approach; as McGeorge Bundy once stated, ―If we guard our toothbrushes and diamonds with equal zeal, we will lose fewer toothbrushes and more diamonds. This document provides guidelines for a risk-based approach to protecting the confidentiality of PII. The recommendations in this document are intended primarily for U.S. Federal government agencies and those who conduct business on behalf of the agencies, but other organizations may find portions of the publication useful. Each organization may be subject to a different combination of laws, regulations, and other mandates related to protecting PII, so an organization‘s legal counsel and privacy officer should be consulted to determine the current obligations for PII protection. For example, the Office of Management and Budget (OMB) has issued several memoranda with requirements for how Federal agencies must handle and protect PII. To effectively protect PII, organizations should implement the following recommendations.

Organizations should identify all PII residing in their environment.

An organization cannot properly protect PII it does not know about. This document uses a broad definition of PII to identify as many potential sources of PII as possible (e.g., databases, shared network drives, backup tapes, contractor sites). PII is ―any information about an individual maintained by an agency, including (1) any information that can be used to distinguish or trace an individual‘s identity, such as name, social security number, date and place of birth, mother‘s maiden name, or biometric records; and (2) any other information that is linked or linkable to an individual, such as medical, educational, financial, and employment information. Examples of PII include, but are not limited to:

- Name, such as full name, maiden name, mother‘s maiden name, or alias

- Personal identification number, such as social security number (SSN), passport number, driver‘s license number, taxpayer identification number, or financial account or credit card number

- Address information, such as street address or email address

- Personal characteristics, including photographic image (especially of face or other identifying characteristic), fingerprints, handwriting, or other biometric data (e.g., retina scan, voice signature, facial geometry)

- Information about an individual that is linked or linkable to one of the above (e.g., date of birth, place of birth, race, religion, weight, activities, geographical indicators, employment information, medical information, education information, financial information).

Organizations should minimize the use, collection, and retention of PII to what is strictly necessary to accomplish their business purpose and mission.

The likelihood of harm caused by a breach involving PII is greatly reduced if an organization minimizes the amount of PII it uses, collects, and stores. For example, an organization should only request PII in a new form if the PII is absolutely necessary. Also, an organization should regularly review its holdings of previously collected PII to determine whether the PII is still relevant and necessary for meeting the organization's business purpose and mission. For example, organizations could have an annual PII purging awareness day.7

OMB M-07-16 specifically requires agencies to:

- Review current holdings of PII and ensure they are accurate, relevant, timely, and complete

- Reduce PII holdings to the minimum necessary for proper performance of agency functions

- Develop a schedule for periodic review of PII holdings

- Establish a plan to eliminate the unnecessary collection and use of SSNs.

Organizations should categorize their PII by the PII confidentiality impact level.

All PII is not created equal. PII should be evaluated to determine its PII confidentiality impact level, which is different from the Federal Information Processing Standard (FIPS) Publication 199 confidentiality impact level, so that appropriate safeguards can be applied to the PII. The PII confidentiality impact level—low, moderate, or high—indicates the potential harm that could result to the subject individuals and/or the organization if PII were inappropriately accessed, used, or disclosed. This document provides a list of factors an organization should consider when determining the PII confidentiality impact level. Each organization should decide which factors it will use for determining impact levels and then create and implement the appropriate policy, procedures, and controls. The following are examples of factors:

- Identifiability. Organizations should evaluate how easily PII can be used to identify specific individuals. For example, a SSN uniquely and directly identifies an individual, whereas a telephone area code identifies a set of people.

- Quantity of PII. Organizations should consider how many individuals can be identified from the PII. Breaches of 25 records and 25 million records may have different impacts. The PII confidentiality impact level should only be raised and not lowered based on this factor.

- Data Field Sensitivity. Organizations should evaluate the sensitivity of each individual PII data field. For example, an individual's SSN or financial account number is generally more sensitive than an individual's phone number or ZIP code. Organizations should also evaluate the sensitivity of the PII data fields when combined.

- Context of Use. Organizations should evaluate the context of use—the purpose for which the PII is collected, stored, used, processed, disclosed, or disseminated. The context of use may cause the same PII data elements to be assigned different PII confidentiality impact levels based on their use. For example, suppose that an organization has two lists that contain the same PII data fields (e.g., name, address, phone number). The first list is people who subscribe to a general-interest newsletter produced by the organization, and the second list is people who work undercover in law enforcement. If the confidentiality of the lists is breached, the potential impacts to the affected individuals and to the organization are significantly different for each list.

- Obligations to Protect Confidentiality. An organization that is subject to any obligations to protect PII should consider such obligations when determining the PII confidentiality impact level. Obligations to protect generally include laws, regulations, or other mandates (e.g., Privacy Act, OMB guidance). For example, some Federal agencies, such as the Census Bureau and the Internal Revenue Service (IRS), are subject to specific legal obligations to protect certain types of PII.

- Access to and Location of PII. Organizations may choose to take into consideration the nature of authorized access to and the location of PII. When PII is accessed more often or by more people and systems, or the PII is regularly transmitted or transported offsite, then there are more opportunities to compromise the confidentiality of the PII.

Organizations should apply the appropriate safeguards for PII based on the PII confidentiality impact level.

Not all PII should be protected in the same way. Organizations should apply appropriate safeguards to protect the confidentiality of PII based on the PII confidentiality impact level. Some PII does not need to have its confidentiality protected, such as information that the organization has permission or authority to release publicly (e.g., an organization's public phone directory). NIST recommends using operational safeguards, privacy-specific safeguards, and security controls, such as:

- Creating Policies and Procedures. Organizations should develop comprehensive policies and procedures for protecting the confidentiality of PII.

- Conducting Training. Organizations should reduce the possibility that PII will be accessed, used, or disclosed inappropriately by requiring that all individuals receive appropriate training before being granted access to systems containing PII.

- De-Identifying PII. Organizations can de-identify records by removing enough PII such that the remaining information does not identify an individual and there is no reasonable basis to believe that the information can be used to identify an individual. De-identified records can be used when full records are not necessary, such as for examinations of correlations and trends.

- Using Access Enforcement. Organizations can control access to PII through access control policies and access enforcement mechanisms (e.g., access control lists).

- Implementing Access Control for Mobile Devices. Organizations can prohibit or strictly limit access to PII from portable and mobile devices, such as laptops, cell phones, and personal digital assistants (PDA), which are generally higher-risk than non-portable devices (e.g., desktop computers at the organization's facilities).

- Providing Transmission Confidentiality. Organizations can protect the confidentiality of transmitted PII. This is most often accomplished by encrypting the communications or by encrypting the information before it is transmitted.

- Auditing Events. Organizations can monitor events that affect the confidentiality of PII, such as inappropriate access to PII.

Organizations should develop an incident response plan to handle breaches involving PII.

Breaches involving PII are hazardous to both individuals and organizations. Harm to individuals and organizations can be contained and minimized through the development of effective incident response plans for breaches involving PII. Organizations should develop plans that include elements such as determining when and how individuals should be notified, how a breach should be reported, and whether to provide remedial services, such as credit monitoring, to affected individuals.

Organizations should encourage close coordination among their chief privacy officers, senior agency officials for privacy, chief information officers, chief information security officers, and legal counsel when addressing issues related to PII.

Protecting the confidentiality of PII requires knowledge of information systems, information security, privacy, and legal requirements. Decisions regarding the applicability of a particular law, regulation, or other mandate should be made in consultation with an organization's legal counsel and privacy officer because relevant laws, regulations, and other mandates are often complex and change over time. Additionally, new policies often require the implementation of technical security controls to enforce the policies. Close coordination of the relevant experts helps to prevent incidents that could result in the compromise and misuse of PII by ensuring proper interpretation and implementation of requirements.[468]

SP 800-128: Guide for Security-Focused Configuration Management of Information Systems

Organizations apply configuration management (CM) for establishing baselines and for tracking, controlling, and managing many aspects of business development and operation (e.g., products, services, manufacturing, business processes, and information technology). Organizations with a robust and effective CM process need to consider information security implications with respect to the development and operation of systems including hardware, software, applications, and documentation. Effective CM of systems requires the integration of the management of secure configurations into the organizational CM process or processes. For this reason, this document assumes that information security is an integral part of an organization's overall CM process; however, the focus of this document is on implementation of the information security aspects of CM, and as such the term *security-focused configuration management* (SecCM) is used to emphasize the concentration on information security. Though both IT business application functions and security-focused practices are expected to be integrated as a single process, *SecCM* in this context is defined as the management and control of configurations for systems to enable security and facilitate the management of information security risk.[469]

---

[468] https://nvlpubs.nist.gov/nistpubs/Legacy/SP/nistspecialpublication800-122.pdf at ES 1-4.
[469] GUIDE FOR SECURITY-FOCUSED CONFIGURATION MANAGEMENT OF INFORMATION SYSTEMS, NAT'L INST. OF STANDARDS AND TECH. 1 (2011), *available at* https://nvlpubs.nist.gov/nistpubs/SpecialPublications/NIST.SP.800-128.pdf.

Information security configuration management requirements are integrated into (or complement) existing organizational configuration management processes (e.g., business functions, applications, products) and information systems. SecCM activities include:

- identification and recording of configurations that impact the security posture of the system and the organization;

- the consideration of security risks in approving the initial configuration;

- the analysis of security implications of changes to the system configuration; and

- documentation of the approved/implemented changes.[470]

Security-focused configuration management of systems involves a set of activities that can be organized into four major phases: Planning; Identifying and Implementing Configurations; Controlling Configuration Changes; and Monitoring. It is through these phases that SecCM not only supports security for a system and its components, but also supports the management of organizational risk. Chapter 3 presents the detailed processes and considerations in implementing the necessary activities in each of these phases.

The four phases of SecCM are illustrated in Figure 2-1 and described below.[471]

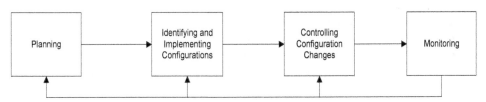

Figure 2-1 – Security-focused Configuration Management Phases

SP 800-137: Information Security Continuous Monitoring (ISCM) for Federal Information Systems and Organizations

Information security continuous monitoring (ISCM) is defined as maintaining ongoing awareness of information security, vulnerabilities, and threats to support organizational risk management decisions. This publication specifically addresses assessment and analysis of security control effectiveness and of organizational security status in accordance with organizational risk tolerance. Security control effectiveness is measured by correctness of implementation and by how adequately the

---

[470] *Id.* at 6.
[471] *Id.* at 7.

implemented controls meet organizational needs in accordance with current risk tolerance (i.e., is the control implemented in accordance with the security plan to address threats and is the security plan adequate). Organizational security status is determined using metrics established by the organization to best convey the security posture of an organization's information and information systems, along with organizational resilience given known threat information. This necessitates:

- Maintaining situational awareness of all systems across the organization;

- Maintaining an understanding of threats and threat activities;

- Assessing all security controls;

- Collecting, correlating, and analyzing security-related information;

- Providing actionable communication of security status across all tiers of the organization; and

- Active management of risk by organizational officials.[472]

SP 800-137A: Assessing Information Security Continuous Monitoring (ISCM) Programs: Developing an ISCM Program Assessment

This publication:

- Offers guidance on the development of an ISCM program assessment process for all organizational risk management levels, i.e., as defined in NIST SP 800-39, *Managing Information Security Risk: Organization, Mission, and Information System View;*

- Describes how an ISCM program assessment relates to important security concepts and processes, such as the NIST Risk Management Framework (RMF), organization-wide risk management levels, organizational governance, metrics applicable to ISCM, and ongoing authorization;

- Describes the properties of an effective ISCM program assessment;

- Presents a set of ISCM program assessment criteria, with references to the sources from which the criteria are derived, that can be adopted by an organization and used for ISCM program assessments or as a

---

[472] INFORMATION SECURITY CONTINUOUS MONITORING (ISCM) FOR FEDERAL INFORMATION SYSTEMS AND ORGANIZATIONS, NAT'L INST. OF STANDARDS AND TECH. (2011), *available at* https://nvlpubs.nist.gov/nistpubs/Legacy/SP/nistspecialpublication800-137.pdf.

starting point for further development of an organization's assessment criteria; and

- Defines a way to conduct ISCM program assessments by using assessment procedures defined in the companion document containing the ISCM Program Assessment Element Catalog and designed to produce a repeatable assessment process.[473]

SP 800-144: Guidelines on Security and Privacy in Public Cloud Computing

Most companies host a least a portion of their business in the cloud because of the efficiencies of doing so. If you are using a SaaS based subscription and you are a single subscriber, you probably don't have any room for negotiating the security of the cloud provider. But if you are a large company customer, you may have some leverage in asking for security additional security controls and audits. Either way reputable cloud providers understand that security is part of their brand and make those security document available for potential customers to review. We suggest you always do that due diligence because your customers will expect you to do so for them if not for yourself. And don't be surprised if you customer asks you if your company complies with SP 800-144. That is easy short-hand for the customer's attorney to take advantage of.

The key guidelines from the report are summarized and listed below and are recommended to federal departments and agencies.

Carefully plan the security and privacy aspects of cloud computing solutions before engaging them.

Public cloud computing represents a significant paradigm shift from the conventional norms of an organizational data center to a deperimeterized infrastructure open to use by potential adversaries. As with any emerging information technology area, cloud computing should be approached carefully with due consideration to the sensitivity of data. Planning helps to ensure that the computing environment is as secure as possible and in compliance with all relevant organizational policies and that privacy is maintained. It also helps to ensure that the agency derives full benefit from information technology spending.

The security objectives of an organization are a key factor for decisions about outsourcing information technology services and, in particular, for decisions about transitioning organizational data, applications, and other resources to a public cloud computing environment. Organizations should take a risk-based approach in analyzing available security and privacy options and deciding about placing organizational functions into a cloud

---

[473] ASSESSING INFORMATION SECURITY CONTINUOUS MONITORING (ISCM) PROGRAMS: DEVELOPING AN ISCM PROGRAM ASSESSMENT, NAT'L INST. OF STANDARDS AND TECH. v (2020), *available at* https://nvlpubs.nist.gov/nistpubs/SpecialPublications/NIST.SP.800-137A.pdf.

environment. The information technology governance practices of the organizations that pertain to the policies, procedures, and standards used for application development and service provisioning, as well as the design, implementation, testing, use, and monitoring of deployed or engaged services, should be extended to cloud computing environments.

To maximize effectiveness and minimize costs, security and privacy must be considered throughout the system lifecycle from the initial planning stage forward. Attempting to address security and privacy issues after implementation and deployment is not only much more difficult and expensive, but also exposes the organization to unnecessary risk.

Understand the public cloud computing environment offered by the cloud provider.

The responsibilities of both the organization and the cloud provider vary depending on the service model. Organizations consuming cloud services must understand the delineation of responsibilities over the computing environment and the implications for security and privacy. Assurances furnished by the cloud provider to support security or privacy claims, or by a certification and compliance review entity paid by the cloud provider, should be verified whenever possible through independent assessment by the organization.

Understanding the policies, procedures, and technical controls used by a cloud provider is a prerequisite to assessing the security and privacy risks involved. It is also important to comprehend the technologies used to provision services and the implications for security and privacy of the system. Details about the system architecture of a cloud can be analyzed and used to formulate a complete picture of the protection afforded by the security and privacy controls, which improves the ability of the organization to assess and manage risk accurately, including mitigating risk by employing appropriate techniques and procedures for the continuous monitoring of the security state of the system.

Ensure that a cloud computing solution satisfies organizational security and privacy requirements.

Public cloud providers' default offerings generally do not reflect a specific organization's security and privacy needs. From a risk perspective, determining the suitability of cloud services requires an understanding of the context in which the organization operates and the consequences from the plausible threats it faces. Adjustments to the cloud computing environment may be warranted to meet an organization's requirements. Organizations should require that any selected public cloud computing solution is configured, deployed, and managed to meet their security, privacy, and other requirements.

Non-negotiable service agreements in which the terms of service are prescribed completely by the cloud provider are generally the norm in public cloud computing. Negotiated service agreements are also possible. Similar to traditional information technology outsourcing contracts used by agencies, negotiated agreements can address an organization's concerns about security and privacy details, such as the vetting of employees, data ownership and exit rights, breach notification, isolation of tenant applications, data encryption and segregation, tracking and reporting service effectiveness, compliance with laws and regulations, and the use of validated products meeting federal or national standards (e.g., Federal Information Processing Standard 140). A negotiated agreement can also document the assurances the cloud provider must furnish to corroborate that organizational requirements are being met.

Critical data and applications may require an agency to undertake a negotiated service agreement in order to use a public cloud. Points of negotiation can negatively affect the economies of scale that a non-negotiable service agreement brings to public cloud computing, however, making a negotiated agreement less cost effective. As an alternative, the organization may be able to employ compensating controls to work around identified shortcomings in the public cloud service. Other alternatives include cloud computing environments with a more suitable deployment model, such as an internal private cloud, which can potentially offer an organization greater oversight and authority over security and privacy, and better limit the types of tenants that share platform resources, reducing exposure in the event of a failure or configuration error in a control.

With the growing number of cloud providers and range of services from which to choose, organizations must exercise due diligence when selecting and moving functions to the cloud. Decision making about services and service arrangements entails striking a balance between benefits in cost and productivity versus drawbacks in risk and liability. While the sensitivity of data handled by government organizations and the current state of the art make the likelihood of outsourcing all information technology services to a public cloud low, it should be possible for most government organizations to deploy some of their information technology services to a public cloud, provided that all requisite risk mitigations are taken.

Ensure that the client-side computing environment meets organizational security and privacy requirements for cloud computing.

Cloud computing encompasses both a server and a client side. With emphasis typically placed on the former, the latter can be easily overlooked. Services from different cloud providers, as well as cloud-based applications developed by the organization, can impose more exacting demands on the client, which may have implications for security and privacy that need to be taken into consideration.

Because of their ubiquity, Web browsers are a key element for client-side access to cloud computing services. Clients may also entail small lightweight applications that run on desktop and mobile devices to access services. The various available plug-ins and extensions for Web browsers are notorious for their security problems. Many browser add-ons also do not provide automatic updates, increasing the persistence of any existing vulnerabilities. Similar problems exist for other types of clients.

Maintaining physical and logical security over clients can be troublesome, especially with embedded mobile devices such as smart phones. Their size and portability can result in the loss of physical control. Built-in security mechanisms often go unused or can be overcome or circumvented without difficulty by a knowledgeable party to gain control over the device. Moreover, cloud applications are often delivered to them through custom-built native applications (i.e., apps) rather than a Web browser.

The growing availability and use of social media, personal Webmail, and other publicly available sites are a concern, since they increasingly serve as avenues for social engineering attacks that can negatively impact the security of the client, its underlying platform, and cloud services accessed. Having a backdoor Trojan, keystroke logger, or other type of malware running on a client device undermines the security and privacy of public cloud services as well as other Internet-facing public services accessed. As part of the overall cloud computing security architecture, organizations should review existing security and privacy measures and employ additional ones, if necessary, to secure the client side.

Maintain accountability over the privacy and security of data and applications implemented and deployed in public cloud computing environments.

Organizations should employ appropriate security management practices and controls over cloud computing. Strong management practices are essential for operating and maintaining a secure cloud computing solution. Security and privacy practices entail monitoring the organization's information system assets and assessing the implementation of policies, standards, procedures, controls, and guidelines that are used to establish and preserve the confidentiality, integrity, and availability of information system resources.

The organization should collect and analyze available data about the state of the system regularly and as often as needed to manage security and privacy risks, as appropriate for each level of the organization (i.e., governance level, mission or business process level, and information systems level) [Dem10]. Continuous monitoring of information security requires maintaining ongoing awareness of privacy and security controls, vulnerabilities, and threats to support risk management decisions. The goal is to conduct ongoing monitoring of the security of an organization's networks, information, and systems, and to respond by accepting, avoiding, or mitigating risk as situations change.

Assessing and managing risk in cloud computing systems can be a challenge, since significant portions of the computing environment are under the control of the cloud provider and may likely be beyond the organization's purview. Both qualitative and quantitative factors apply in a risk analysis. Risks must be carefully weighed against the available technical, management, and operational safeguards and the necessary steps must be taken to reduce risk to an acceptable level. The organization must also ensure that security and privacy controls are implemented correctly, operate as intended, and meet organizational requirements.

Establishing a level of confidence about a cloud service environment depends on the ability of the cloud provider to provision the security controls necessary to protect the organization's data and applications, and also the evidence provided about the effectiveness of those controls [JTF10]. Verifying the correct functioning of a subsystem and the effectiveness of security controls as extensively as with an internal organizational system may not be feasible in some cases, however, and other factors such as third-party audits may be used to establish a level of trust. Ultimately, if the level of confidence in the service falls below expectations and the organization is unable to employ compensating controls, it must either reject the service or accept a greater degree of risk.

Cloud computing depends on the security of many individual components. Besides components for general computing, there are also components that the management backplane comprises, such as those for self-service, resource metering, quota management, data replication and recovery, service level monitoring, and workload management. Many of the simplified interfaces and service abstractions afforded by cloud computing belie the inherent underlying complexity that affects security. Organizations should ensure to the maximum extent practicable that all cloud computing elements are secure and that security and privacy are maintained based on sound computing practices, including those outlined in Federal Information Processing Standards (FIPS) and NIST Special Publications (SP).[474]

SP 800-160 Vol. 1: Systems Security Engineering: Considerations for a Multidisciplinary Approach in the Engineer of Trustworthy Secure Systems

---

[474] https://nvlpubs.nist.gov/nistpubs/Legacy/SP/nistspecialpublication800-144.pdf at vi-x.

After four years of research and development, NIST has published a groundbreaking new security guideline that addresses the longstanding problem of how to engineer trustworthy, secure systems—systems that can provide continuity of capabilities, functions, services, and operations during a wide range of disruptions, threats, and other hazards. In fact, I think that Special Publication 800-160, Systems Security Engineering, is the most important publication that I have been associated with in my two decades of service with NIST.

I want to share what led me to this conclusion.

The Current Landscape

The United States, and every other industrialized nation, is experiencing explosive growth in information technology. These technological innovations have given us access to computing and communications capabilities unparalleled in the history of mankind.

These rapid advancements, and the dramatic growth in consumer demand for them, are occurring alongside a revolutionary convergence of cyber and physical systems, or cyber-physical systems (CPS). The worldwide distribution of these technologies has resulted in a highly complex information technology infrastructure of systems and networks that are difficult to understand and even more difficult to protect.

Today, we are spending more on cybersecurity than ever before. At the same time, we are witnessing an increasing number of successful cyberattacks by nation states, terrorists, hacktivists, and other bad actors who are stealing our intellectual property, national secrets, and private information. Unless we make some kind of radical change to the way we think about and fight these attacks, they are going to have an increasingly debilitating—and potentially disastrous—effect on the economic and national security interests of the United States.

The Basic Problem Is Simple

Our fundamental cybersecurity problem can be summed up in three words—*too much complexity*. There are simply too many bases—all the software, firmware, and hardware components that we rely on to run our critical infrastructure, business, and industrial systems—for us to cover as it is, and we're adding to the number of bases all the time.

Increased complexity translates to increased *attack surface*—providing adversaries a limitless opportunity to exploit vulnerabilities resulting from inherent weaknesses and deficiencies in the components of the underlying systems that we have built and deployed. We can characterize this predicament as the *N+1 vulnerabilities problem*.

According to the Defense Science Board 2013 study done for the U.S. military, there are vulnerabilities that are known; those that are unknown; and those created by your adversaries after they have taken control of your system. Given this reality, there are vulnerabilities that we can find and fix, and a growing number of vulnerabilities that we cannot detect and therefore, remain unmitigated.

While we are making significant improvements in our reactive security measures, including intrusion detection and response capabilities, those measures fail to address the fundamental weaknesses in system architecture and design. These weaknesses can only be addressed with a holistic approach based on sound systems security engineering techniques and security design principles. This holistic approach will make our systems more penetration-resistant; capable of limiting the damage from disruptions, hazards, and threats; and sufficiently resilient so they can continue to support critical missions and business functions after they are compromised.

Engineering-Based Solutions

We have a high degree of confidence our bridges and airplanes are safe and structurally sound. We trust those technologies because we know that they were designed and built by applying the basic laws of physics, principles of mathematics, and concepts of engineering. If bridges were routinely collapsing and airplanes were frequently crashing, the first people we would call would be the scientists and engineers. They would do root-cause failure analysis, find out what went wrong, and fix the problem.

Cybersecurity efforts today are largely focused on what is commonly referred to as "cyber hygiene." Cyber hygiene includes such activities as inventorying hardware and software assets; configuring firewalls and other commercial products; scanning for vulnerabilities; patching systems; and monitoring.

While practicing good cyber hygiene is certainly necessary, it's not enough. This is because these activities don't affect the basic architecture and design of the system. Even if we were to achieve perfection above the water line, we would still be leaving our most critical systems highly vulnerable due to our inability to manage and reduce the complexity of the technology.

The only way to address the N+1 vulnerabilities problem is to incorporate well-defined engineering-based security design principles at every level, from the physical to the virtual. These principles should be driven by mission and business objectives, stakeholder protection needs, and security requirements of the individual organization. While those solutions may not be appropriate in every situation, they should be available to those entities that are critical to the economic and national security interests of the United States including, for example, the electric grid, manufacturing facilities, financial institutions, transportation vehicles, medical devices, water treatment plants, and military systems.

A National Strategy Focused on Trustworthy Systems

Today, the cybersecurity threats to our government, businesses, critical infrastructure, industrial base, and people are as severe as threats of terrorism or the threats we experienced during the Cold War.

Overcoming these threats will require a significant investment of resources and the involvement of government, industry, and the academic community. It will take a concerted effort on a level we haven't seen since President Kennedy dared us to do the impossible and put a man on the moon over a half-century ago.

We can do it again, but the clock is ticking and the time is short. Creating more trustworthy, secure systems requires a holistic view of the problems, the application of concepts, principles, and best practices of science and engineering to solve those problems, and the leadership and will to do the right thing—even when such actions may not be popular.

I think that NIST Special Publication 800-160 is the first step we need to take toward securing the things that matter to us. It will be a grand challenge, but we Americans have a long history of achieving the impossible.[475]

SP 800-171Revision 2: Protecting Controlled Unclassified Information in Nonfederal Systems and Organizations

The purpose of this publication is to provide federal agencies with recommended security requirements for protecting the *confidentiality* of CUI: (1) when the CUI is resident in a nonfederal system and organization; (2) when the nonfederal organization is *not* collecting or maintaining information on behalf of a federal agency or using or operating a system on behalf of an agency; and (3) where there are no specific safeguarding requirements for protecting the confidentiality of CUI prescribed by the authorizing law, regulation, or governmentwide policy for the CUI category listed in the CUI Registry. The requirements

---

[475] Ron Ross, *Rethinking Cybersecurity from the Inside Out*, NAT'L INST. OF STANDARDS AND TECH. (Nov. 15, 2016), https://www.nist.gov/blogs/taking-measure/rethinking-cybersecurity-inside-out.

apply *only* to components of nonfederal systems that process, store, or transmit CUI, or that provide security protection for such components. The requirements are intended for use by federal agencies in appropriate contractual vehicles or other agreements established between those agencies and nonfederal organizations. In CUI guidance and the CUI Federal Acquisition Regulation (FAR), the CUI Executive Agent will address determining compliance with security requirements.[476]

NOTES

Note 1

A group of cybersecurity experts has argued that the NIST Cybersecurity Framework has the potential to serve as the basis of the standard of care in determining whether a cybersecurity breach has occurred. *See* Scott J. Shackelford, Andrew A. Proia, Brenton Martell and Amanda N. Craig, *Toward a Global Cybersecurity Standard of Care? Exploring the Implications of the 2014 NIST Cybersecurity Framework on Shaping Reasonable National and International Cybersecurity Practices*, 50 Tex. Int'l L. J. 305 (2015). The authors state:

> Overall, a critical infrastructure organization could be found to have acted negligently if it is determined that (1) the critical infrastructure organization suffered a cyber attack that resulted in damage or injury; (2) the organization failed to utilize the Framework to address and manage its cybersecurity risks; (3) the Framework is deemed an adequate precaution that, if implemented, would have prevented the harm; and (4) the burden on an organization to utilize the Framework was less than the probability that the cybersecurity incident would occur multiplied by the significance of the incident. *Id.* at 342.

Note 2

President Obama signed the Cybersecurity Information Sharing Act (CISA) in 2015, which encourages private industry to share cybersecurity breach information with the government. For more information on CISA's main features, please see John Heidenreich, *In The Privacy Issues Presented by the Cybersecurity Information Sharing Act*, 91 N.D. L. REV. 395 (2016) (discussing the need for "timely sharing" of information amongst government agencies and private industry).

Note 3

The Cybersecurity and Infrastructure Security Agency [CISA] website states:

---

[476] PROTECTING CONTROLLED UNCLASSIFIED INFORMATION IN NONFEDERAL SYSTEMS AND ORGANIZATIONS, NAT'L INST. OF STANDARDS AND TECH. 2 (2020), *available at* https://nvlpubs.nist.gov/nistpubs/SpecialPublications/NIST.SP.800-171r2.pdf.

[CISA] is the Nation's risk advisor, working with partners to defend against today's threats and collaborating to build more secure and resilient infrastructure for the future. . . .

CISA is at the heart of mobilizing a collective defense as we lead the Nation's efforts to understand and manage risk to our critical infrastructure.

Our partners in this mission span the public and private sectors. Programs and services we provide are driven by our comprehensive understanding of the risk environment and the corresponding needs identified by our stakeholders. We seek to help organizations better manage risk and increase resilience using all available resources, whether provided by the Federal Government, commercial vendors, or their own capabilities.

CISA builds the national capacity to defend against cyber attacks and works with the federal government to provide cybersecurity tools, incident response services and assessment capabilities to safeguard the '.gov' networks that support the essential operations of partner departments and agencies.

We coordinate security and resilience efforts using trusted partnerships across the private and public sectors, and deliver technical assistance and assessments to federal stakeholders as well as to infrastructure owners and operators nationwide.

CISA enhances public safety interoperable communications at all levels of government to help partners across the country develop their emergency communications capabilities.

Working with stakeholders across the country, CISA conducts extensive, nationwide outreach to support and promote the ability of emergency response providers and relevant government officials to continue to communicate in the event of a natural disaster, act of terrorism, or other man-made disaster.

The National Risk Management Center (NRMC) is housed within the Cybersecurity and Infrastructure Security Agency (CISA). NRMC is a planning, analysis, and collaboration center working to identify and address the most significant risks to our nation's critical infrastructure.

NRMC works in close coordination with the private sector and other key stakeholders in the critical infrastructure community to: Identify; Analyze; Prioritize; and Manage the most strategic risks to our National Critical Functions—the functions of government and the private sector so vital to the United States that their disruption, corruption, or dysfunction would have a debilitating impact on security, national economic security, national public health or safety, or any combination. [477]

QUESTION

Why would a company hesitate to share cybersecurity information?

---

[477] *About CISA*, CYBERSECURITY AND INFRASTRUCTURE SEC. AGENCY, https://www.cisa.gov/about-cisa (last visited Oct. 22, 2020).

CHAPTER ELEVEN. LAWS PROHIBITING AND ADDRESSING HACKING

11.1 Introduction

This chapter explores some laws related to the unauthorized access to computers, including the circumvention of technological measures to protect certain types of information. The chapter primarily analyzes the federal Computer Fraud and Abuse Act (CFAA) and the similar California Comprehensive Computer Data Access and Fraud Act and Washington Cybercrime Act. The federal Stored Communications Act and trade secret law is briefly reviewed as well as the Digital Millennium Copyright Act's provisions on anti-circumvention. A common set of facts could result in a violation of the provisions of several of the aforementioned laws.

11.2 Federal Computer Fraud and Abuse Act

The federal Computer Fraud and Abuse Act was passed in 1986. Since its passage, it has been amended multiple times. The substance of the CFAA is numerous potential violations mostly concerning the unauthorized access to protected computers. The law is principally criminal in nature, but also includes civil causes of action. The penalties for violation of the criminal provisions may include prison sentences and fines. A violation of the civil causes of action may result in injunctive relief and damages. The CFAA provides that conspiracy or attempt to violate one of the prohibited actions is also penalized. The CFAA defines the terms "computer" and "protected computer" in 18 U.S.C. section 1030(3)(1)&(2), respectively, as follows:

> (1) the term "computer" means an electronic, magnetic, optical, electrochemical, or other high speed data processing device performing logical, arithmetic, or storage functions, and includes any data storage facility or communications facility directly related to or operating in conjunction with such device, but such term does not include an automated typewriter or typesetter, a portable hand held calculator, or other similar device;

> (2) the term "protected computer" means a computer--

> (A) exclusively for the use of a financial institution or the United States Government, or, in the case of a computer not exclusively for such use, used by or for a financial institution or the United States Government and the conduct constituting the offense affects that use by or for the financial institution or the Government; or

> (B) which is used in or affecting interstate or foreign commerce or communication, including a computer located outside the United States

that is used in a manner that affects interstate or foreign commerce or communication of the United States;

The definition of a protected computer is quite broad in subsection (2)(B) and for the most part is limited only by the Congressional jurisdictional requirement of regulating interstate commerce.

The CFAA includes seven separate subsections which each individually can be violated. Arguably, the broadest subsection is a(2). The other subsections cover additional potential violations. For example, a(1) covers unauthorized access or access that exceeds authority concerning national security or foreign relations. Subsection a(3) generally concerns unauthorized access to federal government computers. Subsection a(4) relates to accessing without authorization or in excess of authorization with intent to defraud. Subsection a(5) has three subparts which concern causing damage or loss to a protected computer through transmission of a program, intentionally accessing it. Subsection a(6) concerns trafficking in passwords used for unauthorized access to a computer. Subsection a(7) relates to communications concerning threats of extortion related to damage to a computer. CFAA section(a) provides:

(a) Whoever--

(1) having knowingly accessed a computer without authorization or exceeding authorized access, and by means of such conduct having obtained information that has been determined by the United States Government pursuant to an Executive order or statute to require protection against unauthorized disclosure for reasons of national defense or foreign relations, or any restricted data, as defined in paragraph y. of section 11 of the Atomic Energy Act of 1954, with reason to believe that such information so obtained could be used to the injury of the United States, or to the advantage of any foreign nation willfully communicates, delivers, transmits, or causes to be communicated, delivered, or transmitted, or attempts to communicate, deliver, transmit or cause to be communicated, delivered, or transmitted the same to any person not entitled to receive it, or willfully retains the same and fails to deliver it to the officer or employee of the United States entitled to receive it;

(2) intentionally accesses a computer without authorization or exceeds authorized access, and thereby obtains--

(A) information contained in a financial record of a financial institution, or of a card issuer as defined in section 1602(n) of title 15, or contained in a file of a consumer reporting agency on a consumer, as such terms are defined in the Fair Credit Reporting Act (15 U.S.C. 1681 et seq.);

(B) information from any department or agency of the United States; or**(C)** information from any protected computer;

(3) intentionally, without authorization to access any nonpublic computer of a department or agency of the United States, accesses such a computer of that department or agency that is exclusively for the use of the Government of the United States or, in the case of a computer not exclusively for such use, is used by or for the Government of the United States and such conduct affects that use by or for the Government of the United States;

(4) knowingly and with intent to defraud, accesses a protected computer without authorization, or exceeds authorized access, and by means of such conduct furthers the intended fraud and obtains anything of value, unless the object of the fraud and the thing obtained consists only of the use of the computer and the value of such use is not more than $5,000 in any 1-year period;

(5)(A) knowingly causes the transmission of a program, information, code, or command, and as a result of such conduct, intentionally causes damage without authorization, to a protected computer;

(B) intentionally accesses a protected computer without authorization, and as a result of such conduct, recklessly causes damage; or

(C) intentionally accesses a protected computer without authorization, and as a result of such conduct, causes damage and loss.1

(6) knowingly and with intent to defraud traffics (as defined in section 1029) in any password or similar information through which a computer may be accessed without authorization, if--

(A) such trafficking affects interstate or foreign commerce; or

(B) such computer is used by or for the Government of the United States;2

(7) with intent to extort from any person any money or other thing of value, transmits in interstate or foreign commerce any communication containing any--

(A) threat to cause damage to a protected computer;

(B) threat to obtain information from a protected computer without authorization or in excess of authorization or to impair the confidentiality of information obtained from a protected computer without authorization or by exceeding authorized access; or

(C) demand or request for money or other thing of value in relation to damage to a protected computer, where such damage was caused to facilitate the extortion;

shall be punished as provided in subsection (c) of this section.

NOTES

Note 1

Subsection (b) provides: "Whoever conspires to commit or attempts to commit an offense under subsection (a) of this section shall be punished as provided in subsection (c) of this section."

Note 2

Criminal Penalties under the CFAA

The CFAA's subsection (C) contains the penalties and fines for violations under subsection (a) as well as aiding and abetting under (b). The statute provides in relevant part:

(c) The punishment for an offense under subsection (a) or (b) of this section is--

(1)(A) a fine under this title or imprisonment for not more than ten years, or both, in the case of an offense under subsection (a)(1) of this section which does not occur after a conviction for another offense under this section, or an attempt to commit an offense punishable under this subparagraph; and

> **(B)** a fine under this title or imprisonment for not more than twenty years, or both, in the case of an offense under subsection (a)(1) of this section which occurs after a conviction for another offense under this section, or an attempt to commit an offense punishable under this subparagraph;

(2)(A) except as provided in subparagraph (B), a fine under this title or imprisonment for not more than one year, or both, in the case of an offense under subsection (a)(2), (a)(3), or (a)(6) of this section which does not occur after a conviction for another offense under this section, or an attempt to commit an offense punishable under this subparagraph;

> **(B)** a fine under this title or imprisonment for not more than 5 years, or both, in the case of an offense under subsection (a)(2), or an attempt to commit an offense punishable under this subparagraph, if--

>> **(i)** the offense was committed for purposes of commercial advantage or private financial gain;

>> **(ii)** the offense was committed in furtherance of any criminal or tortious act in violation of the Constitution or laws of the United States or of any State; or

>> **(iii)** the value of the information obtained exceeds $5,000; and

> **(C)** a fine under this title or imprisonment for not more than ten years, or both, in the case of an offense under subsection (a)(2), (a)(3) or (a)(6) of this

section which occurs after a conviction for another offense under this section, or an attempt to commit an offense punishable under this subparagraph;

(3)(A) a fine under this title or imprisonment for not more than five years, or both, in the case of an offense under subsection (a)(4) or (a)(7) of this section which does not occur after a conviction for another offense under this section, or an attempt to commit an offense punishable under this subparagraph; and

(B) a fine under this title or imprisonment for not more than ten years, or both, in the case of an offense under subsection (a)(4), or (a)(7) of this section which occurs after a conviction for another offense under this section, or an attempt to commit an offense punishable under this subparagraph;

(4)(A) except as provided in subparagraphs (E) and (F), a fine under this title, imprisonment for not more than 5 years, or both, in the case of--

(i) an offense under subsection (a)(5)(B), which does not occur after a conviction for another offense under this section, if the offense caused (or, in the case of an attempted offense, would, if completed, have caused)--

(I) loss to 1 or more persons during any 1-year period (and, for purposes of an investigation, prosecution, or other proceeding brought by the United States only, loss resulting from a related course of conduct affecting 1 or more other protected computers) aggregating at least $5,000 in value;

(II) the modification or impairment, or potential modification or impairment, of the medical examination, diagnosis, treatment, or care of 1 or more individuals;

(III) physical injury to any person;

(IV) a threat to public health or safety;

(V) damage affecting a computer used by or for an entity of the United States Government in furtherance of the administration of justice, national defense, or national security; or

(VI) damage affecting 10 or more protected computers during any 1-year period; or

(ii) an attempt to commit an offense punishable under this subparagraph;

(B) except as provided in subparagraphs (E) and (F), a fine under this title, imprisonment for not more than 10 years, or both, in the case of--

(i) an offense under subsection (a)(5)(A), which does not occur after a conviction for another offense under this section, if the offense caused (or, in the case of an attempted offense, would, if completed, have caused) a harm provided in subclauses (I) through (VI) of subparagraph (A)(i); or

(ii) an attempt to commit an offense punishable under this subparagraph;

(C) except as provided in subparagraphs (E) and (F), a fine under this title, imprisonment for not more than 20 years, or both, in the case of--

(i) an offense or an attempt to commit an offense under subparagraphs (A) or (B) of subsection (a)(5) that occurs after a conviction for another offense under this section; or

(ii) an attempt to commit an offense punishable under this subparagraph;

(D) a fine under this title, imprisonment for not more than 10 years, or both, in the case of--

(i) an offense or an attempt to commit an offense under subsection (a)(5)(C) that occurs after a conviction for another offense under this section; or

(ii) an attempt to commit an offense punishable under this subparagraph;

(E) if the offender attempts to cause or knowingly or recklessly causes serious bodily injury from conduct in violation of subsection (a)(5)(A), a fine under this title, imprisonment for not more than 20 years, or both;

(F) if the offender attempts to cause or knowingly or recklessly causes death from conduct in violation of subsection (a)(5)(A), a fine under this title, imprisonment for any term of years or for life, or both; or

(G) a fine under this title, imprisonment for not more than 1 year, or both, for--

(i) any other offense under subsection (a)(5); or

(ii) an attempt to commit an offense punishable under this subparagraph.

Note 3

Civil Actions

Subsection (g) creates a civil action under the aggravating factors listed under Subsection (c)(4)(A)(i). Subsection (g) provides:

> Any person who suffers damage or loss by reason of a violation of this section may maintain a civil action against the violator to obtain compensatory damages and injunctive relief or other equitable relief. A civil action for a violation of this section may be brought only if the conduct involves 1 of the factors set forth in subclauses (I), (II), (III), (IV), or (V) of subsection (c)(4)(A)(i). Damages for a violation involving only conduct described in subsection (c)(4)(A)(i)(I) are limited to economic damages.

Thus, a violation of subsection (a) or (b) along with the violation of an aggravating factor may, in most cases, create a civil cause of action. Subsection (c)(4)(A)(i) states:

> **(4)(A)** except as provided in subparagraphs (E) and (F), a fine under this title, imprisonment for not more than 5 years, or both, in the case of--
>
> > **(i)** an offense under subsection (a)(5)(B), which does not occur after a conviction for another offense under this section, if the offense caused (or, in the case of an attempted offense, would, if completed, have caused)--
> >
> > > **(I)** loss to 1 or more persons during any 1-year period (and, for purposes of an investigation, prosecution, or other proceeding brought by the United States only, loss resulting from a related course of conduct affecting 1 or more other protected computers) aggregating at least $5,000 in value;
> > >
> > > **(II)** the modification or impairment, or potential modification or impairment, of the medical examination, diagnosis, treatment, or care of 1 or more individuals;
> > >
> > > **(III)** physical injury to any person;
> > >
> > > **(IV)** a threat to public health or safety;
> > >
> > > **(V)** damage affecting a computer used by or for an entity of the United States Government in furtherance of the administration of justice, national defense, or national security; or
> > >
> > > **(VI)** damage affecting 10 or more protected computers during any 1-year period; or

(ii) an attempt to commit an offense punishable under this subparagraph;

Note 4

Statute of Limitations for Civil Actions

Subsection (g) provides, in relevant part, that, "No action may be brought under this subsection unless such action is begun within 2 years of the date of the act complained of or the date of the discovery of the damage."

Note 5

Limitation to Civil Actions

Subsection (g) provides, in relevant part, that, "No action may be brought under this subsection for the negligent design or manufacture of computer hardware, computer software, or firmware."

Note 6

Limitations on the Private Right of Action

Some courts find that the private right of action does not extend vicariously to persons unless they have the requisite criminal intent. *See Doe v. Dartmouth-Hitchcock Med. Ctr.*, 2001 WL 873063 (D.N.H. 2001). ("Expanding the private cause of action created by Congress to include one for vicarious liability against persons who did not act with criminal intent and cannot be said to have violated the statute, like the Dartmouth defendants, would be entirely inconsistent with the plain language of the statute.").

QUESTION

The CFAA has been around for a long time. Do you think it acts as a deterrent to hacking?

11.2[A]   UNAUTHORIZED   ACCESS   OR   ACCESS   EXCEEDING AUTHORIZATION

One of the most important issues concerning the application of the CFAA relates to what is authorized and unauthorized access to a computer. Authorized access is not a violation of the CFAA. Unauthorized access or access exceeding authorization is a violation of the CFAA. For example, 18 USC section 1030(a)(2) provides, in relevant part:

(2) [Whoever] intentionally accesses a computer without authorization or exceeds authorized access, and thereby obtains--

(A) information contained in a financial record of a financial institution, or of a card issuer as defined in section 1602(n) of title 15, or contained in a file of a consumer reporting agency on a consumer, as such terms are defined in the Fair Credit Reporting Act (15 U.S.C. 1681 et seq.);

(B) information from any department or agency of the United States; or

(C) information from any protected computer; . . . shall be punished as provided in subsection (c) of this section.

The following cases explore the question of authorized access and exceeding authorized access in detail. In particular, the U.S. Supreme Court clarified the meaning of exceeding authorized access in 2021 in *Van Buren v. United States*. As you read the following cases, an important question arises as to how the Supreme Court's analysis in that case should influence the analysis of prior court decisions considering related issues. However, first, the Ninth Circuit's former Chief Judge Kozinski provides an analysis of exceeding authorized access before the Supreme Court's *Van Buren* decision.

United States v. Nosal, 676 F.3d 854 (9th Cir. 2012) (en banc).

KOZINSKI, Chief Judge:

Computers have become an indispensable part of our daily lives. We use them for work; we use them for play. Sometimes we use them for play at work. Many employers have adopted policies prohibiting the use of work computers for nonbusiness purposes. Does an employee who violates such a policy commit a federal crime? How about someone who violates the terms of service of a social networking website? This depends on how broadly we read the Computer Fraud and Abuse Act (CFAA), 18 U.S.C. § 1030.

FACTS

David Nosal used to work for Korn/Ferry, an executive search firm. Shortly after he left the company, he convinced some of his former colleagues who were still working for Korn/Ferry to help him start a competing business. The employees used their log-in credentials to download source lists, names and contact information from a confidential database on the company's computer, and then transferred that information to Nosal. The employees were authorized to access the database, but Korn/Ferry had a policy that forbade disclosing confidential information. The government indicted Nosal on twenty counts, including trade secret theft, mail fraud, conspiracy and violations of the CFAA. The CFAA counts charged Nosal with violations of 18 U.S.C. § 1030(a)(4), for aiding and abetting the Korn/Ferry employees in "exceed[ing their] authorized access" with intent to defraud.

Nosal filed a motion to dismiss the CFAA counts, arguing that the statute targets only hackers, not individuals who access a computer with authorization but then misuse information they obtain by means of such access. The district court initially rejected

Nosal's argument, holding that when a person accesses a computer "knowingly and with the intent to defraud ... [it] renders the access unauthorized or in excess of authorization." Shortly afterwards, however, we decided LVRC Holdings LLC v. Brekka, 581 F.3d 1127 (9th Cir.2009), which construed narrowly the phrases "without authorization" and "exceeds authorized access" in the CFAA. Nosal filed a motion for reconsideration and a second motion to dismiss.

The district court reversed field and followed Brekka's guidance that "[t]here is simply no way to read [the definition of 'exceeds authorized access'] to incorporate corporate policies governing use of information unless the word alter is interpreted to mean misappropriate," as "[s]uch an interpretation would defy the plain meaning of the word alter, as well as common sense." Accordingly, the district court dismissed counts 2 and 4–7 for failure to state an offense. The government appeals. We review de novo. United States v. Boren, 278 F.3d 911, 913 (9th Cir.2002).

DISCUSSION

The CFAA defines "exceeds authorized access" as "to access a computer with authorization and to use such access to obtain or alter information in the computer that the accesser is not entitled so to obtain or alter." 18 U.S.C. § 1030(e)(6). This language can be read either of two ways: First, as Nosal suggests and the district court held, it could refer to someone who's authorized to access only certain data or files but accesses unauthorized data or files—what is colloquially known as "hacking." For example, assume an employee is permitted to access only product information on the company's computer but accesses customer data: He would "exceed [ ] authorized access" if he looks at the customer lists. Second, as the government proposes, the language could refer to someone who has unrestricted physical access to a computer, but is limited in the use to which he can put the information. For example, an employee may be authorized to access customer lists in order to do his job but not to send them to a competitor.

The government argues that the statutory text can support only the latter interpretation of "exceeds authorized access." In its opening brief, it focuses on the word "entitled" in the phrase an "accesser is not entitled so to obtain or alter." Id. § 1030(e)(6). Pointing to one dictionary definition of "entitle" as "to furnish with a right," Webster's New Riverside University Dictionary 435, the government argues that Korn/Ferry's computer use policy gives employees certain rights, and when the employees violated that policy, they "exceed[ed] authorized access." But "entitled" in the statutory text refers to how an accesser "obtain[s] or alter[s]" the information, whereas the computer use policy uses "entitled" to limit how the information is used after it is obtained. This is a poor fit with the statutory language. An equally or more sensible reading of "entitled" is as a synonym for "authorized." So read, "exceeds authorized access" would refer to data or files on a computer that one is not authorized to access.

In its reply brief and at oral argument, the government focuses on the word "so" in the same phrase. See 18 U.S.C. § 1030(e)(6) ("accesser is not entitled so to obtain or alter" (emphasis added)). The government reads "so" to mean "in that manner," which it claims must refer to use restrictions. In the government's view, reading the definition narrowly would render "so" superfluous.

The government's interpretation would transform the CFAA from an anti-hacking statute into an expansive misappropriation statute. This places a great deal of weight on a two-letter word that is essentially a conjunction. If Congress meant to expand the scope of criminal liability to everyone who uses a computer in violation of computer use restrictions—which may well include everyone who uses a computer—we would expect it to use language better suited to that purpose. Under the presumption that Congress acts interstitially, we construe a statute as displacing a substantial portion of the common law only where Congress has clearly indicated its intent to do so. . . .

In any event, the government's "so" argument doesn't work because the word has meaning even if it doesn't refer to use restrictions. Suppose an employer keeps certain information in a separate database that can be viewed on a computer screen, but not copied or downloaded. If an employee circumvents the security measures, copies the information to a thumb drive and walks out of the building with it in his pocket, he would then have obtained access to information in the computer that he is not "entitled so to obtain." Or, let's say an employee is given full access to the information, provided he logs in with his username and password. In an effort to cover his tracks, he uses another employee's login to copy information from the database. Once again, this would be an employee who is authorized to access the information but does so in a manner he was not authorized "so to obtain." Of course, this all assumes that "so" must have a substantive meaning to make sense of the statute. But Congress could just as well have included "so" as a connector or for emphasis.

While the CFAA is susceptible to the government's broad interpretation, we find Nosal's narrower one more plausible. Congress enacted the CFAA in 1984 primarily to address the growing problem of computer hacking, recognizing that, "[i]n intentionally trespassing into someone else's computer files, the offender obtains at the very least information as to how to break into that computer system." S.Rep. No. 99–432, at 9 (1986), 1986 U.S.C.C.A.N. 2479, 2487 (Conf. Rep.). The government agrees that the CFAA was concerned with hacking, which is why it also prohibits accessing a computer "without authorization." According to the government, that prohibition applies to hackers, so the "exceeds authorized access" prohibition must apply to people who are authorized to use the computer, but do so for an unauthorized purpose. But it is possible to read both prohibitions as applying to hackers: "[W]ithout authorization" would apply to outside hackers (individuals who have no authorized access to the computer at all) and "exceeds authorized access" would apply to inside hackers (individuals whose initial access to a computer is authorized but who access unauthorized information or files). This is a perfectly plausible construction of the statutory language that maintains the CFAA's focus on hacking rather than turning it into a sweeping Internet-policing mandate.

The government's construction of the statute would expand its scope far beyond computer hacking to criminalize any unauthorized use of information obtained from a computer. This would make criminals of large groups of people who would have little reason to suspect they are committing a federal crime. While ignorance of the law is no excuse, we can properly be skeptical as to whether Congress, in 1984, meant to criminalize conduct beyond that which is inherently wrongful, such as breaking into a computer.

The government argues that defendants here did have notice that their conduct was wrongful by the fraud and materiality requirements in subsection 1030(a)(4), which punishes whoever:

> knowingly and with intent to defraud, accesses a protected computer without authorization, or exceeds authorized access, and by means of such conduct furthers the intended fraud and obtains anything of value, unless the object of the fraud and the thing obtained consists only of the use of the computer and the value of such use is not more than $5,000 in any 1–year period.

18 U.S.C. § 1030(a)(4). But "exceeds authorized access" is used elsewhere in the CFAA as a basis for criminal culpability without intent to defraud. Subsection 1030(a)(2)(C) requires only that the person who "exceeds authorized access" have "obtain[ed] ... information from any protected computer." Because "protected computer" is defined as a computer affected by or involved in interstate commerce—effectively all computers with Internet access—the government's interpretation of "exceeds authorized access" makes every violation of a private computer use policy a federal crime. See id. § 1030(e)(2)(B).

The government argues that our ruling today would construe "exceeds authorized access" only in subsection 1030(a)(4), and we could give the phrase a narrower meaning when we construe other subsections. This is just not so: Once we define the phrase for the purpose of subsection 1030(a)(4), that definition must apply equally to the rest of the statute pursuant to the "standard principle of statutory construction ... that identical words and phrases within the same statute should normally be given the same meaning." Powerex Corp. v. Reliant Energy Servs., Inc., 551 U.S. 224, 232, 127 S.Ct. 2411, 168 L.Ed.2d 112 (2007). The phrase appears five times in the first seven subsections of the statute, including subsection 1030(a)(2)(C). See 18 U.S.C. § 1030(a)(1), (2), (4) and (7). Giving a different interpretation to each is impossible because Congress provided a single definition of "exceeds authorized access" for all iterations of the statutory phrase. See id. § 1030(e)(6). Congress obviously meant "exceeds authorized access" to have the same meaning throughout section 1030. We must therefore consider how the interpretation we adopt will operate wherever in that section the phrase appears.

In the case of the CFAA, the broadest provision is subsection 1030(a)(2)(C), which makes it a crime to exceed authorized access of a computer connected to the Internet without any culpable intent. Were we to adopt the government's proposed interpretation, millions of unsuspecting individuals would find that they are engaging in criminal conduct.

Minds have wandered since the beginning of time and the computer gives employees new ways to procrastinate, by g-chatting with friends, playing games, shopping or watching sports highlights. Such activities are routinely prohibited by many computer-use policies, although employees are seldom disciplined for occasional use of work computers for personal purposes. Nevertheless, under the broad interpretation of the CFAA, such minor dalliances would become federal crimes. While it's unlikely that you'll be prosecuted for watching Reason.TV on your work computer, you could be. Employers wanting to rid themselves of troublesome employees without following proper procedures could threaten to report them to the FBI unless they quit. Ubiquitous, seldom-prosecuted crimes invite arbitrary and discriminatory enforcement.

Employer-employee and company-consumer relationships are traditionally governed by tort and contract law; the government's proposed interpretation of the CFAA allows private parties to manipulate their computer-use and personnel policies so as to turn these relationships into ones policed by the criminal law. Significant notice problems arise if we allow criminal liability to turn on the vagaries of private polices that are lengthy, opaque, subject to change and seldom read. Consider the typical corporate policy that computers can be used only for business purposes. What exactly is a "nonbusiness purpose"? If you use the computer to check the weather report for a business trip? For the company softball game? For your vacation to Hawaii? And if minor personal uses are tolerated, how can an employee be on notice of what constitutes a violation sufficient to trigger criminal liability?

Basing criminal liability on violations of private computer use polices can transform whole categories of otherwise innocuous behavior into federal crimes simply because a computer is involved. Employees who call family members from their work phones will become criminals if they send an email instead. Employees can sneak in the sports section of the New York Times to read at work, but they'd better not visit ESPN.com. And sudoku enthusiasts should stick to the printed puzzles, because visiting www.dailysudoku.com from their work computers might give them more than enough time to hone their sudoku skills behind bars.

The effect this broad construction of the CFAA has on workplace conduct pales by comparison with its effect on everyone else who uses a computer, smart-phone, iPad, Kindle, Nook, X-box, Blu–Ray player or any other Internet-enabled device. The Internet is a means for communicating via computers: Whenever we access a web page, commence a download, post a message on somebody's Facebook wall, shop on Amazon, bid on eBay, publish a blog, rate a movie on IMDb, read www.NYT.com, watch YouTube and do the thousands of other things we routinely do online, we are using one computer to send commands to other computers at remote locations. Our access to those remote computers is governed by a series of private agreements and policies that most people are only dimly aware of and virtually no one reads or understands.

For example, it's not widely known that, up until very recently, Google forbade minors from using its services. See Google Terms of Service, effective April 16, 2007— March 1, 2012, § 2.3, http://www.google. com/intl/en/policies/terms/archive/20070416 ("You may not use the Services and may not accept the Terms if ... you are not of legal age to form a binding contract with Google....") (last visited Mar. 4, 2012). Adopting the government's interpretation would turn vast numbers of teens and pre-teens into juvenile delinquents—and their parents and teachers into delinquency contributors. Similarly, Facebook makes it a violation of the terms of service to let anyone log into your account. See Facebook Statement of Rights and Responsibilities § 4.8 http://www.facebook.com/legal/terms ("You will not share your password, ... let anyone else access your account, or do anything else that might jeopardize the security of your account.") (last visited Mar. 4, 2012). Yet it's very common for people to let close friends and relatives check their email or access their online accounts. Some may be aware that, if discovered, they may suffer a rebuke from the ISP or a loss of access, but few imagine they might be marched off to federal prison for doing so.

Or consider the numerous dating websites whose terms of use prohibit inaccurate or misleading information. See, e.g., eHarmony Terms of Service § 2(I), http://www.eharmony.com/about/terms ("You will not provide inaccurate, misleading or false information to eHarmony or to any other user.") (last visited Mar. 4, 2012). Or eBay and Craigslist, where it's a violation of the terms of use to post items in an inappropriate category. See, e.g., eBay User Agreement, http://pages.ebay.com/help/policies/user-agreement.html ("While using eBay sites, services and tools, you will not: post content or items in an inappropriate category or areas on our sites and services ....") (last visited Mar. 4, 2012). Under the government's proposed interpretation of the CFAA, posting for sale an item prohibited by Craigslist's policy, or describing yourself as "tall, dark and handsome," when you're actually short and homely, will earn you a handsome orange jumpsuit.

Not only are the terms of service vague and generally unknown—unless you look real hard at the small print at the bottom of a webpage—but website owners retain the right to change the terms at any time and without notice. See, e.g., YouTube Terms of Service § 1.B, http://www.youtube.com/t/terms ("YouTube may, in its sole discretion, modify or revise these Terms of Service and policies at any time, and you agree to be bound by such modifications or revisions.") (last visited Mar. 4, 2012). Accordingly, behavior that wasn't criminal yesterday can become criminal today without an act of Congress, and without any notice whatsoever.

The government assures us that, whatever the scope of the CFAA, it won't prosecute minor violations. But we shouldn't have to live at the mercy of our local prosecutor. Cf. United States v. Stevens, 559 U.S. 460, 130 S.Ct. 1577, 1591, 176 L.Ed.2d 435 (2010) ("We would not uphold an unconstitutional statute merely because the Government promised to use it responsibly."). And it's not clear we can trust the government when a tempting target comes along. Take the case of the mom who posed as a 17–year–old boy and cyber-bullied her daughter's classmate. The Justice

Department prosecuted her under 18 U.S.C. § 1030(a)(2)(C) for violating MySpace's terms of service, which prohibited lying about identifying information, including age. See United States v. Drew, 259 F.R.D. 449 (C.D.Cal.2009). Lying on social media websites is common: People shave years off their age, add inches to their height and drop pounds from their weight. The difference between puffery and prosecution may depend on whether you happen to be someone an AUSA has reason to go after.

In United States v. Kozminski, 487 U.S. 931, 108 S.Ct. 2751, 101 L.Ed.2d 788 (1988), the Supreme Court refused to adopt the government's broad interpretation of a statute because it would "criminalize a broad range of day-to-day activity." Id. at 949, 108 S.Ct. at 2763. Applying the rule of lenity, the Court warned that the broader statutory interpretation would "delegate to prosecutors and juries the inherently legislative task of determining what type of ... activities are so morally reprehensible that they should be punished as crimes" and would "subject individuals to the risk of arbitrary or discriminatory prosecution and conviction." Id. By giving that much power to prosecutors, we're inviting discriminatory and arbitrary enforcement.

We remain unpersuaded by the decisions of our sister circuits that interpret the CFAA broadly to cover violations of corporate computer use restrictions or violations of a duty of loyalty. See United States v. Rodriguez, 628 F.3d 1258 (11th Cir.2010); United States v. John, 597 F.3d 263 (5th Cir.2010); Int'l Airport Ctrs., LLC v. Citrin, 440 F.3d 418 (7th Cir.2006). These courts looked only at the culpable behavior of the defendants before them, and failed to consider the effect on millions of ordinary citizens caused by the statute's unitary definition of "exceeds authorized access." They therefore failed to apply the long-standing principle that we must construe ambiguous criminal statutes narrowly so as to avoid "making criminal law in Congress's stead." United States v. Santos, 553 U.S. 507, 514, 128 S.Ct. 2020, 170 L.Ed.2d 912 (2008). . . .

CONCLUSION

We need not decide today whether Congress could base criminal liability on violations of a company or website's computer use restrictions. Instead, we hold that the phrase "exceeds authorized access" in the CFAA does not extend to violations of use restrictions. If Congress wants to incorporate misappropriation liability into the CFAA, it must speak more clearly. The rule of lenity requires "penal laws ... to be construed strictly." United States v. Wiltberger, 18 U.S. (5 Wheat.) 76, 95, 5 L.Ed. 37 (1820). "[W]hen choice has to be made between two readings of what conduct Congress has made a crime, it is appropriate, before we choose the harsher alternative, to require that Congress should have spoken in language that is clear and definite." Jones, 529 U.S. at 858, 120 S.Ct. at 1912 (internal quotation marks and citation omitted).

The rule of lenity not only ensures that citizens will have fair notice of the criminal laws, but also that Congress will have fair notice of what conduct its laws criminalize. We construe criminal statutes narrowly so that Congress will not unintentionally turn ordinary citizens into criminals. "[B]ecause of the seriousness of criminal penalties, and because criminal punishment usually represents the moral condemnation of the community, legislatures and not courts should define criminal activity." United States v. Bass, 404 U.S. 336, 348, 92 S.Ct. 515, 30 L.Ed.2d 488 (1971). "If there is any doubt about whether Congress intended [the CFAA] to prohibit the conduct in which [Nosal] engaged, then 'we must choose the interpretation least likely to impose penalties unintended by Congress.' " United States v. Cabaccang, 332 F.3d 622, 635 n. 22 (9th Cir.2003) (quoting United States v. Arzate–Nunez, 18 F.3d 730, 736 (9th Cir.1994)).

This narrower interpretation is also a more sensible reading of the text and legislative history of a statute whose general purpose is to punish hacking—the circumvention of technological access barriers—not misappropriation of trade secrets—a subject Congress has dealt with elsewhere. Therefore, we hold that "exceeds authorized access" in the CFAA is limited to violations of restrictions on access to information, and not restrictions on its use.

Because Nosal's accomplices had permission to access the company database and obtain the information contained within, the government's charges fail to meet the element of "without authorization, or exceeds authorized access" under 18 U.S.C. § 1030(a)(4). Accordingly, we affirm the judgment of the district court dismissing counts 2 and 4–7 for failure to state an offense. The government may, of course, prosecute Nosal on the remaining counts of the indictment.

AFFIRMED.

Dissent

SILVERMAN, Circuit Judge, with whom TALLMAN, Circuit Judge concurs, dissenting:

This case has nothing to do with playing sudoku, checking email, fibbing on dating sites, or any of the other activities that the majority rightly values. It has everything to do with stealing an employer's valuable information to set up a competing business with the purloined data, siphoned away from the victim, knowing such access and use were prohibited in the defendants' employment contracts. The indictment here charged that Nosal and his co-conspirators knowingly exceeded the access to a protected company computer they were given by an executive search firm that employed them; that they did so with the intent to defraud; and further, that they stole the victim's valuable proprietary information by means of that fraudulent conduct in order to profit from using it. In ridiculing scenarios not remotely presented by this case, the majority does a good job of knocking down straw men—far-fetched hypotheticals involving neither theft nor intentional fraudulent conduct, but innocuous violations of office policy.

. . . I respectfully dissent.

QUESTION

The court makes a distinction between use restrictions and exceeding authorized access. Is this a distinction without a difference? If a user has access to a computer but then exceeds the use permission of that computer should that amount to exceeding authorized access?

Van Buren v. United States, 141 S.Ct. 1648 (2021).

BARRETT, J.,

Nathan Van Buren, a former police sergeant, ran a license-plate search in a law enforcement computer database in exchange for money. Van Buren's conduct plainly flouted his department's policy, which authorized him to obtain database information only for law enforcement purposes. We must decide whether Van Buren also violated the Computer Fraud and Abuse Act of 1986 (CFAA), which makes it illegal "to access a computer with authorization and to use such access to obtain or alter information in the computer that the accesser is not entitled so to obtain or alter."

He did not. This provision covers those who obtain information from particular areas in the computer—such as files, folders, or databases—to which their computer access does not extend. It does not cover those who, like Van Buren, have improper motives for obtaining information that is otherwise available to them.

I A

Technological advances at the dawn of the 1980s brought computers to schools, offices, and homes across the Nation. But as the public and private sectors harnessed the power of computing for improvement and innovation, so-called hackers hatched ways to coopt computers for illegal ends. After a series of highly publicized hackings captured the public's attention, it became clear that traditional theft and trespass statutes were ill suited to address cybercrimes that did not deprive computer owners of property in the traditional sense. See Kerr, Cybercrime's Scope: Interpreting "Access" and "Authorization" in Computer Misuse Statutes, 78 N. Y. U. L. Rev. 1596, 1605–1613 (2003).

Congress, following the lead of several States, responded by enacting the first federal computer-crime statute as part of the Comprehensive Crime Control Act of 1984. § 2102(a), 98 Stat. 2190–2192. A few years later, Congress passed the CFAA, which included the provisions at issue in this case. The Act subjects to criminal liability anyone who "intentionally accesses a computer without authorization or exceeds authorized access," and thereby obtains computer information. 18 U.S.C. § 1030(a)(2). It defines the term "exceeds authorized access" to mean "to access a computer with authorization and to use such access to obtain or alter information in the computer that the accesser is not entitled so to obtain or alter." § 1030(e)(6).

Initially, subsection (a)(2)'s prohibition barred accessing only certain financial information. It has since expanded to cover any information from any computer "used in or affecting interstate or foreign commerce or communication." § 1030(e)(2)(B). As a result, the prohibition now applies—at a minimum—to all information from all computers that connect to the Internet. §§ 1030(a)(2)(C), (e)(2)(B).

Those who violate § 1030(a)(2) face penalties ranging from fines and misdemeanor sentences to imprisonment for up to 10 years. § 1030(c)(2). They also risk civil liability under the CFAA's private cause of action, which allows persons suffering "damage" or "loss" from CFAA violations to sue for money damages and equitable relief. § 1030(g).

B

This case stems from Van Buren's time as a police sergeant in Georgia. In the course of his duties, Van Buren crossed paths with a man named Andrew Albo. The deputy chief of Van Buren's department considered Albo to be "very volatile" and warned officers in the department to deal with him carefully. Notwithstanding that warning, Van Buren developed a friendly relationship with Albo. Or so Van Buren thought when he went to Albo to ask for a personal loan. Unbeknownst to Van Buren, Albo secretly recorded that request and took it to the local sheriff's office, where he complained that Van Buren had sought to "shake him down" for cash.

The taped conversation made its way to the Federal Bureau of Investigation (FBI), which devised an operation to see how far Van Buren would go for money. The steps were straightforward: Albo would ask Van Buren to search the state law enforcement computer database for a license plate purportedly belonging to a woman whom Albo had met at a local strip club. Albo, no stranger to legal troubles, would tell Van Buren that he wanted to ensure that the woman was not in fact an undercover officer. In return for the search, Albo would pay Van Buren around $5,000.

Things went according to plan. Van Buren used his patrol-car computer to access the law enforcement database with his valid credentials. He searched the database for the license plate that Albo had provided. After obtaining the FBI-created license-plate entry, Van Buren told Albo that he had information to share.

The Federal Government then charged Van Buren with a felony violation of the CFAA on the ground that running the license plate for Albo violated the "exceeds authorized access" clause of 18 U.S.C. § 1030(a)(2). The trial evidence showed that Van Buren had been trained not to use the law enforcement database for "an improper purpose," defined as "any personal use." App. 17. Van Buren therefore knew that the search breached department policy. And according to the Government, that violation of department policy also violated the CFAA. Consistent with that position, the Government told the jury Van Buren that access of the database "for a non[-]law[-]enforcement purpose" violated the CFAA "concept" against "using" a computer network in a way contrary to "what your job or policy prohibits." *Id.*, at 39. The jury convicted Van Buren, and the District Court sentenced him to 18 months in prison.

Van Buren appealed to the Eleventh Circuit, arguing that the "exceeds authorized access" clause applies only to those who obtain information to which their computer access does not extend, not to those who misuse access that they otherwise have. While several Circuits see the clause Van Buren's way, the Eleventh Circuit is among those that have taken a broader view.[2] Consistent with its Circuit precedent, the panel held that Van Buren had violated the CFAA by accessing the law enforcement database for an "inappropriate reason." 940 F.3d 1192, 1208 (2019). We granted certiorari to resolve the split in authority regarding the scope of liability under the CFAA's "exceeds authorized access" clause. 590 U. S. ——, 140 S.Ct. 2667, 206 L.Ed.2d 822 (2020).

II A 1

Both Van Buren and the Government raise a host of policy arguments to support their respective interpretations. But we start where we always do: with the text of the statute. Here, the most relevant text is the phrase "exceeds authorized access," which means "to access a computer with authorization and to use such access to obtain ... information in the computer that the accesser is not entitled so to obtain." § 1030(e)(6).

The parties agree that Van Buren "access[ed] a computer with authorization" when he used his patrol-car computer and valid credentials to log into the law enforcement database. They also agree that Van Buren "obtain[ed] ... information in the computer" when he acquired the license-plate record for Albo. The dispute is whether Van Buren was "entitled so to obtain" the record.

"Entitle" means "to give ... a title, right, or claim to something." Random House Dictionary of the English Language 649 (2d ed. 1987). See also Black's Law Dictionary 477 (5th ed. 1979) ("to give a right or legal title to"). The parties agree that Van Buren had been given the right to acquire license-plate information—that is, he was "entitled to obtain" it—from the law enforcement computer database. But was Van Buren "entitled *so* to obtain" the license-plate information, as the statute requires?

Van Buren says yes. He notes that "so," as used in this statute, serves as a term of reference that recalls "the same manner as has been stated" or "the way or manner described." Black's Law Dictionary, at 1246; 15 Oxford English Dictionary 887 (2d ed. 1989). The disputed phrase "entitled so to obtain" thus asks whether one has the right, in "the same manner as has been stated," to obtain the relevant information. And the only manner of obtaining information already stated in the definitional provision is "via a computer [one] is otherwise authorized to access." Reply Brief 3. Putting that together, Van Buren contends that the disputed phrase—"is not entitled *so* to obtain"—plainly refers to information one is not allowed to obtain *by using a computer that he is authorized to access*. On this reading, if a person has access to information stored in a computer—*e.g.,* in "Folder Y," from which the person could permissibly pull information—then he does not violate the CFAA by obtaining such information, regardless of whether he pulled the information for a prohibited purpose. But if the information is instead located in prohibited "Folder X," to which the person lacks access, he violates the CFAA by obtaining such information.

The Government agrees that the statute uses "so" in the word's term-of-reference sense, but it argues that "so" sweeps more broadly. It reads the phrase "is not entitled *so* to obtain" to refer to information one was not allowed to obtain *in the particular manner or circumstances in which he obtained it*. The manner or circumstances in which one has a right to obtain information, the Government says, are defined by any "specifically and explicitly" communicated limits on one's right to access information. Brief for United States 19. As the Government sees it, an employee might lawfully pull information from Folder Y in the morning for a permissible purpose—say, to prepare for a business meeting—but unlawfully pull the same information from Folder Y in the afternoon for a prohibited purpose—say, to help draft a resume to submit to a competitor employer.

The Government's interpretation has surface appeal but proves to be a sleight of hand. While highlighting that "so" refers to a "manner or circumstance," the Government simultaneously ignores the definition's further instruction that such manner or circumstance already will "'ha[ve] been stated,'" "'asserted,'" or "'described.'" *Id.*, at 18 (quoting Black's Law Dictionary, at 1246; 15 Oxford English Dictionary, at 887). Under the Government's approach, the relevant circumstance—the one rendering a person's conduct illegal—is not identified earlier in the statute. Instead, "so" captures *any* circumstance-based limit appearing *anywhere*—in the United States Code, a state statute, a private agreement, or anywhere else. And while the Government tries to cabin its interpretation by suggesting that any such limit must be "specifically and explicitly" stated, "express," and "inherent in the authorization itself," the Government does not identify any textual basis for these guardrails. Brief for United States 19; Tr. of Oral Arg. 41.

Van Buren's account of "so"—namely, that "so" references the previously stated "manner or circumstance" in the text of § 1030(e)(6) itself—is more plausible than the Government's. "So" is not a free-floating term that provides a hook for any limitation stated anywhere. It refers to a stated, identifiable proposition from the "preceding" text; indeed, "so" typically "[r]epresent[s]" a "word or phrase already employed," thereby avoiding the need for repetition. 15 Oxford English Dictionary, at 887; see Webster's Third New International Dictionary 2160 (1986) (so "often used as a substitute ... to express the idea of a preceding phrase"). Myriad federal statutes illustrate this ordinary usage.[3] We agree with Van Buren: The phrase "is not entitled so to obtain" is best read to refer to information that a person is not entitled to obtain by using a computer that he is authorized to access.[478]

---

[478] Editors: Footnote 4 of the Court's opinion states:

> The dissent criticizes this interpretation as inconsistent with "basic principles of property law," and in particular the "familiar rule that an entitlement to use another person's property is circumstance specific." *Post*, at 1664 (opinion of THOMAS, J.). But common-law principles "should be imported into statutory text only when Congress employs a common-law term"—not when Congress has outlined an offense "analogous to a common-law crime without using common-law terms." *Carter v. United States*, 530 U.S. 255, 265, 120 S.Ct. 2159, 147 L.Ed.2d 203 (2000) (emphasis deleted). Relying on the common law is particularly ill advised here because it was the

2

The Government's primary counterargument is that Van Buren's reading renders the word "so" superfluous. Recall the definition: "to access a computer with authorization and to use such access to obtain ... information in the computer that the accesser is not entitled *so* to obtain." § 1030(e)(6) (emphasis added). According to the Government, "so" adds nothing to the sentence if it refers solely to the earlier stated manner of obtaining the information through use of a computer one has accessed with authorization. What matters on Van Buren's reading, as the Government sees it, is simply that the person obtain information that he is not entitled to obtain—and that point could be made even if "so" were deleted. By contrast, the Government insists, "so" makes a valuable contribution if it incorporates all of the circumstances that might qualify a person's right to obtain information. Because only its interpretation gives "so" work to do, the Government contends, the rule against superfluity means that its interpretation wins. See *Republic of Sudan v. Harrison*, 587 U. S. ——, ——, 139 S.Ct. 1048, 1058, 203 L.Ed.2d 433 (2019).

But the canon does not help the Government because Van Buren's reading does not render "so" superfluous. As Van Buren points out, without "so," the statute would allow individuals to use their right to obtain information in nondigital form as a defense to CFAA liability. Consider, for example, a person who downloads restricted personnel files he is not entitled to obtain by using his computer. Such a person could argue that he was "entitled to obtain" the information if he had the right to access personnel files through another method (*e.g.*, by requesting hard copies of the files from human resources). With "so," the CFAA forecloses that theory of defense. The statute is concerned with what a person does on a computer; it does not excuse hacking into an electronic personnel file if the hacker could have walked down the hall to pick up a physical copy.

This clarification is significant because it underscores that one kind of entitlement to information counts: the right to access the information by using a computer. That can expand liability, as the above example shows. But it narrows liability too. Without the word "so," the statute could be read to incorporate all kinds of limitations on one's entitlement to information. The dissent's take on the statute illustrates why.

3

While the dissent accepts Van Buren's definition of "so," it would arrive at the Government's result by way of the word "entitled." One is "entitled" to do something, the dissent contends, only when "'proper grounds'" are in place. *Post*, at 1663 – 1664 (opinion of THOMAS, J.) (quoting Black's Law Dictionary, at 477). Deciding whether a person

---

failure of pre-existing law to capture computer crime that helped spur Congress to enact the CFAA. See *supra,* at 1652. *Id.*

was "entitled" to obtain information, the dissent continues, therefore demands a "circumstance dependent" analysis of whether access was proper. *Post*, at 1663 – 1664. This reading, like the Government's, would extend the statute's reach to any circumstance-based limit appearing anywhere.

The dissent's approach to the word "entitled" fares fine in the abstract but poorly in context. The statute does not refer to "information ... that the accesser is not entitled to obtain." It refers to "information ... that the accesser is not entitled *so to obtain*." 18 U.S.C. § 1030(e)(6) (emphasis added). The word "entitled," then, does not stand alone, inviting the reader to consider the full scope of the accesser's entitlement to information. The modifying phrase "so to obtain" directs the reader to consider a specific limitation on the accesser's entitlement: his entitlement to obtain the information "in the manner previously stated." *Supra*, at 1650. And as already explained, the manner previously stated is using a computer one is authorized to access. Thus, while giving lipservice to Van Buren's reading of "so," the dissent, like the Government, declines to give "so" any limiting function.[479]

The dissent cannot have it both ways. The consequence of accepting Van Buren's reading of "so" is the narrowed scope of "entitled." In fact, the dissent's examples implicitly concede as much: They all omit the word "so," thereby giving "entitled" its full sweep. See *post*, at 1663 – 1664. An approach that must rewrite the statute to work is even less persuasive than the Government's.

4

The Government falls back on what it describes as the "common parlance" meaning of the phrase "exceeds authorized access." Brief for United States 20–21. According to the Government, any ordinary speaker of the English language would think that Van Buren "exceed[ed] his authorized access" to the law enforcement database when he obtained license-plate information for personal purposes. *Id.*, at 21. The dissent, for its part, asserts that this point "settles" the case. *Post*, at 1667.

If the phrase "exceeds authorized access" were all we had to go on, the Government and the dissent might have a point. But both breeze by the CFAA's explicit definition of the phrase "exceeds authorized access." When "a statute includes an explicit definition" of a term, "we must follow that definition, even if it varies from a term's ordinary meaning." *Tanzin v. Tanvir*, 592 U. S. ——, ——, 141 S.Ct. 486, 490, 208 L.Ed.2d 295 (2020) (internal quotation marks omitted). So the relevant question is not whether Van Buren exceeded his authorized access but whether he exceeded his

---

[479] Editors: Footnote 5 of the Court's opinion states: "For the same reason, the dissent is incorrect when it contends that our interpretation reads the additional words "under any possible circumstance" into the statute. *Post*, at 1663 – 1664 (emphasis deleted). Our reading instead interprets the phrase "so to obtain" to incorporate the single "circumstance" of permissible information access identified by the statute: obtaining the information by using one's computer." *Id.*

authorized access *as the CFAA defines that phrase*. And as we have already explained, the statutory definition favors Van Buren's reading.

That reading, moreover, is perfectly consistent with the way that an "appropriately informed" speaker of the language would understand the meaning of "exceeds authorized access." Nelson, What Is Textualism? 91 Va. L. Rev. 347, 354 (2005). When interpreting statutes, courts take note of terms that carry "technical meaning[s]." A. Scalia & B. Garner, Reading Law: The Interpretation of Legal Texts 73 (2012). "Access" is one such term, long carrying a "well established" meaning in the "computational sense"—a meaning that matters when interpreting a statute about computers. American Heritage Dictionary 10 (3d ed. 1992). In the computing context, "access" references the act of entering a computer "system itself" or a particular "part of a computer system," such as files, folders, or databases.[480] It is thus consistent with that meaning to equate "exceed[ing] authorized access" with the act of entering a part of the system to which a computer user lacks access privileges.[481] The Government and the dissent's broader interpretation is neither the only possible nor even necessarily the most natural one.

B

While the statute's language "spells trouble" for the Government's position, a "wider look at the statute's structure gives us even more reason for pause." *Romag Fasteners, Inc. v. Fossil Group, Inc.*, 590 U. S. ——, —— – ——, 140 S.Ct. 1492, 1495, 206 L.Ed.2d 672 (2020).

---

[480] Editors: Footnote 6 of the Court's opinion states:

> 1 Oxford English Dictionary 72 (2d ed. 1989) ("[t]o gain access to ... data, etc., held in a computer or computer-based system, or the system itself"); Random House Dictionary of the English Language 11 (2d ed. 1987) ("*Computers*. to locate (data) for transfer from one part of a computer system to another ..."); see also C. Sippl & R. Sippl, Computer Dictionary and Handbook 2 (3d ed. 1980) ("[c]oncerns the process of obtaining data from or placing data in storage"); Barnhart Dictionary of New English 2 (3d ed. 1990) ("to retrieve (data) from a computer storage unit or device ..."); Microsoft Computer Dictionary 12 (4th ed. 1999) ("[t]o gain entry to memory in order to read or write data"); A Dictionary of Computing 5 (6th ed. 2008) ("[t]o gain entry to data, a computer system, etc."). *Id.*

[481] Editors: Footnote 7 of the Court's opinion states:

> The dissent makes the odd charge that our interpretation violates the "'presumption against'" reading a provision "contrary to the ordinary meaning of the term it defines." *Post*, at 1667. But when a statute, like this one, is "addressing a ... technical subject, a specialized meaning is to be expected." Scalia, Reading Law, at 73. Consistent with that principle, our interpretation tracks the specialized meaning of "access" in the computer context. This reading is far from "'repugnant to'" the meaning of the phrase "exceeds authorized access," *post*, at 1667—unlike, say, a definitional provision directing that "'the word *dog* is deemed to include all horses.'" Scalia, *supra*, at 232, n. 29. *Id.*

The interplay between the "without authorization" and "exceeds authorized access" clauses of subsection (a)(2) is particularly probative. Those clauses specify two distinct ways of obtaining information unlawfully. *First*, an individual violates the provision when he "accesses a computer without authorization." § 1030(a)(2). *Second*, an individual violates the provision when he "exceeds authorized access" by accessing a computer "with authorization" and then obtaining information he is "not entitled so to obtain." §§ 1030(a)(2), (e)(6). Van Buren's reading places the provision's parts "into an harmonious whole." *Roberts v. Sea-Land Services, Inc.*, 566 U.S. 93, 100, 132 S.Ct. 1350, 182 L.Ed.2d 341 (2012) (internal quotation marks omitted). The Government's does not.

Start with Van Buren's view. The "without authorization" clause, Van Buren contends, protects computers themselves by targeting so-called outside hackers—those who "acces[s] a computer without any permission at all." *LVRC Holdings LLC v. Brekka*, 581 F.3d 1127, 1133 (CA9 2009); see also *Pulte Homes, Inc. v. Laborers' Int'l Union of North Am.*, 648 F.3d 295, 304 (CA6 2011). Van Buren reads the "exceeds authorized access" clause to provide complementary protection for certain information within computers. It does so, Van Buren asserts, by targeting so-called inside hackers—those who access a computer with permission, but then "'exceed' the parameters of authorized access by entering an area of the computer to which [that] authorization does not extend." *United States v. Valle*, 807 F.3d 508, 524 (CA2 2015).

Van Buren's account of subsection (a)(2) makes sense of the statutory structure because it treats the "without authorization" and "exceeds authorized access" clauses consistently. Under Van Buren's reading, liability under both clauses stems from a gates-up-or-down inquiry—one either can or cannot access a computer system, and one either can or cannot access certain areas within the system.[482] And reading both clauses to adopt a gates-up-or-down approach aligns with the computer-context understanding of access as entry. See *supra*, at 1657 – 1658.[483]

---

[482] Editors: Footnote 8 of the Court's opinion states: "For present purposes, we need not address whether this inquiry turns only on technological (or "code-based") limitations on access, or instead also looks to limits contained in contracts or policies. Cf. Brief for Orin Kerr as *Amicus Curiae* 7 (urging adoption of code-based approach)."

[483] Editors: Footnote 9 of the Court's opinion states:

> Van Buren's gates-up-or-down reading also aligns with the CFAA's prohibition on password trafficking. See Tr. of Oral Arg. 33. Enacted alongside the "exceeds authorized access" definition in 1986, the password-trafficking provision bars the sale of "any password or similar information through which a computer may be accessed without authorization." § 1030(a)(6). The provision thus contemplates a "specific type of authorization—that is, authentication," which turns on whether a user's credentials allow him to proceed past a computer's access gate, rather than on other, scope-based restrictions. Bellia, A Code-Based Approach to Unauthorized Access Under the Computer Fraud and Abuse Act, 84 Geo. Wash. L. Rev. 1442, 1470 (2016); cf. A Dictionary of Computing, at 30 (defining "authorization" as a "process by which users, having completed an ... authentication stage, gain or are denied access to particular resources based on their entitlement"). *Id.*

By contrast, the Government's reading of the "exceeds authorized access" clause creates "inconsistenc[ies] with the design and structure" of subsection (a)(2). *University of Tex. Southwestern Medical Center v. Nassar*, 570 U.S. 338, 353, 133 S.Ct. 2517, 186 L.Ed.2d 503 (2013). As discussed, the Government reads the "exceeds authorized access" clause to incorporate purpose-based limits contained in contracts and workplace policies. Yet the Government does not read such limits into the threshold question whether someone uses a computer "without authorization"—even though similar purpose restrictions, like a rule against personal use, often govern one's right to access a computer in the first place. See, *e.g., Royal Truck & Trailer Sales & Serv., Inc. v. Kraft*, 974 F.3d 756, 757 (CA6 2020). Thus, the Government proposes to read the first phrase "without authorization" as a gates-up-or-down inquiry and the second phrase "exceeds authorized access" as one that depends on the circumstances. The Government does not explain why the statute would prohibit accessing computer information, but not the computer itself, for an improper purpose.[484]

The Government's position has another structural problem. Recall that violating § 1030(a)(2), the provision under which Van Buren was charged, also gives rise to civil liability. See § 1030(g). Provisions defining "damage" and "loss" specify what a plaintiff in a civil suit can recover. "'[D]amage,'" the statute provides, means "any impairment to the integrity or availability of data, a program, a system, or information." § 1030(e)(8). The term "loss" likewise relates to costs caused by harm to computer data, programs, systems, or information services. § 1030(e)(11). The statutory definitions of "damage" and "loss" thus focus on technological harms—such as the corruption of files—of the type unauthorized users cause to computer systems and data. Limiting "damage" and "loss" in this way makes sense in a scheme "aimed at preventing the typical consequences of hacking." *Royal Truck*, 974 F.3d at 760. The term's definitions are ill fitted, however, to remediating "misuse" of sensitive information that employees may permissibly access using their computers. *Ibid.* Van Buren's situation is illustrative: His run of the license plate did not impair the "integrity or availability" of data, nor did it otherwise harm the database system itself.

---

[484] Editors: Footnote 10 of the Court's opinion states:

> Unlike the Government, the dissent would read both clauses of subsection (a)(2) to require a circumstance-specific analysis. Doing so, the dissent contends, would reflect that "[p]roperty law generally protects against both unlawful entry *and* unlawful use." *Post*, at 1666. This interpretation suffers from structural problems of its own. Consider the standard rule prohibiting the use of one's work computer for personal purposes. Under the dissent's approach, an employee's computer access would be *without* authorization if he logged on to the computer with the purpose of obtaining a file for personal reasons. In that event, obtaining the file would not violate the "exceeds authorized access" clause, which applies only when one accesses a computer "*with* authorization." § 1030(e)(6) (emphasis added). The dissent's reading would therefore leave the "exceeds authorized access" clause with no work to do much of the time—an outcome that Van Buren's interpretation (and, for that matter, the Government's) avoids. *Id.*

C

Pivoting from text and structure, the Government claims that precedent and statutory history support its interpretation. These arguments are easily dispatched.

As for precedent, the Government asserts that this Court's decision in *Musacchio v. United States*, 577 U.S. 237, 136 S.Ct. 709, 193 L.Ed.2d 639 (2016), bolsters its reading. There, in addressing a question about the standard of review for instructional error, the Court described § 1030(a)(2) as prohibiting "(1) obtaining access without authorization; and (2) obtaining access with authorization but then using that access improperly." *Id.*, at 240, 136 S.Ct. 709. This paraphrase of the statute does not do much for the Government. As an initial matter, *Musacchio* did not address—much less resolve in the Government's favor—the "point now at issue," and we thus "are not bound to follow" any dicta in the case. *Central Va. Community College v. Katz*, 546 U.S. 356, 363, 126 S.Ct. 990, 163 L.Ed.2d 945 (2006). But in any event, Van Buren's interpretation, no less than the Government's, involves "using [one's] access improperly." It is plainly "improper" for one to use the opportunity his computer access provides to obtain prohibited information from within the computer.

As for statutory history, the Government claims that the original 1984 Act supports its interpretation of the current version. In a precursor to the "exceeds authorized access" clause, the 1984 Act covered any person who, "having accessed a computer with authorization, uses the opportunity such access provides for purposes to which such authorization does not extend," and thus expressly alluded to the purpose of an insider's computer access. 18 U.S.C. § 1030(a)(2) (1982 ed. Supp. III). According to the Government, this confirms that the amended CFAA—which makes no mention of purpose in defining "exceeds authorized access"—likewise covers insiders like Van Buren who use their computer access for an unauthorized purpose.[11] The Government's argument gets things precisely backward. "When Congress amends legislation, courts must presume it intends the change to have real and substantial effect." *Ross v. Blake*, 578 U. S. 632, 641–642, 136 S.Ct. 1850, 195 L.Ed.2d 117 (2016) (internal quotation marks and brackets omitted). Congress' choice to *remove* the statute's reference to purpose thus cuts *against* reading the statute "to capture that very concept." Brief for United States 22. The statutory history thus hurts rather than helps the Government's position.

III

To top it all off, the Government's interpretation of the statute would attach criminal penalties to a breathtaking amount of commonplace computer activity. Van Buren frames the far-reaching consequences of the Government's reading as triggering the rule of lenity or constitutional avoidance. That is not how we see it: Because the text, context, and structure support Van Buren's reading, neither of these canons is in play. Still, the fallout underscores the implausibility of the Government's interpretation. It is "extra icing on a cake already frosted." *Yates v. United States*, 574 U.S. 528, 557, 135 S.Ct. 1074, 191 L.Ed.2d 64 (2015) (KAGAN, J., dissenting).

If the "exceeds authorized access" clause criminalizes every violation of a computer-use policy, then millions of otherwise law-abiding citizens are criminals. Take the workplace. Employers commonly state that computers and electronic devices can be used only for business purposes. So on the Government's reading of the statute, an employee who sends a personal e-mail or reads the news using her work computer has violated the CFAA. Or consider the Internet. Many websites, services, and databases— which provide "information" from "protected computer[s]," § 1030(a)(2)(C)—authorize a user's access only upon his agreement to follow specified terms of service. If the "exceeds authorized access" clause encompasses violations of circumstance-based access restrictions on employers' computers, it is difficult to see why it would not also encompass violations of such restrictions on website providers' computers. And indeed, numerous *amici* explain why the Government's reading of subsection (a)(2) would do just that—criminalize everything from embellishing an online-dating profile to using a pseudonym on Facebook. See Brief for Orin Kerr as *Amicus Curiae* 10–11; Brief for Technology Companies as *Amici Curiae* 6, n. 3, 11; see also Brief for Reporters Committee for Freedom of the Press et al. as *Amici Curiae* 10–13 (journalism activity); Brief for Kyratso Karahalios et al. as *Amici Curiae* 11–17 (online civil-rights testing and research).

In response to these points, the Government posits that other terms in the statute—specifically "authorization" and "use"—"may well" serve to cabin its prosecutorial power. Brief for United States 35; see Tr. of Oral Arg. 38, 40, 58 ("instrumental" use; "individualized" and "fairly specific" authorization). Yet the Government stops far short of endorsing such limitations. Cf. Brief for United States 37 (concept of "authorization" "may not logically apply"); *id.*, at 38 ("'use'" might be read in a more "limited" fashion, even though it "often has a broader definition"); see also, *e.g.*, *post*, at 1668 – 1669 (*mens rea* requirement "might" preclude liability in some cases). Nor does it cite any prior instance in which it has read the statute to contain such limitations—to the contrary, Van Buren cites instances where it hasn't. See Reply Brief 14–15, 17 (collecting cases); cf. *Sandvig v. Barr*, 451 F.Supp.3d 73, 81–82 (D.D.C. 2020) (discussing Department of Justice testimony indicating that the Government could "'bring a CFAA prosecution based'" on terms-of-service violations causing "'de minimis harm'"). If anything, the Government's current CFAA charging policy shows why Van Buren's concerns are far from "hypothetical," *post*, at 1668 – 1669: The policy instructs that federal prosecution "*may not* be warranted"—not that it would be prohibited—"if the defendant exceed[s] authorized access solely by violating an access restriction contained in a contractual agreement or term of service with an Internet service provider or website."[12] And while the Government insists that the intent requirement serves as yet another safety valve, that requirement would do nothing for those who intentionally use their computers in a way their "job or policy prohibits"—for example, by checking sports scores or paying bills at work. App. 39.

One final observation: The Government's approach would inject arbitrariness into the assessment of criminal liability. The Government concedes, as it must, that the "exceeds authorized access" clause prohibits only unlawful information "access," not downstream information "'misus[e].'" Brief in Opposition 17 (statute does not cover "'subsequen[t] misus[e of] information'"). But the line between the two can be thin on the Government's reading. Because purpose-based limits on access are often designed with an eye toward information misuse, they can be expressed as either access or use restrictions. For example, one police department might prohibit *using a confidential database* for a non-law-enforcement purpose (an access restriction), while another might prohibit *using information from the database* for a non-law-enforcement purpose (a use restriction). Conduct like Van Buren's can be characterized either way, and an employer might not see much difference between the two. On the Government's reading, however, the conduct would violate the CFAA only if the employer phrased the policy as an access restriction. An interpretation that stakes so much on a fine distinction controlled by the drafting practices of private parties is hard to sell as the most plausible.

IV

In sum, an individual "exceeds authorized access" when he accesses a computer with authorization but then obtains information located in particular areas of the computer—such as files, folders, or databases—that are off limits to him. The parties agree that Van Buren accessed the law enforcement database system with authorization. The only question is whether Van Buren could use the system to retrieve license-plate information. Both sides agree that he could. Van Buren accordingly did not "excee[d] authorized access" to the database, as the CFAA defines that phrase, even though he obtained information from the database for an improper purpose. We therefore reverse the contrary judgment of the Eleventh Circuit and remand the case for further proceedings consistent with this opinion.

It is so ordered.

United States v. Nosal, 844 F.3d 1024 (9th Cir. 2016).

McKEOWN, Circuit Judge:

This is the second time we consider the scope of the Computer Fraud and Abuse Act ("CFAA"), 18 U.S.C. § 1030, with respect to David Nosal. The CFAA imposes criminal penalties on whoever "knowingly and with intent to defraud, accesses a protected computer without authorization, or exceeds authorized access, and by means of such conduct furthers the intended fraud and obtains anything of value." Id. § 1030(a)(4) (emphasis added).

Only the first prong of the section is before us in this appeal: "knowingly and with intent to defraud" accessing a computer "without authorization." Embracing our earlier precedent and joining our sister circuits, we conclude that "without authorization" is an unambiguous, non-technical term that, given its plain and ordinary meaning, means accessing a protected computer without permission. Further, we have held that authorization is not pegged to website terms and conditions. This definition has a simple corollary: once authorization to access a computer has been affirmatively revoked, the user cannot sidestep the statute by going through the back door and accessing the computer through a third party. Unequivocal revocation of computer access closes both the front door and the back door. This provision, coupled with the requirement that access be "knowingly and with intent to defraud," means that the statute will not sweep in innocent conduct, such as family password sharing.

Nosal worked at the executive search firm Korn/Ferry International when he decided to launch a competitor along with a group of co-workers. Before leaving Korn/Ferry, Nosal's colleagues began downloading confidential information from a Korn/Ferry database to use at their new enterprise. Although they were authorized to access the database as current Korn/Ferry employees, their downloads on behalf of Nosal violated Korn/Ferry's confidentiality and computer use policies. In 2012, we addressed whether those employees "exceed[ed] authorized access" with intent to defraud under the CFAA. United States v. Nosal (Nosal I), 676 F.3d 854 (9th Cir. 2012) (en banc). Distinguishing between access restrictions and use restrictions, we concluded that the "exceeds authorized access" prong of § 1030(a)(4) of the CFAA "does not extend to violations of [a company's] use restrictions." Id. at 863. We affirmed the district court's dismissal of the five CFAA counts related to Nosal's aiding and abetting misuse of data accessed by his co-workers with their own passwords.

The remaining counts relate to statutory provisions that were not at issue in Nosal I: access to a protected computer "without authorization" under the CFAA and trade secret theft under the Economic Espionage Act ("EEA"), 18 U.S.C. § 1831 et seq. When Nosal left Korn/Ferry, the company revoked his computer access credentials, even though he remained for a time as a contractor. The company took the same precaution upon the departure of his accomplices, Becky Christian and Mark Jacobson. Nonetheless, they continued to access the database using the credentials of Nosal's former executive assistant, Jacqueline Froehlich–L'Heureaux ("FH"), who remained at Korn/Ferry at Nosal's request. The question we consider is whether the jury properly convicted Nosal of conspiracy to violate the "without authorization" provision of the CFAA for unauthorized access to, and downloads from, his former employer's database called Searcher. Put simply, we are asked to decide whether the "without authorization" prohibition of the CFAA extends to a former employee whose computer access credentials have been rescinded but who, disregarding the revocation, accesses the computer by other means.

We directly answered this question in LVRC Holdings LLC v. Brekka, 581 F.3d 1127 (9th Cir. 2009), and reiterate our holding here: "[A] person uses a computer 'without authorization' under [the CFAA] ... when the employer has rescinded permission to access the computer and the defendant uses the computer anyway." Id. at 1135. This straightforward principle embodies the common sense, ordinary meaning of the "without authorization" prohibition.

Nosal and various amici spin hypotheticals about the dire consequences of criminalizing password sharing. But these warnings miss the mark in this case. This appeal is not about password sharing. Nor is it about violating a company's internal computer-use policies. The conduct at issue is that of Nosal and his co-conspirators, which is covered by the plain language of the statute. Nosal is charged with conspiring with former Korn/Ferry employees whose user accounts had been terminated, but who nonetheless accessed trade secrets in a proprietary database through the back door when the front door had been firmly closed. Nosal knowingly and with intent to defraud Korn/Ferry blatantly circumvented the affirmative revocation of his computer system access. This access falls squarely within the CFAA's prohibition on "knowingly and with intent to defraud" accessing a computer "without authorization," and thus we affirm Nosal's conviction for violations of § 1030(a)(4) of the CFAA.

The dissent mistakenly focuses on FH's authority, sidestepping the authorization question for Christian and Jacobson. To begin, FH had no authority from Korn/Ferry to provide her password to former employees whose computer access had been revoked. Also, in collapsing the distinction between FH's authorization and that of Christian and Jacobson, the dissent would render meaningless the concept of authorization. And, pertinent here, it would remove from the scope of the CFAA any hacking conspiracy with an inside person. That surely was not Congress's intent.

We also affirm Nosal's convictions under the EEA for downloading, receiving and possessing trade secrets in the form of source lists from Searcher. . . .

Background

I. Factual Background

Nosal was a high-level regional director at the global executive search firm Korn/Ferry International. Korn/Ferry's bread and butter was identifying and recommending potential candidates for corporate positions. In 2004, after being passed over for a promotion, Nosal announced his intention to leave Korn/Ferry. Negotiations ensued and Nosal agreed to stay on for an additional year as a contractor to finish a handful of open searches, subject to a blanket non-competition agreement. As he put it, Korn/Ferry was giving him "a lot of money" to "stay out of the market."

During this interim period, Nosal was very busy, secretly launching his own search firm along with other Korn/Ferry employees, including Christian, Jacobson and FH. As of December 8, 2004, Korn/Ferry revoked Nosal's access to its computers, although it permitted him to ask Korn/Ferry employees for research help on his remaining open assignments. In January 2005, Christian left Korn/Ferry and, under instructions from Nosal, set up an executive search firm—Christian & Associates—from which Nosal retained 80% of fees. Jacobson followed her a few months later. As Nosal, Christian and Jacobson began work for clients, Nosal used the name "David Nelson" to mask his identity when interviewing candidates.

The start-up company was missing Korn/Ferry's core asset: "Searcher," an internal database of information on over one million executives, including contact information, employment history, salaries, biographies and resumes, all compiled since

1995. Searcher was central to Korn/Ferry's work for clients. When launching a new search to fill an open executive position, Korn/Ferry teams started by compiling a "source list" of potential candidates. In constructing the list, the employees would run queries in Searcher to generate a list of candidates. To speed up the process, employees could look at old source lists in Searcher to see how a search for a similar position was constructed, or to identify suitable candidates. The resulting source list could include hundreds of names, but then was narrowed to a short list of candidates presented to the client. Korn/Ferry considered these source lists proprietary.

Searcher included data from a number of public and quasi-public sources like LinkedIn, corporate filings and Internet searches, and also included internal, non-public sources, such as personal connections, unsolicited resumes sent to Korn/Ferry and data inputted directly by candidates via Korn/Ferry's website. The data was coded upon entry; as a result, employees could run targeted searches for candidates by criteria such as age, industry, experience or other data points. However, once the information became part of the Searcher system, it was integrated with other data and there was no way to identify the source of the data.

Searcher was hosted on the company's internal computer network and was considered confidential and for use only in Korn/Ferry business. Korn/Ferry issued each employee a unique username and password to its computer system; no separate password was required to access Searcher. Password sharing was prohibited by a confidentiality agreement that Korn/Ferry required each new employee to sign. When a user requested a custom report in Searcher, Searcher displayed a message which stated: "This product is intended to be used by Korn/Ferry employees for work on Korn/Ferry business only."

Nosal and his compatriots downloaded information and source lists from Searcher in preparation to launch the new competitor. Before leaving Korn/Ferry, they used their own usernames and passwords, compiling proprietary Korn/Ferry data in violation of Korn/Ferry's computer use policy. Those efforts were encompassed in the CFAA accounts appealed in Nosal I. See 676 F.3d at 856.

After Nosal became a contractor and Christian and Jacobson left Korn/Ferry, Korn/Ferry revoked each of their credentials to access Korn/Ferry's computer system. Not to be deterred, on three occasions Christian and Jacobson borrowed access credentials from FH, who stayed on at Korn/Ferry at Nosal's request. In April 2005, Nosal instructed Christian to obtain some source lists from Searcher to expedite their work for a new client. Thinking it would be difficult to explain the request to FH, Christian asked to borrow FH's access credentials, which Christian then used to log in to Korn/Ferry's computer system and run queries in Searcher. Christian sent the results of her searches to Nosal. In July 2005, Christian again logged in as FH to generate a custom report and search for information on three individuals. Later in July, Jacobson also logged in as FH, to download information on 2,400 executives. None of these searches related to any open searches that fell under Nosal's independent contractor agreement.

In March 2005, Korn/Ferry received an email from an unidentified person advising that Nosal was conducting his own business in violation of his non-compete agreement. The company launched an investigation and, in July 2005, contacted government authorities. . . .

Analysis

I. Convictions Under the Computer Fraud and Abuse Act

A. Background of the CFAA

The CFAA was originally enacted in 1984 as the Counterfeit Access Device and Computer Fraud and Abuse Act, Pub. L. No. 98–473, § 2102(a), 98 Stat. 2190 (1984). The act was aimed at "hackers who accessed computers to steal information or to disrupt or destroy computer functionality." Brekka, 581 F.3d at 1130–31 (citing H.R. Rep. No. 98–894, at 8–9 (1984), reprinted in 1984 U.S.C.C.A.N. 3689, 3694). The original legislation protected government and financial institution computers,2 and made it a felony to access classified information in a computer "without authorization." Counterfeit Access Device and Computer Fraud and Abuse Act § 2102(a).

Just two years later in 1986, Congress amended the statute to "deter[ ] and punish[–] certain 'high-tech' crimes," and "to penalize thefts of property via computer that occur as part of a scheme to defraud," S. Rep. No. 99–432, at 4, 9 (1986), reprinted in 1986 U.S.C.C.A.N. 2479, 2482, 2486–87. The amendment expanded the CFAA's protections to private computers. Computer Fraud and Abuse Act of 1986, Pub. L. No. 99–474, § 2(g)(4), 100 Stat. 1213–15.3

The key section of the CFAA at issue is 18 U.S.C. § 1030(a)(4), which provides in relevant part:

> Whoever ... knowingly and with intent to defraud, accesses a protected computer without authorization, or exceeds authorized access, and by means of such conduct furthers the intended fraud and obtains anything of value ... shall be punished....

A key element of the statute is the requirement that the access be "knowingly and with intent to defraud." Not surprisingly, this phrase is not defined in the CFAA as it is the bread and butter of many criminal statutes. Indeed, the district court borrowed the language from the Ninth Circuit model jury instructions in defining "knowingly" and "intent to defraud" for the jury, and Nosal does not renew any challenges to those instructions on appeal. This mens rea element of the statute is critical because imposing the "intent to defraud" element targets knowing and specific conduct and does not embrace the parade of hypotheticals generated by Nosal and amici.

The CFAA defines "exceeds authorized access" as "access [to] a computer with authorization and [using] such access to obtain or alter information in the computer that the accesser is not entitled so to obtain or alter." Id. § 1030(e)(6). The statute does not, however, define "without authorization." Both terms are used throughout § 1030. Subsection 1030(a)(2), which mirrors (a)(4) but requires that access be intentional, penalizes access without authorization and exceeding authorization. Subsection 1030(a)(1) also incorporates both terms in relation to accessing a computer and obtaining national security information. Subsection 1030(a)(7)(B) criminalizes extortion by threats to obtain information "without authorization or in excess of authorization." The remaining subsections pertain only to access "without authorization." Subsection 1030(a)(3) prohibits access "without authorization" to nonpublic government computers. Subsections 1030(a)(5) and (6) employ the term "without authorization" with respect to, among other things, "transmission of a program, information, code, or command," § 1030(a)(5)(A); intentional access that "causes damage and loss," § 1030(a)(5)(C); and trafficking in passwords, § 1030(a)(6). In construing the statute, we are cognizant of the need for congruence among these subsections.

B. Meaning of "Authorization" Under the CFAA

The interpretive fireworks under § 1030(a)(4) of the CFAA have been reserved for its second prong, the meaning of "exceeds authorized access." Not surprisingly, there has been no division among the circuits on the straightforward "without authorization" prong of this section. We begin with the two Ninth Circuit cases that bind our interpretation of "without authorization"—Brekka and Nosal I—and then move on to address the cases from our sister circuits that are in accord with Brekka, agreeing that "without authorization" is an unambiguous term that should be given its ordinary meaning.

Brekka involved a former employee in circumstances remarkably similar to Nosal: he wanted to compete using confidential data from his former company. Christopher Brekka worked as an internet marketer with LVRC Holdings, LLC ("LVRC"), a residential addiction treatment center. Brekka, 581 F.3d at 1129. LVRC assigned him a computer and gave him access credentials to a third-party website that tracked traffic and other information for LVRC's website. When negotiations to become part owner of LVRC broke down, Brekka left the company. LVRC sued him, claiming that he violated the CFAA by emailing certain confidential company documents to his personal email account while an employee and also by continuing to access LVRC's account on the external website after he left the company.

In Brekka we analyzed both the "without authorization" and "exceeds authorization" provisions of the statute under §§ 1030(a)(2) and (4). Id. at 1132–36. Because the CFAA does not define the term "authorization," we looked to the ordinary, contemporaneous meaning of the term: " 'permission or power granted by an authority.' " Id. at 1133 (quoting Random House Unabridged Dictionary 139 (2001)). In determining whether an employee has authorization, we stated that, consistent with "the plain language of the statute ... 'authorization' [to use an employer's computer] depends on actions taken by the employer." Id. at 1135. We concluded that because Brekka had permission to use his employer's computer, "[t]he most straightforward interpretation of §§ 1030(a)(2) and (4) is that Brekka had authorization to use the computer" while an employee. Id. at 1133.

Brekka's access after LVRC terminated his employment presented a starkly different situation: "There is no dispute that if Brekka accessed LVRC's information on the [traffic monitoring] website after he left the company ..., Brekka would have accessed a protected computer 'without authorization' for purposes of the CFAA." Id. at 1136.4 Stated differently, we held that "a person uses a computer 'without authorization' under §§ 1030(a)(2) and (4) ... when the employer has rescinded permission to access the computer and the defendant uses the computer anyway." Id. at 1135. In Brekka's case, there was no genuine issue of material fact as to whether Brekka actually accessed the website, and thus we affirmed the district court's grant of summary judgment. Id. at 1137.

Not surprisingly, in Nosal I as in this appeal, both the government and Nosal cited Brekka extensively. The focus of Nosal's first appeal was whether the CFAA could be interpreted "broadly to cover violations of corporate computer use restrictions or violations of a duty of loyalty." Nosal I, 676 F.3d at 862. We unequivocally said "no": "For our part, we continue to follow in the path blazed by Brekka and the growing number of courts that have reached the same conclusion. These courts recognize that the plain language of the CFAA 'target[s] the unauthorized procurement or alteration of information, not its misuse or misappropriation.' " Id. at 863 (citations omitted). In line with Brekka, we stated that " '[w]ithout authorization' would apply to outside hackers (individuals who have no authorized access to the computer at all) and 'exceeds authorization access' would apply to inside hackers (individuals whose initial access to a computer is authorized but who access unauthorized information or files)." Id. at 858. Because Nosal's accomplices had authority to access the company computers, we affirmed the district court's dismissal of the CFAA counts related to the period when the accomplices were still employed at Korn/Ferry. Id. at 864.

In Nosal I, authorization was not in doubt. The employees who accessed the Korn/Ferry computers unquestionably had authorization from the company to access the system; the question was whether they exceeded it. What Nosal I did not address was whether Nosal's access to Korn/Ferry computers after both Nosal and his co-conspirators had terminated their employment and Korn/Ferry revoked their permission to access the computers was "without authorization." Brekka is squarely on point on that issue: Nosal and his co-conspirators acted "without authorization" when they continued to access Searcher by other means after Korn/Ferry rescinded permission to access its computer system. As Nosal I made clear, the CFAA was not intended to cover unauthorized use of information. Such use is not at issue here. Rather, under § 1030(a)(4), Nosal is charged with unauthorized access—getting into the computer after categorically being barred from entry.

The text of the CFAA confirms Brekka's approach. Employing classic statutory interpretation, we consider the plain and ordinary meaning of the words "without authorization." See United States v. Stewart, 311 U.S. 60, 63, 61 S.Ct. 102, 85 L.Ed. 40 (1940). Under our analysis in Brekka, "authorization" means " 'permission or power granted by an authority.' " 581 F.3d at 1133 (quoting Random House Unabridged Dictionary 139 (2001)). Other sources employ similar definitions. Black's Law Dictionary defines "authorization" as "[o]fficial permission to do something; sanction or warrant." Black's Law Dictionary 159 (10th ed. 2014). The Oxford English Dictionary defines it as "the action of authorizing," which means to "give official permission for or approval to." Oxford English Dictionary 107 (3d ed. 2014). That common sense meaning is not foreign to Congress or the courts: the terms "authorize," "authorized" or "authorization" are used without definition over 400 times in Title 18 of the United States Code.5 We conclude that given its ordinary meaning, access "without authorization" under the CFAA is not ambiguous. See United States v. James, 810 F.3d 674, 681 (9th Cir. 2016) (concluding that the mere fact that a broad, but otherwise clear, statutory term is "susceptible to application to various factual situations that can come before a jury" does not by itself render a term ambiguous).

That straightforward meaning is also unambiguous as applied to the facts of this case. Nosal and his co-conspirators did exactly what Brekka prohibits—a conclusion that is not affected by the co-conspirators' use of FH's legitimate access credentials. Implicit in the definition of authorization is the notion that someone, including an entity, can grant or revoke that permission. Here, that entity was Korn/Ferry, and FH had no mantle or authority to override Korn/Ferry's authority to control access to its computers and confidential information by giving permission to former employees whose access had been categorically revoked by the company.7 Korn/Ferry owned and controlled access to its computers, including the Searcher database, and it retained exclusive discretion to issue or revoke access to the database. By revoking Nosal's login credentials on December 8, 2004, Korn/Ferry unequivocally conveyed to Nosal that he was an "outsider" who was no longer authorized to access Korn/Ferry computers and confidential information, including Searcher.8 Korn/Ferry also rescinded Christian and Jacobson's credentials after they left, at which point the three former employees were no longer "insiders" accessing company information. Rather, they had become "outsiders" with no authorization to access Korn/Ferry's computer system. One can certainly pose hypotheticals in which a less stark revocation is followed by more sympathetic access through an authorized third party. But the facts before us—in which Nosal received particularized notice of his revoked access following a prolonged negotiation—present no such difficulties, which can be reserved for another day.

Our analysis is consistent with that of our sister circuits, which have also determined that the term "without authorization" is unambiguous. Although the meaning of "exceeds authorized access" in the CFAA has been subject to much debate among the federal courts, the definition of "without authorization" has not engendered dispute. Indeed, Nosal provides no contrary authority that a former employee whose computer access has been revoked can access his former employer's computer system and be deemed to act with authorization.

. . . Our conclusion does nothing to expand the scope of violations under the CFAA beyond Brekka; nor does it rest on the grace of prosecutorial discretion. We are mindful of the examples noted in Nosal I—and reiterated by Nosal and various amici—that ill-defined terms may capture arguably innocuous conduct, such as password sharing among friends and family, inadvertently "mak[ing] criminals of large groups of people who would have little reason to suspect they are committing a federal crime." Nosal I, 676 F.3d at 859. But these concerns are ill-founded because § 1030(a)(4) requires access be "knowingly and with intent to defraud" and further, we have held that violating use restrictions, like a website's terms of use, is insufficient without more to form the basis for liability under the CFAA. See Nosal I, 676 F.3d at 862–63. The circumstance here— former employees whose computer access was categorically revoked and who surreptitiously accessed data owned by their former employer—bears little resemblance to asking a spouse to log in to an email account to print a boarding pass. The charges at issue in this appeal do not stem from the ambiguous language of Nosal I—"exceeds authorized access"—or even an ambiguous application of the phrase "without authorization," but instead relate to the straightforward application of a common, unambiguous term to the facts and context at issue.

The Brekka analysis of the specific phrase "without authorization"—which is consistent with our sister circuits—remains controlling and persuasive. We therefore hold that Nosal, a former employee whose computer access credentials were affirmatively revoked by Korn/Ferry acted "without authorization" in violation of the CFAA when he or his former employee co-conspirators used the login credentials of a current employee to gain access to confidential computer data owned by the former employer and to circumvent Korn/Ferry's revocation of access.

We affirm Nosal's conviction on the CFAA counts. . . .

NOTES

Note 1

Should the Supreme Court's analysis in *Van Buren*, change the result in the Ninth Circuit's 2016 *Nosal* decision?

HiQ Labs, Inc., v. Linkedin Corp., 2022 WL 1132814 (April 18, 2022).

BERZON, Circuit Judge:

We first issued an opinion in this case in September 2019, addressing the question whether LinkedIn, the professional networking website, could prevent a competitor, hiQ, from collecting and using information that LinkedIn users had shared on their public profiles, available for viewing by anyone with a web browser. *hiQ Labs, Inc. v. LinkedIn Corp.*, 938 F.3d 985 (9th Cir. 2019). HiQ, a data analytics company, had obtained a preliminary injunction forbidding LinkedIn from denying hiQ access to publicly available LinkedIn member profiles. At the preliminary injunction stage, we did not resolve the companies' legal dispute definitively, nor did we address all the claims and defenses they had pleaded in the district court. Instead, we focused on whether hiQ had raised serious questions on the merits of the factual and legal issues presented to us, as well as on the other requisites for preliminary relief. We concluded that hiQ had done so, and we therefore upheld the preliminary injunction.

The Supreme Court granted LinkedIn's petition for writ of certiorari, vacated the judgment, and remanded this case for further consideration in light of *Van Buren v. United States*, —— U.S. ——, 141 S. Ct. 1648, 210 L.Ed.2d 26 (2021). *LinkedIn Corp. v. hiQ Labs, Inc.*, —— U.S. ——, 141 S. Ct. 2752, 210 L.Ed.2d 902 (2021). We ordered supplemental briefing and held oral argument on the effect of *Van Buren* on this appeal. Having concluded that *Van Buren* reinforces our determination that hiQ has raised serious questions about whether LinkedIn may invoke the Computer Fraud and Abuse Act ("CFAA") to preempt hiQ's possibly meritorious tortious interference claim, we once again affirm the preliminary injunction.

I.

Founded in 2002, LinkedIn is a professional networking website with over 500 million members. Members post resumes and job listings and build professional "connections" with other members. LinkedIn specifically disclaims ownership of the information users post to their personal profiles: according to LinkedIn's User Agreement, members own the content and information they submit or post to LinkedIn and grant LinkedIn only a non-exclusive license to "use, copy, modify, distribute, publish, and process" that information.

LinkedIn allows its members to choose among various privacy settings. Members can specify which portions of their profile are visible to the general public (that is, to both LinkedIn members and nonmembers), and which portions are visible only to direct connections, to the member's "network" (consisting of LinkedIn members within three degrees of connectivity), or to all LinkedIn members. This case deals only with profiles made visible to the general public.

LinkedIn also offers all members—whatever their profile privacy settings—a "Do Not Broadcast" option with respect to every change they make to their profiles. If a LinkedIn member selects this option, her connections will not be notified when she updates her profile information, although the updated information will still appear on her profile page (and thus be visible to anyone permitted to view her profile under her general privacy setting). More than 50 million LinkedIn members have, at some point, elected to employ the "Do Not Broadcast" feature, and approximately 20 percent of all active users who updated their profiles between July 2016 and July 2017—whatever their privacy setting—employed the "Do Not Broadcast" setting.

LinkedIn has taken steps to protect the data on its website from what it perceives as misuse or misappropriation. The instructions in LinkedIn's "robots.txt" file—a text file used by website owners to communicate with search engine crawlers and other web robots—prohibit access to LinkedIn servers via automated bots, except that certain entities, like the Google search engine, have express permission from LinkedIn for bot access. LinkedIn also employs several technological systems to detect suspicious activity and restrict automated scraping. For example, LinkedIn's Quicksand system detects non-human activity indicative of scraping; its Sentinel system throttles (slows or limits) or even blocks activity from suspicious IP addresses; and its Org Block system generates a list of known "bad" IP addresses serving as large-scale scrapers. In total, LinkedIn blocks approximately 95 million automated attempts to scrape data every day, and has restricted over 11 million accounts suspected of violating its User Agreement, including through scraping.

HiQ is a data analytics company founded in 2012. Using automated bots, it scrapes information that LinkedIn users have included on public LinkedIn profiles, including name, job title, work history, and skills. It then uses that information, along with a proprietary predictive algorithm, to yield "people analytics," which it sells to business clients.

HiQ offers two such analytics. The first, Keeper, purports to identify employees at the greatest risk of being recruited away. According to hiQ, the product enables employers to offer career development opportunities, retention bonuses, or other perks to retain valuable employees. The second, Skill Mapper, summarizes employees' skills in the aggregate. Among other things, the tool is supposed to help employers identify skill gaps in their workforces so that they can offer internal training in those areas, promoting internal mobility and reducing the expense of external recruitment.

HiQ regularly organizes "Elevate" conferences, during which participants discuss hiQ's business model and share best practices in the people analytics field. LinkedIn representatives participated in Elevate conferences beginning in October 2015. At least ten LinkedIn representatives attended the conferences. LinkedIn employees have also spoken at Elevate conferences. In 2016, a LinkedIn employee was awarded the Elevate "Impact Award." LinkedIn employees thus had an opportunity to learn about hiQ's products, including "that [one of] hiQ's product[s] used data from a variety of sources—internal and external—to predict employee attrition" and that hiQ "collected skills data from public professional profiles in order to provide hiQ's customers information about their employees' skill sets."

In recent years, LinkedIn has explored ways to capitalize on the vast amounts of data contained in LinkedIn profiles by marketing new products. In June 2017, LinkedIn's Chief Executive Officer ("CEO"), Jeff Weiner, appearing on CBS, explained that LinkedIn hoped to "leverage all this extraordinary data we've been able to collect by virtue of having 500 million people join the site." Weiner mentioned as possibilities providing employers with data-driven insights about what skills they will need to grow and where they can find employees with those skills. Since then, LinkedIn has announced a new product, Talent Insights, which analyzes LinkedIn data to provide companies with such data-driven information.

In May 2017, LinkedIn sent hiQ a cease-and-desist letter, asserting that hiQ was in violation of LinkedIn's User Agreement and demanding that hiQ stop accessing and copying data from LinkedIn's server. The letter stated that if hiQ accessed LinkedIn's data in the future, it would be violating state and federal law, including the CFAA, the Digital Millennium Copyright Act ("DMCA"), California Penal Code § 502(c), and the California common law of trespass. The letter further stated that LinkedIn had "implemented technical measures to prevent hiQ from accessing, and assisting others to access, LinkedIn's site, through systems that detect, monitor, and block scraping activity."

HiQ's response was to demand that LinkedIn recognize hiQ's right to access LinkedIn's public pages and to threaten to seek an injunction if LinkedIn refused. A week later, hiQ filed an action, seeking injunctive relief based on California law and a declaratory judgment that LinkedIn could not lawfully invoke the CFAA, the DMCA, California Penal Code § 502(c), or the common law of trespass against it. . . .

II.

"A plaintiff seeking a preliminary injunction must establish that he is likely to succeed on the merits, that he is likely to suffer irreparable harm in the absence of preliminary relief, that the balance of equities tips in his favor, and that an injunction is in the public interest." *Winter v. Nat. Res. Def. Council, Inc.*, 555 U.S. 7, 20, 129 S.Ct. 365, 172 L.Ed.2d 249 (2008). All four elements must be satisfied. *See, e.g., Am. Trucking Ass'n v. City of Los Angeles*, 559 F.3d 1046, 1057 (9th Cir. 2009). We use a "sliding scale" approach to these factors, according to which "a stronger showing of one element may offset a weaker showing of another." *Alliance for the Wild Rockies v. Cottrell*, 632 F.3d 1127, 1131 (9th Cir. 2011). So, when the balance of hardships tips sharply in the plaintiff's favor, the plaintiff need demonstrate only "serious questions going to the merits." *Id.* at 1135.

Applying that sliding scale approach, the district court granted hiQ a preliminary injunction, concluding that the balance of hardships tips sharply in hiQ's favor and that hiQ raised serious questions on the merits. We review the district court's decision to grant a preliminary injunction for abuse of discretion. The grant of a preliminary injunction constitutes an abuse of discretion if the district court's evaluation or balancing of the pertinent factors is "illogical, implausible, or without support in the record." *Doe v. Kelly*, 878 F.3d 710, 713 (9th Cir. 2017).

A. Irreparable Harm

We begin with the likelihood of irreparable injury to hiQ if preliminary relief were not granted.

"[M]onetary injury is not normally considered irreparable." *Los Angeles Mem'l Coliseum Comm'n v. Nat'l Football League*, 634 F.2d 1197, 1202 (9th Cir. 1980). Nonetheless, "[t]he threat of being driven out of business is sufficient to establish irreparable harm." *Am. Passage Media Corp. v. Cass Commc'ns, Inc.*, 750 F.2d 1470, 1474 (9th Cir. 1985). As the Second Circuit has explained, "[t]he loss of ... an ongoing business representing many years of effort and the livelihood of its ... owners, constitutes irreparable harm. What plaintiff stands to lose cannot be fully compensated by subsequent monetary damages." *Roso-Lino Beverage Distributors, Inc. v. Coca-Cola Bottling Co. of New York, Inc.*, 749 F.2d 124, 125–26 (2d Cir. 1984) (per curiam). Thus, showing a threat of "extinction" is enough to establish irreparable harm, even when damages may be available and the amount of direct financial harm is ascertainable. *Am. Passage Media Corp.*, 750 F.2d at 1474.

The district court found credible hiQ's assertion that the survival of its business is threatened absent a preliminary injunction. The record provides ample support for that finding.

According to hiQ's CEO, "hiQ's entire business depends on being able to access public LinkedIn member profiles," as "there is no current viable alternative to LinkedIn's member database to obtain data for hiQ's Keeper and Skill Mapper services." Without access to LinkedIn public profile data, the CEO averred, hiQ will likely be forced to breach its existing contracts with clients such as eBay, Capital One, and GoDaddy, and to pass up pending deals with prospective clients. The harm hiQ faces absent a preliminary injunction is not purely hypothetical. HiQ was in the middle of a financing round when it received LinkedIn's cease-and-desist letter. The CEO reported that, in light of the uncertainty about the future viability of hiQ's business, that financing round stalled, and several employees left the company. If LinkedIn prevails, hiQ's CEO further asserted, hiQ would have to "lay off most if not all its employees, and shutter its operations."

LinkedIn maintains that hiQ's business model does not depend on access to LinkedIn data. It insists that alternatives to LinkedIn data exist, and points in particular to the professional data some users post on Facebook. But hiQ's model depends on access to publicly available data from people who choose to share their information with the world. Facebook data, by contrast, is not generally accessible, *see* *infra* p. ——, and therefore is not an equivalent alternative source of data.

LinkedIn also urges that even if there is no adequate alternative database, hiQ could collect its own data through employee surveys. But hiQ is a data analytics company, not a data collection company. Suggesting that hiQ could fundamentally change the nature of its business, not simply the manner in which it conducts its current business, is a recognition that hiQ's current business could not survive without access to LinkedIn public profile data. Creating a data collection system would undoubtedly require a considerable amount of time and expense. That hiQ could feasibly remain in business with no products to sell while raising the required capital and devising and implementing an entirely new data collection system is at least highly dubious.

In short, the district court did not abuse its discretion in concluding on the preliminary injunction record that hiQ currently has no viable way to remain in business other than using LinkedIn public profile data for its Keeper and Skill Mapper services, and that HiQ therefore has demonstrated a likelihood of irreparable harm absent a preliminary injunction.

B. Balance of the Equities

Next, the district court "balance[d] the interests of all parties and weigh[ed] the damage to each in determining the balance of the equities." *CTIA - The Wireless Ass'n v. City of Berkeley, Calif.*, 928 F.3d 832, 852 (9th Cir. 2019) (internal quotation marks and citation omitted). Again, it did not abuse its discretion in doing so.

On one side of the scale is the harm to hiQ just discussed: the likelihood that, without an injunction, it will go out of business. On the other side, LinkedIn asserts that the injunction threatens its members' privacy and therefore puts at risk the goodwill LinkedIn has developed with its members. As the district court observed, "the fact that a user has set his profile to public does not imply that he wants any third parties to collect and use that data for all purposes." LinkedIn points in particular to the more than 50 million members who have used the "Do Not Broadcast" feature to ensure that other users are not notified when the member makes a profile change. According to LinkedIn, the popularity of the "Do Not Broadcast" feature indicates that many members— including members who choose to share their information publicly—do not want their employers to know they may be searching for a new job. An employer who learns that an employee may be planning to leave will not necessarily reward that employee with a retention bonus. Instead, the employer could decide to limit the employee's access to sensitive information or even to terminate the employee.

There is support in the record for the district court's connected conclusions that (1) LinkedIn's assertions have some merit; and (2) there are reasons to discount them to some extent. First, there is little evidence that LinkedIn users who choose to make their profiles public actually maintain an expectation of privacy with respect to the information that they post publicly, and it is doubtful that they do. LinkedIn's privacy policy clearly states that "[a]ny information you put on your profile and any content you post on LinkedIn may be seen by others" and instructs users not to "post or add personal data to your profile that you would not want to be public."

Second, there is no evidence in the record to suggest that most people who select the "Do Not Broadcast" option do so to prevent their employers from being alerted to profile changes made in anticipation of a job search. As the district court stated, there are other reasons why users may choose that option—most notably, many users may simply wish to avoid sending their connections annoying notifications each time there is a profile change. In any event, employers can always directly consult the profiles of users who chose to make their profiles public to see if any recent changes have been made. Employees intent on keeping such information from their employers can do so by rejecting public exposure of their profiles and eliminating their employers as contacts.

Finally, LinkedIn's own actions undercut its argument that users have an expectation of privacy in public profiles. LinkedIn's "Recruiter" product enables recruiters to "follow" prospects, get "alert[ed] when prospects make changes to their profiles," and "use those [alerts] as signals to reach out at just the right moment," without the prospect's knowledge. And subscribers to LinkedIn's "talent recruiting, marketing and sales solutions" can export data from members' public profiles, such as "name, headline, current company, current title, and location."

In short, even if some users retain some privacy interests in their information notwithstanding their decision to make their profiles public, we cannot, on the record before us, conclude that those interests—or more specifically, LinkedIn's interest in preventing hiQ from scraping those profiles—are significant enough to outweigh hiQ's interest in continuing its business, which depends on accessing, analyzing, and communicating information derived from public LinkedIn profiles.

Nor do the other harms asserted by LinkedIn tip the balance of harms with regard to preliminary relief. LinkedIn invokes an interest in preventing "free riders" from using profiles posted on its platform. But LinkedIn has no protected property interest in the data contributed by its users, as the users retain ownership over their profiles. And as to the publicly available profiles, the users quite evidently intend them to be accessed by others, including for commercial purposes—for example, by employers seeking to hire individuals with certain credentials. Of course, LinkedIn could satisfy its "free rider" concern by eliminating the public access option, albeit at a cost to the preferences of many users and, possibly, to its own bottom line.

We conclude that the district court's determination that the balance of hardships tips sharply in hiQ's favor is not "illogical, implausible, or without support in the record." *Kelly*, 878 F.3d at 713.

C. Likelihood of Success

Because hiQ has established that the balance of hardships tips decidedly in its favor, the likelihood-of-success prong of the preliminary injunction inquiry focuses on whether hiQ has raised "serious questions going to the merits." *Alliance for the Wild Rockies*, 632 F.3d at 1131. It has. . . .

2. Computer Fraud and Abuse Act (CFAA)

Our inquiry does not end, however, with the state law tortious interference claim. LinkedIn argues that even if hiQ can show a likelihood of success on any of its state law causes of action, all those causes of action are preempted by the CFAA, 18 U.S.C. § 1030, which LinkedIn asserts that hiQ violated.

The CFAA states that "[w]hoever ... intentionally accesses a computer without authorization or exceeds authorized access, and thereby obtains ... information from any protected computer ... shall be punished" by fine or imprisonment. 18 U.S.C. § 1030(a)(2)(C). The term "protected computer" refers to any computer "used in or affecting interstate or foreign commerce or communication," 18 U.S.C. § 1030(e)(2)(B)—effectively any computer connected to the Internet, *see United States v. Nosal (Nosal II)*, 844 F.3d 1024, 1050 (9th Cir. 2016), *cert. denied*, ——— U.S. ———, 138 S. Ct. 314, 199 L.Ed.2d 207 (2017)—including servers, computers that manage network resources and provide data to other computers. LinkedIn's computer servers store the data members share on LinkedIn's platform and provide that data to users who request to visit its website. Thus, to scrape LinkedIn data, hiQ must access LinkedIn servers, which are "protected computer[s]." *See Nosal II*, 844 F.3d at 1050.

The pivotal CFAA question here is whether once hiQ received LinkedIn's cease-and-desist letter, any further scraping and use of LinkedIn's data was "without authorization" within the meaning of the CFAA and thus a violation of the statute. 18 U.S.C. § 1030(a)(2). If so, LinkedIn maintains, hiQ could have no legal right of access to LinkedIn's data and so could not succeed on any of its state law claims, including the tortious interference with contract claim we have held otherwise sufficient for preliminary injunction purposes.

We have held in another context that the phrase "'without authorization' is a non-technical term that, given its plain and ordinary meaning, means accessing a protected computer without permission." *Nosal II*, 844 F.3d at 1028. *Nosal II* involved an employee accessing without permission an employer's private computer for which access permissions in the form of user accounts were required. *Id.* at 1028–29. *Nosal II* did not address whether access can be "without authorization" under the CFAA where, as here, prior authorization is not generally required, but a particular person—or bot— is refused access. HiQ's position is that *Nosal II* is consistent with the conclusion that where access is open to the general public, the CFAA "without authorization" concept is inapplicable. At the very least, we conclude, hiQ has raised a serious question as to this issue.

First, the wording of the statute, forbidding "access[ ] ... without authorization," 18 U.S.C. § 1030(a)(2), suggests a baseline in which access is not generally available and so permission is ordinarily required. "Authorization" is an affirmative notion, indicating that access is restricted to those specially recognized or admitted. *See, e.g.*, Black's Law Dictionary (11th ed. 2019) (defining "authorization" as "[o]fficial permission to do something; sanction or warrant"). Where the default is free access without authorization, in ordinary parlance one would characterize selective denial of access as a ban, not as a lack of "authorization." *Cf. Blankenhorn v. City of Orange*, 485 F.3d 463, 472 (9th Cir. 2007) (characterizing the exclusion of the plaintiff in particular from a shopping mall as "bann[ing]").

Second, even if this interpretation is debatable, the legislative history of the statute confirms our understanding. "If [a] statute's terms are ambiguous, we may use ... legislative history[ ] and the statute's overall purpose to illuminate Congress's intent." *Jonah R. v. Carmona*, 446 F.3d 1000, 1005 (9th Cir. 2006).

The CFAA was enacted to prevent intentional intrusion onto someone else's computer—specifically, computer hacking. *See United States v. Nosal (Nosal I)*, 676 F.3d 854, 858 (9th Cir. 2012) (citing S. Rep. No. 99-432, at 9 (1986) (Conf. Rep.)).

The 1984 House Report on the CFAA explicitly analogized the conduct prohibited by section 1030 to forced entry: "It is noteworthy that section 1030 deals with an 'unauthorized access' concept of computer fraud rather than the mere use of a computer. Thus, the conduct prohibited is analogous to that of 'breaking and entering' ...'" H.R. Rep. No. 98-894, at 20 (1984); *see also id.* at 10 (describing the problem of "'hackers' who have been able to access (trespass into) both private and public computer systems"). Senator Jeremiah Denton similarly characterized the CFAA as a statute designed to prevent unlawful intrusion into otherwise inaccessible computers, observing that "[t]he bill makes it clear that unauthorized access to a Government computer is a trespass offense, as surely as if the offender had entered a restricted Government compound without proper authorization." 132 Cong. Rec. 27639 (1986) (emphasis added). And when considering amendments to the CFAA two years later, the House again linked computer intrusion to breaking and entering. *See* H.R. Rep. No. 99-612, at 5–6H.R. Rep. No. 99-612, at 5–6 (1986) (describing "the expanding group of electronic trespassers," who trespass "just as much as if they broke a window and crawled into a home while the occupants were away").

In recognizing that the CFAA is best understood as an anti-intrusion statute and not as a "misappropriation statute," *Nosal I*, 676 F.3d at 857–58, we rejected the contract-based interpretation of the CFAA's "without authorization" provision adopted by some of our sister circuits. *Compare Facebook, Inc. v. Power Ventures, Inc.*, 844 F.3d 1058, 1067 (9th Cir. 2016), *cert. denied*, —— U.S. ——, 138 S. Ct. 313, 199 L.Ed.2d 206 (2017) ("[A] violation of the terms of use of a website—without more—cannot establish liability under the CFAA."); *Nosal I*, 676 F.3d at 862 ("We remain unpersuaded by the decisions of our sister circuits that interpret the CFAA broadly to cover violations of corporate computer use restrictions or violations of a duty of loyalty."), *with EF Cultural Travel BV v. Explorica, Inc.*, 274 F.3d 577, 583–84 (1st Cir. 2001) (holding that violations of a confidentiality agreement or other contractual restraints could give rise to a claim for unauthorized access under the CFAA); *United States v. Rodriguez*, 628 F.3d 1258, 1263 (11th Cir. 2010) (holding that a defendant "exceeds authorized access" when violating policies governing authorized use of databases). *Van Buren*, interpreting the CFAA's "exceeds authorized access" clause, approved of *Nosal I* and abrogated *EF Cultural Travel* and *Rodriguez*. 141 S. Ct. at 1653–54 & n.2.

We therefore look to whether the conduct at issue is analogous to "breaking and entering." H.R. Rep. No. 98-894, at 20. Significantly, the version of the CFAA initially enacted in 1984 was limited to a narrow range of computers—namely, those containing national security information or financial data and those operated by or on behalf of the government. *See* Counterfeit Access Device and Computer Fraud and Abuse Act of 1984, Pub. L. No. 98-473, § 2102, 98 Stat. 2190, 2190–91. None of the computers to which the

CFAA initially applied were accessible to the general public; affirmative authorization of some kind was presumptively required.

When section 1030(a)(2)(C) was added in 1996 to extend the prohibition on unauthorized access to any "protected computer," the Senate Judiciary Committee explained that the amendment was designed "to increase protection for the privacy and confidentiality of computer information." S. Rep. No. 104-357, at 7 (emphasis added). The legislative history of section 1030 thus makes clear that the prohibition on unauthorized access is properly understood to apply only to private information—information delineated as private through use of a permission requirement of some sort. As one prominent commentator has put it, "an authentication requirement, such as a password gate, is needed to create the necessary barrier that divides open spaces from closed spaces on the Web." Orin S. Kerr, *Norms of Computer Trespass*, 116 Colum. L. Rev. 1143, 1161 (2016). Moreover, elsewhere in the statute, password fraud is cited as a means by which a computer may be accessed without authorization, *see* 18 U.S.C. § 1030(a)(6), bolstering the idea that authorization is only required for password-protected sites or sites that otherwise prevent the general public from viewing the information.

We therefore conclude that hiQ has raised a serious question as to whether the reference to access "without authorization" limits the scope of the statutory coverage to computers for which authorization or access permission, such as password authentication, is generally required. Put differently, the CFAA contemplates the existence of three kinds of computer systems: (1) computers for which access is open to the general public and permission is not required, (2) computers for which authorization is required and has been given, and (3) computers for which authorization is required but has not been given (or, in the case of the prohibition on exceeding authorized access, has not been given for the part of the system accessed). Public LinkedIn profiles, available to anyone with an Internet connection, fall into the first category. With regard to websites made freely accessible on the Internet, the "breaking and entering" analogue invoked so frequently during congressional consideration has no application, and the concept of "without authorization" is inapt.

The reasoning of *Van Buren* reinforces our interpretation of the CFAA, although it did not directly address the statute's "without authorization" clause. *Van Buren* held that a police sergeant did not violate the CFAA when he "ran a license-plate search in a law enforcement computer database in exchange for money." 141 S. Ct. at 1652. Interpreting the "exceeds authorized access" clause of section 1030(a)(2), the Court held that the CFAA "covers those who obtain information from particular areas in the computer—such as files, folders, or databases—to which their computer access does not extend. It does not cover those who, like Van Buren, have improper motives for obtaining information that is otherwise available to them." *Id.*

Van Buren found the "interplay between the 'without authorization' and 'exceeds authorized access' clauses of subsection (a)(2) ... particularly probative." *Id.* at 1658. "The 'without authorization' clause ... protects computers themselves by targeting so-called outside hackers—those who 'acces[s] a computer without any permission at all.'" *Id.* (quoting *LVRC Holdings LLC v. Brekka*, 581 F.3d 1127, 1133 (9th Cir. 2009)). The "'exceeds authorized access' clause ... provide[s] complementary protection for certain information within computers ... by targeting so-called inside hackers—those who access a computer with permission, but then '"exceed" the parameters of authorized access by entering an area of the computer to which [that] authorization does not extend.'" *Id.* (quoting *United States v. Valle*, 807 F.3d 508, 524 (2d Cir. 2015)). "[L]iability under both clauses stems from a gates-up-or-down inquiry—one either can or cannot access a computer system, and one either can or cannot access certain areas within the system." *Id.* at 1658–59.

Van Buren's "gates-up-or-down inquiry" is consistent with our interpretation of the CFAA as contemplating three categories of computer systems. *See supra* pp. ——— – ———. Discussing the "without authorization" clause, *Van Buren* explained that a computer user who has "authorization" is one who "can ... access a computer system," 141 S. Ct. at 1658, where "access" means "the act of entering a computer 'system itself,'" *id.* at 1657 (citation omitted). In other words, a user with "authorization" is not subject to "limitations on access," whether those limitations are "code-based" or "contained in contracts or policies." *Id.* at 1659 n.8. *Van Buren* stated that the CFAA's password-trafficking provision, section 1030(a)(6), which also uses the word "authorization," "contemplates a 'specific type of authorization—that is, authentication,' which turns on whether a user's credentials allow him to proceed past a computer's access gate, rather than on other, scope-based restrictions." *Id.* at 1659 n.9 (quoting Patricia L. Bellia, *A Code-Based Approach to Unauthorized Access Under the Computer Fraud and Abuse Act*, 84 Geo. Wash. L. Rev. 1442, 1470 (2016)).

Van Buren's distinction between computer users who "can or cannot access a computer system," *id.* at 1658, suggests a baseline in which there are "limitations on access" that prevent some users from accessing the system (i.e., a "gate" exists, and can be either up or down). The Court's "gates-up-or-down inquiry" thus applies to the latter two categories of computers we have identified: if authorization is required and has been given, the gates are up; if authorization is required and has *not* been given, the gates are down. As we have noted, however, a defining feature of public websites is that their publicly available sections lack limitations on access; instead, those sections are open to anyone with a web browser. In other words, applying the "gates" analogy to a computer hosting publicly available webpages, that computer has erected no gates to lift or lower in the first place. *Van Buren* therefore reinforces our conclusion that the concept of "without authorization" does not apply to public websites.

Additionally, neither of the cases LinkedIn principally relies upon casts doubt on our interpretation of the statute. LinkedIn first cites *Nosal II*, 844 F.3d 1024. As we have already stated, *Nosal II* held that a former employee who used current employees' login credentials to access company computers and collect confidential information had acted "'without authorization' in violation of the CFAA." 844 F.3d at 1038. The computer information the defendant accessed in *Nosal II* was thus plainly one which no one could access without authorization.

So too with regard to the system at issue in *Power Ventures*, 844 F.3d 1058, the other precedent upon which LinkedIn relies. In that case, Facebook sued Power Ventures, a social networking website that aggregated social networking information from multiple platforms, for accessing Facebook users' data and using that data to send mass messages as part of a promotional campaign. *Id.* at 1062–63. After Facebook sent a cease-and-desist letter, Power Ventures continued to circumvent IP barriers and gain access to password-protected Facebook member profiles. *Id.* at 1063. We held that after receiving an individualized cease-and-desist letter, Power Ventures had accessed Facebook computers "without authorization" and was therefore liable under the CFAA. *Id.* at 1067–68. But we specifically recognized that "Facebook has tried to limit and control access to its website" as to the purposes for which Power Ventures sought to use it. *Id.* at 1063. Indeed, Facebook requires its users to register with a unique username and password, and Power Ventures required that Facebook users provide their Facebook username and password to access their Facebook data on Power Ventures' platform. *Facebook, Inc. v. Power Ventures, Inc.*, 844 F. Supp. 2d 1025, 1028 (N.D. Cal. 2012). While Power Ventures was gathering user data that was protected by Facebook's username and password authentication system, the data hiQ was scraping was available to anyone with a web browser.

In sum, *Nosal II* and *Power Ventures* control situations in which authorization generally is required and has either never been given or has been revoked. As *Power Ventures* indicated, the two cases do not control the situation present here, in which information is "presumptively open to all comers." *Power Ventures*, 844 F.3d at 1067 n.2. As to the computers at issue in those cases, the authorization gate was "down."

Our understanding that the CFAA is premised on a distinction between information presumptively accessible to the general public and information for which authorization is generally required is consistent with our interpretation of a provision of the Stored Communications Act ("SCA"), 18 U.S.C. § 2701 *et seq.*,[18] nearly identical to the CFAA provision at issue. *Compare* 18 U.S.C. § 2701(a) ("[W]hoever—(1) intentionally accesses without authorization a facility through which an electronic communication service is provided; or (2) intentionally exceeds an authorization to access that facility; and thereby obtains ... unauthorized access to a wire or electronic communication ... shall be punished ....") *with* 18 U.S.C. § 1030(a)(2)(C) ("Whoever ... intentionally accesses a computer without authorization or exceeds authorized access, and thereby obtains ... information from any protected computer ... shall be punished ...."). "The similarity of language in [the SCA and the CFAA] is a strong indication that [they] should be interpreted *pari passu*." *Northcross v. Bd. of Educ. of Memphis City Schs.*, 412 U.S. 427, 428, 93 S.Ct. 2201, 37 L.Ed.2d 48 (1973); *see also United States v. Sioux*, 362 F.3d 1241, 1246 (9th Cir. 2004).

Addressing the "without authorization" provision of the SCA, we have distinguished between public websites and non-public or "restricted" websites, such as websites that "are password-protected ... or require the user to purchase access by entering a credit card number." *Konop v. Hawaiian Airlines, Inc.*, 302 F.3d 868, 875 (9th Cir. 2002); *see also id.* at 879 n.8. As we explained in *Konop*, in enacting the SCA, "Congress wanted to protect electronic communications that are configured to be private" and are " 'not intended to be available to the public.' " *Id.* at 875 (quoting S. Rep. No. 99-541, at 35–36 (1986)). The House Committee on the Judiciary stated, with respect to the section of the SCA at issue, section 2701, that "[a] person may reasonably conclude that a communication is readily accessible to the general public if the ... means of access are widely known, and if a person does not, in the course of gaining access, encounter any warnings, encryptions, password requests, or other indicia of intended privacy." H.R. Rep. No. 99-647, at 62H.R. Rep. No. 99-647, at 62 (1986). The Committee further explained that "electronic communications which the service provider attempts to keep confidential would be protected, while the statute would impose no liability for access to features configured to be readily accessible to the general public." *Id.* at 63.

Both the legislative history of section 1030 of the CFAA and the legislative history of section 2701 of the SCA, with its similar "without authorization" provision, then, support the district court's distinction between "private" computer networks and websites, protected by a password authentication system and "not visible to the public," and websites that are accessible to the general public.

Finally, the rule of lenity favors our narrow interpretation of the "without authorization" provision in the CFAA. The statutory prohibition on unauthorized access applies both to civil actions and to criminal prosecutions—indeed, "§ 1030 is primarily a criminal statute." *LVRC Holdings*, 581 F.3d at 1134. "Because we must interpret the statute consistently, whether we encounter its application in a criminal or noncriminal context, the rule of lenity applies." *Leocal v. Ashcroft*, 543 U.S. 1, 11 n.8, 125 S.Ct. 377, 160 L.Ed.2d 271 (2004). As we explained in *Nosal I*, we therefore favor a narrow interpretation of the CFAA's "without authorization" provision so as not to turn a criminal hacking statute into a "sweeping Internet-policing mandate." 676 F.3d at 858; *see also id.* at 863.

For all these reasons, it appears that the CFAA's prohibition on accessing a computer "without authorization" is violated when a person circumvents a computer's generally applicable rules regarding access permissions, such as username and password requirements, to gain access to a computer. It is likely that when a computer network generally permits public access to its data, a user's accessing that publicly available data will not constitute access without authorization under the CFAA. The data hiQ seeks to access is not owned by LinkedIn and has not been demarcated by LinkedIn as private using such an authorization system. HiQ has therefore raised serious questions about whether LinkedIn may invoke the CFAA to preempt hiQ's possibly meritorious tortious interference claim.[20]

Entities that view themselves as victims of data scraping are not without resort, even if the CFAA does not apply: state law trespass to chattels claims may still be available.[21] And other causes of action, such as copyright infringement, misappropriation, unjust enrichment, conversion, breach of contract, or breach of privacy, may also lie. *See, e.g., Associated Press v. Meltwater U.S. Holdings, Inc.*, 931 F. Supp. 2d 537, 561 (S.D.N.Y. 2013) (holding that a software company's conduct in scraping and aggregating copyrighted news articles was not protected by fair use).

D. Public Interest

Finally, we must consider the public interest in granting or denying the preliminary injunction. Whereas the balance of equities focuses on the parties, "[t]he public interest inquiry primarily addresses impact on non-parties rather than parties," and takes into consideration "the public consequences in employing the extraordinary remedy of injunction." *Bernhardt v. Los Angeles Cnty.*, 339 F.3d 920, 931–32 (9th Cir. 2003) (citations omitted).

As the district court observed, each side asserts that its own position would benefit the public interest by maximizing the free flow of information on the Internet. HiQ points out that data scraping is a common method of gathering information, used by search engines, academic researchers, and many others. According to hiQ, letting established entities that already have accumulated large user data sets decide who can scrape that data from otherwise public websites gives those entities outsized control over how such data may be put to use.

For its part, LinkedIn argues that the preliminary injunction is against the public interest because it will invite malicious actors to access LinkedIn's computers and attack its servers. As a result, the argument goes, LinkedIn and other companies with public websites will be forced to choose between leaving their servers open to such attacks or protecting their websites with passwords, thereby cutting them off from public view.

Although there are significant public interests on both sides, the district court properly determined that, on balance, the public interest favors hiQ's position. We agree with the district court that giving companies like LinkedIn free rein to decide, on any basis, who can collect and use data—data that the companies do not own, that they otherwise make publicly available to viewers, and that the companies themselves collect and use—risks the possible creation of information monopolies that would disserve the public interest.

Internet companies and the public do have a substantial interest in thwarting denial-of-service attacks and blocking abusive users, identity thieves, and other ill-intentioned actors. But we do not view the district court's injunction as opening the door to such malicious activity. The district court made clear that the injunction does not preclude LinkedIn from continuing to engage in "technological self-help" against bad actors—for example, by employing "anti-bot measures to prevent, *e.g.*, harmful intrusions or attacks on its server." Although an injunction preventing a company from securing even the public parts of its website from malicious actors would raise serious concerns, such concerns are not present here.

The district court's conclusion that the public interest favors granting the preliminary injunction was appropriate.

CONCLUSION

We **AFFIRM** the district court's determination that hiQ has established the elements required for a preliminary injunction and remand for further proceedings.

NOTES

Note 1

In a footnote, Judge Berzon discusses the usage of bots:

A web robot (or "bot") is an application that performs automated tasks such as retrieving and analyzing information. *See Definition of "bot,"* Merriam-Webster Dictionary, https://www.merriam-webster.com/dictionary/bot (last visited March 15, 2022). A web crawler is one common type of bot that systematically searches the Internet and downloads copies of web pages, which can then be indexed by a search engine. *See Assoc. Press v. Meltwater U.S. Holdings, Inc.*, 931 F. Supp. 2d 537, 544 (S.D.N.Y. 2013); *Definition of "web crawler,"* Merriam-Webster Dictionary, https://www.merriam-webster.com/dictionary/web%20crawler (last visited March 15, 2022). A robots.txt file, also known as the robots exclusion protocol, is a widely used standard for stating the rules that a web server has adopted to govern a bot's behavior on that server. *See About /robots.txt*, http://www.robotstxt.org/robotstxt.html (last visited March 15, 2022). For example, a robots.txt file might instruct specified robots to ignore certain files when crawling a site, so that the files do not appear in search engine results. Adherence to the rules in a robots.txt file is voluntary; malicious bots may deliberately choose not to honor robots.txt rules and may in turn be punished with a denial of access to the website in question. *See Can I Block Just Bad Robots?*, http://www.robotstxt.org/faq/blockjustbad.html (last visited March 15, 2022); *cf. Assoc. Press*, 931 F. Supp. 2d at 563.

QUESTION

When a user types in a URL, the server responds with populating a web page on the user's local machine. The code and data behind that web page are then available to the user for capturing or scraping. Should there be a law against web page scraping to mine the data from the page?

Domain Name Commission Ltd. v. Domain Name Tools, 449 F. Supp. 2nd 1024 (W.D. Wash. 2020).

ORDER GRANTING IN PART DEFENDANT'S MOTION TO DISMISS

Robert S. Lasnik, United States District Judge

This matter comes before the Court on defendant's "Motion to Dismiss Pursuant to FRCP 12(b)(1) and 12(b)(6)." Dkt. # 64. Plaintiff is a New Zealand non-profit corporation that regulates the use of the .nz top level domain, including registering new domain names and responding to inquiries regarding registrants. Defendant collects domain and registrant information from around the world, stores the information, and uses its current and historic databases to sell monitoring and investigative services and products to the public. Plaintiff alleges that the way defendant accessed .nz domain and registrant information before June 6, 2018, any and all access after that date, and its continuing storage and use of the domain and registrant information violates the Computer Fraud and Abuse Act ("CFAA"). . . . Defendant seeks dismissal of the statutory claim[].

The question for the Court on a motion to dismiss is whether the facts alleged in the complaint sufficiently state a "plausible" ground for relief. *Bell Atl. Corp. v. Twombly*, 550 U.S. 544, 570, 127 S.Ct. 1955, 167 L.Ed.2d 929 (2007). . . .

A. Computer Fraud and Abuse Act, 18 U.S.C. § 1030

As relevant to this litigation, the CFAA prohibits "intentionally access[ing] a computer without authorization or exceed[ing] authorized access," 18 U.S.C. § 1030(a)(2), as well as "intentionally access[ing] a protected computer without authorization" and causing "damage and loss," 18 U.S.C. § 1030(a)(5)(C). Plaintiffs argue that defendant is liable under both provisions because it accessed the .nz servers in ways and for purposes that violated plaintiff's terms of use and continued to access the .nz servers after its right of access had been expressly revoked.

Plaintiff's terms of use prohibited use of Port 43, a communication channel through which users can query plaintiff's servers regarding specific .nz domain names, to send high volume queries to the .nz servers with the effect of downloading or collecting all or part of the .nz register, to access the .nz register in bulk, to store or compile .nz domain data to build up a secondary register, and/or to publish historical or non-current versions of the .nz data. On November 2, 2017, plaintiff sent defendant a cease-and-desist letter notifying defendant that it had violated plaintiff's terms of use and demanding that it "immediately cease and desist accessing .nz WHOIS servers or using and publishing .nz WHOIS data except as permitted by the [terms of use]." When defendant continued to access the .nz servers in ways that plaintiff felt violated the limited license it had granted defendant, plaintiff sent a June 6, 2018, letter revoking defendant's right to access the .nz servers entirely. Plaintiff alleges that defendant accessed the .nz servers after the June 6, 2018, revocation.

Plaintiff argues that defendant's access to the .nz server in ways that violated plaintiff's terms of use prior to June 6, 2018, constitutes both access "without authorization" and in excess of authorized access. Plaintiff also argues that defendant's queries to the .nz servers after plaintiff revoked defendant's right of access was "without authorization." Plaintiff alleges that defendant's unlawful conduct caused plaintiff "loss in an amount far in excess of the $5,000 statutory minimum during each relevant one-year period."

1. "Without Authorization"

The CFAA does not contain a definition of "without authorization." The Ninth Circuit has, therefore, applied the ordinary, common meaning of "authorization," concluding that one is authorized to access a computer when the owner of the computer gives permission to use it. *LVRC Holdings LLC v. Brekka*, 581 F.3d 1127, 1132-33 (9th Cir. 2009). . . . A defendant runs afoul of the "without authorization" provisions of the CFAA "when he or she has no permission to access a computer or when such permission has been revoked explicitly. Once permission has been revoked, technological gamesmanship or enlisting of a third party to aid in access will not excuse liability." *Facebook, Inc. v. Power Ventures, Inc.*, 844 F.3d 1058, 1067 (9th Cir. 2016). The Ninth Circuit has rejected the argument that permission or authorization to access a computer is automatically withdrawn when the user violates a duty owed to the owner of the computer. Rather, whether access is authorized or unauthorized "depends on actions taken by the employer." *Brekka*, 581 F.3d at 1134-35. If the computer owner has not affirmatively rescinded the defendant's right to access the computer, any existing authorization/permission remains. *Id.*

Prior to June 6, 2018, defendant had permission to access the .nz servers, albeit with limitations imposed on the manner in which and purposes for which that access could be exercised. That permission was revoked on June 6, 2018. Taking plaintiff's allegations of access as true, the Court finds that defendant accessed the .nz servers with authorization prior to June 6, 2018, and without authorization after that date.

2. "Exceeds Authorized Access"

The CFAA defines "exceeds authorized access" to mean "to access a computer with authorization and to use such access to obtain or alter information in the computer that the accessor is not entitled to so obtain or alter." 18 U.S.C. § 1030(e)(6). In *United States v. Nosal*, 676 F.3d 854 (9th Cir. 2012), the Ninth Circuit acknowledged that this language could be read in two ways. The first would encompass situations in which a person's authorization to access a computer is limited to certain files, programs, or databases, but he or she "hacks" into other areas of the computer without permission. In the alternative, the language could refer to a person who has unrestricted access to a computer, but who accesses the files, programs, or databases in a way or for a purpose that is proscribed by the owner. *Id.* at 856-57. The Ninth Circuit was concerned that the second interpretation would "transform the CFAA from an anti-hacking statute into an expansive misappropriation statute," making "everyone who uses a computer in violation of computer use restrictions - which may well include everyone who uses a computer" liable under the CFAA. *Id.* at 857.5 The Ninth Circuit held that, whereas the "without authorization" clause of § 1030(c)(2) applies to outside hackers with no rights or authority to access the computer at all, the "exceeds authorized access" clause applies to inside hackers "whose initial access to a computer is authorized but who access unauthorized information or files." *Id.* at 858. It sided with "the growing number of courts" who recognize that the CFAA "target[s] the unauthorized procurement or alteration of information, not its misuse or misappropriation." *Id.* at 863.

Plaintiff argues that once it specifically and individually reminded defendant on November 2, 2017, that its access to the .nz servers was subject to plaintiff's terms of use, further access in violation of the terms of use exceeded defendant's authorization under the analysis set forth in *Facebook, Inc. v. Power Ventures, Inc.*, 844 F.3d 1058 (9th Cir. 2016), and *Ticketmaster LLC v. Prestige Entm't W., Inc.*, 315 F. Supp.3d 1147, 1171 (C.D. Cal. 2018). *Facebook* does not support plaintiff's claim of a CFAA violation prior to June 6, 2018. In that case, Facebook issued a cease-and-desist letter notifying defendant that it was no longer authorized to access Facebook's computers. *Facebook*, 844 F.3d at 1067 n.3. In light of the "explicit revo[cation of the] authorization for *any* access," the Ninth Circuit found that defendant's access following receipt of the notice was without authorization and a violation of the CFAA. *Id.* at 1068 (emphasis in original). Plaintiff's November 2, 2017, letter did not revoke defendant's access to the .nz servers, it simply reminded defendant that access was subject to the terms of use.

Ticketmaster, on the other hand, supports plaintiff's argument, but the Court declines to adopt its analysis. In *Ticketmaster*, the ticket seller made tickets available to the public on its website subject to terms of use that barred the use of robots, programs, and other automated devices ("bots") to make purchases. Defendants used bots to purchase large quantities of tickets for resale. The district court recognized that simply violating Ticketmaster's terms of use did not, standing alone, constitute a violation of the CFAA under *Nosal*. The district court distinguished *Nosal*, however, on the ground that Ticketmaster had sent defendants an individualized cease-and-desist letter informing them that their access was restricted to that which conforms to Ticketmaster's terms of use. In the court's view, this letter "was, in effect, an individualized access policy that revoked authorization upon breach of the policy.... [It was] the violation of the terms of the Letter, not of Ticketmaster's Terms of Use, on which the Court base[d] its finding of a well-pled CFAA claim." 315 F. Supp.3d at 1170-71.

The Court respectfully disagrees. Permission or authorization to access a computer does not evaporate simply because the user has violated a duty owed to the owner of the computer. *See Brekka*, 581 F.3d at 1134-35 (rejecting the Seventh Circuit's reasoning in *Int'l Airport Ctrs., LLC v. Citrin*, 440 F.3d 418 (7th Cir. 2006), and requiring the employer to rescind the defendant's right to use the computer before potential criminal liability under the CFAA will attach). "The CFAA was enacted to prevent intentional intrusion into someone else's computer - specifically, computer hacking." *hiQ*

Labs, 938 F.3d at 1000. The forbidden conduct is analogous to "breaking and entering," where defendant has unlawfully intruded into otherwise inaccessible computers (or portions thereof) in a form of trespass. *Id.*(quoting H.R. Rep. No. 98-894, at 20 (1984)). The Ninth Circuit has already determined that the rule of lenity demands that the "exceeds authorized access" prong of the CFAA be given a narrow interpretation so as to criminalize unauthorized access to a computer (or part thereof), not the misuse of authorized access. *Nosal*, 676 F.3d at 863. *See also hiQ Labs*, 938 F.3d at 1000 (recognizing that the Ninth Circuit has "rejected the contract-based interpretation of the CFAA's prohibitions). This Court is not at liberty to second guess the Ninth Circuit's resolution of the issue, nor is it persuaded that simply repeating or referencing the existing use restrictions in a letter changes the scope of authorized access in a material way.

For all of the foregoing reasons, the Court finds that the allegations of the First Amended Complaint do not support a plausible inference that defendant exceeded its authorization to access the .nz servers (as that phrase has been interpreted by the Ninth Circuit) prior to June 6, 2018. . . .

11.2[B] DAMAGE OR LOSS

Another important issue under the CFAA concerns the question of what constitutes damage or loss, particularly in connection with the CFAA provision creating a civil action. Subsection (g) provides, in relevant part:

> Any person who suffers damage or loss by reason of a violation of this section may maintain a civil action against the violator to obtain compensatory damages and injunctive relief or other equitable relief. A civil action for a violation of this section may be brought only if the conduct involves 1 of the factors set forth in subclauses (I), (II), (III), (IV), or (V) of subsection (c)(4)(A)(i). Damages for a violation involving only conduct described in subsection (c)(4)(A)(i)(I) are limited to economic damages.

Shurgard Storage Centers v. Safe Guard Self Storage, 119 F.Supp.2d 1121 (W.D. Wash. 2000).

ZILLY, District Judge.

INTRODUCTION

Shurgard Storage Centers, Inc. (plaintiff) and Safeguard Self Storage, Inc. (defendant) are competitors in the self-storage business. The plaintiff alleges that the defendant embarked on a systematic scheme to hire away key employees from the plaintiff for the purpose of obtaining the plaintiff's trade secrets. The plaintiff also alleges that some of these employees, while still working for the plaintiff, used the plaintiff's computers to send trade secrets to the defendant via e-mail. The plaintiff's complaint alleges misappropriation of trade secrets, conversion, unfair competition, violations of the Computer Fraud and Abuse Act (CFAA), tortious interference with a business expectancy, and seeks injunctive relief and damages. The defendant has moved to dismiss the CFAA claim pursuant to Fed.R.Civ.P. 12(b)(6)[.] The Court now DENIES the defendant's motion to dismiss the CFAA claim for the reasons set forth in this order.

FACTS

The plaintiff alleges the following facts which the Court accepts as true for the purposes of this motion. The plaintiff is the industry leader in full and self-service storage facilities in both the United States and Europe. The plaintiff's growth in the last 25 years is primarily due to the development and construction of top-quality storage centers in "high barrier to entry" markets. Pursuant to this strategy, the plaintiff has developed a sophisticated system of creating market plans, identifying appropriate development sites, and evaluating whether a site will provide a high return on an investment. The plaintiff invests significant resources in creating a marketing team to carry out these tasks for each potential market. These teams become familiar with the market, identify potential acquisition sites, and develop relationships with brokers and sellers in the market so that the plaintiff has the best opportunity to acquire a preferred site.

The defendant began self-storage operations in 1997. The defendant is a direct competitor of the plaintiff and develops self-storage facilities in the United States and abroad.

In late 1999, the defendant approached Eric Leland, a Regional Development Manager for the plaintiff, and offered him employment with the defendant. Because of his position with the plaintiff, Mr. Leland had full access to the plaintiff's confidential business plans, expansion plans, and other trade secrets. While still employed by the plaintiff, but acting as an agent for the defendant, Mr. Leland sent e-mails to the defendant containing various trade secrets and proprietary information belonging to the plaintiff. Mr. Leland did this without the plaintiff's knowledge or approval. Mr. Leland was later hired by the defendant in October 1999, and he has continued to give the defendant proprietary information belonging to the plaintiff. The defendant has hired away other employees of the plaintiff who have intimate knowledge of the plaintiff's business models and practices, and the defendant continues to recruit employees of the plaintiff.

DISCUSSION

The motion to dismiss raises challenging issues regarding the scope of a civil claim under a criminal statute, the Computer Fraud and Abuse Act, 18 U.S.C. § 1030. In its complaint, the plaintiff asserts that it is entitled to relief under the CFAA. In its opposition to the motion to dismiss, the plaintiff specifies that its claim is sufficient under 18 U.S.C. §§ . . . 1030(a)(4), and 1030(a)(5)(C). . . .

D. Does the plaintiff state a claim under 18 U.S.C. § 1030(a)(5)(C)?

Under 18 U.S.C. § 1030(a)(5)(C), "[w]hoever ... intentionally accesses a protected computer without authorization, and as a result of such conduct, causes damage" violates the CFAA. 18 U.S.C. § 1030(a)(5)(C). The only new issue under this portion of the statute is whether the plaintiff has alleged that "damage" occurred. "The term 'damage' means any impairment to the integrity or availability of data, a program, a system, or information, that ... causes loss aggregating at least $5,000 in value during any 1–year period to one or more individuals...." 18 U.S.C. § 1030(e)(8)(A).

The defendant raises two objections to this claim. First, the defendant asserts that the legislative history of this section of the CFAA shows that it is only intended to apply to "outsiders," and thus would not apply to employees. However, there is no ambiguity in the statute as to when a party is liable, ("*Whoever* ... intentionally accesses....") so this argument lacks merit. *See* 18 U.S.C. § 1030(a)(5)(C).

Second, the defendant argues that the plaintiff has not pled that it incurred "damage" as defined in the statute. Specifically, the defendant argues that the alleged loss of information by the plaintiff is not "damage" under the statute. The statute says damage is *"any impairment* to the integrity ... of data ... or information." 18 U.S.C. § 1030(e)(8)(A) (emphasis added). The unambiguous meaning of "any" clearly demonstrates that the statute is meant to apply to "any" impairment to the integrity of data. However, the word "integrity" is ambiguous in this context. Webster's New International Dictionary (3d ed.1993), defines "integrity" as, "an unimpaired or unmarred condition: entire correspondence with an original condition." The word "integrity" in the context of data necessarily contemplates maintaining the data in a protected state. Because the term may be ambiguous, the Court examines the legislative history to determine if "integrity" and thus "damage" could include the alleged access and disclosure of trade secrets in this case.

The term "damage" was addressed in the Senate Report regarding the 1996 amendments to the CFAA:

The 1994 amendment required both "damage" and "loss," but it is not always clear what constitutes "damage." For example, intruders often alter existing log-on programs so that user passwords are copied to a file which the hackers can retrieve later. After retrieving the newly created password file, the intruder restores the altered log-on file to its original condition. Arguably, in such a situation, neither the computer nor its information is damaged. Nonetheless, this conduct allows the intruder to accumulate valid user passwords to the system, requires all system users to change their passwords, and requires the system administrator to devote resources to resecuring the system. Thus, although there is arguably no "damage," the victim does suffer "loss." If the loss to the victim meets the required monetary threshold, the conduct should be criminal, and the victim should be entitled to relief.

The bill therefore defines "damage" in new subsection 1030(e)(8), with a focus on the harm that the law seeks to prevent. S.Rep. No. 104–357, at 11 (1996). This example given in the report is analogous to the case before the Court. The "damage" and thus violation to the "integrity" that was caused in the example is the accumulation of passwords and subsequent corrective measures the rightful computer owner must take to prevent the infiltration and gathering of confidential information. Similarly, in this case, the defendant allegedly infiltrated the plaintiff's computer network, albeit through different means than in the example, and collected and disseminated confidential information. In both cases no data was physically changed or erased, but in both cases an impairment of its integrity occurred. From the legislative history it is clear that the meaning of "integrity" and thus "damage" apply to the alleged acts of the defendant in this case and thus the plaintiff has stated a claim under 18 U.S.C. § 1030(a)(5)(C).

NetApp v. Nimble Storage, 2015 WL 400251 (N.D. Cal. 2015)

LUCY H. KOH, District Judge

Plaintiff NetApp, Inc. ("NetApp") has filed this suit against Defendants Nimble Storage, Inc. ("Nimble"), and Michael Reynolds ("Reynolds") (collectively, "Defendants"). *See* ECF No. 71 (Second Am. Compl.). Defendants move to dismiss all the claims that NetApp asserts against Nimble and Reynolds, except for a state law breach of contract claim and claims under 18 U.S.C. §§ 1030(a)(2)(C) and (a)(4). *See* ECF No. 74 ("Mot.Dismiss"). . . .

I. BACKGROUND

A. The Parties' Relationship

NetApp and Nimble are competing companies in the data storage industry. . . . Defendant Reynolds is an Australian citizen and resident who works at Nimble Storage Australia Pty Limited ("Nimble AUS"), an entity related to Defendant Nimble. . . . This lawsuit stems from NetApp's belief that "Nimble targeted NetApp talent and valuable confidential and non-confidential information to compete unfairly in the marketplace.". . . NetApp alleges that "Nimble has achieved rapid growth and customer adoption" by "rely[ing] heavily on foundational information as to the internal working of NetApp's products and its proprietary business processes.". . .

According to NetApp, Reynolds previously worked at Thomas Duryea Consulting ("TDC"), an "IT infrastructure consultancy business" in Australia. . . . NetApp contracted with TDC for certain services, provided Reynolds with access to NetApp's computer systems, and offered Reynolds training courses available to NetApp employees, all subject to NetApp's restrictions on unauthorized access to and use of its systems. . . . Reynolds left TDC in April 2013, and took a job with Nimble AUS, where—NetApp alleges—Reynolds accessed NetApp databases repeatedly from June through August 2013 and used confidential and proprietary information to solicit business for Nimble. . . .

II. LEGAL STANDARDS

A. Motion to Dismiss Under Rule 12(b)(6)

A complaint may be dismissed as a matter of law due to lack of a cognizable legal theory, or insufficient facts to support a cognizable legal claim. *Robertson v. Dean Witter Reynolds, Inc.*, 749 F.2d 530, 534 (9th Cir.1984). A complaint must contain "a short and plain statement of the claim showing that the pleader is entitled to relief." Fed.R.Civ.P. 8(a)(2).

. . .

The Court next addresses Nimble's motion to dismiss certain of NetApp's claims under the Computer Fraud and Abuse Act, 18 U.S.C. § 1030 ("CFAA"). "The CFAA prohibits a number of different computer crimes, the majority of which involve accessing computers without authorization or in excess of authorization, and then taking specified forbidden actions, ranging from obtaining information to damaging a computer or computer data." LVRC Holdings LLC v. Brekka, 581 F.3d 1127, 1131 (9th Cir.2009) (citing 18 U.S.C. § 1030(a)(1)-(7)). Here, Nimble moves to dismiss NetApp's claims under § 1030(a)(5). Unlike the CFAA's other causes of action, § 1030(a)(5) requires that the accused cause "damage" to data, system, information, or a program. In relevant part, the CFAA imposes liability on whomever:

> (A) knowingly causes the transmission of a program, information, code, or command, and as a result of such conduct, intentionally causes damage without authorization, to a protected computer;

> (B) intentionally accesses a protected computer without authorization, and as a result of such conduct, recklessly causes damage; or

> (C) intentionally accesses a protected computer without authorization, and as a result of such conduct, causes damage and loss.

18 U.S.C. § 1030(a)(5). Section 1030(e)(8) defines "damage" as "any impairment to the integrity or availability of data, a program, a system, or information." 18 U.S.C. § 1030(e)(8).

NetApp alleges that Reynolds caused "damage" to NetApp's computers, and thereby violated § 1030(a)(5), in three ways: (1) that Reynolds "cop[ied] certain information from NetApp's protected computers and transferr[ed] it to a non-secure area or device"; (2) that Reynolds "diminish[ed] the value of NetApp's data by compromising its exclusivity, for which it derives value because it is not available to competitors"; and (3) that Reynolds "alter[ed] or modif[ied] NetApp's performance data contained on its protected computers." Defendants argue that none of these allegations plead a cognizable claim of "damage" within the meaning of the CFAA because NetApp has not alleged that Reynolds' alleged actions "impair[ed] the integrity or availability of any part of NetApp's systems—he did not crash NetApp's systems, delete data, or prevent any other user's access." NetApp counters that merely "rendering a computer system less secure should be considered 'damage' under § 1030(a)(5)[ ], even when no data, program, or system is damaged or destroyed." The Court will address the sufficiency of each of NetApp's allegations in turn.

First, NetApp alleges that Reynolds "cop[ied] certain information from NetApp's protected computers and transferr[ed] it to a non-secure area or device." The Ninth Circuit has not addressed whether the copying of information, without more, states a cognizable claim of "damage" under the CFAA. In addition, district courts are divided on this issue. The majority of district courts to have considered the question agree that the mere copying of information does not plead a recognizable claim of "damage" under § 1030(a)(5). See, e.g., Capitol Audio Access, Inc. v. Umemoto, 980 F.Supp.2d 1154, 1157–58 (E.D.Cal.2013) (rejecting claim that "access to a publication and the disclosure of its information satisfies the CFAA's definition of damage"); Garelli Wong & Associates, Inc. v. Nichols, 551 F.Supp.2d 704, 710 (N.D.Ill.2008) (where information has been misappropriated through the use of a computer, "we do not believe that such conduct alone can show 'impairment to the integrity or availability of data, a program, a system, or information.'"); Landmark Credit Union v. Doberstein, 746 F.Supp.2d 990, 993 (E.D.Wis.2010) (allegation that "defendant accessed and disclosed information from Landmark's computer" does not plead a cognizable claim of "damage"). . . .

Moreover, these courts have decided the mere copying of information does not constitute "damage" where, as NetApp alleges here, a former employee is accused of taking information from his former employer to give to a competitor. See, e.g., Del Monte Fresh Produce, 616 F.Supp.2d at 811 (no cognizable claim of "damage" under the CFAA where an ex-employee e-mails former employer's files to a competitor); Keener, 989 F.Supp.2d at 530 (no cognizable claim of "damage" under the CFAA where ex-employee copied employer's information to an external hard drive and shared it with a competitor); Speed, 2006 WL 2683058, at *8 (no cognizable claim of "damage" under the CFAA where former employees copied employer's information to CDs and personal digital assistants to give to competitor).

Courts that have decided that the copying of information is not "damage" within the scope of the CFAA base their holdings on at least one of three premises. First, these courts point out that the CFAA "is not intended to expansively apply to all cases where a trade secret has been misappropriated by use of a computer." U.S. Gypsum Co., 670 F.Supp.2d at 744. . . . Finally and relatedly, these courts have generally required that there be actual damage to data, information, a program, or system in order to state a claim under the relevant provision of the CFAA. Such damage occurs where there is "the destruction, corruption, or deletion of electronic files, the physical destruction of a hard drive, or any diminution in the completeness or usability of the data on a computer system." Keener, 989 F.Supp.2d at 529. . . . Typically, the mere copying of information does not result in such destruction. See Keener, 989 F.Supp.2d at 529.

On the other side of the issue, some district courts have found that the copying of information, without more, can constitute a claim of damage within the meaning of the CFAA. Shurgard Storage Centers, Inc. v. Safeguard Self Storage, Inc. is the leading case in this Circuit on this question. 119 F.Supp.2d 1121. . . . NetApp, in support of its position that Reynolds' alleged copying of information caused "damage" within the meaning of the CFAA, cites to Shurgard, as well as several cases with similar holdings. Nearly all of these cases also cite and rely on the reasoning in Shurgard. . . . Multiven v. Cisco, 725 F.Supp.2d 887, 894–95 (N.D.Cal. Jul. 20, 2010) (citing Shurgard for the proposition that it is "not necessary for data to be physically changed or erased to constitute damage"). . . .

The Court finds that the mere copying of information does not constitute a claim of "damage" within the meaning of the CFAA. As previously discussed, the statutory definition of "damage" in the CFAA is "any impairment to the integrity of data, a program, a system, or information." 18 U.S.C. § 1030(e)(8). NetApp contends that the copying of information impairs that information's "integrity." Opp'n Mot Dismiss at 14. The legislative history of the CFAA does not define the term "integrity." However, district courts that have considered the meaning of "integrity" in the CFAA have noted that the word typically means "an unimpaired or unmarred condition" or "soundness." See Worldspan, 2006 WL 1069128, at *5; see also Resdev, 2005 WL 1924743, at *5 ("integrity ... ordinarily means 'wholeness' or 'soundness' "). Therefore, the copying of information could damage that information's integrity if, for instance, the information's wholeness or soundness was affected. However, simply copying information, as NetApp alleges here, without otherwise affecting the wholeness or soundness of the information, would not impair the information's "integrity" as that term is commonly defined. Moreover, in this Court's prior order dismissing NetApp's claim under § 1030(a)(5), the Court stated that NetApp failed to plead that Reynolds "damaged any systems or destroyed any data." NetApp's amendment to the effect that Reynolds copied information from NetApp's computer systems similarly fails to plead that Reynolds damaged or destroyed any data, systems, program, or information. Finally, the Court notes that while the Ninth Circuit has not addressed the definition of "damage" within the CFAA, the Ninth Circuit has cautioned against interpreting the CFAA in a way that would "transform the CFAA from an anti-hacking statute into an expansive misappropriation statute." United States v. Nosal, 676 F.3d 854, 857 (9th Cir.2012) (en banc). Interpreting the term "damage" within the CFAA to encompass the simple copying of information risks doing precisely that. Any digital misappropriation necessarily involves the copying of information, and therefore any digital misappropriation of information would result in liability under § 1030(a)(5). This is the outcome against which the Ninth Circuit, as well as other courts, warned.

The Court is also ultimately unpersuaded by the reasoning of the Shurgard line of cases. Shurgard and its progeny rely on the Senate report which accompanied the 1996 amendments to the CFAA for support of the proposition that copying and disseminating information, without more, constitutes a claim of damage. However, the Senate report gave a specific example of conduct that, while it "arguably" causes "no 'damage,' " was punishable by the CFAA, and that is where hackers "alter existing log-on programs so that user passwords are copied to a file which the hackers can retrieve later." S.Rep. No. 104–357, at 11 (1996). The Senate Report says nothing about imposing liability under § 1030(a)(5) for the taking of information. In addition, the Court is not convinced that the taking of passwords is analogous to the taking of information. Stealing passwords necessarily compromises the security of a computer system and increases the risk of further damage, because it enables hackers to later access password-protected computer systems, information, programs, and data. See S.Rep. No. 104–357, at 11 (1996) (noting that the conduct of copying and retrieving password files "allows the intruder to accumulate valid user passwords to the system"). Therefore, it is not surprising that Congress would want to impose liability for the copying of passwords. In contrast, copying information does not necessarily render computer systems less secure, because copying information on its own does not necessarily allow a hacker to access other systems, programs, or data. Furthermore, neither NetApp, nor the Shurgard court, nor this Court identified any legislative history indicating Congressional intent to impose § 1030(a)(5) liability for misappropriating information.

For the above reasons, the Court finds that NetApp's allegation that Reynolds "cop[ied] certain information from NetApp's protected computers and transferr [ed] it to a non-secure area or device" fails to state a cognizable claim of "damage" within the meaning of the CFAA.

NetApp's remaining two allegations likewise fail to claim the requisite "damage." First, NetApp contends that Reynolds' actions caused damage to NetApp because they "diminish[ed] the value of NetApp's data by compromising its exclusivity, for which it derives value because it is not available to competitors."

The CFAA's definition of "damage," however, requires that there be "impairment to the integrity or availability" of data. 18 U.S.C. § 1030(e)(8). Moreover, NetApp cites no authority for the proposition that diminishment in value equates to an "impairment to ... integrity." Therefore, the harm alleged here falls outside the statute's definition of damage. In addition, the Court notes that this claim is essentially the same as the allegation that NetApp raised in its First Amended Complaint, which this Court previously dismissed with leave to amend. . . . Furthermore, if NetApp's allegation that diminishing the value of data by "compromising its exclusivity" stated a cognizable claim of damage, any misappropriation of trade secrets or confidential information would also state a claim of "damage," as misappropriation necessarily diminishes the value of confidential information by impairing its confidentiality. As previously stated, the Ninth Circuit has frowned upon such a broad interpretation of the CFAA. Nosal, 676 F.3d at 857. Therefore, NetApp fails to plead a claim of "damage" within the meaning of the CFAA by simply alleging that Reynolds diminished the value of NetApp's data by compromising its exclusivity.

Finally, NetApp alleges that Reynolds caused "damage" because Reynolds "alter [ed] or modif[ied] NetApp's performance data contained on its protected computers." As discussed previously, the CFAA's definition of "damage" requires "impairment to the integrity or availability" of data. 18 U.S.C. § 1030(e)(8). Here, NetApp does not describe how Reynolds altered or modified NetApp's performance data. The only facts NetApp alleges in support of its claim is that Reynolds "accessed NetApp's protected computers on a variety of occasions" and "downloaded" NetApp information. Therefore, according to NetApp's operative Complaint, the only basis upon which Reynolds could have altered or modified NetApp's performance data was by accessing and downloading information. See id. NetApp makes no allegation that Reynolds deleted information, or otherwise altered or modified the information he accessed. Thus, on these facts, NetApp fails to plead any "impairment" as required by statute.

For the reasons stated above, the Court finds NetApp does not allege a claim of "damage" under the CFAA and GRANTS Defendants' motion to dismiss NetApp's claims under § 1030(a)(5). Moreover, this is the second time that this Court has dismissed NetApp's claims under § 1030(a)(5) for failure to adequately plead "damage" as required by statute. Furthermore, this is NetApp's third complaint, and NetApp has twice had the opportunity to amend its claim under the CFAA in response to motions to dismiss. Yet, NetApp still fails to assert a viable claim. . . .

NOTES

Note 1

In the *Van Buren* Supreme Court decision, Justice Barrett discusses the "damage" and "loss" provisions:

> The Government's position has another structural problem. Recall that violating § 1030(a)(2), the provision under which Van Buren was charged, also gives rise to civil liability. See § 1030(g). Provisions defining "damage" and "loss" specify what a plaintiff in a civil suit can recover. "'[D]amage,'" the statute provides, means "any impairment to the integrity or availability of data, a program, a system, or information." § 1030(e)(8). The term "loss" likewise relates to costs caused by harm to computer data, programs, systems, or information services. § 1030(e)(11). The statutory definitions of "damage" and "loss" thus focus on technological harms—such as the corruption of files—of the type unauthorized users cause to computer systems and data. Limiting "damage" and "loss" in this way makes sense in a scheme "aimed at preventing the typical consequences of hacking." *Royal Truck*, 974 F.3d at 760. The term's definitions are ill fitted, however, to remediating "misuse" of sensitive information that employees may permissibly access using their computers. *Ibid.* Van Buren's situation is illustrative: His run of the license plate did not impair the "integrity or availability" of data, nor did it otherwise harm the database system itself.

Does *Van Buren* foreclose a *Shugard* type claim?

Note 2

In *Sandvig v. Barr*, 2020 WL 1494065 (D.D.C. 2020), the Court adopted an interpretation of the scope of the CFAA that does not criminalize the plaintiff academic researchers research by "providing false information to target websites, in violation of these websites' terms of service." Because of that interpretation, the Court decided that it did not need to reach the as applied First Amendment constitutional challenge to their alleged criminal conduct under the CFAA. Several authors have questioned whether the CFAA is unintentionally prohibiting the ability to root out bias. *See* Bradley Williams, *Preventing Unintended Internet Discrimination: An Analysis of the Computer Fraud and Abuse Act for Algorithmic Racial Steering*, 2018 Univ. of Ill. L. Rev. 847 (2018) (discussing CFAA and use of scrapers to identify racial discrimination); Brian Z. Mund, *Protecting Deceptive Academic Research Under the Computer Fraud and Abuse Act*, 37 Yale L. Pol'y Rev. 385 (2018) (arguing that obtaining access to data through deception for academic research purposes should not violate the CFAA). That issue appears to have been avoided for now by *Sandvig v. Barr*.

Note 3

Several organizations and individuals have filed amicus briefs in *Van Buren v. United States*. Notably, the Computer Security Researchers, Eletronic Frontier Foundation, Center for Democracy & Technology, Bugcrowd, Rapid, Scythe, and Tenable filed an amicus brief making the following arguments:

> the work of the computer security research community is vital to the public interest, including computer security benefits from the involvement of independent researchers, security researchers have made important contributions to the public interest by identifying security threats in essential infrastructure, voting systems, medical devices, vehicle software and more; and the broad interpretation of the CFAA adopted by the Eleventh Circuit chills valuable security research, including the Eleventh Circuit's interpretation of the CFAA would extend to violations of website terms of service and other written restrictions on computer use, standard computer security research methods can violate written access restrictions, the broad interpretation of the CFAA discourages researchers from pursuing and disclosing security flaws, voluntary disclosure guidelines and industry sponsored bug bounty programs are not sufficient to mitigate the chill, and malicious actors seeking security flaws are not dissuaded by the CFAA.

Note 4

In the Eleventh Circuit's *United States v. Rodriguez*, which predates the Supreme Court's *Van Buren* decision, Mr. Rodriguez alleged that he wanted to access protected files for the purpose of determining whether a friend was being underpaid based on gender. Should that type of "hactivism" be allowed under the statute? Surely, he would be addressing a harm specifically addressed by other federal statutes. What if

Mr. Rodriguez wanted to determine people's salaries to ascertain whether they were giving a "suitable" amount to his church? What types of "hactivism" should be allowed and not allowed? Should a person be allowed to hack into your computer for a purpose consistent with their values, but not your values? Should the CFAA be amended to address certain forms of hactivism?

Note 5

Even though the CFAA has been amended many times, do you believe the CFAA is out-of-date? The question of whether a person has access or not has become more complicated as the technology and its delivery have evolved. *See e.g.*, Amanda B. Gottlieb, *Reevaluating the Computer Fraud and Abuse Act: Amending the Statute to Expressly Address the Cloud*, 86 Ford. L. Rev. 767 (2017) (arguing that the CFAA should be amended to exempt access to cloud services under certain circumstances); Marcelo Triana, *Is Selling Malware a Federal Crime*, 93 N.Y.U. L. Rev. 1311 (2018) (asserting that the selling of malware is not adequately covered under the CFAA); Andrew Sellars, *Twenty Years of Web Scraping and the Computer Fraud and Abuse Act*, 24 Boston Univ. J. of Sci. & Tech. L. 372 (2018) (discussing how 9th Circuit case law recognizes that authorization may be "revoked"); *See also*, Melissa Anne Springer, *Social Media and Federal Prosecution: A Circuit Split on Cybercrime and the Interpretation of the Computer Fraud and Abuse Act*, 86 U. Cin. L. Rev. 315 (2018) (arguing for a narrow interpretation of the CFAA). Given the speed of technological change, are anti-hacking laws doomed to failure? Or, are narrow and very specific laws that prohibit certain conduct and are amended frequently the answer?

Note 6

In *Available, Granted, Revoked: A New Framework for Assessing Unauthorized Access Under the Computer Fraud and Abuse Act*, 87 U. Chi. L. Rev. 1437 (2020), Samuel Kane argues that the circuit split before the Supreme Court's *Van Buren* decision concerning interpreting the "authorized access" provisions of the CFAA should be resolved as follows:

> Leveraging concepts from CFAA case law and offering applicability across a wide range of factual and technological contexts, this Comment's Available-Granted-Revoked (AGR) Framework sequentially evaluates (1) whether the computer in question is publicly *available* or private; (2) whether the computer's owner had, at any point, *granted* the accesser permission to access the computer; and (3) whether the computer owner had affirmatively *revoked* the accesser's permission, if any, prior to the purportedly unauthorized access.
>
> This approach serves the interests underlying both the broad and narrow approaches. By limiting the scope of the CFAA's unauthorized access provisions to private computers (via Step 1) and adopting a permission-focused inquiry in Steps 2 and 3, the Framework will help to restrain the scope of CFAA liability--a key aim of narrow-approach advocates. At the

same time, by allowing computer owners to terminate access authorization by affirmatively revoking permission (via Step 3), the Framework will advance the broad-approach goal of allowing computer owners to protect their systems.

Note 7

Companies are reportedly becoming increasingly willing to accept the help of grey and white hat hackers in finding and disclosing vulnerabilities. For example, some companies offer bug bounty programs to incentivize the finding and disclosure of vulnerabilities. Moreover, as previously alluded to, society also has an interest in perhaps encouraging hacktivism for social justice or the protection of individual liberties. Moreover, an expansive statute criminalizing all hacking activities could be problematic given the arguable need to encourage grey and white hat activities. What about entities who were hacked, but want to hack back to recover data? Should the CFAA be amended to expressly state that those activities are exempt from liability? *See* Adam J. Goebel, *The Computer Fraud and Abuse Act is Stifling Security and Individual Rights, Digital Diplomacy* (July 15, 2020), https://medium.com/digital-diplomacy/the-computer-fraud-and-abuse-act-is-stifling-security-and-individual-rights-51ffc25bf784 ("Hack-tivists use digital town squares to spread messages of social change, including promoting free speech, human rights, and freedom of information among other political and social agendas. Yet our system of laws has yet to catch up to these myriads of new variations of the word hack resulting in absurd often draconian prosecutions of some, while others face no prosecution at all."). *See also* Eric Goldman, *The Computer Fraud and Abuse Act Is a Failed Experiment*, Forbes (March 28, 2013), https://www.forbes.com/sites/ericgoldman/2013/03/28/the-computer-fraud-and-abuse-act-is-a-failed-experiment/#345269665e90 (providing a list of potential amendments including a clause preempting state laws).

Notably, on May 19, 2022, the U.S. Department of Justice announced that it would be prosecute CFAA violations for "good faith security research." This is good news for white hat, ethical hackers; however, state laws criminalize similar behavior. The Press Release from the U.S. Department of Justice states:

> The policy for the first time directs that good-faith security research should not be charged. Good faith security research means accessing a computer solely for purposes of good-faith testing, investigation, and/or correction of a security flaw or vulnerability, where such activity is carried out in a manner designed to avoid any harm to individuals or the public, and where the information derived from the activity is used primarily to promote the security or safety of the class of devices, machines, or online services to which the accessed computer belongs, or those who use such devices, machines, or online services. . . .

The new policy states explicitly the longstanding practice that "the department's goals for CFAA enforcement are to promote privacy and cybersecurity by upholding the legal right of individuals, network owners, operators, and other persons to ensure the confidentiality, integrity, and availability of information stored in their information systems." Accordingly, the policy clarifies that hypothetical CFAA violations that have concerned some courts and commentators are not to be charged. Embellishing an online dating profile contrary to the terms of service of the dating website; creating fictional accounts on hiring, housing, or rental websites; using a pseudonym on a social networking site that prohibits them; checking sports scores at work; paying bills at work; or violating an access restriction contained in a term of service are not themselves sufficient to warrant federal criminal charges. The policy focuses the department's resources on cases where a defendant is either not authorized at all to access a computer or was authorized to access one part of a computer — such as one email account — and, despite knowing about that restriction, accessed a part of the computer to which his authorized access did not extend, such as other users' emails.

However, the new policy acknowledges that claiming to be conducting security research is not a free pass for those acting in bad faith. For example, discovering vulnerabilities in devices in order to extort their owners, even if claimed as "research," is not in good faith. The policy advises prosecutors to consult with the Criminal Division's Computer Crime and Intellectual Property Section (CCIPS) about specific applications of this factor. *See* U.S. Department of Justice, *Department of Justice Announces New Policy for Charging Cases under the Computer Fraud and Abuse Act* (May 19, 2022), available at Department of Justice Announces New Policy for Charging Cases under the Computer Fraud and Abuse Act | OPA | Department of Justice.

Note 8

The U.S. State Department is offering rewards for information concerning cybersecurity issues:

Commensurate with the seriousness with which we view these cyber threats, the Rewards for Justice program has set up a Dark Web (Tor-based) tips-reporting channel to protect the safety and security of potential sources. The RFJ program also is working with interagency partners to enable the rapid processing of information as well as the possible relocation of and payment of rewards to sources. Reward payments may include payments in cryptocurrency.

More information about this reward offer is located on the Rewards for Justice website at www.rewardsforjustice.net . We encourage anyone with information on malicious cyber activity, carried out against U.S. critical infrastructure in violation of the CFAA by actors at the direction of or under the control of a foreign government, to contact the Rewards for Justice office via our Tor-based tips-reporting channel at: he5dybnt7sr6cm32xt77pazmtm65flqy6irivtflruqfc5ep7eiodiad.onion (Tor browser required).

See Rewards for Justice – Reward Offer for Information on Foreign Malicious Cyber Activity Against U.S. Critical Infrastructure, Department of State (July 15, 2021), available at https://www.state.gov/rewards-for-justice-reward-offer-for-information-on-foreign-malicious-cyber-activity-against-u-s-critical-infrastructure/.

Note 9

In *HiQ v. Linkedin*, Judge Berzon noted that several plausible causes of action could exist based on HiQ's scraping of Linkedin's website. One of the causes of action mentioned is trespass to chattels. Notably, some courts have recognized trespass to chattels as a potential cause of action involving bombarding a computer system with email or spyware. *See e.g., CompuServ v. Cyber Promotions*, 962 F.Supp. 1015 (1997). In 2003, the California Supreme Court in *Intel v. Hamidi*, 30 Cal.4th 1342 (2003) rejected a trespass to chattels claim based on a former employee of Intel who sent emails to former colleagues critiquing Intel. The Court stated:

> Intel Corporation (Intel) maintains an electronic mail system, connected to the Internet, through which messages between employees and those outside the company can be sent and received, and permits its employees to make reasonable nonbusiness use of this system. On six occasions over almost two years, Kourosh Kenneth Hamidi, a former Intel employee, sent e-mails criticizing Intel's employment practices to numerous current employees on Intel's electronic mail system. Hamidi breached no computer security barriers in order to communicate with Intel employees. He offered to, and did, remove from his mailing list any recipient who so wished. Hamidi's communications to individual Intel employees caused neither physical damage nor functional disruption to the company's computers, nor did they at any time deprive Intel of the use of its computers. The contents of the messages, however, caused discussion among employees and managers.

> On these facts, Intel brought suit, claiming that by communicating with its employees over the company's e-mail system Hamidi committed the tort of trespass to chattels. The trial court granted Intel's motion for summary judgment and enjoined Hamidi from any further mailings. A divided Court of Appeal affirmed.

> After reviewing the decisions analyzing unauthorized electronic contact with computer systems as potential trespasses to chattels, we conclude

that under California law the tort does not encompass, and should not be extended to encompass, an electronic communication that neither damages the recipient computer system nor impairs its functioning. Such an electronic communication does not constitute an actionable trespass to personal property, i.e., the computer system, because it does not interfere with the possessor's use or possession of, or any other legally protected interest in, the personal property itself. . . . The consequential economic damage Intel claims to have suffered, i.e., loss of productivity caused by employees reading and reacting to Hamidi's messages and company efforts to block the messages, is not an injury to the company's interest in its computers—which worked as intended and were unharmed by the communications—any more than the personal distress caused by reading an unpleasant letter would be an injury to the recipient's mailbox, or the loss of privacy caused by an intrusive telephone call would be an injury to the recipient's telephone equipment.

Under the reasoning of *Hamidi*, do you think a trespass to chattels claim would be successful under the facts of *HiQ v. Linkedin*?

11.2[C] CONSTITUTIONAL CHALLENGES AND THE SCOPE OF THE CFAA

The CFAA has recently been constitutionally challenged. The following case raises issues concerning the constitutional viability of some of Congress' efforts to regulate the Internet and cybersecurity issues.

Sandvig v. Sessions, 315 F.Supp. 3d 1 (D.D.C. 2018).

MEMORANDUM OPINION

JOHN D. BATES, United States District Judge

It's a dangerous business, reading the fine print. Nearly every website we visit features Terms of Service ("ToS"), those endless lists of dos and don'ts conjured up by lawyers to govern our conduct in cyberspace. They normally remain a perpetual click away at the bottom of every web page, or quickly scrolled past as we check the box stating that we agree to them. But to knowingly violate some of those terms, the Department of Justice tells us, could get one thrown in jail. This reading of federal law is a boon to prosecutors hoping to deter cybercrime. Yet it also creates a dilemma for those with more benign intentions. Plaintiffs in this case, for instance, are researchers who wish to find out whether websites engage in discrimination, but who have to violate certain ToS to do so. They have challenged the statute that they allege criminalizes their conduct, saying that it violates their free speech, petition, and due process rights. First, however, they must show that they have a sufficient injury to make it through the courthouse door, and that their suit is plausible enough to continue. For the following reasons, the Court finds that plaintiffs have standing, and that they can bring one (but not the rest) of their claims.

I. BACKGROUND

This case centers on a few sections of the Computer Fraud and Abuse Act (CFAA), a law dedicated to "deterring the criminal element from abusing computer technology." H.R. Rep. No. 98–894, at 4 (1984). Plaintiffs directly challenge one section, referred to here as the Access Provision, which sweeps in the greatest amount of conduct. The Access Provision states that "[w]hoever ... intentionally accesses a computer without authorization or exceeds authorized access, and thereby obtains ... information from any protected computer ... shall be punished as provided in subsection (c) of this section." 18 U.S.C. § 1030(a)(2)(C). The CFAA defines "protected computer" to mean, among other things, "a computer ...which is used in or affecting interstate or foreign commerce or communication." Id. § 1030(e)(2)(B). This definition encompasses just about all computers hooked up to the Internet—including computers that house website servers. See, e.g., United States v. Nosal, 676 F.3d 854, 859 (9th Cir. 2012). The statute also defines "exceeds authorized access" as "to access a computer with authorization and to use such access to obtain or alter information in the computer that the accesser is not entitled so to obtain or alter." 18 U.S.C. § 1030(e)(6). Thus, the Access Provision applies to anyone who purposely accesses an Internet-connected computer without authorization, or uses a legitimate authorization to receive or change information that they are not supposed to, and thereby obtains information from the computer.

The CFAA provides for a fine and/or imprisonment for up to one year upon a first violation of the Access Provision, or up to ten years for any further offenses. Id. § 1030(c)(2)(A), (C). However, the punishment for an initial violation rises to a sentence of up to five years' imprisonment if the offense (1) "was committed for purposes of commercial advantage or private financial gain," (2) was "in furtherance of any criminal or tortious act in violation of the Constitution" or state or federal law, or (3) involved obtaining information valued at more than $5,000. Id. § 1030(c)(2)(B). Thus, meeting one of these three conditions makes a first violation a felony; if none are met, the first violation is a misdemeanor.

Plaintiffs in this case are four professors and a media organization: Christian W. Sandvig of the University of Michigan; Kyratso "Karrie" Karahalios of the University of Illinois; Alan Mislove of Northeastern University; Christopher "Christo" Wilson of Northeastern University; and First Look Media Works, Inc. ("Media Works"), which publishes the online news platform The Intercept. Plaintiffs are conducting studies to respond to new trends in real estate, finance, and employment transactions, which increasingly have been initiated on the Internet. Data brokers assemble consumers' information from myriad sources and place consumers into models that include racial, ethnic, socioeconomic, gender, and religious inferences about them. After brokers create consumer profiles, those profiles follow consumers around online through tracking technologies such as cookies. Tracking allows websites and advertisers to display content targeted at particular groups, based on consumers' inferred characteristics or the sorts of websites they visit. But plaintiffs are concerned, "[g]iven the ... history of racial discrimination in housing and employment," that this technology may be "harnessed for discriminatory purposes." They are also concerned that, "when algorithms automate decisions, there is a very real risk that those decisions will unintentionally have a prohibited discriminatory effect."

One way to determine whether members of protected classes are being discriminated against is to engage in "outcomes-based audit testing." Such testing commonly involves accessing a website or other network service repeatedly, generally by creating false or artificial user profiles, to see how websites respond to users who display characteristics attributed to certain races, genders, or other classes. This method is similar to classical paired testing procedures, in which multiple people—identical but for one legally protected trait—apply for the same house or job. Such procedures are often used to uncover violations of housing and employment discrimination laws in the physical world.

Plaintiffs plan to engage, and are engaging, in such audit testing. Sandvig and Karahalios are investigating whether computer programs that decide what to display on real estate websites discriminate against users based on race or other factors. They are writing a computer program that will create bots—automated agents that will each browse the Internet and interact with websites as a human user might. Each bot will create a number of distinct user profiles, each of which is called a "sock puppet." Sandvig and Karahalios will program the bots to visit real estate websites and search for properties, while also engaging in behaviors correlated with members of a particular race. Sandvig and Karahalios will use an automatic data recording technique known as scraping to record the properties that each bot sees on the real estate sites. They can then examine their data to determine whether race-associated behaviors caused the sock puppets to see different sets of properties.

Similarly, Mislove and Wilson plan to conduct a study to see whether hiring websites' algorithms end up discriminating against job seekers based on protected statuses like race or gender. They will first use bots to crawl the profiles of a random selection of job-seekers to obtain baseline demographic data, then create fake employer profiles so that they can search for candidates and record how the algorithms rank those candidates. They will also create fictitious sock-puppet job seeker profiles, and have the fictitious seekers—who will vary along different demographic axes—apply for fictitious jobs, to examine how the algorithms rank the candidates. Mislove and Wilson will prevent real people from applying for the false jobs by giving them titles that say "[t]his is not a real job, do not apply," and will delete the fictitious accounts and jobs when they finish. Media Works and its journalists seek to investigate online companies, websites, and platforms, including by examining any discriminatory effects of their use of algorithms.

Mislove and Wilson plan to publish their findings in academic papers, and to bring the results of their research to the public. Media Works intends to use the results of its journalistic investigations to inform the public about online business practices. Sandvig and Karahalios do not explicitly claim that they will publish their work, but state that their findings "would produce important new scientific knowledge about the operation of computer systems, discrimination, and cumulative disadvantage."

Plaintiffs are all aware that their activities will violate certain website ToS. All intend to use scraping to record data, which is banned by many of the websites plaintiffs seek to study. Many of the housing websites that Sandvig and Karahalios will study prohibit the use of bots. All of the hiring websites that Mislove and Wilson will study prohibit the use of sock puppets, and most prohibit crawling. Additionally, some websites control when and how visitors may speak about any information gained through the site—even in other forums—by including non-disparagement clauses in their ToS. Some sites also have ToS that require advance permission before using the sites for research purposes, which, plaintiffs allege, creates the possibility of viewpoint-discriminatory permission schemes. Aside from their ToS violations, plaintiffs' experiments will have at most a minimal impact on the operations of the target websites. All plaintiffs but Media Works have already begun some of the activities involved in their research plans, including activities that require violating websites'.

Plaintiffs claim that they must either refrain from conducting research, testing, and investigations that (they argue) constitute protected speech or expressive activity, or else expose themselves to the risk of prosecution under the Access Provision of the CFAA. Plaintiffs therefore filed this suit against the Attorney General, raising four causes of action: (1) a facial overbreadth and as-applied challenge under the Free Speech and Free Press Clauses of the First Amendment; (2) a First Amendment Petition Clause challenge; (3) a vagueness claim under the Fifth Amendment's Due Process Clause; and (4) a claim of unconstitutional delegation to private parties under the Fifth Amendment. The government has moved to dismiss under Federal Rules of Civil Procedure 12(b)(1) and 12(b)(6) for lack of standing and failure to state a claim.

II. DISCUSSION

. . .

A. The Internet as Public Forum

At the outset, it is necessary to answer a question that affects both the standing and the merits inquiries in this case: what is the First Amendment status of the Internet? And, more particularly, what powers does the government possess to regulate activity on individual websites?

The government bases much of its argument that plaintiffs do not have standing, and that they have not alleged a First Amendment violation, on the premise that this case is about "a private actor's abridgment of free expression in a private forum." This argument finds some support in Supreme Court case law, which has rejected the First Amendment claims of individuals who wished to distribute handbills or advertise a strike in shopping centers against the wishes of the property owners. See Hudgens v. NLRB, 424 U.S. 507, 520, 96 S.Ct. 1029, 47 L.Ed.2d 196 (1976). Private property, the

Court determined, does not "lose its private character merely because the public is generally invited to use it for designated purposes." Lloyd, 407 U.S. at 569, 92 S.Ct. 2219. Why, then, would it violate the First Amendment to arrest those who engage in expressive activity on a privately owned website against the owner's wishes?

The answer is that, quite simply, the Internet is different. The Internet is a "dynamic, multifaceted category of communication" that "includes not only traditional print and news services, but also audio, video, and still images, as well as interactive, real-time dialogue." Reno v. Am. Civil Liberties Union, 521 U.S. 844, 870, 117 S.Ct. 2329, 138 L.Ed.2d 874 (1997). Indeed, "the content on the Internet is as diverse as human thought." Id. Only last Term, the Supreme Court emphatically declared the Internet a primary location for First Amendment activity: "While in the past there may have been difficulty in identifying the most important places (in a spatial sense) for the exchange of views, today the answer is clear. It is cyberspace ...." Packingham v. North Carolina, —— U.S. ——, 137 S.Ct. 1730, 1735, 198 L.Ed.2d 273 (2017).

With this special status comes special First Amendment protection. The Packingham Court applied public forum analysis to a North Carolina law that banned former sex offenders from using social media websites, employing intermediate scrutiny because the law was content-neutral. The fact that the statute restricted access to particular websites, run by private companies, did not change the calculus. Consider: on one of the sites the Court treated as an exemplar of social media, LinkedIn, "users can look for work, advertise for employees, or review tips on entrepreneurship," id. at 1735— the same activities in which Mislove and Wilson wish to engage for their research. As the Court warned, the judiciary "must exercise extreme caution before suggesting that the First Amendment provides scant protection for access to vast networks in [the modern Internet]." The government's proposed public/private ownership distinction cannot account for the Court's determination in Packingham that privately-owned sites like Facebook, LinkedIn, and Twitter are part of a public forum, government regulation of which is subject to heightened First Amendment scrutiny. The Internet "is a forum more in a metaphysical than in a spatial or geographic sense, but the same principles are applicable." Rosenberger v. Rector & Visitors of Univ. of Virginia, 515 U.S. 819, 830, 115 S.Ct. 2510, 132 L.Ed.2d 700 (1995).

An analogy to the real world, while necessarily imperfect, may help illustrate the point. Stroll out onto the National Mall on any day with decent weather and you will discover a phalanx of food trucks lining the streets. Those food trucks are privately owned businesses. Customers interact with them for the private purpose of buying a meal. If they were a brick-and-mortar store on private property, they would encounter no First Amendment barrier to removing a patron who created a ruckus. Yet if a customer standing on a public sidewalk tastes her food and then yells at those in line behind her that they should avail themselves of the myriad other culinary options nearby, the truck could not call the police to arrest her for her comments. She is in a public forum, and her speech remains protected even when she interacts with a private business located within that forum.

It makes good sense to treat the Internet in this manner. "Each medium of expression ... must be assessed for First Amendment purposes by standards suited to it, for each may present its own problems." Se. Promotions, Ltd. v. Conrad, 420 U.S. 546, 557, 95 S.Ct. 1239, 43 L.Ed.2d 448 (1975). Regulation of the Internet presents serious line-drawing problems that the public/private distinction in physical space does not. The decisions in Lloyd and Hudgens concerned "property privately owned and used nondiscriminatorily for private purposes only." Lloyd, 407 U.S. at 568, 92 S.Ct. 2219. It is difficult to argue that most websites readily meet this description. As the Supreme Court has recognized, the Internet "provides relatively unlimited, low-cost capacity for communication of all kinds." Reno, 521 U.S. at 870, 117 S.Ct. 2329. Much of this communication takes place on websites that, in the physical world, would be seen solely as private, commercial spaces. Take Amazon.com. As a "popular retail website," Amazon undoubtedly has a private use "as a seller of products." Packingham, 137 S.Ct. at 1741 (Alito, J., concurring in the judgment). Yet the site also "facilitates the social introduction of people for the purpose of information exchanges," since it "allows a user to create a personal profile" and, "[w]hen someone purchases a product on Amazon, the purchaser can review the product and upload photographs, and other buyers can then respond to the review." Id. Conversely, Facebook—to which the Court pointed in Packingham as a quintessential site for protected First Amendment activity—allows users to buy and sell products in its Marketplace, and, like many social media sites, sells ads to make revenue. Simply put: the public Internet is too heavily suffused with First Amendment activity, and what might otherwise be deemed private spaces are too blurred with expressive spaces, to sustain a direct parallel to the physical world.

At the same time, however, it would be ill-advised to "equate the entirety of the [I]nternet with public streets and parks." To do so would "gloss[ ] over the dual public and private nature of digital arenas," and subject to heightened scrutiny regulations on even the Internet's most secluded nooks and crannies. Note, First Amendment—Freedom of Speech—Public Forum Doctrine—Packingham v. North Carolina, 131 Harv. L. Rev. 233, 238 (2017). Rifling through a business's confidential files is no less a trespass merely because those files are located in the cloud. A hacker cannot legally break into a Gmail account and copy the account-holder's emails, just as a busybody cannot legally reach into someone else's mailbox and open her mail. The First Amendment does not give someone the right to breach a paywall on a news website any more than it gives someone the right to steal a newspaper.

What separates these examples from the social media sites in Packingham is that the owners of the information at issue have taken real steps to limit who can access it. But simply placing contractual conditions on accounts that anyone can create, as social media and many other sites do, does not remove a website from the First Amendment protections of the public Internet. If it did, then Packingham—which examined a law that limited access to websites that require user accounts for full functionality—would have come out the other way. 137 S.Ct. at 1737; see also Orin S. Kerr, Cybercrime's Scope: Interpreting "Access" and "Authorization" in Computer Misuse Statutes, 78

N.Y.U. L. Rev. 1596, 1658 (2003) ("Applying a contract-based theory of authorization in a criminal context ... may be constitutionally overbroad, criminalizing a great deal beyond core criminal conduct, including acts protected by the First Amendment."). Rather, only code-based restrictions, which "carve[ ] out a virtual private space within the website or service that requires proper authentication to gain access," remove those protected portions of a site from the public forum. Orin S. Kerr, Essay, Norms of Computer Trespass, 116 Colum. L. Rev. 1143, 1171 (2016). Stealing another's credentials, or breaching a site's security to evade a code-based restriction, therefore remains unprotected by the First Amendment.

To return to the National Mall example, suppose that a food truck remains stationed on the Mall but boards up for the night, and the owner returns home. By shutting the food in a truck, perhaps along with her cooking instructions, the owner has placed a barrier between that property and the public forum outside. Thus, while the police could not arrest a customer for telling others in line that the food tastes terrible, or for reading the menu on the truck's exterior, they could arrest that customer for breaking into the boarded-up truck seeking confidential culinary information. This is true even if the customer claimed she was doing so in order to broadcast to the world the truck's substandard ingredients and ill-conceived recipes. While the First Amendment has free rein on the Mall generally, it does not protect those who circumvent barriers that demarcate private areas, even if those private areas are surrounded by an otherwise public forum. This distinction guides the Court's analysis here.

. . . C. Interpreting the Statute

Plaintiffs allege only constitutional claims in this case. Likely because they are bringing a pre-enforcement challenge, they are not claiming that the statute, properly read, does not apply to them. However, nearly all of their claims require the Court to determine the reach of the Access Provision before deciding the constitutional question. Since the Court does not accept plaintiffs' legal conclusions as true for purposes of a motion to dismiss under Rule 12(b)(6), see Doe v. Rumsfeld, 683 F.3d 390, 391 (D.C. Cir. 2012), plaintiffs' reading of the statute to cover their conduct does not control. Instead, the Court must interpret the law.

Courts are split as to how to read the relevant provisions. The CFAA defines the phrase "exceeds authorized access" as "to access a computer with authorization and to use such access to obtain or alter information in the computer that the accesser is not entitled so to obtain or alter." 18 U.S.C. § 1030(e)(6). The Second, Fourth, and Ninth Circuits have held that this language prohibits only unauthorized access to information. See United States v. Valle, 807 F.3d 508, 523–28 (2d Cir. 2015); WEC Carolina Ener. Solutions LLC v. Miller, 687 F.3d 199, 206 (4th Cir. 2012); Nosal, 676 F.3d at 863; see also Pulte Homes, Inc. v. Laborers' Int'l Union of N. Am., 648 F.3d 295, 304 (6th Cir. 2011) (stating, based on Ninth Circuit precedent, that "an individual who is authorized to use a computer for certain purposes but goes beyond those limitations ... has 'exceed[ed] authorized access' " (citation omitted) (alteration in original)). Meanwhile, the First, Fifth, and Eleventh Circuits have held that it also covers (at least in some instances) unauthorized use of information that a defendant was authorized to access only for specific purposes. See EF Cultural Travel BV v. Explorica, Inc., 274 F.3d 577, 583 (1st Cir. 2001); United States v. John, 597 F.3d 263, 271 (5th Cir. 2010); United States v. Rodriguez, 628 F.3d 1258, 1263 (11th Cir. 2010); see also Int'l Airport Centers, LLC v. Citrin, 440 F.3d 418, 420–21 (7th Cir. 2006) (holding that an employee who deleted his employer's files in violation of his employment contract had terminated the agency relationship that authorized him to access the information). Courts have also split over whether violating a website's ToS exceeds authorized access for purposes of the CFAA.9 The D.C. Circuit has never opined on either question. Several district judges in this Circuit, however, have held that the provision only applies to unauthorized access to information, not to unauthorized use of properly accessed material. See Hedgeye Risk Mgmt., LLC v. Heldman, 271 F.Supp.3d 181, 194–95 (D.D.C. 2017) (collecting cases).

At one point in their briefing, plaintiffs suggest a different dividing line: a limiting construction that carves out harmless ToS violations from the statute. Pls.' Mem. at 31–33, 35. However, "[t]he text will not bear such a reading." INS v. Yueh-Shaio Yang, 519 U.S. 26, 30, 117 S.Ct. 350, 136 L.Ed.2d 288 (1996). It is one thing to carve out such violations by determining that the statute is unconstitutional as applied, but the text of the statute itself—"exceeds authorized access"—and its statutory definition do not appear to allow for such a surgical slicing off of conduct. How does the text differentiate between ToS violations and violations of employers' computer use policies, for instance? And how does the text distinguish between "[ToS] violations alone," Pls.' Mem. at 35, and ToS violations that cause damage or involve fraud, which plaintiffs admit are covered by §§ 1030(a)(4) and (a)(5), id. at 31–32? One can just as easily "use [authorized] access to obtain or alter information in the computer that the accesser is not entitled so to obtain or alter," § 1030(e)(6), whether it is a website or some other entity that is doing the authorizing, and whether the violation is harmful or harmless.

The question thus remains whether "exceeds authorized access" refers to access alone or to access, use, and other violations. The Court finds the narrow interpretation adopted by the Second, Fourth, and Ninth Circuits—and by numerous other district judges in this Circuit—to be the best reading of the statute. First, the text itself more naturally reads as limited to violations of the spatial scope of one's permitted access. To "exceed[ ] authorized access," one must have permission to access the computer at issue, and must "use such access"—i.e., one's authorized presence on the computer—"to obtain or alter information in the computer." Id. Thus, unlike the phrase "unauthorized access" used alongside it in several CFAA provisions, the phrase "exceeds authorized access" refers not to an outside attack but rather to an inside job. See, e.g., Nosal, 676 F.3d at 858. The rest of the definition requires that the information at issue be information "that the accesser is not entitled so to obtain or alter." Id. The key word here is "entitled." "And, in context, the most 'sensible reading of "entitled" is as a synonym for "authorized.' " " Hedgeye, 271 F.Supp.3d at 194 (quoting Nosal, 676 F.3d at 857). The focus is thus on whether someone is allowed to access a computer at all, in the case of "unauthorized access," or on whether someone is authorized to obtain or alter particular information, in the case of "exceeds authorized access." In neither instance does the statute focus on how the accesser plans to use the information. . . .

All of these factors, therefore, lead the Court to adopt a narrow reading of the term "exceeds authorized access." Just as an individual "accesses a computer 'without authorization' when he gains admission to a computer without approval," an individual " 'exceeds authorized access' when he has approval to access a computer, but uses his access to obtain or alter information that falls outside the bounds of his approved access." WEC Carolina, 687 F.3d at 204.

This interpretation gets us far, but not all the way. At oral argument, both parties agreed that the Access Provision applies only to access restrictions. See Tr. of Mot. Hr'g at 19:17–20:3, 34:10–35:22. But they have very different ideas about what that means. The government treats this difference as a largely temporal one. It argues that "the moment the violation occurs is on access," so that subsequent usage of information lawfully obtained does not constitute a CFAA violation. Id. at 20:12–:18. But the government also claims that "it's appropriate to analyze the issue of whether access is authorized according to a broad context of background facts that could include limitations on the purpose for which information is accessed," such as "access restrictions that are contained in the [ToS] that the website itself has prepared." Id. at 19:21–20:2. Plaintiffs, on the other hand, argue that the distinction between access and use turns on the conduct being prohibited, rather than whether the website attempts to cast the conduct as related to access rather than use. Id. at 61:17–:23. Plaintiffs' reading is the more natural one, and better reflects the constitutional avoidance concerns that support the Court's interpretation of the statute. Therefore, the Court must make an objective inquiry into the conduct alleged to violate websites' ToS. The focus is on what information plaintiffs plan to access, not on why they wish to access it, the manner in which they use their authorization to access it, or what they hope to do with it.

Applying this standard, it becomes clear that most of plaintiffs' proposed activities fall outside the CFAA's reach. Scraping or otherwise recording data from a site that is accessible to the public is merely a particular use of information that plaintiffs are entitled to see. The same goes for speaking about, or publishing documents using, publicly available data on the targeted websites. The use of bots or sock puppets is a more context-specific activity, but it is not covered in this case. Employing a bot to crawl a website or apply for jobs may run afoul of a website's ToS, but it does not constitute an access violation when the human who creates the bot is otherwise allowed to read and interact with that site. See Kerr, Norms of Computer Trespass, supra, at 1170. The website might purport to be limiting the identities of those entitled to enter the site, so that humans but not robots can get in. See Star Wars: Episode IV—A New Hope (Lucasfilm 1977) ("We don't serve their kind here! ... Your droids. They'll have to wait outside."). But bots are simply technological tools for humans to more efficiently collect and process information that they could otherwise access manually. Cf. Star Wars: Episode II—Attack of the Clones (Lucasfilm 2002) ("[I]f droids could think, there'd be none of us here, would there?").

Out of plaintiffs' proposed activities, then, only Mislove and Wilson's plan to create fictitious user accounts on employment sites would violate the CFAA. Unlike plaintiffs' other conduct, which occurs on portions of websites that any visitor can view, creating false accounts allows Mislove and Wilson to access information on those sites that is both limited to those who meet the owners' chosen authentication requirements and targeted to the particular preferences of the user. Creating false accounts and obtaining information through those accounts would therefore fall under the Access Provision. With that in mind, the Court must turn to the government's motion to dismiss plaintiffs' constitutional claims.

D. Freedom of Speech and Freedom of the Press

Plaintiffs first claim that the Access Provision violates the First Amendment's guarantees of freedom of speech and of the press. They assert that the provision is both facially overbroad and unconstitutional as applied to their own conduct. The Court will analyze these claims in turn.

1. Facial Overbreadth

Plaintiffs allege that the Access Provision "creates virtually limitless restrictions on speech and expressive activity," such that the statute "is unconstitutionally overbroad on its face." In a typical facial challenge, plaintiffs must show "'that no set of circumstances exists under which [the Access Provision] would be valid,' ... or that the statute lacks any 'plainly legitimate sweep.'" Stevens, 559 U.S. at 472, 130 S.Ct. 1577 (citations omitted). However, First Amendment cases allow for "'a second type of facial challenge,' whereby a law may be invalidated as overbroad if 'a substantial number of its applications are unconstitutional, judged in relation to the statute's plainly legitimate sweep.'" Id. at 473, 130 S.Ct. 1577. This second, lower bar is the one against which plaintiffs—and the Court—measure their challenge.

The government argues that plaintiffs have failed to state a plausible overbreadth claim. The Court agrees. "The first step in overbreadth analysis is to construe the challenged statute; it is impossible to determine whether a statute reaches too far without first knowing what the statute covers." United States v. Williams, 553 U.S. 285, 293, 128 S.Ct. 1830, 170 L.Ed.2d 650 (2008). The Court has now done so. Plaintiffs have operated under the assumption that the Access Provision covers all ToS violations; but, properly read, the Access Provision incorporates only those ToS that limit access to particular information. This fact alone is enough to dispose of plaintiffs' overbreadth claim. "Invalidation for overbreadth is strong medicine," id. (citation omitted), to be "employed ... sparingly and only as a last resort," Broadrick v. Oklahoma, 413 U.S. 601, 613, 93 S.Ct. 2908, 37 L.Ed.2d 830 (1973). A court should not invalidate a provision for overbreadth "when a limiting construction has been or could be placed on the challenged statute."

Plaintiffs concede that a limiting construction would address their overbreadth concerns—though they contend that the Access Provision would need to be "construed not to reach [ToS] violations alone." While the Court's reading of "exceeds authorized access" is not as narrow as the reading plaintiffs might prefer, it does eliminate many of the potentially unconstitutional applications of the Access Provisions. To be overbroad, a statute's unconstitutional scope must be "substantial, not only in an absolute sense, but also relative to the statute's plainly legitimate sweep." Williams, 553 U.S. at 292, 128 S.Ct. 1830. As purpose, use, or manner restrictions fall outside the Access Provision's reach, plaintiffs have not plausibly alleged that the provision's potentially unconstitutional applications are substantial relative to its legitimate ones. Moreover, plaintiffs also bring an as-applied claim, and facial challenges are disfavored when a case "may be disposed of on narrower grounds." Texas v. Johnson, 491 U.S. 397, 403 n.3, 109 S.Ct. 2533, 105 L.Ed.2d 342 (1989). Hence, Plaintiffs' overbreadth claim will be dismissed.

2. As-Applied Challenge

Plaintiffs allege that, "[a]s applied to the[m]," the Access Provision "unconstitutionally restricts their protected speech." Compl. ¶ 184. "[T]o prevail on an as-applied First Amendment challenge," plaintiffs "must show that the [Access Provision is] unconstitutional as applied to their particular speech activity." Edwards v. District of Columbia, 755 F.3d 996, 1001 (D.C. Cir. 2014). " '[T]he distinction between facial and as-applied challenges ... goes to the breadth of the remedy employed by the Court, not what must be pleaded in a complaint.' ...The substantive rule of law is the same for both challenges." Id. (citations omitted).

Aside from the overarching objections that the Court has already rejected, the government's primary response to plaintiffs' as-applied claim is that the Access Provision regulates conduct, rather than speech, and is therefore subject to limited scrutiny. But even if a law "says nothing about speech on its face," it is "subject to First Amendment scrutiny" if "it restricts access to traditional public fora." McCullen v. Coakley, —— U.S. ——, 134 S.Ct. 2518, 2529, 189 L.Ed.2d 502 (2014). As the Access Provision both limits access to and burdens speech in the public forum that is the public Internet, see supra Part II.A, heightened First Amendment scrutiny is appropriate. "In particular, the guiding First Amendment principle that the 'government has no power to restrict expression because of its message, its ideas, its subject matter, or its content' applies with full force in a traditional public forum." Content- or viewpoint-based restrictions receive strict scrutiny. See Reed v. Town of Gilbert, —— U.S. ——, 135 S.Ct. 2218, 2226, 192 L.Ed.2d 236 (2015). On the other hand, if a statute is content-neutral and only "impose[s] reasonable restrictions on the time, place, or manner of protected speech," McCullen, 134 S.Ct. at 2529, it is subjected to intermediate scrutiny. "In order to survive intermediate scrutiny, a law must be 'narrowly tailored to serve a significant governmental interest,' " Packingham, 137 S.Ct. at 1736 (citation omitted), and must "leave open ample alternative channels for communication of the information," McCullen, 134 S.Ct. at 2529.14

Plaintiffs claim that the Access Provision allows websites to impose direct speech restrictions, including content-based restrictions, and that it is therefore subject to strict scrutiny. However, the statute itself does not target speech, or impose content-based regulations, on its face. Nor have plaintiffs plausibly alleged that the government's purpose is to restrict speech based on its content or viewpoint. Indeed, while the government has not yet been able to proffer much evidence of the purposes behind the provision, the legislative history indicates that Congress was interested in passing the Access Provision to prevent the digital equivalent of theft. See S. Rep. 104–357, at 7 ("The proposed subsection 1030(a)(2)(C) is intended to protect against the interstate or foreign theft of information by computer.... This subsection would ensure that the theft of intangible information by the unauthorized use of a computer is prohibited in the same way theft of physical items are protected [sic]."). Therefore, strict scrutiny does not apply. See Pursuing America's Greatness v. FEC, 831 F.3d 500, 509 (D.C. Cir. 2016) (stating that courts must determine content neutrality based on text, and then purpose).

From the information available so far, significant interests appear to underlie the Access Provision. In addition to the legislative history regarding theft prevention, the government suggests that the Court analogize the CFAA to trespass law, arguing that Congress was also trying to prohibit the digital equivalent of trespassing. While plaintiffs dispute the trespass analogy, they recognize that the CFAA was passed to prevent computer theft and other cybercrime, and have not disputed that this is a significant interest. The question is thus whether the statute fails narrow tailoring as applied to Mislove and Wilson's plan to "creat[e] profiles containing false information," Compl. ¶ 124, and "access[ ] websites using artificial tester profiles, in violation of [ToS] that prohibit providing false information."

"To satisfy narrow tailoring, the [government] must prove the challenged regulations directly advance its asserted interests." Edwards, 755 F.3d at 1003. This means "the government must show 'a close fit between ends and means,'" such "that the regulation 'promotes a substantial government interest that would be achieved less effectively absent the regulation,'" and does "not 'burden substantially more speech than is necessary to further the government's legitimate interests.'" A.N.S.W.E.R. Coalition v. Basham, 845 F.3d 1199, 1213–14 (D.C. Cir. 2017) (citations omitted). At this early stage, the government has not put forward any evidence to show that prosecuting those who provide false information when creating accounts, without more, would advance its interest in preventing digital theft or trespass.

Indeed, presuming the allegations in the complaint to be true, it appears that the government's interest "is not implicated on these facts" at all. Johnson, 491 U.S. at 410, 109 S.Ct. 2533. Plaintiffs allege that their conduct "will not cause material harm to the target websites' operations," and that "they have no intent to commit fraud or to access any data or information that is not made available to the public." It is difficult to argue that trespass or theft concerns can justify restricting—or even apply to—viewing information that a website makes available to anyone who chooses to create a username and password. Cf. Kerr, Cybercrime's Scope, supra, at 1646. And any inadvertent "fraud" plaintiffs may perpetrate against the target websites by creating fictitious accounts will be, plaintiffs allege, harmless. The CFAA already punishes harmful, intentional fraud in a separate section, see 18 U.S.C. § 1030(a)(4), providing additional evidence that the government can further its legitimate interests just as well without applying the Access Provision to plaintiffs' bare false statements. At this stage, "absent any evidence that the speech [would be] used to gain a material advantage," Alvarez, 567 U.S. at 723, 132 S.Ct. 2537, plaintiffs' false speech on public websites retains First Amendment protection, see id. at 722, 132 S.Ct. 2537, and rendering it criminal does not appear to advance the government's proffered interests. Hence, plaintiffs have plausibly alleged an as-applied First Amendment claim, and the motion to dismiss that claim will be denied.

E. Right to Petition

In addition to their free speech and press claims, plaintiffs allege that the Access Provision violates their rights under the Petition Clause of the First Amendment. That clause states: "Congress shall make no law ... abridging ... the right of the People ... to petition the Government for a redress of grievances." U.S. Const. amend. I. Plaintiffs assert that the Access Provision, by criminalizing websites' prohibitions on critical speech or publishing, prevents people from using any information they might gain from plaintiffs' planned research to inform Congress or agencies about potential discrimination by those websites. They also assert that, for the same reasons, the Access Provision prevents people from accessing the courts to enforce Title VII or the Fair Housing Act: nobody who had visited a website with a non-disparagement clause in its ToS could bring discrimination claims against that site in court without opening him- or herself up to a potential CFAA prosecution.

These allegations are focused on ToS that restrict subsequent speech: disparagement, for instance, or use of the sites' information in court. However, such ToS constitute restrictions on the use of information, not on access to it. They therefore do not fall within the Access Provision's ambit, as properly interpreted. But even if one assumes that plaintiffs allege that access restrictions criminalized by the Access Provision violate the Petition Clause, plaintiffs' petition challenge is, at best, no stronger than their free speech challenge. Speech and petition rights are "generally subject to the same constitutional analysis," Wayte v. United States, 470 U.S. 598, 610 n.11, 105 S.Ct. 1524, 84 L.Ed.2d 547 (1985), unless "the special concerns of the Petition Clause would provide a sound basis for a distinct analysis," Borough of Duryea v. Guarnieri, 564 U.S. 379, 389, 131 S.Ct. 2488, 180 L.Ed.2d 408 (2011). Here, the rights appear to overlap: plaintiffs' Petition Clause claim focuses on speech restrictions that could then affect the petitioning process. Thus, plaintiffs "just as easily could have alleged"—and do, in fact, allege—a Speech Clause violation on the same set of facts.

And it is on that free speech claim that plaintiffs' First Amendment case must rise or fall. The Speech and Press Clauses, rather than the Petition Clause, provide the more natural home for plaintiffs' concerns about the Access Provision. Plaintiffs assert that the CFAA "prevents them from engaging in" petitioning because some websites' ToS (and thus the Access Provision) "prohibit the speech necessary to engage in ...

petitioning." The real concern, then, is the Access Provision's alleged restrictions on speech, which have ripple effects in a variety of contexts. The application of the Access Provision to the petitioning process constitutes one small subset of the speech and conduct the provision allegedly prohibits. Any effect the statute might have on plaintiffs' petition rights, then, is an extra step removed from the central speech harm, and is thus too attenuated to state a plausible claim for relief.

Ultimately, "the Petition Clause protects the right of individuals to appeal to courts and other forums established by the government for resolution of legal disputes," and "[i]nterpretation of the Petition Clause must be guided by the objectives and aspirations that underlie the right." Borough of Duryea, 564 U.S. at 387–88, 131 S.Ct. 2488. As the government notes, the clause is not aimed at the right to gather facts, or to speak while doing so, as a preliminary step to help prepare that petition in a preferred way. See Def.'s Mem. at 28. That right is more naturally the province of the Speech and Press Clauses than of the Petition Clause. See Burt Neuborne, Madison's Music: On Reading the First Amendment 11–12, 89 (2015) (arguing that the First Amendment's protected rights form "a rigorous chronological narrative of free citizens governing themselves in an ideal democracy," and that the Petition Clause "concludes Madison's narrative, protecting [an] idea's introduction into the formal democratic process, forcing the legislature to place the issue on its agenda"). Hence, plaintiffs' Petition Clause claim will be dismissed.

F. Vagueness

Plaintiffs next allege that the Access Provision violates the Due Process Clause because it is unconstitutionally vague. A statute is void if it is "[1] so vague that it fails to give ordinary people fair notice of the conduct it punishes, or [2] so standardless that it invites arbitrary enforcement." Johnson v. United States, —— U.S. ——, 135 S.Ct. 2551, 2556, 192 L.Ed.2d 569 (2015). Plaintiffs allege that the Access Provision meets both prongs of this test.

Because of potential chilling effects, "a more stringent vagueness test" applies when a law "interferes with the right of free speech." Vill. of Hoffman Estates v. Flipside, Hoffman Estates, Inc., 455 U.S. 489, 499, 102 S.Ct. 1186, 71 L.Ed.2d 362 (1982). Properly interpreted, however, the Access Provision is not unconstitutionally vague. "A plaintiff whose speech is clearly proscribed cannot raise a successful vagueness claim" based on a lack of fair notice. Expressions Hair Design v. Schneiderman, —— U.S. ——, 137 S.Ct. 1144, 1151–52, 197 L.Ed.2d 442 (2017). Nor can that plaintiff bring a facial vagueness challenge "based on the speech of others." Humanitarian Law Project, 561 U.S. at 20, 130 S.Ct. 2705. As we have already seen, the Access Provision plainly proscribes the creation of false accounts, but does not prohibit plaintiffs' other activities. Indeed, plaintiffs allege that they are aware that their proposed conduct would violate their target websites' ToS restrictions on creating false accounts. As the Court has determined that the Access Provision applies to one of their activities but not to the others, and as plaintiffs admit that they have the requisite mens rea to commit the crime, no facial claim or as-applied notice claim can go forward.

Nor can plaintiffs plausibly allege that the Access Provision invites arbitrary enforcement. "[A] statute's vagueness is either susceptible to judicial construction or is void for vagueness based on the application of traditional rules for statutory interpretation." United States v. Bronstein, 849 F.3d 1101, 1106 (D.C. Cir. 2017). Thus, "before striking a federal statute as impermissibly vague," courts must "consider whether the prescription is amenable to a limiting construction." Welch v. United States, —— U.S. ——, 136 S.Ct. 1257, 1268, 194 L.Ed.2d 387 (2016). The Court has already determined that a more limited construction is not only possible, but is in fact more natural than the broad reading that raises vagueness concerns. Read to apply only to access, and not to use, restrictions, the Access Provision severely curtails both websites' ability to define the law and prosecutors' freedom arbitrarily to enforce it. Plaintiffs' Fifth Amendment vagueness claim will be dismissed.

. . .

CONCLUSION

This case raises important questions about the government's ability to criminalize vast swaths of everyday activity on the Internet. However, the Court need not answer all of them today, because it concludes that the CFAA prohibits far less than the parties claim (or fear) it does. For the reasons explained above, plaintiffs have plausibly alleged that they have standing to sue, and that the Access Provision violates the Free Speech and Free Press Clauses of the First Amendment as applied to them. The government's motion to dismiss for lack of standing and on this single as-applied claim will therefore be denied. But the Access Provision, as the Court reads it, does not sweep widely enough to render plausible plaintiffs' First Amendment overbreadth and petition claims, or their Fifth Amendment vagueness . . . claims. The government's motion to dismiss those claims, therefore, will be granted. . . .

11.2[D] FOREIGN SOVEREIGN IMMUNITY FOR HACKING

An important issue concerns the liability for hacking or facilitating hacking by foreign governments. Foreign governments are often granted sovereign immunity. However, additional important questions include whether a private company working on behalf of a foreign government or with its explicit or implicit permission also receives sovereign immunity. The next clase explores those issues.

WhatsApp, Inc. v. NSO Group Technologies Ltd., 17 F.4th 930 (2021).

FORREST, Circuit Judge

The question presented is whether foreign sovereign immunity protects private companies. The law governing this question has roots extending back to our earliest history as a nation, and it leads to a simple answer—no. Indeed, the title of the legal doctrine itself—*foreign sovereign* immunity—suggests the outcome.

Plaintiffs-Appellees WhatsApp Inc. and Facebook, Inc. (collectively WhatsApp) sued Defendants-Appellants NSO Group Technologies Ltd. and Q Cyber Technologies Ltd. (collectively NSO), alleging that NSO, a privately owned and operated Israeli corporation, sent malware through WhatsApp's server system to approximately 1,400 mobile devices, breaking both state and federal law. NSO argues foreign sovereign immunity protects it from suit and, therefore, the court lacks subject matter jurisdiction. Specifically, NSO contends that even if WhatsApp's allegations are true, NSO was acting as an agent of a foreign state, entitling it to "conduct-based immunity"—a common-law doctrine that protects foreign officials acting in their official capacity.

The district court rejected NSO's argument, concluding that common-law foreign official immunity does not protect NSO from suit in this case. We agree that NSO is not entitled to immunity in this case, but we reach this conclusion for a different reason than did the district court. We hold that the Foreign Sovereign Immunity Act (FSIA or Act) occupies the field of foreign sovereign immunity as applied to *entities* and categorically forecloses extending immunity to any entity that falls outside the FSIA's broad definition of "foreign state." And we reject NSO's argument that it can claim foreign sovereign immunity under common-law immunity doctrines that apply to foreign officials—i.e., natural persons. *See Samantar v. Yousuf*, 560 U.S. 305, 315–16, 130 S.Ct. 2278, 176 L.Ed.2d 1047 (2010). There is no indication that the Supreme Court intended to extend foreign *official* immunity to entities. Moreover, the FSIA's text, purpose, and history demonstrate that Congress displaced common-law sovereign immunity doctrine as it relates to entities. *See Native Vill. of Kivalina v. ExxonMobil Corp.*, 696 F.3d 849, 856 (9th Cir. 2012) ("Federal common law is subject to the paramount authority of Congress.").

I. BACKGROUND

NSO is an Israeli company that designs and licenses surveillance technology to governments and government agencies for national security and law enforcement purposes. One of NSO's products—a program named Pegasus—"enables law enforcement and intelligence agencies to remotely and covertly extract valuable intelligence from virtually any mobile device." Pegasus users may intercept messages, take screenshots, or exfiltrate a device's contacts or history. NSO claims that it markets and licenses Pegasus to its customers,[485] which then operate the technology themselves. According to NSO, its role "is limited to ... providing advice and technical support to assist customers in setting up—not operating—the Pegasus technology."

---

[485] Editors: Footnote 1 of the Court's opinion states: "WhatsApp contends that NSO's customers are not limited to foreign governments. Whether this is true or not is immaterial to the outcome of this case." *Id.*

WhatsApp provides an encrypted communication service to the users of its application. Because of its encryption technology, every type of communication (telephone calls, video calls, chats, group chats, images, videos, voice messages, and file transfers) sent using WhatsApp on a mobile device can be viewed only by the intended recipient. WhatsApp asserts that NSO used WhatsApp's servers without authorization to send "malicious code" to approximately 1,400 WhatsApp users. The malicious code was allegedly designed to infect the targeted devices for the purpose of surveilling the device users.

In October 2019, WhatsApp sued NSO in federal district court. WhatsApp asserted claims under the Computer Fraud and Abuse Act, 18 U.S.C. § 1030, and the California Comprehensive Computer Data Access and Fraud Act, Cal. Penal Code § 502, as well as claims for breach of contract and trespass to chattels. WhatsApp alleged that NSO intentionally accessed WhatsApp servers without authorization to figure out how to place Pegasus on WhatsApp users' devices without detection. WhatsApp sought an injunction restraining NSO from accessing WhatsApp's servers, violating WhatsApp's terms, and impairing WhatsApp's service. WhatsApp also sought compensatory, statutory, and punitive damages.

NSO moved to dismiss the complaint. As relevant here, NSO asserted that the court lacked subject matter jurisdiction because NSO was acting at the direction of its foreign government customers and is protected from suit under foreign sovereign immunity. The district court denied NSO's motion. Relying on the Restatement (Second) of Foreign Relations Law § 66, the district court concluded that NSO was not entitled to common-law conduct-based foreign sovereign immunity because it failed to show that exercising jurisdiction over NSO would serve to enforce a rule of law against a foreign state. This interlocutory appeal followed.

II. DISCUSSION

. . .

B. Foreign Sovereign Immunity

1. Origins of the Doctrine

Chief Justice John Marshall's opinion in *Schooner Exchange v. McFaddon*, 11 U.S. 116, 7 Cranch 116, 3 L. Ed. 287 (1812), is credited with establishing foreign sovereign immunity in American law. *See Opati v. Republic of Sudan*, —— U.S. ——, 140 S. Ct. 1601, 1605, 206 L.Ed.2d 904 (2020); *see also Schooner Exchange*, 7 Cranch at 136 (noting the Court was "exploring an unbeaten path, with few, if any, aids from precedents or written law"). Writing for the Court, he reasoned that a nation's jurisdiction within its own boundaries is "exclusive and absolute" and any limitations on such jurisdiction "must be traced up to the consent of the nation itself. They can flow from no other legitimate source." *Schooner Exchange*, 7 Cranch at 136. Chief Justice Marshall further explained that respecting, and claiming, the "perfect equality and absolute independence of sovereigns," the nations of the world have "wave[d] the exercise of a part of that complete exclusive territorial jurisdiction" in cases brought within their jurisdiction against a foreign sovereign and ministers of a foreign sovereign. *Id.* at 137–39; *Republic of Austria v. Altmann*, 541 U.S. 677, 688 & n.9, 124 S.Ct. 2240, 159 L.Ed.2d 1 (2004).

From this origin—described as "the classical or virtually absolute theory of sovereign immunity," *Permanent Mission of India to the U.N. v. City of New York*, 551 U.S. 193, 199, 127 S.Ct. 2352, 168 L.Ed.2d 85 (2007)—"[t]he doctrine of foreign sovereign immunity developed as a matter of common law." *Samantar*, 560 U.S. at 311, 130 S.Ct. 2278. During our early years as a country, the State Department took the lead in applying foreign sovereign immunity. *Id.*; *see also* Br. of Foreign Sovereign Immunity Scholars, 4–7, No. 20-16408. Essentially, when faced with an immunity claim brought by a foreign state or official, if the State Department suggested immunity, a court would acquiesce. *Samantar*, 560 U.S. at 311–12, 130 S.Ct. 2278. And if the State Department did not suggest immunity, the court's inquiry consisted of asking whether the State Department had a policy for recognizing sovereign immunity in similar circumstances. *Id.* So, the State Department, not the courts, was the primary arbiter of foreign sovereign immunity. And the State Department's general practice was to suggest immunity "in all actions against friendly sovereigns." *Id.* at 312, 130 S.Ct. 2278.

2. The Foreign Sovereign Immunity Act

In the early 1950s, the State Department abandoned the absolute theory of foreign sovereign immunity and "join[ed] the majority of other countries by adopting the 'restrictive theory' of sovereign immunity." *Permanent Mission of India to the U.N.*, 551 U.S. at 199, 127 S.Ct. 2352. Under this theory, foreign sovereign "'immunity is confined to suits involving the foreign sovereign's public acts, and does not extend to cases arising out of a foreign state's strictly commercial acts.'" *Samantar*, 560 U.S. at 312, 130 S.Ct. 2278 (quoting *Verlinden B.V. v. Cent. Bank of Nigeria*, 461 U.S. 480, 487, 103 S.Ct. 1962, 76 L.Ed.2d 81 (1983)). Congress recognized that "[u]nder international law, states are not immune from the jurisdiction of foreign courts insofar as their commercial activities are concerned." 28 U.S.C. § 1602. Unsurprisingly, the politics of international diplomacy, at times, caused the State Department to suggest granting immunity in cases where its new, restrictive theory would have dictated denial. *Samantar*, 560 U.S. at 312, 130 S.Ct. 2278; *Verlinden B.V.*, 461 U.S. at 487, 103 S.Ct. 1962. Inconsistent outcomes also occurred depending on whether an immunity claim was presented to the State Department or a court. *Verlinden B.V.*, 461 U.S. at 487–88, 103 S.Ct. 1962.

Congress disapproved of this inconsistency and enacted the FSIA to promote uniformity. *Samantar*, 560 U.S. at 313, 130 S.Ct. 2278. As the Act explains, its purpose was twofold: (1) "endorse and codify the restrictive theory of sovereign immunity" that existed under international law, and (2) "transfer primary responsibility for deciding claims of foreign states to immunity from the State Department to the courts." *Id.* (internal quotation marks omitted); 28 U.S.C. § 1602. In Congress's view, placing the responsibility for deciding foreign sovereign immunity claims with courts "would serve the interests of justice and would protect the rights of both foreign states and litigants in the United States courts." 28 U.S.C. § 1602. And so, immunity determinations were no longer made in the Secretary's office but a courtroom.

The Supreme Court has addressed the purpose and scope of the FSIA on multiple occasions. In *Verlinden B.V.*, the Court addressed whether the FSIA exceeded the scope of Article III of the Constitution and concluded that the FSIA "contains a comprehensive set of legal standards governing claims of immunity in every civil action against a foreign state or its political subdivisions, agencies or instrumentalities." 461 U.S. at 488, 103 S.Ct. 1962. Likewise, in *Republic of Austria*, the Court considered whether the FSIA governed pre-enactment conduct and stated that the FSIA "established a comprehensive framework for resolving *any* claim of sovereign immunity." 541 U.S. at 699, 124 S.Ct. 2240 (emphasis added). Six years later, the Court addressed whether a foreign *official* comes within the FSIA's definition of "foreign state" and is, therefore, subject to the Act. *Samantar*, 560 U.S. at 313–14, 130 S.Ct. 2278. Backing away from its prior expansive pronouncements concerning the scope of the FSIA, the Court interpreted the Act's definition of "foreign state" as not including *individual foreign officials* seeking immunity. *Id.* at 315–20, 130 S.Ct. 2278. But the Court reiterated that the FSIA does govern the immunity of foreign state entities: "The FSIA was adopted ... to address a modern world where foreign state enterprises are every day participants in commercial activities, and to assure litigants that decisions regarding claims against states *and their enterprises* are made purely on legal grounds." *Id.* at 323, 130 S.Ct. 2278 (emphasis added). Considering that foreign sovereign immunity cases involving foreign officials were "few and far between" prior to the FSIA's enactment, the Court's initial expansive pronouncements concerning the scope of the Act are not surprising. *Id.*

For purposes of resolving the present case, it is worth retracing the Court's interpretative analysis in *Samantar*. The FSIA established that "'a foreign state shall be immune from the jurisdiction of the courts of the United States and of the States' except as provided in the Act." *Id.* at 313, 130 S.Ct. 2278 (quoting 28 U.S.C. § 1604). Where it applies, the FSIA takes the entire field regarding application of immunity. If a party seeking immunity is a "foreign state," as defined in the Act, the FSIA "is the sole basis for obtaining jurisdiction" over that party. *Id.* at 314, 130 S.Ct. 2278. In such a case, it is improper for courts to consider common-law principles. *Native Vill. of Kivalina*, 696 F.3d at 856 ("[W]hen federal statutes directly answer the federal question, federal common law does not provide a remedy because legislative action has displaced the common law."). While "foreign state" could be defined as including only "a body politic that governs a particular territory," Congress defined it more broadly. *Samantar*, 560 U.S. at 314, 130 S.Ct. 2278. Under the FSIA, "foreign state" includes a body politic, as well as its "political subdivisions, agencies, and instrumentalities." *Id.*; 28 U.S.C. § 1603(a). And "agency or instrumentality" is defined to include "*any entity* [that] is a separate legal person, corporate or otherwise and ... which is an organ of a foreign state or political subdivision thereof, or a majority of whose shares or other ownership interest is owned by a foreign state or political subdivision thereof." 28 U.S.C. § 1603(b) (emphasis added); *Samantar*, 560 U.S. at 316, 130 S.Ct. 2278 ("Congress had corporate formalities in mind."); *see also EIE Guam Corp. v. Long Term Credit Bank of Japan, Ltd.*, 322 F.3d 635, 640 (9th Cir. 2003) (noting that an entity can be an organ of a foreign state even if it is involved in some commercial affairs). Given these defined terms, and the absence of *any* reference to individual foreign officials,[486] the Supreme Court held that Congress did not intend for the FSIA to govern immunity of foreign officials in part because "the types of defendants listed [in the FSIA] are *all entities.*" *Samantar*, 560 U.S. at 317, 130 S.Ct. 2278.

3. Foreign Sovereign Immunity & Private Entities

Neither the Supreme Court nor this Court has answered whether an entity that does not qualify as a "foreign state" can claim foreign sovereign immunity under the common law. It is clear under existing precedent that such an entity cannot seek immunity under the FSIA. Whether such entity can sidestep the FSIA hinges on whether the Act took the entire field of foreign sovereign immunity as applied *to entities*, or whether it took the field only as applied to foreign *state* entities, as NSO suggests. The answer lies in the question. The idea that foreign sovereign immunity could apply to non-state entities is contrary to the originating and foundational premise of this immunity doctrine. Moreover, there is no indication that Congress, in codifying the restrictive theory of foreign sovereign immunity to promote uniformity and ensure that immunity decisions are based on law rather than politics, intended to exempt an entire category of entities from its "comprehensive" regime. *See* 28 U.S.C. § 1603(b); *Republic of Austria*, 541 U.S. at 699, 124 S.Ct. 2240. While the FSIA was silent about immunity for individual officials, that is not true for entities—quite the opposite. Thus, we hold that an entity is entitled to foreign sovereign immunity, if at all, only under the FSIA. If an entity does not fall within the Act's definition of "foreign state," it cannot claim foreign sovereign immunity. Period.

Before diving into the details, we go back to the beginning. Chief Justice Marshall explained that foreign sovereign immunity arises from the recognition of the "perfect equality and absolute independence of sovereigns." *Schooner Exchange*, 7 Cranch at 137. We give sovereign immunity to other nations as an act of "grace and comity," *Verlinden B.V.*, 461 U.S. at 486, 103 S.Ct. 1962, so they will do the same for us. This cooperative acknowledgement that each nation has equal autonomy and authority promotes exchange and good relationships between nations. *See Schooner Exchange*, 7 Cranch at

---

[486] Editors: Footnote 2 of the Court's opinion states:

We recognize that the FSIA literally includes "person" in the definition of "agency or instrumentality," but as the Supreme Court has explained, the phrase "separate legal person, corporate or otherwise" in § 1603(b)(1) "typically refers to the legal fiction that allows an entity to hold personhood separate from the natural persons who are its shareholders or officers." *Samantar*, 560 U.S. at 315, 130 S.Ct. 2278. "It is similarly awkward to refer to a person as an 'organ' of the foreign state .... [And] the terms Congress chose simply do not evidence the intent to include individual officials within the meaning of 'agency or instrumentality.'" *Id.* at 315–16, 130 S.Ct. 2278. *Id.*

137; *see also Siderman de Blake v. Republic of Argentina*, 965 F.2d 699, 718 (9th Cir. 1992) (quoting Chief Justice Marshall's discussion of the origins of sovereign immunity); *Butters v. Vance Int'l, Inc.*, 225 F.3d 462, 465 (4th Cir. 2000) ("[Sovereign] acts often have political, cultural, and religious components. Judicial interference with them would have serious foreign policy ramifications for the United States."). None of the purposes for recognizing foreign sovereign immunity are served by granting immunity to entities and actors that are neither sovereigns themselves nor are not acting on behalf of a sovereign. Again, the very name of the doctrine—*foreign sovereign* immunity—reflects this truth. Congress did not displace this foundational premise when it enacted the FSIA. *See Samantar*, 560 U.S. at 320 n.13, 130 S.Ct. 2278 ("Congress is understood to legislate against a background of common-law ... principles").

As noted above, Congress could have limited the FSIA's reach to only "a body politic that governs a particular territory." *Id.* at 314, 130 S.Ct. 2278. It did not. It expanded the FSIA's reach to "*any entity* [that] is a separate legal person, corporate or otherwise and ... which is an organ of a foreign state or political subdivision thereof, or a majority of whose shares or other ownership interest is owned by a foreign state of political subdivision thereof." 28 U.S.C. § 1603(b) (emphasis added). In defining what qualifies as a "foreign state," the FSIA necessarily defines the scope of foreign sovereign immunity. An entity must be a sovereign or must have a sufficient relationship to a sovereign to claim sovereign-based immunity. Without such status or relationship, there is no justification for granting sovereign immunity. It is odd indeed to think that by not including a category of entity within its definition of "foreign state," Congress intended for such entities to have the ability to seek immunity outside its "comprehensive" statutory scheme. *See Republic of Austria*, 541 U.S. at 699, 124 S.Ct. 2240.

This reasoning is supported by the *expressio unius exclusio alterius* interpretive canon. In creating a "comprehensive set of legal standards governing claims of immunity ... against a foreign state or its political subdivisions, agencies or instrumentalities," *Verlinden B.V.*, 461 U.S. at 488, 103 S.Ct. 1962, Congress defined the types of foreign entities—including, specifically, foreign corporate entities[487] —that may claim immunity. 28 U.S.C. § 1603(b). The most reasonable interpretation then is that the definition of "foreign state" forecloses immunity for any entity falling outside such definition, particularly where "foreign state" is defined broadly.[488] *See Pfizer, Inc. v. Gov't*

---

[487] Editors: Footnote 4 of the Court's opinion states: "The Supreme Court has recognized that in enacting the FSIA, "Congress was aware of settled principles of corporate law and legislated within that context." *Dole Food Co. v. Patrickson*, 538 U.S. 468, 474, 123 S.Ct. 1655, 155 L.Ed.2d 643 (2003)." *Id.*

[488] Editors: Footnote 5 of the Court's opinion states:

> The D.C. Circuit recently relied on the common law in denying foreign sovereign immunity to three United States citizens and a United States limited liability corporation. *Broidy Cap. Mgmt. LLC v. Muzin*, 12 F.4th 789, 798 (D.C. Cir. 2021). When summarizing *Samantar*, the court presumed without explanation that the common law applied to "private entities or individuals." *Id.* at 802. Unlike here, the parties in *Broidy* agreed that the FSIA did not apply; the defendants made only common-law arguments, and the defendant-entity was domestic, not foreign. *Id.* at 792; *see also NML Cap., Ltd.*, 573 U.S. at 142, 134 S.Ct. 2250. The D.C. Circuit did not

of India, 434 U.S. 308, 312–13, 98 S.Ct. 584, 54 L.Ed.2d 563 (1978) (noting that expansive statutory language matched the underlying statute's comprehensive nature); *Ingersoll-Rand Co. v. McClendon*, 498 U.S. 133, 138–39, 111 S.Ct. 478, 112 L.Ed.2d 474 (1990) (explaining that defining a term broadly underscored Congress's intent that the underlying statutory term be expansively applied). And the Supreme Court's holding in *Samantar* that individual foreign officials are not subject to the FSIA does not defeat this interpretation because, as the Court explained, the FSIA did not address, *at all*, immunity for individuals or natural persons. 560 U.S. at 319, 130 S.Ct. 2278 ("Reading the FSIA as a whole, there is nothing to suggest we should read 'foreign state' in § 1603(a) to include an official acting on behalf of the foreign state, and much to indicate that this meaning was not what Congress enacted.").

Moreover, the Act's definition of "foreign state" cannot be divorced from the context that "[t]he FSIA was adopted ... to address a modern world where foreign state enterprises are everyday participants in commercial activities." *Id.* at 323, 130 S.Ct. 2278 (emphasis added) (internal quotation marks and citation omitted). Congress prohibited applying foreign sovereign immunity to "strictly commercial acts." *Id.* at 312, 130 S.Ct. 2278. So, a plaintiff who can show that a foreign entity—even a direct sovereign like the Welsh Government—was engaged in "a regular course of commercial conduct or a particular commercial transaction or act," 28 U.S.C. § 1603(d), may defeat a claim of immunity, *see Pablo Star Ltd. v. Welsh Gov't*, 961 F.3d 555, 560 (2d Cir. 2020), *cert. denied*, —— U.S. ——, 141 S. Ct. 1069, 208 L.Ed.2d 531 (2021); 28 U.S.C. § 1605(a)(2). It makes little sense to conclude that the FSIA leaves open the possibility that a corporate entity *less* connected to a sovereign than those meeting the statutory definition of "foreign state" could seek immunity for commercial conduct under a different immunity doctrine while entities *more* connected to a sovereign—even a body politic itself—could not. Especially where the other immunity doctrine proffered, *foreign official* immunity, is as narrowly focused on natural persons as the FSIA is broadly focused on entities. *See Samantar*, 560 U.S. at 323, 130 S.Ct. 2278 (finding "no reason to believe that Congress saw as a problem, or wanted to eliminate, the State Department's role in determinations regarding individual official immunity."). Instead, the omission of entities like NSO from the FSIA's definition of foreign states and their "political subdivisions, agencies, and instrumentalities" reflects a threshold determination about the availability of foreign sovereign immunity for such entities: they never qualify.[489]

---

make an explicit finding that foreign sovereign immunity claims from foreign private entities should be analyzed under the common law, and it did not explain its summary assertion that a private *entity* can seek immunity under the common law despite the FSIA. *See Broidy*, 12 F.4th at 802. *Id.*

[489] Editors: Footnote 6 in the Opinion states:
In *Butters*, the Fourth Circuit extended the doctrine of domestic derivative sovereign immunity, applicable to United States contractors, to a United States corporation acting as an agent of a foreign state. 225 F.3d at 466. *Butters* did not discuss whether this common-law doctrine also extends to *foreign* contractors acting on behalf of foreign

4. NSO's Foreign Sovereign Immunity Claim

Concluding that the FSIA governs all foreign sovereign immunity claims brought by entities, as opposed to individuals, makes this an easy case. NSO is a private corporation that designs spyware technology used by governments for law enforcement purposes. According to NSO, its Pegasus technology is a program that was "marketed only to and used only by sovereign governments" and it allowed those governments "to intercept messages, take screenshots, or exfiltrate a device's contacts or history."[490] NSO's clients choose how and when to use Pegasus, not NSO. NSO simply licenses the technology and provides "advice and technical support" at its customers' direction.

NSO does not contend that it meets the FSIA's definition of "foreign state," and, of course, it cannot. It is not itself a sovereign. 28 U.S.C. § 1603(a). It is not "an organ ... or political subdivision" of a sovereign. *Id.* § 1603(b)(2). Nor is a foreign sovereign its majority owner. *Id.* NSO is a private corporation that provides products and services to sovereigns—several of them. NSO claims that it should enjoy the immunity extended to sovereigns because it provides technology used for law-enforcement purposes and law enforcement is an inherently sovereign function. Whatever NSO's government customers do with its technology and services does not render NSO an "agency or instrumentality of a foreign state," as Congress has defined that term. Thus, NSO is not entitled to the protection of foreign sovereign immunity. And that is the end of our task. There is no need to analyze whether NSO is entitled to immunity under the common law and inquire how the State Department would resolve this case. *See WhatsApp Inc. v. NSO Grp. Techs. Ltd.*, 472 F. Supp. 3d 649, 665 (N.D. Cal. 2020). Nor is it necessary to explain that neither the State Department nor any court has ever applied foreign official immunity to a foreign private corporation under the common law, although this is a compelling fact indeed.[491] The proper analysis begins and ends with the FSIA, the comprehensive framework Congress enacted for resolving any entity's claim of foreign sovereign immunity. *See Republic of Austria*, 541 U.S. at 699, 124 S.Ct. 2240; *Samantar*, 560 U.S. at 319, 130 S.Ct. 2278.

---

states. In any event, it is unclear what remains of such reasoning where the Supreme Court has instructed that "any sort of immunity defense made by a foreign sovereign in an American court must stand on the Act's text. Or it must fall." *Republic of Argentina v. NML Cap., Ltd.*, 573 U.S. 134, 142, 134 S.Ct. 2250, 189 L.Ed.2d 234 (2014). *Id.*

[490] Editors: Footnote 7 in the opinion states: "NSO alleges that its customers include the Kingdom of Bahrain, the United Arab Emirates, and Mexico." *Id.*

[491] Editors: Footnote 8 in the opinion states:

There is not a single documented instance of the State Department recommending conduct-based immunity for a foreign private corporation. *See, e.g.*, Digest of U.S. Practice in International Law 2020, at 403–09 (CarrieLyn D. Guymon, ed.); Digest of U.S. Practice in International Law 2019, at 344–55 (CarrieLyn D. Guymon, ed.); Digest of U.S. Practice in International Law 2018, at 410–13 (CarrieLyn D. Guymon, ed.); Digest of U.S. Practice in International Law 2017, at 444–55 (CarrieLyn D. Guymon, ed.); Digest of U.S. Practice in International Law 2016, at 450–61 (CarrieLyn D. Guymon, ed.). Nor have we found any case contemplating the same. *Id.*

AFFIRMED

NOTES

Note 1

A petition for certiorari to the U.S. Supreme Court has been filed in April of 2022 for *WhatsApp, Inc. v. NSO Group Technologies Ltd.*, 17 F.4th 930 (2021).

Note 2

The NSO Group has released a document, titled, "NSO Group Transparency and Responsibility Report."

> In addition to detailing the legal and compliance framework that NSO Group has established, the Report also identifies the most salient human rights risks associated with potential customer misuse of our products, and it outlines the concrete steps that the company has taken to mitigate and prevent future instances of misuse, including our human rights due diligence process, in which customer prospects are evaluated prior to any final sales or licensing agreements. The Report also highlights NSO's contractual terms, the company's human rights-focused training programs for employees and customers, and describes how customer engagements can be terminated in the event product misuse is confirmed by our investigative processes. To date, NSO has rejected over US $300 million in sales opportunities as a result of its human rights review processes.
>
> Additional layers of approval are provided by select government regulatory authorities. NSO Group is closely regulated by export control authorities in the countries from which we export our products: Israel, Bulgaria and Cyprus. The Defense Export Controls Agency ("DECA") of the Israeli Ministry of Defense strictly restricts the licensing of some of our products and it conducts its own analysis of potential customers from a human rights perspective.[492]

Note 3

The Washington Post and others launched the Pegasus Project, which involved in investigation into the use of the Pegasus spyware. The Washington Post noted:

> Military-grade spyware leased by the Israeli firm NSO Group to governments for tracking terrorists and criminals was used in attempted and successful hacks of 37 smartphones belonging to journalists, human

---

[492] NSO GROUP, NSO GROUP TRANSPARENCY AND RESPONSIBILITY REPORT (June 30, 2021), available at https://www.nsogroup.com/wp-content/uploads/2021/06/ReportBooklet.pdf.

rights activists, business executives and the two women closest to murdered Saudi journalist Jamal Khashoggi, according to an investigation by The Washington Post and 16 media partners led by the Paris-based journalism nonprofit Forbidden Stories.[493]

An additional issue concerns waivers of sovereign immunity. In the following case concerning a U.S. government data breach, the question arose as to whether sovereign immunity had been waived.

In re Office of Personnel Management Data Security Breach Litigation, 928 F.3d 42 (DC Cir. 2019).

Per Curiam:

In 2014, cyberattackers breached multiple U.S. Office of Personnel Management ("OPM") databases and allegedly stole the sensitive personal information—including birth dates, Social Security numbers, addresses, and even fingerprint records—of a staggering number of past, present, and prospective government workers. All told, the data breaches affected more than twenty-one million people. Unsurprisingly, given the scale of the attacks and the sensitive nature of the information stolen, news of the breaches generated not only widespread alarm, but also several lawsuits. . . . Both sets of plaintiffs alleged that OPM's cybersecurity practices were woefully inadequate, enabling the hackers to gain access to the agency's treasure trove of employee information, which in turn exposed plaintiffs to a heightened risk of identity theft and a host of other injuries. The district court dismissed both complaints for lack of Article III standing and failure to state a claim. For the reasons set forth below, we reverse in part and affirm in part.

I

As its name suggests, the U.S. Office of Personnel Management serves as the federal government's chief human resources agency. In that capacity, OPM maintains electronic personnel files that contain, among other information, copies of federal employees' birth certificates, military service records, and job applications identifying Social Security numbers and birth dates.

The agency also oversees more than two million background checks and security clearance investigations per year. To facilitate these investigations, OPM collects a tremendous amount of sensitive personal information from current and prospective federal workers, most of which it then stores electronically in a "Central Verification System." The investigation-related information stored by OPM includes birth dates, Social Security numbers, residency details, passport information, fingerprints, and other records pertaining to employees' criminal histories, psychological and emotional health, and finances. In recent years, OPM has relied on a private investigation and security firm, KeyPoint Government Solutions, Inc. ("KeyPoint"), to conduct the lion's share of

---

[493] *Takeaways from the Pegasus Project*, WASHINGTON POST (February 2, 2022).

the agency's background and security clearance investigation fieldwork. KeyPoint investigators have access to the information stored in OPM's Central Verification System and can transmit data to and from the agency's network through an electronic portal.

It turns out that authorized KeyPoint investigators have not been the only third parties to access OPM's data systems. Cyberattackers hacked into the agency's network on several occasions between November 2013 and November 2014. Undetected for months, at least two of these breaches resulted in the theft of vast quantities of personal information. According to the complaint, after breaching OPM's network "using stolen KeyPoint credentials" around May 2014, the cyberintruders extracted almost 21.5 million background investigation records from the agency's Central Verification System. They gained access to another OPM system near the end of 2014, stealing over four million federal employees' personnel files. Among the types of information compromised were current and prospective employees' Social Security numbers, birth dates, and residency details, along with approximately 5.6 million sets of fingerprints. The breaches also exposed the Social Security numbers and birth dates of the spouses and cohabitants of those who, in order to obtain a security clearance, completed a Standard Form 86. According to the complaints, since these 2014 breaches, individuals whose information was stolen have experienced incidents of financial fraud and identity theft; many others whose information has not been misused—at least, not yet—remain concerned about the ongoing risk that they, too, will become victims of financial fraud and identity theft in the future.

After announcing the breaches in the summer of 2015, OPM initially offered individuals whose information had been compromised fraud monitoring and identity theft protection services and insurance at no cost for either eighteen months or three years, depending on whether their Social Security numbers had been exposed. But OPM's offer failed to address the concerns of all such parties, and the agency soon found itself named as a defendant in breach-related lawsuits across the country. . . .

Arnold Plaintiffs allege that KeyPoint's "information security defenses did not conform to recognized industry standards" and that the company unreasonably failed to protect the security credentials that the hackers used to unlawfully access one of OPM's systems in mid-2014. Specifically, they assert that "KeyPoint knew or should have known that its information security defenses did not reasonably or effectively protect Plaintiffs' and Class members' [personal information] and the credentials used to access it on KeyPoint's and OPM's systems." As for OPM, Arnold Plaintiffs allege that the agency had long been on notice that its systems were prime targets for cyberattackers. OPM experienced data breaches related to cyberattacks in 2009 and 2012, and it is no secret that its network is regularly subject to a strikingly large number of hacking attempts. Despite this, say Arnold Plaintiffs, OPM repeatedly failed to comply with the Federal Information Security Management Act of 2002, 44 U.S.C. §§ 3541 et seq. (repealed 2014), and its replacement, the Federal Information Security Modernization

Act of 2014, 44 U.S.C. §§ 3551 et seq. (collectively, "Information Security Act"), which require agencies to "develop, implement, and maintain a security program that assesses information security risks and provides adequate security for the operations and assets of programs and software systems under agency and contractor control."

As early as 2007, Information Security Act compliance audits conducted by OPM's Office of the Inspector General regularly identified major information security deficiencies that left the agency's network vulnerable to attack. Such problems included "severely outdated" security policies and procedures, understaffed and undertrained cybersecurity personnel, and a lack of a centralized information security management structure. As a result, in every year from 2007 through 2013, the Inspector General identified "serious concerns that * * * pose an immediate risk to the security of assets or operations"—termed "material weaknesses"—in the agency's information security governance program. Although in 2014 the Inspector General, acting on the basis of "imminently planned improvements," reclassified OPM's security governance program as a "significant deficiency" (an improvement over the more serious "material weakness"), other serious issues resurfaced at that time. Specifically, in 2014, the agency failed to complete an Information Security Act-required Security Assessment and Authorization for eleven of the twenty-one OPM systems due for reauthorization. Because the agency was unable to ensure the functionality of security controls for the systems that lacked a valid authorization—one of which was "a general system that supported and provided the electronic platform for approximately two-thirds of all information systems operated by OPM"—the Inspector General advised the agency to shut them down. Despite the Inspector General's recommendation, OPM continued to operate the systems. The agency compounded existing security vulnerabilities by failing to encrypt sensitive data—including Social Security numbers—and failing to enforce multifactor authentication requirements. To make matters worse, when the 2014 data breaches occurred, the agency lacked a centralized network security operations center from which it could continuously and comprehensively monitor all system security controls and threats.

The 2014 cyberattacks were "sophisticated, malicious, and carried out to obtain sensitive information for improper use." Arnold Plaintiffs assert that as a result of these attacks, they have suffered from a variety of harms, including the improper use of their Social Security numbers, unauthorized charges to existing credit card and bank accounts, fraudulent openings of new credit card and other financial accounts, and the filing of fraudulent tax returns in their names. At least three named Arnold Plaintiffs purchased credit monitoring services after falling victim to such fraud; others have spent time and money attempting to unwind fraudulent transactions made in their names. And some Arnold Plaintiffs who have yet to experience a fraud incident purchased credit monitoring services and spent extra time monitoring their accounts to mitigate the "increased risk" of identity theft caused by the breaches.

Arnold Plaintiffs assert several claims against OPM, but they press only one on appeal: that the agency "willfully failed" to establish appropriate safeguards to ensure the security and confidentiality of their private information, in violation of Section 552a(e)(10) of the Privacy Act of 1974. [S]ee also 5 U.S.C. § 552a(e)(10) (requiring the agency to "establish appropriate administrative, technical, and physical safeguards to insure the security and confidentiality of records and to protect against any anticipated threats or hazards to their security or integrity which could result in substantial harm, embarrassment, inconvenience, or unfairness to any individual on whom information is maintained"). They also bring a variety of common-law and statutory claims against KeyPoint, alleging that the company's "actions and inactions constitute[d] negligence, negligent misrepresentation and concealment, invasion of privacy, breach of contract, and violations of the Fair Credit Reporting Act and state statutes." Arnold Plaintiffs seek damages from OPM under the Privacy Act; from KeyPoint, they request money damages and an order requiring the company to extend free lifetime identity theft and fraud protection services to all putative class members, among other things.

The other complaint, filed by the National Treasury Employees Union, seeks declaratory and injunctive relief against the Acting Director of OPM in her official capacity based on essentially the same set of facts. NTEU Plaintiffs assert that when they provided OPM with the sensitive personal information ultimately exposed in the breaches, they did so upon the agency's assurance that it "would be safeguarded" and kept confidential. They allege that OPM's "reckless failure to safeguard [NTEU Plaintiffs'] personal information," which ultimately "resulted in [its] unauthorized disclosure" during the 2014 attacks, amounted to a violation of what they describe as their "constitutional right to informational privacy[.]"

NTEU Plaintiffs further allege that, despite the fallout from the 2014 breaches, OPM has yet to make the cybersecurity improvements necessary to protect their personal information from future attacks. According to the complaint, the agency's Inspector General warned at the end of 2015 that OPM was ill-equipped to protect itself from another attack, given "the overall lack of compliance that seems to permeate the agency's IT security program." NTEU Plaintiffs' Compl. ¶ 88, J.A. 182 (quoting United States Office of Pers. Mgmt., Office of the Inspector General, Office of Audits, Final Audit Report: Federal Information Security Modernization Act Audit FY 2015, at 5 (Nov. 10, 2015)). NTEU Plaintiffs seek a declaration that OPM's failure to protect their information violated their putative constitutional right to informational privacy and an order requiring the agency to provide them with free lifetime credit monitoring and identity theft protection. They also request an injunction requiring OPM "to take immediately all necessary and appropriate steps to correct deficiencies in [its] IT security program so that NTEU members' personal information will be protected from unauthorized disclosure" in the future.

OPM and KeyPoint moved to dismiss Arnold Plaintiffs' complaint, arguing that they lacked Article III standing, that their claims were barred by sovereign immunity, and that they failed to state valid claims under the state and federal statutes and common-law theories invoked. OPM moved to dismiss NTEU Plaintiffs' complaint for lack of standing and failure to state a claim upon which relief could be granted—that is, failure to allege a cognizable constitutional violation. The district court granted both motions to dismiss on the ground that neither Arnold Plaintiffs nor NTEU Plaintiffs pled sufficient facts to demonstrate Article III standing. . . .

The district court went on to explain that it also lacked subject matter jurisdiction over Arnold Plaintiffs' claims for the additional reasons that (i) they failed to plead the actual damages necessary to bring them within the Privacy Act's waiver of sovereign immunity; and (ii) as a government contractor, KeyPoint enjoyed derivative sovereign immunity from suit. Finally, the court concluded that Arnold Plaintiffs failed to plausibly allege a Privacy Act claim and that NTEU Plaintiffs' complaint failed to state a constitutional claim. Both sets of plaintiffs have appealed.

We reverse in part and affirm in part the district court's judgment. We hold that both sets of plaintiffs have alleged facts sufficient to satisfy Article III standing requirements. Arnold Plaintiffs have stated a claim for damages under the Privacy Act, and have unlocked OPM's waiver of sovereign immunity, by alleging OPM's knowing refusal to establish appropriate information security safeguards. KeyPoint is not entitled to derivative sovereign immunity because it has not shown that its alleged security faults were directed by the government, and it is alleged to have violated the Privacy Act standards incorporated into its contract with OPM. Finally, we agree with the district court that, assuming a constitutional right to informational privacy, NTEU Plaintiffs have not alleged any violation of such a right.

. . .

III

It is "axiomatic" that a waiver of sovereign immunity is a jurisdictional "prerequisite" for Arnold Plaintiffs' claims against OPM to get out of the starting gate. United States v. Mitchell, 463 U.S. 206, 212, 103 S.Ct. 2961, 77 L.Ed.2d 580 (1983). The Privacy Act, 5 U.S.C. § 552a, provides just such a waiver of sovereign immunity. That statute "safeguards the public from unwarranted collection, maintenance, use and dissemination of personal information contained in agency records." Henke v. Department of Commerce, 83 F.3d 1453, 1456 (D.C. Cir. 1996). As part of that obligation, the Act mandates that federal agencies "protect the privacy of individuals identified in information systems maintained by [them]." Pub. L. No. 93-579, § 2(a)(5), 88 Stat. 1896, 1896 (1974). The Privacy Act waives sovereign immunity by expressly authorizing a cause of action for damages against federal agencies that violate its rules protecting the confidentiality of private information in agency records.

The district court nonetheless ruled that OPM's sovereign immunity remained intact, reasoning that Arnold Plaintiffs failed to allege the type of harms covered by the Privacy Act. Reviewing the district court's dismissal of the Privacy Act claim de novo, Skinner v. Department of Justice, 584 F.3d 1093, 1096 (D.C. Cir. 2009), we reverse. OPM's allegedly willful failure to protect Arnold Plaintiffs' sensitive personal information against the theft that occurred falls squarely within the Privacy Act's ambit.

To unlock the Privacy Act's waiver of sovereign immunity and state a cognizable claim for damages, a plaintiff must allege that (i) the agency "intentional[ly] or willful[ly]" violated the Act's requirements for protecting the confidentiality of personal records and information; and (ii) she sustained "actual damages" (iii) "as a result of" that violation. At this threshold stage of the litigation, Arnold Plaintiffs have plausibly alleged each of those elements.

A

To start, Arnold Plaintiffs have straightforwardly alleged a "willful" violation of the Privacy Act's requirements. 5 U.S.C. § 552a(g)(4). OPM was necessarily aware that the Privacy Act requires it to "establish appropriate administrative, technical, and physical safeguards" that "insure the security and confidentiality of records," and to "protect against any anticipated threats or hazards to their security or integrity which could result in substantial harm, embarrassment, inconvenience, or unfairness to any individual on whom information is maintained." 5 U.S.C. § 552a(e)(10).

The complaint alleges in no uncertain terms that OPM dropped that ball because appropriate safeguards were not in place. See, e.g., Arnold Plaintiffs' Compl. ¶ 134, J.A. 74 ("OPM's decisions not to comply with [Information Security Act] requirements for critical security safeguards enabled hackers to access and loot OPM's systems for nearly a year without being detected."); id. ¶ 178, J.A. 87 ("Despite known and persistent threats from cyberattacks, OPM allowed multiple 'material weaknesses' in its information security systems to continue unabated. As a result, Plaintiffs' and Class members' [government investigation information] under OPM's control was exposed, stolen, and misused.").

Of course, violating the Privacy Act is not by itself enough. The agency's transgression must have been "intentional or willful." 5 U.S.C. § 552a(g)(4). Under the Privacy Act, willfulness means more than "gross negligence." Maydak v. United States, 630 F.3d 166, 179 (D.C. Cir. 2010). Allegations that the agency's conduct was "disjointed" or "confused," or that errors were "inadvertent[ ]" will not suffice.

Instead, a complaint must plausibly allege that the agency's security failures were "in flagrant disregard of [their] rights under the Act," were left in place "without grounds for believing them to be lawful," or were "so patently egregious and unlawful that anyone undertaking the conduct should have known it unlawful." Maydak, 630 F.3d at 179.

Arnold Plaintiffs' complaint clears that hurdle by plausibly and with specificity alleging that OPM was willfully indifferent to the risk that acutely sensitive private information was at substantial risk of being hacked. According to the complaint, at the time of the breach, OPM had long known that its electronic record-keeping systems were prime targets for hackers. The agency suffered serious data breaches from hackers in 2009 (millions of users' personal information stolen) and 2012 (OPM access credentials stolen and posted online), and is subject to at least ten million unauthorized electronic intrusion attempts every month.

Despite that pervading threat, OPM effectively left the door to its records unlocked by repeatedly failing to take basic, known, and available steps to secure the trove of sensitive information in its hands. Information Security Act audits by OPM's Inspector General repeatedly warned OPM about material deficiencies in its information security systems. Among the identified flaws were

- severely outdated security policies and procedures;

- permitting employees to leave open, or to not terminate, remote access;

- understaffed and undertrained cybersecurity personnel;

- failure to implement or enforce multi-factor identification in any of its major information systems;

- declining to patch or install security updates for its systems promptly;

- lacking a mature vulnerability scanning program to find and track the status of security weaknesses in its systems;

- failure to maintain a centralized information security management structure that would continuously monitor security events and controls;

- lacking the ability to detect unauthorized devices connected to its network; and

- failure to engage in appropriate oversight of its contractor-operated systems.

So forewarned, OPM chose to leave those critical information security deficiencies (and more) in place. On top of that, in the year that the hacks occurred, OPM (allegedly) also left undone mandated security assessments and authorizations for half of its electronic record-keeping systems. Arnold Plaintiffs' Compl. ¶¶ 101–102, J.A. 69 (no information security assessments conducted for eleven of the twenty-one systems). The risk created by these lapses was so serious that the Inspector General took the unprecedented step of advising OPM to shut down all the systems lacking valid authorizations until adequate security measures could be put in place. OPM declined, choosing instead to continue operating these systems.

The complaint's plausible allegations that OPM decided to continue operating in the face of those repeated and forceful warnings, without implementing even the basic steps needed to minimize the risk of a significant data breach, is precisely the type of willful failure to establish appropriate safeguards that makes out a claim under the Privacy Act. See American Fed'n of Gov't Employees v. Hawley, 543 F. Supp. 2d 44, 52 (D.D.C. 2008) (Department of Homeland Security's failure to establish appropriate safeguards to prevent losing a computer hard drive was "intentional and willful" given the Inspector General's repeated warnings of "recurring, systemic, and fundamental deficiencies" in the agency's information security); In re Department of Veterans Affairs

(VA) Data Theft Litig., No. 06-0506 (JR), 2007 WL 7621261, at *4–5 (D.D.C. Nov. 16, 2007) (Department of Veterans Affairs' failure to establish appropriate safeguards to protect against theft of laptop and hard drive was "intentional and willful" in light of the Government Accountability Office's repeated warnings of "deficiencies" in the agency's "information security").

B

Arnold Plaintiffs' lawsuit is not in the clear yet. The complaint must also allege facts showing that they suffered "actual damages" as "a result of" OPM's Privacy Act violation. 5 U.S.C. § 552a(g)(4). The complaint rises to that task as well.

1

"Actual damages" within the meaning of the Privacy Act are limited to proven pecuniary or economic harm. The district court concluded that only two Arnold Plaintiffs had properly alleged that they suffered "actual damages": Jane Doe, who incurred legal fees when she retained a law firm to close fraudulent accounts opened in her name, and Charlene Oliver, whose electricity account had been fraudulently accessed and saddled with unauthorized charges.

While those harms certainly qualify as actual damages, the complaint contains still more relevant allegations of injury.

First, nine of the named Arnold Plaintiffs purchased credit protection and/or credit repair services after learning of the breach. Paul Daly, for example, purchased credit monitoring services after a fraudulent 2014 tax return was filed in his name. And Teresa J. McGarry subscribed to a monthly credit and identity protection service to prevent identity theft. Those reasonably incurred out-of-pocket expenses are the paradigmatic example of "actual damages" resulting from the violation of privacy protections.

OPM counters that those individual purchases were unnecessary because Congress provided credit monitoring services for potentially affected individuals. Congress, though, did not offer credit repair services. Anyhow, the argument wrongly assumes facts in OPM's favor at the complaint stage, such as that the services offered were equal or superior to those obtained privately, or that they took effect in a timely manner and for a sufficient period of time. Notably, at least one named plaintiff purchased credit monitoring services before OPM's offered services were "up and running."

Second, seven of the named Arnold Plaintiffs had accounts opened and purchases made in their names. For example, Kelly Flynn and her husband had several new credit card accounts fraudulently opened in their names. They also discovered that two separate loans totaling $ 6,400 had been taken out in their names without their permission and were now delinquent. Those financial losses qualify as "actual damages."

The district court deemed those damages insufficient because Arnold Plaintiffs did not further allege that their costs went unreimbursed. That was error. At this stage of the litigation, all facts and reasonable inferences must be drawn in favor of Arnold Plaintiffs, and the complaint provides no basis for disregarding the claimed financial losses based on OPM's speculation that Arnold Plaintiffs were indemnified.

. . . Lastly, one Plaintiff, Lillian Gonzalez-Colon, spent more than 100 hours to resolve the fraudulent tax return filing and to close a fraudulently opened account. Those efforts "required her to take time off work[ ]" to address the consequences of the OPM breach. Arnold Plaintiffs' Compl. ¶ 31, J.A. 50–51; see Beaven, 622 F.3d at 557–559 (concluding that plaintiffs could claim damages for "lost time" spent "dealing with the disclosure" of their Bureau of Prison personnel files).

. . . For all of those reasons, Arnold Plaintiffs have adequately alleged actual damages within the meaning of the Privacy Act.

2

The complaint also explains how Arnold Plaintiffs' actual damages were the "result of" OPM's Privacy Act violations. 5 U.S.C. § 552a(g)(4)(A).

To meet the Privacy Act's causation requirement, Arnold Plaintiffs must plausibly allege that the OPM hack was the "proximate cause" of their damages. Dickson v. Office of Pers. Mgmt., 828 F.2d 32, 37 (D.C. Cir. 1987). That is, OPM's conduct must have been a "substantial factor" in the sequence of events leading to Arnold Plaintiffs' injuries, and those injuries must have been "reasonably foreseeable or anticipated as a natural consequence" of OPM's conduct. Owens v. Republic of Sudan, 864 F.3d 751, 794 (D.C. Cir. 2017). To be the proximate cause is not necessarily to be the sole cause. OPM was the proximate cause of the harm befalling Arnold Plaintiffs so long as its conduct created a foreseeable risk of harm through the hackers' intervention.

The complaint alleges facts demonstrating proximate cause. Arnold Plaintiffs contend that OPM's failure to establish appropriate information security safeguards opened the door to the hackers, giving them ready access to a storehouse of personally identifiable and sensitive financial information. In particular, the complaint explains that OPM's failure to adopt basic protective measures "foreseeably heightened the risk of a successful intrusion into OPM's systems." And its decisions to disregard the Inspector General's repeated warnings and "not to comply with [Information Security Act] requirements for critical security safeguards enabled hackers to access and loot OPM's systems for nearly a year without being detected."

The proof is in the pudding: Numerous Arnold Plaintiffs suffered forms of identity theft accomplishable only with the type of information that OPM stored and the hackers accessed. That directly links the hack to the theft of the victims' private information, the pecuniary harms suffered, and the ongoing increased susceptibility to identity theft or financial injury. To argue, as OPM does, that the presumed occurrence of other data breaches defeats a causal connection as a matter of law at this early stage again wrongly construes inferences drawn from generic assertions about the general risk of data breaches in the government's favor. The law would embody quite a "perverse incentive" were it to hold at this threshold stage of litigation that, "so long as enough data breaches take place," agencies "will never be found liable." In re Equifax, Inc., Customer Data Security Breach Litig., 362 F. Supp. 3d 1295, 1318 (N.D. Ga. 2019); accord In re Anthem, Inc. Data Breach Litig., 162 F. Supp. 3d 953, 988 (N.D. Cal. 2016).

In any event, OPM makes no claim that these particular plaintiffs have been subjected to hacks of equivalent breadth and depth, sweeping in such acutely sensitive personal information as Social Security numbers, fingerprints, and birth certificates.

In sum, Arnold Plaintiffs have adequately alleged (i) that OPM willfully chose not to establish basic and necessary information security safeguards in violation of Section 552a(e)(10) of the Privacy Act, and (ii) that those actions proximately caused (iii) actual damages in multiple, specific ways. Because the complaint, at this threshold stage, states a viable Privacy Act claim, OPM's sovereign immunity has been waived.

IV

In addition to their Privacy Act claim against OPM, Arnold Plaintiffs assert statutory and common law claims against OPM's contractor, KeyPoint Government Solutions. Arnold Plaintiffs' Compl. ¶¶ 208–275, J.A. 94–110 (alleging negligence, negligent misrepresentation and concealment, invasion of privacy, violation of the Fair Credit Reporting Act, 15 U.S.C. § 1681, violation of "State Statutes Prohibiting Unfair and Deceptive Trade Practices," violation of "State Data Breach Acts," and breach of contract).

OPM tasked KeyPoint with performing background and security clearance investigations and inputting the sensitive information it collected into OPM's electronic recordkeeping system. The hackers allegedly were able to obtain KeyPoint credentials and then used them to gain access to OPM's network.

The district court held that, as OPM's contractor, KeyPoint enjoyed "derivative sovereign immunity" from those claims. We review the applicability of derivative sovereign immunity de novo, and find no basis for its application in this case. OPM's contract obligated KeyPoint to meet the same standards for protecting personal information that the Privacy Act imposes directly on OPM. Because the improper conduct alleged would have violated the Privacy Act if committed by OPM itself and because KeyPoint's challenged misconduct was not directed by OPM, there is no sovereign immunity for KeyPoint to derive.4

As a private company, KeyPoint ordinarily would not enjoy immunity against the statutory and tort claims asserted by Arnold Plaintiffs. But government contractors may sometimes "obtain certain immunity in connection with work which they do pursuant to their contractual undertakings with the United States."

Derivative sovereign immunity, though, is less "embracive" than the immunity a sovereign enjoys. It applies only when a contractor takes actions that are "authorized and directed by the Government of the United States," and "performed pursuant to the Act of Congress" authorizing the agency's activity. In that way, derivative sovereign immunity ensures that " 'there is no liability on the part of the contractor' who simply performed as the Government directed." Said another way, a government contractor that "violates both federal law and the government's explicit instructions" loses the shield of derivative immunity and is subject to suit by those adversely affected by the contractor's violations.

Like the plaintiff in Campbell-Ewald, Arnold Plaintiffs have plausibly alleged that KeyPoint's failure to secure its credentials ran afoul of both OPM's explicit instructions and federal law standards, rendering derivative sovereign immunity unavailable.

At the outset, KeyPoint's failure to place in the record its contract with OPM makes it particularly difficult for it to establish, on a motion to dismiss, that its alleged security lapses were "authorized and directed" by OPM.

In fact, Privacy Act regulations require OPM, when contracting "for the operation * * * of a system of records to accomplish an agency function," to "cause the requirements" of the Privacy Act to be "applied to such system." 5 U.S.C. § 552a(m)(1); see 48 C.F.R. §§ 24.102(a), 24.104, 52.224-2. KeyPoint does not deny that. So KeyPoint was obligated by contract and regulation to, among other things, establish "appropriate safeguards to insure the security and confidentiality of records." 5 U.S.C. § 552a(e)(10).

The complaint expressly asserts that KeyPoint failed to fulfill those obligations, which led to the break-in. KeyPoint allegedly violated its regulatory and contractual obligations, among other things, to (i) "secure its systems for gathering and storing" government investigation information despite "knowing of [its] vulnerabilities;" (ii) "comply with industry-standard data security practices;" (iii) "perform requisite due diligence and supervision in expanding its workforce;" (iv) "encrypt [government investigation information] at collection, at rest, and in transit;" (v) "employ adequate network segmentation and layering;" (vi) "ensure continuous system and event monitoring and recording;" and (vii) "otherwise implement security policies and practices sufficient to protect * * * [government investigation information] from unauthorized disclosure." Notably, it was KeyPoint's alleged failure to secure and protect its employees' log-in credentials that allowed the hackers to access OPM's system in May 2014, and it was from there that the hackers ultimately stole 21.5 million background investigation records.

Unsurprisingly, KeyPoint does not argue that OPM "authorized and directed" it to design its system with the security flaws that Arnold Plaintiffs identify. So KeyPoint cannot wrap itself in derivative immunity garb on the ground that it "simply performed as the Government directed." Id.

. . . In sum, derivative sovereign immunity has its limits. KeyPoint exceeded those limits, and for that reason cannot don the cloak of derivative sovereign immunity.

11.3 State Anti-Hacking Laws: Washington and California

Numerous states have enacted laws which are similar to the CFAA. The following materials include the Washington Cybercrime Act, and the California Comprehensive Computer Data Access and Fraud Act.

11.3[A] WASHINGTON STATE LAW

Washington Cybercrime Act

RCWA 9A.90.010

The legislature finds that the rapid pace of technological change and information computerization in the digital age generates a never ending sequence of anxiety inducing reports highlighting how the latest device or innovation is being used to harm consumers. The legislature finds that this generates an ongoing pattern of legislation being proposed to regulate each new technology. The legislature finds that a more systemic approach is needed to better protect consumers and address these rapidly advancing technologies. The legislature finds that the application of traditional criminal enforcement measures that apply long-standing concepts of trespass, fraud, and theft to activities in the electronic frontier has not provided the essential clarity, certainty, and predictability that regulators, entrepreneurs, and innovators need. The legislature finds that an integrated, comprehensive methodology, rather than a piecemeal approach, will provide significant economic development benefits by providing certainty to the innovation community about the actions and activities that are prohibited. Therefore, the legislature intends to create a new chapter of crimes to the criminal code to punish and deter misuse or abuse of technology, rather than the perceived threats of individual technologies. This new chapter of crimes has been developed from an existing and proven system of computer security threat modeling known as the STRIDE system.

The legislature intends to strike a balance between public safety and civil liberties in the digital world, including creating sufficient space for white hat security research and whistleblowers. The state whistleblower and public record laws prevent this act from being used to hide any deleterious actions by government officials under the guise of security. Furthermore, this act is not intended to criminalize activity solely on the basis that it violates any terms of service.

The purpose of the Washington cybercrime act is to provide prosecutors the twenty-first century tools they need to combat twenty-first century crimes.

9A.90.030. Definitions

The definitions in this section apply throughout this chapter unless the context clearly requires otherwise.

(1) "Access" means to gain entry to, instruct, communicate with, store data in, retrieve data from, or otherwise make use of any resources of electronic data, data network, or data system, including via electronic means.

(2) "Cybercrime" includes crimes of this chapter.

(3) "Data" means a digital representation of information, knowledge, facts, concepts, data software, data programs, or instructions that are being prepared or have been prepared in a formalized manner and are intended for use in a data network, data program, data services, or data system.

(4) "Data network" means any system that provides digital communications between one or more data systems or other digital input/output devices including, but not limited to, display terminals, remote systems, mobile devices, and printers.

(5) "Data program" means an ordered set of electronic data representing coded instructions or statements that when executed by a computer causes the device to process electronic data.

(6) "Data services" includes data processing, storage functions, internet services, email services, electronic message services, web site access, internet-based electronic gaming services, and other similar system, network, or internet-based services.

(7) "Data system" means an electronic device or collection of electronic devices, including support devices one or more of which contain data programs, input data, and output data, and that performs functions including, but not limited to, logic, arithmetic, data storage and retrieval, communication, and control. This term does not include calculators that are not programmable and incapable of being used in conjunction with external files.

(8) "Electronic tracking device" means an electronic device that permits a person to remotely determine or monitor the position and movement of another person, vehicle, device, or other personal possession. As used in this definition, "electronic device" includes computer code or other digital instructions that once installed on a digital device, allows a person to remotely track the position of that device.

(9) "Identifying information" means information that, alone or in combination, is linked or linkable to a trusted entity that would be reasonably expected to request or provide credentials to access a targeted data system or network. It includes, but is not limited to, recognizable names, addresses, telephone numbers, logos, HTML links, email addresses, registered domain names, reserved IP addresses, user names, social media profiles, cryptographic keys, and biometric identifiers.

(10) "Malware" means any set of data instructions that are designed, without authorization and with malicious intent, to disrupt computer operations, gather

sensitive information, or gain access to private computer systems. "Malware" does not include software that installs security updates, removes malware, or causes unintentional harm due to some deficiency. It includes, but is not limited to, a group of data instructions commonly called viruses or worms, that are self-replicating or self-propagating and are designed to infect other data programs or data, consume data resources, modify, destroy, record, or transmit data, or in some other fashion usurp the normal operation of the data, data system, or data network.

(11) "White hat security research" means accessing a data program, service, or system solely for purposes of good faith testing, investigation, identification, and/or correction of a security flaw or vulnerability, where such activity is carried out, and where the information derived from the activity is used, primarily to promote security or safety.

(12) "Without authorization" means to knowingly circumvent technological access barriers to a data system in order to obtain information without the express or implied permission of the owner, where such technological access measures are specifically designed to exclude or prevent unauthorized individuals from obtaining such information, but does not include white hat security research or circumventing a technological measure that does not effectively control access to a computer. The term "without the express or implied permission" does not include access in violation of a duty, agreement, or contractual obligation, such as an acceptable use policy or terms of service agreement, with an internet service provider, internet web site, or employer. The term "circumvent technological access barriers" may include unauthorized elevation of privileges, such as allowing a normal user to execute code as administrator, or allowing a remote person without any privileges to run code.

9A.90.040. Computer trespass in the first degree

(1) A person is guilty of computer trespass in the first degree if the person, without authorization, intentionally gains access to a computer system or electronic database of another; and

 (a) The access is made with the intent to commit another crime in violation of a state law not included in this chapter; or

 (b) The violation involves a computer or database maintained by a government agency.

(2) Computer trespass in the first degree is a class C felony.

9A.90.050. Computer trespass in the second degree

(1) A person is guilty of computer trespass in the second degree if the person, without authorization, intentionally gains access to a computer system or electronic database of another under circumstances not constituting the offense in the first degree.

(2) Computer trespass in the second degree is a gross misdemeanor.

9A.90.060. Electronic data service interference

(1) A person is guilty of electronic data service interference if the person maliciously and without authorization causes the transmission of data, data program, or other electronic command that intentionally interrupts or suspends access to or use of a data network or data service.

(2) Electronic data service interference is a class C felony.

9A.90.070. Spoofing

(1) A person is guilty of spoofing if he or she, without authorization, knowingly initiates the transmission, display, or receipt of the identifying information of another organization or person for the purpose of gaining unauthorized access to electronic data, a data system, or a data network, and with the intent to commit another crime in violation of a state law not included in this chapter.

(2) Spoofing is a gross misdemeanor.

9A.90.080. Electronic data tampering in the first degree

(1) A person is guilty of electronic data tampering in the first degree if he or she maliciously and without authorization:

(a)(i) Alters data as it transmits between two data systems over an open or unsecure network; or

(ii) Introduces any malware into any electronic data, data system, or data network; and

(b)(i) Doing so is for the purpose of devising or executing any scheme to defraud, deceive, or extort, or commit any other crime in violation of a state law not included in this chapter, or of wrongfully controlling, gaining access to, or obtaining money, property, or electronic data; or

(ii) The electronic data, data system, or data network is maintained by a governmental [government] agency.

(2) Electronic data tampering in the first degree is a class C felony.

9A.90.090. Electronic data tampering in the second degree

(1) A person is guilty of electronic data tampering in the second degree if he or she maliciously and without authorization:

(a) Alters data as it transmits between two data systems over an open or unsecure network under circumstances not constituting the offense in the first degree; or

(b) Introduces any malware into any electronic data, data system, or data network under circumstances not constituting the offense in the first degree.

(2) Electronic data tampering in the second degree is a gross misdemeanor.

9A.90.100. Electronic data theft

(1) A person is guilty of electronic data theft if he or she intentionally, without authorization, and without reasonable grounds to believe that he or she has such authorization, obtains any electronic data with the intent to:

       (a) Devise or execute any scheme to defraud, deceive, extort, or commit any other crime in violation of a state law not included in this chapter; or

       (b) Wrongfully control, gain access to, or obtain money, property, or electronic data.

(2) Electronic data theft is a class C felony.

9A.90.110. Commission of other crime

A person who, in the commission of a crime under this chapter, commits any other crime may be punished for that other crime as well as for the crime under this chapter and may be prosecuted for each crime separately.

QUESTION

       The law does not define "computer system" or "electronic database," yet the trespass law uses both of these terms. Do you find it odd that neither of these terms are defined? Does this give a potential defendant some wiggle room if the defendant attacks a router instead of a server?

NOTES

Note 1

       At the time of the publication of this casebook, there have not been any published decisions interpreting and applying Washington's cybercrime law.

Note 2

       Do you think that definition 11 concerning "without authorization" resolves the controversy under the CFAA concerning the scope of "exceeds authorization?" Should

Congress amend the CFAA to adopt a similar definition under the CFAA? Why or why not?

11.3[B] CALIFORNIA STATE LAW

11.3[B][I] CALIFORNIA PENAL CODE SECTION 502.
COMPREHENSIVE COMPUTER DATA ACCESS AND FRAUD ACT

The California Penal Code Section 502 has 14 separate subsections that somewhat mirror the CFAA, but also appear to provide broader protection for unauthorized access to computers, computer systems and computer data. Section 502(c) provides:

(c) Except as provided in subdivision (h), any person who commits any of the following acts is guilty of a public offense:

(1) Knowingly accesses and without permission alters, damages, deletes, destroys, or otherwise uses any data, computer, computer system, or computer network in order to either (A) devise or execute any scheme or artifice to defraud, deceive, or extort, or (B) wrongfully control or obtain money, property, or data.

(2) Knowingly accesses and without permission takes, copies, or makes use of any data from a computer, computer system, or computer network, or takes or copies any supporting documentation, whether existing or residing internal or external to a computer, computer system, or computer network.

(3) Knowingly and without permission uses or causes to be used computer services.

(4) Knowingly accesses and without permission adds, alters, damages, deletes, or destroys any data, computer software, or computer programs which reside or exist internal or external to a computer, computer system, or computer network.

(5) Knowingly and without permission disrupts or causes the disruption of computer services or denies or causes the denial of computer services to an authorized user of a computer, computer system, or computer network.

(6) Knowingly and without permission provides or assists in providing a means of accessing a computer, computer system, or computer network in violation of this section.

(7) Knowingly and without permission accesses or causes to be accessed any computer, computer system, or computer network.

(8) Knowingly introduces any computer contaminant into any computer, computer system, or computer network.

(9) Knowingly and without permission uses the internet domain name or profile of another individual, corporation, or entity in connection with the sending of one or more electronic mail messages or posts and thereby damages or causes damage to a computer, computer data, computer system, or computer network.

(10) Knowingly and without permission disrupts or causes the disruption of government computer services or denies or causes the denial of government computer services to an authorized user of a government computer, computer system, or computer network.

(11) Knowingly accesses and without permission adds, alters, damages, deletes, or destroys any data, computer software, or computer programs which reside or exist internal or external to a public safety infrastructure computer system computer, computer system, or computer network.

(12) Knowingly and without permission disrupts or causes the disruption of public safety infrastructure computer system computer services or denies or causes the denial of computer services to an authorized user of a public safety infrastructure computer system computer, computer system, or computer network.

(13) Knowingly and without permission provides or assists in providing a means of accessing a computer, computer system, or public safety infrastructure computer system computer, computer system, or computer network in violation of this section.

(14) Knowingly introduces any computer contaminant into any public safety infrastructure computer system computer, computer system, or computer network.

A violation of one of these provisions may result in criminal penalties. Moreover, subsection (e) creates a civil action based on a violation of one of the 14 provisions of subsection (c):

"(e)(1) In addition to any other civil remedy available, the owner or lessee of the computer, computer system, computer network, computer program, or data who suffers damage or loss by reason of a violation of any of the provisions of subdivision (c) may bring a civil action against the violator for compensatory damages and injunctive relief or other equitable relief. Compensatory damages shall include any expenditure reasonably and necessarily incurred by the owner or lessee to verify that a computer system, computer network, computer program, or data was or was not altered, damaged, or deleted by the access. For the purposes of actions authorized by this subdivision, the conduct of an unemancipated minor shall be imputed to the parent or legal guardian having control or custody of the minor, pursuant to the provisions of Section 1714.1 of the Civil Code.

(2) In any action brought pursuant to this subdivision the court may award reasonable attorney's fees."

California Penal Code section 502 includes numerous definitions and contains a provision concerning the award of punitive damages.

QUESTION

Does (7) Knowingly and without permission accesses or causes to be accessed any computer, computer system, or computer network put grey hats at risk?

11.3[B][II] CASES CONCERNING CALIFORNIA PENAL CODE SECTION 502

In *United States v. Christensen*, 828 F.3d 763 (9th Cir. 2015), the Ninth Circuit noted differences between the scope between the federal CFAA and California Penal Code section 502. The Ninth Circuit stated:

1. Computer Fraud and Unauthorized Computer Access Claims

2. Identity Theft Claims

Turner, Arneson, and Pellicano contend that their convictions for certain other offenses cannot stand once the CFAA computer fraud and unauthorized computer access convictions have been set aside. The convictions at issue are for identity theft under 18 U.S.C. § 1028 and racketeering (both the conspiracy and the substantive offense) under 18 U.S.C. § 1962(c)–(d).

Identity theft is defined as the knowing possession, use, or transfer of a means of identification with the intent to commit another crime under either federal or state law.7 18 U.S.C. § 1028. Similarly, a racketeering conviction requires the jury to find certain other criminal violations. Here, to support a conviction for identity theft, the government alleged criminal intent in the form of either computer fraud under CFAA or unauthorized computer access under the California Penal Code. Identity theft was then identified as an underlying predicate act for the RICO conviction. Defendants argue that the need to vacate their CFAA convictions requires that the identity theft and RICO convictions also be set aside.

Defendants' arguments fail. The alleged errors are subject to plain error review because timely objections were not made at trial. Defendants cannot establish that the CFAA error prejudiced them or affected their substantial rights in connection with the identity theft and racketeering convictions.

To return a guilty verdict for identity theft, the jurors were instructed that they had to find criminal intent under either the CFAA, 18 U.S.C §

1030(a)(4), or under California Penal Code § 502(c)(2). While the jury instructions relating to the CFAA were plainly erroneous, the instructions relating to the California statute were not. Although a verdict that may be based on a legally invalid ground must ordinarily be set aside, *see Griffin v. United States*, 502 U.S. 46, 58, 112 S.Ct. 466, 116 L.Ed.2d 371 (1991), reversal is not required "if it was not open to reasonable doubt that a reasonable jury would have convicted" the defendant on the valid ground. *Pelisamen*, 641 F.3d at 406 (quoting *United States v. Black*, 625 F.3d 386, 388 (7th Cir. 2010)). . . .

We do not doubt that the jury would have convicted Turner, Arneson, and Pellicano for identity theft on the valid ground of underlying intent to violate the California Penal Code. The statute provides:

(c) Except as provided in subdivision (h), any person who commits any of the following acts is guilty of a public offense ... (2) Knowingly accesses and without permission takes, copies, or makes use of any data from a computer, computer system, or computer network, or takes or copies any supporting documentation, whether existing or residing internal or external to a computer, computer system, or computer network.

Cal. Penal Code § 502.8 "Access" is defined as "to gain entry to, instruct, ... or communicate with, the logical, arithmetical, or memory function resources of a computer, computer system, or computer network." Cal. Penal Code § 502(b)(1).

Defendants argue that we should interpret the state statute consistent with the federal statute as interpreted by *Nosal*, but we disagree. The statutes are different. In contrast to the CFAA, the California statute does not require *unauthorized* access. It merely requires *knowing* access. *Compare* 18 U.S.C. § 1030(a)(2) *with* Cal. Penal Code § 502(c)(2). What makes that access unlawful is that the person "without permission takes, copies, or makes use of" data on the computer. Cal. Penal Code § 502(c)(2). A plain reading of the statute demonstrates that its focus is on unauthorized taking or use of information. In contrast, the CFAA criminalizes unauthorized *access*, not subsequent unauthorized *use*. *Nosal*, 676 F.3d at 864.

Defendants argue that the state statute's definition of "access" does not cover mere use of the computer. They cite *Chrisman*, 155 Cal.App.4th at 34–35, 65 Cal.Rptr.3d 701, in which the California Court of Appeal held that a police officer who logged in to a police database to satisfy personal curiosity did not violate the statute because § 502 "defines 'access' in terms redolent of 'hacking,' " and "[o]ne cannot reasonably describe [Chrisman's] improper computer inquiries about celebrities, friends, and others as hacking." Other California Court of Appeal decisions point to a different conclusion, however. For example, in *Gilbert v. City of Sunnyvale*, 130 Cal.App.4th 1264, 1281, 31 Cal.Rptr.3d 297 (2005), the court cited § 502(c)(2) in upholding a police officer's termination after he accessed a police database and revealed to a third party the results of the searches he ran. In another case, the court never doubted that the defendant "accessed" information when he made a copy of his employer's proprietary source code and used it to found a competing business. *People v. Hawkins*, 98 Cal.App.4th 1428, 99 Cal.App.4th 1333A, 121 Cal.Rptr.2d 627 (2002).

We conclude that the term "access" as defined in the California statute includes logging into a database with a valid password and subsequently taking, copying, or using the information in the database improperly. We base that conclusion primarily on the plain language of the statute. Otherwise, the words "without permission" would be redundant, since by definition hackers lack permission to access a database. The exception carved out in subdivision (h) provides further support for our position. If access were by definition unauthorized, there would be no need to exempt employees acting within the scope of their lawful employment. Accordingly, we find no error in the jury instructions regarding unauthorized computer access under California law.

Oracle USA v. Remini Street, 879 F.3d 848 (9th Cir. 2018), rev'd on other grounds in Remini Street v. Oracle USA, 139 S.Ct. 873 (2019).

FOGEL, District Judge:

Oracle . . . licenses its proprietary enterprise software for a substantial one-time payment. Oracle also sells its licensees maintenance contracts for the software that are renewed on an annual basis. The maintenance work includes software updates, which Oracle makes available to purchasers of the contracts through its support website.

At all relevant times, Rimini Street, Inc. ("Rimini") provided third-party support for Oracle's enterprise software, in lawful competition with Oracle's direct maintenance services. But in order to compete effectively, Rimini also needed to provide software updates to its customers. Creating these software updates inherently required copying Oracle's copyrighted software, which, unless allowed by license, would be copyright infringement. With Oracle's knowledge, Rimini in fact did copy the software to provide the updates. At least from late 2006 to early 2007, Rimini obtained software from Oracle's website with automated downloading tools in direct contravention of the terms of use of the website.

Oracle filed suit against Rimini and Rimini's CEO, Seth Ravin ("Ravin"), in the District of Nevada in 2010. . . . The jury also found against both Rimini and Ravin with respect to Oracle's claims under the California Comprehensive Data Access and Fraud Act ("CDAFA") and the Nevada Computer Crimes Law ("NCCL") (collectively, the "state computer laws"). . . . The jury awarded damages in the sum of $50,027,000 which, when prejudgment interest, attorneys' fees and costs were added, resulted in a total monetary judgment of $124,291,396.82. The district court also issued an extensive permanent injunction. Rimini subsequently filed this timely appeal. The Electronic Frontier Foundation ("EFF") has filed an amicus brief with respect to the state computer law claims.

. . . The second principal dispute is whether Rimini and Ravin violated applicable state laws intended to prevent computer-based fraud by flouting Oracle's restrictions against the use of automated tools to download software from its website. . . . We reverse the judgment with respect to Oracle's claims under the state computer laws . . ..

II. State Computer Law Claims

A. The CDAFA and the NCCL

The CDAFA is California's computer abuse law. It states, in relevant part, that:

any person who commits any of the following acts is guilty of a public offense:

....

(2) Knowingly accesses and without permission takes, copies, or makes use of any data from a computer, computer system, or computer network, or takes or copies any supporting documentation, whether existing or residing internal or external to a computer, computer system, or computer network.

(3) Knowingly and without permission uses or causes to be used computer services.

Cal. Penal Code § 502(c). It provides a cause of action to "the owner or lessee of the computer, computer system, computer network, computer program, or data who suffers damage or loss by reason of a violation." *Id.* § 502(e)(1). . . .

B. Accused Acts

The ultimate question as to whether Rimini and Ravin (referred to collectively in this section as "Rimini") violated the state computer laws by downloading content from Oracle's website was submitted to the jury, which found in favor of Oracle. In denying Rimini's renewed motion for judgment as a matter of law, the district court observed that Oracle had for some time "encouraged its customers to use automated downloading tools as a means to obtain" large numbers of customer support files in a timely manner. *Oracle USA, Inc. v. Rimini St., Inc.*, 191 F.Supp.3d 1134, 1139 (D. Nev. 2016) ("*Oracle III*"). Rimini had been doing just that when, "in response to an increased volume of mass downloads through the use of automated tools, and other server and database pressures, Oracle America changed its website's Terms of Use to specifically prohibit the use of 'any software routines commonly known as robots, spiders, scrapers, or any other automated means to access [the site] or any other Oracle accounts, systems or networks,' " a change which "prohibited the use of previously allowed automated downloading tools." *Id.* at

1139–40 (alteration in original). The evidence showed that, in response, Rimini stopped using automatic downloading tools for about a year but then "began reusing automated tools on the website in violation of the Terms of Use (terms which it had to specifically agree to when logging on to the website) in order to download full libraries of support documents and files for entire software products lines—each involving hundreds of thousands of different files." *Id.* at 1140.

C. Positions of the Parties

Rimini and EFF contend that the statutory language "without permission" should not be read in a way that criminalizes violation of a website's terms of use. As EFF puts it, "[n]either statute ... applies to bare violations of a website's terms of use— such as when a computer user has permission *and* authorization to access *and* use the computer or data at issue, but simply accesses or uses the information in a manner the website owner does not like."

Oracle, on the other hand, urges us to read the state statutes as not requiring unauthorized access for a violation, which appears to be how the district court construed them. *See id.* at 1143–44 (holding that Rimini's "claim that they had permission from their clients to access Oracle['s] ... website is irrelevant" under the state statutes).

D. Analysis

We review the denial of Rimini's motion for judgment as a matter of law de novo. *Castro v. Cty. of Los Angeles*, 833 F.3d 1060, 1066 (9th Cir. 2016) (en banc).

The district court treated the two statutes as essentially identical, and for purposes of this appeal, we will take the CDAFA as representative. As the district court observed, "[w]hile the case law on the NCCL is limited, the statute covers the same conduct as the CDAFA and the same legal reasoning should apply." *Oracle III*, 191 F.Supp.3d at 1144. The parties appear to agree with this approach; indeed, their arguments about liability do not differentiate between the two statutory schemes.

Here, there is no question that Rimini "t[ook]" and "m[ade] use of" "data."... The central issue here is whether, by using automated tools to take data in direct contravention of Oracle's terms of use, Rimini violated the statutes.

We hold that taking data using a *method* prohibited by the applicable terms of use, when the taking itself generally is permitted, does not violate the CDAFA. Because the same reasoning applies to the NCCL claim, we reverse the judgment as to both claims.

Oracle obviously disapproved of the method—automated downloading—by which Rimini took Oracle's proprietary information. But the key to the state statutes is whether Rimini was authorized in the first instance to take and use the information that it downloaded. *See United States v. Christensen*, 828 F.3d 763, 789 (9th Cir. 2015) (emphasis added) ("A plain reading of the [CDAFA] demonstrates that *its focus is on unauthorized taking or use of information*.").

Because it indisputably had such authorization, at least at the time it took the data in the first instance, Rimini did not violate the state statutes. This result is consistent with our decision in *Facebook, Inc. v. Power Ventures, Inc.*, 844 F.3d 1058, 1069 (9th Cir. 2016), *cert. denied*, —— U.S. ——, 138 S.Ct. 313, 199 L.Ed.2d 206 (2017) (affirming the district court's holding that the defendant violated the CDAFA on the ground that the defendant "*without permission* took, copied, and made use of [the downloaded] data" (emphasis added)).

11.4 Defend Trade Secrets Act and Economic Espionage Act

This section discusses the Federal Defend Trade Secrets Act and Economic Espionage Acts concerning trade secrecy.

11.4[A] DEFEND TRADE SECRETS ACT

The federal Defend Trade Secrets Act was enacted in 2016 and provides a federal civil cause of action for trade secret misappropriation. The federal Defend Trade Secrets Act was based on the Uniform Trade Secrets Act, which has been adopted in many states; however, there are some notable differences. Occasionally, trade secret causes of action may be brought based on the same set of facts as anti-hacking claims. *See* Iacovacci v. Brevet Holdings, 437 F.Supp.3d 367 (S.D. N.Y. 2020); ATS Group v. Legacy Tank and Industrial Services, 407 F.Supp.3d 1186 (W.D. O.K. 2019). Indeed, prior to the enactment of the Defend Trade Secrets Act, a CFAA claim was used to acquire federal jurisdiction over state trade secret claims in some cases. Importantly, a trade secret is generally some information subject to reasonable efforts of secrecy, derives independent economic value from not being generally known and readily ascertainable. Trade secret misappropriation generally involves acquisition or use of the trade secret through an improper mean, which may be broadly defined. Importantly, trade secret misappropriation ordinarily does not include discovering the trade secret independently or through reverse engineering. Importantly, the federal Defend Trade Secrets Act includes an *ex parte* seizure order and procedural safeguards for seized materials, particularly digital materials.

11.4[A][I] TRADE SECRET CASES

Physicians Interactive v. Lathian Systems Inc., 2003 WL 23018270 (E.D. Va. 2003).

LEE, J.

THIS MATTER is before the Court on Plaintiff Physicians Interactive's Motion for a Temporary Restraining Order and Preliminary Injunction, and Plaintiff's Motion for Limited Expedited Discovery. This is a case where the host of an interactive website for medical professionals contends that Lathian Systems, Inc.'s ("Lathian") information technology employee, Mr. Martinez, secretly hacked Physicians Interactive's website and stole their confidential customer lists and computer software code. The question presented is whether an injunction should issue where Physicians Interactive has shown probable cause to believe that Lathian's information technology employee used both a Lathian computer and his home computer to hack into Physicians Interactive's web site using computer software to secretly collect Physicians Interactive's customer lists and proprietary software. An injunction will be issued because Physicians Interactive has made a preliminary showing of an invasion of its computer system, unauthorized copying of its customer list, and theft of its trade secrets. Lathian may not use this confidential information to gain an unfair trade advantage; therefore, the Court will enjoin this activity. The Court will also enjoin Lathian, its employee Stephen Martinez, and any other agents of Lathian from any future attacks on the Physicians Interactive website. Finally, the Court will enjoin Lathian and its agents from using any of Physicians Interactive's information previously obtained by Lathian or its employee(s).

FACTUAL BACKGROUND

Physicians Interactive alleges that Defendants Lathian and Stephen Martinez hacked its website by sending "electronic robots" to steal its customer list, computer code, and confidential data. Physicians Interactive runs a website for physicians, <*www.physinteractive.com* >, featuring medical product and pharmaceutical data. *See* Mem. of P. & A. in Supp. of Pl's Mot. for a T.R.O. and Prelim. Inj. ("Pl.'s Prelim. Inj. Mem.") at 1-5. Lathian runs a similar type of service, <*www.mydrugrep.com*>. *Id.* Physicians Interactive maintains its file servers in Sterling, Virginia, which is located in the Eastern District of Virginia. *Id.* On its file server, Physicians Interactive maintains an extensive confidential electronic database of the physicians and other medical professionals who use its service. *Id.* Specifically, Physicians Interactive's database contains the names, street addresses, and e-mail addresses of all of its medical professional clients. Physicians Interactive's file server is connected to the Internet, and is accessible by others via the Internet. *Id.* The public, however, does not have access to Physicians Interactive's client lists. In order to make full use of the Physicians Interactive website, a medical professional must have a user password and personal identification number that has been issued by the Plaintiff. *Id.* The website's most valuable asset is its data lists on medical professionals. These client lists consist of the medical professional's name, title, occupation, speciality, mailing address, e-mail address, telephone number, and fax number. *Id.* at 5.

Physicians Interactive alleges that Defendants launched three "attacks" on its file servers to surreptitiously steal confidential data from its website. The attacks were carried out by Lathian's technology employee, Stephan Martinez, to obtain the proprietary medical professional information stored on Physicians Interactive's website. *Id.* at 7-11. The first alleged attack occurred on January 24, 2003. According to Plaintiff's Preliminary Injunction Memorandum, the computer that accessed Physicians Interactive's computer on that date "began to issue a series of commands to the Physicians Interactive Website Servers in which the URL and query string used by the Physicians Interactive Website Servers had been intentionally altered ... These modifications appeared as part of a calculated effort to discover-through a process of experimentation-the elements of the query string that the Physicians Interactive Website Servers use to ensure that a user logged onto the site accesses only the information on the Website intended for that Medical Professional ... Approximately 50 of these commands were issued." *Id.* at 8. Physicians Interactive did an investigatory audit of this alleged attack, and concluded that the computer which initiated this action had an Internet Provider ("IP") address of 4.18.53.195. *Id.* According to the registration records maintained by the American Registry for Internet Numbers ("ARIN"), this address is registered to <*www.mydrugrep.com* >, Lathian's website. *Id.*

The Defendants second alleged attack occurred on January 27, 2003. This attack, according to Physicians Interactive, lasted over 30 hours and "flooded [Physicians Interactive's] servers with a constant stream of commands issued at a rate of approximately 2.4 commands per second. *Id.* at 9. This alleged attack, according to Physicians Interactive, succeeded in accessing a significant number of Plaintiff's proprietary medical professional information. According to Physicians Interactive, because of the nature of the attack, the alleged hacker used a "software robot" or "extraction software" program. *Id.* The purpose of such a program, according to Plaintiff, is to "operat[e] across the Internet to perform searching, copying, and retrieving functions on the websites of others...." *Id.* The IP address involved in this alleged attack, 68.4.173.153, was registered to Cox Communications, Inc. ("Cox"), an Internet Service Provider ("ISP"). Physicians Interactive subpoenaed Cox to determine what person used this IP address at the time of the alleged attack. However, Cox no longer had the user information from this time period. *Id.*

The Defendants third alleged attack took place on September 10, 2003. The third attack, according to Physicians Interactive, was similar to the second, and succeeded in accessing an even more greater number of Physicians Interactive's proprietary medical professional information. *Id.* at 10. According to Physicians Interactive, the alleged attack originated from IP address 69.99.188 .51. This IP address was also registered to Cox. According to Cox, this IP address was assigned to Defendant Stephan Martinez of Lake Forest, California. Mr. Martinez is an information technology employee of Lathian Systems. Lake Forest, California, according to Physicians Interactive, is approximately 14 miles from Lathian's Newport Beach offices. *Id.*

After Physicians Interactive determined the place and nature of these computer hacking attacks, its information technology professionals implemented a software patch to protect its website from unauthorized access. The purpose of this software patch is to "prevent such unauthorized access from recurring." *Id.* at 12.

Physicians Interactive is suing Lathian Systems, Stephan Martinez, and John Doe(s) 1-10 for a private right of action under the federal Computer Fraud and Abuse Act, 18 U.S.C. § 1030, the Virginia Computer Crimes Act, Va.Code Ann. §§ 18.2-152.3,-153.4, the Virginia Uniform Trade Secret Act, Va.Code Ann. §§ 59.1-336 *et seq.*, and a common law trespass on chattels claim. In its Motion for Temporary Restraining Order and Preliminary Injunction, Physicians Interactive moves this Court to enjoin Defendants from (1) accessing Plaintiff's website file servers; (2) obtaining confidential proprietary and trade secret information belonging to Plaintiff; (3) using or disclosing any information that Defendants acquired by their allegedly unauthorized and illegal intrusions into Plaintiff's website file servers; and (4) destroying or altering any evidence of such acts. *See* Pl.'s Prelim. Inj. Mem. at 1. . . .

STANDARD OF REVIEW

In deciding whether to grant a motion for a preliminary injunction, this Court must apply the four part test set forth in *Blackwelder Furniture Co. v. Seilig Mfg. Co.,* 550 F.2d 189 (4th Cir.1977); *see also Manning v. Hunt,* 119 F.3d 254, 263 (4th Cir.1997); *Microstrategy Inc. v. Motorola, Inc.,* 245 F.3d 335 (4th Cir.2001). The four-part test involves a consideration of the following factors: (1) the likelihood of irreparable harm to the plaintiff if the preliminary injunction is denied; (2) the likelihood of harm to the defendant if the requested relief is granted; (3) the likelihood that the plaintiff will succeed on the merits; and (4) the public interest. *Id.* at 195-96. The Fourth Circuit has held that in a *Blackwelder* analysis, harm to both parties is the most important consideration. *See Direx Israel, Ltd. v. Breakthrough Medical Corp.,* 952 F.2d 802, 812 (4th Cir.1992); *see also Wilson v. Office of Civilian Health & Medical Program of the Uniformed Services (CHAMPUS),* 866 F.Supp. 903, 905 (E.D.Va.1994). The plaintiff bears the burden of establishing that each of the *Blackwelder* factors support granting the injunction. *See id.* In addition, if the probable irreparable harm to the plaintiff in the absence of injunctive relief greatly outweighs the likely harm to the defendant if the Court should grant injunctive relief, then "it is not enough that grave or serious questions are presented; and plaintiff need not show a likelihood of success." *Blackwelder,* 550 F.2d at 196. Conversely, "[t]he importance of probability of success increases as the probability of irreparable harm diminishes." *Blackwelder,* 550 F.2d at 195.

. . .

ANALYSIS

A) *Irreparable Harm to Plaintiff*

The Fourth Circuit has held that a plaintiff must make a clear showing of the irreparable harm it will suffer from the denial of injunctive relief. *Dan River, Inc. v. Icahn,* 701 F.2d 278, 284 (4th Cir.1983). In accordance with *Blackwelder,* Physicians Interactive has demonstrated that there is a likelihood of irreparable harm to it if this Court denies the injunction. To date, Physicians Interactive has alleged three computer attacks against its file server. The origin of the second attack is unknown. However, Physicians Interactive has provided affidavits of its information technology staff, which trace the source of the first attack to <*www.mydrugrep.com* >, Lathian's website. Further, Physicians Interactive has alleged that it has traced the third attack to an IP address registered to Mr. Martinez. Physicians Interactive has shown probable cause to establish that the three hacking attacks described above are directly linked to the

Defendants. This preliminary showing demonstrates irreparable harm to Physicians Interactive. Defendants argue that Physicians Interactive fails to show irreparable harm regarding future attacks because Physicians Interactive has, by its own admission, installed a software patch to protect Physicians interactive's computer file server. Defendants' argument has little merit. Although Physicians Interactive has indeed stated that it has installed a software patch that corrects its file server's current security vulnerabilities, such electronic security systems are not foolproof. The possibility still remains that Physicians Interactive's system could continue to be the target of Lathian's computer hackers. Such future Lathian attacks, if successful, would cost Physicians Interactive time and money through investigation and clean up.

B) *HARM TO DEFENDANTS*

The Court holds that the likelihood of irreparable harm to defendant, if the Court grants injunctive relief, is non-existent compared to the likelihood of harm to the plaintiff if the Court does not grant injunctive relief. Under the second prong of *Blackwelder,* the Court must balance the likelihood of irreparable harm to the plaintiff against the likelihood of harm to the defendant. *See Blackwelder,* 550 F.2d at 195. Physicians Interactive argues that the likelihood of irreparable harm to the Defendants is slim, because "defendants Martinez and Lathian will suffer no legally cognizable harm if they are required to stop accessing the PI Website Servers and to stop using or disclosing Physicians Interactive trade secrets and other confidential and proprietary information they have illegally obtained." *See* Pl.'s Prelim. Inj. Mem. at 28. The Court agrees with this argument. Injunctive relief is proper in this case for two reasons. First, injunctive relief is proper because any injunctive relief that this Court will grant will not prohibit the Defendants from using the authorized, public functions of Physicians Interactive's website. Second, any injunctive relief that the Court will issue will not infringe upon Lathian's right to legally compete within the marketplace for its services. Additionally, the Court recognizes some merit in Defendants' assertion that Physicians Interactive's proposed injunction request is vague. Indeed, the Court finds that Physicians Interactive's proposed injunctive request is overbroad and accordingly will issue a more narrowly tailored form of injunctive relief in a separate order.

C) *LIKELIHOOD OF SUCCESS ON THE MERITS*

The Court holds that Physicians Interactive has sufficiently shown a likelihood of success on the merits at this stage of the pleadings on all of its Counts. The third prong of *Blackwelder* requires Physicians Interactive to demonstrate to the Court that it is likely to succeed on the merits of all claims. Counts One, Two, and Three of Plaintiff's First Amended Complaint allege that Defendants violated subsections (a)(2)(C), (a)(4), and (a)(5) of the Computer Fraud and Abuse Act ("CFAA"), 18 U.S.C. § 1030. Counts Four and Five of Plaintiff's First Amended Complaint allege that Defendants violated the Virginia Computer Crimes Act ("VCCA"), Va.Code Ann. §§ 18.2-152.3, -153.4. Count Six of Plaintiff's First Amended Complaint allege a violation of the Virginia Uniform Trade Secrets Act (the "VUTSA"), Va.Code Ann. §§ 59.1-336 *et seq.* Finally, Count Seven of Plaintiff's First Amended Complaint allege a trespass on chattels under Virginia common law.

. . .

iii) *Count Six (VUTSA)*

Physicians Interactive has demonstrated a likelihood of success on the merits of its VUTSA claim because Physicians Interactive has shown unauthorized copying of customer lists and proprietary software codes. Physicians Interactive has also shown that customer lists and proprietary software taken in the previously described computer attacks are trade secrets. Physicians Interactive has also shown a likelihood that these trade secrets were misappropriated by Lathian or its agent, Mr. Martinez.

To succeed on a claim under the VUTSA, a plaintiff must demonstrate that (1) the defendant has acquired or disclosed a "trade secret" and (2) that the trade secret has been "misappropriated," meaning that the person knows or has reason to know that the information was acquired by improper means. A trade secret is information that derives economic value from its secrecy and is subject to reasonable attempts to be maintained as secret. *See Fordham v. Onesoft, Corp.,* No. 00 Civ. 1078-A, 2001 U.S. Dist. LEXIS 22918, *13 (E.D.Va.2001); *Newport News Indus. v. Dynamic Test'g, Inc.,* 130 F.Supp.2d 745, 750-51 (E.D.Va.2001).

In order to demonstrate the existence of a trade secret, a plaintiff must demonstrate that the information derives economic value from its secrecy and that it was subject to reasonable attempts to maintain it as a secret. Information that would economically benefit competitors, were it to become known to them, satisfies the standard if that information is safeguarded from disclosure in a manner that is reasonable under the circumstances. *See Dionne v. Southeast Foam Conv'g & Pack'g, Inc.,* 240 Va. 297, 302-03, 397 S.E.2d 110, 113-14 (1990). Numerous courts have held that customer lists and customer information are classic examples of trade secrets. *See, e.g., North Atl. Instr., Inc. v. Haber,* 188 F.3d 38, 44 (2d Cir.1999); *Four Seasons Hotels and Resorts B.V. v. Consorcio Barr, S.A,* 267 F.Supp.2d 1268, 1325 (S.D.Fla.2003).

Physicians Interactive's information stored on its computer file server was not meant for the public domain and, therefore, was not stored in the public area of the website. Physicians Interactive created significant electronic safeguards to protect this information. Indeed, since the alleged attacks, Physicians Interactive has taken additional steps to safeguard this information through a software patch.

Under the VUTSA, "misappropriation" is defined to include the use of "improper means" to acquire knowledge of the trade secret, and the "improper means" are defined to include "theft", "misrepresentation" and "espionage through electronic or other means." Va Code Ann. § 59.1-336; *see Fordham,* 2001 U.S. Dist. LEXIS 22918 at *13; *Newport News,* 130 F.Supp.2d at 751.

There can be no doubt that the use of a computer software robot to hack into a computer system and to take or copy proprietary information is an improper means to obtain a trade secret, and thus is misappropriation under the VUTSA. Defendants again argue that their access to Physicians Interactive's website was authorized because of Physicians Interactive's failure to place a usage restriction on its website. Again, for the reasons stated earlier, this argument fails to negate Plaintiff's likelihood to succeed on the merits. . . .

D) *Public Interest*

This Court holds that there is a strong public interest in granting preliminary injunctive relief in this action. The facts alleged by Physicians Interactive, if true, violate several federal and state criminal and civil statutes. This Court has an obligation to enjoin any alleged computer hackers from continuing to attack and steal Physicians Interactive's proprietary information.

. . .

As discussed above, Physicians Interactive meets its burden under *Blackwelder* and thus the Court will grant it preliminary injunctive relief. Physicians Interactive has shown irreparable harm. Defendants have failed to show they will suffer irreparable harm by the Court's grant of injunctive relief. Physicians Interactive has overwhelmingly shown a likelihood of success on the merits. Finally, there is a strong public interest in granting this injunctive relief.

For the foregoing reasons, Plaintiff's Motion for a Temporary Restraining Order and Preliminary Injunction is GRANTED.

. . .

The Court ORDERS Plaintiff to pay a bond in the amount of One Hundred Thousand ($100,000) Dollars, pursuant to Fed.R.Civ.P. 65(c). The Clerk is directed to forward a copy of this Order to counsel.

Iacovacci v. Brevet Holdings, 437 F.Supp.3d 367 (S.D. N.Y. 2020).

WILLIAM H. PAULEY III, Senior United States District Judge:

Plaintiff Paul Iacovacci moves to dismiss the Amended Counterclaims of Defendants Brevet Holdings, LLC ("BH"), Brevet Capital Management, LLC ("BCM"), Brevet Short Duration Partners, LLC ("BSDP"), Brevet Short Duration Holdings, LLC ("BSDH"), Douglas Monticciolo, and Mark Callahan (collectively "Defendants") pursuant to Rules 12(b)(1) and 12(b)(6) of the Federal Rules of Civil Procedure. Iacovacci avers that Defendants' counterclaims for misappropriation of trade secrets under New York law and the Defend Trade Secrets Act ("DTSA") fail as a matter of law. For the following reasons, Iacovacci's motion is denied.

BACKGROUND

I. The State Action

In October 2016, Iacovacci commenced an action in New York Supreme Court (the "State Action") asserting state law claims arising out of his termination by Brevet. In the State Action, Iacovacci alleges that after he announced his retirement, Brevet engaged in a fraudulent scheme to deprive him of payments under certain agreements and prevent him from obtaining future business opportunities in the financial industry. He also alleges that Brevet impermissibly accessed his personal home computer, external hard drives, and Yahoo! email account. Brevet then terminated Iacovacci and took possession of his interests in BSDP and BSDH. . . .

II. The Federal Action

Iacovacci filed this action on September 4, 2018, alleging violations of the Computer Fraud and Abuse Act, 18 U.S.C. § 1030(a)(2)(C), the Federal Wiretap Act, 18 U.S.C. § 2511(1)(a), and the Stored Communications Act, 18 U.S.C. § 2701. . . . Defendants assert ten counterclaims against Iacovacci: . . . (9) misappropriation of trade secrets; and (10) violation of the DTSA. . . .

DISCUSSION . . .

III. Motion to Dismiss Trade Secret Counterclaims under Rule 12(b)(6)

Iacovacci next argues that this Court should dismiss Defendants' counterclaims for misappropriation of trade secrets under the DTSA and New York law pursuant to Rule 12(b)(6). This argument lacks merit.

To state a claim for misappropriation under the DTSA, a plaintiff must allege that it possessed a trade secret that the defendant misappropriated. 18 U.S.C. § 1836(b)(1). The elements for a misappropriation claim under New York law are fundamentally the same. Since "[t]he requirements are similar," courts have found that a "[c]omplaint sufficiently plead[ing] a DTSA claim ... also states a claim for misappropriation of trade secrets under New York law." "[D]istrict courts often rely on cases discussing misappropriation under New York law to analyze DTSA claims."

A. Possession of Trade Secrets

The DTSA defines "trade secret" to include "all forms and types of financial, business, scientific, technical, economic, or engineering information, including patterns, plans, compilations, program devices, formulas, designs, prototypes, methods, techniques, processes, procedures, programs, or codes," so long as: (1) "the owner thereof has taken reasonable measures to keep such information secret"; and (2) "the information derives independent economic value ... from not being generally known to, and not being readily ascertainable through proper means by, another person who can obtain economic value from the disclosure or use of the information." 18 U.S.C. § 1839(3). Although there is "no heightened pleading requirement on actions brought under the DTSA," "district courts in this circuit routinely require that plaintiffs plead their trade secrets with sufficient specificity to inform the defendants of what they are alleged to have misappropriated."

New York courts consider the following factors in determining whether information qualifies as a trade secret:

> (1) the extent to which the information is known outside of [the] business; (2) the extent to which it is known by employees and others involved in [the] business; (3) the extent of measures taken by [the business] to guard the secrecy of the information; (4) the value of the information to [the business] and to [its] competitors; (5) the amount of effort or money expended by [the business] in developing the information; (6) the ease or difficulty with which the information could be properly acquired or duplicated by others.

Integrated Cash Mgmt. Servs., Inc. v. Digital Transactions, Inc., 920 F.2d 171, 173 (2d Cir. 1990) (citation omitted). "These factors are guideposts, not elements, and it is not necessary to plead every single factor to state a claim."

Here, Defendants allege that the purportedly misappropriated trade secrets include: (1) non-public sourcing information for over 2,000 clients; (2) business-specific non-disclosure agreements; and (3) certain specifically identified documents, such as "Brevet's Direct Lending Presentation," "Brevet's Valuation Methodology, Principles and Procedures," "Brevet's Deal Scoring Template," and "Brevet's Underwriting and Closing Guidelines." Although Iacovacci contends that the above materials are "a hodgepodge of generic categories of routine information," these types of documents and information can constitute trade secrets.

An assessment of the above six factors bolsters the conclusion that Defendants have adequately pled trade secrets. For example, Defendants claim that the allegedly misappropriated sourcing network contained "non-public information," to which not even Iacovacci had complete access, (Am. Countercls. ¶ 20 ("[A]s a Managing Director of BCM and Member of the LLCs, [Iacovacci] was entrusted with access to some, but not all, of this information.")). Defendants took steps to protect the putative trade secrets by using—among other things—a "firewall" and "log-in and password protect[ion]." Moreover, Defendants represent that they "expended considerable resources, both financial and in personnel time, developing this non-public information," which is an "extremely valuable asset[ ] of the company." These claims are sufficient to defeat a motion to dismiss. See, e.g., Medidata Sols., Inc., 2018 WL 6173349, at *4 ("The Complaint plausibly alleges that the trade secrets derive independent economic value from being kept secret. The Complaint alleges that Medidata spent a great deal of time and money, $500 million, developing its technology, [and] that Medidata went to great lengths to protect its confidential business information."); Bancorp Servs., LLC v. Am. Gen. Life Ins. Co., 2016 WL 4916969, at *11 (S.D.N.Y. Feb. 11, 2016) (plaintiff adequately pled trade secret where "it ha[d] a proprietary accounting methodology" that it "took measures to guard" and "spent five years and $10 million to develop").

B. Misappropriation

Defendants adequately allege misappropriation by Iacovacci. Defendants allege that Iacovacci stole Brevet's sourcing network information and forwarded several documents to his personal email and disseminated them. Defendants also allege that Iacovacci modified other Brevet documents, ostensibly for his own use. Additionally, Defendants claim that Iacovacci attempted to execute business transactions using Defendants' trade secrets. Again, these allegations are sufficient at this stage. . . .

CONCLUSION

For the foregoing reasons, Iacovacci's motion to dismiss is denied. . . .

QUESTION

For trade secrets tied to a computer system, should the company take physical, administrative, and technical measures to protect those trade secrets from inside threats?

The following case involves the question of whether scraping may constitute misappropriation of trade secrets under Florida's Uniform Trade Secrets Law.

Compulife Software v. Newman, 959 F.3d 1288 (11th Cir. 2020).

NEWSOM, Circuit Judge:

There's nothing easy about this case. The facts are complicated, and the governing law is tangled. At its essence, it's a case about high-tech corporate espionage. The very short story: Compulife Software, Inc., which has developed and markets a computerized mechanism for calculating, organizing, and comparing life-insurance quotes, alleges that one of its competitors lied and hacked its way into Compulife's system and stole its proprietary data. The question for us is whether the defendants crossed any legal lines—and, in particular, whether they infringed Compulife's copyright or misappropriated its trade secrets, engaged in false advertising, or violated an anti-hacking statute. . . .

In the case, Compulife alleges that the defendants hired a hacker, Natal, to "scrape" data from its server. Scraping is a technique for extracting large amounts of data from a website. The concept is simple; a hacker requests information from a server using ordinary HTTP commands similar to those that a legitimate client program of the server might employ in the ordinary course. Although a hacker could obtain the data manually by entering each command as a line of code and then recording the results, the true power of a scraping attack is realized by creating a robot—or "bot," for short—that can make many requests automatically and much more rapidly than any human could. A bot can request a huge amount of data from the target's server—technically one query at a time, but several queries per second—and then instantaneously record the returned information in an electronic database. By formulating queries in an orderly fashion and recording the resulting information, the bot can create a copy—or at least a partial copy—of a database underlying a website.

Natal used this scraping technique to create a partial copy of Compulife's Transformative Database, extracting all the insurance-quote data pertaining to two zip codes—one in New York and another in Florida. That means the bot requested and saved all premium estimates for every possible combination of demographic data within those two zip codes, totaling more than 43 million quotes. Doing so naturally required hundreds of thousands of queries and would have required thousands of man-hours if performed by humans—but it took the bot only four days. The HTML commands used in the scraping attack included variables and parameters—essentially words (or for that matter any string of characters) used to designate and store values—from Compulife's copyrighted HTML code. For example, the parameter "BirthMonth" in Compulife's code stores a number between one and twelve, corresponding to a prospective purchaser's birth month.)

Compulife alleges that the defendants then used the scraped data as the basis for generating quotes on their own websites. The defendants don't disagree, except to claim that they didn't know the source of the scraped data but, rather, innocently purchased the data from a third party. Moses Newman testified, however, that he watched Natal collect the requested data in a manner consistent with a scraping attack. David Rutstein also testified that when the defendants instructed Natal to obtain insurance-quote information, they fully intended for her to "extract[ ] data" from an existing website.

. . .

To prove a claim under the Florida Uniform Trade Secrets Act (FUTSA), Compulife "must demonstrate that (1) it possessed a trade secret and (2) the secret was misappropriated." Florida law defines a trade secret as

> information ... that: (a) [d]erives independent economic value ... from not being generally known to, and not being readily ascertainable by proper means by, other persons who can obtain economic value from its disclosure or use; and (b) [i]s the subject of efforts that are reasonable under the circumstances to maintain its secrecy.

Fla. Stat. § 688.002(4). "[W]hether something is a trade secret is a question typically 'resolved by a fact finder after full presentation of evidence from each side.'" The magistrate judge found that Compulife's Transformative Database was a trade secret, a finding that is not clearly erroneous and that, in any event, doesn't seem to be contested on appeal. We can therefore move straight to the question of misappropriation.

One party can misappropriate another's trade secret by either acquisition, disclosure, or use. Compulife alleges misappropriation both by acquisition and by use—but not by improper disclosure. A person misappropriates a trade secret by acquisition when he acquires it and "knows or has reason to know that the trade secret was acquired by improper means." Id.§ 688.002(2)(a). A person misappropriates a secret by use if he uses it "without express or implied consent" and either:

> 1. Used improper means to acquire knowledge of the trade secret; or

> 2. At the time of disclosure or use, knew or had reason to know that her or his knowledge of the trade secret was:

> a. Derived from or through a person who had utilized improper means to acquire it;

> b. Acquired under circumstances giving rise to a duty to maintain its secrecy or limit its use; or

> c. Derived from or through a person who owed a duty to the person seeking relief to maintain its secrecy or limit its use; or

> 3. Before a material change of her or his position, knew or had reason to know that it was a trade secret and that knowledge of it had been acquired by accident or mistake.

Id. § 688.002(2)(b).

The concept of "improper means"—which under FUTSA may apply in both the acquisition and use contexts—is significant here, so we should pause to unpack it. As used in FUTSA, "[i]mproper means" is defined to include "theft, bribery, misrepresentation, breach or inducement of a breach of a duty to maintain secrecy, or espionage through electronic or other means." In the law of trade secrets more generally, "theft, wiretapping, or even aerial reconnaissance" can constitute improper means, but "independent invention, accidental disclosure, or ... reverse engineering" cannot. Kewanee Oil Co. v. Bicron Corp., 416 U.S. 470, 476, 94 S.Ct. 1879, 40 L.Ed.2d 315 (1974). Actions may be "improper" for trade-secret purposes even if not independently unlawful. See E. I. duPont deNemours & Co. v. Christopher, 431 F.2d 1012, 1014 (5th Cir. 1970) (rejecting the argument "that for an appropriation of trade secrets to be wrongful there must be a trespass, other illegal conduct, or breach of a confidential relationship"). Moreover, the inadequacy of measures taken by the trade-secret owner to protect the secret cannot alone render a means of acquisition proper. So long as the precautions taken were reasonable, it doesn't matter that the defendant found a way to circumvent them. Indeed, even if the trade-secret owner took no measures to protect its secret from a certain type of reconnaissance, that method may still constitute improper means.

In one case from the former Fifth Circuit, for example, DuPont claimed that trade secrets had been misappropriated by photographers who took pictures of its methanol plant from a plane. See Christopher, 431 F.2d at 1013. These aerial photographs, DuPont contended, threatened to reveal its secret method of manufacturing methanol. See id. at 1013–14. The photographers sought summary judgment, emphasizing that "they conducted all of their activities in public airspace, violated no government aviation standard, did not breach any confidential relation, and did not engage in any fraudulent or illegal conduct." Id. at 1014. The Fifth Circuit rejected their contention and held that the aerial photography constituted improper means even though DuPont had left the its facility open to inspection from the air.   Under the broad definition adopted in Christopher, misappropriation occurs whenever a defendant acquires the secret from its owner "without his permission at a time when he is taking reasonable precautions to maintain its secrecy."

. . .

Although the magistrate judge found Compulife's Transformative Database to be a trade secret, he determined that the defendants hadn't misappropriated it. The magistrate judge's analysis, however, contains two flaws. First, in both in the 08 case and in the 42 case, he failed to consider the several alternative varieties of misappropriation contemplated by FUTSA. Second, in the 42 case, he erred in reasoning that the public availability of quotes on Compulife's Term4Sale site automatically precluded a finding that scraping those quotes constituted misappropriation.

A

The magistrate judge rejected the misappropriation-by-use claims in the 08 case because he found that Compulife had "failed to prove the existence of the duty critical to its claims of trade secret misappropriation through use.". The judge erred in considering only varieties of misappropriation by use that require a violation of some legal "duty" external to the statute. To be sure, some types of use-misappropriation do require proof of an external duty under the Florida statute, see Fla. Stat. § 688.002(2)(b)2.b., c. Just as surely, though, the same statute describes other kinds of use-misappropriation that do not depend on the existence of an external duty. When, for instance, a defendant knows that his knowledge of a trade secret was acquired using "improper means," or that he has acquired knowledge of a trade secret "by accident or mistake" and still uses it, such use is actionable misappropriation. Moreover, while not defined in the statute, the bar for what counts as "use" of a trade secret is generally low. See Penalty Kick Mgmt. v. Coca Cola Co., 318 F.3d 1284, 1292 (11th Cir. 2003) ("[A]ny exploitation of the trade secret that is likely to result in injury to the trade secret owner or enrichment to the defendant is a 'use.'" (quoting Restatement (Third) of Unfair Competition § 40 cmt. c (1995))). Even assuming that the defendants had no external "duty" not to use Compulife's trade secret, they nonetheless may have used the secret in violation of the statute.

The magistrate judge never considered these possibilities, although they are plainly contemplated in the Florida statute. And there was clearly enough evidence of these other, non-duty-based varieties of use-misappropriation that the magistrate judge should have discussed them before dismissing them. In the 08 case, the defendants plausibly engaged in "misrepresentation"—and thus "improper means" within meaning of the statute—given the way that David Rutstein explained the defendants' affiliation with McSweeney and Savage to Compulife's Jeremiah Kuhn when Rutstein initially sought access to the Transformative Database. Fla. Stat. § 688.002(1), (2)(b) 1. Alternatively, even if the email exchange between Rutstein and Kuhn didn't amount to "improper means," it could have been understood as an "accident or mistake" of which the defendants knew or had reason to know and by which they gained knowledge of the Transformative Database. Id. § (2)(b)3. In either case, the defendants' use would amount to misappropriation—without respect to the presence (or absence) of any external duty. The magistrate judge's failure to consider either possibility requires vacatur and remand. See Swint, 456 U.S. at 291, 102 S.Ct. 1781 (explaining that failure "to make a finding because of an erroneous view of the law" generally requires remand "to permit the trial court to make the missing findings").

The magistrate judge should also have considered misappropriation by use in the 42 case. The judge seems to have considered only misappropriation by acquisition as to that case—more on that momentarily—but there was no justification for truncating the analysis in this way. If the scraping attack constituted "improper means"—a question that the magistrate judge also failed to address—it would be difficult to escape the conclusion that the defendants either (1) used a trade secret of which they had improperly acquired knowledge or (2) used a trade secret of which they had acquired knowledge from a person whom they knew or had reason to know had improperly acquired the knowledge. See Fla. Stat. § 688.002(2)(b) 1., 2.a. The defendants admitted both to hiring the hacker and to observing her take actions consistent with a scraping attack. It's hard to see how the defendants didn't at least "have reason to know" that Natal had acquired knowledge of a trade secret for them by improper means—if, indeed, the scraping attack amounted to improper means. The magistrate judge's failure to consider this possibility must also be rectified on remand.

B

In addition to improperly ignoring the possibility of misappropriation by use in the 42 case, the magistrate judge erred in his treatment of misappropriation by acquisition. He reasoned—improperly, we conclude—that the Transformative Database couldn't have been misappropriated by acquisition in the 42 case because the individual quotes that Natal scraped were freely available to the public. True, the quotes' public availability is important to the first prong of trade-secret misappropriation—the initial determination whether a protectable secret exists. Public availability creates a vulnerability, which—if unreasonable—could be inconsistent with the reasonable precautions requisite to trade-secret protection. See Fla. Stat.§ 688.002(4)(b). But here the magistrate judge found that the Transformative Database was a trade secret; he gave judgment for the defendants because he believed that the public availability of the quotes precluded a finding of misappropriation. The magistrate judge reasoned that all "claims in the 42 case, alleging misappropriation of these quotes, necessarily fail" simply because the individual quotes were available to the public and thus did "not constitute trade secrets."

That is incorrect. Even granting that individual quotes themselves are not entitled to protection as trade secrets, the magistrate judge failed to consider the important possibility that so much of the Transformative Database was taken—in a bit-by-bit fashion—that a protected portion of the trade secret was acquired. The magistrate judge was correct to conclude that the scraped quotes were not individually protectable trade secrets because each is readily available to the public—but that doesn't in and of itself resolve the question whether, in effect, the database as a whole was misappropriated. Even if quotes aren't trade secrets, taking enough of them must amount to misappropriation of the underlying secret at some point. Otherwise, there would be no substance to trade-secret protections for "compilations," which the law clearly provides. See Fla. Stat. § 688.002(4) ("'Trade secret' means information, including a ... compilation.").

Nor does the fact that the defendants took the quotes from a publicly accessible site automatically mean that the taking was authorized or otherwise proper. Although Compulife has plainly given the world implicit permission to access as many quotes as is humanly possible, a robot can collect more quotes than any human practicably could. So, while manually accessing quotes from Compulife's database is unlikely ever to constitute improper means, using a bot to collect an otherwise infeasible amount of data may well be—in the same way that using aerial photography may be improper when a secret is exposed to view from above. See Christopher, 431 F.2d at 1013. In the most closely analogous case of which we are aware, a district court held that hacking a public-facing website with a bot amounted "improper means." Physicians Interactive v. Lathian Sys., Inc., No. CA 03-1193-A, 2003 WL 23018270, at *8 (E.D. Va. Dec. 5, 2003) ("There can be no doubt that the use of a computer software robot to hack into a computer system and to take or copy proprietary information is an improper means to obtain a trade secret, and thus is misappropriation under the VUTSA."). In that case, the trade-secret owner's "failure to place a usage restriction on its website" did not automatically render the hacking proper. So too, here.

Consider how broadly the magistrate judge's reasoning would sweep. Even if Compulife had implemented a technological limit on how many quotes one person could obtain, and even if the defendants had taken all the data, rather than a subset of it, each quote would still be available to the public and therefore not entitled to protection individually. On the magistrate judge's logic, Compulife couldn't recover even in that circumstance, because even there—in the magistrate judge's words—"any member of the public [could] visit the website of a Compulife customer to obtain a quote" with "no restriction" on the subsequent use of the quote. But under the plain terms of the governing statute, the defendants would be liable in this scenario; they would have acquired a compilation of information that "[d]erives independent economic value ... from ... not being readily ascertainable" and "[i]s the subject of efforts that are reasonable under the circumstances to maintain its secrecy" by means which plainly amount to "espionage through electronic ... means." Fla. Stat.§ 688.002(1), (4).

The magistrate judge treated the wrong question as decisive—namely, whether the quotes taken were individually protectable. He left undecided the truly determinative questions: (1) whether the block of data that the defendants took was large enough to constitute appropriation of the Transformative Database itself, and (2) whether the means they employed were improper. Having found that the Transformative Database was protectable generally, the magistrate judge was not free simply to observe that the portions taken were not individually protectable trade secrets.

We express no opinion as to whether enough of the Transformative Database was taken to amount to an acquisition of the trade secret, nor do we opine as to whether the means were improper such that the acquisition or use of the quotes could amount to misappropriation. We merely clarify that the simple fact that the quotes taken were publicly available does not automatically resolve the question in the defendants' favor. These issues must be addressed on remand. . . .

NOTES

Note 1

In *Out of Thin Air: Trade Secrets, Cybersecurity and the Wrongful Acquisition Tort*, Professor Sharon Sandeen explains limitations of trade secret law and how a wrongful acquisition tort may not remedy those limits. See Sharon K. Sandeen, *Out of Thin Air: Trade Secrets, Cybersecurity and the Wrongful Acquisition Tort*, 19 Minn. J.L. Sci. & Tech. 373 (2018) (discussing concerns with conflict with policies underlying patent, trade secret and copyright law, including concerns with competition and innovation in recognizing a wrongful acquisition tort).

Note 2

In an unpublished opinion, the Court of Chancery of Delaware determined that a plaintiff failed to demonstrate reasonable efforts to keep information secret disclosed in a Zoom call by not utilizing some Zoom features to control access to the call and making the call-in information widely available. The Court stated:

> Assuming for the sake of analysis that Smash had protectable trade secrets, Smash did not take reasonable steps to protect their secrecy. Smash freely gave out the Zoom information for the Franchisee Forum Calls and the Founder Calls to anyone who had expressed interest in a franchise and completed the introductory call. Smash used the same Zoom meeting code for all of its meetings. Smash did not require that participants . . . enter a password and did not use the waiting room

feature to screen participants. Anyone who had expressed interest and received the code could join the calls, and participants could readily share the code with others.

Smash Franchise Partners v. Kanda Holdings, Inc., 2020 WL 4692287 *15 (Ct. Chan. Del. 2020).

11.4[B] Economic Espionage Act

11.4[B][1] Selected Provisions of the Economic Espionage Act

§ 1831. Economic espionage

(a) In general.--Whoever, intending or knowing that the offense will benefit any foreign government, foreign instrumentality, or foreign agent, knowingly--

1) steals, or without authorization appropriates, takes, carries away, or conceals, or by fraud, artifice, or deception obtains a trade secret;

(2) without authorization copies, duplicates, sketches, draws, photographs, downloads, uploads, alters, destroys, photocopies, replicates, transmits, delivers, sends, mails, communicates, or conveys a trade secret;

(3) receives, buys, or possesses a trade secret, knowing the same to have been stolen or appropriated, obtained, or converted without authorization;

(4) attempts to commit any offense described in any of paragraphs (1) through (3); or

(5) conspires with one or more other persons to commit any offense described in any of paragraphs (1) through (3), and one or more of such persons do any act to effect the object of the conspiracy,

shall, except as provided in subsection (b), be fined not more than $5,000,000 or imprisoned not more than 15 years, or both.

(b) Organizations.--Any organization that commits any offense described in subsection (a) shall be fined not more than the greater of $10,000,000 or 3 times the value of the stolen trade secret to the organization, including expenses for research and design and other costs of reproducing the trade secret that the organization has thereby avoided.

§ 1832. Theft of trade secrets

(a) Whoever, with intent to convert a trade secret, that is related to a product or service used in or intended for use in interstate or foreign commerce, to the economic benefit of anyone other than the owner thereof, and intending or knowing that the offense will, injure any owner of that trade secret, knowingly--

(1) steals, or without authorization appropriates, takes, carries away, or conceals, or by fraud, artifice, or deception obtains such information;

(2) without authorization copies, duplicates, sketches, draws, photographs, downloads, uploads, alters, destroys, photocopies, replicates, transmits, delivers, sends, mails, communicates, or conveys such information;

(3) receives, buys, or possesses such information, knowing the same to have been stolen or appropriated, obtained, or converted without authorization;

(4) attempts to commit any offense described in paragraphs (1) through (3); or

(5) conspires with one or more other persons to commit any offense described in paragraphs (1) through (3), and one or more of such persons do any act to effect the object of the conspiracy, shall, except as provided in subsection (b), be fined under this title or imprisoned not more than 10 years, or both.

(b) Any organization that commits any offense described in subsection (a) shall be fined not more than the greater of $5,000,000 or 3 times the value of the stolen trade secret to the organization, including expenses for research and design and other costs of reproducing the trade secret that the organization has thereby avoided.

11.4[B][II] ECONOMIC ESPIONAGE CASE

U.S. v. Hanjuan Jin, 833 F.Supp.2d 977 (N.D. Ill. 2012).

RUBEN CASTILLO, District Judge.

On December 9, 2008, a Grand Jury returned a superseding indictment charging Hanjuan Jin ("Defendant" or "Jin") with three counts of theft of trade secrets and three counts of economic espionage in violation of the Economic Espionage Act, 18 U.S.C. § 1831 et seq. ("EEA"). (R. 37, Superseding Indictment.). . . . The Court, having reviewed all of the evidence, its trial notes, the testimony of the witnesses to determine the credibility of each witness, and the parties' post-trial submissions, hereby concludes that Jin criminally betrayed Motorola by stealing its trade secrets. The Court also concludes that there was not enough evidence to find that Jin criminally betrayed the United States by committing economic espionage for the Peoples' Republic of China ("PRC"). . ..

BACKGROUND

A criminal complaint was filed against Jin on March 3, 2008. On April 1, 2008, Jin was indicted by the Grand Jury. On December 9, 2008, the Grand Jury returned a superseding indictment (the "indictment").

The indictment alleged that Jin began working as a software engineer for Motorola, a telecommunications company based in Chicago, in 1998. In February 2006, Jin took a one-year medical leave of absence from Motorola. According to the indictment, during this time, Jin negotiated and ultimately accepted employment with Sun Kaisens, a telecommunications company in China that develops telecommunications technology and products for the Chinese military. The indictment further alleged that after accepting employment with Sun Kaisens, Jin briefly returned to work at Motorola at the end of February 2007, downloaded numerous Motorola proprietary technical documents, and was in possession of those documents as she attempted to board a flight to China on February 28, 2007.

According to the indictment, three of the documents in Jin's possession, Moto 1, Moto 2, and Moto 3, were trade secrets. Counts One through Three—one count for each document—charged Jin with possession of trade secrets with intent to convert them to the economic benefit of someone other than the owner, intending or knowing that the offense would injure the owner, in violation of 18 U.S.C. § 1832(a)(3) ("Section 1832(a)(3)"). (Id. at 1–6.) Counts Four through Six—again, one count for each document—charged Jin with possession of trade secrets, knowing the trade secrets were obtained and converted without authorization, intending or knowing that the offense would benefit a foreign Government, in violation of 18 U.S.C. § 1831(a)(3) In sum, the indictment alleged that Jin stole trade secrets pertaining to telecommunications technology from Motorola, and intended to convert those trade secrets to the benefit of herself, Sun Kaisens, and the PRC.

. . .

CONCLUSIONS OF LAW

1. The EEA criminalizes two principal categories of trade secret misappropriation, "economic espionage" as defined by 18 U.S.C. § 1831, and "theft of trade secrets" as defined by 18 U.S.C. § 1832. Jin has been charged with three counts under each section.

2. Section 1832(a)(3), the theft of trade secrets provision, provides:

> (a) Whoever, with intent to convert a trade secret, that is related to or included in a product that is produced for or placed in interstate or foreign commerce, to the economic benefit of anyone other than the owner thereof, and intending or knowing that the offense will, injure any owner of that trade secret, knowingly ... (3) receives, buys, or possesses such information, knowing the same to have been stolen or appropriated, obtained, or converted without authorization ... shall ... be fined under this title or imprisoned not more than 10 years, or both.

18 U.S.C. § 1832(a)(3). In order to prove a violation of the theft of trade secrets provision of the EEA in this case, the Government must prove beyond a reasonable doubt that: (1) the information at issue—Moto 1, Moto 2, and Moto 3—were trade secrets; (2) Jin knowingly possessed the trade secrets; (3) Jin knew the trade secret information was stolen or appropriated, obtained, or converted without authorization; (4) Jin intended to convert the trade secrets to the economic benefit of anyone other than Motorola; (5) Jin

intended or knew that the offense would injure Motorola; and (6) the trade secrets were related to a product placed in interstate or foreign commerce.

3. Section 1831(a)(3), the economic espionage provision, provides:

> (a) Whoever, intending or knowing that the offense will benefit any foreign Government, foreign instrumentality, or foreign agent, knowingly ... (3) receives, buys, or possesses a trade secret, knowing the same to have been stolen or appropriated, obtained, or converted without authorization ... shall ... be fined not more than $500,000 or imprisoned not more than 15 years, or both.

18 U.S.C. § 1831(a)(3). In order to establish a violation of Section 1831(a)(3) in this case, the Government must prove beyond a reasonable doubt that: (1) the information at issue—Moto 1, Moto 2, and Moto 3—were trade secrets; (2) Jin knowingly possessed the trade secrets; (3) Jin knew the trade secrets were "stolen or appropriated, obtained, or converted without authorization"; and (4) Jin intended or knew that the offense would benefit "any foreign Government, foreign instrumentality, or foreign agent[.]" Id.

The Court will first analyze whether the Government met its burden in proving the first three elements common to Sections 1831(a)(3) and 1832(a)(3), and will then turn to the remaining elements under each section.

Elements Common to Sections 1831(a)(3) and 1832(a)(3)

Whether Moto 1, Moto 2, and Moto 3 were trade secrets

A threshold question under both sections of the EEA is whether each charged document qualifies as a trade secret. As an initial matter, instead of merely "point[ing] to broad areas of technology and assert[ing] that something there must have been secret[,]"the Government highlighted specific information in each document related to the technology at issue that qualifies as trade secrets. In Moto 1, the Government pointed to information contained in Table 2 on page 29 of the document relating to hDACs, hardware with iDEN-specific software, and the process by which audio is conveyed over the iDEN internet protocol through the interconnection of hDACs. Regarding Moto 2, the Government focused on the information about the iDEN base radio channel control structure found in Figure 3 of the document. In Moto 3, the Government pointed to the information that illustrates the decoding of messages used within the iDEN protocol found in Table 119 of the document. Consequently, the Court's analysis will focus on these specific areas of information in determining whether Moto 1, Moto 2, and Moto 3 qualify as trade secrets.

The EEA defines a trade secret as:

> [A]ll forms and types of financial, business, scientific, technical, economic, or engineering information ... whether tangible or intangible, and whether or how stored, compiled, or memorialized physically, electronically, graphically, photographically, or in writing if—(A) the

owner thereof has taken reasonable measures to keep such information secret; and (B) the information derives independent economic value, actual or potential, from not being generally known to, and not being readily ascertainable through proper means by, the public[.]

18 U.S.C. § 1839(3). Thus, the Government must have proven the following elements as to each of the three documents at issue in this case: "(1) that the information [in the charged documents] [was] actually secret because it [was] neither known to, nor readily ascertainable by, the public; (2) that [Motorola] took reasonable measures to maintain that secrecy; and (3) that independent economic value derived from that secrecy." See United States v. Chung, 659 F.3d 815, 824–25 (9th Cir.2011). Whether information qualifies as a trade secret is a fact-specific inquiry that "requires an ad hoc evaluation of all the surrounding circumstances."

Not known or readily ascertainable

Regarding the first element of a trade secret, whether the information is "not known to" or "readily ascertainable through proper means by the public," the Seventh Circuit has noted that there is some dispute as to whom "the public" includes. While the Third Circuit assumed that "general" belongs in front of "public" in United States v. Hsu, 155 F.3d 189, 196 (3d Cir.1998), the Seventh Circuit has suggested that "public" could just as plausibly be implicitly preceded by "educated" or "economically important." Lange, 312 F.3d at 266–67 (noting that "the public" could be shorthand for the longer phrase found in the UTSA of all "persons who can obtain economic value from its disclosure or use"). In Lange, the Seventh Circuit also observed that the phrase "readily ascertainable" can be "understood to concentrate attention on either potential users of the information, or proxies for them (which is to say, persons who have the same ability to 'ascertain' the information)." Ultimately, the Seventh Circuit declined to decide whether "general" precedes "public" because even if it did, the information at issue in the case before it was not " 'readily ascertainable' to the general public, the educated public, the economically relevant public, or any sensible proxy for these groups."

The Court concludes that the Government proved beyond a reasonable doubt that the information in the charged documents was "not known" or "readily ascertainable" to the public, whether defined as the general public or the economically relevant public. Regarding Moto 1, although some of the information in the document has been disclosed to customers, certain technical information has not been shared outside of Motorola. In particular, the technical information relating to the formatting of the voice as it traverses that internet protocol and the interconnection of hDACs has not been disclosed outside of Motorola. Thus, even though certain information in Moto 1 has been disclosed, Moto 1 still contains information—specifically the information about the hDACs on page 29 of the document—that was secret.

Similarly, with Moto 2, certain technical information found in the document has been disclosed to customers and RadioFrame. Importantly, though, the information in

Figure 3 about the iDEN broadcast control channel structure has only been shared pursuant to a nondisclosure agreement, which does not forfeit trade secret protection. Rockwell Graphic Sys., 925 F.2d at 178. As for Moto 3, the information in Table 119 that decodes the messages used in the iDEN protocol has never been shared outside of Motorola. Accordingly, the relevant sections in Moto 1, Moto 2, and Moto 3 meet the first element of a trade secret.

Reasonable measures to maintain secrecy

Under the second element of a trade secret, whether the precautionary steps taken by the owner of the purported trade secret were reasonable, the Court must balance "the costs and benefits" of a given precautionary measure, which will "vary from case to case." Rockwell Graphic Sys. v. DEV Indust., 925 F.2d 174, 179 (7th Cir.1991). On the one hand, failure to take steps to protect a secret "is persuasive evidence that the secret has no real value" and is undeserving of the law's protection. Additionally, "[i]f the owner fails to attempt to safeguard his or her proprietary information, no one can be rightfully accused of misappropriating it." H.R.Rep. No. 104–788, at 7 (1996), 1996 U.S.C.C.A.N. 4021, 4026. On the other hand, taking precautionary measures to protect secrets imposes both direct and indirect costs on the owner of the secret, and thus "perfect security is not optimum security." Rockwell Graphic Sys., 925 F.2d at 180 (noting that "[i]f trade secrets are protected only if their owners take extravagant, productivity-impairing measures to maintain their secrecy, the incentive to invest resources in discovering more efficient methods of production will be reduced, and with it the amount of invention"). Thus, while a trade secret owner need not take "every conceivable step to protect the property from misappropriation," H.R.Rep. No. 104–788, at 7, the owner must employ precautionary measures that are reasonable under the circumstances.

The government proved beyond a reasonable doubt that Motorola took reasonable measures to protect the secrecy of the purported trade secrets. As outlined above, the Court was presented with extensive evidence regarding Motorola's physical security. The evidence showed that Motorola carefully controlled access to the Motorola campus as well as each building on the campus. Security cameras and alarms abounded on the campus, and there was a small force of 40 security employees to monitor the cameras and patrol the campus.

The Court was also presented with detailed evidence regarding Motorola's network and computer security. Motorola employed typical measures such as passwords and firewalls to prevent hackers and other outside threats from infiltrating the Motorola network. Motorola also had measures in place to protect confidential and proprietary information internally, including restricting access within the Motorola network depending on the user's authorization and the classification status of a document or file. Users of the Motorola network were reminded every time they logged onto the Motorola network that their use of the network was subject to monitoring, and that it could only be used for authorized purposes.

Motorola also employed a specific program, POPI, to protect its proprietary information. This program entailed detailed policies regarding the classification of proprietary documents, access to the documents, and the physical handling of the documents. Under these policies, documents containing confidential and proprietary information were marked as such, including the documents at issue here. The POPI program also provided for the training of new hires and current employees, as well as audits to promote compliance with the program's policies.

Motorola's final level of security consisted of agreements with Motorola employees. Motorola employees signed an employment agreement, a code of conduct understanding that contained a confidentiality provision, and a policy on the appropriate use of computer resources. Upon hiring, employees were also informed of the Motorola policy regarding the protection of proprietary information, including classification levels and their concomitant handling requirements. Employees were reminded of their obligation to maintain the secrecy of Motorola's proprietary information through regular trainings and POPI audits.

The Court concludes that this multi-pronged approach to security—controlled and monitored physical access to Motorola facilities, limited access to the Motorola computer network and Motorola network equipment, a specific policy for the protection of proprietary information, and confidentiality agreements and trainings for Motorola employees—was a reasonable way to maintain the secrecy of the information in Moto 1, Moto 2, and Moto 3. In reaching this conclusion, the Court notes that this case highlighted some gaps in Motorola's security program, as well as the ineffectiveness of some of the measures it did employ. The evidence also indicated that there were measures Motorola could have utilized to improve its security, including the monitoring of Compass and MVP for abnormal use, the regular review of employees' access authorizations, the disabling of USB ports, and the search of all bags leaving Motorola's facilities. These additional protections, however, would have come at an additional cost, and that there were other precautions Motorola could have taken does not mean that the measures it did take were not reasonable. See Rockwell Graphic Sys., 925 F.2d at 180. The Court accordingly concludes that the Government proved beyond a reasonable doubt that the charged documents satisfy the second element of a trade secret.

Independent economic value

When evaluating the last required element of a trade secret under the EEA, courts have considered many factors in determining whether the information at issue derives independent economic value from its secrecy. Courts often consider "the degree to which the secret information confers a competitive advantage on its owner." Other courts have considered the cost and effort necessary to develop the secret information. In some cases, the value of the trade secret is evident in the circumstances of the offense, such as a defendant's acknowledgment that the secret is valuable or the asking price set by a defendant for the trade secret. As with the other elements of a trade secret under the EEA, this is a fact-intensive analysis for which there are no bright-line rules.

The Court concludes that the information in the charged documents derived economic value from its secrecy. Although the evidence before the Court indicates that the use of iDEN technology is overall on the decline, its customer base and coverage areas are still growing in certain regions of the world. When a new customer is added on the iDEN network, that customer must purchase iDEN-specific hardware from Motorola, including base stations and switching equipment. When an existing iDEN customer expands its coverage area, it must, at a minimum, purchase more base stations. This is relevant here because the information in Moto 1, Moto 2, and Moto 3 that the Court identified as secret above would be necessary for a competitor to build competing versions of these iDEN products that are sold globally. Additionally, the secret information identified above could be used to intercept messages or audio over the iDEN network. Thus, it is clear to the Court that this information derived value from its secrecy.

The Court has carefully evaluated each document separately and independently and certainly acknowledges that the overall economic value of each document is markedly different in the world marketplace. In particular, the overall market value of Moto 2 is rather weak because it largely details a failed project. Yet even Moto 2 describes enough useful information to have some independent economic value.

Jin argues that the Government also needed to prove that the information in the charged documents was not within her own personal knowledge, skill, or ability because the EEA does not apply "to individuals who seek to capitalize on the personal knowledge, skill, or abilities they may have developed" in moving from one job to another. H.R.Rep. No. 104–788, at 7. The Court agrees that the EEA allows employees to economically benefit from the general skills and knowledge that they acquired while working for a former employer. What is not permitted, however, is for employees to take confidential information about "products or processes" from their former employers to use for their own, or a third party's, economic benefit. See id.; United States v. Martin, 228 F.3d 1, 11 (1st Cir.2000) ("§ 1832(a) was not designed to punish competition, even when such competition relies on the know-how of former employees of a direct competitor. It was, however, designed to prevent those employees (and their future employers) from taking advantage of confidential information gained, discovered, copied, or taken while employed elsewhere.") Jin was accused of taking very specific technical data unique to iDEN, not broad information about telecommunications generally or skills she acquired while at Motorola. The technical data in the charged documents cannot be classified as personal or generic knowledge; it is clearly the type of "confidential information" the EEA prohibits employees from taking from their former employers.

Jin lastly argues that the charged trade secret documents do not qualify as trade secrets because they are labeled as "Motorola Confidential and Proprietary" instead of "Motorola Registered Secret Proprietary," and under Motorola's proprietary information classification system, a trade secret falls in the latter category. This argument fails because the statutory definition of a trade secret in the EEA—not Motorola's classification of the documents—governs the determination of whether the documents qualify as trade secrets. Of course, the definitions of the classification categories and the label ultimately given a document are evidence that is relevant to the elements of a trade secret. Motorola, however, defined "Motorola Confidential and Proprietary" information as that which an unauthorized disclosure of would cause "substantial detrimental effect" to Motorola. And, as discussed above, Motorola took many steps to protect "Motorola Confidential and Proprietary" information. That the documents at issue here are labeled as "Motorola Confidential and Proprietary" is thus not inconsistent with them being trade secrets under the statutory definition. Accordingly, because Moto 1, Moto 2, and Moto 3 each contain some information that was not known to the public and derived value from its secrecy, and Motorola took reasonable precautions to maintain the secrecy of the information, the Court concludes that the charged documents are in fact trade secrets under the EEA.

Knowledge of the trade secrets

In addition to proving that the charged information qualifies as a trade secret, the Government must have proven that Jin had the requisite mens rea in order to establish a violation of Sections 1831(a)(3) and 1832(a)(3). Although the sections vary slightly in their mens rea requirements, one element the parties agree is required under both sections is that Jin had knowledge of what she possessed. What specifically Jin needs to have known about the information in her possession, however, is disputed. Jin argues that both sections require the Government to prove that she knew that the documents in her possession contained trade secrets. She does not argue that the Government needed to prove that she knew her actions were illegal under the EEA, but rather that she knew "that what she took was in fact a trade secret, as a factual matter." The Government, on the other hand, contends that it only needed to prove that Jin knew the information was proprietary in order to satisfy this knowledge requirement.

As an initial matter, the Court notes that this dispute arises from the lack of clarity in the case law interpreting the EEA's mens rea requirements. Many courts, as well as the parties here, treat the knowledge requirements in Sections 1831(a)(3) and 1832(a)(3) as one and the same despite differences in the statutory text. The Court will accordingly analyze the sections separately.

Statutory interpretation begins with the plain language of the statute. United States v. LaFaive, 618 F.3d 613, 616 (7th Cir.2010) (citation omitted). The Court may refer to "'the language itself, the specific context in which that language is used, and the broader context of the statute as a whole.'" The Court will consider the legislative history of a statute only "when necessary to decode an ambiguous enactment; it is not a sine qua non for enforcing a straightforward text.". If the statute remains ambiguous after this analysis, the rule of lenity requires the statute to be interpreted in favor of the defendant.

The element of Section 1831(a)(3) at issue here requires that the defendant "knowingly ... receives, buys, or possesses a trade secret, knowing the same to have been stolen, appropriated, obtained or converted without authorization." 18 U.S.C. § 1831(a)(3). The question here is whether "knowingly" modifies "trade secret," or only "receives, buys, or possesses." The Supreme Court was faced with an analogous question regarding a similarly structured statute in Flores–Figueroa v. United States, 556 U.S. 646, 129 S.Ct. 1886, 173 L.Ed.2d 853 (2009). In Flores–Figueroa, the Supreme Court interpreted a federal criminal statute forbidding "[a]ggravated identity theft" that imposes a mandatory consecutive two-year prison term upon individuals convicted of certain crimes "if, during (or in relation to) the commission of those other crimes, the offender 'knowingly transfers, possesses, or uses, without lawful authority, a means of identification of another person.' The Supreme Court concluded that under a plain reading of the statute, "knowingly" modifies not only the transitive verbs of "transfers, possesses, or uses," but also the object of those verbs—"a means of identification of another person." Because courts ordinarily interpret criminal statutes in a manner that is "fully consistent with this ordinary English usage," a phrase that introduces the elements of a crime with the word "knowingly" applies that word to each element in most criminal statutes. Accordingly, the Supreme Court held that the statute required the Government to show that the defendant knew that the means of identification at issue belonged to another person.

The Court concludes that "knowingly" in Section 1831(a)(3) modifies "trade secret," and that Section 1831(a)(3) therefore requires the Government to prove that a defendant knew, as a factual matter, that the information she possessed had the general attributes of a trade secret. The district court in the Central District of California reached the same conclusion in United States v. Chung, 633 F.Supp.2d 1134 (C.D.Cal.2009). Noting that the Supreme Court "has long recognized a presumption in favor of an intent requirement for 'the crucial element' that separates lawful from unlawful conduct," the district court concluded that it "would be unjust and inconsistent with the purpose of the criminal law to hold [the defendant] accountable for possession of what he honestly believed was publicly available information." Id. at 1144–45. The district court thus held that under Section 1831(a)(3), "the Government must prove that [the defendant] knew that the information he possessed was trade secret information."

The Court is not convinced, as the Government argues, that Chung is "an outlier" and that other cases on this issue contradict its holding that knowledge of the trade secret is a required element under Section 1831(a)(3). (R. 203, Govt. Resp. at 6.) The Government is correct in noting that many courts discussing the knowledge requirement under the EEA state that the defendant must have knowledge of the proprietary nature of the information. The Government fails to acknowledge, however, that these cases deal with Section 1832(a)(3) and that the defendants were arguing that the Government needed to prove that the defendants had knowledge of the illegality of their conduct. Here, Jin does not argue and the Court does not conclude that the Government is required to prove that Jin knew that her conduct was illegal or that the information she possessed met the statutory definition of a trade secret. . . .

Although the Court agrees with Jin that Section 1831(a)(3) requires the Government to prove that she knew that Moto 1, Moto 2, and Moto 3 contained trade secrets, this heightened knowledge requirement is easily met in this case. Jin knew that this information was not readily accessible; had she thought otherwise she would not have gone to the effort of returning to work for the few days it took her to download the documents. Jin was also aware, starting with her first day of employment with Motorola, of the many measures employed by Motorola to protect its proprietary information, and she knew that the relevant documents were marked "Confidential and Proprietary." Finally, that Jin knew this information derived economic value from its secrecy can easily be inferred from other facts. First, she had worked on iDEN and was aware of the years of research and development that went into iDEN technology. Second, Jin went through the ruse of returning to work in order to obtain the information, something she would not have done had she thought the documents were worthless. These facts make it clear that Jin was aware that the charged documents had the attributes of a trade secret.

Turning now to the theft of trade secrets provision of the EEA, the statutory language employed in Section 1832(a)(3) is less clear in requiring that the defendant have knowledge that the information she possesses is a trade secret. Under Section 1832(a)(3), a defendant must "inten[d] to convert the trade secret," and "knowingly ... receive[ ], buy[ ], or possess[ ] such information, knowing the same to have been stolen or appropriated, obtained, or converted without authorization[.]" 18 U.S.C. § 1832(a)(3). That Section 1832(a)(3) requires knowledge of "such information" instead of "a trade secret" may be a distinction without a difference, but this is an issue the Court need not decide because the Court has already concluded that the Government proved beyond a reasonable doubt that Jin knew that the charged documents were trade secrets as a factual matter.

Misappropriation of the trade secrets

For both theft of trade secrets and economic espionage, the Government must prove that the defendant misappropriated the trade secrets through one of the prohibited acts in Sections 1831 and 1832. Here, Jin was charged with possessing Moto 1, Moto 2, and Moto 3, knowing that they were "stolen or appropriated, obtained, or converted without authorization." 18 U.S.C. §§ 1831(a)(3), 1832(a)(3). Thus, under this element, the Government must first prove that the trade secrets at issue were actually "stolen, appropriated, or converted without authorization," and next, that Jin knew the trade secrets were "stolen, appropriated, or converted without authorization."

This element was met in this case. Jin downloaded and copied thousands of documents when they were clearly outside the scope of her limited duties upon her return from sick leave. She continued to download documents even after sending her email resignation to Bach. This was in clear contravention of the Motorola policies that

Jin had agreed to follow. Given the training she received as an employee of Motorola regarding the care of confidential and proprietary information, her excellent employment record and educational training, the manner in which she obtained the documents, and the lies she told the CBP and FBI agents about the documents when she was caught with them at O'Hare, the Court easily concludes that this was not an innocent mistake. The Court finds beyond a reasonable doubt that Jin knew that she had taken the documents without authorization.

The Court now turns to the unique elements of Sections 1832(a)(3) and 1831(a)(3).

Remaining theft of trade secret elements

As detailed herein, the Government met its burden with regards to the first three elements of Section 1832(a)(3) for Moto 1, Moto 2, and Moto 3, specifically that: the charged documents contained trade secrets; Jin knowingly possessed the charged documents, knowing they were trade secrets; and Jin knew the trade secrets were obtained without authorization. It was also undisputed at trial that the trade secrets related to a product placed in interstate commerce. The Court now turns to the two remaining elements under Section 1832(a)(3).

Intent to provide an economic benefit to the defendant or a third party

The fourth element under Section 1832(a)(3)—that the defendant intended for the offense to economically benefit anyone other than the owner—ensures that mere possession of trade secrets is not unlawful. Instead, the Government must have proven that Jin possessed the trade secrets with the intent to convert the trade secrets to the economic benefit of herself or someone else who is not the trade secret's owner.

Jin contends that this element requires the Government to "prove an economic benefit to the end user—whether the end user is the defendant herself or a third party to whom the Government has proven the defendant intended to provide the materials." Based on this premise, Jin maintains that if the Government's theory of the case was that Jin took the documents for her own benefit, then the Government needed to prove that the trade secrets provided Jin with information she did not already possess. If the Government's theory was that Jin intended to benefit a third party by taking the charged documents, Jin argues that the Government "needed to prove that the third party stood to profit in some manner from the three charged documents."

The Court concludes that this argument overstates the Government's burden under Section 1832(a)(3). The statutory language and the case law interpreting it establish that the key inquiry is the defendant's intent at the time of the offense, not whether there was an actual benefit to a party other than the owner of the trade secret. See Hsu, 155 F.3d at 196 ("[P]rosecutions under § 1832 uniquely require that the defendant intend to confer an economic benefit on the defendant or another person or entity."). Additionally, while the Court agrees that the EEA permits an employee to use the general skills and knowledge she acquired working for a previous employer to her economic benefit, as previously discussed, what is at issue here is not general information or knowledge that Jin possessed but rather specific technical information unique to iDEN.

In this case, the Court concludes that this element was proven beyond a reasonable doubt because Jin took the trade secrets to help her prepare for her future employment. It is clear that when Jin was stopped with the documents on February 28, 2007, she had planned to move to China for an indefinite duration and work for Sun Kaisens. Although Jin had been an excellent employee at Motorola throughout most of her time there, after her prolonged and serious illness, Jin had decided to return to China to be closer to her husband and her ailing mother. The evidence clearly showed that employment at Sun Kaisens was key to this plan. There is no doubt that Jin had done work for Sun Kaisens in the past, and her emails with Sun Kaisens management and her former supervisor at Lemko establish that she planned to work for Sun Kaisens upon her return to China.

Jin also clearly believed that the documents she took from Motorola—including the trade secrets—would help her prepare for her future employment at Sun Kaisens. While the evidence did not establish that someone at Sun Kaisens had requested the documents or that Jin planned to give the documents to Sun Kaisens, the evidence demonstrated beyond a reasonable doubt that, at a minimum, Jin planned to use the documents to prepare herself for her position at Sun Kaisens. She admitted numerous times, including in her written statement, that she sought to refresh her memory with the documents and to use them to help her get her next job. After being on medical leave from Motorola for 15 of the preceding 21 months, Jin could not arrive at Sun Kaisens unfamiliar with the very areas of technology that she had told Gengshan Liu she had worked on at Motorola. Thus, while there was no evidence regarding what the actual economic benefit to Jin would be in terms of a dollar amount, it is clear that she planned to use the documents to her economic benefit by using them to prepare for her next job at Sun Kaisens. Jin's planned use of these documents would also indirectly benefit Sun Kaisens.

In reaching this conclusion, the Court notes that there was no evidence that Sun Kaisens sought this information, and in fact, the evidence indicated that Sun Kaisens would likely not be directly interested in iDEN technology because it was focused on more advanced CDMA technology. The focus here, however, is on Jin's intent, and the evidence showed that Jin had made representations about her work at Motorola to Gengshan Liu, and that she sought to be a productive, helpful member of his team. Thus, even though in the end Jin's knowledge of iDEN technology and the stolen trade secrets may not have directly benefitted Sun Kaisens, she believed at the time she took the documents that they would, at a minimum, help prepare her for her new job with Sun Kaisens and meet the expectations of her new employer.

The conclusion that Jin planned to use the documents for this improper purpose is also supported by the many misrepresentations she made leading up to and following her arrest, the sheer quantity of documents she took, and the manner in which she took them. First, Jin lied to Motorola employees in the course of her phony return to work. The evidence showed that Jin never intended to return to work for Motorola and instead returned from medical leave solely to obtain the documents that were found in her possession on February 28, 2007. Jin also lied repeatedly to CBP and FBI officials about her employment with Motorola, the source of the documents, and her contacts in China.

Jin's vast downloading of thousands of documents over the course of a few days also indicates that she did not merely clean out her desk in a haphazard manner. She had multiple copies of Moto 1, Moto 2, and Moto 3 in her possession when she was stopped at O'Hare. She used multiple storage devices to store the documents, and possessed many of the documents in paper form. These facts indicate a concerted effort on the part of Jin to obtain information she believed would help her in her future job.

The elaborate steps taken by Jin to obtain the documents also show that she was acting with the improper purpose of obtaining an economic benefit for herself. Her prior purchase of a one-way ticket to China indicates that she had no intention of staying when she returned to Motorola. As soon as she knew she had access to the Motorola buildings and the Motorola network, she began accessing and saving thousands of documents, and did so late into the night and after she sent her email resignation. There simply was no legitimate reason for these multiple deceptive acts, which firmly establish Jin's criminal intent. The Court concludes that the Government proved beyond a reasonable doubt that Jin took the trade secrets with the purpose of economically benefitting herself and indirectly benefitting Sun Kaisens.

Intent to injure the owner of the trade secret

A defendant guilty of theft of trade secrets must have intended or known that her conduct would harm the owner of the trade secret. The legislative history of the EEA suggests that this requires that the defendant "knew or was aware to a practical certainty" that her conduct would cause injury to the trade secret's owner. Hsu, 155 F.3d at 196 (quoting S.Rep. No. 104–359, at 15). This does not mean that the Government must "prove malice or evil intent, but merely that the actor knew or was aware to a practical certainty that his conduct would cause some disadvantage to the rightful owner." H.R.Rep. No. 104–788, at 11; see also Aleynikov, 785 F.Supp.2d at 59 (intent to harm trade secret owner established by evidence that the stolen trade secrets could be used to directly compete with the trade secret owner, the defendant knew of the highly secretive nature of the business area and of the measures taken to protect the trade secrets, and that the defendant took steps to circumvent the security measures).

Here, this element is satisfied because Jin was well-informed that her conduct would harm Motorola. First, as discussed above, Jin knew the charged documents were trade secrets because she was aware that information within the documents was not available to the public, that the information derived value from its secrecy, and that Motorola took many precautions to maintain the secrecy of the information. All of the charged documents are marked as "Motorola Confidential and Proprietary," and

Motorola's policy regarding the protection of proprietary information, a copy of which was in Jin's possession on February 27, 2007, states that the unauthorized disclosure of "Motorola Confidential and Proprietary" information "would cause substantial detrimental effect" to Motorola. Additionally, the following statement is found on the covers of both Moto 1 and Moto 2: "The information contained in this document is classified Company Confidential. The use and divulgence of any part of this information can seriously affect the welfare and financial security of the company."

Second, Jin, as a former Motorola employee, knew of the effort and resources that went into developing and protecting the technology described in the trade secrets, and she therefore knew that the use or disclosure of the information could give an unfair advantage to a Motorola competitor, thereby harming Motorola. Additionally, even if the trade secret information never reached the hands of a competitor, the possibility that it could would cause Motorola to take preventative measures to reduce the damage a potential disclosure might cause. Thus, the Court concludes that the Government proved the final element under the theft of trade secrets statute. The Court therefore finds that the Government proved beyond a reasonable doubt that Jin is guilty of Counts One, Two, and Three of the indictment.

Remaining economic espionage element

As discussed above, the Government proved the first three elements under Section 1831(a)(3) beyond a reasonable doubt. The remaining issue under Section 1831(a)(3) is an additional mens rea element necessary to establish a violation of the economic espionage provision of the EEA—that Jin knew or intended that her conduct would benefit a foreign Government or a foreign instrumentality. This element has two related parts: the intended beneficiary and the intended benefit. The Government must first prove that the intended beneficiary was a "foreign Government, instrumentality, or agent." 18 U.S.C. § 1831(a). Here, the Government alleged that Jin intended for her conduct to benefit the PRC, which is clearly a foreign Government.

Second, the Government must prove that Jin intended or knew that her conduct would benefit the PRC. While Section 1832 limits the type of "benefit" intended to economic benefits, "benefit in Section 1831 is intended to be interpreted broadly." H.R.Rep. No. 104–788, at 11. The defendant need not intend to confer an economic benefit; rather the Government need only prove that the defendant intended that her actions would benefit the foreign Government, instrumentality, or agent "in any way." "Therefore, in this circumstance, benefit means not only an economic benefit but also reputational, strategic, or tactical benefit."

Here, the government did not prove beyond a reasonable doubt that Jin intended or knew her conduct would benefit the PRC in any way. The Government put forth no evidence that Jin was asked or directed to take the trade secrets, and as discussed above, the evidence did not establish that Jin planned to give the trade secrets to Sun Kaisens, let alone the PRC. Instead, the Government argued that Jin knew her conduct would benefit the PRC because Sun Kaisens develops telecommunications technology for the Chinese military, Jin knew that Sun Kaisens developed telecommunication projects for the Chinese military, and the trade secrets pertained to telecommunications technology.

The inferential chain from the facts to the Government's conclusion fails to establish the required proof beyond a reasonable doubt. First, the same evidence that the Government relied on to show that Jin knew that Sun Kaisens develops technology for the Chinese military also showed that the Chinese military was seeking telecommunications technology that was superior to and incompatible with iDEN. Nearly all of the documents found in Jin's possession pertain to telecommunications systems that use CDMA, soft switching technology, or have other technological requirements that could not be met using iDEN. Additionally, the evidence before the Court established that while iDEN technology was still generating revenue for Motorola in 2007, it was 2G technology that had been surpassed by other telecommunications technology and would likely be phased out of use in the not-too-distant future. Thus, this was not cutting-edge technology that would necessarily give the PRC any tactical, reputational, or other benefit.

Second, the only purported evidence of any connection or link between the Chinese military and the trade secrets in the documents does not meet the Government's burden. The Government pointed to two Chinese military documents that contain a total of three brief references to telecommunications systems using channel widths of 25 and 50 kilohertz. While iDEN technology is hypothetically compatible with those channel widths, the Government failed to show why the Chinese military would want to use iDEN when the publicly available and technologically superior TETRA technology could also be used in such systems. There was also a passing mention of Israel's "Secure Cellular Phone Applications" on a slide in a Chinese military telecommunications presentation, but the slide does not mention anything about iDEN and the same presentation discusses China's GSM and CDMA mobile communication networks. That these minor references to technology that could possibly relate to iDEN indicate a connection between the Chinese military or the PRC and iDEN is a stretch at best. Given the superiority of other available telecommunications technology to iDEN, the Chinese military documents' focus on technologies that are incompatible with iDEN, and, at best, minimal evidence of a connection between the Chinese military documents Jin had in her possession and Moto 1, Moto 2, and Moto 3, the Court concludes that the evidence failed to establish beyond a reasonable doubt that Jin intended or knew that her conduct would benefit the PRC. There is certainly plenty of speculative proof that the PRC may have benefitted from Jin's conduct, but such speculation does not equate to proof beyond a reasonable doubt. The Court therefore finds that the Government did not prove beyond a reasonable doubt that Jin is guilty of Counts Four, Five, and Six of the pending indictment.

CONCLUSION

For the foregoing reasons, the Court finds that the Government proved beyond a reasonable doubt that Jin is guilty of theft of trade secrets under Section 1832(a)(3) of the EEA. The Government's evidence failed to prove beyond a reasonable doubt that Jin is guilty of economic espionage under Section 1831(a)(3) of the EEA. The Court hereby enters a judgment of guilty against Jin on Counts One, Two, and Three, and a judgment of not guilty on Counts Four, Five, and Six of the pending indictment.

NOTES

Note 1

The Federal Bureau of Investigation (FBI) released an article which discussed comments FBI Director Christopher Wray made concerning China and intellectual property theft on February 1, 2022:

> The threat's complexity is rooted in the intrinsic entanglement of the American and Chinese economies, which is fueled by a high U.S. demand for Chinese-made products and a steady exchange of students between American and Chinese borders. Wray stressed that China has pulled no punches about capitalizing on this interconnectedness to chase economic superiority.

> "When we tally up what we see in our investigations—over 2,000 of which are focused on the Chinese government trying to steal our information or technology—there is just no country that presents a broader threat to our ideas, our innovation, and our economic security than China," Wray said, adding that the Bureau opens a new counterintelligence case against China about twice a day.

> FBI Director Christopher Wray discussed the myriad threats our nation faces from the Chinese government and Chinese Communist Party during a speech at the Ronald Reagan Presidential Library and Museum in Simi Valley, California, on January 31, 2022.

> China's strategy is especially dangerous because it pursues economic espionage on multiple fronts—some so subtle that they don't set off alarms. But once China sets its sights on a technology, Wray explained, it uses every available resource to try to steal it. He pointed to a foiled Chinese plot to use a combination of industrial espionage and hacking to steal trade secrets from GE Aviation to illustrate this approach.

> This theft not only gives China an unfair advantage in the global marketplace but also directly harms American companies and workers.

> Yet the Chinese government's thirst for power can't be quenched by economic dominance alone, Wray noted. China also ultimately seeks to undermine and infiltrate the U.S. government and silence dissent whenever possible.

The Chinese Communist Party (CCP) aims to win American leaders' loyalty through money or intimidation and "to undermine our democratic process by influencing our elected officials." Wray said. The CCP is patient in this pursuit, aiming to recruit early-career politicians—often at the state and local level—who can then be called on to do Beijing's bidding when their power and influence grow.

The Chinese government is also increasingly using a program it calls Fox Hunt to target, threaten, intimidate, and ultimately repatriate former Chinese citizens living overseas whom it sees as a political or financial threat. Many of them are green card holders and naturalized citizens here in the United States.

Through Fox Hunt, the Chinese government has sought to intimidate and silence Chinese and Chinese American students who are studying at U.S. universities. If a student voices or posts an opinion critical of the Chinese government, their family members back in China may receive threats.

"China may be the first government to combine authoritarian ambitions with cutting-edge technical capability," Wray said. "It's like the surveillance nightmare of East Germany combined with the tech of Silicon Valley."

Fortunately, as China's thirst for power has grown, the FBI's strategy and capabilities have evolved to deter it.

One such advance has been the FBI's use of intelligence to identify and disrupt threats early, as it did in response to China's recent compromise of Microsoft Exchange email servers.

The FBI also now shares information with domestic and international partners to help them defend against future plots and has boosted private-sector engagement.

Additionally, the Bureau has repurposed lessons learned from the counterterrorism arena to deter China. This included standing up Cyber Task Forces and Counterintelligence Task Forces in every FBI field office and forming a National Counterintelligence Task Force.

America's democratic and legal processes also play a role, Wray explained, since our ability to make substantiated allegations can move allies to act, and indictments can inspire increased public scrutiny of bad actors.

"So, we're confronting this threat and winning important battles, not just *while* adhering to our values, but *by* adhering to our values,"

Wray said. "I believe that in the course of doing so, we're showing why the Chinese government needs to change course—for all our sakes."[494]

11.5 Stored Communications Act

The Stored Communications Act ("SCA") generally addresses voluntary and compelled disclosure of stored wire and electronic communications. One violates the SCA if they intentionally access without authorization a facility the provides electronic communication service, intentionally exceeds authorization to access these facilities, and obtains, alters, or prevents authorized access to a wire or electronic communications while it is in electronic storage. Criminal penalties attach for violations of the SCA, and severity of such penalties depend on whether this is a first or subsequent offense.

11.5[A] SELECTED PROVISIONS OF THE STORED COMMUNICATIONS ACT

18 U.S.C.A. § 2701

§ 2701. Unlawful access to stored communications

(a) Offense.--Except as provided in subsection (c) of this section whoever--

(1) intentionally accesses without authorization a facility through which an electronic communication service is provided; or

(2) intentionally exceeds an authorization to access that facility; and thereby obtains, alters, or prevents authorized access to a wire or electronic communication while it is in electronic storage in such system shall be punished as provided in subsection (b) of this section.

(b) Punishment.--The punishment for an offense under subsection (a) of this section is--

(1) if the offense is committed for purposes of commercial advantage, malicious destruction or damage, or private commercial gain, or in furtherance of any criminal or tortious act in violation of the Constitution or laws of the United States or any State--

(A) a fine under this title or imprisonment for not more than 5 years, or both, in the case of a first offense under this subparagraph; and

(B) a fine under this title or imprisonment for not more than 10 years, or both, for any subsequent offense under this subparagraph; and

---

[494] FEDERAL BUREAU OF INVESTIGATION, *China's Quest for Economic, Political Domination Threatens America's Security* (February 1, 2022), available at https://www.fbi.gov/news/stories/director-wray-addresses-threats-posed-to-the-us-by-china-020122.

(2) in any other case--

(A) a fine under this title or imprisonment for not more than 1 year or both, in the case of a first offense under this paragraph; and

(B) a fine under this title or imprisonment for not more than 5 years, or both, in the case of an offense under this subparagraph that occurs after a conviction of another offense under this section.

(c) Exceptions.--Subsection (a) of this section does not apply with respect to conduct authorized--

(1) by the person or entity providing a wire or electronic communications service;

(2) by a user of that service with respect to a communication of or intended for that user; or

(3) in section 2703, 2704 or 2518 of this title.

18 U.S.C.A. § 2707

§ 2707. Civil action

(a) Cause of action.--Except as provided in section 2703(e), any provider of electronic communication service, subscriber, or other person aggrieved by any violation of this chapter in which the conduct constituting the violation is engaged in with a knowing or intentional state of mind may, in a civil action, recover from the person or entity, other than the United States, which engaged in that violation such relief as may be appropriate.

(b) Relief.--In a civil action under this section, appropriate relief includes--

(1) such preliminary and other equitable or declaratory relief as may be appropriate;

(2) damages under subsection (c); and

(3) a reasonable attorney's fee and other litigation costs reasonably incurred.

(c) Damages.--The court may assess as damages in a civil action under this section the sum of the actual damages suffered by the plaintiff and any profits made by the violator as a result of the violation, but in no case shall a person entitled to recover receive less than the sum of $1,000. If the violation is willful or intentional, the court may assess punitive damages. In the case of a successful action to enforce liability under this section, the court may assess the costs of the action, together with reasonable attorney fees determined by the court.

(d) Administrative discipline.--If a court or appropriate department or agency determines that the United States or any of its departments or agencies has violated any provision of this chapter, and the court or appropriate department or agency finds that the circumstances surrounding the violation raise serious questions about whether or not an officer or employee of the United States acted willfully or intentionally with respect to the violation, the department or agency shall, upon receipt of a true and correct copy of the decision and findings of the court or appropriate department or agency promptly initiate a proceeding to determine whether disciplinary action against the officer or employee is warranted. If the head of the department or agency involved determines that disciplinary action is not warranted, he or she shall notify the Inspector General with jurisdiction over the department or agency concerned and shall provide the Inspector General with the reasons for such determination.

(e) Defense.--A good faith reliance on--

(1) a court warrant or order, a grand jury subpoena, a legislative authorization, or a statutory authorization (including a request of a governmental entity under section 2703(f) of this title);

(2) a request of an investigative or law enforcement officer under section 2518(7) of this title; or

(3) a good faith determination that section 2511(3), section 2702(b)(9), or section 2702(c)(7) of this title permitted the conduct complained of;

is a complete defense to any civil or criminal action brought under this chapter or any other law.

(f) Limitation.--A civil action under this section may not be commenced later than two years after the date upon which the claimant first discovered or had a reasonable opportunity to discover the violation.

(g) Improper disclosure.--Any willful disclosure of a "record", as that term is defined in section 552a(a) of title 5, United States Code, obtained by an investigative or law enforcement officer, or a governmental entity, pursuant to section 2703 of this title, or from a device installed pursuant to section 3123 or 3125 of this title, that is not a disclosure made in the proper performance of the official functions of the officer or governmental entity making the disclosure, is a violation of this chapter. This provision shall not apply to information previously lawfully disclosed (prior to the commencement of any civil or administrative proceeding under this chapter) to the public by a Federal, State, or local governmental entity or by the plaintiff in a civil action under this chapter.

18 U.S.C.A. § 2711

§ 2711. Definitions for chapter

As used in this chapter-- . . .

(2) the term "remote computing service" means the provision to the public of computer storage or processing services by means of an electronic communications system; . . . .

11.5[B] Cases Concerning Stored Communications Act

Hately v. Watts, 917 F.3d 770 (2019).

. . .

WYNN, Circuit Judge:

Patrick Hately brought this action alleging that David Watts unlawfully accessed messages in Hately's web-based email account in violation of the Virginia Computer Crimes Act and the federal Stored Communications Act. But the district court found that Hately failed to demonstrate the requisite statutory injury under state law, and that Hately's previously opened and delivered emails stored by a web-based email service were not in statutorily protected "electronic storage" under federal law. We disagree with both determinations and therefore reverse and remand this case to the district court for further proceedings consistent with this opinion.

I. A.

In August 2008, Hately enrolled at Blue Ridge Community College, a constituent institution of the Virginia Community College System. At Blue Ridge College, Hately had a student email account that he continued to use after he graduated in 2013.

Blue Ridge College uses a web-based email client with branding specific for Blue Ridge College. Google hosts all emails. Account holders can access the copies stored on their web-based email page as long as the student does not delete those copies. Blue Ridge College also stores at least one additional copy of all student emails, which can be used to recover any email that is accidentally deleted. Students may access these stored copies only by requesting them from Blue Ridge College's technical support personnel.

From August 2011 to February 2015, Hately had an intimate relationship with Nicole Torrenzano, with whom Hately has two children. During their relationship, Hately and Nicole shared login and password information for their email accounts—including Hately's Blue Ridge College email account. But when, about March 2015, Nicole informed Hately that she also was involved in an intimate relationship with Watts, who was her co-worker and married to Audrey Hallinan Watts, Hately and Nicole separated. Pertinent to this action, Hately did not change the password that he shared with Nicole for his Blue Ridge College email account.

Watts and Nicole continued their personal relationship, and during the fall of 2015, Watts and Audrey initiated divorce proceedings. In an effort to help Watts in his divorce proceedings, Nicole told Watts that Hately and Audrey were having an affair. Nicole said she knew of emails between Hately and Audrey that Watts could obtain by using the password that she had to Hately's Blue Ridge College email account.

Watts stated that he used the password Nicole gave him to browse through Hately's emails but contended that he "did not open or view any email that was unopened, marked as unread, previously deleted, or in the [student email account]'s 'trash' folder." Watts also said that he did not "change the status of, or modify, any email in any way." *Id.* . . .

C.

In April 2017, Hately refiled his action against Watts, again alleging that Watts unlawfully accessed his email, in violation of the Computer Fraud and Abuse Act, the Stored Communications Act, and the Virginia Computer Crimes Act.

Unlike his initial action against Watts, which was voluntarily dismissed without prejudice, Hately's refiled action supported his Virginia Computer Crimes Act claims by reciting additional factual allegations bearing on damages. For example, whereas Hately's initial complaint alleged that Hately "incurred many hours of valuable time away from day-to-day responsibilities in attempting to determine the source of the computer breach," Hately's complaint in the refiled action provided greater detail as to the time he lost as a result of the breach, alleging that he "was forced to identify" and make "several calls to" Blue Ridge College's technical support personnel "in order to ascertain the individual(s) that owns the domain for his school-related email account, as well as the individual(s) that manages the exchange servers for his school-related email account." And Hately's refiled complaint alleged that he "review[ed]" "hundreds or thousands of email messages" and "restore[d]" "deleted but unread email messages" that "were previously unknown to [Hately]." Also, the refiled complaint alleged that Hately was "forced to download and run programs that scanned his mobile telephone for viruses."

. . . Thereafter, in January 2018, Hately and Watts filed cross-motions for summary judgment on the remaining Stored Communications Act claim. In an order entered March 14, 2018, the district court denied Hately's motion, granted Watts' motion, and dismissed the case. In an accompanying opinion, the court held that "previously opened and delivered emails" stored "in a web-based email client" were not in protected "electronic storage" for purposes of the Stored Communications Act. According to the court, the statutory definition of "electronic storage" "covers emails only up to the point where the emails have been initially transmitted to their recipient and read or initially downloaded."

The district court also held that Hately's emails were not protected under the statute because they were not stored by an "electronic communication service" and were not stored "for purposes of backup protection." According to the court, Blue Ridge College was acting, for purposes of the Stored Communications Act, as a "remote computing service"—not as an "electronic communication service"—because the emails Watts accessed were "service copies" maintained by Blue Ridge College "for the purposes of transmitting them to a single user's account upon that user's command." Furthermore, the emails were not stored for purposes of backup protection because, the court maintained, they were stored for *Hately's* backup purposes rather than *Blue Ridge College's* "own backup or administrative purposes." Because Hately's accessed emails were not protected "electronic storage," Watts was entitled to judgment as a matter of law on the Stored Communications Act claim.

Hately timely appealed . . . the grant of summary judgment on the Stored Communications Act claim. . . .

III.

Hately next contends that the district court erred in granting Watts summary judgment on Hately's Stored Communications Act claim. In particular, Hately argues that the court erred by concluding that "previously opened and delivered emails" stored "in a web-based email client" were not in protected "electronic storage" within the meaning of the Stored Communications Act. "We review the district court's grant of a motion for summary judgment de novo." Summary judgment is appropriate only when "there is no genuine dispute as to an issue of material fact and the moving party is entitled to summary judgment as a matter of law."

Before construing the meaning of the relevant statutory language, it is useful to recount Congress's purpose in enacting the Stored Communications Act. "Enacted in 1986, the Stored Communications Act was born from congressional recognition that neither existing federal statutes nor the Fourth Amendment protected against potential intrusions on individual privacy arising from illicit access to 'stored communications in remote computing operations and large data banks that stored e-mails.' " In re Google Inc. Cookie Placement Consumer Privacy Lit., 806 F.3d 125, 145 (3d Cir. 2015).

To Congress, this "legal uncertainty pose[d] potential problems in a number of areas." First, it "unnecessarily discourage[d] potential customers from using innovative communications systems.".Next, it "encourage[d] unauthorized users to obtain access to communications to which they are not a party." "Most importantly," Congress recognized that the uncertainty surrounding the legal protections, if any, afforded to electronic communications would "promote the gradual erosion of th[e] precious right [to privacy]."

Senator Patrick Leahy first introduced a bill to remedy this legal uncertainty in 1985. Shortly thereafter, the Congressional Office of Technology Assessment "released a long-awaited study on the privacy implications of electronic surveillance." That report led to additional hearings and to the drafting of a new version of the bill, which Congress ultimately enacted.

In its report, the Office of Technology Assessment emphasized the lack of legal protection for email. The report, which the legislative history of the Stored Communications Act references at length, concluded that the "current legal protections for electronic mail are 'weak, ambiguous, or non-existent,' and that 'electronic mail remains legally as well as technically vulnerable to unauthorized surveillance.' " S. Rep. No. 99-541, at 4 (quoting Office of Technology Assessment, Federal Government Information Technology: Electronic Surveillance and Civil Liberties 44 (Oct. 1985) ("OTA Report")). The report further identified the "stages at which an electronic mail message could be intercepted and its contents divulged to an unintended receiver."

Among the identified stages was the point at which the message was "in the electronic mailbox of the receiver." Appreciating the legal uncertainty that existed, the report further noted that "electronic mail companies can reveal a great deal of information about an individual" and "[r]egardless of what [legal protection] the courts may decide [to grant] based on the facts [of the] case, the issue requires [congressional] attention."

Less than a year after the report was published, Congress enacted the Stored Communications Act. In so doing, Congress expressed its "judgment that users have a legitimate interest in the confidentiality of communications in electronic storage at a communications facility." The Stored Communications Act protects this interest in three principal ways. First, the Stored Communications Act limits the knowing disclosure of "electronic communications" by "electronic communication services" and "remote computing services." See 18 U.S.C. § 2702(a). Second, the statute circumscribes the government's power to compel the disclosure of electronic communications. See 18 U.S.C. § 2703. Third, the statute protects electronic communications from unauthorized access by third-parties. See 18 U.S.C. § 2701.

Section 2701 of the Stored Communications Act—under which Hately seeks relief—criminalizes and provides a private civil cause of action against anyone who "intentionally accesses without authorization a facility through which an electronic communication service is provided ... and thereby obtains, alters, or prevents authorized access to a wire or electronic communication while it is in electronic storage in such system[.]" 18 U.S.C. § 2701(a)(1); see also 18 U.S.C. § 2707 (providing a civil cause of action). The Stored Communications Act defines "electronic storage" as follows:

(A) any temporary, intermediate storage of a wire or electronic communication incidental to the electronic transmission thereof; and

(B) any storage of such communication by an electronic communication service for purposes of backup protection of such communication[.]

18 U.S.C. § 2510(17). The majority of courts have held—and we agree—that the two subsections recognize two discrete types of protected electronic storage. That understanding conforms to the provision's legislative history, in which Congress stated that the definition of "electronic storage" encompasses "two types": (1) storage "incidental to transmission" and (2) "backup" storage. H.R. Rep. No. 99-647, at 68H.R. Rep. No. 99-647, at 68; see also S. Rep. 99-541, at 35 ("The term 'electronic storage' ... includes both temporary, intermediate storage of a wire or electronic communication incidental to the transmission of the message, and any storage of such communication by the electronic communication service for purposes of backup protection of the communication."

The district court concluded that Hately's emails that Watts allegedly accessed unlawfully—all of which the undisputed evidence establishes were previously delivered and opened—were not in "electronic storage" under either Subsection (A) or Subsection (B). Accordingly, we must interpret the Stored Communications Act to determine whether either Subsection (A) or Subsection (B) encompasses previously delivered and opened emails stored by a web-based email service.

"When interpreting a statute, we begin with the plain language." In doing so, "we give the terms their ordinary, contemporary, common meaning, absent an indication Congress intended [it] to bear some different import." "To determine a statute's plain meaning, we not only look to the language itself, but also 'the specific context in which the language is used, and the broader context of the statute as a whole.' " "If the plain language is unambiguous, we need look no further." "On the other hand, if the text of a statute is ambiguous, we look to 'other indicia of congressional intent such as the legislative history' to interpret the statute."

A.

Whether Hately's previously opened and delivered emails stored by a web-based email service were in "electronic storage" within the meaning of Subsection (A) is a question of first impression in this Circuit. That provision encompasses "temporary, intermediate storage of a[n] ... electronic communication incidental to the electronic transmission thereof[.]" 18 U.S.C. § 2510(17)(A).

Congress broadly defined "electronic communication" to include, with a few inapposite exceptions, "any transfer of signs, signals, writing, images, sounds, data, or intelligence of any nature transmitted in whole or in part by a wire, radio, electromagnetic, photoelectric or photo optical system that affects interstate or foreign commerce[.]" 18 U.S.C. § 2510(12). The plain language of this definition encompasses email. And the legislative history confirms that Congress intended this definition to encompass email. See H.R. Rep. No. 99-647, at 34H.R. Rep. No. 99-647, at 34 (recognizing that the definition of "electronic communications" provides "electronic mail" "with protection against interception"). Thus, email is a form of "electronic communication" within the meaning of the Stored Communications Act. . . .

Even so, the district court held that previously delivered and opened emails— like Hately's emails at issue—"are no longer in 'temporary, intermediate storage ... incidental to the[ir] electronic transmission' " and therefore do not fall within the scope of Subsection (A). We agree.

Dictionaries define "temporary" as "existing or continuing for a limited time," Temporary, Webster's Third New International Dictionary 2353 (1961), and "intermediate" as "lying or being in the middle[,]" Intermediate, Webster's Third New International Dictionary 1180; see also The American Heritage Dictionary 914, 1781 (4th ed. 2000) (defining "temporary" as "lasting, used, serving, or enjoyed for a limited time" and "intermediate" as "lying or occurring between two extremes or in a middle position or state"). These definitions indicate that electronic communications are protected by Subsection (A) while they are stored "for a limited time" "in the middle" of transmission.

But previously opened and delivered emails stored by a web-based email service do not fall within the plain language of Subsection (A). Such emails already have been "transmitted" to the recipient and therefore no longer are "in the middle" of transmission. See Councilman, 418 F.3d at 81 (holding that Subsection (A) "refers to temporary storage, such as when a message sits in an email user's mailbox after transmission but before the user has retrieved the message from the mail server"). Likewise, a recipient's decision not to delete an email after receiving and opening the message suggests that the recipient does not intend to keep the message for a "limited" amount of time. Thus, previously received and accessed emails are in not protected "electronic storage" under Subsection (A).

B.

In the alternative, Hately contends that previously opened and delivered emails stored in a web-based email client are in "electronic storage" within the meaning of Subsection (B), which encompasses "any [1] storage of [2] such communication [3] by an electronic communication service [4] for purposes of backup protection of such communication." 18 U.S.C. § 2510(17)(B). This too is a question of first impression in this Circuit. As further explained below, we conclude that previously opened and delivered emails fall within each element of this definition.

1.

To be in protected "electronic storage" under Subsection (B), previously opened and delivered emails must be in "storage." See 18 U.S.C. § 2510(17)(B). Ordinarily, something is "stored" when it is "reserved for future use." Store, The American Heritage Dictionary 1708; see also Store, Webster's Third New International Dictionary 2252 ("[T]o record (information) in an electronic device (as a computer) from which the data can be obtained as needed."). Congress indicated it intended for courts to construe the meaning of "storage" broadly, stating that it did not intend to limit the term to particular mediums, forms, or locations.

In light of the ordinary meaning of storage and Congress's intent that the term be interpreted broadly, we agree with the Ninth Circuit that "prior access is irrelevant" to whether an email is in "storage," "reserved for future use" or available to "be obtained as needed." When a user of a web-based email client, like Hately, opens a message and then chooses not to delete the message after he reads it, the message remains "reserved" on the host server for "future use"—i.e., in the event the user needs to view the message again. See Pure Power Boot Camp v. Warrior Fitness Boot Camp, 587 F.Supp.2d 548, 555 (S.D.N.Y. 2008) ("[T]he majority of courts which have addressed the issue have determined that e-mail stored on an electronic communication service provider's systems after it has been delivered ... is a stored communication subject to the [Stored Communications Act].").

Regardless of whether Hately had previously opened and accessed his web-based emails, those emails were nevertheless "reserved for future use" by the Blue Ridge

College email host in the event that Hately would need to access them in the future. Accordingly, Hately's emails were in "storage" within the meaning of Subsection (B).

2.

Next, to be in protected "electronic storage" under Subsection (B), previously opened and delivered emails must be included within the meaning of the phrase "such communication." See 18 U.S.C. § 2510(17)(B). The phrase "such communication" relates back to Subsection (A), which provides: "any temporary, intermediate storage of a wire or electronic communication incidental to the electronic transmission thereof."

Watts argues—and the district court agreed—that to fall under Subsection (B) a "communication" must be both "wire or electronic" and in "temporary, intermediate storage" because both of those phrases precede the term "communication" in Subsection (A). Hately, 309 F.Supp.3d at 413 ("'[S]uch communication' in § 2510(17)(B) refers to communication 'temporar[ily and] intermediate[ly]' stored 'incidental to the electronic transmission thereof."). By contrast, Hately contends that Congress intended the term "such" in Subsection (B) to serve as a shorthand for the phrase "wire or electronic" in Subsection (A). We agree with Hately.

As the Ninth Circuit explained, "Subsection (A) identifies a type of communication ('a wire or electronic communication') and a type of storage ('temporary, intermediate storage ... incidental to the electronic transmission thereof')." Theofel, 359 F.3d at 1076. "The phrase 'such communication' in [S]ubsection (B) does not, as a matter of grammar, reference attributes of the type of storage defined in subsection (A)." Put simply, the phrase "temporary, intermediate" modifies the noun "storage," but does not modify the noun "communication"—the term referred to in Subsection (B). Therefore, "as the statute is written, 'such communication' is nothing more than shorthand for 'a wire or electronic communication."

Our interpretation also conforms to the principle of statutory construction that "if possible, a court should avoid an interpretation that renders any 'clause, sentence, or word ... superfluous, void, or insignificant.'" Were we to construe "such communication" as encompassing only wire or electronic communications in "temporary, intermediate storage," Subsection (B) would be rendered "essentially superfluous, since temporary backup storage pending transmission would already seem to qualify as 'temporary, intermediate storage' within the meaning of [S]ubsection (A)." Theofel, 359 F.3d at 1075–76.

Hately's emails constitute "wire or electronic communication" as the Stored Communications Act uses that term. Accordingly, the district court erred in holding that Hately's emails did not constitute "such communication" within the meaning of Subsection (B).

3.

Third, to constitute "electronic storage" for purposes of Subsection (B), the wire or electronic communication must be stored by an "electronic communication service." 18 U.S.C. § 2510(17)(B). The Stored Communications Act defines "electronic communication service," as "any service which provides to users thereof the ability to send or receive wire or electronic communications." Id. § 2510(15). As explained above, email is a form of "electronic communication" for purposes of the Stored Communications Act. Under the plain language of Section 2510(17)(B), therefore, "any service which provides to users thereof the ability to send or receive" email messages constitutes an electronic communication service. Because Blue Ridge College's email service enables account holders, like Hately, to "send or receive" email messages, it falls within the plain language of the Stored Communications Act's definition of electronic communication service.

Notably, the Stored Communications Act's legislative history supports this conclusion, stating that "electronic mail companies are providers of electronic communication services." S. Rep. No. 99-541, at 14. And in accordance with the plain language of the Stored Communications Act and the statute's legislative history, courts have concluded that email services—like Hately's College email account—are electronic communication services.

Watts nevertheless argues—and the district court agreed—that, at least for purposes of the email copies in question, Blue Ridge College's email service was functioning not as an electronic communication service, but solely as a "remote computing service"—a term not used in the Stored Communications Act's definition of electronic storage. The Stored Communications Act defines "remote computing service" as "the provision to the public of computer storage or processing services by means of an electronic communications system." 18 U.S.C. § 2711(2). According to the district court, Blue Ridge College's email service "was not acting as an [electronic communication service] with respect to" the copies of Hately's "delivered and opened" emails accessed by Watts but was instead providing "storage or processing" of the emails, and therefore was acting as a remote computing service.

The district court's reasoning rests on the premise that, for purposes of the emails in question, Blue Ridge College's email service could not simultaneously function as both an electronic communication service and a remote computing service. But nothing in the plain language of the definitions of electronic communication service and remote computing service precludes an entity from simultaneously functioning as both. There is no logical or technological obstacle to an entity "provid[ing] to users thereof the ability to send or receive wire or electronic communications"—i.e., functioning as an electronic communication service—while, and as part of the same service, "provi[ding] the public [with] computer storage or processing services by means of an electronic communications system"—i.e., functioning as a remote computing service. And the relevant legislative history expressly contemplates as much, stating that "remote computing services may also provide electronic communication services." S. Rep. No. 99-541, at 14.

Notably, other aspects of the district court's opinion appear to contradict its conclusion that an entity cannot simultaneously function as an electronic communication service and a remote computing service. In particular, the district court held—and Watts does not dispute—that the email provider was acting as an electronic communication service as to unread or not downloaded emails. When, as here, emails are accessed through a web-based email service, then the provider of the email service necessarily would, under the district court's reasoning, also seem to be providing "remote computing services" as to "unread or not downloaded" emails because it is providing "storage ... by means of an electronic communications system." 18 U.S.C. § 2711(2).

The legislative history also supports the conclusion that Congress viewed email providers as simultaneously functioning as both a remote computing service and an electronic communication service when such providers store "unread or not downloaded" messages. . . .

Significantly, because the plain language of the Stored Communications Act, the statute's legislative history, and the district court's own reasoning contemplates that entities can simultaneously function as both an electronic communication service and a remote computing service, the House Report's statement that a user's opened messages "continue to be covered" by remote computing service provisions in no way precludes a finding that the entity also "continue[d] to" act as an electronic communication service after the user opened the messages. And because an entity can simultaneously function as an electronic communication service and a remote computing service, an entity's status as a remote computing service in no way precludes a determination that the entity also was acting as an electronic communication service.

To be sure, "the statutory definitions of [electronic communication service] and [remote computing service] are functional and context sensitive." Therefore, an entity that acts as an electronic communication service in one context may act as only a remote computing service in another context or, in still other contexts, may not act as either an electronic communication service or a remoting computing service. Id. For example, we conclude today that companies such as Microsoft and Google function as an electronic communication services when they provide email services through their proprietary web-based email applications. But that does not mean that Microsoft and Google necessarily function as electronic communication services regarding other applications and services they offer, like cloud-based data processing and analytics services, or goods or products they sell or license, like hardware or software.

Because (1) email providers fall squarely within the statutory definition of electronic communication service and (2) the terms electronic communication service and remote computing service are not mutually exclusive, the district court erred in holding Hately's College email account did not amount to an electronic communication service.

4.

Finally, to constitute "electronic storage" under Subsection (B), an electronic communication must be stored "for purposes of backup protection." 18 U.S.C. §

2510(17)(B). Notwithstanding that the Stored Communications Act defines numerous terms, the statute does not define the term "backup protection." Accordingly, we must look to the term's plain meaning and Congress's intent in enacting the Stored Communications Act and Section 2701(a), in particular, to determine whether previously delivered and opened emails stored by a web-based email service are stored for "purposes of backup protection."

The most relevant definition of "backup" is "a copy of computer data (such as a file or the contents of a hard drive)." Backup, Merriam-Webster.com. A "copy" is a "duplicate." Copy, Merriam-Webster.com More general definitions of "backup" include "substitute" or "support." Backup, Merriam-Webster.com. "Protection" is defined as "the act of protecting," Protection, Merriam-Webster.com, which means "cover[ing] or shield[ing] from exposure, injury, damage, or destruction," Protect, Merriam-Webster.com. Accordingly, a wire or electronic communication is stored for "purposes of backup protection" if it is a "copy" or "duplicate" of the communication stored to prevent, among other things, its "destruction."

The copies of previously delivered and opened emails retained on the server of the host of a web-based email service—like Hately's emails at issue—fall within this understanding of electronic communication stored "for purposes of backup protection." To understand why such emails fall within the definition of "backup," it is useful to explain the typical manner in which a web-based email service functions.

To begin, after the sender drafts and sends a message, a copy of the message is transmitted to the recipient's web-based email service. Such services typically (including Google, which hosted Blue Ridge College's email service) "utilize completely redundant systems consisting of multiple data servers." See Br. of Amici Curiae the Ctr. for Dem. & Tech., the Elec. Frontier Found. "In redundant systems, a single email is stored on multiple servers, likely in different locations around the country, and possibly around the world." Web-based email services store copies of messages on multiple servers in order "to decrease email downtime (i.e., users being unable to access their email) or loss of information" in the event any one server fails. Id. Accordingly, when a web-based email service receives an email, it typically generates numerous copies of the email, the existence of which ensures that the inaccessibility or failure of a particular server or the errant destruction of any one copy will not lead to the loss of a message. Put differently, in a web-based email service, each "copy" serves as a "substitute" or "support" for the many other copies stored by the service. See id.; see also Reliability, Google Cloud Support ("[A]ll Google systems are inherently redundant by design, and each subsystem is not dependent on any particular physical or logical server for ongoing operation. Data is replicated multiple times across Google's clustered active servers so that, in the case of a machine failure, data will still be accessible through another system."); Christopher Soghoian, Caught in the Cloud: Privacy, Encryption, and Government Back Doors in the Web 2.0 Era, 8 J. Telecomm. & High Tech. L. 359, 361 (2010) ("Cloud computing services provide consumers with vast amounts of cheap, redundant storage and allow them to instantly access their data from a web-connected computer anywhere in the world.").

When the recipient chooses to view the email via a web browser or application on a computer, smartphone, or other internet-connected device, one of the web-based email service's servers sends a copy of the message to the user's device for the user to view through the browser or application. That copy is temporarily stored in the device's short-term memory. The user's device also might download a copy for retention in the device's long-term memory. Accordingly, the "copies" retained by the host of the web-based email service also serve as a "substitute" or "support" for the copies of the message the recipient downloads to his device's short-term or long-term memory. Accord Cheng, 2013 WL 6814691, at *3 ("[R]egardless of the number of times [the plaintiff] or [the defendant] viewed [the plaintiff's] email (by downloading web page representations of those emails into their person computer's web browser) the Yahoo! server continued to store copies of those same emails that previously had been transmitted to [the plaintiff's] web browsers, and again to [the defendant's] web browser.").

Numerous other copies may exist as well. For example, the sender may retain a copy of the message in her outbox. The sender's email service also may retain copies of the message on one or more servers for the sender to access. And during the transmission process, intermediate computers may retain one or more copies as well.

Notably, notwithstanding that some courts have lamented that "[i]t is not always easy to square the decades-old [Stored Communications Act] with the current state of email technology," the way modern web-based email services function is closely analogous to how Congress described the "most common form" of email used at the time it enacted the Stored Communications Act: "[M]essages are typed into a computer terminal, and then transmitted over telephone lines to a recipient computer operated by an electronic mail company. If the intended addressee subscribes to the service, the message is stored by the company's computer 'mail box' until the subscriber calls the company to retrieve its mail, which is then routed over the telephone system to the recipient's computer." S. Rep. No. 99-541, at 8. Just as in the system Congress described, in a modern web-based email service, a sender's email service transmits a message to the addressee's web-based email service. Also like the system Congress described, the web-based email service then "stores" the message until the addressee "retrieves" it, by routing the message through the addressee's internet provider to the browser or application on the addressee's internet-connected device in which the addressee views the message.

The copies of emails retained by a user in his web-based account also are stored by the web-based email service—i.e., the electronic communication service—for purposes of its own and its users' "protection." As set forth above, web-based email services—including Google, which hosted the copies Hately's emails accessed by Watts—retain multiple copies of the messages in a user's account for the web-based email service's own backup protection. Such services use "redundant" systems "to decrease email downtime (i.e., users being unable to access their email) or loss of information due to component failure," CDT Br. at 22—i.e., to ensure the product the web-based email service markets functions as intended, expected, and demanded by users. Put simply, by storing copies of messages on multiple servers and in multiple locations, the web-based email service protects itself against the failure of one or more of its servers.

Additionally, the web-based email service stores previously opened and delivered emails for the "protection" of their users. When the user of a web-based email service, like Hately, opens and reviews an email message and then chooses not to delete the message from his account, the user is likely retaining that message to prevent its destruction. There are numerous reasons a recipient may not want to destroy a message he already has read. For example, a user who receives an email setting up a meeting may choose not to delete the email after first reading it because the user wants to keep a copy readily available in case the user forgets the time or place of the meeting. Or, a user who reaches a business agreement over email may choose to retain in his web-based account messages concerning the agreement to document the agreement's existence and terms. Or, a user who receives a message from a friend or loved one may choose not to delete the message because it has sentimental value and the user wishes to reread the message of future. Or, a user may choose not to delete a message after reading it simply because the user does not know whether the user will need the message in the future and therefore wishes to preserve it. In each of these examples, the user chooses not to delete the message because the user does not want the message to be "destroyed."

But importantly, the meaning of "backup protection" does not turn on whether a user subjectively chose not to delete the email after reading the message because the user wanted to keep the message for backup protection. That is because the purpose of the web-based email service in providing storage for the message—storage that is a feature of the product the web-based email service offers—is to afford the user a place to store messages the user does not want destroyed. The web-based email service does not need to know why the user has elected not to delete particular message. Rather, the web-based email service recognizes that users who choose to use a web-based email platform desire storage for read and unread messages and therefore the web-based email service provides such storage to meet user demand. That is why providers of web-based email services like Google, Microsoft, and Yahoo! market the amount of storage their services provide. See, e.g., Nicholas Behrens, Gmail, now with 10 GB of Storage (and counting), Official Gmail Blog (April 24, 2012). Put simply, the web-based email service is storing the message for the purpose of providing backup protection to its users because that is a feature users desire.

Our conclusion that previously delivered and opened emails stored on a web-based email client are in "electronic storage"—and therefore actionable under Section 2701(a)—also finds support in the statute's legislative history. . . .

Watts nevertheless argues that previously delivered and opened emails stored by a web-based email service do not fall within the meaning of "backup protection" for three reasons: (1) the term encompasses only copies "made for the service provider's own administrative purposes"; (2) the term encompasses only copies retained "for use in the event that the original is rendered unusable"; and (3) the emails were stored for Hately's backup protection and not for Blue Ridge College's backup protection.

Watts' first argument—that the term "backup protection" encompasses only copies "made for the service provider's own administrative purposes"—principally rests on his contention, with which the district court agreed, that the meaning of "backup protection" in Subsection (B) should be construed in accordance with the meaning of "backup copy" in 18 U.S.C. § 2704. See Hately, 309 F.Supp.3d at 413 n.9 (quoting Kerr, supra, at 1217 n.61 ("Section 2704 makes clear that the Stored Communications Act uses the phrase 'backup copy' in a very technical way to mean a copy made by the service provider for administrative purposes.")). Section 2704 provides that the government "may include in its subpoena or court order [requesting communications stored by a remote computing service] a requirement that the service provider to whom the request is directed create a backup copy of the contents of the electronic communications sought in order to preserve the communications." Accordingly, the term "backup copy" in Section 2704 means a copy of an electronic communication created by a service provider pursuant to a court order.

Section 2704's use of the term "backup copy" does not bear the interpretive weight Watts claims. Nothing in the Stored Communications Act's definition of electronic storage, Section 2704, or the statute's legislative history provides any indication that Congress intended "backup protection" and "backup copy" to have the same meaning. On the contrary, Section 2704(a) deals with a specific type of "backup copy"—one created pursuant to court order—and therefore does not, and cannot, establish the general definition of "backup." Notably, Watts and the district court concede as much, concluding that the definition of "backup protection" encompasses all "backup" copies created for an electronic communication service's "administrative purposes," not just any backup copies created pursuant to a court order issued under Section 2704(a). Indeed, the "backup copies" at issue in Section 2704(a) arguably are not created for "administrative purposes" at all—they are created to comply with the court order.

More significantly, even assuming Watts and the district court are correct that the term "backup protection" encompasses only copies that are "made for the service provider's own administrative purposes," Hately's emails in question would fall within the meaning of "backup protection." "Administrative" means "relating to the running of a business, organization, etc." Administrative, Merriam-Webster.com. As explained above, web-based email services—including Google, which hosted Hately's College email account—create numerous copies of emails for their own administrative purposes, such as decreasing email downtime, protecting against loss of data in the event a particular server fails, and for their own commercial purposes, such as to more effectively target advertisements. Accordingly, the copies of Hately's emails at issue were created for Blue Ridge College email service's "administrative purposes" under the common meaning of that term.

In support of his second argument—that the term "backup protection" encompasses only copies retained "for use in the event that the original is rendered unusable"—Watts asserts that the definition of backup presupposes the existence of an "original." According to Watts, the emails accessed by users of a web-based email service are "originals," rather than "copies," and therefore do not fall within the meaning of "backup."

To be sure, some definitions of "backup" suggest a distinction between "backups" and "originals." See Backup, The American Heritage Dictionary 132. But not all definitions of "backup" draw such a distinction. And relying on definitions of "backup" that define the term relative to an "original" makes little sense in the context of messages stored by electronic communication services, and email services, in particular. That is because the "original" would seem to be most readily understood as the copy of a message that a sender types into his email client. The sender's email service then sends a copy of that original to the recipient's email service, meaning that the recipient's email service never receives, much less stores, the "original" message. See S. Rep. No. 99-541, at 8 (stating that in the "most common form" of email "messages are typed into a computer terminal, and then transmitted over telephone lines to a recipient computer operated by an electronic mail company. If the intended addressee subscribes to the service, the message is stored by the company's computer 'mail box' until the subscriber calls the company to retrieve its mail"). Put differently, all copies of an email held by a recipient's email service, web-based or otherwise, are "copies," rather than "originals."

Additionally, even if an addressee's email service did receive an "original," in the context of "redundant" web-based email services—like Blue Ridge College's email service hosted by Google—even the "original" serves as a "backup." In particular, each of the numerous copies of the messages created and stored on the service's server acts as a "substitute" or "support" for every other copy stored on the service's servers. See id. Accordingly, even if one of those numerous copies was an "original," that "original" would still serve as a "backup" for all the other copies stored by the service.

Third, Watts argues—and the district court agreed—that Hately's emails were not stored "for purposes of backup protection" because the court determined those emails were stored for Hately's backup protection and not for Blue Ridge College email service's backup protection. See Hately, 309 F.Supp.3d at 413 (holding that Subsection (B) "refers to a copy of a communication ... stored by the [electronic communication service] for its own backup or administrative purposes" (emphasis added)). But, as explained above, messages stored by a web-based email service are stored for purposes of the web-based email service's own backup protection as well as the user's backup protection. Equally important, "nothing in the [Stored Communications Act] requires that the backup protection be for the benefit of the [electronic communication service] rather than the user." On the contrary, the statute's legislative history expressly contemplates that the requisite backup protection may be for the benefit of the user. H.R. No. 99-647, at 68

("Back up protection preserves the integrity of the electronic communication system and to some extent preserves the property of the users of such a system." (emphasis added)).

* * * * *

We conclude that previously delivered and opened emails stored by an electronic communication service are stored for "purposes of backup protection," under the plain and ordinary meaning of those terms. And because such emails amount to "wire or electronic communications" in "storage" by an "electronic communication service," such emails are in "electronic storage" for purposes of Subsection (B). See supra Parts III.B.1–3.9

5.

Our conclusion that previously delivered and opened emails fall within the meaning of Subsection (B) also accords with Congress's purpose in enacting the Stored Communications Act. Congress sought to fill in a "gap" in then-existing law as to the "protect[ion of] the privacy and security of communications transmitted by new non-common carrier communications services or new forms of telecommunications and computer technology," including email. S. Rep. No. 99-541, at 5; H.R. Rep. No. 99-647, at 17H.R. Rep. No. 99-647, at 17 (noting that statutory framework that existed prior to enactment of the Stored Communications Act "appear[ed] to leave unprotected an important sector of the new communications technologies," including email); id. at 18 (noting "[t]he statutory deficiency ... with respect to non-voice communications"). As noted above, Congress expressed concern that the absence of such protection "unnecessarily discourage[s] potential customers from using innovative communications systems" and "encourages unauthorized users to obtain access to communications to which they are not a party." S. Rep. No. 99-541, at 5; H.R. Rep. No. 99-647, at 19H.R. Rep. No. 99-647, at 19.

The district court's construction of Subsection (B)—that previously delivered and opened emails stored by a web-based email service are not in "electronic storage" and therefore not actionable under Section 2701(a)(1)—would materially undermine these objectives. Potential users of web-based-email services—like Blue Ridge College's email service—would be deterred from using such services, knowing that unauthorized individuals and entities could access many, if not most, of the users' most sensitive emails without running afoul of federal law. Likewise, without the prospect of liability under federal law, unauthorized entities will face minimal adverse consequences for accessing, and using for their own benefit, communications to which they are not a party. The legislative history establishes that Congress did not intend such a result.

The district court's interpretation of Subsection (B)—which would protect only unread emails stored in by web-based email service—also leads to an arbitrary and untenable "gap" in the legal protection of electronic communications. Under the district court's reading, the Stored Communications Act renders unlawful unauthorized access of unopened messages stored by web-based email services, whereas unauthorized access of opened and saved messages stored by such services would not violate the Stored

Communications Act. But the messages a user of a web-based email service chooses not to delete—the messages the district court's construction of Subsection (B) leaves unprotected—are likely precisely the types of messages Congress sought to protect. By choosing to save such messages after reading them, the user indicates that the messages have sufficient personal, commercial, or other significance that they want to be able to access them again in the future. It defies logic that the unopened junk and spam email messages that a user leaves in his or her inbox or designated folder without opening would be entitled to more protection than those messages the user chooses to open and retain. We do not believe Congress intended such an absurd result when it enacted a statute intended to fill in the gaps in the then-existing privacy protections for electronic communications and therefore spur adoption of new communication technologies, like email.

IV.

. . . [T]he district court erroneously granted Watts's motion for summary judgment by concluding that previously opened and delivered emails stored in a web-based email client were not "electronic storage" for purposes of the Stored Communications Act. Accordingly, we reverse the district court's dismissals of [the] . . . Stored Communications Act claims and remand the case to the district court for further proceedings consistent with this opinion.

REVERSED AND REMANDED

Garcia v. City of Laredo, Texas, 702 F.3d 788 (5th Cir. 2012).

W. EUGENE DAVIS, Circuit Judge:

In this appeal, Plaintiff–Appellant Fannie Garcia ("Garcia") contends the district court's interpretation of the Stored Communications Act was erroneous. Garcia alleges that the statute applies and protects all text and data stored on her personal cell phone which the Defendants accessed without Garcia's permission. We conclude that the Stored Communications Act, which prohibits accessing without authorization a facility through which an electronic communication service is provided and thereby obtaining access to an electronic communication while it is in electronic storage, does not apply to data stored in a personal cell phone. For the reasons more fully set forth below, we AFFIRM.

I.

Garcia, a former police dispatcher for the City of Laredo, claims Defendants accessed the contents of her cell phone without permission in violation of the Stored Communications Act. On November 15, 2008, a police officer's wife removed Garcia's cell phone from an unlocked locker in a substation of the Laredo Police Department, and she accessed text messages and images found on Garcia's phone. Believing she had discovered evidence of violations of a department policy, she then set up a meeting with

Cynthia Collazo, the deputy assistant city manager, and Gilbert Navarro, the interim/assistant police chief. At the meeting, she utilized Garcia's cell phone to access and to share with Collazo and Navarro the text messages sent from and received by the phone and the photographs stored on the phone. Later, investigators Gilbert Magaña and Steven Moncevais successfully downloaded one video recording and thirty-two digital images from the cell phone; they were unable to download any of the text messages.

A subsequent internal investigation concluded, based in whole or in part upon images and text messages retrieved from her cell phone, that Garcia had violated police department rules and regulations and Garcia was terminated from her employment.

The district court granted summary judgment for Defendants and denied Garcia's motion for partial summary judgment on the Stored Communications Act, finding that the statute did not apply to Defendants' actions in this case. We affirm.

II.

We review summary judgment rulings *de novo*. Summary judgment is appropriate when there is no genuine dispute as to any material fact and the movant is entitled to judgment as a matter of law. Fed.R.Civ.P. 56(a). A question of statutory interpretation is reviewed *de novo*.

III.

Garcia first argues that the district court erred in granting summary judgment for Defendants because the Stored Communications Act ("SCA") protects all text and data stored on Garcia's cell phone which Defendants accessed without her consent. Defendants argue the SCA does not apply to images and text messages accessed from and stored in an ordinary cell phone.

Prior to 1986, the United States Code provided no protection for stored communications in remote computing operations and large data banks that stored e-mails. In response, Congress passed the SCA as part of the Electronic Communications Privacy Act to protect potential intrusions on individual privacy that the Fourth Amendment did not address. Orin S. Kerr, *A User's Guide to the Stored Communications Act, and a Legislator's Guide to Amending It*, 72 Geo. Wash. L. Rev. 1208, 1209–13 (2004). The SCA prohibits unauthorized access to wire and electronic communications in temporary and back-up storage and provides in relevant part:

[W]hoever—

(1) intentionally accesses without authorization a *facility* through which an *electronic communication service* is provided; or

(2) intentionally exceeds an authorization to access that facility;

and thereby obtains, alters, or prevents authorized access to a wire or electronic communication while it is in *electronic storage* in such system shall be punished as provided in subsection (b) of this section.

18 U.S.C. § 2701(a) (2006) (emphasis added). Accordingly, for Defendants to be liable under the SCA, they must have gained unauthorized access to a facility through which electronic communication services are provided (or the access must have exceeded the scope of authority given) and must thereby have accessed electronic communications while in storage. Garcia argues that her personal cell phone is a "facility" in which electronic communication is kept in electronic storage in the form of text messages and pictures stored on the cell phone.

While the SCA does not define the term "facility," it does define the terms "electronic communication service" and "electronic storage." The statute defines an "electronic communication service" ("ECS") as "any service which provides to users thereof the ability to send or receive wire or electronic communications." 18 U.S.C. § 2510(15). "Electronic storage" is defined as "(A) any temporary, intermediate storage of a wire or electronic communication incidental to the electronic transmission thereof; and (B) any storage of such communication by an electronic communication service for purposes of backup protection of such communication." *Id.* § 2510(17).

Courts have interpreted the statute to apply to providers of a communication service such as telephone companies, Internet or e-mail service providers, and bulletin board services. For example, in *Steve Jackson Games, Inc. v. United States Secret Service,* we found that the SCA applied to cover the seizure of a computer used to operate an electronic bulletin board system. Other circuits have applied the SCA to Internet service providers.

These cases, however, are not helpful to Garcia in establishing that an individual's computer, laptop, or mobile device fits the statutory definition of a "facility through which an electronic communication service is provided." The Eleventh Circuit's decision in *United States v. Steiger* provides useful guidance. 318 F.3d 1039, 1049 (11th Cir.2003). In *Steiger,* when a hacker accessed an individual's computer and obtained information saved to his hard drive, the court held such conduct was beyond the reach of the SCA. The court found that "the SCA clearly applies ... to information stored with a phone company, Internet Service Provider (ISP), or electronic bulletin board system," but does not, however, "appear to apply to the source's hacking into Steiger's computer to download images and identifying information stored on his hard-drive." It noted that "the SCA may apply to the extent the source accessed and retrieved any information *stored with Steiger's Internet service provider." Id.* (emphasis added).

A number of district courts that have considered this question have also concluded that "the relevant 'facilities' that the SCA is designed to protect are not computers that *enable* the use of an electronic communication service, but instead are facilities that are *operated by* electronic communication service providers and used to store and maintain electronic storage." *Freedom Banc Mortg. Servs., Inc. v. O'Harra,* No. 2:11–cv–01073, 2012 WL 3862209, at *9 (S.D.Ohio Sept. 5, 2012). Recently, the Northern District of California held that a class of iPhone plaintiffs had no claim under the SCA because their iPhones did not "constitute 'facilit[ies] through which an electronic communication service is provided.'" *In re iPhone Application Litig.,* 844 F.Supp.2d 1040, 1057–58 (N.D.Cal.2012).

Thus these courts agree that a "home computer of an end user is not protected by the SCA." Kerr, *supra,* at 1215. As explained by Orin Kerr in his widely cited law review article, the words of the statute were carefully chosen: "[T]he statute envisions a *provider* (the ISP or other network service provider) and a *user* (the individual with an account with the provider), with the *user's communications in the possession of the provider.*" *Id.* at 1215 n. 47 (emphasis added).

This reading of the statute is consistent with legislative history, as "Sen. Rep. No. 99–541 (1986)'s entire discussion of [the SCA] deals only with facilities operated by electronic communications services such as 'electronic bulletin boards' and 'computer mail facilit[ies],' and the risk that communications temporarily stored in these facilities could be accessed by hackers. It makes no mention of individual users' computers ...." *In re DoubleClick Inc. Privacy Litig.,* 154 F.Supp.2d 497, 512 (S.D.N.Y.2001).

Even if Garcia's cell phone were somehow considered a "facility," this stops short of demonstrating that storage of text messages and pictures on Garcia's cell phone fits within 18 U.S.C. § 2510(17)'s definition of "electronic storage." "Electronic storage" as defined encompasses only the information that has been stored by an electronic communication service provider. Thus, information that an Internet provider stores to its servers or information stored with a telephone company—if such information is stored temporarily pending delivery or for purposes of backup protection—are examples of protected electronic storage under the statute. But information that an individual stores to his hard drive or cell phone is not in electronic storage under the statute. *Freedom Banc,* 2012 WL 3862209, at *8–9; *see Hilderman v. Enea TekSci, Inc.,* 551 F.Supp.2d 1183, 1205 (S.D.Cal.2008) ("E-mails stored on the laptop computer are not in 'temporary, intermediate storage' [as required by § 2510(17)(A)]. Furthermore, the e-mails on the laptop are not stored 'by an electronic communication service for purposes of backup protection' as required by subsection (B)."); *Bailey v. Bailey,* No. 07–11672, 2008 WL 324156, at *6 (E.D.Mich. Feb. 6, 2008) (unpublished) ("Stored Communications Act protection does not extend to emails and messages stored only on Plaintiff's personal computer.").

An individual's personal cell phone does not *provide* an electronic communication service just because the device *enables* use of electronic communication services, and there is no evidence here that the Defendants ever obtained any information from the cellular company or network. Accordingly, the text messages and photos stored on Garcia's phone are not in "electronic storage" as defined by the SCA and are thus outside the scope of the statute.

. . .

For the above reasons, the judgment of the district court is AFFIRMED.

NOTES

Note 1

In *Surveillance Intermediaries*, Professor Alan Z. Rozenshtein provides an analysis of the role of surveillance intermediaries such as technology companies in modulating and impacting surveillance generally, including by the government. See Alan Rozenshtein, *Surveillance Intermediaries*, 70 Stan. L. Rev. 99 (2018).

Note 2

Electronic Communications Privacy Act

The Stored Communications Act is considered part of the broader Electronic Communications Privacy Act (ECPA). The ECPA provides some protection for electronic communications when made, in transit and stored, including emails. The Congressional Research Service describes the ECPA as follows:

> It is a federal crime to wiretap or to use a machine to capture the communications of others without court approval, unless one of the parties has given his prior consent. It is likewise a federal crime to use or disclose any information acquired by illegal wiretapping or electronic eavesdropping. Violations can result in imprisonment for not more than five years; fines up to $250,000 (up to $500,000 for organizations); civil liability for damages, attorneys' fees and possibly punitive damages; disciplinary action against any attorneys involved; and suppression of any derivative evidence. Congress has created separate, but comparable, protective schemes for electronic communications (e.g., email) and against the surreptitious use of telephone call monitoring practices such as pen registers and trap and trace devices.
>
> Each of these protective schemes comes with a procedural mechanism to afford limited law enforcement access to private communications and communications records under conditions consistent with the dictates of the Fourth Amendment. The government has been given narrowly confined authority to engage in electronic surveillance, conduct physical searches, and install and use pen registers and trap and trace devices for law enforcement purposes under ECPA and for purposes of foreign intelligence gathering under the Foreign Intelligence Surveillance Act.

Charles Doyle, *Privacy: An Overview of the Electronic Communications Privacy Act*, Congressional Research Service 1 (October 9, 2012). Notably, the ECPA is criticized as out of date given changes in technology. *See* Deirdre K. Mulligan, *Reasonable Expectations in Electronic Communications: A Critical Perspective on the Electronic*

Communications Privacy Act, 72 Geo. Wash. L. Rev. 1557 (2004). Additionally, the ECPA also regulates the use of Pen Registers, which may be used to collect basic information data concerning emails, such as date, time, recipient and sender. Some commentators have criticized the ECPA for making the tracing of cyberattacks more difficult.

Note 3

The U.S. Constitution's Fourth Amendment provides: "The right of the people to be secure in their persons, houses, papers, and effects, against unreasonable searches and seizures, shall not be violated, and no Warrants shall issue, but upon probable cause, supported by Oath or affirmation, and particularly describing the place to be searched, and the persons or things to be seized." In *Carpenter v. United States*, the U.S. Supreme Court held that the government's obtaining of cell phone location information—"personal information maintained by a third party"--was a search and subject to the Fourth Amendment's requirement for a warrant supported by probable cause and that the information obtained pursuant to the Stored Communications Act's "reasonable grounds" standard did not meet the probable cause mandate. The U.S. Supreme Court stated:

> As technology has enhanced the Government's capacity to encroach upon areas normally guarded from inquisitive eyes, this Court has sought to "assure [ ] preservation of that degree of privacy against government that existed when the Fourth Amendment was adopted." *Kyllo v. United States,* 533 U.S. 27, 34, 121 S.Ct. 2038, 150 L.Ed.2d 94 (2001). For that reason, we rejected in *Kyllo* a "mechanical interpretation" of the Fourth Amendment and held that use of a thermal imager to detect heat radiating from the side of the defendant's home was a search. *Id.* Because any other conclusion would leave homeowners "at the mercy of advancing technology," we determined that the Government—absent a warrant— could not capitalize on such new sense-enhancing technology to explore what was happening within the home. *Ibid.*

> Likewise in *Riley,* the Court recognized the "immense storage capacity" of modern cell phones in holding that police officers must generally obtain a warrant before searching the contents of a phone. We explained that while the general rule allowing warrantless searches incident to arrest "strikes the appropriate balance in the context of physical objects, neither of its rationales has much force with respect to" the vast store of sensitive information on a cell phone. *Id. . . .*

> We decline to grant the state unrestricted access to a wireless carrier's database of physical location information. In light of the deeply revealing nature of CSLI, its depth, breadth, and comprehensive reach, and the inescapable and automatic nature of its collection, the fact that such information is gathered by a third party does not make it any less deserving of Fourth Amendment protection. The Government's

acquisition of the cell-site records here was a search under that Amendment.[495]

In *United States v. Felton*, the District Court distinguished the *Carpenter* case from *Felton* wherein the government obtained information concerning "content of the communications between [Felton's] IP address and the USPS server and the information obtained from Comcast regarding his IP address" and stated:

> The government argues that even if Felton had standing to challenge the law enforcement activities regarding the searches, these activities do not constitute a search within the meaning of the Fourth Amendment. The government is correct; the IP address and tracking logs obtained from the USPS and Comcast were not owned, nor possessed by Felton. The third-party doctrine partly stems from the notion that an individual has a reduced expectation of privacy in information knowingly shared with another.
>
> "Prior to the digital age, law enforcement might have pursued a suspect for a brief stretch, but doing so "for any extended period of time was difficult and costly and therefore rarely undertaken. For that reason, 'society's expectation has been that law enforcement agents and others would not—and indeed, in the main, simply could not—secretly monitor and catalogue every single movement of an individual's car for a very long period of time." However, the Court in *Carpenter* concluded that because the cell-phone data allowed law enforcement to track Carpenter's every movement and to retrace his whereabouts, it invaded Carpenter's reasonable expectation of privacy in the whole of his physical movements.
>
> Such is not the case here. There is no doubt that the IP address and tracking logs were obtained from a third-party. By identifying Felton as the IP address owner and analyzing the data obtained from the USPS server, the government was able to determine that Felton's IP address requested tracking information, such as the location of the packages and the delivery to their final destination.
>
> This Court finds that first, the third-party doctrine is relevant in part because Felton's use of the IP address is not so closely related to his "home" that the Court can say that there is a privacy interest as to his papers and personal effects. Second, the logs obtained from the USPS do not track Felton's every movement of every day; they only identify the fact that Felton was tracking the packages. The Court further recognizes the very narrow ruling in *Carpenter* and finds that it does not govern this case. Thus, the Court concludes that there was no reasonable expectation of privacy as to the information provided by Comcast (Felton's IP address)

---

[495] Carpenter v. United States, 138 S. Ct. 2206, 2214, 2223(2018).

and the content of the communication between Felton's IP address and the USPS server.[496]

For additional discussion concerning the Fourth Amendment, privacy and new technology, please see Laura K. Donohue, *The Fourth Amendment in the Digital World*, 71 N.Y.U. Ann. Surv. Am. L. 533-685 (2017) ("This Article postulates that four Fourth Amendment dichotomies (private vs. public space; personal vs. third party data; content vs. non-content; and domestic vs. international) are breaking down in light of new and emerging technologies. The distinctions are becoming blurred.") and Rebecca Levin, *"Alexa, can you keep a secret?" An Analysis of 4th Amendment Protection Regarding Smart Home Devices*, Timely Tech, Univ. Ill. J. L. & Pol'y (Feb. 18, 2019), http://illinoisjltp.com/timelytech/alexa-can-you-keep-a-secret-an-analysis-of-4th-amendment-protection-regarding-smart-home-devices/ ("[S]mart home device data also contains this kind of deeply personal information such as what music one listens to and what books and articles they read [and, thus] smart home device information should be afforded the same protection as cell phone location data and the Third-Party Doctrine should also not apply in the case of smart home devices."). While the Supreme Court noted that the holding in *Carpenter* was relatively narrow, it will be interesting to see how Supreme Court jurisprudence continues to evolve in light of the growing ubiquity of the Internet of Things and developing cybersecurity expertise.

11.6 Digital Millennium Copyright Act

The section 1201 of the Digital Millennium Copyright Act (DMCA) does not allow the circumvention of "technological measures that effectively controls access to a [copyrighted] work." The DMCA also prohibits trafficking or importing technology which is used to circumvent technological measures under certain circumstances. Section 1201 is relatively lengthy and contains exemptions for security testing, encryption research and reverse engineering. Moreover, section 1201 includes detailed exemptions for libraries, archives and educational institutions. The following materials explore some of the important parts of Section 1201.

11.6[A] SELECTED PROVISIONS OF THE DIGITAL MILLENNIUM COPYRIGHT ACT

The following contains an edited excerpt of the DMCA section 1201.

17 U.S.C.A. § 1201

§ 1201. Circumvention of copyright protection systems

(a) Violations regarding circumvention of technological measures.–(1)(A) No person shall circumvent a technological measure that effectively controls access to a work protected under this title. The prohibition contained in the preceding sentence shall

---

[496] United States v. Felton, 367 F.Supp.3d 569, 570, 573–575 (W.D. La. 2019).

take effect at the end of the 2-year period beginning on the date of the enactment of this chapter.

. . .

(2) No person shall manufacture, import, offer to the public, provide, or otherwise traffic in any technology, product, service, device, component, or part thereof, that--

    (A) is primarily designed or produced for the purpose of circumventing a technological measure that effectively controls access to a work protected under this title;

    (B) has only limited commercially significant purpose or use other than to circumvent a technological measure that effectively controls access to a work protected under this title; or

    (C) is marketed by that person or another acting in concert with that person with that person's knowledge for use in circumventing a technological measure that effectively controls access to a work protected under this title.

(3) As used in this subsection--

(A) to "circumvent a technological measure" means to descramble a scrambled work, to decrypt an encrypted work, or otherwise to avoid, bypass, remove, deactivate, or impair a technological measure, without the authority of the copyright owner; and

(B) a technological measure "effectively controls access to a work" if the measure, in the ordinary course of its operation, requires the application of information, or a process or a treatment, with the authority of the copyright owner, to gain access to the work.

(b) Additional violations.--(1) No person shall manufacture, import, offer to the public, provide, or otherwise traffic in any technology, product, service, device, component, or part thereof, that--

    (A) is primarily designed or produced for the purpose of circumventing protection afforded by a technological measure that effectively protects a right of a copyright owner under this title in a work or a portion thereof;

    (B) has only limited commercially significant purpose or use other than to circumvent protection afforded by a technological measure that effectively protects a right of a copyright owner under this title in a work or a portion thereof; or

    (C) is marketed by that person or another acting in concert with that person with that person's knowledge for use in circumventing protection afforded by a technological measure that effectively protects a right of a copyright owner under this title in a work or a portion thereof.

(2) As used in this subsection--

(A) to "circumvent protection afforded by a technological measure" means avoiding, bypassing, removing, deactivating, or otherwise impairing a technological measure; and

(B) a technological measure "effectively protects a right of a copyright owner under this title" if the measure, in the ordinary course of its operation, prevents, restricts, or otherwise limits the exercise of a right of a copyright owner under this title.

(c) Other rights, etc., not affected.—(1) Nothing in this section shall affect rights, remedies, limitations, or defenses to copyright infringement, including fair use, under this title.

(2) Nothing in this section shall enlarge or diminish vicarious or contributory liability for copyright infringement in connection with any technology, product, service, device, component, or part thereof.

(3) Nothing in this section shall require that the design of, or design and selection of parts and components for, a consumer electronics, telecommunications, or computing product provide for a response to any particular technological measure, so long as such part or component, or the product in which such part or component is integrated, does not otherwise fall within the prohibitions of subsection (a)(2) or (b)(1).

(4) Nothing in this section shall enlarge or diminish any rights of free speech or the press for activities using consumer electronics, telecommunications, or computing products.

. . .

(e) Law enforcement, intelligence, and other government activities.--This section does not prohibit any lawfully authorized investigative, protective, information security, or intelligence activity of an officer, agent, or employee of the United States, a State, or a political subdivision of a State, or a person acting pursuant to a contract with the United States, a State, or a political subdivision of a State. For purposes of this subsection, the term "information security" means activities carried out in order to identify and address the vulnerabilities of a government computer, computer system, or computer network.

(f) Reverse engineering.—(1) Notwithstanding the provisions of subsection (a)(1)(A), a person who has lawfully obtained the right to use a copy of a computer program may circumvent a technological measure that effectively controls access to a particular portion of that program for the sole purpose of identifying and analyzing those elements of the program that are necessary to achieve interoperability of an independently created computer program with other programs, and that have not previously been readily available to the person engaging in the circumvention, to the extent any such acts of identification and analysis do not constitute infringement under this title.

(2) Notwithstanding the provisions of subsections (a)(2) and (b), a person may develop and employ technological means to circumvent a technological measure, or to circumvent protection afforded by a technological measure, in order to enable the identification and analysis under paragraph (1), or for the purpose of enabling interoperability of an independently created computer program with other programs, if such means are necessary to achieve such interoperability, to the extent that doing so does not constitute infringement under this title.

(3) The information acquired through the acts permitted under paragraph (1), and the means permitted under paragraph (2), may be made available to others if the person referred to in paragraph (1) or (2), as the case may be, provides such information or means solely for the purpose of enabling interoperability of an independently created computer program with other programs, and to the extent that doing so does not constitute infringement under this title or violate applicable law other than this section.

(4) For purposes of this subsection, the term "interoperability" means the ability of computer programs to exchange information, and of such programs mutually to use the information which has been exchanged.

(g) Encryption research.--

(1) **Definitions.**--For purposes of this subsection--

(A) the term "encryption research" means activities necessary to identify and analyze flaws and vulnerabilities of encryption technologies applied to copyrighted works, if these activities are conducted to advance the state of knowledge in the field of encryption technology or to assist in the development of encryption products; and

(B) the term "encryption technology" means the scrambling and descrambling of information using mathematical formulas or algorithms.

(2) **Permissible acts of encryption research.**--Notwithstanding the provisions of subsection (a)(1)(A), it is not a violation of that subsection for a person to circumvent a technological measure as applied to a copy, phonorecord, performance, or display of a published work in the course of an act of good faith encryption research if--

(A) the person lawfully obtained the encrypted copy, phonorecord, performance, or display of the published work;

(B) such act is necessary to conduct such encryption research;

(C) the person made a good faith effort to obtain authorization before the circumvention; and

(D) such act does not constitute infringement under this title or a violation of applicable law other than this section, including section 1030 of title

18 and those provisions of title 18 amended by the Computer Fraud and Abuse Act of 1986.

(3) Factors in determining exemption.--In determining whether a person qualifies for the exemption under paragraph (2), the factors to be considered shall include--

(A) whether the information derived from the encryption research was disseminated, and if so, whether it was disseminated in a manner reasonably calculated to advance the state of knowledge or development of encryption technology, versus whether it was disseminated in a manner that facilitates infringement under this title or a violation of applicable law other than this section, including a violation of privacy or breach of security;

(B) whether the person is engaged in a legitimate course of study, is employed, or is appropriately trained or experienced, in the field of encryption technology; and

(C) whether the person provides the copyright owner of the work to which the technological measure is applied with notice of the findings and documentation of the research, and the time when such notice is provided.

(4) Use of technological means for research activities.--Notwithstanding the provisions of subsection (a)(2), it is not a violation of that subsection for a person to--

(A) develop and employ technological means to circumvent a technological measure for the sole purpose of that person performing the acts of good faith encryption research described in paragraph (2); and

(B) provide the technological means to another person with whom he or she is working collaboratively for the purpose of conducting the acts of good faith encryption research described in paragraph (2) or for the purpose of having that other person verify his or her acts of good faith encryption research described in paragraph (2).

. . .

(i) Protection of personally identifying information.--

(1) Circumvention permitted.--Notwithstanding the provisions of subsection (a)(1)(A), it is not a violation of that subsection for a person to circumvent a technological measure that effectively controls access to a work protected under this title, if--

(A) the technological measure, or the work it protects, contains the capability of collecting or disseminating personally identifying information reflecting the online activities of a natural person who seeks to gain access to the work protected;

(B) in the normal course of its operation, the technological measure, or the work it protects, collects or disseminates personally identifying information about the person who seeks to gain access to the work protected, without providing conspicuous notice of such collection or dissemination to such person, and without providing such person with the capability to prevent or restrict such collection or dissemination;

(C) the act of circumvention has the sole effect of identifying and disabling the capability described in subparagraph (A), and has no other effect on the ability of any person to gain access to any work; and

(D) the act of circumvention is carried out solely for the purpose of preventing the collection or dissemination of personally identifying information about a natural person who seeks to gain access to the work protected, and is not in violation of any other law.

(2) Inapplicability to certain technological measures.--This subsection does not apply to a technological measure, or a work it protects, that does not collect or disseminate personally identifying information and that is disclosed to a user as not having or using such capability.

(j) Security testing.--

(1) Definition.--For purposes of this subsection, the term "security testing" means accessing a computer, computer system, or computer network, solely for the purpose of good faith testing, investigating, or correcting, a security flaw or vulnerability, with the authorization of the owner or operator of such computer, computer system, or computer network.

(2) Permissible acts of security testing.--Notwithstanding the provisions of subsection (a)(1)(A), it is not a violation of that subsection for a person to engage in an act of security testing, if such act does not constitute infringement under this title or a violation of applicable law other than this section, including section 1030 of title 18 and those provisions of title 18 amended by the Computer Fraud and Abuse Act of 1986.

(3) Factors in determining exemption.--In determining whether a person qualifies for the exemption under paragraph (2), the factors to be considered shall include--

(A) whether the information derived from the security testing was used solely to promote the security of the owner or operator of such computer, computer system or computer network, or shared directly with the developer of such computer, computer system, or computer network; and

(B) whether the information derived from the security testing was used or maintained in a manner that does not facilitate infringement under this title or a violation of applicable law other than this section, including a violation of privacy or breach of security.

(4) Use of technological means for security testing.--Notwithstanding the provisions of subsection (a)(2), it is not a violation of that subsection for a person to develop, produce, distribute or employ technological means for the sole purpose of performing the acts of security testing described in subsection (2),[1] provided such technological means does not otherwise violate section[2] (a)(2).

11.6[B] DMCA CASES

MDY Industries v. Blizzard Entertainment, 629 F.3d 928 (9th Cir. 2010).

CALLAHAN, Circuit Judge:

Blizzard Entertainment, Inc. ("Blizzard") is the creator of World of Warcraft ("WoW"), a popular multiplayer online role-playing game in which players interact in a virtual world while advancing through the game's 70 levels. MDY Industries, LLC and its sole member Michael Donnelly ("Donnelly") (sometimes referred to collectively as "MDY") developed and sold Glider, a software program that automatically plays the early levels of WoW for players.

MDY brought this action for a declaratory judgment to establish that its Glider sales do not infringe Blizzard's copyright or other rights, and Blizzard asserted counterclaims under the Digital Millennium Copyright Act ("DMCA"), 17 U.S.C. § 1201 et seq. . . .. The district court found MDY and Donnelly liable for . . . violations of DMCA § 1201(a)(2) and (b)(1). . . . We reverse the district court except as to MDY's liability for violation of DMCA § 1201(a)(2).

I.

A. World of Warcraft

In November 2004, Blizzard created WoW, a "massively multiplayer online role-playing game" in which players interact in a virtual world. WoW has ten million subscribers, of which two and a half million are in North America. The WoW software has two components: (1) the game client software that a player installs on the computer; and (2) the game server software, which the player accesses on a subscription basis by connecting to WoW's online servers. WoW does not have single-player or offline modes.

WoW players roleplay different characters, such as humans, elves, and dwarves. A player's central objective is to advance the character through the game's 70 levels by participating in quests and engaging in battles with monsters. As a player advances, the character collects rewards such as in-game currency, weapons, and armor. WoW's virtual world has its own economy, in which characters use their virtual currency to buy and sell items directly from each other, through vendors, or using auction houses. Some players also utilize WoW's chat capabilities to interact with others.

B. Blizzard's use agreements

Each WoW player must read and accept Blizzard's End User License Agreement ("EULA") and Terms of Use ("ToU") on multiple occasions. The EULA pertains to the game client, so a player agrees to it both before installing the game client and upon first running it. The ToU pertains to the online service, so a player agrees to it both when creating an account and upon first connecting to the online service. Players who do not accept both the EULA and the ToU may return the game client for a refund.

C. Development of Glider and Warden

Donnelly is a WoW player and software programmer. In March 2005, he developed Glider, a software "bot" (short for robot) that automates play of WoW's early levels, for his personal use. A user need not be at the computer while Glider is running. As explained in the Frequently Asked Questions ("FAQ") on MDY's website for Glider:

> Glider ... moves the mouse around and pushes keys on the keyboard. You tell it about your character, where you want to kill things, and when you want to kill. Then it kills for you, automatically. You can do something else, like eat dinner or go to a movie, and when you return, you'll have a lot more experience and loot.

Glider does not alter or copy WoW's game client software, does not allow a player to avoid paying monthly subscription dues to Blizzard, and has no commercial use independent of WoW. Glider was not initially designed to avoid detection by Blizzard.

The parties dispute Glider's impact on the WoW experience. Blizzard contends that Glider disrupts WoW's environment for non-Glider players by enabling Glider users to advance quickly and unfairly through the game and to amass additional game assets. MDY contends that Glider has a minimal effect on non-Glider players, enhances the WoW experience for Glider users, and facilitates disabled players' access to WoW by auto-playing the game for them.

In summer 2005, Donnelly began selling Glider through MDY's website for fifteen to twenty-five dollars per license. Prior to marketing Glider, Donnelly reviewed Blizzard's EULA and client-server manipulation policy. He reached the conclusion that Blizzard had not prohibited bots in those documents.

In September 2005, Blizzard launched Warden, a technology that it developed to prevent its players who use unauthorized third-party software, including bots, from connecting to WoW's servers. Warden was able to detect Glider, and Blizzard immediately used Warden to ban most Glider users. MDY responded by modifying Glider to avoid detection and promoting its new anti-detection features on its website's FAQ. It added a subscription service, Glider Elite, which offered "additional protection from game detection software" for five dollars a month.

Thus, by late 2005, MDY was aware that Blizzard was prohibiting bots. MDY modified its website to indicate that using Glider violated Blizzard's ToU. In November 2005, Donnelly wrote in an email interview, "Avoiding detection is rather exciting, to be sure. Since Blizzard does not want bots running at all, it's a violation to use them." Following MDY's anti-detection modifications, Warden only occasionally detected Glider. As of September 2008, MDY had gross revenues of $3.5 million based on 120,000 Glider license sales.

D. Financial and practical impact of Glider

Blizzard claims that from December 2004 to March 2008, it received 465,000 complaints about WoW bots, several thousand of which named Glider. Blizzard spends $940,000 annually to respond to these complaints, and the parties have stipulated that Glider is the principal bot used by WoW players. Blizzard introduced evidence that it may have lost monthly subscription fees from Glider users, who were able to reach WoW's highest levels in fewer weeks than players playing manually. Donnelly acknowledged in a November 2005 email that MDY's business strategy was to make Blizzard's anti-bot detection attempts financially prohibitive:

The trick here is that Blizzard has a finite amount of development and test resources, so we want to make it bad business to spend that much time altering their detection code to find Glider, since Glider's negative effect on the game is debatable.... [W]e attack th[is] weakness and try to make it a bad idea or make their changes very risky, since they don't want to risk banning or crashing innocent customers.

E. Pre-litigation contact between MDY and Blizzard

In August 2006, Blizzard sent MDY a cease-and-desist letter alleging that MDY's website hosted WoW screenshots and a Glider install file, all of which infringed Blizzard's copyrights. Donnelly removed the screenshots and requested Blizzard to clarify why the install file was infringing, but Blizzard did not respond. In October 2006, Blizzard's counsel visited Donnelly's home, threatening suit unless MDY immediately ceased selling Glider and remitted all profits to Blizzard. MDY immediately commenced this action.

II.

. . . After a January 2009 bench trial, the district court held MDY liable under DMCA § 1201(a)(2) and (b)(1). . . . On May 12, 2009, Blizzard timely cross-appealed the district court's holding that MDY did not violate DMCA § 1201(a)(2) and (b)(1) as to the game software's source code.

. . .

V.

After MDY began selling Glider, Blizzard launched Warden, its technology designed to prevent players who used bots from connecting to the WoW servers. Blizzard used Warden to ban most Glider users in September 2005. Blizzard claims that MDY is liable under DMCA § 1201(a)(2) and (b)(1) because it thereafter programmed Glider to avoid detection by Warden.

A. The Warden technology

Warden has two components. The first is a software module called "scan.dll," which scans a computer's RAM prior to allowing the player to connect to WoW's servers. If scan.dll detects that a bot is running, such as Glider, it will not allow the player to connect and play. After Blizzard launched Warden, MDY reconfigured Glider to circumvent scan.dll by not loading itself until after scan.dll completed its check. Warden's second component is a "resident" component that runs periodically in the background on a player's computer when it is connected to WoW's servers. It asks the computer to report portions of the WoW code running in RAM, and it looks for patterns of code associated with known bots or cheats. If it detects a bot or cheat, it boots the player from the game, which halts the computer's copying of copyrighted code into RAM.

B. The Digital Millennium Copyright Act

Congress enacted the DMCA in 1998 to conform United States copyright law to its obligations under two World Intellectual Property Organization ("WIPO") treaties, which require contracting parties to provide effective legal remedies against the circumvention of protective technological measures used by copyright owners. See Universal City Studios, Inc. v. Corley, 273 F.3d 429, 440 (2d Cir.2001). In enacting the DMCA, Congress sought to mitigate the problems presented by copyright enforcement in the digital age. Id. The DMCA contains three provisions directed at the circumvention of copyright owners' technological measures. The Supreme Court has yet to construe these provisions, and they raise questions of first impression in this circuit.

The first provision, 17 U.S.C. § 1201(a)(1)(A), is a general prohibition against "circumventing a technological measure that effectively controls access to a work protected under [the Copyright Act]." The second prohibits trafficking in technology that circumvents a technological measure that "effectively controls access" to a copyrighted work. 17 U.S.C. § 1201(a)(2). The third prohibits trafficking in technology that circumvents a technological measure that "effectively protects" a copyright owner's right. 17 U.S.C. § 1201(b)(1). . . .

We turn to consider whether Glider violates DMCA § 1201(a)(2) and (b)(1) by allowing users to circumvent Warden to access WoW's various elements. MDY contends that Warden's scan.dll and resident components are separate, and only scan.dll should be considered as a potential access control measure under § 1201(a)(2). However, in our view, an access control measure can both (1) attempt to block initial access and (2) revoke access if a secondary check determines that access was unauthorized. Our analysis considers Warden's scan.dll and resident components together because the two components have the same purpose: to prevent players using detectable bots from continuing to access WoW software.

D. Construction of § 1201

One of the issues raised by this appeal is whether certain provisions of § 1201 prohibit circumvention of access controls when access does not constitute copyright infringement. To answer this question and others presented by this appeal, we address the nature and interrelationship of the various provisions of § 1201 in the overall context of the Copyright Act.

We begin by considering the scope of DMCA § 1201's three operative provisions, §§ 1201(a)(1), 1201(a)(2), and 1201(b)(1). We consider them side-by-side, because "[w]e do not ... construe statutory phrases in isolation; we read statutes as a whole. Thus, the [term to be construed] must be read in light of the immediately following phrase...."

1. Text of the operative provisions

"We begin, as always, with the text of the statute." Section 1201(a)(1)(A) prohibits "circumvent[ing] a technological measure that effectively controls access to a work protected under this title." . . . .

2. Our harmonization of the DMCA's operative provisions

For the reasons set forth below, we believe that § 1201 is best understood to create two distinct types of claims. First, § 1201(a) prohibits the circumvention of any technological measure that effectively controls access to a protected work and grants copyright owners the right to enforce that prohibition. Cf. Corley, 273 F.3d at 441 ("[T]he focus of subsection 1201(a)(2) is circumvention of technologies designed to prevent access to a work"). Second, and in contrast to § 1201(a), § 1201(b)(1) prohibits trafficking in technologies that circumvent technological measures that effectively protect "a right of a copyright owner." Section 1201(b)(1)'s prohibition is thus aimed at circumventions of measures that protect the copyright itself: it entitles copyright owners to protect their existing exclusive rights under the Copyright Act. Those exclusive rights are reproduction, distribution, public performance, public display, and creation of derivative works. 17 U.S.C. § 106. Historically speaking, preventing "access" to a protected work in itself has not been a right of a copyright owner arising from the Copyright Act.

Our construction of § 1201 is compelled by the four significant textual differences between § 1201(a) and (b). First, § 1201(a)(2) prohibits the circumvention of a measure that "effectively controls access to a work protected under this title," whereas § 1201(b)(1) concerns a measure that "effectively protects a right of a copyright owner under this title in a work or portion thereof." (emphasis added). We read § 1201(b)(1)'s language—"right of a copyright owner under this title"—to reinforce copyright owners' traditional exclusive rights under § 106 by granting them an additional cause of action against those who traffic in circumventing devices that facilitate infringement. Sections 1201(a)(1) and (a)(2), however, use the term "work protected under this title." Neither of these two subsections explicitly refers to traditional copyright infringement under § 106. Accordingly, we read this term as extending a new form of protection, i.e., the right to prevent circumvention of access controls, broadly to works protected under Title 17, i.e., copyrighted works.

Second, as used in § 1201(a), to "circumvent a technological measure" means "to descramble a scrambled work, to decrypt an encrypted work, or otherwise to avoid, bypass, remove, deactivate, or impair a technological measure, without the authority of the copyright owner." 17 U.S.C. § 1201(a)(3)(A). These two specific examples of unlawful circumvention under § 1201(a)—descrambling a scrambled work and decrypting an encrypted work—are acts that do not necessarily infringe or facilitate infringement of a copyright. Descrambling or decrypting only enables someone to watch or listen to a work without authorization, which is not necessarily an infringement of a copyright owner's traditional exclusive rights under § 106. Put differently, descrambling and decrypting do not necessarily result in someone's reproducing, distributing, publicly performing, or publicly displaying the copyrighted work, or creating derivative works based on the copyrighted work.

The third significant difference between the subsections is that § 1201(a)(1)(A) prohibits circumventing an effective access control measure, whereas § 1201(b) prohibits trafficking in circumventing devices, but does not prohibit circumvention itself because such conduct was already outlawed as copyright infringement. The Senate Judiciary Committee explained:

> This ... is the reason there is no prohibition on conduct in 1201(b) akin to the prohibition on circumvention conduct in 1201(a)(1). The prohibition in 1201(a)(1) is necessary because prior to this Act, the conduct of circumvention was never before made unlawful. The device limitation on 1201(a)(2) enforces this new prohibition on conduct. The copyright law has long forbidden copyright infringements, so no new prohibition was necessary.

S.Rep. No. 105–90, at 11 (1998). This difference reinforces our reading of § 1201(b) as strengthening copyright owners' traditional rights against copyright infringement and of § 1201(a) as granting copyright owners a new anti-circumvention right.

Fourth, in § 1201(a)(1)(B)–(D), Congress directs the Library of Congress ("Library") to identify classes of copyrighted works for which "noninfringing uses by persons who are users of a copyrighted work are, or are likely to be, adversely affected, and the [anti-circumvention] prohibition contained in [§ 1201(a)(1)(A)] shall not apply to such users with respect to such classes of works for the ensuing 3–year period." There is no analogous provision in § 1201(b). We impute this lack of symmetry to Congress' need to balance copyright owners' new anti-circumvention right with the public's right to access the work. Cf. H.R.Rep. No. 105–551, pt. 2, at 26 (1998) (specifying that the House Commerce Committee "endeavored to specify, with as much clarity as possible, how the right against anti-circumvention (sic) would be qualified to maintain balance between the interests of content creators and information users."). Sections

1201(a)(1)(B)–(D) thus promote the public's right to access by allowing the Library to exempt circumvention of effective access control measures in particular situations where it concludes that the public's right to access outweighs the owner's interest in restricting access. In limiting the owner's right to control access, the Library does not, and is not permitted to, authorize infringement of a copyright owner's traditional exclusive rights under the copyright. Rather, the Library is only entitled to moderate the new anti-circumvention right created by, and hence subject to the limitations in, DMCA § 1201(a)(1).

Our reading of § 1201(a) and (b) ensures that neither section is rendered superfluous. A violation of § 1201(a)(1)(A), which prohibits circumvention itself, will not be a violation of § 1201(b), which does not contain an analogous prohibition on circumvention. A violation of § 1201(a)(2), which prohibits trafficking in devices that facilitate circumvention of access control measures, will not always be a violation of § 1201(b)(1), which prohibits trafficking in devices that facilitate circumvention of measures that protect against copyright infringement. Of course, if a copyright owner puts in place an effective measure that both (1) controls access and (2) protects against copyright infringement, a defendant who traffics in a device that circumvents that measure could be liable under both § 1201(a) and (b). Nonetheless, we read the differences in structure between § 1201(a) and (b) as reflecting Congress's intent to address distinct concerns by creating different rights with different elements.

3. Our construction of the DMCA is consistent with the legislative history

Although the text suffices to resolve the issues before us, we also consider the legislative history in order to address the parties' arguments concerning it. Our review of that history supports the view that Congress created a new anticircumvention right in § 1201(a)(2) independent of traditional copyright infringement and granted copyright owners a new weapon against copyright infringement in § 1201(b)(1). For instance, the Senate Judiciary Committee report explains that § 1201(a)(2) and (b)(1) are "not interchangeable": they were "designed to protect two distinct rights and to target two distinct classes of devices," and "many devices will be subject to challenge only under one of the subsections." S.Rep. No. 105–190, at 12 (1998). That is, § 1201(a)(2) "is designed to protect access to a copyrighted work," while § 1201(b)(1) "is designed to protect the traditional copyright rights of the copyright owner." Thus, the Senate Judiciary Committee understood § 1201 to create the following regime:

> [I]f an effective technological protection measure does nothing to prevent access to the plain text of the work, but is designed to prevent that work from being copied, then a potential cause of action against the manufacturer of a device designed to circumvent the measure lies under § 1201(b)(1), but not under § 1201(a)(2). Conversely, if an effective technological protection measure limits access to the plain text of a work only to those with authorized access, but provides no additional protection against copying, displaying, performing or distributing the work, then a

potential cause of action against the manufacturer of a device designed to circumvent the measure lies under § 1201(a)(2), but not under § 1201(b).

Id. The Senate Judiciary Committee proffered an example of § 1201(a) liability with no nexus to infringement, stating that if an owner effectively protected access to a copyrighted work by use of a password, it would violate § 1201(a)(2)(A)

> [T]o defeat or bypass the password and to make the means to do so, as long as the primary purpose of the means was to perform this kind of act. This is roughly analogous to making it illegal to break into a house using a tool, the primary purpose of which is to break into houses.

Id. at 12. The House Judiciary Committee similarly states of § 1201(a)(2), "The act of circumventing a technological protection measure put in place by a copyright owner to control access to a copyrighted work is the electronic equivalent of breaking into a locked room in order to obtain a copy of a book." See H.R.Rep. No. 105–551, pt. 1, at 17 (1998). We note that bypassing a password and breaking into a locked room in order to read or view a copyrighted work would not infringe on any of the copyright owner's exclusive rights under § 106.

We read this legislative history as confirming Congress's intent, in light of the current digital age, to grant copyright owners an independent right to enforce the prohibition against circumvention of effective technological access controls.9 In § 1201(a), Congress was particularly concerned with encouraging copyright owners to make their works available in digital formats such as "on-demand" or "pay-per-view," which allow consumers effectively to "borrow" a copy of the work for a limited time or a limited number of uses. As the House Commerce Committee explained:

> [A]n increasing number of intellectual property works are being distributed using a "client-server" model, where the work is effectively "borrowed" by the user (e.g., infrequent users of expensive software purchase a certain number of uses, or viewers watch a movie on a pay-per-view basis). To operate in this environment, content providers will need both the technology to make new uses possible and the legal framework to ensure they can protect their work from piracy.

See H.R.Rep. No. 105–551 pt. 2, at 23 (1998).

Our review of the legislative history supports our reading of § 1201: that section (a) creates a new anticircumvention right distinct from copyright infringement, while section (b) strengthens the traditional prohibition against copyright infringement.10 We now review the decisions of the Federal Circuit that have interpreted § 1201 differently.

4. The Federal Circuit's decisions

The Federal Circuit has adopted a different approach to the DMCA. In essence, it requires § 1201(a) plaintiffs to demonstrate that the circumventing technology infringes or facilitates infringement of the plaintiff's copyright (an "infringement nexus requirement"). See Chamberlain Group, Inc. v. Skylink Techs., Inc., 381 F.3d 1178, 1203 (Fed.Cir.2004).

The seminal decision is Chamberlain, 381 F.3d 1178 (Fed.Cir.2004). In Chamberlain, the plaintiff sold garage door openers ("GDOs") with a "rolling code" security system that purportedly reduced the risk of crime by constantly changing the transmitter signal necessary to open the door. Id. at 1183. Customers used the GDOs' transmitters to send the changing signal, which in turn opened or closed their garage doors. Id.

Plaintiff sued the defendant, who sold "universal" GDO transmitters for use with plaintiff's GDOs, under § 1201(a)(2). The plaintiff alleged that its GDOs and transmitters both contained copyrighted computer programs and that its rolling code security system was a technological measure that controlled access to those programs. Accordingly, plaintiff alleged that the defendant—by selling GDO transmitters that were compatible with plaintiff's GDOs—had trafficked in a technology that was primarily used for the circumvention of a technological measure (the rolling code security system) that effectively controlled access to plaintiff's copyrighted works.

The Federal Circuit rejected the plaintiff's claim, holding that the defendant did not violate § 1201(a)(2) because, inter alia, the defendant's universal GDO transmitters did not infringe or facilitate infringement of the plaintiff's copyrighted computer programs. The linchpin of the Chamberlain court's analysis is its conclusion that DMCA coverage is limited to a copyright owner's rights under the Copyright Act as set forth in § 106 of the Copyright Act. Id. at 1192–93. Thus, it held that § 1201(a) did not grant copyright owners a new anti-circumvention right, but instead, established new causes of action for a defendant's unauthorized access of copyrighted material when it infringes upon a copyright owner's rights under § 106. Id. at 1192, 1194. Accordingly, a § 1201(a)(2) plaintiff was required to demonstrate a nexus to infringement—i.e., that the defendant's trafficking in circumventing technology had a "reasonable relationship" to the protections that the Copyright Act affords copyright owners. Id. at 1202–03. The Federal Circuit explained:

> Defendants who traffic in devices that circumvent access controls in ways that facilitate infringement may be subject to liability under § 1201(a)(2). Defendants who use such devices may be subject to liability under § 1201(a)(1) whether they infringe or not. Because all defendants who traffic in devices that circumvent rights controls necessarily facilitate infringement, they may be subject to liability under § 1201(b). Defendants who use such devices may be subject to liability for copyright infringement. And finally, defendants whose circumvention devices do not facilitate infringement are not subject to § 1201 liability.

Id. at 1195 (emphasis added). Chamberlain concluded that § 1201(a) created a new cause of action linked to copyright infringement, rather than a new anti-circumvention right separate from copyright infringement, for six reasons.

First, Chamberlain reasoned that Congress enacted the DMCA to balance the interests of copyright owners and information users, and an infringement nexus requirement was necessary to create an anti-circumvention right that truly achieved that balance. Second, Chamberlain feared that copyright owners could use an access control right to prohibit exclusively fair uses of their material even absent feared foul use. Id. at 1201. Third, Chamberlain feared that § 1201(a) would allow companies to leverage their sales into aftermarket monopolies, in potential violation of antitrust law and the doctrine of copyright misuse. Id. (citing Eastman Kodak Co. v. Image Tech. Servs., 504 U.S. 451, 455, 112 S.Ct. 2072, 119 L.Ed.2d 265 (1992) (antitrust); Assessment Techs. of WI, LLC v. WIREdata, Inc., 350 F.3d 640, 647 (7th Cir.2003) (copyright misuse)). Fourth, Chamberlain viewed an infringement nexus requirement as necessary to prevent "absurd and disastrous results," such as the existence of DMCA liability for disabling a burglary alarm to gain access to a home containing copyrighted materials.

Fifth, Chamberlain stated that an infringement nexus requirement might be necessary to render Congress's exercise of its Copyright Clause authority rational. Id. at 1200. The Copyright Clause gives Congress "the task of defining the scope of the limited monopoly that should be granted to authors ... in order to give the public appropriate access to their work product." Id. (citing Eldred v. Ashcroft, 537 U.S. 186, 204–05, 123 S.Ct. 769, 154 L.Ed.2d 683 (2003)). Without an infringement nexus requirement, Congress arguably would have allowed copyright owners in § 1201(a) to deny all access to the public by putting an effective access control measure in place that the public was not allowed to circumvent.

Finally, the Chamberlain court viewed an infringement nexus requirement as necessary for the Copyright Act to be internally consistent. It reasoned that § 1201(c)(1), enacted simultaneously, provides that "nothing in this section shall affect rights, remedies, limitations, or defenses to copyright infringement, including fair use, under this title." The Chamberlain court opined that if § 1201(a) creates liability for access without regard to the remainder of the Copyright Act, it "would clearly affect rights and limitations, if not remedies and defenses."

Accordingly, the Federal Circuit held that a DMCA § 1201(a)(2) action was foreclosed to the extent that the defendant trafficked in a device that did not facilitate copyright infringement.

5. We decline to adopt an infringement nexus requirement

While we appreciate the policy considerations expressed by the Federal Circuit in Chamberlain, we are unable to follow its approach because it is contrary to the plain language of the statute. In addition, the Federal Circuit failed to recognize the rationale for the statutory construction that we have proffered. Also, its approach is based on policy concerns that are best directed to Congress in the first instance, or for which there appear to be other reasons that do not require such a convoluted construction of the statute's language.

i. Statutory inconsistencies

Were we to follow Chamberlain in imposing an infringement nexus requirement, we would have to disregard the plain language of the statute. Moreover, there is significant textual evidence showing Congress's intent to create a new anticircumvention right in § 1201(a) distinct from infringement. As set forth supra, this evidence includes: (1) Congress's choice to link only § 1201(b)(1) explicitly to infringement; (2) Congress's provision in § 1201(a)(3)(A) that descrambling and decrypting devices can lead to § 1201(a) liability, even though descrambling and decrypting devices may only enable non-infringing access to a copyrighted work; and (3) Congress's creation of a mechanism in § 1201(a)(1)(B)–(D) to exempt certain non-infringing behavior from § 1201(a)(1) liability, a mechanism that would be unnecessary if an infringement nexus requirement existed.

Though unnecessary to our conclusion because of the clarity of the statute's text, we also note that the legislative history supports the conclusion that Congress intended to prohibit even non-infringing circumvention and trafficking in circumventing devices. Moreover, in mandating a § 1201(a) nexus to infringement, we would deprive copyright owners of the important enforcement tool that Congress granted them to make sure that they are compensated for valuable non-infringing access—for instance, copyright owners who make movies or music available online, protected by an access control measure, in exchange for direct or indirect payment.

The Chamberlain court reasoned that if § 1201(a) creates liability for access without regard to the remainder of the Copyright Act, it "would clearly affect rights and limitations, if not remedies and defenses." This perceived tension is relieved by our recognition that § 1201(a) creates a new anti-circumvention right distinct from the traditional exclusive rights of a copyright owner. It follows that § 1201(a) does not limit the traditional framework of exclusive rights created by § 106, or defenses to those rights such as fair use. We are thus unpersuaded by Chamberlain's reading of the DMCA's text and structure.

ii. Additional interpretive considerations

Though we need no further evidence of Congress's intent, the parties, citing Chamberlain, proffer several other arguments, which we review briefly in order to address the parties' contentions. Chamberlain relied heavily on policy considerations to support its reading of § 1201(a). As a threshold matter, we stress that such considerations cannot trump the statute's plain text and structure. Even were they permissible considerations in this case, however, they would not persuade us to adopt an infringement nexus requirement. Chamberlain feared that § 1201(a) would allow companies to leverage their sales into aftermarket monopolies, in tension with antitrust law and the doctrine of copyright misuse. Concerning antitrust law, we note that there is no clear issue of anti-competitive behavior in this case because Blizzard does not seek to put a direct competitor who offers a competing role-playing game out of business and the parties have not argued this issue. If a § 1201(a)(2) defendant in a future case claims that a plaintiff is attempting to enforce its DMCA anti-circumvention right in a manner that violates antitrust law, we will then consider the interplay between this new anti-circumvention right and antitrust law.

Chamberlain also viewed an infringement nexus requirement as necessary to prevent "absurd and disastrous results," such as the existence of DMCA liability for disabling a burglary alarm to gain access to a home containing copyrighted materials. In addition, the Federal Circuit was concerned that, without an infringement nexus requirement, § 1201(a) would allow copyright owners to deny all access to the public by putting an effective access control measure in place that the public is not allowed to circumvent. Both concerns appear to be overstated, but even accepting them, arguendo, as legitimate concerns, they do not permit reading the statute as requiring the imposition of an infringement nexus. As § 1201(a) creates a distinct right, it does not disturb the balance between public rights and the traditional rights of owners of copyright under the Copyright Act. Moreover, § 1201(a)(1)(B)–(D) allows the Library of Congress to create exceptions to the § 1201(a) anticircumvention right in the public's interest. If greater protection of the public's ability to access copyrighted works is required, Congress can provide such protection by amending the statute.

In sum, we conclude that a fair reading of the statute (supported by legislative history) indicates that Congress created a distinct anti-circumvention right under § 1201(a) without an infringement nexus requirement. Thus, even accepting the validity of the concerns expressed in Chamberlain, those concerns do not authorize us to override congressional intent and add a non-textual element to the statute. See In Re Dumont, 581 F.3d 1104, 1111 (9th Cir.2009) ("[W]here the language of an enactment is clear or, in modern parlance, plain, and construction according to its terms does not lead to absurd or impracticable consequences, the words employed are to be taken as the final expression of the meaning intended."). Accordingly, we reject the imposition of an infringement nexus requirement. We now consider whether MDY has violated § 1201(a)(2) and (b)(1).

E. Blizzard's § 1201(a)(2) claim

1. WoW's literal elements and individual non-literal elements

We agree with the district court that MDY's Glider does not violate DMCA § 1201(a)(2) with respect to WoW's literal elements and individual non-literal elements, because Warden does not effectively control access to these WoW elements. First, Warden does not control access to WoW's literal elements because these elements—the game client's software code—are available on a player's hard drive once the game client software is installed. Second, as the district court found:

> [WoW's] individual nonliteral components may be accessed by a user without signing on to the server. As was demonstrated during trial, an

owner of the game client software may use independently purchased computer programs to call up the visual images or the recorded sounds within the game client software. For instance, a user may call up and listen to the roar a particular monster makes within the game. Or the user may call up a virtual image of that monster.

Since a player need not encounter Warden to access WoW's individual non-literal elements, Warden does not effectively control access to those elements.

Our conclusion is in accord with the Sixth Circuit's decision in Lexmark International v. Static Control Components, 387 F.3d 522 (6th Cir.2004). In Lexmark, the plaintiff sold laser printers equipped with an authentication sequence, verified by the printer's copyrighted software, that ensured that only plaintiff's own toner cartridges could be inserted into the printers. Id. at 530. The defendant sold microchips capable of generating an authentication sequence that rendered other manufacturers' cartridges compatible with plaintiff's printers.

The Sixth Circuit held that plaintiff's § 1201(a)(2) claim failed because its authentication sequence did not effectively control access to its copyrighted computer program. Rather, the mere purchase of one of plaintiff's printers allowed "access" to the copyrighted program. Any purchaser could read the program code directly from the printer memory without encountering the authentication sequence. Id. The authentication sequence thus blocked only one form of access: the ability to make use of the printer. However, it left intact another form of access: the review and use of the computer program's literal code. Id. The Sixth Circuit explained:

> Just as one would not say that a lock on the back door of a house "controls access" to a house whose front door does not contain a lock and just as one would not say that a lock on any door of a house "controls access" to the house after its purchaser receives the key to the lock, it does not make sense to say that this provision of the DMCA applies to otherwise-readily-accessible copyrighted works. Add to this the fact that the DMCA not only requires the technological measure to "control access" but requires the measure to control that access "effectively," 17 U.S.C. § 1201(a)(2), and it seems clear that this provision does not naturally extend to a technological measure that restricts one form of access but leaves another route wide open.

Id. at 547.

Here, a player's purchase of the WoW game client allows access to the game's literal elements and individual non-literal elements. Warden blocks one form of access to these elements: the ability to access them while connected to a WoW server. However, analogously to the situation in Lexmark, Warden leaves open the ability to access these elements directly via the user's computer. We conclude that Warden is not an effective access control measure with respect to WoW's literal elements and individual non-literal elements, and therefore, that MDY does not violate § 1201(a)(2) with respect to these elements.

2. WoW's dynamic non-literal elements

We conclude that MDY meets each of the six textual elements for violating § 1201(a)(2) with respect to WoW's dynamic non-literal elements. That is, MDY (1) traffics in (2) a technology or part thereof (3) that is primarily designed, produced, or marketed for, or has limited commercially significant use other than (4) circumventing a technological measure (5) that effectively controls access (6) to a copyrighted work. See 17 U.S.C. § 1201(a)(2).

The first two elements are met because MDY "traffics in a technology or part thereof"—that is, it sells Glider. The third and fourth elements are met because Blizzard has established that MDY markets Glider for use in circumventing Warden, thus satisfying the requirement of § 1201(a)(2)(C).16 Indeed, Glider has no function other than to facilitate the playing of WoW. The sixth element is met because, as the district court held, WoW's dynamic non-literal elements constitute a copyrighted work. See, e.g., Atari Games Corp. v. Oman, 888 F.2d 878, 884–85 (D.C.Cir.1989) (the audiovisual display of a computer game is copyrightable independently from the software program code, even though the audiovisual display generated is partially dependent on user input).

The fifth element is met because Warden is an effective access control measure. To "effectively control access to a work," a technological measure must "in the ordinary course of its operation, require[ ] the application of information, or a process or a treatment, with the authority of the copyright owner, to gain access to the work." 17 U.S.C. § 1201(a)(3)(B). Both of Warden's two components "require[ ] the application of information, or a process or a treatment ... to gain access to the work." For a player to connect to Blizzard's servers which provide access to WoW's dynamic non-literal elements, scan.dll must scan the player's computer RAM and confirm the absence of any bots or cheats. The resident component also requires a "process" in order for the user to continue accessing the work: the user's computer must report portions of WoW code running in RAM to the server. Moreover, Warden's provisions were put into place by Blizzard, and thus, function "with the authority of the copyright owner." Accordingly, Warden effectively controls access to WoW's dynamic non-literal elements. We hold that MDY is liable under § 1201(a)(2) with respect to WoW's dynamic non-literal elements. Accordingly, we affirm the district court's entry of a permanent injunction against MDY to prevent future § 1201(a)(2) violations.

F. Blizzard's § 1201(b)(1) claim

Blizzard may prevail under § 1201(b)(1) only if Warden "effectively protect[s] a right" of Blizzard under the Copyright Act. Blizzard contends that Warden protects its reproduction right against unauthorized copying. We disagree.

First, although WoW players copy the software code into RAM while playing the game, Blizzard's EULA and ToU authorize all licensed WoW players to do so. We have explained that ToU § 4(B)'s bot prohibition is a license covenant rather than a condition. Thus, a Glider user who violates this covenant does not infringe by continuing to copy code into RAM. Accordingly, MDY does not violate § 1201(b)(1) by enabling Glider users to avoid Warden's interruption of their authorized copying into RAM.

Second, although WoW players can theoretically record game play by taking screen shots, there is no evidence that Warden detects or prevents such allegedly infringing copying. This is logical, because Warden was designed to reduce the presence of cheats and bots, not to protect WoW's dynamic non-literal elements against copying. We conclude that Warden does not effectively protect any of Blizzard's rights under the Copyright Act, and MDY is not liable under § 1201(b)(1) for Glider's circumvention of Warden. . . .

We vacate the district court's decision because we determine that MDY . . . is liable under the DMCA only for violation of § 1201(a)(2) with respect to WoW's dynamic non-literal elements. . . .

Each side shall bear its own costs.

Philips North America v. Summit Imaging, 2020 WL 1515624 (W.D. Wash. 2020).

JAMES L. ROBART, United States District Judge

I. INTRODUCTION

Before the court is Defendants Summit Imaging Inc. ("Summit") and Lawrence R. Nguyen (collectively, "Defendants") Federal Rule of Civil Procedure 12(b)(6) motion to dismiss. Plaintiffs Philips North America LLC, Koninklijke Philips N.V., and Philips India Ltd. (collectively, "Philips") oppose the motion. . . . [T]he court GRANTS in part and DENIES in part Defendants' motion to dismiss.

II. BACKGROUND

Philips manufactures, sells, and services medical imaging systems—including ultrasound systems, computed tomography scanners, positron emission tomography scanners, X-ray machines, magnetic resonance scanners, and nuclear medicine scanners—for hospitals and medical centers. The vast majority of the allegations in the complaint relate to Philips' ultrasound imaging devices. Philips sells and services ultrasound imaging devices under the "CX," "HD," "ClearVue," "Sparq," "VISIQ," "Xperius," "Affiniti," and "EPIQ" brand names (collectively, the "Ultrasound Systems"). In addition to the Ultrasound Systems, Philips manufactures and sells related ultrasound hardware devices. The Ultrasound Systems are driven by one of two software platforms that Philips developed and owns: (1) Philips Voyager Platform and (2) Philips Common Platform.

Each Ultrasound System Philips sells includes certain software and hardware features that may only be used when Philips enables a particular licensable feature for the specific Ultrasound System. For each Ultrasound System, Philips enables only the licensed features and tools that their customers purchased for that specific system, and only the specific authorized users of the machine can access the enabled features and software options. Philips has registered the copyright in the software for the different Ultrasound Systems they sell, and allege that they "use[] multiple layers of technological controls to protect" their copyrighted works from unauthorized access. Philips alleges that their software and access control systems are trade secrets and that those systems contain other trade secret information.

Philips alleges that Summit hacks into Philips' software and alters the Ultrasound Systems using a program Summit developed called Adepto in order to enable features or options for which Philips' customers have not paid Philips. Philips claims that Summit trains its customers on how to circumvent Philips' access controls. Summit allegedly advertises that its Adepto tool is a "legal solution" or a "legal alternative" to working with Philips in order to enable additional features and options. Mr. Nguyen is the "principal owner, Governor, Chief Executive Officer, and Chief Technology Officer of Summit." Philips alleges that Mr. Nguyen designed, directed, and carried out Summit's hacking scheme.

Philips brings seven causes of action against Defendants: (1) circumventing a technological measure in violation of the Digital Millennium Copyright Act ("DMCA"), 17 U.S.C. § 1201; (2) modifying copyright management information ("CMI") in violation of the DMCA, 17 U.S.C. § 1202; (3) trade secret misappropriation in violation of the Defend Trade Secrets Act ("DTSA"), 18 U.S.C. § 1836; (4) trade secret misappropriation in violation of the Washington Uniform Trade Secrets Act ("UTSA"), RCW ch. 19.108; . . . and (7) copyright infringement in violation of the Copyright Act, 17 U.S.C. §§ 101, 501.

III. ANALYSIS

Pursuant to Rule 12(b)(6), Defendants move to dismiss the following claims for failure to state a claim: Philips' DMCA claims, DTSA claim, UTSA claim, false advertising claim, CPA claim, and any portion of their copyright infringement claim that alleges contributory copyright infringement. The court sets forth the applicable legal standard before addressing Philips' causes of action in turn.

. . .

B. Summit's Motion to Dismiss

1. Circumventing a Technological Measure

Defendants argue that Philips' claim for circumventing a technological measure in violation of the DMCA, 17 U.S.C. § 1201 should be dismissed because Philips failed to "allege sufficient facts supporting that a technological measure that effectively controls access to a copyrighted work has been circumvented." (*See* Mot. at 13.) The Ninth Circuit explains that § 1201 of the DMCA sets forth "two distinct types of claims." *MDY Indus., LLC v. Blizzard Entm't, Inc.*, 629 F.3d 928, 944 (9th Cir. 2010); *see also* 17 U.S.C. § 1201. "First, § 1201(a) prohibits the circumvention of any technological measure that effectively controls access to a protected work and grants copyright owners the right to enforce that prohibition." *Id.* Section 1201(a)(1)(A) contains a general prohibition against "circumventing a technological measure that effectively controls access to a work protected under [the Copyright Act]," *see* 17 U.S.C. § 1201(a)(1)(A), while § 1201(a)(2) prohibits trafficking in technology that circumvents a technological measure that "effectively controls access" to a copyrighted work, *see* 17 U.S.C. § 1201(a)(2). "Second, and in contrast to § 1201(a), § 1201(b)(1) prohibits trafficking in technologies that circumvent technological measures that effectively protect 'a right of a copyright owner.' " *MDY Indus., LLC*, 629 F.3d at 944 (quoting 17 U.S.C. § 1201(b)(1)). In other words, § 1201(a) is focused on prohibiting "circumvention of technologies designed to prevent access to a work" while § 1201(b) "prohibits trafficking in devices that facilitate circumvention of measures that protect against copyright infringement." *See id.* at 944, 946 (citations omitted). Although Philips' response to Defendants' motion fails to explicitly state whether Philips' first cause of action alleges a § 1201(a) claim, a § 1201(b) claim, or both (*see, e.g.*, Resp. at 8 (concluding that "the [complaint] provides Defendants with sufficient notice of facts supporting Plaintiffs' DMCA Section 1201 claims" without detailing what subsection of § 1201 those claims are filed under)), the complaint appears to plead claims under both § 1201(a)(1) and (a)(2).

Philips has sufficiently pleaded that their Ultrasound Systems are protected by "a technological measure that effectively controls access to a work" under §§ 1201(a)(1) and (a)(2). Under § 1201(a), "a technological measure 'effectively controls access to a work' if the measure, in the ordinary course of its operation, requires the application of information, or a process or a treatment, with the authority of the copyright owner, to gain access to the work." 17 U.S.C. § 1201(a)(3)(B). The complaint identifies "multiple layers of technological controls" that Philips employs on their Ultrasound Systems "to protect Philips' copyright-protected works from unauthorized access." Specifically, the complaint identifies the following technological measures: (1) user-specific codes; (2) user-specific hardware keys; (3) machine-specific codes and hardware keys; (4) software files with licensed features and optional add-on controls; (5) machine-specific configuration files that control compatibility between the systems and software and/or the systems and replacement parts; and (6) software disabling if a user attempts to make use of an unlicensed feature.

The complaint also explains how these technological measures work. (*See id.*) User-specific access codes and hardware keys "enable the software access and control features for a particular registered user" by permitting "access to enabled Philips tools and features based on a user's registered access authorization level." Machine-specific controls "only permit user access to the features and tools that have been enabled on a specific machine." Licensed feature controls limit what features users can access on a specific machine, control access to protected software, and limit the options available for use on a specific machine.

The court concludes that these allegations sufficiently plead that Philips' Ultrasound Systems are protected by "a technological measure that effectively controls access to a work" as required by §§ 1201(a)(1) and (a)(2). *See, e.g., Synopsys, Inc. v. AzurEngine Techs., Inc.,* 401 F. Supp. 3d 1068, 1072 (S.D. Cal. 2019) (finding sufficient allegations that "the software will not run without the licensee 'checking out' a license key from a server that is designed to only grant such keys to approved licensees" and stating that "[e]very court to consider the issue has found that similar methods of license-control satisfy the 'effectively controls' requirement of the DMCA"); *Synopsys, Inc. v. InnoGrit, Corp.,* No. 19-CV-02082-LHK, 2019 WL 4848387, at *7 (N.D. Cal. Oct. 1, 2019) ("Synopsys's license key system requires the use of an encrypted control code to access Synopsys software. The license key system therefore 'requires the application of information ... to gain access to the' Synopsys software.") (quoting 17 U.S.C. § 1201(a)(3)(B)).

Philips has also adequately alleged that Defendants took actions to "circumvent" Philips' access controls. Under § 1201(a), "to 'circumvent a technological measure' means to descramble a scrambled work, to decrypt an encrypted work, or otherwise to avoid, bypass, remove, deactivate, or impair a technological measure, without the authority of the copyright owner." 17 U.S.C. § 1201(a)(3)(A). Numerous paragraphs in the complaint detail the steps Defendants allegedly took to circumvent and modify Philips' access controls. At a high level, Philips alleges that Defendants remove the hard drive from the Ultrasound Systems and run the Adepto program on the hard drive. The Adepto program changes configuration files and software files in order to enable unlicensed options on the hard drive. Philips also alleges that Defendants use Adepto to hack onboard tools to force compatibility with otherwise incompatible transducer parts. These allegations sufficiently plead that Defendants took actions to "circumvent" Philips' access controls under § 1201(a). *See, e.g., Davidson & Assocs. v. Jung,* 422 F.3d 630, 640 (8th Cir. 2005) (finding a DMCA violation where the defendant developed and used an "emulator" that "allowed ... access [to] Battle.net mode features without a valid or unique CD key"); *Dish Network, L.L.C. v. Vicxon Corp.,* No. 12-CV-9-L WVG, 2013 WL 3894905, at *7 (S.D. Cal. July 26, 2013) (finding that use of "piracy software" to circumvent a television provider's security measures satisfied the "circumvention" requirement of § 1201(a)).

Because Philips has sufficiently alleged that Defendants "circumvent[ed] a technological measure that effectively controls access to a work," *see* 17 U.S.C. § 1201(a)(1)(A); *see also id.* § 1201(a)(2), the court DENIES Defendants' motion to dismiss Philips first cause of action.

Davidson & Associates v. Jung, 422 F.3d 630 (8ᵗʰ Cir. 2005).

SMITH, Circuit Judge.

Davidson & Associates, Inc. d/b/a Blizzard Entertainment ("Blizzard") and Vivendi Universal Games, Inc. ("Vivendi"), owner of copyrights in computer game software and online gaming service software sued Ross Combs ("Combs"), Rob Crittenden ("Crittenden"), Jim Jung ("Jung"), and Internet Gateway, Inc. ("Internet Gateway") (collectively referred to as "Appellants"), for . . . circumvention of copyright protection system, and trafficking in circumvention technology. Both parties moved for summary judgment. The district court granted summary judgment in favor of Blizzard and Vivendi, and determined that: . . . (4) Appellants violated the anti-circumvention and anti-trafficking provisions of the Digital Millennium Copyright Act ("DMCA"). We affirm.

I. Background

A. Factual Background

Blizzard, a California corporation and subsidiary of Vivendi, creates and sells software games for personal computers. This appeal concerns the particular Blizzard games "StarCraft," "StarCraft: Brood War," "WarCraft II: Battle.net Edition," "Diablo," and "Diablo II: Lord of Destruction." Combs and Crittenden are computer programmers, Jung is a systems administrator, and Internet Gateway is an Internet service provider based in St. Peters, Missouri. Jung is also the president, co-owner, and day-to-day operator of Internet Gateway.

In January 1997, Blizzard officially launched "Battle.net," a 24–hour online-gaming service available exclusively to purchasers of its computer games. The Battle.net service has nearly 12 million active users who spend more that 2.1 million hours online per day. Blizzard holds valid copyright registrations covering Battle.net and each of its computer games at issue in this litigation. Battle.net is a free service that allows owners of Blizzard games to play each other on their personal computers via the Internet. Battle.net mode allows users to create and join multi-player games that can be accessed across the Internet, to chat with other potential players, to record wins and losses and save advancements in an individual password-protected game account, and to participate with others in tournament play featuring elimination rounds. Players can set up private "chat channels" and private games on Battle.net to allow players to determine with whom they wish to interact online. These Battle.net mode features are only accessible from within the games.

Like most computer software, Blizzard's games can be easily copied and distributed over the Internet. Blizzard has taken steps to avoid piracy by designing Battle.net to restrict access and use of the Battle.net mode feature of the game. Each time a user logs onto Battle.net, a Battle.net server examines the user's version of the game software. If a Blizzard game does not have the latest software upgrades and fixes, the Battle.net service updates the customer's game before allowing the game to play in Battle.net mode.

With the exception of "Diablo," each authorized version of a Blizzard game comes with a "CD Key." A CD Key is a unique sequence of alphanumeric characters printed on a sticker attached to the case in which the CD–ROM was packaged. To log on to Battle.net and access Battle.net mode, the game initiates an authentication sequence or "secret handshake" between the game and the Battle.net server.3 In order to play the Blizzard game contained on a CD–ROM, a user must first install the game onto a computer and agree to the terms of the End User License Agreement ("EULA")4 and Terms of Use ("TOU"), both of which prohibit reverse engineering. At the end of both the EULA and TOU, Blizzard includes a button with the text, "I Agree" in it, which the user must select in order to proceed with the installation. Users are also required to enter a name and the CD Key during installation of Battle.net and Blizzard games.

The outside packaging of all Blizzard games, except for Diablo, contains a statement that use of the game is subject to the EULA and that use of Battle.net is subject to the terms of the TOU. The terms of neither the EULA nor the TOU appear on the outside packaging. If the user does not agree to these terms, the game may be returned for a full refund of the purchase price within thirty (30) days of the original purchase. Combs, Crittenden, and Jung installed Blizzard games and agreed to the terms of the EULA. Crittenden and Jung logged onto Battle.net and agreed to the TOU.

The users of Battle.net have occasionally experienced difficulties with the service. To address their frustrations with Battle.net, a group of non-profit volunteer game hobbyists, programmers, and other individuals formed a group called the "bnetd project." The bnetd project developed a program called the "bnetd.org server" that emulates the Battle.net service and permits users to play online without use of Battle.net. The bnetd project is a volunteer effort and the project has always offered the bnetd program for free to anyone. Combs, Crittenden, and Jung were lead developers for the bnetd project.

The bnetd project was organized and managed over the Internet through a website, www.bnetd.org, that was made available to the public through equipment provided by Internet Gateway. The bnetd.org emulator provides a server that allows gamers unable or unwilling to connect to Battle.net to experience the multi-player features of Blizzard's games. The bnetd.org emulator also provides matchmaking services for users of Blizzard games who want to play those games in a multi-player environment without using Battle.net. Bnetd.org attempted to mirror all of the user-visible features of Battle.net, including online discussion forums and information about the bnetd project, as well as access to the program's computer code for others to copy and modify.

To serve as a functional alternative to Battle.net, bnetd.org had to be compatible with Blizzard's software. In particular, compatibility required that bnetd.org speak the same protocol language that the Battle.net speaks. By speaking the same protocol language, the bnetd programs would be interoperable with Blizzard games. Once game play starts, a user perceives no difference between Battle.net and the bnetd.org.

By necessity, Appellants used reverse engineering to learn Blizzard's protocol language and to ensure that bnetd.org worked with Blizzard games. Combs used reverse engineering to develop the bnetd.org server, including a program called "tcpdump" to log communications between Blizzard games and the Battle.net server. Crittenden used reverse engineering to develop the bnetd.org server, including using a program called "Nextray." Crittenden also used a program called "ripper" to take Blizzard client files that were compiled together in one file and break them into their component parts. Crittenden used the ripper program to determine how Blizzard games displayed ad banners so that bnetd.org could display ad banners to users in the format that Blizzard uses on the Battle.net service. Combs tried to disassemble a Blizzard game to figure out how to implement a feature that allowed bnetd.org to protect the password that a user enters when creating an account in Battle.net mode. Crittenden made an unauthorized copy of a Blizzard game in order to test the interoperability of the bnetd.org server with multiple games.

Blizzard designed its games to connect only to Battle.net servers. To enable a Blizzard game to connect to a bnetd.org server instead of a Battle.net server, bnetd had to modify the computer file that contained the Internet address of the Battle.net servers. As part of the bnetd project, Combs participated in the development of a utility program called "BNS" to allow Blizzard games to connect to bnetd.org servers more easily. Through the BNS program, the game sends the bnetd.org server information about its CD Key. An individual can thus play one of the Blizzard games at issue over the Internet via bnetd.org rather than Battle.net. According to Blizzard, the EULAs and TOUs prohibit this activity.

Bnetd.org has important operational differences from Battle.net. When bnetd.org receives the CD Key information, unlike Battle.net, it does not determine whether the CD Key is valid or currently in use by another player. The bnetd.org server computer code always sends the game an "okay" reply regardless of whether the CD Key is valid or currently in use by another player. The bnetd .org emulator always allows the Blizzard games to access Battle.net mode features even if the user does not have a valid or unique CD Key. Blizzard did not disclose the methods it used to generate CD Keys or to confirm the validity of CD Keys.

Combs, Crittenden, and Jung used Blizzard games to log into bnetd .org. Crittenden was aware that unauthorized versions of Blizzard games were played on bnetd.org. Jung knew that the bnetd.org emulator did not require that Blizzard games provide valid CD Keys. Combs suspected that the bnetd.org emulator would not know the difference between a real game and a pirated game. Combs and Crittenden either sent portions of the bnetd software to Jung to place on the www.bnetd.org website for download or put the software on the website themselves. Combs made the bnetd software available on his website located at www.cs.nmsu.edu /~rcombs/sc/. Also distributed was the BNS utility program which allowed Blizzard games to connect to bnetd.org. The source code was made available as an "open source" application, meaning that others were free to copy the source code and distribute it with or without modifications. Because the bnetd.org source code was freely available, others developed additional Battle.net emulators based on the bnetd.org source code. Binary versions of the bnetd.org were distributed which made it more convenient for users to set up and access the emulator program. Internet Gateway has donated space on its computers for use by the bnetd project. Internet Gateway also hosted a bnetd.org server that anyone on the Internet could access and use to play Blizzard games in Battle.net mode. . . .

II. Discussion

. . .

B. DMCA Claims and Interoperability Exception

Congress enacted the DMCA in 1998 to implement the World Intellectual Property Organization Copyright Treaty ("WIPO Treaty"). WIPO requires contracting nations to "provide adequate legal protection and effective legal remedies against the circumvention of effective technological measures that are used by authors in connection with the exercise of their rights under this Treaty or the Berne Convention and that restrict acts, in respect of their works, which are not authorized by the authors concerned or permitted by law." WIPO Treaty, Apr. 12, 1997, art. 11, S. Treaty Doc. No. 105–17 (1997), available at 1997 WL 447232.10 The DMCA contains three provisions targeted at the circumvention of technological protections.

The first is § 1201(a)(1), the anti-circumvention provision. This provision prohibits a person from "circumvent[ing] a technological measure that effectively controls access to a work protected under [Title 17, governing copyright]." The Librarian of Congress is required to promulgate regulations every three years exempting from this subsection individuals who would otherwise be "adversely affected" in "their ability to make noninfringing uses." 17 U.S.C. § 1201(a)(1)(B)-(E). Section 1201(a)(1) differs from the second and third provisions in that it targets the use of a circumvention technology, not the trafficking in such a technology.

The second and third provisions are §§ 1201(a)(2) and 1201(b)(1), the "anti-trafficking provisions." These sections are similar, except that § 1201(a)(2) covers those who traffic in technology that can circumvent "a technological measure that effectively controls access to a work protected under" Title 17, whereas § 1201(b)(1) covers those who traffic in technology that can circumvent "protection afforded by a technological measure that effectively protects a right of a copyright owner under" Title 17. 17 U.S.C. §§ 1201(a)(2) & (b)(1). (Emphases added.) In other words, although both sections prohibit trafficking in a circumvention technology, the focus of § 1201(a)(2) is circumvention of technologies designed to prevent access to a work, and the focus of § 1201(b)(1) is circumvention of technologies designed to permit access to a work but prevent copying of the work or some other act that infringes a copyright. See S.Rep. No. 105–190, at 11–12 (1998).

The district court determined that Appellants's reverse engineering violated § 1201(a)(1) as well as § 1201(a)(2). We agree.

1. Anti–Circumvention Violation

Section 1201(a)(1) provides that "[n]o person shall circumvent a technological measure that effectively controls access to a work protected under this title." The term "circumvent a technological measure" "means to descramble a scrambled work, to decrypt an encrypted work, or otherwise to avoid, bypass, remove, deactivate, or impair a technological measure, without the authority of the copyright owner." 17 U.S.C. § 1201(3)(A). "Effectively controls access to a work" means that the measure, in the ordinary course of its operation, requires the application of information, or a process or a treatment, with the authority of the copyright owner, to gain access to the work. 17 U.S.C. § 1201(3)(B).

Blizzard games, through Battle.net, employed a technological measure, a software "secret handshake" (CD key), to control access to its copyrighted games. The bnetd.org emulator developed by Appellants allowed the Blizzard game to access Battle.net mode features without a valid or unique CD key. As a result, unauthorized copies of the Blizzard games were played on bnetd.org servers. After Appellants distributed the bnetd program, others developed additional Battle.net emulators based on the bnetd source code. Appellants's distribution of binary versions of the bnetd program facilitated set up and access to the emulator program.

Relying on Lexmark Int'l, Inc. v. Static Control Components, Inc., 387 F.3d 522 (6th Cir.2004), Appellants argue that Battle.net mode is a strictly functional process that lacks creative expression, and thus DMCA protections do not apply. Lexmark Int'l, Inc., concerned two computer programs: the first was known as the "Toner Loading Program" and the second was known as the "Printer Engine Program." Id. at 528. DMCA anti-circumvention claims were brought after Lexmark's authentication sequence contained in its printer cartridges were allegedly circumvented. Id. at 528–29. The district court in that case held that Lexmark's authentication sequence effectively controlled access to the programs because it controlled the consumers' ability to make use of those programs. Id. at 546. The Sixth Circuit reversed, holding that it was not Lexmark's authentication sequence that controlled access to the programs, but the purchase of a Lexmark printer that allowed access to the program. Id. "No security device, in other words, protects access to the ... program and no security device accordingly must be circumvented to obtain access to that program code." Id. at 547.

Here, Battle.net's control measure was not freely available. Appellants could not have obtained a copy of Battle.net or made use of the literal elements of Battle.net mode without acts of reverse engineering, which allowed for a circumvention of Battle.net and Battle.net mode. Unlike in Lexmark Int'l, Inc., Battle.net mode codes were not accessible by simply purchasing a Blizzard game or logging onto Battle.net., nor could data from the program be translated into readable source code after which copies were freely available without some type of circumvention. Appellants misread Lexmark Int'l, Inc. and we are unpersuaded that summary judgment on the anti-circumvention violations was improperly granted in favor of Blizzard and Vivendi.

2. Anti-trafficking Violations

Section 1201(a)(2) provides that:

> No person shall manufacture, import, offer to the public, provide, or otherwise traffic in any technology, product, service, device, component, or part thereof, that ... is primarily designed or produced for the purpose of circumventing a technological measure that effectively controls access to a work protected under this title; ... has only limited commercially significant purpose or use other than to circumvent a technological measure that effectively controls access to a work protected under this title; or ... is marketed by that person or another acting in concert with that person with that person's knowledge for use in circumventing a technological measure that effectively controls access to a work protected under this title.

17 U.S.C. § 1201(a)(2). The bnetd.org emulator had limited commercial purpose because its sole purpose was to avoid the limitations of Battle.net. There is no genuine issue of material fact that Appellants designed and developed the bnetd.org server and emulator for the purpose of circumventing Blizzard's technological measures controlling access to Battle.net and the Blizzard games. Summary judgment was properly granted in favor of Blizzard and Vivendi on the anti-trafficking violations.

3. Interoperability Exception

The DMCA contains several exceptions, including one for individuals using circumvention technology "for the sole purpose" of trying to achieve "interoperability" of computer programs through reverse engineering. See 17 U.S.C. § 1201(f). Subsection (f)(4) defines interoperability as "the ability of computer programs to exchange information, and such programs mutually to use the information which has been exchanged." 17 U.S.C. § 1201(f)(4). Appellants argue that the interoperability exception applies to any alleged infringement of Blizzard games and Battle.net. To successfully prove the interoperability defense under § 1201(f), Appellants must show: (1) they lawfully obtained the right to use a copy of a computer program; (2) the information gathered as a result of the reverse engineering was not previously readily available to the person engaging in the circumvention; (3) the sole purpose of the reverse engineering was to identify and analyze those elements of the program that were necessary to achieve interoperability of an independently created computer program with other programs; and (4) the alleged circumvention did not constitute infringement. See 17 U.S.C. § 1201(f).

Appellants's circumvention in this case constitutes infringement. As detailed earlier, Blizzard's secret handshake between Blizzard games and Battle.net effectively controlled access to Battle.net mode within its games. The purpose of the bnetd.org project was to provide matchmaking services for users of Blizzard games who wanted to play in a multi-player environment without using Battle.net. The bnetd.org emulator enabled users of Blizzard games to access Battle.net mode features without a valid or unique CD key to enter Battle.net. The bnetd.org emulator did not determine whether the CD key was valid or currently in use by another player. As a result, unauthorized copies of the Blizzard games were freely played on bnetd.org servers. Appellants failed to establish a genuine issue of material fact as to the applicability of the interoperability exception. The district court properly granted summary judgment in favor of Blizzard and Vivendi on the interoperability exception.

Summary judgment in favor of Blizzard and Vivendi is affirmed.

NOTES

Note 1

Subsection a(1)(a) is subject to the following exception:

(B) The prohibition contained in subparagraph (A) shall not apply to persons who are users of a copyrighted work which is in a particular class of works, if such persons are, or are likely to be in the succeeding 3-year period, adversely affected by virtue of such prohibition in their ability to make noninfringing uses of that particular class of works under this title, as determined under subparagraph (C).

(C) During the 2-year period described in subparagraph (A), and during each succeeding 3-year period, the Librarian of Congress, upon the recommendation of the Register of Copyrights, who shall consult with the Assistant Secretary for Communications and Information of the Department of Commerce and report and comment on his or her views in making such recommendation, shall make the determination in a rulemaking proceeding for purposes of subparagraph (B) of whether persons who are users of a copyrighted work are, or are likely to be in the succeeding 3-year period, adversely affected by the prohibition under subparagraph (A) in their ability to make noninfringing uses under this title of a particular class of copyrighted works. In conducting such rulemaking, the Librarian shall examine--

(i) the availability for use of copyrighted works;

(ii) the availability for use of works for nonprofit archival, preservation, and educational purposes;

(iii) the impact that the prohibition on the circumvention of technological measures applied to copyrighted works has on criticism, comment, news reporting, teaching, scholarship, or research;

(iv) the effect of circumvention of technological measures on the market for or value of copyrighted works; and

(v) such other factors as the Librarian considers appropriate.

(D) The Librarian shall publish any class of copyrighted works for which the Librarian has determined, pursuant to the rulemaking conducted under subparagraph (C), that noninfringing uses by persons who are users of a copyrighted work are, or are likely to be, adversely affected, and the prohibition contained in subparagraph (A) shall not apply to such users with respect to such class of works for the ensuing 3-year period.

(E) Neither the exception under subparagraph (B) from the applicability of the prohibition contained in subparagraph (A), nor any determination made in a rulemaking conducted under subparagraph (C), may be used as a defense in any action to enforce any provision of this title other than this paragraph.

The Librarian of Congress has issued exemptions concerning the above-mentioned exception. The exemptions include, but is not limited to, the following works:

- Literary works consisting of compilations of data generated by implanted medical devices and corresponding personal monitoring systems

- Computer programs that operate the following types of devices, to allow connection of a new or used device to an alternative wireless network ("unlocking"):

    o Cellphones

    o Tablets

    o Mobile hotspots

    o Wearable devices (*e.g.*, smartwatches)

- Computer programs that operate the following types of devices, to allow the device to interoperate with or to remove software applications ("jailbreaking"):

    o Smartphones

    o Tablets and other all-purpose mobile computing devices

    ○ Smart TVs

    ○ Voice assistant devices

- Computer programs that control motorized land vehicles, including farm equipment, for purposes of diagnosis, repair, or modification of the vehicle, including to access diagnostic data

- Computer programs that control smartphones, home appliances, or home systems, for diagnosis, maintenance, or repair of the device or system

- Computer programs for purposes of good-faith security research

- Computer programs other than video games, for the preservation of computer programs and computer program-dependent materials by libraries, archives, and museums

- Video games for which outside server support has been discontinued, to allow individual play by gamers and preservation of games by libraries, archives, and museums (as well as necessary jailbreaking of console computer code for preservation uses only), and preservation of discontinued video games that never required server support

- Computer programs that operate 3D printers, to allow use of alternative feedstock.[497]

Note 2

In June 2017, the U.S. Copyright Office Register issued a report titled, "Section 1201 of Title 17: A Report of the Register of Copyrights" [Report]. The Report provides a discussion of the provisions of Section 1201. In discussing the exemption for encryption research, the Report states:

> Section 1201(g) exempts from section 1201(a)(1)(A) and (2)—but not section 1201(b)— certain circumvention activities done for purposes of "encryption research," i.e., "activities necessary to identify and analyze flaws and vulnerabilities of encryption technologies applied to copyrighted works, if these activities are conducted to advance the state of knowledge in the field of encryption technology or to assist in the development of encryption products." Congress adopted section 1201(g) to ensure that U.S. Copyright Office Section 1201 of Title 17 the anticircumvention laws would not have "the undesirable and unintended consequence of chilling legitimate research activities in the area of encryption."

---

[497] *See Frequently Asked Questions About the Section 1201 Rulemaking*, U.S. COPYRIGHT OFFICE, https://www.copyright.gov/1201/2018/faqs.html (last visited Oct. 28, 2020).

The statute defines "encryption technology" as "the scrambling and descrambling of information using mathematical formulas or algorithms." The exemption to subsection (a)(1)(A) allows circumvention of a TPM "in the course of an act of good faith encryption research," provided (1) the copy was lawfully obtained, (2) the act is "necessary to conduct" the research, (3) the researcher made a good faith effort to obtain authorization before the circumvention, and (4) the act does not constitute infringement or a violation of other applicable law. The statute includes a "non-exhaustive list of factors a court shall consider in determining whether a person properly qualifies" for this exemption, including whether and how the information derived from the encryption research was distributed, whether the researcher has been trained or experienced, or is engaged in a legitimate course of study, in the field of encryption technology, and whether the researcher provided the copyright owner with the results of the research. With respect to subsection (a)(2), section 1201(g)(4) permits a person to develop and employ technological means to circumvent a TPM for the sole purpose of performing the permitted acts of encryption research. In addition, that person may provide such means "to another person with whom he or she is working collaboratively" for the purpose of conducting the permitted research, "or for the purpose of having that other person verify his or her acts of good faith encryption research." The legislative history notes, however, that "generally available encryption testing tools" would not be prohibited in the first place by subsection (a)(2).

CHAPTER TWELVE. INTERNET OF THINGS

12.1 Introduction

This chapter reviews cybersecurity issues related to the Internet of Things (IoT). In prior chapters, we have reviewed cases involving internet connected devices such as WiFi routers. Indeed, with the advent of the ubiquitous home WiFi router, "things" have been connected to the internet for a long time in the form of laptops, pads, and smart phones. Today, those "things" have exponentially increased with the continuous rising adoption of smart home devices. In this chapter, we review materials specifically directed to the IoT such as NIST documents and the Complaint filed against Ring concerning cybersecurity deficiencies.

12.2 Background Information Concerning the IoT

A major concern of security departments is Denial of Service (DOS) attacks on a company's infrastructure. Basically, a DOS is caused by overloading a service or device with so much network traffic that the service or device becomes unavailable. Distributed Denial of Service (DDOS) attacks are similar and are caused by traffic from a distribution of sources.

It is a common goal of many hackers to take control of computing resources in order to harness as much computing power as possible. This can come in very handy if a hacker wanted expanded computer power for searching for bit coins or other efforts that become easier with enhanced computing power. Thus, the hacker forms a network of time-slices of computing power from many computing sources without the computer owner even knowing their computer is being used by someone else. These are known as botnets. With the miniaturization of the components of a laptop computer, powerful miniaturized computing power has moved into a smart phone, and from the smart phone into other miniaturized devices that can also contain sensors and WiFi connection capability. In short it has become technologically easy to put a microprocessor with Wi-Fi capability into almost any device, such as:

- TVs
- thermostats
- wireless cameras
- doorbells with cameras
- ovens
- refrigerators
- cars
- printers
- alarm sensors
- watches
- light bulbs
- light switches
- smart meters for water, etc.
- lawn sprinkler system controller

- door locks
- washer/dryer
- garage openers

And the above are smart devices used mainly for the home. Outside of the home, cities are also adding smart device technologies that may include:

- various meters (water, electrical, parking)
- signaling for traffic and train control
- various sensors that feed into apps such as bus arrival time apps

"The IoT is experiencing what some might describe as hypergrowth. Gartner forecasts that the number of IoT devices will reach 25 billion by 2021, while Forbes forecast that the market will exceed $457 billion before 2021."[498]

The National Institute of Science and Technology (NIST) provides the following take that focuses on IoT devices throughout the business enterprise in addition to the home:

"The Internet of Things (IoT) is a rapidly evolving and expanding collection of diverse technologies that interact with the physical world. IoT devices are an outcome of combining the worlds of information technology (IT) and operational technology (OT). Many IoT devices are the result of the convergence of cloud computing, mobile computing, embedded systems, big data, low-price hardware, and other technological advances. IoT devices can provide computing functionality, data storage, and network connectivity for equipment that previously lacked them, enabling new efficiencies and technological capabilities for the equipment, such as remote access for monitoring, configuration, and troubleshooting. IoT can also add the abilities to analyze data about the physical world and use the results to better inform decision making, alter the physical environment, and anticipate future events.

While the full scope of IoT is not precisely defined, it is clearly vast. Every sector has its own types of IoT devices, such as specialized hospital equipment in the healthcare sector and smart road technologies in the transportation sector, and there is a large number of enterprise IoT devices that every sector can use. Versions of nearly every consumer electronics device, many of which are also present in organizations' facilities, have become connected IoT devices—kitchen appliances, thermostats, home security cameras, door locks, light bulbs, and TVs."[499]

Imagine a commuter train that is approaching a busy crossroad that requires the gates to come down and block the road. This requires sensors communicating with sensors. A mistake here could mean the loss of life. Or imagine a power grid that feeds

---

[498] SECURING SMALL-BUSINESS AND HOME INTERNET OF THINGS (IOT) DEVICES: MITIGATING NETWORK-BASED ATTACKS USING MANUFACTURER USAGE DESCRIPTION (MUD), NAT'L INST. OF STANDARDS AND TECH. & NAT'L CYBERSECURITY CTR. OF EXCELLENCE 2 (2020), *available at* https://www.nccoe.nist.gov/sites/default/files/library/sp1800/iot-ddos-nist-sp1800-15-draft.pdf.

[499] CONSIDERATIONS FOR MANAGING INTERNET OF THINGS (IOT) CYBERSECURITY AND PRIVACY RISKS, NAT'L INST. OF STANDARDS AND TECH. iv (2019), *available at* https://nvlpubs.nist.gov/nistpubs/ir/2019/NIST.IR.8228.pdf.

a manufacturing plant that contains machinery sensitive to voltage. Sensors within the power grid talk to other sensors that control the grid voltage to that particular plant. An uncontrolled spike in voltage could cause damage to expensive manufacturing equipment. Security of these sensors also known as things is obviously important.

The NIST identifies three IoT risk areas for business entities:

"Cybersecurity and privacy risks for IoT devices can be thought of in terms of three high-level risk mitigation goals:

1.   **Protect device security**. In other words, prevent a device from being used to conduct attacks, including participating in distributed denial of service (DDoS) attacks against other organizations, and eavesdropping on network traffic or compromising other devices on the same network segment. This goal applies to all IoT devices.

2.   **Protect data security.** Protect the confidentiality, integrity, and/or availability of data (including personally identifiable information [PII]) collected by, stored on, processed by, or transmitted to or from the IoT device. This goal applies to each IoT device except those without any data that needs protection.

3.   **Protect individuals' privacy.** Protect individuals' privacy impacted by PII processing beyond risks managed through device and data security protection. This goal applies to all IoT devices that process PII or that directly or indirectly impact individuals."[500]

Per a recent NIST study:

"Gartner predicts there will be 25 billion Internet of Things (IoT) devices by 2021. While such rapid growth has the potential to provide many benefits, it is also a cause for concern because IoT devices are tempting targets for attackers. State-of-the-art security software protects full-featured devices, such as laptops and phones, from most known threats, but many IoT devices, such as connected thermostats, security cameras, and lighting control systems, have minimal security or are unprotected. Because they are designed to be inexpensive and limited purpose, IoT devices may have unpatched software flaws. They also often have processing, timing, memory, and power constraints that make them challenging to secure. Users often do not know what IoT devices are on their networks and lack means for controlling access to them over their life cycles. However, the consequences of not addressing the security of IoT devices can be catastrophic. For instance, in typical networking environments, malicious actors can detect and attack an IoT device within minutes of it connecting to the internet. If it has a known vulnerability, this weakness can be exploited at scale, enabling an attacker to commandeer sets of compromised devices, called *botnets*, to launch large-scale distributed denial of service (DDoS) attacks, such as Mirai, as well as other network-based attacks. DDoS attacks can significantly harm an organization, rendering it

---

[500] *Id.* at v.

impossible for the organization's customers to reach it and thereby resulting in revenue loss, potential liability exposure, reputation damage, and eroded customer trust."[501]

"The Mirai malware, which launched a large DDoS attack on the internet infrastructure firm Dyn that took down many of the internet's top destinations offline for much of a day, relied heavily on hard-coded administrative access to assemble botnets consisting of more than 100,000 devices."[502]

But an increase in DDoS attacks and size of the attacks are only two of the cybersecurity threats caused by the proliferation of the IoT. Most of these smart devices for the home come with a free app with which to access and configure the smart device. But traffic to the user is not all that goes across the internet. Data can also be pulled down and logged to the manufacturer's server. The manufacturer can then send monthly usage data back to the owner as a service. Accordingly, this creates a data source at the manufacturer or seller of the device that must be protected by reasonable security measures.

Another aspect of IoT devices that can make it difficult to secure IoT devices is that some devices such as security cameras and security sensors do not communicate directly with the WiFi hub but instead with its own aggregator. And then the aggregator communicates with the WiFi. Compounding the aggregator issue is that the communication protocol between the devices and the aggregator is not a standard communication protocol. Thus, it is possible to have multiple aggregators in one home and each communicating over a different protocol. This presents a challenge for cybersecurity professionals.

Another issue with smart devices is that some of the built-in security features are lacking. For example, some smart devices have been sold, all with the same password, and the user is not required to change the password after startup. Some smart devices are sold with different passwords, but there is no requirement to change the password after startup. Thus, these devices have been an easy target for hackers to take over and then point at a particular IP address to cause a DDoS.

Many devices require an app for control of the device and the user is instructed to download a particular app during the installation of the device. After the app is downloaded, normally to a smart phone or tablet, an account must be opened through the app for control. Normally, the account requires, at minimum, a username and a password with setup options after the initial login for more robust security in the way of two-step verification security. Two-step verification, also known as multi-factor authorization, is normally not mandatory, and many users choose to not implement the two-step verification. Some device manufacturers have started to mandate two-step verification.

---

[501] SECURING SMALL-BUSINESS AND HOME INTERNET OF THINGS (IoT) DEVICES: MITIGATING NETWORK-BASED ATTACKS USING MANUFACTURER USAGE DESCRIPTION (MUD), NAT'L INST. OF STANDARDS AND TECH. & NAT'L CYBERSECURITY CTR. OF EXCELLENCE 1 (2020), *available at* https://www.nccoe.nist.gov/sites/default/files/library/sp1800/iot-ddos-nist-sp1800-15-draft.pdf.
[502] *Id.* at 11.

Unfortunately, the same poor password creation and management techniques that a user can apply to a laptop password can be applied to device app accounts. Indeed, the human behavior in setting up an app password may be worse because the user may be more focused on getting the device to work and not on good password management.

Another aspect that may affect device security is the security setup of the WiFi router, with which the device or device aggregator communicates. Has the WiFi been placed into a secure mode or is it open to the driving by public? How many people have been given the password to the WiFi? If a guest network feature exists on the WiFi, has it been set up for visitors? Has the original WiFi password been changed? If a hacker can access the WiFi traffic, then the hacker and sniff the IoT traffic.

12.3 NIST Guidance Document: Foundational Cybersecurity Activities for IoT Device Manufacturers

The NIST has released a guidance document titled, "Foundational Cybersecurity Activities for IoT Device Manufacturers," in May 2020. The document provides cybersecurity counseling for IoT device manufacturers concerning the development of devices to be sold to consumers. The Executive Summary provides, in relevant part:

"The purpose of this publication is to give manufacturers recommendations for improving how securable the IoT devices they make are. This means the IoT devices offer device cybersecurity capabilities—cybersecurity features or functions the devices provide through their own technical means (i.e., device hardware and software)—that customers, both organizations and individuals, need to secure the devices when used within their systems and environments. IoT device manufacturers will also often need to perform actions or provide services that their customers expect and/or need to plan for and maintain the cybersecurity of the device within their systems and environments. From this publication, IoT device manufacturers will learn how they can help to create a baseline of cybersecurity capabilities for IoT devices, and to publish cybersecurity practices for IoT device manufacturers. IoT device customers by carefully considering which device cybersecurity capabilities to design into their devices for customers to use in managing their cybersecurity risks.

This publication describes six recommended foundational cybersecurity activities that manufacturers should consider performing to improve the securability of the new IoT devices they make. Four of the six activities primarily impact decisions and actions performed by the manufacturer before a device is sent out for sale (pre-market), and the remaining two activities primarily impact decisions and actions performed by the manufacturer after device sale (postmarket). Performing all six activities can help manufacturers provide IoT devices that better support the cybersecurity-related efforts needed by IoT device customers, which in turn can reduce the prevalence and severity of IoT device compromises and the attacks performed using compromised IoT devices. These activities are intended to fit within a manufacturer's existing development process and may already be achieved in whole or part by that existing process.

Note that this publication is intended to inform the manufacturing of new devices and not devices that are already produced or in production, although some of the information in this publication might also be applicable to such devices.

Activities with Primarily Pre-Market Impact

• Activity 1: Identify expected customers and users, and define expected use cases. Identifying the expected customers and users, as well as the end users' expected use cases for an IoT device early in its design is vital for determining which device cybersecurity capabilities the device should implement and how it should implement them.

• Activity 2: Research customer cybersecurity needs and goals. Customers' risks drive their cybersecurity needs and goals. Manufacturers cannot completely understand or anticipate all of their customers' risks. However, manufacturers can make their devices at least minimally securable by those they expect to be customers of their product and who use them consistent with the expected use cases.

• Activity 3: Determine how to address customer needs and goals. Manufacturers can determine how to address those needs and goals by having their IoT devices provide particular device cybersecurity capabilities in order to help customers mitigate their cybersecurity risks. To provide a starting point to use in identifying the necessary device cybersecurity capabilities, a companion publication is provided, which is a set of device cybersecurity capabilities that customers are likely to need to achieve their goals and fulfill their needs.

• Activity 4: Plan for adequate support of customer needs and goals. Manufacturers can help make their IoT devices more securable by appropriately provisioning device hardware and software resources to support the desired device cybersecurity capabilities. They should also consider business resources necessary to support development and continued support of the IoT device in ways that support customer needs and goals (e.g., secure coding practices, vulnerability response and flaw remediation).

Activities with Primarily Post-Market Impact

• Activity 5: Define approaches for communicating to customers. Many customers will benefit from manufacturers communicating to them more clearly about cybersecurity risks involving the IoT devices the manufacturers are currently selling or have already sold. This communication could be targeted at the customer directly or others acting on the customers' behalf, such as an internet service provider or a managed security services provider, depending on context and roles.

• Activity 6: Decide what to communicate to customers and how to communicate it. There are many potential considerations for what information a manufacturer communicates to customers for a particular IoT product and how that information will be communicated. Examples of topics are:

o Cybersecurity risk-related assumptions that the manufacturer made when designing and developing the device

o Support and lifespan expectations, such as expected term of support, what process will guide end-of-life, will any functions of the device remain after its end-of-life, how customers can communicate with the manufacturer about suspected vulnerabilities during and even after the end of device support, and how customers may be able to maintain securability after support ends and at end-of-life

o Device composition and capabilities, such as information about the device's software, hardware, services, functions, and data types

o Software updates, such as if updates will be available, when, how and by whom they will be distributed, and how customers can verify source and content of a software update

o Device retirement options, such as if and how a customer can securely transfer ownership of the device, and whether the customer can render the device inoperable for disposal

o Device cybersecurity capabilities that the device provides, as well as cybersecurity functions that can be provided by a related device or a manufacturer service or system."

The publication also states:

"Improving the securability of an IoT device for customers means helping customers meet their risk mitigation goals, which involves identifying and addressing a set of risk mitigation areas. Even customers without formal risk mitigation goals, such as home consumers, often have informal and indirect cybersecurity goals, like having their IoT device provide the desired functionality as expected (e.g., automatically), that are dependent to some extent on addressing risk mitigation areas. Based on an analysis of existing NIST publications such as the SP 800-53 [5] and the Cybersecurity Framework [6] and the characteristics of IoT devices, NISTIR 8228 [7] identified the common risk mitigation areas for IoT devices as:

• Asset Management: Maintain a current, accurate inventory of all IoT devices and their relevant characteristics throughout the devices' lifecycles in order to use that information for cybersecurity risk management purposes. Being able to distinguish each IoT device from all others is needed for the other common risk mitigation areas— vulnerability management, access management, data protection, and incident detection.

• Vulnerability Management: Identify and mitigate known vulnerabilities in IoT device software throughout the devices' lifecycles in order to reduce the likelihood and ease of exploitation and compromise. Vulnerabilities can be eliminated by installing updates (e.g., patches) and changing configuration settings. Updates can also correct IoT device operational problems, which can improve device availability, reliability, performance, and other aspects of device operation. Customers often want to alter a device's configuration settings for a variety of reasons, including cybersecurity, interoperability, privacy, and usability.

• Access Management: Prevent unauthorized and improper physical and logical access to, usage of, and administration of IoT devices throughout the devices' lifecycles by people, processes, and other computing devices. Limiting access to interfaces reduces the attack surface of the device, giving attackers fewer opportunities to compromise it.

• Data Protection: Prevent access to and tampering with data at rest or in transit that might expose sensitive information or allow manipulation or disruption of IoT device operations throughout the devices' lifecycles.

• Incident Detection: Monitor and analyze IoT device activity for signs of incidents involving device and data security throughout the devices' lifecycles."[503]

NOTES

Note 1

In *Open Source Software and Hardware for the Internet of Things*, Brian Ray explains how open source is being utilized for the Internet of Things. *See* Brian Ray, *Open Source Software and Hardware for the Internet of Things*, Medium (June 8, 2017), https://medium.com/iotforall/open-source-software-and-hardware-for-the-internet-of-things-eca2aa728fa4. Do you think open source software is more or less secure than proprietary software? *See* Sentinel One, *How Secure is Open Source Software*, Sentinel One Blog (January 30, 2019), https://www.sentinelone.com/blog/open-source-security/ (noting ubiquity of open source software, and discussing transparency benefits of exposed open source code and mentioning downsides such as the software may not be maintained).

12.4 California's Internet of Things Legislation

California has passed legislation concerning cybersecurity and the Internet of Things. SB-327 Information privacy: connected devices is enacted as:

TITLE 1.81.26. Security of Connected Devices

1798.91.04.

(a) A manufacturer of a connected device shall equip the device with a reasonable security feature or features that are all of the following:

(1) Appropriate to the nature and function of the device.

---

[503] FOUNDATIONAL CYBERSECURITY ACTIVITIES FOR IOT DEVICE MANUFACTURERS, NAT'L INST. OF STANDARDS AND TECH. 4 (2020), *available at* https://nvlpubs.nist.gov/nistpubs/ir/2020/NIST.IR.8259.pdf.

(2) Appropriate to the information it may collect, contain, or transmit.

(3) Designed to protect the device and any information contained therein from unauthorized access, destruction, use, modification, or disclosure.

(b) Subject to all of the requirements of subdivision (a), if a connected device is equipped with a means for authentication outside a local area network, it shall be deemed a reasonable security feature under subdivision (a) if either of the following requirements are met:

(1) The preprogrammed password is unique to each device manufactured.

(2) The device contains a security feature that requires a user to generate a new means of authentication before access is granted to the device for the first time.

1798.91.05.

For the purposes of this title, the following terms have the following meanings:

(a) "Authentication" means a method of verifying the authority of a user, process, or device to access resources in an information system.

(b) "Connected device" means any device, or other physical object that is capable of connecting to the Internet, directly or indirectly, and that is assigned an Internet Protocol address or Bluetooth address.

(c) "Manufacturer" means the person who manufactures, or contracts with another person to manufacture on the person's behalf, connected devices that are sold or offered for sale in California. For the purposes of this subdivision, a contract with another person to manufacture on the person's behalf does not include a contract only to purchase a connected device, or only to purchase and brand a connected device.

(d) "Security feature" means a feature of a device designed to provide security for that device.

(e) "Unauthorized access, destruction, use, modification, or disclosure" means access, destruction, use, modification, or disclosure that is not authorized by the consumer.

1798.91.06.

(a) This title shall not be construed to impose any duty upon the manufacturer of a connected device related to unaffiliated third-party software or applications that a user chooses to add to a connected device.

(b) This title shall not be construed to impose any duty upon a provider of an electronic store, gateway, marketplace, or other means of purchasing or downloading software or applications, to review or enforce compliance with this title.

(c) This title shall not be construed to impose any duty upon the manufacturer of a connected device to prevent a user from having full control over a connected device, including the ability to modify the software or firmware running on the device at the user's discretion.

(d) This title shall not apply to any connected device the functionality of which is subject to security requirements under federal law, regulations, or guidance promulgated by a federal agency pursuant to its regulatory enforcement authority.

(e) This title shall not be construed to provide a basis for a private right of action. The Attorney General, a city attorney, a county counsel, or a district attorney shall have the exclusive authority to enforce this title.

(f) The duties and obligations imposed by this title are cumulative with any other duties or obligations imposed under other law, and shall not be construed to relieve any party from any duties or obligations imposed under other law.

(g) This title shall not be construed to limit the authority of a law enforcement agency to obtain connected device information from a manufacturer as authorized by law or pursuant to an order of a court of competent jurisdiction.

(h) A covered entity, provider of health care, business associate, health care service plan, contractor, employer, or any other person subject to the federal Health Insurance Portability and Accountability Act of 1996 (HIPAA) (Public Law 104-191) or the Confidentiality of Medical Information Act (Part 2.6 (commencing with Section 56) of Division 1) shall not be subject to this title with respect to any activity regulated by those acts.

(i) This title shall become operative on January 1, 2020.[504]

This law requires manufacturers to provide reasonable security features with the device. It actually spells out how to meet the "reasonable security feature or features." But the law does not require the homeowner to take action on the devices it already owns. And the law does not appear to require any retroactive actions by the owner. Also, the potential problem of poor password selection still exists.

Also, it is worth noting that this law applies to devices that would enter California. Thus, even if a device is made in Texas but enters California for use, the Texas manufacturer is subject to the laws of California.

QUESTION

The California IoT law does not require two-step verification or Multi-Factor authorization. Should it?

---

[504] CAL. CIV. CODE §§ 1798.91.04–1798.91.06 (West 2018).

12.5 Complaint Concerning Internet of Things and Cybersecurity

There has been an emphasis on securing internet devices so that they cannot be used as botnets in a DDOS. But if the device can be hacked, the functionality of the device can be controlled by an outside threat in the form of an unknown person. This is particularly concerning when the device contains a camera or listening device that can be hijacked. Camera's today are ubiquitous, even TVs contain cameras. And listening devices include Siri and Alexa among others.

The following document is the complaint filed against Ring concerning cybersecurity deficiencies in its product. Notably, the complaint was filed by attorneys Francis J. "Casey" Flynn, Jr. of the Law Office of Francis J. Flynn, Jr. and John A. Yanchunis of Morgan and Morgan. Please note that this complaint was filed in 2019 before the California IoT law went into effect on January 1, 2020.

Complaint in Orange et al., v. Ring filed in the U.S. District Court, Central District of California, No. 19-10899

Plaintiff John Baker Orange, Philip Tillapaugh, Jason Caldwell, and Megan Skuese ("Plaintiffs"), by and through their undersigned counsel, individually and on behalf of all others similarly situated, bring this class action lawsuit against Ring LLC ("Defendant," or "Ring") and alleges, based upon information and belief and the investigation of his counsel as follows:

JURISDICTION AND VENUE

1. This Court has subject matter jurisdiction over this action under the Class Action Fairness Act, 28 U.S.C. § 1332(d)(2) because (a) the aggregated claims of putative class members exceeds $5 million, exclusive of interest and costs; (b) there are at least hundreds of putative class members; and (c) at least one of the members of the putative class is a citizen of a different state than Defendant. . . .

INTRODUCTION

2. Ring is a security and safety company which manufactures, markets and sells alarms, video doorbells, security systems, and cameras. At its core, Ring's products are designed to promote the safety of its customers and to protect their privacy.

3. Wi-Fi cameras are among Ring's most popular offerings. They are designed to be strategically placed throughout a property, enabling authorized users to see covered areas in high definition and to communicate directly with occupants via a two-way speaker-microphone system.

4. Ring promises its customers "peace of mind" with its Wi-Fi enabled smart security systems. Unfortunately, Ring's cameras fail to deliver on its most basic promise. Lax security standards and protocols render its camera systems vulnerable to cyber-attack. Indeed, over the past several months numerous Ring customers reported that their camera systems had been hacked by malicious third parties who gained access to

the video and two-way speaker-microphone system which they used to invade the privacy of customers' homes and terrorize unsuspecting occupants, many of whom are children.

5.   While Ring quickly attempted to distance itself from liability by blaming customers for failing to create strong security passwords, it is Ring who failed to provide sufficiently robust security measures such as two-factor authentication and other protocols necessary to maintain the integrity and inviolability of its cameras. As a result of Ring's defective design, and its failure to imbue its Wi-Fi cameras with sufficient security protocols, its customers' most basic privacy rights were violated along with the security and sanctity of their homes.

6.   Plaintiff, on behalf of all others similarly situated, alleges claims for negligence, invasion of privacy, breach of implied contract, breach of implied warranty and unjust enrichment. In addition, Plaintiff seeks damages, injunctive and declaratory relief.

PARTIES

7.   Plaintiff John Baker Orange is a resident of Jefferson County Alabama. He purchased a Ring outdoor camera for his house in July 2019 for approximately $249.00. The Ring camera was installed over his garage with a view of the driveway. Mr. Orange purchased the Ring camera to provide additional security for him and his family which include his wife and three children aged 7, 9, and 10. Recently, Mr. Orange's children were playing basketball when a voice came on through the camera's two-way speaker system. An unknown person engaged with Mr. Orange's children commenting on their basketball play and encouraging them to get closer to the camera. Once Mr. Orange learned of the incident, he changed the password on the Ring camera and enabled two-factor authentication. Prior to changing his password, Mr. Orange protected his Ring camera with a medium-strong password.

8.   Prior to the recent hacking incidents, Mr. Orange was unaware of and believes that Ring did not provide users the ability to secure their systems with two-factor authentication.

9.   Plaintiff Jason Caldwell is a resident of Wayne County, Michigan. Plaintiff Caldwell purchased four (4) Ring cameras for his house. One Ring camera was installed in the kitchen. . . . Mr. Caldwell purchased the Ring camera to provide additional security for him his family. On January 2, 2020, a hacker gained access to his Ring camera and began make noises and threaten Mr. Caldwell, singing the chorus to Pumped Up Kicks by the Foster People, which included:

"All the other kids with the pumped up kicks **You'd better run, better run, out run my gun** All the other kids with the pumped up kicks You'd better run, better run, faster than my bullet." Ring acknowledged the security breach, but has otherwise been unhelpful."

10.   Prior to the recent hacking incidents, Mr. Caldwell was unaware of and

believes that Ring did not provide users the ability to secure their systems with two-factor authentication.

11.   . . . Plaintiff [Megan] Skeuse purchased a Ring camera for her house Ms. Skeuse purchased the Ring camera to provide additional security for her and her family, which includes children. Recently, a hacker gained access to her Ring camera and began yelling at her children and scared them. Ring acknowledged the security breach, but has otherwise been unhelpful.

12.   Prior to the recent hacking incidents, Ms. Skeuse was unaware of and believes that Ring did not provide users the ability to secure their systems with two-factor authentication.

13.   Plaintiff Philip Tillapaugh . . . purchased a Ring camera for his house[.] . . . Mr. Tillapaugh purchased the Ring camera to provide additional security for him and his family[.] Once Mr. Tillapaugh learned of the security issues with Ring, he changed the password on the Ring camera and enabled two-factor authentication.

14.   Prior to the recent hacking incidents, Mr. Tillapaugh was unaware of and believes that Ring did not provide users the ability to secure their systems with two-factor authentication.

15.   Defendant Ring LLC is a home security and smart home company that manufactures a range of home security products including Wi-Fi enabled smart cameras. Ring LLC is a wholly owned subsidiary of Amazon.com with its place of business located at 1523 26th St, Santa Monica, California 90404.

STATEMENT OF FACTS

A.   *Ring Products and Wi-Fi Connectivity*

16.   Ring offers a variety of Wi-Fi enabled security and safety devices, most notably video doorbells and cameras. The Ring video doorbell is the company's flagship product. It is a smart doorbell that contains a high-definition camera, a motion sensor, a microphone and speaker for two-way audio communication. It integrates with an associated mobile app, which allows users to view real-time video from the camera, receive notifications when the doorbell is rung, and communicate with visitors at the door via the integrated speaker.

17.   In 2015, Ring released the first of its internal wireless IP cameras. Like the video doorbell, the cameras provide high definition video and microphone-speaker functionality for two-way communication. Since 2015, Ring has expanded its selection to include a range of indoor and outdoor cameras, each with video and two-way audio communication.

18.   Ring products are designed to operate through a users' Wi-Fi network. Once connected, the cameras enable users to see a high definition video stream in the camera's range and listen to and/or communicate with nearby occupants.

19.   Creating a Ring account to fully enable the system involves a 4 step process: (1) download the Ring App; (2) Launch the app and click on the Setup Device button; (3) Create an Account at the bottom of the screen; (4) Enter your first and last name, email address and password.

20.   Ring cameras are relatively affordable, easy to install, simple to use, and heavily marketed by Amazon, making them one of the best-selling home security and surveillance devices on the market.

21.   In addition to their own direct-to-consumer marketing efforts, Ring has signed partnership agreements with hundreds of police departments around the country, many of which have marketed and sold Ring devices on the company's behalf.

22.   Ring promises its customers "peace of mind" with "smart security here, there, everywhere."

At the core of Ring, and guiding every action we take, is respect for the privacy and security of our neighbors (what we call our customers). This includes giving our neighbors effective, easy-to-use and affordable products and services to help protect their homes. It also means taking extremely seriously the privacy, security and control of their devices and personal information. Below you will find Ring's guiding principles.

We know you have many options to choose from so protecting your privacy and data security is a job we take seriously. We know that you place a huge amount of trust in us and we have every intention of continuing to earn that trust.

23.   Unfortunately, Ring does not fulfill its core promise of providing privacy and security for its customers, as its camera systems are fatally flawed. The Ring system is Wi-Fi enabled, meaning that it will not work without internet connectivity. Once connected, however, any internet device can be seen by the on-line community, making it incumbent upon its manufacturer to design the device such that it can be properly secured for only intended use. This obligation is even more critical in instances where the device, like the Ring camera, is related to the safety and security of person and property.

24.   Ring failed to meet this most basic obligation by not ensuring its Wi-Fi enabled cameras were protected against cyber-attack. Notably, Ring only required users enter a basic password and did not offer or did not compel two-factor authentication.

25.   Dual factor or two-factor authentication ("2FA") is a security process in which the user provides two different authentication factors to verify themselves to better protect both the user's credentials and the resources the user can access. 2FA provides a higher level of assurance than authentication methods that depend on single-factor authentication, in which the user provides only one factor -- typically a password. 2FA adds an additional layer of security to the authentication process by making it harder for attackers to gain access to a person's devices or online accounts, because knowing the victim's password alone is not enough to pass the authentication check. Two-factor authentication has long been used to control access to sensitive systems and

data, and online service providers are increasingly using 2FA to protect their users' credentials from being used by hackers who have stolen a password database or used phishing campaigns to obtain user passwords.

26.   Ring was certainly aware of the infirmity of its cameras and the necessity to employ good security practices which included, at a minimum, insistence on robust passwords and dual factor authentication.

B.   Hacking Incidents

27.   Over the past several weeks, news media has been inundated with reports of hackers gaining unauthorized access to homes across the country via insecure Ring devices. Once in, hackers routinely terrorizing occupants, invade their privacy and undermine their sense of safety and security. While the dramatic nature of these hacking incidents, which involved interactions between the hackers and occupants of the home, many of whom were children, caught the attention of mainstream media, the insecurity of the cameras poses an additional and more looming threat. Hackers who choose not to interact with occupants have gone unnoticed for days, month and even years during which time they spied on occupants and their homes, gathering an array of private which can subsequently be sold and used for a host of nefarious purposes:

(a)   Mississippi Incident

Pedophile Hacker Hacked 8yo Girl's Room – Told Her That He Is Santa Claus

Parents will do anything to keep their child safe. This includes installing a CCTV inside the child's room so that they can monitor their child while at work. However, for a couple in US, this move has caused their 8-year-old daughter to be harassed by a hacker.

The mother, Ashley LeMay told CNN that she installed the camera so that she could make sure that they are OK while she's at the overnight shift but four days after the camera was installed, a hacker managed to get through the system.

From the CCTV footage, it can be seen that their daughter went into her room after hearing song being played from inside her room. Alyssa went on to ask who was playing the song and a voice came through the speaker of the camera. He said, "I'm your best friend. I'm Santa Claus. Don't you want to be my best friend?"

When the couple's 8-year-old daughter, Alyssa, checked on the music and turned on the lights, a man started speaking to her, repeatedly calling her a racial slur and saying he was Santa Claus. She screamed for her mother.

"She won't even sleep in her room," Ms. LeMay said on Saturday. "She actually spent the night with a friend the other night because she didn't want to be here." "I did a lot of research on these before I got them. You know, I really felt like it was safe,"

A big part of Ring's marketing strategy revolves around making customers feel like their own homes are unsafe, so that they'll turn to surveillance devices to ease those fears.

(b)   Waterbury, Connecticut Incident

Ed Slaughter told NBC Connecticut last week that he felt "violated" after a hacker started yelling obscenities and woke up his mother-in-law, who had been sleeping in the basement where he had installed a Ring camera.

(c)   Cape Coral, Florida Incident

Josefine Brown told NBC 2 that she was frightened by an episode in which a hacker could be heard in footage from a Ring security camera provided to the station asking the interracial couple if their son was a "baboon."

In an email on Sunday, Ms. Brown said: "We are very concerned about our safety and privacy because we thought having a security camera will keep us safe. We don't know how long someone has been watching us. It is very scary."

(d)   Staten Island, New York Incident

Gina Scarlato's 13-year-old son, was terrorized by a hacker who followed the boy from camera to camera throughout the house.

(e)   North Texas Incident

"The first thing that they heard was like a siren that went off," said Lue Mayora of Forney. Wednesday night, while Mayora and her husband were coming home from work, someone hacked into their Ring cameras.

They were shouting profanities, racial slurs and threats at their 9-year-old and 11-year-old children who they said ran out of the house in terror.

"I heard real, real screaming and I came out and said what's going on," Mayora's neighbor Johnny Davila said. "They said someone is in house yelling they're going to kill us."

Mayora's neighbor got his gun and ran next door thinking someone was inside the home.

As he heard the voice coming from the camera, he eventually realized it had been hacked.

"It made me so mad that they're targeting our kids," he said. "They don't want to sleep by themselves," Mayora said. "They don't want to be in the house." Mayora has now deactivated her Ring cameras and said she will be getting rid of them this weekend.

(f)   Georgia Incident

A Georgia woman was given a terrifying wake-up call by a man who hacked into her Ring security camera and began speaking to her in the middle of the night.

The woman was in bed when an unidentified man called to her through the camera, which she and her boyfriend installed to keep an eye on their new puppy, Beau, during working hours.

In footage of the encounter, which a friend of the woman's shared on Twitter, the stranger can be heard clapping, calling to the puppy and telling the woman to "wake up!"

"Hello? Hello? Come here, puppy," he shouts.

"Hello? Hello?" he says after multiple ignored commands. "I can see you in the bed, come on, wake the f*** up."

(g) Texas Incident

Ring hackers demand $350,000 in Bitcoin from Texas Couple

One of the most bizarre recent reports comes from Grand Prairie, Texas, where a couple says they awoke in the middle of the night to an alarm coming from their Ring camera. But that's not all they heard; After the couple came to investigate, a voice over the Ring's built-in speaker claimed that the couple's Ring account had been terminated, and that they themselves would be "terminated" if they didn't fork over a hefty haul of cryptocurrency.

The "hackers" demanded a whopping 50 bitcoins. Going by the current conversion rate, that's over $350,000.

* * *

[W]hat makes this whole thing scary is that they also gained control over the home's Ring doorbell. They used their access to the doorbell to spoof their presence outside of the couple's home, making the homeowners believe that someone was actually stalking their property while demanding the ransom.

Ring's Response

28.   In response to the swath of hacking incidents across the country, Ring said only that it takes the security of its devices seriously, and then proceeded to blame Ring users for the hacking.

"Our security team has investigated this incident and we have no evidence of an unauthorized intrusion or compromise of Ring's systems or network," the statement said. "Recently, we were made aware of an incident where malicious actors obtained some Ring users' account credentials (e.g., username and password) from a separate, external, non-Ring service and reused them to log in to some Ring accounts."

29.   According to Ring, the hacked cameras were accessed when unauthorized

third parties were able to login as authentic users with a proper password. Ring places the blame squarely on its customers suggesting these hacks are possible because people are using weak passwords that have previously been compromised.

30.   By so doing, however, Ring ignores the fact that it allows its products – whose very purpose is to provide customers with safety and security – to be setup in a manner that makes it unreasonably susceptible to hacking.

31.   Although Ring is in the business of home security and was certainly aware that its Wi-Fi enabled product, was vulnerable to attack, it took no steps to "require camera owners to use two-factor authentication, which could help prevent these types of attacks..." Moreover, it knew, or should have known, in an era of pervasive data breaches, that logging in with user emails instead of unique account names, and not requiring at least 2FA, put its Wi-Fi enabled product at an unreasonable risk of being compromised.

32.   Not only was Ring aware that its cameras were inadequately secured, it was also aware of the existence of "online forums where hackers discussed how to break into Ring accounts connected to the cameras."

33.   According to *Motherboard,*

Ring was aware that the hacking community developed dedicated software for breaking into Ring security cameras. Indeed, several posts on different crime forums where hackers discuss creating tools for breaking into the Ring accounts which are connected to cameras.

'Ring Video Doorbell Config,' one thread on a hacking forum reads. A config is a file use to drive special software for rapidly churning through usernames or email addresses and passwords and trying to use them to log into accounts. Hackers have developed configs for a wide variety of websites and online services, from Uber to Facebook.

The thread title adds that the config has a "High CPM," or high "check per minute," meaning it can test if a username and password allows access to a Ring camera quickly. In a different thread, one hacker is offering a Ring.com checker for $6.

34.   Sadly, Ring hacking events have become so common place that there is even a podcast dedicated to live and recorded hacking events wherein malevolent third parties take control of Ring devices and terrorize occupants for entertainment. "The NulledCast is a podcast livestreamed to Discord. It's a show in which hackers take over people's Ring and Nest smart home cameras and use their speakers to talk to and harass their unsuspecting owners." "'Sit back and relax to over 45 minutes of entertainment,' an advertisement for the podcast posted to a hacking forum called Nulled reads. 'Join us as we go on completely random tangents such as; Ring & Nest Trolling, telling shelter owners we killed a kitten, Nulled drama, and more ridiculous topics. Be sure to join our Discord to watch the shows live.'" As reported in Slashgear:

Reality [] has taken on a frightening turn for owners of Ring security cameras who suddenly find virtual intruders in their homes, thanks to hackers who break into the security system and live stream their harassment for the entertainment of a few.

The irony is probably lost on no one that the very devices that are supposed to keep homes and their owners safe have become the very vehicle for violations of their privacy. Tools to hack Ring security cameras have unfortunately become widespread enough to become almost common. And to show off their abilities and get a few kicks, some of these hackers have taken to live streaming their activities in bold defiance to authorities.

35.   The podcast and other online hacker forums even feature software specifically designed to hack Ring cameras. The software churns through previously compromised email addresses and passwords to break into Ring cameras at scale.

36.   Despite active knowledge of such forums Ring continued to blame these hacking incidents on poor security practices by users. Ring contends that in each of the hacking incidents, "credentials stolen during a data breach are sold on the black market and used for hacking into accounts.... Due to the fact that customers often use the same username and password for their various accounts and subscriptions, bad actors often re-use credentials stolen or leaked from one service on other services." Ring's explanation, however, neither eliminates its responsibility, nor accurately attributes the fault. As one hacking victim, Tania Amador, explained, her Ring password is 21 characters long and only used for that account.

37.   Moreover, "Ring's status as a maker of home security cameras makes it much more sensitive than most accounts. Ring could probably do more to encourage users to choose strong passwords and set up two-factor authentication. For example, Google-owned Nest recently switches to Google logins, which have industry-leading security features. It also pesters people in the app to configure two-factor if they haven't already."

38.   "Additionally, Ring does not alert users of attempted log-in from an unknown IP address, or tell users how many others are logged into an account at one time. Because of this, there is no obvious way to know whether any bad actors have logged into people's compromised Ring accounts without their consent."

39.   Ring's failure to employ good security practices in the design and implementation of its camera systems has directly resulted in the unlawful exposure of Plaintiff and Class Members' person and property and has damaged them thereby.

C.   **Plaintiff and Class Members Suffered Damages**

40.   The ramifications of Defendant's failure to properly secure their cameras and attendant access protocols may be felt for years to come. While the immediate in terrorem effects resulting from unauthorized access may be assuaged by disconnecting the camera, hackers have had access to information derived from those cameras for years, including but not limited to intimate details of household members, work

schedules, and property contents. This information can be sold and used for a host of nefarious purposes.

41.   The hacking was a direct and proximate result of Ring's failure to: (a) properly secure its camera systems in order to prevent, or at least minimize, the ability of unauthorized third parties to gain access; (b) establish and implement appropriate administrative, technical, and physical safeguards to ensure the security and confidentiality of their cameras; and (c) protect against reasonably foreseeable threats to the security or integrity of such cameras.

42.   Defendant had the resources necessary to properly secure its cameras but neglected to do so. Had Defendant taken such steps and adopted basic security measures (e.g. 2FA), it would have prevented the intrusions suffered by Plaintiff and Class Members.

43.   As a direct and proximate result of Defendant's wrongful actions and inactions, Plaintiff and Class Members have been placed at an imminent, immediate, and continuing increased risk of harm from malicious third parties who gained unauthorized access to their homes and highly sensitive details of their lives.

44.   As a result of the Defendant's actions, Plaintiff and Class Members have been damages and can no longer trust the integrity of the Ring cameras or believe in security it claims to provide.

CLASS ACTION ALLEGATIONS

45.   Plaintiff seeks relief on behalf of herself and as representatives of all others who are similarly situated. Pursuant to Fed. R. Civ. P. Rule 23(a), (b)(2), (b)(3) and (c)(4), Plaintiff seeks certification of a Nationwide class defined as follows:

All persons in the United States whose purchased a Ring camera within the applicable statute of limitations periods (the "Class").

46.   Excluded from the Class are Ring and any of its affiliates, parents or subsidiaries; all persons who make a timely election to be excluded from the Class; government entities; and the judges to whom this case is assigned, their immediate families, and court staff.

47.   Plaintiff hereby reserves the right to amend or modify the class definitions with greater specificity or division after having had an opportunity to conduct discovery.

48.   The proposed Class meets the criteria for certification under Rule 23(a), (b)(2), (b)(3) and (c)(4).

49.   **Numerosity. Fed. R. Civ. P. 23(a)(1).** Consistent with Rule 23(a)(1), the members of the Class are so numerous and geographically dispersed that the joinder of all members is impractical. Ring sells tens of thousands of cameras throughout the United States every year. Ring has physical and/or email addresses for Class Members

who therefore may be notified of the pendency of this action by recognized, Court-approved notice dissemination methods, which may include U.S. mail, electronic mail, internet postings, and/or published notice.

50.   **Commonality. Fed. R. Civ. P. 23(a)(2) and (b)(3).** Consistent with Rule 23(a)(2) and with 23(b)(3)'s predominance requirement, this action involves common questions of law and fact that predominate over any questions affecting individual Class members. The common questions include:

a.   Whether Ring knew or should have known of the susceptibility of its camera systems to hacking;

b.   Whether Ring's security measures to protect their camera systems were reasonable;

c.   Whether Ring was negligent in failing to implement reasonable and adequate security procedures and practices;

d.   Whether Ring's failure to implement adequate security measures rendered its camera systems subject to hacking;

e.   Whether Plaintiff and Class Members were injured and suffered damages or other losses because of Ring's failure to reasonably secure its camera systems; and;

f.   Whether Plaintiff and Class members are entitled to relief.

51.   **Typicality. Fed. R. Civ. P. 23(a)(3).** Consistent with Rule 23(a)(3), Plaintiff's claims are typical of those of other Class members. Plaintiff is a purchaser of a Ring camera. Plaintiff's damages and injuries are akin to other Class Members, and Plaintiff seeks relief consistent with the relief sought by the Class. The claims of the Plaintiff and the respective Class are based on the same legal theories and arise from the same unlawful and willful conduct of Defendant, resulting in the same injury to the Plaintiff and the respective Class. Plaintiff and all members of the Class are similarly affected by Defendant's wrongful conduct and were damaged in the same way. Plaintiff's interests coincide with, and are not antagonistic to, those of the other Class members. Plaintiff have been damaged by the same wrongdoing set forth in this Complaint. Plaintiff's damages and injuries are akin to other Class Members, and Plaintiff seeks relief consistent with the relief sought by the Class.

52.   **Adequacy. Fed. R. Civ. P. 23(a)(4).** Consistent with Rule 23(a)(4), Plaintiff is an adequate representative of the Class because Plaintiff is a member of the Class he seeks to represent; is committed to pursuing this matter against Ring to obtain relief for the Class; and has no conflicts of interest with the Class. Moreover, Plaintiff's Counsel are competent and experienced in litigating class actions, including privacy litigation of this kind. Plaintiff intends to vigorously prosecute this case and will fairly and adequately protect the Class's interests.

53.   **Superiority. Fed. R. Civ. P. 23(b)(3).** Consistent with Rule 23(b)(3), a

class action is superior to any other available means for the fair and efficient adjudication of this controversy, and no unusual difficulties are likely to be encountered in the management of this class action. The quintessential purpose of the class action mechanism is to permit litigation against wrongdoers even when damages to an individual plaintiff may not be sufficient to justify individual litigation. Here, the damages suffered by Plaintiff and the Class are relatively small compared to the burden and expense required to individually litigate their claims against Ring, and thus, individual litigation to redress Ring's wrongful conduct would be impracticable. Individual litigation by each Class member would also strain the court system. Individual litigation creates the potential for inconsistent or contradictory judgments and increases the delay and expense to all parties and the court system. By contrast, the class action device presents far fewer management difficulties and provides the benefits of a single adjudication, economies of scale, and comprehensive supervision by a single court.

54. **Injunctive and Declaratory Relief.** Class certification is also appropriate under Rule 23(b)(2) and (c). Defendant, through Defendant's uniform conduct, acted or refused to act on grounds generally applicable to the Class as a whole, making injunctive and declaratory relief appropriate to the Class as a whole.

55. Likewise, particular issues under Rule 23(c)(4) are appropriate for certification because such claims present only particular, common issues, the resolution of which would advance the disposition of this matter and the parties' interests therein.

56. **Ascertainability.** Finally, all members of the proposed Classes are readily ascertainable. Ring has access to customer names and addresses. Additionally, Ring videos contain hidden geographic coordinates, including latitude and longitude with up to six decimal points of precision. Using this information, Class Members can be identified and ascertained for the purpose of providing notice.

FIRST CAUSE OF ACTION

NEGLIGENCE

57. Plaintiff realleges and incorporates by reference each preceding paragraph as though set forth at length herein.

58. Defendant had full knowledge of the purpose for which its security cameras were being used and the sensitivity of the people and things the cameras were designed to secure and protect. Defendant also knew the types of harm that Plaintiff and Class Members could and would suffer if the integrity of the cameras were compromised.

59. Defendant had a duty to exercise reasonable care in ensuring its cameras were secure, safe to use and inviolable by unauthorized parties. This duty includes, among other things, ensuring that reasonable and proper protocols and safeguards are in place, so that the Wi-Fi enabled cameras are not easily compromised by unauthorized users.

60.   Plaintiff and Class Members were the foreseeable and probable victims of any inadequate security practices and procedures. Defendant knew of or should have known of the inherent risks of allowing Ring cameras to be set up and used without adequate security protocols and safeguards.

61.   Defendant's own actions and inactions created a foreseeable risk of harm to Plaintiff and Class Members. Defendant's misconduct included, but was not limited to, its failure to sell cameras with sufficiently robust security protocols to prevent unauthorized users from gaining access to the cameras and to provide users with sufficient instructions and tools to properly secure their Wi-Fi enabled cameras.

62.   Plaintiff and the Class Members had no idea Ring cameras were vulnerable to misappropriated and therefore had not ability to properly protect their cameras from unauthorized use.

63.   In contrast, Defendant was in a position to protect against the harm suffered by Plaintiff and Class Members and had a duty to do so.

64.   Defendant, through their actions, unlawfully breached their duty to Plaintiff and Class Members by failing to ensure their cameras and set up procedures were sufficiently robust to protect against unauthorized use.

65.   But for Defendant's wrongful and negligent breach of duties owed to Plaintiff and Class Members, Plaintiff's and Class Members' would not have used or purchased a product that is so readily compromised.

66.   As a result of Defendant's negligence, Plaintiff and the Class Members have suffered and will continue to suffer damages and injury including, but not limited to: the cost of replacement cameras; cost of additional surveillance and protective devices and services; time spent monitoring, addressing the current and future consequences of the exposure enabled by Ring; and the necessity to engage legal counsel and incur attorneys' fees, costs and expenses.

SECOND CAUSE OF ACTION

INVASION OF PRIVACY

67.   Plaintiff realleges and incorporates by reference each preceding paragraph as though set forth at length herein.

68.   Plaintiff and Class Members had a legitimate expectation of privacy with respect to the people, location and subject matter of what their Ring cameras were observing and were accordingly entitled to the protection of this information against disclosure to unauthorized third parties.

69.   Defendant owed a duty to their customers, including Plaintiff and Class Members, and the general public to ensure that its cameras and the data they observed and recorded remained confidential and secure.

70.   The failure to ensure the cameras had sufficiently robust security features and were accompanied by sufficient security practices is highly offensive to a reasonable person.

71.   The intrusion was into a place or thing, which was private and is entitled to be private. Plaintiff and Class Members purchased and used Ring cameras with the expectation that people, places and information seen and heard by the camera would be private and would not be subject to disclosure without their authorization.

72.   The failure to ensure the camera and its setup features provided adequate security constitutes an intentional interference with Plaintiff and Class Members' interest in solitude or seclusion, either as to their persons or as to their private affairs or concerns, of a kind that would be highly offensive to a reasonable person.

73.   Defendant acted with a knowing state of mind when they permitted the cameras to be marketed and sold in such a fashion because they knew their security practices were inadequate.

74.   Acting with this knowledge, Defendant had notice and knew that their inadequate security practices would cause injury to Plaintiff and Class Members.

75.   As a proximate result of Defendant's acts and omissions, Plaintiff's and Class Members' privacy was violated causing Plaintiff and Class Members to suffer damages.

76.   Unless and until enjoined, and restrained by order of this Court, Defendant's wrongful conduct will continue to cause great and irreparable injury to Plaintiff and Class Members.

77.   Plaintiff and Class Members have no adequate remedy at law for the injuries in that a judgment for monetary damages will not end the invasion of privacy for Plaintiff and the Class.

THIRD CAUSE OF ACTION

BREACH OF THE IMPLIED WARRANTY OF MERCHANTABILITY

78.   Plaintiff realleges and incorporates by reference each preceding paragraph as though set forth at length herein.

79.   Defendant is in the business of manufacturing, designing, supplying, marketing, advertising, warranting, and selling security cameras. Defendant impliedly warranted to Plaintiff and Class Members that the Product was of a certain quality, free from defects, fit for the ordinary purpose of observing and recording events for the purpose of securing property and maintaining safety of its residents.

80.   The Ring cameras were and are unfit for ordinary use and not of merchantable quality as warranted by Defendant because the Products are defective in that they are not secure and can easily be hacked by unauthorized third parties. Before

purchase, Plaintiff and Class Members could not have readily discovered that the cameras were not merchantable for use to protect their homes and occupants.

81.   Defendant has failed to provide adequate remedies under their limited warranty, which have caused that warranty to fail of its essential purpose, thereby permitting remedies under these implied warranties.

82.   Defendant had unequal bargaining power and misrepresented the Products' reliability and performance properties, and the limited remedies unreasonably favor Defendant and fail Plaintiff's reasonable expectations for product performance.

83.   As a direct and proximate result of the breaches of these implied warranties, Plaintiff and Class Members suffered damages, injuries in fact and ascertainable losses in an amount to be determined at trial, including repair and replacement costs and damages to other property.

FOURTH CAUSE OF ACTION

BREACH OF IMPLIED CONTRACT

84.   Plaintiff realleges and incorporates by reference each preceding paragraph as though set forth at length herein.

85.   . . . Defendant has acknowledged the benefit and accepted or retained the benefit conferred.

86.   Implicit in the agreement between the Defendant and Plaintiff and Class Members was to provide cameras that were suitable for their purpose and not designed with flaws that render them vulnerable to hacking resulting in the compromise of user safety and security.

87.   Without such implied contracts, Plaintiff and Class Members would not have paid for and conferred a benefit upon Defendant, but rather chosen one of the numerous alternative cameras that were available to them and which did not present a hidden safety risk.

88.   Plaintiff and Class Members fully performed their obligations under the implied contracts with Defendant, however, Defendant did not.

89.   Defendant breached the implied contracts with Plaintiff and Class Members by failing to acknowledge the inherent vulnerability in their cameras. These circumstances are such that it would be inequitable for Defendant to retain the benefit received.

90.   As a direct and proximate result of Defendant's breach of their implied contracts with Plaintiff and Class Members, Plaintiff and Class Members have suffered and will suffer injury, including but not limited to: the cost of replacement cameras; the cost of additional surveillance and protective devices and services; and time spent

monitoring, addressing the current and future consequences of the exposure enabled by Ring.

FIFTH CAUSE OF ACTION

UNJUST ENRICHMENT

91.   Plaintiff realleges and incorporates by reference each preceding paragraph as though set forth at length herein.

92.   As the intended and expected result of their conscious wrongdoing, Defendant has profited and benefited from the purchase of the Product by Plaintiff and the Class.

93.   Defendant has voluntarily accepted and retained these profits and benefits, with full knowledge and awareness that, as a result of Defendant's misconduct, Plaintiff and the Class did not receive Product of the quality, nature, fitness, or value that had been represented by Defendant, and that reasonable consumers expected.

94.   Defendant has been unjustly enriched by Defendant's fraudulent and deceptive withholding of benefits to Plaintiff and the Class at the expense of these parties.

95.   Equity and good conscience militate against permitting Defendant to retain these profits and benefits.

As a direct and proximate result of Defendant's unjust enrichment, Plaintiff and Class Members suffered injury and seek an order directing Defendant's disgorgement and the return to Plaintiffs and the classes of the amount each improperly paid to Defendant.

SIXTH CAUSE OF ACTION

VIOLATION OF CALIFORNIA'S UNFAIR COMPETITION LAW ("UCL")

Cal. Bus. Prof. Code § 17200

96.   Plaintiff realleges and incorporates by reference each preceding paragraph as though set forth at length herein.

97.   Plaintiff has standing to pursue this cause of action as Plaintiff has suffered injury in fact and has lost money or property as a result of Defendant's actions as delineated herein.

98.   The UCL defines unfair business competition to include any "unlawful, unfair or fraudulent" act or practice, as well as any "unfair, deceptive, untrue or misleading" advertising. Cal. Bus. Prof. Code § 17200.

99.   A business act or practice is "unlawful" if it violates any established state

or federal law.

100.   Defendant's business practices, as alleged herein, violate the "unlawful" prong by:

(a)   breaching implied warranty of merchantability as to purchasers of the Ring camera;

(b)   By engaging in negligent acts and practices by failing to take one or more acts when it should have acted or by taking one or more affirmative actions that it should not have taken as described herein;

(c)   By violating the Privacy Policy available at https://shop.ring.com/pages/privacy-notice and/or engaging in misrepresentations and/or omissions of fact;

(d)   By violating the FTC;

(e)   By being unjustly enriched;

(f)   By knowingly and intentionally concealing from Plaintiff and the Class material information; and/or

(g)   By breaching an implied contract (e.g., Privacy Policy available at https://shop.ring.com/pages/privacy-notice)

(h)   By violating other common or statutory law.

101.   Defendant's business practices, as alleged herein, violate the "unfair" prong of California Business & Professions Code §§ 17200, *et seq.* Defendant's business practices are unfair business practice under the UCL because they "either 'offend[] an established public policy' or [are] 'immoral, unethical, oppressive, unscrupulous or substantially injurious to consumers.'" *Evenchik v. Avis Rent A Car Sys., LLC*, 2012 WL 4111382, at *8 (S.D. Cal. Sept. 17, 2012) *(quoting McDonald v. Coldwell Banker*, 543 F.3d 498, 506 (9th Cir.2008) (quoting *People v. Casa Blanca Convalescent Homes, Inc.*, 159 Cal.App.3d 509, 530, 206 Cal.Rptr. 164 (1984)).

102.   A business act or practice is also, "unfair" under the Unfair Competition Law if the reasons, justifications, and motives of the alleged wrongdoer are outweighed by the gravity of the harm to the alleged victims. The injury resulting from Defendant's acts and practices is substantial, not outweighed by any countervailing benefits to consumers or to competition, and not an injury that the consumers themselves could reasonably have avoided.

103.   Defendant's business practices, as alleged herein, also violate the "unfair" prong of the UCL because Defendant (a) misrepresented the source, sponsorship, approval, or certification of goods or services; (b) represented that goods or services have sponsorship, approval, characteristics, ingredients, uses, quantities that they did not have or that a person has a sponsorship, approval, status, affiliation, or connection that

he or she does not have; (c) representing that goods or services are of a particular standard, quality, or grade [...] if they are of another; (d) advertising goods or services with intent not to sell them as advertised; (e) representing that a transaction confers or involves rights, remedies, or obligations that it does not involve, or that are prohibited by law; (f) representing that the subject of a transaction has been supplied in accordance with a previous representation when it has not; and/or (g) inserting an unconscionable provision in a contract.

104.   As a direct and proximate result of Defendant's unlawful and unfair, business practices, Plaintiff and the Class have suffered injury in fact and lost money or property.

105.   The basis for Plaintiff's claims emanated from California as one or more decisions regarding security regarding the Ring cameras occurred at the Ring Headquarters. Additionally, Ri*ng LLC claims that "if you have any questions about this Privacy Notice, or if you would like us to update information we have about you, change your preferences or exercise other applicable data protection rights, please contact us by e-mail at privacy@ring.com or write to us at: Ring LLC 1523 26th Street Santa Monica, CA 90404."

PRAYER FOR RELIEF

WHEREFORE, Plaintiff, on behalf of herself and all others similarly situated, respectfully requests the following relief:

a.   An Order certifying this case as a class action;

b.   An Order appointing Plaintiff as the class representative;

c.   An Order appointing undersigned counsel as class counsel;

d.   A mandatory injunction directing the Defendant to hereinafter adequately safeguard the PII of the Class by implementing improved security procedures and measures;

e.   An award of damages;

f.   An award of costs and expenses;

g.   An award of attorneys' fees; and

h.   Such other and further relief as this court may deem just and proper.

DEMAND FOR JURY TRIAL

Plaintiff demands a jury trial as to all issues triable by a jury.

NOTES

Note 1

The Ring Help Page[505] states the following, in relevant part:

Enhancing Security with Two-Step Verification

The purpose of Two-Step Verification is to protect you from unauthorized logins into your Ring account.

Every time you log into Ring (any app, ring.com or Ring Community) you will receive a One-Time Passcode via your email address on file, and you will have to enter a six-digit code to successfully log in.

- The passcode expires after 10 minutes.

- You can request "Resend code" after 60 seconds if you haven't received it.

- If you continue to use your mobile apps every 30 days, you will not have to login via Two-Step Verification (unless you log out, or "Remove All" authorized devices from Control Center).

Note: A feature on the sign-in page will allow you to choose to remember the browser you logged in with. By agreeing to identify your browser, you will not be challenged by Two-Step Verification for 30 days.

Troubleshooting

If you are receiving an "error occurred" or "bad connection" similar error message when logging into your Ring App, this is because your app requires an update to continue. You can update your app by following this link: https://ring.com/gettheapp.

The following Ring app versions do not have the ability to utilize Two-Step   Verification:

iOS 5.12 or earlier

- You may receive an error message stating, "Your internet connection   is   not   currently   working.   Please   try   again."

Android 3.12 or earlier

---

[505] Editors: It is unclear when the text of this page was created. It was likely created after the incidents in the complaint.

- You may receive an error message stating, "An error occurred trying to perform the operation. Try again later.

What happens if I'm unable to receive, or cannot locate, the Two-Step Verification email?
Search your email for the subject line, "New Login Attempt". This email should include the 6-digit code necessary to log in to your account.

Note: Codes expire 10 minutes after the login attempt.

Double-check spam folders, or other filters that might be active on your email account.
FAQs

What is Two-Step Verification?

Two-Step Verification is a mandatory, enhanced security feature that helps keep your account secure and prevents unauthorized users from gaining access to your Ring account. With every new login to your Ring account, you will receive a six-digit code to verify your login attempt. That one-time code needs to be entered within 10 minutes before you can access your Ring account. If you are already logged into your account, in the Ring app for instance, you will not be asked to enter a code. If you log into your account from another device, you will be asked to enter a verification code.

We have added an additional measure of security for you and also require any Shared Users on your account to use Two-Step Verification. The same code entry process happens for any Shared Users that you have on the account. They will receive a one-time code, which expires in 10 minutes, and will have to enter it in order to get access to their Ring account.

You or your Shared Users can choose to receive the one-time passcode via the email address listed on the Ring account or on a phone as a text message (SMS). Requiring this code helps ensure that the person trying to log into your account is actually you and that your Shared Users are also authorized to access information from your Ring account.

Is this feature available for every Ring user? Is it mandatory?
Yes. Upon every Ring account login, you will be prompted to enter a one-time, six-digit code to verify the login attempt. This applies to primary account Owners as well as Shared Users. If you already have SMS (text) verification enabled, you will receive the one-time six digit code through a text message instead of an email to verify your login.

Why is Ring doing this?

The Two-Step Verification is a way of securing your account from bad actors by making sure that you know and can identify any browser or device that is being used to access your account.

Am I going to have to do this every time I log into my account?

No. If you continue to use your mobile apps every 30 days, you will not have to login via Two-Step Verification (unless you log out or "Remove All" authorized devices).

How long does the six-digit code last?

The code will last for 10 minutes. After that, you'll need to attempt to log back in to get a new code.

What happens if I don't receive the code at my email address?

Be sure to check your spam filter for the code. If you still haven't received it, you can ask for the code to be re-sent after 60 seconds have elapsed.

I don't see this feature in my app / I am not being prompted to enter the six digit code in my app, why can't I use this feature?

If you received the Two-Step Verification email, but are unable to enter the six-digit code in the Ring app, you will need to update your Ring app to the latest version.

Are users being forced to log out of their accounts because of this feature?

No.

Can you opt out of Two-Step Verification?

No.

If I have text message verification turned on, will I still receive the Two-Step Verification email?

No. If you already have text message verification enabled, you will receive the one-time six digit code through a text message instead of an email.

What if I set up my Ring account with an email I no longer use / have access to?

If you have an email tied to a Ring account that you no longer use or have access to, you should call Ring Community Support for assistance.

Will Shared Users receive Two-Step Verification emails as well?

Yes. All Ring accounts, including shared users, will need to authenticate all logins to their Ring account by using Two-Step Verification. All new shared user logins must be authenticated by entering the one-time, six-digit code in the Ring app. If a shared user already has text verification enabled, they will receive the one-time six digit code through a text message instead of an email.

What about the Neighbors app or Rapid Ring app?
Yes, Two-Step Verification is mandatory for all logins on the Neighbors app, Rapid Ring app, Ring.com, and Ring Community as well.[506]

QUESTIONS

1) Plaintiff does not list the new California IoT law discussed immediately before this complaint. Would the new law apply?

2) In 2019, multi-factor authentication was not the norm for most smart home devices. It was not required by California IoT and is still not required by California IoT law. Will these facts aid the defendant?

3) What other agencies' position on multi-factor law could also help the defendants?

4) When a baseball fan attends a baseball game it is understood that the baseball fan is taking on some risk of being hit by a foul ball. That is known as assumption of the risk and is a well-known defense in tort law. When a person connects a smart device to the internet, is that person taking on an assumption of the risk that the device is now available for hacking?

5) If a vendor provides security features for its smart device such as password protection and multi-factor authentication, what responsibility should the vendor have for educating the customer on the use of password protection and/or multi-factor authentication? Should the vendor force the customer to use multi-factor authentication?

6) What responsibility does the user have for implementing security? Can a user be negligent in today's society for not better understanding security for things connected to the internet or for implementing poor security measures such as a "123456" password?

7) Can two-step verification aka multi-factor authentication still be hacked?

---

[506] *Enhancing Security with Two-Step Verification*, RING, https://support.ring.com/hc/en-us/articles/360039693891-Enhancing-Security-with-Two-Step-Verification (last visited Oct. 23, 2020).

12.6 NIST SPECIAL PUBLICATION 1800-15 Securing Small-Business and Home Internet of Things (IoT) Devices: Mitigating Network-Based Attacks Using Manufacturer Usage Description (MUD)

Protecting the Network in Lieu of Adding Complex Security to IoT Devices

There are often many technical solutions available for a technical issue. The technical issue of concern with the Internet of Things (IoT) is how to keep billions of smart internet devices from becoming used for a distributed denial of service attack. These smart devices are normally small without complex operating systems. The devices are made from a multitude of manufacturers, the devices are normally not expensive to stay market competitive and adding complex security measures to these devices could add cost that makes the devices unattractive on the marketplace. So perhaps, focusing on implementing robust security in these smart devices is not cost effective. Instead of looking at the devices that can be overtaken for a DDOS, perhaps there is a better defense for taking into consideration. The components of the DDOS attack are the smart devices (assumed overtaken), the network (i.e. the internet) and the target (a server or other large and valuable computing device).

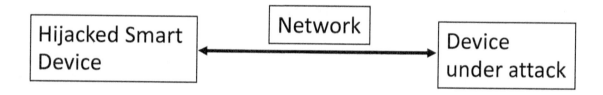

Would it be possible for the Network to stop or control the attack? Actually, industry is already working towards that goal and as expected the National Institute of Technology and Standards (NIST) and the National Cybersecurity Center of Excellence (NCCOE) is also taking an active role.

Because IoT devices are designed to be low cost and for limited purposes, it is not realistic to try to solve the problem of IoT device vulnerability by requiring that all IoT devices be equipped with robust, state-of-the-art security mechanisms. Instead, we are challenged to develop ways to improve IoT device security without requiring costly or complicated improvements to the devices themselves.

A second challenge lies in the need to develop security mechanisms that will be effective even though IoT devices will, by their very nature, remain vulnerable to attack, and some will inevitably be compromised. These security mechanisms should protect the rest of the network from any devices that become compromised.

Given the widespread use of IoT devices by consumers who may not even be aware that the devices are accessing their network, a third challenge is the practical need for IoT security mechanisms to be easy to use. Ideally, security features should be so transparent that a user need not even be aware of their operation.

To address these challenges, the National Cybersecurity Center of Excellence (NCCoE) and its collaborators have demonstrated the practicality and effectiveness of using the Internet Engineering Task Force's Manufacturer Usage Description (MUD) standard to reduce both the vulnerability of IoT devices to network-based attacks and the potential for harm from any IoT devices that become compromised.[507]

The National Cybersecurity Center of Excellence (NCCoE), a part of the National Institute of Standards and Technology (NIST), is a collaborative hub where industry organizations, government agencies, and academic institutions work together to address businesses' most pressing cybersecurity issues. This public-private partnership enables the creation of practical cybersecurity solutions for specific industries, as well as for broad, cross-sector technology challenges. Through consortia under Cooperative Research and Development Agreements (CRADAs), including technology partners— from Fortune 50 market leaders to smaller companies specializing in information technology security—the NCCoE applies standards and best practices to develop modular, easily adaptable example cybersecurity solutions using commercially available technology. The NCCoE documents these example solutions in the NIST Special Publication 1800 series, which maps capabilities to the NIST Cybersecurity Framework and details the steps needed for another entity to re-create the example solution. The NCCoE was established in 2012 by NIST in partnership with the State of Maryland and Montgomery County, Maryland.[508]

The goal of the Internet Engineering Task Force's Manufacturer Usage Description (MUD) specification is for Internet of Things (IoT) devices to behave as intended by the manufacturers of the devices. MUD provides a standard way for manufacturers to indicate the network communications that a device requires to perform its intended function. When MUD is used, the network will automatically permit the IoT device to send and receive only the traffic it requires to perform as intended, and the network will prohibit all other communication with the device, thereby increasing the device's resilience to network-based attacks.[509]

The primary technical elements of this project include components that are designed and configured to support the MUD protocol. We describe these components as being *MUD-capable*. The components used include MUD-capable network gateways, routers, and switches that support wired and wireless network access; MUD managers; MUD file servers; MUD-capable Dynamic Host Configuration Protocol (DHCP) servers; update servers; threat-signaling servers; MUD-capable IoT devices; and MUD files and their corresponding signature files. We also used devices that are not capable of supporting the MUD protocol, which we call *non-MUD-capable* or *legacy* devices, to

---

[507] SECURING SMALL-BUSINESS AND HOME INTERNET OF THINGS (IoT) DEVICES: MITIGATING NETWORK-BASED ATTACKS USING MANUFACTURER USAGE DESCRIPTION (MUD), NAT'L INST. OF STANDARDS AND TECH. & NAT'L CYBERSECURITY CTR. OF EXCELLENCE 1 (2020), *available at* https://www.nccoe.nist.gov/sites/default/files/library/sp1800/iot-ddos-nist-sp1800-15-draft.pdf.

[508] *Id.* at ii.

[509] *Id.*

demonstrate the security benefits of the demonstrated approach that are independent of the MUD protocol, such as threat signaling and device onboarding. Non-MUD-capable devices used include laptops, phones, and IoT devices that cannot emit or otherwise convey a uniform resource locator (URL) for a MUD file as described in the MUD specification.[510]

The demonstrated approach, which deploys MUD as an additional security tool rather than as a replacement for other security mechanisms, shows that MUD can make it more difficult to compromise IoT devices on a home or small-business network by using a network-based attack. While MUD can be used to protect networks of any size, the scenarios examined by this National Cybersecurity Center of Excellence (NCCoE) project involve IoT devices being used in home and small-business networks. Owners of such networks cannot be assumed to have extensive network administration experience. This makes plug-and-play deployment a requirement. Although the focus of this project is on home and small-business network applications, the home and small-business network users are not the guide's intended audience. This guide is intended primarily for IoT device developers and manufacturers, network equipment developers and manufacturers, and service providers whose services may employ MUD-capable components. MUD-capable IoT devices and network equipment are not yet widely available, so home and small-business network owners are dependent on these groups to make it possible for them to obtain and benefit from MUD-capable equipment and associated services.[511]

The project architecture is intended for home and small-business networks that are composed of both IoT components and fully featured devices (e.g., personal computers). The architecture is designed to provide three forms of protection:
- use of the MUD specification to automatically permit an IoT device to send and receive only the traffic it requires to perform as intended, thereby reducing the potential for the device to be the victim of a communications-based malware exploit or other network-based attack, and reducing the potential for the device, if compromised, to be used in a DDoS or other network- based attack
- use of network-wide access controls based on threat signaling to protect legacy (non-MUD- capable) IoT devices and fully featured devices, in addition to MUD-capable IoT devices, from connecting to domains that are known current threats
- automated secure software updates to all devices to ensure that operating system patches are installed promptly.[512]

The following text walks the reader through the project architecture:
- The IoT device emits a MUD URL by using a mechanism such as DHCP, LLDP, or X.509 certificate (step 1).
- The router extracts the MUD URL from the protocol frame of whatever mechanism was used to convey it and forwards this MUD URL to the MUD manager (step 2).

---

[510] *Id.* at 1.

[511] *Id.* at 1–2.

[512] *Id.* at 12.

•   Once the MUD URL is received, the MUD manager uses hypertext transfer protocol secure (https) to request the MUD file from the MUD file server by using the MUD URL provided in the previous step (step 3a); if successful, the MUD file server at the specified location will serve the MUD file (step 3b).

•   Next, the MUD manager uses https to request the signature file associated with the MUD file (step 4a) and upon receipt (step 4b) verifies the MUD file by using its signature file.

•   The MUD file describes the communications requirements for the IoT device. Once the MUD manager has determined the MUD file to be valid, the MUD manager converts the access control rules in the MUD file into access control entries (e.g., access control lists—ACLs, firewall rules, or flow rules) and installs them on the router or switch (step 5).[513]

MUD is an interesting approach but will it be universally adopted to a point where it can be effective? Unfortunately, the technical landscape is littered with useful inventions that did not go mainstream. The adoption will likely come down to a cost/benefit analysis.

Regardless of which security measures are adopted to control IoT risk, IoT is here to stay and growing exponentially. As of today, the benefits outweigh the risks. The current adoption rate of IoT would indicate that there will continue to be a place in society for IoT devices and that security efforts to control IoT shortcomings will be a profitable endeavor.

NOTES

Note 1

In February of 2022, the NIST released guidance concerning cybersecurity and connected health devices that remotely transmit patient health information. The guidance is based upon previously developed risk assessment frameworks as well as industry comment: https://www.nccoe.nist.gov/healthcare/securing-telehealth-remote-patient-monitoring-ecosystem.

---

[513] *Id.* at 14.

CHAPTER THIRTEEN. RANSOMWARE

13.1 Overview

Normally, the authors would not single out ransomware from the myriad of cybersecurity threats and give ransomware a dedicated chapter, but recent events have directed the spotlight on ransomware, and it now deserves its own dedicated chapter.

Ransomware and ransomware attacks are not new. Ransomware attacks have been around for a long time. What is new is the visibility of ransomware and the effect of successful ransomware attacks on a broad swath of society. The Colonial Pipeline ransomware attack caused long gas lines in certain states touching everyone who uses gasoline in those states. Ransomware attacks that had been previously localized to smaller targets, such as city governments, hospitals, schools, and law firms could no longer be ignored by politicians and the federal government, and of course, the general public. The danger of ransomware was made all too clear. Ransomware can no longer be pushed to the back burner to be dealt with at a later time.

The application of ransomware is quite simple. After obtaining access to a data source, ransomware encrypts that data with an encryption key. Without the key, the data is unreadable and thus, unavailable. Encryption is not the issue. Most of us safely use encryption every day without even knowing it. Many systems already encrypt data, cell phone, laptops, to name a few. But the user (or more likely the software that completed the encryption for the user) retains the encryption key, which allows the user to use the data. The data is only locked out from those that don't have access to the key. Encryption is good. Encryption provides a safe harbor against many data protection laws for dealing with breached data. The hacker accesses the data, but cannot read the data because the hacker does not have the encryption key. We can also use encryption to destroy data in the cloud at the end of its life cycle. The process is known as crypto-shredding. The data is encrypted, then encrypted again and then the key is destroyed so the data is effectively inaccessible and thus, destroyed. Physically, the data is still available but without the key it cannot be read. Normally, with the word ransom, we think of a person or asset being withheld from the owner or family. But with ransomware, the data is not being withheld, the data is still in the same location it was in before the attack. The encryption key is being withheld.[514]

An encryption key is normally a string of numbers and letters that are required to unlock the encryption coded data. It may look something like: AXXA-UQYD-YERF-7DF6-XBMH-GWDS. The encryption key is what the perpetrators are holding for the ransom payment. And the perpetrators are only willing to provide the key for the payment of the ransom amount. The popularity of crypto currency such as bitcoin has made it easy for the bad guys to receive payment without getting caught.

---

[514] Critical information may also be exfiltrated.

It was not that long ago that the common criminal was restricted to more traditional methods of ransom: people and assets. Initially, the creation of ransomware required a skilled programmer to design, write, and implement the software for ransomware. That is no longer the case. Today, ransomware is available as Ransomware-as-a-Service (RaaS) in the same manner that that word processor software is available as Software-as-a-Service (SaaS). Thus, just as a lay person can use a word processer, a non-programming criminal can now subscribe to and use ransomware.

The operation of ransomware is fairly straight forward, gain access to data, encrypt the data and return the encryption key to the user of the ransomware. The owner of the data is then notified of the ransom demand. Of course, as soon as the data is encrypted, the user normally knows that the data is unavailable because every system trying to access the data is not successful in gaining access to readable data. The perpetrators gaining access to the data is accomplished through penetrating vulnerabilities, either human or system. A common vulnerability is a human who has authorized access to a system clicking a link that gives the ransomware access to the system's data and thus, the ability to encrypt and exfiltrate the data.

Not having access to its data is devastating for most entities. Without data, hospitals cannot serve its patients. Not only is the hospital not collecting fees for its service, but patients may suffer without access to their records that now are mostly all online. As a society we have moved most of our data online. HIPAA, as discussed in a later chapter, encouraged the moving of records online for the medical profession to be able to better serve patients. Without data, law firms cannot serve their clients. All the documents and court management data is online. Attorneys cannot work if they cannot access their documents and court dates could be missed if the court docket system data is not available. For a large firm, millions of dollars in billables can be lost in a single day without access to data. Both examples are quite painful to those involved with those entities. But the major risk is critical infrastructure. What if a nuclear power plant operations center cannot access its data? What if an electrical grid cannot access its data to manage power flows to areas needed because it cannot access its data? What if a gasoline pipeline that supplies the East Coast of America cannot access the data it needs to operate its pipeline? We know the answer to this last question from the Colonial Pipeline ransomware incident.

In an effort to inform the nation on ransomware, the Cybersecurity and Infrastructure Security Agency ("CISA") and the Multi-State Information Sharing & Analysis Center (MS-ISAC) released the "Ransomware Guide" in September 2020 that "includes industry best practices and a response checklist that can serve as a ransomware-specific addendum to organization response plans."[515] The Secret Service[516] and NIST[517] have also released helpful information.

The U.S. Treasury Department Financial Crimes Enforcement Network released a report on October 15, 2021, concerning Bank Secrecy Act Suspicious Activity Reports from financial institutions which may indicate the scope and depth of ransomware

---

[515] https://www.cisa.gov/stopransomware/ransomware-101 (last visited May 15, 2022).

[516] https://www.secretservice.gov/investigation/Preparing-for-a-Cyber-Incident (last visited May 15, 2022).

[517] https://csrc.nist.gov/publications/detail/nistir/8374/final (last visited May 15 2022).

attacks and payments made by victim entities.[518] The Executive Summary states, in relevant part:

> FinCEN analysis of ransomware-related SARs filed during the first half of 2021 indicates that ransomware is an increasing threat to the U.S. financial sector, businesses, and the public. The number of ransomware-related SARs filed monthly has grown rapidly, with 635 SARs filed and 458 transactions reported between 1 January 2021 and 30 June 2021 ("the review period"), up 30 percent from the total of 487 SARs filed for the entire 2020 calendar year. The total value of suspicious activity reported in ransomware-related SARs during the first six months of 2021 was $590 million, which exceeds the value reported for the entirety of 2020 ($416 million). Trends represented in this report illustrate financial institutions' identification and reporting of ransomware events and may not reflect the actual dates associated with ransomware incidents. FinCEN's analysis of ransomware-related SARs highlights average ransomware payment amounts, top ransomware variants, and insights from FinCEN's blockchain analysis:

> Average Monthly Suspicious Amount of Ransomware Transactions: According to data generated from ransomware-related SARs, the mean average total monthly suspicious amount of ransomware transactions was $66.4 million and the median average was $45 million. FinCEN identified bitcoin (BTC) as the most common ransomware-related payment method in reported transactions. Top Ransomware Variants: Ransomware actors develop their own versions of ransomware, known as "variants," and these versions are given new names based on a change to software or to denote a particular threat actor behind the malware. FinCEN identified 68 ransomware variants reported in SAR data for transactions during the review period. The most commonly reported variants were REvil/Sodinokibi, Conti, DarkSide, Avaddon, and Phobos. Insights from Blockchain Analysis: FinCEN identified and analyzed 177 unique convertible virtual currency (CVC) wallet addresses used for ransomware-related payments associated with the 10 most commonly reported ransomware variants in SARs during the review period. Based on blockchain analysis of identifiable transactions with the 177 CVC wallet addresses, FinCEN identified approximately $5.2 billion in outgoing BTC transactions potentially tied to ransomware payments. FinCEN Identified Ransomware Money Laundering Typologies: FinCEN identified several money laundering typologies common among ransomware variants in 2021 including threat actors increasingly requesting payments in Anonymity-enhanced Cryptocurrencies (AECs) and avoiding reusing wallet addresses, "chain hopping" and cashing out

---

[518] FINANCIAL TREND ANALYSIS: RANSOMWARE TRENDS IN BANK SECRECY ACT DATA BETWEEN JANUARY 2021 AND JUNE 2021, U.S. DEP'T OF TREASURY FINANCIAL CRIMES ENFORCEMENT NETWORK, available at Financial Trend Analysis (fincen.gov).

at centralized exchanges, and using mixing services and decentralized exchanges to convert proceeds. . . .

Attacks on small municipalities and healthcare organizations have also increased, typically due to perceived weaker security controls and higher propensity of these victims to pay the ransom because of the criticality of their services, particularly during a global health pandemic. Additionally, since at least late 2019, ransomware groups have adopted new extortion tactics to maximize revenue and create an additional incentive for victims to pay. In one such tactic, known as "double extortion," ransomware operators exfiltrate massive amounts of a victim's data encrypting it and then threaten to publish the stolen data if ransom demands are not met. Lastly, ransomware attackers are finding new ways to obfuscate their identities by requesting payment in AECs.

Ransomware Variants: FinCEN identified 68 ransomware variants reported in SAR data for transactions during the review period. Ransomware variant analysis can help determine potential threat actors behind an attack. Ninety SARs did not name the ransomware variant used in the attack, and some SARs reported multiple incidents involving more than one variant. . . . The top 10 variants with the highest cumulative payment amounts identified in SARs during the review period accounted for $217.56 million in suspicious activity. The highest total suspicious payment amounts for individual variants reported in SARs range from $30 to $76 million. Monthly suspicious payment amounts reported in SARs for the top 10 variants range from $3,095 to $43.06 million with a median average of $27 million and mean average of $36.26 million. In June 2021, the highest cumulative suspicious payment amounts were associated with Variant 1 ($11.78 million) and Variant 2 ($8.53 million), according to SAR data.[519]

As mentioned *supra*, relatively small city governments have been the subject of ransomware attacks by hackers.

On October 1, 2020, the U.S. Department of Treasury released a document titled, "Advisory on Potential Sanctions Risks for Facilitating Ransomware Payments," which warns that ransomware payments to certain individuals or entities may run afoul of laws and regulations concerning, for example, transactions with certain blocked entities and individuals, or countries with sanctions against them.[520] The ransomware space will continue to develop. The U.S. Department of Justice has announced a new task

---

[519] *Id.*

[520] U.S. DEP'T OF TREASURY, *Advisory on Potential Sanctions Risks for Facilitating Ransomware Payments* (Oct. 1, 2020), https://home.treasury.gov/system/files/126/ofac_ransomware_advisory_10012020_1.pdf.

force addressing ransomware[521] and the U.S. government co-hosted a counter-ransomware initiative with many countries.[522]

13.2 Ransomware Prevention

The best prevention against ransomware is to take your laptop, unplug the laptop from any ethernet cables and turn off the Wi-Fi connection, and then place the laptop in a locked drawer. Obviously, this is not a viable solution. Likely just as hard is to keep employees from visiting dangerous websites and from clicking on unknown links that are links to malware such as ransomware.

Training can go a long way in addressing ransomware attacks. But even with adequate training there might be that one bad hyperlink that looks official, and an employee clicks on the link considering it a valid link. Thus, training can only go so far as protection against ransomware attacks. There are also technical solutions available for minimizing ransomware attacks such firewalls that do not permit traffic from black-listed IP address; segmenting the network to protect at least parts of a network from attack; and the best solution, create a backup that is protected from the ransomware attack and that can be used in place of the encrypted data. This requires a well-thought-out backup solution because attackers have started using the tactic of "deleting system backups, that make restoration and recovery more difficult or infeasible for impacted organizations."[523]

13.2[A] AWARENESS AND COMMUNICATION

Awareness and communication are also helpful in combating ransomware. CISA recommends that organizations join an information sharing group such as one of the following:

o Multi-State Information Sharing and Analysis Center (MS-ISAC)[524]

o Election Infrastructure Information Sharing and Analysis Center (EI-ISAC)[525]

o Sector-based ISACs – National Council of ISACs[526]

o Information Sharing and Analysis Organization (ISAO) Standards Organization[527]

CISA also invites building "a lasting partnership and collaborat[ion] on information sharing, best practices, assessments, exercises, and more" through

---

[521] Dustin Volz, *Ransomware Targeted by New Justice Department Task Force*, WALL STREET JOURNAL (April 21, 2021).
[522] David E. Sanger, *U.S. Holds Global Meeting to Fight Ransomware, Minus the World's No. 1 Culprit*, N.Y. TIMES (October 14, 2021).
[523] https://www.cisa.gov/sites/default/files/publications/CISA_MS-ISAC_Ransomware%20Guide_S508C_.pdf at page 2.
[524] https://learn.cisecurity.org/ms-isac-registration
[525] https://learn.cisecurity.org/ei-isac-registration
[526] https://www.nationalisacs.org
[527] https://www.isao.org/information-sharing-groups/

CyberLiaison_SLTT@cisa.dhs.gov   for   SLTT   organizations   and
CyberLiaison_Industry@cisa.dhs.gov for private sector organizations.[528]

CISA advises that "[i]t is critical to maintain offline, encrypted backups of data
and to regularly test your backups. Backup procedures should be conducted on a regular
basis. It is important that backups be maintained offline as many ransomware variants
attempt to find and delete any accessible backups. Maintaining offline, current backups
is most critical because there is no need to pay a ransom for data that is readily accessible
to your organization."[529] A risk analysis should be performed to determine how often
data should be backed up. In other words, how many minutes / hours of data can an
organization afford to give up to restore service from backups, one hour, two hours, three
hours? It depends on the business model. Some organizations run hot backups, which
means backing up each record to a fully functional offsite system so that the organization
can fail over to that system without losing any data. For organizations that run hot
backups, care should be taken to secure that system from ransomware attacks from the
operational system. For entities that backup data in the cloud, the entities should
understand the protection provided by the cloud provider for maintaining backups.

Organizations should also maintain base-line configurations for systems and
hardware should hackers also affect those areas. This would apply to organizations'
legacy systems that are maintained on company premises. In the event that the
company uses cloud-based infrastructure and services, the company should review its
cloud-based contracts to verify the cloud providers are taking the appropriate measure
to ensure recovery from attack.

13.2[B] ADDRESS RANSOMWARE INFECTION VECTORS

Infection vectors are basically the paths that ransomware uses to infiltrate a
system and encrypt the data. Without getting into the weeds of the technical
applications, here are the infection vectors identified by CISA.[530]

- Identify and fix internet-facing vulnerabilities and misconfigurations of
software and hardware. This can often be accomplished with available cybersecurity
tools to discover the vulnerabilities and then applying software and operating system
patches to fix the vulnerability

- Implement a training and awareness program, and technical controls to combat
phishing

- Look for precursor malware infections

- Determine the risk of using third parties and managed service providers

---

[528] https://www.cisa.gov/sites/default/files/publications/CISA_MS-
ISAC_Ransomware%20Guide_S508C_.pdf at page 2.

[529] *Id.* at 3.

[530] *Id.* at 4-6.

13.2[C] CREATE AND MAINTAIN AN INCIDENT RESPONSE PLAN

Assume that the ransomware attack will occur on a Friday evening after a majority of the work force has left for a long weekend. The attacker has the benefit of choosing the time of the attack. An incident response plan (IRP) will provide the guidance needed at this moment and can be followed by those trained on how to use. An often-exercised IRP is even better. The exercise can be a tabletop exercise carried out by the designed participants. A tabletop exercise is a made-up scenario that is war-gamed at a conference table by those designated as IRP team members. All teams perform better if they practice.

13.3 Post-Ransomware Attack

A good IRP always includes a checklist of tasks and actions to perform. A good starting place for checklist content is provided by CISA.[531] The checklist should be modified to fit the particular entity. Also, the checklist as well as any IRP should always be evaluated after an incident and modified with lessons learned.

The incident response team should understand its legal obligations after an attack. On June 3, 2021, the Department of Justice (DOJ), in the wake of the Colonial Pipeline attack, issued the following memo: "Guidance Regarding Investigations and Cases Related to Ransomware and Digital Extortion"[532] The memo establishes new requirements "relating to ransomware or digital extortion attacks and investigations and cases with a nexus to ransomware and digital extortion."[533] The memo requires additional notifications and coordination within the Justice Department.

It is important to understand whether a payment to retrieve the encryption key after an attack is illegal. Currently, the FBI provides the following guidance: "The FBI does not support paying a ransom in response to a ransomware attack. Paying a ransom doesn't guarantee you or your organization will get any data back. It also encourages perpetrators to target more victims and offers an incentive for others to get involved in this type of illegal activity."[534] And the FBI has recommended to Congress on July 27 that the United States should not forbid payment of ransom after a ransomware attack.[535]

Indeed, the General Assembly of North Carolina has taken budget action to cut off ransomware payments through budget limitations on state agencies.

GENERAL ASSEMBLY OF NORTH CAROLINA

SESSION LAW 2021-180

SECTION 1.1. This act shall be known as the "Current Operations Appropriations Act of 2021." . . .

---

[531] *Id.* at 11-5.
[532] https://www.justice.gov/dag/page/file/1401231/download
[533] *Id.*
[534] https://www.fbi.gov/scams-and-safety/common-scams-and-crimes/ransomware
[535] https://www.cnn.com/2021/07/27/politics/senate-judiciary-ransomware-hearing/index.html.

CYBERSECURITY/STATE AGENCIES PROHIBITED FROM MAKING RANSOMWARE PAYMENTS

SECTION 38.13.(a)

§ 143-800. State entities and ransomware payments.

(a)   No State agency or local government entity shall submit payment or otherwise communicate with an entity that has engaged in a cybersecurity incident on an information technology system by encrypting data and then subsequently offering to decrypt that data in exchange for a ransom payment.

(b)   Any State agency or local government entity experiencing a ransom request in connection with a cybersecurity incident shall consult with the Department of Information Technology in accordance with G.S. 143B-1379.

(c)   The following definitions apply in this section:

(1)   Local government entity. – A local political subdivision of the State, including, but not limited to, a city, a county, a local school administrative unit as defined in G.S. 115C-5, or a community college.

(2)   State agency. – Any agency, department, institution, board, commission, committee, division, bureau, officer, official, or other entity of the executive, judicial, or legislative branches of State government. The term includes The University of North Carolina and any other entity for which the State has oversight responsibility.

SECTION 38.13.(b) G.S. 143B-1320 . . .:

§ 143B-1320. Definitions; scope; exemptions.

(a)   Definitions. – The following definitions apply in this Article:

…

(4a)   Cybersecurity incident. – An occurrence that:

a.   Actually or imminently jeopardizes, without lawful authority, the integrity, confidentiality, or availability of information or an information system; or

b.   Constitutes a violation or imminent threat of violation of law, security policies, privacy policies, security procedures, or acceptable use policies.

…

(14a)   Ransomware attack. – A cybersecurity incident where a malicious actor introduces software into an information system that encrypts data and renders the systems that rely on that data unusable, followed by a demand for a ransom payment in exchange for decryption of the affected data.

...

(16a)   Significant cybersecurity incident. – A cybersecurity incident that is likely to result in demonstrable harm to the State's security interests, economy, critical infrastructure, or to the public confidence, civil liberties, or public health and safety of the residents of North Carolina. A significant cybersecurity incident is determined by the following factors:

a.   Incidents that meet thresholds identified by the Department jointly with the Department of Public Safety that involve information:

1.   That is not releasable to the public and that is restricted or highly restricted according to Statewide Data Classification and Handling Policy; or

2.   That involves the exfiltration, modification, deletion, or unauthorized access, or lack of availability to information or systems within certain parameters to include (i) a specific threshold of number of records or users affected as defined in G.S. 75-65 or (ii) any additional data types with required security controls.

b.   Incidents that involve information that is not recoverable or cannot be recovered within defined time lines required to meet operational commitments defined jointly by the State agency and the Department or can be recovered only through additional measures and has a high or medium functional impact to the mission of an agency.

....

SECTION 38.13.(c) G.S. 143B-1379(c). . . :

(c)   Local government entities, as defined in G.S. 143-800(c)(1), shall report cybersecurity incidents to the Department. Information shared as part of this process will be protected from public disclosure under G.S. 132-6.1(c). Private sector entities are encouraged to report cybersecurity incidents to the Department."

SECTION 38.13.(d) G.S. 143B-1322(c). . . :

(c)   Administration. – The Department shall be managed under the administration of the State CIO. The State CIO shall have the following powers and duty to do all of the following:

...

(22)   Coordinate with the Department of Public Safety to manage statewide response to cybersecurity incidents, significant cybersecurity incidents, and ransomware attacks as defined by G.S. 143B-1320.

SECTION 38.13.(e) This section is effective when it becomes law.[536]

How to report:

§ 143B-1379. State agency cooperation and training; liaisons; county and municipal government reporting.

(a)   The head of each principal department and Council of State agency shall cooperate with the State CIO in the discharge of the State CIO's duties by providing the following information to the Department:

(1)   The full details of the State agency's information technology and operational requirements and of all the agency's significant cybersecurity incidents within 24 hours of confirmation.

(2)   Comprehensive information concerning the information technology security employed to protect the agency's data, including documentation and reporting of remedial or corrective action plans to address any deficiencies in the information security policies, procedures, and practices of the State agency.

(3)   A forecast of the parameters of the agency's projected future cybersecurity and privacy needs and capabilities.

(4)   Designating an agency liaison in the information technology area to coordinate with the State CIO. The liaison shall be subject to a criminal background report from the State Repository of Criminal Histories, which shall be provided by the State Bureau of Investigation upon its receiving fingerprints from the liaison. Military personnel with a valid secret security clearance or a favorable Tier 3 security clearance investigation are exempt from this requirement. If the liaison has been a resident of this State for less than five years, the background report shall include a review of criminal information from both the State and National Repositories of Criminal Histories. The criminal background report shall be provided to the State CIO and the head of the agency. In addition, all personnel in the Office of the State Auditor who are responsible for information technology security reviews shall be subject to a criminal background report from the State Repository of Criminal Histories, which shall be provided by the State Bureau of Investigation upon receiving fingerprints from the personnel designated by the State Auditor. For designated personnel who have been residents of this State for less than five years, the background report shall include a review of criminal information from both the State and National Repositories of Criminal Histories. The criminal background reports shall be provided to the State Auditor. Criminal histories provided pursuant to this subdivision are not public records under Chapter 132 of the General Statutes.

---

[536] https://www.ncleg.gov/EnactedLegislation/SessionLaws/HTML/2021-2022/SL2021-180.html.

(5)   Completing mandatory annual security awareness training and reporting compliance for all personnel, including contractors and other users of State information technology systems.

(b)   The information provided by State agencies to the State CIO under this section is protected from public disclosure pursuant to G.S. 132-6.1(c).

(c)   County and municipal government agencies shall report cybersecurity incidents to the Department. Information shared as part of this process will be protected from public disclosure under G.S. 132-6.1(c). Private sector entities are encouraged to report cybersecurity incidents to the Department. (2015-241, s. 7A.2(b); 2019-200, s. 6(e).)[537]

NOTES

Note 1

As discussed *supra* in Chapter Seven Additional Federal Regulation, President Biden recently signed a law requiring cybersecurity incident and ransomware payment reporting concerning critical infrastructure.

13.4 Ransomware Related Laws and Lawsuits

As discussed *infra*, a ransomware attack may indicate that cybersecurity related laws have been violated. Depending on the business model of the victim as well as the federal regulator, a specific federal regulation may have been violated which may lead to an enforcement action. In some cases, a state agency may be able to enforce a federal regulation such as HIPAA. Notably, the federal Computer Fraud and Abuse Act likely will apply to a ransomware situation as well. Additionally, many states have enacted laws similar to the federal Computer Fraud and Abuse Act which may also apply. Importantly, several states have enacted laws specifically dealing with extortion and the access to computers without authorization. These laws are discussed, *infra*. As an example, West Virginia has a specific law addressing computer fraud and ransomware:

(a) Any person who, knowingly and willfully, directly or indirectly, accesses or causes to be accessed any computer, computer services, or computer network for the purpose of: (1) Executing any scheme or artifice to defraud; or (2) obtaining money, property, or services by means of fraudulent pretenses, representations, or promises is guilty of a felony and, upon conviction thereof, shall be fined not more than $10,000 or imprisoned in a state correctional facility for a determinate sentence of not more than 10 years, or both fined and imprisoned.

---

[537] https://www.ncleg.gov/EnactedLegislation/Statutes/HTML/BySection/Chapter_143B/GS_143B-1379.html.

(b) Any person who, with intent to extort money or other consideration from another, introduces ransomware into any computer, computer system, or computer network is guilty of a felony and, upon conviction thereof, shall be fined not more than $100,000 or imprisoned in a state correctional facility for a determinate sentence of not more than 10 years, or both fined and imprisoned.

(c) A person is criminally responsible for placing or introducing ransomware into a computer, computer system, or computer network if the person directly places or introduces the ransomware or directs or induces another person to do so, with the intent of demanding payment or other consideration for removing, restoring access, or other remediation of the impact of the ransomware.

(d)(1) Any person who, knowingly and willfully, directly or indirectly, accesses, attempts to access, or causes to be accessed any data stored in a computer owned by the Legislature without authorization is guilty of a felony and, upon conviction thereof, shall be fined not more than $5,000 or imprisoned in a state correctional facility for a determinate sentence of not more than five years, or both fined and imprisoned.

(2) Notwithstanding the provisions of § 61-3C-17 of this code to the contrary, in any criminal prosecution under this subsection against an employee or member of the Legislature, it shall not be a defense: (A) That the defendant had reasonable grounds to believe that he or she had authorization to access the data merely because of his or her employment or membership; or (B) that the defendant could not have reasonably known he or she did not have authorization to access the data: *Provided,* That the Joint Committee on Government and Finance shall promulgate rules for the respective houses of the Legislature regarding appropriate access of members and staff and others to the legislative computer system.[538]

A ransomware attack may also give rise to a data breach. As discussed *infra,* there are numerous potential causes of action that arise out of data breaches. The requirements for these lawsuits, such as standing and class action prerequisites, as well causes of action such as negligence are discussed in Chapter Nine. There have been several cases involving data breaches and ransomware.[539] The following is an example of a ransomware case.

Keach III v. BST & CO. and Murray, on behalf of herself and all others similarly situated v. Community Care Physicians, P.C. 142 N.Y.S.3d 790 (March 30, 2021).

Richard M. Platkin, J.

---

[538] W. Va. Code, § 61-3C-4.

[539] *See, e.g., Graham v. Universal Health Service, Inc.,* __ F.3d __, 2021 WL 1962865 (E.D. Penn. May 17, 2021); *Blahous v. Sarrell Reg. Dental Ctr. For Public Health, Inc.,* 2020 WL 4016246 (M.D. Ala. July 16, 2020).

The above-captioned actions arise from a December 2019 "ransomware" attack on the computer systems of BST & Co. CPAs, LLP ("BST"), an accounting and consulting firm. As a result of the data breach, hackers obtained access to BST's client data, which included the personal information of 170,000 current and former patients of Community Care Physicians, P.C. ("CCP"), a large medical practice.

On May 27, 2020, Elmer R. Keach III commenced Action No. 1 on behalf of himself and others similarly situated, seeking damages, restitution and injunctive relief from BST based on the firm's alleged failure to adequately safeguard the personal information of CCP members (see Action No. 1, NYSCEF Doc No. 1 ["Keach Compl"]). Eleanor Murray then commenced Action No. 2 on July 31, 2020, seeking similar relief from both BST and CCP on behalf of herself and others similarly situated (see Action No. 2, NYSCEF Doc No. 1 ["Murray Compl"]).

As both actions arise from the same facts and circumstances, the parties stipulated, "in the interest of simplifying motion practice," that BST and CCP would "jointly file a single motion to dismiss applicable to both the *Keach* Action and the *Murray* Action, with joint response and reply briefs to follow" (Action No. 1, NYSCEF Doc No. 13, p. 2). The instant motion practice ensued.

BACKGROUND

CCP is a large multi-specialty medical group with offices throughout the greater Capital District. BST is an accounting, tax and advisory firm retained by CCP.

Plaintiffs Keach and Murray are CCP patients and, in that connection, disclosed certain personal, financial and insurance information to the medical practice. CCP, in turn, provided information concerning its current and former patients to BST in connection with a professional consulting engagement.

On December 7, 2019, BST learned that a portion of its computer network had been infected with "ransomware" that prevented the firm from accessing certain electronically stored information. BST retained a forensic investigations firm to determine the nature and scope of the data breach and eventually learned: a computer virus was active on BST's network from December 4, 2019 to December 7, 2019; the virus was introduced by unknown individuals outside of BST who gained access to a portion of the network where client data, including member data provided by CCP, was hosted; and, as a result of the foregoing data breach ("Data Breach"), certain personal information of current and former CCP patients "was accessed or acquired without authorization, including individuals' names, dates of birth, medical record numbers, medical billing codes, and insurance descriptions".

On February 14, 2020, BST issued a "Notice of Data Privacy Event" to potentially affected individuals, including plaintiffs. The notice advised CCP members of the following:

> ... On December 7, 2019, BST learned that part of its network was infected with a virus that prohibited access to its files. BST quickly restored its systems and engaged an industry-leading forensic investigation firm to determine the nature and scope of this incident. After a thorough analysis of all available forensic evidence, the investigation determined the virus

> was active on BST's network from December 4, 2019, to December 7, 2019. The virus was introduced by an unknown individual or individuals outside of BST who gained access to part of the network where certain client files are stored, including files from CCP.

Because of the risk that data may have been accessed, acquired, or otherwise disclosed from its network without authorization due to the virus, BST reviewed the files in detail to determine what, if any, personal health information they contained. By February 5, 2020, in conjunction with CCP, BST confirmed the files contained some personal information for certain individuals and ascertained the addresses of these patients to communicate the security incident to them directly.

... The investigation determined that, as a result of this incident, certain personal or protected health information for individuals may have been accessed or acquired without authorization, including individuals' names, dates of birth, medical record numbers, medical billing codes, and insurance descriptions. Patient medical records and Social Security numbers were not impacted by this incident.

Although BST cannot confirm that any individual's personal information was actually accessed, or viewed without permission, BST is providing this notice out of an abundance of caution and to mitigate risk to individuals (https://web.archive.org/web/2021 0120161627/www.bstco.com/notice -of-data-privacy-event/ [web archive as of Jan. 20, 2021, last accessed Mar. 30, 2021 ("Privacy Event Notice")]).

In addition, BST offered "potentially impacted individuals access to complimentary credit monitoring services [for one year] as an added precaution and to mitigate risk".

After receiving the Privacy Event Notice, plaintiffs commenced suit against BST and CCP based on their alleged "collective failure" to prevent the Data Breach and safeguard the personal information that they entrusted to CCP, which included their names, dates of birth and medical billing and health insurance information.

Plaintiffs assert that they have been "significantly injured by the Data Breach". "Armed with the [compromised personal information], data thieves can commit a variety of crimes," including opening new financial accounts in the names of CCP members, taking out fraudulent loans, filing false tax returns, filing false medical claims, giving false information to police during an arrest, and obtaining bogus drivers' licenses.

Plaintiffs therefore contend that, "[a]s a result of the Ransomware Attack, [they] are exposed to a heightened and imminent risk of fraud and identity theft". Plaintiffs further allege that they may incur out-of-pocket costs from the Data Breach, such as the cost of credit monitoring services, credit freezes, credit reports and other measures directed at detecting and preventing identity theft. Additionally, plaintiffs cite the time and expense associated with mitigation efforts, the loss of their "benefit of the bargain" with CCP, and the alleged diminution in value of their personal information.

The Keach Complaint alleges four causes of action against BST: (1) negligence; (2) negligence *per se*; (3) violation of General Business Law ("GBL") § 349; and (4) breach of fiduciary duty. The Murray Complaint alleges seven causes of action: (1) negligence; (2) breach of contract (CCP only); (3) trespass to chattels; (4) bailment (CCP only); (5) violation of GBL § 349; (6) unjust enrichment (CCP only); and (7) conversion (BST only).

Defendants now move for dismissal of the Keach and Murray complaints ("Complaints") on two grounds. First, defendants argue that plaintiffs did not, and cannot, allege that they have sustained an injury-in-fact from the Data Breach. According to defendants, "[p]laintiffs rely exclusively on the speculative possibility of harm that could occur in the future". As a second, independent ground for dismissal, defendants contend that each cause of action alleged in the Complaints must be dismissed for pleading insufficiency.

Plaintiffs oppose the motion, except as to Keach's claims for negligence *per se* and breach of fiduciary duty.

Remote oral argument on the motions was held on January 29, 2021, a certified copy of the argument transcript was provided to the Court on February 22, 2021 (*see* Action No. 1, NYSCEF Doc No. 30 ["Transcript"]), and this Consolidated Decision & Order follows.

ANALYSIS

"Whether a person seeking relief is a proper party to request an adjudication is an aspect of justiciability which, when challenged, must be considered at the outset of any litigation" (*Society of Plastics Indus. v County of Suffolk*, 77 NY2d 761, 769 [1991] [citation omitted]).

"On a defendant's motion to dismiss the complaint based upon the plaintiff's alleged lack of standing, the burden is on the moving defendant to establish, *prima facie*, the plaintiff's lack of standing as a matter of law" (*New York Community Bank v McClendon*, 138 AD3d 805, 806 [2d Dept 2016] [citations omitted]; *see* CPLR 3211 [a] [3]). The "motion will be defeated if the plaintiff's submissions raise a question of fact as to its standing" (*U.S. Bank N.A. v Clement*, 163 AD3d 742, 743 [2d Dept 2018] [internal quotation marks and citation omitted], *appeal dismissed and lv denied* 32 NY3d 1197 [2019]).

To have standing to sue, plaintiffs must allege the "existence of an injury in fact — an actual legal stake in the matter being adjudicated" that "ensures that [they have] some concrete interest in prosecuting the action" (*Society of Plastics*, 77 NY2d at 772-773). Each of the named plaintiffs therefore must allege that he or she has suffered, or will suffer, an actual injury-in-fact by reason of the Data Breach (*see New York State Assn. of Nurse Anesthetists v Novello* , 2 NY3d 207, 211 [2004] ; *see also Warth v Seldin* , 422 US 490, 502 [1975] ; *Murray v Empire Ins. Co.* , 175 AD2d 693, 695 [1st Dept 1991] ; *Raske v Next Mgt., LLC* , 40 Misc 3d 1240[A], 2013 NY Slip Op 51514[U], *8 [Sup Ct, NY County 2013] [class representative must have "individual standing," which "means that the class representative must have an individual injury that is cognizable at law" (internal quotation marks and citation omitted)]).

"The injury in fact element must be based on more than conjecture or speculation" (*Matter of Animal Legal Defense Fund, Inc. v Aubertine*, 119 AD3d 1202, 1203 [3d Dept 2014] [citations omitted]; *see Matter of Brennan Ctr. for Justice at NYU Sch. of Law v New York State Bd. of Elections* , 159 AD3d 1299, 1301 [3d Dept 2018], *lv denied* 32 NY3d 912 [2019]), and the claimed injury cannot be "tenuous" or "ephemeral" (*Novello* , 2 NY3d at 214 [internal quotation marks and citation omitted]). Plaintiffs must allege an " 'actual or imminent' " injury (*Matter of Association for a Better Long Is., Inc. v New York State Dept. of Envtl. Conservation*, 23 NY3d 1, 7 [2014], quoting *Lujan v Defenders of Wildlife*, 504 US 555, 564 [1992]) — one that is "impending" rather than "speculative"

(*Whalen v Michaels Stores, Inc.*, 689 Fed Appx 89, 90 [2d Cir 2017] [internal quotation marks and citation omitted]).

In evaluating whether plaintiffs in a data breach case have alleged an actual injury or the imminent prospect thereof, the New York courts have looked to five principal factors: (1) the type of personal information that was compromised; (2) whether hackers were involved in the data breach or personal information otherwise was targeted; (3) whether personal information was exfiltrated, published and/or otherwise disseminated; (4) whether there have been any incidents of, or attempts at, identity theft or fraud using the compromised personal information; and (5) the length of time that has passed since the data breach without incidents of identity theft or fraud.

The first factor looks to the type of personal information that was compromised and the extent to which the disclosure of such information renders individuals susceptible to identity theft or fraud. The personal information at issue here consists of names, dates of birth, medical record numbers, medical billing codes and health insurance descriptions.

While the foregoing collection of information about an individual certainly can be misused, particularly in connection with medical identity theft or other healthcare fraud, the instant cases are unlike those involving the disclosure of social security numbers or financial account information (*see Smahaj*, 69 Misc 3d at 599 ["names, dates of birth, social security numbers, and other information so that (collection agency) could collect on (plaintiff's) debt"]; *Manning*, 56 Misc 3d at 791 ["customers' names, Social Security numbers, street addresses, and some account and debit card numbers"]).

As plaintiffs recognize, the disclosure of social security numbers leaves individuals at a considerably greater risk of identity theft or fraud, and the same is true of information concerning active financial accounts. The instant cases also differ from *Lynch*, where the compromised personal information belonged to New York Police Department officers, who are subject to heightened risks by reason of their official position (*see Lynch*, 2018 NY Slip Op 32962[U], *4 ["(i)n light of the risks faced daily by police officers, the dissemination of their personal information presents more risk"]).

The second factor looks to whether computer hackers were involved in the data breach or personal information otherwise was targeted. In this regard, case law recognizes that the involvement of computer hackers "creates an inference of malicious intent to steal private information, supporting an increased risk of identity theft" (*Smahaj* , 69 Misc 3d at 599, 601; *see Sackin v TransPerfect Global, Inc.* , 278 F Supp 3d 739, 747 [SD NY 2017] [distinguishing authorities involving "plaintiffs (who) did not allege or could not show that obtaining their (information) was the motivation for the theft"]; *cf. Manning* , 56 Misc 3d at 791 [laptop computer stolen from vehicle contained personal and banking information of customers]).

Plaintiffs specifically allege that the attack on BST's computer systems "was the work of the notorious Maze ransomware ring". On the other hand, the Complaints repeatedly characterize the Data Breach as a "ransomware attack", which, by plaintiffs' own definition, "is a type of malicious software that blocks access to a computer system or data, usually by encrypting it, until the victim pays a fee to the attacker". Thus, while ransomware deprives the victim of access to electronically stored information, the information itself ordinarily is not the object of the hackers' attack. Nonetheless, plaintiffs do allege that "the Maze ransomware gang has been known to extort businesses by publicly posting breached data on the Internet — and threatening full dumps of stolen data if the ring's 'customers' don't pay for their files to be unencrypted".

The third factor looks to whether the compromised personal information was exfiltrated, published and/or otherwise disseminated (*see Smahaj*, 69 Misc 3d at 599 ["Plaintiff alleges that the hackers attempted to 'place a batch of 200,000 payment card numbers for sale on a popular Darknet Market.' Plaintiff claims that due to the data breach, it is likely that she and other class members' private information 'will or has been disclosed already on the Darknet,' though there is 'uncertainty as to the nature and extent' of the information that was compromised."]).

Here, plaintiffs allege that their personal information was "stolen", citing the Maze ransomware gang's history of "extort[ing] businesses by publicly posting breached data on the Internet — and threatening full dumps of stolen data if the ring's 'customers' don't pay for their files to be unencrypted". Relatedly, the Complaints cite a Florida data breach incident where hackers publicly released a portion of the stolen data as part of their extortion scheme. Plaintiffs also allege that the "Maze ransomware gang published the Private Data online for all cyberthieves to access", but the Complaints do not include any particulars concerning this alleged publication, only a vague and conclusory allegation.

Fourth, courts look to whether there have been any incidents of identity theft or fraud using the compromised personal information or any attempts to do so (*see Smahaj*, 69 Misc 3d at 603 ["the complaint fails to allege any actual suspicious activity that directly harmed plaintiff"]; *Manning*, 56 Misc 3d at 797 ["neither named plaintiff specifically identifies an actual or attempted identity theft or indicates any fraudulent charges"]). Plaintiffs do not allege any incidents of, or attempts at, identity theft or fraud using the compromised personal information of CCP members.

Finally, in cases like these, where there are no allegations of actual or attempted misuse of the compromised personal information, "a temporal component may factor into determining whether a threatened harm is sufficient for standing" (*Smahaj*, 69 Misc 3d at 601). In other words, "a lengthy passage of time without any suspicious activity weighs against finding an injury in fact" (*id.* at 602).

The intrusion into BST's computer systems occurred in early December 2019. Thus, nearly 16 months have passed without incidents of identity theft, fraud or similar misuse of the compromised personal information of CCP members (*cf. Smahaj*, 69 Misc 3d at 602 [almost 18 months since conclusion of data breach]; *Manning*, 56 Misc 3d at 791 [17.5 months]; *Jantzer v Elizabethtown Cmty. Hosp.*, 2020 WL 2404764, *1, 2020 US Dist LEXIS 83207, *2 [ND NY, May 12, 2020, No. 8:19-cv-00791 (BKS/DJS)] [almost 19 months]). This lengthy period without incident counsels against finding injuries that are imminent or substantially likely to occur.

Upon consideration of the foregoing factors, as well as the other arguments and contentions raised by the parties in their written submissions and at oral argument, the Court concludes that the two named plaintiffs, Keach and Murray, have not sufficiently alleged an injury-in-fact sustained from the Data Breach.

Even assuming that the personal information of plaintiffs, which did not include social security numbers or financial account information, was exfiltrated from BST's computer systems as part of the ransomware attack, plaintiffs have alleged no acts of identity theft, fraud or other suspicious activity involving their personal information. Nor have plaintiffs alleged any attempts to commit identity theft, fraud or other wrongdoing using their personal information.

Instead, plaintiffs are left to speculate about the prospect of future harms that may or may not come to pass. As in *Smahaj,* plaintiffs rely on allegations of:

> (1) an increased risk of suffering from identity theft and fraud; (2) time, money, and other resources spent to mitigate against risks, both now and in the future, by cancelling credit cards, ability to open new bank accounts, reversing fraudulently imposed charges, and incurring high interest rates due to the inevitable decline in credit score when plaintiff and class members reasonably do not pay for items and services they did not purchase; and (3) the diminution of the value and/or loss of the benefits or products and services purchased directly or indirectly from defendants (*Smahaj*, 69 Misc 3d at 599-600).

But the passage of a lengthy period following the Data Breach with no suspicious activity weighs heavily against finding that the injuries claimed by the named plaintiffs are imminent or substantially likely to occur (*see id.* at 602-603).

"Amorphous allegations of potential future injury do not suffice" (*Lynch*, 2018 NY Slip Op 32962[U], *3), and plaintiffs "cannot manufacture standing merely by inflicting harm on themselves based on their fears of hypothetical future harm that is not certainly impending" Thus, "[w]hile injury [from the Data Breach] is possible, as it was in [*Smahaj, Lynch* and *Manning*], it remains only a risk, too speculative to constitute injury".

As well articulated by the *Jantzer* Court in dismissing a similar data breach case against a healthcare institution:

> Those who are entrusted with details about an individual's health care should guard against even the inadvertent disclosure of that confidential information and those duties were allegedly breached in this case when hackers secured access to confidential health care information through a cyberattack. Nonetheless, while legal remedies may be pursued by those who were injured, the law only allows for the pursuit of ... claims ... only by those who have standing based on an alleged legally compensable injury. The Court finds the harm of increased risk of future identity fraud too speculative to support standing in this case (*Jantzer*, 2020 WL 2404764).

The Court therefore concludes that the named plaintiffs have failed to allege particularized and concrete injuries that are impending, imminent or substantially likely to occur. For this reason, their Complaints must be dismissed.

In conclusion, the Court recognizes that the case law from outside of the New York State courts concerning the standing of data breach plaintiffs is far from uniform, and some federal courts and courts of other jurisdictions have found standing on facts somewhat similar to those presented here (*see* Opp Mem, pp. 5-6 & n 4; *see generally* Mitchell J. Surface, *Civil Procedure — Article III Cause-in-Fact Standing: Do Data Breach Victims Have Standing Before Compromised Data Is Misused?* , 43 Am J Trial Advoc 503 [2020]). The Court further recognizes that *Smahaj, Lynch* and *Manning* — decisions from courts of coequal jurisdiction — are not binding precedent.

But the Court finds the multi-factor analysis taught by *Smahaj, Lynch* and *Manning* to be a sound approach to identifying whether the injuries alleged by data breach plaintiffs are "actual or imminent" (*Matter of Association for a Better Long Is.*, 23 NY3d at 7), rather than "based on ... conjecture or speculation" (*Matter of Animal Legal Defense Fund*, 119 AD3d at 1203). Indeed, under New York law, the bulk of plaintiffs' claims do not even accrue and become legally enforceable until plaintiffs have sustained actual and ascertainable damages (*see Kronos, Inc. v AVX Corp.*, 81 NY2d 90, 96 [1993] ["It is the incurring of damage that engenders a legally cognizable right."]).

The ubiquitous nature of data breaches further counsels in favor of a cautious approach to standing. More than six years ago, a federal Judge addressing a data breach lawsuit observed: "There are only two types of companies left in the United States, according to data security experts: those that have been hacked and those that don't know they've been hacked" (*Storm v Paytime, Inc.*, 90 F Supp 3d 359, 360 [MD Pa 2015] [internal quotation marks and footnote omitted]). As illustrated by the reference sources copiously cited in plaintiffs' Complaints, the prevalence of data breaches has only increased since then.

CONCLUSION

For all of the foregoing reasons, it is **ORDERED** that defendants' motions to dismiss the complaints in Action Nos. 1 and 2 are granted; and it is further **ORDERED** that the complaints in Action Nos. 1 and 2 are dismissed.

NOTES

Note 1

Should the result in *Keach* changed based on the U.S. Supreme Court's decision in *Transunion v. Ramirez*?

CHAPTER FOURTEEN. CYBERSECURITY: AN INTERNATIONAL PERSPECTIVE

14.1 Introduction

This Chapter reviews some international issues concerning cybersecurity and privacy. However, it is not a comprehensive examination of all related issues. This Chapter provides a general overview of the following subjects: 1) Movement Toward a Comprehensive Cybersecurity Treaty; 2) the European Union's General Data Protection Regulation (GDPR); 3) the European Convention on Cybercrime; 4) the Tallinn Manual (2.0) concerning cyberwar; 5) U.S. Cyberspace Solarium Commission Report; and 6) Regional Free Trade Agreements.

14.2 Movement Toward a Comprehensive Cybersecurity Treaty

An important topic concerning cybersecurity law concerns the adoption of a comprehensive multi-lateral treaty relating to the subject. There are several reasons why a comprehensive treaty has not been adopted. The group of issues include, but are not limited to 1) the borderless nature of the Internet; 2) ideological differences amongst stakeholder countries; 3) national security; 4) definitional problems; and 5) the nature of unregulated markets for vulnerabilities. This section also discusses efforts at the United Nations to regulate cybersecurity.

The first group of issues concerns the borderless nature of the Internet. First, the interconnected nature of the Internet raises issues with a cyberattack that may originate in one country impacting the citizens of another country. This raises difficult questions with respect to sovereignty. Second, a related issue to the first issue concerns the anonymous nature of the Internet. It can be difficult to confirm the source of a cyberattack. This raises issues with regards to ensuring that the alleged source of the attack is actually the source. There are obvious issues with respect to countries and private actors making it appear that another country was the responsible party.[540] Third, countries may utilize private parties either through express or tacit agreements

---

[540] *See* RICHARD A. CLARKE AND ROBERT K. KANE, CYBER WAR: THE NEXT THREAT TO NATIONAL SECURITY AND WHAT TO DO ABOUT IT 249 (Harper Collins 2010) ("One way to address the attribution problem is to shift the burden from the investigator and accuser to the nation in which the attack software was launched. This same burden shifting has been used in dealing with international crime and with terrorism."); Jack Goldsmith, *Cybersecurity Treaties: A Skeptical View*, Hoover Institution, Stanford University (2011) ("Verification is hard because attribution is hard."); Kristen E. Eichensehr, *The Law and Politics of Cyberattack Attribution*, 67 UCLA L. REV. 520 (2020) ("Instead of blocking the development of evidentiary standards for attribution, as the United States, France, the Netherlands, and the United Kingdom are currently doing, states should establish an international law requirement that public attributions must include sufficient evidence to enable crosschecking or corroboration of the accusations.").

to conduct cybersecurity attacks on the resources of other countries. This allows countries to deny responsibility for those acts particularly with respect to tacit agreements. For example, some have alleged that the Russian government has tacit agreements with private parties in Russia that if they attack or destabilize democratic institutions in the West that they will be essentially left alone in Russia. The United States has recently accused China of entering contracts with hackers who attack the West. Fourth, there is a question with regards to the ability of private actors to claim some form of sovereign immunity if they are working with a foreign government. This question would likely need to be clarified in a comprehensive treaty. Fifth, there is a problem concerning extradition of the sources of cyberattacks for criminal prosecution to another country where the harm occurred.

The second group of issues relates to ideology. A fundamental obstacle to the adoption of a comprehensive treaty concerns the different ideological approach between some Western countries and Russia and China, in particular. Some Western countries, specifically the United States, have favored a multi-stakeholder approach to issues related to cybersecurity and Internet. Importantly, this approach is favored by the United States because a significant portion of U.S. critical infrastructure is owned by private companies. The multi-stakeholder approach ensures that private companies and other groups are included in deciding how the Internet is regulated and protects the separation between the government and private sector.[541] A significant private sector provides a check on government abuse. Moreover, the U.S. approach likely favors the spread of information, including democratic ideals through various forms of media. The U.S. approach may also result in greater protection for privacy and other democratic values, including protecting internationally recognized rights.[542] Additionally, the U.S. position includes a bottom-up norms driven approach rather than a top-down one.[543]

---

[541] *See* Microsoft, *Protecting People in Cyberspace: The Vital Role of the United Nations in 2020* ("Given current trends, it is clear that international law either (a) does not sufficiently prohibit some of the most egregious and unwanted cyberactivity, including systemic cyber operations targeting individual users or their infrastructure below the use of force threshold, or (b) provides a "patchwork" of contested rules (and meanings) resulting in insufficient and/or ineffective regulation or deterrence of or consequences for unwanted activity."); Ido Kilovaty, *Privatized Cybersecurity*, 10 UC IRVINE L. REV. 1181 (2020) ("These private actors, while not yet on an equal footing to states, are increasingly displacing states as they seek to create their own privatized and unaccountable version of cybersecurity law.").

[542] *See* UNITED NATIONS, DEVELOPMENTS IN THE FIELD OF INFORMATION AND TELECOMMUNICATIONS IN THE CONTEXT OF INTERNATIONAL SECURITY: REPORT OF THE FIRST COMMITTEE, A/74/363 (November 18, 2019) (noting difference in voting on two proposed resolutions, including China and Russia's rejection of a resolution reaffirming the applicability of the UN Charter and other international law to cyberspace); *see also* UNITED NATIONS, DEVELOPMENTS IN THE FIELD OF INFORMATION AND TELECOMMUNICATIONS IN THE CONTEXT OF INTERNATIONAL SECURITY: REPORT OF THE FIRST COMMITTEE, A/75/394 (November 16, 2020) (also noting difference in voting by China and Russia versus United States on resolutions); UNITED NATIONS, OPEN-ENDED WORKING GROUP ON DEVELOPMENTS IN THE FIELD OF INFORMATION AND TELECOMMUNICATIONS IN THE CONTEXT OF INTERNATIONAL SECURITY: CHAIR'S REPORT, A/AC.290/2021/CRP.3 (March 10, 2021) (noting differing views on binding international law on cybersecurity).

[543] In the development of standards, China has a top-down approach. *See* Shin Yi Peng, *"Private" Cybersecurity Standards? Cyberspace Governance, Multistakeholderism, and the (Ir)relevance of the*

The Snowden leaks resulted in the release of information confirming the U.S. government's involvement in hacking underwater cables to access information among other sins. Further, the Schrems dispute concerning cross-border data flows and the rejection of the U.S. Privacy Shield highlights how the European Union has decided that there are insufficient protections for European citizens' data from the U.S. government.

Additionally, the private ownership and control of intellectual property may be favored under a multi-stakeholder approach to regulating cybersecurity issues. China's and Russia's approach favors state control of networks and would result in government control and surveillance of private citizens.[544] This would result in the ability of the current Russian government to retain power and ensure stability. Additionally, the Russian approach would likely result in the disclosure of intellectual property to the government in order for the government to regulate cybersecurity issues. Notably, exposing intellectual property as well as technology may result in less cybersecurity protection in Western countries. China had a requirement that financial institutions doing business in China disclose their source code to the Chinese government. A cynical person may find it humorous that the Russian government may sponsor or approve of cyberattacks against the West to undermine democracy and then utilize intergovernmental processes to then allow them to use those attacks to justify increased control over their own citizenry. Moreover, the state sanctioned cyberattacks against Western countries results in a destabilizing of the West's economic system as the costs to do business of cyberattack victims are raised because of the resulting expense of data breaches. This is also damaging because it then provides a competitive advantage to competitors of those companies. Finally, there is a dispute concerning the proper forum to resolve issues concerning cybersecurity.

A third group of issues related to the second group concerns national security. The United States as well as other countries have asserted that national security justifies the intrusion into computer networks to thwart, for example, terrorism.[545]

TBT Regime, 51 CORNELL INT'L L.J. 445 (2018) ("In this context, perhaps China's top-down, government-centered standardization system represents the most outstanding case. In the Chinese ICT market, the government assumes primary responsibility in standardization development, with the policy rationale that state-led standardization creates the most efficient national economy.").

[544] *See e.g.*, UNITED NATIONS, OPEN-ENDED WORKING GROUP ON DEVELOPMENTS IN THE FIELD OF INFORMATION AND TELECOMMUNICATIONS IN THE CONTEXT OF INTERNATIONAL SECURITY: CHAIR'S REPORT, A/AC.290/2021/CRP.3 (March 10, 2021) (China proposed the following language: "States should exercise jurisdiction over the ICT infrastructure, resources as well as ICT-related activities within their territories.").

[545] The U.S. Government under the Trump Administration has pushed for some Chinese social media companies to leave the U.S. market such as Tik Tok or WeChat, in part, because of cybersecurity concerns. Those concerns seem to revolve around the collection and use of data of U.S. citizens by those companies for or provided to the Chinese Government. China has been criticized for market protection and potential intellectual property theft because of conditioning access to the Chinese market for foreign countries on access to, for example, financial institutions source code for their software. China has also required or desired that foreign companies doing business in China have a Chinese business partner. This could lead to the disclosure of trade secrets or sensitive personal data to the Chinese business partner.

Moreover, reportedly, the United States government and other governments have engaged in purchasing zero-day vulnerabilities. The United States and other governments, reportedly, have also developed hacking tools. Unfortunately, there are reports that hacking tools have been stolen by rival governments and private parties. There is arguably not effective legislation or practice which protects these tools. There are also reports of more governments ramping up their ability to engage in cybersecurity attacks. Every government may use national security as a reason why they must engage in cybersecurity breaches.[546] Governments have also engaged in hacking back and defend forward strategies to address cybersecurity attacks.[547] Additionally, a difficult issue exists as to defining national security. The protection of critical infrastructure as well as protecting private intellectual property likely fall within the umbrella of national security.

A fourth group of issues concerns definitional problems. The international community has not found agreement on the meaning of terms such as "cyberattack" and what may constitute an act of war.[548] This is related to the definitional issue with respect to national security. Importantly, information technology can have civilian and military applications.

A fifth group of issues concerns the inability to avoid vulnerabilities in software given the motivation of most private software companies to be first to market and the complexity of software. The lack of effective laws incentivizing software companies to ensure that their software is adequately tested and protected will also continue to lead to the presence of vulnerabilities.

A sixth group of issues, also related to the third group of issues, concerns the relatively unregulated nature of markets for zero-day vulnerabilities and hacking tools.[549] This market includes participants including governments and private parties.

With regard to requiring access to source code of financial institutions, China argued that was necessary to combat terrorism—essentially national security reasons.

[546] In October of 2020, Sweden decided to ban Chinese companies Huawei and ZTE from its 5G networks. Notably, the reason for the ban concerned security. *See* Richard Milne, *Sweden Bans China's Huawei and ZTE from Its 5G Networks*, L. A. TIMES (Oct. 20, 2020), https://www.latimes.com/business/story/2020-10-20/sweden-bans-china-huawei-zte-5g-networks.

[547] *See* Amanda N. Craig, Scott J. Shackelford and Janine S. Hiller, *Proactive Cybersecurity: A Comparative Industry and Regulatory Analysis*, 52 AM. BUS. L. J. 721 (2015) (discussing potential emerging norm of proactive cybersecurity).

[548] See Oona A. Hathaway, Rebecca Crootof, Philip Levitz, Haley Nix, Aileen Nowlan, William Predue & Julie Spiegel, *The Law of Cyber-Attack*, 100 CALIF. L. REV. 817 (2012) (addressing need for agreement on defining terms "cyber-attack," "cyber-crime," and "cyber-warfare"); David Satola & Henry L. Judy, *Towards a Dynamic Approach to Enhancing International Cooperation and Collaboration in Cybersecurity Legal Frameworks: Reflections on the Proceedings of the Workshop on Cybersecurity Legal Issues at the 2010 United Nations Internet Governance Forum*, 37 WM. MITCHELL L. REV. 1745 (2011) (Cybersecurity does not necessarily mean cyberware or cyber crime.).

[549] *See* Mailyn Fidler, *Regulating the Zero-Day Vulnerability Trade: A Preliminary Analysis*, 11 I/S: J. L. & POL'Y FOR INFO. SOC'Y 405 (2015). Near the time of publication of this book, the U.S. Department of Commerce released a rule for public comment concerning the export and sale of certain hacking tools. *See* Ellen Nakashima, *Commerce Department announces new rule aimed at stemming sale of hacking*

Governmental disclose of zero-day vulnerabilities may also be an issue.[550] Moreover, the cybersecurity environment likely benefits from having gray hat hackers who may find and disclose vulnerabilities. The promulgation of regulation prohibiting gray hat hacker activity, and more importantly, enforcement of those regulations, may result in a loss of the benefit of gray hat hackers and pushing gray hat hackers towards the black hat space.

These issues as well as others have hindered the efforts to adopt a comprehensive cybersecurity law treaty. Commentators have made several proposals to address the international state of cybersecurity law.[551] For example, one commentator has proposed a global regulatory agency.[552] Another commentator has proposed that states enter a treaty regarding critical infrastructure.[553] The materials *infra* discuss international attempts to develop norms and confidence building measures related to cybersecurity law.

---

tools to Russia and China, WASHINGTON POST (October 20, 2021), available at https://www.washingtonpost.com/national-security/commerce-department-announces-new-rule-aimed-at-stemming-sale-of-hacking-tools-to-repressive-governments/2021/10/20/ecb56428-311b-11ec-93e2-dba2c2c11851_story.html?utm_campaign=wp_the_cybersecurity_202&utm_medium=email&utm_source=newsletter&wpisrc=nl_cybersecurity202. The Summary concerning the proposed rule states:

> This interim final rule outlines the progress the United States has made in export controls pertaining to cybersecurity items, revised Commerce Control List (CCL) implementation, and requests from the public information about the impact of these revised controls on U.S. industry and the cybersecurity community. Specifically, this rule establishes a new control on these items for National Security (NS) and Anti-terrorism (AT) reasons, along with a new License Exception Authorized Cybersecurity Exports (ACE) that authorizes exports of these items to most destinations except in the circumstances described. These items warrant controls because these tools could be used for surveillance, espionage, or other actions that disrupt, deny or degrade the network or devices on it.

Information Security Controls, BUREAU OF INDUSTRY AND SECURITY, U.S. DEPARTMENT OF COMMERCE (October 20, 2021), available at https://public-inspection.federalregister.gov/2021-22774.pdf.

[550] *See* Dakota Cary, *China's New Software Policy Weaponizes Cybersecurity Research*, THE HILL (July 22, 2021). ("China's new policies would allow its hacking teams to free ride on cybersecurity research conducted outside its borders, turning defensive research into offensive capabilities. Article 2 and Article 7(2) of http://www.cac.gov.cn/2021-07/13/c_1627761607640342.htm require companies operating within China to report known software vulnerabilities to the Ministry of Industry and Information Technology (MIIT) within two days of becoming aware of the issue.").

[551] *See* RICHARD A. CLARKE AND ROBERT K. KANE, CYBER WAR: THE NEXT THREAT TO NATIONAL SECURITY AND WHAT TO DO ABOUT IT 240 (Harper Collins 2010) (proposing a treaty with a no first use pledge regarding cyberattacks – still allows development of cyber weapons, but places stigma on first violator.).

[552] *See* Susanna Bagdasarova, *Brave New World: Challenges in International Cybersecurity Strategy and the Need for Centralized Governance*, 199 PENN. ST. L. REV. 1005 (2015).

[553] Mark Barrera, *The Achievable Multinational Cyber Treaty: Strengthening Our Nation's Critical Infrastructure* (2019), available at https://media.defense.gov/2017/Jun/19/2001764798/-1/-1/0/CPP_0003_BARRERA_MULTINATIONAL_CYBER_TREATY.PDF.

14.2[A]   UNITED   NATIONS   EFFORTS   TOWARDS   REGULATING CYBERSECURITY

The United Nations has given attention to cybersecurity for quite some time. This has included resolutions as well as the formation of working groups to address cybersecurity issues. The following discussion provides an overview of some of those efforts.

14.2[A][I] UNITED NATIONS RESOLUTIONS CONCERNING CYBERSECURITY

The United Nations has issued numerous resolutions related to cybersecurity. For example, in 1999, the United Nations General Assembly passed Resolution A/RES/53/70 titled, "Developments in the field of information and telecommunications in the context of international security." That Resolution expressly recognized that technology may have civilian and military purposes and noted concerns with stability and terrorism. The Resolution stated, in part:

> Expressing concern that these technologies and means can potentially be used for purposes that are inconsistent with the objectives of maintaining international stability and security and may adversely affect the security of States, Considering that it is necessary to prevent the misuse or exploitation of information resources or technologies for criminal or terrorist purposes, 1. Calls upon Member States to promote at multilateral levels the consideration of existing and potential threats in the field of information security; 2. Invites all Member States to inform the Secretary-General of their views and assessments on the following questions: (a) General appreciation of the issues of information security; (b) Definition of basic notions related to information security, including unauthorized interference with or misuse of information and telecommunications systems and information resources; (c) Advisability of developing international principles that would enhance the security of global information and telecommunications systems and help to combat information terrorism and criminality . . ..

Since that time, the United Nations has adopted additional resolutions and formed governmental expert groups to address issues related to cybersecurity. In 2009, the General Assembly of the United Nations adopted Resolution A/RES/64/25 titled, "Developments in the field of information and telecommunications in the context of international security." That Resolution states, in part: "Calls upon Member States to promote further at multilateral levels the consideration of existing and potential threats in the field of information security, as well as possible measures to limit the threats emerging in this field, consistent with the need to preserve the free flow of information . . .." Another example is Resolution A/RES/74/28 titled, "Advancing responsible State behaviour in cyberspace in the context of international security." Importantly, this Resolution references the reports of the U.N. Group of Governmental Experts on Developments in the Field of Information and Telecommunications in the Context of

International Security.   The Resolution affirms the work of the U.N. Group of Governmental Experts and states, in part:

> Stressing the importance of the assessments and recommendations contained in the reports of the Group of Governmental Experts, Confirming the conclusions of the Group of Governmental Experts, in its 2013 and 2015 reports, that international law, and in particular the Charter of the United Nations, is applicable and essential to maintaining peace and stability and promoting an open, secure, stable, accessible and peaceful information and communications technology environment, that voluntary and non-binding norms, rules and principles of responsible behaviour of States in the use of information and communications technologies can reduce risks to international peace, security and stability, and that, given the unique attributes of such technologies, additional norms can be developed over time,

> Confirming also the conclusions of the Group of Governmental Experts that voluntary confidence-building measures can promote trust and assurance among States and help to reduce the risk of conflict by increasing predictability and re ducing misperception and thereby make an important contribution to addressing the concerns of States over the use of information and communications technologies by States and could be a significant step towards greater international security,

> Confirming further the conclusions of the Group of Governmental Experts that providing assistance to build capacity in the area of information and communications technology security is also essential for international security, by improving the capacity of States for cooperation and collective action and promoting the use of such technologies for peaceful purposes,

> Stressing that, while States have a primary responsibility for maintaining a secure and peaceful information and communications technology environment, effective international cooperation would benefit from identifying mechanisms for the participation, as appropriate, of the private sector, academia and civil society organizations.

The Resolution further calls on members to act consistently with the U.N. Group of Governmental Experts recommendations as well as provide information concerning "[e]fforts taken at the national level to strengthen information security and promote international cooperation in this field." The Resolution also recognizes the beginning of the work of the Open-ended Working Group on Developments in the Field of Information and Telecommunications in the Context of International Security. The Open-ended Working Group includes a much broader membership of stake holders. Resolution A/RES/74/29 titled, "Developments in the field of information and telecommunications in the context of international security," recognizes that the U.N. Group of Governmental Experts and the Open-ended Working Group are intended to be complementary, but essentially independent. That Resolution further expresses the importance of capacity building and bridging in the field, and potential differences between countries relative to their individual capacity. The Resolution also notes that, "the United Nations should encourage regional efforts, promote confidence-building and transparency measures and support capacity-building and the dissemination of best practices."

The U.N. Human Rights Council has also adopted resolutions related to cybersecurity. For example, Resolution A/HRC/RES/23/17 titled, "The promotion, protection and enjoyment of human rights on the Internet," specifically recognizes the applicability of existing human rights obligations to online activity such as the Universal Declaration of Human Rights, International Covenant on Civil and Political Rights and the International Covenant on Economic, Social and Cultural Rights. In addressing cybersecurity, the Resolution states in part, "Recognizing that, for the Internet to remain global, open and interoperable, it is imperative that States address security concerns in accordance with their international human rights obligations, in particular with regard to freedom of expression, freedom of association and privacy[.]" The Resolution further notes that:

> Calls upon all States to address security concerns on the Internet in accordance with their international human rights obligations to ensure protection of freedom of expression, freedom of association, privacy and other human rights online, including through national democratic, transparent institutions, based on the rule of law, in a way that ensures freedom and security on the Internet so that it can continue to be a vibrant force that generates economic, social and cultural development[.]

The U.N. General Assembly has also passed resolutions indirectly relating to cybersecurity. For example, Resolution A/RES/69/166 titled, "The Right to Privacy in the Digital Age," provides, in part:

> Emphasizing that States must respect international human rights obligations regarding the right to privacy when they intercept digital communications of individuals and/or collect personal data and when they require disclosure of personal data from third parties, including private companies, Recalling that business enterprises have a responsibility to respect human rights as set out in the Guiding Principles on Business and Human Rights: Implementing the United Nations "Protect, Respect and Remedy" Framework[.]

The Resolution also "[c]alls on upon all States[,] . . . To respect and protect the right to privacy, including in the context of digital communication."

14.2[A][II] THE U.N. GROUP OF GOVERNMENTAL EXPERTS AND OPEN ENDED WORKING GROUP REPORTS

As mentioned *supra*, the U.N. has convened, at least, two groups to address cybersecurity issues. The first is the U.N. Group of Governmental Experts, and the second is the Open Ended Working Group. The U.N. Group of Governmental Experts has released multiple reports. The reports include the 2010, 2013 and 2015 reports. In 2017, the U.N. Group of Governmental Experts was unable to reach a consensus.[554] The Open Ended Working Group released a recent report in 2021. The reports generally set forth a framework for considering issues related to cybersecurity in the international context. For example, the reports tend to discuss and favor norm development in the cybersecurity space, confidence building measures and the sharing of information. Exploration and agreement on these concepts help define expectations and prevent conflict between states regarding cybersecurity. This section will review highlights of the 2010, 2013 and 2015 reports and the recent 2021 report.

The 2010 U.N. Group of Governmental Experts report consisted of the contributions of experts from 15 different states. The states included, "Belarus, Brazil, China, Estonia, France, Germany, India, Israel, Italy, Qatar, the Republic of Korea, the Russian Federation, South Africa, the United Kingdom of Great Britain and Northern Ireland and the United States of America." The 2010 report notes that cooperation, capacity building and additional norms in the context of security and the Internet should be developed. The 2010 report makes numerous recommendations:

> 18. Taking into account the existing and potential threats, risks and vulnerabilities in the field of information security, the Group of Governmental Experts considers it useful to recommend further steps for the development of confidence-building and other measures to reduce the risk of misperception resulting from ICT disruptions: (i) Further dialogue among States to discuss norms pertaining to State use of ICTs, to reduce collective risk and protect critical national and international infrastructure; (ii) Confidence-building, stability and risk reduction measures to address the implications of State use of ICTs, including exchanges of national views on the use of ICTs in conflict; (iii) Information exchanges on national legislation and national information and communications technologies security strategies and technologies, policies and best practices; [and] (iv) Identification of measures to support capacity-building in less developed countries . . . [.]

The 2013 U.N. Group of Governmental Experts report builds on the contributions of the 2010 report. The 2013 report notes several existing threats, risks and vulnerabilities, including the dual use nature of information communication technologies and "[t]he combination of global connectivity, vulnerable technologies and anonymity facilitates the use of ICTs for disruptive activities." Anonymity raises the problem with false and mistaken attribution. Moreover, the report expresses that, "States are concerned that embedding harmful hidden functions in ICTs could be used

---

[554] *See* UNITED NATIONS, GROUP OF GOVERNMENTAL EXPERTS ON DEVELOPMENTS IN THE FIELD OF INFORMATION AND TELECOMMUNICATIONS IN THE CONTEXT OF INTERNATIONAL SECURITY REPORT OF THE SECRETARY-GENERAL, RESOLUTION A/72/327 (August 14, 2017) ("No consensus was reached on a final report.").

in ways that would affect secure and reliable ICT use and the ICT supply chain for products and services, erode trust in commerce and damage national security." The report also states that risk exists with respect to the "use of ICTs in critical infrastructures and industrial control systems." The report further notes:

> Different levels of capacity for ICT security among different States can increase vulnerability in an interconnected world. Malicious actors exploit networks no matter where they are located. These vulnerabilities are amplified by disparities in national law, regulations and practices related to the use of ICTs.

The 2013 report also makes numerous recommendations concerning rules, principles and norms development relating to responsible behavior amongst states, including:

> 19. International law, and in particular the Charter of the United Nations, is applicable and is essential to maintaining peace and stability and promoting an open, secure, peaceful and accessible ICT environment. 20. State sovereignty and international norms and principles that flow from sovereignty apply to State conduct of ICT-related activities, and to their jurisdiction over ICT infrastructure within their territory. 21. State efforts to address the security of ICTs must go hand-in-hand with respect for human rights and fundamental freedoms set forth in the Universal Declaration of Human Rights and other international instruments. 22. States should intensify cooperation against criminal or terrorist use of ICTs, harmonize legal approaches as appropriate and strengthen practical collaboration between respective law enforcement and prosecutorial agencies. 23. States must meet their international obligations regarding internationally wrongful acts attributable to them. States must not use proxies to commit internationally wrongful acts. States should seek to ensure that their territories are not used by non-State actors for unlawful use of ICTs. 24. States should encourage the private sector and civil society to play an appropriate role to improve security of and in the use of ICTs, including supply chain security for ICT products and services. 25. Member States should consider how best to cooperate in implementing the above norms and principles of responsible behaviour, including the role that may be played by private sector and civil society organizations. These norms and principles complement the work of the United Nations and regional groups and are the basis for further work to build confidence and trust.

The 2013 report also makes recommendations concerning voluntary confidence building measures between states to enhance transparency, predictability and cooperation, including:

> (a) The exchange of views and information on a voluntary basis on national strategies and policies, best practices, decision-making

processes, relevant national organizations and measures to improve international cooperation. The extent of such information will be determined by the providing States. This information could be shared bilaterally, in regional groups or in other international forums; (b) The creation of bilateral, regional and multilateral consultative frameworks for confidence-building, which could entail workshops, seminars and exercises to refine national deliberations on how to prevent disruptive incidents arising from State use of ICTs and how these incidents might develop and be managed; (c) Enhanced sharing of information among States on ICT security incidents, involving the more effective use of existing channels or the development of appropriate new channels and mechanisms to receive, collect, analyse and share information related to ICT incidents, for timely response, recovery and mitigation actions. States should consider exchanging information on national points of contact, in order to expand and improve existing channels of communication for crisis management, and supporting the development of early warning mechanisms; (d) Exchanges of information and communication between national Computer Emergency Response Teams (CERTs) bilaterally, within CERT communities, and in other forums, to support dialogue at political and policy levels; (e) Increased cooperation to address incidents that could affect ICT or critical infrastructure that rely upon ICT-enabled industrial control systems. This could include guidelines and best practices among States against disruptions perpetrated by non-State actors; (f) Enhanced mechanisms for law enforcement cooperation to reduce incidents that could otherwise be misinterpreted as hostile State actions would improve international security.

The 2013 report makes additional recommendations regarding international capacity building, including the following:

> (a) Supporting bilateral, regional, multilateral and international capacity-building efforts to secure ICT use and ICT infrastructures; to strengthen national legal frameworks, law enforcement capabilities and strategies; to combat the use of ICTs for criminal and terrorist purposes; and to assist in the identification and dissemination of best practices; (b) Creating and strengthening incident response capabilities, including CERTs, and strengthening CERT-to-CERT cooperation; (c) Supporting the development and use of e-learning, training and awareness-raising with respect to ICT security to help overcome the digital divide and to assist developing countries in keeping abreast of international policy developments; (d) Increasing cooperation and transfer of knowledge and technology for managing ICT security incidents, especially for developing countries; (e) Encouraging further analysis and study by research institutes and universities on matters related to ICT security.

The 2015 report further builds on the 2010 and 2013 reports. The 2015 report examines the development of norms, rules and principles as well as confidence building measures in more depth. Importantly, the 2015 report provides recommendations for voluntary norms for consideration by states:

(a) Consistent with the purposes of the United Nations, including to maintain international peace and security, States should cooperate in developing and applying measures to increase stability and security in the use of ICTs and to prevent ICT practices that are acknowledged to be harmful or that may pose threats to international peace and security; (b) In case of ICT incidents, States should consider all relevant information, including the larger context of the event, the challenges of attribution in the ICT environment and the nature and extent of the consequences; (c) States should not knowingly allow their territory to be used for internationally wrongful acts using ICTs; (d) States should consider how best to cooperate to exchange information, assist each other, prosecute terrorist and criminal use of ICTs and implement other cooperative measures to address such threats. States may need to consider whether new measures need to be developed in this respect; (e) States, in ensuring the secure use of ICTs, should respect Human Rights Council resolutions 20/8 and 26/13 on the promotion, protection and enjoyment of human rights on the Internet, as well as General Assembly resolutions 68/167 and 69/166 on the right to privacy in the digital age, to guarantee full respect for human rights, including the right to freedom of expression; (f) A State should not conduct or knowingly support ICT activity contrary to its obligations under international law that intentionally damages critical infrastructure or otherwise impairs the use and operation of critical infrastructure to provide services to the public; (g) States should take appropriate measures to protect their critical infrastructure from ICT threats, taking into account General Assembly resolution 58/199 on the creation of a global culture of cybersecurity and the protection of critical information infrastructures, and other relevant resolutions; (h) States should respond to appropriate requests for assistance by another State whose critical infrastructure is subject to malicious ICT acts. States should also respond to appropriate requests to mitigate malicious ICT activity aimed at the critical infrastructure of another State emanating from their territory, taking into account due regard for sovereignty; (i) States should take reasonable steps to ensure the integrity of the supply chain so that end users can have confidence in the security of ICT products. States should seek to prevent the proliferation of malicious ICT tools and techniques and the use of harmful hidden functions; (j) States should encourage responsible reporting of ICT vulnerabilities and share associated information on available remedies to such vulnerabilities to limit and possibly eliminate potential threats to ICTs and ICT-dependent infrastructure; (k) States should not conduct or knowingly support activity to harm the information systems of the authorized emergency response teams (sometimes known as computer emergency response teams or cybersecurity incident response teams) of another State. A State should not use authorized emergency response teams to engage in malicious international activity. 14. The Group observed that, while such measures may be essential to promote an open, secure, stable, accessible and peaceful ICT environment, their implementation may not immediately be possible, in particular for developing countries, until they acquire adequate capacity.

The 2015 report examines how international law should apply in the cybersecurity context. Notably, the report states:

> (a) States have jurisdiction over the ICT infrastructure located within their territory; (b) In their use of ICTs, States must observe, among other principles of international law, State sovereignty, sovereign equality, the settlement of disputes by peaceful means and non-intervention in the internal affairs of other States. Existing obligations under international law are applicable to State use of ICTs. States must comply with their obligations under international law to respect and protect human rights and fundamental freedoms; (c) Underscoring the aspirations of the international community to the peaceful use of ICTs for the common good of mankind, and recalling that the Charter applies in its entirety, the Group noted the inherent right of States to take measures consistent with international law and as recognized in the Charter. . . ."

The 2015 report additionally refers to confidence building measures that could be adopted, including:

> Establish a national computer emergency response team and/or cybersecurity incident response team or officially designate an organization to fulfil this role. States may wish to consider such bodies within their definition of critical infrastructure. States should support and facilitate the functioning of and cooperation among such national response teams and other authorized bodies; (d) Expand and support practices in computer emergency response team and cybersecurity incident response team cooperation, as appropriate, such as information exchange about vulnerabilities, attack patterns and best practices for mitigating attacks, including coordinating responses, organizing exercises, supporting the handling of ICT-related incidents and enhancing regional and sector based cooperation[.]

The 2015 report was adopted generally by the United Nations General Assembly in Resolution A/RES/70/237 and provides guidance to member states concerning cybersecurity issues. This report and its predecessors provide the outline for addressing cybersecurity issues.

The Open Ended Working Group released a Final Substantive Report in March of 2021. The process of developing the report included input from non-governmental entities. The report reviewed the existing threats and risks, including the potential for escalating conflicts and damage to critical infrastructure. The report also addressed the rules, norms and principles of responsible state behavior and recommended that:

> 30. States, on a voluntary basis, survey their national efforts to implement norms, develop and share experience and good practice on norms implementation, and continue to inform the Secretary-General of their national views and assessments in this regard. 31. States should not conduct or knowingly support ICT activity contrary to their obligations under international law that intentionally damages critical infrastructure or otherwise impairs the use and operation of critical infrastructure to provide services to the public. Furthermore, States should continue to strengthen measures to protect of all critical infrastructure from ICT threats, and increase exchanges on best practices with regard to critical infrastructure protection. 32. States, in partnership with relevant organizations including the United Nations, further support the implementation and development of norms of responsible State behaviour by all States. States in a position to contribute expertise or resources be encouraged to do so. 33. States, recalling General Assembly resolution 70/237 and acknowledging General Assembly resolution 73/27 take note of proposals made by States on the elaboration of rules, norms and principles of responsible behaviour of States in future discussions on ICTs within the United Nations, noting that resolution 75/240 established an Open-ended Working Group on security of and in the use of information and communications technologies 2021-2025.

The report further addressed international law noting that the U.N. Charter as well as other international law continues to apply in cyberspace. The report recommends that:

> 38. States, on a voluntary basis, continue to inform the Secretary-General of their national views and assessments on how international law applies to their use of ICTs in the context of international security, and continue to voluntarily share such national views and practices through other avenues as appropriate. 39. States in a position to do so continue to support, in a neutral and objective manner, additional efforts to build capacity, in accordance with the principles contained in paragraph 56 of this report, in the areas of international law, national legislation and policy, in order for all States to contribute to building common understandings of how international law applies to the use of ICTs by States, and to contribute to building consensus within the international community. 40. States continue to study and undertake discussions within future UN processes on how international law applies to the use

of ICTs by States as a key step to clarify and further develop common understandings on the issue.

The report also discussed confidence building measures, including:

> 45. Building on their essential assets of trust and established relationships, States concluded that regional and sub-regional organizations have made significant efforts in developing CBMs, adapting them to their specific contexts and priorities, raising awareness and sharing information among their members. In addition, regional, cross-regional and inter-organizational exchanges can establish new avenues for collaboration, cooperation, and mutual learning. As not all States are members of a regional organization and not all regional organizations have CBMs in place, it was noted that such measures are complementary to the work of the UN and other organizations to promote CBMs.

> 46. Drawing from the lessons and practices shared at the OEWG, States concluded that the prior existence of national and regional mechanisms and structures, as well as the building of adequate resources and capacities, such as national Computer Emergency Response Teams (CERTs), are essential to ensuring that CBMs serve their intended purpose.

> 47. As a specific measure, States concluded that establishing national Points of Contact (PoCs) is a CBM in itself, but is also a helpful measure for the implementation of many other CBMs, and is invaluable in times of crisis. States may find it useful to have PoCs for, inter alia, diplomatic, policy, legal and technical exchanges, as well as incident reporting and response.

The report discussed capacity building measures such as process and purpose, partnerships, and people. Specifically, the report pointed toward institutional building, increased cooperation, and building technical, legal, legislative and regulatory skills. Importantly, states also agreed to continue to work under the auspices of the United Nations on cybersecurity related issues.[555] Numerous nongovernmental organizations

---

[555] Russia and China recently announced a new treaty. *See* THE EMBASSY OF THE RUSSIAN FEDERATION TO THE UNITED KINGDOM OF GREAT BRITAIN AND NORTHERN IRELAND, *Press Release: Joint Statement of the Russian Federation and the People's Republic of China on the Twentieth Anniversary of the Treaty of Good Neighbourliness and Friendly Cooperation between the Russian Federation and the People's Republic of China, 28 June 2021* (June 29, 2021), available at https://www.rusemb.org.uk/fnapr/7007. The treaty includes issues relevant to cybersecurity:

> The Parties reaffirm their commitment to strengthen international information security both at bilateral and multilateral levels, and they will further contribute to establishing a global international information security system based on such principles as prevention of conflicts in information space and promotion of the use of information and

were permitted to comment on an earlier draft of the report, including Microsoft, the International Red Cross and the International Chamber of Commerce. The International Chamber of Commerce specifically applauded "the recognition of the

---

communication technologies for peaceful purposes. In this context, they underline the applicability of international law, in particular the UN Charter, to information space, however, a common understanding on how it is used given the specifics of information and communication technologies is required, express their support for the work being done within the UN to elaborate new rules, norms and principles of responsible behaviour of States in information space and reiterate the key role of the UN in countering threats in the field of international information security.

The Parties emphasize the need to ensure an ongoing and continuous specialized negotiation process under the aegis of the United Nations within the new UN Open-Ended Working Group 2021–2025, set up at the initiative of Russia with active support from the People's Republic of China.

Russia and China strongly support the work of the Ad Hoc Intergovernmental Committee of Experts established under UN General Assembly resolutions 74/247 and 75/282, promote the early adoption of a comprehensive UN convention on combating the use of information and communication technologies for criminal purposes, and call on all parties to engage constructively in negotiations.

The Parties underscore their unity on issues related to Internet governance, which include ensuring that all States have equal rights to participate in global-network governance, increasing their role in this process and preserving the sovereign right of States to regulate the national segment of the Internet. Russia and China emphasize the need to enhance the role of the International Telecommunication Union and strengthen the representation of the two countries in its governing bodies.

Russia supports the Global Initiative on Data Security launched by China, and both Parties intend to continue promoting the development of possible joint measures to counter threats to international information security, including data security, within the UN Open-Ended Working Group 2021–2025.The Parties are determined to continue deepening bilateral cooperation on the basis of the joint statement of the President of the Russian Federation and the President of the People's Republic of China on cooperation in the development of information space of 25 June 2016 and the Agreement between the Government of the Russian Federation and the Government of the People's Republic of China on Cooperation in Ensuring International Information Security of 8 May 2015. *Id.*

In an Opinion article in the Washington Post, David Ignatius states that the move to the U.N.'s International Telecommunications Union is an attempt to increase their influence over the Internet while at the same time controlling content in their respective countries. *See* David Ignatius, *Opinion: Russia and China's hypocritical attempt to control cyberspace*, WASHINGTON POST (July 20, 2021), available at https://www.washingtonpost.com/opinions/2021/07/20/russia-china-are-trying-control-internet-even-they-censor-it/.

fundamental role of private companies in developing and deploying the technologies necessary to safeguard the lives and livelihoods of people around the world."556

As discussed *infra*, the EU Convention on Cybercrime (Budapest Convention) directly concerns cybercrime, but Russia and China are not members of the convention. Importantly, the United Nations is working on a Comprehensive International Convention on Countering the Use of Information and Communications Technologies for Criminal Purposes.557 In May 18, 2022, the European Data Protection Supervisor released comments concerning their participation in the negotiations of the convention:

> The EDPS is concerned that, if not specifically addressed, the future UN convention risks weakening the protection of individuals' fundamental rights, including the rights to data protection and privacy guaranteed under EU law, given the large number of countries, which each have their own legal system, that are partaking in its negotiations. As such, the EDPS advises the EU not to become party to the future UN convention on cybercrime, if its final draft does not guarantee these fundamental rights.558

---

556 ICC, INTERNATIONAL CHAMBER OF COMMERCE STATEMENT ON ZERO DRAFT OEWG (February 22, 2021), available at https://front.un-arm.org/wp-content/uploads/2021/02/ICC-statement_OEWG-ZeroDraft.pdf.

557 *See* UNITED NATIONS, COUNTERING THE USE OF INFORMATION AND COMMUNICATIONS TECHNOLOGIES FOR CRIMINAL PURPOSES, A/RES/74/247 (December 17, 2021) ("Decides to establish an open-ended ad hoc intergovernmental committee of experts, representative of all regions, to elaborate a comprehensive international convention on countering the use of information and communications technologies for criminal purposes, taking into full consideration existing international instruments and efforts at the national, regional and international levels on combating the use of information and communications technologies for criminal purposes, in particular the work and outcomes of the open-ended intergovernmental Expert Group to Conduct a Comprehensive Study on Cybercrime."). In January of 2022, the United Nations Office on Drugs and Crime released a FAQs document concerning work on the convention. UNITED NATIONS, FAQS—NEW UNITED NATIONS CONVENTION ON CYBERCRIME (January 2022), available at https://www.unodc.org/documents/Cybercrime/AdHocCommittee/FAQ_Jan2022.pdf. The United Nations Office on Drugs and Crime has a website for the Ad Hoc Committee to Elaborate a Comprehensive International Convention on Countering the Use of Information and Communications Technologies for Criminal Purposes available at https://www.unodc.org/unodc/en/cybercrime/ad_hoc_committee/home. There are scheduled meetings through 2022. *Id.*

558 EUROPEAN DATA PROTECTION SUPERVISOR, *A New United Nations Convention on Cybercrime: Fundamental Rights Come First* (May 18, 2022), available at https://edps.europa.eu/press-publications/press-news/press-releases/2022/new-united-nations-convention-cybercrime_en?mkt_tok=MTM4LUVaTS0wNDIAAAGEgWVzR_jkLLNPEUqy0gUttCvN4b2MObiK5HOnhMkgml7goASmPQOuXxREFHq3awkYSaEueJmdaeHFnXGv4--cE7aUoa-_nIb-vZlQfuGP2CoU; EUROPEAN DATA PROTECTION SUPERVISOR, OPINION 9/2022 ON THE RECOMMENDATION FOR A COUNCIL DECISION AUTHORISING THE NEGOTIATIONS FOR A COMPREHENSIVE INTERNATIONAL CONVENTION ON COUNTERING THE USE OF INFORMATION AND COMMUNICATIONS TECHNOLOGIES FOR CRIMINAL PURPOSES (May 18, 2022), available at https://edps.europa.eu/system/files/2022-05/2022-05-18-opinion_on_international_convention_en.pdf. The EDPS states:

14.2[B]   Other State Efforts to Create International Consensus Regarding Cybersecurity Law

States have also acted either independently or with other states, including within the United Nations, to create international consensus regarding cybersecurity law outside of the context of bilateral or multilateral agreements.[559] This section provides

> In its Opinion, the EDPS reaffirms that EU data protection law allows transfers of personal data to non-EU countries without additional requirements only if the non-EU country in question provides an adequate level of protection for individuals' personal data. If a non-EU country does not provide an adequate level of protection for individuals' personal data, specific transfers of personal data may be allowed exceptionally, providing that appropriate safeguards are put in place.
>
> The EDPS makes four additional recommendations to ensure that individuals' rights to data protection and privacy are upheld. Firstly, the cooperation, and therefore exchange of personal data, between countries should be limited to the crimes defined in the future UN convention. Secondly, the access to and exchange of personal data should be monitored carefully. In particular, the sharing of data should only take place between the law enforcement authorities of the countries concerned. Thirdly, future agreements between EU countries and non-EU countries that ensure a higher level of protection of individuals' privacy rights than the UN convention, should apply instead. Fourthly and finally, an EU Member State should, in certain cases, be allowed not to cooperate under the international convention with a non-EU country party to the future UN convention. *Id.*

[559] There have been numerous efforts by collections of various groups such as private institutions, government and others to develop principles, norms and frameworks for cybersecurity. One such effort is the Global Commission on the Stability of Cyberspace (GCSC). The GCSC produced a report in November of 2019 titled, "Advancing Cybersecurity." *See* GCSC, ADVANCING CYBERSECURITY (November 2019), available at https://cyberstability.org/report/. The Report sets forth a framework for addressing and norms related to cybersecurity issues. The Report provides four principles:

> Responsibility: Everyone is responsible for ensuring the stability of cyberspace.
> Restraint: No state or non-state actor should take actions that impair the stability of cyberspace.
> Requirement to Act: State or non-state actors should take reasonable and appropriate steps to ensure the stability of cyberspace.
> Respect for Human Rights: Efforts to ensure the stability of cyberspace must respect human rights and the rule of law. *Id.*

The Report also provides numerous norms:

1. State and non-state actors should neither conduct nor knowingly allow activity that intentionally and substantially damages the general availability or integrity of the public core of the Internet, and therefore the stability of cyberspace.
2. State and non-state actors must not pursue, support or allow cyber operations intended to disrupt the technical infrastructure essential to elections, referenda or plebiscites.
3. State and non-state actors should not tamper with products and services in development and production, nor allow them to be tampered with, if doing so may substantially impair the stability of cyberspace.
4. State and non-state actors should not commandeer the general public's ICT resources for use as botnets or for similar purposes.

some examples of those efforts.[560] First, China has proposed a Global Initiative on Data Security. Second, France and other countries have proposed creating a "Programme of

---

5.   States should create procedurally transparent frameworks to assess whether and when to disclose not publicly known vulnerabilities or flaws they are aware of in information systems and technologies. The default presumption should be in favor of disclosure.

6.   Developers and producers of products and services on which the stability of cyberspace depends should (1) prioritize security and stability, (2) take reasonable steps to ensure that their products or services are free from significant vulnerabilities, and (3) take measures to timely mitigate vulnerabilities that are later discovered and to be transparent about their process. All actors have a duty to share information on vulnerabilities in order to help prevent or mitigate malicious cyber activity.

7.   States should enact appropriate measures, including laws and regulations, to ensure basic cyber hygiene.

8.   Non-state actors should not engage in offensive cyber operations and state actors should prevent such activities and respond if they occur. *Id.*

The Report also provides recommendations for consideration, including:

1.   State and non-state actors adopt and implement norms that increase the stability of cyberspace by promoting restraint and encouraging action.

2.   State and non-state actors, consistent with their responsibilities and limitations, respond appropriately to norms violations, ensuring that those who violate norms face predictable and meaningful consequences.

3.   State and non-state actors, including international institutions, increase efforts to train staff, build capacity and capabilities, promote a shared understanding of the importance of the stability of cyberspace, and take into account the disparate needs of different parties.

4.   State and non-state actors collect, share, review, and publish information on norms violations and the impact of such activities.

5.   State and non-state actors establish and support Communities of Interest to help ensure the stability of cyberspace.

6.   A standing multistakeholder engagement mechanism be established to address stability issues, one where states, the private sector (including the technical community), and civil society are adequately involved and consulted. *Id.*

[560] There have been numerous attempts to address cybersecurity related issues at the global level. For example, the GCSC lists the efforts:

> Global Forum on Cyber Expertise . . ., World Summit on the Information Society, the Global Commission on Internet Governance (the Bildt Commission), the Internet Governance Forum . . ., the Global Conference on CyberSpace (GCCS/the London Process), the NETmundial Initiative, the Organization for Security and Co-operation in Europe . . ., the African Union Commission . . ., the Charter of Trust, the Cybersecurity Tech Accord, The Hague Program for Cyber Norms, the United Nations Institute for Disarmament Research . . ., the Paris Call for Trust and Security in Cyberspace . . ., and the UN Secretary-General's High-level Panel on Digital Cooperation. *Id.*

Action for advancing responsible State behaviour in cyberspace." Third, Russia, China and others have created an International Code of Conduct for Information Security.

In September of 2020, China released a Global Initiative on Data Security designed to stimulate agreement on issues related to cybersecurity.[561] The initiative is directed to countries and private companies. The initiative proposes:

-States should handle data security in a comprehensive, objective and evidence-based manner, and maintain an open, secure and stable supply chain of global ICT products and services.

-States should stand against ICT activities that impair or steal important data of other States' critical infrastructure, or use the data to conduct activities that undermine other States' national security and public interests.

-States should take actions to prevent and put an end to activities that jeopardize personal information through the use of ICTs, and oppose mass surveillance against other States and unauthorized collection of personal information of other States with ICTs as a tool.

-States should encourage companies to abide by laws and regulations of the State where they operate. States should not request domestic companies to store data generated and obtained overseas in their own territory.

-States should respect the sovereignty, jurisdiction and governance of data of other States, and shall not obtain data located in other States through companies or individuals without other States' permission.

-Should States need to obtain overseas data out of law enforcement requirement such as combating crimes, they should do it through judicial assistance or other relevant multilateral and bilateral agreements. Any bilateral data access agreement between two States should not infringe upon the judicial sovereignty and data security of a third State.

-ICT products and services providers should not install backdoors in their products and services to illegally obtain users' data, control or manipulate users' systems and devices.

-ICT companies should not seek illegitimate interests by taking advantage of users' dependence on their products, nor force users to upgrade their systems and devices. Products providers should make a

---

[561] Ministry of Foreign Affairs of the People's Republic of China, *Global Initiative on Data Security* (September 8, 2020), available at https://www.fmprc.gov.cn/mfa_eng/zxxx_662805/t1812951.shtml.

commitment to notifying their cooperation partners and users of serious vulnerabilities in their products in a timely fashion and offering remedies.

France, the EU and other states have proposed creating a "Programme of Action for advancing responsible State behaviour in cyberspace."[562]   Essentially, the Programme would discard the UN Group of Governmental Experts and the Open Ended Working Group processes and create a single permanent program similar to the existing United Nations "Programme of Action to Prevent, Combat and Eradicate the Illicit Trade in Small Arms and Light Weapons in All Its Aspects." The program would basically continue with discussions regarding the following items: "Create a framework and a political commitment based on recommendations, norms and principles already agreed;" "Have regular working-level meetings, focused on implementation;" "Step up cooperation and capacity building;" "Have regular Review conferences to make sure that the PoA is still fully adapted to needs and threats;" and "Organize consultations with other stakeholders (private companies, NGOs, civil society...), regional organizations, representatives of other UN processes, and relevant multi-stakeholder initiatives dealing with cyber-related issues in the context of international security."

In 2015, China, Kazakhstan, Kyrgyzstan, the Russia, Tajikistan and Uzbekistan (members of the Shanghai Cooperation Organization) proposed an International Code of Conduct for Information Security.[563] The Code of Conduct provides that adhering states much pledge:

> (1) To comply with the Charter of the United Nations and universally recognized norms governing international relations that enshrine, inter alia, respect for the sovereignty, territorial integrity and political independence of all States, respect for human rights and fundamental freedoms and respect for the diversity of history, culture and social systems of all countries; (2) Not to use information and communications technologies and information and communications networks to carry out activities which run counter to the task of maintaining international peace and security; (3) Not to use information and communications technologies and information and communications networks to interfere in the internal affairs of other States or with the aim of undermining their political, economic and social stability; (4) To cooperate in combating criminal and terrorist activities that use information and communications technologies and information and communications networks, and in curbing the dissemination of

---

[562] France et al, *The future of discussions on ICTs and cyberspace at the UN* (October 8, 2020), available at https://front.un-arm.org/wp-content/uploads/2020/10/joint-contribution-poa-future-of-cyber-discussions-at-un-10-08-2020.pdf.

[563] *See* United Nations, Letter dated 9 January 2015 from the Permanent Representatives of China, Kazakhstan, Kyrgyzstan, the Russian Federation, Tajikistan and Uzbekistan to the United Nations addressed to the Secretary-General (January 13, 2015), available at https://digitallibrary.un.org/record/786846?ln=en.

information that incites terrorism, separatism or extremism or that inflames hatred on ethnic, racial or religious grounds; (5) To endeavour to ensure the supply chain security of information and communications technology goods and services, in order to prevent other States from exploiting their dominant position in information and communications technologies, including dominance in resources, critical infrastructures, core technologies, information and communications technology goods and services and information and communications networks to undermine States' right to independent control of information and communications technology goods and services, or to threaten their political, economic and social security; (6) To reaffirm the rights and responsibilities of all States, in accordance with the relevant norms and rules, regarding legal protection of their information space and critical information infrastructure against damage resulting from threats, interference, attack and sabotage; (7) To recognize that the rights of an individual in the offline environment must also be protected in the online environment; to fully respect rights and freedoms in the information space, including the right and freedom to seek, receive and impart information, taking into account the fact that the International Covenant on Civil and Political Rights (article 19) attaches to that right special duties and responsibilities. It may therefore be subject to certain restrictions, but these shall only be such as are provided by law and are necessary: (a) for respect of the rights or reputations of others; (b) for the protection of national security or of public order (ordre public), or of public health or morals; (8) All States must play the same role in, and carry equal responsibility for, international governance of the Internet, its security, continuity and stability of operation, and its development in a way which promotes the establishment of multilateral, transparent and democratic international Internet governance mechanisms which ensure an equitable distribution of resources, facilitate access for all and ensure the stable and secure functioning of the Internet; (9) All States must cooperate fully with other interested parties in encouraging a deeper understanding by all elements in society, including the private sector and civil-society institutions, of their responsibility to ensure information security, by means including the creation of a culture of information security and the provision of support for efforts to protect critical information infrastructure; (10) To develop confidence-building measures aimed at increasing predictability and reducing the likelihood of misunderstanding and the risk of conflict. Such measures will include, inter alia, voluntary exchange of information regarding national strategies and organizational structures for ensuring a State 's information security, the publication of white papers and exchanges of best practice, wherever practical and advisable; (11) To assist developing countries in their efforts to enhance capacity building on information security and to close the digital divide; (12) To bolster bilateral, regional and international cooperation, promote a prominent role for the United Nations in areas such as encouraging the development of international legal norms for information security, peaceful settlement of international disputes, qualitative improvements in international cooperation in the field of information security; and to enhance coordination among relevant international organizations; (13) To settle any dispute resulting from the application of this code of conduct through peaceful means, and to refrain from the threat or use of force.

Commentators critique the Code of Conduct as an attempt to erode international human rights protections, such as privacy.[564]

NOTES

Note 1

In 2022, Russia invaded the Ukraine. The implications of Russia's action continue to develop. How do you think the invasion has impacted the likelihood of the establishment of a comprehensive treaty on cybersecurity with Russia as a signatory? One interesting development involved Conti, a well-known ransomware group. Conti apparently voiced support for Russia after the invasion and was apparently subsequently hacked resulting in a leak of information concerning Conti.[565] Notably, the hack was reportedly by Ukrainian supporters.[566]

14.3 GDPR

The GDPR is fundamentally a privacy regulation as demonstrated by the beginning of the first two recitals of the regulation:

"The protection of natural persons in relation to the processing of personal data is a fundamental right."[567]

"The principals of, and rules on the protection of natural persons with regard to the processing of their personal data should, whatever their nationality or residence, respect their fundamental rights and freedoms, in particular their right to the protection of personal data."[568]

---

[564] *See* Sarah McKune, *An Analysis of the International Code of Conduct for Information Security*, THE CITIZEN LAB (September 28, 2015), available at https://citizenlab.ca/2015/09/international-code-of-conduct/.

[565] *See* Monica Buchanan Pitrelli, *Leaked Documents Show Notorious Ransomware Group has an HR Department, Performance Reviews and an 'Employee of the Month'*, CNBC (April 13, 2022), available at https://www.cnbc.com/amp/2022/04/14/conti-ransomware-leak-shows-group-operates-like-normal-tech-company.html.

[566] *Id.*

[567] Regulation 2016/679, 2016 O.J. (L 119) 1.

[568] *Id.*

But with that said, the GDPR does provide a cybersecurity enforcement mechanism that we will explore further in a few paragraphs.   But first a little background.

As per Article 2 of the GDPR, the GDPR covers processing "by automated means" and "personal data which form part of a filing system."[569] For purposes of the GDPR, "'personal data' means any information relating to an identified or identifiable natural person ('data subject'); an identifiable natural person is one who can be identified, directly or indirectly, in particular by reference to an identifier such as a name, an identification number, location data, an online identifier or to one or more factors specific to the physical, physiological, genetic, mental, economic, cultural or social identity of that natural person[.]"[570]

Article 9 of the GDPR further addresses personal data by enumerating special categories of personal data: "Processing of personal data revealing racial or ethnic origin, political opinions, religious or philosophical beliefs, or trade union membership, and the processing of genetic data, biometric data for the purpose of uniquely identifying a natural person, data concerning health or data concerning a natural person's sex life or sexual orientation shall be prohibited."[571]

The GDPR first touches on security of data in Article 5: "Personal data shall be: f. processed in a manner that ensures appropriate security of the personal data, including protection against unauthorized or unlawful processing and against accidental loss, destruction or damage, using appropriate technical or organizational measures ('integrity and confidentiality')."[572]

It is interesting that Article 5 mentions two parts of CIA (confidentiality and integrity) but does not refer to "Availability." Availability remains important in the goals of the GDPR because a natural person needs to be able to review its data and to review its data, it must be available.

There are two concepts that are key to understanding the GDPR, the 'controller' and the 'processor'. "'[C]ontroller' means the natural or legal person, public authority, agency or other body which, alone or jointly with others, determines the purposes and means of the processing of personal data; where the purposes and means of such processing are determined by Union or Member State law, the controller or the specific criteria for its nomination may be provided by Union or Member State law;"[573] "'[P]rocessor' means a natural or legal person, public authority, agency or other body

---

[569] *Id.* at 32.
[570] *Id.* at 33.
[571] *Id.* at 38.
[572] *Id.* at 35–36.
[573] *Id.* at 33.

which processes personal data on behalf of the controller;"[574] Both the controller and processor "shall implement appropriate technical and organizational measures . . .."[575]

The GDPR outlines the security required in process in Article 32:

Article 32 Security of processing

1.　　Taking into account the state of the art, the costs of implementation and the nature, scope, context and purposes of processing as well as the risk of varying likelihood and severity for the rights and freedoms of natural persons, the controller and the processor shall implement appropriate technical and organisational measures to ensure a level of security appropriate to the risk, including inter alia as appropriate:

(a) the pseudonymisation and encryption of personal data;

(b) the ability to ensure the ongoing confidentiality, integrity, availability and resilience of processing systems and services;

(c) the ability to restore the availability and access to personal data in a timely manner in the event of a physical or technical incident;

(d) a process for regularly testing, assessing and evaluating the effectiveness of technical and organisational measures for ensuring the security of the processing.

　　2.　In assessing the appropriate level of security account shall be taken in particular of the risks that are presented by processing, in particular from accidental or unlawful destruction, loss, alteration, unauthorised disclosure of, or access to personal data transmitted, stored or otherwise processed.

　　3.　Adherence to an approved code of conduct as referred to in Article 40 or an approved certification mechanism as referred to in Article 42 may be used as an element by which to demonstrate compliance with the requirements set out in paragraph 1 of this Article.

　　4.　The controller and processor shall take steps to ensure that any natural person acting under the authority of the controller or the processor who has access to personal data does not process them except on instructions from the controller, unless he or she is required to do so by Union or Member State law.[576]

Article 32 is where resilience is added to CIA. It is interesting that this is the only mention of resilience.

As with many U.S. state breach notification laws, encryption can be a silver bullet:

---

[574] *Id.*
[575] *Id.* at 47.
[576] *Id.* at 51–52.

"The communication to the data subject [of a breach] shall not be required if any of the following conditions are met:

a. the controller has implemented appropriate technical and organizational protection measures, and those measures were applied to the personal data affected by the personal data breach, in particular those that render the personal data unintelligible to any person who is not authorised to access it, such as encryption."[577]

NOTES

Note 1

So how does Article 32 fit into the GDPR enforcement efforts? According to an American Bar Association article, Article 32 is the third most cited article in the GDPR for enforcement.

II. Regulators Focused on Four Articles to Substantiate Most GDPR Fines

EU data regulators focused on four GDPR Articles, Articles 5, 6, 15, and 32, to substantiate the bulk of levied fines. By far the most often cited was Article 5 (principles relating to processing of personal data). Article 5 principles include protecting personal data by ensuring appropriate levels of security to reduce the risk of unauthorized or unlawful processing and against accidental loss, destruction or damage, using appropriate technical or organizational measures ("integrity and confidentiality"). Article 5 also ensures personal data are collected in a limited manner, for a specific, explicit, and legitimate purpose. Article 5 violations were cited an estimated 30 times from among the 91 fines levied. Many regulators from across the EU found to Article 5 infringements such as failure to: process personal data lawfully, fairly, and in a transparent manner; prevent use of personal data for new purposes incompatible with the purpose for which the data were initially collected; delete personal data; and prevent indiscriminate access to an excessive number of user data.

In addition, Article 6 (lawfulness of processing) was the second most often cited infringement with a total of twelve violations. Under Article 6, lawful processing of personal data requires one (or more) of six factors: (1) obtained consent of the data subject; (2) data processed in performance of a contract; (3) data processed to comply with a legal obligation of the Member State or EU; (4) data processed to protect vital interests (i.e., interests essential for the life of the data subject or for humanitarian purposes); (5) data processed to perform a task that is in the public interest (e.g., a local government authority using personal data to collect taxes); or (6) data processed where necessary to fulfill legitimate controller (individual or entity that determines the purpose and means of

---

[577] *Id.* at 53.

processing personal data, such as a payroll management company) or third-party interests.

Articles 32 (security of processing personal data) and 15 (right of access by the data subject) were the third-most- often-cited infringements with a total of 7 violations each. Under Article 32, for example, appropriate technical and organizational measures must be implemented to ensure security appropriate to the risk including, but not limited to, the pseudonymization and encryption of personal data. Article 15 provides a right of access whereby the data subject may request information about how personal data are being processed. Data subjects have a right to request a copy of data being processed, the purpose for processing the data, categories of data being processed (e.g., name, address, phone number) and any third-party recipients of the personal data, among others. Generally, regulators tend to levy fines for failures related to the lawful processing of personal data, including security measures to protect personal data.[578]

It is not surprising that Article 32 would be cited because if an entity is lax in processing data it would be a reasonable assumption that the entity would also be lax in its security measures.

A more interesting question is how many cases used only Article 32 to take enforcement action against an entity. A review of the case source used by the ABA article reveals that out of 391 entries, 85 included a cite to Article 32.[579]

Out of those 85 that cited Article 32, the number of cases that cited only Article 32 are as follows:

Romania – 15; Spain – 8; Germany – 4; Norway – 3; Czech Republic – 3; UK – 2; Netherlands – 2; Slovakia – 2; Bulgaria – 2; France – 2; Cyprus – 1; Italy – 1 and Poland – 1.

There is a total of 46 cases, which is approximately 12 percent of all of the cases. One of the more interesting cases occurred in the Czech Republic:

The operator of an online game was exposed to several DDoS attacks which caused the malfunctioning of the servers. The attacker blackmailed the operator stating that the attacks will not stop unless he pays money. As part of the blackmail, the attacker offered the operator that he will create an upgraded and better firewall protection to the servers of the

---

[578] Catherine Barrett, *Emerging Trends from the First Year of EU GDPR Enforcement*, AM. BAR ASS'N (Feb. 28, 2020), https://www.americanbar.org/groups/science_technology/publications/scitech_lawyer/2020/spring/emerging-trends-the-first-year-eu-gdpr-enforcement/.

[579] *GDPR Enforcement Tracker*, ENFORCEMENT TRACKER, https://www.enforcementtracker.com (last visited Nov. 2, 2020) (with a further search on '32' to arrive at 85).

operator. The operator agreed and paid the attacker. The operator implemented the new code from the attacker which proved better than the old one but there was a "backdoor" in the code. The attacker used the backdoor to steal all the data from the server about the players and uploaded these details to his website. The Office for Personal Data Protection concluded that the operator did not take appropriate security measures.[580]

It appears, based on the case facts, that many of the cases that contain only a cite to Article 32, could have added cites to other articles. We can only speculate as to why the authorities for that country did not. One speculation is that once Article 32 is established it may be easier to proceed on that article without adding other articles.

Note 2

The European Cybersecurity Act was adopted by the European Members of Parliament in 2019. The European Cybersecurity Act essentially:

strengthens the [European Union Agency for Network and Information Security Agency] by granting to the agency a permanent mandate, reinforcing its financial and human resources and overall enhancing its role in supporting EU to achieve a common and high level cybersecurity.

establishes the first EU-wide cybersecurity certification framework to ensure a common cybersecurity certification approach in the European internal market and ultimately improve cybersecurity in a broad range of digital products (e.g. Internet of Things) and services.[581]

Note 3

On May 13, 2022, the European Commission released a press release concerning the agreement by the European Parliament and member states concerning a new "**Directive on measures for a high common level of cybersecurity across the Union (NIS 2 Directive)** proposed by the Commission in December 2020." The Press Release states:

The existing rules on the security of network and information systems (NIS Directive),[582] have been the first piece of EU-wide legislation on cybersecurity and paved the way for a significant change in mind-set, institutional and regulatory approach to cybersecurity in many Member States. In spite of their notable achievements and positive impact, they had to be updated because of the increasing degree of

---

[580] Id.

[581] *The Cybersecurity Act Strengthens Europe's Cybersecurity*, E.U. COMM'N (Mar. 19, 2019), https://ec.europa.eu/digital-single-market/en/news/cybersecurity-act-strengthens-europes-cybersecurity.

[582] Available at https://eur-lex.europa.eu/legal-content/EN/TXT/HTML/?uri=CELEX:32016L1148&from=EN (last visited May 25, 2022).

digitalisation and interconnectedness of our society and the rising number of cyber malicious activities at global level.

To respond to this increased exposure of Europe to cyber threats, the **NIS 2 Directive**[583] now covers medium and large entities from more sectors that are critical for the economy and society, including providers of public electronic communications services, digital services, waste water and waste management, manufacturing of critical products, postal and courier services and public administration, both at central and regional level. It also covers more broadly the healthcare sector, for example by including medical device manufacturers, given the increasing security threats that arose during the COVID-19 pandemic. The expansion of the scope covered by the new rules, by effectively obliging more entities and sectors to take cybersecurity risk management measures, will help increase the level of cybersecurity in Europe in the medium and longer term.

The NIS 2 Directive also strengthens cybersecurity requirements imposed on the companies, addresses security of supply chains and supplier relationships and introduces accountability of top management for non-compliance with the cybersecurity obligations. It streamlines reporting obligations, introduces more stringent supervisory measures for national authorities, as well as stricter enforcement requirements, and aims at harmonising sanctions regimes across Member States. It will help increase information sharing and cooperation on cyber crisis management at a national and EU level.[584]

Note 4

Standard Contractual Clauses

The transfer of data under the GDPR is subject to "appropriate safeguards."[585] An effective method for companies outside of the EEA to prove that they have appropriate safeguards is to implement standard contractual clauses (SCC) as part of their data processing contracts. The Commission Implementing Decision (EU) 2021/914 of 4 June 2021 on standard contractual clauses for the transfer of personal data to third countries pursuant to Regulation (EU) 2016/679 of the European Parliament and of the Council provided the latest SCC approved for use. Annex II: Technical and Organisational Measures Including Technical Organisational Measures to Ensure the Security of the Data declares that the "technical and organizational measure must be

---

[583] Available at https://eur-lex.europa.eu/legal-content/EN/TXT/HTML/?uri=CELEX:52020PC0823&from=EN (last visited May 25, 2022).

[584] *Commission Welcomes Agreement on New Rules on Cybersecurity on Network and Information Systems*, E.U. COMM'N (March 13, 2022), available at https://ec.europa.eu/commission/presscorner/detail/en/IP_22_2985.

[585] *Id.* at Article 46.

described in specific (and not generic) terms."[586] A nonexclusive list of possible measures includes the following examples:

Measures of pseudonymization and encryption of personal data

Measures for ensuring ongoing confidentiality, integrity, availability and resilience of processing systems and services

Measures for ensuring the ability to restore the availability and access to personal data in a timely manner in the event of a physical or technical incident

Processes for regularly testing, assessing and evaluating the effectiveness of technical and organisational measures in order to ensure the security of the processing

Measures for user identification and authorisation

Measures for the protection of data during storage

Measures for ensuring physical security of locations at which personal data are processed

Measures for ensuring events logging

Measures for ensuring system configuration, including default configuration

Measures for internal IT and IT security governance and management

Measures for certification/assurance of processes and products

Measures for ensuring data minimisation

Measures for ensuring data quality

Measures for ensuring limited data retention

Measures for ensuring accountability

Measures for allowing data portability and ensuring erasure[587]

14.4 European Convention on Cybercrime

The European Convention on Cybercrime (also know as the Budapest Convention on Cybercrime) is a treaty which provides provisions concerning cybercrime. It also

---

[586] The Commission Implementing Decision (EU) 2021/914 of 4 June 2021 on standard contractual clauses for the transfer of personal data to third countries pursuant to Regulation (EU) 2016/679 of the European Parliament and of the Council.

[587] *Id. Annex II.*

contains provisions concerning discovery of electronic data and systems, extradition and mutual assistance.

Convention on Cybercrime

Budapest, 23.XI.2001

Preamble

The member States of the Council of Europe and the other States signatory hereto,

. . . Convinced of the need to pursue, as a matter of priority, a common criminal policy aimed at the protection of society against cybercrime, *inter alia*, by adopting appropriate legislation and fostering international co-operation;

Conscious of the profound changes brought about by the digitalisation, convergence and continuing globalisation of computer networks;

Concerned by the risk that computer networks and electronic information may also be used for committing criminal offences and that evidence relating to such offences may be stored and transferred by these networks;

Recognising the need for co-operation between States and private industry in combating cybercrime and the need to protect legitimate interests in the use and development of information technologies;

Believing that an effective fight against cybercrime requires increased, rapid and well-functioning international co-operation in criminal matters;

Convinced that the present Convention is necessary to deter action directed against the confidentiality, integrity and availability of computer systems, networks and computer data as well as the misuse of such systems, networks and data by providing for the criminalisation of such conduct, as described in this Convention, and the adoption of powers sufficient for effectively combating such criminal offences, by facilitating their detection, investigation and prosecution at both the domestic and international levels and by providing arrangements for fast and reliable international co-operation;

Mindful of the need to ensure a proper balance between the interests of law enforcement and respect for fundamental human rights as enshrined in the 1950 Council of Europe Convention for the Protection of Human Rights and Fundamental Freedoms, the 1966 United Nations International Covenant on Civil and Political Rights and other applicable international human rights treaties, which reaffirm the right of everyone to hold opinions without interference, as well as the right to freedom of expression, including the freedom to seek, receive, and impart information and ideas of all kinds, regardless of frontiers, and the rights concerning the respect for privacy;

Mindful also of the right to the protection of personal data, as conferred, for example, by the 1981 Council of Europe Convention for the Protection of Individuals with regard to Automatic Processing of Personal Data;

. . . Have agreed as follows:

Chapter I – Use of terms

Article 1 – Definitions

For the purposes of this Convention:

a "computer system" means any device or a group of interconnected or related devices, one or more of which, pursuant to a program, performs automatic processing of data;

b "computer data" means any representation of facts, information or concepts in a form suitable for processing in a computer system, including a program suitable to cause a computer system to perform a function;

c "service provider" means:

i any public or private entity that provides to users of its service the ability to communicate by means of a computer system, and

ii any other entity that processes or stores computer data on behalf of such communication service or users of such service.

d "traffic data" means any computer data relating to a communication by means of a computer system, generated by a computer system that formed a part in the chain of communication, indicating the communication's origin, destination, route, time, date, size, duration, or type of underlying service.

Chapter II – Measures to be taken at the national level

Section 1 – Substantive criminal law

Title 1 – Offences against the confidentiality, integrity and availability of computer data and systems

Article 2 – Illegal access

Each Party shall adopt such legislative and other measures as may be necessary to establish as criminal offences under its domestic law, when committed intentionally, the access to the whole or any part of a computer system without right. A Party may require that the offence be committed by infringing security measures, with the intent of obtaining computer data or other dishonest intent, or in relation to a computer system that is connected to another computer system.

Article 3 – Illegal interception

Each Party shall adopt such legislative and other measures as may be necessary to establish as criminal offences under its domestic law, when committed intentionally, the interception without right, made by technical means, of non-public transmissions of computer data to, from or within a computer system, including electromagnetic emissions from a computer system carrying such computer data. A Party may require that the offence be committed with dishonest intent, or in relation to a computer system that is connected to another computer system.

Article 4 – Data interference

1 Each Party shall adopt such legislative and other measures as may be necessary to establish as criminal offences under its domestic law, when committed intentionally, the damaging, deletion, deterioration, alteration or suppression of computer data without right.

2 A Party may reserve the right to require that the conduct described in paragraph 1 result in serious harm.

Article 5 – System interference

Each Party shall adopt such legislative and other measures as may be necessary to establish as criminal offences under its domestic law, when committed intentionally, the serious hindering without right of the functioning of a computer system by inputting, transmitting, damaging, deleting, deteriorating, altering or suppressing computer data.

Article 6 – Misuse of devices

1 Each Party shall adopt such legislative and other measures as may be necessary to establish as criminal offences under its domestic law, when committed intentionally and without right:

a the production, sale, procurement for use, import, distribution or otherwise making available of:

i a device, including a computer program, designed or adapted primarily for the purpose of committing any of the offences established in accordance with Articles 2 through 5;

Title 2 – Computer-related offences

Article 7 – Computer-related forgery

Each Party shall adopt such legislative and other measures as may be necessary to establish as criminal offences under its domestic law, when committed intentionally and without right, the input, alteration, deletion, or suppression of computer data, resulting in inauthentic data with the intent that it be considered or acted upon for legal purposes as if it were authentic, regardless whether or not the data is directly readable and intelligible. A Party may require an intent to defraud, or similar dishonest intent, before criminal liability attaches.

Article 8 – Computer-related fraud

Each Party shall adopt such legislative and other measures as may be necessary to establish as criminal offences under its domestic law, when committed intentionally and without right, the causing of a loss of property to another person by:

a any input, alteration, deletion or suppression of computer data,

b any interference with the functioning of a computer system, with fraudulent or dishonest intent of procuring, without right, an economic benefit for oneself or for another person.

with fraudulent or dishonest intent of procuring, without right, an economic benefit for oneself or for another person.

Title 5 – Ancillary liability and sanctions

Article 11 – Attempt and aiding or abetting

1 Each Party shall adopt such legislative and other measures as may be necessary to establish as criminal offences under its domestic law, when committed intentionally, aiding or abetting the commission of any of the offences established in accordance with Articles 2 through 10 of the present Convention with intent that such offence be committed.

. . . .

NOTES

Note 1

In an article titled, *"The Council of Europe Convention on Cybercrime,"* Michael A. Vatis notes the expansive scope of the Budapest Convention on Cybercrime:

> One critical, but often overlooked, aspect of the Convention is that many of its procedural provisions are not limited to cybercrimes. Rather, they extend to any crimes for which it is necessary to collect evidence "in electronic form.[588]

He also notes that the Convention was intended to operate as a framework providing flexibility for the changing nature of cybercrimes and not as a model law for adopting states. *Id.* Moreover, he points out that the United States was influential in the creation of the Convention because of its experience with cybersecurity issues. *Id.*

Note 2

The Council of Europe in a report titled, "The Budapest Convention on Cybercrime: Benefits and Impact in Practice," points to the success of the Convention as a framework for national legislation concerning cybercrime around the world and

---

[588] NAT'L RES. COUNCIL, PROCEEDINGS OF A WORKSHOP ON DETERRING CYBERATTACKS: INFORMING STRATEGIES AND DEVELOPING OPTIONS FOR U.S. POLICY 208 (2010), *available at* http://static.cs.brown.edu/courses/csci1800/sources/lec16/Vatis.pdf.

allowing cooperation amongst parties around the world. In May of 2020, there were 76 countries who were either parties to the treaty, invited to join the treaty or were signatories. The report notes that 153 members of the United Nations utilized the Convention in drafting their own national laws.[589]

Note 3

The Council of Europe notes that there are increased concerns with cybercrime since the COVID-19 global pandemic:

> Phishing campaigns and malware distribution through seemingly genuine websites or documents providing information or advice on COVID-19 are used to infect computers and extract user credentials.
>
> Ransomware shutting down medical, scientific or other health-related facilities where individuals are tested for COVID-19 or where vaccines are being developed in order to extort ransom.
>
> Attacks against critical infrastructures or international organizations, such as World Health Organization.
>
> Ransomware targeting the mobile phones of individuals using apps that claim to provide genuine information on COVID-19 in order to extract payments.
>
> . . . Misinformation or fake news are spread by trolls and fake media accounts to create panic, social instability and distrust in governments or in measures taken by their health authorities.[590]

Note 4

There is also a Protocol to the Budapest Convention on Cybercrime concerning racial and xenophobic acts on computer systems. An additional protocol is being negotiated concerning electronic evidence and international cooperation.

Note 5

In *Transnational Government Hacking*, Professor Jennifer Daskal discusses Federal Rules of Criminal Procedure, Rule 41. *See* Jennifer Daskal, *Transnational Government Hacking*, 10 J. Nat'l Security L. & Pol'y 677 (2020). Federal Rules of Criminal Procedure, Rule 41 relates to the ability of a magistrate to issue a warrant to use remote access to search electronic storage media and to seize or copy electronically stored information located within or outside that district if: "**(A)** the district where the

---

[589] COUNCIL OF EUR., THE BUDAPEST CONVENTION ON CYBERCRIME: BENEFITS AND IMPACT IN PRACTICE 5 (2020), *available at* https://rm.coe.int/t-cy-2020-16-bc-benefits-rep-provisional/16809ef6ac.
[590] *Cybercrime and COVID-19*, COUNCIL OF EUR. (Mar. 27, 2020), https://www.coe.int/en/web/cybercrime/-/cybercrime-and-covid-19.

media or information is located has been concealed through technological means; or **(B)** in an investigation of a violation of 18 U.S.C. § 1030(a)(5), the media are protected computers that have been damaged without authorization and are located in five or more districts." See Federal Rules of Criminal Procedure, Rule 41. Professor Daskal argues "that governments should . . . when reasonably possible, seek consent from foreign governments when accessing devices or computer systems known to be located in a foreign jurisdiction [except in certain situations, such as] jeopardiz[ing] the investigation . . . or when law enforcement has physical access to a device and is merely accessing, via that device, data that automatically downloads from the cloud. . . ." *Id.* at 679. For additional analysis on governmental law enforcement hacking and international relations, please see Ahmed Ghappour, *Searching Places Unknown: Law Enforcement Jurisdiction on the Dark Web*, 69 Stan. L. Rev. 1075 (2017) ("[This article] is intended to offer a policymaking framework for this new surveillance technology that minimizes immediate foreign relations and national security risks and allocates the authority to make new decisions on appropriate procedures to the institutions most competent to address them.")

14.5 Tallinn Manual

The Tallinn Manual essentially restates the international law as applied to cyberwarfare. There are two Tallinn Manuals. The following article by Professor Eric Talbot Jensen discusses some of the issues addressed in Tallinn Manual 2.0.

Eric Talbot Jensen, *Tallinn Manual 2.0: Highlights and Insights*, 48 Geo. J. Int'l L. 735 (2017).[591]

I. INTRODUCTION

. . .

[T]he vast majority of malicious cyber activity has taken place far below the threshold of armed conflict between states, and has not risen to the level that would trigger such a conflict. Rather, the majority of cyber activities so prevalent in the news involve the stealing of corporate secrets, the spreading of false information, or the breach of government computers in an attempt to steal state secrets.

Nevertheless, the significance of cyber hacking has become a reality for millions of individuals whose personal information has been compromised through cyber means. The prevalence of these cyber events, along with the risks they raise to states individually and to the international community as a whole, have forced both states and multinational organizations to take notice and seek solutions. Among those multinational organizations is the North Atlantic Treaty Organization (NATO) whose

---

[591] This article was partially presented at a symposium on International Justice in the US Context: Where We Stand, Where We Fall, and Where We Need To Be. The article was originally published in the Georgetown Journal of International Law.

Cooperative Cyber Defense Center of Excellence (CCD COE) in Tallinn, Estonia, helped facilitate the original Tallinn Manual on the International Law Applicable to Cyber Warfare (Tallinn Manual 1.0) and the newly released Tallinn Manual 2.0 on the International Law Applicable to Cyber Operations. The substance of Tallinn 1.0 appears in Tallinn 2.0, though slightly altered to reflect points of clarification since its original publication.

This Article will briefly summarize the key points in the Tallinn Manual 2.0 (the Manual), including identifying some of the most important areas of non-consensus among the legal experts who wrote the Manual. The Article will also attempt some insights into where international law on cyber operations will need to go in the future.

II. THE PROCESS

Both Tallinn Manuals were written by groups of international legal experts (the Experts) gathered by the CCD COE and Michael N. Schmitt, a prominent global cyber expert. . . .

The intent of the project was never to make law or to produce a manual that would have the force of law. As the introduction makes clear:

Ultimately, Tallinn Manual 2.0 must be understood only as an expression of the opinions of the two International Groups of Experts as to the state of the law .... This Manual is meant to be a reflection of the law as it existed at the point of the Manual's adoption by the two International Groups of Experts in June 2016. It is not a 'best practices' guide, does not represent 'progressive development of the law', and is policy and politics-neutral. In other words, Tallinn Manual 2.0 is intended as an objective restatement of the *lex lata*. . . .

III. THE MANUAL

The Manual is divided into four parts. Part I deals with general international law and cyberspace. Part II covers specialized regimes of international law and cyberspace. Part III concerns international peace and security and cyber activities, which is drawn mostly from Tallinn 1.0. And Part IV is the rest of Tallinn 1.0 and applies to the law of cyber armed conflict. As Tallinn 1.0 has already been extensively commented on, this Article will draw exclusively on Parts I and II and a small portion of Part III.

A. *Sovereignty*

The Manual begins with a discussion of sovereignty and makes the point in its first rule that "[t]he Principle of Sovereignty applies to cyberspace." The subsequent two rules differentiate between internal and external sovereignty, and Rule 4 says that "[a] State must not conduct cyber operations that violate the sovereignty of another State."

The assumption underlying the Expert's conclusion in Rule 4 is that sovereignty is a rule of international law, the violation of which is an internationally wrongful act. The commentary to Rule 4 states:

In the cyber context, therefore, it is a violation of territorial sovereignty for an organ of a State, or others whose conduct may be attributed to the State, to conduct cyber operations while physically present on another State's territory against that State or entities or persons located there. For example, if an agent of one State uses a USB flash drive to introduce malware into cyber infrastructure located in another State, a violation of sovereignty has taken place.

This "sovereignty-as-rule" approach is not universally accepted. . . .

Historically, sovereignty predates the establishment of the modern state and originates in the Prince as Sovereign. With the rise of the modern state, international law has been formed by states applying the doctrine of sovereignty to particular sets of facts or instances of state interaction. For example, considering land territory, sovereignty has been applied differently to diplomats and spies from other state nationals. With respect to espionage, states have not found espionage to be a per se violation of sovereignty, even when those actions take place in and/or have effects in another state. States routinely outlaw the methods of espionage as a matter of domestic law, but not as a violation of sovereignty. Similarly, long before the Vienna Convention on the Law of Treaties was promulgated, customary international law provided immunities to diplomatic premises and persons on the territory of other states. Though states adapted the application of the principle of sovereignty with respect to land territory differently in these two cases, they support the assertion that sovereignty is a principle that gets applied based on the practical imperatives of states, rather than as a uniform rule of international law.

Contrasting the application of sovereignty in the domains of air, space, and sea is also instructive. In these cases, sovereignty has been applied differently by the international community depending on the practice of states across these domains, resulting in disparate legal paradigms. The lack of legal consistency across these domains makes the formulation of a rule that will apply to cyberspace especially difficult. It appears, based on state practice to date, that states are applying sovereignty with respect to cyberspace in a way that does not preclude cyber activities on the infrastructure and territory of another state to include actions taken by one state that do not impinge on the inherently governmental functions of another state.

What seems clear is that, as stated by former Department of State Legal Advisor Brian Egan, the international community is currently "faced with a relative vacuum of public State practice." Mike Schmitt echoed this at the U.S. launch of the Tallinn Manual 2.0. When asked what part of the Manual is most likely to change in the next five years, he answered that he thought it would be that states would need to clarify their positions on sovereignty. Again, as Brian Egan argued, "[s]tates should publicly state their views on how existing international law applies to State conduct in cyberspace to the greatest extent possible in international and domestic forums." It is only through the elucidation of state positions on the interaction of sovereignty and cyber capabilities that this question will be answered.

B. *Due Diligence*

Due diligence is not a substantive provision of international law, but rather the standard that states must apply in preventing their territory from being used to cause transboundary harm. As stated in Rule 6 of the Tallinn Manual, "a State must exercise due diligence in not allowing its territory, or territory or cyber infrastructure under its governmental control, to be used for cyber operations that affect the rights of, and produce serious adverse consequences for, other States."

There are several important aspects to this rule. First, the Rule recognizes that states' obligation to apply due diligence is in fact a rule of international law. When that standard must be applied and to what degree is still a matter of discussion, but the fact that the rule exists and applies to states was uncontested with the Experts.

States are not required to remedy all transboundary harm; only that harm resulting in serious adverse consequences. Some level of harm is assumed to be below the threshold that would trigger the due diligence principle. Despite using this language in the Rule, the Tallinn Experts could not fully describe what "serious adverse consequences" meant. In fact, they concluded that international law on this point was unclear. However, the Experts did argue that no "physical damage to objects or injuries to individuals" was required.

For a state to be responsible for applying due diligence to prevent transboundary harm, the state must have knowledge of the harm. That knowledge may be constructive knowledge if the state, in the normal course of events, would or objectively should have known about the harm. However, such a view does not require a state to take preventive measures with its cyber infrastructure, or even monitor infrastructure in an effort to be apprised of any potential transboundary harm.

At the point where a state knows of the transboundary harm, it is required to take "all measures that are feasible in the circumstances to put an end to the cyber operations." In other words, the state must take measures that are "reasonably available and practical," though the means whereby this is accomplished is at the discretion of the state from which the harm is emanating.

States are not generally fond of the due diligence principle because it places some amount of responsibility on them. In the United Nations Group of Governmental Experts (UN GGE), states were only willing to admit that they "should" exercise due diligence, rather than that they "must" as the Rule states. However, when analyzed in conjunction with the previous principle of sovereignty, even the standard proposed by the Experts leaves a large gap where victims of cyber harm are left with few remedies.

For example, assume that a terrorist organization in State A is conducting harmful cyber activities against entities in State C through State B. Both States A and B have no affirmative obligation until they know the harm is taking place. Because they have no obligation to monitor or prevent, States A and B are likely to come to the knowledge of the harm only after State C has suffered sufficient harm to conduct computer forensics and determine where the harm is coming from.

Even when State C knows from where the harm is originating, it is unable to take any proactive measures, such as countermeasures which will be discussed below, because the harm is being caused by a non-state actor. This leaves State C completely reliant on State A's and State B's acceptance of the assertion by State C, State A's and State B's determination that it is true and that the harm is coming from within their territory (including whatever time and process they feel is necessary to ascertain the facts), their analysis of what would be feasible to do to block the harm, and their determination of what feasible measures they will implement to stop the transboundary harm.

Some might argue in response that this is no different than the application of the due diligence principle in other areas of international law, such as international environmental law. However, the fundamental differences include that environmental transboundary harm is often more transparently manifest and often easier to allocate responsibility. Additionally, environmental harm often has effects in the host state on its way to the victim state, providing greater encouragement for the host state to take action. Environmental harm is usually contiguous and involves neighbors which might share more vested interests. And finally, there is little evidence of states using proxies to cause environmental harm to their neighbors, leaving little incentive to deny the harm or delay the remedy. However, with malicious cyber activities, the situation is quite different, with a host of allegations that states use proxies to conduct cyber activities, specifically with the intent of being able to deny attribution.

Given the fact that sovereignty is one of the principles most under pressure and due diligence is one of the principle means of applying pressure, this is an area of great interest to follow over the next few years as greater state practice develops.

C. Jurisdiction

The chapter of the Manual on jurisdiction encompasses six rules and extensive commentary. Jurisdiction is defined as "the competence of States to regulate persons, objects, and conduct under their national law, within the limits imposed by international law." The first rule on jurisdiction states, "[s]ubject to limitations set forth in international law, a State may exercise territorial and extraterritorial jurisdiction over cyber activities." This means that "in principle, cyber activities and the individuals who engage in them are subject to the same jurisdictional prerogatives and limitations as any other form of activity."

The Manual addresses the three traditional types of jurisdiction--prescriptive, enforcement, and adjudicative--and discusses key aspects of each one. With respect to prescriptive jurisdiction, the Manual explains that states are basically unfettered with respect to prescriptive jurisdiction within their sovereign territory and can exercise prescriptive jurisdiction extraterritorially (meaning based on either location of the cyber activity or its effects) if based on one of the traditional bases for extraterritorial jurisdiction.

Rule 9 discusses territorial jurisdiction and confirms that both subjective and objective territorial jurisdiction apply to cyber activities. In most cases, this was a non-controversial rule. However, the group split on the question of cyber activities with only a minimum connection, such as transiting data. Some of the group thought a state could exercise jurisdiction on transiting data and others did not think so. This point is illustrated by an example from the Manual.

Consider a scenario where data from a cyber operation initiated in State A transits State B on its way to State C, where it actually has effects. State A can exercise prescriptive territorial jurisdiction as the state where the cyber activity originated; State C can as well as the state where the effects occur; but can State B exercise jurisdiction? The Experts split on that question. In determining an answer, of course it is important to resolve who determines what is a minimum connection, or de minimis. And, of course, however this question is resolved does not prejudice a state from exercising other bases of jurisdiction, such as nationality. Further, this determination has important repercussions on the issue of due diligence discussed above.

Rule 10 acknowledges that states can also assert extraterritorial jurisdiction through nationality, the protective principle, passive personality, and universality with respect to cyber activities outside their territory. With respect to nationality jurisdiction, one of the interesting questions that remains unresolved concerns the cyber activities of a state's nationals and whether a state can exercise jurisdiction only over the individual abroad or also the data created by the individual. In other words, if the national of State A creates data in State B, it is unclear if State A can exercise jurisdiction over that data as well as the individual.

Rule 11 deals with enforcement jurisdiction. As with prescriptive jurisdiction, states can exercise enforcement jurisdiction in their territory but have a more limited ability to exercise extraterritorial enforcement jurisdiction, such an exercise is generally allowed only upon consent of the territorial state. This is also one of the areas where cyber activities present a number of interesting issues.

Rule 11 presents a narrow view of enforcement jurisdiction and there are certainly some who have argued for a broader view. The Tallinn Manual view is that international law, including specific treaties such as the law of the sea, outer space, and treaties concerning aviation activities, might support the exercise of enforcement jurisdiction abroad. It was the opinion of the Experts that where these grants of jurisdiction occur, they would include cyber related activities. In fact, some treaties may specifically invoke certain extraterritorial enforcement privileges, such as the Convention on Cybercrime.

Given the nature of cyber data, the Tallinn Group (Group) acknowledged that there may be times when it is unclear in which state data or other digital evidence resides. The Group determined that international law currently doesn't address this issue clearly so the Group was unable to come to any kind of consensus on that case. Assumedly, in such a case, a state which decided to exercise its enforcement jurisdiction would do so subject to some amount of risk.

The Experts also noted that there may be difficulty in assessing whether electronic data that is widely available on the internet, but hosted on servers in another state is an exercise of territorial or extraterritorial enforcement jurisdiction. Ultimately, the Group decided that it was an exercise of territorial jurisdiction because the data is available in the concerned state. This is true even if the data is non-public and password-protected as long as it is accessed from the state's territory. In contrast, data that may be accessible via the internet but is not intended to be available to individuals in the concerned state requires an exercise of extraterritorial enforcement jurisdiction and either consent or specific authorization by international law.

The Manual also recognizes that adjudicative jurisdiction is generally co-extensive with prescriptive jurisdiction but its exercise may be limited by the consent of a territorial state. With respect to situations of military members abroad, Status of Forces Agreements often have specific grants of consent to the sending state to allow adjudicative jurisdiction over members of the force. Other agreements might have similar effects in specific situations.

Of course, none of these types of jurisdiction is exclusive. States may often have concurrent jurisdiction and this applies in the cyber realm as well. Note one of the illustrations from the Manual--"a criminal who is a national of State A, but located in State B, may conduct a cyber operation against a web server in State C in order to steal the bank information of individuals located in State D." In that instance, each state would have the ability to exercise jurisdiction. Of course, such a scenario emphasizes the need for international cooperation.

The chapter on jurisdiction concludes with a rule on immunity and a rule about international cooperation. This chapter, while identifying some areas where there is no international consensus on an issue or where international law is as yet unclear, is unlikely to cause much controversy.

D. *Law of International Responsibility*

Because of the nature of current cyber activities, this is an extremely important chapter in the Manual. It applies the doctrine of state responsibility, codified mainly in the International Law Commission's Articles on State Responsibility to cyber actors and cyber activities. There was complete agreement among the Experts that the customary law of state responsibility applies to cyber activities. Rule 14, therefore states that "[a] State bears international responsibility for a cyber-related act that is attributable to the State and that constitutes a breach of an international legal obligation." Neither physical damage nor injury is required for a cyber act to be an internationally wrongful act, and geography is not determinative in determining state responsibility.

The concept of attribution for cyber acts has generated a great deal of discussion and consternation. Rules 15 through 17 address this issue with respect to cyber operations. Rule 15 echoes Articles 4 and 5 of the Articles of State Responsibility and notes that the cyber actions of state organs, such as the CIA or NSA in the United States, are attributable to the state, even if outside that organization's approved authority, or *ultra vires*. For this purpose, organs of the state would also include actors that are not organs by law, but that have "complete dependence" on the state, and persons or entities that are empowered to exercise elements of governmental authority.

Even though these statements reflect international law in non-cyber situations, their application to cyber activities is not without controversy. For example, the Experts noted that traditionally the use of government assets such as tanks or warships was a near irrefutable indication of attribution of an activity to a state. The same cannot be said of cyber activities. Indeed, given the ability to capture or spoof cyber infrastructure, including where the cyber activities might originate from, "the mere fact that a cyber operation has been launched or otherwise originates from governmental cyber infrastructure, or that malware used against hacked cyber infrastructure is designed to 'report back' to another State's governmental cyber infrastructure, is usually insufficient evidence for attributing the operation to that State."

In the case where an organ of the state is put at the disposal of another state, if that organ functions exclusively under the control of the receiving state and takes actions for the purposes and on behalf of that that state, the organ's acts are attributable to the receiving state.

The most difficult legal question in the area of attribution comes from non-state actors who may be working as proxies for a state or who are in some way acting on behalf of a state without clear legal authority to do so. This is addressed by Rule 17, and reflects Article 8 of the Rules of State Responsibility. Many of the discussions around recent cyber events have revolved around the attempt to attribute the actions of private actors to states with whom those actors were aligned. In accordance with international law, cyber operations conducted by non-state actors, but carried out under the "effective control" of a state, are attributable to the state. Mere encouragement or support for the actions of the non-state actor are insufficient to reach attribution. In contrast to the actions of state organs, *ultra vires* acts of non-state actors in these situations are not attributable to the state as they would be acts outside the "effective control" of the state. Finally, if a state does not effectively control a non-state actor, but subsequently adopts the cyber actions of that non-state actor as its own, those acts are also attributable to the state.

As with attribution more generally, it is much easier to identify and state the rule than it is to apply it in factual situations. For example, as noted by the Experts, "a State's preponderant or decisive participation in the 'financing, organizing, training, supplying, and equipping ..., the selection of its military or paramilitary targets, and the planning of the whole of its operation' has been found insufficient to reach the 'effective control' threshold." In the cyber realm, that might be translated as a state providing the cyber tools, identifying the targets, and selecting the date for the cyber operation to take place and it would still not implicate state responsibility. Some allege this is exactly the scenario with Russia and Russian hacktivists who cyber-assaulted Estonia in the wake of the movement of a Russian war memorial.

Over time, it will be interesting to see how states continue to respond to the high threshold for attribution. As states continue to be the victims of cyber activities that are unattributable to a state, and the rules of sovereignty and due diligence don't allow victim states to require effective action by the host state, the pressure on the attribution standard will increase as a method of allowing victim states to have broader access to countermeasures (discussed below).

Rule 18 covers the doctrines of aiding and assisting, and responsibility for the acts of other states. With respect to aid and assistance, it is vital that the state know that it is actually providing aid and assistance to the internationally wrongful act, and that the state intends to do so. It is also important to note that the aiding state is only responsible for aiding and assisting, not the actual wrongful act. Though not directly dealt with by the Experts, it seems clear that aiding and assisting would require more than allowing transit of harmful data through its cyber infrastructure, even if it did so knowingly. It would defy logic that the standard to trigger the due diligence requirement would be similar or even less than that of the standard of aiding and assisting.

The Manual argues that all the normal circumstances precluding wrongfulness apply to cyber activities. The Manual then embarks on a fairly lengthy discussion of countermeasures. Because countermeasures must not rise to the level of a use of force, cyber activities seem to fit the paradigm well. It is important to note that countermeasures are only available against states and will not preclude the wrongfulness of an act if targeted against non-state actors, unless their actions are attributable to a state. However, the cyber countermeasure need not target the specific organ of the state that is violating international law as the state itself is the target. Additionally, cyber countermeasures are not limited to "in-kind" response. In other words, a state can respond to a non-cyber violation with a cyber countermeasure, and to a cyber violation with a non-cyber countermeasure.

Cyber countermeasures raise several interesting issues. One of the requirements of a countermeasure is that it be temporary in nature and reversible as far as possible. The Experts understood that requirement broadly and argued in the context of cyber that the deletion of data, even if it prevented some later, post-countermeasure activity, would not bar the countermeasure. The Experts were unable to agree on whether, given two cyber countermeasure options, there was a requirement to utilize the one that was most reversible.

Another element of countermeasures that the Experts found particularly noteworthy is the requirement to notify and potentially seek to negotiate resolution prior to taking a countermeasure. The Experts noted that this requirement was not absolute and agreed that if notifying the target state prior to taking the cyber countermeasure would render the countermeasure ineffective, notification need not be provided. Given the nature of cyber operations, this is a pragmatic approach.

The Experts agreed that cyber countermeasures cannot violate a peremptory norm and must be proportionate to the injury to which they respond, though there is no requirement that the cyber countermeasure target the exact state organ violating international law.

The Experts split on the issue of collective countermeasures with the majority arguing it was not lawful for a non-injured state to take countermeasures on behalf of an injured state. However, the majority then split on the issue of whether a non-injured state may assist the injured state in taking countermeasures.

The remainder of the chapter in the Manual contains rules and commentary on the effect of countermeasures on third parties, the plea of necessity, several rules on the obligations of states for internationally wrongful acts, and a rule on the responsibility of international organizations.

These rules and commentary on countermeasures highlight the difference between applying a countermeasure, particularly in cyberspace, as opposed to taking an action in self-defense. The rules and constraints on countermeasures detailed above act as a greater constraint on a state's ability to act in response to actions that do not amount to use of force than actions in response to an armed attack. Importantly, the standards for applying countermeasures are much less discretionary in that certain actual steps must be taken as opposed to a discretionary decision by a state that an action amounts to an armed attack or that an armed attack is imminent. With respect to cyber, this is a particularly important point because so much of the unfriendly cyber interaction between states does not amount to an armed attack.

Perhaps this imbalance is exactly what states desire with respect to cyber countermeasures. This Author has argued elsewhere that easing the ability to use countermeasures may lead to unintended harmful consequences. Nevertheless, it will be interesting to see if in the future, states evolve international law to either lessen the constraints on cyber countermeasures or soften the threshold of an armed attack in order to provide more effective response measures to a greater variety of cyber activities.

E. *Cyber Operations Not Per Se Regulated*

This section of the Manual recognizes that some actions by states are not specifically regulated by international law, but finds a narrow set of actions that fall into this category. As mentioned above with respect to sovereignty, there is a view that this category of unregulated cyber activities is broader. However, the Tallinn Experts took a strict reading of cyber operations not regulated *per se* by international law.

Rule 32 applies to peacetime cyber espionage and takes an almost apologetic tone. Without actually stating that cyber espionage is permitted by international law, the Rule says "[a]lthough peacetime cyber espionage by States does not per se violate international law, the method by which it is carried out might do so." For the purposes of the rule, cyber espionage is defined as "any act undertaken clandestinely or under false pretenses that uses cyber capabilities to gather, or attempt to gather, information." The rule only applies to espionage conducted by states, and the Experts recognized that not only do many states make espionage illegal as a matter of domestic law when carried out against them, but also that there are a number of states that have specifically authorized certain forms of espionage against other states.

Despite the agreement that even though there is no prohibition *per se*, the Experts agreed that "espionage may be conducted in a manner that violates international law due to the fact that certain methods employed to conduct cyber espionage are unlawful." However, the Experts could not reach a consensus as to whether remote cyber espionage violated international law. The majority believed that the exfiltration of data violated no rule of international law. Conversely, a few of the experts believed that at some point the exfiltration might be so severe as to make it illegal. Similarly, the Experts did not agree on close-access operations, such as operations where an individual in the territory of the target state inserts a USB drive into a government system and exfiltrates data. None of the Experts argued that the exfiltration was a violation of international law, but a majority believed it was violative of the target state's sovereignty. The remainder of the Experts viewed espionage as an exception to sovereignty.

The Experts agreed that "honeypots"--valuable data or network segments designed to lure in malicious hackers in order to identify them and examine their methods, but not actually reveal any useful data--were not illegal as a matter of international law. Weaponized honeypots, where the data designed to be exfiltrated contains malware that is then executed on the infiltrator's own system, caused a division among the Experts, with the majority finding them completely permissible.

The treatment of espionage in the Tallinn Manual is tied closely to the view of sovereignty. In many of the cases presented where the "method" of espionage might make it illegal, the Experts determined the rule violated was that of sovereignty. Evidence seems to be mounting that cyber-capable nations are engaging in cyber espionage. Increasing cyber espionage is likely to put pressure on the current understanding of how sovereignty applies to the domain of cyberspace, perhaps affecting Rule 32 in the future.

The other rule in this section of unregulated cyber operations says "[i]nternational law regulates cyber operations by non-State actors only in limited cases." With the exception of international law regimes specifically applicable to individuals such as human rights law and the law of armed conflict, the Experts believed that international law did not regulate non-state actors. This is left to be regulated by states through domestic law.

As with espionage, this is an area of international law where the rule is likely to come under pressure. The combination of the volume of incidents caused by non-state actors, the restrictive application of the due diligence rule to states, and the proscription of the use of countermeasures against non-state actors may force states to reconsider the effectiveness of international law with respect to enforcement measures against non-state actors.

F. *International Human Rights Law*

This part of the Manual and those that follow in this Article are separated into what the Experts refer to as Specialized Regimes. These regimes are specialized in that they have developed over time to become their own, somewhat self-contained regimes that govern a narrow range of activities. The Manual applies those regimes to cyber activities.

The first specialized regime covered in the Manual is international human rights law. Many of the difficulties in crafting this portion of the Manual can be directly tied to the lack of clarity with respect to international human rights law more generally. Combined with the vagaries of cyber operations, this chapter contains perhaps the most disagreement among the Experts. Along these lines, one of the important points made with respect to the application of human rights law to cyber operations is that "although a State's activity may interfere with a specific international human right, such as the right to privacy, this fact does not answer the question of whether that right has been violated." In other words, the determination that human rights apply to a cyber activity does not mean that the cyber activity has violated human rights. The potential violation is a separate and additional analysis.

Rule 34 states the general rule of applicability. It says "[i]nternational human rights law is applicable to cyber-related activities." In defining the applicability, the Experts agreed, "as a general principle, customary international human rights law applies in the cyber context beyond a State's territory in situations in which that State exercises 'power or effective control', as it does offline." However, the Experts were split on whether "power or effective control" required "physical" control, with the majority believing physical control was required. The Experts were also split on whether a human rights treaty that was silent on its extraterritorial application should be interpreted as applying extraterritorially. The majority believed that it should be applied extraterritorially in the absence of some provision that limited its scope.

Rule 35 states that "Individuals enjoy the same international human rights with respect to cyber-related activities that they otherwise enjoy." This includes the freedom of expression, though the experts could not agree on the precise parameters of that right. The right to hold an opinion and the right to privacy are also protected.

With respect to the right to privacy, the Experts believed that this right "encompasses the confidentiality of communications." The Experts agreed that this protected an individual's private communications from human inspection, but were divided on how the right applied to cases of algorithmic inspections by machines. However, the majority believed that such an inspection did not implicate the individual's right unless and until the state accessed the communications in some way, including data processing. Of course, information available to the public generally does not implicate the right to privacy, even if collected through cyber means, while those available to only a small group could. The Experts were unclear on where these lines actually are drawn between these two situations. The Experts could not agree on how the expectation of privacy applied generally to this right.

The Experts agreed that the right to privacy also protected individuals' "personal data," though the Experts acknowledged that this term is not well defined in international law. With respect to metadata, the Experts agreed that metadata would be considered "personal data" and therefore protected for the purposes of this rule at the point where it was "linked to an individual and relates to that individual's private life." With respect to other metadata, the Experts could not reach a consensus.

The Experts further noted that the customary nature of economic, social, and cultural rights remains unsettled in international law, but agreed that to the extent that they are recognized as rights, cyber operations could certainly implicate those rights. Finally, the Experts noted the claim that there is an international human right of access to the internet and a "right to be forgotten." None of the Experts acknowledged these as rights under current customary law.

Rule 36 states that "[w]ith respect to cyber activities, a State must: (a) respect the international human rights of individuals; and (b) protect the human rights of individuals from abuse by third parties." The obligation to respect human rights applies generally to those rights discussed in the previous rule and applies extraterritorially to applicable rights.

The obligation to protect, or ensure respect for human rights is an affirmative obligation on states, though the Experts acknowledged that some states do not agree that such a rule exists and that the parameters of the rule are at least contested. However, the Experts agreed that such a rule exists, despite its lack of clear definition. For example, the Experts could not agree on the "precise territorial circumstances in which a State has an obligation to protect a particular individual's human rights from interference by third parties."

The Experts agreed that this right included the requirement to take preventive measures such as preventing terrorist impacts on human rights. Relating back to the Experts opinion that there is no right to the internet discussed above, the Experts divided on the issue in which access to the internet was necessary to exercise a human right such as voting. However, the majority of Experts believed that states have no customary right to provide remedies when violations of individual human rights occur.

Rule 37 discusses limitations on the obligation to respect and protect and states "[t]he obligations to respect and protect international human rights, with the exception of absolute rights, remain subject to certain limitations that are necessary to achieve a legitimate purpose, non-discriminatory, and authorized by law." This rule acknowledges that States must strike a balance concerning cyber activities between individual rights and other important responsibilities, such as public order and national security, though some rights such as protection from slavery and torture are absolute in nature and cannot be limited. The Manual illustrates this point by stating "it is generally considered necessary to restrict the online freedom of expression or right to privacy in order to eliminate child pornography and child exploitation, protect intellectual property rights, and stop incitement to genocide."

In exercising limitations on human rights, the Experts divided on the applicability of the principle of proportionality, with the majority arguing that it did apply. All the Experts believed that whatever limitations were imposed, they must be done non-discriminatorily.

In addition to limitations, states may also derogate from certain human rights obligations, as discussed in Rule 38. This rule is centered completely on treaty law and depends entirely on the specific provisions of the treaty under consideration.

The amount of disagreement among the Experts in this chapter reflects not only the cyber application to human rights law, but the general acceptance of human rights law across states. The Experts noted in many instances that states simply diverge in their views, sometimes dramatically, on the application to human rights law. This is reflected in the application of cyber operations to human rights law. As greater clarity emerges with respect to the primary rules of human rights law, the application to cyber activities will undoubtedly also become clearer.

G. *Diplomatic and Consular Law*

The Chapter on Diplomatic and Consular Law draws heavily from the 1961 Vienna Convention on Diplomatic Relations and the 1963 Vienna Convention on Consular Relations as substantially reflective of customary international law. The first rule reflects one of the foundational principles of diplomatic and consular law, the inviolability of premises. Though all the Experts agreed with the rule, the application of the rule caused some divided opinions.

The majority believed this protection precluded remote cyber operations on infrastructure located in the premises, as well as diplomatic or consular equipment not located on the premises but used for diplomatic or consular purposes. The Experts were evenly divided on the question of whether third states have an obligation to respect the inviolability of premises or whether that obligation only lies on the host state.

Consideration of Rule 39 prompted discussion of virtual embassies and online diplomatic presences. The Experts did not believe the inviolability extended to these virtual presences, except to the extent that being hosted on the premises as discussed above protected them.

Rule 40 requires that "[a] receiving State must take all appropriate steps to protect cyber infrastructure on the premises of a sending State's diplomatic mission or consular post against intrusion or damage." The application of this rule is dependent on "the magnitude of the threat to the premises, the extent to which the receiving State is aware of a specific threat, and the capacity of the receiving State to take action in the circumstances."

Rule 41 applies the protection given to diplomatic and consular archives, documents, and official correspondence to electronic versions of the same. The Experts were split, however, with respect to private submissions to a mission or consular post, with the majority believing they were covered by extension of the rule. As with premises, the Experts were split with respect to the obligation of third states to diplomatic or consular archives, documents, and correspondence, with the majority again extending the protections. The Experts were also split on whether the protection continued to apply to communications other than those between the mission and the sending state, such as between the mission and third states. The majority believed that all such communications were protected. Finally, the question was raised concerning normally protected communications that have been disclosed by third parties. In this case, the majority believed that the protection no longer applied.

Rule 42 concerns the right to freedom of communication and states that "[a] receiving State must permit and protect the free cyber communication of a diplomatic mission or consular post for all official purposes." The Experts agreed that receiving states "may not interfere with access to a diplomatic mission's or consular post's website that is used to convey essential information to its citizens in the country, interrupt or slow the Internet connection of a diplomatic mission or consular post, or block or interfere with its cell phones or other telecommunications equipment." The "protect" requirement in this rule is similar to the due diligence rule in that there is still no duty to monitor or take proactive measures to prevent, but merely to remediate when the receiving state has knowledge.

Rule 43 deals with the premises and personnel of states and says:

(a) [t]he premises of a diplomatic mission or consular post may not be used to engage in cyber activities that are incompatible with diplomatic or consular functions,: and (b) Diplomatic agents and consular officials may not engage in cyber activities that interfere in the internal affairs of the receiving State or are incompatible with the laws.

The section then lists some cyber activities that would be permissible under this rule in a cyber context. Importantly, the Experts concluded that conducting cyber espionage would not be allowed. The section concludes with a rule concerning privileges and immunities of diplomatic and consular personnel, and concludes that the same privileges and immunities apply to cyber related activities.

There are obviously a number of unanswered questions with respect to cyber operations and diplomatic and consular law, particularly with respect to communications. Because so many of those communications now occur via cyber modalities, the application of international law to this area is going to be an important area of legal development.

H. *Law of the Sea*

The law of the sea is a specialized regime with a long history and significant recent codification. The Experts agreed that much of the United Nations Convention on the Law of the Sea reflected customary international law and consequently, the Experts relied on it heavily.

Rule 45 states the general principle of applicability and confirms that "[c]yber operations on the high seas may be conducted only for peaceful purposes, except as otherwise provided for under international law." As an example, the Experts concluded that "[o]f particular note in the cyber context are the high seas freedoms of navigation, overflight, and the laying of submarine cables. Based on, for example, the first two freedoms, both aircraft and vessels are entitled to conduct cyber operations over and in the high seas so long as they do not violate applicable international law." With respect to military cyber operations, the Experts "saw no reason to deviate from the general principle that military activities not involving a prohibited use of force are within the scope of high seas freedoms and other internationally lawful uses of the sea, as set forth in Article 87(1) of the Law of the Sea Convention."

The Experts confirmed the "right of visit" with respect to cyber activities but divided on the permissibility of a "virtual visit," meaning using cyber modalities to conduct the visit. The Experts further confirmed the application of the due regard standard to cyber actions taken in the Exclusive Economic Zone (EEZ), though the Experts split on the legality of conducting military operations in the EEZ with the majority arguing they were permissible.

With respect to the territorial sea and the right of innocent passage, the Experts agreed to Rule 48, which states, "[i]n order for a vessel to claim the right of innocent passage through a coastal State's territorial sea, any cyber operations conducted by the vessel must comply with the conditions imposed on that right." The Experts helpfully listed a number of examples of cyber activities that would render the passage non-innocent. The Experts considered the impact on innocent passage of a state vessel from State A in the territorial waters of State B, conducting cyber operations against State C. The majority of Experts determined this would not be compatible with innocent passage.

Despite the Manual reserving most rules concerning international armed conflict to later in the Manual, Rule 49 says "[d]uring an international armed conflict, a neutral coastal State may not discriminate between the belligerents with respect to cyber operations in that State's territorial sea." Rule 50 returns to more general rules and deals with enforcement jurisdiction in the territorial sea. The Experts divided on the scale of the potential consequences necessary to trigger the right of enforcement jurisdiction. The majority argued that any violation was sufficient, but the minority thought *de minimis* effects would not trigger the right.

The Experts argued that the standard provisions of the law of the sea apply to cyber operations in the contiguous zone, international straits, archipelagic waters, and to submarine cables. With respect to submarine cables, the Experts could not agree on the application of jurisdiction "between the coastal State and the State laying the submarine communication cable on the coastal State's continental shelf or in its EEZ." Though the Experts agreed that it was violative of international law to damage submarine communication cables, they also agreed that such cables can be tapped to collect and transmit data.

The Manual itself points out areas where the law of the sea is unsettled with respect to cyber operations, such as the need for states to find a method to criminalize willful or negligent damage to submarine communication cables under the high seas. Given the vast amount of data that passes through submarine communication cables, and the increasing ability of states to access them, this is almost certainly an area where state practice will continue to develop.

I. *Air Law*

As with the law of the sea, the Experts determined that international law was generally reflected in the provisions of the most prominent treaty in the area--in this case the 1944 Convention on International Civil Aviation (ICAO), or "Chicago Convention" as it has come to be known. Indeed the terms used throughout the section are governed by definitions in the ICAO.

Rule 55 states the rule of general applicability of airspace law to cyber operations on aircraft in national airspace. The Experts noted that this specialized regime only governs the aircraft, and not the cyber operations it is engaged in. Those operations would be governed by other laws, such as those of the subjacent state. With respect to military aircraft--those most likely to be involved in airborne cyber operations--the Experts noted that the Convention requires the permission of the subjacent state for overflight, and allows the subjacent state the right to set the conditions of that overflight, conditions which might include a proscription on cyber operations.

The Experts divided on how to characterize a violation of a state's airspace by another state's military aircraft that is engaged in cyber operations. A minority believed the combination of unconsented presence and the conduct of cyber operations was enough to be an armed attack and trigger the right of self-defense. The majority thought the characterization depended on the nature of the cyber operation. Some of the Experts were also of the view that the mere unconsented presence of a military aircraft authorized the use of force to expel the aircraft from the state's territory.

As opposed to national airspace, cyber operations in international airspace are generally allowed. Rule 56 says "[s]ubject to restrictions thereon contained in international law, a State may conduct cyber operations in international airspace." States may not claim sovereignty over international airspace. Moreover, when conducting cyber operations in international air space, states are only limited by international law proscriptions such as the prohibition on intervention and the use of force, or accepted navigation regimes such as flying over international straits. Additionally, when flying subject to a navigation regime that requires transport in normal mode, the majority of Experts deemed that this did not include active cyber operations, even for aircraft whose purpose is to conduct offensive cyber operations. Finally, states are precluded from conducting any cyber operations that might jeopardize the safety of the international aviation.

As mentioned earlier, at least with respect to sovereignty, state practice has not taken as restrictive a view toward cyberspace as it has toward airspace. Increasing state capabilities to conduct cyber operations from platforms in the air will potentially result in a clash of paradigms, with the less restrictive cyberspace paradigm giving way to the more restrictive airspace rules. When contrasted with the more liberal space regime discussed below, this difference in legal regulation may push cyber development, particularly with respect to the principle of sovereignty, to space rather than air assets.

J. *Space Law*

Though the spatial differentiation between the law governing airspace and space is not precisely defined, the differences between the two regimes are quite distinct, particularly with respect to the exercise of sovereign authority. The Experts drew a distinction between space-enabled cyber operations, to which space law has only limited application, and cyber-enabled space operations. In drafting the rules, the Experts noted that the applicable treaty law is less complete and less recognized as codifying customary law. However, in the cases where the Experts relied on the language of various space treaties, they did so using provisions they believed were considered customary.

Rule 58 notes the difference in legal proscriptions on the use of cyber on the moon and other celestial bodies and in space more generally. The rule states "(a) [c]yber operations on the moon and other celestial bodies may be conducted only for peaceful purposes. (b) Cyber operations in outer space are subject to international law limitations on the use of force." The Experts concluded as a result of this rule that offensive cyber capabilities could not be placed on the moon, whereas no similar prohibition exists for outer space more generally. With respect to space more generally, the proscription is on the use of cyber capabilities and is governed by the same standards as on earth, including the U.N. Charter.

Rule 59 says "(a) [a] State must respect the right of States of registry to exercise jurisdiction and control over space objects appearing on their registries. (b) A State must conduct its cyber operations involving outer space with due regard for the need to avoid interference with the peaceful space activities of other States."

In accord with this rule, the Experts agreed that states have jurisdiction over their satellites and other space objects and persons thereon, but also noted that this jurisdiction might not be exclusive. For example, if the activities of one state's space objects affect another state's space objects, those states may share concurrent jurisdiction. The Experts also noted that the term "due regard" in this rule carried the same meaning as it does in the law of the sea context.

Finally, respecting the responsibilities of states for cyber activities in outer space, Rule 60 says "(a) [a] State must authorize and supervise the cyber 'activities in outer space' of its non-governmental entities. (b) Cyber operations involving space objects are subject to the responsibility and liability regime of space law."

As more and more private entities begin to operate in outer space, including placing persons in space, this rule will increase in importance. The rule follows treaty law in describing the governance regime as "national" in nature. States must accept responsibility to monitor and approve the actions of non-government entities.

Accordingly, states are generally responsible for their actions under the space law regime which incorporates some of the principles from the Articles of State Responsibility. For example, launching states are liable for damage caused to another state based on a space launch. However, damage caused to space objects by other space objects is based on "fault". The Experts determined these principles apply to cyber operations in space as well.

The continued expansion into space will include the increased employment of cyber capabilities. The law surrounding the space regime was formulated when few states had access to space and is fairly permissive, particularly when compared to the rules governing airspace. As more states, including private entities within those states, begin to conduct operations including cyber operations in outer space, the permissive regime may give way to a more limiting regime. At least one major transnational effort is underway now to look more closely at the legal regime applicable to space and it will undoubtedly provide extremely useful input on this important subject.

K. *International Telecommunications Law*

Unlike prior sections of the Manual, which relied primarily on customary international law to support the rules contained therein, in this section of the Manual the Experts note the lack of customary law and explicitly base the following rules on the treaty regime of the International Telecommunications Union. The Experts felt comfortable doing so because "nearly all States are Parties to the treaty regime."

Rule 61 states that "[a] State must take measures to ensure the establishment of international telecommunication infrastructure that is required for rapid and uninterrupted international telecommunications. If, in complying with this requirement, the State establishes cyber infrastructure for international telecommunications, it must maintain and safeguard that infrastructure." The treaty regime establishes three distinct obligations for member states: "to ensure the establishment of infrastructure that facilitates rapid and uninterrupted international telecommunications; to safeguard that infrastructure; and to maintain it." The Experts noted that these are obligations of conduct, not of result, and therefore based on feasibility. Thus, a state need not fulfill its obligation through cyber means, but if it decides to do so, it must safeguard and maintain that cyber infrastructure. As this obligation is a state obligation, the majority of Experts believed it was not lawful for one state to establish communications in another state without the second state's consent.

The Experts determined that states may generally exercise their sovereign authority to suspend or stop communications. Rule 62 says:

(a) [a] State may suspend, either in part or in full, international cyber communication services within its territory. Immediate notice of such suspension must be provided to other States. (b) A State may stop the transmission of a private cyber communication that appears contrary to its national laws, public order, or decency, or that is dangerous to national security.

However, the Experts note in the commentary that "[t]his right is without prejudice to any international law obligations the State concerned may shoulder prohibiting it from doing so in a particular case" such as diplomatic communications. Assuming communications are suspended, the Experts divided as to the lawfulness of another state restoring communications without the consent of the territorial state. The majority agreed that such action would not be lawful without the consent of the territorial state.

With respect to specific communications, the Experts agreed that stopping specific private cyber communications could include "an instant message, email, or a Tweet."

Rule 63 says "[a] State's use of radio stations may not harmfully interfere with other States' protected use of radio frequencies for wireless cyber communications or services." The Experts accepted the definition of harmful interference to mean interference which "endangers the functioning of a radio navigation service or ... or seriously degrades, obstructs or repeatedly interrupts a radio communication service operating in accordance with the [International Telecommunication Union] Radio Regulations." They further agreed that the rule "applies exclusively to interference caused by one State with another's use of frequencies that enable cyber communications or services, wherever those communications or services take place, including in outer space."

Finally, Rule 64 exempts military radio stations and says "[a] State retains its entire freedom under international telecommunication law with regard to military radio installations." Though the rule is limited to radio installations, the Experts agreed that it also included "devices that enable the wireless transmission of data over radio waves." The Experts specified that the exemption only applies to truly "military" installations and not other radio installations put to use by the military in a dual military and civilian capacity.

Though this regime is almost completely treaty-based and not, therefore, viewed as binding customary international law, the practice of inter-state telecommunications will build norms and practices that will undoubtedly help formulate rules with respect to cyberspace. For example, the interaction of a state's right to stop or suspend telecommunications under this regime with emerging human rights expectations concerning individual internet access will continue to refine what state's accept as their legal obligations with respect to cyberspace in the future.

L. *Peaceful Settlement of Disputes*

This section marks the beginning of the transition of the Manual to "International Peace and Security and Cyber Activities." The first three Rules of this section act as a lead-in to the rules on the use of force (*just ad bellum*) and the rules governing armed conflict (*jus in bello*). Because the first three rules are not dealt with in Tallinn 1.0, they deserve some comment here.

Rule 65 concerns states' obligation to peacefully settle their disputes and is based on UN Charter paragraphs 2(3) and 33(1) and is generally accepted as customary international law. The Rule states: "(a) States must attempt to settle their international disputes involving cyber activities that endanger international peace and security by peaceful means; (b) If States attempt to settle international disputes involving cyber activities that do not endanger international peace and security, they must do so by peaceful means."

The Experts agreed that this rule only applies to international disputes and "not to purely internal ones." However, the Experts disagreed on the application to a transnational dispute between a state and a non-state actor with only a minority believing such conflicts were covered. Despite this disagreement, the Experts agreed that "peaceful means," when required, did not limit a resort to lawful means such as countermeasures or the use of force in self-defense, or any measure authorized by the United Nations Security Council.

States must exercise good faith in attempting to peacefully settle their cyber disputes, but need neither be successful, nor exhaust all possible peaceful means in order to comply with this obligation. The Experts also agreed that this obligation continues even in times of hostilities if peaceful means remain open as to a specific cyber dispute. The Experts further agreed that states must still use peaceful means if they endeavor to solve international disputes that do not endanger international peace and security, but that states are under no obligation to attempt to solve international disputes if they choose not to do so.

Given the increasing number of international and transnational cyber disputes, this rule is extremely important. Recent cyber disputes between states and between states and non-state actors have generally been resolved by peaceful means, but as the severity of the cyber interventions increases, this rule will likely be tested. Russian President Putin's seemingly dismissive acknowledgement of "patriotic" Russians intervening in U.S. elections, discussed in the next section, highlights the importance of clarity in applying principles of sovereignty, due diligence, and the remedies of retorsion and countermeasures to cyber activities. The more effective various "peaceful means" prove to be at resolving cyber disputes, the more content states will be to rely on them.

K. *Prohibition of Intervention*

The customary prohibition on intervention is divided into two rules in the Manual, the first dealing with States and the second with the United Nations.

Rule 66 states the well-recognized international law principle: "A State may not intervene, including by cyber means, in the internal or external affairs of another State." The rule only applies to relations between states, and only proscribes coercive interference. Though the Experts felt the "precise contours and application of the prohibition of intervention are unclear in light of ever-evolving and increasingly intertwined international relations," they concurred in the definition provided by the International Court of Justice that a prohibited intervention must bear on a state's *domaine réservé*, meaning such matters are the "choice of a political, economic, social, and cultural system, and the formulation of foreign policy."

The Experts also agreed that "the scope of *domaine réservé* may shrink as States commit issues related to cyberspace to international law regulation," but concluded that the "matter most clearly within a State's *domaine réservé* appears to be the choice of both the political system and its organization." With respect to coercion, the Experts split on whether the coercion must be "designed to influence outcomes in, or conduct with respect to, a matter reserved to a target State," with the majority agreeing that it did. They also split on whether the coercive act had to directly cause the effect, with the majority arguing it did not, "so long as there is a causal nexus."

Similarly, the Experts did not agree on whether the state had to actually know it was being coerced for the intervening state to be violating international law. The majority decided such knowledge was not a necessary precondition. On the other hand, the Experts agreed that knowledge that the cyber coercion was coming from a state (or an entity attributable to a state) was not required for a violation, though intent to coerce was required. Further, the effectiveness of the coercion was immaterial as to whether there was an intervention.

The Experts split on whether cyber operations designed to protect its nationals that were in the target state would amount to intervention, with the majority deciding that they generally would not. Though the Experts agreed that economic measures, such as unilateral economic sanctions, would not amount to an intervention, they were split concerning cyber operations in support of humanitarian intervention in the absence of a United Nations Security Council authorization, with the Experts divided along the lines of whether they believed humanitarian intervention itself was lawful.

Rule 67 continues the discussion of intervention but focuses on actions by the United Nations. The rule states "The United Nations may not intervene, including by cyber means, in matters that are essentially within the domestic jurisdiction of a State. This principle does not prejudice the taking of enforcement measures decided upon by the UN Security Council under Chapter VII of the United Nations Charter." A few Experts believed this rule should apply to international organizations generally, but consensus could only be achieved on applying it to the United Nations.

The basis of this rule is Article 2(7) of the United Nations Charter which prohibits the United Nations from intervening in "matters which are essentially within the domestic jurisdiction of any state." As a result, the Experts agreed that this rule would not limit actions concerning international peace and security. While the Experts agreed that the matters that fell in the scope of article 2(7) has been constricting, they agreed that despite the rule being phrased in terms of intervention, for matters truly within the domestic jurisdiction of any state, even non-coercive interference by the United Nations would violate this rule.

The prohibition on cyber intervention has become very important in light of recent allegations of Russian cyber intervention into elections in both the United States and Europe. While no target of Russian hacking has yet declared such activities to be a violation of international law, President Obama did make a somewhat veiled threat to President Putin in October 2016 over the famous "red phone," by telling President Putin that "[i]nternational law, including the law of armed conflict, applies to actions in cyber space."

The tepid international response to what has long been understood as the stereotype of a prohibited intervention may be pushing the boundaries of previously recognized norms. The Manual's strong statement will hopefully be one clear articulation of the prohibition as applied to cyber activities that states can begin to use to push back against Russian cyber operations.

Of course, as long as President Putin can simply attribute the cyber meddling to "patriotic hackers," and then accept no responsibility to control them or limit their activities, international law will have little impact on cyber intervention. This, once again, highlights the importance of the future evolution of the due diligence principle and its potential to more strictly impose responsibility on states for the cyber actions of those within their borders or under their control.

The remainder of the Manual provides rules with respect to the *jus ad bellum* and the *jus in bello*, and is only slightly amended from the rules as published in the Tallinn Manual 1.0. Therefore, no highlights will be provided here.

IV. CONCLUSION

It is important to remember that the Experts who participated in the Tallinn Manuals were committed to stating the law as it was and to producing Manuals that would be understood to be their own views and not those of states. The Experts were humbler in their intention for the project than some others who have commented on it. In fact, as noted at the U.S. launch of the Manual by Mr. Rutger van Marrising from the Ministry of Foreign Affairs of the Kingdom of the Netherlands, Tallinn 2.0 is really designed to be the beginning of a longer and more significant discussion.

Nevertheless, Tallinn 2.0 will be the starting point for the discussion for the next several years and perhaps longer. Its comprehensive nature, informed analysis and conclusions, and incorporation of both state and peer comments all make it the most valuable reference and starting point for a discussion on the international law applicable to cyber operations.

As this Article notes, there are still many areas of disagreement and lack of clarity, even amongst the Experts who wrote the Tallinn Manuals. There are also many situations where states have not spoken or acted publically with respect to cyber operations. This is still a growing area of the law and one in which there exists a great need for insight and understanding to create new approaches to existing problems. However, until states clarify exactly where the law is headed, Tallinn 2.0 will serve as the starting point for moving forward with the law on cyber operations.

NOTES

Note 1

For an overview of some of the provisions of the Tallinn Manual, please see Kirsten E. Eichensehr's review of the TALLINN MANUAL ON THE INTERNATIONAL LAW

APPLICABLE TO CYBER-WARFARE, Cambridge University Press 2013 (ed. Michael N. Schmitt).[592]

14.6 U.S. Cyberspace Solarium Commission Report

The following document is the Executive Summary of the U.S. Cyberspace Solarium Commission Report issued in March of 2020. The US Cyberspace Solarium Commission was formed by Congress to develop a strategy to confronting cyberattacks. The notes following the Executive Summary discuss some challenged facing the United States concerning cybersecurity and warfare.

U.S. Cyberspace Solarium Commission Report Executive Summary

AN URGENT CALL TO ACTION

For over 20 years, nation-states and non-state actors have used cyberspace to subvert American power, American security, and the American way of life. Despite numerous criminal indictments, economic sanctions, and the development of robust cyber and non-cyber military capabilities, the attacks against the United States have continued. The perpetrators saw that their onslaught damaged the United States without triggering a significant retaliation. Chinese cyber operators stole hundreds of billions of dollars in intellectual property to accelerate China's military and economic rise and undermine U.S. military dominance.2 Russian operators and their proxies damaged public trust in the integrity of American elections and democratic institutions.3 China, Russia, Iran, and North Korea all probed U.S. critical infrastructure with impunity.

Criminals leveraged globally connected networks to steal assets from individuals, companies, and governments. Extremist groups used these networks to raise funds and recruit followers, increasing transnational threats and insecurity. American restraint was met with unchecked predation.4

The digital connectivity that has brought economic growth, technological dominance, and an improved quality of life to nearly every American has also created a strategic dilemma. The more digital connections people make and data they exchange, the more opportunities adversaries have to destroy private lives, disrupt critical infrastructure, and damage our economic and democratic institutions. The United States now operates in a cyber landscape that requires a level of data security, resilience, and trustworthiness that neither the U.S. government nor the private sector alone is currently equipped to provide. Moreover, shortfalls in agility, technical expertise, and unity of effort, both within the U.S. government and between the public and private sectors, are growing.

---

[592] Kirsten E. Eichensehr, *Tallinn Manual on the International Law Applicable to Cyber-Warfare*, 108 AM. J. INT'L L. 585 (2014); *see* INTERNATIONAL GROUP OF EXPERTS, TALLINN MANUAL ON THE INTERNATIONAL LAW APPLICABLE TO CYBER WARFARE (2013) (studying how international law applies to cyber conflicts and cyber warfare).

The 2019 National Defense Authorization Act chartered the U.S. Cyberspace Solarium Commission to address this challenge. The President and Congress tasked the Commission to answer two fundamental questions:

What strategic approach will defend the United States against cyberattacks of significant consequences? And what policies and legislation are required to implement that strategy?

THE STRATEGY

After conducting an extensive study including over 300 interviews, a competitive strategy event modeled after the original Project Solarium in the Eisenhower administration, and stress tests by external red teams, the Commission advocates a new strategic approach to cybersecurity: layered cyber deterrence. The desired end state of layered cyber deterrence is a reduced probability and impact of cyberattacks of significant consequence. The strategy outlines three ways to achieve this end state:

EXECUTIVE SUMMARY

1. Shape behavior. The United States must work with allies and partners to promote responsible behavior in cyberspace.

2. Deny benefits. The United States must deny benefits to adversaries who have long exploited cyberspace to their advantage, to American disadvantage, and at little cost to themselves. This new approach requires securing critical networks in collaboration with the private sector to promote national resilience and increase the security of the cyber ecosystem.

3. Impose costs. The United States must maintain the capability, capacity, and credibility needed to retaliate against actors who target America in and through cyberspace.

Each of the three ways described above involves a deterrent layer that increases American public- and private-sector security by altering how adversaries perceive the costs and benefits of using cyberspace to attack American interests. These three deterrent layers are supported by six policy pillars that organize more than 75 recommendations. These pillars represent the means to implement layered cyber deterrence.

While deterrence is an enduring American strategy, there are two factors that make layered cyber deterrence bold and distinct. First, the approach prioritizes deterrence by denial, specifically by increasing the defense and security of cyberspace through resilience and public- and private-sector collaboration. Reducing the vulnerabilities adversaries can target denies them opportunities to attack American interests through cyberspace.

Second, the strategy incorporates the concept of "defend forward" to reduce the frequency and severity of attacks in cyberspace that do not rise to a level that would warrant the full spectrum of retaliatory responses, including military responses. Though the concept originated in the Department of Defense, the Commission integrates defend forward into a national strategy for securing cyberspace using all the instruments of power.

Defend forward posits that to disrupt and defeat ongoing adversary campaigns, the United States must proactively observe, pursue, and counter adversaries' operations and impose costs short of armed conflict. This posture signals to adversaries that the U.S. government will respond to cyberattacks, even those below the level of armed conflict that do not cause physical destruction or death, with all the tools at its disposal and consistent with international law.

THE IMPLEMENTATION

Foundation: Government Reform

The three layers of cyber deterrence rest on a common foundation: the need to reform how the U.S. government is organized to secure cyberspace and respond to attacks. The U.S. government is currently not designed to act with the speed and agility necessary to defend the country in cyberspace. We must get faster and smarter, improving the government's ability to organize concurrent, continuous, and collaborative efforts to build resilience, respond to cyber threats, and preserve military options that signal a capability and willingness to impose costs on adversaries. Reformed government oversight and organization that is properly resourced and staffed, in alignment with a strategy of layered cyber deterrence, will enable the United States to reduce the probability, magnitude, and effects of significant attacks on its networks.

Pillar: Reform the U.S. Government's Structure and Organization for Cyberspace. While cyberspace has transformed the American economy and society, the government has not kept up. Existing government structures and jurisdictional boundaries fracture cyber policymaking processes, limit opportunities for government action, and impede cyber operations. Rapid, comprehensive improvements at all levels of government are necessary to change these dynamics and ensure that the U.S. government can protect the American people, their way of life, and America's status as a global leader. Major recommendations in this pillar are:

• The executive branch should issue an updated National Cyber Strategy (1.1) that reflects the strategic approach of layered cyber deterrence and emphasizes resilience, public-private collaboration, and defend forward as key elements.

• Congress should establish House Permanent Select and Senate Select Committees on Cybersecurity (1.2) to provide integrated oversight of the cybersecurity efforts dispersed across the federal government.

• Congress should establish a Senate-confirmed National Cyber Director (NCD) (1.3), supported by an Office of the NCD, within the Executive Office of the President. The NCD will be the President's principal advisor for cybersecurity-related issues, as well as lead national-level coordination of cybersecurity strategy and policy, both within government and with the private sector.

• Congress should strengthen the Cybersecurity and Infrastructure Security Agency (CISA) (1.4) in its mission to ensure the national resilience of critical infrastructure, promote a more secure cyber ecosystem, and serve as the central coordinating element to support and integrate federal, state and local, and private-sector cybersecurity efforts. Congress must invest significant resources in CISA and provide it with clear authorities to realize its full potential.

• Congress and the executive branch should pass legislation and implement policies designed to better recruit, develop, and retain cyber talent (1.5) while acting to deepen the pool of candidates for cyber work in the federal government.

Layer 1: Shape Behavior

In the first layer, the strategy calls for shaping responsible behavior and encouraging restraint in cyberspace by strengthening norms and non-military instruments. Effective norms will not emerge without American leadership. For this reason, the United States needs to build a coalition of partners and allies to secure its shared interests and values in cyberspace.

Pillar: Strengthen Norms and Non-military Tools. A system of norms, built through international engagement and cooperation, promotes responsible behavior and, over time, dissuades adversaries from using cyber operations to undermine any nation's interests. The United States and others have agreed to norms of responsible behavior for cyberspace, but they go largely unenforced today. The United States can strengthen the current system of cyber norms by using non-military tools, including law enforcement actions, sanctions, diplomacy, and information sharing, to more effectively persuade states to conform to these norms and punish those who violate them. Such punishment requires developing the ability to quickly and accurately attribute cyberattacks. Building a coalition of like-minded allies and partners willing to collectively use these instruments to support a rules-based international order in cyberspace will better hold malign actors accountable. The major recommendations in this pillar are:

• Congress should create an Assistant Secretary of State (2.1) in the Department of State, with a new Bureau of Cyberspace Security and Emerging Technologies, who will lead the U.S. government effort to develop and reinforce international norms in cyberspace. This will help promote international norms that support and reflect U.S. interests and values while creating benefits for responsible state behavior through engagement with allies and partners.

• The executive branch should engage actively and effectively in forums setting international information and communications technology standards (2.1.2). Specifically, the National Institute of

Standards and Technology should facilitate robust and integrated participation by the federal government, academia, professional societies, and industry.

• Congress should take steps to improve international tools for law enforcement activities in cyberspace (2.1.4), including streamlining the Mutual Legal Assistance

Treaty and Mutual Legal Assistance Agreement process and increasing the number of FBI Cyber Assistant Legal Attachés.

Layer 2: Deny Benefits

In the second layer, the strategy calls for denying benefits to adversaries by promoting national resilience, reshaping the cyber ecosystem, and advancing the government's relationship with the private sector to establish an enhanced level of common situational awareness and joint collaboration. The United States needs a whole-of-nation approach to secure its interests and institutions in cyberspace.

Pillar: Promote National Resilience. Resilience—the capacity to withstand and quickly recover from attacks that could cause harm or coerce, deter, restrain, or otherwise shape U.S. behavior—is key to denying adversaries the benefits of their operations and reducing confidence in their ability to achieve their strategic ends.

National resilience efforts rely on the ability of the United States, in both the public and private sectors, to accurately identify, assess, and mitigate risk across all elements of critical infrastructure. The nation must be sufficiently prepared to respond to and recover from an attack, sustain critical functions even under degraded conditions, and, in some cases, restart critical functionality after disruption. Major recommendations in this pillar are:

• Congress should codify responsibilities and ensure sufficient resources (3.1) for the Cybersecurity and Infrastructure Security Agency and sector-specific agencies in the identification, assessment, and management of national and sector-specific risk.

• Congress should direct the U.S. government to develop and maintain Continuity of the Economy planning (3.2) in consultation with the private sector to ensure continuous operation of critical functions of the economy in the event of a significant cyber disruption.

• Congress should codify a Cyber State of Distress tied to a Cyber Response and Recovery Fund (3.3) to ensure sufficient resources and capacity to respond rapidly to significant cyber incidents.

• Congress should improve the structure and sustain the funding of the Election Assistance Commission (3.4), enabling it to increase its operational capacity to support states and localities in defense of the digital election infrastructure that underpins federal elections and to ensure the widest use of voter-verifiable, auditable, and paper-based voting systems.

• The U.S. government should promote digital literacy, civics education, and public awareness (3.5) to build societal resilience to foreign, malign cyber-enabled information operations.

Pillar: Reshape the Cyber Ecosystem toward Greater Security. Raising the baseline level of security across the cyber ecosystem—the people, processes, data, and technology that constitute and depend on cyberspace—will constrain and limit adversaries' activities.

Over time, this will reduce the frequency, scope, and scale of their cyber operations. Because the vast majority of this ecosystem is owned and operated by the private sector, scaling up security means partnering with the private sector and adjusting incentives to produce positive outcomes. In some cases, that requires aligning market forces. In other cases, where those forces either are not present or do not adequately address risk, the U.S. government must explore legislation, regulation, executive action, and public- as well as private-sector investments. Major recommendations in this pillar are:

• Congress should establish and fund a National Cybersecurity Certification and Labeling Authority(4.1) empowered to establish and manage a program on security certifications and labeling of information and communications technology products.

• Congress should pass a law establishing that final goods assemblers of software, hardware, and firmware are liable for damages from incidents that exploit known and unpatched vulnerabilities (4.2) for as long as they support a product or service.

• Congress should establish a Bureau of Cyber Statistics (4.3) charged with collecting and providing statistical data on cybersecurity and the cyber ecosystem to inform policymaking and government programs.

• Congress should resource and direct the Department of Homeland Security to fund a federally funded research and development center (4.4) to work with state-level regulators to develop certifications for cybersecurity insurance products.

• The National Cybersecurity Certification and Labeling Authority should develop a cloud security certification (4.5), in consultation with the National Institute of Standards and Technology, the Office of Management and Budget, and the Department of Homeland Security.

• Congress should direct the U.S. government to develop and implement an industrial base strategy for information and communications technology to ensure trusted supply chains (4.6) and the availability of critical information and communications technologies.

• Congress should pass a national data security and privacy protection law (4.7) establishing and standardizing requirements for the collection, retention, and sharing of user data.

Pillar: Operationalize Cybersecurity Collaboration with the Private Sector. Unlike in other physical domains, in cyberspace the government is often not the primary actor. Instead, it must support and enable the private sector. The government must build and communicate a better understanding of threats, with the specific aim of informing private-sector security operations, directing government operational efforts to counter malicious cyber activities, and ensuring better common situational awareness for collaborative action with the private sector. Further, while recognizing that private-sector entities have primary responsibility for the defense and security of their networks, the U.S. government must bring to bear its unique authorities, resources, and intelligence capabilities to support these actors in their defensive efforts. Major recommendations in this pillar are:

• Congress should codify the concept of "systemically important critical infrastructure" (5.1), whereby entities responsible for systems and assets that underpin national critical functions are ensured the full support of the U.S. government and shoulder additional security requirements befitting their unique status and importance.

• Congress should establish and fund a Joint Collaborative Environment (5.2), a common and interoperable environment for sharing and fusing threat information, insights, and other relevant data across the federal government and between the public and private sectors.

• Congress should direct the executive branch to strengthen a public-private, integrated cyber center in CISA (5.3) to support its critical infrastructure security and resilience mission and to conduct a one-year, comprehensive systems analysis review of federal cyber and cybersecurity centers.

• The executive branch should establish a Joint Cyber Planning Cell (5.4) under CISA to coordinate cyber- security planning and readiness across the federal government and between the public and private sectors.

Layer 3: Impose Costs

In the final layer, the strategy outlines how to impose costs to deter future malicious behavior and reduce ongoing adversary activities short of armed conflict through the employment of all instruments of power in the defense of cyberspace, including systemically important critical infrastructure. A key, but not the only, element of cost imposition is the military instrument of power. Therefore, the United States must maintain the capacity, resilience, and readiness to employ cyber and non-cyber capabilities across the spectrum of engagement from competition to crisis and conflict. The United States needs ready and resilient capabilities to thwart and respond to adversary action.

Pillar: Preserve and Employ the Military Instrument of Power—and All Other Options to Deter Cyberattacks at Any Level. Cyberspace is already an arena of strategic competition, where states project power, protect their interests, and punish their adversaries. Future contingencies and conflicts will almost certainly contain a cyber component. In this environment, the United States must defend forward to limit malicious adversary behavior below the level of armed attack, deter conflict, and, if necessary, prevail by employing the full spectrum of its capabilities, using all the instruments of national power. Examples of adversary actions below armed attack include cyber-enabled attacks on the U.S. election systems or cyber-enabled intellectual property theft. To achieve these ends, the U.S. government must demonstrate its ability to impose costs, while establishing a clear declaratory policy that signals to rival states the costs and risks associated with attacking the United States in cyberspace. Furthermore, conventional weapons and nuclear capabilities require cybersecurity and resilience to ensure that the United States preserves credible deterrence and the full range of military response options. The United States must be confident that its military capabilities will work as intended. Finally, across the spectrum of engagement from competition to crisis and conflict, the United States must ensure that it has sufficient cyber forces to accomplish strategic objectives in and through cyberspace. This demands sufficient capacity, capabilities, and streamlined decision-making processes to enable rapid and effective cyber response options to impose costs against adversaries. Major recommendations in this pillar include:

• Congress should direct the Department of Defense to conduct a force structure assessment of the Cyber Mission Force (6.1) to ensure that the United States has the appropriate force structure and capabilities in light of growing mission requirements and increasing expectations, in both scope and scale. This should include an assessment of the resource implications for the National Security Agency in its combat support agency role.

• Congress should direct the Department of Defense to conduct a cybersecurity vulnerability assessment of all segments of the nuclear control systems and continually assess weapon systems' cyber vulnerabilities (6.2).

• Congress should require Defense Industrial Base (DIB) participation in threat intelligence sharing programs (6.2.1) and threat hunting on DIB networks (6.2.2).

THE WAY FORWARD

The status quo in cyberspace is unacceptable. The current state of affairs invites aggression and establishes a dangerous pattern of actors attacking the United States without fear of reprisal. Adversaries are increasing their cyber capabilities while U.S. vulnerabilities continue to grow. There is much that the U.S. government can do to improve its defenses and reduce the risk of a significant attack, but it is clear that government action alone is not enough. Most of the critical infrastructure that drives the American economy, spurs technological innovation, and supports the U.S. military resides in the private sector. If the U.S. government cannot find a way to seamlessly collaborate with the private sector to build a resilient cyber ecosystem, the nation will never be secure. And, eventually, a massive cyberattack could lead to large-scale physical destruction, sparking a response of haphazard government overreach that stifles innovation in the digital economy and further erodes American strength. To avoid these outcomes, the U.S. government must move to adopt the new strategy detailed in this report—layered cyber deterrence—and the more than 75 recommendations designed to make this approach a reality.

The executive branch and Congress should give these recommendations and the associated legislative proposals close consideration. Congress should also consider ways to monitor, assess, and report on the implementation of this report's recommendations over the next two years.

LAYER 3.

Impose Costs

LAYER 2.

Deny Benefits

LAYER 1.

Shape Behavior

Reform the U.S. Government

Build Partnerships

Ensure Continuity of the Economy

Generate Cyber Capabilities & Capacity

Leverage Non-military Instruments

Secure Elections

Protect Critical Infrastructure

Desired End State

Reduce the frequency and severity of cyber attacks of significant consequence.

Limit the ability of great powers, rogue states, extremists, and criminals to under-mine American power and influence.

Layered Cyber Deterrence

PILLAR 1: REFORM THE U.S. GOVERNMENT'S STRUCTURE AND ORGANIZATION FOR CYBERSPACE

Key Recommendation 1.1: Issue an Updated National Cyber Strategy

Enabling Recommendation 1.1.1: Develop a Multitiered Signaling Strategy

Enabling Recommendation 1.1.2: Promulgate a New Declaratory Policy

Key Recommendation 1.2: Create House Permanent Select and Senate Select Committees on Cybersecurity

Enabling Recommendation 1.2.1: Reestablish the Office of Technology Assessment

Key Recommendation 1.3: Establish a National Cyber Director

Key Recommendation 1.4: Strengthen the Cybersecurity and Infrastructure Security Agency

Enabling Recommendation 1.4.1: Codify and Strengthen the Cyber Threat Intelligence Integration Center

Enabling Recommendation 1.4.2: Strengthen the FBI's Cyber Mission and the National Cyber Investigative Joint Task Force

Key Recommendation 1.5: Diversify and Strengthen the Federal Cyberspace Workforce

Enabling Recommendation 1.5.1: Improve Cyber-Oriented Education

PILLAR 2: STRENGTHEN NORMS AND NON-MILITARY TOOLS

Key Recommendation 2.1: Create a Cyber Bureau and Assistant Secretary at the U.S. Department of State

Enabling Recommendation 2.1.1: Strengthen Norms of Responsible State Behavior in Cyberspace

Enabling Recommendation 2.1.2: Engage Actively and Effectively in Forums Setting International Information and Communications Technology Standards

Enabling Recommendation 2.1.3: Improve Cyber Capacity Building and Consolidate the Funding of Cyber Foreign Assistance

Enabling Recommendation 2.1.4: Improve International Tools for Law Enforcement Activities in Cyberspace

Enabling Recommendation 2.1.5: Leverage Sanctions and Trade Enforcement Actions

Enabling Recommendation 2.1.6: Improve Attribution Analysis and the Attribution-Decision Rubric

Enabling Recommendation 2.1.7: Reinvigorate Efforts to Develop Cyber Confidence-Building Measures

PILLAR 3: PROMOTE NATIONAL RESILIENCE

Key Recommendation 3.1: Codify Sector-specific Agencies into Law as "Sector Risk Management Agencies" and Strengthen Their Ability to Manage Critical Infrastructure Risk

Enabling Recommendation 3.1.1: Establish a Five-Year National Risk Management Cycle Culminating in a Critical Infrastructure Resilience Strategy

Enabling Recommendation 3.1.2: Establish a National Cybersecurity Assistance Fund to Ensure Consistent and Timely Funding for Initiatives That Underpin National Resilience

Key Recommendation 3.2: Develop and Maintain Continuity of the Economy Planning

Key Recommendation 3.3: Codify a "Cyber State of Distress" Tied to a "Cyber Response and Recovery Fund"

Enabling Recommendation 3.3.1: Designate Responsibilities for Cybersecurity Services under the Defense Production Act

Enabling Recommendation 3.3.2: Clarify Liability for Federally Directed Mitigation, Response, and Recovery Efforts

Enabling Recommendation 3.3.3: Improve and Expand Planning Capacity and Readiness for CyberIncident Response and Recovery Efforts

Enabling Recommendation 3.3.4: Expand Coordinated Cyber Exercises, Gaming, and Simulation

Enabling Recommendation 3.3.5: Establish a Biennial National Cyber Tabletop Exercise

Enabling Recommendation 3.3.6: Clarify the Cyber Capabilities and Strengthen the Interoperability of the National Guard

Key Recommendation 3.4: Improve the Structure and Enhance Funding of the Election Assistance Commission

Enabling Recommendation 3.4.1: Modernize Campaign Regulations to Promote Cybersecurity

Key Recommendation 3.5: Build Societal Resilience to Foreign Malign Cyber-Enabled Information

Operations

Enabling Recommendation 3.5.1: Reform Online Political Advertising to Defend against Foreign Influence in Elections

PILLAR 4: RESHAPE THE CYBER ECOSYSTEM TOWARD GREATER SECURITY

Key Recommendation 4.1: Establish and Fund a National Cybersecurity Certification and Labeling Authority

Enabling Recommendation 4.1.1: Create or Designate Critical Technology Security Centers

Enabling Recommendation 4.1.2: Expand and Support the National Institute of Standards and Technology Security Work

Key Recommendation 4.2: Establish Liability for Final Goods Assemblers

Enabling Recommendation 4.2.1: Incentivize Timely Patch Implementation

Key Recommendation 4.3: Establish a Bureau of Cyber Statistics

Key Recommendation 4.4: Resource a Federally Funded Research and Development Center to Develop Cybersecurity Insurance Certifications

Enabling Recommendation 4.4.1: Establish a Public-Private Partnership on Modeling Cyber Risk

Enabling Recommendation 4.4.2: Explore the Need for a Government Reinsurance Program to Cover Catastrophic Cyber Events

Enabling Recommendation 4.4.3: Incentivize Information Technology Security through Federal Acquisition Regulations and Federal Information Security Management Act Authorities

Enabling Recommendation 4.4.4: Amend the Sarbanes-Oxley Act to Include Cybersecurity Reporting Requirements

Key Recommendation 4.5: Develop a Cloud Security Certification

Enabling Recommendation 4.5.1: Incentivize the Uptake of Secure Cloud Services for Small and

Medium-Sized Businesses and State, Local, Tribal, and Territorial Governments

Enabling Recommendation 4.5.2: Develop a Strategy to Secure Foundational Internet Protocols and Email

Enabling Recommendation 4.5.3: Strengthen the U.S. Government's Ability to Take Down Botnets

Key Recommendation 4.6: Develop and Implement an Information and Communications Technology Industrial Base Strategy

Enabling Recommendation 4.6.1: Increase Support to Supply Chain Risk Management Efforts

Enabling Recommendation 4.6.2: Commit Significant and Consistent Funding toward Research and Development in Emerging Technologies

Enabling Recommendation 4.6.3: Strengthen the Capacity of the Committee on Foreign Investment in the United States

Enabling Recommendation 4.6.4: Invest in the National Cyber Moonshot Initiative

Key Recommendation 4.7: Pass a National Data Security and Privacy Protection Law

Enabling Recommendation 4.7.1: Pass a National Breach Notification Law

PILLAR 5: OPERATIONALIZE CYBERSECURITY COLLABORATION WITH THE PRIVATE SECTOR

Key Recommendation 5.1: Codify the Concept of "Systemically Important Critical Infrastructure"

Enabling Recommendation 5.1.1: Review and Update Intelligence Authorities to Increase Intelligence Support to the Broader Private Sector

Enabling Recommendation 5.1.2: Strengthen and Codify Processes for Identifying Broader Private-Sector Cybersecurity Intelligence Needs and Priorities

Enabling Recommendation 5.1.3: Empower Departments and Agencies to Serve Administrative Subpoenas in Support of Threat and Asset Response Activities

Key Recommendation 5.2: Establish and Fund a Joint Collaborative Environment for Sharing and Fusing Threat Information

Enabling Recommendation 5.2.1: Expand and Standardize Voluntary Threat Detection Programs

Enabling Recommendation 5.2.2: Pass a National Cyber Incident Reporting Law

Enabling Recommendation 5.2.3: Amend the Pen Register Trap and Trace Statute to Enable Better Identification of Malicious Actors

Key Recommendation 5.3: Strengthen an Integrated Cyber Center within CISA and Promote the Integration of Federal Cyber Centers

Key Recommendation 5.4: Establish a Joint Cyber Planning Cell under the Cybersecurity and Infrastructure Security Agency

Enabling Recommendation 5.4.1: Institutionalize Department of Defense Participation in Public-Private Cybersecurity Initiatives

Enabling Recommendation 5.4.2: Expand Cyber Defense Collaboration with Information and Communications Technology Enablers

PILLAR 6: PRESERVE AND EMPLOY THE MILITARY INSTRUMENT OF POWER

Key Recommendation 6.1: Direct the Department of Defense to Conduct a Force Structure Assessment of the Cyber Mission Force

Enabling Recommendation 6.1.1: Direct the Department of Defense to Create a Major Force Program Funding Category for U.S. Cyber Command

Enabling Recommendation 6.1.2: Expand Current Malware Inoculation Initiatives

Enabling Recommendation 6.1.3: Review the Delegation of Authorities for Cyber Operations

Enabling Recommendation 6.1.4: Reassess and Amend Standing Rules of Engagement and Standing Rules for Use of Force for U.S. Forces

Enabling Recommendation 6.1.5: Cooperate with Allies and Partners to Defend Forward

Enabling Recommendation 6.1.6: Require the Department of Defense to Define Reporting Metrics

Enabling Recommendation 6.1.7: Assess the Establishment of a Military Cyber Reserve

Enabling Recommendation 6.1.8: Establish Title 10 Professors in Cyber Security and Information Operations

Key Recommendation 6.2: Conduct a Cybersecurity Vulnerability Assessment of All Segments of the NC3 and NLCC Systems and Continually Assess Weapon Systems' Cyber Vulnerabilities

Enabling Recommendation 6.2.1: Require Defense Industrial Base Participation in a Threat Intelligence Sharing Program

Enabling Recommendation 6.2.2: Require Threat Hunting on Defense Industrial Base Networks

Enabling Recommendation 6.2.3: Designate a Threat-Hunting Capability across the Department of Defense Information Network

Enabling Recommendation 6.2.4: Assess and Address the Risk to National Security Systems Posed by Quantum Computing

NOTES

Note 1

The Solarium Commission has recommended 54 specific legislative proposals in a 257 page document.[593]   The Commission has supplemented those proposals with pandemic-related or inspired legislative proposals.[594]

Note 2

In 2018, the U.S. Department of Defense released the Summary: Department of Defense Cyberstrategy [DOD Cyberstrategy].[595] The DOD Cyberstrategy states:

> We are engaged in a long-term strategic competition with China and Russia. These States have expanded that competition to include persistent campaigns in and through cyberspace that pose longterm strategic risk to the Nation as well as to our allies and partners. China is eroding U.S. military overmatch and the Nation's economic vitality by persistently exfiltrating sensitive information from U.S. public and private sector institutions. Russia has used cyber-enabled information operations to influence our population and challenge our democratic processes. Other actors, such as North Korea and Iran, have similarly employed malicious cyber activities to harm U.S. citizens and threaten U.S. interests. Globally, the scope and pace of malicious cyber activity continue to rise. The United States' growing dependence on the cyberspace domain for nearly every essential civilian and military function makes this an urgent and unacceptable risk to the Nation.

---

[593] U.S. CYBERSPACE SOLARIUM COMM'N, LEGISLATIVE PROPOSALS (2020), *available at* https://drive.google.com/file/d/1S5N7KvjFfxow19kCnPl0nx7Mah8pK0uG/view.

[594] U.S. CYBERSPACE SOLARIUM COMM'N, CYBERSECURITY LESSONS FROM THE PANDEMIC: LEGISLATIVE PROPOSALS (2020), *available at* https://drive.google.com/file/d/11jk6QrHwBBtwCaUPJt7Vdonv_vIcTZxI/view.

[595] U.S. DEP'T OF DEF., SUMMARY: CYBER STRATEGY (2018), *available at* https://media.defense.gov/2018/Sep/18/2002041658/-1/-1/1/CYBER_STRATEGY_SUMMARY_FINAL.PDF.

The Department must take action in cyberspace during day-to-day competition to preserve U.S. military advantages and to defend U.S. interests. Our focus will be on the States that can pose strategic threats to U.S. prosperity and security, particularly China and Russia. We will conduct cyberspace operations to collect intelligence and prepare military cyber capabilities to be used in the event of crisis or conflict. We will defend forward to disrupt or halt malicious cyber activity at its source, including activity that falls below the level of armed conflict. We will strengthen the security and resilience of networks and systems that contribute to current and future U.S. military advantages. We will collaborate with our interagency, industry, and international partners to advance our mutual interests.

During wartime, U.S. cyber forces will be prepared to operate alongside our air, land, sea, and space forces to target adversary weaknesses, offset adversary strengths, and amplify the effectiveness of other elements of the Joint Force. Adversary militaries are increasingly reliant on the same type of computer and network technologies that have become central to Joint Force warfighting. The Department will exploit this reliance to gain military advantage. The Joint Force will employ offensive cyber capabilities and innovative concepts that allow for the use of cyberspace operations across the full spectrum of conflict.

STRATEGIC COMPETITION IN CYBERSPACE

First, we must ensure the U.S. military's ability to fight and win wars in any domain, including cyberspace. This is a foundational requirement for U.S. national security and a key to ensuring that we deter aggression, including cyber attacks that constitute a use of force, against the United States, our allies, and our partners. The Department must defend its own networks, systems, and information from malicious cyber activity and be prepared to defend, when directed, those networks and systems operated by non-DoD Defense Critical Infrastructure (DCI)1 and Defense Industrial Base (DIB)2 entities. We will defend forward to halt or degrade cyberspace operations targeting the Department, and we will collaborate to strengthen the cybersecurity and resilience of DoD, DCI, and DIB networks and systems. Second, the Department seeks to preempt, defeat, or deter malicious cyber activity targeting U.S. critical infrastructure that could cause a significant cyber incident regardless of whether that incident would impact DoD's warfighting readiness or capability. Our primary role in this homeland defense mission is to defend forward by leveraging our focus outward to stop threats before they reach their targets. The Department also provides public and private sector partners with indications and warning (I&W) of malicious cyber activity, in coordination with other Federal departments and agencies. Third, the Department will work with U.S. allies and partners to strengthen cyber capacity, expand combined cyberspace operations, and increase bi-directional information sharing in order to advance our mutual interests.

The Department's cyberspace objectives are: 1. Ensuring the Joint Force can achieve its missions in a contested cyberspace environment; 2. Strengthening the Joint Force by conducting cyberspace operations that enhance U.S. military advantages; 3. Defending U.S. critical infrastructure from malicious cyber activity that alone, or as part of a campaign, could cause a significant cyber incident; 4. Securing DoD information and systems against malicious cyber activity, including DoD information on non-DoD-owned networks; and 5. Expanding DoD cyber cooperation with interagency, industry, and international partners.

DEFENDING CIVILIAN ASSETS THAT ENABLE U.S. MILITARY ADVANTAGE

The Department must be prepared to defend non-DoD-owned Defense Critical Infrastructure (DCI) and Defense Industrial Base (DIB) networks and systems. Our chief goal in maintaining an ability to defend DCI is to ensure the infrastructure's continued functionality and ability to support DoD objectives in a contested cyber environment. Our focus working with DIB entities is to protect sensitive DoD information whose loss, either individually or in aggregate, could result in an erosion of Joint Force military advantage. As the Sector Specific Agency (SSA) for the DIB and a business partner with the DIB and DCI, the Department will: set and enforce standards for cybersecurity, resilience, and reporting; and be prepared, when requested and authorized, to provide direct assistance, including on non-DoD networks, prior to, during, and after an incident.

The Strategic Approach

Our strategic approach is based on mutually reinforcing lines of effort to build a more lethal force; compete and deter in cyberspace; expand alliances and partnerships; reform the Department; and cultivate talent.

BUILD A MORE LETHAL JOINT FORCE

Accelerate cyber capability development: The Department will accelerate the development of cyber capabilities for both warfighting and countering malicious cyber actors. Our focus will be on fielding capabilities that are scalable, adaptable, and diverse to provide maximum flexibility to Joint Force commanders. The Joint Force will be capable of employing cyberspace operations throughout the spectrum of conflict, from day-to-day operations to wartime, in order to advance U.S. interests. Innovate to foster agility: The Department must innovate to keep pace with rapidly evolving threats and technologies in cyberspace. We will accept and manage operational and programmatic risk in a deliberate manner that moves from a "zero defect" culture to one that fosters agility and innovation because success in this domain requires the Department to innovate faster than our strategic competitors.

Leverage automation and data analysis to improve effectiveness: The Department will use cyber enterprise solutions to operate at machine speed and large-scale data analytics to identify malicious cyber activity across different networks and systems. The Department will leverage these advances to improve our own defensive posture and to ensure that our cyber capabilities will continue to be effective against competitors armed with cutting edge technology.

Employ commercial-off-the-shelf (COTS) cyber capabilities: The Department excels at creating cyber capabilities tailored for specific operational problems. In addition to these capabilities, we will make greater use of COTS capabilities that can be optimized for DoD use. ›

COMPETE AND DETER IN CYBERSPACE

Deter malicious cyber activities: The United States seeks to use all instruments of national power to deter adversaries from conducting malicious cyberspace activity that would threaten U.S. national interests, our allies, or our partners. The Department will prioritize securing sensitive DoD information and deterring malicious cyber activities that constitute a use of force against the United States, our allies, or our partners. Should deterrence fail, the Joint Force stands ready to employ the full range of military capabilities in response.

Persistently contest malicious cyber activity in day-to-day competition: The Department will counter cyber campaigns threatening U.S. military advantage by defending forward to intercept and halt cyber threats and by strengthening the cybersecurity of systems and networks that support DoD missions. This includes working with the private sector and our foreign allies and partners to contest cyber activity that could threaten Joint Force missions and to counter the exfiltration of sensitive DoD information.

Increase the resilience of U.S. critical infrastructure: The Department will work with its interagency and private sector partners to reduce the risk that malicious cyber activity targeting U.S. critical infrastructure could have catastrophic or cascading consequences. We will streamline our publicprivate information-sharing mechanisms and strengthen the resilience and cybersecurity of critical infrastructure networks and systems.

STRENGTHEN ALLIANCES AND ATTRACT NEW PARTNERSHIPS

Build trusted private sector partnerships: The private sector owns and operates the majority of U.S. infrastructure and is on the frontlines of nation-state competition in cyberspace. In coordination with other Federal departments and agencies, the Department will build trusted relationships with private sector entities that are critical enablers of military operations and carry out deliberate planning and collaborative training that enables mutually supporting cybersecurity activities.

Operationalize international partnerships: Many of the United States' allies and partners possess advanced cyber capabilities that complement our own. The Department will work to strengthen the capacity of these allies and partners and increase DoD's ability to leverage its partners' unique skills, resources, capabilities, and perspectives. Information-sharing relationships with allies and partners will increase the effectiveness of combined cyberspace operations and enhance our collective cybersecurity posture.

Reinforce norms of responsible State behavior in cyberspace: The Department will reinforce voluntary, non-binding norms of responsible State behavior in cyberspace during peacetime. The United States has endorsed the work done by the UN Group of Governmental Experts on Developments in the Field of Information and Telecommunications in the Context of International Security (UNGGE) to develop a framework of responsible State behavior in cyberspace. The principles developed by the UNGGE include prohibitions against damaging civilian critical infrastructure during peacetime and against allowing national territory to be used for intentionally wrongful cyber activity. The Department will work alongside its interagency and international partners to promote international commitments regarding behavior in cyberspace as well as to develop and implement cyber confidence building measures (CBM). When cyber activities threaten U.S. interests, we will contest them and we will be prepared to act, in conjunction with partners, to defend U.S. interests.

REFORM THE DEPARTMENT

Incorporate cyber awareness into DoD institutional culture: The Department will adapt its institutional culture so individuals at every level are knowledgeable about the cyberspace domain and can incorporate that knowledge into their day-to-day activities. Leaders and their staffs need to be "cyber fluent" so they can fully understand the cybersecurity implications of their decisions and are positioned to identify opportunities to leverage the cyberspace domain to gain strategic, operational, and tactical advantages.

Increase cybersecurity accountability: Reducing the Department's "attack surface" requires an increase in cybersecurity awareness and accountability across the Department. We will hold DoD personnel and our private sector partners accountable for their cybersecurity practices and choices. Seek material solutions that are affordable, flexible, and robust: The Department will reduce the time it takes to procure software and hardware in order to keep pace with the rapid advance of technology. We will identify opportunities to procure scalable services, such as cloud storage and scalable computing power, to ensure that our systems keep pace with commercial information technology and can scale when necessary to match changing requirements. We will also leverage COTS capabilities where feasible to reduce our reliance on expensive, custom-built software that is difficult to maintain or upgrade. Expand crowd-sourced vulnerability identification: The Department will continue to identify crowdsourcing opportunities, such as hack-a-thons and bug-bounties, in order to identify and mitigate vulnerabilities more effectively and to foster innovation.

CULTIVATE TALENT

Sustain a ready cyber workforce: The Department's workforce is a critical cyber asset. We will invest in building future talent, identifying and recruiting sought-after talent, and retaining our current cyber workforce. We will provide ample opportunities—both inside and outside the Department—for the professional development and career progression of cyber personnel. We will create processes for maintaining visibility of the entire military and civilian cyber workforce and optimizing personnel rotations across military departments and commands, including maximizing the use of the Reserve Components. The Department will also ensure that its cyber requirements are filled by the optimal mix of military service members, civilian employees, and contracted support to serve mission requirements.

Enhance the Nation's cyber talent: The Department plays an essential role in enhancing the Nation's pool of cyber talent in order to further the goal of increasing national resilience across the private and public sectors. To that end, we will increase our efforts alongside other Federal departments and agencies to promote science, technology, engineering, mathematics, and foreign language (STEM-L) disciplines at the primary and secondary education levels throughout the United States. The Department will also partner with industry and academia to establish standards in training, education, and awareness that will facilitate the growth of cyber talent in the United States.

Embed software and hardware expertise as a core DoD competency: To make it attractive to skilled candidates, the Department will establish a career track for computer science related specialties (including hardware engineers, software developers, and data analysts) that offers meaningful challenges, rotational billets at other Federal departments and agencies, specialized training opportunities tied to retention commitments, and the expansion of compensation incentives for the Cyber Excepted Service (CES).

Establish a cyber top talent management program: The Department will establish a cyber talent management program that provides its most skilled cyber personnel with focused resources and opportunities to develop key skills over the course of their careers. The Department will use competitive processes, including individual and team competitions, to identify the most capable DoD military and civilian cyber specialists and then empower those personnel to solve the Department's toughest challenges.

Note 3

In *COVID-19 Proves How Dangerously We Misjudged China*, published by The Hill, the author argues that the United States response to rivals such as Russia and China has failed because of a lack of understanding their approach. For example, Mr. Cropsey points to how intellectual property theft ostensibly by China and Russian cyberattacks on banks are part of a comprehensive warfare strategy unlike the traditional interaction between traditional war and politics. In understanding China, Mr. Cropsey points to the writing of Prussian General Clausewitz who viewed politics and warfare as similar with only "different means."[596]

Note 4

In a RAND publication titled, *The Emerging Risk of Virtual Societal Warfare: Social Manipulation in a Changing Information Environment*, the authors attempt to discern the future of social manipulation through the provision of electronic information in light of new technologies after the manipulation of the 2016 U.S. presidential election.[597] In addition to traditional cyberattacks, the authors list a number of potential harms that may continue and occur in the future, which include, in part:

[1] deploying classic propaganda, influence, and disinformation operations through multiple channels, including social media[; 2] generating massive amounts of highly plausible fabricated video and audio material to reduce confidence in shared reality[; 3] discrediting key mediating institutions that are capable of distinguishing between true and false information[; 4] corrupting or manipulating the databases on which major components of the economy increasingly rely[; 5] manipulating or degrading systems of algorithmic decision making, both

---

[596] Seth Cropsey, *COVID-19 Proves How Dangerously We Misjudged China*, THE HILL (Sept. 2, 2020, 1:30 PM), https://thehill.com/opinion/national-security/514758-covid-19-proves-how-dangerously-we-misjudged-china.

[597] Michael J. Mazarr, et al., *The Emerging Risk of Virtual Societal Warfare*, RAND CORP. (2019), *available at* https://www.rand.org/pubs/research_reports/RR2714.html.

to impair day-to-day government and corporate operations and to intensify loss of faith in institutions, as well as increase social grievances and polarization. . . [.]

According to the authors, the ultimate targeted harm is truly a loss of confidence and trust in institutions—economic or political "and generating a persistent sense of insecurity and anxiety." From a cybersecurity perspective, please remember the CIA: Confidentiality, Integrity and Availability. What is the future importance of the role of the cybersecurity professional and counselor? Indeed, the authors also point to increasing need for cooperation between public and private sectors, which is a foundation upon which the NIST Risk Assessment Framework is built. On October 19, 2020, the New York Times reported that the U.S. Department of Justice had brought charges against Russian government hackers who have targeted many countries, including the United States.[598]

Note 5

In a RAND publication titled, *The Emerging Risk of Virtual Societal Warfare: Social Manipulation in a Changing Information Environment*, the authors point to how cyberattacks can eventually lead to a lessening of the territorial integrity norm:

> Begin working toward international norms constraining the use of virtual societal aggression. . . . To the extent that nations begin attacking one another in virtual but highly damaging ways, the prevailing consensus on territorial nonaggression could collapse, leading eventually to large-scale armed adventurism.[599]

Note 6

An expert panel at the U.S. Department of Defense emphasized how women and minorities are not sufficiently represented in the cyber security field.[600]

Note 7

In an article titled, *To Succeed in Its Cybersecurity Mission, the Defense Department Must Partner with Academia (For Real)*, Monica M. Ruiz, Jacquelyn G. Schneider and Eli Sugarman essentially argue that the Defense Department should develop closer ties with academia. In particular, a close partnership is needed to ensure

---

[598] *See* Michael S. Schmidt & Nicole Perlroth, *U.S. Charges Russian Intelligence Officers in Major Cyberattacks,* N. Y. TIMES (Oct. 19, 2020), https://www.nytimes.com/2020/10/19/us/politics/russian-intelligence-cyberattacks.html ("The prosecutors focused on seven breaches that together showed how Russia sought in recent years to use its hacking abilities to undermine democratic institutions and ideals, retaliate against enemies and destroy rival economies.").

[599] Michael J. Mazarr, et al., *The Emerging Risk of Virtual Societal Warfare*, RAND CORP. (2019), *available at* https://www.rand.org/pubs/research_reports/RR2714.html.

[600] *See* Terri Moon Cronk, *Women, Minorities Underrepresented in Cyber Security*, U.S. DEP'T OF DEF. (Sept. 2, 2020), https://www.defense.gov/Explore/News/Article/Article/2334909/women-minorities-underrepresented-in-cyber-security-dod-expert-says/.

that academia is continuing to produce necessary research as well as trained students in law, social sciences and computer science.[601]

Note 8

In *How to Compete in Cyberspace: Cyber Command's New Approach*, Paul M. Nakasone and Michael Sulmeyer explain how the proactive approach of the U.S. military in investigating cyber security issues in other countries has led to the "inoculation" of private sector computer systems from malware. Paul M. Nakasone is Commander of U.S. Cyber-Command, Director of the National Security Agency, and Chief of the Central Security Service. Michael Sulmeyer is Senior Advisor to the Commander of U.S. Cyber Command.[602]

Note 9

The U.S. Government reportedly collects cybersecurity vulnerabilities for national security reasons. If the U.S. Government is utilizing a vulnerability to "hack" a computer system to monitor for example, potentially terroristic activities by users of the system, should the U.S. Government also have to disclose to the company with the vulnerability that there is a vulnerability?

Note 10

The U.S. Government under the Trump Administration has pushed for some Chinese social media companies to leave the U.S. market such as Tik Tok or WeChat, in part, because of cybersecurity concerns. Those concerns seem to revolve around the collection and use of data of U.S. citizens by those companies for or provided to the Chinese Government. China has been criticized for market protection and potential intellectual property theft because of conditioning access to the Chinese market for foreign countries on access to, for example, financial institutions source code for their software. China has also required or desired that foreign companies doing business in China have a Chinese business partner. This could lead to the disclosure of trade secrets or sensitive personal data to the Chinese business partner. Is the United States essentially adopting Chinese policy regarding doing business in the United States? With regard to requiring access to source code of financial institutions, China argued that was necessary to combat terrorism—essentially national security reasons.

Note 11

---

[601] Monica M. Ruiz, Jacquelyn G. Schneider, & Eli Sugarman, *To Succeed in Its Cybersecurity Mission, the Defense Department Must Partner With Academia (For Real)*, LAW FARE (Sept. 8, 2020, 2:34 PM), https://www.lawfareblog.com/succeed-its-cybersecurity-mission-defense-department-must-partner-academia-real.

[602] Paul M. Nakasone & Michael Sulmeyer, *How to Compete in Cyberspace: Cyber Command's New Approach*, FOREIGN AFF. (Aug. 25, 2020), https://www.foreignaffairs.com/articles/united-states/2020-08-25/cybersecurity.

In October of 2020, Sweden decided to ban Chinese companies Huawei and ZTE from its 5G networks. Notably, the reason for the ban concerned security.[603]

14.7 Regional Free Trade Agreements

Numerous regional free trade agreements address cybersecurity related issues. For example, the Asia-Pacific Economic Cooperation Cross-Border Privacy Rules System, Comprehensive and Progressive Agreement for Trans-Pacific Partnership, and the United States-Mexico-Canada Agreement all address cybersecurity issues. The following restates some of the relevant provisions in those agreements. However, first, a Brookings Institute Report outlines some of the issues associated with cybersecurity and trade.

14.7[A] OVERVIEW OF TRADE AND CYBERSECURITY

Joshua P. Meltzer and Cameron F. Kerry, Cybersecurity and Digital Trade: Getting it right, The Brookings Institution Report (September 18, 2019).[604]

INTRODUCTION: THE INTERACTION OF CYBERSECURITY AND TRADE

Trade and cybersecurity are increasingly intertwined. The expansion of the internet globally and use of data flows globally by businesses and consumers for communication, e-commerce, and as a source of access to information and innovation, is transforming international trade. The spread of artificial intelligence, the "internet of things," and cloud computing will work to increase global connectivity of businesses, governments, and supply chains.

As global interconnectivity grows, however, so does exposure to the risks and costs of cyberattacks. For example, formjacking—using JavaScript to steal credit card details from e-commerce sites—or supply chains hacks which exploit third party services and software to compromise a final target, undermine business and consumer trust in using the internet for commerce. The WannaCry ransomware attributed to North Korea infected more than 200,000 computers across 153 countries, costing hundreds of millions of dollars damage. What is clear is a lack of cybersecurity is costly and can undermine the trust of consumers and business in engaging in digital trade. Protecting trust in a digitally connected world necessarily involves collaboration across borders between the public and private sectors because global networks, organizations, and supply chains rely on the same systems and software, most of it supplied by enterprises, and they face the same threats.

---

[603] Richard Milne, *Sweden Bans China's Huawei and ZTE from Its 5G Networks*, L. A. TIMES (Oct. 20, 2020, 8:25 AM), https://www.latimes.com/business/story/2020-10-20/sweden-bans-china-huawei-zte-5g-networks.

[604] Joshua P. Meltzer & Cameron F. Kerry, *Cybersecurity and Digital Trade: Getting It Right*, BROOKINGS (Sept. 18, 2019), https://www.brookings.edu/research/cybersecurity-and-digital-trade-getting-it-right/. This article originally was published by the Brookings Institution.

The importance of cybersecurity is leading countries to adopt cybersecurity policies. According to one estimate at least 50 countries have adopted cybersecurity policies and regulation. Some of these cybersecurity policies recognize a need for international cooperation: the EU identified "a need for closer cooperation at a global level to improve security standards, improve information, and promote a common global approach to network and information security issues ...."and the most recent U.S. Cybersecurity Strategy reaffirms the need to "strengthen the capacity and interoperability of those allies and partners to improve our ability to optimize our combined skills, resources, capabilities, and perspectives against shared threats.

A common approach can enhance cybersecurity and protect digital trade. Conversely, divergent or obstructive approaches risk creating barriers to digital trade. These can include unique standards, requirements for localization of data or technology supply, and overreaching national security protections may violate obligations under the WTO and free trade agreements. A recent Brookings roundtable among cybersecurity and trade experts from government, civil society, and the private sector identified a need to unpack broad or restrictive measures from reasonable practices and policies designed to enhance the security of network infrastructure.

This brief will discuss how trade policy can be an instrument to support good cybersecurity practices and to build cooperation on cybersecurity among governments. We explore ways that trade agreements and trade policy can be used to unpack meaningful cybersecurity from artificial trade barriers. In particular, we look at the extent to which these can differentiate between cybersecurity and more restrictive measures in the name of national security. The challenge of adapting trade rules developed in an analog era to today's digital world economy is an ongoing project, and managing cybersecurity effectively needs to be part of that project.

CYBERSECURITY, THE WTO NATIONAL SECURITY, AND OTHER WTO EXCEPTIONS

The WTO security exception. Article XXI of GATT allows for a number "security exceptions" from WTO obligations. Until recently, this exception has been used infrequently, not only because parties have been reluctant to put national security interests to the test of dispute settlement but in part out of concern that the exception could blow a very large hole in the trading system.

Now, however, the growth in connectivity and parallel rise in cybersecurity concerns presents a real risk that cybersecurity becomes a catch-all to justify political control or to protect domestic industry from online competitors. For instance, Vietnam's cybersecurity law prohibits, among other things "distorting history, denying revolutionary achievements, or destroying the fine tradition and customs of the people, social ethics or health of the community." A statement by the Shanghai Cooperation Organization on Cooperation in the Field of International Information Security considers as a threat the "dissemination of information harmful to social and political, social and economic systems, as well as spiritual, moral and cultural sphere of other states." The vague definition in China's cybersecurity law of what constitutes critical infrastructure could be used to limit access of foreign firms to key sectors or require access to source code under the justification of security as a condition of entering a market, yet exposing foreign companies to IP theft.

The Trump administration's decision to use a national security rationale to justify tariffs not only on imports of steel and aluminum but also possibly tariffs on automobiles heightened concerns over abuse of the national security exception. Russia relied on the national security exception to justify blockages on goods from Ukraine transiting its territory, and the UAE is relying on the exception to justify barriers on imports from Qatar.

A 2019 WTO panel in the Russia/Ukraine case made clear that the GATT national security exception is not self-judging and that panels will make an objective assessment as to whether there were qualifying events such as "an emergency in international relations."https://www.brookings.edu/research/cybersecurity-and-digital-trade-getting-it-right/ - footnote-11 This assessment is complicated in the cybersecurity context because the exceptions for national security and the general exceptions provisions in the WTO and in free trade agreements (FTAs) blur with a proliferation of cyber risks from state and non-state actors and where measures to address cyber risks are increasingly economy-wide. Setting boundaries will require a common global definition of the cybersecurity domain.

The U.S. National Institute of Standards and Technology (NIST) provides a reference point for such a definition. It defines cybersecurity as "the prevention of damage to, unauthorized use of, exploitation of, and—if needed—the restoration of electronic information and communications systems, and the information they contain, in order to strengthen the confidentiality, integrity and availability of these systems." In turn, the White House National Cyber Strategy focuses on increasing the security and resilience of the nation's information and information systems.

This definition reflects two key elements of cyberattacks: On information and on information systems. It does not differentiate between action by states as well as criminals and its impact on public and private information, networks, and infrastructure. Thus, for example, it includes Russian use of false accounts and addresses to seed false information as well as malware to intrude on systems.

Critically, this focus on the integrity of information and information systems does not encompass broader purposes such as development of national industries, preserving law enforcement access to information on citizens, regulation of information content, or social controls that are not directly related to these core elements. Such laws should stand or fall on aspects of trade agreements other than the security exception.

Other WTO exceptions. The global networks of trade are vulnerable to attacks along supply chains. In some cases, government may determine that the best policy response to this vulnerability is to prevent certain companies or governments from participating in the supply of key technologies. For instance, a recent White House Executive Order prohibits the importation of information and communication technology and services from entities controlled by a foreign adversary and where the import poses various risks—including of cyberattack. Recent draft regulations out of China regarding its cybersecurity review process also identify services and products controlled by foreign governments as potentially being subject to cybersecurity review.

Actions like these raise fundamental questions about consistency with WTO MFN commitments and would have to be justified as either necessary for national security or under the more general exceptions provision. While national security would seem the most logical exception, this provision was crafted in 1948 during the Cold War and its references to national security, such as trafficking in arms or relating to fissionable material, are not well suited to the cyber context, where the attacks might concern malware that affects how electrical grids operate.

The WTO GATT Article XX and GATS Article XIV general exception provisions are also available to justify such trade restrictions for cybersecurity purposes, and measures to protect critical infrastructure and supply chains could be considered necessary for public order or to protect human life or health. Yet, in these cases, the government would be subject to the more rigorous (compared to the national security exception) disciplines of these other provisions, which include requiring that the cybersecurity measures are least trade-restrictive and that there is a no less trade-restrictive alternative available to achieve the members desired level of protection. In addition, the chapeau to these exception provisions requires that the cyber measures are not arbitrary or unjustifiable or a disguised restriction on international trade. Applying such disciplines to cybersecurity measures that restrict trade would help distinguish between measures to protect information and information systems versus disguised restrictions on trade. However, whether governments are prepared to subject what they see as a national security measure to the disciplines of the general exception disciplines remains to be tested.

Yet, where governments seek to rely on the national security exception instead, the risk is this could lead to a large increase in trade restrictions. Given the step-up in aggressiveness in the cyber domain, it appears that cybersecurity will challenge how the trading system has traditionally balanced rights of access to markets with rights of governments to restrict trade for legitimate policy reasons. Fresh thinking and cooperation among like-minded trading partners on how to provide scope for legitimate cybersecurity policy that does not unnecessarily restrict trade is needed.

USING TRADE POLICY TO IMPROVE CYBERSECURITY

Although digital trade increases cybersecurity risks, trade and cybersecurity policy can also work in tandem to support growth in digital trade as well as strengthen cybersecurity outcomes.

Access to data. As cybersecurity defense becomes more sophisticated, use of analytics and machine learning to monitor network activity plays a growing role in the analysis of risks and anomalies. In fact, requiring data to be localized reduces opportunities for companies to use big data analytics to assess risk across global operations and supply chains. Forcing data into specific locations also increases the risk and cost of a data breach.The CPTPP and USMCA commitments to information flows across borders (subject to appropriate exceptions) and to avoiding data localization requirements, advances digital trade opportunities and cybersecurity outcomes.

Information sharing. As reflected in the U.S. Cybersecurity Information Sharing Act, real-time sharing of information on threats and vulnerabilities to promote awareness, plan responses, and help targets adapt and respond has become an important feature of cybersecurity policies. The trust issues in sharing proprietary or classified information in the domestic context are compounded when dealing with governments or organizations across national borders. Nevertheless, the U.S. is seeking to improve information sharing with international partners and allies and along supply chains. Trade agreements can include commitments to building public and private sector information sharing mechanisms. For example, the U.S.-Mexico-Canada trade agreement includes a commitment to sharing information and best practices as a means of addressing and responding to cyberattacks.

Cybersecurity standards. Cybersecurity standards can build a common approach to addressing cybersecurity risks based on best practice. For instance, the International Standards Organization (ISO) and the International Electrotechnical Commission (IEC) have developed a number of cybersecurity-related standards, including the jointly developed ISO/IEC 27000 series as well as sector specific-standards for electric utilities, healthcare, and shipping. Standards are most effective when they don't proscribe a particular approach but instead are frameworks for managing risk, relying on business and government to design cybersecurity measures most suitable to their business practices and risk profiles. In turn, the NIST Cyber Framework relies on international standards such as ISO 27001 as references for its cyber risk management framework, with the result that the framework is not U.S. specific and can be adopted globally. Trade agreements can be used to reinforce the role of consensus-based standards with commitments to develop international standards and to use international standards where they exist as a basis for domestic regulation, which also supports the development of globally consistent and least trade-restrictive approaches to cybersecurity. Using international standards as a basis for cybersecurity policy can also help address concerns that cybersecurity regulation is a disguised restriction on trade aimed instead at supporting domestic industry.

Certification of compliance with cybersecurity standards. Compliance certification can give consumers and business confidence in the cybersecurity of organizations and government. Under the EU Cybersecurity Act which came in to force in June 2019, the European Union Agency for Cybersecurity (ENISA) will establish an EU-wide cybersecurity certification scheme. NIST has developed a different approach in the Baldridge Performance Excellence Program, which encourages self-assessment of compliance. Trade agreements can support conformity assessment regimes and seek to minimize such regimes becoming unnecessarily burdensome on trade by requiring governments to allow other parties to demonstrate and undertake in the country of export conformity assessment of products with the country of imports cybersecurity regulations. In addition, commitments that conformity assessment requirements are non-discriminatory and not disguised restrictions on international trade provide additional disciplines that lead to the consideration of trade impacts on the development of cybersecurity regulation.

Risk-based approach to cybersecurity. According to the OECD, cybersecurity should "aim to reduce the risk to an acceptable level relative to the economic and social benefits expected from those activities, while taking into account the legitimate interests of others." Similarly, the NIST framework relies on risk assessments tailored to each organization's needs, and the EU's Network and Information System Directive requires security measures "appropriate and proportionate … to manage the risks posed to the security of network and information systems." A risk assessment should then inform decisions as to what measures to adopt, what risk reduction can be expected, and at what cost. The rapidly changing nature of cybersecurity threats means that addressing risk is a dynamic process that requires regular reassessment of risk and consideration of what else might be needed to reduce risk to acceptable levels. By contrast, an overly prescriptive regulation can become quickly outdated or lead to box-checking instead of thoughtful assessment whether the steps taken are in fact reducing risk.

Building an effective approach to cybersecurity also requires engaging government and business leaders and building cyber risk management into the core of corporate and government practice. The USMCA includes a recognition of the importance of taking a risk-based approach to cybersecurity instead of proscriptive approaches, including risk-based approaches that rely on consensus-based international standards and best practices.

CONCLUSION

The scope for trade policy to support cybersecurity outcomes presents a complex set of issues that are only beginning to be explored. Today, cybersecurity risk is growing more acute as business, government, and people become more interconnected and reliant on technology. On the one hand, the risk that governments increasingly will restrict access to data and networks merits attention, since it could potentially result in adverse consequences for digital trade and impair the potential for the free flow of data to drive growth and welfare. On the other hand, getting cybersecurity policy wrong will undermine trust in the digital economy. Therefore, new trade rules that can both support risk based effective cybersecurity regulation, build bridges between the cybersecurity policy in different countries to maximize synergies, and minimize barriers to trade are needed.

14.7[B] ASIA-PACIFIC ECONOMIC COOPERATION CROSS-BORDER PRIVACY RULES SYSTEM

IV. Promotion of technical measures to protect privacy

46. Technical measures can make a significant contribution to the overall effectiveness and impact of domestic privacy regimes, by supplementing and complementing legal

protections of privacy. Therefore, when considering approaches to give effect to the Framework, member economies should promote technical measures which help to protect privacy.

47. Member economies may, for example, encourage personal information controllers to make full use of readily available technical safeguards and measures. In addition, they may promote research and development, encourage further privacy innovation and support the development of technical standards that embed best privacy practice into systems engineering.

Part IV. Implementation

A. Guidance for Domestic Implementation

VII. Providing for appropriate remedies in situations where privacy protections are violated

53. A member economy's system of privacy protections should include appropriate remedies for privacy violations, which could include redress, the ability to stop a violation from continuing, and other remedies. In determining the range of remedies for privacy violations, member economies should take a number of factors into account including: a) the particular system in that member economy for providing privacy protections (e.g., legislative enforcement powers, which may include rights of individuals to pursue legal action, industry self-regulation, or a combination of systems); and b) the importance of having a range of remedies commensurate with the extent of the actual or potential harm to individuals resulting from such violations.

54. A member economy should consider encouraging or requiring personal information controllers to provide notice, as appropriate, to Privacy Enforcement Authorities and/or other relevant authorities in the event of a significant security breach affecting personal information under its control. Where it is reasonable to believe that the breach is likely to affect individuals, timely notification directly to affected individuals should be encouraged or required, where feasible and reasonable.

14.7[C] COMPREHENSIVE AND PROGRESSIVE AGREEMENT FOR TRANS-PACIFIC PARTNERSHIP

Chapter 14 of the Comprehensive and Progressive Agreement for Trans-Pacific Partnership contains a section on Electronic Commerce. The relevant articles related to cybersecurity and privacy follow:

Article 14.1 Definitions

. . .

electronic authentication means the process or act of verifying the identity of a party to an electronic communication or transaction and ensuring the integrity of an electronic communication;

electronic transmission or transmitted electronically means a transmission made using any electromagnetic means, including by photonic means;

personal information means any information, including data, about an identified or identifiable natural person;

. . .

Article 14.6: Electronic Authentication and Electronic Signatures

1. Except in circumstances otherwise provided for under its law, a Party shall not deny the legal validity of a signature solely on the basis that the signature is in electronic form.

2. No Party shall adopt or maintain measures for electronic authentication that would: (a) prohibit parties to an electronic transaction from mutually determining the appropriate authentication methods for that transaction; or (b) prevent parties to an electronic transaction from having the opportunity to establish before judicial or administrative authorities that their transaction complies with any legal requirements with respect to authentication.

3. Notwithstanding paragraph 2, a Party may require that, for a particular category of transactions, the method of authentication meets certain performance standards or is certified by an authority accredited in accordance with its law.

4. The Parties shall encourage the use of interoperable electronic authentication.

Article 14.8: Personal Information Protection

1. The Parties recognise the economic and social benefits of protecting the personal information of users of electronic commerce and the contribution that this makes to enhancing consumer confidence in electronic commerce.

2. To this end, each Party shall adopt or maintain a legal framework that provides for the protection of the personal information of the users of electronic commerce. In the development of its legal framework for the protection of personal information, each Party should take into account principles and guidelines of relevant international bodies.6

3. Each Party shall endeavour to adopt non-discriminatory practices in protecting users of electronic commerce from personal information protection violations occurring within its jurisdiction.

4. Each Party should publish information on the personal information protections it provides to users of electronic commerce, including how: (a) individuals can pursue remedies; and (b) business can comply with any legal requirements.

5. Recognising that the Parties may take different legal approaches to protecting personal information, each Party should encourage the development of mechanisms to promote compatibility between these different regimes. These mechanisms may include the recognition of regulatory outcomes, whether accorded autonomously or by mutual arrangement, or broader international frameworks. To this end, the Parties shall endeavour to exchange information on any such mechanisms applied in their jurisdictions and explore ways to extend these or other suitable arrangements to promote compatibility between them.

Footnote 6 For greater certainty, a Party may comply with the obligation in this paragraph by adopting or maintaining measures such as a comprehensive privacy, personal information or personal data protection laws, sector-specific laws covering privacy, or laws that provide for the enforcement of voluntary undertakings by enterprises relating to privacy

Article 14.16: Cooperation on Cybersecurity Matters

The Parties recognise the importance of: (a) building the capabilities of their national entities responsible for computer security incident response; and (b) using existing collaboration mechanisms to cooperate to identify and mitigate malicious intrusions or dissemination of malicious code that affect the electronic networks of the Parties.

Article 14.17: Source Code

1. No Party shall require the transfer of, or access to, source code of software owned by a person of another Party, as a condition for the import, distribution, sale or use of such software, or of products containing such software, in its territory.

2. For the purposes of this Article, software subject to paragraph 1 is limited to mass-market software or products containing such software and does not include software used for critical infrastructure.

3. Nothing in this Article shall preclude: (a) the inclusion or implementation of terms and conditions related to the provision of source code in commercially negotiated contracts; or (b) a Party from requiring the modification of source code of software necessary for that software to comply with laws or regulations which are not inconsistent with this Agreement.

4. This Article shall not be construed to affect requirements that relate to patent applications or granted patents, including any orders made by a judicial authority in relation to patent disputes, subject to safeguards against unauthorised disclosure under the law or practice of a Party.

14.7[D] UNITED STATES-MEXICO-CANADA AGREEMENT (ARTICLE 19 ET SEQ.).

Article 19.1: Definitions

electronic authentication means the process or act of verifying the identity of a party to an electronic communication or transaction and ensuring the integrity of an electronic communication; . . .

personal information means information, including data, about an identified or identifiable natural person; . . .

Article 19.6: Electronic Authentication and Electronic Signatures

1. Except in circumstances provided for under its law, a Party shall not deny the legal validity of a signature solely on the basis that the signature is in electronic form.

2. No Party shall adopt or maintain measures for electronic authentication and electronic signatures that would: (a) prohibit parties to an electronic transaction from mutually determining the appropriate authentication methods or electronic signatures for that transaction; or (b) prevent parties to an electronic transaction from having the opportunity to establish before judicial or administrative authorities that their transaction complies with any legal requirements with respect to authentication or electronic signatures.

3. Notwithstanding paragraph 2, a Party may require that, for a particular category of transactions, the electronic signature or method of authentication meets certain performance standards or is certified by an authority accredited in accordance with its law.

4. Each Party shall encourage the use of interoperable electronic authentication.

Article 19.8: Personal Information Protection

1. The Parties recognize the economic and social benefits of protecting the personal information of users of digital trade and the contribution that this makes to enhancing consumer confidence in digital trade.

2. To this end, each Party shall adopt or maintain a legal framework that provides for the protection of the personal information of the users of digital trade. In the development of this legal framework, each Party should take into account principles and guidelines of relevant international 19-5 bodies, such as the APEC Privacy Framework and the OECD Recommendation of the Council concerning Guidelines governing the Protection of Privacy and Transborder Flows of Personal Data (2013).

3. The Parties recognize that pursuant to paragraph 2, key principles include: limitation on collection; choice; data quality; purpose specification; use limitation; security safeguards; transparency; individual participation; and accountability. The Parties also recognize the importance of ensuring compliance with measures to protect personal

information and ensuring that any restrictions on cross-border flows of personal information are necessary and proportionate to the risks presented.

4. Each Party shall endeavor to adopt non-discriminatory practices in protecting users of digital trade from personal information protection violations occurring within its jurisdiction.

5. Each Party shall publish information on the personal information protections it provides to users of digital trade, including how: (a) a natural person can pursue a remedy; and (b) an enterprise can comply with legal requirements.

6. Recognizing that the Parties may take different legal approaches to protecting personal information, each Party should encourage the development of mechanisms to promote compatibility between these different regimes. The Parties shall endeavor to exchange information on the mechanisms applied in their jurisdictions and explore ways to extend these or other suitable arrangements to promote compatibility between them. The Parties recognize that the APEC CrossBorder Privacy Rules system is a valid mechanism to facilitate cross-border information transfers while protecting personal information.

Article 19.15: Cybersecurity

1. The Parties recognize that threats to cybersecurity undermine confidence in digital trade. Accordingly, the Parties shall endeavor to: (a) build the capabilities of their respective national entities responsible for cybersecurity incident response; and (b) strengthen existing collaboration mechanisms for cooperating to identify and mitigate malicious intrusions or dissemination of malicious code that affect electronic networks, and use those mechanisms to swiftly address cybersecurity incidents, as well as for the sharing of information for awareness and best practices.

2. Given the evolving nature of cybersecurity threats, the Parties recognize that risk-based approaches may be more effective than prescriptive regulation in addressing those threats. Accordingly, each Party shall endeavor to employ, and encourage enterprises within its jurisdiction to use, risk-based approaches that rely on consensus-based standards and risk management best practices to identify and protect against cybersecurity risks and to detect, respond to, and recover from cybersecurity events.

Article 19.16: Source Code

1. No Party shall require the transfer of, or access to, a source code of software owned by a person of another Party, or to an algorithm expressed in that source code, as a condition for the import, distribution, sale or use of that software, or of products containing that software, in its territory.

2. This Article does not preclude a regulatory body or judicial authority of a Party from requiring a person of another Party to preserve and make available the source code of software, or an algorithm expressed in that source code, to the regulatory body for a

specific investigation, inspection, examination, enforcement action, or judicial proceeding, subject to safeguards against unauthorized disclosure.